The Wiley Handbook of Art Therapy

The Wiley Handbook of Art Therapy

Edited by

David E. Gussak and Marcia L. Rosal

WILEY Blackwell

Dedications

For my children, Samantha and Joseph. DEG
For my sister, Ana—you will always be in my heart. MLR

Dedications

For my children, Samantha and Joseph. DEG
For my sister, Ana—you will always be in my heart. MLR

Contents

Part II   Understanding Art Media in Therapy   133

Part III   Developmental Spectrum and Therapeutic
Considerations   199

Part IX   Current and Contemporary Issues in Art Therapy   775

Editors

David E. Gussak, PhD, ATR-BC, is professor and chairperson for the Florida State University's Department of Art Education. Prior to his teaching for the Florida State University, Gussak was the director of the Graduate Art Therapy Program in the Department of Psychology and Special Education at Emporia State University in Kansas. He has also been an adjunct and visiting professor for many art therapy programs across the United States.

Gussak has presented extensively—internationally, nationally, and regionally—on forensic art therapy, art therapy in forensic settings, working with aggressive and violent clients, working with clients who have substance abuse issues, the work of the art therapist, and supervision for art therapists. He has published extensively on various topics, but most significantly on art therapy within the forensic milieu. Gussak is the co-editor and contributing author for the books *Drawing Time: Art Therapy in Prisons and Other Correctional Settings* (with Evelyn Virshup; Magnolia Street Publishers, 1997) and *Art Education for Social Justice* (with Tom Anderson, Kara Hallmark, and Alison Paul; National Art Education Association, 2010). His latest book is *Art on Trial: Art Therapy in Capital Murder Cases*, which was published by Columbia University Press in 2013. He is also the author of the *Psychology Today* blog titled *Art on Trial: Confessions of a Serial Art Therapist*.

Gussak has served the art therapy field in many capacities, including as director-at-large on the board of directors for the American Art Therapy Association, and as treasurer for the Art Therapy Credentials Board. He is currently on the editorial board for the *Art Therapy: Journal of the American Art Therapy Association*, and was the chairperson of the Nominating Committee. He is also guest editor for several other journals, including *The International Journal of Offender Treatment and Criminology*.

Marcia L. Rosal, PhD, ATR-BC, HLM, is a director of the Florida State University's (FSU) art therapy program. She received a master's degree in art therapy from the University of Louisville and a doctorate in educational psychology from the University of Queensland. Prior to joining the faculty at FSU in 1999, Marcia taught for 14 years at the University of Louisville in the Expressive Therapies Program, where she received the 1998 Distinguished Teacher Award. She has been an adjunct or visiting professor in several other art therapy programs at various colleges and universities in the United States and abroad, including Australia, Britain, and Taiwan. In addition, she has presented frequently at state, national, and international conferences.

She was a Fulbright Scholar in 2008, and as such conducted lectures and research in Taiwan. She is currently working on professional connections with Taiwan, South Korea, and Latvia through the Fulbright Foundation.

Rosal is active professionally. She served as the executive secretary of the Kentucky Art Therapy Association for several years prior to her move to Florida. On the national level, she served and chaired on what is now called the Educational Program Approval Board of the American Art Therapy Association, and was active on several other committees, including programs committees for the national conferences prior to her election to the board of directors. Her 8-year tenure on the board culminated with a 2-year term as president (1999–2001). She is active as an editorial board member for the international journal *The Arts in Psychotherapy*, is the senior editor for *Journal of Art for Life*, and is a member of the editorial board of *Journal of Clinical Art Therapy*. She continues to work on various committees with American Art Therapy Association and the Art Therapy Credentials Board.

Contributing Authors

Josie Abbenante, ATR-BC, LPAT, has practiced archetypal art therapy for 35 years. For 30 years, she taught in various graduate art therapy programs, and directed those at the University of New Mexico and Seton Hill College. She coordinated and taught at Pratt Institute' summer program, and taught for Eastern Virginia Medical School and Vermont College. She works as an art therapist with the New Mexico School for the Deaf, the UNM Children's Hospital, and continues her private practice in art therapy and sandplay. She has presented nationally and internationally on archetypal art therapy, transition, deaf culture, art therapy and feminist theory, and the language of aesthetics and metaphor.

Susan Ainlay Anand, MA, ATR-BC, ATCS, LPAT, joined the faculty in the Department of Psychiatry at the University of Mississippi Medical Center after receiving her master's degree in art therapy from New York University. Her clinical interests relate to art therapy of medically ill and psychiatric patients, and she co-leads art therapy groups with PGYIII psychiatry residents as part of residency training. She also provides art therapy services to cancer patients in an outpatient setting and conducts training workshops in the United States and abroad.

Frances E. Anderson, EdD, ATR-BC, HLM, is the DVD and non-print editor of *The Arts in Psychotherapy*. A distinguished professor of art, emerita, at Illinois State University, she is affiliate faculty at the College of Charleston, Charleston, South Carolina. Author of 70 articles, monographs, and two seminal books on art with disabled children, she has received five Fulbright Awards (Argentina, 2002; Taiwan, 2005; Thailand, 2008; Pakistan twice, 2010).

Doris Arrington, EdD, ATR-BC, HLM, artist, author, administrator, educator, and licensed psychologist, has served 30 years as founding director and professor of the Art Therapy Psychology Department at Notre Dame de Namur University. A Fulbright Senior Specialist to the Ukraine, Arrington has keynoted and taught caregivers worldwide on how to rehabilitate the abused and traumatized using art. Author of two books and many chapters and articles, she exhibits art through the Peninsula Art Institute in Burlingame, California.

Paige Asawa, PhD, ATR-BC, is a faculty member at Loyola Marymount University since 1998, and is the director of the Helen B. Landgarten Art Therapy Clinic, which provides art therapy for underserved populations in Los Angeles. In the clinic, she developed the Resilient & Ready Program, ART First Trauma Training & Response Program, and Family Art Assessment Program. Maintaining a private practice for over 20 years, she provides art therapy for families, children, individuals, and couples.

Kevin Bailey, MS, received his MS in art therapy from Florida State University, and since that time has provided art therapy services in hospitals, outpatient clinics, public school settings, and intermediate care facilities. He is currently employed as the administrator for a 63-bed residential facility that services adults with developmental disabilities. Kevin is also the proud father of two sons, one with cerebral palsy, from whom he draws much inspiration.

Mercedes Ballbéter Maat, PhD, ATR-BC, LPC, is an associate professor in counselor education. She teaches and provides supervision in counseling principles, theory and skills, ethics, and multicultural competence to master's-level students. She has over 28 years of combined art therapy and counseling experience with children and adults from diverse backgrounds and in a variety of settings. She is a national and international speaker who has published numerous articles and has received research grants to work with immigrant students and their families.

Katy Barrington, PhD, ATR-BC, CT, is an associate professor at the Masters of Counseling Psychology: Art Therapy program at Adler University, Chicago, Illinois. She earned her doctorate from Florida State University and a Certificate of Aging Studies from the Claude Pepper Institute on Public Policy. She is a Certified Thanatologist (CT). She has presented nationally and internationally; authored the book chapter "Creative Expression for Social Justice with Older Adults" (2010) for Anderson, Gussak, Hallmark, and Paul's *Art Education for Social Justice* (National Art Education Association, 2010); volunteers for hospice; and continues to advocate for seniors.

Amar Abdulla Behbehani, PhD, MSc, MFA, ATR, defines herself as a life scientist who devotes her passion for the sciences of art therapy, design, well-being, and education. She believes in the power of art in analyzing the depth of human psychology; as a result, she uses the creative path in multiple research and learning arenas. She is an educator, art therapist, and life coach in the State of Kuwait, Middle East.

Lesli-Ann M. Belnavis, MS, ATR, is a graduate of Florida State University. Her experience includes conducting sessions with children and adults with various physical and psychological disabilities in different educational settings in Jamaica. She has co-authored the publication She has co-authored the book *Art: A Healing Tool for Children. A Look at Caribbean Clinicians and Arts and Crafts* with Dr. Claudia Williams (2011), and maintains a private practice. She is the president of the Caribbean Art Therapy Association.

Donna Betts, PhD, ATR-BC, is a research professor in the Graduate Art Therapy Program at George Washington University, Washington, DC, and president-elect of the American Art Therapy Association. Betts' doctoral research culminated in the seminal 2006 article titled "Art Therapy Assessments and Rating Instruments: Do They Measure Up?" An authority on art therapy assessments, she has authored several publications, including a 2014 book chapter co-written with psychologist Gary Groth-Marnat.

Gaelynn P. Wolf Bordonaro, PhD, ATR-BC, is the director of the Emporia State University Art Therapy Program, and associate professor in the Department of Counselor Education. Passionate about international art therapy responses to natural and human-created disasters, pediatric medical art therapy, and therapeutic uses of photography, she has presented throughout the world. She is the clinical director of Communities Healing through Art, and has served on the board of directors of the American Art Therapy Association.

Charlotte Boston, MA, ATR-BC, has served in roles such as director of expressive therapy, clinical director, supervisor, consultant, presenter, and author. Her career includes work with psychiatric inpatients and residents. She has presented and published on multicultural issues. In 2010, she débuted the film *Wheels of Diversity: Pioneers of Color*. She is currently secretary of the American Art Therapy Association and adjunct faculty of the George Washington University.

Richard Carolan, EdD, ATR-BC, is a licensed psychologist and a board-certified art therapist. He has taught at Notre Dame de Namur University for 20 years, developing the research program, serving as department chair, and currently serving as program director of the PhD program in art therapy. Carolan previously served as director of the internship program and director of training at Thunder Road Adolescent Treatment Centers, Inc., in Oakland, California. He also works in private practice.

Selma Ciornai, PhD, ATR, holds a doctorate in clinical psychology (Saybrook University, San Francisco), an MA in art therapy (California State University), and is a Gestalt therapist. She is the founder and coordinator of the Art Therapy Training Program at Instituto Sedes Sapientiae, São Paulo, and Instituto da Família, Porto Alegre. She is also an honorary member of UBAAT (Brazilian Union of Art Therapy Associations), and author and editor of *Percursos em Arteterapia* (*Paths in Art Therapy*), a three volume series on art therapy theory and practice.

Barry M. Cohen, MA, ATR-BC, primary creator of the Diagnostic Drawing Series, is the author/co-author of numerous journal articles and chapters. He also co-authored/co-edited three books, including *Telling Without Talking: Art as a Window into the World of Multiple Personality* (W. W. Norton, 1995), and the workbook *Managing Traumatic Stress through Art* (Sidran Traumatic Stress Ins, 1995). He is the executive director of Expressive Media, and he founded the annual Expressive Therapies Summit in 2010. In 2013, he co-founded, with Eliana Gil, the Mid-Atlantic Play Therapy Training Institute.

Marcia Sue Cohen-Liebman, MCAT, ATR-BC, LPC, is an adjunct assistant clinical professor in the Department of Creative Arts Therapies at Drexel University in Philadelphia, Pennsylvania. She is a forensic art therapist, specializing in child sexual abuse investigations and custodial matters. She teaches a course entitled "Forensic Art Therapy," and has published on related topics. Cohen-Liebman is a PhD candidate at Drexel University in the Department of Creative Arts Therapies.

Elizabeth Coss, ATR-BC, AThR, LCAT, is an educator, researcher, writer, painter, and activist, in addition to being an art therapist. She helped develop the art therapy field in Singapore at LASALLE College of the Arts, and has presented throughout the Asia-Pacific region. She was a co-researcher for a University of Melbourne study on epilepsy, and has worked with a variety of populations. She has also taught for the New York University, the School of Visual Arts, and the New York Institute of Technology College of Osteopathic Medicine. She is currently writing about art, social justice, and transformation based on her documentation of Occupy Wall Street, Free Cooper Union, and other recent activism.

Annette M. Coulter, DipFA, PgDipATh, MAAEd(ATh), AThR, ATR, KATR, is a British-trained and Australian-based art psychotherapist, interactive drawing therapy (IDT) practitioner, and published author with 38 years clinical experience, specializing in child, adolescent, family, and couple work. She is a trained and accredited IDT teacher and supervisor. She taught post-graduate art therapy in Australia, Great Britain and Southeast Asia, and has completed further training in child psychotherapy, family therapy, and group work. Through the Centre for Art Psychotherapy, she provides consultation, supervision, education, and customized training.

Tracy Councill, MA, ATR-BC, serves as program director for Tracy's Kids (www. tracyskids.org), and is the lead art therapist in the Tracy's Kids program at Georgetown University Hospital's Lombardi Cancer Center. She earned her MA in art therapy from the George Washington University in 1988, and her BFA in painting and printmaking from Virginia Commonwealth University in 1978. She teaches medical art therapy at the George Washington University, and served as a director of the American Art Therapy Association from 2009 to 2011.

Cynthia Cox, MEd, OT/L, has been an occupational therapist for 25 years, specializing in the treatment of patients with traumatic brain injury and neurological deficits. She received her bachelor's degree from the University of Wisconsin and her master's degree from the University of Florida. She is an advocate and mentor for patients, families, and students, both within the healthcare system and the community at large.

Maria d'Elia, MA, was born in 1963 near Boston, Massachusetts, in the United States. She is German, has an Italian husband, and currently lives in Luxembourg. She studied art education, art history, and psychology in Munich, Germany, and received her MA in art therapy from Vermont College of Norwich University. She has worked in psychiatry in Germany and Luxembourg. She is the co-founder and president of Luxembourgish

Arts Therapies Association (ALAtD) and co-coordinator of an art therapists' network with members from 27 EU states. She has several publications in German.

Irene Rosner David, PhD, ATR-BC, LCAT, HLM, is director of therapeutic arts at Bellevue Hospital in New York, where she has practiced medical art therapy since 1973. Her work has focused on the contributory role of artistic expression in coping with illness and disability. Her specializations have included trauma, stroke, paralysis, brain injury, dementia, oncology, and palliative care. She has served on the board of the American Art Therapy Association, and has received numerous awards for her clinical work and advocacy of the field.

Michelle L. Dean, MA, ATR-BC, LPC, CGP, has 20 years experience in treating individuals with addictions, eating disorders, relationship issues, and traumatic experiences. She co-founded the Center for Psyche & the Arts, LLC (http://psychearts. org) in Philadelphia. In addition, she is an author, supervisor, educator, and consultant. She has been an adjunct professor at Arcadia University since 1997, and has several publications to her credit, including the children's book titled *Taking Weight Issues to School* (JayJo Books, 2005). She has received many distinguished awards, including the Honorary Life Member Award from DVATA.

Sarah P. Deaver, PhD, ATR-BC, has been an art therapy educator, researcher, and clinician for over 30 years. A professor in the Eastern Virginia Medical School Department of Psychiatry and School of Health Professions, her scholarly interests include art therapy educational theory and practice and art therapy assessment and efficacy research. She is currently president of the American Art Therapy Association.

Cheryl Earwood, MA, ATR-BC, a Florida native, received her BFA degree from Virginia Commonwealth University, and her MA in art therapy from George Washington University. She then worked at the Virginia Treatment Center for Children, followed by the Appalachian Hall, a private psychiatric hospital. She currently works for the Miami-Dade County Public Schools, where she has worked for over 20 years. Her research and case studies have been included in books by Rawley Silver.

Deborah Elkis-Abuhoff, PhD, LCAT, ATR-BC, ATCS, BCPC, is an associate professor in the Creative Arts Therapy program at Hofstra University. Elkis-Abuhoff also holds an appointment to the North Shore-Long Island Jewish Health System's Feinstein Institute for Medical Research, in the Center of Neuroscience. Her research interests bring together medical art therapy and behavioral medicine with individuals diagnosed with Parkinson's disease, and those actively receiving chemotherapy or blood transfusions.

Maria Espinola, PsyD, is a postdoctoral clinical fellow at McLean Hospital and the Department of Psychiatry at Harvard Medical School. Her areas of interest are psychological trauma and multicultural issues. Espinola completed her predoctoral psychology internship at the Center for Multicultural Training in Psychology at Boston Medical Center and Boston University School of Medicine. She received her bachelor's (BS), master's (MS), and doctoral degrees in clinical psychology from Nova Southeastern University, Fort Lauderdale, Florida.

Melinda Fedorko, MA, ATR-BC, received an MA in art therapy from the University of Louisville Institute of Expressive Therapies. She is a registered art therapist, licensed marriage and family therapist, and National Board Certified teacher. Fedorko has assisted Rawley Silver in her research and writing.

Holly Feen-Calligan, PhD, ATR-BC, earned her doctoral degree at the University of Michigan, where she studied service-learning in higher education. She has directed the art therapy program at Wayne State University for 25 years, and is a founding member and research director of *ArtsCorpsDetroit*, providing volunteer opportunities to help revitalize the City of Detroit through the arts. Holly has been associate editor of *Art Therapy: Journal of the American Art Therapy Association* for 9 years.

Lariza B. Fenner, MS, ATR, NCC, is most invested in teaching excellence in the areas of art therapy research, assessment, and interventions for the treatment of trauma. She has directed collaborative social service projects that aim to reduce violence through the use of creative expression in the communities of south Chicago, and has dedicated herself to serving American Art Therapy Association local chapter and national committees. She is a passionate advocate for the art therapy profession in Illinois.

Michael A. Franklin, coordinator of the Naropa University graduate art therapy program, has practiced and taught in various academic and clinical settings since 1981. The author of numerous articles, he is an international lecturer and founder of the Naropa Community Art Studio, a project dedicated to researching service as a spiritual practice, training socially engaged artists, and serving marginalized community members through the studio arts. His research focuses on integrating art-based research methods with contemplative East–West traditions.

Linda Gantt, PhD, HLM, ATR-BC, has an MA in art therapy from the George Washington University, and a doctorate in interdisciplinary studies from the University of Pittsburgh. She and Carmello Tabone developed the Formal Elements Art Therapy Scale (FEATS). Linda owns Intensive Trauma Therapy, in Morgantown, West Virginia, an outpatient clinic for trauma-related disorders where art therapy is the primary means of treatment. She and her late husband Louis Tinnin have written and presented widely on trauma.

Nancy Gerber, PhD, ATR-BC, LPC, is an art psychotherapist, author, clinical associate professor and director of the PhD program in creative arts therapies, and former director of the master's degree program in art therapy at Drexel University. She has presented and published on art therapy assessment, art therapy and doctoral education, mixed methods research, and arts-based research. Gerber was the first recipient of the Distinguished Educator's Award from the American Art Therapy Association.

Deborah A. Good, PhD, ATR-BC, ATCS, LPAT, LPCC, is a board-certified art therapist and New Mexico–licensed professional art therapist and clinical counselor. She has worked in outpatient and hospital settings in the mental health field for 42 years. Deborah is a past president of both the American Art Therapy Association and the Art Therapy Credentials Board. She has authored several book chapters, introductions, and articles on art therapy, and speaks nationally and internationally on various art therapy and counseling topics.

Laura Greenstone, ATR-BC, LPC, has extensive experience working with children, adults, and families coping with trauma, domestic violence, and disasters. She has been honored for her expertise in government affairs by both the American Art Therapy Association and New Jersey Art Therapy Association, and has served as past chair of the National Coalition of Creative Arts Therapies Associations and on the national policy planning committee for Arts Advocacy Day.

Meirav Haber, MA, MFTI, is an art therapist and artist in Los Angeles. She earned her BFA from the University of California, Los Angeles, and master's degree in marriage and family therapy/clinical art therapy from Loyola Marymount University. She works with adults with severe mental illness at Sherman Oaks Hospital's intensive outpatient program. She is a strong advocate of a family system's approach to art therapy, and is currently building a private practice with children and families.

Lisa D. Hinz, PhD, ATR, is a licensed clinical psychologist and a registered art therapist who has been helping people achieve their goals of optimal health:—body, mind, and spirit—for 25 years. Hinz is an adjunct professor of art therapy at the Saint Mary-of-the-Woods College, and the author of many professional publications, including the book titled *Expressive Therapies Continuum: A Framework for Using Art in Therapy* (Routledge, 2009).

Sarah A. Soo Hon, MA, ATR, is a graduate of Long Island University and a doctoral student at Queen Margaret University. She has provided art therapy services for persons with autism, children living with HIV/AIDS, and persons with psychiatric illness. She currently serves as PRO of the Autistic Society of Trinidad and Tobago, and also as the vice president of the Caribbean Art Therapy Association.

Ellen G. Horovitz, PhD, ATR-BC, LCAT, E-RYT, LFYP, is a professor/director of art therapy at the Nazareth College in Rochester, New York. Her books include *Spiritual Art Therapy: An Alternate Path* (Charles C. Thomas Publisher, 2002); *A Leap of Faith: The Call to Art* (Charles C. Thomas Publisher, 1999); *Art Therapy As Witness: A Sacred Guide* (Charles C. Thomas Publisher, 2005); *Visually Speaking: Art Therapy and the Deaf* (Charles C. Thomas Publisher, 2007); *Digital Image Transfer: Creating Art With Your Photography* (Pixiq, 2011); *The Art Therapists Primer: A Clinical Guide to Writing Assessments, Diagnosis and Treatment* (Charles C. Thomas Publisher, 2009); and *Yoga Therapy: Theory and Practice* (Routledge, 2015).

Janice Hoshino, PhD, ATR-BC, ATCS, LMFT, chairs the art and drama therapy programs at Antioch University Seattle, Washington. She is a co-author of *Family Art Therapy: Foundations of Theory and Practice* (Routledge, 2007)), in addition to other articles and chapters. She serves on the board of directors for the Art Therapy

Credentials Board, and received the 2013 Distinguished Service Award from the American Art Therapy Association. Her clinical focus is primarily with couples and families.

Paula Howie, ATR-BC, LPC, is a registered, board-certified art therapist and a licensed counselor in Washington, DC, and Virginia. She directed the Art Therapy Service at Walter Reed for over 25 years. She is currently an associate professorial lecturer at the George Washington University in Washington, DC. She served as president of the American Art Therapy Association from 2005 to 2007, and currently maintains a private practice in Washington, DC.

Margaret Hunter, LMFT, ATR, is an art therapist working in Central Valley, California. She is a co-founder of Meghan's Place Eating Disorder Center in Modesto, California, and has 13 years of experience in prevention and treatment of eating disorders. She is the author of the book *Reflections of Body Image in Art Therapy: Exploring Self Through Metaphor and Multi-Media* (Jessica Kingsley Publishers, 2012). She uses popular cultural metaphors in her body image workshops to facilitate awareness and transformation.

Patricia D. Isis, PhD, LMHC, ATR-BC, ATCS, holds her doctoral degree in the expressive therapies, with an emphasis on art therapy. Isis is a licensed mental health counselor and a registered board-certified art therapist and credentialed supervisor. Since 1980, she has practiced art psychotherapy in South Florida. Currently, she provides art therapy services full time in the public schools, maintains a part-time private practice, and facilitates mindfulness-based stress-reduction classes and trainings. More information is available on her website, www.MiamiArtTherapy.com.

Maxine Borowsky Junge, PhD, LCSW, ATR-BC, HLM, has been an art therapist for 40 years. She is professor emerita at Loyola Marymount University, where she was chair of the art therapy master's degree program. She also taught at the Immaculate Heart College in Los Angeles, Goddard College in Vermont, and Antioch University Seattle, in Washington. She is the author of seven books on art therapy and creativity. For the last 13 years, her personal artwork has focused on mass murderers. She lives on Whidbey Island, in Washington.

Donna H. Kaiser, PhD, ATR-BC, LPC, LMFT, is associate clinical professor and director of the graduate art therapy program in the Hahnemann Creative Arts Therapies Department at Drexel University. She is an experienced art therapist, educator, and researcher, and is editor-designate of *Art Therapy: Journal of the American Art Therapy Association*.

Debra Kalmanowitz, MA, RATh, has worked extensively in the context of trauma, political violence, and social change—locally, internationally, and in countries of conflict. She is a research postgraduate in the Department of Social Work and Social Administration, and an honorary clinical associate at the Centre on Behavioural

Health, University of Hong Kong. Debra works with refugees and asylum seekers, continues to co-direct ATI (www.atinitiative.org), and works in her own studio. She has published several articles and books in the field.

Frances F. Kaplan, MPS, DA, ATR-BC, has served as supervisor of creative arts therapies at Carrier Clinic, New Jersey, and as director of the graduate art therapy program at Hofstra University, New York. She spent a sabbatical year at Edith Cowan University, Perth, Western Australia, and is a past editor of *Art Therapy: Journal of the American Art Therapy Association*. Currently, she is an adjunct professor in the graduate art therapy counseling program at Marylhurst University, Oregon. She is author of *Art, Science and Art Therapy: Repainting the Picture* (Jessica Kingsley Publishers, 2000) and many other publications.

Lisa Kay, EdD, ATR-BC, is an assistant professor in art education and community arts practices, Tyler School of Art, Temple University, Philadelphia. Kay's interest in narrative storytelling—which encourages personal reflection, self knowledge, and healing in the context of making art—is evidenced in her scholarly publications, her devotion to art therapy and art education, her selection of focus for her Fulbright Scholarship, and her own art. She has exhibited her art in both the United States and Europe.

Seong-in Kim, PhD, is a professor emeritus of industrial management engineering at Korea University. His research interests include applied statistics, artificial intelligence, and quality control. He developed a computer sentencing system for criminal justice cases. His recent focus has been on developing computer systems in art therapy, including the C_CREATES (Computer Color Related Art Therapy Evaluation System), and an app for free drawings, mandalas, and kinetic family drawings.

Juliet L. King, MA, ATR-BC, LPC, is currently the director of the graduate art therapy program at Herron School of Art and Design in Indianapolis, Indiana, and has spent the last 16 years as a clinician, administrator, and professor. She researches on art therapy treatment in a neuroscience context, helping healthcare practitioners understand the value and importance of the profession. Putting theory to practice, she currently volunteers at the Richard L. Roudebush VA Medical Center, Indianapolis, Indiana.

Rachel Lev-Wiesel, PhD, is professor and chair of the Graduate School of Creative Arts Therapies and the Emili Sagol Creative Arts Therapies Research Center, both at the University of Haifa, in Haifa, Israel. Lev-Wiesel has published more than 125 scientific papers and chapters and eight books on topics such as trauma, posttraumatic growth, childhood sexual abuse, intervention techniques, and analysis of drawings for assessment and therapeutic purposes.

Myra F. Levick, PhD, ATR-BC, is an exhibiting artist and art psychotherapist. She founded Hahnemann University's graduate art therapy program in 1967 and graduated the first art therapists with an MS in art therapy. Until her retirement and move to Florida in 1986, she was professor and director of its Creative Arts in Therapy

Program. A founder and first president of the American Art Therapy Association, Levick is editor-in-chief emeritus of the journal *The Arts in Psychotherapy*. Levick has published a textbook, two books for parents and teachers defining art therapy and on the LECATA, and many journal articles and book chapters. She founded and directs the South Florida Art Psychotherapy Institute.

Debra Linesch, PhD, LMFT, ATR-BC, is currently professor and department chairperson of the Graduate Department of Marital and Family Therapy at Loyola Marymount University in Los Angeles, specializing in clinical art therapy. She has authored five books and many articles, and has helped her program and the field expand its thinking about research methodologies, contextualized cultural awareness, and community-based learning. She is committed to exploring and impacting the perceived boundaries of the field.

Sheila Lorenzo de la Peña, MS, is an art therapist at a forensic psychiatric hospital. She has served as an adjunct professor and internship supervisor. She has spent several years providing art therapy and dialectical behavior therapy to clients with severe mental illness. Her research interests include provider burnout and self-care, and the therapeutic use of mandalas. She has presented at national and regional meetings of the American Art Therapy Association and the American Music Therapy Association.

Vija B. Lusebrink, PhD, ATR, HLM, professor emerita, is the author of the book *Imagery and Visual Expression in Therapy* (Plenum Press, 1990), several book chapters, and many articles on art therapy, including on art therapy and brain functions, and also on imagery and sandtray therapy. Prior to her retirement, she was the director of the expressive therapies program at the University of Louisville, Kentucky.

Donald C. Mattson, PhD, ATR, LPC, is a practicing psychotherapist and active researcher. His current interests include constructing art therapy apps, computerizing art-based instruments, and digitizing art therapy documentation. He is a pioneer in the computerized assessment of art-based instruments (CAABI), and continues to explore ways to merge technology with art therapy.

Mary Ellen McAlevey, MA, LPC, ATR-BC, ATCS, ACS, is a graduate of Marywood College in Scranton, Pennsylvania. She has worked with people with severe mental illness for over 10 years. A past president of the New Jersey Art Therapy Association and recipient of its Honorary Life Member award, she is an adjunct faculty member at Caldwell University and Montclair State University, both in New Jersey. She is currently president-elect of the Art Therapy Credentials Board.

Einat Metzl, PhD, LMFT, ATR-BC, RYT, is an assistant professor of art therapy and marital family therapy at the Loyola Marymount University in Los Angeles, California. After working in psychiatric hospitals, residential facilities, schools, and elderly adult centers, she currently works predominantly with couples in private practice. Her topics of publication include resilience and creativity after natural disasters, art therapy research methodology, inter-generational transmission of trauma, and sexuality education for art therapists. Her current research interests explore the meeting places of art therapy, play, and cultural diversity.

Anne Mills, MA, ATR-BC, LPC, maintains a private practice in Washington, DC, and is director of the Diagnostic Drawing Series Archive. Her areas of specialization include supervision/consultation, hypnotherapy, and the treatment of survivors of severe early trauma, particularly those who are highly dissociative. She provides resiliency-focused treatment for adolescents and adults who have experienced difficult transitions such as illness, bereavement, and loss of culture (refugees, expatriates, international students, transnational workers). More details are available on her website, www.anne-mills.com.

Catherine Hyland Moon, ATR-BC, is a professor in the Art Therapy Department at the School of the Art Institute of Chicago; author of *Studio Art Therapy: Cultivating the Artist Identity in the Art Therapist* (Jessica Kingsley Publishers, 2001); and editor of *Materials & Media in Art Therapy: Critical Understandings of Diverse Artistic Vocabularies* (Routledge, 2010). She has practiced art therapy for over 30 years, and is currently involved in the collaborative development of community studios in Chicago and therapeutic art programs for children in East Africa.

Penny Orr, PhD, ATR-BC, ATCS, is a director of the master's degree program in counseling/art therapy program at Edinboro University, Pennsylvania. She served as an Art Therapy Credentials Board director from 2008 to 2014, and as its president from 2013 to 2014. Orr has presented, published articles, and written book chapters on digital media, film, and online education as it applies to the profession of art therapy.

Joan Phillips, PhD, ATR-BC, has been a practicing art therapist for 30 years, maintaining a private practice in Norman, Oklahoma, where she is also faculty at the University of Oklahoma. She is a visiting lecturer at New York University, Florida State University, and several other universities. Phillips has served on the boards of the American Art Therapy Association and the Art Therapy Credentials Board. She was a Fulbright Scholar in Ireland (2011), and is active in the Irish Association of Creative Arts Therapists.

Amanda Alders Pike, PhD, ATR-BC, has exhibited, published, and taught internationally on topics related to creativity in locations such as Finland, Mexico, and Chile. Amanda has served as president of the Florida Art Therapy Association, and currently works as a clinical art therapist. She is also founder of Art Therapy Consulting and Services, a group practice of art therapists. Pike welcomes collaboration, and can be contacted at amanda@arttherapyconsulting.com.

Jordan S. Potash, PhD, ATR-BC, is also a licensed creative arts therapist (LCAT) and registered expressive arts therapist (REAT). He is primarily interested in the applications of art and art therapy in community development and social change, with an emphasis on reducing stigma, confronting discrimination, and promoting cross-cultural relationships. He is co-editor of *Art Therapy in Asia: To the Bone or Wrapped in Silk* (Jessica Kingsley, 2012).

Dafna Regev, PhD, is the head of the art therapy track and a member in the Emili Sagol CAT Research Center in the Graduate School of Creative Art Therapies in the University of Haifa, Israel. She specializes in dyadic parent–child art therapy and working in private clinics.

Dina L. Ricco, PhD, ATR, LMHC, works as a clinical art therapist in Jacksonville, Florida. Her approach includes family systems, cognitive behavioral, and art therapy techniques. She has experience in a variety of clinical and instructional settings, including various agencies, correctional facilities, school systems, community colleges, and universities. Ricco conducted research on the use of the Gottman model with couples, and now specializes in marital/couple art therapy. She presents statewide and nationally on the use of art therapy to treat depression, anxiety, and relationship issues.

Jane Ferris Richardson, ATR-BC, is also a registered play therapist; a supervisor, mental health counselor, and core faculty member in art therapy at Lesley University in Massachusetts; and an exhibiting artist. Her work with expressive "languages" for children with autism has led to collaboration, nationally and internationally, in Africa, Asia, and Europe. She has published and presented her work on autism and art therapy; play therapy and autism; and the importance of multiple languages for expression.

Megan Robb, MA, ATR-BC, is an art therapist, educator, and researcher who has presented nationally and published on the intersections of culture in education, leadership, therapy, medical settings, and work/life balance. Her research is based on pedagogy and art therapy practice with children and adults in medical and mental hospitals, school settings, and private practice. Robb earned her MA in art therapy from the George Washington University in 2002. Currently, she is a professor of art therapy counseling at Southern Illinois University Edwardsville, in Illinois.

Judith A. Rubin, PhD, ATR-BC, HLM, former Art Lady on "Mister Rogers' Neighborhood," is also a psychologist and psychoanalyst. A past president and Honorary Life Member of the American Art Therapy Association, she has authored six books, made 10 films, and is on the faculty of the Psychiatry Department, University of Pittsburgh, and the Pittsburgh Psychoanalytic Center. She has presented widely, and is currently working on a film about Fred Rogers, and on the creation and dissemination of a Teaching Film Library.

María Cristina Ruiz, MA, teaches at Universidad del Valle, in Cali-Colombia; belongs to its research team on popular education; and coordinates the master's program on popular education and community development. She is also co-founder of the Colombian Association of Art Therapy. She holds a BA in transpersonal counseling psychology; an MA in art therapy concentration from Naropa University; and is a PhD candidate in arts education at the Simon Fraser University, in Canada. Her current dissertation work explores portrait as a genre and its connection with social and cultural identities.

Libby Schmanke, ATR-BC, is an artist whose first career included counseling and administration in a range of addiction treatment settings, from women's long-term residential to community outpatient to prison programs. She incorporated art activities into treatment. She has been on the faculty of the graduate art therapy program at Emporia State University, Kansas, since 2002, and a director of the Art Therapy Credentials Board since 2010. Specialties in her art therapy private practice include trauma, adolescents, and addictions.

Craig A. Siegel, MA, ATR-BC, is a graduate of the George Washington University. Siegel serves as the chairperson of the Clinical Art Therapy Department at Miami-Dade County Public Schools, where he has worked since 1995. He has also maintained a private practice in Boca Raton, Florida, since 1999. Siegel has served the profession in various capacities in the American Art Therapy Association, on both state and national levels.

Jessica Woolhiser Stallings, ATR-BC, LPC, joined the faculty of the Emporia State University, Kansas, in 2008, and was promoted to associate professor in 2014. Jessica served as lead clinician for an autism social skills project at the University of Nebraska Medical Center. She teaches courses in multiculturalism, research, ethics, and supervision. She also operates a private practice, specializing in working with children and adolescents with autism. She has served as the conference chair and is president-elect for the Kansas Art Therapy Association.

Patricia St John, EdD, ATR-BC, LCAT, professor and graduate art therapy programs director at the College of New Rochelle, New Rochelle, New York, since 1986, is a researcher and thesis mentor. For the American Art Therapy Association, she is past research committee chair; current education committee chair; Task Force for Education Standards Revision co-chair; and research roundtable convener. A published author, she reviews for *Art Therapy: Journal of the American Art Therapy Association*, *Arts in Psychotherapy*, and *Art for Life*.

Savneet Talwar, PhD, is an associate professor and chair of the graduate art therapy program at the School of the Art Institute of Chicago. Her current research examines feminist politics, critical theories of difference, social justice, and questions of resistance. Using an interdisciplinary approach, she is interested in community-based art practices; cultural trauma; performance art; and public cultures as they relate to art therapy theory, practice, and pedagogy.

Laurel Thompson, PhD, ATR-BC, DMT-BC, LCAT, is a faculty member for the Pratt Institute's Creative Arts Therapy Department, teaching classes that integrate theory and practice, and also serving as a thesis advisor since 1993. She has an extensive history of presentations; has served on various committees for the American Dance Therapy Association and American Art Therapy Association; and has been on the editorial boards of a range of journals addressing creative arts therapy. She also has a private practice, specializing in individuals with eating disorders and dissociative disorders.

Janis Timm-Bottos, PhD, ATR-BC, ATPQ, an Associate Professor in the Department of Creative Arts Therapies at the Concordia University in Montreal, Quebec. She initiated six community art studios, including community-university's La Ruche d'Art and Studio d'Art St Sulpice. Her research team is involved in investigating the qualities of healing spaces on learning, and is launching the national art hive initiative, which promotes small and sustainable art hubs for mutual recovery of creativity and health in every community across Canada. More details are available at www.arthives.org.

Terry Towne, ATR-BC, has provided art therapy services in a variety of treatment settings; has served as an assistant professor and clinical coordinator of the graduate art therapy program at Albertus Magnus College in New Haven, Connecticut; and is the founder of *Drawing on Our Strengths*®, an art therapy consulting firm. She is a frequent presenter on various topics related to the profession and practice of art therapy.

Carolyn Brown Treadon, PhD, ATR-BC, ATCS, is an adjunct professor at Florida State University. Carolyn provided art therapy in alternative schools and outpatient settings before becoming clinical supervisor of a community-based mental health clinic. She supervises art therapy interns and interns from other disciplines. She has published and presented on using art museums in the therapeutic process, on the use of constructivist models for teaching, and on using the art therapy process to alter perceptions and attitudes toward individuals with disabilities. She is currently a board member for the Art Therapy Credentials Board.

Ana Laura Treviño, MA, holds a bachelor's degree in psychology and a master's degree in psychoanalysis and family therapy. She has provided art therapy services for different populations—street kids, left-behind families, adolescent pregnant woman, and domestic violence couples—and has had a private practice for 23 years. Founder of the Instituto Mexicano de Psicoterapia de Arte, she was a visiting professor at the Loyola Marymount University in Los Angeles, California; Mexican director of the Loyola Marymount University summer program; and part-time faculty at Universidad Iberoamericana in Mexico City.

Randy M. Vick, MS, ATR-BC, LCPC, is an associate professor in the art therapy department at the School of the Art Institute of Chicago, where he teaches history, theory, and research courses. With over 30 years in the profession, he has worked in a variety of inpatient and community settings. In his current research, writing, and presentations, he connects the areas of art therapy, outsider art, and studios for artists with disabilities.

Harriet Wadeson, PhD, LCSW, ATR-BC, HLM, worked as a clinician/researcher in art therapy at the National Institutes of Health; directed the art therapy graduate program at the University of Houston, the University of Illinois, and its Annual Summer Institute; directed the art therapy certificate program at the Northwestern University in Illinois; and maintained a private practice throughout her career. She has published eight books on art therapy, 70 papers, and numerous chapters in related texts. She is an international guest speaker, having given numerous keynote speeches.

Her honors include the American Art Therapy Association's HLM and its First Prize for Research; first prize for art from the Smithsonian Institute; the Benjamin Rush Award from the American Psychiatric Association; a Resolution of Commendation from the Illinois State Legislature; and a Distinguished Teaching Award from the Northwestern University in Illinois.

Jill Westwood, PhD, is a registered art psychotherapist in Great Britain and Australia. She is the programme convener of the MA programme in art psychotherapy at Goldsmiths, University of London, and an adjunct fellow at the School of Social Sciences and Psychology at the University of Western Sydney, Australia, where she completed her PhD on art therapy education in Australia. Her interests include art therapy and contemporary art, art therapy in organizations, and art therapy education.

Laurie Wilson, PhD, ATR-BC, HLM, is a practicing New York City psychoanalyst, art historian, author, and art therapist. She is also a clinical associate professor of psychiatry at the New York University Medical Center; a faculty member of the Psychoanalytic Institute, affiliated with New York University Medical Center; and Professor Emerita at the New York University, where she directed the graduate art therapy program for 23 years. She was awarded American Art Therapy Association's HLM in 2008. Her book *Alberto Giacometti: Myth, Magic and the Man* was published by Yale University Press in 2003, and her biography of Louise Nevelson is scheduled to be published by Monacelli Press in 2015.

Stephanie Wise, ATR-BC, LCAT, is a licensed creative arts therapist, practicing in New York. She received her master's degree in art therapy from New York University, and her certificate in international trauma studies from the International University Center for Human Rights and the International Trauma Studies Program at New York University. She is currently a clinical assistant professor at the Marywood University in Scranton, Pennsylvania, and a former member of the Art Therapy Credentials Board.

Linney Wix, PhD, ATR-BC, is a professor at the University of New Mexico. Her teaching and research in art therapy and art education are steeped in archetypal psychological thought. She is the author of *Through a Narrow Window: Friedl Dicker-Brandeis and Her Terezín Students* (University of New Mexico Press, 2010), and her recent Fulbright-funded research concerns art and memory in the context of children's art classes in the Terezín concentration camp near Prague.

John Wong, CM, is the head, associate professor, and senior consultant psychiatrist for the Department of Psychological Medicine, Yong Loo Lin School of Medicine, National University of Singapore, and the National University Hospital in Singapore, respectively.

Acknowledgments

We would like to thank the visionaries at Wiley Blackwell for their foresight in making this art therapy handbook possible. Among all the psychological topics identified for handbooks developed by this publisher, art therapy could have easily been overlooked. Yet, Wiley Blackwell decided that our profession deserved a comprehensive volume. We were pleased and grateful when we were asked to edit the handbook, and we are honored to be included among the cadre of the editors of the Wiley Blackwell psychology handbook series. The support and flexibility that Wiley Blackwell and its editors offered during the development of this multiyear project is most appreciated.

We are also indebted to Florida State University for supporting us through the time it took us to complete this project. The Department of Art Education and the Art Therapy Program lent its support by assigning four art therapy graduate assistants to help with this undertaking: Anna Campbell (Flowers), Frances Morris, Jaimie Burkewitz, and Amber "Jamie" Nelson. These students offered their organizational, technological, and creative skills to help with this massive undertaking. If there is one thing that demonstrates the length of time it took to complete this program, it is the number of graduate assistants needed over the years. At the beginning of each new academic year, a new assistant was assigned to this project, with the previous one passing on information about the responsibilities and expertise required to assist us in this effort. Thank you all!

The book would be nothing without the 88 authors who agreed to work with us on this project, and interacting with each writer was an exciting learning experience. We learned so much not only from their writings, but also from dialoguing about the topics and ideas that each person wanted to explore in his or her chapter.

We are indebted to each other as partners who kept each other going. At the time of this writing, we have worked together in one capacity or another for almost 20 years. While stressful and challenging at times, this project reinforced the respect, admiration, and friendship that we have for each other—we could not have done it without the other.

Finally, support from our spouses and family members was not only necessary but of utmost importance during the final days of the project.

An Introduction

David E. Gussak and Marcia L. Rosal

The American Art Therapy Association defined *art therapy* as:

> … a mental health profession that uses the creative process of art making to improve and enhance the physical, mental and emotional well-being of individuals of all ages. It is based on the belief that the creative process involved in artistic self-expression helps people to resolve conflicts and problems, develop interpersonal skills, manage behavior, reduce stress, increase self-esteem and self-awareness, and achieve insight (http://www.americanarttherapyassociation.org)

A profession that is now complicated in breadth, depth, and scope, art therapy was originally practiced within two distinct theoretical orientations: art as therapy, focusing on the process of art making; and art psychotherapy, focusing on the finished created product and relying on the triangulated relationship between therapist, artist, and the artwork. Contemporary art therapy flows along a continuum of numerous approaches and has become so much more nuanced than the original perspectives. No longer are there only two ways to think about our work.

Over the past 50 years, many forces drove the profession forward. First, art therapists interacted with related specialists within the numerous clinical, educational, medical, and other organizational systems where they worked. The cross-pollination of ideas that occurred when working with other professionals sparked new ways of thinking about the use of art therapy. The manner in which art therapy is now practiced is dependent upon the population, the setting, and the clinician's theoretical orientation. Educational programs for art therapists proliferated. Research in the field developed, and today there is evidence that several approaches have merit. Finally, the expansion of art therapy across the globe increased our understanding of practicing art therapy with cultural and societal sensitivity.

Because of the diversity and intricacy of the practice of art therapy, there are really very few texts—if any—that have comprehensively captured all aspects of the field. While it is true that there is a great deal of literature about art therapy already on the market, most texts seem to fall into two distinct categories—breadth *or* depth.

The Wiley Handbook of Art Therapy, First Edition. Edited by David E. Gussak and Marcia L. Rosal.
© 2016 John Wiley & Sons, Ltd. Published 2016 by John Wiley & Sons, Ltd.

Early in the development of the profession, a number of books were published that provided an overview of the field, either as a historical account or an extensive examination of the various theoretical perspectives. Analyses of the benefits of art therapy were also published. Other books focused on specific populations or diagnostic groups. Some examined the numerous philosophical, theoretical, or pragmatic issues of the field.

A number of books relied on edited chapters to explore the diverse perspectives in the profession. This literature is peppered with case vignettes that illustrated a particular perspective. There are other books that explored the value of art-based assessments and art therapy research; some focused on a particular type of research method or assessment procedure. There are texts that concentrated on a particular artistic medium and illustrated the various therapeutic benefits of that material on diverse populations. All of these books were, remain, and will continue to be valuable.

When we were asked by Wiley-Blackwell to develop an extensive handbook on art therapy, and were given few limitations, we knew this was a rare opportunity to capture a contemporary, holistic picture of our profession. We proposed an ambitious project that would be a compendium of the historic, current, and innovative clinical, theoretical, and research approaches in the field. We wanted to create a source book for students, novice therapists, and seasoned professionals. Creating a manuscript that has breadth *and* depth was our aim.

As a result, this volume, titled *The Wiley Handbook of Art Therapy*, is comprised of nine sections, each featuring an important aspect of the field to provide breadth. To provide depth, each section has 7–12 chapters, each written by an expert in his or her particular area. Although we were cognizant of the scope of the handbook, even we were surprised when the project expanded to include 84 chapters and the writings of 90 authors. Nonetheless, we realize that *despite* the scope of this book, no single volume will ever come close to being totally inclusive of the field.

As we were organizing subject areas for the book, fresh ideas emerged. We spoke to potential authors who suggested innovative topics. From developing the outline to submitting completed chapters, the book took 4 years to complete; and this does not include the time it took the publisher to print and disseminate the text. During this time, the profession continued to evolve and other issues and perspectives emerged. Social media platforms allowed for the immediate dissemination of new ideas. It was impossible for us to cover all emerging perspectives in this one project.

What we accomplished is a single resource with an unprecedented combination of depth and breadth. The format of this text is aligned with the vision of the publisher's online psychology series of handbooks—offering a comprehensive book available in both hard and electronic copy formats; yet, each chapter or section is available for readers who only need access to certain aspects of the text.

The Sections

As indicated, this book is comprised of nine distinct sections. As the book project progressed, these sections coalesced into distinct and overarching themes: the first two sections provide the building blocks on which the field is built (theory and media); the next three sections encompass the scope of the art therapists' practice—clients with whom art therapists provide treatment and the settings where services are rendered; the next two sections present chapters on assessment and evaluation as well as the realm of research inquiry; and the final two sections demonstrate just how far our field has expanded, and address issues that may emerge as the profession continues to develop (global and contemporary issues). Each section has its own introduction, which provides details of the dedicated chapters contained within.

Section I: Historical and Theoretical Frameworks

The 12 chapters that form this section focus on the field's scaffolding—its history and the various theories that inform the art therapists' practice.

Section II: Understanding Art Media in Therapy

Seven chapters provide theoretical and application overviews of art media and other tools that make us distinct from other therapeutic professions.

Section III: Developmental Spectrum and Therapeutic Considerations

The nine chapters that make up this section address art therapy along the developmental continuum—from early childhood to death—and offer suggestions for various therapeutic approaches to address expected life changes.

Section IV: Art Therapy with Various Populations

Since the development of the field, the types of clients with whom art therapists work has expanded. The wisdom of the art therapist now includes practice with a wide-array of populations. Each of these 12 chapters addresses approaches to art therapy with a particular population.

Section V: Practicing Art Therapy in Interdisciplinary Settings

Originally art therapists found limited settings in which to work. This has changed considerably over the decades. Each of these seven chapters focuses on a particular setting in which art therapists now practice.

Section VI: Art Therapy Assessments

The literature on art-based assessments, what Stephanie Brooks called the "tools of the trade," is abundant. Yet, a comprehensive text would not be complete without addressing this aspect of art therapy. The 10 chapters in this section not only examine a particular assessment tool, but several authors present arguments for developing and using art therapy assessments.

Section VII: Research Models in Art Therapy

The field has come a long way from the narrative case studies that informed our field early in its history. The seven chapters in this section provide a number of art therapy research designs that include qualitative, quantitative, and mixed-method models.

Section VIII: Art Therapy Around the World

The field continues to expand and has reached most corners of the globe. These 11 chapters are only a small sample of the countries where art therapy is now practiced.

Section IX: Current and Contemporary Issues in Art Therapy

As the profession expands, art therapists face a number of growing pains—from pragmatic issues to questions of identity—that may impact the future of our field. These final nine chapters explore the concerns of the authors, and some address controversies present in our profession.

Through the wealth of knowledge, wisdom, experiences, and perspectives presented in this *Handbook*, the reader is meant to be exposed to the countless applications and uses of art therapy and to gain an appreciation for the ever-expanding development of the field. The 90 authors who were chosen for this project are emerging or established experts in their respective specializations. These exemplary authors have dispensed unique and important knowledge relevant to their fields. Perhaps the ideas presented herein will not only provide a comprehensive understanding of art therapy, but also spark a thoughtful debate on the contemporary issues that face our profession.

Part I
Historical and Theoretical Frameworks

Introduction

Since the inception of the profession, art therapists have debated the basic tenets of how art therapy works and pondered on the therapeutic value of art processes. As stated in the introduction of this handbook, two perspectives formed the basis of art therapy in the mid-twentieth century. Through the decades, other theoretical orientations have advanced the knowledge base of the profession. Deeper analysis and broader experiences have even led to revisions of the two original viewpoints. The steady progression from our historical roots to the numerous current theoretical models practiced today reveals professionals who value intellectual curiosity and who rarely settle for easy answers. The field simultaneously fragments and becomes stronger through examinations of these various theoretical foci. This section presents a sample of the historical and theoretical frameworks upon which our profession has been built.

A historical overview is essential for a reader to put the theories examined in this section in context. M. Junge provides a foundation for examining art therapy theory through her analysis of the history of art therapy. Wilson also finds history to be vital to the practice of art therapy, but on a micro level. In her chapter titled *Psychoanalytic Study of Artists and Their Art: Its Relevance for Art Therapists*, Wilson posits that uncovering a client's personal history informs her work. Through what she terms *psychobiography*, psychoanalytic understanding of a person and his or her art is vital to the practice of art therapy.

Rubin's chapter, *Psychoanalytic Art Therapy*, explores the foundational psychodynamic perspective and its incarnations as the field advanced through the twentieth and into the twenty-first century. In *Archetypal Art Therapy*, Abbenante and Wix re-introduce archetypal thinkers Hillman, Watkins, and McConeghy, and explore how archetypes can be used in art therapy. These authors rely on the structure and content of the image to inform practice. Archetypal practice embodies the notion that "… the image is core to archetypal art therapy's commitment to art's primacy in art therapy."

Ciornai's chapter, *Gestalt Art Therapy: A Path to Consciousness Expansion*, provides the philosophical, theoretical, and methodological foundation of the Gestalt model.

The Wiley Handbook of Art Therapy, First Edition. Edited by David E. Gussak and Marcia L. Rosal.
© 2016 John Wiley & Sons, Ltd. Published 2016 by John Wiley & Sons, Ltd.

Drawing upon authors such as Arnheim, Rhyne, and Gombrich, Ciornai focuses on the primary goal of Gestalt work: "consciousness expansion through the use of creative and artistic resources."

Lusebrink's chapter, *Expressive Therapies Continuum*, outlines an interactionist model of art therapy that informs the therapist's understanding of the interactions between the artist, the art medium and its process, and the product. Lusebrink revisits this relationship and re-examines the ETC model in this chapter.

Next, Rosal explores cognitive behavioral theoretical perspectives through her chapter *Cognitive Behavioral Art Therapy Revisited*. She discusses early cognitive behavioral art therapy (CBAT) thinkers and examines how this theory is used in practice today. King provides information about how brain science is impacting the practice of art therapy in her chapter titled *Art Therapy: A Brain-based Profession*. In the chapter, King argues:

> The fields of art therapy and neuroscience are inextricably linked—akin to the conscious-ness and unconsciousness, mind and body, limbic system and cerebral cortex. Applying art therapy theory, treatment, and research within a neuroscience framework is necessary, and as expansive and limitless as the mind itself.

In *Positive Art Therapy*, Isis argues that art and art therapy, when used correctly, can contribute to life experiences and to well-being through mindfulness and art-making. In his chapter *Essence, Art, and Therapy: A Transpersonal View*, Franklin reminds the reader that "transpersonal" refers to "moving through or beyond the personal." His chapter explores the intersection where spirituality, creativity, and psychology meet to help facilitate a person's well-being.

The last two chapters espouse diverse practices and perspectives to inform the practitioner. Moon argues in her contribution, *Open Studio Approach to Art Therapy*, that when allowing free and open expression in a studio environment, the focus is on health rather than pathology, is less hierarchical, and more dynamic. Moon emphasizes both the art-making process *and* the product.

Lastly, in the chapter titled *An Eclectic Approach to Art Therapy—Revisited*, Wadeson revisits the chapter she wrote for Rubin's 2001 volume *Approaches to Art Therapy*. Wadeson expands on her philosophy that any number of theories can be applied by an effective clinician. She encourages clinicians to encompass and to be open to all theoretical perspectives. She concentrates on how the eclectic approach contributes to contemporary issues such as trauma-based treatment, community mental health, and working from a multicultural perspective.

Together, these chapters form a foundation, a scaffold upon which all the following sections are built. Art therapists are guided by these important theories. The practice of art therapy would not be as robust without these rich and varied perspectives.

1

History of Art Therapy

Maxine Borowsky Junge

Art therapy is an interdisciplinary mix of visual arts and psychology. In the United States, it dates from the 1940s when Margaret Naumburg (called by many the "mother of art therapy") began publishing clinical cases and, in 1943, gave a name to the new field by calling her work "dynamically oriented art therapy." The term "art therapy" was used in England as far back as the 1930s (Waller, 1991, 1998), and artist Adrian Hill formally coined it in 1942—about the same time as Naumburg in America. Such use of art is not new.

Since prehistoric times, the arts have played a crucial role in human history, development, culture, and consciousness. Such an understanding goes as far back as cave paintings, when people used imagery to express and master the world. Therapeutic rituals using the visual arts can be found in ancient cultures from hundreds of years ago, such as Navajo sand paintings and African sculpture. These ideas were the precursors of contemporary understanding of art therapy.

Intellectual and sociological developments of the 1940s later provided ground for this new profession. Evolving ideas about psychology, recognition of the unconscious, and the growing acknowledgement of art as an expression of a person's inner mind gave rise to important notions that led directly to art therapy as an innovative and original mental health discipline. This chapter will provide a brief overview of the evolution of the field.

Ancestors and Influences

Art therapy did not emerge from a vacuum. There were numerous predecessors and cultural influences that eventually lead to the emergent profession we now call art therapy. Several of the influences are discussed here.

Outsider artists and the art of psychiatric patients

"Outsider art" is the term for self-taught artists and the art of the insane. Early on, European psychiatrists such as Lombroso, Tardiu, and Simon were interested in the art of the insane because of its *aesthetic value* (MacGregor, 1989).

The Wiley Handbook of Art Therapy, First Edition. Edited by David E. Gussak and Marcia L. Rosal.
© 2016 John Wiley & Sons, Ltd. Published 2016 by John Wiley & Sons, Ltd.

Few considered that art might contain diagnostic clues or treatment potential. A Heidelberg art historian and psychiatrist, Hans Prinzhorn, collected more than 5,000 pieces of artwork of psychiatric patients and published a book on his collection in 1922, titled *Artistry of the Mentally Ill.* (His work was published in the United States in 1974.) Although Prinzhorn's extensive collection of art of the insane influenced the art therapy community, he was primarily interested in the artwork as compelling and expressive, but not necessarily as potential indicators for diagnosis or treatment.

In the early part of the twentieth century, European psychiatrists Kraepelin, Jaspers, and Aschaffenburg came to believe that the art of institutionalized patients might offer clues to psychiatric and diagnostic knowledge. Later, the Swiss psychiatrist Sechehaye (1951) and the Australian psychiatrist Ainslie Meares (1958) understood the importance of personal symbols by institutionalized and regressed patients.

The American psychologist Tarmo Pasto, a direct precursor of the art therapy movement, argued that artists "had stopped providing the 'one great means of experiencing emotion', but in children's art and the art of the insane, inner meaning could be expressed" (Junge, 2010). In the 1960s, Pasto found the institutionalized Martin Ramirez at De Witt State Hospital in Auburn, California, saved his artwork, (which at the hospital was typically confiscated and burned), gave Ramirez art materials, and organized his first exhibit.

Freud and Jung

Sigmund Freud and Carl Gustav Jung are considered by many to be art therapy's primary ancestors. Theories and methods of psychoanalysis were the bedrock from which the new field grew. Freud's powerful description of an active unconscious and his personality theory pervading intellectual thought in the twentieth century provided a useful jump-start for art therapists. His fascination with life histories of artists as sources of aesthetic creativity, his recognition of dream imagery as important messages from the unconscious, and even his long-discredited ideas of the connection between creativity and madness served to link psychological and psychoanalytical processes to visual art. However, while Freud prominently recognized the importance of dream imagery, he never asked his patients to draw their dreams. Jung did.

Jung's ideas have greatly influenced art therapy as he believed the image itself was central, rather than a clue or symbol to be deciphered: "To paint what we see before us is a different art from painting what we see within" (1954, p. 253). Jung's concept of the "collective unconscious" as a universal, cross-culturally shared symbolic language is often cherished by art therapists; this includes the *mandala,* a term that simply means "magic circle" in Sanskrit. This symbol has been adopted by some art therapists as a *structure* to contain personality chaos or disintegration.

Although art therapy has proven adaptable over the years to a wide variety of differing psychological theories (including those which are behaviorally-based), there are some today who still primarily associate it with psychodynamic theory and psychoanalytic techniques. However, art therapy's contemporary applications are considerably broader.

Psychological tests

Projective psychological tests—such as the Rorschach Inkblot Test, Thematic Apperception Test (TAT), Draw-a-Man, Draw-a-Person (DAP) and House-Tree- Person (HTP)—developed in the first half of the twentieth century, were important influences on the evolution of art therapy as a diagnostic tool. With a single image as a stimulus, psychological tests indicated that imagery could be a clinical tool to reveal human personality. Unlike the single image, however, art therapists have since learned to use *a sequence of drawings*, rather than just a single drawing, to provide indications of inner psychic processes.

Influences from England

Art therapy in Great Britain followed a different evolutionary path. The term "art therapy" was first used there as early as the 1930s (Waller, 1991, 1998). After World War II, Adrian Hill, a professional artist, recuperating from tuberculosis in a sanatorium, began to use his paintings as therapy for himself, and introduced art to other patients. Hill has been credited with originating the term "art therapy." In 1946, artist Edward Adamson was hired to research the effects of lobotomy on patients in a psychiatric hospital. "His research was the first 'rigorous attempt in British psychiatry to ascertain the usefulness of art as therapy'" (Junge, 2010, p. 10). In the United Kingdom, art therapy has primarily found its roots in the theories of Carl Jung. In 1942, Gilbert and Irene Champernowne, who both followed the Jungian perspective, founded Withymead House in Devon, the first therapeutic center dedicated to art therapy. Since then, art therapy is included in the National Health Service.

Education and the arts

Art has also found its way into the educational arena. The scientific study of childhood began in the late nineteenth century, out of which grew the idea that education should consider "the whole child." Called "Progressive Education" (Dewey, 1958), this philosophy advocates *learning through doing*. New teaching methods were developed based on a respect for the child's creativity, and included an emphasis on the arts.

Pioneers of modern art education such as Franz Cizek, Viktor Lowenfeld, and Florence Cane were major influences in the development of art therapy. Cizek was the first to study spontaneous art in children. He recognized that child art revealed the inner workings of the mind and had about it aesthetic and creative properties. Lowenfeld studied analysis in Vienna with Cizek, and, in 1947, in the United States, published his influential book in art education. Conceptualizing an artistic developmental process of six stages, Lowenfeld argued that a child's intellectual development was integrally correlated to creative development. Cane was the older sister of Margaret Naumburg. An artist and art educator, she taught at the Walden School (originally called the Children's School) in New York City, founded and directed by Margaret. Cane developed methods to free children's creativity. Along with drawing and painting, they included movement and sound.

International Society for Psychopathology of Expression and the
American Society of Psychopathology of Expression

Seldom recognized in art therapy history, the societies were an important driving force in the establishment of the first and the most important professional organization for art therapists, the American Art Therapy Association. The International Society for Psychopathology of Expression was established by psychiatrist Irene Jakab in 1959 and the American Society of Psychopathology of Expression incorporated in 1964. Many art therapists were members. They attended conferences, presented papers, and published their work in the volumes edited by Jakab. Importantly, the societies became meeting places for art therapists who eventually decided to form their own organizations, which propelled art therapy forward as a separate profession.

Art Therapy Profession Evolves as a Separate
Mental Health Discipline

Within the flourishing cultural and intellectual milieu of psychoanalysis, many artists and art educators studied analytic theory and undertook personal analyses. Eventually, the synergy between art and psychology became known as "art therapy." Milestones in the evolution of the field in America include: (1) artist's connections with psychiatric clinicians resulting in their employment in mental health institutions; (2) two theories for the new profession; (3) the establishment of the first art therapy journal; and (4) the founding of the professional organization, the American Art Therapy Association, which brought art therapists together to share knowledge and to develop standards of education and practice.

Mentors and supporters of art therapy and art therapists
in the American psychiatric community

Intrigued with the juxtaposition of art and psychiatry, many well-respected mental health professionals recognized the talents of artists and art therapists and the potential of art therapy as an exciting new tool for the treatment of mental dysfunction. They found uncredentialed artists and set them to work in mental health institutions. They trained them in psychiatry and often encouraged further formal education.[1] In 1941, Nolan D. C. Lewis hired Margaret Naumburg at the New York State Psychiatric Institute. Beginning in the early 1960s, university departments of psychiatry and psychiatric institutes provided classes showcasing the intersection of art and psychiatry. Sometimes taught by art therapists, these courses were precursors of art therapy education and functioned to further awareness and value of the evolving field. Roger White began an art therapy program in 1959 at the University of Louisville, which closed after graduating two students. In Philadelphia, two psychiatrists, Morris J. Goldman and Paul Fink, were instrumental in beginning the first art therapy master's program in the country, at Hahnemann Medical College (now Drexel University), with art therapist Myra Levick as director.

Early art therapy clinicians

Until contemporary times, the art therapy profession has largely been one of clinicians. Art therapy was an idea whose time had come. Many art therapists working alone in different places thought they had invented the practice themselves. The following information is from my book, *A History of Art Therapy in the United States* (Junge, 1994).

Midwestern America

The origins of the field of art therapy in the United States are usually thought of as an East Coast phenomenon. However, as early as the 1930s and 1940s, art therapy was beginning to have a presence on the plains of Kansas at the Menninger Foundation. Established in the 1920s in Topeka, the Menninger Clinic was a psychoanalytically based milieu therapy facility. At the time, it was widely considered that the only option for a severely disturbed mental patient was long-term custodial care in an asylum. The Menningers believed that a person with mental problems could be treated and helped, a radical notion at the time. Karl Menninger was a psychiatrist who loved art. His interest inspired Menninger staff members to include the arts in therapeutic treatment. From the start, Menninger patients were treated with psychoanalytically based psychotherapy and activity therapies including art. In 1937, an article was published by two Menninger staff members, Jeanette Lyle and Ruth Faison Shaw (Friedman, 1990). It concerned children's finger paintings and drawings revealing and externalizing the child's inner experience and is considered an early description of art therapy. The authors proposed that, combined with the child's history, the drawings could be used to interpret intrapsychic processes.

In 1946, Mary Huntoon, artist and printmaker who worked at Winter General Hospital, connected with the Menninger Clinic, and later with the Menninger Foundation. First, she was an "art instructor"; in 1949, she was called a "therapist"; and in 1956 a "manual arts therapist." She was never a psychotherapist, but functioned as a *recreational* therapist. Early on, Huntoon named what she did "dynamically oriented art therapy" or "following the patient's dynamics." In this, she may have preceded Margaret Naumburg in her definition.

Don Jones, a Conscientious Objector during World War II, was assigned to Marlboro State Hospital in New Jersey, where he became interested in and collected patient artwork. After the war, he came to Rossville, Kansas, as an artist/pastor. He taught art in Topeka, and many Menninger staff members were his students. Through this connection, he met Karl Menninger. He began employment at the Menninger Clinic in 1951, developing an expressive arts program that would employ and train many art therapists, Robert Ault among them. At first an *activities therapy*, art therapy eventually became a *psychotherapy* option for patients at the Menninger Clinic.

In 1959, Pedro Corrons, a Spanish psychiatrist interested in art and music, visited Mary Huntoon at The Menninger Clinic and then established an art psychotherapy unit at the Columbus State Hospital in Ohio. This was the first state-supported art psychotherapy program. With Bernard Stone, by 1967–1968, there were 12 art psychotherapy programs in Ohio.

Eastern art therapy clinicians

In the Eastern United States, Naumburg's groundbreaking work at the New York State Psychiatric Institute was a significant influence, and in 1940, perhaps the single most important occurrence in the early history of art therapy occurred when she defined art therapy as a distinct profession. Although her first art therapy book was published in 1947, it was not until 1960 that Naumburg's description of her theory was published in *Dynamically Oriented Art Therapy*. She was 84 years old. In 1970, Naumburg was the first to receive the highest award in art therapy, the Honorary Life Member (HLM) from the American Art Therapy Association.

In the 1950s, art therapists Ulman, Kramer, Naumburg, and others presented their work to psychiatric groups and institutions. From 1964 on, Judith Rubin consulted in New York with Naumburg and Kramer. Having been an art teacher and having worked with schizophrenic children, she wanted to receive training to become a "real" art therapist.

The National Institutes of Health (NIH) in Bethesda, Maryland, outside of Washington, DC, an agency of the United States Department of Health, is a leading medical research center. In 1958, Hanna Yaxa Kwiatkowska was hired as a researcher at the NIH. There, she "accidentally" invented family art therapy and developed a six-step procedure for evaluating families. Harriet Wadeson came to NIH in 1961 and trained with Kwiatkowska. Before that, in 1949, her art therapy career began when she worked at St. Elizabeth's Hospital, a psychiatric facility in Washington, DC.

The driving force behind the founding of the American Art Therapy Association was Myra Levick, its first president, who began work as an art therapy clinician in 1963 at the Albert Einstein Medical Center in Philadelphia.

Western art therapy clinicians

In 1964, Helen Landgarten taught art to geriatrics in a community center in Los Angeles, California, and became an art therapist in a psychiatric inpatient unit at USC/County General Hospital. In 1968, she came to Mt. Sinai Hospital (later Cedars/Sinai Hospital) in the Child and Family Division, Department of Psychiatry. Here, Landgarten trained art therapists as *primary therapists* knowledgeable enough to carry full case responsibility. Her art therapy master's program, established at Immaculate Heart College, reflected this philosophy and was called "Clinical Art Therapy."

Janie Rhyne was a Gestalt art therapist living in San Francisco. The Human Potential Movement of the 1960s, of which Rhyne was a part, eschewed diagnosis and the medical model in favor of a humanistic psychology focus aiming to aid an individual's personal growth.

The first art therapy journal

The first art therapy journal was established by Elinor Ulman in 1961. Called the *Bulletin of Art Therapy*, Ulman's journal gave art therapists a forum in which to communicate and debate their ideas. Before the publication of the journal, art therapists had worked alone, often making it up as they went along. Perhaps most important, the *Bulletin* offered art therapists a way to find out about each other. In 1963, Ulman conducted a survey of art therapists in the United States and Canada and found 30. In 1970, the *Bulletin* changed its name to the *American Journal of Art Therapy*. It existed for 41 years until 2002 when it ceased publication. Ulman's journal was a crucial milestone in driving the rapidly evolving field toward becoming a professional organization.

Art therapy theorists: Margaret Naumburg and Edith Kramer

Despite acknowledgment that art therapy can be effectively intertwined with almost any contemporary theory (cf. Rubin's *Approaches to Art Therapy*, 1987), there are two major theories in the field—both deriving from Freudian psychoanalytic thought and methods. On one side of the art therapy theoretical spectrum, stemming from Margaret Naumburg's ideas, are art psychotherapists, employing art *mostly as a method of non-verbal imagistic communication or "symbolic speech."* On the other side of the spectrum are the art therapists, originating from Edith Kramer's notions— psychologically informed and close to art educators who believe that it is *the creative process itself that is healing*.

In 1940, Naumburg was the first to define art therapy as a separate mental health discipline and as a different form of psychotherapy. She lived in the lively intellectual zeitgeist of New York City, underwent both Jungian and Freudian analysis, and studied with the educational visionaries of the time such as Maria Montessori and John Dewey. Naumburg went to work for the psychiatrist Nolan D. C. Lewis at the New York State Psychiatric Institute and published her first art therapy book in 1947, titled *Studies of the "Free" Expression of Behavior Problem Children as a Means of Diagnosis and Therapy*.

Edith Kramer, a painter, fled Hitler's Germany for New York City in 1938. With Friedl Dicker, Kramer had conducted art classes in Prague for refugee children and recognized that art could alleviate trauma. Her book, *Art Therapy in a Children's Community*, was published in 1958. In it, she described a second major theory for art therapy, focusing on the importance of how the creative process and product is healing. Similar to Naumburg, Kramer's theory is based on Freudian ideas. She delineates Freud's defense mechanism of "sublimation" as key to art therapy. She postulates that inappropriate id and aggressive impulses can be sublimated into socially acceptable behaviors through creative work, and that the "completeness" of the art product is indicative of successful sublimation. Unlike Naumburg, Kramer argues that art therapists are not psychotherapists, and should not aim to be. Her work relies very little, if any, on *talking*, whereas Naumburg, through verbal inquiry, intends to further the patient's conscious exploration of the unconscious.

Formation of the American Art Therapy Association

Founding of the American Art Therapy Association was the most important step in the establishment of a separate identity for art therapy. With its formation, art therapy became a distinct and significant field of trained practitioners with special expertise.

In 1966, Naumburg's book *Dynamically Oriented Art Therapy* laid out the theoretical constructs of art therapy. Although discussed earlier in her other books and presentations, this was the first formal publication of art therapy theory, and it was a major influence in the formation of art therapy as a separate mental health discipline. Kramer's theoretical ideas were first published in 1958.

The British Art Therapy Association was formed in 1964. In the United States, against the background of the turbulent 1960s and with the coalescing force of Ulman's *Bulletin of Art Therapy* and Naumburg's theoretical foundation, art therapists wanted to form their own professional society and focus not only on pathology in art but on diagnosis and treatment.

In 1968, art therapists met in Boston at the American Psychiatric Association to discuss forming a separate organization. Myra Levick, director of the art therapy master's program at Hahnemann Hospital in Philadelphia, was the driving force and energy for founding the new organization, and was its first president.

In late 1968, along with Paul Fink, Levick convened an organizational meeting. All the art therapists they could find were invited, and 50 attended. It was clear from the start that many definitions of art therapy would be included in the new organization, but the hybrid nature of the new field was evident as some feared that an association would define art therapy as *art psychotherapy*. From this split began the great argument—with noisy proponents on both sides—which would dominate the field for decades: *art psychotherapy versus art as therapy*.

On June 27, 1969, in Louisville, Kentucky, the American Art Therapy Association was voted into being. Only art therapists could be voting members. The first conference was held in September 1970, and 100 people attended. The association established a system of standards for art therapists and began awarding the "A.T.R." (Art Therapist Registered) for those who met the standards.[2] Later, the ability of art therapists to attain state licensing for employment became a central focus. However, the small numbers of art therapists make licensing a difficult proposition in state's political climate, and art therapy has sometimes found itself aligning with other mental health disciplines, bringing to fore the perpetual challenge of professional identity.

The immense importance of the American Art Therapy Association to the evolution of the field is obvious. Providing an arena where art therapists could come together to debate the major issues of the new field, it had a tremendous influence on the evolving profession, and, without it, arguably, there would not have been an art therapy profession at all. For a long time, the American Art Therapy Association *was* art therapy. From the early days when Ulman's survey found 30 art therapists in the United States and Canada, and 100 people attended the first conference, there are now about 4,000 members in the American Art Therapy Association.

Art therapy master's training programs

Soon after the founding of the American Art Therapy Association, and sometimes even before, many art therapy pioneers, mostly self-taught, founded art therapy education and training programs across the country. These programs tended to bear the philosophical and theoretical stamp of their founders and were quite different from each other. With master's-level education, it was the role of the programs to develop art therapists with a certain curriculum and internship experience. In 1975, "Guidelines for Education and Training" were established by the

American Art Therapy Association. A program assessment process began—a form of accreditation—known as "approval" for those programs that met the standards. As with all accreditation procedures, the intention of the American Art Therapy Association was to improve education through curriculum standardization, but establishing acceptable education standards while still allowing for creativity was and remains a difficult balance.

Art Therapy: Milestones and the Future

Since its beginnings, art therapy has established an expansive literature documenting clinical work, art therapy's many definitions, and the wide philosophy and approaches to it. The literature has saluted art therapy's history and pioneers and suggested a number of underlying ideas and practices that contribute to theory. In addition, there are books and articles that survey the field, focusing on special techniques, populations, and specific issues. In the early days, art was thought to be relegated to children and special people called "artists." Art therapy's literature reveals the many ages, populations, and problems amenable. Computers and the Internet have resulted in art therapy e-books and CD-ROMs. Research has come to be understood as important to art therapy, although contemporary art therapy primarily remains a profession of clinicians. Advances in neuroscience and technological advances may potentially help explain the mind/body connection and how art and creativity work on the brain.

Great Britain and the United States are well known for highly developed art therapy professions. They are often models for the rest of the world. However, the development and spread of the Internet have given voice and presence to art therapists internationally through the International Art Therapy Organization (IATO). Not unlike Ulman's original art therapy journal, the IATO intends to be inclusive and socially conscious, and functions as a virtual "place" to argue, to discuss, and to celebrate. In the global village, the idea of the integration of art and therapy has taken hold. A few years ago, it was said that only 33 countries had art therapy or arts therapies associations. In many of these countries, unfortunately, the establishment of education for art therapists was not easy, and, therefore, development of the field was difficult. *The Modern History of Art Therapy in the United States* (Junge, 2010) lists the following as contemporary issues: the Question of Art Therapy Assessment, Multiculturalism, Centrality of the Art in Art Therapy, Registration, Certification, Licensing, Research, and the International development of Art Therapy.

Since the last half of the twentieth century, art therapy has expanded and, in a sense, "grown up." Establishing widespread practice standards while simultaneously allowing for creativity is, and will always be, a central challenge. With more recognition comes public confusion about what an art therapist is. While it will always remain a small field, the expertise of a skillful professional art therapist is quite different from a mental health professional, who sometimes uses art in clinical practice. Rubin (2010) wrote, "Art therapy is a unique profession, in that it combines a deep understanding of art and the creative process with an equally sophisticated comprehension of psychology and psychotherapy" (p. xxvi). Art therapists are people with an artist's identity and creativity who strive to help people heal and grow.

Endnotes

1   An exception is the experience of art therapist Judith Rubin, who was admonished not to seek further education by the eminent developmental psychologist Erik Erikson. He was afraid it would hinder her intuition.
2   In 1993, the awarding of ATRs was housed in the newly formed Art Therapy Certification Board (ATCB). It became "ATR" (without periods). In the early 1990s, Board Certification as an art therapist began.

References

Dewey, J. (1958). *Art as experience*. London: Putnam.
Friedman, L. (1990). *Menninger: The family and the clinic*. New York, NY: Alfred A. Knopf.
Jung, C. (1954). *The aims of psychotherapy. The practice of psychotherapy, Bollingen Series XX*. New York, NY: Pantheon.
Junge, M. (1994). *A history of art therapy in the United States*. Mundelein, IL: AATA.
Junge, M. (2010). *The modern history of art therapy*. Springfield, IL: Charles C. Thomas.
Kramer, E. (1958). *Art therapy in a children's community*. New York, NY: Charles C. Thomas.
MacGregor, J. (1989). *The discovery of the art of the insane*. Lawrenceville, NJ: Princeton University.
Meares, A. (1958). *The door of serenity*. Springfield, IL: Charles C. Thomas.
Naumburg, M. (1947/1973). *Studies of the "free" expression of behavior problem children and adolescents as a means of diagnosis and treatment*. New York & London: Teacher's College Press, Columbia University.
Naumburg, M. (1966). *Dynamically oriented art therapy: Its principles and practice*. New York, NY: Grune & Stratton. (Reprinted in 1987, Chicago, IL: Magnolia Street.)
Prinzhorn, H. (1922, 1974). *Artistry of the mentally ill* (E. von Brockdorff, Trans.). New York, NY: Springer-Verlag. (Originally published as *Bildnerei der Geisteskranken*. Berlin: Verlag Julius Springer.)
Rubin, J. (1987). *Approaches in art therapy*. New York, NY: Brunner/Mazel.
Rubin, J. (2010). *Introduction to art therapy, sources and resources* (Rev. ed.). New York, NY: Routledge.
Sechehaye, M. (1951). *Symbolic realization*. New York, NY: International Universities Press.
Waller, D. (1991). *Becoming a profession*. London, England: Routledge.
Waller, D. (1998). *Towards a European art therapy*. Buckingham, UK: Open University Press.

Additional Suggested Readings

Cane, F. (1951/1983). *The artist in each of us*. Craftsbury Common, VT: Art Therapy Publications. (Originally published by Pantheon, New York.)
Freud, S. (1963). In J. Strachey (Ed. & Trans.), *New introductory lectures on Psychoanalysis, Vol XV, Part II*. London, England: Hogarth Press.
Junge, M., & Wadeson, H. (2008). *Architects of art therapy, memoirs and life stories*. Springfield, IL: Charles C. Thomas.
Lowenfeld, V. (1964). *Creative and mental growth* (5th ed.). New York, NY: MacMillan.
Malchiodi, C. (2003). *Handbook of art therapy*. New York & London: The Guilford Press.
Malchiodi, C. (2007). *The art therapy sourcebook*. New York, NY: McGraw-Hill.

Professional Organizations

American Art Therapy Association, www.arttherapy.org
International Art Therapy Association, www.internationalarttherapy.org

2

Psychoanalytic Study of Artists and Their Art: Its Relevance for Art Therapists

Laurie Wilson

Art therapists work with patients for a relatively limited period of time—if we are lucky, weeks or months rather than days. We learn the main events of their lives from team meetings, records, and initial interviews. We discover more during the course of our clinical work with them and through the artwork they make with us. However much we learn, it is exceptionally limited in light of their accumulated personal history. It is a nanosecond compared with an entire lifetime.

We can greatly enhance our work by learning to think as biographers even with very sparse amounts of data. By stretching our perspective to encompass the whole life of a person, we can more accurately pinpoint the issues of concern during the brief time we have with patients. Even though we will never have the necessary information for a genuine biography of our patients, the effort to imagine the entire scope of a person's life immeasurably enriches our time with that person. Just attempting to imagine the early history of an individual is both humbling and useful. Obviously, we cannot "know" very much about that early history, but we can think about it and recognize how much it has affected the people sitting right in front of us. Curiosity about that early history can inspire us to ask patients a few pertinent questions that may not have been answered in the charting about an individual. What were the parents like? Are there siblings? Older or younger? What were the circumstances of his or her childhood and adolescence? What is this person's earliest memory? The answer to that question can open the door to a person's key concerns and/or pleasures. Just thinking about any of these questions expands our awareness of the present moment. Becoming aware of how each of us carries the past inside us is enlightening.

My focus on the biography of artists makes it somewhat easier to consider the artwork of our patients. Artists are concerned with the visual world throughout their entire life. By examining the life of one artist, we can begin to understand how the visual world affects all people. For an artist, the effect of the visual world is profound. What they see early is bound to appear later in their work. Likewise, with our patients,

The Wiley Handbook of Art Therapy, First Edition. Edited by David E. Gussak and Marcia L. Rosal.

what they see as children makes a big impression and will appear later in how they see the world and themselves, but not necessarily in the art they will make.

In researching and writing two psychoanalytic/biographical studies of artists (Alberto Giacometti and Louise Nevelson), I have been able to see startling connections between their early life experience and the sculpture, paintings, and drawings they made as adults. This realization has immeasurably enriched my work as an art therapist, but it came to me in different ways.

With Giacometti, I could study his art, his writing, his extensive correspondence, and a sizable amount of biographical information (Wilson, 2003). I could interview many relatives and friends who had known him well. I had access to the many letters written by his mother and father during his childhood and youth, as both parents penned detailed anecdotes about their children. Unfortunately, Alberto Giacometti lived a fairly short life—a mere 65 years—from 1901 to 1966.

This chapter focuses on Louise Nevelson's life narrative, as she saw it and as others understood it around her (Wilson, in press). I will be connecting her childhood with her adult behavior and artwork, and I will be expanding on the main themes in her work and life: royalty, death, and marriage.

In addition, I shall be spelling out what her persona—her *public* face—meant and where it originated. All people have a public face, our patients included. Nevelson's was outrageous and highly noticeable; examining Nevelson's persona will encourage readers to think about the differences between the person inside and the public presentation. Because she chose to be a very public person for the last 40 years of her life, there is much evidence of her inner life. She was willing to talk to many people about her thoughts and dreams and actions. What I was able to learn about Nevelson through a careful, long-term study can serve as a kind of macrocosm of the microcosmic work we do with patients in the much shorter time we have with them. Once I had seen and understood the complexity and depth of one person's story, I could never again be too quick to decide what lay beneath the surface of any patient I would see. I knew I would have to look and listen very carefully to their words and artwork and be prepared for surprises and complex understandings that honored both the patient's present and past.

Biographical Information

Louise Nevelson was born in 1899 and died in 1988 at the age of 89. She was born in Ukraine, the second oldest child in a Russian Jewish family, and grew up in Rockland, Maine, where her parents and siblings had emigrated when she was aged 5 years. At 20, she married and moved to New York City, where she lived—with brief interruptions— for the rest of her life. A mother at 22, she found she disliked the conventional life of an upper-middle-class, relatively wealthy Jewish wife and mother and began to explore outlets for her energy and creativity. By 30, she had left her husband and son and started on the path that would—after almost three more decades—lead to success as an artist and worldwide acclaim. She kept making art until the last few months of life.

Because she did not keep diaries and wrote few letters, there is a limited amount of archival material in her own hand. But there is her artwork, dating back to her early years, which became more voluminous and varied as the years passed. After she became famous as one of the first art-world celebrities in the 1960s and 1970s, she was frequently interviewed. Because she had a gift for witty and wise remarks as well as a long-standing desire to be known and admired, she became a hot item for journalists. Hence, there are tens of thousands of her spoken words available about her childhood, her family, her search to discover her creative core, her views about world events, politics, and the women's movement; and, of course, she spoke at length about her art, which filled her life with energy and meaning. As she told an interviewer in her 1977 documentary *Portrait of an Artist: Nevelson in Process*:

> It's funny, no matter what one does in life, it hasn't got the vitality of the excitement of really living except when you're really working. … No matter what you are doing. You can be dancing on your head in any position. But when you're creating, there's added energy that surpasses anything else.

Most people, artists included, misremember their childhoods as either better or worse than the actual experience. For example, Giacometti and all his siblings recalled "a perfectly happy childhood," and the only memories that were accessible were the good ones. In the course of my research, however, I discovered his reluctance—or inability—to tell or know the truth about the sadness, loss, tragedy, hostile feelings, and repressed rage that ran like a river through his *unhappy* childhood. Also, Giacometti's mother, who would surely have been a prime subject of these painful memories and a target for his hostile feelings, was the enforcer of the family idealization. She died only a few years before her son, so he never had time to tell the truth about his early life.

Louise Nevelson, on the other hand, could and did recall the pain of her early years; indeed, she was hard-pressed to remember the good times. However, in the mid-1970s, when I first started doing research on her for my art history dissertation, she and her siblings were quite willing to talk about their childhood. As a result, I have been able to put together a rich and reasonably reliable set of stories about growing up in the Berliawsky family in Rockland, Maine, during the first few decades of the twentieth century.

In addition to Nevelson and her siblings, over 50 people who had known her, worked with her, loved and hated her were interviewed. The focus of my dissertation, *Louise Nevelson: Iconography and Sources* (1981), was about how she became who she became. I also explored what meaning—conscious and unconscious—could be attributed to her first major thematic exhibits in the 1950s, which led to her signature style of walls of black or white boxes of wood.

As with many artists, she denied having influences (other than Picasso) and absolutely denied that her work had any meaning other than formal. In trying to understand her life and work, I did what I do with patients. I looked for patterns and anomalies. I was interested in her unconscious fantasies and how they informed her work, her black boxes. The titles of the thematic exhibitions were used to track her unfolding ideas during the late 1950s that culminated in her breakthrough show in 1958, *Moon Garden + One*. Themes such as royalty, marriage, and death kept resonating. They appeared in the titles of her sculpture and exhibitions as well as in her poetry. These themes could then be connected to what I eventually learned about her life.

Her family's low status in Rockland, combined with her mother's high hopes for her children, made Nevelson susceptible to grandiose fantasies about her own "family romance" and to identify with accomplished women artists. In her 20s, her dramatics teacher, Norina Matchabelli, a beautiful actress married to a Russian Georgian prince, entranced her. In her 60s, her ego ideal was Edith Sitwell, the acclaimed English writer who descended from an ancient and royal lineage. Both women were visually striking. Matchabelli was "a great mind, a great beauty ... she and Garbo were the two greatest beauties that I have ever seen" (Nevelson, personal communication, January 8, 1976), and Sitwell was famous for wearing large chunky jewelry and bizarre clothes.

Current Research

In 2006, I continued my research on Nevelson, intending to write her biography. Nevelson was no longer alive, but she had worked pretty much nonstop until her death in 1988. Since the focus of my dissertation had been on her work up to and through 1960, there was now almost 30 years of her art and life to study. In many cases, I could not find out exactly who said what to whom when she was working on her art piece, *Zag XXXIV*. However, given the overall length of her life, I had time on my side.

Fortunately, Nevelson was a pat rack and kept everything that had her name on it, filling 25 chronologically ordered notebooks with clippings, correspondence, and photographs. In addition, in the late 1950s, she gave 30 boxes of autobiographical material to the Archives of American Art and later gave an almost equal amount of material to the Farnsworth Museum and the Library Berliawsky—Nevelson Archives— in 1979. I also met with her art dealer and good friend, Arne Glimcher, numerous times to discuss her almost three decades of work with him. Likewise, her assistant, Diana MacKown, generously shared her archives, photographs, and memories of Nevelson's life and work during that same period. In addition to these and many other interviews, I have had access to all the files and photos concerning her work in metal (aluminum and steel) from Donald Lippincott, sculpture fabricator for most of the large-scale sculpture produced in America from 1966 to 1994.

What was learned during this later stage of research—combined with what was learned earlier but not used for my dissertation—has helped me form a clear picture of what was going on in her life while she was making various sets of works. This opened an entirely new way of understanding the person of Louise Nevelson and her art.

For example, I discovered that the woman who did not go to her parents' or her favorite youngest sister's funerals, whose exhibition *Moon Garden + One* was set in the funeral surround of a church, and whose most famous works were black, absolutely denied the connection of black with death. As I continued to study her, I began to suspect—and then went on to conclude—that her feelings about death, though mostly unconscious, were psychologically and artistically central. For example, her mother was a lifelong hypochondriac and depressive who was mostly unavailable to her children except as an iconic figure, a sad queen.

One of the phenomena not studied earlier was Nevelson's development of a persona, what her friend Edward Albee called "The Nevelson." In her early 60s, Nevelson took advantage of her newly won success and celebrity to "repackage" her- self in an unconventional way that suited her needs and aesthetic tastes. Having been for many years an attractive woman, used to being admired, she began wearing dramatic—often outrageous—outfits as a way to stave off old age and still get noticed. She knew the power of good looks in an indifferent world; and by making what she wore fascinating, even spectacular, she got the press and the public, as well as critics and fellow artists, to take her and her sculpture seriously.

A fringe of two or three false eyelashes, which during the 1960s were quite fashionable, became part of her increasingly elaborate self-creation. She made a spectacle of herself layering levels of clothes, calling herself an "atmospheric dresser" and a collagist. She wore exquisite Chinese embroidered robes over a lumber-jacket shirt, over a silk night-gown, topping it off with a jockey hat and gold-painted space shoes. The new "look" worked for her as a comfortable and eye-catching disguise, and she carried it off with a regal air. Indeed, her exotic, otherworldly sense of herself is reflected in the titles of some of her most original works, such as *Royal Voyage*, *Royal Tides*, or *Mrs. N's Palace*.

As with many other scholars, I initially saw Nevelson's charismatic, highly structured persona as an example of narcissism run wild. It took me a while to realize that it had been developed over decades, originally as a result of her childhood experience. Her mother, a Jewish immigrant in a hostile Yankee town, had had a wonderful sense of fashion and had dressed all her children in the best clothes that could be found in New England. After buying the most beautiful outfits available, she saved them carefully in tissue paper. "Fancy dress" had been a defense for her mother, and it became a shield for Louise Nevelson, a woman artist determined to make it in a man's world. A Chicago art dealer who greatly admired both the woman and the artist, when asked about Nevelson's tough persona, observed, "She doesn't exist now and won't again. There was no one like her and doesn't have to be now since it no longer matters on the art scene whether you are a man or a woman artist" (Richard Gray, personal communication, July 29, 2009).

Further research suggested that, for young Louise, dressing up initially seemed a useful defense against her shyness. In fact, she often claimed that she had studied dramatics and dance for this same reason. During the time that she was becoming an actress, she came across the ideas of Jiddu Krishnamurti, whom she heard speak at Carnegie Hall. His teachings convinced her that pursuing a career as an artist would allow her to achieve her most realized self. Focusing on her drawing and sculpture to the exclusion of most other conventional activities, including motherhood and marriage, seemed to her not selfish but actually generous. As she said in an interview in 1980:

> I felt that my great search was for myself, the inner being of myself and [making sculpture] was the best way I knew to project how I was feeling about everything in the world. Consequently, it wasn't that I made anything for anybody. Now we call it "work," and I don't like to call it work at all. It really is a projection of awareness, a consciousness. People don't understand that when you project yourself you are really at the height of your awareness, and that means you're at your best. So I have never moved from the awareness.[1]

Louise had received considerable recognition for her creative gifts as a child. The art teacher in Rockland, Lena Cleveland, had promoted her as the best artist in the school, and once she started exhibiting in New York she often won prizes and positive critical attention—especially as a sculptor—that gave her external and internal gratification.

During several long decades, she received little financial gain for her work, but her family supported her, and her needs were few. Apart from her dressing up clothes, space to work, and art supplies, everything else was incidental. After she ended her marriage at age 31, she never again let herself become entangled in a romantic relationship with someone who might make demands on her time or interfere with her work. She had lovers, who were stevedores, alcoholic artists, or poetry-writing junk dealers, and she liked sex and flirting, but she liked her independence more.

To Nevelson, creativity was the highest value, and she encouraged all the people around her to do their own thing—to write, to paint, to sing. She set a good example by working on her art as much as and as often as she could. She was aware that she was happiest when she was in her studio making something new. "In my studio I'm as happy as a cow in her stall. That's the only place where everything is all right" (Nevelson, 1976, p. 115).

> Work is to my life like breathing is to my body. It is the spirit of my life. If someone asked me what part of success means most to me, I would say that success means I can have a loft big enough to work in I can have help with my work and I can have all the materials I need whatever they are, to express that work. You see, I'm lucky. We're lucky on this earth if we can find something to identify with and my work is the total mirror of me. There has never been a moment when it hasn't given me my life, even in all those years when I wanted to jump out of a window from neglect. (Sullivan, 1974, p. 3)

Throughout her life, Louise collected wood scraps and pieces and saved them for years until she found exactly the right way to use them. Her friends also collected for her, and there is scarcely a single account by someone going out to dinner with Louise in her downtown neighborhood that did not include retrieving some piece of scrap wood from the street at Louise's insistence, dragging it along to the restaurant and then back to her studio after dinner. Nevelson saw her life and her artwork as all of a piece. "I'm not making art," she told her interviewer, Connie Goldman, in the late fall of 1973. "That's not what I want. I just do what I know. You can only do what you are. My work is a mirror of myself. I use visual harmonies to express my knowingness of life. That's the livingness of living" (Goldman, 1973, p. 282).

Though she was known for her candid comments, Nevelson was not usually so outspoken about her inner life—especially with a journalist. When I recently talked with Goldman about the conversation she had had with Nevelson so many years ago, Goldman said she had developed a new perspective on the artist's comments. After writing six books about aging in the last 40 years, Goldman's research had persuaded her that everyone—especially older people—need to find their inner or real self and not just go along with the way we have been defined by the outer world. Goldman reflected about her interviews with the artist:

> I was so surprised that Nevelson was so verbal and able to maintain a self-centered focus on what was going on inside her. At the time I thought "what a self-centered person she is." If I did that interview today, instead of being put off or angered, I would admire the fact that she realized she couldn't do her art honestly unless she kept the focus on the inner Louise Nevelson. Though it seemed that she was being rude and

self-centered, Nevelson had what I now see as elder wisdom. If she hadn't gone inside herself and cut out the rest of the world, she could not have made her art. ... I didn't understand Nevelson at all then, but now I accept that she had a perfect right to be what she was. (Goldman, personal communication, 2013)

As Nevelson's biographer, I focused on her entire life experience. In looking at her childhood to discover possible links to her later work and life, I learned that all the Berliawsky children had regular chores, and that Louise's were cleaning the house and keeping it orderly. Not surprisingly, creating "order" became her lifelong passion. As an adult, not only did she start each day sweeping or cleaning her house (which was also her studio), she kept her workspace scrupulously neat. She could find any one of the thousands of wood fragments she had collected whenever she needed it, and was famous for noticing if someone had moved a single piece.

Her childhood passion for order was refined and then transformed during her 20s and 30s when she studied Picasso's work, especially paintings from his cubist period. From his earliest years as an artist, Picasso combined a powerful gift as a draftsman with an uncanny compositional aptness. Lacking Picasso's brilliance in drawing, Louise honed her natural talent for composition, which became a distinguishing aspect of her art. Decades later, she adopted a "metaphysical" explanation for her search for compositional harmony. She believed that, with her sculpture, she was bringing a cosmic order, which she called "the fourth dimension," down to the three-dimensional world.

Since she both loved her work and loved to work, the almost infinite repetition of tasks that might bore someone else helped her refine her eye. In the 1930s, for example, she made hundreds of drawings, mostly figurative with a Matisse-like quality, in which she endlessly tried out compositional ways to play with figures and with fluid lines. In the late 1940s, she began making hundreds of terracotta sculptures. The more cats, people, and cows she made, the more interesting they became, and the more she refined her style.

In the early 1940s, buoyed by the European surrealists who came to Manhattan, she also made a series of witty wood sculptures and followed that with a collection of abstract wood pieces using scraps she had found on the street. It was wartime, and no one had money for much else; bronze, even terracotta, was in limited supply.

Visits to Mexico and Guatemala taught her that low was high and vice versa, and the burst of confidence she gained from this insight helped her achieve her breakthrough signature style. As a child in Rockland, Maine, she had observed that the Native Americans, the gypsies, and the Jews were all treated as low-class outsiders, usually reviled and dismissed, while the white, Anglo-Saxon Protestants were accorded social prominence and high status. Seeing the extraordinary art and architectural accomplishments of the Mayans, Aztecs, and Toltecs made her realize how upside-down the New England version of hierarchy was. She was inspired by the ancient pre-Colombian peoples, who had used common stones to build their massive temples out of the most available, non-precious material, much in the same way that she used scrap wood, which she transformed with a coat of black, white, or gold paint.

For therapists as well as patients, childhood matters. Louise had much in common with her handsome, charming, highly energetic father. Endowed with a strong aesthetic sense, he collected antiques, which his more conventional wife made him keep in the barn. He was also a contractor, and owned forests and lumberyards.

As already presented, Louise's mother shaped her life and work in significant ways. Minna Berliawsky was also the silent partner in one of the key relationships of Louise's life: her relationship with a young man named Arnold Glimcher. In fact, Louise's career came together in the early 1960s when she met Glimcher, an exceptionally gifted young dealer who knew how to promote and sell art and artists. He adored Louise and treated her like a queen, providing anything she wanted, including a chinchilla coat. More important, he gave her everything she could possibly want as an artist. He arranged for her to have whatever art supplies and assistance she might need, all the travel plans connected to her exhibitions, anything that would help her work and working life. He even once offered to buy her an airplane. Glimcher and Louise shared a similar sense and talent for arranging objects in space, and his installations of her exhibitions at the Pace Gallery in New York City were always excellent. The artist and her dealer were a perfectly synchronous pair, and they made each other rich and famous.

She called him her little lover boy, and he was, in fact, a far better son to her than her biological offspring. With the Glimcher family, Nevelson also found a family that in many ways resembled the family of her childhood: close-knit and totally supportive of her creativity and unconventionality. Arne's mother Eva was exactly Nevelson's age and had come from the same part of the Ukraine. She became a successful saleswoman in the United States, with an abiding belief in creativity and hard work. Eva Glimcher was religious; Louise was spiritual. But they were both gutsy women, way ahead of their times. Similar to the Berliawsky family, the Glimcher family enabled her to keep going through years of minimal recognition and even more minimal financial success.

Conclusion

Looking at the artwork of patients, and thinking about their behavior during the art therapy session as well as their life history, an art therapist is bound to find connections. Even if they cannot be seen, the links—between past and present, individual and art, the conscious and the unconscious—are certain to be present.

This is the biggest lesson for me as a therapist—and one that I have learned from the psychobiographical works I did with Alberto Giacometti and Louise Nevelson. I was gradually able to put both art and life puzzle pieces together. I hoped that might be the case when I first started working as an art therapist. After all, Edith Kramer and Margaret Naumburg had told me it was so.

Endnote

1   Louise Nevelson, interview with Barbaralee Diamondstien, 1980.

References

Goldman, C. (1973). Interview with Louise Nevelson. *Northwest Architect, 37*(7), 282.

Nevelson, L. (1976). *Dawns and dusks.* New York, NY: Charles Scribner's Sons.

Sullivan, M. (1974). Louise Nevelson, one of art world's most noted. *Courier Gazette.* (July 18, Sect. B, p. 3).

Wilson, L. (1981). *Louise Nevelson: Iconography and sources [Outstanding dissertation in the fine arts series].* New York, NY: Garland Publishers.

Wilson, L. (2003). *Alberto Giacometti: Myth, magic, and the man.* New Haven, CT: Yale University Press.

Wilson, L. (in press). *Louise Nevelson, Art is Life.* New York, NY and London, England: Thames & Hudson.

3

Psychoanalytic Art Therapy

Judith A. Rubin

Art therapy was born at a time when psychoanalysis dominated mental health. It therefore makes sense that the earliest formulations of how and why art is therapeutic were couched in psychoanalytic terms (Kramer, 1958; Naumburg, 1947). Moreover, the psychiatrists instrumental in the development of art therapy in the United States were also analysts—Nolan D. C. Lewis, who wrote a paper on using art in 1925 and invited Margaret Naumburg to work at the New York State Psychiatric Institute in 1941; Irene Jakab (1998), founder of both the International Society of Psychopathology of Expression and the American Society of Psychopathology of Expression; Karl Menninger, who hired art therapists Mary Huntoon in the 1930s, Don Jones in the 1940s, and Bob Ault in the 1950s; and Paul Fink, who employed artist Myra Levick in the 1960s, and was the driving force behind the founding of both the first art therapy training program and the American Art Therapy Association.

Not only was psychoanalysis the dominant orientation for individual psychotherapy, but family (Ackerman, 1966; Minuchin, 1974) and group therapy (Bion, 1961; Moreno, 1994) were also developed by analysts. It is no surprise then that the pioneers of both family (Kwiatkowska, 1978; Landgarten, 1987) and group art therapy (McNeilly, 2005; Waller, 1993) were trained and supervised by analysts.

Psychoanalytic ideas have continued to play a central role in art therapy, in both the United States (Robbins, 1987; Shore, 2013) and the United Kingdom (Hogan & Coulter, 2013; Schaverien, 2009), the two countries where the profession has developed most extensively. In New York City, the Institute for Expressive Analysis, founded in 1978 by Dr. Arthur Robbins, art therapist and analyst, offers both training and treatment.[1]

Even today, over a century since the publication of *The Interpretation of Dreams* (1900), the writings of Sigmund Freud are still widely studied. Moreover, many of his hypotheses are being confirmed by contemporary research—such as the neurobiological interpersonal foundations of psychological development and mental functioning (Green, 2003; Kandel, 2012; Schore, 2011; Siegel, 2012).

In fact, far from being the static doctrinaire discipline often caricatured, twenty-first-century analysis is teeming with exciting developments. Among these are a deepening understanding of the role of *attachment* (Cassidy & Shaver, 2010), the

The Wiley Handbook of Art Therapy, First Edition. Edited by David E. Gussak and Marcia L. Rosal.

centrality of *mentalization* (Fonagy, Gergely, Jurist, & Target, 2005), and the importance of a *relational* approach to therapeutic work (Aron & Harris, 2011). Although it is no longer the only game in town, psychoanalysis continues to influence clinicians from all backgrounds (Bateman & Fonagy, 2012).

Its founder, Sigmund Freud (1949), was convinced that the causes of patients' problems were *unconscious*. His first model of the mind (*topographic*) emphasized the difference between what is *conscious*, what is *preconscious* (available to consciousness through attention and effort), and what is *unconscious* (unknown). Freud believed that recovering repressed memories of traumatic events would permit *catharsis*, which would lead to symptom relief. The goal of early psychoanalytic treatment therefore was to "make the unconscious conscious."

Unconscious contents are accessible only indirectly—through clues provided by what Freud called *free association*. This method, of allowing the mind to produce thoughts and images without the usual constraints of logic or propriety, was not new. Freud cited a manuscript by a creative writer on the process of freely listening to spontaneous inner voices as a way of generating ideas for a composition, and artists like Leonardo da Vinci had used such techniques for centuries.

Over time, Freud developed a *tripartite* theory, involving an internal struggle between three metaphorical parts of the mind—*Id* (unconscious strivings), *Superego* (conscience), and *Ego* (executive function). Freud suggested an image of the Ego as a rider on the horse of the Id, taming, controlling, and directing the powerful *drives* inside in a manner that results in feelings of pleasure, at the same time satisfying the demands of the Superego.

Freud also postulated a *dynamic* battle between forbidden wishes and the equally unconscious defenses against them—"*internalized conflict*." He theorized that the pressure for discharge—for satisfaction—was so strong that the elements of unconscious conflict would invade mental products best under conditions of relaxed censorship, such as *free association* or sleep—where *dreams* were seen as a "royal road to the unconscious." Although Freud commented that his patients often complained about having to translate waking or sleeping *imagery* into words, he never made drawing a regular part of analytic technique.

The integration of Freud's insights about unconscious communication through imagery and the use of art in therapy was made by Margaret Naumburg, widely acknowledged as the founder of art therapy in the United States. One of the first Americans to undergo psychoanalysis, she brought pictures of her dreams and fantasies to her analyst, finding them useful in her own therapy.

In 1914, Naumburg founded Walden School, based on psychoanalytic principles and emphasizing the arts. Her sister Florence Cane (1951) became the art teacher there. Both stressed the *release* of unconscious imagery through *spontaneous* art expression, believed to prevent emotional problems through *catharsis*.

Naumburg and Cane were also influenced by the teachings of psychiatrist Carl Jung (1964), who developed his own theory of *analytical psychology* following a disagreement with Freud. Jung turned to painting as part of his self-analysis, and recommended it as one way to get in touch with the unconscious through *active imagination*, a kind of "free association" using all forms of creative expression—movement, imagery, art, drama, music, writing, etc. (Jung & Chodorow, 1997).

Many psychoanalytic therapists were excited by the rich potential of art in both diagnosis and therapy. Human figure drawings were used to assess intellectual ability, emotional distress, and interpersonal relationships (Hammer, 1958). The pioneers of child analysis—Anna Freud (1927) and Melanie Klein (1932)—were also the first play therapists and, as today, they offered drawing materials along with toys.

Margaret Naumburg (1966) was not alone in her use of art for either diagnosis or therapy, but she was the first to identify its role as a primary agent rather than an auxiliary tool. She called her approach *dynamically oriented art therapy*. A scholar knowledgeable about many schools of thought regarding symbolism, she insisted that the only valid meaning of anyone's art came from the artist. She was skeptical about formulas for decoding symbolic meaning, a position consistent with Freud's teachings about dream analysis—one still held by psychoanalysts and most art therapists.

As a therapist who understood the patient's art as "symbolic speech," Margaret Naumburg remained within the communicative framework of her verbal model. Her approach to art therapy, in which art expression is used as a tool in therapy, evolved into what is sometimes called *art psychotherapy*.

The other major art therapy pioneer, Edith Kramer (1958), developed an approach she called *art as therapy* (1971). Kramer knew psychoanalytic theory well, growing up in Vienna during the development of *ego psychology*. In this evolution of Freudian theory, the emphasis was on the function of the ego in regulating the personality, using a wide array of defense mechanisms (A. Freud, 1936).

Kramer's approach to art therapy focused not on uncovering unconscious conflicts, but rather on the role of creative work in the service of a specific coping mechanism that Freud called *sublimation*. When successful, conflicted impulses are "tamed" (neutralized) by being channeled into artwork. For Kramer, sublimation explained the healing power of the creative process.

Elinor Ulman, another American pioneer, published the first art therapy journal in 1961. She also believed in Freudian theory, but was convinced that *both* "art psychotherapy" *and* "art as therapy" were valid, the particular approach to be chosen depending on the individual circumstance (Ulman, 2001).

Because my best supervisors were analysts, I decided to study psychoanalysis rather than pursue a doctorate in clinical psychology. Having used art in both child and adult analysis and psychotherapy since the mid-1970s, I believe that, in analytic art therapy, it is often necessary to shift gears from one mode to the other—even with the same person, and sometimes in the course of a single session (Rubin, 2005). There are a variety of psychoanalytic approaches to art therapy, evident in the second and third editions of *Approaches to Art Therapy* (Rubin, 2001; 2016).

All art therapists who work analytically, however, share certain beliefs, in addition to the assumption of a dynamic unconscious. Central is a conviction that the past influences the present, so that an understanding of normal and abnormal *development* is essential. A generally accepted framework begins with Freud's formulations of successive *psychosexual phases* (oral, anal, phallic), and includes Erik Erikson's (1950) description of *psychosocial stages* throughout the life span, as well as Anna Freud's (1965) elaboration in the *developmental profile*.

In addition, based on psychoanalytic observations of child–parent interactions (Mahler, Pine, & Bergman, 1975), analytic art therapists are also concerned with the resolution of *developmental tasks* such as *separation–individuation*, including navigating the *rapprochement crisis* and achieving *self and object constancy*. In addition to dyadic issues of parent–child interaction, in regard to both *attunement* (Stern, 2000) and *attachment* (Bowlby, 1969), analytic art therapists also consider triadic issues such as what Freud called the *oedipal conflict*. This fantasy is named for the Greek drama *Oedipus Rex*, in which Oedipus unknowingly slays his father and marries his mother. During his self-analysis, Freud discovered a universal wish for an *oedipal victory*. The fantasy involves wanting to have each parent all to oneself, which inevitably entails getting rid of the primary rival—the other parent. Since the other parent is also deeply loved, and someone on whom the child depends, this creates a situation of conflict, for which the child struggles to find a safe resolution.

Psychoanalytic art therapists also agree on the importance of the patient's internal world, especially its representation in what Freud called "*transference*." This ubiquitous phenomenon, magnified in analytic therapy, refers to the symbolic ways in which the patient perceives and responds to the therapist, while "*counter-transference*" refers to what is being evoked in the therapist by the patient.

Both are extremely useful in analytic art therapy, where they are expressed in both art and behavior. Transference helps to identify distorted perceptions, which are presumably based on unresolved conflicts from the past. Counter-transference also reflects the patient's attempts to re-enact unsettled issues with the new person of the therapist, while trying to make the drama end differently—what Freud called the "*repetition compulsion*."

He also reasoned that people are constantly striving for some kind of equilibrium and good feeling—seeking pleasure and avoiding pain. He called this the *pleasure "principle"*. This is, parenthetically, another reason for art therapy's effectiveness—that it is intrinsically pleasurable to work with art materials and to create. It also accounts for the strenuous efforts made by every patient to avoid conscious awareness of forbidden impulses and ideas, manifest in something he called "*resistance*." Indeed, this is an inevitable aspect of "*working through*," giving up maladaptive wishes and fears and accepting the self and the world, thus freeing energy formerly spent defensively for constructive aims.

Related to the idea of *transference*, and implicit in analytic ideas about *symbolism*, is that we try to make sense of the world by giving meaning to what we experience; and that in so doing we express our own needs—what Freud called "*projection*." People of all ages project meaning onto unstructured visual stimuli, such as seeing images in clouds. *Projective tests*, whether responsive like Rorschach inkblots or expressive like Person drawings, are assumed to reflect ideas and impulses of which the artist is not aware.

Characteristics of Psychoanalytic Art Therapy

Art therapists who consider their work to be analytic believe in the existence and importance of unconscious conflict and in the presence of both transference and resistance. They behave somewhat differently, however, depending on whether they are doing *art psychotherapy* or *art as therapy*.

In *art as therapy*, where the goal is *sublimation* through the creative process, there is usually less discussion and more emphasis on helping the patient to create a finished and satisfying artistic product. In *art psychotherapy*, where the goal is *uncovering and insight*, there is generally less emphasis on the product, and more interviewing about the art, as well as an attempt to help the individual to relate it to him or herself.

In *art as therapy*, the transference is noted, but is not encouraged or analyzed; in *art psychotherapy*, it is encouraged and sometimes explored with the patient. Analytic art therapists who utilize the transference as part of their work usually meet with patients more often than once a week, primarily to promote a more intense involvement. They also behave in as neutral a fashion as possible, so that patients can more easily project ideas and feelings onto them and the relationship.

Technique: Psychoanalytic Art Therapy

Although there are individual differences, there are also commonalities among analytic art therapists because of the value placed on the importance of expressing unconscious material through art. Whether the focus is on art *as* therapy or art *in* psychotherapy, the following statements apply to individual, family, and group art therapy when it is psychoanalytic in approach.

- **The Setting**—The art therapist establishes a physical and psychological space in which it is safe to be freely creative. British psychoanalyst Donald W. Winnicott (1972) described what he named *"transitional space,"* the play space within which therapy happens. He called the provision of such a space a *"holding environment."* A similar concept of a space in which it is safe to be creative is what I have called a *"framework for freedom"* (Rubin, 2005).

- **The Therapeutic Alliance**—The art therapist works to forge what analysts call a *therapeutic alliance*. This is a real relationship that is sturdy and trusting enough to withstand the inevitable strains of the transference and resistance. With youngsters, it includes an alliance with the parents, to ensure their sustained support for the treatment. The collaborative nature of this alliance has been further reinforced by recent developments in *intersubjective* and *relational psychoanalysis* (Aron & Mitchell, 1999).

- **The Task**—What is requested in art is as open-ended as possible, so that the patient can truly express what is pressing for release. This is usually reflected in a *free choice of materials, topic*, or *both*, as in my diagnostic art interview (Rubin, 2005). If *specific media* are offered, it is assumed that using each will reveal a different aspect of the person's inner world, as in Kramer's (2000) assessment, which involves drawing, painting, and modeling. And if particular *topics* are requested, it is assumed that they will reveal critical aspects of the individual's perception of self and others, such as the family drawings included in Kwiatkowska's (1978) family art evaluation.

- **Stimulation**—If stimulation is provided, whether it is an activity such as relaxation and mental imagery, or a visual "starter" such as a *scribble*, it is designed to help patients get in touch with unconscious imagery. Winnicott (1971) used small pencil drawings in an interactive *squiggle game*. Cane (1951) developed a *scribble technique* using large rhythmic movements and chalk on big sheets of paper attached to easels to liberate creativity. In both, the patient is asked to project an image onto the scribble and to develop it artistically.

- **Observation**—Because of the psychoanalytic assumption of *psychic determinism*—that all behavior has meaning, and that the *sequence* itself carries meaning—the analytic art therapist observes carefully throughout the entire process. All verbal and nonverbal behaviors are significant, as is the order in which they occur.

- **Activity**—If the art therapist is active, it is to facilitate the patient's authentic expression. This can take many forms, from "*extending the frame of reference*" (Lowenfeld, 1957), to technical instruction, working alongside, or actively helping, as in Kramer's (2000) use of the art therapist's "*third hand.*"

- **Interviewing**—Interviewing, whether during or after the working process, is as open-ended as possible. All questions, comments, and suggestions are designed to help patients to associate as freely as they can to their artwork.

- **The Art Product**—The artwork produced in therapy is treated with care and respect, understood as an extension of the person's self. How the individual treats the art that he or she has created is also seen as a reflection of the state of their self-perception and self-esteem. A related idea is *healthy narcissism*, named by Freud after the Greek god Narcissus, who fell in love with his own reflection in a pool of water. All children begin life with a primary narcissism which, if responded to warmly by a "*gleam in the mother's eye*" (Kohut, 1971), grows and evolves into a love for others as well. The child's first *gifts* of (bodily) products, if valued, lead to pleasure in producing (art) as well.

- **Confidentiality**—In order for patients to feel free to express any and all ideas and fantasies, it is vital to be secure in the privacy of the verbal and creative work with the art therapist. This means that nothing is disclosed, nor is artwork shown, to others, including parents or teachers, without the artist's permission.

- **Patience**—Although it is possible to conduct short-term analytic art therapy, this approach works best when more time is available. It takes time to develop trust, to express previously hidden ideas and impulses, to figure out their meanings and origins, to give up defenses, and to *work through* the conflicts behind symptoms, not simply to ease or modify the symptoms themselves.

Looking at the Material

How analytic art therapists view and understand what patients "say" in art, words, and body language depends on their particular orientation. The lenses through which the patient's expressions are viewed by psychoanalytic art therapists are varied and variable—object relations, symbolization, insight, sublimation, self psychology, and other ways of understanding. How art and behavior are perceived is determined by the nature of the material (Hedges, 1983), as well as by the individual therapist's preferred way of understanding.

Whatever the particular way of seeing and hearing, the analytic art therapist is guided in behavior by what he or she feels will help the patient to improve. The emphasis is on freeing the personality to grow, and to be able to live, love, and play in a more creative fashion.

Saying Goodbye

Analytic art therapists view termination, like the work itself, as something best planned by both partners in the therapeutic endeavor. There is also a belief that the patient needs to be able to continue the growth achieved in art therapy on his or her own. This includes being able to recognize patterns of thought, feeling, and behavior, and to understand one's own dreams, art, or slips of the tongue.

And because art is a "normal" activity, it offers a concrete way for the patient to carry on. Sometimes the individual literally continues to create in art, working independently, taking classes, even exhibiting. This may represent a transitional activity—a way of keeping the therapist present—or an identification with the lost object of the art therapist. On the other hand, it may simply be a reflection of the fact that involvement in the creative process during art therapy was so rewarding that the patient wants to continue it.

Vignette: Jackie and Post-Traumatic Stress Disorder (PTSD)

At age 5, Jackie had not only been sexually abused by her father, but had also witnessed a horrifying event: her mother shooting and killing her younger brother. She could not talk about either, and was clearly suffering from PTSD. She had scary nightmares and intrusive waking imagery.

She was also miserable, because her grumpy behavior with everyone left her feeling very lonely. She had been in play therapy for almost a year with no change in her symptoms. Her childcare worker, who had attended an art therapy workshop, decided to see if art therapy might help.

Like most children with abusive parents, Jackie could not safely know or acknowledge anger at her mother. She was too afraid of losing what little good feeling she clung to on her infrequent visits to the jail. But she could safely direct her rage at me—as the mother in the transference—in "ugly" drawings of *Dr. Rubin's Face* (Figure 3.1).

For several weeks, she put signs on my office door, warning other children not to believe what I said, and—projecting her own envy and neediness onto me—accusing me of being "a beggar" (Figure 3.2).

Over time, using art and the relationship, Jackie was able to work through her confused feelings about herself and others. She eventually integrated good and bad images of both of us in a happy *Bunny Family* (Figure 3.3). She was eventually able to leave therapy and to feel a warm attachment, giving me a loving Valentine card to say goodbye (Figure 3.4). Thus, Jackie was able to *work through* her rage at her parents by using me and her art in the *transference*.[2]

Figure 3.1 Dr. Rubin's Ugly Face.

Figure 3.2 Warning Sign.

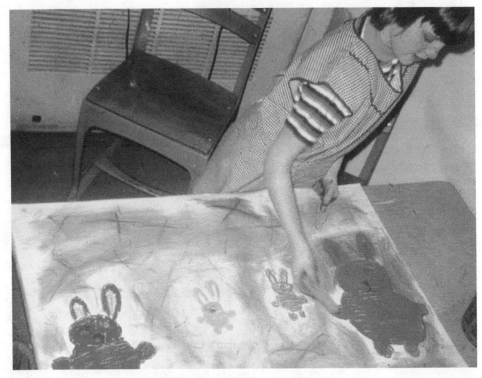

Figure 3.3 Jackie in Art Therapy.

Figure 3.4 Jackie's Goodbye Valentine.

Endnotes

1 Information about the Institute can be found at www.ieanyc.org.
2 The reader is referred to Chapter 1 of *Introduction to Art Therapy* and Part I of *Approaches to Art Therapy* for additional examples of psychoanalytic art therapy with patients of different ages conducted by myself (Rubin, 2010) and by colleagues (Rubin, 2001).

References

Ackerman, N. W. (1966). *Treating the troubled family.* New York, NY: Basic Books.
Aron, L., & Harris, A. (Eds.) (2011). *Relational psychoanalysis* (Vol. 5). New York, NY: Routledge.
Aron, L., & Mitchell, S. A. (Eds.) (1999). *Relational psychoanalysis* (Vol. 1). New York, NY: Routledge.
Bateman, A. W., & Fonagy, P. (Eds.) (2012). *Handbook of mentalizing in mental health practice.* Arlington, VA: American Psychiatric Association.
Bion, W. R. (1961). *Experiences in groups.* London: Tavistock.
Bowlby, J. B. (1969). *Attachment.* London: Tavistock Publications.
Cane, F. (1951/1983). *The artist in each of us.* Craftsbury Common, VT: Art Therapy Publications.
Cassidy, J., & Shaver, P. R. (2010). *Handbook of attachment* (2nd ed.). New York, NY: Guilford Press.
Erikson, E. H. (1950). *Childhood and society.* New York, NY: W.W. Norton.
Fonagy, P., Gergely, G., Jurist, E., & Target, M. (2005). *Affect regulation, mentalization, and the development of the self.* New York, NY: Other Press.
Freud, A. (1927/1974). The methods of child analysis. *The writings of Anna Freud* (pp. 19–35). New York, NY: International Universities Press.
Freud, A. (1936/1985). The ego and the mechanisms of defense. *The writings of Anna Freud* (Vol. 2). New York, NY: International Universities Press.
Freud, A. (1965). *Normality and pathology in childhood.* New York, NY: International Universities Press.
Freud, S. (1900). *The interpretation of dreams* (Standard edition, Vols. 4 & 5). London: Hogarth Press.
Freud, S. (1949). *An outline of psycho-analysis.* New York, NY: W.W. Norton.
Green, V. (Ed.) (2003). *Emotional development in attachment theory and neuroscience.* NY: Routledge.
Hammer, E. F. (Ed.). (1958). *The clinical application of projective drawings.* Springfield, IL: Charles C. Thomas.
Hedges, L. E. (1983). *Listening perspectives in psychotherapy.* New York, NY: Jason Aronson.
Hogan, S., & Coulter, A. (2013). *The introductory guide to art therapy.* London: Routledge.
Jakab, I. (1998). *Pictorial expression in psychiatry.* Budapest, Hungary: Akademiai Kiado.
Jung, C. G. (1964). *Man and his symbols.* New York, NY: Doubleday.
Jung, C. G., & Chodorow, J. (Eds.) (1997). *Jung on active imagination.* Princeton: Princeton University Press.
Kandel, E. (2012). The age of insight. New York, NY: Random House.
Klein, M. (1975/1932). *The psycho-analysis of children.* New York, NY: Delacorte.
Kohut, H. (1971). *The analysis of the self.* New York, NY: International Universities Press.
Kramer, E. (1958). *Art therapy in a children's community.* Springfield, IL: Charles C. Thomas.
Kramer, E. (1971). *Art as therapy with children.* New York, NY: Schocken Books.
Kramer, E. (2000). *Art as therapy* (Lani Gerrity, Ed.). Philadelphia: Jessica Kingsley.

Kwiatkowska, H. Y. (1978). *Family therapy and evaluation through art.* Springfield, MA: Charles C. Thomas.

Landgarten, H. B. (1987). *Family art psychotherapy.* New York, NY: Brunner/Mazel.

Lowenfeld, V. (1957). *Creative and mental growth.* New York, NY: Macmillan.

Mahler, M. S., Pine, F., & Bergman, A. (1975). *The psychological birth of the human infant.* New York, NY: Basic Books.

McNeilly, G. (2005). *Group analytic art therapy.* London: Jessica Kingsley Publishers.

Minuchin, S. (1974). *Families and family therapy.* Cambridge: Harvard University Press.

Moreno, J. L. (1994). *Psychodrama and group psychotherapy* (4th ed.). New York, NY: Mental Health Resources.

Naumburg, M. (1947). Studies of the "free" art expression of behavior problem children and adolescents as a means of diagnosis and therapy. *Nervous and Mental Disease Monograph,* No. 17 (*An Introduction to art therapy* (2nd ed.). NY: Teachers College Press, 1973).

Naumburg, M. (1966). *Dynamically oriented art therapy.* New York, NY: Grune & Stratton.

Robbins, A. (1987). *The artist as therapist.* Philadelphia: Jessica Kingsley.

Rubin, J. A. (Ed.) (2001). *Approaches to art therapy* (2nd Ed.). New York, NY: Routledge.

Rubin, J. A. (2005). *Child art therapy* (3rd ed.). New York, NY: Wiley.

Rubin, J. A. (2010). *Introduction to art therapy.* New York, NY: Routledge.

Rubin, J. A. (2016). *Approaches to art therapy* (3rd Ed.) New York, NY: Routledge.

Schaverien, J. (2009). *The revealing image.* London: Jessica Kingsley.

Schore, A. N. (2011). *The science of the art of psychotherapy.* New York, NY: W. W. Norton.

Shore, A. (2013). *The practitioner's guide to child art therapy.* New York, NY: Routledge.

Siegel, D. J. (2012). *The developing mind* (2nd ed.). New York, NY: Guilford Press.

Stern, D. N. (2000). *The interpersonal world of the human infant.* New York, NY: Basic Books.

Ulman, E. (2001). Variations on a Freudian theme. In J. A. Rubin (Ed.), *Approaches to art therapy* (2nd ed.). New York, NY: Routledge.

Waller, D. (1993). *Group interactive art therapy.* New York, NY: Routledge.

Winnicott, D. W. (1971). *Therapeutic consultations in child psychiatry.* New York, NY: Basic Books.

Winnicott, D. W. (1972). *Playing and reality.* New York, NY: Basic Books.

4

Archetypal Art Therapy
Josie Abbenante and Linney Wix

Ours is an image-focused therapy.

J. Hillman

In this chapter, the authors, archetypal art therapists and educators, present the theory and practice of art therapy as based in the writings of archetypal thinkers James Hillman (1975, 1977, 1978, 1979), Patricia Berry (1982), Mary Watkins (1984), and Howard McConeghey (1981, 2003). Three ideas essential to the theory and practice of archetypal art therapy are presented:

1. Archetypal art therapy focuses on paying close attention to the structure and content of images.
2. Archetypal art therapy is an imaginal rather than a symbolic approach to working with images.
3. Archetypal art therapists use metaphorical language to hear images in their own words.

Paying Close Attention to the Structure and Content of Images

As noted by Hillman (1975), archetypal art therapy values the making of art and what is made. It trusts that the skills that give form to images enhance the skills that give form to the soul, and that the soul and the created image reflect each other. Archetypal art therapy trusts the image and the form in which it arrives is presented, and demands attention. Therapists and makers in archetypal art therapy sessions work hard to see just what emerges in the artwork and use language with care to describe the image. The therapist guides the client in paying close attention to describing the details in order to hear the image in metaphorical or poetic language rather than literal or declarative language. Metaphorical and poetic responses to images are core to practicing archetypal art therapy. Practitioners aim to imagine precisely and support clients in doing the same, even when the words may sound unfamiliar and may not "click" (Hillman, 1977) or "ring a bell" (Betensky, 1995).

The Wiley Handbook of Art Therapy, First Edition. Edited by David E. Gussak and Marcia L. Rosal.
© 2016 John Wiley & Sons, Ltd. Published 2016 by John Wiley & Sons, Ltd.

Archetypal art therapists rely on the client to give form to images, and they understand that there is no other way of knowing than watching and listening to the image as it unfolds. They understand that "an image is complete just as it presents itself ... that everything there is necessary, which further suggests that everything necessary is there" (Hillman, 1977, p. 68). In his 1993 keynote address to the American Art Therapy Association annual conference, Hillman indicated that form in art therapy is just as important as feeling, as emotional content, as expressive power, and that form shows art therapists what shape things are in. Furthermore, forming images skillfully and carefully helps a chaotic psyche settle down and present its intentions in the making of an image.

McConeghey (2003) wrote:

> It is essential for art therapists to think of form as an active force, as an image doing something. A painting speaks but it speaks in images through form ... true communication cannot be a contrived attempt to convey an already formed idea ... If one already knows what will be communicated, then it is more like propaganda than true communication. (p. 28)

While careful forming is an underlying idea in art therapy (Dicker-Brandeis cited in Wix, 2010; Kramer, 1972; Shafer-Simmern, 1948), archetypal art therapists pay particular attention to form through language that is based in a "syntax of the imaginal: the parts of speech freed from their narrational obligations which link them into time sequences for storytelling" (Hillman, 1978, p. 165). The work of archetypal art therapists is to see and hear artworks imaginally rather than literally or rationally, with the aim of making them matter. The working process is not one of interpreting images but rather one of working with words to hear what is seen in the artwork. Imaginative precision is the aim. Trusting the images to inform and guide the therapy involves noticing them very closely. "Close noticing" (Hillman, 1979, p. 143) preserves the integrity of the image and encourages therapists and clients to ask, "What does the image want?" and "How do we give voice to the artwork and the art making in order to hear the imagination?"

An Imaginal Rather than a Symbolic Approach to Working with Images

While most therapies, including art therapies, take a symbolic approach to working with visual images, counting on the interpreter's knowledge of symbols to determine meaning, archetypal art therapists "particularize" symbols to allow them to be seen and heard as images. Particularizing a symbol reduces its universality by focusing specifically on the way the symbol appears. For example, while there may be an oak tree in the picture, it must be described exactly as it appears rather than 'read' as oak tree in the symbol dictionary. They count on the image itself to reveal its multiple meanings through close focus on structure, content, and medium. Hillman (1977) wrote that "symbols give grandeur" (p. 65); they universalize, generalize, and conventionalize rather than focus on specifics.

While symbols stand in for concepts and thus abstract into universal meaning, working archetypally, or imaginally, takes one back to the artwork. Hillman (1977) cautioned therapists that, in working with images, "There is nowhere else to go. Only [the image] can tell us about itself" (p. 68). Paying particular attention to the content and structure of the artwork helps therapists and clients "stick to the image" (Lopez-Pedraza in Berry, 1982, p. 57).

Margulies (1984) encouraged suspending judgment, allowing the therapist and client not to know in order to know more. In referencing Keats (cited in Margulies, 1984), he indicated, "Negative capability … is when man is capable of being in uncertainties, mysteries, doubts, without any irritable reaching after fact and reason" (p. 1029). Margulies asserted that what we think we know gets in the way of empathy; we assert that it gets in the way of understanding images. Unable to sit with and accept the mystery of not knowing, art therapists tend to seek fact and reason to make rational sense of clients' artwork. While interpretations depart from the image for intellectual meanings, that may have little to do with the artwork, working imaginally requires suspending what one thinks one knows in order to remain with what may not initially make sense. McConeghey (1981) noted that therapists and educators who cling to traditional techniques do so:

> [B]ecause it is a comfortable way to neutralize the disturbing effects and metaphorical ambiguity of imaginal expression. … The imaginal approach requires a truly radical reorientation [in which] sharp sight becomes insight and clarity becomes awareness of the internal relations within the psychic image. (p. 132–133)

While the word *therapy* derives from the Greek *therapeia*, which has to do with serving and witnessing (Ayto, 1990), therapists often think their role is to "fix" clients. When fixing becomes the goal, the art often falls through the cracks. Focusing on the problem rather than the image can easily shift the art therapist's role into one of being a counselor, thus usurping the opportunity to witness and serve through the art. Maintaining the focus on the image to serve clients is core to archetypal art therapy's commitment to art's primacy in art therapy. The session's focus is on art, which holds the attention of the therapist and the client. When working imaginally, art therapists do not amplify, symbolize, moralize, sexualize, pathologize, personalize, generalize, correct, add emotion in or abstract it out, turn the image into a narrative, devise a course of action from, apply negative or positive value, use a developmental model, or confine the image to a single meaning (Hillman, 1977). Instead, archetypal art therapists stick to the image, trusting it, rather than the ego, to inform. They use language that circles the art with an ear toward metaphor and poetics.

Using Metaphorical Language to Hear Images in their Own Words

Using descriptive, concrete, poetic language to hear images is called "image work." In discussing Arnheim's views on language, Franklin (1994), citing Arnheim, indicated that the poet:

> … draws deeply on the expressive properties of language. … In the poetic mode, the meanings of words interpenetrate with sensuous properties. And the poet, like the visual artist, works toward creating structural equivalents of ideas and feelings in a medium. … Language rooted in a concrete, sensuous base is a language of possibilities. (p. 263)

As noted above language of archetypal art therapy "stick[s] to the image" (Lopez-Pedraza in Berry, 1982, p. 57) and is thus "rooted in a concrete, sensuous base of possibilities" (Franklin, 1994, p. 263). If the client and therapist cannot hear what they are seeing, then it is time to change the language so that images are seen and heard poetically—in their own language. Franklin (1994) presented three modes of language use: pragmatic language for getting things done (a language often used in therapy sessions); conceptual language for labeling ideas (also common in sessions, this distances therapists and clients from concrete sensuous language and from the art itself); and poetic language "through which ideas and feelings are given body and transformed, and through which relationships among parts are displayed and understood" (p. 263). Language that sticks to the image, the language core to archetypal art therapy practice, falls into the third category.

Betensky (1995), in presenting verbal articulation in art therapy, defined the phenomenological approach which, while sharing similarities with archetypal art therapy differ significantly in that language leaves the image to return to the client's problem. Her focus on description leads back to the client's reality, thus privileging the ego's rationality while ignoring other, quieter parts of self. Betensky's description involves what describers think they see rather than what they actually see because the aim is to hear the ego talking rather than to listen to the image for what it has to offer. She insisted that the initial description "leads to the client's inner reality" (p. 17), supporting the therapist in "connect[ing] the art work with the inner experience" (p. 17). While her approach seeks integration of art and client, an archetypal approach allows the images to be separate from the client, and even encourages the images to stand on their own, insisting that they have lives of their own. Deepening into the image through the senses has the potential to help therapists and clients see and hear images anew in the process of giving form to soul.

Betensky's (1995) conscious effort to connect the images made during therapy sessions to the artists' inner experience detracts from art's own ability to inform and to contribute new insights. While she encouraged clients to look closely for observations that "ring a bell"—which most often indicates an ego identification with the image rather than a deeper soul identification—archetypal art therapists encourage clients to stay with the image long enough and closely enough to be stained by it. While archetypal art therapy focuses on phenomena involved in the making process and what is made, its consideration of these phenomena differs from that of Betensky's phenomenological approach.

In regard to metaphor, Abbenante (2007) noted that it is "a difficult concept and often misunderstood" (p. vii). The difficulty comes in therapists' need to literalize metaphor, making them stand for something in the client's situation. In archetypal practice, artwork is not a metaphor of or for anything but itself. As Hillman (1979) stated, "The act of ... metaphorical insight ... does not dissolve what is there, the image, into what is not there, a meaning" (p. 138). Working to hear the description metaphorically can lead to discovering the necessity within the image, what it wants (in contrast to what I want), in turn increasing its value. Berry (1982) encouraged therapists to "discover what the image wants and from that determine our therapy" (p. 78).

Hillman (1975) further insisted that metaphors are not solutions to personal problems, but flourish in ambiguity. Rather than making moves that link the artwork through metaphor with the person or the problem, archetypal art therapists use metaphor to enter imagination in order to deepen their understanding of the image. Imagining demands a step away from practical life; it deviates from continuity. Metaphors are perfect lead-ins to knowing, perceiving, feeling, and being differently.

Archetypal art therapists shy away from interpreting, and instead "stay faithfully close" to what is actually presented (Hillman, 1977, p. 78). In practice, archetypal art therapists use "gadgets" (as defined by Hillman, 1977, 1978, 1979; and Berry, 1982) which help therapists and clients see and hear more deeply into the image, into the heart of the matter. Their use allows for hearing images metaphorically. (For use of gadgets in an art therapy case, see Wix, 1997.)

Underlying all the gadgets is description, which involves describing what one sees, not what one thinks one sees. Describing requires all the senses. Hillman (1979) wrote about synesthesia, and how it goes on all the time "when we talk imaginatively or of imagining. ... Evidently, synesthesia is how imagination imagines. ... [c]onsequently, synesthesia plays a special role in the arts because it helps art's intention—metaphorical insight, awakening of sensibility—freeing it from depiction and representation" (p. 133). Describing also involves suspending judgment, letting go of determining what is good or bad or looking for what is pathological in the image. Client and therapist need only stay true to the artwork, sensing the subtleties therein by hearing what is seen through careful description.

As therapist and client describe the image fully and listen for metaphors, they move away from literal and linear readings of the image (see example). They begin to expand their language to include analogizing, which allows for hearing possibilities in the image: What is it like? For example, "What is the blue, the heavy line, the pictured animal like?" Finding essential similarities and using associations that stay with the image (unlike free association, which leaves the image) help hear multiple meanings already there. "When ... then" statements, used in the gadget of simultaneity, establish ongoing internal relationships and help therapists and clients hear that everything in the image belongs. Repetition and restatement invite seeing and hearing the ways in which the image repeats itself and call therapists and clients to listen to the language of the image. Restating with different emphases (emphasizing different words in the description), and restating without punctuation, chanting, and changing word order moves listeners away from the literal, from "this means that," and opens the door to hearing the actual image. Playing with prepositions, adjectives, adverbs, and reversing parts of speech further de-literalizes the description and gives a sense of positioning and placement. For example, "What is at the edge, in the middle, underneath, over, or above?" Hillman (1977) further suggested modifying nouns with adjectives, and adjectives with adverbs to increase precision and stir up hearing and seeing.

Another gadget is punning, wherein the client and therapist hear the puns in the artwork; however, Hillman (1978) cautioned not to get caught up in irrelevance. Contrasting encourages asking questions. For example, "Why the sun and not the moon? Why green and not blue? Why mother, not father?" Exploring etymology, checking on roots of words that arise from describing, offers opportunity to see what's underneath the word.

Close work with images through gadgetry helps "keep the image around for a while" (Hillman, 1978, p. 180). Keeping images around is a way of tending them. It invites sedimentation rather than interpretation; it does not insist on a meaning and does not leave the image for a problem or a life story. Journaling, creating series, carrying the image psychically or physically are ways to keep images. Watkins (1984) indicated, "In an imaginal psychology one would try to help the journeyer keep returning to the image" (p. 102).

Working imaginally has to do with loving images, with entering them in reverie. Assisting someone into places of reverie is more useful than interpretation or diagnosis, which stops the reverie, the imagination, and the images. While working with gadgets can feel technical, working precisely yet expansively for a long enough time leads to understanding the images metaphorically. Encouraging play with the possibility in an image opens up more possibilities and slows the desire for an answer.

> Start close in,
> don't take the second step
> or the third,
> start with the first
> thing
> close in,
> the step you don't want to take.
> David Whyte (2007, p. 362)

Case example of image work

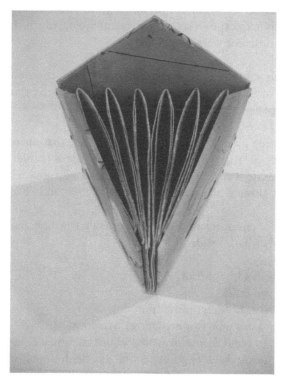

Process

Must making books be making something to read? Painting huge sheets, staining sheets and more sheets. Soaking sheets in paint and ink. Painting/staining/soaking. Hanging out to dry. Waiting. Lettering over. Precise rendering of writing, of letters that can't be read. Waiting. Working big, cutting up and away. Chancing it in the cutting up. What will show up? Using it all, no waste. Nothing cast away. It's all there whether readable or not. Drawing on.

Artwork

Books stand like houses. Like three-sided houses that open.
Three sided, not four sided.
Sides are like doors that open and close, revealing what's inside.
Inside are pages in sections/sections of pages.
Sections divide the space like rooms.
There's stitching and folding and writing that can't be read, like an ancient language. Another language.
Unknown letters spell unrecognizable words.
There are hard and soft edges, well-defined edges and less well-defined edges (description with analogy, contrasting).
When what's like doors close at the front, there's a glimpse of edges that are soft, fore-edging softly. What's at that fore-edge that you can barely see? What's at the fore? At the edge? (description with analogy, simultaneity, prepositioning).
Closing what is hard exposes soft edges (restatement, which could be repeated and re-heard in different ways).
Closing reveals.
Closing reveals softness at the edge (description, pre-positioning).
Opening above allows for seeing into but to really see in, the hard edges/doors have to open.
Opening hard edges opens seeing.
There's a holding place that opens/holding a place that opens (restatement).
When doors open, then what's held inside also opens (simultaneity).
What's held inside is what's unknown, another language (description).
Opening and closing: what does it sound like? Sounds like a bird's wings flapping.
(expanding the senses, relating inside to outside through analogy).
Stitching holds what's inside inside.
Thread binds.
The insides are held by thread.
Held by a thread inside.
Hanging by a thread (description, punning).
Why thread and not tape (for attaching)? (contrast)
Looking up *stitch* and *bound* in word origins dictionary (etymology): *stitch* relates to sting, prick; *bound* relates to obliged or destined; intending to go;

border, edge, limit: leap: boundary, bundle; *religio* relates to bind, being bound to something through ligature (Ayto, 1990). Stitching binds. Is it the sting of the prick that binds? That holds things together?

Inside is still space/still a space inside, (restatement, reversal) like a place to walk around (analogy). Wanting to trace lines moving through … <u>when</u> lines move through, <u>then</u> there's wanting to follow (simultaneity).

Inside, texture varies: paint feathers, brushes dryly, bleeds.

Paint bleeds.

When paint bleeds, lines contain and break away (simultaneity).

There's both containing and breaking away (description).

Inside there are edges and boundaries and no edges and no boundaries (description, pre-positioning).

When three books stand like houses, roofs peak.

One roof peaks steeply, like the steeple of a church (adverb modifies verb to note the way the roof peaks; analogy).

Steep/steeple/steeply relates to precipitous, very high; also soak (etymology). While these roofs peak, one steeply, I wonder about soaking, the way the paint and ink soaked the paper.

What else is soaking?

Ambiguity inside hard-edged structure.

When structure is firm and hard-edged, then there's ambiguity.

What backs and grounds (both inside and out) is subtle, a background for unknown words and letters.

Subtlety backgrounds.

Looking up *subtle* (etymology): sub-tela, a weaving term, "beneath the lengthwise threads in a loom … finely woven" (Ayto, 1990, p. 509).

Stained, soaked, hung out to dry. Waiting. Taking chances, nothing cast away. Opening and closing reveal another language, a glimpse of softness. To really see in, hard edges have to open. Like birds' wings, hanging by a thread. Is it the sting of the prick that binds? Wanting to follow the still space inside, contained and breaking away. When standing together, then peaking steeply, peeking in, wondering about soaking. Soaking in. Firm hard-edged ambiguity. Subtlety backs and grounds. Or, finely weaves underneath it all. Revealing.

Summary

In summary, archetypal art therapy values the making of art and what is made. Sticking to the image is core to archetypal art therapy's commitment to art's primacy in art therapy. Therapists and clients pay close attention to describing the details in artwork to hear the image imaginally, in metaphorical or poetic language. Close focus on content and structure, as well as medium and process, gives the image its own voice, and avoids interpretation. Working imaginally requires suspending what we think we know in order to instead "stay faithfully close" to what is actually presented (Hillman, 1977, p. 78).

References

Abbenante, J. (2007). Foreword. In B. Moon, *The role of metaphor in art therapy: Theory, method and experience* (pp. v–ix). Springfield, IL: Charles C. Thomas.

Ayto, J. (1990). *Dictionary of word origins*. New York, NY: Arcade.

Berry, P. (1982). *Echo's subtle body: Contributions to an archetypal psychology*. Dallas: Spring Publications.

Betensky, M. (1995). *What do you see: Phenomenology of therapeutic art expression*. London: Jessica Kingsley.

Franklin, M. (1994). A feeling for words: Arnheim on language. *The Arts in Psychotherapy, 21*(4), 261–267.

Hillman, J. (1975). *Revisioning psychology*. New York, NY: Harper Colophon.

Hillman, J. (1977). Inquiry into image. *Spring: An Annual of Archetypal Psychology and Jungian Thought* (pp. 62–88). Zurich: Spring.

Hillman, J. (1978). Further notes on images. *Spring: An Annual of Archetypal Psychology and Jungian Thought* (pp. 152–182). Irving, TX: Spring.

Hillman, J. (1979). Image sense. *Spring: An Annual of Archetypal Psychology and Jungian Thought* (pp. 130–143). Irving, TX: Spring.

Hillman, J. (1993, November). *If it ain't broke, don't fix it*. Keynote address at the 24th annual conference of the American Art Therapy Association, Atlanta, GA.

Kramer, E. (1972). *Art as therapy with children*. New York, NY: Schocken Books.

Margulies, A. (1984). Toward empathy: The uses of wonder. *American Journal of Psychiatry, 141*(9), 1025–1033.

McConeghey, H. (1981). Art education and archetypal psychology. *Spring: An Annual of Archetypal Psychology and Jungian Thought* (pp. 127–136). Irving, TX: Spring.

McConeghey, H. (2003). *Art and soul*. Thompson, CT: Spring.

Shafer-Simmern, H. (1948). *The unfolding of artistic activity*. Berkeley: University of California Press.

Watkins, M. (1984). *Waking dreams*. Dallas: Spring Publications.

Whyte, D. (2007). *River flow: New and selected poems, 1984–2007*. Langley, WA: Many Rivers.

Wix, L. (1997). Picturing the relationship. *American Journal of Art Therapy, 35,* 74–82.

Wix, L. (2010). *Through a narrow window: Friedl Dicker-Brandeis and her Terezín students*. Albuquerque, NM: University of New Mexico Press.

5

Gestalt Art Therapy: A Path to Consciousness Expansion
Selma Ciornai

This chapter focuses on the theoretical and methodological basis of Gestalt art therapy, and on what I perceive as its main goal: consciousness expansion through the use of creative and artistic resources. As Gestalt art therapy has its theoretical and philosophical basis in Gestalt therapy, this chapter will begin with its philosophical foundations.

Gestalt therapy is considered part of the existential–phenomenological school of therapy. Therefore, this chapter will explore and focus on the ultimate goals of any existential–phenomenological-based therapy: awareness and awareness expansion and how these are applied. Furthermore, some of the contributions of Gestalt psychology will be described. One of these later elaborations—the works of Rudolph Arnheim— of utmost importance to understanding the Gestalt approach to art therapy, will be highlighted. Finally, I'll present the work of some therapists who developed their practice based on these premises.

Defining Gestalt Art Therapy

Gestalt art therapy is a way of using art resources *in* and *as* therapy under a Gestalt therapy–based theoretical and philosophical understanding. It is a process-oriented approach in which both the creation of art and the reflection upon what is produced is seen as having potential therapeutic value.

Gestalt art therapy understands that people can be agents of their own health and growth processes, finding for themselves meanings that are personally relevant. Therefore, in the Gestalt approach to art therapy, therapists do not use their knowledge in order to interpret a client's artwork. Rather, the goal is to be facilitators and companions of the client's process, at times suggesting experiments as a way to help the exploration and unveiling of people's inner dynamics and realities as well as the discovery of new paths and directions.

Furthermore, Gestalt art therapists rely on the belief that creativity is intrinsically connected with the process of life, and that the ability to express oneself through different verbal and non-verbal languages is a natural potential of all human beings. Its affinity with art is deeply embedded in Gestalt therapy's philosophical foundations, its

The Wiley Handbook of Art Therapy, First Edition. Edited by David E. Gussak and Marcia L. Rosal.
© 2016 John Wiley & Sons, Ltd. Published 2016 by John Wiley & Sons, Ltd.

perspective of human beings, its model of healthy functioning as creative functioning, and in its methodology—all of which are extended to the work of Gestalt art therapy.

The Existential Philosophical Basis

Embedded in Gestalt therapy's foundation is that humans are always able to creatively construct, choose, and organize their paths.

According to Sartre (1943), human beings have to submit only to four condemnations: to be born, to die, to be sociable, and to be free. In the existential vision, human beings are seen as being always in a possible state of remaking themselves—if awareness is present—and of choosing and organizing their own existence, that is, of being subjects of their own history.

Based on these premises, in psychotherapeutic terms, the objective of such therapy is to work toward constant awareness expansion to facilitate people becoming creators and agents of their own transformations.

The volume titled *Gestalt Therapy: Excitement and Growth in Human Personality*, by Perls, Hefferline, and Goodman (1951), demonstrates the aesthetic dimension that this existential fundament takes. Constant parallels are established between creative processes and healthy human functioning, between art and therapy.

Both in art as in therapy, the human ability to perceive, figure out, and reconfigure relations with oneself, with others, and with the world is manifested. By taking human experience away from the stream of the routine (at times, automatic) of daily life, and putting it under new lights, establishing new relations among its elements, mixing the old with the new, the known with the dreamed, the feared with the envisioned. both art and therapy have the potential to bring forth new integrations, possibilities, and growth. This belief in the sparkle of divine in each and every one of us, the faith in humans' capacity to be "the artist of their own existence," or, in Paulo Coelho's words (1988), "the alchemist of our own existence," is *embedded* in Gestalt thinking.

Gestalt therapy became well known in the 1960s, as it actively engaged in recovering human spontaneity and authenticity, in reestablishing a more creative, full, and pleasurable dimension of human existence. For Perls (1969), Gestalt therapy was a way to help people free themselves of their internal tyrannies, preparing the way to deep social changes. In this sense, the potential ability to express oneself through different languages (verbal and non-verbal), and the view that perception and expression are not only mental activities, but experiences that involve all senses, were seen as a way to extend humans' capacity of awareness, expression, and creativeness.

In Gestalt therapy, as well as in Gestalt art therapy, there is distrust for quick interpretations that proceed from references external to the person. This does not mean that Gestalt therapists avoid searching for meanings, but that:

> We want to hear the story first and let the meaning unfold. ... Though the search for meaning is a human reflex, the compulsion to meaning frequently drowns out experience itself. ... Instead of playing intellectual games, we prefer that a patient get inside his own experience... (Polster & Polster, 1974, p. 16–17)

Hence, the Gestalt art therapist will pay attention to the client's presence and behavior through direct sensory perceptions. Therapists will help clients get in touch with their sensations, and use their own sensations while in therapeutic contact. This process leads to meaningful insights.

In Gestalt art therapy, the same approach is used to observe the art-making behavior and process, and to pay attention to the visual language. This might include the order and rhythm in which materials, colors, and forms are chosen; the characteristics of lines, forms, and compositions; and the relation between figure and ground, and between parts and the whole.

This kind of observation is practiced during each contact and over longer periods of time. Thus, changes in visual language are recognized, and the therapist can recognize how these reflect changes in mood, self-esteem, existential perspectives, and styles of contact. This type of observation can be done with an individual client or in a therapy group.

Finally, therapists *will privilege the relationship*. This means that possible or inferred meanings of artwork or behavior can only be understood in the *context* of the therapeutic relationship.

The emphasis on therapeutic relationship as a two-way human engagement is called "therapist as his/her own instrument of work" (Polster & Polster, 1974, p. 19). Gestalt therapists are trained to be tuned to their own feelings, sensations, and intuitions and to use them in the therapeutic encounter.

> It is as if the therapist becomes a resonating chamber to what is going on between himself and the patient. He receives and reverberates to what happens in the interaction and he amplifies it so that it becomes part of the dynamic of the therapy... (Polster & Polster, 1974, p. 18)

In Gestalt art therapy, this attitude is manifested by creating mutual works or in the mutual sharing of feelings and perceptions about a client's artistic expression.

Healthy Functioning as Creative Functioning

In Gestalt therapy, individuals are conceived as open systems. Health is conceived as being related to the creative processes in life, to the vision of human beings as beings-in-relation, beings-in-the-world, whose particular nature it is to be creators; as beings who interact with people around them and the environment they live in, using their resources to recognize and creatively deal with it. This view of the interconnections between health and creativity, and healthy functioning and creative functioning, and the understanding of healthy contact as ones' openness to contact with the new, and good contact as those with *pragnanz* (the quality of good forms) is basic in Gestalt thinking and brings an aesthetic paradigm to the understanding of human beings and aesthetics to psychotherapy (Ciornai, 1994; Perls et al., 1951; Zinker, 1978, 1994).

Why Art in and as Therapy?

Making sense through our senses/mobilization in action

When the quality of contact is poor, the figures that appear in awareness are weak, cloudy, undefined, or opaque. In turn, the person may feel confused, unhappy, anxious, anguished, or depressed. Contact needs to be heightened, and energy brought up to the experience in order to facilitate new insights and understandings, eventually leading to reconfigurations and new openness in one's inner world.

In these cases, the profusion of "talking about" can lead to mere rationalizations. Real insight—a new "inner-sight"—is always accompanied by a change of energy. There is a sense of vitalization that comes with unblocking hidden barriers, the disclosure of hidden or unfinished gestalts, and with achieving strong and clear figures of awareness. Art processes can be a valuable resource to help heighten the quality of contact.

Contact has its roots in contact functions: seeing, smelling, sensing, and moving. Talking comes later in order to organize what we contacted with our senses into words. As Arnheim (1974) indicated, "Art may seem to be in danger of being drowned by talk":

> We have neglected the gift of comprehending things through our senses. Concept is divorced from percept, and thought moves among abstractions. Our eyes have been reduced to instruments with which to identify and to measure, hence we suffer a paucity of ideas that can be expressed in images and an incapacity to discover meaning in what we see. ... Words can wait and must wait until our mind distills, from the uniqueness of the experience, generalities that can be grasped by our senses, conceptualized and labeled. ...
> It often happens that we see and feel certain qualities in a work of art but cannot express them in words. The reason for our failure is not that we use language, but that we have not succeeded in casting those perceived qualities into suitable categories. Language cannot do the job directly because it is no direct avenue for sensory contact with reality. (p. 2)

Janie Rhyne (1978b) indicated:

> Through our senses we become aware, we perceive in action, we gain insight about the nature of the world and of our place in it by contacting what's out there directly with our basic, innate organismic perceptual system. Thus Gestaltists encourage exploration through sensory-motor activation, believing that this often facilitates recognition and clarification of problems.

One of Gestalt therapy's basic tenets, "epistemology of direct sensorial experience," implies the understanding that knowledge, information, and wisdom are not synonymous, and that real knowledge has to be learned "organismically." Art can be a powerful way to engage the person's whole being, as it engages the sensory-motor, the emotional, the cognitive, and the intuitive levels of our functioning.

It is possible for a person to sometimes feel dull, without energy, with no contact whatsoever with what lies underneath this mood. In art, there is a mobilization of energy and emotion *in action*, where consciousness is formed in the process of the act itself. Perceptions and transformations may happen in the course of experience. Senses, emotion, awareness, perception, imagination, and cognition can all be mutually co-activated. At the same time, new possibilities can be really experienced and tried out and not only imagined.

Art expression as a human language

Words are sometimes not the best means to express what is contacted within oneself. Plastic, poetic, musical, and other artistic languages might be more adequate for the expression and elaboration of what is barely glimpsed or too complex. This is generally the quality of what happens in our psychic intimacy, a world of constant perceptions and sensations, thoughts, fantasies, dreams, and visions that do not respect the logic and temporal order of language. Art provides the possibility for the expression of these phenomena. Art is a phenomenon of the soul (Bachelard, 1989). For this reason, it can help develop and refine senses and sensibility.

The quality of concreteness/art as an alternative reality

Gestalt therapy emphasizes learning through experience. In art therapy, inner representations, feelings, and experiences gain concreteness. This quality is very useful in working with people who have difficulty dealing with abstractions in that it helps to eventually heal, transform, and reconstruct through tangible representation of what feels incurable or lost.

As an alternative reality, art allows the expression of feelings and experiences that individuals hardly dare to express in their daily lives (Kreitler & Kreitler, 1972). Art can relax defenses and allow one to feel, elaborate, and express what otherwise would be threatening or dangerous. Art allows the individual to express, try, and experiment with what is unusual. By doing this, a new knowledge about oneself, others, or the world might be gained.

When Therapy Helps: Goals of Gestalt Art Therapy

Sometimes the figures of our physiological, emotional, or spiritual needs do not stand out clearly and are not satisfactorily completed.

> When the figure is dull, confused, graceless, lacking of energy (a weak gestalt), something in the environment is blocked out, some vital organic need is not being expressed: the person is not "all there"... (Perls et al., 1951, p. 231–232)

It is common that clients come to therapy feeling anguished, anxious, or sad, but with no clear idea of why. There may sometimes be incongruence between what they say and how they appear. A therapist's job, then, may be to help them focus their energy on the emerging figure, and heighten contact with their inner realities, the hidden gestalts. When this contact is achieved, clarity, unity, vigor, and release emerge. Awareness leads to insights and transformations.

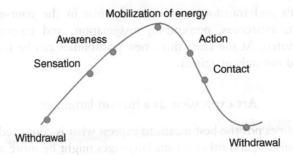

Figure 5.1 Cycle of Contact. Zinker (1978). Reproduced with permission of J. Zinker.

Zinker (1978) described figuratively the cycle of contact, the process of figure/ground formation, as follows (Figure 5.1):

Energy can get stuck in one part of this cycle. Sometimes it characteristically gets stuck in the same part of the process. Some have a difficult time becoming aware of their sensations or contacting their wishes and needs, letting a clear figure emerge from the ground of their experiences. Or, they may be aware of them, but cannot mobilize themselves in order to act in a satisfying direction. For example, a person may know and be aware of feeling lonely, and yet not be able to reach out for nurturing human contact.

When something such as this happens, the energy may be stuck in "unfinished business" of the past. It is as if the individual were using an old colored pair of glasses, and new situations are seen as a repetition of older ones. This old situation may be partially or totally out of awareness. There may be an expectation, an "inner myth," that the story will always be the same. There is no freshness or openness to relate to and evaluate new situations. The person may relate to others without vitality. Energy is scarce, locked somewhere else in a past situation never resolved—a fixed or crystalized gestalt.

In cases such as these, therapy may help expand the crippled flux of energy, unblock the energy stuck in old, incomplete gestalts, and bring it to the here-and-now. This leads to the recovery of vitality and freshness to relate to new situations with good quality of contact. Art therapy can help in several ways. It can heighten sensations through activities with a sensory-motor component, through activities that will stimulate perception and the emergence of feelings, or through ones that will activate symbolic and cognitive processes raising awareness (Kagin & Lusebrink, 1978).

Therefore, Gestalt art therapy's goals may be:

- The mobilization of energy and emotion that occurs in present experiences, which call for energized involvement of the sensorial, cognitive, and emotional levels of functioning of the person.
- The perceptions and transformation possibilities that are foreseen and experienced through experiments and experiences.
- The understandings and insights that emerge from reflections after and during the experiences lived in the therapeutic setting.

The Strong Relationship Between Gestalt Psychology and Gestalt Art Therapy

Form and structure became the key to all psychic phenomena for Gestalt therapists. Affirming the universality of structural properties of all things and the isomorphism between psychological and physical structures, they saw in form's structural properties the basic unit of all experience phenomena.

> Gestalt psychology originated as a theory of perception that included the interrelationships between the form of the object and the processes of the perceiver. … Gestalt thinking emphasized "leaps" of insight, closure, figure/ground characteristics, fluidity of perceptual processes and the perceiver as an active participant in his perceptions rather than a passive recipient of the qualities of form. (Fagan & Shepherd, 1970, p. 3, cited in Rhyne, 1976, p. 483)

Gestalt therapy took from Gestalt psychology some of its most basic concepts, such as "system organism–environment," "figure–ground formation," "figure of good contact," and the concept of "gestalt" itself, establishing analogies between psychic and physical phenomena. In art therapy:

> We do not have to talk *about* configurations, figure/ground relationships, dynamic movement, contact/boundaries, coherence and fragmentation in the abstract, rather we speak of these phenomena in the very act of perceiving and becoming aware of what is obviously there. (Rhyne, 1980, p. 77)

Implicit in Gestalt thinking is the acceptance that physical and psychological phenomena are *isomorphic*, that is, their forms are structurally similar. An image is structurally similar to the behavior of the organism that created it.

> The willow is not "sad" because it looks like a sad person. Rather, because the shape, direction and flexibility of the branches convey passive hanging, a comparison with the structurally similar state of mind and body that we call sadness imposes itself secondarily. (Arnheim, 1974, p. 452)

This has an implication of utmost importance to therapists, in relation to the observation and understanding of their clients' gestural, tonal, postural, and rhythmic behaviors that appear as figure or as ground, in their contact with them, as in relation to the observation and understanding of their artistic and expressive manifestations. Gestalt psychology asserts that the meaning is *embedded* in form that it is indeed *inherent* to it, and that, therefore, in order to apprehend meanings, it is important to learn to see them. To see and recognize underlying structures, lines, forms, and composition is related to the language of form.

> People perceive the slow, listless, "droopy" movements of one person as contrasted to the brisk, straight, vigorous movements of another, but do not necessarily go beyond the appearance to think of psychic weariness or alertness behind it. Weariness and alertness are contained in the physical behavior itself, they are not distinguished in any

essential way from the weariness of a slow floating tar or the energetic ring of the phone bell. (Arnheim, 1974, p. 451)

Nevertheless, it is important to remember that a single visual pattern can lead to two different perceptions, literally two different organizations of visual stimuli. One famous and classic example is the figure that is either a young woman with a hat or an old woman with a big chin and scarf over her head. This once again underscores the importance of the clarified relationship between client and therapist and of the phenomenological approximation in the artistic manifestations of clients.

On the other hand, the isomorphic approach has its limitations. No formal analysis can explain the strong effect of themes such as love or familial relations over human beings (Gombrich, 1980).

Arnheim greatly contributed in bringing "the theory of isomorphism out of academic isolation, insisting that the image is similar in structure to the behavior of the organism that creates it, and that the expression is structured similarly to the working of the mind" (Rhyne, 1978b). His works are basically about the importance of paying attention to the "language of art."

It is easy to recognize how some of Gestalt therapy's most usual methods and techniques, such as asking a person to "give a voice," "gesture," or "sound" to a feeling, for example, has its roots in Gestalt psychology's theory of isomorphism. In Gestalt art therapy, this understanding and type of experiment is extended to the created art forms.

Another important aspect of the theory of isomorphism addresses past history:

> Natural objects often possess strong visual dynamics because their shapes are the traces of the physical forces that created the objects. ... The highly dynamic curve of an ocean wave is the result of the upward thrust of the water bent by the counter-pull of gravity. The traces of waves on the wet sand of a beach owe their sweeping contours to the motion of the water and in expansive convexities of clouds and the rising and breaking outlines of mountains, we directly perceive the nature of the mechanical forces that generated them. The winding, twisting, swelling shapes of tree trunks, branches, leaves and flowers, retain and repeat the motions of growth. (Arnheim, 1974, p. 416–417)

Gestalt therapy's emphasis on the present experience does not mean that past experiences or future expectations are not dealt with, but that it is in the present that they are recalled, remembered, or foreseen. In the same way, the "here-and-now" is emphasized, in plastic expression, "the past history is not merely inferred intellectually from clues, but directly experienced as forces and tensions present and active in the visible shape." (Arnheim, 1974, p. 417)

Many times then, it is by re-doing—in action or imagination—the movement of the arm or the body that created the trait or the form, that the deepest meaning of the internal movement of the client who created it is derived. Sometimes, this process is mutually realized as a way to explore the contents and emotions present in the work of art.

Finally, Gestalt psychology emphasizes the importance of always considering the whole "gestalt," not reducible in parts that could be separately analyzed. A therapist will always consider the other as a whole. Consonantly, "Gestalt art therapy deals with the whole configuration of personal expressiveness in visual messages, in voice tone, body language and in verbal content as well" (Rhyne, 1978b, p. 2).

Final Remarks

The aim of this chapter is to expose the philosophical, ideological, theoretical, and methodological foundations that underlie the Gestalt approach to art therapy and how they are transposed to practice. Other Gestalt therapists have come to be known for the use of artistic media and expression in their work, such as Violet Oaklander (1978) and myself. However, the scope of this chapter does not allow me to cover all of these experiences.

I have been teaching and working with Gestalt art therapy for 30 years, and find it a very useful and passionate path to work with individuals, groups and community, and social programs. For me, art therapy is not only the space for creating, expressing, discovering, unveiling, elaborating, and perceiving. It is foremost the space of mystery, where therapists and clients meet beyond their roles to share the unique experience of wonder and fascination, in the presence of that which "invents itself and invents me every day" (Octavio Paz, 1975, p. 5).

References

Arnheim, R. (1974). *Art and visual perception*. Berkeley: University of California Press.

Bachelard, G. (1989). *A poética do espaço* [The poetics of space] (2nd ed.). São Paulo: Martins Fontes Editora Ltda.

Ciornai, S. (1994). Arteterapia Gestaltica: Um caminho para expansão de Consciência [Gestalt art therapy: A path to consciousness expansion]. Revista de Gestalt 3, Vol 1. Instituto Sedes Sapientiae, SP, Brazil.

Coelho, P. (1988). *O alquimista* [The alchemist]. Rio de Janeiro: Editora Rocco Ltda.

Fagan, J., & Shepherd, I. L. (1970). *Gestalt therapy now*. New York, NY: Harper & Row.

Gombrich, E. H. (1980). *On physiognomic perception*. Deadalus, 11.

Kagin, S., & Lusebrink, V. (1978). *The Expressive Therapies Continuum. The Arts in Psychotherapy* (Vol. 5, pp. 171–180). New York: Pergamon Press.

Kreitler, H., & Kreitler, S. (1972). *Psychology of the arts*. Durham, NC: Duke University Press.

Oaklander, V. (1978). *Windows to our children*. Moab, Utah: Real People Press.

Paz, O. (1973). *Early poems 1935–1955*. New York, NY: New Directions Paper Book.

Perls, F. (1969). *Gestalt therapy verbatim*. Lafayette, CA: Real People Press.

Perls, F., Hefferline, H., & Goodman, P. (1951). *Gestalt therapy: Excitement and growth in human personality*. New York, NY: Dell Publication Co.

Polster, E., & Polster, M. (1974). *Gestalt therapy integrated: Contours of theory and practice*. New York, NY: Vintage Books.

Rhyne, J. (1976). *The gestalt approach to experience, art and art therapy*. In C. Hatcher & P. Himelstein (Eds.), *The handbook of Gestalt therapy*. New York, NY: Jason Aronson.

Rhyne, J. (1978a). *Expanding our comprehension of visual imagery*. Proceedings of the Ninth Annual Conference of the American Art Therapy Association, 95–97.

Rhyne, J. (1978b). *Theoretical backgrounds for art therapy*. Unpublished paper presented at panel at the American Association of Art Therapy.

Rhyne, J. (1980). Gestalt psychology/Gestalt therapy: forms/ contexts. *The Gestalt Journal, III*(1), 76–83.

Sartre, J. P. (1943). *L'Etre et le néant* [Being and nothingness]. Paris, Fr: Gallimard, Pub.

Zinker, J. (1978). *Creative process in Gestalt therapy*. New York, NY: Vintage Books.

Zinker, J. (1994). *In search of good form: Gestalt-therapy with couples and families*. Cleveland, OH: GIC Press.

Additional Suggested Readings

Ciornai, S. (1983). Art therapy with working class Latino women. *The Arts in Psychotherapy*, 10(2), 63–76.

Ciornai, S. (1995). The importance of the background in Gestalt therapy. *The Gestalt Journal*, XVIII(2), 7–34.

Ciornai, S. (2003). L'Art—thérapie gestaltiste: Une approche expérientielle, phénoménologique et existentielle. *Cahiers de Gestalt Thérapie*, 13, 139–151. Paris: College Français de Gestalt Therapie.

Ciornai, S. (2004). Arteterapia Gestáltica [Gestalt art therapy]. In *Percursos em Arteterapia* [Paths in art therapy] (pp. 20–197). São Paulo: Summus Editorial.

Dartigues, A. (1973). *O que é fenomenologia?* [What is phenomenology?]. Rio de Janeiro: Livraria Eldorado.

Feinstein, D., & Krippner, S. (1988). *Personal mythology.* Los Angeles, CA: Jeremy Tarcher, Inc.

Rhyne, J. (1973). *The gestalt art experience.* Monterey, CA: Brooks & Cole.

Rhyne, J. (1977). *Drawings as personal constructs: a study in visual dynamics.* Unpublished doctoral dissertation, University of California, Santa Cruz.

Yontef, G. (1979). Gestalt therapy: clinical phenomenology. *The Gestalt Journal*, II(1), 27–45.

6

Expressive Therapies Continuum
Vija B. Lusebrink

Art therapy relies on diverse theoretical approaches to therapy. The Expressive Therapies Continuum (ETC), with its emphasis on the elements specific to art therapy—namely, expression of sensations, perceptions, feelings, thoughts, and ideas in visual images using art media—offers an approach to art therapy based on the multifaceted characteristics of visual expressions. Specific to the ETC is its stepwise structure of three levels of visual information processing and expression of increasing complexity.

Introduction

Originally the ETC, as formulated by Kagan (now Graves-Alcorn) and Lusebrink (1978), was based on their respective observations in their work in art therapy with patients with acute psychosis (Lusebrink, 1974) and mental retardation (Kagin, 1969). The concept of the ETC incorporated the main existing approaches to art therapy: art as therapy (Cane, 1951; Kramer, 1971); dynamically oriented art therapy (Naumburg, 1950, 1953, 1966); phenomenological art therapy (Betensky, 1973, 1995); and Gestalt art therapy (Rhyne, 1973, 1979, 1987). Lusebrink (1990, 1991) elaborated this model by including information related to imagery and visual expression from other disciplines. Based on Pascual-Leone's (2006) work on the plasticity of the brain, Lusebrink (2004, 2010) also hypothesized that artistic expression can contribute to changes in the pathways or create new pathways used in processing visual information. Her studies of visual imagery and its psychophysiological components (Lusebrink, 1986, Lusebrink & McGuigan, 1989) led Lusebrink (2004, 2010) to propose possible different areas and functions of the brain associated with different levels of visual information processing and visual expression. The structural basis of the three stepwise levels of the ETC has been further discussed by Lusebrink, Martinsone, and Dzilna-Silova (2013).

The Wiley Handbook of Art Therapy, First Edition. Edited by David E. Gussak and Marcia L. Rosal.
© 2016 John Wiley & Sons, Ltd. Published 2016 by John Wiley & Sons, Ltd.

Description of ETC

The expression and the use of media and techniques in art therapy can be seen as taking place on different levels. These levels represent information processing from spontaneous reaction to the expression of feelings and thought through art media. Each level of the ETC is described as a continuum between two opposite poles, whereby the extreme end of each pole represents variations as an indication of possible psychopathology found in visual expressions on that level. The sequence of the three levels (kinesthetic/sensory, perceptual/affective, and cognitive/symbolic) reflects the mental and graphical development in progression from simple to more complex levels of information processing (Lusebrink, 1990; Lusebrink et al., 2013).

A creative expression can occur at any single level of the ETC, or can represent the integration of functioning on all levels (see Figure 6.1). The levels of the ETC and their polarities can be regarded as separate systems in relation to each other. These levels are organized in a stepwise order, whereby the expression on a particular level of the ETC incorporates the characteristics of a system at a lower level (Lusebrink, 1990, p. 113).

Kinesthetic/sensory (K/S) level   On the K/S level, the kinesthetic (K) component represents simple motor expressions with art media and their corresponding visual manifestations of energy.

An emphasis on kinesthetic activity on the kinesthetic level decreases awareness of the sensory component of the expression, whereas on the sensory level the emphasis on the sensory component decreases and slows down kinesthetic action because the focus is directed to the experience of sensations. The variations of the K component are characterized by agitated actions and disregard for boundaries and limits, such as frantic scribbling, throwing or destruction of materials, or marked lack of energy. Lusebrink (2010) hypothesized that the K component appears to reflect the predominant involvement of the basal ganglia and the primary motor cortex (Christian, 2008) of the brain.

The sensory (S) component of the visual expression focuses attention on the sensory exploration of materials, surfaces, and textures. The variations of the S component are typified as over-absorption in the sensory experience, extreme sensory sensitivity, and marked slowing down of movements involved in the expression. The S component

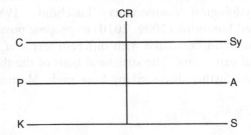

Figure 6.1   Schematic drawing of the ETC. From: Vija B. Lusebrink (1990). *Imagery and visual expression in therapy* (Figure 5.1, p. 92). New York, NY: Plenum Press. With kind permission from Springer Science +Business Media B. V.

appears to reflect an emphasis of involvement of primary somato-sensory cortex. The creative transition of this level of ETC encompasses kinesthetic expression integrated with sensory awareness of the movement involved in art making.

Perceptual/affective level (P/A) The perceptual (P) component of the P/A level focuses on forms and their differentiation. Perceptual processing of visual expression is characterized by figure/ground differentiation, whereby forms are defined by lines as boundaries and/or by color to mark defined areas. The variations of the P component are characterized by disintegration of forms, incomplete forms, figure and ground reversal, geometrization of forms, and overemphasis of details or lack of details. Very small forms, minimal or no color to define forms, and constricted use of space indicate a restricted affective involvement.

The perceptual component appears to reflect an emphasis on the processes of the ventral stream of the visual information processing in the inferior temporal lobe with its emphasis on differentiation and clarification of features and shapes, or the question "what is it?," whereas the dorsal stream in the multimodal association cortex in the parietal lobe indicates where the form is located in space in relation to other forms, or "where is it?" (Christian, 2008; Fuster, 2003; Lusebrink, 2010).

The affective (A) component of the P/A level is characterized by increased involvement with, and expression of, affect and affective modification of forms. The presence, differentiation, and change of affect are indicated by the increased use of hues and their values. The variations of the A component are marked by disintegration of form, indiscriminate mixing of color, clashing colors or colors inappropriate to the subject matter, interpenetration of forms, and/or merging of figure and ground.

The affective component appears to primarily reflect the processing of emotions in the amygdala and its influence on the ventral visual stream (Christian, 2008; Lusebrink, 2010).

The creative transition area of this ETC level encompasses good and/or differentiated gestalts (Kreitler & Kreitler, 1972, pp. 81–96), dynamic forms enlivened with color, and aesthetical ordering of forms.

Cognitive/Symbolic level (C/SY) The cognitive (C) component of the cognitive/ symbolic level emphasizes cognitive operations. It is characterized by the cognitive integration of forms and lines leading to concept formation, categorization, problem solving, spatial differentiation and integration, word inclusion, differentiation of meaning of objective images, and abstractions. The variations of the C component are characterized by disintegration of surface and spatial structure, illogical relations between forms, loss of conceptual meaning, and over-inclusion of words.

The cognitive component appears to involve the regulatory "top–down" influences of the prefrontal cortex, especially the dorsolateral prefrontal cortex and possibly the anterior part of the cingulate cortex (Christian, 2008; Lusebrink, 2010).

The symbolic (Sy) component of this level emphasizes global processing by involving input from sensory and affective sources, processing of autobiographic material, and symbolic expressions. It is characterized by affective images, the symbolic use of color, symbolic abstractions, and intuitive integrative concept formation. Large symbolic images may be associated with loss of reflective distance. The variations of the symbolic component are characterized by obscure or idiosyncratic meaning of symbols, over-identification with symbols, symbolic manifestations of defenses, and figure/ground reversal.

The symbolic component appears to primarily reflect the "top–down" processes of the orbitofrontal cortex and possibly the posterior part of the cingulate cortex (Christian, 2008; Lusebrink, 2010). The integrative function of the orbitofrontal cortex includes the retrieval of autobiographical consciousness (Carr, 2008).

The creative transition area between the cognitive and symbolic poles encompasses intuitive problem solving, images of self-discovery, and spiritual insight.

The three-leveled structure of the ETC can be applied in therapy with the other modalities of arts therapies, namely, music, dance, and drama (Lusebrink, 1991).

Influence of interdisciplinary sources on the structure of the ETC

The structural aspects and stepwise sequence of the ETC levels (Lusebrink et al., 2013) are based on several authors' concepts of the different stages of graphical development (Lowenfeld & Brittain, 1970), stages of imagery formation and cognitive development (Bruner,1964; Horowitz, 1970), and the sequence of visual information processing in different brain structures (Fuster, 2003).

Lowenfeld and Brittain (1970) conceptualized several developmental stages in children's artwork based on general principles of cognitive development. The stages of graphic development (scribbling, pre-schematic, schematic, dawning realism, and pseudo-naturalistic) emerge parallel to a child's biopsychosocial development.

Bruner (1964) formulated three types of representation: active, iconic, and symbolic. Active-type representation reflects events through a response with movement; iconic-type representation selectively organizes individuals' perceptions and images; and symbolic-type representation names and transforms the experience through abstraction and other complex mental processes.

Horowitz (1970, 1983) expanded Bruner's model by proposing three modes of representation of thought: enactive, image, and lexical. The first two modes represent thought based on movement and perceptions, including inputs form all sensory channels, memories, and fantasies, whereas the lexical or verbal mode serves in abstraction and concept formation.

According to Fuster (2003, p. 109), sensory information is processed in the brain on hierarchical levels of perceptual knowledge in a "bottom–up" manner, proceeding from simpler to more complex processes, namely from primary sensory and motor cortex to unimodal association cortex, to polymodal association cortex, and then to the prefrontal zones of the brain. Fuster points out that neural pathways are accessible in both parallel processing and coordination of information and its dissemination happens in both directions—upwards and downwards or bottom-up and top-down (p. 67). Fuster and others (Horowitz, 1970; Marks, 1983) indicate that when the brain processes the images, it uses the same pathways and areas as the corresponding sensory modalities of perception.

Common to the preceding concepts and the ETC are their stepwise increase in the complexity of information processing.

Application of the ETC in therapy

Inherent in the application of the ETC concept in art therapy are the transitions between the different levels and their polarities. The levels of the ETC can be regarded as different but interconnected systems reflecting the different brain processes and functions, whereby "the expression and interaction with media on the different levels of the ETC function as a whole and changes occurring of separate levels are interrelated" (Lusebrink, 1990, p. 113). Difficulties with or blockage of a particular component of the ETC indicate a disconnection between the systems and/or difficulties in the transitions between them.

Possible steps toward integrated functioning on the different levels, as well as suggestions for interventions through the application of different media in art therapy, are based on the influences that media exert generally on visual expression. The characteristics of media in art therapy range from resistive to fluid (Hinz, 2009; Kagin, 1969; Lusebrink, 1990). These media qualities can influence and enhance visual expressions on different levels of the ETC. Generally, the left-side components of the ETC schema (see Figure 6.1), namely kinesthetic, perceptual, and cognitive, may indicate left hemispheric predominance in information processing, and are enhanced through the use of resistive media, such as pencil, crayons, or markers. The right-side components of the ETC schema, namely, sensory, affective, and symbolic, may indicate right hemispheric predominance in information processing and are evoked and enhanced through the use of fluid media, such as poster paint, water color, or finger paint (Hinz, 2009; Lusebrink, 1990). The influence of media enhances the change of ETC levels in visual expression, and possibly contributes to the changes in the pathways used in processing information based on the plasticity of the brain.

Visual expressions in art therapy reflect the predominant level(s) of ETC present and display the client's strengths and weaknesses or difficulties. The client's strengths are manifested in their visual expressions on any level(s) of the ETC that correspond to the normal descriptions on that particular level(s). The client's weaknesses are displayed when their visual expressions correspond to the descriptions of variations possibly indicating psychopathology on any level of the ETC.

The predominant level in the visual expression may offer a starting point in the therapy, in that the client presumably feels relatively comfortable on this level of expression and would display the least resistance. If the predominant level coincides with the client's strengths on this level, this entry point would provide a solid foundation from which to proceed in dealing with the weaknesses and/or psychopathology displayed on other level(s) of ETC.

The weaknesses or difficulties represent a "missing link" in the fluid process of information processing. If the predominant level in the expression displays weakness, steps need to be taken to explore it while reinforcing levels that reflect the client's strengths. The weaknesses are explored gradually using different media to enhance the vertical and/or horizontal transitions between levels and the components of the ETC (Lusebrink et al., 2013).

The schematic representation of the ETC becomes a ladder indicating movement from lower levels to higher levels and vice versa in the client's visual expressions, and,

correspondingly, his/her functioning (Lusebrink, 2010). The ETC schematic representation (Figure 6.1) can be used for charting the levels of visual expression for each
step in therapy and also in the review process over a period of time.

The ETC directly addresses the use of media in art therapy, and at the same time
can be used concurrently with other approaches to psychotherapy appropriate to the
corresponding levels of the ETC, or with the therapist's preferred approach (Hinz,
2009). Hinz discusses the application of ETC in art therapy with different client
groups and presenting problems.

In art therapy, the structure of ETC with its three different levels can help to
facilitate, enhance, and understand the underlying art therapy process, as illustrated
by the following excerpts from a case study.

A Case Vignette[1]

Robert, a 17-year-old adolescent, was referred to short-term art therapy for his
hostile interactions with peers and the diagnosis of adjustment reaction. The
following discussion of his art expressions focuses on the process of art therapy.
As part of his assessment, Robert executed a freehand drawing of an "Automaton"
(Figure 6.2).

In the next session, Robert elaborated on his drawing by creating, in modeling
clay, "Decadron," the good guy, and Automaton, the bad guy, with his son
(Figure 6.3), who were ready to fight.

Figure 6.2 Automaton.

Figure 6.3 Decadron, Automaton, and Automaton's son.

Figure 6.4 Finger painting of a volcano.

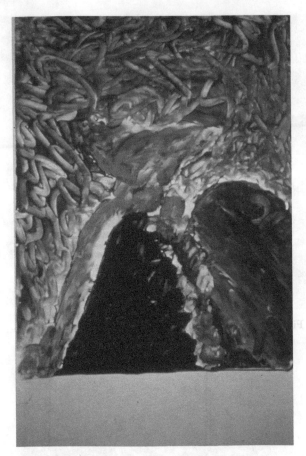

Figure 6.5 Robert's good and bad feelings.

Next time, the therapist suggested to Robert the use of finger paint to express how the figures felt.

After several amorphous finger paintings Robert painted a volcano (Figure 6.4) as an expression of his anger.

After several weeks, Robert made a drawing differentiating his good and bad feelings in six images. The good feelings, identified by a smiling mask, were represented by climbing a mountain and helping an old woman to walk across a street, whereas angry finger painting, an angry mask, and a realistic-looking young man who was ready to "punish" the bad guy, were associated with his bad feelings (Figure 6.5).

In the context of the concept of ETC, Robert's images were at first on the symbolic level, and showed a strong sense of form on the perceptual level, but indicate possible restriction or repression of his feelings on the affective level. His first expressions with finger paint were on the sensory level, followed by the expression of his feelings on the affective pole of the perceptual/affective level, whereas the painting of a volcano reflected the transition to the perceptual side

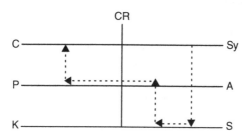

Figure 6.6 Representation of Robert's sequence of visual expressions on the ETC schema.

of this level. The final six drawings represent Robert's differentiation of feelings, and are predominantly on the cognitive level, whereby the figure drawings are on the cognitive level, masks on the perceptual level, and the inclusion of the finger painting refers back to the sensory and affective levels. This process is schematically presented in Figure 6.6.

Based on the proposed areas and functions associated with the different levels of the ETC (Lusebrink, 2004, 2010), this sequence of the art expression appears to reflect a transition between areas and functions of the brain involved in visual expression. The initial symbolic displacement and activity in the right prefrontal cortex was transformed through the kinesthetic/sensory activity and associated feelings that evoked the image of a volcano in the inferior temporal cortex, and was eventually followed by cognitive activity in the left prefrontal cortex. Negative emotions are associated with a predominantly right hemispheric activity, whereas positive emotions with a predominantly left hemispheric activity (Lusebrink, 2004; Davidson with Begley, 2012).

In a recent summary of cognitive influences on emotions and the underlying activity of brain processes, Davidson (Davidson with Begley, 2012) points out that the activation of the left prefrontal cortex shortens the period of amygdala activation, and that greater left-versus-right activation in the prefrontal cortex is associated with a greater resilience to distress.

The ETC schematic representation of the visual expressions in the preceding case example highlights the change of a predominantly symbolic activity to the predominance of cognitive activity through the process of art therapy

Conclusions

The ETC differentiates visual expressions of images, thoughts, and feelings into three stepwise levels: kinesthetic/sensory, perceptual/affective, and cognitive/symbolic, whereas a creative expression can be present on any of these levels. Its interdisciplinary-based structure of increasing complexity parallels the stages of cognitive development, the increasing complexity of visual information processing in the brain, and reflects the multifaceted character of visual images.

The stepwise structure of the ETC provides a conceptual framework for planning therapeutic interventions and for reviewing the process of art therapy as expressed in images over a period of time. Specific to using the different levels of the ETC and their polarities in art therapy is the recognition of blocked information processing on specific level(s) and their integration through the use of different media.

The different levels of the ETC can also provide a basis for research in art therapy on the effects of interventions on a particular level on the other aspects of information processing and expression.

Endnote

1 Case study by intern while student at the Expressive Therapies program, University of Louisville, Kentucky, United States.

References

Betensky, M. G. (1973). *Self-discovery through self-expression*. Springfield, IL: Charles C. Thomas.

Betensky, M. G. (1995). *What do you see: Phenomenology of therapeutic art expression*. London: Jessica Kingsley Publishers.

Bruner, J. S. (1964). The course of cognitive growth. *American Psychologist, 19*, 1–15.

Cane, F. (1951). *The artist in each of us*. New York, NY: Pantheon Books.

Carr, R. (2008). Sensory processes and responses. In Noah Hass-Cohen & Richard Carr (Eds.), *Art therapy and clinical neuroscience* (pp. 43–61). London: Jessica Kingsley.

Christian, D. (2008). The cortex: Regulation of sensory and emotional experience. In N. Hass-Cohen & R. Carr (Eds.), *Art therapy and clinical neuroscience* (pp. 62–75). London: Jessica Kingsley.

Davidson, R. J. with Begley, S. (2012). *The emotional life of your brain*. New York, NY: Hudson Street Press.

Fuster, J. M. (2003). *Cortex and mind: Unifying cognition*. New York, NY: Oxford University Press.

Hinz, L. D. (2009). *Expressive Therapies Continuum: A framework for using art in therapy*. New York, NY: Routledge.

Horowitz, M. J. (1970). *Image formation and cognition*. New York, NY: Appleton-Century-Crofts.

Horowitz, M. J. (1983). *Image formation and cognition* (rev. ed.). New York, NY: Jason Aronson.

Kagin, S. L. (1969). *The effects of structure on the painting of retarded youth*. Unpublished master's thesis, University of Tulsa, Tulsa, Oklahoma.

Kagin, S. L., & Lusebrink, V. B. (1978). The Expressive Therapies Continuum. *Art Psychotherapy, 5*(4), 171–180.

Kramer, E. (1971). *Art as therapy with children*. New York, NY: Schocken Press.

Kreitler, H., & Kreitler, S. (1972). *Psychology of the arts*. Durham, NC: Durham University Press.

Lowenfeld, V., & Brittain, W. M. (1970). *Creative and mental growth* (5th ed.). New York, NY: Macmillan.

Lusebrink, V. B. (1974). Visual expression and creativity in psychosis. Paper presented at the 5th Annual Conference of the American Art Therapy Association, New York, NY.

Lusebrink, V. B. (1986). Visual imagery: Its psychophysiological components and information processing. *Imagination, Cognition, and Personality, 6*(3), 205–218.

Lusebrink, V. B. (1990). *Imagery and visual expression in therapy*. New York, NY: Plenum Press.

Lusebrink, V. B. (1991). A systems oriented approach to the expressive therapies: The Expressive Therapies Continuum. *The Arts in Psychotherapy, 18*(5), 395–403.

Lusebrink, V. B. (2004). Art therapy and the brain: An attempt to understand the underlying processes of art expression in therapy. *Art therapy: Journal of American Art Therapy Association, 21*(3), 125–135.

Lusebrink, V. B. (2010). Assessment and therapeutic application of the Expressive Therapies Continuum: Implications for brain structures and functions. *Art Therapy: Journal of American Art Therapy Association, 27*(4), 168–77.

Lusebrink, V. B., Martinsone, K., & Dzilna-Silova, I. (2013). The expressive therapies continuum (ETC): Interdisciplinary bases of the ETC. *International Journal of Art Therapy, 18*(2), 75–85.

Lusebrink, V. B., & McGuigan. J. F. (1989). Psychophysiological components of visual imagery. *Pavlovian Journal of Biological Science, 24*(2), 58–62.

Marks, D. F. (1983). Mental imagery and consciousness: A theoretical review. In A. Sheikh (Ed.), *Imagery: Current theory, research, and application* (pp. 96–130). New York, NY: Wiley.

Naumburg, M. (1950). *Schizophrenic art: It's meaning in art therapy.* New York, NY: Grune & Stratton.

Naumburg, M. (1953). *Psychoneurotic art: Its function in psychotherapy.* New York, NY: Grune & Stratton.

Naumburg, M. (1966). *Dynamically oriented art therapy: Its principles and practice.* New York, NY: Grune & Stratton.

Pascual-Leone, A. (2006). Disrupting the brain to guide plasticity and improve behavior. *Progress in Brain Research, 157*, 315–329.

Rhyne, J. (1973). *The gestalt art therapy experience.* Monterey, CA: Brooks/Cole Publishing Company.

Rhyne, J. (1979). Drawings as personal constructs: A study of visual dynamics. *Dissertation Abstracts International, 40*(5), 2411B (University Microfilms International No. Tx, 375–487).

Rhyne, J. (1987). Gestalt art therapy. In J. Rubin (Ed.), *Approaches to art therapy* (pp. 167–187). New York, NY: Brunner/Mazel, Publishers.

7

Cognitive-behavioral Art Therapy Revisited

Marcia L. Rosal

Cognitive-behavioral therapies (CBTs), which encompass a constellation of treatment variants, have been around for about 50 years. According to some psychologists, it is still regarded as a relatively new theoretical approach to therapy (when compared to psychodynamic approaches; Davey, 2013). Based on numerous studies, including randomized controlled studies, CBT is a highly effective and useful therapeutic approach for anxiety disorders including post-traumatic stress disorder (PTSD), depression, eating disorders, schizophrenia, personality disorders, criminality, substance abuse disorders, etc. In fact, some even tout cognitive therapy as one of the most important advances in medical treatment in the past 50 years (Altman as cited in Hofmann, Asmundson, & Beck, 2013). The foundation of CBT is rooted in social learning theory (Bandura, 1969; Miller & Dollard, 1941; Rotter, 1966). This theory arose at a time when psychologists were exploring theories to accommodate not only how humans behave but how we think about issues, emotions, events, and ourselves, and how we perceive these important aspects of being.

Cognitive-behavioral art therapy (CBAT) first appeared in art therapy literature during the late 1970s when two important thinkers wrote about their work: (1) Ellen Roth (1978) discussed the idea of using behavioral therapy techniques and "reality shaping" as a means of conceptualizing art therapy for children with both developmental and psychiatric disorders; and (2) Janie Rhyne (1979) explored personal construct theory (Kelly, 1955) as a base for helping individuals to explore emotional states. Thus, CBAT has only been around for 25 years, or one-half as long as CBT. Neither Roth nor Rhyne realized just how pivotal their work would become.

I was introduced to CBT in the early 1980s while working on a doctoral degree. My research interest involved treating children with two serious problems: external locus of control (Rotter, 1966.) and learned helplessness (Maier & Seligman, 1976). While researching these two psychological constructs, it became evident that CBT was the most effective strategy for alleviating the effects of these issues on problematic behavior and for restoring overall functioning. My challenge was to develop an art therapy program for children experiencing these difficulties. Based on the evidence that CBT was a powerful, efficacious treatment, I created and tested a CBAT program for children with serious behavioral problems (Rosal, 1986, 1993).

The Wiley Handbook of Art Therapy, First Edition. Edited by David E. Gussak and Marcia L. Rosal.
© 2016 John Wiley & Sons, Ltd. Published 2016 by John Wiley & Sons, Ltd.

In this chapter, I would like to reimagine CBAT. To do this, I will: (1) examine CBT today; (2) review historical and recent developments in CBAT as well as provide examples from the art therapy literature; and (3) rediscover CBAT in our work as art therapists.

CBT Today

CBT is one of the dominant approaches to therapy today. There are several treatment models that fall under the CBT umbrella, and these variants have commonalities. Mennin, Ellard, Fresco, and Gross (2013) found that the unifying goal of CBTs is *behavioral adaptation*. According to these authors, CBT therapists "direct interventions towards cultivating more *behaviorally adaptive* [emphasis added] responses in order to survive and thrive in these important [life] domains" (p. 236). They cited three guiding principles of CBT: (1) context engagement or re-examining problematic situations in order to imagine novel responses; (2) attention change or helping clients to sustain or shift attention in order to better adapt to various situations; and (3) cognitive change or gain perspective or alter meanings of emotionally significant situations (p. 237). Other important CBT traditions include helping clients recognize and disengage from ruminations, negative patterns of thinking and behaving, and damaging self-talk so entwined with devastating consequences.

Hofmann and Asmundson (2008) identified six essential steps or foci in the practice of CBT: (1) establishing a good therapeutic rapport; (2) having a problem focus; (3) identifying irrational thoughts; (4) challenging irrational thoughts; (5) testing the validity of thoughts; and (6) substituting irrational thoughts with rational ones (p. 4). Specific CBT protocols have been developed for various diagnostic groups. For example, Ehlers and Clark (2000) developed a protocol for PTSD that includes identification and remediation of triggers as well as cognitive and behavioral variables that maintain PTSD.

There are discussions among CBT theorists about the importance of emotions and emotional responses in cognitive theory. Gross (2002) found that regulating emotional distress and targeting CBT approaches for emotional regulation are both parts of CBT. Hofmann and Asmundson (2008) affirmed that effective CBT includes the examination of emotional experiences. According to Mennin et al. (2013), CBT therapists "target a change in existing emotional responses to achieve symptom reduction and distress relief" (p. 237). This is because "cognitions causally influence emotions" (Hofmann, Asmundson, & Beck, 2013, p. 200), and "the relationship between emotions and cognitions is bidirectional because changes in emotions can lead to changes in cognitions" (p. 200). In her understanding of personal construct therapy, Rhyne (1979) found that both cognitive and emotional components of experiences uncovered in treatment are interwoven, and both need attention.

As indicated in the preceding text, there are numerous treatment variants within CBT. Three recent variants—dialectical behavioral therapy (Linehan, 1993), mindfulness-based cognitive therapy (Segal, Williams, &Teasdale, 2002), and motivational interviewing (Miller & Rollnick, 1991)—are familiar to art therapists and are often misconstrued as being separate from CBT. Yet, these recent CBTs have many of the same components (e.g., intervention characteristics, goals, principles, and processes) as traditional CBTs; they have a common framework with CBT and are, in reality, under the CBT umbrella (Mennin et al., 2013). What is of particular importance to this discussion is that art therapists seem to embrace DBT and MBCT with more ease than more traditional CBTs. In 2001, I commented that, "[t]he misconception that CBT focuses only on the thinking process may be one of the reasons that art therapists have not embraced it more fully" (p. 213). The other reasons for this phenomenon are multidimensional and too numerous to address in this chapter. With a detailed discussion of CBAT, a renewed appreciation for this approach among art therapists may be possible.

CBAT Yesterday and Today

CBT and CBAT have common elements: (1) developing healthy and flexible adaptation strategies in order to enhance the chances of survival and improve life; (2) understanding cognitions, including inner speech and mental imagery, as antecedents to behavior; and (3) promoting pragmatic solution generation for helping individuals under duress and as an efficient way to relieve stress and enhance coping. In addition, uncovering mental images and emotion states, as part of the cognitive framework, is an important component of CBAT.

As stated previously, CBAT began with Roth and Rhyne. Other art therapists experimented with incorporating CBT into their work. Some CBT principles useful to art therapists are: (1) problem-solving (Packard, 1977); (2) modeling (Roth, 1978; Rozum, 2001); (3) relaxation techniques and mental imagery (Lusebrink, 1990; Rosal, 1986, 1993); (4) stress reduction (Lusebrink, 1990); and (5) systematic desensitization and/or flooding (De Francisco, 1983; Gerber, 1994; Matto, 1997; Reynolds, 1999). These CBAT principles will be discussed in the following text using examples from both historic and current writers.

Reality shaping

Reality shaping involves identifying a concept that eludes the understanding of the client (Roth, 2001). First, the art therapist helps the client bring representational form to that concept by creating a shape; and second, the child constructs and reconstructs these structures. This can be a repetitive process; also, the child is encouraged to use more complex materials to explore the form through both two-dimensional (2D) and three-dimensional (3D) materials. The goal of reality shaping is based on the principle that developing and constructing a schema (through both mental and graphic images) for complex, psychologically sensitive issues is a means to organize confused, dysfunctional thinking and can be useful in helping a client gain control of the problems at hand. Roth (2001) used reality shaping with Larry, a child with destructive behavior, who set fire to the family home. Using craft sticks, Roth formed a flat model of a house, which Larry used as a template to re-create houses; after several sessions of using the 2D house, Larry was ready to build 3D houses. He became protective of the houses he drew and constructed, which coincided with a shift in this destructive behavior in his family home.

In a recent study of learning-disabled children with a poor sense of self, Freilich and Shechtman (2010) presented the case of Dina. They described her first human figures, made using modeling clay, as poorly shaped. After creating several human figures over a number of sessions, the shapes became more clearly articulated. This corresponded with an improvement in her trust of adults, including therapists and teachers.

Personal constructs analysis

Personal constructs, or an individual's hypotheses on how aspects of the world work (Kelly, 1955), were used by Rhyne (1979) for helping individuals understand emotions and emotionally charged situations and events. Rhyne proposed 15 common feelings or mind states and encouraged individuals to create small black-and-white drawings of each mind state or personal construct of emotions. Through the process of finding commonalities and differences among the drawn personal constructs, individuals (1) uncovered how the emotionally charged situations in their life became out of control; (2) used the mind state drawings to understand which feeling states preceded uncomfortable periods in their life; and (3) learned how to use mind states to regulate their emotional well-being.

Recently, Pifalo (2007) used a similar concept for trauma processing with sexually abused children. She used a box to afford "a concrete vehicle for separating and expressing emotions that are appropriate for sharing with the world in general on the outside of the box and, on the inside of the box, those feelings that are shared only with someone who is trusted" (p. 172). Not only were the children provided opportunities to identify feeling states, but they also learned to distinguish what feelings might be best discussed in private versus in public. In 2002, Pifalo reported another art therapy experience reminiscent of Rhyne's work. She had children who had been sexually abused create two puppets: one that had been abused and one that was the perpetrator. Speaking through the puppets, the girls "were able to try on different personas and look at the event from different perspectives" (p. 18). This was one way for the children to regain control of the abusive situation.

Problem-solving

Central to CBAT is problem-solving. The generation of solutions helps clients adapt to new situations and solve dilemmas. Packard (1977) interjected problem-solving in her CBAT work with children with learning disabilities. She assisted children to create maps or mental layouts to organize information. The newly organized information would lead to finding solutions to both simple and complex problems.

An updated use of problem-solving can be seen in the work of Breiner, Tuomisto, Bouyea, Gussak, and Aufderheide (2011). They developed an anger management treatment protocol for male inmates in a state prison. The protocol was steeped in the CBT tradition, as is typical in the US prison system, but they added art therapy to engage the inmates and help them visualize and alter rigid, stereotypical cognitive constructs. First, the inmates were instructed to visualize and create a 3D model of a vehicle using only colored construction paper and glue. Second, these constructions were used in a guided imagery, which took the inmates on a trip in their vehicle that led to a large body of water. The inmates had to problem-solve overcoming a large body of water using their land-based vehicles. Finally, the ability to re-imagine and reconstruct their vehicles for use over water was related to the aggression cycle. Two of the goals for this CBAT intervention were solution-generation and creating a shift in dysfunctional thinking.

Modeling

Several art therapists have discussed the CBT principle of modeling. Rozum (2001) considered the importance of modeling when working with groups of children with behavioral disorders. In her groups, positive, pro-social behavior was modeled by the group art therapist; children modeled positive behaviors for each other; and seasoned members modeled pro-group behaviors for new members so that they, too, could adjust to group culture. Rozum realized that modeling the use of art materials was a natural function of most group and individual art therapy work with children.

More recently, Pifalo (2007) integrated modeling in her work with abused children. In her report of *parallel activity*, Pifalo recommended that the art therapist work alongside the child. Using the modeling method, information could be imparted in a less threatening manner.

Relaxation techniques and mental imagery

People think in words *and* in images. Mental images often drive behavior, particularly mental images of one's self. Lusebrink (1990) stated, "The assessment of the client's *self-image* is an important part of using imagery in healing" (p. 228). Art therapists have long asked clients to draw how they see themselves. The CBAT technique of having clients draw what they see "in their mind's eye" is facilitated by being in a relaxed state (Lusebrink, 1990). These two techniques, when coupled, can create fertile ground for art therapists to explore difficult, emotion-laden material. Lusebrink found that art therapy can bring the chaos of some mental images into focus through a drawn form of these images. Rosal (1986, 1993) used relaxation and mental images to help children and young adolescents with behavior disorders to uncover how they see themselves and problematic areas of their life. Through a guided imagery and subsequent drawn images of a problematic classroom event, a young male student realized that *his* behavior was the root cause of classmates seeing him in a poor light.

More recently, Rankin and Taucher (2003), in an article on art therapy and trauma treatment, recommended clients *imagine* the scene of a traumatic event as part of creating the trauma narrative. In a 2010 study of teens preparing for high school, Spier asked the participants to draw, "Me in the Ninth Grade." After a series of six other CBAT interventions, the students were once again asked to draw themselves in high school. The pre- and post-test drawings of one participant were remarkable, illustrating changes in both organization and drawing detail.

Stress reduction and adaptive coping strategies

Reducing stress and helping clients identify and employ new coping strategies is a major goal of CBAT. Imagery and relaxation aid in stress reduction, and, as Lusebrink (1990) affirmed, "Stress and relaxation are incompatible with each other" (p. 233). Stress reduction is one result of learning new ways to cope. Using art therapy to uncover coping strategies might be as simple as engaging a client in art-making itself. Creating art can release tensions, especially when scribbling with markers or throwing clay. Karen, who suffered from depression, learned some simple coping strategies through a simple timeline drawing (Rosal, 2001). She was directed to use a line to chart the highs and lows of her life. When thinking about circumstances that preceded her lows, she realized that serious and difficult events always triggered the depressive episodes. After drawing out several mood states (see Rhyne, 1979), Karen realized that stress and then anxiety were associated with these disturbing events. When her stress heightened, depression soon followed. Subsequent treatment sessions focused on coping with stress. Karen found relief when she learned to identify the bodily sensations of stress. She also drew out a number of ways to cope with stress, including informing her doctor before the stress and anxiety spiked.

Chapman, Morabito, Ladakakos, Schreier, and Knudson (2001) developed a short-term art therapy protocol for post-traumatic stress. She began with a graphic kines-thetic activity "to stimulate the formation of images" (p. 102). Next, she directed a series of drawings to help the child tell the trauma story. In this protocol, stress was released in the motor activity and then further contained through the drawn narrative. In their trauma work, Rankin and Taucher (2003) used "art-making to self-soothe by choosing calming and comforting colors, shapes, lines, and images while relaxing the shoulders and slowing hand movement" (p. 140). Curl (2008) agreed that the external expression of stress through art-making decreased anxiety states. Spier (2010) found that addressing inappropriate responses to stress was a first step toward learning coping strategies for difficult events in the school environment.

Systematic desensitization

Systematic desensitization (SI), which is often paired with flooding, is useful in coping with stressors and fears. DeFrancisco (1983) and Gerber (1994) both used images to desensitize clients experiencing stress associated with a specific situation. Matto (1997) found that women with eating disorders had difficulty identifying and dealing with intense emotions. She encouraged the women to deal with emotions by examining the least troublesome feelings first. As they became accustomed to lesser evocative emotions, Matto would have the clients explore more difficult feeling states. This systematic exposure to increasingly threatening material serves as a finely tuned example of SI.

A more recent example of SI comes from Rankin and Taucher (2003). When working with individuals who had traumatic losses, the authors had "clients identify and process lesser loses before addressing the more devastating ones" (p. 143). They recommended the use of collage images to begin this process. After the client found a representation of a loss, they would ask the client to tear the image in half to represent the loss. This was followed by having clients identify the feelings associated with the loss and finding other images to represent the impact of the loss on their current life.

Reimagining CBAT

CBAT is alive and well. Illustrations of CBAT interventions pepper the art therapy literature. There are many exciting and specific CBAT processes employed by art therapists. Authors may not have identified their approach as CBAT, but it is clear that many art therapy interventions have a CBT base. One way to grasp just how important CBAT is to our field is by reading art therapy literature through a CBAT lens and looking for key terms such as *stress reduction, problem-solving, regulating emotions, developing self-efficacy, modifying perceptions, coping strategies,* etc.

Embracing the fact that CBT has a central place in the practice of art therapy is important and timely. For example, CBAT is now recognized as an important component of PTSD treatment. Finding treatment paradigms for PTSD has recently gained momentum due to the number of veterans returning from wars in Afghanistan and Iraq with trauma symptoms, as well as the renewed focus on societal problems such as childhood physical and sexual abuse and the after-effects of human trafficking. PTSD treatment includes a number of CBT approaches including desensitization, coping, identification and reactivation of positive emotions, and enhancing self-efficacy (Collie, Backos, Malchiodi, & Spiegel, 2006). These authors theorized that art therapy shows promise for the treatment of PTSD, and other art therapists certainly agree (Chapman et al., 2001; Pifalo, 2002, 2007; Rankin & Taucher, 2003).

Anxiety and stress are components of PTSD; anxiety is also a disorder in itself. Working with clients who experience anxiety is a challenge, as anxiety disorders typically begin in childhood and can be lifelong. Morris (2014) studied CBAT with two individuals, one with panic disorder and agoraphobia (PDA), and the other with generalized anxiety disorder (GAD). She found support for CBAT with both diagnostic groups. Morris specified that "Art therapy may be one way in which some people with PDA and GAD can be empowered to literally create their own image of their fears and envision solutions" (p. 120).

Sarid and Huss (2010) compared the tenets of CBT to art therapy principles. They examined two individuals with traumatic stress and anxiety. They found that both modalities provided a safe space to explore sensory experiences, modulate traumatic memories, construct new cognitions, and improve "the potential of creating new connections and pathways between the physical, emotional, and cognitive components of traumatic memory" (p. 10). The authors were surprised about how two seemingly different approaches included parallel components. Their work substantiates the importance of CBAT.

CBAT is also congruent with art therapy in the schools (particularly with behaviorally disordered students; Rozum, 2001) and in the prison system (Breiner et al., 2011). In these two arenas, increasing positive, prosocial behavior is valuable for both the clients and the settings. CBAT participants develop a sense of personal success and self-efficacy, and these settings can become safer and more productive places to inhabit.

A strong case for the power of CBAT is now established. CBAT does not negate the importance of the sensory, emotive capacity of art therapy. CBAT embraces the significance of these concepts for envisioning new and adaptive patterns of thinking, behaving, problem-solving, and coping. Visualizing and reframing stressful, traumatic, disturbing thoughts, actions, and events is the domain of CBAT. I imagine art therapists embracing the CBAT concepts discussed not only in this chapter and but in other CBAT literature as well. Grasping, using, and reimagining CBAT constructs will benefit our clients for years to come.

References

Bandura, A. (1969). *Principles of behavior modification.* New York, NY: Holt, Rinehart, and Winston.

Breiner, M. J., Tuomisto, L., Bouyca, E., Gussak, D. E., & Aufderheide, D. (2011). Creating an art therapy treatment anger management protocol for male inmates through a collaborative relationship. *International Journal of Offender Therapy and Comparative Criminology, 1–20.* doi:10.1177/0306624X11417362

Collie, K., Backos, A., Malchiodi, C., & Spiegel, C. (2006). Art therapy for combat-related PTSD: Recommendations for research and practice. *Art Therapy: Journal of the American Art Therapy Association, 23*(4), 157–164.

Chapman, L., Morabito, D., Ladakakos, C., Schreier, H., & Knudson, M. M. (2001). The effectiveness of art therapy interventions in reducing post traumatic stress disorder (PTSD) symptoms in pediatric trauma patients. *Art Therapy: Journal of the American Art Therapy Association, 18*(2), 100–104.

Curl, K. (2008). Assessing stress reduction as a function of artistic creation and cognitive focus. *Art Therapy: Journal of the American Art Therapy Association, 25*(4), 164–169.

Davey, G. (2013). Review of cognitive behavioural therapy in mental health care. *Asia Pacific Journal of Counselling and Psychotherapy, 4*(1), 102–103.

DeFrancisco, J. (1983). Implosive art therapy: A learning-theory based, psychodynamic approach. In L. Gantt & S. Whitman (Eds.), *Proceedings of the Eleventh Annual Conference of the American Art Therapy Association* (pp. 74–79). Baltimore: AATA.

Ehlers, A., & Clark, D. M. (2000). A cognitive model of posttraumatic stress disorder. *Behaviour Research and Therapy, 38,* 319–345.

Freilich, R., & Shechtman, Z. (2010). The contribution of art therapy to the social, emotional, and academic adjustment of children with learning disabilities. *The Arts in Psychotherapy, 37,* 97–105.

Gerber, J. (1994). The use of art therapy in juvenile sex offender specific treatment. *The Arts in Psychotherapy, 21,* 367–374.

Gross, J. J. (2002). Emotional regulation: Affective, cognitive, and social consequences. *Psychophysiology, 39,* 281–291.

Hofmann, S. G., & Asmundson, G. J. G. (2008). Acceptance and mindfulness-based therapy: New wave or old hat? *Clinical Psychology Review, 28,* 1–16. doi: 10.1016/j.cpr.2007.09.003

Hofmann, S. G., Asmundson, G. J. J., & Beck, A. (2013). The science of cognitive therapy. *Behavior Therapy, 44,* 199–212.

Kelly, G. A. (1955). *The psychology of personal constructs.* New York, NY: W. W. Norton.

Linehan, M. (1993). *Skills training manual for treating borderline personality disorder.* New York, NY: Guildford Press.

Lusebrink, V. B. (1990). *Imagery and visual expression in therapy.* New York, NY: Plenum Press.

Maier, S. F., & Seligman, M. E. (1976). Learned helplessness: Theory and evidence. *Journal of Experimental Psychology: General, 105*(1), 3–46. doi: 10.1037/0096-3445.105.1.3

Matto, H. C. (1997). An integrative approach to the treatment of women with eating disorders. *The Arts in Psychotherapy, 24,* 347–354.

Mennin, D. S., Ellard, K. K., Fresco, D. M., & Gross, J. J. (2013). United we stand: Emphasizing commonalities across cognitive-behavioral therapies. *Behavior Therapy, 44*, 234–238.

Miller, N. E., & Dollard, J. (1941). *Social learning and imitation*. New Haven, CT: Yale University Press.

Miller, W. R., & Rollnick, S. (1991). *Motivational interviewing: Preparing people to change addictive behavior*. New York, NY: Guildford Press.

Morris, F. J. (2014). Should art be integrated into cognitive behavioral therapy for anxiety disorders? *The Arts in Psychotherapy, 41*, 343–352.

Packard, S. (1977). Learning disabilities: Identification and remediation through creative art activity. In R. H. Shoemaker & S. E. Gonick-Barris (Eds.), *Proceedings of the Seventh Annual Conference of the American Art Therapy Association* (pp. 57–61). Baltimore: AATA.

Pifalo, T. (2002). Pulling out the thorns: Art therapy with sexually abused children and adolescents. *Art Therapy: Journal of the American Art Therapy Association, 19*(1), 12–22.

Pifalo, T. (2007). Jogging the cogs: Trauma-focused art therapy and cognitive behavioral therapy with sexually abused children. *Art Therapy: Journal of the American Art Therapy Association, 24*(4), 170–175.

Rankin, A. B., & Taucher, L. C. (2003). A task-oriented approach to art therapy in trauma treatment. *Art Therapy: Journal of the American Art Therapy Association, 20*(3), 138–147.

Reynolds, R. (1999). Cognitive behavioral counseling of unresolved grief through the therapeutic adjunct of tapestry-making. *The Arts in Psychotherapy, 26*, 165–171.

Rhyne, J. (1979). *Drawings as personal constructs: A study in visual dynamics*. Unpublished doctoral dissertation, University of California, Santa Cruz.

Rosal, M. L. (1986). *The use of art therapy to modify the locus of control and adaptive behavior of behavior disordered children*. Unpublished doctoral dissertation, University of Queensland, Brisbane, Australia.

Rosal, M. L. (1993). Comparative group art therapy research to evaluate changes in locus of control. *The Arts in Psychotherapy, 20*, 231–241.

Rosal, M. (2001). Cognitive-behavioral art therapy. In J. Rubin (Ed.), *Approaches to art therapy* (pp. 210–225). Philadelphia, PA: Bruner/Routledge.

Roth, E. (1978). Art therapy with emotionally disturbed-mentally retarded children: A technique of reality shaping. In B. K. Mandel, R. H. Shoemaker, & R. E. Hays (Eds.), *The dynamics of creativity* (pp. 168–172). Baltimore: American Art Therapy Association.

Roth, E. (2001). Behavioral art therapy. In J. Rubin (Ed.), *Approaches to art therapy* (pp. 195–102). Philadelphia, PA: Bruner/Routledge.

Rotter, J. B. (1966). Generalized expectancies for internal versus external control of reinforcements. *Psychological Monographs: General and Applied, 80*(1), Whole No. 609.

Rozum, A. (2001). Integrating the language of art into a creative cognitive-behavioral program with behavior-disordered children. In S. Riley (Ed.), *Group Process Made Visible* (pp. 115–138). Philadelphia, PA: Brunner/Routledge.

Sarid, O., & Huss, E. (2010). Trauma and acute stress disorder: A comparison between cognitive behavioral intervention and art therapy. *The Arts in Psychotherapy, 37*, 8–10.

Segal, Z. V., Williams, J. M. G., & Teasdale, J. D. (2002). *Mindfulness-based cognitive therapy for depression*. New York, NY: Guildford Press.

Spier, E. (2010). Group art therapy with eighth-grade students transitioning to high school. *Art Therapy: Journal of the American Art Therapy Association, 27*(2), 75–83.

8

Art Therapy: A Brain-based Profession

Juliet L. King

One of the principal physical characteristics that separate *Homo sapiens* from all the other studied life forms is the presence of the cerebral cortex. This part of the brain distinguishes human thought and reasoning from all other animals; it forms the human psyche with a complexity not found in other sentient species. Throughout the course of evolution, we have come to understand the mind and psyche as separate from the brain, the processes of which are intricate and complicated, yet can be understood symbolically and supported with science. Art psychotherapists interested in cognitive processes as well as sensory and emotional processes consider understanding the brain to be a crucial area of study. Recent research on the brain has provided the profession with a framework to substantiate what has been hypothesized: art therapy is a brain-based profession.

Overview

Among contemporary schools of psychology, many credit Freud, a neuroscientist, as the first to develop a conceptually intricate theory of the mind that sought to answer complex psychological questions (DeSousa, 2011). Jung (1968) expounded on this theory, and emphasized that, due to its expansive nature, unconscious processes must be understood in relation to consciousness. In his work with patients and his own artistic exploration, Jung learned that the symbolic communication offered through the creative process was a meaningful and important way to understand the subjective experience of being human. The basic constructs of many evolving theories have similarities to this first psychological school of thought; for example, memories, perceptions, judgment, affect, and motivations are not always consciously accessible (Shedler, 2010).

Throughout the twentieth century, psychoanalytic theory has been challenged, mostly due to a lack of empirical evidence to support its claims. Present-day analysts have recognized the failure of psychoanalysis to keep up with science, and are making appeals to re-energize the field by developing a closer relationship with biology and cognitive neuroscience (Kandel, 2012). For example, neuroscience technology is now

The Wiley Handbook of Art Therapy, First Edition. Edited by David E. Gussak and Marcia L. Rosal.
© 2016 John Wiley & Sons, Ltd. Published 2016 by John Wiley & Sons, Ltd.

being used to correlate Freudian constructs with neurobiological substrates to develop validity for the primary and secondary processes as originally defined by Freud (Carhart-Harris & Friston, 2010). Allan Schore (1994, 2002, 2011, 2012) has written extensively from the perspective of neuropsychoanalysis, and through his work has described with intricate detail that the unconscious appears to be a hierarchal system that is situated in the right brain and evolves, very simply stated, from the inside out and on a developmental continuum.

Just as it is for all psychotherapeutic approaches, the use of a neuroscience framework and its applications to explore and explain our work as art therapists is essential for the evolution and survival of our profession.

An Integrative Approach

Art therapy is a profession that facilitates psychic integration through the creative process and within the context of the therapeutic relationship. Conscious and unconscious mental activity, mind–body connectedness, the use of mental and visual imagery, bilateral stimulation, and communication between the limbic system and cerebral cortex functioning underscore and illuminate the healing benefits of art therapy—none of which could take place without the flexibility of neuronal processes, otherwise known as *neuroplasticity*.

Although our early childhood experiences of attachment are imprinted somatically and remembered in our bodies (Bowlby, 1969), because the brain is not a static organ, humans have the capacity to change and shift both intra- and interpersonally. Hubel and Wiesel discovered the concept of neuroplasticity in the 1960s, finding that the brain is malleable from infancy through adulthood (Doidge, 2007). Significant experiences, including positive relationships, can restructure attachments and change neural pathways, which provide opportunities for rehabilitation and change (Doidge, 2007).

These concepts are central to a developmental approach to art therapy, which correlates child development with stages of artistic expression and matches interventions with brain regions in neurosequential art therapy practice. This theory also applies to all ages, in that "art making evokes early sensory experiences and taps into symbolic expression that is found throughout the developmental continuum" (Malchiodi, Kim, & Choi, 2003, p. 93).

Art therapist Linda Chapman has utilized a neurodevelopmental approach to inform a substantial body of work and has created interventions to address both short- and long-term experiences of trauma with the Chapman Art Therapy Treatment Intervention (CATTI) and Neurodevelopmental Art Therapy (NDAT), respectively (Chapman, 2014). Additionally, Hass-Cohen and Findlay (2009) explained how early relational attachment affects the adult's ability to cope with real or threatened pain by looking at interpersonal neurobiological aspects of the pain experience from information gleaned in the Art Therapy Relational Neuroscience Assessment Protocol (ATR-N).

The educational standards for the American Art Therapy Association state that art therapists must be trained as artist practitioners who incorporate the "soft science" foundations of psychology. To embrace the topic of art therapy and neuroscience with ideological certainty may be counterproductive and may risk a rigid perspective, making it difficult to connect with clients, peers, and empirically minded colleagues. To incorporate an adaptive plasticity is useful, and the art therapist is positioned to remain flexible when approaching assessment, intervention, and research strategies.

The call for an integrative and neuroscience-minded approach to art therapy research and practice is not new (Gantt & Mills, 1998; Kapitan, 2010; Kaplan, 2000, 2004; Malchiodi, 2003), and the ways of considering research are "as broad and rich as the profession itself" (Deaver, 2011, p. 24). Rather than relying on theories borrowed from other psychotherapy models, Kaplan (2000) urged the art therapy profession to develop a theory of its own that keeps from forcing its work into "ill-fitting molds" (p. 18).

This stance is supported by McNiff (1998, 2011), whose writing on arts-based research is nestled in the premise that the creative process and artistic expression help to further our understanding of the self and others in ways that language (and strictly verbal therapies) cannot. McNiff (2011) theorized that, by focusing on the artistic process, research would become more accurate, and, "like a scientist in a lab," one could become more committed to the physical and psychological qualities of the artistic process (p. 12).

Belkofer and Konopka (2008) took this premise to "the lab" in a different context, seeking to measure aspects of the artistic process with an electroencephalogram (EEG). They were interested in capturing a shift in brainwave patterns pre– and post–art-making, and found that the neurobiological activity after an art-making exercise was statistically different from that at rest.

Belkofer (2012) expanded this research using a brain-mapping technology called *qualitative electroencephalogram* (qEEG) to study the neurological effects of art-making. He observed differences in all subjects after the art-making experience, and also found that the art-making process created changes in activity in many parts of the brain. While cautioning the tendency to overgeneralize the findings due to the complexities of the human mind, his research supported the use of neuroscience technology as a tool to measure the efficacy of art therapy interventions.

The groundbreaking relevance of these studies are exemplary of subjective arts-based research ideas housed in an objective and quantitative experiment, which offers a new and energized method of collecting data that draws the link between the "hard" science of neurobiology and the "softer" science of psychology. The study supports the evolutionary understanding that both hemispheres are engaged in creativity and sublimation as opposed to specific lateralization of structures and functions.

Sublimation and Flow

Art therapists are successfully using the principle of sublimation through art-making as a revelatory process to discover the synthesis between the conscious and unconscious minds of their patients (Rubin, 1987). There is little debate that the creative process taps into the unconscious of an individual and plays an enormous role in the processes of self-expression and healing. Chilton (2013) noted how improved well-being and creativity have been empirically linked to what Csikszentmihalyi (1996) called *flow*: the "designing or discovering something new" (p. 108) within a psychological state of optimal attention and engagement. Chilton (2013) suggested that, as a "flow-facilitating art therapist" (p. 67), she was able to assess her client's artistic skills and potentially alleviate anxiety while they attended to the tasks at hand.

Chilton (2013) framed the flow experience in a neuroscience context, referencing the seminal work of Lusebrink (1990, 2010). Chilton articulated a theory of artistic visual expression, which involves cerebral systems that process sensory information and are related to the functions and structures of the brain. The exchanges between conscious and unconscious mental activities are paramount to this discourse and can be referred to as an explicit and implicit dialogue that takes place within the psyche when a person makes art. In essence, explicit information systems involve higher-level cognition, and implicit information systems are concerned with the more archaic, sensory, and emotional centers in the brain (Krebs, Weinberg, & Akesson, 2011). Making art in the context of the therapeutic relationship facilitates an integration of cognitive and emotional processes.

Mind–Body Dualism

Riley (2004) purported that sharing basic information about brain development with clients helped them progress through treatment. She emphasized the importance of the "body memory" that is "based on the concept that the body informs the mind and the mind informs the body—there is no division" (p. 185). In his discussion of the construction of self and the *Quest to Understand Consciousness*, Damasio (2011) explained this certainty with science, indicating that consciousness encompasses much more than previously surmised, and that it does not exist without an interaction between the cerebral cortex, brain stem, and the body.

Kaplan (2000) emphasized this point, claiming that there is no mind–body dualism, and that consciousness is "simply (or not so simply) the aggregate of participating neural circuits at any given time" (p. 38). Art therapists understand that our bodies respond to mental imagery in a very real way (Malchiodi, 2003), and are naturally inclined to incorporate this theory. Hass-Cohen and Carr (2008) framed how art therapists use the mind–body relationship to understand and inform assessment and treatment from a comprehensive and detailed neurological foundation that outlines the structures and functions of neurological systems.

Imagery

Just as the body responds to mental imagery, the brain responds to conscious experiences, and a correlation exists between the two. Humans think in images and use symbol and metaphor to communicate both abstract and concrete concepts. Lusebrink (2004, 2010) asserted that it is through imagery that art therapists navigate internal and external worlds, a process that relies on the isomorphic principle. Simply put, what we feel on the inside is represented through a similar form externally, and simultaneously, external forms create an internal, feeling response. Arnheim (1969) described the relationship that exists between what we see and how we respond as a fluid and organic process that can be seen in the formal elements of art productions, in that "different strokes tell different stories" (Lusebrink, 1990, p. 71).

Neuroimaging techniques such as positron emission tomography (PET) and magnetic resonance imaging (MRI) have expanded the understanding of the different structures within the brain and supported assumptions about the connections between visual expression and the brain (Lusebrink, 2004). The process of creating the image elicits physical, physiological, and emotional changes at the structural level of the brain, which performs all of the functions for the body and mind (Lusebrink 1990, 2004, 2010; Lusebrink & McGuigan, 1989).

Understanding and working with imagery is a component of most psychotherapeutic practices, and developments in neuroscience are helping to provide a psychobiological context to explain the nature of human experience and expression. Schore (as cited in Chapman, 2014) explained how internal imagery is a property of the more unconscious right brain and is imprinted by a range of senses and psychobiological self-states, processes that take place primarily through the work of the amygdala. The amygdala, located in the limbic system (primary brain), is considered key to emotional learning and memory and plays a critical role in the processing of drive-related behavior and the emotions related to these behaviors (Krebs, Weinberg, & Akesson, 2011). The externalization of preverbal internal feeling states is central to the work of the art therapist and can now be further articulated with scientific findings.

The objectivity that artwork affords makes it easier to connect with and understand clients (Wadeson, 2010), and, through the expression of internal imagery, a safe space is provided to discuss aspects of the self. Art therapists have always used graphic productions of clients as communicative tools to assist in understanding the holistic nature of the individual and to facilitate connectedness and empathy in the therapeutic relationship.

Empathy

Being emotionally aware of another person is a simple way of describing empathy, an important part of the therapeutic puzzle. Empathy is also a component of the aesthetic experience, as there is often a physical and emotional response to artwork observed and created (Belkofer, 2012). Relational processes are a healing factor in most psychotherapeutic approaches, and a greater appreciation of the integration of neuroscience, genetics, and the biology of relational processes allows for increased communication between different schools of thought. (Beach et al., 2006).

Franks and Whitaker (2007) found positive outcomes when working with a group of personality-disordered clients by using neuroscience and attachment theory as a framework for understanding how individuals function internally and within relationships. By engaging their clients in the process of "mentalization," they found that the use of the image helped to generate empathy and understanding throughout the group process. Canty's (2009) work with clients in drug rehabilitation facilities found that, through visual imagery, group members were able to empathize with the anger felt by others. Awareness of the client's capacity to empathize, combined with an understanding the neurological processes of creative activity, helped to increase the therapist's understanding of client and group dynamics. Consideration of neurological components involved in the relational process has been enhanced with research on the mirror neuron system and affords the opportunity to present clinical case examples in a new way.

Mirror Neurons

Neurophysiologists found that certain groups of neurons fired in the brains of macaque monkeys when they performed an action *and* when they watched and heard someone else performing the action (Rizzolatti, Fadiga, Gallese, & Fogassi, 1996). These are known as mirror neurons. It is theorized that the mirror neuron system is involved in the observation and motor activity of others and has implications for understanding and integrating interpersonal experiences. The closely related concept of embodied simulation was described by Gallese (2009), who explained that the feeling states attached to behavioral observations are a part of an embodied simulation that allows people to connect to one another primarily through sensory-motor systems.

Franklin (2010) highlighted the mirror neuron system to support an empathic art intervention to assist clients with emotional regulation and the development of interpersonal relatedness. Buk (2009) asserted that the mirror neuron system may enhance the art therapist's understanding of the therapeutic relationship, in that the therapist has greater ability to support the client emotionally. Both authors used a physiological framework to describe their observations and help to explain effective interventions with a language and theory that is understood and accepted by the science community at large.

Understanding the mirror neuron system and embodied simulation informs the treatment of mental disorders such as autism. Martin (2008) described the difficulty that autistic clients often have when trying to maintain focus on human faces. She connected easier with clients when they drew portraits of one another, highlighting the importance of art therapy as an alternate form of communication. Martin's work considered the potential deficits in cognitive processing of social recognition and facial cues, a fundamental problem that research has found to be related to a neural or "social circuit" that exists in the brain (Beach et al., 2006). Although Martin did not mention mirror neurons or neural/social circuits specifically, she wrote within their context. This is an example of how art therapists are naturally inclined to call upon interpersonal neurobiology as a way to understand the therapeutic relationship and interventions therein.

Parallel Processes

Lusebrink's quest to identify the brain processes involved in myriad aspects of art therapy assessment and treatment have provided the profession with a comprehensive *way of knowing* called the Expressive Therapies Continuum (ETC). Further explained by Hinz (2009), the different levels of visual information processing (kinesthetic/ sensory, perceptual/affective, and cognitive/symbolic) "parallel the three hierarchal levels of sensory information processing in the occipital, temporal and parietal lobes..." (Lusebrink, 2004, p. 170). The use of artistic media to elicit expression along the ETC assists in the development of therapeutic goals and interventions. The art media facilitates expression of symbols and metaphor beyond what is afforded through verbal expression alone (Chapman, 2014).

The ETC provides implications for a deeper understanding of various art materials used in treatment and helps to inform research from a neuroscience perspective. For example, Elkis-Abuhoff, Goldblatt, Gaydos, and Corrato (2008) studied the effectiveness of using clay manipulation with patients suffering from Parkinson's disease. The authors found a decrease in somatic and emotional symptoms and a reduction in physical tremors after engaging in the use of clay.

Kruk (submitted) utilized the qEEG as a tool to study the impact of several art materials on various areas of the brain during the art-making process. Using healthy adult women as participants, the data indicated that the lateral frontal and parietal lobes, mostly in the right hemisphere, were activated during art-making. Providing empirical support for the ETC, Kruk asserted that the results of the study suggest that art processes such as clay sculpting "promote visual spatial working memory processes which may enhance therapeutic effect and emotional regulation in individuals with various psychological illnesses" (p. 21).

Linda Chapman has built upon the theoretical model of the ETC in the development of neurologically informed intervention protocols of the aforementioned CATTI and NDAT, both of which serve to help children and adolescents access, express, and synthesize traumatic experiences. This important work is exemplary of her years of clinical experience working with trauma survivors and the congruence that exists between art therapy treatment and the neurobiology of trauma (Chapman, 2014).

Trauma and the Brain

The bulk of art therapy research with patients who have experienced a trauma is supported with neuroscientific findings. Traumatic experiences are psychically complex, and gaining conscious access to trauma events is difficult because of psychological defenses and difficulty in accessing the neurological processes responsible for coding the event (Johnson, 1987). Within a neurobiological framework, Gantt and Tinnin (2009) suggested that the theory of defensive functioning be re-examined. They proposed that art therapy is an effective treatment because it establishes neural pathways that connect language and emotional content.

Recent developments in neuroscience have provided information about areas of the brain responsible for the verbal processing of traumatic event(s). Brain imaging illustrates that, when traumatized patients are exposed to scripts of their traumatic event, Broca's area (language) shuts down and, at the same time, the amygdala becomes aroused (Tripp, 2007). Expression of traumatic events and the accompanying emotions become blocked because the memories are stored in an area of the brain where there is little ability to communicate them logistically and linearly. Right brain activation through art media and process allows for less reliance on the verbal languages areas, an important aspect of the expressive therapies that provides substantiation for why non-verbal therapies might be more effective when working with trauma (Klorer, 2005).

According to Arrington (2007), "traumatic images from unresolved trauma may allow implicit memory [emotional] processing but block explicit memory [cognitive] storage, resulting in negative flashbacks, flooded emotions, bad memories and dreams" (p. 23). Art therapy practice encourages the healthy expression and integration of imprinted memories as they are brought to consciousness within the safety of the therapeutic relationship.

Art-based interventions stimulate the senses, thus memories can be more easily explored when the sensory components in the brain have been activated (Lusebrink, 2004). There is growing research published in both peer-reviewed journals and noteworthy texts that substantiate the neurological effects of traumatic experiences on memory. Art therapists have written about the use of expressing the nonverbal and symbolic aspects of traumatic experiences through art, and have provided evidence about the impact of art processes on symptom reduction and improved health (Avrahami, 2005; Buschel & Madsen, 2006; Crenshaw, 2006; Loumeau-May, 2011; Malchiodi, 2011; Pifalo, 2007; Sarid & Huss, 2010; Spiegel, Malchiodi, Bakos, & Collie, 2006).

Tripp (2007) studied the integration of art therapy interventions with eye movement desensitization reprocessing (EMDR) to enhance the therapeutic relationship and decrease negative symptoms of traumatic experiences. To engage both the left and right hemispheres, bilateral stimulation encourages insight and integration and leads to greater self-awareness. McNamee (2004, 2005, 2006) created a bilateral art protocol that has provided quantifiable results and can be applied therapeutically when working with individuals, families, and even in clinical supervision (McNamee & McWey, 2004). Greenwood (2011) attributed the key factors of success with clients to the integrative aspects of the right and left brain, and many art therapists reference the bilateral processes to underscore their work with traumatized patients, making hemispheric synthesis more fluid (Gerteisen, 2008; Spring, 2004; Tripp, 2007).

Neuroscience contributions inform our understanding of clinical symptoms and the effects of early childhood attachment, trauma, and abuse, and help in determining the multiple ways of conceptualizing treatment. Art therapists have developed specific protocols to test the efficacy of art therapy and treatment interventions with the traumatized populations (Chapman, Morabito, Ladakakos, Schreier, & Knudson, 2001; Hass-Cohen & Carr, 2008; McNamee, 2005, 2006; O'Brian, 2004; Tripp, 2007). The data collected indicates that art therapy is an effective intervention. These authors have demonstrated that art therapy: (1) facilitates the organization and integration of traumatic memories; (2) reactivates positive emotions and serves as a vehicle for exposure and externalization of difficult content; (3) reduces heightened arousal responses; (4) enhances emotional self-efficacy and maintains a space for the exploration of self perception and psychic integration; and (5) enhances the development of identity.

Traumatic brain injury and disorders caused by abnormal brain changes, such as Alzheimer's disease and dementia, are other areas where art therapists can naturally synthesize a neuroscience framework with direct practice and research. Improving cognitive function by understanding and identifying the areas of the brain affected through the art therapy process is a common goal of art therapists who work with people with brain injuries. Incorporating a neuropsychological perspective of neurodegenerative illness provides a more in-depth understanding of what the client is experiencing and a context for behavioral and emotional changes. Art therapy can help address and exercise areas of the brain that are functioning well and increase quality of life through self-expression and sensory stimulation (Stewart, 2004).

Observations of artwork help to clarify diagnosis and assist with neurologically informed intervention strategies (Safer & Press, 2011). The use of art productions to assist in diagnosis and treatment is not new to the art therapist, but an area of great research potential is how graphic productions may track neurological changes throughout the course of an illness when correlated with brain wave activity. Garner (1996, 2000) used cognitive, psychological, and emotional components in developing the neuropsychological art therapy protocol (NAT) for those with traumatic brain imagery. He suggested the use of brain scans along with neuropsychological assessment to measure physical changes and specific neurological deficits.

New Technology and New Tools

Current technologies that measure brain activity during art-making hold promise for art therapists by gathering the empirical evidence needed to substantiate the efficacy of interventions. These tools include positron emission tomography (PET), magnetic resonance imaging (MRI), fMRI (functional magnetic resonance imaging), the EEG and qEEG (electroencephalogram and qualitative electroencephalogram), and the fNIRS (functional near infrared spectroscopy). Methods such as galvanic skin response (GSR) can also be used to measure psychological and physical arousal, which can be an effective tool for both psychiatric and medical populations. Use of these tools will help correlate the results of art therapy assessments and interventions with physical, physiological, and neurobiological changes in the mind and body.

Combining forces with neuropsychologists and biofeedback practitioners who use this type of equipment in their practice is a logical step in conducting future research. Implications for these collaborations also include integrative treatment, such as the use of art therapy to help clients understand and verbalize the changes they experience during neurofeedback training (brainwave biofeedback). Graphic productions may track neurological changes during neurofeedback training, and, conversely, the technology can show the impact of the addition of art therapy treatment on the brain.

The use of technology such as the qEEG might help in identifying what media will work best with certain conditions, and might also help identify brain functions in relation to basic media used in art therapy. From this, art therapy protocols for certain populations might be developed and tested, providing the field with much needed evidence-based and outcomes research.

Future Research and Conclusion

In a recent Delphi study conducted by Kaiser and Deaver (2013), art therapy researchers prioritized art therapy and neuroscience as the second most important priority for the field. The top priority is studies that provide outcomes, efficacy, and evidence-based research.

Understanding and applying art therapy principles and practices within a neuroscience framework is essentially a "no brainer." The profession is positioned to continue the quest for scientific confirmation of art therapy theory and intervention through the neurosciences, which is necessary for the quality and comprehensive care of patients. Not all art therapists need to *walk the walk* of research, but all have a duty to *talk the talk* when it comes to explaining the work within a context based in scientific principles.

Articulating the work of the art therapist in a neuroscience framework is crucial for the survival of the profession, in that the general and healthcare public increasingly requires evidence-based language when considering the efficacy of intervention strategies and insurance reimbursement. Explaining the work of the art therapist from a scientific perspective helps to clarify the depth of art therapist training and works to further develop a professional identity. This assists in the advocacy for independent licensure at both state and national levels and helps to distinguish the profession among other mental healthcare practitioners.

The fields of art therapy and neuroscience are inextricably linked—akin to the consciousness and unconsciousness, mind and body, limbic system and cerebral cortex. Applying art therapy theory, treatment, and research within a neuroscience framework is necessary, and as expansive and limitless as the mind itself.

References

Arnheim, R. (1969). *Visual thinking*. London, England: University of California Press, Ltd.

Arrington, D. (2007). *Art, angst, and trauma: Right brain interventions with developmental issues*. Springfield, IL: Charles C. Thomas Publisher.

Avrahami, D. (2005). Visual art therapy's unique contribution in the treatment of post-traumatic stress disorder. *Journal of Trauma & Dissociation, 6*(4), 5–38.

Beach, S., Wamboldt, M., Kaslow, N., Heyman, R., First, M., Underwood, L., & Reiss, D. (2006). *Relational processes and DSM-V: Neuroscience, assessment, prevention, and treatment*. Washington, DC: American Psychiatric Publishing Inc.

Belkofer, C. M. (2012). *The impact of visual art-making on the brain* (Unpublished doctoral dissertation). Lesley University, Cambridge, MA.

Belkofer, C. M., & Konopka, L. (2008). Conducting art therapy research using Quantitative EEG measures. *Art Therapy: Journal of the American Art Therapy Association, 25*(2), 56–63. doi: 10.1080/07421656.2008.10129412

Bowlby, J. (1969). *Attachment*. New York, NY: Basic Books.

Buk, A. (2009). The mirror neuron system and embodied simulation: Clinical implications for art therapists working with trauma survivors. *The Arts in Psychotherapy, 36*(2), 61–74. doi:10.1016/j.aip.2009.01.008

Buschel, B., & Madsen, L. (2006). Strengthening connections between mothers and children: Art therapy in a domestic violence shelter. *Journal of Aggression, Maltreatment & Trauma, 13*(1), 87–108.

Canty, J. (2009). The key to being in the right mind. *International Journal of Art Therapy: Formerly Inscape, 14*(1), 11–16.

Carhart-Harris, R. L., & Friston, K. J. (2010). The default-mode, ego-functions and free-energy: A neurobiological account of Freudian ideas. *Brain, 133*(4), 1265–1283. doi: 10.1093/brain/awq010

Chapman, L. (2014). *Neurobiologically informed trauma therapy with children and adolescents: Understanding the mechanisms of change*. New York, NY: W.W Norton & Company, Inc.

Chapman, L., Morabito, D., Ladakakos, C. Schreier, H., & Knudson, M. (2001). The effectiveness of art therapy interventions in reducing post traumatic stress disorder (PTSD) symptoms in pediatric trauma patients. *Art Therapy: Journal of the American Art Therapy Association, 18*(2), 100–104.

Chilton, G. (2013). Art therapy and flow: A review of the literature and applications. *Art Therapy: Journal of the American Art Therapy Association, 30*(2), 64–70. doi: 10.1080/07421656.2013.787211

Crenshaw, D. (2006). Neuroscience and trauma treatment implications for creative art therapists. In L. Carey (Ed.), *Expressive and creative arts methods for trauma survivors* (pp. 21–38). London: Jessica Kingsley Publishers.

Csikszentmihalyi, M. (1996). *Creativity: Flow and the psychology of discovery and invention.* New York, NY: Harper Collins Publishers, Inc.

Damasio, A. (2011, March). The quest to understand consciousness. Retrieved from http://www.ted.com/talks/antonio_damasio_the_quest_to_understand_consciousness.html

Deaver, S. P. (2011). What constitutes art therapy research? *Art Therapy: Journal of the American Art Therapy Association, 19*(1), 23–27. doi: 10.1080/07421656.2002.10129721

DeSousa, A. (2011). Freudian theory and consciousness: A conceptual analysis. *Mens Sana Monograph, 9*(1), 210–217. doi: 10.4103/0973-1229.77437

Doidge, N. (2007). *The brain that changes itself: Stories of personal triumph from the frontiers of brain science.* New York, NY: Penguin Group.

Elkis-Abuhoff, D. L., Goldblatt, R. B., Gaydos, M., & Corrato, S. (2008). Effects of clay manipulation on somatic dysfunction and emotional distress in patients with Parkinson's disease. *Art Therapy: Journal of the American Art Therapy Association, 25*(3), 122–128.

Franklin, M. (2010). Affect regulation, mirror neurons, and the third hand: Formulating mindful empathic art interventions. *Art Therapy: Journal of the American Art Therapy Association, 27*(4), 160–167. doi: 10.1080/07421656.2010.10129385

Franks, M., & Whitaker, R. (2007). The image, mentalisation and group art psychotherapy. *International Journal of Art Therapy: Formerly Inscape, 12*(1), 3–16.

Gallese, V. (2009). Mirror neurons, embodied simulation, and the neural basis of social identification. *Psychoanalytic Dialogues, 19*(5), 519–536.

Gantt, L. M., & Mills, B. (1998). A discussion of art therapy as a science. *Art Therapy: Journal of the American Art Therapy Association, 15*(1), 3–12.

Gantt, L. M., & Tinnin, L. W. (2009). Support for a neurobiological view of trauma with implications for art therapy. *The Arts in Psychotherapy, 36*, 148–153.

Garner, R. (1996). The NAT model: Factors in neuropsychological art therapy. *American Journal of Art Therapy, 34*(4), 107–111.

Garner, R. (2000). *Neuropsychological art therapy treatment protocol: An intervention utilizing portraiture, computer-based data analysis, and a discipline based art education framework* (Unpublished doctoral dissertation). Florida State University, Tallahassee, FL.

Gerteisen, J. (2008). Monsters, monkeys, & mandalas: Art therapy with children experiencing the effects of trauma and fetal alcohol spectrum disorder (FASD). *Art Therapy Journal of the American Art Therapy Association, 25*(2), 90–93.

Greenwood, H. (2011). Long-term individual art psychotherapy. Art for art's sake: The effect of early relational trauma. *International Journal of Art Therapy: Inscape, 16*(1), 41–51.

Hass-Cohen, N., & Carr, R. (2008). *Art therapy and clinical neuroscience.* London: Jessica Kingsley Publishers.

Hass-Cohen, N., & Findlay, J. C. (2009). Pain, attachment, and meaning making: Report on an art therapy relational neuroscience assessment protocol. *The Arts in Psychotherapy, 36*, 175–184.

Hinz, L. (2009). *Expressive therapies continuum: A framework for using art in therapy.* New York, NY: Routledge.

Johnson, D. R. (1987). The role of the creative arts therapies in the diagnosis and treatment of psychological trauma. *The Arts in Psychotherapy, 14*, 7–13.

Jung, C. G. (1968). *Man and his symbols.* New York, NY: Dell Publishing.

Kaiser, D., & Deaver, S. (2013). Establishing a research agenda for art therapy: A Delphi study. *Art Therapy: Journal of the American Art Therapy Association, 30*(3), 114–121. doi: 10.1080/07421656.2013.819281

Kandel, E. R. (2012). Biology and the future of psychoanalysis: A new intellectual framework for psychiatry revisited. *Psychoanalytic Review, 99*(4), 2–39.

Kapitan, L. (2010). The empathic imagination of art therapy: Good for the brain? *Art Therapy: Journal of the American Art Therapy Association, 27*(4), 158–159. doi: 10.1080/07421656.2010.10129384

Kaplan, F. F. (2000). *Art, science and art therapy: Repainting the picture.* London: Jessica Kingsley Publishers.

Kaplan, F. F. (2004). Inner space. *Art Therapy: Journal of the American Art Therapy Association, 21*(3), 122–123. doi: 10.1080/07421656.2004.10129502

Klorer, P. G. (2005). Expressive therapy with severely maltreated children: Neuroscience contributions. *Art Therapy: Journal of the American Art Therapy Association, 22*(4), 213–220.

Krebs, C., Weinberg, J., & Akesson, E. (2011). *Neuroscience.* Baltimore, MD: Lippincott, Williams & Wilkins.

Kruk, K. (submitted). *Frontoparietal artmaking.* Manuscript submitted for publication.

Loumeau-May, L. V. (2011). Art therapy with traumatically bereaved children. In S. Ringel & J. R. Brandell (Eds.), *Trauma: Contemporary directions in theory, practice, and research* (pp. 98–129). Thousand Oaks, CA: SAGE Publications.

Lusebrink, V. B. (1990). *Imagery and visual expression in therapy. Emotions, personality, and psychotherapy.* New York, NY: Plenum Press.

Lusebrink, V. B. (2004). Art therapy and the brain: An attempt to understand the underlying processes of art expression in therapy. *Art Therapy: Journal of the American Art Therapy Association, 21*(3), 125–135.

Lusebrink, V. B. (2010). Assessment and therapeutic application of the expressive therapies continuum: Implications for brain structures and functions. *Art Therapy: Journal of the American Art Therapy Association, 27*(4), 168–177.

Lusebrink, V. B., & McGuigan, F. J. (1989). Psychophysiological components of imagery. *Pavlonian Journal of Biological Science, 24*(2), 58–63.

Malchiodi, C. A. (2003). Art therapy and the brain. In C. A. Malchiodi (Ed.), *Handbook of art therapy* (pp. 16–24). New York, NY: Guilford Press.

Malchiodi, C. (2011). Trauma informed art therapy and sexual abuse in children. In P. Goodyear-Brown (Ed.), *Handbook of child sexual abuse: Identification, assessment, and treatment* (pp. 341–354). Hoboken, NJ: Wiley.

Malchiodi, C. A., Kim, D. Y., & Choi, W. S. (2003). Developmental art therapy. In C. A. Malchiodi (Ed.), *Handbook of art therapy* (pp. 93–105). New York, NY: Guilford Press.

Martin, N. (2008). Assessing portrait drawings created by children and adolescents with Autism Spectrum Disorder. *Art Therapy: Journal of the American Art Therapy Association, 25*(1), 15–23. doi: 10.1080/07421656.2008.10129348

McNamee, C. M. (2004). Using both sides of the brain: Experiences that integrate art and talk therapy through scribble drawings. *Art Therapy Journal of the American Art Therapy Association, 21*(3), 136–142.

McNamee, C. M. (2005). Bilateral art: Integrating art therapy, family therapy, and neuroscience. *Contemporary Family Therapy, 27*(4), 545–557.

McNamee, C. M. (2006). Experiences with bilateral art: A retrospective study. *Art Therapy Journal of the American Art Therapy Association, 23*(1), 7–13.

McNamee, C. M., & McWey, L. M. (2004). Using bilateral art to facilitate clinical supervision. *The Arts in Psychotherapy, 31*, 229–243.

McNiff, S. (1998). *Art-based research*. London: Jessica Kingsley Publishers.

McNiff, S. (2011). Artistic expressions as primary modes of inquiry. *British Journal of Guidance and Counseling, 39*(3), 385–396.

O'Brian, F. (2004). The making of mess in art therapy: Attachment, trauma and the brain. *Inscape, 9*(1), 2–13.

Pifalo, T. (2007). Jogging the cogs: Trauma-focused art therapy with cognitive behavioral therapy with sexually abused children. *Art Therapy Journal of the American Art Therapy Association, 24*(4), 170–175.

Riley, S. (2004). The creative mind. *Art Therapy: Journal of the American Art Therapy Association, 21*(4), 184–190. doi: 10.1080/07421656.2004.10129694

Rizzolatti, G., Fadiga, L., Gallese, V., & Fogassi, L. (1996). Premotor cortex and the recognition of motor actions. *Cognitive Brain Research, 3*(2), 131–141.

Rubin, J. (1987). *Approaches to art therapy: Theory and technique*. New York, NY: Routledge.

Safer, L. T., & Press, D. Z. (2011). Art and the brain: Effects of dementia on art production in art therapy. *Art Therapy: Journal of the American Art Therapy Association, 28*(3), 96–103.

Sarid, O., & Huss, E. (2010). Trauma and acute stress disorder: A comparison between cognitive behavioral intervention and art therapy. *The Arts in Psychotherapy, 37*, 8–12.

Schore, A. N. (1994). *Affect regulation and the origin of the self*. Mahwah, NJ: Erlbaum.

Schore, A. N. (2002). The right brain as the neurobiological substratum of Freud's dynamic unconscious. In D. Scharff (Ed.), *The psychoanalytic century: Freud's legacy for the future* (pp. 61–88). New York, NY: Other Press.

Schore, A. N. (2011). The right brain implicit self lies at the core of psychoanalysis. *Psychoanalytic Dialogues, 21*, 75–100.

Schore, A. N. (2012). *The science of the art of psychotherapy*. New York, NY: Norton.

Shedler, J. (2010). The efficacy of psychodynamic psychotherapy. *American Psychologist, 65*(2), 98–109. American Psychological Association. doi: 10.1037/a0018378

Spiegel, D., Malchiodi, C., Bakos, A., & Collie, K. (2006). Art therapy for combat-related PTSD: Recommendations for research and practice. *Art Therapy Journal of the American Art Therapy Association, 23*(4), 157–164.

Spring, D. (2004). Thirty-year study links neuroscience, specific trauma, PTSD, image conversion, and language translation. *Art Therapy Journal of the American Art Therapy Association, 21*(4), 200–209.

Stewart, E. G. (2004). Art therapy and neuroscience blend: Working with patients who have dementia. *Art Therapy: Journal of the American Art Therapy Association, 21*(3), 148–155.

Tripp, T. (2007). A short term therapy approach to processing trauma: Art therapy and bilateral stimulation. *Art Therapy Journal of the American Art Therapy Association, 24*(4), 176–183.

Wadeson, H. (2010). *Art Psychotherapy*. Hoboken, NJ: John Wiley and Sons, Inc.

9

Positive Art Therapy

Patricia D. Isis

"I hate this and you!" shouted the self-proclaimed ringleader of my art therapy group for male teenagers in an addiction treatment unit. Though pummeled with insults, abrasive comments, and derogatory remarks, I insisted on maintaining the group for the duration of the time originally contracted. "How am I going to survive this?" I thought as I stared at the provocative sculpture of a dead tree just completed by the most hostile member of the group (see Figure 9.1).

As a novice art therapist, I was convinced that I would have to "tough it out," regardless of the situation until the full hour was up. With that belief system, I set myself and the group members up for a disastrous experience. I later realized that, during the group, the patients were letting me know through their abusive behavior that they were not ready to allow the art making and group process to alleviate their suffering. On the contrary, my decision to continue the group served to reinforce and extend the painful proceedings, which, in turn, extended the negativity. Consequently, there were no opportunities for them to increase their insight and or sense a feeling of accomplishment. Had I chosen not to continue the group further, I could have set limits on the abusive behavior and modeled realistic consequences that result from such behavior. The focus could then have been highlighting the group's abundance of passion, energy, and creativity, which could be harnessed for collaboration and support rather than for ongoing conflict and agitation.

In 32 years of art therapy practice, I can think of several times when I wondered why I was putting myself through a particularly torturous session such as the one mentioned here. With the insight I have gained through these challenging experiences along with increased knowledge of positive psychology, I have come to realize how critical it is to first cultivate positivity and well-being in my personal and professional life. Only then can I engage my clients in discovering and promoting their own well-being. Positive psychology encompasses the notion of cultivating and sustaining a fulfilling life.

Provided in this chapter is a brief definition of positive psychology, along with a list of the five elements found to be critical to well-being and a chart identifying the six virtues and 24 "signature strengths" that support these five elements (Seligman, 2011). Three case examples—a child, an adolescent, and an adult—will illustrate the integration of positive psychology theory with art therapy practice. The intention is

The Wiley Handbook of Art Therapy, First Edition. Edited by David E. Gussak and Marcia L. Rosal.

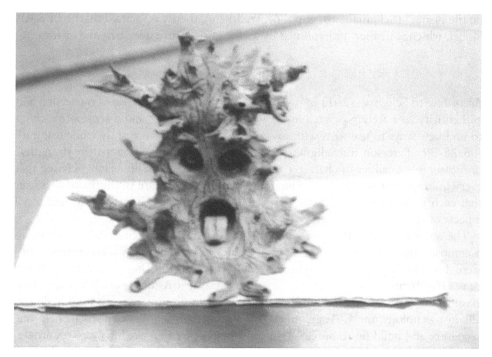

Figure 9.1 Untitled.

to inform and inspire other art therapists and related professionals to consider utilizing this approach personally and professionally. Enhancing one's own experience of living requires deliberate moment-to-moment non-judgmental self-awareness (mindfulness), self and social compassion, kindness, and a willingness to move beyond self and promote well-being globally.

Positive Psychology

Over the past two decades, Martin Seligman developed a new theory called positive psychology (2002), originally known as *"authentic happiness."* More recently, with feedback from his students, Seligman realized that the original theory, which focused solely on authentic happiness, omitted the significance of success and mastery, as it only attended to positive mood and limited the reasons people make choices for life satisfaction. As a result, he published *Flourish: A Visionary Understanding of Happiness and Well-being* (2011), in which he provided a revised theory of what he defined as a "full life" through the increase of five measurable and distinctive elements to gain well-being and flourish. These include positive emotions, engagement, positive relationships, meaning, and accomplishment(s) (PERMA). No individual element can characterize well-being alone. Rather, each contributes toward maximizing its construction. "The goal of positive psychology in well-being theory ... is plural and importantly different: it is to increase the amount of flourishing in your own life and on the planet" (Seligman, 2011, p. 26). Well-being theory is focused on the PERMA model, which is further underpinned by a host of signature strengths and virtues.

Signature strengths

According to Seligman (2011), "a signature strength has ... a sense of ownership and authenticity ... a feeling of excitement while displaying it ... and a sense of yearning to find new ways to use it ... with joy, zest, enthusiasm, even ecstasy while using it" (pp. 38–39). Peterson and Seligman (2005) carefully researched "signature strengths" or measurable qualities of character that enable flourishing in life. They believed that every individual possesses many signature strengths. These are strengths of character that each person owns, celebrates, and engages in effortlessly every day, and in all aspects of life.

The authors created the Values in Action (VIA-IS) character strengths survey to accompany the Character Strengths and Virtues Handbook (CSV); both these items were developed as a positive psychology complement to the *Diagnostic and Statistical Manual of Mental Disorders* (DSM; American Psychiatric Association). While the DSM classifies and describes pathology and diagnostic identification, which is used traditionally in psychology, the CSV identifies human strengths and is designed to help one recognize and build on resources and positivity in order to make life more rewarding. The inventory identifies particular strengths, and identifies how to utilize them to enhance well-being, and successfully cope with challenges and weaknesses.[1] The data is also used to contribute to research and reliability studies. Table 9.1 provides the names and descriptions of the six virtue categories and the accompanying signature strengths.

Developing Strengths through Art Making and Art Therapy

Measuring personal signature strengths requires a genuine self-appraisal of how happy one believes he or she is presently. To promote a state of flourishing, one must start with increased self-awareness. Knowing one's strengths promotes a willingness to further expand the positivity of the strengths to enhance relationships toward self and others.

Table 9.1 Virtues and signature strengths

Wisdom/ Knowledge	Curiosity	Creativity	Judgment	Love of learning	Perspective
Courage	Bravery	Perseverance	Honesty	Zest	
Humanity	Love	Kindness	Social intelligence		
Justice	Teamwork	Fairness	Leadership		
Temperance	Forgiveness Mercy	Humility/ modesty	Prudence	Self-regulation	
Transcendence	Appreciation of beauty	Gratitude	Hope	Humor	**Spirituality**

In the scenario described in the opening of this chapter, the group's focus could have been more positive by verbalizing the conflict. This would have provided an opportunity to underscore the intense emotions expressed in the session. The sculpture of the dead angry tree was a powerful piece of expression and outrage. The fact that the group member was able to create such work in the midst of so much hostility demonstrated a willingness to express his inner world and vulnerability with the group. With such knowledge, instead of regret about that group, I can now feel positive about seeing the beauty within the challenges and uncertainty of the process and outcome.

Art therapy is defined by the American Art Therapy Association (2013) as using:

> the creative process, and the resulting artwork to explore their feelings, reconcile emotional conflicts, foster self-awareness, manage behavior and addictions, develop social skills, improve reality orientation, reduce anxiety, and increase self-esteem. A goal in art therapy is to improve or restore a client's functioning and his or her sense of personal well-being. ... Art therapy helps people resolve conflicts, improve interpersonal skills, manage problematic behaviors, reduce negative stress, and achieve personal insight. Art therapy also provides an opportunity to enjoy the life-affirming pleasures of art making. (www.americanarttherapy association.org)

It seems clear that art therapy naturally complements positive psychology. The art making process by itself gives a new perspective on how a client, group, or family might experience familiar and unique signature strengths.

Positive Art Therapy

Much like positive psychotherapy, art therapy requires "a set of techniques that are most effectively delivered with basic therapeutic essentials such as warmth, accurate empathy, basic trust, genuineness, and rapport" (Seligman, 2011, p. 40). Concurrently, a number of the exercises developed to enhance flourishing can easily be expanded upon and embellished through a therapeutic art-making directive. For example, in an initial positive psychotherapy session, the client is often invited to "write a one-page ... 'positive introduction', in which one tells a concrete story showing her at her best and illustrating how she used her highest character strengths" (Seligman, 2011, p. 41). This exercise could be elaborated further in an art therapy session with a directive to create a positive self-object with any media of choice. The client would be invited to focus on the personal strengths that he or she is currently aware of and then create symbols to represent those strengths. The artwork can become a rich container of images that represent how the clients view themselves at their best in their life now.

Similarly, art therapists could offer clients another positive psychotherapy experience by asking them to create positive tangible responses with line, shape, and color to the question "what went well" (recording at least three daily things that went well). These are just two examples of positive art therapy interventions that have been effective in school settings with adolescents with emotional and behavioral difficulties and in a private office with bereaved children and adults suffering from depression. The following case examples briefly illustrate the value of positive art therapy as a catalyst for increasing feelings of well-being amidst tremendous challenges.

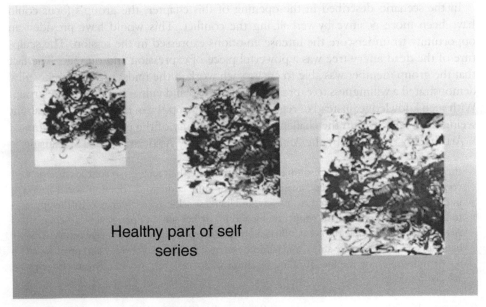

Healthy part of self
series

Figure 9.2   Wellness painting.

Chris

In a school art therapy session, Chris (a pseudonym) admitted his desire to kill his father. As a result, he was hospitalized for homicidal ideation. He went back on psychotropic medication and returned to high school post discharge. Chris is a talented musician and artist. He actively painted and wrote songs about the demons that lived in his mind during his art therapy sessions. In an effort to help Chris view himself through a positive perspective, he was asked to paint how he felt when he was "at his best." He created Figure 9.2. Through this work, he demonstrated signature strengths of zest, vitality, appreciation of beauty and excellence, creativity, and perseverance.

Through the images of himself playing his guitar and the trust established in the therapy sessions, he was able to access and validate his strengths and abilities to gain some serenity.

In his graduation drawing (see Figure 9.3), Chris organized the composition to display the complicated and successful array of equipment he had created to record music in his bedroom. This drawing again shows his passion, curiosity, and vitality in the process of making and sharing his music and artwork. With this focus, he can find hope and acknowledgement for his creative genius and talent despite his emotional disabilities.

Allan

Allan was 9 years old when his dad abruptly died one morning. Allan was a quiet boy, and yet his artwork within private art therapy sessions allowed him to scream out his feelings safely. He later used his strengths of creativity and curiosity to illustrate a dream about his dad coming back to life. The goals established in his art therapy sessions were to give Allan a safe opportunity to express and move through his grief toward

Figure 9.3　Termination drawing/plans after high school.

reconciliation by finding intermittent joy and well-being despite his devastating loss. Nearly a year into this process, he took up baseball. Shortly after discovering his passion for the sport, he spontaneously created a drawing with his dad as the pitcher and himself at bat. Through art, Allan comforted himself and used his vivid imagination to increase feelings of well-being in the wake of his grief. In his final art therapy session, Allan made a ceramic baseball bat and ball (see Figure 9.4).

Allan demonstrated through these symbols how he was moving toward reconciliation despite the tragic loss of his father. The artwork also served as evidence for his resilience, bravery, courage, and persistence in the wake of so much challenge.

Anna

Anna, a middle-aged woman, came to art therapy sessions privately to treat her depression. She had difficulty dealing with her demanding husband and adult son, who relied on her financially. As a result, she felt trapped and chronically agitated. Using clay, she created several sculptures over a period of 2 years, working through issues of independence, poor self-esteem, and self-acceptance. In her final ceramic piece (Figure 9.5), Anna exhibited and acknowledged her strengths of hope, creativity, spirituality, persistence, and appreciation of beauty. She realized that she did not need to financially enable her son any longer and chose instead to fortify a strong support for her marriage while growing in her own individuality.

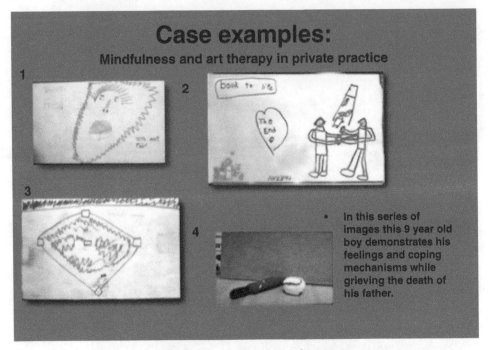

Figure 9.4   Process of grief work.

Figure 9.5   Hanging together beautifully; separate but united.

Conclusion

The integration of art therapy with positive psychology is a rich and valuable collaboration toward the pursuit of well-being and optimal functioning. Art therapy has the potential of motivating clients to reveal more of who they are to themselves. Much needs to be researched and written on this vital work.

In my own personal and professional process, I have realized the importance of contributing one's skills as a positive art therapist beyond self-awareness and clinical treatment strategies. It is crucial for art therapists and related professionals to take an active role as catalysts for positive change and growth. Together, helping professionals can find and invigorate ways to promote and guide others to discover their extraordinary talents and strengths through leadership, community service, art activism, and ongoing research.

Endnote

1 To determine strengths and virtues, several assessment tools are available free of charge on the website www.authentichappiness.org.

References

American Art Therapy Association (2013). *About Art Therapy*. Retrieved from http://www.americanarttherapyassociation.org/#About.

Peterson, C., & Seligman, M. E. P. (2005). Orientations to happiness and life satisfaction: The full life versus the empty life. *Journal of Happiness Studies, 6,* 25–41.

Seligman, M. E. P. (2002). *Authentic happiness: Using the new positive psychology to realize your potential for lasting fulfillment.* New York, NY: Free Press.

Seligman, M. E. P. (2011). *Flourish: A visionary new understanding of happiness and well-being.* New York, NY: Free Press.

Additional Suggested Readings

Csikszentmihalyi, M. (1990). *Flow: The psychology of optimal experience.* New York, NY: Harper and Row.

Csikszentmihalvi, M. (1997). *Flow: The psychology of engagement with everyday life.* New York, NY: Basic Books.

Isis, P. (2007). Using art therapy with troubled adolescents. *ANZJAT: Australian and New Zealand Journal of Art Therapy, 2*(1), 28–33.

Isis, P. (2011). The case of Leon: An adolescent study in school art therapy. *American Art Therapy Association Newsletter, XLIV*(2), 1–7.

Isis, P. (2012). Mindfulness-based stress reduction (MBSR) and the expressive therapies in a hospital-based community outreach program. In L. Rappaport (Ed.), *Mindfulness and Arts Therapies*. London: Jessica Kingsley.

Isis, P., Bush, J., Siegal, C. A., & Ventura, Y. (2010). Empowering students through creativity: Art therapy in Miami-Dade County Public Schools. *Art Therapy: Journal of the American Art Therapy Association, 27*(2), 56–61.

Kabat-Zinn, J. (1990). *Full catastrophe living: How to cope with stress, pain and illness using mindfulness meditation.* New York, NY: Delacorte.

Langer, E. (2005). *On becoming an artist: Reinventing yourself through mindful creativity.* New York, NY: Ballantine Books.

Nansok, P., Peterson, C., & Seligman, M. (2006). Character strengths in fifty-four nations and the fifty US states. *The Journal of Positive Psychology, 1*(3), 118–129.

Niemiec, R. M., Rashid, T., & Spinella M. (2012). Strong mindfulness: Integrating mindfulness and character strengths. *Journal of Mental Health Counseling, 34,* 240–253.

Park, N., & Peterson, C. (2005). The values in action inventory of character strengths for youth. In K. A. Moore & L. H. Lippman (Eds.), *What do children need to flourish? Conceptualizing and measuring indicators of positive development* (pp. 13–23). New York, NY: Springer.

Park, N., & Peterson, C. (2009). Character strengths: Research and practice. *Journal of College and Character, 10,* np.

Peterson, C. (2006). *Primer in positive psychology.* New York, NY: Oxford University Press.

Peterson, C., & Seligman, M. E. P. (2004). *Character strengths and virtues: A handbook and classification.* New York, NY: Oxford University Press/Washington DC: American Psychological Association.

Peterson, C., & Seligman, M. E. P. (2005). Orientations to happiness and life satisfaction: The full life versus the empty life. *Journal of Happiness Studies, 6,* 25–41.

Peterson, C., Park, N., & Seligman, M. E. P. (2005). Assessment of character strengths. In G. P. Koocher, J. C. Norcross, & S. S. Hill (Eds.), *Psychologists; desk reference* (2nd ed. pp. 93–98). New York, NY: Oxford University Press.

Peterson, C., Ruch, W., Beerman, U., Park, N., & Seligman, M. E. P. (2007). Strengths of character, orientations to happiness and life satisfaction. *The Journal of Positive Psychology, 2,* 149–156.

Schueller, S. M., & Seligman, M. E. P. (2006). Pursuit of pleasure, and meaning: Relationships to subjective and objective measures of well-being. *The Journal of Positive Psychology, 5*(4), 253–263.

Seligman, M. E. P. (2002). *Authentic happiness: Using the new positive psychology to realize your potential for lasting fulfillment:* New York, NY: Free Press.

Seligman, M. E. P., Rashid, T., & Parks, A. C. (2006). Positive psychotherapy. *American Psychology, 61,* 774–788.

10

Essence, Art, and Therapy:
A Transpersonal View©
Michael A. Franklin

As I sit down to write this chapter on transpersonal art therapy, the latest news that the world media is celebrating is the discovery of Higgs boson, popularly known as the "God particle." Between the predicted existence of this elusive particle and the latest statistical data implying its evidential certainty. Concerning this chapter, this news is significant for several reasons. First, as sophisticated research tools probe deeper into subjects such as physics and consciousness, we can skillfully study the obscure territories that have existed between science and theology. These regions were previously understood in the ancient and indigenous worlds through observation, and therefore practice-based informed intuition and observation.

We live in a time when we are discovering finer delineations of the conscious universe and consequently need a refined scientific yet numinous psychology to study the resulting questions. Second, there always seems to be more beyond what we can see, measure, and statistically forecast. It is at this ineffable edge of the body, mind, and spirit equation that science, mathematics, psychology, and metaphysics intersect. This is also the territory from which many intelligent, enduring philosophical questions emerge. There is a need for psychology researchers to study the questions emerging from the perennial philosophy (Huxley, 1944), indigenous wisdom traditions (Harner, 1980), consciousness studies (Weisberg, 2011), and religious experience (James, 2002), including the influence of Eastern traditions on human potential (Boorstein, 1996; Tart, 1992; Welwood, 2002). Indeed, there are many paths beyond limiting ego constructs of self (Walsh & Vaughan, 1993b).

Beginning with a succinct history of transpersonal psychology and its relationship to art and art therapy, this chapter provides a brief discussion of several core subjects within the field. Since transpersonal psychology, as considered in this chapter, stands at the crossroads between art, spirituality, and psychology, these subjects are worth mentioning: the historical roots of transpersonal psychology, transpersonal practices including art, transpersonal research methods including art-based research, and art historical and therapy themes related to spirituality.

The Wiley Handbook of Art Therapy, First Edition. Edited by David E. Gussak and Marcia L. Rosal.
© 2016 John Wiley & Sons, Ltd. Published 2016 by John Wiley & Sons, Ltd.

Historical Roots of Transpersonal Psychology

Arguably the first author to use the term "transpersonal" and study related phenomena was William James in the early twentieth century (Ryan, 2008). The foremost transpersonal model of psychology is attributed to Carl Jung (Scotton, Chinen, & Battista, 1996). First called "transhumanistic," then "transpersonal" (Ryan, 2008), the field emerged out of the edgy soil of the 1960s (Ruzek, 2007). Between Maslow's original work on peak experiences, self-exploration through spiritual traditions such as yoga (Feuerstein, 2003; Johnsen, 1994; Muktananda, 1994; Yogananda, 2003), shamanic practices (Harner, 1980), meditation (Benson, 1975; Trungpa, 1976; Walsh & Shapiro, 2006), use of psychedelic substances and transformative breath work (Groff, 1993), ecopsychology (Roszak, Gomes, & Kanner, 1995), and the overall socio-political unrest plaguing the daily moral life of the times, a hopeful fourth force (or perspective) in psychology emerged. This new field focused on the transformative cultural revolution taking place (Ruzek, 2007). In addition to the three main established models of psychology—psychoanalysis, cognitive-behavioral, and humanistic—additional perspectives were needed. From the beginning, transpersonal psychology recognized the value inherent in all three earlier psychological approaches (Scotton et al., 1996). Therefore, the field continues to revisit the importance of established theory and practice.

Beginnings

Founded by Anthony Sutich and Abraham Maslow (Ruzek, 2007), the *Journal of Transpersonal Psychology* (JTP) was born in the late 1960s. Shortly earlier, *The Bulletin of Art Therapy*, later to become the *American Journal of Art Therapy* (AJAT), began in the early 1960s. Although the early content of AJAT was far from transpersonal, there was interest in how art could access, manifest, and heal interior life. Initial North American forays into transpersonal art therapy can be seen in McNiff's (1988) investigations into shamanism, Garai's (1984) interest in humanistic psychology, and the work of Cane and Naumburg (Detre et al., 1983). European influences in transpersonal art therapy can be linked to influential philosophers such as Rudolf Steiner (2003) and Carl Jung (2009).

Early on, the field of transpersonal psychology recognized the need for an expanded view of human developmental potential and health (Davis, 2003). Researchers studied the psychological change process in subjects—such as non-ordinary states of consciousness, spiritual life, and mystical practices (Boorstein, 1996). Transpersonal psychologists asked questions such as: What is true pathology, and how can sacred, transcendent experience impersonate pathology? What is the role of spirituality in psychotherapy? From this came an understanding of the boundaries between benign emerging spiritual experiences and when those experiences become spiritual emergencies. Thus, the terms "spiritual emergence" and "spiritual emergency" entered the transpersonal vocabulary and clinical methodology for dealing with forms of psycho-spiritual crisis (Grof & Grof, 1989).

Previous conservative models did not account for the expansive, full capacity of human potential. Few Western theories of development described the ability to achieve the non-dual, unity awareness of an illuminated, even enlightened mind

(Aurobindo, 2001). From the beginning, transpersonal psychology was poised to empirically investigate subjects such as near-death experiences:

> ... peak experiences, B-values, mystical experience ... self-actualization ... transcendence of the self ... cosmic awareness, individual and species-wide synergy, maximal interpersonal encounter, sacralization of everyday life, transcendental phenomena ... maximal sensory awareness, responsiveness in expression; and related concepts, experiences, and activities that comprise transpersonal studies. (Ruzek, 2007, p. 155)

When considering subjects such as transcendence of the self or trans-ego states, additional developmental questions emerge. Ken Wilber (1997) persuasively argued that a fallacy exists when confusing pre-personal states (sensorimotor or pre-operational) with transpersonal or trans-ego states. Moving beyond the limited views of a separate self toward self-transcendence is often the goal of a disciplined spiritual or contemplative practice, and is different from those in the pre-personal state. Thus, adults who nonchalantly view young children as enlightened beings are engaged in a developmental fallacy. Essentially, one needs to cultivate an ego based self before attempting to transcend it. Wilber has since distanced himself from transpersonal psychology proper in favor of developing a far-reaching integral model of consciousness that encompasses multiple disciplines, including art (Wilber, 1997, 2000).

Transpersonal Practices, Experiences, and Research

The two roots of the word "transpersonal" refer to moving through or beyond the personal. In this case, "personal" usually means limited, solid views of the ego-identified self (Walsh & Vaughan, 1993b). Although our daily life patterns manifest in various ways, such as defense mechanisms (e.g., suppression and reaction formation), we are certainly more than these bounded views of human behavior (Caplan, Hartelius, & Rardin, 2003). As embodied consciousness, at our optimal potential, we are unlimited awareness contemplating itself. Conceptually, this is a heady view of the human potential. Therefore, transpersonal counseling also focuses on general health and well-being, along with personal and interpersonal structures of the ego (ego strengths/resources, ego ideals, ego defense mechanisms, ego boundaries, observing ego). It is important to understand the mechanisms of the ego if the ultimate goal is to relax its primacy, or to regress in the service of transcendence (Washburn, 1995). Toward this end, an implicit premise in transpersonal psychology is non-duality, or a unified view that transcends subject–object splits. Davis (2000) noted that Western psychological theory is primarily based on conditioning, "reductionism, and separateness," and that our fundamental well-being implies self-transcendence from a "conditioned personality to a sense of spiritual identity," which is non-dual unification with the cosmos (p. 4).

Additionally, transpersonal experiences expand our usual categories of understanding beyond the personal, to include a larger view of awareness (Walsh & Vaughan, 1993a). Therefore, transpersonal practices consist of "structured activities that focus on inducing transpersonal experiences" (p. 203). Transpersonal research includes disciplines that study transpersonal phenomena. In order to investigate this material, dimensional techniques for gathering and examining this data are needed (Braud & Anderson, 1998), especially when considering psychological diagnoses (Ingersoll, 2002). These authors note different methods for acquiring information such as intuitive inquiry, organic research, and analyzing exceptional human experiences such as near-death encounters. Additionally, within transpersonal research methods is a running conviction that transformation of the researcher is inevitable and worth studying as an epistemological theme.

Investigating subjects such as self-actualization and spiritual experiences are challenging to research with meticulous, one-dimensional scientific techniques, and therefore requires "methodological pluralism" (Davis, 2009, p. 4). Since its inception, the field has struggled to adequately research the points between transpersonal phenomena and noumena such as transcendent events (Friedman, 2002).

As with art therapy, defining the field of transpersonal psychology as a scientific discipline has been difficult. At times, the lines have been blurred between transpersonal psychology as a science and the study of personal transcendent experiences (Friedman, 2002). Locating transpersonal psychology as a science is crucial for the evolution of the field and our planet. For example, technology alone cannot modify human behavior. Instead, as in the case of overpopulation, by joining technology with applied, culturally attuned psychological science, human behavior can be altered in order to change population growth patterns. Friedman believes that transpersonal psychology can offer legitimate solutions to our planetary social and ecological challenges.

Similarly, in the nascent field of art-based research (ABR), important questions emerge concerning how to study subjective experience (Franklin, 2012b; McNiff, 1998; Sullivan, 2010). Consciousness studies have grappled with similar questions when it comes to methods for studying introspective data (Weisberg, 2011).

The study of consciousness, or the introspective, felt properties of states of awareness, is another focus of transpersonal psychology and art therapy. The Latin roots of the word "consciousness" are "con" (together or with) and "scire" (to know), implying subjective knowing by being with. First-person awareness of inner events (knowing) further suggests various forms of reflective awareness (being with). Direct sensory observation and perceptual awareness of subjective states, as in art, imply inner processes of both encounter and reflective understanding. When studying consciousness, questions emerge such as: What are concepts? Some believe that concepts are "mental representations" such as components of thought. Within this view, "concepts are to thoughts as words are to sentences" (Gennaro, 2007, p. 1). In terms of art, this quality of awareness could imply that visual content is to thoughts what images are to narratives.

Overall, studying states of consciousness expands the dialogue of consensus reality. A Eurocentric lens primarily observes consciousness from a monophasic point of view, specifically the waking state. Additionally, sleep and mind/body-numbing drug use or alcohol abuse are part of a monophasic worldview. Polyphasic or multiple states of consciousness, viewed from the perspective of indigenous and wisdom traditions, considers many states beyond consensus reality (Walsh & Shapiro, 2006). Artistic inquiry that fosters immersion in the process of using art materials, and dialoguing with—and amplification of—symbols, opens the door into unique states of awareness based on absorbed concentration. Complete immersion in a process such as art can lead to the flow state whereby intrinsic reward occurs, linear time becomes blurred, and one's sense of self temporarily recedes (Csikszentmihalyi, 1977).

There is a lot of curiosity about the expansive dimensions of consciousness. Carefully guided experiences with trained professionals—such as art-based absorption, vision quests, yoga/tantra/yantra meditation techniques including mindfulness, use of psychedelic substances (LSD, yajé, peyote), and breath work (*pranayama* and holotropic)—can offer access to non-ordinary states of consciousness for study. However, this may invite controversy, as this is potentially dangerous territory for the uninformed individual practitioner, and also a lightening rod for disdain from the orthodoxy of the academy. At the very least, professional guidance is necessary. As suggested by M. Esther Harding (1961), when one goes fishing in the deep waters of the unconscious, if not carefully anchored to reality, it is possible to be swallowed whole.

Concerning future research, consciousness studies will undergo a dramatic shift when medical imaging technologies become sophisticated enough to clearly see the life force exiting the body at the time of death. When this happens, theology and science will transcend their historical splits and join together unlike never before. Words such as "soul" and "spirit" will take on new meaning, as their subtle reality becomes the domain of physical science research. Art-based research methods will enhance these merging subjects as new indelible images of the human spirit will peel away from the physical body, and become known and folded into probing creative work. Literally seeing matter change form from solid to subtle essence while migrating to even subtler destinations will forever alter our maps around dying and death. New questions will emerge, and the arts will be right there with science to play a pivotal role in probing these great eternal subjects.

Content–context–process

While working with clients on perceptions of identity, habitual cognitive distortions, or matters like those related to death and dying, the transpersonal therapist can silently hold the contextual view that the client is a divine being rather than a cluster of diagnostic pathologized categories. A core principle of Chögyam Trungpa's (2005) numerous publications asserts that, at an elemental level, we are born with the fundamental sanity of basic goodness. This fundamental substratum is the ground of the human psyche and is quite different from a worldview of original sin.

In a related way, Vaughan (1979) further contextualized Trungpa's view with a triadic model of context, content, and process, to help articulate the role of the therapist working from a transpersonal orientation. Transpersonal context, as just mentioned, consists of the inner orientation, values, and presence of the art therapist. For example, a therapist who has a consistent meditation practice and silently cultivates open-minded, open-hearted presence along with a view of basic goodness might be experienced by the client as unusually non-judgmental and relationally available. The art therapist would certainly not disclose this sort of personal information, but instead would bring the fruits of presence cultivated from a disciplined meditation practice to work in a non-intrusive way.

The content part of this triadic model addresses whatever the client brings to therapy. Core transpersonal themes such as near-death experiences or spiritual emergencies are possible areas for exploration. Within a content perspective then, the client brings transpersonal material to the therapeutic relationship, while the art therapist skillfully addresses this subject matter discerning, for example, what is a potentially pathological or sacred experience. Lastly, process refers to the adage that Jungians often espouse, which is that one must go through shadow to get to Self (archetype). Put another way, art therapists process and practice through potent, perhaps irrational, identifications to dis-identification with our tangled cognitive–emotional–behavioral grasping, and onto transcendence of these limiting perceptions of self. As this chapter suggests, art offers many pathways for supporting personal transformation.

In hindsight, the combination of art with therapy easily nests within a discussion of transpersonal psychology. A cross-cultural history of art includes references to the transformative nature of creativity (Arieti, 1976; Mahony, 1998; Rothenberg & Hausman, 1976), imagination (Berry, 1982; Chodorow, 1997; Hillman, 1978; McNiff, 1992; Watkins, 1984), and symbols, rites, and rituals (Dissanayake, 1992). Studying the phenomenology of artistic consciousness also implies an examination of the phenomenology of creativity from Western romantic, modernist movements to indigenous wisdom traditions.

The Transpersonal Roots of Art Therapy

For some time now, several in the field of art therapy have considered art to be a spiritual practice (Allen, 2001; Cane, 1951; Farrelly-Hansen, 2001; Garai, 2001; Kellogg, 2002). This is because art communicates layered, symbolic themes from our imaginal interior self that can unite latent/unconscious and manifest/conscious realms (Harding, 1961; McNiff, 1992; Naumburg, 1987). These and other authors have produced literature on the several subjects: spirituality (Cane, 1951; Farrelly-Hansen, 2001; Garai, 2001; Horovitz-Darby, 1994); transpersonal applications (Franklin, 1999a; Franklin, Farrelly-Hansen, Marek, Swan-Foster, & Wallingford, 2000; Hocoy, 2005; Kossak, 2009; Lewis, 1997); contemplative applications (Franklin, 1999b; Monti et al., 2006; Rappaport, 2009); existentialism (Moon, 1990); and shamanism (McNiff, 1988, 1992).

Florence Cane (1951) was likely one of the first visionaries in the emerging, yet-to-be-defined field of US art therapy and art education. She actively engaged with art, yoga, and meditation, including interest in the philosophical–spiritual work of Jiddu Krishnamurti (Detre et al., 1983). Cane integrated her esoteric interests into a series of multi-modal art exercises that engaged the body, breath, and voice. She keenly observed how art could unite body with mind and spirit by balancing opposites through various art processes. Cane felt that the resulting outcome of these procedures could integrate the personality and awaken spiritual awareness through the core functions of movement, feeling, and thought.

If Florence Cane were alive today, she may very well embrace a transpersonal view of psychology and art. For example, her open-minded, progressive approach to art

Figure 10.1   Florence Cane. Gift to Naropa University's Art Therapy Department.

can be seen in the following painting (Figure 10.1), which hangs in Naropa University's art therapy program's office, and was gifted by her daughters (Figure 10.1). She indicated that:

> ... this painting developed from the idea of the small self in the state of becoming, and the greater self, or universal being, as in the state of Immanence, being eternally the same. The little figure is in a lotus flower, which is opened through great tenderness received from the spirit. The upper part of the painting is treated in reds and yellows and represents sunlight and the lower part night, or the moon and the darkness of night. The central triangle of light symbolizes a state of peace, and the smaller triangles to the left and right represent the terrifying force of the everyday world.

This painting highlights Cane's knowledge of Eastern, likely Hindu/yoga iconography. The relationship between the small, or ego-based, self and the greater expansive Self of universal consciousness underscores the essence of spiritual life and spiritual work, as both are always simultaneously present. The integration of opposites is also observed as the sun and moon, perhaps masculine and feminine principles, harmonize together. It is stunning that this was painted in 1923 (New York City) when such ideas were still fresh in early modernist circles. Cane's sister, Margaret Naumburg, had similar interests that influenced her work as an educator and later as an art therapist (Detre et al., 1983).

Joseph Garai (1979, 2001), an early practitioner and educator, studied humanistic psychology and holistic healing and how these progressive subjects integrated with art therapy. He formulated methods for cultivating the human potential that included meditation and art as means to developing a healthy mind–body–spirit connection.

Another farsighted pioneer in the field of art therapy was Joan Kellogg, who was interested in the spiritual dimensions of artwork. This led to her collaborating with transpersonal practitioners and pioneers such as Stanislav Grof. During this period, she collected stacks of mandala drawings from clients and developed codified ideas on the 12 categories of the Great Round utilized in the Mandala Assessment Research Instrument (MARI; Thayer, 1994).

An early spokeswoman for the Jungian perspective in art therapy, Edith Wallace (2001), was a physician and analyst interested in utilizing methods such as active imagination in her clinical work. Wallace boldly proclaimed that "all art" is related to meditation (p. 100). Within this declaration and her views on active imagination, Wallace conveyed that art exposes the presence of the ego while inviting this quality of mind to relax its influence. Once achieved, unconscious content can emerge fresh and unencumbered. She advocated for a state of receptive emptiness (p. 98) along with Winnicott's notion of a "non-purposive state" (p. 100) that defines a quality of playful openness to emerging imagery. In addition to Wallace, there are other art therapists who have pursued Jungian analytic training—such as Ethne Gray in Boston, Massachusetts, Sondra Geller in Washington DC, Nora Swan-Foster in Boulder, Colorado, and Roberta Shoemaker in Austin, Texas, in the United States; and Michael Edwards in the United Kingdom.

Ellen Horovitz (1994, 1999, 2012) has written about the clinical relationships between art and spirituality. She asserted that spiritual elements should not be ignored in clinical practice. The art process also inspired her to return to the studio as a deep well to dip into and find healing solutions to life's challenges (Horovitz, 1999).

In addition to the authors mentioned so far, other art therapists have addressed the subject of spirituality from various perspectives. For example, Chickerneo (1993) and Feen-Calligan (1995) have integrated spiritual aspects of substance abuse treatment with art therapy. Most important is that this brief survey reveals that transpersonal ideas have been present in art therapy for some time. This momentum continues today with ongoing interest in transpersonal education (Franklin et al., 2000), yoga (Franklin, 1999a), meditation (Monti et al., 2006), expressive therapies (Kossack, 2009; Lewis, 1997), near-death experiences (Rominger, 2010), and social action (Hocoy, 2005). Contemporary researchers increasingly see the seamless connections between art, creation, and contemplative practices such as mindfulness meditation and focusing (Rappaport, 2009, 2014).[1]

In addition, some in the field view art and image work as soul work. Although their references to the word *soul*, as it relates to art, are subtle and at times difficult to define, McNiff (1992), Moon (1997), and Allen (1995, 2001, 2005) are passionate that art reconnects us to soul. McNiff (1992) made an effort to describe soul with terms such as "kinesis, process, creation, interplay, and continuous motion" (p. 54). For him, soul and psyche are synonymous, and when in trouble, the psyche will minister to the self through the imaginal language of the arts. Creating images and staying close to their unique autonomous presence can directly influence the imaginal experience of soul. The urge of the psyche to articulate its contents in images (Chodorow, 1997; McNiff, 1992) and imaginal movements (Watkins, 1984) is a consistent theme of archetypal and imaginal psychology (Berry, 1982; Hillman, 1978) as well as transpersonal art therapy.

Lastly, sublimation through art addresses how art is inherently transformative (Knafo, 2002). According to Kramer (1971), artistic sublimation is a way to visually redirect chaotic urges into symbolic equivalents. Curiously, even though forceful behavior has been temporarily circumvented, prominent harmful thoughts can still exist. Even so, "as the authors of our own destiny" in terms of resolve, action, and therefore karma, methods to handle impetuous behaviors related to personal freedoms is essential (Shantideva, 1997, p. 6). Toward this end, artistic sublimation is a helpful practice to skillfully develop free will and practice ahimsa or doing less or no harm in the world (Franklin, 2012a). It is better to manage the urges to act out aggressive behaviors through the arts than to externalize dishonorable behavior and possibly hurt others.

Future trends in transpersonal art therapy

Many in the field of art therapy do not necessarily identify as transpersonal practitioners. However, many of these colleagues do include transpersonal material in their clinical-, studio-, and community-based work. Currently, art therapy conferences and journal articles include papers on subjects such as yoga, meditation, ecopsychology, and various spiritual applications. It is assumed that these presentations and articles will grow as connections between art, neuroscience, meditation (Rappaport, 2014), and spirituality increases, especially in healthcare and particularly in counseling (Corey, Corey, & Callanan, 2011; Rose, Westefeld, & Ansley, 2008). Importantly, some liberally bend the word "transpersonal" to mean many things and end up bypassing the messiness of spiritual work. A term coined by John Welwood (2002), "spiritual bypassing," or "premature transcendence," occurs when people ascribe to spiritual desires while sidestepping the "developmental tasks" (p. 12) necessary to achieve long-lasting transcendent outcomes.

Conclusion

It seems that quality research in either art therapy or transpersonal psychology emerges in part from a practice life that informs the work. Additionally, in order to be an art therapist, one has to be dialectically astute by straddling both art and the behavioral/social sciences. Transpersonal psychology also straddles numerous fields and, in tandem with art therapy, offers further cross-pollination that harbors great promise. As methodologies to awaken consciousness, contemplative ethics, and spiritual blueprints for cultivating moral living, the promise of continual synergistic collaboration abounds between these two fields.

For example, since the inception of the Naropa University Art Therapy Program in 1992, meditation training remains a core value of throughout its curriculum. And since 2001, the Naropa Community Art Studio, and more recently its international arm, has been researching service as a spiritual practice including the interface between studio-based art therapy, civic engagement, service learning, and the spiritual dimensions of seva (selfless service) and karma yoga (Franklin, Rothaus, & Schpock, 2005).

Still, both art therapy and transpersonal psychology are emerging disciplines within the academy. One only has to look at the dearth of research institutions offering advanced degrees in either profession. Until this changes, academics in both fields will continue to strive to gain scholarly recognition. The arts, which tend to be less scientific and more subjective, continue to support the exploration of contemplative, spiritual, and transpersonal content from the point of view of self-referential exploration (Franklin, 2012b). While legitimate research, more science is needed. Human beings have the capacity of awareness—to become aware that we are aware—and therefore art in combination with meditation is a sensible avenue for researching the states and traits of contemplative practices (Cahn & Polich, 2006). As more art therapists receive PhDs and study the efficacy of our field, and transpersonal psychologists research the contemplative/spiritual importance of the arts, the exhilarating synergy between both fields will continue to surface exciting connections.

Endnote

1   For a more complete review of art therapists practicing from a spiritual perspective, see Farrelly-Hansen's 2001 publication, *Spirituality and Art Therapy: Living the Connection*.

References

Allen, P. (1995). *Art is a way of knowing.* Boston: Shambhala Publications.

Allen, P. B. (2001). Art making as spiritual path: The open studio process as a way to practice art therapy. In J. A. Rubin (Ed.), *Approaches to art therapy* (pp. 178–188). Philadelphia, PA: Brunner-Routledge.

Allen, P. (2005). *Art is a spiritual path: Engaging the sacred through the practice of art and writing.* Boston: Shambhala.

Arieti, S. (1976). *Creativity: The magic synthesis.* New York, NY: Basic Books.

Aurobindo, S. (2001). *The essential Aurobindo* (R. A. McDermott, Ed.). Great Barrington, MA: Lindisfarne Books.

Benson, H. (1975). *The relaxation response.* New York, NY: Avon Books.

Berry, P. (1982). *Echo's subtle body: Contributions to an archetypal psychology.* Dallas, TX: Spring.

Boorstein, S. (1996). *Transpersonal psychotherapy.* Albany: State University of New York Press.

Braud, W., & Anderson, R. (1998). *Transpersonal research methods for the social sciences: Honoring human experience.* Thousand Oaks, CA: Sage.

Cahn, B. R., & Polich, J. (2006, March). Meditation states and traits: EEG, ERP, and neuroimaging studies. *Psychological Bulletin, 13*(2), 180–211.

Cane, F. (1951). *The artist in each of us.* New York, NY: Pantheon Books.

Caplan, M., Hartelius, G., & Rardin, M. (2003). Contemporary viewpoints on transpersonal psychology. *Journal of Transpersonal Psychology, 35*(2), 143–162.

Chickerneo, N. B. (1993). *Portraits of spirituality in recovery: The use of art in recovery from co-dependency and/or chemical dependency.* Springfield, IL: Charles C. Thomas.

Chodorow, J. (1997). *Jung on active imagination.* Princeton, NJ: Princeton University Press.

Corey, G., Corey, M. S., & Callanan, P. (2011). *Issues and ethics in the helping professions.* Belmont, CA: Brooks/Cole, Cengage Learning.

Csikszentmihalyi, M. (1997). *Finding flow: The psychology of engagement with everyday life.* New York, NY: Basic Books.

Davis, J. (2000). We keep asking ourselves, what is transpersonal psychology? *Guidance and Counseling, 15*(3), 3–8.

Davis, J. (2003, Spring). An overview of transpersonal psychology. *The Humanistic Psychologist, 31*(2–3), 6–21.

Davis, J. (2009). Complementary research methods in humanistic and transpersonal psychology: A case for methodological pluralism. *The Humanistic Psychologist, 37*, 4–23.

Detre, K. C., Frank, T., Kniazzeh, C. R., Robinson, M. C., Rubin, J. A., & Ulman, E. (1983). Roots of art therapy: Margaret Naumburg (1890–1983) and Florence Cane (1882–1952): A family portrait. *The American Journal of Art Therapy, 22*(4), 111–123.

Dissanayake, E. (1992). Art for life's sake. *Art Therapy Journal of the American Art Therapy Association, 9*, 169–177.

Farrelly-Hansen, M. (2001). *Spirituality and art therapy: Living the connection.* Philadelphia: Kingsley.

Feen-Calligan, H. (1995). The use of art therapy in treatment programs to promote spiritual recovery form addiction. *Art Therapy: The Journal of the American Art Therapy Association, 12*(1), 46–50.

Feuerstein, G. (2003). *The deeper dimension of yoga: Theory and practice.* Boston, MA: Shambhala.

Franklin, M. (1999a). Becoming a student of oneself: Activating the Witness in meditation, art, and super-vision. *The American Journal of Art Therapy, 38*(1), 2–13.

Franklin, M. (1999b). Art practice/psychotherapy practice/meditation practice: Sitting on the dove's tail. *Guidance and Counseling, 15*(3), 18–22.

Franklin, M. (2012a). Karuna—ahimsa—and relational aesthetics: Empathic art interventions for contemplative approaches to psychotherapy. In P. de Silva (Ed.), *Buddhist psychotherapy* (pp. 145–154). Ayuthaya, Thailand: Mahachulalongkornrajavidyalaya University.

Franklin, M. A. (2012b). Know thyself: Awakening self-referential awareness through art-based research. *Journal of Applied Arts and Health: Special Issue on Art-Based Research: Opportunities & Challenges, 3*(1), 87–96.

Franklin, M., Farrelly-Hansen, M., Marek, B., Swan-Foster, N., & Wallingford, S. (2000). Transpersonal art therapy education. *Art Therapy, 17*(2), 101–110.

Franklin, M., Rothaus, M., & Schpock, K. (2005). Unity in diversity: Communal pluralism in the art studio and the classroom. In F. Kaplan (Ed.), *Art therapy and social action: Treating the world's wounds.* London and Philadelphia: Jessica Kingsley Publishers.

Friedman, H. (2002). Transpersonal psychology as a scientific field. *The Journal of Transpersonal Psychology, 21*, 175–187.

Garai, J. E. (1979). New horizons of the humanistic approach to expressive therapies and creativity development. *Art Psychotherapy, 6*, 177–183.

Garai, J. (1984). New horizons of holistic healing through creative expression. *Art Therapy: The Journal of the American Art Therapy Association, 1*(2), 76–82.

Garai, J. (2001). Humanistic art therapy. In J. A. Rubin (Ed.), *Approaches to art therapy* (pp. 149–162). Philadelphia, PA: Brunner-Routledge.

Gennaro, R. J. (2007). Consciousness and concepts: An introductory essay. *Journal of Consciousness Studies, 14*(9–10), 1–19.

Grof, S. (1993). *The holotropic mind: The three levels of human consciousness and how they shape our lives.* New York, NY: HarperCollins.

Grof, S., & Grof, C. (1989). *Spiritual emergency.* Los Angeles, CA: Tarcher.

Harding, M. E. (1961). What makes the symbol effective as a healing agent? In G. Adler (Ed.), *Current trends in analytical psychology* (pp. 1–18). London, UK: Tavistock.

Harner, M. (1980). *The way of the Shaman: A guide to power and healing.* New York, NY: Harper and Row.

Hillman, J. (1978). Further notes on images. *Spring,* 152–182.

Hocoy, D. (2005). Art therapy and social action: A transpersonal framework. *Art Therapy,* *22*(1), 7–16.

Horovitz-Darby, E. (1994). *Spiritual art therapy: An alternate path.* Springfield, IL: Charles C. Thomas.

Horovitz, E. G. (1999). *A leap of faith: A call to art.* Springfield, IL: Charles C. Thomas.

Horovitz, E. G. (2012). American Art Therapy Association 43rd Annual Conference, Savannah, GA., July 10, 2012, *Psycho-spiritual Considerations: Integrating Yoga Therapy and Art Therapy with Cancer Survivors.*

Huxley, A. (1944). *The perennial philosophy.* New York, NY: Harper.

Ingersoll, E. R. (2002). An integral approach for teaching and practicing diagnosis. *The Journal of Transpersonal Psychology, 34*(2), 115–127.

James, W. (2002). *The varieties of religious experience: A study in human nature.* New York, NY: Modern Library.

Johnsen, L. (1994). *Daughters of the Goddess: The women saints of India.* Saint Paul Minnesota: Yes International Publishers.

Jung, C. G. (2009). *The red book* (S. Shamdasani, Ed. & Trans.). New York, NY: Norton.

Kellogg, J. (2002). *Mandala: Path of beauty* (3rd ed., 2nd printing). Belleair, FL: ATMA, Inc.

Knafo, D. (2002). Revisiting Ernst Kris's concept of regression in the service of the ego in art. *Psychoanalytic Psychology, 19*(1), 24–49.

Kossack, M. S. (2009). Therapeutic attunement: A transpersonal view of expressive arts therapy. *The Arts in Psychotherapy, 36*(1), 13–18.

Kramer, E. (1971). *Art as therapy with children.* New York, NY: Schocken Books.

Lewis, P. (1997). Transpersonal arts psychotherapy: Toward an ecumenical worldview. *The Arts in Psychotherapy, 24*(3), 243–254.

Mahony, W. K. (1998). *The artful universe: An introduction to the Vedic imagination.* New York, NY: State University of New York Press.

McNiff, S. (1988). The shaman within. *The Arts in Psychotherapy, 15*(4), 285–291.

McNiff, S. (1992). *Art as medicine.* Boston, MA: Shambhala.

McNiff, S. (1998). *Art-based research.* Philadelphia, PA: Kingsley.

Moon, B. (1990). *Existential art therapy: The canvas mirror.* Springfield, IL: Charles C. Thomas.

Moon, B. (1997). *Art and soul.* Springfield, IL: Charles C. Thomas.

Monti, D. A., Peterson, C., Shankin-Kunkel, E. J., Hauk, W. W., Pequignot, E., Rhodes, L., et al. (2006). A randomized trial of mindfulness-based art therapy (MBAT) for women with cancer. *Psycho-Oncology, 15,* 363–373.

Muktananda, S. (1994). *The play of consciousness.* South Fallsburg, NY: SYDA Foundation.

Naumburg, M. (1987). *Dynamically oriented art therapy: Its principals and practice (pp. 1–25).* Chicago, IL: Magnolia Street Publishers.

Rappaport, L. (2009). *Focusing oriented art therapy: Accessing the body's wisdom and creative intelligence.* Philadelphia, PA: Kingsley.

Rappaport, L. (ed.) (2014). *Mindfulness and the arts therapies: Theory and practice.* London: Jessica Kingsley.

Rominger, R. (2010). Postcards from heaven and hell: Understanding the near-death experience through art. *Art Therapy: The Journal of the American Art Therapy Association, 27*(1), 18–25.

Rose, M. R., Westefeld, J. S., & Ansley, T. N. (2008). Spiritual issues in counseling: Clients' beliefs and preferences. *Psychology of Religion and Spirituality, S*(1), 18–33.

Roszak, T., Gomes, M. E., & Kanner, A. D. (1995). *Ecopsychology: Restoring the earth and healing the mind.* San Francisco: Sierra Club Books.

Rothenberg, A., & Hausman, C. R. (1976). *The creativity question.* Durham, NC: Duke University Press.

Ruzek, N. (2007). Transpersonal psychology in context: Perspectives from its founders and historians of American psychology. *The Journal of Transpersonal Psychology, 39*(2), 153–174.

Ryan, M. B. (2008). The transpersonal William James. *The Journal of Transpersonal Psychology, 40*(1), 20–40.

Scotton, B. W., Chinen, A. B., & Battista, J. R. (1996). *Textbook of transpersonal psychiatry and psychology.* New York, NY: Basic Books.

Shantideva. (1997). *The way of the Bodhisattva: The Padmakara translation group.* Boston: Shambhala Press.

Steiner, R. (2003). *Art: An introductory reader* (C. von Arnim, Trans). Forest Row: Sophia Books.

Sullivan, G. (2010). *Art practice as research: Inquiry in the visual arts.* Los Angeles: Sage.

Tart, C. T. (1992). Transpersonal psychologies: Perspectives on the mind form seven great spiritual traditions. New York, NY: Harper Collins.

Thayer, J. A. (1994). An interview with Joan Kellogg. *Art Therapy: Journal of the American Art Therapy Association, 11*(3), 200–205.

Trungpa, C. (1976). *The myth of freedom.* Boston, MA: Shambhala.

Trungpa, C. (1996). *Dharma art.* Boston, MA: Shambhala.

Trungpa, C. (2005). *The sanity we are born with: A Buddhist approach to psychotherapy.* Boston, MA: Shambhala.

Vaughan, F. (1979). Transpersonal psychotherapy: Context, content, and process. *Journal of Transpersonal Psychology, 11*(1), 25–30.

Wallace, E. (2001). Healing through the visual arts. In J. A. Rubin (Ed.), *Approaches to art therapy* (pp. 95–108). Philadelphia, PA: Brunner-Routledge.

Walsh, R., & Shapiro, S. L. (2006). *The meeting of meditative disciplines and Western psychology, 61*(3), 227–239.

Walsh, R., & Vaughan, F. (1993a). On transpersonal definitions. *The Journal of transpersonal Psychology, 25*(2), 199–207.

Walsh, R., & Vaughan, F. (1993b). *Paths beyond ego: A transpersonal vision.* New York, NY: Tarcher-Putnam.

Washburn, M. (1995). *The ego and the dynamic ground: A transpersonal theory of human development.* New York, NY: State University of New York press.

Watkins, M. (1984). *Waking dreams.* Dallas, TX: Spring.

Weisberg, J. (2011). Introduction. *Journal of Consciousness Studies, 18*(1), 7–20.

Welwood, J. (2002). *Toward a psychology of awakening: Buddhism, psychotherapy, and the path of personal and spiritual transformation.* Boston: Shambhala.

Wilber, K. (1997). *The eye of spirit: An integral vision for a world gone slightly mad.* Boston: Shambhala.

Wilber, K. (2000). *Integral psychology: Consciousness, spirit, psychology, therapy.* Boston: Shambhala.

Yogananda, P. (2003). *Autobiography of a yogi.* Los Angeles, CA: Self Realization Fellowship.

Additional Suggested Readings

Cortright, B. (1997). *Psychotherapy and spirit: Theory and practice in transpersonal psychotherapy.* Albany: State University of New York Press.

Ulman, E. (1975). Art therapy: Problems of definition. In E. Ulman & P. Dachinger (Eds.), *Art therapy.* New York, NY: Schocken Books.

11

Open Studio Approach to Art Therapy

Catherine Hyland Moon

Introduction

A studio approach to art therapy might be defined as one in which engagement with art products and processes constitute the core of the work (C. Moon, 2010). However, what happens when the word *open* is added to that definition? Open to what?

Such an approach to art therapy might indicate openness in regard to participants' free choice of materials, processes, and thematic content. Or *open studio* might denote a drop-in program where participants can come and go at will (Hogan, 2001). It might refer to community-based programs that are open to anyone from the general public, without discrimination. Possibly, the openness of the studio might be in relation to the therapist, as this type of practice tends to be characterized by a high level of transparency, a "mutual exchange of self-discovery between [participant] and therapist" (B. Moon, 2009, p. 98).

This chapter briefly addresses the historical development of an open studio approach to art therapy and describes the multiple and sometimes contested characteristics of this approach.

Brief History of Open Studio Approach

Conveying even a brief history of the open studio approach to art therapy is an acknowledgement that history is constructed from multiple perspectives and voices, as the account of open studio approaches deviates from the dominant psychodynamic and organizationally focused history of the field. Instead, it is the story of how the process of art-making has been used for therapeutic aims, particularly within the context of community. Wix (2010) believes that art therapy's bias toward its psychological over its artistic roots has diminished our field's theoretical and philosophical groundings in the practices of art and their potential for meaning making and healing. It is important to note this alternative history, so that those who identify with non-dominant approaches can recognize and claim their lineage (Potash, 2005).

The Wiley Handbook of Art Therapy, First Edition. Edited by David E. Gussak and Marcia L. Rosal.
© 2016 John Wiley & Sons, Ltd. Published 2016 by John Wiley & Sons, Ltd.

The concept of the open studio approach in art therapy began with people such as Mary Huntoon in the United States in the late 1930s and Edward Adamson in Britain in the mid-1940s. Each of them worked in community studios within psychiatric hospitals, and each viewed their role as a facilitator, rather than someone directing the patients' output (Adamson, 1984; Hogan, 2001; Waller, 1991; Wix, 2000). Adamson (1984) did not believe in making suggestions, criticizing, praising, or interpreting the patients' art. Instead, he welcomed what patients made and accorded them the "dignity of helping to cure themselves" (p. 2). Huntoon believed that art draws upon health, not pathology (Wix, 2000, p. 172).

In the United States, art therapists of color, who made significant contributions to the establishment of art therapy approaches, focused on meeting participants within the contexts of their communities and cultures. In the 1930s, Georgette Powell, who would later become an art therapist, engaged in community and activist arts as part of the Works Project Administration, painting positive images of African Americans in direct opposition to Harlem Hospital's ban on "Negro" subject matter (Boston & Short, 2006). Cliff Joseph, a muralist, academic, and politically engaged art therapist, worked primarily with racially and economically oppressed communities (Doby-Copeland, 2006; Farris, 2006; Joseph, 2006). He was adamant about contextualizing the interpersonal within larger social contexts and, in the 1960s, even advocated for psychiatric patients' involvement in community activism, proposing that it was an expression of collective health (Joseph, 2006). Lucile Venture, working in the 1970s, suggested that an art- and community-based approach to art therapy made it more accessible to those who were socially marginalized based on race or class (Potash, 2005).

Edith Kramer, primarily due to her scholarly publications from the 1950s to the 1980s, remains the person most strongly identified with approaches to art therapy that locate the primary therapeutic benefit within the act of making art (Junge & Asawa, 1994). Kramer's strong identity as an artist influenced the art-centered approach to her work and prompted her critique of art therapists who, in their attempts to be "baby psychoanalysts," left behind their unique artistic skills and knowledge (as cited in Wix, 2010, p. 179). Other early proponents of an art-based approach included Don Jones, who began his work in the 1940s, followed by Bob Ault in the 1960s. Jones not only maintained an active art practice, but also made art alongside the patients with whom he worked (Feen-Calligan & Sands-Goldstein, 1996; Jones, 1983). Ault thought of his artist and therapist roles as complementary (Feen-Calligan & Sands-Goldstein, 1996), and worried when the focus on developing the field's knowledge base led to psychologizing the art process (Ault, 1994).

Since those early days of the field, other art therapists have been strong advocates of art therapists' ties to the fundamental benefits of art-making. These art therapists include: Millie Lachman-Chapin (1983, 2000), who related to clients by making art with them and presenting herself as someone also striving to create meaning through art; Mickie McGraw (1995), who in 1967 created the still operating open art studio at Metro Health Medical Center in Cleveland, Ohio; Shaun McNiff, whose numerous publications over the years have emphasized an integrated arts-based approach; Pat Allen (1992), whose seminal paper on the "clinification" of art therapy warned of the danger of over-identification with clinicians from related fields and the simultaneous loss of connection to the artist identity; Bruce Moon, whose stories about work with clients captured the vibrancy of the exchange between artist therapist and artist client (McNiff, 1998); Janis Timm-Bottos (1995, 2011, 2012), who has been a leader in developing community-based art therapy studios in the United States and Canada; Lani Gerity (Chilton, Gerity, LaVorgna-Smith, & MacMichael, 2009; Gerity, 2010), who advocated for the egalitarian platform of the virtual environment; and this author, who has articulated some of the unique theoretical and practical contributions of an artist's identity to therapeutic practice (C. Moon, 2002).

Characteristics of an open studio approach

An open studio approach signifies a commitment to art made within a communal context. At its core is a belief in relational aesthetics, the "capacity of art to promote healthy interactions within and among people and the created world" (C. Moon, 2002, p. 140). In a studio setting, art is "the way" rather than simply a tool for uncovering and depicting problems (Wix, 1995, p. 175). Multiple aims for—and modes of—art production are embraced (Huss, 2010; C. Moon, 2010).

In contrast to a conventional model of art therapy, participation in an open art therapy studio often is informal, occurring through word of mouth and on a drop-in basis, particularly at sites where there are no criteria for participation and no intake procedures. Attendees may be comprised of networks of friends and family members, many of whom find traditional mental health services financially or socially inaccessible. There is likely no guarantee or expectation of confidentiality, and the role of "helper" is often shared among multiple participants rather than located primarily with the therapist (Allen, 1995; Kapitan, 2008; Malchiodi, 1995; McGraw, 1995). However, in having a human service or pathology focus, the open art therapy studio may still be subtly aligned with art therapy's clinical history and thus be distinguished from the vocational, aesthetic, or arts marketing emphases associated with the art world (Vick & Sexton-Radek, 2008).

There are other features that characterize an open studio approach to art therapy. What follows are descriptions of the dominant characteristics of this approach.

Aligned with health

In an open studio approach to art therapy, the arts are viewed democratically, based on the idea that everyone has an equal right to access and representation in the cultural life of a community (Moon & Shuman, 2013). Involvement in communal creative endeavors tends to downplay social differences and to accentuate health, and for some it reorients identity from social service recipient to artist or maker (Allen, 2008; Thompson, 2009). This shift in identity, along with the correspondence that occurs between processes of art-making and life's challenges and struggles, can lead to participants' enhanced self-esteem (Franklin, 1992). Even in situations of community stress and trauma, art-making in the context of community can reinforce a sense of normalcy by strengthening social bonds and recontextualizing symptomatology as a normal response to an abnormal situation (Czamansky-Cohen, 2010).

Role of art therapist

In contrast to institutional settings that often privilege analytical and therapeutic skills, a studio setting enables the art therapist to simply offer, through art, the chance for participants to be seen, acknowledged, and understood (Lachman-Chapin, 2000). The therapist is not the expert who interprets or fixes, but rather is a collaborator and co-participant (Allen, 2008; Gray, 2012). The art therapist can exploit the positive impacts of working alongside clients (Allen, 1992; Haeseler, 1989; Lachman-Chapin, 1983; B. Moon, 2009; C. Moon, 2002) without privileging the individualistic, heroic image of the fine artist (Cahn, 2000). The art therapist models investment in the art-making process and confidence in its benefits (Block, Harris, & Laing, 2005; McNiff, 1995), but at times also is the recipient of mentorship by other participants (Franklin, Rothaus, & Schpok, 2007). The aim is not to disown the expertise of the art therapist—such as knowledge about art materials and processes, or skill with facilitating group communication—but rather to contextualize that expertise within the ecology of the studio, where participants hold an array of skills, knowledge areas, and abilities.

There are many potential roles for the art therapist in an open studio setting, depending on the studio's context and structure: fellow artist, educator, co-mentor, guest, curator, community member, administrator, consultant, collaborator, marketing designer, organizer, activist, interloper, grant writer, etc. (Block et al, 2005; Franklin, Rothaus, & Schpok, 2007; C. Moon & Shuman, 2013; Timm-Bottos, 1995). Because these roles can occur simultaneously and shift over time, the flexibility of the art therapist is key. In an environment that prioritizes collaboration, it is also important for the art therapist to acknowledge and address power differentials, which are typically minimized but never eliminated.

Studio environment

The ambiance and functionality of the studio space are undeniably important to an open studio approach. The space immediately conveys that art is pivotal to what happens there (Henley, 1995; Wix, 1995). Not only does the studio consist of the physical space, equipment, and materials to make artistic production possible, it also contains an "ecology of mutual influences" (McNiff, 1995, p. 181) that both shape and are shaped by those who participate in it. Variously described as atmosphere, ambiance, or vibe, the feel of the environment is something that art therapists co-create every time they work with others. Ideally, the studio generates novelty, imagination, flexibility, and interchanges between personal and collective content (McNiff, 2009). Whitaker (2005, 2012) envisions the studio as a flexible, dynamic site of activation where people, projects, materials, sensory encounters, artworks, and the environment are assembled and reassembled by the art therapy participants in an improvisatory exploration of subjectivity. The studio is a sensory and relational playground/workspace where interactions occur between and with media, between people working in the space, between the maker and his or her art-making process, and between the artist and art product (Seiden, 2001; Wix, 1995, 2010).

Kalmanowitz and Lloyd (2005, 2011) coined the term *portable studio* based on their work in less-than-ideal contexts in multiple countries. The portability of their approach refers not to transporting tangible materials from place to place, but rather to the internal structures of the art therapist who creates dynamic studios out of whatever is at hand, including his or her own beliefs in participants' personal and cultural resources. A quiet, tranquil sanctuary may not be possible, or perhaps even desirable, depending on the cultural context (McElroy, 2005). Instead, the open studio might reflect and respond to the vibrant, fluid, or even chaotic environments within which it is situated (C. Moon, 2010; Whitaker, 2012).

Structure

An open art therapy studio might be a freestanding entity, a project carried out in collaboration with a social service agency, or a program located within an institutional setting. Its affiliations and administrative structures will inevitably impact everything from whether and how much participants pay for services, to how the program is documented and evaluated, to who picks out the wall paint colors.

In general, art therapy studio programs tend to have more open-ended time structures than traditional mental health settings where art-making is constricted by fixed session times and length of stay limits (Malchiodi, 1995). Thus, an open studio approach "foregrounds the therapeutic value of sustained attention to making art" (Cahn, 2000, p. 178). In an open studio, the process of creating something tends to correspond with the normal processes of a working artist, including having time to contemplate, responding in a natural way to the urge to create (McNiff, 1988), and experiencing variability in output due to fluctuations in inspiration and motivation. In a similar way, life issues and concerns tend to arise organically, out of the conversations that happen while people are making art.

An open studio approach often is equated with a non-directive and unstructured way of working. However, directed skill-building workshops are common, and some open studio practices employ approaches to art-making that are highly structured (e.g., see Allen, 2001).

Art exhibitions tend to be common components of the structure provided by open studios. Exhibits serve to emphasize the health, creativity, and capability of participants, and to position participants as assets to the community. They also make art more accessible to the public and can help challenge public perceptions of stigmatized populations (Block et al., 2005; Gray, 2012; McGraw, 1995; Potash & Ho, 2011). Exhibitions, including performance and activist art, also can be used in an overtly political way to express and critique social stigma and marginalization related to illness and disability (Frostig, 2011; Hogan, 2001).

Process and product

An emphasis on process is often cited as a hallmark of art therapy, yet the "tenacious, irascible attribute of the art product constantly reappears in art therapy theory and practice" (Thompson, 2009, p. 160). In a studio approach, the product is generally considered at least as important as the process of art-making. Some studio settings, similar to conventional art therapy, focus on art-making with simple materials as a means to gain insight, yet they do so within a decidedly studio framework in which the art product is also valued (e.g., see Block et al., 2005). Other open studio sites make available a range of art materials and processes for experimentation and skill development, as well as provide opportunities to use art for emotional expression, development of self-awareness, and group interaction (e.g., see McGraw, 1995).

When art is the focus of discussions, it is understood through its own language—imagery, metaphor, aesthetics, and perception—and not merely used as a catalyst for a discussion about a problem (Wix, 1995, 2010).

However, even in the context of studio-based models, art therapists tend to privilege individualized self-expression (C. Moon, 2005), even though the current scope of art practices extends far beyond private, intuitive exploration and expression of the unconscious. Of particular relevance to art therapy, art practices are used for community building through collective expressions of ritual, myth, and spirituality (Hocoy, 2005), and for engaging critical citizenship and activism (Frostig, 2011). Open studio venues can provide ideal environments for expanding art therapy's reach, enabling participants to explore a range of art practices—from individual self-expression to community building to political activism.

As the open studio model develops, the place of critique requires further exploration. Models that refrain from any commentary on the art have their place. But lowered expectations and a judgment-free environment might also be perceived as patronizing and deprive participants of the critical discernment to which they are entitled (Lentz, 2008). Henley (2004) offers an approach to critique that is empathic and supportive of the artists' intentions, while also calling the artist to be accountable to challenging and communicating with the viewer.

Ethical considerations

The word *open* in an open studio approach does not sit well with the concept of safety in therapy, which is correlated with clear boundaries, privacy, and confidentiality. How does an art therapist negotiate the use of ethical guidelines that were written for more conventional art therapy practices? For example, what are the ethical responsibilities of art therapists in studio settings that are not explicitly identified as art therapy? In open studio settings, dual relationships are common (e.g., art therapists are often both participants and facilitators). There may be no formal procedures for establishing consent, no structures for developing goals with individual participants, no ability to ensure privacy or confidentiality in relation to participants' artistic or verbal self-disclosures, and no written documentation of sessions. Elmendorf (2010) suggested that community-based art therapists must question and clarify their intentions and agenda, work to stay clear about those intentions, determine how best to keep a space safe, become aware of their potential for causing harm, consider in advance how to exit with integrity, and be aware of power relationships among multiple stakeholders.

It is not enough to consider ethics in relation to individual participants; the community-based studio practitioner must also take into consideration the potential beneficial and harmful effects on the community at large (Lu & Yuen, 2012; Toporek & Chope, 2006). One strategy for lessening the potential for community harm is to work with community members in developing locally relevant, sustainable models of practice. Such a strategy acknowledges that psychological states and social realities are intertwined, that personal and collective suffering is a communal responsibility, that the social context is an important dimension of health, and that social ties and support promote collective coping and well-being (Czamansky-Cohen, 2010; Hocoy, 2005; Timm-Bottos, 2011; Wix, 1995).

Emphasis on collectivity

Of all the features of an open studio approach to art therapy, the most central characteristic, aside from art, is a focus on collectivity. An emphasis on working in the context of community reinforces and builds upon what is commonly understood in relation to group art therapy—that making art with others fosters connection, serves as an antidote to social isolation, and generates positive group energy (B. Moon, 2010). A collective focus is reinforced when everyone is valued for what he or she brings to the community and is viewed as capable of contributing to decision-making and care of the space. In such an atmosphere, a sense of belonging, empowerment, and responsibility develops (Moon & Shuman, 2013). Art-making becomes a means by which "communities name and understand their realities, identify their needs and strengths, and transform their lives in ways that contribute to individual and collective well-being and social justice" (Golub, 2005, p. 17).

A social justice agenda is not an inherent feature of an open studio art therapy approach; however, a practice focusing on collectivity and community makes it difficult to disregard the social, economic, and political realities of participants and to deny the links between individual and social change. Working from a social justice agenda requires shifting from an ameliorative approach, whereby one provides individualized help or support, to a transformational approach, focused on social change. It requires that art therapists engage in both the containment of the studio and the messiness of the wider world, to challenge the social structures that reinforce imbalances of power, perpetuate marginalization based on social differences, and contribute to unjust social conditions. The studio provides the perfect location for working in creative solidarity to address issues that undermine our collective humanity.

Conclusion

In this chapter, the open studio approach to art therapy has been recognized as having an alternative history to that of dominant psychodynamic and organizational perspectives. While not an approach congruent with every art therapist's professional identity, or an approach appropriate to every circumstance, the open studio model has enhanced the field's theoretical, philosophical, and practical grounding in artistic practice, and raised awareness of the importance of the social context as an aspect of health.

An open studio approach is not one unified method of working, but rather an array of diverse practices that place art and social engagement at their core. The dominant characteristics of this approach include a more informal atmosphere than conventional therapy, a focus on health rather than pathology, a less hierarchical and more flexible role for the therapist than is typical, a dynamic studio environment conducive to artistic production, an open structure that allows both the artistic process and conversation among participants to unfold naturally, an emphasis on both the processes and products of art-making, and an awareness of the interrelationship between personal and social well-being and change. While this approach raises unique ethical challenges, it also positions the field of art therapy to more effectively engage with and challenge the social forces that shape the lives of those who make use of our services.

References

Adamson, E. (1984). *Art as healing.* Boston: Coventure.

Allen, P. B. (1992). Artist-in-residence: An alternative to "clinification" for art therapists. *Art Therapy: Journal of the American Art Therapy Association, 9,* 22–29.

Allen, P. B. (1995). Coyote comes in from the cold: The evolution of the open studio concept. *Art Therapy: Journal of the American Art Therapy Association, 12,* 161–166.

Allen, P. B. (2001). Art making as spiritual path: The open studio process as a way to practice art therapy. In Judith A. Rubin (Ed.), *Approaches to art therapy: Theory and technique* (2nd ed., pp. 178–188). Philadelphia: Brunner-Routledge.

Allen, P. B. (2005). *Art is a spiritual path: Engaging the Sacred through the practice of art and writing.* Boston: Shambhala.

Allen, P. B. (2008). Commentary on community-based art studios: Underlying principles. *Art Therapy: Journal of the American Art Therapy Association, 25,* 11–12.

Ault, B. (1994). How Will the profession of art therapy change in the next 25 years? Responses by past award winners: In search of the wisdom of a vision. *Art Therapy: Journal of the American Art Therapy Association, 11,* 251–253.

Block, D., Harris, T., & Laing, S. (2005). Open studio process as a model of social action: A Program for at-risk youth. *Art Therapy. Journal of the American Art Therapy Association, 22,* 32–38.

Boston, C., & Short, G. (2006). Notes: Georgette Seabrook Powell. *Art Therapy. Journal of the American Art Therapy Association, 23,* 89–90.

Cahn, E. (2000). Proposal for a studio-based art therapy education. *Art Therapy: Journal of the American Art Therapy Association, 17,* 177–182.

Chilton, G., Gerity, L., LaVorgna-Smith, M., & MacMichael, H. N. (2009). An online art exchange group: 14 secrets for a happy artist's life. *Art Therapy: Journal of the American Art Therapy Association, 26,* 66–72.

Czamansky-Cohen, J. (2010). "Oh! now I remember": The use of a studio approach to art therapy with internally displaced people. *The Arts in Psychotherapy, 37,* 407–413.

Doby-Copeland, C. (2006). Things come to me: Reflections from an art therapist of color. *Art Therapy: Journal of the American Art Therapy Association, 23,* 81–85.

Elmendorf, D. (2010). Minding our P's and Q's: Addressing possibilities and precautions of community work through new questions. *Art Therapy: Journal of the American Art Therapy Association, 27,* 40–43.

Farris, P. (2006). Mentors of diversity: A tribute. *Art Therapy: Journal of the American Art Therapy Association, 22,* 86–88.

Feen-Callahan, H., & Sands-Goldstein, M. (1996). A picture of our beginnings: The artwork of art therapy pioneers. *American Journal of Art Therapy, 35,* 43–59.

Franklin, M. (1992). Art therapy and self-esteem. *Art Therapy: Journal of the American Art Therapy Association, 9,* 78–84.

Franklin, M., Rothaus, M. E., & Schpok, K. (2007). Unity in diversity: A communal pluralism in the art studio and the classroom. In F. Kaplan (Ed.), *Art therapy and social action* (pp. 213–230). London: Jessica Kingsley.

Frostig, K. (2011). Arts activism: Praxis in social justice, critical discourse, and radical modes of engagement. *Art Therapy: Journal of the American Art Therapy Association, 28*(2), 50–56.

Gerity, L. (2010). Fourteen secrets for a happy artist's life: Using art and the internet to encourage resilience, joy, and a sense of community. In C. H. Moon (Ed.), *Materials and Media in Art Therapy: Critical Understandings of Diverse Artistic Vocabularies* (pp. 155–182). New York, NY: Routledge.

Golub, D. (2005). Social action art therapy. *Art Therapy: Journal of the American Art Therapy Association, 22,* 17–23.

Gray, B. L. (2012). The Babushka project: Mediating between the margins and wider community through public art creation. *Art Therapy: Journal of the American Art Therapy Association, 29,* 113–119.

Haeseler, M. P. (1989). Should art therapist create art alongside their clients? *American Journal of Art Therapy, 27,* 70–79.

Henley, D. (1995). A consideration of the studio as therapeutic intervention. *Art Therapy: Journal of the American Art Therapy Association, 12,* 188–190.

Henley, D. (2004). The meaningful critique: Responding to art from preschool to postmodernism. *Art Therapy: Journal of the American Art Therapy Association, 21,* 79–87.

Hocoy, D. (2005). Art therapy and social action: A transpersonal framework. *Art Therapy: Journal of the American Art Therapy Association, 22,* 7–16.

Hogan, S. (2001). *Healing arts: The history of art therapy.* London: Jessica Kingsley.

Huss, E. (2010). Bedouin women's embroidery as female empowerment: Crafts as culturally embedded expression within art therapy. In C. H. Moon (Ed.), *Materials and media in art therapy: critical understandings of diverse artistic vocabularies* (pp. 215–229). New York, NY: Routledge.

Jones, D. (1983). An art therapist's personal record. *Art Therapy: Journal of the American Art Therapy Association, 1,* 22–25.

Joseph, C. (2006). Creative alliance: The healing power of art therapy. *Art Therapy: Journal of the American Art Therapy Association, 23,* 30–33.

Junge, M. B., & Asawa, P. P. (1994). *A history of art therapy in the United States.* Mundelein, IL: The American Art Therapy Association.

Kalmanowitz, D., & Lloyd, B. (2005). *Art therapy and political violence: With art, without illusions.* London: Routledge.

Kalmanowitz, D., & Lloyd, B. (2011). Inside-out outside-in: Found objects and portable studio. In E. G. Levine & S. K. Levine (Eds.), *Art in action: Expressive arts therapy and social change* (pp. 104–127). London: Jessica Kingsley.

Kapitan, L. (2008). "Not art therapy": Revisiting the therapeutic studio in the narrative of the profession. *Art Therapy: Journal of the American Art Therapy Association, 25,* 2–3.

Lachman-Chapin, M. (1983). The artist as clinician: An interactive technique. *American Journal of Art Therapy, 23,* 13–25.

Lachman-Chapin, M. (2000). Is art therapy a profession or an idea? *Art Therapy: Journal of the American Art Therapy Association, 17,* 11–13.

Lentz, R. (2008). What we talk about when we talk about art therapy: An outsider's guide to identity crisis. *Art Therapy: Journal of the American Art Therapy Association, 25,* 13–14.

Lu, L., & Yuen, F. (2012). Journey women: Art therapy in a decolonizing framework. *The Arts in Psychotherapy, 39,* 192–200.

Malchiodi, C. (1995). Studio approaches to art therapy. *Art Therapy: Journal of the American Art Therapy Association, 12,* 154–156.

McElroy, S. (2005). A soldier's story: An art therapy intervention in Sri Lanka. In D. Kalmanowitz & B. Lloyd (Eds.), *Art Therapy and Political Violence: With Art, Without Illusions* (pp. 187–199). London: Routledge.

McGraw, M. (1995). The art studio: A studio based art therapy program. *Art Therapy: Journal of the American Art Therapy Association, 12,* 167–174.

McNiff, S. (1988). *Fundamentals of art therapy.* Springfield, IL: Charles C. Thomas.

McNiff, S. (1995). Keeping the studio. *Art Therapy: Journal of the American Art Therapy Association, 12,* 179–183.

McNiff, S. (1998). *Art-based research.* London: Jessica Kingsley.

McNiff, S. (2009). *Integrating the arts in therapy: History, theory, and practice.* Springfield, IL: Charles C. Thomas.

Moon, B. (2009). *Existential art therapy: The canvas mirror* (3rd ed.). Springfield, IL: Charles C. Thomas.

Moon, B. (2010). *Art-based group therapy: Theory and practice.* Springfield, IL: Charles C. Thomas.

Moon, C. H. (2002). *Studio art therapy: Cultivating the artist identity in the art therapist.* London: Jessica Kingsley.

Moon, C. H. (2005). Call and response: Exploring diverse artistic vocabularies. *Canadian Art Therapy Association Journal, 18,* 2–8.

Moon, C. H. (2010). *Materials and media in art therapy: Critical understandings of diverse artistic vocabularies.* New York, NY: Routledge.

Moon, C. H., & Shuman, V. (2013). The community art studio: Creating a space of solidarity and inclusion. In P. Howie, S. Prasad, & J. Kristel (Eds.), *Using Art Therapy with Diverse Populations: Crossing Cultures and Abilities.* London: Jessica Kingsley.

Potash, J. (2005). Rekindling the multicultural history of the American Art Therapy Association, Inc. *Art Therapy: Journal of the American Art Therapy Association, 22,* 184–188.

Potash, J., & Ho, R. T. H. (2011). Drawing involves caring: Fostering relationship building through art therapy for social change. *Art Therapy: Journal of the American Art Therapy Association, 28,* 74–81.

Seiden, D. (2001). *Mind over matter: The uses of materials in art, education and therapy.* Chicago: Magnolia Street.

Thompson, G. (2009). Artistic sensibility in the studio and gallery model: Revisiting process and product. *Art Therapy: Journal of the American Art Therapy Association, 26,* 159–166.

Timm-Bottos, J. (1995). Artstreet: Joining community through art. *Art Therapy: Journal of the American Art Therapy Association, 12,* 184–187.

Timm-Bottos, J. (2011). Endangered threads: Socially committed community art action. *Art Therapy: Journal of the American Art Therapy Association, 28,* 57–63.

Timm-Bottos, J. (2012). The "five and dime:" Developing a community's access to art-based research. In H. Burt (Ed.), *Art Therapy and Postmodernism: Creative Healing through a Prism* (pp. 97–117). London: Jessica Kingsley.

Toporek, R. L., & Chope, R. C. (2006). Individual, programmatic and entrepreneurial approaches to social justice: Counseling psychologists in career and vocational counseling. In R. L. Toporek, L. H. Gerstein, N. A. Fouad, G. Roysircar, & T. Israel (Eds.), *Handbook for social justice in counseling psychology* (pp. 276–293). Thousand Oaks, CA: Sage.

Vick, R. M., & Sexton-Radek, K. (2008). Community-based art studios in Europe and the United States: A comparative study. *Art Therapy: Journal of the American Art Therapy Association, 25,* 4–10.

Waller, D. (1991). *Becoming a profession: The history of art therapy in Britain 1940–1982.* London: Tavistock/Routledge.

Whitaker, P. (2005). Moving art, moving worlds: performing the body in visual arts and art therapy. *Canadian Art Therapy Association Journal, 18,* 27–34.

Whitaker, P. (2012). The art therapy assemblage. In Helene Burt (Ed.), *Art therapy and postmodernism: Creative healing through a prism* (pp. 344–366). London: Jessica Kingsley.

Wix, L. (1995). The intern studio: A pilot study. *Art Therapy: Journal of the American Art Therapy Association, 12,* 175–178.

Wix, L. (2000). Looking for what's lost: The artistic roots of art therapy: Mary Huntoon. *Art Therapy: Journal of the American Art Therapy Association, 17,* 168–176.

Wix, L. (2010). Studios as locations of possibility: Remembering a history. *Art Therapy: Journal of the American Art Therapy Association, 27,* 178–183.

12

An Eclectic Approach to Art Therapy—Revisited

Harriet Wadeson

In the early 1990s, Judith Rubin said to me, "Harriet, I'd like to include you in the book I'm putting together on various approaches to art therapy, but I don't identify you with any particular approach."

"You're right," I replied, "I guess I'm sort of eclectic."
"That's it. You'll write the chapter on The Eclectic Approach to Art Therapy."
And so I did (Rubin, 2001).

When I look back at that chapter, I am struck by how much the field has changed in the past decade. So when I was asked to write a chapter on the eclectic approach for this book, I agreed, knowing that I would write a completely different chapter. In the Rubin book, I spoke of the importance of the recognition that the art therapist brings her whole person to the therapeutic encounter so that her art therapy beliefs must be consonant with her own life experience. I wrote of the value of familiarity with major psychological developmental theories, and gave examples of how I utilized Freudian, Jungian, Gestalt, and behavioral theoretical concepts and practices in my own work. I advocated for art therapists' unique development of their own ways of working, utilizing the wisdom from their studies to fashion their own approach to the work. I saw this as a dynamic process that would evolve and develop with the therapists' experience in both their profession and in their lives.

I do not disagree with any of this today. However, my focus now is vastly different, coinciding with the change in focus we see in present psychological services in general and in art therapy in particular. That lens has expanded from pinpointing the individual to encompassing larger societal influences, recognitions of previously unrecognized pathology causes, and physiological underpinnings of emotional states and behavior.

Specifically, I will concentrate on three areas that I believe an eclectic approach should include today: (1) trauma and its physiological effects; (2) community treatment; and (3) multicultural issues. Although these areas are covered in more detail in other chapters of this book, I want to focus on how they inform an eclectic approach, and how the development of increased understanding of each is essential to the practice of art therapy.

The Wiley Handbook of Art Therapy, First Edition. Edited by David E. Gussak and Marcia L. Rosal.
© 2016 John Wiley & Sons, Ltd. Published 2016 by John Wiley & Sons, Ltd.

Trauma and Its Physiological Effects

Regardless of one's theoretical approach to art therapy—Freudian, Jungian, humanistic, behavioristic, etc.—it is imperative to recognize the results of studies that show trauma in the backgrounds of many patients suffering from psychological disorders. Herman (1997) stated that as many as 60% of psychiatric patients and 70% of psychiatric emergency room patients report a background of childhood abuse. In an examination of 384,000 psychiatric hospital records between 1997 and 1998, Macy (1998) found that post-traumatic stress disorder (PTSD), along with depression, was the most common diagnosis. According to Kulka et al., "about half of the general population will experience a traumatic stress at some time in their lives. Of these, about 15% will develop chronic symptoms of post-traumatic stress disorder" (cited in Bremmer, 2005, p. 19). Kessler, Sonnega, Bromet, Hughes, and Nelson (1995) stated that, in the United States, 15% of the population reported having been physically assaulted, raped, or involved in combat. Those figures are probably higher today, as a result of years of wars in the twenty-first century.

Exposure to a traumatic stressor, however, does not necessarily result in PTSD. Such a diagnosis is made when there are repeated experiences of reliving the trauma, increased arousal, and avoidance of reminders of the trauma, which may include numbing, detachment, and dissociation, sometimes mixed with intrusive recollections (van der Kolk, 2003).

Traumatic memories are often stored in images and other sensations, rather than in words, especially those memories formed in early childhood. According to Herman (1997), who is not an art therapist, they may be more accessible in images, rather than through verbalization. Of particular importance to art therapists is the related significance of some of the physiological effects of trauma-based disorders. Psychophysiological studies have demonstrated that the development of a trauma-based disorder is qualitatively different from a simple exaggeration of the normal stress response, in that excessive stimulation of the central nervous system during trauma appears to cause permanent neuronal changes. When recalling traumatic experiences, subjects evidenced significant decrease in activation in Boca's area of the frontal lobe of the brain, which is thought to be responsible for translating personal experiences into communicable language, thus causing difficulty in verbalizing the traumatic experience (van der Kolk, 2003). For all these reasons, art therapy is often an effective means for dealing with trauma. Given its prevalence in the backgrounds of so many psychiatric patients, art therapists should be prepared to deal with PTSD, even in cases where such a diagnosis is not the presenting problem.

Many art therapists have observed how making art has released memories inaccessible previously. For Anna, a woman with a history of incest, creating art stimulated memories of ritual sexual abuse by a group of perpetrators (Wadeson, 2010).

Another example of art releasing memories of a traumatic experience and the feelings it engendered can be seen in work with Jennifer, a young woman who was raped in an alley near her home (Wadeson, 2010). For the first 6 weeks, she made pleasant pictures of flowers and birds, saying that art therapy helped her relax and get out of herself. She did not speak of the rape, saying she couldn't. I realized that it was important to give her the time she needed to build trust in me, which is often longer for

Figure 12.1   Feelings shattering a young woman's calm appearance.

those who have been traumatized than others. I eventually suggested that she draw a picture of herself illustrating how she was feeling. She drew a placid face and after staring at it for a while, added a red gash slashing the face (see Figure 12.1).

"She's trying to keep it all inside her," she explained, "but it's cracking her open, shattering her calm appearance. I'm having horrible nightmares."

I suggested that she draw one of them. She drew the alley. Next, she drew the shower she took after returning home from the alley, showing the blood pooling around her. This was the beginning. Jennifer drew many pictures of the rape, her rage, fear, and vulnerability. Making art enabled her to get in touch with her feelings and to express them. Eventually, she was able to return to work, overcome her fear of sex, and to marry.

Whatever the art therapist's theoretical approach, it is possible that he or she will be confronted with clients who have suffered trauma. It is important, therefore, to understand the effects of trauma, its stages, and the symptoms of PTSD, along with the conditions necessary for its treatment.

Community Treatment

Art therapy has expanded in recent decades, from its early focus on the individual and the nuclear family to the larger community as well. Community work can take many different forms and serve very different purposes. I will cite three examples to show the possible range of these programs.

Closely related to problems of trauma are community crises that stress large numbers of individuals. Such crises may result from natural disasters, such as Hurricane Katrina, which struck New Orleans in 2005, and the tsunami in Southeast Asia in 2004. Particularly catastrophic are crises generated deliberately by humans in wars and terrorist attacks.

Thousands of years ago in ancient Greece, Seneca wrote of the destruction of Troy with the feeling that could have easily been aroused by the 9/11 attack:

> Whoever believes in wealth, power, the state,
> those fragile toys of man's contrivance, whoever
> puts his trust in such things and does not fear
> the whimsical gods, let him look upon me,
> and this, behind me—all that remains of Troy.
> Never did we imagine the ground we stood on
> could give way, shudder, gape open, and swallow
> all we had and were. We supposed that gods
> had built this city—
> We believed ourselves to be safe.
> But Pergamon is fallen, devastated,
> her high walls toppled down into dust.
> *Trojan Women* (Slavitt, 1992)

In the aftermath of the catastrophe that forever changed Americans' worldview, human service providers were called upon for trauma debriefings, answering crisis phones, counseling bereaved families, advising school personnel, working with airline personnel, firefighters, and families of lost rescue workers. In less than 2 days following the attack, hundreds of creative arts therapists throughout the world responded to the need for many kinds of help. Some worked with the Red Cross. Others worked in schools and shelters. Art was used to unite and support communities in their shared grief.[1]

The point is that art therapists, whatever their fundamental training and understandings of human development, must be prepared to respond to community crises. As the twenty-first century progresses, our awareness that we live in a global community that is increasingly impacted by natural and human disasters makes us realize that, as responsible human service providers, we are called upon not only to help, but to develop our skills to enable us to respond to community crises.

A very different example of community work began with a call for help to the Illinois Art Therapy Association from a residential continuing life care facility whose elderly residents were distraught over the construction of part of their building that eliminated their lobby and entrance, forcing them to use a stairwell exit. Their activities therapist asked us to paint a mural to brighten it up. As art therapists, we did not want to be merely artists doing a job. We wanted to involve the residents. They resisted, asking us to do all the painting, but we were able to involve them gradually, beginning with discussions of what they wanted in the mural. They specified an outdoor scene with a fountain and a picket fence. As we started to paint, they gathered around to watch. We got to know one another. Some staff as well as residents began painting the walls. Others who had difficulty standing worked at tables, painting

Figure 12.2   Part of a mural painted at a senior center.

cutout hydrangea bushes that were then attached to the walls. The mural was lively and colorful, covering the walls and proceeding up the stairs (see Figure 12.2). Upon completion, we celebrated together with a festive party (Wadeson, 2010). Although it might be a stretch to consider this work as therapy, it is an example of art therapists responding to community needs.

Another example, from a different segment of society that also called upon art therapists for help, was the hockey/art alliance that art therapist Gail Wirtz and I formed (Wadeson, 2010). A boys' ice hockey team was having problems, mostly focused on the behavior of one of its best players. Gail was asked to help him, but she recognized that difficulties existed for the whole team, including the coach. We set up a structured 10-session program for the team that emphasized on self-respect and respect for others among these 13-year-old boys and their coach. The program centered on the creation of a city made from wood scraps. Although the boys were making individual structures, they eventually joined them together (see Figure 12.3). The culmination was attendance at a professional hockey game with dinner in the stadium's skybox. Motivation was high among the boys, and parents reported positive changes in their sons' behavior. There was less fighting on the ice and in the locker room. As a result of increased cooperation, an additional benefit was that the team began winning games and captured the league championship.

Because of the success of the hockey/art alliance, we repeated the program during the following year's hockey season. This time, the project was a book made by each

Figure 12.3 The hockey/art alliance city construction project.

boy from various art activities. We focused more on feelings, and the results were even more impressive than the previous year, building upon what was accomplished in the first year. We saw possibilities for future programs that would utilize art for sports groups to help young people to develop positive feelings about themselves and to function more cooperatively in their relationships with one another.

In an eclectic approach to art therapy, the traditional session structure for an individual, family, or small group can be expanded to include whole communities. The possibilities here are enormous, and many such opportunities are now being provided throughout the country by art therapists.

A Multicultural Community

Awareness that we live in a global community is not confined to moments of crisis. The insular lives of tribes and later nations has been transformed by more recent migrations of peoples, so that most societies in which art therapists work today are composed of a polyglot of peoples. Many of these migrations are sufficiently recent, so that acculturation is incomplete, and there remains a great variety in backgrounds, traditions, customs, values, and worldviews within many societies. Other subcultures are based, not on ethnic differences, but on other aspects of lifestyle, such as sexual preference, physical disability, and age. In many communities, such subgroups have their own distinctive cultures.

In recent decades, norms for psychological services have shifted to recognize that a one-size-fits-all understanding of human functioning is inappropriate and often harmful in dealing with subcultures with values and customs that differ from those in the dominant culture. Most obvious is the previous view, that what deviates from the mainstream is pathological. Art therapists today are required to study multiculturalism to develop both sensitivity and competence. Because prejudice is such an integral part of life in Western counties, it is imperative for art therapists to examine their own attitudes and the lens through which they view others. They should try to become knowledgeable about the values and customs of their culturally diverse clients and learn the best ways to approach them. This may mean reformatting the traditional ways in which clients are seen and addressed. The meaning of therapy and the place of art in the client's culture of origin may be especially significant.

An example of the meaning of art in a culture may be seen in the work of Naoko Takano, a native of Japan who came to the United States to study art therapy. While working with Cambodian refugees who had suffered extreme torture, she learned the significance of making paper flowers as a spiritual offering. Flower-making was particularly helpful for a one suicidal woman. After Naoko taught her how to make them from tissue paper, the woman began coming early to the group sessions, and taught the other women to make them, providing a shared spiritual experience (Wadeson, 2010).

Culturally, Sue Lee was the ideal art therapist to work with a group of Korean adolescents dealing with identity problems, as she had emigrated from Korea herself. The artwork was a sensitive medium for the expression and exploration for this issue. Group members were pressured by their parents to adopt the American dominant culture. Most of them had moved to this country in order to give their children advantages that they did not have. An 18-year-old girl who had come to the United States when she was 10 was even discouraged by her parents from making Korean friends, because they wanted her to adapt to the American culture quickly. For some time, she thought that she had actually become "white" by dying and perming her hair and using heavy makeup. However, finally, she realized that would never happen. Depicting her stress of being Korean–American, she drew herself screaming with her hair half black and half curly blonde (see Figure 12.4). In the middle of her body is her real self, scared and trapped inside her. All the others in the group responded with feelings of also being torn by their parents' expectations (Wadeson, 2010).

As a mature white woman working with African American young people, many of whom were involved in a drug culture, I was at times seen as a threat.

Rocky, a handsome young man weighted down with gold jewelry, announced upon seeing me, "I don't want no white old woman with glasses. That's just like all my teachers, the principal, and even the school counselor." I believe he saw me as his traditional enemy, white women who were always critical of his behavior. I knew little of his highflying lifestyle of luxury trips to Acapulco, fancy cars, and death threats from competing drug dealers. I assured him that I would refer him to one of the clinic's black male therapists as soon as there was an opening. In the meantime, I tried to see his life from his point of view and encouraged him to draw it.

When I asked him what brought him to therapy, he said, "My bitch won't marry me." I asked why not, and he said, "She says she don't want to be no widow." When I asked what made her think he would die, he responded, "I can't talk to no white woman

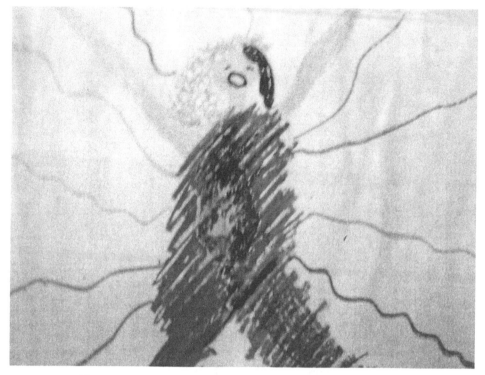

Figure 12.4   Confused identity of a Korean/American teenager.

about that shit." Nevertheless, he was willing to draw it. His drawing of his girlfriend shows her leading him like a dog on a leash. Rocky enjoyed making pictures of his life and talking about them. At the end of each session, he rolled them up to take home to show his girlfriend. When a black male therapist's schedule opened, Rocky decided to stay in art therapy, so he "wouldn't have to start all over again," he said. Through his artwork, he came to sort out what he wanted for his life, gave up drug dealing, and went into the construction business with his brother. Not long afterward, I received an invitation to his wedding. Rocky taught me much about the drug world that he inhabited. Although he had seen me initially as the traditional enemy who would judge him, I think my openness to his lifestyle, and genuine interest in his world and in what was important to him, overcame his mistrust of me as a white woman (Wadeson, 2010).

As is the case in the other topics covered in this chapter, multicultural sensitivity and competence are essential, despite the other aspects of one's art therapy approach and training.

Art for Professional Self-processing

I have not listed the art therapist's use of his or her own artwork for professional self-processing because I see it as more of a recommendation than a necessity. Nevertheless, I am including it here because I believe it is very valuable. Many art

Figure 12.5   "Babies Having Babies."

therapy training programs include art-making as integral to training, especially in supervision where the student is called upon to reflect on work with clients, not only in discussion and writings, but in making art, which can readily tap into non-verbal aspects of the student's experience in practicum work. In addition to using the art extensively in both individual supervision and in supervision seminars myself, I have encouraged student art-making in the exploration of concepts as well. Although many art therapists may be grounded in this sort of processing through their education, they often find themselves too busy to take the time to do so, once they are holding jobs.

An example of response art that was very helpful in expressing a student's feelings about his internship work was made by Terry Lavery, who had been an illustrator before studying art therapy. He drew Figure 12.5 at his internship in response to his anguish in dealing with teenage mothers not much younger than himself (Wadeson, 2010).

The importance of processing challenges through art became clear for me when I was diagnosed with cancer several years ago. During my treatment, I created an altered book of around 70 pictures of my cancer experience. Making art was the most helpful thing that I did for myself in dealing with all the medical procedures, nausea, fatigue, and constant dread of that period. Making art throughout this time reinforced my faith in the healing power of art and the importance of art therapy for our clients. The eclectic approach that I am advocating would include the art therapist's use of art for self-processing.

Conclusion

In this chapter, I enlarged upon our understanding of an eclectic approach to art therapy. In the past, this term has been applied to the art therapist's theoretical orientation. As we look at art therapy practice today, societal influences appear to be more important in governing the direction of work than whether the art therapist operates out of a psychoanalytic, Jungian, behavioristic, or other framework. Of greater prominence is the need for the understanding of and skill in working within a socio-cultural context. This framework is much wider than the narrow constructs of individual development. I focused on only three of the many possible understandings that are necessary for an art therapist practicing today. There are many others that are more specialized. For example, art therapists working in a prison system must understand how that system operates and how it impacts their clients. Those working with the elderly need to understand the challenges older people face, physically, emotionally, socially, and economically. And, finally, art therapists can be well served by utilizing the coin of our realm, making art, not only for our clients, but for ourselves.

Although I do not believe that art therapy has ever been an ivory-tower profession (as psychoanalysis was in its early days), as I attempt to define our work, I believe that we must continue to enlarge our canvas. An eclectic approach requires the necessary study and practice needed to paint this larger picture.

Endnote

1 For more details of immediate responses of art therapists, see *Art Therapy: Journal of the American Art Therapy Association, 18*(4), 179–189.

References

Bremmer, J. D. (2005). *Does stress damage the brain? Understanding trauma-related disorders from a mind-body perspective.* New York, NY: W. W. Norton.

Herman, J. L. (1997). *Trauma and recovery.* New York, NY: Basic Books.

Kessler, R. C., Sonnega, A., Bromet, E., Hughes, M., & Nelson, C. B. (1995). Posttraumatic stress disorder in the national comorbidity survey. *Archives of General Psychiatry, 52*(12), 1048–1060.

Macy, R. D. (1998). Prevalence rates for PTSD and utilization of rates of behavioral health services for an adult Medicaid population. Unpublished doctoral dissertation.

Rubin, J. (2001). *Approaches to art therapy, theory and technique* (2nd ed.). Philadelphia: Brunner-Routledge.

Slavitt, D. (Trans.) (1992). *Seneca: The tragedies.* Baltimore: Johns Hopkins University Press.

van der Kolk, B. (2003). Post-traumatic stress disorder and the nature of trauma. In M. Solomon & D. Siegel (Eds.), *Healing trauma: Attachment—mind, body, brain* (pp. 168–196). New York, NY: W.W. Norton.

Wadeson, H. (2010). *Art psychotherapy* (2nd ed.). Hoboken, NJ: John Wiley & Sons.

Additional Suggested Reading

Wadeson, H. (2011). *Journaling cancer in words and images, caught in the clutch of the crab.* Springfield, IL: Charles Thomas.

Part II
Understanding Art Media in Therapy

Introduction

One factor that separates art therapists from other healing and mental health professionals is the tools they use—visual art media. Art materials are so integral to art therapy practice that practitioners are dedicated to understanding the uses, intricacies, and therapeutic power of various visual art tools. As a result, numerous studies, monographs, and texts exploring the therapeutic properties and efficacy of various art-making materials are available. In fact, there have been entire books that have focused on only one particular material.

In this section, several types of art media are discussed. With a myriad of art materials at the fingertips of art therapists today, it was not possible to include discussions of all media in this text. The chapters in this section do address many of the most common materials utilized in art therapy practice today.

In the introductory chapter, *Media Considerations in Art Therapy: Directions for Future Research*, Hinz expands upon the concept of media dimensions variable, originally developed by Kagin and Lusebrink in 1978. In the conclusion, Hinz calls for robust, empirical research to demonstrate the benefits of each tool. What follows in this section are a set of chapters in which the therapeutic uses of various art materials are examined in depth.

In *2D Expression is Intrinsic*, Lorenzo de la Peña introduces various "mark-making" materials along several dimensions, including dry to wet and simple to complex. Ever mindful of the client, she urges careful, therapeutic application of 2D materials in practice. Fenner argues, in her chapter titled *Constructing the Self: Three-dimensional Form*, that creating sculptural form is equitable to a client constructing one's subjective self. She found 3D materials to be natural tools for constructing and reconstructing personal experiences.

The next three chapters focus on specific materials and directives. For example, a material commonly used by art therapists is collage. Collage materials are easily collected, used, and are cost-effective. Yet, Stallings, in her chapter titled *Collage as an Expressive Medium in Art Therapy*, says that collage-making is a complicated artistic medium that, when used properly, can address a myriad of therapeutic needs. In the

The Wiley Handbook of Art Therapy, First Edition. Edited by David E. Gussak and Marcia L. Rosal.
© 2016 John Wiley & Sons, Ltd. Published 2016 by John Wiley & Sons, Ltd.

chapter titled *Printmaking: Reflective and Receptive Impressions in the Therapeutic Process*, Dean explores one of the more traditional and varied forms of art-making. In doing so, she explains various printmaking techniques, from simple to complex, and the therapeutic benefits that these techniques offer. In *Photography as Therapy: Through Academic and Clinical Explorations*, Horovitz offers a personal and scholarly reflection on how a variety of photographic techniques can be applied in an academic setting as a teaching tool and in a clinical environment to address client needs.

This section concludes with Orr's chapter, *Art Therapy and Digital Media*. Digital media represents the latest set of tools in the art therapist's arsenal. In this chapter, Orr discusses the pros and cons of digital formats in therapy. She also provides an overview of current practices and offers several thoughtful considerations for using emerging digital technology in therapy sessions.

The art media included in this section is limited. This introduction to the art materials used in art therapy practice is designed to provide a basic understanding of the tools that art therapists use to address a client's needs. These chapters may launch the reader's appreciation of the complex thinking it takes to apply art materials therapeutically and effectively.

Reference

Kagin, S. L., & Lusebrink, V. B. (1978). The expressive therapies continuum. *Art Psychotherapy*, 5(4), 171–179.

13

Media Considerations in Art Therapy: Directions for Future Research

Lisa D. Hinz

The word *medium* has various meanings, all of which have implications for art therapy. Medium can be defined as: (1) something in a middle position; (2) a means of effecting or conveying something: as a mode of artistic expression or communication; and (3) a condition or environment in which something may function or flourish (Merriam-Webster, 2012). Media in art therapy have functioned in all aspects of the definition: as objects in the middle of the relationship between client and therapist, and as a bridge between client's inner self and the outer world (Peterson, 2010). Media have been a means of expression and communication for those who are unable or unwilling to talk (Cruz, 2011; Rubin, 2011). Art media provide the conditions through which clients may flourish (Moon, 2010). Given the pivotal role of media in art therapy, elucidating their healing properties is essential for advancing the field. Research must support art therapists' choices of media and their differential applications in therapy.

Art therapy is not always benign; materials and processes can be harmful (Springham, 2008; Vick & Sexton-Radek, 2009). Consequently, ongoing attention to the choice and implementation of media is an ethical responsibility (Moon, 2006). Art therapists are obliged to understand media properties in order to safeguard clients' well-being and to promote excellent therapeutic outcomes. Understanding media properties will aid art therapists in choosing optimal materials for each unique client or situation, as well as in opening minds to alternative media that best fit client needs. This chapter explores media properties, media fit, and unconventional media uses in art therapy. Directions for future research are proposed in each subject area.

Media Properties

Early in the history of art therapy, media were described as possessing inherent qualities that affect the way they are perceived and used (Betensky, 1973; Kagin & Lusebrink, 1978; Robbins & Sibley, 1976). Pioneer art therapist Margaret Naumburg

The Wiley Handbook of Art Therapy, First Edition. Edited by David E. Gussak and Marcia L. Rosal.
© 2016 John Wiley & Sons, Ltd. Published 2016 by John Wiley & Sons, Ltd.

believed that positive therapeutic outcomes could be achieved solely through the use of pastels and poster paints (Naumburg, 1966). Robbins and Sibley (1976) on the other hand, stressed the importance of offering an ample assortment of media and of appreciating the "psychology of materials" (p. 207). The authors explained that each material has a stimulus potential, or capacity to activate a unique response in the user. They suggested that art therapists become familiar with the potential for media to stimulate through texture, color, movement and rhythm, and boundaries. In addition, they counseled art therapists to attend to the risk-taking potential of media, their concrete or abstract potential, and their ability to evoke mastery and control. These themes have been elaborated by others (Hinz, 2009; Horowitz & Eksten, 2009; Kagin & Lusebrink, 1978; Lusebrink, 1990; Rubin, 2011), but very little research confirms such media properties.

Most commonly, art therapists have referenced a continuum of fluid to resistive media characteristics capable of evoking thought, behavior, and emotion (Kagin, 1969, as cited in Lusebrink, 1990). Media with more inherent structure are called *resistive* because they resist easy alteration. The use of resistive materials in art therapy is likely to promote a considered and thoughtful experience. Media that are easily manipulated and altered, and thus more difficult to control, are termed *fluid*. Using fluid media, such as watercolor paints and chalk pastels, is likely to arouse emotion (Betensky, 1973; Horowitz & Eksten, 2009; Robbins & Sibley, 1976; Rubin, 2011). Fluid media also are hypothesized to access unconscious processes, mediated on a preverbal level by the right hemisphere of the brain, and thus aid in the integration of long-term memory (Morley & Duncan, 2007) and trauma recovery (Gantt & Tinnin, 2009). When using 2D materials, fluid/resistive media properties interact with paper texture to modify the emotional/cognitive nature of the expression (Robbins & Sibley, 1976; Seiden, 2001). The fluid/ resistive continuum is a foundation upon which the work of art therapy is built and, as new media become more widely used, art therapists might have to augment its definition. Computer artists may face a particular type of resistance as they endeavor to translate their ideas into computer programs and resulting products (Austin, 2010).

The discussion of media characteristics was expanded to include the fundamental structure of materials (Kagin & Lusebrink, 1978). Media with a solid composition, such as wood or mosaic tiles, are called highly structured or *boundary-determined media*, and are hypothesized to provide a safe, controlled, and nonthreatening art therapy experience. Materials with no inherent boundaries, such as watercolor paint, are *quantity-determined*. The amount of the medium limits their use, and therefore if an individual is responsive to the emotional qualities of a fluid medium, adding more of the medium would increase the emotional experience. In addition, paper has fundamental boundaries that furnish a limit-setting function (Lusebrink, 1990). Smaller paper can be provided as one way to limit or contain the ideas or affects expressed (Hinz, 2006). Orr (2010) extended the discussion of media properties to include time, accessibility, and social significance, which are especially important in digital media applications. Providing evidence to support the existence of inherent media properties is a direction for future study; understanding these dimensions will guide effective treatment.

Researchers have demonstrated the general efficacy of art therapy interventions to relieve anxiety and reduce negative mood (e.g., Bell & Robbins, 2007; Curl, 2008; Curry & Kasser, 2005; Drake, Coleman & Winner, 2011; Drake & Winner, 2012; Henderson, Rosen, & Mascaro, 2007; Kersten & van der Vennet, 2010; Kimport & Robbins, 2012; Sandmire, Gorham, Rankin, & Grimm, 2012; van der Vennet & Serice, 2012; Wood, Molassiotis, & Payne, 2011). In one study, creating collage images was associated with decreased negative mood, but merely viewing and sorting pictures was not (Bell & Robbins, 2007). Drake et al. (2011) compared writing and drawing (both with black pen) to ameliorate negative mood and found significantly more positive effects for drawing than writing. Curl (2008) studied the effects of drawing and collage, carried out with either a positive or negative mental framework, and found that both art tasks, paired with a positive cognitive focus, reduced stress. The lack of a differential effect of medium could be attributed to the art tasks studied: both were relatively cognitive tasks unlikely to evoke differential emotional (i.e., stress-reducing) responses. In another study, students anticipating final exams who created art for 30 minutes demonstrated significantly less anxiety than a control group. Although students were allowed a free choice of art materials (mandala coloring, painting, collage, clay, drawing), no main effect of media was noted, probably due to the small and uneven numbers of students in each condition (Sandmire et al., 2012).

Trying to understand more fully the effects of media properties themselves, Crane (2010) studied the stress-reducing effects of working with pencil, clay, and watercolor paint. She found that after 20 minutes of working with materials, all subjects rated themselves as significantly less anxious than prior to the task. The smallest effect was seen in the pencil condition, which the author hypothesized was due to its resistive nature. The greatest reduction in self-rated anxiety was seen in the clay condition, which was attributed to its tension-releasing properties. In another attempt to understand specific media properties, Ichiki (2012) surveyed 74 American art therapists and 106 Japanese psychologists using art in therapy (Japan does not have an art therapy specialization) about media preferences, media use, and media properties. Analysis of the data demonstrated three distinct healing factors operating through media: one involved movement, sensation, rhythm, and playfulness; the second involved cognitive control and conscious thought, and the last, use of symbols. The research documented that different art media were associated with each factor. Clay was most highly associated with movement and playfulness, and pencil with cognitive control. These studies indicate that art therapists are beginning to provide evidence for the unique healing effects of various materials. Because media and materials are fundamental to the field of art therapy, this is an area of research that deserves significant further inquiry. When media properties are established, art therapists will be closer to confirming evidence-based treatments.

Media Fit

The Expressive Therapies Continuum (ETC) is a theoretical framework describing and prescribing how clients interact with media to process information and form images (see Chapter 6, titled "Expressive Therapies Continuum," by Vija B. Lusebrink in this volume). This structure can help therapists determine which media clients are drawn to and therefore will work best in the initial art therapy sessions. Other considerations in media fit include, but are not limited to, gender, culture, and age.

Gender Differences

Gender differences in the content of art images have been demonstrated (Silver, 1993, 2003), but there has been little attention to other gender differences or preferences in art therapy. Art therapy proved effective in decreasing depression in male and female prison inmates, with interesting gender differences noted (Gussak, 2009). Therapeutic effects were stronger for females who benefitted from the cooperative art therapy *process*. In contrast, males were competitive with one another about the art *product*, and received fewer therapeutic effects. According to Trombetta (2007), males prefer making comic strips, tattoo art, and graffiti-like images. He added that the use of clay with men allows for the release and expression of pent-up aggression related to depression, and that scribble drawings can contain anxiety as well as help discharge and transform previously unexpressed aggression.

Writing about how to engage boys in treatment, Cruz (2011) discussed the use of graffiti as a particularly effective intervention. The author further explained that boys like to observe how things work and become enthusiastic about using tools such as metal sheers, drills, saws, and hammers. Cruz (2011) added that wood and stone have a natural appeal to boys who enjoy sculpture and construction with found objects from neighborhoods, cities, or nature.

The use of fiber arts in therapy has focused on the healing nature of these traditional materials and processes with women (Collier, 2011a, 2011b; Huss, 2010; Moxley, Feen-Calligan, Washington, & Garriott, 2011; Reynolds, 1999, 2000, 2002). Fiber arts have been shown to increase relaxation, soothe fears, distract from intrusive thoughts, build self-esteem, increase perceived control and social support, and transform illness experiences (Reynolds, 1999, 2000, 2002). Collier (2011a) found that women reported the spontaneous use of textile arts such as knitting and weaving to decrease negative mood, distract, and rejuvenate. The use of fiber arts can increase meditative, communication, and problem-solving skills (Huss, 2010). Art therapists can assist women in making their fiber art deliberately metaphorical and personally expressive through the combined use of guided imagery and expressive writing (Collier, 2011b).

This brief review of the different responses of women and men to media could be interpreted to mean that the majority of media work effectively with all clients. However, determining gender-related media preferences should not be based solely on clinical experience. It is an empirical question that deserves further examination to determine how to construct best practices.

Cultural Applications

It is essential that art therapists are educated about the specific cultural groups that they will come into contact with and about how art therapy can be uniquely helpful to them. For the disenfranchised client, art potentially can offer a powerful voice that previously has been disregarded, ignored, or intentionally silenced (Hinz, 2006). Further, it is imperative that art therapists explore and understand how cultural differences influence clients' comfort level with art media and, to the best of their ability, supply culturally sensitive materials (Moon, 2006). In addition, art therapists should be aware that clients' level of acculturation can affect media choices as much as primary culture (Shaked, 2009). Cultural competence includes using easily accessible and obtainable materials, so that participants will continue to engage in art making after therapy is terminated (Moon, 2010). Acculturation, art therapist cultural competence, and client cultural preferences in media are topics deserving of further exploration to ensure the provision of excellent art therapy services.

Age Differences

Alders and Levine-Madori (2010) achieved improved cognitive functioning in elderly adults using a variety of materials; the logical next step in the research process would be to distinguish differential effects of media on cognitive performance. For example, elderly clients with dementia respond well to sensory-stimulating materials that can reduce sensory deprivation and aid memory reconstitution (Hinz, 2009; Lusebrink, 1990).

Child and adolescent clients enjoy various media, particularly digital applications: digital photography, video production, video gaming, and computer-assisted art applications (Austin, 2010; Orr, 2005). Children and adolescents can be particularly responsive to the use of film to stimulate metaphorical art related to life themes (Gramaglia et al., 2011; Marsick, 2010). Austin (2010) urges art therapists working with adolescents to adopt and embrace technological applications that are relevant to adolescents and to be at the forefront of their development.

Unconventional Media

Moon (2010) noted that media in art therapy usually have been confined to long-established domains such as drawing, painting and sculpture. However, a recent survey demonstrated that art therapists believe that any medium that can safely produce change should be considered for use (Peterson, 2010). Moon (2010) added that the use of nontraditional materials is more sustainable in countries where art supplies are not readily available and where even trash is devoid of useable materials such as old magazines. In addition, Moon (2010) attempted to raise awareness that sometimes alternative media better convey meaning even when more traditional supplies are at hand. Art therapists are encouraged to discover, document, and disseminate information on the healing properties of diverse materials.

Certain qualities of unconventional media can make them more suitable than traditional media for the expression of unique concerns and conflicts. For example, Hunter (2012) suggested the use of handbags, shoes, and Barbie dolls as some of the media through which complex body image work can best be undertaken. According to Feen-Calligan, McIntyre, and Sands-Goldstein (2009), identity and body image issues easily arise through the use of dolls. Moreover, dolls can help female clients connect with mothering, nurturing, and femininity concerns. Working with homeless adults, Davis (1997) encouraged participants to create house sculptures using scrap wood from demolished houses. For the participants, scraps from demolished buildings powerfully represented the destruction that had taken place, both literally and symbolically, in their lives.

Found objects are contemporary and sustainable. Their use in art can convey the ordinary turned extraordinary, and reduce the pressures of perfection (Seiden, 2001). In a recent review, Camic, Brooker, and Neal (2011) reported that found objects can increase therapeutic engagement, emotional identification, and transformation. They hypothesized that the functions of found objects in art therapy are to help establish a sense of self, increase confidence and containment, evoke memories and emotions, and act as symbols for healing. Also, in their quests for useable objects, clients are active *in* the environment and act as positive agents *on* the environment.

Discarded books are a form of found object transformed to new life through painting, drawing, or collaging pages (Chilton, 2007). Words can be highlighted as poetry or prose to enhance the experience (Cobb & Negash, 2010). Because of their association with history, biography, and memoir, using books as media can help clients reflect on their lives and organize their personal stories (Cobb & Negash, 2010; Kohut, 2011). Books have an inherent and expected structure that can guide their use as media, and, at the same time, reworking books can afford a safe way to rebel against convention. Their structure invites opening and closing and can supply a sense of containment (Chilton, 2007).

Findlay, Latham, and Hass-Cohen (2008) found that the use of textiles in art therapy calls forth tactile sensory experiences embodied in attachment styles: blankets were used by children to demonstrate the warmth of secure attachment, whereas unpredictable textures were indicative of insecure parent–child bonds. Beyond their individually therapeutic applications, textiles have been used in community action programs (Timm-Bottos, 2011).

Weiser (2004) has been an advocate for the use of photographs in art therapy to capture the immediacy of affective experiences. According to the author, photos as media are the most publicly familiar and emotionally powerful of all artistic media. Photos can provide alternate views of the self, and they are perceived as both "realistic illusion and illusory reality" (p. 26). Although photos have been used for quite some time in therapy, little research exists to support their use. The advent of digital photography and editing software allows for simple and nearly instantaneous creative manipulation of images, and these new applications require renewed research efforts (Wolf, 2007).

Although computers are an essential part of the lives of many clients and art therapists, their use in art therapy has been greatly debated (Orr, 2010). Computers have been alternately derided as impersonal and lacking important tactile qualities, and lauded for their use in helping disabled or isolated persons access the creative process (Orr, 2005). In two recent surveys, art therapists who were asked to consider adopting digital media were less concerned with their digital nature and more concerned with their therapeutic possibilities (Mihailidis et al., 2010; Peterson, 2010). New computer applications being developed include handheld devices with finger paint, collage, and flipbook animation, as well as distance art therapy groups (Collie & Čubranić, 2002). Collie and Čubranić used a computer-based painting program as the medium through which group members created art. Audio and video connections were the platforms through which artwork was processed and shared. The authors assumed that the impersonal nature of computers and the lack of face-to-face contact would reduce participant engagement in computer-assisted distance group art therapy, but found the opposite. They concluded that computers increasingly will be used to reach isolated and disabled elderly clients.

It is possible that contemporary art therapy consumers, expecting to influence their world through digital participation, will actively engage in digital art therapy processes (Orr, 2010). The use of computers for gaining and sharing information, and for artistic purposes, can increase self-respect, communication, and social bonding among formerly homeless clients, and also serve as a powerful facilitator of social justice (Stotrocki, Andrews, & Saemundsdottir, 2004). Spring et al. (2011) successfully used computers to remotely include chronically ill group members when they were no longer physically able to participate.

Although their use in art therapy has been contested, computers will likely see greater use in the future. Austin (2010) discusses a time when the interface between product and user will mimic more traditional art media, not involving a mouse or keyboard. He urges art therapists to champion the use of computers and to be on the cutting edge of development.

Conclusion

Art therapy is founded upon the use of media; however, there exists surprisingly little research demonstrating the differential effects of materials. Until quite recently, material use has remained relatively constant and unquestioned. Materials were assumed to possess certain characteristics that determined their choice for use in therapy (Lusebrink, 1990; Seiden, 2001). The field currently operates on the basis of clinical observations regarding the nature of media: fluid vs. resistive, boundary vs. quantity determined, traditional vs. alternative materials; and some of these assumptions are beginning to be tested (e.g., Crane, 2010; Ichiki, 2012). As the discipline matures, art therapy is in need of empirical evidence to direct and support the use of media. Expanding this research will provide the required foundation for evidenced-based practice. In addition, the number of materials used in art therapy has increased and expanded, and will continue to evolve. Art therapists should be at the forefront of providing evidence for the uses of media—new and old.

References

Alders, A., & Levine-Madori, L. (2010). The effect of art therapy on cognitive performance of Hispanic/Latino older adults. *Art Therapy: Journal of the American Art Therapy Association, 27*(3), 127–135. doi:10.1080/07421656.2010.10129661

Austin, B. (2010). Technology, art therapy, and psychodynamic theory: Computer animation with an adolescent in foster care. In C. H. Moon (Ed.), *Materials and media in art therapy: Critical understandings of diverse artistic vocabularies* (pp. 199–213). New York, NY: Routledge.

Bell, C. E., & Robbins, S. J. (2007). Effect of art production on negative mood: A randomized, controlled trial. *Art Therapy: Journal of the American Art Therapy Association, 24*(2), 71–75. doi: 10.1080/07421656.2007.10129589

Betensky, M. (1973). Self-discovery through self-expression: Use of art psychotherapy with children and adolescents. Springfield, IL: Charles C. Thomas Publisher.

Camic, P. M., Brooker, J., & Neal, A. (2011). Found objects in clinical practice: Preliminary evidence. *The Arts in Psychotherapy, 38,* 151–159. doi: 10.1016/j.aip.2001.04.002

Chilton, G. (2007). Altered books in art therapy with adolescents. *Art Therapy: Journal of the American Art Therapy Association, 24*(2), 59–63. doi: 10.1080/07421656.2007.10129588

Cobb, R. A., & Negash, S. (2010). Altered book making as a form of art therapy: A narrative approach. *Journal of Family Psychotherapy, 21*(1), 54–69. doi: 10.1080/0897535 1003618601

Collie, K., & Čubranić, D. (2002). Computer-supported distance art therapy: A focus on traumatic illness. *Journal of Technology in Human Services, 20,* 155–171. doi: 10.1300/ J017v20n01_12

Collier, A. F. (2011a). The well-being of women who create with textiles: Implications for art therapy. *Art Therapy: Journal of the American Art Therapy Association, 28*(3), 104–112. doi: 10.1080/07421656.2011.597025

Collier, A. F. (2011b). Using textile arts and handcrafts in therapy with women: Weaving lives back together. London: Jessica Kingsley Publishers.

Curl, K. (2008). Assessing stress reduction as a function of artistic creation and cognitive focus. *Art Therapy: Journal of the American Art Therapy Association, 25*(4), 164–169. doi: 10.1080/07421656.2008.10129550

Curry, N. A., & Kasser, T. (2005). Can coloring mandalas reduce anxiety? *Art Therapy: Journal of the American Art Therapy Association, 22*(2), 81–85. doi: 10.1080/07421 656.2005.10129441

Crane, R. (2010). *Impact of art materials on symptoms of stress.* Unpublished master's thesis, Albertus Magnus College, East Hartford, CT.

Cruz, J. (2011). Breaking through with art: Art therapy approaches for working with at-risk boys. In C. Haen (Ed.), *Engaging boys in treatment: Creative approaches to the therapy process* (pp. 177–194). New York, NY: Routledge.

Davis, J. (1997). Building from the scraps: Art therapy within a homeless community. *Art Therapy: Journal of the American Art Therapy Association, 14*(3), 210–213.

Drake, J. E., Coleman, K., & Winner, E. (2011). Short-term mood repair through art: Effects of medium and strategy. *Art Therapy: Journal of the American Art Therapy Association, 28*(1), 26–30. doi: 10.1080/07421656.2011.557032

Drake, J. E., & Winner, E. (2012, January, 30). Confronting sadness through art-making: Distraction is more beneficial than venting. Advance online publication. *Psychology of Aesthetics, Creativity, and the Arts.* doi: 10.1037/a0026909

Feen-Calligan, H., McIntyre, B., & Sands-Goldstein, M. (2009). Art therapy applications of dolls in grief recovery, identity and community service. *Art Therapy: Journal of the American Art Therapy Association, 26*(4), 167–173. doi: 10.1080/07421656.2009.10129613

Findlay, J. C., Latham, M. E., & Hass-Cohen, N. (2008). Circles of attachment: Art therapy albums. In N. Hass-Cohen & R. Carr (Eds.), *Art therapy and clinical neuroscience* (pp. 191–206). London: Jessica Kingsley Publishers.

Gantt, L., & Tinnin, L. W. (2009). Support for a neurobiological view of trauma with implications for art therapy. *The Arts In Psychotherapy, 36*(3), 148–153. doi:10.1016/ j.aip.2008.12.005

Gramaglia, C., Abbate-Daga, G., Amianto, F., Brustolin, A., Campisi, S., De-Bacco, C., & Fassino, S. (2011). Cinematherapy in the day hospital treatment of patients with eating disorders. Case study and clinical considerations. *The Arts in Psychotherapy*, *38*(4), 261–266. doi:10.1016/j.aip.2011.08.004

Gussak, D. (2009). The effects of art therapy on male and female inmates: Advancing the research base. *The Arts in Psychotherapy*, *36*, 5–12. doi: 10.1016/j.aip.2008.10.002

Henderson, P., Rosen, D., & Mascaro, N. (2007). Empirical study on the healing nature of mandalas. *Psychology of Aesthetics, Creativity, and the Arts*, *1*(3), 148–154. doi: 10.1037/1931-3896.1.3.148

Hinz, L. D. (2006). *Drawing from within: Using art to treat eating disorders*. London: Jessica Kingsley Publishers.

Hinz, L. D. (2009). Expressive therapies continuum: A framework for using art in therapy. New York, NY: Routledge.

Horowitz, E. G., & Eksten, S. L. (2009). *The art therapists' primer*. Springfield, IL: Charles C. Thomas Publisher.

Hunter, M. R. (2012). Reflections of body imagery in art therapy: Exploring self through metaphor and multi-media. London: Jessica Kingsley Publishers.

Huss, E. (2010). Bedouin women's embroidery as female empowerment: Crafts as culturally embedded expressions within art therapy. In C. H. Moon (Ed.), *Materials and media in art therapy: Critical understandings of diverse artistic vocabularies* (pp. 215–229). New York, NY: Routledge.

Ichiki, Y. (2012). *The significance of art materials in psychotherapy and assessment*. Unpublished doctoral dissertation, Koshien University, Takarazuka, Hyōgo, Japan.

Kagin, S. L. (1969). *The effects of structure on the painting of retarded youth*. Unpublished master's thesis, University of Tulsa, Tulsa, Oklahoma.

Kagin, S. L., & Lusebrink, V. B. (1978). The expressive therapies continuum. *Art Psychotherapy*, *5*(4), 171–179.

Kersten, A., & van der Vennet, R. (2010). The impact of anxious and calm emotional states on color usage in pre-drawn mandalas. *Art Therapy: Journal of the American Art Therapy Association*, *27*(4), 184–189. doi: 10.1080/07421656.2010.10129387

Kimport, E. R., & Robbins, S. J. (2012). Efficacy of creative clay work for reducing negative mood: A randomized controlled trial. *Art Therapy: Journal of the American Art Therapy Association*, *29*(2), 74–79. doi: 10.1080/07421656.2012.680048

Kohut, M. (2011). Making art from memories: Honoring deceased loved ones through a scrapbooking bereavement group. *Art Therapy: Journal of the American Art Therapy Association*, *28*(3), 123–131. doi: 10.1080/07421656.2011.599731

Lusebrink, V. B. (1990). Imagery *and visual expressions in therapy*. New York, NY: Springer.

Marsick, E. (2010). Cinematherapy with preadolescents experiencing parental divorce: A collective case study. *The Arts in Psychotherapy*, *37*(4), 311–318. doi:10.1016/j.aip.2010.05.006

Merriam-Webster. (2012, Retrieved January 15) from http://www.merriam-webster.com/dictionary/media

Mihailidis, A., Blunsden, S., Boger, S., Richards, B., Zuntis, K., Young, L., & Hoey, J. (2010). Towards the development of a technology for art therapy for dementia: Definition of needs and design constraints. *The Arts in Psychotherapy*, *37*, 293–300. doi: 10.1016/j.aip.2010.05.004

Moon, B. L. (2006). *Ethical issues in art therapy* (2nd ed.). Springfield IL: Charles C. Thomas.

Moon, C. (2010). A history of materials and media in art therapy. In C. H. Moon (Ed.), *Materials and media in art therapy: Critical understandings of diverse artistic vocabularies* (pp. 3–47). New York, NY: Routledge.

Morley, T., & Duncan, A. C. (2007). Recovered memories: An arts program designed for patients with dementia. In D. B. Arrington (Ed.), *Art, angst, and trauma: Right brain interventions with developmental issues* (pp. 230–243). Springfield, IL: Charles C. Thomas Publisher.

Moxley, D. P., Feen-Calligan, H. R., Washington, O. G. M., & Garriott, L. (2011). Quilting in self-efficacy group work with older African American women leaving homelessness. *Art Therapy: Journal of the American Art Therapy Association, 28*(3), 113–122. doi: 10.1080/07421656.2011.599729

Naumburg, M. (1966). Dynamically *oriented art therapy: Its principles and practice*. New York, NY: Grune and Stratton.

Orr, P. (2005). Technology media: An exploration for inherent qualities. *The Arts in Psychotherapy, 32*, 1–11. doi: 10.1016/j.aip.2004.12.003

Orr, P. (2010). Social remixing: Art therapy media in the digital age. In C. H. Moon (Ed.), *Materials and media in art therapy: Critical understandings of diverse artistic vocabularies* (pp. 89–100). New York, NY: Routledge.

Peterson, B. C. (2010). The media adoption stage model of technology for art therapy. *Art Therapy: Journal of the American Art Therapy Association, 27*(1), 26–31. doi: 10.1080/07421656.2010.10129565

Reynolds, F. (1999). Cognitive behavioral counseling of unresolved grief through the therapeutic adjunct of tapestry making. *The Arts in Psychotherapy, 26*(3), 165–171. doi: 10.1016/S0197-4556(98)00062-8

Reynolds, F. (2000). Managing depression though needlecraft creative activities: A qualitative study. *The Arts in Psychotherapy, 27*(2), 107–114. doi: 10.1016/S0197-4556(99)00033-7

Reynolds, F. (2002). Symbolic aspects of coping with chronic illness through textile arts. *The Arts in Psychotherapy, 29*, 99–106. doi: 10.1016/S0197-4556(01)00140-X

Robbins, A., & Sibley, L. B. (1976). Creative *art therapy*. New York, NY: Brunner/Mazel.

Rubin, J. A. (2011). The *art of art therapy: What every art therapist needs to know* (2nd ed.). New York, NY: Routledge.

Sandmire, D. A., Gorham, S. R., Rankin, N. E., & Grimm, D. R. (2012). The influence of art making on anxiety: A pilot study. *Art Therapy: Journal of the American Art Therapy Association, 29*(2), 68–73. doi: 10.1080/07421656.2012.683748

Seiden, D. (2001). Mind over matter: The uses of materials in art, education and therapy. Chicago: Magnolia Street Publishers.

Shaked, R. (2009). *The influence of culturally familiar art materials on the effectiveness of art therapy with multicultural clients.* Unpublished master's thesis, Saint Mary-of-the-Woods College, Saint Mary-of-the-Woods, IN.

Silver, R. (1993). Age and gender differences expressed through drawings: A study of attitudes toward self and others. *Art Therapy: Journal of the American Art Therapy Association, 10*(3), 159–168.

Silver, R. (2003). Cultural differences and similarities in responses to the Silver Drawing Test in the USA, Brazil, Russia, Estonia, Thailand, and Australia. *Art Therapy: Journal of the American Art Therapy Association, 20*(1), 16–20. doi: 10.1080/07421656.2003.10129638

Spring, J. A., Baker, M., Dauya, L., Ewemade, I., Marsh, N., Patel, P., Scott, A., Stoy, N., Turner, H., Viera, M., & Will, D. (2011). Gardening with Huntington's disease clients—creating a programme of winter activities. *Disability and Rehabilitation, 33*(2): 159–164. doi: 10.3109/09638288.2010.487924

Springham, N. (2008). Through the eyes of the law: What is it about art that can harm people? *International Journal of Art Therapy, 13*(2), 65–73.

Stotrocki, M., Andrews, S. S., & Saemundsdottir, A. (2004). The role of art for homeless women and survivors of domestic violence. *Visual Arts Research, 29*(58), 73–82.

Timm-Bottos, J. (2011). Endangered threads: Socially committed community arts action. *Art Therapy: Journal of the American Art Therapy Association, 28*(2), 57–63. doi: 10.1080/07421656.2011.578234

Trombetta, R. (2007). Art therapy, men, and the expressivity gap. *Art Therapy: Journal of the American Art Therapy Association, 24*(1), 29–32. doi:10.1080/07421656.2007.101293 62 DOI:10.1080%25252F07421656.2007.10129362

van der Vennet, R., & Serice, S. (2012). Can coloring mandalas reduce anxiety? A replication study. *Art Therapy: Journal of the American Art Therapy Association, 29*(2), 87–92. doi: 10.1080/07421656.2012.680047

Vick, R. M., & Sexton-Radek, K. (2009). Art and migraine: Researching the relationship between art making and pain experience. *Art Therapy: Journal of the American Art Therapy Association, 26*(3), 114–123. doi: 10.1080/07421656.2005.10129518

Weiser, J. (2004). Phototherapy techniques in counselling and therapy—Using ordinary snapshots and photo-interactions to help clients heal their lives. *Canadian Art Therapy Association Journal, 17*(2), 23–53.

Wolf, R. I. (2007). Advances in phototherapy training. *The Arts in Psychotherapy, 34*(2), 124–133. doi: 10.1016/j.aip.2006.11.004

Wood, M. M., Molassiotis, A., & Payne, S. (2011). What research evidence is there for the use of art therapy in the management of symptoms in adults with cancer? A systematic review. *Psycho-Oncology, 20*(2), 135–145. doi:10.1002/pon.1722

14

2D Expression is Intrinsic

Sheila Lorenzo de la Peña

In its most basic form, creative expression is present within everyone (Dissanayake, 2000); both clients and therapists benefit from the experience of creating art (Moon, 2002; Robbins, 2000). As indicated in the other chapters in this book, the expressive act of creating is revealing, whether it is for the purpose of processing the lived experience for one's self or to communicate within social groups. Individuals naturally turn toward their environment when translating the emotive experience into concrete form (Dissanayake, 2000). Regardless of artistic experience, background, or affiliation, what matters most is *how* something is said. Toward understanding the visual expression of emotive content, this chapter will provide a glimpse of how 2D media may impact clients in art therapy. By understanding media dimensions variables (MDVs), or media properties, art therapists are able to think about the impact that various art materials have on clients (Hinz, 2010; Lusebrink, 1990). The wealth of information about mark-making dry and wet media is summarized in this chapter. Some consideration of the types of surfaces upon which 2D materials are used will be offered. Case vignettes will be presented to illustrate the dialectic exchange between the participant and the media.

2D Visual Representation

For most people, the principal means of expression is in 2D format—a flat surface onto which media can be applied toward creating a visual representation of an experience. The flat surface is versatile in construction, size, and means of engagement. Of all surfaces, paper is the most readily accessible, available in a variety of sizes, colors, textures, and translucency. The 2D format is not restricted to paper; leather, bark, cloth, cardboard, wood, clay, or even stone can be quite appropriate.

Surfaces

A surface provides a starting point, a place on which emotive marks are made. While media properties have a direct impact on the creative process, the surface onto which marks are made plays a subtler role. Choosing the work surface requires an

The Wiley Handbook of Art Therapy, First Edition. Edited by David E. Gussak and Marcia L. Rosal.
© 2016 John Wiley & Sons, Ltd. Published 2016 by John Wiley & Sons, Ltd.

understanding of the clients' goals and choices, the media being used, budgetary constraints, and environmental factors. At times, it may be necessary to reconsider or downgrade an activity in lieu of having an appropriate surface for mark-making. When considering work surfaces for 2D work, size is not the only thing that matters. Although artist-quality white paper will suffice in most instances, both the art therapist and the client may at times want or need to branch out further. It is, however, not the only option.

Paper   Paper is the most common type of surface used for expression, owing to its availability and affordability; it is also portable and inconspicuous. Paper choice varies, depending on media specifications and client need. While environmental and budgetary constraints may call for the use of white 8.5 x 11 inch paper, it is not always ideal, due to the constrained size and inferior quality. A higher *pound* or weight of paper indicates the potential for the paper to withstand wear and tear before it begins to breakdown. Consideration can also be given to texture, chemical additives, and longevity.

For the most part, participants in art therapy will not request for *Arches® cold press* when working with watercolors; it is nevertheless important to understand the influence that a surface has on planned directives. In most art stores, paper will be clearly labeled and categorized in relation to the media it is associated with: watercolor paper, charcoal paper, drawing paper, and decorative papers. Paper will also be labeled as single sheets, bundles, or books. Most papers will be sized with a chemical coating on the surface, allowing for even and crisp watercolor distribution and lifting techniques; sizing also affects the adherence of dry media, allowing for the option of having clean erasures. For occasions when sizing is unwanted, some brands offer unsized sheets, affecting the media application and not the longevity of the paper.

Whereas the work of an artist is expected to outlast its maker, the work completed in art therapy sessions may or may not need an expansive timeline. Papers with high contents of wood pulp such as construction paper, newsprint, and Manila paper degrade quickly and change color and pliability within months. A high content of cotton rag will increase durability for those directives where longevity is preferred. Archival-quality paper will have a high percentage of cotton rag, is acid free, and has a neutral pH. While in some cases paper degradation is a desired trait, it must be considered before beginning a project, as it will not always be evident from direct observation.

Textured surfaces   Exposure to surface textures may increase creativity. Textured surfaces range from fine and barely visible such as charcoal and pastel paper, visibly rough. Cold-press papers have rough surface texture and work well with soft and fluid media. Although not ideal for painting or drawing with pencils, some papers provide a surface coated with micro-abrasive granules akin to fine sandpaper that is great for pastels. An alternative to paper, raw or gessoed canvas and canvas boards can be used with softer media and thick paints. In accordance with the goals of the client, the texture of any surface can be enhanced or decreased. Although textured surfaces tend to be well suited for soft dry media, their rough qualities make it difficult to add fine detail. In such cases, smoother surfaces are preferred.

Smooth surfaces Low-weight smooth white paper tends to be the most accessible. Heavier, thicker, more durable paper known as *cardstock* can be found in office supply stores in a variety of colors and tones. Bristol paper, while similar to cardstock, is denser and available in a variety of sizes. It is heavy enough for use with light-to-medium paint applications and well suited for mixed-media work. Hardboards can be found with enough grout for pastel use, are otherwise great for painting, and take-up virtually no space when storing. Painting and drawing surfaces, however, are not limited to paper and canvas.

Other 2D surfaces Although paper and paper-based surfaces are the most common for casual visual expression, illustrative media can adorn any flat, relief, and 3D surface while remaining a 2D expression. Sanded prepared wood panels sold in art stores offer smooth surfaces and are ready to hang or frame once complete. Untreated planks are rougher and have natural imperfections, knots and cracks, but can be cheaply obtained from home improvement stores. More exotic surfaces can be acquired through art stores, found, or made. In selecting a work surface, familiarity with media properties will facilitate effective pairing between surface and media toward the desired outcome.

Mark-making Tools Along the Continuum

For the art therapist, mark-making is the focus. The most common tools are pencils, pens, and markers—I will label these as *dry media*. *Wet media* are those often used with water (such as water colors or tempera paints) or thicker media such as acrylic paints.

Dry media

While pens come in every shape, size, and color, their prices do not dictate their effectiveness. The pen is often cast aside due to its commonality and permanence; it can be an effective mediator for reflective distance from affect and sensory tactile experiences. While a pen can be the starting point of a doodle, it can also bring closure to a collage, a painting or a designated mixed-media piece or art. Most pens work best on smooth surfaces such as Bristol or card stock, and can be applied under paint or after it has dried.

Working in a forensic ward, I have heard the all-too-familiar plea from clients to borrow art media "just this once … or for the weekend, I can't do anything otherwise!" Flex pens or golf pencils are often the only tools allowed in certain forensic mental health wards; a golf pencil is a 3-inch stub, and a flex pen is a single-cartridge pen. Both offer no capacity for erasing mistakes, and are uncomfortable to hold over long periods of time. Despite the media constraints of the forensic setting, clients should be encouraged to experiment with these materials and visual examples of pen techniques might be offered. Working with the permanence of the marks created with these inflexible tools necessitates the development of frustration tolerance. Clients learn to conceal their mistakes. Juxtaposing a qualitatively resistive tool within a restrictive environment encourages creative expression and problem-solving.

Similar to pens, pencils are resistive and mediated tools, yet pencil marks can be erased. Pencils are as diverse as pens and are rated from soft to hard, depending on the lead used in manufacturing it. While harder leads will allow for increased distance between the participant and his or her image due to increased resistance, the softer leads with smoother application can provide a greater sensory experience. While pencils are the norm, solid graphite sticks with their lack of exterior coverings allow for a direct sensory experience, as all its sides can be used to make marks; they are best used with large gestural expressions on oversized surfaces. Soluble graphite, available in pencil and stick form, can be handled dry or wet.

Transitioning from a resistive-dry application to a fluid manipulation only necessitates a moist soft-bristle brush. Through this transition, the art therapist provides the client with the possibility of moving from the cognitive/symbolic level of the Expressive Therapies Continuum (ETC) to the perceptual/affective or the kinesthetic/sensory levels (Hinz, 2010; Lusebrink, 1990). Developed by Kagin and Lusebrink (1978), the ETC provides a framework for the therapist to understand the interactions taking place between the client and media.

The therapist ought to lead by example when introducing soluble graphite sticks or any new materials to clients, bringing awareness to the tool's surface, its weight, the sound it makes on contact with the sheet, and the mark left behind. Once comfortable with these properties, clients can be encouraged to further explore with brushes and water. A silent "Ahh" can often be heard as the broken dry-marks made by the graphite saturate and deepen in hue, the resistive marks transformed into fluid sensual movements. With this unexpected change, clients become immersed in a new sensory experience and may move toward the lower levels of the ETC (Hinz, 2010; Lusebrink, 1990). Graphite and charcoal powders are further removed from the resistive end of the MDV toward the fluid (Hinz, 2010; Lusebrink, 1990); the hands-on and unmediated expression can promote expressive gestures akin to finger painting, but with a dry media.

A vast variety of other drawing media is available, including charcoal and pastels. Available in an assortment of types with distinctive properties, charcoal can inhabit varying areas of the MDV continua (Hinz, 2010; Lusebrink, 1990). While the most resistive of charcoal types is in its pencil form, the compressed and vine charcoal are more mid-range on the fluid/resistive continuum. Once in powdered form, charcoal, attains fluidity akin to paint.

After all the monochromatic media, clients may be eager to try colorful chalk pastels. The dust of these can be minimized, if not eliminated, by using saturated coldpress paper with damp pastels or by brushing over a pastel mark with a wet brush. The latter would allow for a second tracing of the entire image with the possibility of further processing and editing by means of painting; once dry, the image will revert to its natural chalky qualities. The client response to the dust of the chalk pastels or the charcoal, or the bits left behind when using oil pastels, may allow for developing frustration tolerance and creative problem-solving.

Conté crayons®, on the other hand, are nearly residue free and may produce bold dark lines. These crayons have a clear external coating that keeps fingers relatively clean until the coating is removed through friction, and then marks can be made with all sides. Conté crayons, similar to graphite sticks, work best for expressive sketches that require minimal color, since they primarily come in black, white, and terracotta. Art therapists should consider using Conté crayons on colored surfaces. The variability in the color of the drawing surface will give visibility to the full range of media values from dark to light, also making it possible for the client to notice the most minimal of marks.

From graphite, charcoal, and Conté crayons to vibrant soft pastels, oil pastels, and hard pastels such as *NuPastels®* and *Polychromos®*, art therapists can add colorful media to their repertoire. Chalky soft pastels behave much like semi-resistive compressed charcoal; their best performance will be on paper surfaces with some tooth with which to grab the soft powder after repeated passes. Easily blended with rags, napkins, brushes, or bare hands, chalk pastels have a tendency to appear smooth when blended but can also be bold and striking when applied with force. The degree to which mediation tools are used or attention given to the nuances of application from resistive to fluid will transition a client through the various levels of the ETC (Hinz, 2010; Lusebrink, 1990). As with powdered graphite and charcoal, chalk pastels can also be manipulated with a wet brush providing a prelude to fluid media (Hinz, 2010).

Wet media

Wet media is an expansive and broad category of art materials that exists either in liquid state or in solid state prior to use, but is in fluid state at application. While the most familiar wet media are tempera, watercolors, acrylics, and oil paints, there is enough variety and complexity in these media families to engage a variety of clients at any level of the ETC (Hinz, 2010; Lusebrink, 1990). Where some media have minimal differences between the child grade, the student grade, and the hobbyist grade, paints have great variability in quality. Facilitating the transition between ETC levels from kinesthetic/sensory finger paints, to perceptual/affective wet-on-wet watercolor applications, to cognitive/symbolic for detailed acrylic expressions, fluid media has a wide range of applicability (Hinz, 2010; Lusebrink, 1990). Several wet media offer flexibility in media properties that in turn provide variability in their application. In addition to the inherent qualities of the media, the use of brushes (i.e., foam-tipped, soft-bristle, hard-bristle) or palette knives mediate and add complexity to the painting process.

Dry watercolor cake pans may pose a great challenge to participants. The use of dry watercolor cakes is complex, requiring sequencing of the multi-step process of wetting a brush, tapping off excess, saturating the desired color cake, loading the brush, painting, and rinsing the brush before switching to another color. Once learned, the procedure can be tailored for other wet media such as dry-tempera cakes. Tempera paints provide opaque primary and secondary hues; the oversized pans are user-friendly, portable, and ideal for beginning learners and those with special needs.

Media choice is often not intuitive; at times it can be intimidating or overwhelming. How much skill-coaching must art therapists provide for their clients to be successful, and under what contexts? Introducing participants to brush types (flat or round), and their care, may provide important learning experiences. Media techniques might be presented in conjunction with directives. I sometimes pair basic brush use with a breathing watercolor exercise where I lead by example and the client follows. In this way, clients learn some tenets of brushwork such as the application of varied pressure and color saturation in conjunction with an increased awareness of how our bodies respond to media application.

In working with a particularly challenging group of men with mixed diagnoses, the watercolor activity was presented as a relaxation lesson. Participants began by taking deep breaths and moving their arms in the air; these moves were transposed onto paper by making long strokes with a loaded brush. As mastery was achieved, participants were coached on how differences in brush pressure impact line quality: making dark lines or light lines, thick lines or thin ones. After some practice, the round brushes were traded out for flat ones. Slowly twisting the brush between the index and thumb to draw attention to line variations, participants were again encouraged to practice and explore. Providing lessons on using the tools as part of a directive may allow the art therapy provider to build a rapport with the client for future interactions.

Introducing clients to fluid media allows for versatility in relation to MDV levels (Hinz, 2010; Lusebrink, 1990). In choosing a playful, minimalistic, yet structured approach, manageable pieces of watercolor paper (e.g., bookmark strips, squares 3 x 3, or ATCs 2.5 x 3.5) are saturated in water one at a time and placed in a containment area (e.g., a plastic plate with sides to serve as concrete boundaries). For a simple semistructured approach, clients are given small squeeze bottles with the watercolors and instructed to mindfully trickle two to three drops onto their saturated paper and observe the movements created by the surface tension as the paint spreads. The portable size of artist trading cards (ATCs) makes them ideal for this activity and leaves the client with multiple completed pieces by the end of the session.

Adding breathing awareness and biophysiological feedback to any directive will build on the degree of complexity. After clients have completed at least one observation of the properties of the paint on saturated paper, directions can be given to begin a second piece just as the first. Once the paint is dropped, participants can be encouraged to influence the pattern by picking-up the plate and exploring movement. Another variation may involve blowing the paint drops through straws or further manipulating the surface tension by gingerly applying water drops with a brush. Semi-moist brushes can be used to push and pull at the puddles of fluid on the paper surface. Another inexpensive and easy means to obtain the push and pull of paint is by crumbling sea salt onto the saturated surface; when given ample space, each crystal will pull water and create a halo effect. Successful exploratory activities familiarize the clients with the media, while increasing self-awareness. By inviting and modeling a play-like exploration of unfamiliar media, the stage is set for the development of the relationship between the client, media, and therapist.

The following section focuses on acrylic paints (oil paints, although similar to acrylic paints, require careful consideration prior to use with clients). While working with acrylic paint, the most noticeable properties in contrast to watercolors will be its viscosity and opacity. Acrylics are available from the traditional to the easy-to-use craft acrylics that boast an assortment of ready-to-use affordable varieties: outdoor, indoor, glass, ceramic, glittery, and puffy (extra-thick paint in a squeeze bottle with applicator tip). With the addition of modifiers, paints can increase in fluidity, or gain viscosity, resulting in shifts in its relative placement on the MDV (Hinz, 2010; Lusebrink, 1990). Due to client needs, such as at the developmental level, it may be necessary to adjust the plasticity of an affordable media, such as craft acrylics, in order to effectively complete a project. In some cases, it may be necessary to add Elmer's School Glue to craft acrylics, or tempera, to increase the viscosity and flexibility in order to prevent later cracking and chipping.

Historically, organic modifiers have been added to paints to change their textural properties: sand, dirt, hair, straw, shell fragments, seeds, etc. Similar qualities can be added by using pre-mixed acrylic mediums, available in a wide range—from thickening paste, which adds volume and can be applied with palette knives, to pouring mediums, which dilute the acrylic hue so that it can be poured onto a surface with marbling-like effects. Pre-mixed mediums can also contain textural additives such as glass micro-beads, fibers, sandy grit, and even crackle paste. For diversity, and to some extent an exciting change from the norm, additives can be purposely utilized for creating 2D expressions on a variety of surfaces. Adding tactile components raises complexity, as the use of the material may no longer be a basic process; yet, the opportunity for challenges and modifications may increase the complexity and therapeutic value of experiences.

Mixed media

When the artist uses two or more media, with or without intent, he or she is using mixed media. Considering the number and various types of media and their prop-erties, the combinations are infinite and can range from simple to complex. Most cli-ents intuitively use mixed media when seeking to modify an art expression. Introducing how and when a second media is offered to a client can add to a successful creative experience. Consider the earlier example of the introduction to painting via brush maintenance and watercolor breathing mindfulness. Building on the new sensitivity to brush work, acrylics are introduced, by means of an impasto application of paint, with a focus on the kinesthetic/sensory level of the ETC (Hinz, 2010; Lusebrink, 1990). Using the raised surface of the dried paint for tactile sensory exploration before accent-ing with dry media (i.e., chalks) allows for a gradual climb from the lower ETC level toward the perceptual/affective, whereby the expression is seen anew (Hinz, 2010; Lusebrink, 1990).

Unwanted art pieces can be recycled by cutting them down into ATC pieces such as doodle cards and decorative cheerleading notes. While the initial work may be in ballpoint pen or a *Sharpie*®, adding layers of other materials will add complexity (e.g., tissue paper, cut-out words, paint, oil pastels, organic material, etc.). By experiencing and exploring art media, clients become receptive to the concepts of using fresh and different materials for their art (Hinz, 2010). Part of the work of the art therapist is to facilitate confidence in their clients' selection of art materials. This is often achieved through the careful selection and sequencing of directives and periodically exposing the client to new and different art media and techniques.

Considerations for the Art Therapist

Art therapists need to be mindful of the client, the art therapy directive, the influences of the media, and their ability to facilitate the overall art therapy experience. From the moment the client/participant enters the therapeutic space, everything matters.

As the provider interacts with the space and the media, the client observes, noticing non-verbal cues and modeling what is witnessed. As media properties affect the participant, the effectiveness of the directive toward the desired goal will affect the participant–provider relationship. Being knowledgeable about media properties as theorized by MDV will facilitate therapeutic intervention planning (Hinz, 2010; Lusebrink, 1990). In guiding the client toward well-being, the tools of the trade (the ETC and the MDV) will be indispensable; appropriate media selection will have the effect of building the client–therapist and the client–media relationships that are necessary for lasting change (Hinz, 2010; Lusebrink, 1990; Robbins, 2000).

Conclusion

In considering the needs and goals of the participant and the setting, the therapist needs to be able to select the appropriate media for a session. It is the therapist who has control over the degree of structure provided by the art therapy directive. The art therapist provides boundaries within the session by means of size and texture of the 2D surface, along with the effective pairing of surface properties with media attributes. A positive pairing increases the potential for intended results. Resistive drawing media, such as graphite, charcoal, and solid-state color pigments, may offer safety to the emotive expression. Fluid media, with their amorphous boundaries, challenge control of the art expression. Use of resistive or fluid 2D materials needs to be carefully considered.

The MDV will guide art therapists in choosing the most effective art materials for addressing the needs of the client (Hinz, 2010; Lusebrink, 1990). Utilizing the ETC also offers art therapists guidelines for developing therapeutic art directives (Hinz, 2010; Lusebrink, 1990). Both the ETC and the MDV provide means of conceptualizing the potentiality of the creative experience for therapeutic gain. Having direct experience with the media furnishes the art therapist with the knowledge to select, use, and understand the value of 2D materials in art therapy.

References

Dissanayake, E. (2000). *Art and intimacy: How the arts began.* Seattle: University of Washington Press.

Hinz, L. (2010). *Expressive therapies continuum: A framework for using art in therapy* [Kindle for Android version 3.6.0.87]. New York, NY: Routledge, Taylor & Francis Group. Retrieved from Amazon.com

Kagin, S. L., & Lusebrink, V. B. (1978). The expressive therapies continuum. *Art Psychotherapy*, 5(4), 171–179.

Lusebrink, V. (1990). *Imagery and visual expression in therapy.* New York, NY: Plenum Press.

Moon, C. H. (2002). *Studio art therapy.* Philadelphia, PA: Jessica Kingsley Publishers.

Robbins, A. (2000). *The artist as therapist.* Philadelphia, PA: Jessica Kingsley Publishers.

15

Constructing the Self: Three-Dimensional Form

Lariza B. Fenner

Three-dimensional objects and forms occupy a large portion of our lived experience. Objects, from the corporeal to ethereal, connect us to our constructed reality. We engage in a continual dialogue about our existence through these inevitable interactions. Through this dialogue, sculpture and three-dimensional processes in art therapy "set up connections and differentiations among our experiences, and synthesize structures of shape that refer to structures of analogical form within our lived human experience" (Rawson, 1997, pp. 8–9). The way in which a material is shaped, assembled, or constructed relates back to the story of the creator. As the sculptural object is made, individual reflections, motivations, and visions are most likely influenced by a number of factors.

A theoretical approach well suited to understanding the act of creating in three dimensions is constructivism. As a person fields the innumerable sensory inputs of lived experience, one cannot help but be "affected by the self-knowledge that he or she has been able to conjure" as a result of this constant influx of stimuli (Guidano, 1995, p. 94). What is perceived is then sorted into *constructs* that allow a person to create themes, predict outcomes, and guide behavior (Kelly, 1955/1991). While conjuring notions of self, constructivists believe that these personal constructs constantly shift and change because the self is not viewed as a unitary structure but as including many facets (Neimeyer, 1995, 2000). Defining the self is a dynamic, non-teleological process. Assembling, shaping, reshaping, and reflecting are, in sculpture, all aspects of the media that lend to constant redefinition of space and personal narrative.

Mahoney (1995) noted three interwoven tenets of constructivist theory relating to human experience: active engagement, tacit understanding, and the social construction of meaning. These principles of the theory can also be used to understand the sculptural and therapeutic art process. When creating an object sculpturally, the artist is *active* and engaged in a multimodal task that calls upon the use of several cognitive capacities and methods of knowing. It is this fact that also influences a *tacit* level of awareness employed during art making. Although there may be a plan and process in approaching the chosen sculptural media, the maker is not always aware of the message communicated through the art object.

The Wiley Handbook of Art Therapy, First Edition. Edited by David E. Gussak and Marcia L. Rosal.
© 2016 John Wiley & Sons, Ltd. Published 2016 by John Wiley & Sons, Ltd.

In viewing the object after the experience of creating it, the maker may attempt to explain the newly constructed phenomena via this dialectic (Guidano, 1995). In doing so, a level of awareness about the individual's method of ordering experience may be internalized. In viewing the object, the artist may also initiate a dialogue among differing self-constructs, which may eventually lead to understanding why one may be more or less prominent. Finally, the individual creator seeks to maintain patterns of action that are consistent with his or her *social system*, and these are invariably reflected in the sculptural object (Mahoney, 1995; Neimeyer, 1995). Many aspects of the self are conveyed through, and linked to, the sculptural object. In this chapter, salient elements of the constructed self will be mentioned as they relate to three-dimensional form and the sculptural process.

Active Engagement

When working with sculptural media, the creator is active and engaged on many levels of consciousness. In the process of "translating a mass of material from one area of significance to another" (Rawson, 1997, p. 5), the mind, body, and soul work in concert to reflect some aspect of the self. Sculpture also "shapes and generates its own inner spatial content along with its environment, by articulating rhythmically closed and open volumes, solids and voids" to which the observer can respond (p. 5). Sculpture has the potential to engage kinesthetic, sensory, perceptual, affective, cognitive, and symbolic capacities as it spans the entire Expressive Therapies Continuum (ETC; Hinz, 2010). Although the media used may delineate which capacity is at the fore, working in three dimensions offers great diversity of response.

The kinesthetic function is characterized mostly by bodily movement and action, and is called forth readily by sculptural processes (Hinz, 2010). Pounding and molding clay, banging nails into a piece of wood, and chipping pieces of soft stone are all actions that release bodily energy and require marked physical activity. Although this faculty may be the most engaged by the process, other methods of knowing and understanding experience are active as well. The sensory function is also prominent, especially when using a material such as clay. When exploring the sensations of weight, grit, and earth, the creator's focus enters the haptic realm, and the experience may even lead to an affective response (Hinz, 2010, p. 77; Sholt & Gavron, 2006). Affect is also elicited when perceiving the created object. Stepping back and looking at the finished object offers an opportunity for the viewer to understand it for the process used and the entity that actually displaces physical space. The object embodies imaginal and structural components that eventually lead to personal symbol formation (Lusebrink, 1990).

Finally, sculptural processes are inherently cognitive and can facilitate a form of literacy (Rawson, 1997). This literacy enables the creator and observer to think in three dimensions and create abstractions from physical reality, and fosters cognitive growth. A person can hold the percepts of physical space in their mind's eye and reiterate them through the process of modeling. In doing so, reality is abstracted and presented in sculptural form. Abstraction is a cognitive capacity that has been shown time and again to foster cognitive growth and aid in the attainment of learning objectives (Efland, 2002). In addition, these abstractions in physical form can be used as a conduit of meaning from one human, and one modality, to another.

Hagan, Lewis, and Smilansky (1988) demonstrated how creating in clay can enhance verbal and sculptural fluency. The Clay Project, a study that incorporated over 1,600 children in two countries, explored the cognitive process of creating with clay and examined if the learning in one type of media could transfer to gains in other areas of cognition. The expressive qualities of clay use, as well as various aspects of skill acquisition, were assessed through the clay sculptures and then correlated to tests of intelligence, verbal ability, and drawing reasoning. An important independent variable was the type of instruction provided to reach the learning objectives. Essential conclusions from this study revealed that a directive form of clay instruction yielded analogous positive gains in several intelligence tests (WPPSI I.Q., Goodenough-Harris Draw a Man Test, and Clay Verbs Inventory; Hagan et al., 1988, pp. 102–103).

Art therapists working in special education may see the unique benefits of clay instruction in addressing emotional needs and both behavioral and learning goals. For instance, the clay "increases language: and there is a natural flow of talk around the table," which may aid in reducing the social isolation of many children (Hagan et al., 1988, p. 105). Frustration tolerance may be taught more readily as the actual flexibility of the substance allows for errors that can be corrected immediately by reforming. Furthermore, clay reduces tension and allows for a kinesthetic release that calms and maintains attention span. Children who often have little investment in two-dimensional materials will become immediately engaged in clay sculpture (p. 106). This investment is also noticed in the way that children become attached to the objects. Children follow the process of sculpting, drying, and firing with great patience as they anticipate their final product.

Tacit Understanding

Cognitive qualities of the material are but one attribute that is accentuated during the creation of sculptural objects. In describing her work with clay and pottery, Richards (1964) stated that, "In touch, our inner eye stands quick in the membrane of the flesh, and thus we may more wholly see" (p. 131); there is a tacit understanding that precedes cognition and comprises our first modality of experiencing the world—our sense of touch. Before our cognitive centers for language and formal thought develop fully—usually before 7 years of age—touch and object play are primary modes of understanding experience and subsequently the self (Sholt & Gavron, 2006).

One of the earliest experiences that contribute to the construction of a sense of self is the relationship to a primary caregiver. Feelings of safety, fear, rage, and anxiety are all regulated by this vital early relationship (Crittenden, 1990). Not only does the relationship with a primary attachment figure solidify an internal working model of the self, but it paves certain patterns of interactions with others in relationships (Shaver & Mikulincer, 2006). If a person did not have a positive, safe, and affirming experience with this initial figure, strategies for reducing affective distress may be enacted within adult relationships to ensure a sense of perceived safety.

Consequently, sculptural modalities and clay are uniquely suited to investigating these early constructions of the self and other. They can be used as a bridge to understanding preverbal emotions, thoughts, and interactions in an attempt at formulating new self-awareness at any age. In a constructivist vein, this is accomplished in the process of experiencing (creating in sculptural media) and explaining (the process, the product, and the therapeutic relationship) (Guidano, 1995). This reflective distance and dialogue with the art piece is a common practice among art therapists. Through the dialectic of experience and explanation, personal meaning is constructed, and notions of the self are intrinsically altered. The following case exemplifies the ability of the sculptural process to elucidate the tensions that may exist among competing aspects of the self. The sculptural piece communicates a struggle for the understanding and expression of emotion related to tacit experience.

Mary had been in therapy for several months with an initial complaint of difficulty with interpersonal and romantic relationships. She was able to verbally identify that she was coping with an insecure attachment style and exhibited hyper-activating strategies in a string of long-term relationships. In each, she had patterned a style of relating that would ensure consistent support and love in addition to intense reactions to rejection and disapproval. She could trace the intense discomfort to continued neglect and censure by primary caregivers through early adulthood. As a result of the neglect, she was also exposed to perpetrators in the community who had sexually abused her at a young age. In her trauma work, there was continued rationalization and recanting of numerous scenarios that rarely elicited an emotional response.

Although Mary had a fine arts background and had the opportunity to use artistic media in therapy, she often refused and put the experience off for several sessions at a time. When she did create, she often chose collage and creative writing in lieu of more fluid materials. When she was ready, she chose to work in clay to understand her relationship with her mother. She was questioning why, in all of her relationships she was so preoccupied with the love and affection of others, as well as embodying an insatiable need for the positive appraisal of intimate others. It was as if the pain of abandonment and lack of the necessary early support left her in a state of constant seeking, and she was not able to be content in relationships. This sculpture (see Figure 15.1) embodied the realization that her mother's love was never enough, and that she was looking for this in her relationships. The base is a void that wind can travel through and its contents were described as ephemeral. The dead tree was perceived as the potential for "growth" that she felt had been taken from her. The pain communicated through the sculpture allowed for a lesser-known feeling and belief system to be expressed. It also created an opportunity for Mary to expand upon her constructs related to her primary attachment figure and to intimate partners. As a result, she felt capable of approaching new relationships with a more flexible understanding of her emotional needs.

It is important to recognize that clay work can be a direct conduit to emotional experience, and this quality of the media should not be approached lightly. Mary had been in therapy for quite some time and had established a therapeutic alliance. She felt safe to express the emotions embodied in her sculpture, but this course was not set forth by the therapist. It was the trust that she had in her therapist and the healing process that led her to create in such a way. As a result of creating this piece, her

Figure 15.1 "It's Never Enough."

anxieties and preoccupations subsided greatly. Her question was answered, and this sense of self that she felt was driving her was demystified.

Sculpture facilitates a communion with intrapersonal dialogue, cognitive processes, and primary attachment figures, and can play a pivotal role in how an individual constructs a personal narrative. Just outside our bodies and primary intimate relations lie several systems that also contribute to the whole selves that we attempt to conjure. In the following section, several such social and cultural systems will be discussed, in tandem with sculptural processes, which also contribute to the formation of a comprehensive sense of the self.

Social and Cultural Systems

In responding to an objectivist perspective of mind–body dualism, radical constructivists claim that humans "are not free-floating 'heads' that can think whatever they like or collections of feelings that well up from unknown depths to cause mischief ... lines of thought are context dependent and are always propped up by environmental and bodily supports" (Efran & Fauber, 1995, p. 283). This is not to say that human behavior or beliefs are entirely determined by social influences, but rather that they "couple with the social and natural environment in unique ways" (p. 287). Whether a person is a part of a specific racial or ethnic group, socioeconomic status, or gender queer variance; has a life-altering medical condition; or belongs to a large family, the individual strives to order experience in light of a constant stream of influence from outside systems and environmental human conditions.

The family

Family interactions are a means of social learning and language acquisition, verbal and non-verbal. Symbolic exchanges and referents are constructed in the home that may have relevance only for its members. Despite this somewhat isolated mode of communication, the exchange within the home is not without wide-ranging cultural referents. While filtering various cultural influences, individuals express communication patterns in the home that may contribute to the distress of its members. Examples of such factors include, but are definitely not limited to: cultural and ethnic identity; immigration status; socioeconomic status; multigenerational violence; gender role expression; intra-familial hierarchies; and differing familial definitions (Rosenblum & Travis, 2012).

Two notable techniques that have been employed by family therapists rely on space, gesture, and sculpture to exemplify family dynamics. *Family Sculpture* is seen as a powerful method of symbolizing familial interactions (Bell, 1986; Duhl, Kantor, & Duhl, 1973). Each member is asked to portray other members in "terms of space, posture, and attitude" (Nichols & Schwartz, 2001, p. 191). Some sculptural activities are directed at a particular time of tension in the home in order to offer members other avenues to share individual perceptions of problematic scenarios. Additionally, members can more fully define their roles and personal construction of the family as a result of engaging in such an active process.

Bell's (1986) *Family Paper Sculpture* is a directive that allows space to express relationship dynamics and the degree of perceived proximity or separation among members. It also aims to assess agreement among members around a specific issue. Although the use of yarn and chips (preferred media for this intervention) resemble a mixed media collage, the action and spatial placement component of the exercise give it sculptural attributes. Relationships play out in physical space and are manipulated and changed by the participating family members throughout the activity. In discussing boundaries and proximity, the conversation relies on a structural understanding that fusion and emotional cutoff lead to disunity in a family system (Nichols & Schwartz, 2001, p. 239). Engaging in sculptural processes may allow for the development of an awareness of the self within the system.

Cultural and environmental considerations

Physical and environmental aspects of sculpture may also link directly to the psyche of the individual and present a reflective aspect of the self in an environment. When discussing his transition into Bauhaus Architecture and Design, Max Bill (as quoted in Steele, B., 2010) stated that:

> The Bauhaus became for me the epicenter, with its overlapping of disciplines and its insistence that in everything we design we have a personal responsibility towards society or, as the later formulation would have it, the whole environment created by us, from the spoon

to the city, had to be brought into harmony with social conditions, which implied shaping those conditions too. (p. 9)

These collectively created objects were intrinsically linked to society's wants and needs, and Bill channeled cultural and societal phenomenon through his work.

The relevance of the environment with regard to sculptural objects and architectural treatments is also mentioned by Smith (1973). In arguing about the psychological impact of larger environmental structures and buildings, he indicated that they have not accommodated well to our advancing society. He proposed that sculptural design was not as effective in creating an impact because people have a threshold for absorbing information in their environment. Structures can potentially over- or underwhelm our consciousness, and as a result the urban landscape is doing humankind a psychological disservice. His resolution was that, through maximizing the system by which sculptural objects were presented in the environment, individuals would ultimately be more engaged and fulfilled.

Beyond the corporeal existence is the ethereal. Rawson (1997) explained that the energy that is embodied in a sculptural object's force may be better accounted for by that which is outside of the individual or culture. Best explained by a transpersonal perspective, objects created by sculptors were seen as an act of spirit. Sculpture, through the ages, has been seen as "providing bodies or dwellings for spirit-beings or forces" (p. 21). Sacred objects such as masks have been used in rituals, clay figurines have inspired fertility, and sculptural materials are often used for the purpose of expressing an objects' permanence on this earth. Finally, sculpted spirals and labyrinths have been used to imbue power and mysticism to the objects on which they were placed (p. 22). In observing or making sculptural objects, people have the opportunity to convene with forces that offer strength beyond the self. It is this experience that informs and inspires the construction of personal and universal mythology.

Conclusion—Therapist as Witness

The constructivist lens asserts that reality is socially and individually constructed, and therefore the creator of the sculptural object is the narrator of their subjective experience. The art therapist may be present to witness various aspects of the process while endeavoring to withhold assertions of objective truth or absolute interpretation. It is the challenge of the therapist to help the client expand upon these individual narratives and possibly gain more flexible and expanded storylines (Neimeyer, 1997; Neimeyer & Raskin, 2001).

While acknowledging the fact that the creator is the author of his or her experience, it is nearly impossible to be an art therapist without bias or personally constructed presence. Co-constructing the relationship in every interaction is a quest for the people involved. A therapist may strive to relinquish the "expert" role, but the space is still constructed by the art therapist and, at times, the materials are pre-selected as well. Furthermore, with sculptural media, in-depth instruction is almost always necessary, owing to the advanced properties of the material and process for transformation. Most important is the relationship established while engaging in the experience of making and reflecting on such powerful objects. From ameliorating cognitive challenges, assisting in the development of the self concept, unfolding attachment and relationship dynamics, understanding familial roles, or addressing spirituality, the use of three-dimensional materials have the potential to express many aspects of the lived experience.

References

Bell, L. G. (1986). Using the family paper sculpture technique for education, therapy, and research. *Contemporary Family Therapy, 8*(4), 291–300.

Crittenden, P. M. (1990). Internal representational models of attachment relationships. *Infant Mental Health Journal, 11*(3), 259–277.

Duhl, F., Kantor, D., & Duhl, B. (1973). Learning space and action in family therapy: A primer of sculpture. *Seminars in Psychology, 5*, 167–183.

Efland, A. D. (2002). *Art and cognition: Integrating the visual arts in the curriculum.* New York, NY: Teachers College Press.

Efran, J. S., & Fauber, R. L. (1995). Radical constructivism: Questions and answers. In R. A. Neimeyer & M. J. Mahoney (Eds.), *Constructivism in psychotherapy* (pp. 275–304). Washington, DC: American Psychological Association.

Guidano, V. F. (1995). Constructivist psychotherapies: A theoretical perspective. In R. A. Neimeyer & M. J. Mahoney (Eds.), *Constructivism in psychotherapy* (pp. 93–108). Washington, DC: American Psychological Association.

Hagan, J., Lewis, L., & Smilansky, S. (1988). *Clay in the classroom: Helping children develop cognitive and affective skills for learning.* New York, NY: Teacher's College Press.

Hinz, L. (2010). *The expressive therapies continuum.* New York, NY: Taylor & Francis Group.

Kelly, G. (1955/1991). *The psychology of personal constructs.* London: Routledge.

Lusebrink, V. B. (1990). Imagery and visual expression in therapy. New York, NY: Plenum Press.

Mahoney, M. J. (1995). Continuing evolution of the cognitive sciences and psychotherapies. In R. A. Neimeyer & M. J. Mahoney (Eds.), *Constructivism in psychotherapy* (pp. 39–67). Washington, DC: American Psychological Association.

Neimeyer, R. A. (1995). Constructivist theories: Features, foundations and future directions. In R. A. Neimeyer & M. J. Mahoney (Eds.), *Constructivism in psychotherapy* (pp. 11–38). Washington, DC: American Psychological Association.

Neimeyer R. A. (1997). Problems and prospects in constructivist psychotherapy. *Journal of Constructivist Psychology, 10*, 51–74.

Neimeyer, R. A. (2000). Narrative disruptions in the construction of the self. In R. A. Neimeyer & J. D. Raskin (Eds.), *Constructions of disorder: Meaning Making frameworks for psychotherapy* (pp. 207–241). Washington, DC: American Psychological Association.

Neimeyer, R. A., & Raskin, J. D. (2001). Varieties of constructivism in psychotherapy. In K. S. Dobson (Ed.), *Handbook of cognitive-behavioral therapies.* New York, NY: The Guilford Press.

Nichols, M. P., & Schwartz, R. C. (2001). *Family therapy: Concepts and methods* (5th ed.). Boston, MA: Pearson Education, Allyn & Bacon.

Rawson, P. (1997). Sculpture. Philadelphia, PA: University of Pennsylvania Press.

Richards, M. C. (1964). *Centering: In pottery, poetry and the person.* Middletown, CT: Wesleyan University Press.

Rosenblum, K. E., & Travis, T. C. (Eds.). (2012). *The meaning of difference: American constructions of race, sex and gender, social class, sexual orientation, and disability* (6th ed.). New York, NY: McGraw-Hill.

Shaver, P. R., & Mikulincer, M. (2006). Attachment theory, individual psychody-namics, and relationship functioning. In A. L. Vangelisti & D. Perlman (Eds.), *Cambridge handbook of personal relationships*. Retrieved from http://ezproxy.adler.edu/login?qurl=http%3A%2F%2Fwww.credoreference.com/entry/cuppr/attachment_theory_individual_psychodynamics_and_relationship_functioning)

Sholt, M., & Gavron, T. (2006). Therapeutic qualities of clay-work in art therapy and psycho-therapy: A review. *Art Therapy, 23*(2), 66–72. doi: 10.1080/07421656.2006.10129647

Smith, P. F. (1973). Urban sculpture: A kind of therapy. *Leonardo, 6*(3), 227–232.

Steele, B. (Ed.) (2010). *Max Bill: Form, function, beauty = gestalt. Architecture words* (Vol. 5). Great Britain: Architectural Association.

16

Collage as an Expressive Medium in Art Therapy
Jessica Woolhiser Stallings

There are several methods in which to create a collage—gluing objects or surfaces together including photomontage (photo collage), assemblage (sculptural collage), and decoupage (collage with paper; Leland & Williams, 1994; Malchiodi, 2007, 2010). Paper collage emerged as an art form as early as the twelfth century in Japan to provide dynamic backgrounds for calligraphy. Using collage to enhance other images continued throughout the medieval period, with jewels and other flourishes on religious imagery, as well as in the Renaissance period when artists embellished coats of arms with collaged fabric and paper (Leland & Williams, 1994). Collage continued into the nineteenth century through stamp collections and early scrapbooks (Kohut, 2011; Leland & Williams, 1994), in theater posters, and even in the illustrations of Hans Christian Anderson's books. Photomontage emerged during this same era with the advent of the camera. In the twentieth century, collage emerged among the fine art community, notably Picasso and Braque, who used it as an extension of their paintings. Debuffet utilized collage to add texture and form, and pop artists such as Rauschenberg used this process to reflect on the role of media in the modern world (Kachur, 2009). Contemporary artist Sarah Lucas, among others, utilized collage as political commentary (The Museum of Modern Art, 2004). Futurists, Dadaists, abstract expressionists, nouveau realists, pop artists and contemporary artists all embraced collage (Leland & Williams, 1994; Kachur, 2009). In the early twentieth century, collage began to break with traditional fine art (Leland & Williams, 1994). Whether it was through the addition of scraps to a painting or a composition entirely of collage material, it challenged art world norms. The art world fully embraced the expressive potential of collage by the end of the twentieth century (Leland & Williams, 1994).

Collage as Therapeutic Tool

Art therapists see collage as one of many media at their disposal (Landgarten, 1993; Malchiodi, 2007; Vick, 1999), extending its expressive potential beyond the fine arts world to therapeutic settings. Moriarty (1973) used collage with a group of female

The Wiley Handbook of Art Therapy, First Edition. Edited by David E. Gussak and Marcia L. Rosal.
© 2016 John Wiley & Sons, Ltd. Published 2016 by John Wiley & Sons, Ltd.

patients with chronic schizophrenia in a psychiatric ward, indicating that "It was suitable for the group ... because it is ... structured and less threatening" (Moriarty, 1973, p. 153), while simultaneously allowing patients to develop autonomy and decreased dependence on the therapist. Many art therapists use collage for its potential to provide structure to a session while simultaneously promoting freedom of choice and creative artistic expression (Elkis-Abuhoff, 2008; Foster, 1992; Vick, 1999; Stallings, 2009). Clients often embrace collage because it does not demand the ability or perceived ability to draw (Buchalter, 2011; Elkis-Abuhoff, 2008; Landgarten, 1981; Malchiodi, 2010; Moriarty, 1973; Rubin, 2005; Stallings, 2009). Linesch (1988) stressed that such structured materials limit clients "and offer little opportunity for regression or over-stimulation" (p. 72).

One important consideration is whether to provide precut images for clients to choose from or to allow them to thumb through magazines. Some see magazines as a big distraction, as clients have a tendency to read the articles or fixate on material not related to the art directives (Capri-Orsini, 1996). However, for some populations in highly controlled environments, such as older adults with dementia, allowing them to thumb through magazines can provide a much-needed sense of freedom and choice (Foster, 1992).

If clients are easily distracted, a clinician can do several things—for instance, precutting collage items and sorting them into labeled boxes (Landgarten, 1993). Other art therapists suggest sorting cut and torn items into labeled folders, in order to minimize distractors and allow for easy selection of themed material (Knapp, n.d.).

Collage as Projective Assessment

Projective assessments are common in psychoanalytic-based therapies, including psychoanalytic art therapy. Landgarten (1993) created a multicultural projective assessment called the Magazine Photo Collage (MPC). Landgarten believed that projective assessments were ethnically and racially biased, created by and normed on mostly white Euro-American subjects, making their reliability and validity questionable for minority populations.

Landgarten's MPC necessitates some advance preparation on the part of the clinician, to tear or cut out pictures from magazines (1993). The clinician then sorts these images into two labeled boxes, one for images of people and the other for miscellaneous items. The clinician is careful to include people from diverse cultures, varied ages, and gender, in mostly realistic and diverse environments, with various facial expressions and body placements. Also, the clinician may include black and white as well as color imagery.

> If the therapist has a special agenda in mind, then images related to that goal may be planted in the box. For example, pictures that hint at: chemical or alcohol dependency; physical or sexual abuse; fire setting; eating disorders; suicidal ideation; guilt around parental divorce; repressed mourning; conflicting value systems; a delusional system, and so on. (p. 6)

Regardless of agenda, a detailed protocol exists for conducting the MPC. The protocol has four tasks:

1. Look through the box of miscellaneous items and pick out pictures that catch your attention. Paste them onto the paper. ... Write directly onto the page, or tell me [the therapist], anything that comes to mind about each picture.
2. Select approximately a half-dozen pictures of people, paste them down, and then comment on what the people are thinking and saying.
3. Select another half-dozen images from the miscellaneous items box that "stand for something GOOD and something BAD" (p. 11), paste them down, and tell the meaning of the images.
4. Select and paste down one image of a person and "tell what is HAPPENING to that person" (p. 11), then consider whether the "situation will CHANGE" (p. 11), and if so then the client is directed to select an image depicting "WHAT will make it change (pp. 9–11).

In addition to the four tasks, Landgarten also provided observation guidelines:

1. How are the photographs handled?
2. Were the images torn out, cut away, trimmed, or left in their original state before being pasted down?
3. How was the glue handled?
4. Was the placement carefully thought out, reasonable, or haphazard?
5. What was the gist of the pictorial content?
6. Did specific messages appear? (p. 9)

As stated in her book, *Magazine Photo Collage: A Multicultural Assessment And Treatment Technique*, Landgarten (1993) found collage to be an important vehicle for assessment, and described the process discussed here in much greater detail; she also included examples.

Vick (1999), who also believed that collage and other pre-structured art elements allowed clients to create and reflect on their own projective images, utilized pre-structured elements, such as collage, to work with adolescents in a short-term treatment setting. Although he utilized a less structured process, often employing a free directive rather than a predetermined theme, he observed that clients reveal significant themes about their lives. Vick believed, as did the creators of structured projective assessments, that client choice of material and/or image instructs clinicians about the clients' inner world, "... even the simplest production of a single image glued on the paper and titled can offer material for discussion since all the choices in selection, placement, and text are those of the maker" (p. 70).

Collage as Alternative to and Enhancer of Verbal Communication

Stallings (2009) used a modified version of the MPC to enhance the ability of older adults with dementia to participate in reminiscence through life review. The modified process included two boxes filled with images, one labeled as "people" and the other labeled as "things," the latter container filled with images of miscellaneous objects. She worked with clients individually for two sessions. In the first session, she asked clients to complete a "collage of things you like"; in the second, she requested that they complete "a collage about yourself" (Stallings, 2009, p. 137). "These directives were [made] ... in order to evaluate collage as a medium for personal reminiscence, self-expression and the recovery of dignity and control" (Stallings, 2009, p. 137). She found that collage, in this small qualitative sample, provided adults with dementia a way to communicate visually, an opportunity to reminisce, and "allowed for expression beyond the verbal and cognitive abilities of the clients" (Stallings, 2009, p. 140).

Elkis-Abuhoff (2008) used collage with an adolescent suffering from Asperger's syndrome (AS), believing that it was a therapeutic medium "for allowing adolescents with AS to be expressive without the anxiety that drawing and painting may trigger" (p. 266), and considered it less threatening for her client, "Emma." Her initial directive—"using cut or torn out pictures from the magazines, create a collage that represents who Emma is" (p. 266)—is similar to Stallings' directive outlined earlier. Through this process, she was able to address many of Emma's external problems related to her AS, including difficulty empathizing with other people; the collage provided a springboard for both therapeutic communication and development.

Both of these examples illustrate how collage can serve as an enhancer of—and alternative to—verbal communication. In addition, collage can also assist clients in making decisions and promoting sound decision-making skills.

Collage and the Decision-Making Process

Horay (2006) used a *Pro–Con* collage directive to encourage individuals undergoing substance abuse treatment to explore their drug use. She borrowed elements of stages of change (SOC) theory and motivational interviewing (MI), which aim to assist clients in finding internal motivation for sobriety through self-exploration and evaluation (DiClemente & Velasquez, 2002). The Pro–Con collage encourages clients to explore the positive and negative aspects of their substance use, acknowledging that most clients would not use if they did not get some benefit. "This directive ... was designed to foster some acknowledgement of why substances were abused, thus strengthening the chances for avoiding relapse and continuing sobriety long term" (Horay, 2006, p. 18). SOC and MI are contrary to older styles of addictions counseling, which often focused solely on the negative aspects of substance use.

Horay presented a case study in which the client, David, was initially uncomfortable with conveying these aspects of his drug use. David reported that completion of the Pro–Con collage about his drug use allowed him to see emptiness in his life when he used substances and to identify the oppressive power of drug use. Although his Pro–Con collage on sobriety revealed some ambivalence toward getting clean, it also revealed a desire for a happy and healthy life that he saw as attainable through sobriety, and as such assisted David in choosing the path of sobriety. The Pro–Con collage as described here illustrates collage as a decision-making tool and could be used in a variety of settings, not just substance abuse treatment.

Foster (1992), an artist and professor of architectural design, taught design elements and collage in a care center for older adults. Although not an art therapist, Foster believed that:

> The psychological aspects of the design process, perception (sensing and intuition) and judgment (thinking and feeling) are inherent in the collage-making procedure. The participants' unique life experiences, memories and present concerns generate concepts capable of producing well-defined creative visual statements, as problem solutions—works of art. (p. 29)

She instructed older adults in design elements, such as form, line, space, and content. Beyond that instruction, she empowered participants to find their own themes and concepts. Foster encouraged a process akin to life review, guiding participants to pull themes and concepts from their diverse life experiences. She found that those who participated in the collage-making were provided "control through decision-making," and a sense of fulfillment and improvement in self-concept (p. 29).

Collage can help clients examine previous decisions and chose new paths. It can also allow individuals with limited choice, such as those in nursing homes, an opportunity to freely express themselves without the pressure of coming to a specific presupposed outcome. In addition, it provides clients with opportunities to share with others, learn about themselves, and regain control in their lives. Creating a collage can assist clients in processing events beyond their control and can be a tool for healing.

Collage as a Tool for Coping with Grief

Robbins (1998) pointed out that collage parallels the mourning and healing process as it "is a process of construction, reconstruction, and rehabilitation" (p. 41). The process of making a collage, "collecting, sorting, assembling, adjusting, recovering, replacing, and adhering" (pp. 40–41), is akin to the four phases in Bowlby's attachment theory of mourning that include numbing, yearning and searching, disorganization, and reorganization (Bowlby, 1980; Robbins, 1998). Completing collages, through organizing and reorganizing to create new compositions, reflects adjusting to the loss of a loved one. Robbins (1998) suggested using box collages with those in mourning as they provide "controlled environments" (p. 42). By using a box collage to explore the multiple phases of the grief process, art therapists help clients to connect with the past and present in a safe, contained environment. "Collage is beneficial in this restructuring by providing the medium for experimentation, discovery, and protest. Just as collage connects materials it connects the past and the present" (p. 43).

Kohut (2011) believed that "the organization of scrapbooking may be compared to collage work, given that both activities provide a structured means to organize images and words" (p. 125). Similar to Robbins' description of collage-making, Kohut believed that scrapbooking also allows for reorganizing life. It actively encourages the use of personal images and photos as well as journaling, which enhances its therapeutic potential. She felt that the process allowed for a finished product that could acknowledge the deceased, accept the death, and assist the artist in healing.

New Avenues in Therapeutic Collage

Use of collage in therapy continues to evolve. In recent years, clinicians have developed new ways to incorporate collage into their practice. Although the goals are similar to those mentioned in the preceding text, these new avenues in therapeutic collage incorporate novel media as well as other alternate ways of working with collage.

Digital collage

According to Malchiodi (2010), "Digital art therapy is, in part, the contemporary descendant of magazine photo collage, offering another way to 'cut, move, and paste' without the sharps or Elmer's glue" (para. 5). Thong (2007) acknowledged that some clients may miss the physical interaction with the tactile media; others may prefer the no-mess opportunities provided by digital collage. Digital collage provides endless imagery options, thanks to the ability to access the Internet's vast digital image repositories, such as through Google Images, and to the use of digital cameras.

SoulCollage®

SoulCollage® (2013) is a trademarked process developed by psychotherapist Seena Frost. The process is meant to be ongoing and involves the creation of a "deck" of collaged cards, limitless in number and usually done on 5 x 8 inch mat board, each representing an aspect of the creator. The deck is comprised of four suits: (1) representations of the inner parts or aspects of the personality; (2) representations of persons who have influenced the creator's life; (3) archetypes of interest to the creator; and (4) animal totem or physical energies. Unlike other types of collage that may combine many concepts in one piece, each SoulCollage® card is limited to a specific aspect or being, such as the angry inner child, the artist self, the Great Mother archetype, etc. In this way, the spiritual concept of "the One and the many" finds a parallel in the one deck/person and the many cards or attributes (SoulCollage®).

In addition to the pleasurable process of making the collages, the cards may be used for journaling, meditation, or non-divinatory "readings" (SoulCollage®, 2013). The reader focuses on a particular question or need, draws a card blindly from the deck, then speaks first person, in a Gestalt manner, referencing the question and speaking as the aspect in that card. SoulCollage® (2013) borrows heavily from Jungian concepts such as archetypal energies, synchronicity, and active imagination.

Many art therapists have incorporated SoulCollage® into their work—including with patients suffering from trauma, eating disorders, substance abuse, bereavement, and dementia, and also with veterans, adolescents, prisoners, and hospice patients.

Altered books

Altered books are books that have been recycled or *upcycled* into something new; the technique is similar to both scrapbooking and journaling (Brazelton, 2004; Chilton, 2007). "Altered book making is an option for art therapists who are looking for a means to provide containment while promoting creativity" (Chilton, 2007, p. 59).

Altered books stimulate creation, influenced by the book's content as well as notions and ideas that clients may have pertaining to books (Chilton, 2007). Due to the nature of books, collage is often an art form used in their alteration.

Conclusion

Collage is a diverse medium that works well with a variety of client populations and settings. It can be used as an assessment tool and as a therapeutic art directive. It excels as a medium to calm clients' fears about the art-making process. Collage provides a less threatening starting point for art therapy and is a useful tool throughout the art therapy process. Art therapists and other clinicians continue to find new media for collage-making, including the use of digital images.

References

Buchalter, S. I. (2011). *Art therapy and creative coping techniques for older adults*. London: Jessica Kingsley Publishers.

Bowlby, J. (1980). *Loss: Sadness & depression. Attachment and Loss* (Vol. 3). New York, NY: Basic Books.

Brazelton, B. (2004). *Altered books workshop*. Cincinnati, OH: North Light Books.

Capri-Orsini, C. (1996). *A thousand words: Healing through art for people with developmental disabilities*. Eastman, Quebec: Diverse City Press.

Chilton, G. (2007). Altered books in art therapy with adolescents. *Art Therapy: Journal of the American Art Therapy Association, 24*(2), 59–63.

DiClemente, C. C., & Velasquez, M. M. (2002). Motivational interviewing and the stages of change model. In W. R. Miller & S. Rollnick (Eds.), *Motivational interviewing: Preparing people for change* (pp. 201–216). New York, NY: Guilford Press.

Elkis-Abuhoff, D. I. (2008). Art therapy applied to an adolescent with Asperger's Syndrome. *The Arts in Psychotherapy, 35*, 262–270.

Foster, M. T. (1992). Experiencing a "creative high." *The Journal of Creative Behavior, 26*(1), 29–39.

Frost, S. B. (2003–2010). *The principles of SoulCollage®* Retrieved from http://www.soulcollage.com/principles-of-soulcollage

Horay, B. J. (2006). Moving towards gray: Art therapy and ambivalence in substance abuse treatment. *Art Therapy: Journal of the American Art Therapy Association, 23*(1), 14–22.

Kachur, L. (2009). Collage. *Oxford Art Online*. Retrieved from http://www.oxfordartonline.com/subscriber/article/grove/art/T018573?q=collage&search=quick&pos=1&_start=1#firsthit

Knapp, N. (n.d.). Collage. Unpublished handout. Emporia State University, Emporia, KS.

Kohut, M. (2011). Making art from memories: Honoring deceased loved ones through a scrapbooking bereavement group. *Art Therapy: Journal of the American Art Therapy Association, 28*(3), 123–131.

Landgarten, H. (1981). *Clinical art therapy: A comprehensive guide*. New York, NY: Brunner/Mazel.

Landgarten, H. (1993). *Magazine photo collage: A multicultural and assessment technique*. New York, NY: Bruner/Mazel.

Leland, N., & Williams, V. L. (1994). *Creative collage techniques: A step-by-step guide including 52 demonstrations and the work of over 60 artists*. Cincinnati, OH: North Light Books.

Linesch, D. G. (1988). *Adolescent art therapy*. New York, NY: Routledge.

Malchiodi, C. A. (2007). *The art therapy sourcebook*. New York, NY: McGraw Hill.

Malchiodi, C. (2010, February 16). Cool art therapy intervention #10: Magazine Photo Collage. Retrieved from http://www.psychologytoday.com/blog/the-healing-arts/201002/cool-art-therapy-intervention-10-magazine-photo-collage

Moriarty, J. (1973). Collage group therapy with female chronic schizophrenic inpatients. *Psychotherapy: Theory and Practice, 10*(2), 153–154.

Rubin, J. A. (2005). *Artful therapy*. Hoboken, NJ: John Wiley & Sons, Inc.

Robbins, T. (1998). Collage: The language of love and loss. *Pratt Institute: Creative Arts Therapy Review, 19*, 40–47.

SoulCollage®. (2013). *SoulCollage® FAQ*. Retrieved from http://www.soulcollage.com/about-soulcollage/soulcollage-faq

Stallings, J. W. (2009). Collage as a therapeutic modality for reminiscence in patients with dementia. *Art Therapy: Journal of the American Art Therapy Association, 27*(3), 136–140.

The Museum of Modern Art. (2004). *MoMA highlights*. New York, NY: The Museum of Modern Art.

Thong, S. A. (2007). Redefining the tools of art therapy. *Art Therapy: Journal of the American Art Therapy Association, 24*(2), 52–58.

Vick, R. M. (1999). Utilizing prestructured art elements in brief group art therapy with adolescents. *Art Therapy: Journal of the American Art Therapy Association, 16*(2), 68–77. doi: 10.1080/07421656.1999.10129670.

17

Printmaking: Reflective and Receptive Impressions in the Therapeutic Process

Michelle L. Dean

An *imprint* may be defined as:

- An impression or stamp
- A mark or line on a surface or body
- A verb meaning to make an impression (a feeling or opinion about someone or something)
- A mark on someone
- Or, to simply fix an idea firmly in one's mind

Animals create an internal imprint of their mothers at birth through their primordial attachment. Imprint is also used to identify a printmaker's mark and is a term used when creating an impression or "an indelible distinguishing effect or influence" (Merriam-Webster, 1994, p. 584). Just as imprinting creates inextricable connections between the object, image of the object, and associated feelings, art expression is able to hold and weave together multiple associations due to its polyvalent nature.

To create a print as an art production is to weave the artist's experience and perception, insight, and differentiation into one (Neumann, 1974). It allows for the expression of internal thoughts, affect, and experiences to be put forth in an observable form. Printmaking as a therapeutic process enables a suspended mirroring, which both distorts and amplifies an internal and contextually relevant reality that allows for reflection and the working of the divine through place and time.

This chapter will provide an historical overview of printmaking, the characteristics of printmaking that lend itself to the therapeutic process, and various printmaking techniques and directives that can be adopted within a therapeutic milieu. While printmaking can be a complex process that may involve materials not suited for all settings and populations, this chapter will focus on printmaking processes that would be best suited for the most common therapeutic situations.

The Wiley Handbook of Art Therapy, First Edition. Edited by David E. Gussak and Marcia L. Rosal.
© 2016 John Wiley & Sons, Ltd. Published 2016 by John Wiley & Sons, Ltd.

Impressions by Design: History and Overview of Printmaking

Printmaking, arguably, may be the first art expression of our earliest ancestors. It is now believed that printmaking dates back to between 30,000 and 32,000 years ago through imprints discovered in the Chauvet Cave in Southern France in 1994 (Herzog et al., 2010). On its walls are what appear to be the earliest art productions of early humans. Sets of handprints in this cave accompany the haunting images of pre-historic ice-age animals, markings believed to be part of a spiritual practice. They are unique and identifiable to a single artist, and, as such, carry the identity of the artist across the millennia.

When creating handprints, footprints, and nose prints—pressed into plaster, sand, or on a steamy window—children delight and marvel in their own printmaking and partake in the earliest forms of art expressions. Printmaking provides an opportunity for reflection and mirroring, and can record progression and growth, clearly seen in the prints of children's hands in ink on paper or as plaster casts in trays. As a therapeutic process, printmaking provides ample opportunities for expression and can be an effective medium as it can be modified for the particular needs of an individual or group. As with any medium, it is best to let the context of the therapist–patient relationship lead the therapist's choice of material rather than to apply the technique systematically.

The Mirror Image in the Printmaking Process

Reflective processes are inherent in all artwork. Just as the early cave prints established a record of the identity of the creator, announcing one's existence to others, so too does the print reflect that identity back to the creator, similar to a mirror. Thus, it is a self-mirroring process that expresses that which can be seen by the creator as well as by others. There is abundant literature available on the potential for symbolic expression, possibly more so than other forms of art, due to the reversals of image and text inherent in many of the methods; this can be seen prevalently in Da Vinci's journals, which contained notes in reversed script as a means to conceal its contents (Chastel, 1961).

Reversed images hold symbolic expression much in the same way a person sees himself or herself in a mirror. The "… creative process by which the artist sinks deep inside of her inner world and picks up shapeless images from which to make concrete art works has something to do with the all-encompassing wisdom that touches the root of human existence … wisdom in the formative process" (Yama, 2010, pp. 15–16). Printmaking has the potential to tap into both sophisticated intellectual abilities as well as into the emerging primal process, spanning the formed and unformed aspects of the self.

The Surrendering to the Oracle: The Unpredictable in Printmaking

Printmaking, even with the most well conceived and thoughtfully executed designs, still has an element of chance to it. With most methods, once the plate has been carved and inked and the paper placed on top, the image is concealed; after a strong rub, in the climactic moment, the print is pulled off the plate. This moment is akin to the moment when the magician exclaims "Voilà!" at the revealing of his magic trick and "Presto!" The image is revealed. Bagilhoe (1983) agreed: "It [printmaking] will always have a magical quality" (p. 6). This process is akin to surrendering to a creative muse, the wisdom of an oracle of a higher power. There is a receptivity that is required in the wisdom of the process.

Much of what happens is out of the control of those who experience it, but it is their response to the situation that determines their outlook and general sense of well-being (von Franz, 1980). Some therapeutic interventions rely on acknowledging and coming to terms with such chance. For example, some 12-step programs include surrendering to chance and lack of control as a part of their doctrine:

> In Step One, the addict must equally acknowledge that the problem of and the addiction is more powerful than he or she is in order to admit complete defeat. Jungians describe this as "relativizing the ego." Step Two involves recognizing a divine archetypal power that can restore one to sanity. (Grynbaum, 2010, p. 80)

It may be chance that one has a predisposition to addictive behaviors and to chemical dependency, but it is the response, including the receptivity of the divine, and the subsequent actions that are taken that determine one's recovery. This surrendering includes receptivity to a power greater than oneself who aids in the recovery process. This is true for many spiritual and religious beliefs, which hold the divine as a means of holding both the rational and those things that defy rational beliefs, and may be seen in such practices as consulting the *I Ching* (Wilhelm & Baynes, 1976) or other professorial practices and beliefs. It is an image of life, which is something that one can organize to a certain extent with intelligence and reason (von Franz, 1980). This is reflected in printmaking, where one can organize and apply intellectual process to the creation; however, there is always an aspect of receptivity that must occur for satisfaction.

Multiplicity and Sociological Considerations of Printmaking

One of the greatest advantages in printmaking is the ability to create multiple images from the same plate. Early printmaking techniques relied on wood blocks or bone pressed into clay and wax in China in the second century (Ross & Romano, 1972). However, the Europeans brought great fame to printmaking with the popularity of the invention the Gutenberg Press (Peterdi, 1959; Schachner, 1970; White, 2002). Gutenberg revolutionized the process by including exchangeable images and movable type. Religious materials were among the first and most important printings produced and disseminated en masse, including the *Gutenberg Bible*.

The new technology capitalized on what was already known about propagating self-image and instilling significance and unifying a nation. Industrialized printing was an efficient and rapid way to share material about political leaders, self-image, and other types of what we would consider public relations materials. It had been a long-standing practice for rulers to have their images pressed onto coins as a way of spreading their images and importance across the lands they ruled. It was meaningful in terms of uniting an empire, which may have stretched across numerous cultures and diverse people. These same principles may be utilized within a therapeutic context with individuals and groups.

Multiplicity in the therapeutic process can be helpful in working with self-image, group dynamics, and connectivity spanning time. Multiple prints reduce the preciousness of a single art production and lend themselves to sharing more freely, uniting a group. The sharing of one's image in a therapeutic context may help develop greater group cohesiveness. For example, group members may each create an individual stamp and share this with other group members, either by creating a collective image as in a mural, or in multiple images so that each member has his or her own graphic representation of the group contained in one sheet. Likewise, if the theme of the stamp is about future goals, wishes, and dreams, a stamp may be created that is used on cardstock to create stationary. The individual or group members may then be encouraged to write a letter to their future selves reminding them where they are and what they intend to put forth as goals for themselves in the future. Then the group facilitator mails the letters to the group members in the specified amount of time (e.g., 3 months).

A variation with more immediate results, but with the ability to carry a message well into the future, would be one in which the group members would create printed cards highlighting the other group members' positive attributes and gift it to one another. For example, Figure 17.1 illustrates a young woman's self-image portrait that she created while in an inpatient setting, admitted for trauma symptoms and eating-disorder behaviors.

She was one of several participants who successfully utilized a collagraph to create a self-image utilizing a relief printmaking process. This image was printed on the front of a card in which she wrote a letter to herself, highlighting her hopes and dreams and words of encouragement for her future. This card was mailed to her 3 months after her discharge from the facility.

Types of Printmaking Suitable for Therapeutic Settings

While all printmaking methods may be possible for particular individuals or groups, commonsense and sound clinical judgment are imperative when considering the setting and population. For example, the patients' health may be compromised, so potentially harmful materials must be avoided. Consideration has also been given to work that must fall within rigid time increments, such as a 1-hour individual or 1.5-hour group sessions. Of course, adaptations of the following suggestions are encouraged to best meet specific considerations of the situation and institution. Hence, methods that commonly employ the use of hazardous materials have been purposely omitted.

Monoprints: a painterly process

Monoprints are considered one of the "most painterly" methods of printmaking, and it allows for a great range of fluid possibilities in an image. They can also be considered a "*natural* way of working due to the viscous quality of the ink and its glorious

Figure 17.1 This self-image was created by a young woman while engaged in treatment for trauma symptoms and eating-disorder behaviors.

uncontrollability, which provides an experience of unequaled immediacy" (Nissen, 2008, p. 17). The images are considered one-off productions, as a second image from the same plate is typically compromised and faded, resulting in a ghostly image, which in some cases may be desired. The monoprint allows for a truly individual artistic production with an aspect of the mysterious for the creator, and can be used with diverse populations, ranging from the very young to the elderly, and in a multitude of situations that would be appropriate for painting.

Monoprints are created by spreading juicy paint or ink directly on a Plexiglas® or similar slick substrate. The ability to directly paint on a rigid surface allows for a degree of control over the final picture, but also allows for a direct painterly experience. The image is created by pulling off a piece of paper laid on top of the painted surface. Traditionally, oil-based paints or inks are used for this process. However, successful results may be achieved by using water-soluble inks as well as acrylic paints and, if needed, acrylic paint mixed with a drying retarder or methylcellulose, a liquid adhesive commonly used in bookbinding. Substituting water-based paints or inks for

Figure 17.2 *The Wayward Crow* (detail), created by the author, was a second-run monoprint in which the eyes and other prominent features of the bird were painted directly. Painting into the image does change the surface quality of the print but may offer a good compromise between the unpredictability of the print and the directness of additive painting.

oil minimizes the inherent hazards associated with the chemicals found in oil-based paints and inks. A drying retarder compensates for the shorter drying time of water-soluble media and allows for longer and more detailed painting sessions. It can also be helpful to dampen the paper because the dampness will draw in the color from the plate. A press may be used for greater transfer of paint to paper, but it is not necessary in most cases. If needed, a hand-held roller such as a brayer, a bone folder, or one's hand may be used gently to burnish the back of the paper.

The pulled image is in reverse and can range in vibrancy. Typically, thicker paint and greater pressure applied result in a darker and more vibrant image transfer. Since most monoprints yield only one successful image, each is unique. Additionally, the image may be later worked into a painting, bringing details into greater clarity. Painting into the image does change the surface quality of the print but may offer a good compromise between the unpredictability of the print and the directness of additive painting, as seen in the detail of The *Wayward Crow* (Figure 17.2).

Collagraph: relief printing

Typically, relief printing conjures up images of detailed wood or linoleum block printing in which elaborate designs are carved into the surface, covered in ink, and pressed on paper or fabric to reproduce a reversed imprint (Schachner, 1970). While this method produces beautiful and detailed results, the use of sharp tools is not practical in most clinical settings. However, there are many alternatives to the traditional techniques that provide this experience while avoiding the need for sharp carving instruments.

Many vendors carry soft panels that can be carved with a wooden stylus, pencil, plastic spoon, or other blunt instrument. Trade names for such products include E-Z-Cut printing blocks®, Scratch–Art Scratch–Foam Soft Surface Printing Boards®, and InovartPrintfoam®. Additionally, Styrofoam trays, used by supermarkets to hold fruit and vegetables, may also be used (Weiss, 1976); the food itself—potatoes, broccoli, mushrooms, and apples—can be carved and used as printing blocks. The quality of the image will vary depending on the material used, but all produce satisfactory results without the need for sharp cutting tools or a press. Likewise, premade foam and rubber stamps can be incorporated into other drawing or collage work.

In addition to using a reductionist or subtractive method (carving into a block) to create an imprint, additive constructions—assembled blocks—may be used to create the printing surface image. This is done by employing found objects and adhering them to the foundation. Clay such as Model Magic® can be sculpted and glued onto a board. The sculpted shapes can then be inked and printed. Rubbings can also be made from these blocks by placing a sheet of paper on them and rubbing the raised areas with wax crayons or an inked brayer.

Additionally, found objects may be assembled in a similar fashion, such as gluing pieces of spaghetti, macaroni, dry alphabet noodles, doilies, bottle tops, string, rubber bands, hairpins, fabric, lace, and pieces of cardboard to a substrate board such as chipboard. Such a directive would best be spread over two or more sessions to give adequate time for the glue to dry. This method can be particularly helpful with sight-impaired clients. Depending on the setting and population, a hot-glue gun can be used to expedite the drying time. Likewise, one may "draw" with liquid glue, such as Sobo® or Elmer's® White Glue (polyvinyl acetate, aka PVA), onto a board, let it set, and then use the board to ink or create similar rubbings.

Cyanotype: the blue sun print

Sun printing, also known as *blue printing* or *cyanotype*, is an easy method to create prints from objects or photos. The printing method lends itself to a huge range of abilities, from simple one-step and two-step directions to complicated, multifaceted applications. The continuum spans from relying on prepared kits to creating elaborate multi-step projects using quilts, books, and fabrics. The sun-printing process begins with a prepared sun-sensitive surface and high-contrast black-and-white photographs or prints, pictures drawn with a permanent marker on a transparency sheet or scratched with Clear-Scratch™ Art Film sheets. The sun-sensitive paper's surface is prepared with a solution of potassium ferricyanide and ferric ammonium citrate. This photo-reactive surface turns blue when exposed to light, leaving a monotone print of blue and white.

Kits with prepared paper can be purchased at most art supply vendors, and fabric as well as other papers types and sizes may be prepared with the solution to provide a more individualized result. Along with the prepared papers, the only other material needed to complete this process is a small vat of water, as large as the sheet of paper, to rinse the sheets after 3–10 minutes of sun exposure. Objects such as leaves, keys, lace, or shells may be placed on top of the paper to create patterns or compositions. While this process is easily done outdoors or on a windowsill, producing higher-contrast images is dependent on keeping the objects still on the page for the duration of the exposure.

Figure 17.3 *The Blue Fern Book*, created by the author, is a simple accordion book made from blank greeting cards and three cyanotype, or sun prints, on alternating pages, and was later used to hold a poem of similar title.

To use photographs, print an image of high contrast in black and white onto everyday copy paper—the thinner or lighter the paper, the better. Alternatively, one can print or copy directly onto a transparency sheet using the appropriate setting of the printer or copier. Place the image on the prepared paper. Placing a piece of Plexiglas™ on top of the image as it is exposed to the sun will help prevent the photo from moving, and it also minimizes the distance between the image and photosensitive paper sheets as excessive distance or curling of the sheets can reduce the contrast in the final image of the sun print.

Similar to the process outlined in the preceding text, light-sensitive dyes can be painted directly onto fabric. The fabric may need to be exposed to light for as long as 30 minutes, but all other methods of exposing the cloth are similar to the process discussed earlier. The printed fabric can be incorporated into other projects—such as printed images from old negatives of ancestors; heirloom fabrics from christening garments, wedding gowns, and silk ties of deceased relatives; or books as in *The Blue Fern Book* (Figure 17.3).

Additional Printmaking Methods to Consider

There are numerous techniques that may not immediately come to mind when thinking about printmaking. However, the following methods deserve mention due to their ease as well as ability to convey content, pattern, and image through a variety of everyday supplies. Prints do not need to be confined to paper; pressing objects into a slab of clay to make a textured tile creates a lively panel and a detailed relief. Working with clay slabs adds another dimension to printmaking. The clay itself provides a more tactile experience. Likewise, stenciling is another printmaking technique useful in the painting or glazing of two-dimensional or three-dimensional objects. Rubbings can be made from found objects, gravestones, or other group members' tiles once they have dried.

Printmaking in its many forms is a viable and creative way to work with imagery in a therapeutic situation. The ability to use intellectual skills as well as surrendering to the creative process—the divine—invites working with that which is unpredictable for a wide range of therapeutic situations. Printmaking in groups may foster greater group cohesiveness and sharing opportunities. And, as is true with the prints created several millennia ago by our earliest ancestors, printmaking today can continue to span time and place, creating bridges to oneself and to others.

References

Chastel, A. (1961). *The genius of Leonardo da Vinci: Leonardo da Vinci on art and artist.* New York, NY: The Orion Press.

Grynbaum, G. (2010). Addiction: A world of demons and daimons. *Jung Journal: Culture & Psyche*, 4(4), 78–81.

Herzog, W. (Director), & Nelson, E., Ciuffo, A., Harding, D., Hobbs, J., & McKillop, D. (Producers). (2010). *Cave of forgotten dreams* [Motion picture]. France: Creative Differences, History Films, Ministère de la Culture et de la Communication, Arte France, Werner Herzog, Filmproduktion, More4.

Merriam-Webster. (1994). *Merriam-Webster's dictionary of English usage.* Springfield, MA: Merriam-Webster, Inc.

Neumann, E. (1974). *Art and the creative unconscious: Four essays.* Bollingen Series LXI. Translated from the German by Ralph Manheim. Princeton, NJ: Princeton University Press.

Nissen, D. (2008). Stalking the feral artist: A Series of monoprints in which the artist has an unforeseen encounter with Habuman. *Jung Journal: Culture & Psyche*, 2(4), 17–33.

Peterdi, G. (1959). *Printmaking: Methods old and new.* New York, NY: The Macmillan Company.

Ross, J., & Romano, C. (1972). *The complete PRINTMAKER: The art and technique of the relief print, the intaglio print, the collagraph, the lithograph, the screen print, the dimensional print, photographic prints, children's prints, collecting prints, print workshop.* New York, NY: The Free Press.

Schachner, E. (1970). *Step-by-step printmaking: A complete introduction to the craft of relief printing.* New York, NY: Golden Press.

von Franz, M. L. (1980). *On divination and synchronicity: The psychological meaning of chance.* Toronto: Inner City Books.

Weiss, P. (1976). *Simple printmaking.* New York, NY: Lothrop, Lee & Shepard Co.

White, L. M. (2002). *Printmaking as therapy: Frameworks for freedom.* London: Jessica Kingsley Publishers.

Wilhelm, R., & Baynes, C. F. (Trans.) (1976). *I Ching or Book of Changes* (3rd ed., 13th printing). Bollingen Series XIX. Princeton, NJ: Princeton University Press.

Yama, M. (2010). The artist's experience of formative work: Japanese painter Yasuo Kazuki and his Siberian Series. *Jung Journal: Culture & Psyche*, 4(4), 15–31.

18

Photography as Therapy: Through Academic and Clinical Explorations

Ellen G. Horovitz

In the mid-1990s, I enrolled in a 5-day poetry workshop led by Carol Barrett. For one of Dr. Barrett's exercises, she handed out 2 × 3 inch index cards, each containing one random line of text from various publications such as journals, newspapers, and magazines. From these cards, participants were instructed to create a poem in less than 10 minutes. I received the sentences "I used to come here as a child" and "But what of the things we left." My poem reflected my work in phototherapy, containing hidden clues of how I made sense of my childhood by reflecting on pictures of my youth and family:

> **The mahogany drawer**
> I used to come here as a child—
> that long, dank narrow space,
> looming inside my mind.
> I sorted through pictures of your memory,
> the only thing worth preserving that I kept.
> I used to come here as a child—
> that mahogany, bottom drawer,
> replete with glossy photos, embedded
> with your history.
> I used to come here as a child—
> and pretend that your black and
> white existence would lend glossy
> texture to my tattered and broken heart.
> I used to come here as a child—
> and sift through the sea of photographs
> that lined the walnut-stained images
> of my sepia-toned hues of your color.
> I used to come here as a child—
> and bury myself in the comfort of your memory,
> more real than any

The Wiley Handbook of Art Therapy, First Edition. Edited by David E. Gussak and Marcia L. Rosal.
© 2016 John Wiley & Sons, Ltd. Published 2016 by John Wiley & Sons, Ltd.

that you left me.
Yes, I used to come here as a child—
always hoping, praying, to find you
real in those long-ago places,
now buried in your institutionalized,
and vapid mind.
I used to come here as a child—
but no longer do I visit that ebony rimmed,
mahogany container that was you.
But what of the things we left?
© *Ellen G. Horovitz*

The poem was evocative and concretized my understanding of how photographic images reveal our history.

I taught my first phototherapy class shortly after that workshop. The historical texts of Krauss and Fryear (1983) and Fryear and Corbit (1992) contributed much to the course development, but it was not until I read Weiser's (1993) work that I really understood phototherapy. Phototherapy can be understood from a variety of perspectives, which includes examining photographs of one's past to creating pictures, sculptures, and videos to reflect one's current perspective. Phototherapy has the inherent "ability to immediately trigger memories, trigger affect, put the client back into that feeling state" (Krauss as cited in Horovitz, 2005), more so than any other medium. For patients with complex etiologies such as Asperger's syndrome, autism, and aphasia of varying typologies, using photographic images often accelerates recovery in these difficult-to-reach clients. This success is understandable. As Weiser (1993) suggested:

> We can only be aware of ourselves to the extent that we can self-reflect; our existence at any moment is a summary of selective memory and, within the distortive nature of that process, also a partial fiction created only by what we can know of ourselves and have introjected from others. (1993, p. 20)

This is especially true when working with people who have temporarily lost their memory, such as through traumatic brain injury and for those enduring various stages of Alzheimer's disease and dementia.

Phototherapy can be used for almost any kind of affliction, from trauma-related disorders to bereavement. Familial photographs have been used to address mourning and loss issues because the evocative power of these images can break through the most hardened defenses. Photographs can be used either as the primary focus in grief therapy or as an initial medium used to begin delving into deeper concerns, which may help the bereaved move toward wellness and recovery.

The old maxim "a picture is worth a thousand words," although true for many of us, may be particularly relevant to nonverbal clients. Individuals who do not speak or who choose not to do so can communicate volumes when they bring a meaningful photograph to therapy or when they are asked to select an picture from a collection of images. Incorporating the photo into a larger artwork can illuminate the meaning with few or no words.

The reason behind the power of photographic images may be explained through understanding archetypal psychology. Archetypes, or mythic ideas and images, were first identified by Jung (1964) as holding psychological power for human beings. Archetypal images are resonant with universal meaning for us humans. It is not surprising then that photographic images have been used throughout the history of psychology as one aspect of assessment and diagnosis.

Additionally, the image is and always will be a powerful and therapeutic avenue for exploring emotions. A photographic image may take a person back to the time, place, and state of mind when the image was taken. Little else can move a person so close to recovering memory.

Academic Applications

When teaching phototherapy, learning various techniques offers students both the numerous perspectives of this powerful medium and its applications for working with various clients. The methods range from varying transfer techniques; cyanotype printing; luminous emulsions on paper, wood, metal, and ceramic; and the use of specialty papers (e.g., Lazertran and Sheer Heaven papers; Horovitz, 2011). Landgarten's (1993) photographic collage is important to teach as well. Although Landgarten found the collage to be an important assessment tool, it can also be used therapeutically.

The real advantage of learning various phototherapy techniques for students may be the opportunity to explore one's own issues. To begin, students have found that creating a visual photographic genogram (a three-generation diagram of a person's familial history; McGoldrick & Gerson, 1985) revealed important personal information that may be important to explore therapeutically. This snapshot of one's family tree may hold more symbolic knowledge than a simple line drawing. For example, the photographs or even magazine cutouts selected to represent each family member may provide symbolic material not otherwise discovered. Variations of the family pho-togenogram (e.g., cut out photographs of animals that represent each of your family members) can uncover newfound perspectives.

Whether working with students or clients, a family system diagram is a powerful starting point for further examination of the self; it allows the artist to see the self as part of a larger system and not just as an "identified patient." When clients understand that their problems exist within the family system, less guilt and blame may prevail. Clients see themselves as a symptom of family issues, and learn that they may be the catalyst for moving the family toward recovery.

In another phototherapy exercise that may address family issues, students are asked to find an image of themselves when they were under 6 years of age. They are asked to manipulate the image *any way they desire*, such as with image-editing software (e.g., Photoshop) and transfer methods, and then write a letter to that image (Horovitz, 2011). For example, KC scanned an image into the computer and then used a laser printer to transfer it onto Lazertran silk paper. She burnished the image onto Scupley polyform clay®, and allowed it to sit for 30 minutes. She then placed the clay in water and the backing paper lifted off. After adding more imagery, she baked it in a toaster oven at 325 degrees for 15 minutes to harden it into the final form (see Figure 18.1).

Figure 18.1   KC on polyform Clay (Sculpey) using Lazertran silk paper for output.

When discussing the artwork and reading the letter, tears cascaded down her cheeks as she talked about her mother and her grief over how badly she had treated her mother during her adolescent years. It was pointed out to KC that she could resolve these feelings and mend whatever chasm she felt existed.

Another early-childhood phototherapy example illustrates how individuals continue to carry around parts of themselves that are disliked. JF removed the emulsion backing from an old Polaroid image (with warm water) and then rubbed off areas that she wished to be viewed as transparent. Next, she folded this image up and placed a string through it and contained it with a snap, making it appear to be a tiny, sealed pocketbook (see Figure 18.2). The transformation into a small yet tightly sealed container for emotions is the epitome of a transitional object (Winnicott, 1953). According to Winnicott, transitional objects represent a good enough mother and/or the first internalized experience. In this case, JF's internal compass was now a tangible object, albeit one representative of her negative self-introjection. Moreover, the psychological value of the art piece was perceptible even to her. By creating this object, JF began to value that which she *liked least* about herself. Based on the importance of this piece, JF and her classmates were able to ponder her negative relationship with her mother and her resulting negative sense of self.

Figure 18.2　JF's purse 1" x 2".

Another assignment required students to create a personal box from any image and medium. One student created a box that was a functional pincushion disguised as a bed (see Figure 18.3). The cyanotype image chosen was of her mother, flanked on both sides by the student and her sibling. From the beginning of the course, the student and her images exposed the pain created by her parents' divorce. The student's mother was a seamstress and the box was created as a gift for her mother. Through class discussion, the student realized that, by creating this piece, she was finally putting the pain of the divorce to bed.

In yet another assignment, students were asked to take five Polaroid or digital images of themselves by directing a partner to photograph them. The opportunity to "direct" the shot as well as be the object is rather different from being behind the camera. While there are healthy dissociative properties that an artist moves through when creating a work of art (Horovitz, 1999), adding a camera to the artistic arsenal may expose voyeuristic perspectives. When asked to be on the other side of the camera, issues may arise from the art directive itself. For example, a person can rework difficult feelings by being the photo-orator and directing how a photograph is crafted. In directing how photos are taken, a client might find himself or herself in a commanding role. For example, a shy, passive person who rejects close relationships may obtain control over his or her environment by directing the distance from which he or she is photographed and can decide if the photographer zooms in on specific parts of the shot.

Figure 18.3 Putting darker issues to bed.

The photographer can hide behind the camera, which provides comfort, or helps him or her safely approach a personal encounter that heretofore was not palatable.

Clinical Applications

Photographic images, old movies, and slides are often used with clients in order to retrieve memories long buried. These images may lead clients to create pillows, tee shirts, or quilts to honor people who have passed on. Photographic images can be digitized and stored on a computer in order to rework images with digital software programs such as Photoshop, Painter, Studio Artist, and Artmatic. Remaking images can be a restorative process. For example, when working with a client who is self-abusive, the process of enhancing, manipulating, and discussing images can be quite empowering. Three phototherapy techniques useful with clients are explored in the following text.

Intervention 1

Working outside the confines of a therapeutic office can also be quite valuable. BH, an adolescent client in residential treatment center for self-injurious behavior (SIB), used phototherapy techniques and a digital camera supplied by his therapist to capture the world around him. Individual sessions consisted of taking walks in the woods and photographing nature as well as each other. It seemed restorative and productive. When taking BH out to a local donut shop, he developed a relationship with another patron. Every Tuesday when visiting the shop, BH interacted with a woman who told the saga of her husband's recent hospitalization and his unconscious state. BH photographed her. One day, he approached her with some of the photographs that he had taken of her as well as other photos taken during his walks. They talked for an hour, and both were engaged and animated. Watching BH in this alternative environment was important and revealing. At the donut shop, he was polite, appropriate, and charming. When he returned to the treatment center, he returned to being angry and resistant.

Of all the photos he took, one of the most unusual was of his own eye. He directed that his eye be photographed; it was not until later that he confessed that its importance had to do with how I was reflected in the photograph of his eye. This seemed to be BH's way of revealing that my "vision" of him was what mattered, no matter how others viewed his behavior.

Through further manipulation of the digital photo, BH changed the eye so that it appeared blackened, much like an eye would after being battered. He had been terribly beaten by his biological father when he was 3 years old; creating this image seemed to be cathartic for BH. He decided to carry around these photos between sessions; these images possibly became transitional objects between therapy sessions (Horovitz, 1999).

Intervention 2

Other simpler applications can be used by practitioners who do not have access to digital equipment and/or computer software. A simple photocopy machine can be used to distort images by moving them over the glass when the light photographs the images to be copied. These images can then be reworked with various media. Photocopies can be used pasted down on paper, and a clinician need only suggest the simple directive, "*if those images could say something what would that be?*" A dialogue between images may ensue. This simple directive reduced a client with aphasia caused by a stroke, troubled by her marriage, to tears. After discussing her reaction to this directive, she found strength to discuss her feelings with her husband. In this example, the client wrote down the dialogue between the images. She wrote:

> "I used to like the way we talked together."
> "We have so much to live for."
> "I wish I could tell you these things but I can't form the words."

These words unlocked introspection about the marital relationship, and she was able to admit the struggle she felt after her stroke.

Intervention 3

Still another client, CS, diagnosed with Asperger's syndrome and an intellectual disability, used countless phototherapy methods to create images of her family system. Many resulted in gifts for others as well as transitional objects for herself. In one session, while viewing slides from CS's past, she cried for the first time. She sobbed for 10 minutes and declared, "I promise I will be good, if only they'll take me back." After this heartbreaking confession, CS worked toward forgiving and reconciling with her family of origin. Creating gifts of her works of art reflected increased self-worth and her progression toward individuation.

CS's creations, while perhaps crude in their artistry, were completely crafted by the client. Such activities were not only affirming but also comforting to the client in ways that other art media have not been. Photographic pieces, embedded with emotions from the past, have restorative properties that can be coddled, held, and can be so reassuring that people such as CS want to sleep with them. It is difficult to sleep with a painting or a sculpture, but images such as these are meaningful in an altogether different fashion.

Conclusion

As outlined in the preceding text, photographic imagery of all types can be incorporated in both learning and clinical environments. The emotionally charged quality of these images can captivate and motivate the human psyche in ways that other media simply cannot. Perhaps it is the evocative power of a photographic image that can stir the soul back into a time long forgotten. Coupled with the power of technological advances, such as those discussed herein, people can rework past images and themselves in the process. Phototherapy continues to evolve as a therapeutic modality. As technology advances, so does the practice of phototherapy. As Henry James (1893) once said, "We work in the dark, we do what we can. Our doubt is our passion, and our passion is our task. The rest is the madness of art" (p. 315).

References

Fryear, J. L., & Corbit, I. E. (1992). *Photo art therapy: A Jungian perspective.* Springfield, IL: Charles C. Thomas.

Horovitz, E. G. (1999). *A leap of faith: the call to art.* Springfield, IL: Charles C. Thomas.

Horovitz, E. G. (2005). Art therapy as witness: A sacred guide. Springfield, IL: Charles C. Thomas.

Horovitz, E. G. (2011). *Digital image transfer: Creating art with your photography.* New York, NY: Pixq: Sterling Publishers.

James, H. (1893/1945). The middle years. In C. Fadiman (Ed.), *The short stories of Henry James* (pp. 293–315). New York, NY: Random House.

Jung, C. (Ed.). (1964). *Man and his symbols.* New York, NY: Doubleday.

Landgarten, H. B. (1993). *Magazine photo collage: A multicultural assessment and treatment technique.* New York, NY: Brunner/Mazel Publishers.

Krauss, D. A., & Fryear, J. L. (1983). *Phototherapy in mental health.* Springfield, IL: Charles C. Thomas.

McGoldrick, M., & Gerson, R. (1985). *Genograms in family assessment.* New York, NY: Norton.

Weiser, J. (1993). *Phototherapy techniques.* San Francisco, CA: Jossey-Bass Publishers.

Winnicott, D. W. (1953). Transitional objects and transitional phenomena—A study of the first not-me possession. *International Journal of Psycho-Analysis, 34,* 89–97.

19

Art Therapy and Digital Media

Penny Orr

> Sometimes I feel that as art therapists we can get stuck with paint and paper not only
> because we are usually short of space but because we may be a little trapped in the
> conventions of the traditional "studio" and the convention of "Art as expression," when
> it refers to art therapy. (Waller, 1993, p. 55)

At the time of this statement, traditional materials such as paint, clay, and pencil were
still dominant in the practice of art therapy. However, traditional film and photography were also being used as creative "technology" tools within art therapy as early
as 1972 (Arnott & Gushin, 1976; Fox & Wortman, 1975; McNiff & Cook, 1975;
Muller & Bader, 1972; Nelson-Gee, 1976; Wolf, 1976; Zwick, 1978). By the 1980s,
digital media in the form of computer art making, digital photography, and film-
making were being explored (Canter, 1987; Weinberg, 1985). However, by the early
1990s, at the time of Waller's comment, these new media were still in an exploratory
stage of use in the field of art therapy.

Art therapists, as with all artists, are influenced by—and work with—new creative
media and innovations as they arise. Because they have the added responsibility of
maintaining client confidentiality and well-being while working with these new innovations, art therapists are more cautious in adopting new media. In this chapter, how
new media, specifically digital, are used in art therapy is explored.

Historical and Theoretical Underpinnings

Photography was invented in 1839, and was seen primarily as a documentation tool
and not an art medium. It was used by the American photographer Mathew Brady
during the American Civil War for documentation, and by the English photographer Eadweard Maybridge to scientifically understand how a horse runs. It was not
until 1879, 40 years after photography's invention, that Jacob Riss used photography in an intentionally artistic and social manner and was recognized by the
society at large as having created art (Newhall, 1982). It took another 70 years for

The Wiley Handbook of Art Therapy, First Edition. Edited by David E. Gussak and Marcia L. Rosal.
© 2016 John Wiley & Sons, Ltd. Published 2016 by John Wiley & Sons, Ltd.

art therapists to pick up the camera to determine how to use it artistically and therapeutically within practice.

The time gap between the invention of photography and its use in art therapy may seem large at first glance, but to be fair, one has to recognize that art therapy was not a named concept until 1940, almost a hundred years after photography was invented (Junge & Asawa, 1994). Once art therapy was recognized as a form of therapy, its focus for the first 30 years was on traditional drawing, painting, and clay media. By focusing on these three media, art therapists had a starting point for understanding the dynamics of art therapy and the role of media. These were the materials with which art therapists were most familiar, and these therapists inherently understood their therapeutic value. It makes sense that early art therapists would stick to what they understood best.

When the Expressive Therapies Continuum (ETC) was developed in the late 1970s, art therapists gained a systems approach framework for beginning to understand and intentionally use media within art therapy (Kagin & Lusebrink, 1978; Lusebrink, 1990, 1992). During the early stages of art therapy theory development, media was limited. As art therapists were able to develop a clearer framework for understanding and choosing materials, experimentation with additional types of media expanded, while drawing, painting, and clay remained a solid foundation. Thus, photography was addressed as an art therapy tool as early as 1974 (Hogan, 1981; Maciag, 1976; Milford, Fryrear, & Swank, 1983; McNiff & Cook, 1975; Nelson-Gee, 1976; Wolf, 1976; Zwick, 1978). Other newer media, such as video and color photography, were to follow quickly (Canter, 1987; Fryrear & Stephens, 1988; Weinberg, 1985).

The world's first commercially available general-purpose computers were deployed in 1951, used to create art in 1963, and used by art therapists with clients in 1985. The time lag between its use in the art world and the art therapy world is still large (34 years), but it had a shorter adoption time period than photography. With the availability of the digital camera in the early 1980s and digital image manipulation software in the early 1990s, access to digital media, and the ability to use it within sessions, became easier and more prevalent. At the same time, due to the widespread deployment and growth of the Internet and its symbiotic relationship with digital media, the social and confidential aspects of using it beyond the therapeutic environment became a new issue that art therapists had to work through. The Internet allowed clients easy access for sharing their work, and the social boundaries among clients, therapists, and the larger world became murky. Art therapists began to write less about what technology-based or digital media was used and how it was used in practice, and more about why that particular media was or was not used and the related ethical ramifications (Peterson, 2010).

Art therapists wrote about the therapeutic value of digital media (Barbee, 2002; Hartwich & Brandecker, 1997; Horovitz, 1999; Martin, 1997; McLeod, 1999; Orr, 2005; Parker-Bell, 1999; Rutherford, 2002; Seiden, 2001; Thong, 2007; Wolf, 2007); what was not therapeutic (Williams, Kramer, Henley, & Gerity, 1997); the potential ethics issues involved with using digital media in art therapy practice (Alders, Beck, Allen, & Mosinski, 2011; Jacobs, 1994; Moon, 2006; Orr, 2011a, 2011b, 2011c); its social implications (Belkofer & McNutt, 2011; Kapitan, 2011; Orr, 2011a, 2011b, 2011c); and the training needed to address the complicated theoretical and ethical aspects of digital media for future art therapists (Moon, 2006; Orr, 2012). From these conceptual and research writings on digital media use, the following *principles* have emerged:

Principle 1: Digital media has limitations. However, with knowledge of those limitations, art therapists can mitigate them and use digital media ethically in practice.

(a) *Confidentiality and security:* No matter how great the encryption or firewall that is in place, there are always limitations to the ability to maintain confidentiality and security when working, transmitting, or storing data within an electronic environment. Art therapists are responsible for informing clients of these limitations prior to working with digital media within an electronic environment, and for learning about and using updated security measures.

(b) *Digital impressions never disappear.* It is difficult and sometimes impossible for information and imagery created or placed in digital format to be completely erased or removed from digital storage, networks, and the Internet. The Internet cannot be destroyed, and there is a very good chance that any imagery placed on the Internet will always be on it somewhere. Art therapists, when gaining consent from clients for using their art on the Internet, need to inform the clients that they will not be able to revoke their consent at a later date, as the imagery can never be totally removed.

(c) *Technology fails.* When working with digital media, it is always possible, and likely, that the physical hardware will fail at some point, causing loss of work and—in the online environment—loss of connection with clients. Art therapists should always have backups of important information (such as client records) in different locations and on different devices. Art therapists should also have alternative means of communication with clients if the technology should fail.

(d) *Digital media is not for everyone.* Digital media, similar to other art media, have inherent therapeutic benefits for some clients, but can also be detrimental to others. When choosing media to use with a client, it is always important to determine client interests, personal associations, and experience with any medium before working with it. Most of all, any medium should be chosen (or provided as an option for choice) for clients based on what is going to help or meet the needs of that individual client at that point in their therapeutic process. As a result, there will be particular times when it is therapeutically beneficial to work with digital media with a particular client, and times when it is not; it may even be harmful. As with all art materials, it is not a question of whether or not digital media is helpful or harmful when used in art therapy practice; it is a question of *when* it is helpful or harmful.

(e) *Digital media and the Internet are not limited by physical space and time, but people and regulations are.* It is possible to communicate, socially interact, provide therapy, collaborate on creations, and show your art to anyone anywhere at anytime in the world through the Internet. Art therapists should be aware of who they are working with, the location in which they are working, and should have a clear understanding of the type of relationship implied in communication. It is easy to develop dual relationships with clients in the online environment due to the profusion of social media and the ease with which a person can misrepresent himself online. There are macro and micro regulations for counselors that differ between countries and even states. An art therapist should be aware of these regulations and of how they may apply to each online relationship, and the physical locations of the client and the therapist.

Kapitan (2011) stated that working within the specific codes of practice for art therapists (AATA, 2011; ATCB, 2011) will help guide them in the ethical practice of art therapy, no matter what media or environment they are working within.

Principle 2: Digital media is limitless. Art therapists' continued exploration into specific digital media (e.g., digital video, digital assessment, computer art, mobile art) has revealed that we are more limited in our imagination than digital media is in its possibilities.

(a) *Digital media is fluid in its symbolic and conceptual meanings.* Ottiger (2004) explored the meaning of the computer medium in art psychotherapy. She stated:

The computer is a paradox, and full of opposites: it is real yet unreal, a physical object (material) yet a mental space (immaterial), visible yet invisible, subject and object, or neither. This constant switching in the computer's meaning and position, from which it is regarded, is a fundamental difference that traditional art mediums used in art therapy do not have. The speed and the diversity in the technique of the computer is phenomenal. (p. 53)

Ottinger posits that the paradoxical nature of digital media allows the client to associate meaning with their product, their relationship to it, and the its impact on them as viewer in a malleable way that can change as the client's needs change. It is only limited by the client's needs.

(b) *Art therapy assessment translates well to digital structure in its administration, collection, analysis, and implementation.* In the late 1980s, art therapists began to experiment with the possibility that computers could analyze art therapy images to provide more consistency and less bias in these evaluations (Canter, 1987; Weinberg, 1985). Later, the program Expert System for Diagnosis in Art Psychotherapy (ESDAP) was developed using "if–then" statements to connect drawing characteristics with diagnosis (Kim, Kim, Lee, & Yoo, 2007; Kim, Kang, & Kim, 2009).

Mattson (2011) explored creating a revised face stimulus assessment to measure the formal elements to be adapted for computer analysis. He modified technology already developed for the analysis of biomedical imagery to analyze the artwork. He concluded with continued improvement in the technology, and felt that there was much promise in the development of using computers to standardize assessment in art therapy. Art therapists are just at the beginning of being able to realize the potential and pitfalls of computer assessment of art-based images (Mattson, 2011).

(c) *Digital media is developing toward more human-responsive interfaces.* One concern that many art therapists have cited about using digital media rather than traditional materials is that it lacks sensual and tactile qualities. With advances in technology—touch sensitivity, 3D imagery, and virtual worlds—the cold technology is becoming more integrated with human interactions, human senses, and human emotions in an intuitive and responsive way (Austin, 2010, personal communication). The dimensions of possibilities that may evolve from these innovations and the art making that could result is beyond what art therapists can imagine.

Use of Digital Media in Art Therapy Practice

Orr (2012) explored the changes in attitudes, use, and adoption rates of technology by art therapists between 2004 and 2011. The survey she conducted showed that, in 2011, art therapists were adopting technology in their practice, and increasing their knowledge, at a parallel rate with that of the general population. However, because art therapists started at a lower adoption level in 2004 than did the general public, they remained lower in their use of technology within their practice as compared to the general public. However, there are a number of art therapists who have been working with digital media, as indicated in their presentations and writings. This helped close the gap between their clients' digital media use and the media that they used in their own practice.

The following section introduces the projects of three pioneering art therapists working in digital media: Leonhardt, Austin, and Mosinski. The summaries of their projects have been conveyed through their own words.

Leonhardt on using iPads in hospitals (Leonhardt, 2012)

Ginger Pool and Bridget Pemberton-Smith use art apps to help treat children in the pediatric oncology ward at UNC Hospitals. Working with the North Carolina Art Therapy Institute, they provide art therapy for children staying in hospitals and are working to expand their services to other clients in the health care system. They find that iPads are easy to use, and that patients can spend more time creating art and talking about it rather than learning how to use a program. iPads are a sterile art medium that works well in a hospital setting. They realized that working with iPads while undergoing procedures helped to reduce stress for patients.

Austin on The Animation Project

The Animation Project's (TAP) mission is to nurture the social, emotional, and cognitive growth of at-risk teenagers, using digital art technology as a therapeutic medium and a work force development tool. We capitalize on teenagers' natural interest in new media to engage them in group therapy sessions, cultivating self

Figure 19.1   iPad art.

expression, improving self esteem, and enhancing social and emotional coping skills, while simultaneously fostering the development of practical computer competencies that transfer to many career and education paths. Those who participate in the TAP believe that, in order to effect change in the lives of youth, we must first build the emotional coping skills, especially impulse control, necessary to ensure that they make good choices. Second, we must improve their interpersonal skills by promoting collaboration, healthy self-esteem, and self-governance, enabling the autonomy needed to fulfill adult roles and responsibilities. Third, by capitalizing on the emotional and social growth of our initial steps, we are able to create an environment whereby youth are able to effectively learn and make use of practical technical skills (in our case, digital art technology).

These multiple returns begin with our core program, *3D Computer Animation Therapy Group*. In these hands-on, direct service groups, youth work as a team to produce an original, computer-animated video. Co-led by a computer animator and an art therapist, these sessions allow youth to practice self-governance and learn social skills through making creative decisions as a group. Simultaneously, they learn professional-level computer animation skills (such as Autodesk 3ds Max) and use them as an expressive means of revealing and managing their aspirations and frustrations (Austin, 2012; personal communication).

Mosinski on database development

In 2009, when I was hired as an art therapist at Gay Men's Health Crisis (GMHC), a nonprofit agency in New York, I noticed racks of artwork made during art therapy sessions with several art therapists, some of whom no longer worked at GMHC. The artwork accumulated over time and was relegated to the top of file cabinets located in a secured "staff only" area of the Mental Health Program. It was apparent that a

Figure 19.2 TAP.

system for returning artwork to clients or for cataloging the artwork had not been developed. Consequently, the artwork was not available or useful to anyone, except maybe the art therapist who put the art there in the first place, or the curious clinician who might take a look at a drawing or painting that was partially visible through the wire racks. The art therapy team created a database on a stand-alone hard drive of all the artwork created in sessions. The database was designed so that it could easily be searched, and each piece was clearly identified in several key areas: artwork, client code, therapist, and date of the session (Mosinski, 2012; personal communication).

The contents of this hard drive were moved to a designated drive housed within the Information Systems department of GMHC. The art therapy database is accessible using any computer if the user has permission to access the drive at GMHC. The images are now accessible to the entire team of clinicians, no matter where in the building they are located. Non-art-therapy clinicians have been using client imagery, electronic communications, Facebook, etc., as part of the therapy sessions. With prior approval, those electronic media can be downloaded and catalogued as part of the therapeutic session.

Making Decisions

As illustrated through these examples, there are many options that art therapists can choose and a multitude of decisions they must make. If an art therapist should choose to use traditional paints with a client, they should consider the different qualities that different types of paint (watercolor, acrylic, oil, finger paint, etc.) inherently possess. They also have to decide what tools to use for transferring and manipulating the paint (fingers, broad brushes, thin brushes, sponges, palette knife, etc.). All of these choices fall under the category of "painting" with art therapy clients, because of similar fluid qualities in all paints, but each type of paint, each type of tool, can change the therapeutic quality of art experience.

The same idea applies to digital media. The main thing that all digital media have in common is that they are binary-based, which makes them extremely flexible. The underlying binary structure of digital media always remains the same; what changes over time are the programs and the hardware. Despite the similar qualities among all digital media due to this binary foundation, each type of digital media (drawings, photos, film, animation, collage, etc.) and tool (computer, mouse, touch screen, stylus, camera, etc.) brings unique variations to each therapeutic experience. The art therapist has to take into account the overall qualities and differences in these tools.

Manipulation of the product is endlessly possible. Digital media is easy to store, share, and use in conjunction with other materials. It can record process as well as product, and multiple outcomes are possible for any project and all outcomes can be saved as separate final products. However, as with any strength, such flexibility is also its main weakness. Digital media can be stolen, shared without permission, is continually evolving, difficult to stay up to date with, and once shared often difficult to permanently erase.

As with any materials, art therapists, when thinking about working with digital media, should have experience working with that media prior to using it with the client. This will help in the decision-making process as to whether or not a particular sub-media of digital media and particular tools will best meet the client's needs and goals. An exception to this rule would be if the goal of the session was to allow the client to teach the therapist about a particular media, or if a shared learning experience would be most beneficial.

Conclusion

When a new media for art therapy is discovered or created, art therapists should not reject it because it is unknown to them. Rather, they should systematically explore them to see how such new tools can best benefit clients. Art therapists are currently exploring the possibility of using digital media in practice. Art therapists are adopting and exploring these new tools in parallel with the general public, but are a step behind in making sure they understand its qualities and how it can help clients in a safe and confidential manner.

References

Alders, A., Beck, L., Allen, P., & Mosinski, B. (2011). Technology in art therapy: Ethical challenges. *Art Therapy: Journal of the American Art Therapy Association, 28*(4), 165–170.

American Art Therapy Association (AATA). (2011). *Ethical principles for art therapists.* Retrieved from http://www.americanarttherapyassociation.org/upload/ethicalprinciples.pdf

Arnott, B., & Gushin, J. (1976). Film making as a therapeutic tool. *American Journal of Art Therapy, 16*(1), 29–33.

Art Therapy Credentials Board (ATCB). (2011). *Code of professional practice.* http://atcb. org/export/sites/atcb/resources/author_files/2011-ATCB-Code-of-Professional-Practice.pdf

Barbee, M. (2002). A visual-narrative approach to understanding transsexual identity. *Art Therapy: Journal of the American Art Therapy Association, 19*(2), 53–61.

Belkofer, C., & McNutt, J. (2011). Understanding social media culture and its ethical challenges for art therapists. *Art Therapy: Journal of the American Art Therapy Association, 28*(4), pp. 159–164.

Canter, D. S. (1987). The therapeutic effects of combining Apple Macintosh computers and creativity software in art therapy sessions. *American Journal of Art Therapy, 4*(1), 17–26.

Fox, C., & Wortman, C. B. (1975). A therapeutic use of film with university students. *American Journal of Art Therapy, 15*(1), 19–21.

Fryrear, J. L., & Stephens, B. C. (1988). Group psychotherapy using masks and video to facilitate intrapersonal communication. *The Arts in Psychotherapy, 15*(3), 227–234.

Hartwich, P., & Brandecker, R. (1997). Computer-based art therapy with inpatients: Acute and chronic schizophrenics and borderline cases. *The Arts in Psychotherapy, 24*(4), 367–373.

Hogan, P. T. (1981). Phototherapy in the educational setting. *The Arts in Psychotherapy, 8*(3/4), 193–199.

Horovitz, E. G. (1999). *A leap of faith: The call to art.* Springfield, IL: Charles C. Thomas.

Jacobs, L. J. (1994). Photography and confidentiality. *Art Therapy: Journal of the American Art Therapy Association, 11*(4), 296–297.

Junge, M. B., & Asawa, P. P. (1994). *A history of art therapy in the United States.* Mundelein, IL: American Art Therapy Association.

Kagin, S. L., & Lusebrink, V. B. (1978). The expressive therapies continuum. *Art Psychotherapy, 5*(4), 171–179.

Kapitan, L. (2011). "But is it ethical?" Articulating an art therapy ethos. *Art Therapy: Journal of the American Art Therapy Association, 28*(4), 150–151.

Kim, S. I., Kang, H. S., & Kim, Y. H. (2009). A computer system for art therapy assessment of elements in structured mandala. *The Arts in Psychotherapy, 36*, 19–28.

Kim, S. I., Yoo, S., Kim, K. E., & Lee, Y. (2007). A framework for expert system knowledge base in art psychotherapy. In A. R. Tyler (Ed.), *Expert systems research trends* (pp. 323–339). Haupauge, NY: Nova Science.

Leonhardt, T. (2012). UNC hospitals using iPads, art to treat children. http://reesenews.org/2012/01/31/unc-hospitals-using-ipads-apps-to-treat-children/30453/?goback=%2Eanb_2172516_*2_*1_*1_*1_*1_*1

Lusebrink, V. B. (1990). *Imagery and visual expression in therapy.* New York, NY: Plenum Press.

Lusebrink, V. B. (1992). A systems oriented approach to the expressive therapies: The expressive therapies continuum. *Arts in Psychotherapy, 18*(5), 395–403.

Maciag, B. (1976). The use of film, photography and art with ghetto adolescents. In A. Robbins & L. B. Sibley (Eds.), *Creative art therapy* (pp. 154–173). New York, NY: Brunner/Mazel.

Martin, R. (1997). Looking and reflecting: Returning the gaze, re-enacting memories and imagining the future through phototherapy. In S. Hogan (Ed.), *Feminist approaches to art therapy* (pp. 150–176). London: Routledge.

Mattson, D. (2011). *Constructing a revised version of the Face Stimulus Assessment to measure formal elements: A pilot study.* Unpublished Doctoral dissertation: Florida State University.

McLeod, C. (1999). Empowering creativity with computer-assisted art therapy: An introduction to available programs and techniques. *Art therapy: Journal of the American Art Therapy Association, 16*(4), 201–205.

McNiff, S., & Cook, C. (1975). Video art therapy. *Art psychotherapy, 2*(1), 55–63.

Milford, S. A., Fryrear, J. L., & Swank, P. (1983). Phototherapy with disadvantaged boys. *The Arts in Psychotherapy, 10*(4), 221–228.

Moon, B. L. (2006). *Ethical issues in art therapy* (2nd ed.). Springfield, IL: Charles C. Thomas.

Muller, C., & Bader, A. (1972). Therapeutic art programs around the world—IX: Film making in a Swiss psychiatric hospital. *American Journal of Art Therapy, 11*(4), 185–189.

Nelson-Gee, E. (1976). Play, art and photography in a therapeutic nursery school. In A. Robbins & L. B. Sibley (Eds.), *Creative art therapy* (pp. 103–127). New York, NY: Brunner/Mazel.

Newhall, B. (1982). *The history of photography: From 1839 to the present* (5th ed.). New York, NY: Museum of Modern Art.

Orr, P. (2005). Technology media: An exploration for "inherent qualities." *The Arts in Psychotherapy, 32*(1), 1–11.

Orr, P. (2011a). Ethics in the age of social media: Electronic means. *Art Therapy Credential Board Review, 18*(3), 4–7.

Orr, P. (2011b). Ethics in the age of social media: Confidentiality. *Art Therapy Credential Board Review, 18*(2), 3–5.

Orr, P. (2011c). Ethics in the age of social media: Multiple relationships. *Art Therapy Credential Board Review, 18*(1), 7–9.

Orr, P. (2012). Technology use in art therapy practice: 2004 and 2011 comparisons. *The Arts in Psychotherapy, 39*(4), 234–238.

Ottiger, P. (2004). Digital Fetish: The meaning of the computer medium in art psychotherapy—A case study. Unpublished Masters Thesis: Goldsmiths College University of London.

Parker-Bell, B. (1999). Embracing a future with computers and art therapy. *Art Therapy: Journal of the American Art Therapy Association, 16*(4), 180–185.

Peterson, B. C. (2010). The media adoption stage model of technology for art therapy, *Art Therapy: Journal of the American Art Therapy Association, 27*(1), 26–31.

Rutherford. (2002). The shadow of the photographer: Using photographic snapshots in our search for meaning and fulfillment. *The Canadian Art Therapy Association Journal, 15*(2), 14–32.

Seiden, D. (2001). *Mind over matter: The uses of materials in art, education and therapy.* Chicago: Magnolia Street.

Thong, S. A. (2007). Redefining the tools of art therapy. *Art Therapy: Journal of the American Art Therapy Association, 24*(2), 52–58.

Waller, D. (1993). *Group interactive art therapy: Its use in training and treatment.* London, Routledge.

Weinberg, D. J. (1985). The potential of rehabilitative computer art therapy for the quadriplegic cerebral vascular accident and brain trauma patient. *American Journal of Art Therapy, 2*(2), 66–72.

Williams, K., Kramer, E., Henley, D., & Gerity, L. (1997). Art, art therapy, and the seductive environment. *American Journal of Art Therapy, 35*(4), 106–117.

Wolf, R. I. (1976). The Polaroid technique: Spontaneous dialogues from the unconscious. *Art Psychotherapy, 3*(3), 197–201.

Wolf, R. I. (2007). Advances in phototherapy training. *The Arts in Psychotherapy, 34*(2), 124–133.

Zwick, D. S. (1978). Photography as a tool toward increased awareness of the aging self. *Art Psychotherapy: An International Journal, 5*(3), 135–141.

Part III

Developmental Spectrum and Therapeutic Considerations

Introduction

There is a common misconception by those outside the field that art therapy is used primarily with children. In this section, the authors demonstrate that art therapy can be used across the entire life span and in various therapeutic configurations. This section begins with Arrington's chapter, *The Developmental Journey*. Through this general overview, Arrington hypothesizes that art therapy is "able to impact the lives of humans at any and all stages of development."

The three chapters after Arrington's overview are examinations of three formats within which art therapy can be practiced: family, couples, and group art therapy. These formats are often used to help individuals with intimacy, social, and communication skills. Incorporating art into family therapy is a natural fit as often the subtle issues troubling a family may be difficult to put into words. Hoshino's chapter, *Getting the Picture: Family Art Therapy*, provides historical and contemporary perspectives on weaving art therapy into the intricate work of family therapy. Ricco addresses marriage and couples' issues by combining art therapy with a well-known marital therapy model in her chapter, *A Treatment Model for Marital Art Therapy: Combining Gottman's Sound Relationship House Theory with Art Therapy Techniques*. In the chapter, she theorizes, "Art therapy as part of couple's counseling helps make complex, sensitive relationship interactions and patterns of behavior visible." Lastly, Rosal investigates art therapy as part of group work in her chapter, *Rethinking and Reframing Group Art Therapy: An Amalgamation of British and US Models*. She includes ideas from both sides of the Atlantic to explore the intricacies of using art in group practice.

Five chapters cover the developmental stages of human life. In *Art Therapy with Children*, Councill presents the benefits of art therapy on children. Based on her extensive experience, she explores the tenets of art therapy with kids in various settings and with varying issues. Linesch tackles therapy work with teens in her chapter, *Art Therapy with Adolescents*. She identifies the main principles of art therapy with this difficult age group and illustrates these goals through thought-provoking case

The Wiley Handbook of Art Therapy, First Edition. Edited by David E. Gussak and Marcia L. Rosal.
© 2016 John Wiley & Sons, Ltd. Published 2016 by John Wiley & Sons, Ltd.

material. In *Adult Art Therapy: Four Decades, 20–60 Years,* Good reviews her expansive experience to identify the main tenets of adult art therapy. Discussions of difficult yet creative clients illuminate her ideas.

The following two chapters address the final years. In *Art Therapy with Older Adults: A Focus on Cognition and Expressivity,* Alders, drawing upon cognitive perspectives and neuroscience, demonstrates how art therapy is useful in serving older adults with cognitive impairments. This section concludes with Barrington's chapter, *Art Therapy and Thanatology: A Unified Approach.* Barrington highlights various philosophical and theoretical perspectives of life in its later stages. She weaves these perspectives into art therapy techniques of working with adults struggling with end-of-life issues.

The nine chapters in this section address only a few ways in which art therapy may be useful throughout a person's lifespan. In these chapters, the authors convey the complexity of the developmental process and how art therapy may be of benefit when developmental roadblocks impede one's evolution.

20

The Developmental Journey
Doris Arrington

From birth onward, people develop through their experiences with varying degrees of energy and information. Developmental theory, an interdisciplinary study, concerns itself with phases of human experience. "Developmental psychology offers a view of how [human] minds grow within families [and environments] across time." (Siegel, 1999, p. 1). This chapter will provide an overview of the human life cycle identified by theorists, and an "insight into how experience shapes and is shaped by mental processes" of memory, emotion, attachment, and self-awareness (p. 2). Patterns of art development are included.

The Life Cycle Journey and Developmental Psychology

Developmental psychology includes a wide variety of disciplines (i.e., procreation, attachment, child and adolescent development, etc.). In normal development, with some cultural variations, the ages associated with developmental stages are consistent across the life cycle journey (see Table 20.1).

Human development

Although conception has many variations, both sperm and egg are still required. The normal human embryo spends the first 9 months in intrauterine life and begins the journey to individuation after often long, painful, and dangerous rhythms that facilitate mother and child's first separation. According to Arrington (2007), the first goal of the infant (ages 0–1) is to "develop trust in his world through a secure attachment with his primary caregiver" (p. 5), usually identified as the mother. Thoughtfulness, care, and consistent interactions allow this unique human "to develop ease in living, eating, sleeping, and eliminating so that he grows in hope of reaching his maximum complexity physically, cognitively, and affectively" (Arrington, 2007, p. 5).

The Wiley Handbook of Art Therapy, First Edition. Edited by David E. Gussak and Marcia L. Rosal.

Table 20.1 Comparison Table of Developmental Theories

Physical Age	Psychosexual (Freud)	Jungian (Jung)	Object Relations (Mahler)	Psychosocial (Erikson)	Cognitive (Piaget)	Artistic (Lowenfeld)
0–1 year	Oral	Childhood	Autistic/symbiosis	Trust/mistrust	Sensory/motor	Random
2–3 years	Anal		Separation Individuation Differentiation Practicing Rapprochement Object and self constancy	Autonomy/shame Initiative/guilt		Scribble Circular and horizontal forms
4–6 years	Phallic			Industry/inferiority Preoperational	Concrete operations	Sun shapes
7–11 years	Latency				Formal operations	Preschematic Schematic Realism
Puberty and adolescent	Genital	Puberty		Identity/role confusion		
Young adult		Before 40		Intimacy/isolation		
Adulthood		Maturity		Generativity/stagnation		
Seniors				Ego Integrity/despair		

Note: Developed by Doris Arrington, published in *Home Is Where the Art Is* (2001); reprint permission by Charles C. Thomas.

Implicit memory

From life's beginning implicit memory, patterns of emotional communication—such as facial expressions, physical and voice tonality, satisfying tastes and smells, or "self-states," as referred to by Siegel (1999, p. 8)—are "mediated [during the first 3 years] predominantly by the right side of the brain" as it processes "nonverbal signals in a holistic, parallel and visual–spatial manner" (Solomon & Siegel, 2003, p. 14). Emotions link the internal and interpersonal worlds of the human mind and serve as a central organizing process within the brain. The left side of the brain develops later and is "about linear processing using linguistics in a logical fashion" (p. 15). Memory, an active set of processes, is combined with past implicit features and the construction of new and future explicit memories shaped by emotion and attachment. Stimulating both sides of the brain activates explicit elements of the prefrontal cortex, autobiographical (early memories of self) and time-oriented information (age or place).

Solomon and Siegel (2003) found that, "a child's attachment to caregivers seems to involve the sharing of a wide range of dependent representational processes from both sides of the brain" (p. 7). Emotions serve as a central organizing process within the brain as they link internal and interpersonal worlds. Explicit elements of early memory are transferred bi-laterally through the corpus collosum to the left side of the brain (Siegel & Hartzell, 2003). By the child's first birthday, implicit learning patterns have been deeply etched into his brain. The child now encodes and "retrieves facts from experiences and semantic memory, in which knowledge of specific events can be recalled even after a long delay" (p. 44).

Human relationships are molded by culture, language, and values, as well as how the local collective views the child's gender, individuality, and development, all of which can be a "matter of life and death" (Neumann, 1973, p. 8). An infant's primary tasks are to develop a healthy body, a strong sense of self, and trust in another person. The infant does this by relying on his or her primary caregiver for food, shelter, nurturance, and affection needs. If the mother does not provide adequate nurturing, the infant's sense of trust does not develop. Knowledge is acquired in Freud's (1949) oral psychosexual stage through repeated and pleasant or unpleasant oral experiences such sucking on toys, fingers, bottles, and the breast. The infant's preference throughout early life is that she and mother are "an omnipotent system, a dual unity within one common boundary" (Mahler et al., 1975, p. 45). Ego construction occurs throughout life but is most crucial during the early years of childhood when the child assumes knowledge of trust and mistrust (Erikson, 1980; Siegel, 1999; Siegel & Hartzell, 2003).

The child's normal life begins in an autistic/symbiotic period when the infant works with his or her physiological rather than psychological processes. His waking life centers on his continuous attempts "to achieve homeostasis through tension-reducing processes of his own such as urinating, defecating, coughing, sneezing, spitting, regurgitating and vomiting" (Mahler et al., 1975, p. 43). According to Arrington (1986), Jung saw this as the origins of intelligence and the beginning of a long mother-dominated childhood.

Developmental Markers and Art throughout the Life Span

Preschool

Once the toddler (ages 2–3) learns to lay, sit, and run comfortably, she has tasted independence and now wills to make it her own. She is constantly separating from her primary caregivers, and exploring ways to manipulate her immediate environment. Freud referred to this as the *anal stage*, noting that it centers on eliminative activities (as cited in Hall, Lindzey, & Campbell, 1997). While "she wills to both learn to know and to hold on," she also wills to let go. That means to "let go of mother, chairs, toys, and bowel movements" (Arrington, 2007, p. 5). Yet, in seeking to maintain attachment with her primary caregiver, she will not go far without seeking the mother's attention. This is the "mine" stage. She longs for independence by feeding herself, playing alone, and making personal choices. Mahler et al. (1975) noted that this object and self-constancy period includes separation/individuation, differentiation, practicing, and rapprochement behaviors. Erikson (1980) referred to this stage as the initiative-versus-guilt stage.

The toddler, through observing family members and peers, learns social behavior or accepted misbehavior. Equally important is the climate of the child's living environment. Lewis, Osofsky, and Moore (1997) indicated that clinical studies of children living in areas with high rates of violence report that simply witnessing or having knowledge of a local violent event can negatively affect a child.

Preschool art   Kramer (1971) noted that, for children, "art is a means of supporting the ego, fostering the development of a sense of identity, and promoting maturation in general" (p. xiii). Through art, we can identify feelings and emotions and communicate them to others. "Art does not have to be verbalized, it is a way of expression that transcends words" (Virshup, Eslinger, & Arrington, 1977, p. 25). Artwork created by children during this trust-and-mistrust period of Erikson is identified by early art educators Lowenfeld (1953), Kellogg (1967), Uhlin (1972), and Drachnik (1995) as random scribbles. These uncontrolled chaotic arches lack hand–eye coordination. The child waves the crayon or pencil back and forth on the paper in a push–pull motion. This is the stage of rhythmic and kinesthetic exploration, the beginning of pattern. In the 2-year-old period, the child, emotionally bound up with the mother, makes circular forms, attempting integration by making clusters of suns and circular shapes. The child begins to draw more in the center of the page, adding vertical and horizontal lines that represent arms and legs on his first human person. He begins naming his scribbles and art projects. As the child reaches 3–3½ years of age, he creates his first figures with circular body heads with stick-like arms and legs.

Preoperational stage

Freud's (1949) developmental period for 4–6-year-olds is the psychosexual phallic stage. Erikson's psychosocial stage is *industry versus inferiority* (1980). Piaget (1951) called this stage *preoperational*. The child plays dress-up, copies and practices adult tasks, takes risks, and recognizes the differences between boys and girls.

For ego development, the child still needs her primary caregiver to recognize her newly acquired abilities. "Mommie, mommie, look at me," she yells from the top of the slide. When 4–6-year-olds interact with their world, they learn about their own power. They ask questions and seek answers about everything that they see, touch, taste, hear, and smell.

Preschematic art   Early art educators note that children of this age, with a growing awareness of the self, begin drawing preschematic compositions with a variety of body images. As a way of distancing from the self, these drawings may include animal forms (Lowenfeld, 1953). Kramer stressed that "play is the prerogative of childhood" (1971, p. 28). In this stage, children begin using colors realistically and make up stories about their drawings (Drachnik, 1995).

Latency age

Freud's next psychosexual stage, latency (ages 7–11), is a time of competitive peer play (1949). Children in Erikson's psychosocial stage acquire a sense of industry and fend off feelings of inferiority (1980). Theorists note that life is a practice of competence. In latency, the child wards off failure at any price by measuring her skills and her self-worth with her friends and society. Piaget (1951) identified this stage as *concrete-operational*, noting that "If the child is unable to meet her own demands or those of significant others, inferiority will reign, making life difficult for her and those close to her in her next stage, youth" (Arrington, 2007, p. 9).

Latency and schematic art   Children use art as a nonverbal language. In latency, the child makes art in recognizable forms and establishes a baseline. Her preschematic drawings of people, trees, animals, and structures progress to more schematic forms. She makes associative color choices and becomes aware of perspective.

Adolescence

Adolescence is the stage from about age 13 to the early 20s. Connected to the genital stage, Freud (1949) believed that changes during adolescence were primarily sexual. Jung identified this stage as *puberty*, where a rapid unfolding process occurs, with clear changes in secondary sex characteristics (Arrington, 1986). By 1950, adolescence as a life stage had come of age. G. Stanley Hall played a major role in the encouragement of adolescent conformity, in the encouragement of school spirit, as well as in the loyalty and hero worship of athletic team members (as cited in Santrock, 2008). The physical growth of adolescents that often adds to their confusion continues today. Adolescents may grow 3–8 inches a year for several years, reacting and adjusting to changes in shape and proportion of hands, feet, and bodies. Erikson (1980), in his psychosocial theory, saw these mental and physical changes as a crisis of identity resulting in role confusion, as youth ask the question "how do I make this transition from being dependent to being independent." One way adolescents discover who they are and become separate, independent people from their parents is through rebellion. Defending against role diffusion, adolescents become cliquish, accepting little deviances in dress, thought, or behavior. Many adolescents find themselves in a moratorium, forestalling their need for identity in a commitment to a person, a belief, or a purpose. Piaget called this period *concrete operations*, noting the qualitative changes in the development of intelligence and abstract thought in adolescents. As a result of brain development, most adolescents move into Piaget's (1951) *formal operations stage*, where they develop the capacity for deductive reasoning. With both physical and moral changes, adolescents find more commonalities with their peers than with their families. From Freud's perspective, the move through the latency stage and into the genital stage activates libidinal energy, which must be appropriately channeled. Identity formed from past experiences helps shape who the adolescent is, but current interests and behaviors redefine him or her (Bee & Boyd, 2005).

Adolescent art   Linesch (1988) found that "for some youngsters that creative expression provides the only vehicle for their social participation" (p. 5). She noted that adolescent artistic productions are often recognizably autobiographical and reach their height during phases of libidinal withdrawal from the object world.

Early adulthood

Until the last half of the twentieth century, adulthood had been an unidentified area on the developmental journey throughout the world. With limited adolescence, in America, women and men often married early, birthed children early, and worked at the same job throughout their adulthood, supporting the family. Today, however, adulthood emerges over years rather than arriving at a specific time. "Finding a life partner is a major milestone of early adult development with profound consequences for self-concept and psychological well-being" (Berk, 2010, p. 372). Conformity to or departure from the social clock of marrying, having babies, and establishing independence can all be a major source of adult personality change. Today, the dominant family form is the dual-earner couple, with the woman experiencing moderate-to-high levels of stress in trying to succeed in both work and family worlds. Finding full-time work and attaining economic independence are often difficult for the young adult.

Berk (2010), writing on "middle adulthood," noted that it "is a productive time of life where people attain their highest accomplishments and satisfactions" (p. 406). Often, middle adults succeed at work, but at the expense of their physical health. Today, careers and full-time work in mid-life may leave little time for proper body and leisure care.

Adult art   In 1971, Kramer noted that art superseded play as one of the few areas of symbolic living that remain accessible to adults, but today it is much broader than that. Play still exists for adults as they participate in or view the arts, sports, travel, and volunteer experiences.

Late adulthood

What does it mean to be an older person in the United States? Compared to young adult or middle-aged adult people, the elderly—with more wrinkles, body part replacements, and pain medicines—are as diverse a group as the younger people.

Today, the *baby boomers* (those born between 1946 and 1964) are swelling the ranks of seniors. The wealthy or affluent seniors can live wherever they want. They pay for their own retirement, leisure, and health care. Middle-class seniors are healthier and better educated than previous cohort groups. They generally have retirement income in social security or pensions and think of themselves as middle aged. Seniors in the lower social economic status (SES), however, find themselves more vulnerable in income, living conditions, and health care. In all classes, there is an increasing focus on inner processes.

A recent decade-long study of 18–91-year-olds found that the subjects became happier with more stable emotions as they aged (Carstensen, 2011). In helping mid-life adults plan for a long and bright future, Carstensen proposed a framework that included four basic principles: envision, design, diversify, and invest. She recommended that adults daydream about ways to enjoy the years that lie ahead and diversify their expertise because they may try more than one career or fulfill many volunteer or civic roles. She theorized that the key for the mid-life adult is to design social and physical environments to reinforce goals. Finally, Carstensen encouraged individuals and families to invest in ways that can help the children of today look forward to an old age more promising than what is currently expected.

Today, communities and cities throughout America sponsor senior centers providing opportunities for building meaningful relationships. Thus, many seniors have a confidant spouse, child, or friend with whom they share their daily concerns. If they are fortunate enough to have met most of Erikson's (1980) developmental goals in each psychosocial stage of life (trust, autonomy, initiative, industry, identity, intimacy, and generativity), seniors will move into this final stage with wisdom and ego integrity, having lived uniquely and yet interrelated with others. If they have not been able to integrate life's developmental goals, life's ending may be one of loss, sadness, and despair.

Death

As mentioned at the beginning of this chapter, life is filled with experiences, energies, and both pleasant and unpleasant emotions. It is also filled with death. Death is a natural part of life: death of experiences, of relationships, and finally, the end of life itself. Mourning is the coming to terms with the reality of death and loss not as essential changes in the self.

> The psychological mourning process involves the review of and many other aspects of the lost relationship in order that the bonds binding the bereaved to the dead partner may gradually be relinquished, freeing the emotional investment for ongoing life and further relationships ... the process is inevitable painful, yet must progress. (Raphael, 1994, p. 187)

"In industrialized countries, opportunities to witness the physical aspects of death are less available today than in previous generations. Most people in the developed world die in hospitals, where doctors and nurses, not loved ones, attend their last moments" (Berk, 2010, p. 503). Grief and loss are experienced differently in each case.

The Impact of Violence on Development

Today, between birth and death, far too many people experience violence in their developmental path. People may experience violence in the home or the neighborhood or as a spontaneous interruption in their journey. Violence is unhealthy. It erodes a person's "sense of personal safety and security" (Lewis et al., 1997). According to Lewis et al., violence depersonalizes the people involved in it or witnessing it, while at the same time it "diminishes their future orientation" (p. 279).

According to the developmental journey, the lifespan perspective is influenced by multiple forces: biological, historical, social, and cultural. As art therapists, we work with people throughout this developmental pathway. As professional clinicians, we must question how to assist others in their struggles along life's journey.

Conclusion

For many reasons, from infants to seniors, humans age at different rates, and therefore chronological age is an imperfect indicator of functional age. Carstensen (2011) saw the new *old age* as 60–91 years of age. Added years of longevity and health plus financial stability have granted an active, opportunistic time of life for many contemporary seniors. Today, men and women, regardless of culture, care for their families, their communities, and give back to all parts of the world. Regardless of their sexual preferences or identity, as people age, it is evident that the family cycle remains important. Individuals are affected by both implicit and explicit memories of the values, culture, and environment experienced in their early childhood. Divorce, addictions, poor physical or mental health, poor economy, and even military service affect the family, the couple, and the child–parent relationships. Single-parenting and step-parenting lifestyles are prominent. But, they are also difficult and, in many cases, economically debilitating, affecting family and individual lifestyles and possibilities.

Art therapists are able to impact the lives of humans at any and all stages of development. Each stage offers its own set of challenges for the art therapist. With a finely tuned understanding of human development, art therapists can develop caring and thoughtful treatment strategies for each period of life.

Author's Note

While writing this chapter, I had to take my body into the body shop for general repair; an experience not available to my parents. It began in the fall with a complete knee replacement of the left leg that I had broken years earlier. Replacement surgery threw my heart out of rhythm, derailing my daily walks. Three months of swimming rehab and recovery found my right shoulder, broken on a ski slope years earlier, also needing replacement. I never thought my senior disability would be my right arm, my art arm, my typing arm, my dressing and make up arm, but it is. With my replacements, I am doing well. My forever partner is speeding down the highway of retirement connecting needy communities with available funds and willing volunteers. We are fortunate. Daily, we get to envision, design, diversify, and invest in the life that lies before us. We have lived through hard work, illness, and the death of friends, family, and a precious grandson. We have experienced both joy and sadness, but what I miss most in my senior years is that exciting energy that allowed me to dance all evening with loved ones and friends.

References

Arrington, D. (1986). A Jungian-based study of selected visual constructs preferred by women. *Doctoral dissertation, University of San Francisco. University Microfilm International.* Ann Arbor, MI. No. 87-13, 271.

Arrington, D. (2001). *Home is where the art is: An art therapy approach to family therapy.* Springfield, IL: Charles C. Thomas.

Arrington, D. (2007). *Art, angst, and trauma: Right brain interventions with developmental issues.* Springfield, IL: Charles C. Thomas.

Bee, H., & Boyd, D. (2005). *Lifespan development* (4th ed.). Boston, MA: Allyn & Bacon.

Berk, L. (2010). *Exploring lifespan development* (2nd ed.). Boston, MA: Allyn & Bacon.

Carstensen, L. (2011). *A long bright future.* New York, NY: Public Affairs.

Drachnik, C. (1995). *Interpreting metaphors in children's drawings.* Burlingame, CA: Abbeygate Press.

Erikson, E. (1980). *Childhood and society* (2nd ed.). New York, NY: W. W. Norton.

Freud, S. (1949). *An outline of psycho-analysis* (Rev. ed.). New York, NY: W. W. Norton.

Hall, C., Lindzey, G., & Campbell, J. (1997). *Theories of personality* (4th ed.). New York, NY: John Wiley.

Kellogg, R. (1967). *The psychology of children's art.* New York, NY: Random House.

Kramer, E. (1971). *Art as therapy with children.* New York, NY: Schocken Books.

Lewis, M., Osofsky, J., & Moore, M. S. (1997). Violent cities, violent streets. Children draw their neighborhoods. In J. Ofosky (Ed.), *Children in a violent society* (pp. 277–299). New York, NY: The Guilford Press.

Linesch, D. (1988). *Adolescent art therapy.* New York, NY: Brunner/Mazel.

Lowenfeld, V. (1953). *Creative and mental growth.* New York, NY: MacMillan.

Mahler, M., Pine, F., & Bergman, A. (1975). *The psychological birth of the human infant: Symbiosis and individuation.* New York, NY: Basic Books.

Neumann, E. (1973). *The child.* New York, NY: Harper Colophon Books.

Piaget, J. (1951). *Play, dreams, and imitation in childhood* (Trans. C. Gattegno & F. Hodgso). New York, NY: W. W. Norton.

Raphael, B. (1994). *The anatomy of bereavement.* Lanham, MD: Jason Aranson, Inc.

Santrock, J. (2008). *Adolescence* (12th ed.). New York, NY: McGraw-Hill.

Siegel, D. (1999). *The developing mind: Toward a neurobiology of interpersonal experience.* New York, NY: Guilford Press.

Siegel, D., & Hartzell, M. (2003). *Parenting from the inside out; How a deeper self-understanding can help you raise children who thrive.* New York, NY: Jeremy P. Tarcher.

Solomon, M., & Siegel, D. (2003). *Healing trauma: attachment, mind, body and brain.* New York, NY: W.W. Norton.

Uhlin, D. (1972). *Art for exceptional children* (2nd ed.). Dubuque, IA: Wm. C. Brown.

Virshup, E., Eslinger, S., & Arrington, D. (1977). *In touch through art.* Fresno CA: Fresno Art Center.

21

Getting the Picture:
Family Art Therapy

Janice Hoshino

"It's unbelievable how much you don't know about the game you've been playing all your life." (Mickey Mantle)

This chapter provides an overview of the family and art therapy theory, integrating a systemic art therapy framework. A case vignette involving a family with adopted children is presented through an intergenerational view—particularly the Bowen family systems theory lens.

"Family therapy and art therapy encompass a number of interesting parallels. Both professions emerged through the work of passionate, committed professionals who simultaneously but independently began to explore unchartered territories..." (Hoshino, 2003, p. 25). Nichols (2010) discussed the evolution of family therapists: "While they were struggling for legitimacy, family clinicians emphasized their common beliefs and downplayed their differences" (p. 36). Interestingly, this counters the evolution of art therapists, who often seemed to emphasize their differences and downplay their common beliefs. The common thread was that both art therapy and family therapy were perceived as non-traditional and alternative approaches that were not readily embraced by the larger circle of mental health professionals.

Nichols (2010) delineated classic schools of family therapy including Bowen family systems theory; strategic, structural, experiential, psychoanalytic, cognitive behavioral, solution-focused, narrative family therapy; and, more recently, integrative models. Family art therapists are frequently integrative, but favor a particular approach.

It has been said that those who are ignorant of history are doomed to repeat it—perhaps this is most true for family systems. My former professor James Framo often reminded our class that we were not just working with the current family, but rather with also the ghosts from generations past who were remarkably present in the session as well. As such, my training and approach in working with families stems from an intergenerational lens, wherein existing symptomology and presenting issues exist, in part, from influences, belief systems, patterns, and the equilibrium of any particular family system. The challenge in working from this systemic lens is that it often counters why the family sought therapy, which is often relief from the issues that bring the family into therapy, most commonly through a symptomatic family member.

While some may argue that symptom reduction or alleviation provides a reprieve, the family art therapist is attuned that the symptom is often an indicator of larger systemic issues. Consider a family who brings a defiant child, wanting help to "fix this child." While beneficial to develop appropriate behaviors, the larger systemic issue often includes marital tension, conflict, and/or parenting styles. Therefore, the presenting problem (the defiant child) is not necessarily the overarching issue (marital discord); the family art therapist helps shift this perception by providing new alternatives.

Art therapy provides families with an effective and unique treatment option offering a distinctive, balanced process. Since art transcends language, it spans the cultural, language, and age barriers that influence family power and balance. Engaging the family through art levels the playing field, providing a new venue for each family member to communicate equally. Language provides an unbalanced power differential, especially in families with younger children, from diverse cultures that may not value language, and with English as a second language (ESL).

Next, families find that art therapy navigates through what can be coined as "verbal stuck-ness." A system is an organized assemblage of components that form a complex whole that is greater than the sum of its parts. Likewise, a family is more than an assortment of individuals; it is a network of interactions and relationships. Families learn to regulate interactions among its members and their behavior to ensure its constancy results, with some families becoming stuck in repetitive loops of unproductive behavior in the process (Nichols, 2010).

Family Art Therapy Pioneers

Hanna Yaxa Kwiatkowska is considered to be the pioneer of family art therapy. In the 1960s, she began using art therapy with families at the National Institute of Mental Health.

> The richness, freshness and variety of pictorial and behavioral material obtained from accidental participation of family members in patient's individual art sessions led me to recognize how much we could gain from a mode of communication with the family that was not exclusively verbal. (Kwiatkowska, 1978, p. 3)

Consequently, she developed a sequence of six art directives, the family art evaluation, that expanded the boundaries of diagnostic and therapeutic perception from the individual patient to the larger family system (Kwiatkowska, 1978).

While much of the family art therapy research and publications have been focusing on image analysis and indicators within the art, family art therapist Maxine Junge has been working and writing about art therapy with families for decades. In *Mourning, Memory and Life Itself* (2008), Junge dedicated several chapters to utilizing art therapy with grieving families. Junge characterized the nature of systems thinking with an artist as:

> A painting is a system in which all parts must work together to make a whole. To change one thing is to change the whole. For example, to change a bit of color is to change the whole painting and the rest must be adjusted to fit the change. (cited in Kaplan, 2006, p. 41)

Notably, other prominent art therapists developed couple and family art therapy assessments. July Rubin developed four directives with families who had a child or adolescent in treatment. These included a scribble drawing, family portrait (which could be realistic or abstract), family murals, and a free drawing. Rubin noted that, "Engaging in creative tasks—especially those that require family members to work together and those which invite them to represent the family—provides a storehouse of information in a natural kind of atmosphere" (Hoshino, 2003, p. 24).

Harriet Wadeson worked with many well-known clinicians at the National Institute of Health, which led to the development of an assessment for couples who were hospitalized when one spouse was diagnosed with manic depression. Her directives were: joint picture without talking, an abstract of the marital relationship, and a self-portrait given to spouse. These directives extended beyond her work at NIH, as she used them in private practice. A more detailed description of her work with couples can be found in her numerous publications and in *Family Art Therapy* (Kerr, Hoshino, Sutherland, Parashak, & McCarley, 2008, pp. 45–48).

Helen Landgarten began her work in family art therapy while the art therapy field was developing. Landgarten's colleagues found her approach to be "amazingly successful ... in the initial session as the entire family drew pictures together, the family system and the roles each member played was immediately revealed." (Hoshino, 2003, p. 48). Her directives were: the nonverbal team art task; the nonverbal family art task; and the verbal family art task.

Family art therapist Shirley Riley considered herself integrative by weaving constructs from structural, strategic, social constructivist, family of origin, and post-modern approaches. Riley did not develop specific assessments for couples and families, but noted the need for a "philosophy that allowed the clients to model their own treatment, illustrate their own invented truth and find, with the support of the art therapist, a more acceptable reality to embrace their lives" (Riley & Malchiodi, 2003, p. 36).

Doris Arrington (2001) developed a directive of family landscapes that provided family members a venue to explore boundary issues and compassion between family members. Clients are asked to draw a symbolic landscape between the ages 3 and 12 years, place a legend that identifies family members, consider significant changes during this time, and create alternative landscapes to depict various emotional climates.

Current Trends in Family Art Therapy

A 6-year review of family art therapy literature illustrates an interesting shift; approximately half of the articles are from outside the United States, including Korea, Australia, Israel, Iran, Columbia, and Brazil. Almost two-thirds of the articles were clinically based, including art therapy techniques with specific populations (Kim, Kirchoff, & Whitsett, 2011; Kohut, 2011; Pifalo, 2009; Saneei & Haghayegh, 2011; Shafer, 2008; Snir & Hazut, 2012; Sutherland, 2011), while others were research-based (Goldner & Scharf, 2011; Holt & Kaiser, 2001; Im et al., 2010; Leon, Wallace, & Rudy, 2007).

Systemic framework

Art therapists find their creative and clinical cadence in conjunction with their philosophical lens, clinical training, and their particular practice and population. While many rely heavily on working from an intuitive lens, it is important to couple intuition with conceptualization. Jungian therapist Ann Blake suggested that the consequence of practicing without the foundation of theory, such as working only from intuition, might create ungrounded therapeutic conceptualization and interventions, and cautioned that a one-sided stance can be a liability (A. B. Blake, personal communication, June 20, 2012). While a systemic lens is expansive and perhaps daunting to the innumerable schools of thought, I would like to offer some overarching and relevant guidelines that influence my work with families.

Multigenerational patterns   Michael Kerr (1981) noted that it is generally difficult for families to recognize that one generation's problems are related to the previous generation. This occurs with many families from diverse backgrounds. Consider the following example.

Juliana was the twelfth of 13 children, one of many siblings who spanned 20 years. One of the most pivotal moments of Juliana's life occurred when she had just turned 14. It was the last night she would get to see and connect with her mother, age 48, who was dying of heart failure. Aware that this was a chapter quickly closing in her life, Juliana found herself in a quandary. She desperately wanted to tell her mother she loved her … but this was simply never done in her family of origin. Her mother never told any of the children she loved them. As she watched her mother dying, she pondered. Should she break tradition and protocol and tell her mother she loved her and will truly miss her? Or should she not take the risk and maintain the acceptable status quo. Her mother died that night, and Juliana never did tell her mother she loved her. But a watershed moment transpired as Juliana vowed that, should she ever have children, they would know they were loved, and she would never hesitate to say, "I love you." At just 14 years of age, Juliana had successfully broken a multigenerational family pattern.

McGoldrick (2011) wrote, "to make sense of what we experience in the present—to understand our symptoms, cutoffs, and even the multiple characterizations of different family members—we must understand our family's history" (p. 34). Some of the challenges families face when examining multigenerational patterns include: awareness of, but resistance to, changing the familiar patterns, regardless of the impact to the family system; loyalty to the parental system; and family legacies, traditions, and rituals.

Current family patterns   One of the most compelling components of working with families is to examine how their current family structure and subsequent patterns correlate with their family of origin. While some theorists purport that individuals may seek out in a partner what they lack in themselves (i.e., an introvert may seek out an extrovert), it is equally compelling to consider the degree to which individuals may blindly and unknowingly recreate what is familiar from their family of origin. Some patterns are obvious, if not simplistic; however, more often, the complexity of the system and emergent patterns may reveal themselves from working with families over time. Patterns and themes may include family secrets, triangulation, cut-off, family roles, loyalties, traditions, rituals, and myths to cite a few; these patterns are often found across generations, but are not obvious to the family system. Awareness into the current patterns that have been absorbed across generations enlightens and informs families, thereby enabling them to more freely choose a new family blueprint.

Genograms When working with families, it is beneficial to do a three-generation family genogram in an effort to understand the history and legacy of the family. McGoldrick (2011) stated, "genograms map out the basic biological and legal structure of the family … [they] remind us about what parts of the family we know already but also alert us to what we don't yet know" (p. 33). In addition to creating a genogram with the family, engaging families in art-making to create their family trees is beneficial. By providing a variety of materials and an unstructured approach, families often reflect on how they define family; it also opens up a space for storytelling, memories, and dialogue.

Creating genograms with families is best done collaboratively and with transparency. Using a large sheet of paper set on an easel allows all members to witness and recognize patterns within their own family of origin, and their partner's family of origin. Despite how long a person has been in a committed relationship, genogram work inevitably helps families develop and expand their understanding of how patterns emerge and continue from generations past. The inclusion of relationship lines helps provide a visual template of cross-generational understanding.

Case Study

Families seek therapy for a plethora of reasons. Some arrive in crisis, seeking therapy after a particular event occurs with one or more family members. Others, while not in crisis, have awareness that part of the system is not fully functioning. Other families may seek therapy to validate their stance on the presenting issue, hoping to elicit change through the therapist's interpretation of the situation. While therapists historically have been trained to look at symptomology and diagnoses, family therapists were forerunners in adopting a strength-based resiliency framework. This departure from a diagnosis-based framework allows families to not only recognize their growing edges and challenges, but also provides a structure to examine the family system from the ability to work through and endure hardship, and recognize the assets and contributions of both individuals and the family system. This more positive and useful approach empowers and enlightens family systems.

The Reynolds family was referred for family art therapy for challenges they were experiencing with their middle child. The family consisted of: the father Dan, 60 years old, who was in management; the mother Ashley, 50 years old, who also worked in management; biological daughter Nicole, age 16; adopted son Ricky, age 15, who was adopted at age 1 year from Lithuania; and adopted daughter Chrissy, age 13, adopted from Korea at age 10 months (see Figure 21.1).

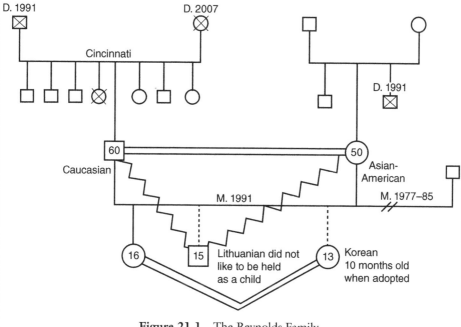

Figure 21.1   The Reynolds Family.

Figure 21.2   Touring the Country.

The family was asked to create a kinetic family portrait. Interestingly, all family members drew the family as a unit doing some activity together that they reported was realistic. Mom's drawing depicted a cross-country trip with the entire family (see Figure 21.2). She reported that, in an effort to keep calm with the family system, each person was given a roll of nickels daily, from which they had to give up some nickels if they were mouthy and talked back. Dad drew the family at the dinner table, which was a common event (see Figure 21.3). Dad noted that the family was generally "nice to each other 70% of the time, with tension at the table the other 30% of the time," due to one of the children, particularly Ricky, being mouthy. Ricky's drawing depicted the family together every Friday night, when they went out to dinner. Ricky liked this weekly family outing since the children got to decide alternatively, where to go to dinner.

AT

DINNER 10/8/07

Figure 21.3 At Dinner.

The family interacted in a manner that illustrated both their strengths and resiliency as a system. Everyone participated in both discussion and art-making, and seemed genuinely interested in what the others had to say or what they created. Furthermore, they were respectful of each other during the discussion; unlike families who present with high chaos or drama, this family listened to each other, and offered opinions, even if they differed from the other. The family also agreed upon the challenges they were having; they cited communication challenges, particularly with Ricky, fighting among the children, pushback around chores, and not showing respect. Overall, they felt they had strong support systems through their family, their church, and that, despite the challenges, they spent time together as a family. Their reflection seemed honest, and frankly not dissimilar to many typical and relatively healthy family systems.

The issue that brought them into family art therapy centered around Ricky's increasing and significant anger and hostility, which seemed to have escalated within the prior 2 months. Both parents agreed that things had both deteriorated and intensified, and his increasing lack of respect, particular with Mom, ended up with sometimes all parties saying things that were harmful. Subsequent sessions with the parents alone revealed some thought-provoking information on the early lives of the two adopted children, Ricky and Chrissy. Both had been adopted at roughly the same age. However, Ricky never liked to be held or cuddled as a baby, and was often stiff and resistant to snuggling. To the contrary, Chrissy, although adopted at the same age, liked affection, cuddling, and attention. The parents noted that the orphanage they adopted Ricky from had a system where the children were kept clean and fed, but were not cuddled or nurtured and were basically left to their own accord.

Subsequent sessions indicated that Ricky's early environment may have contributed to current behaviors. Zilberstein (2006) noted that children with secure attachments have awareness that their caregivers are available to them emotionally and physically, which fosters safe exploration and learning. Those that do not have emotionally available or intermittently available caregivers may result in insecure attachment, which has the subtypes "anxious-avoidant," "anxious-resistant," and "disorganized."

Traditionally, individuals have been classified by their attachment styles into categories of "secure," "anxious avoidant," "anxious resistant," and "disorganized." Securely attached individuals are "more equipped to regulate negative emotions." Individuals showing signs of being "anxious avoidant" are noted as traditionally being "more aggressive than securely attached (individuals)" (Termini, Golden, Lyndon, & Sheaffer, 2009), particularly as seen in males. When separated from their parents, children with this attachment style traditionally do not "acknowledge" the separation. Individuals with a history of being "anxious resistant" respond to separation through "passive-withdrawn behaviors" and are traditionally viewed as children who are "difficult to console, displaying anger and crying during reunion scenarios (with caretakers)." The "disorganized" attachment style has been noted as most detrimental, with individuals, "exhibiting contradictory behaviors, attempting to interact with the caregiver, but failing to approach the caregiver out of fear" (Termini et al., 2009).

Working with families entails examining multigenerational patterns, including attachment issues across generations. With this family, potential early attachment issues with the adopted children became evident. As sessions progressed, it also became transparent that the father Dan was determined to not recreate what he experienced in his family of origin, particularly around his own attachment challenges. Recalling the pain, rejection, and criticism he experienced in his family of origin, most often with his mother, brought him to tears. Dan described himself as a "good kid, people pleaser" who felt invisible; he had ample freedom, no limits, no container, and "no one that held me tight." He questioned if his mother's behavior, particularly the lack of emotional connection, could have resulted from her unresolved grief from the loss of a 9-month-old baby girl who had died prior to Dan's birth.

He titled his geometric family of origin portrait "fairly dysfunctional," describing his dad as a soft, gentle, kind yellow sun, and his mom as a red square, as an intense disciplinarian, with sharp edges and definitive ideas (see Figure 21.4). While the drawing appears somewhat simplistic, the process allowed Dan to process the experiences of his and his siblings childhood to their current relationships. Ashley felt she learned a few things from this drawing that she was previously unaware of. The art provided a venue to look at his-story, as Takaki (personal communication, 2002–lecture at University of Washington) would say.

Dan openly wept during painful moments, such as that described previously, and Ashley would throw her arms around him and gently hold him, soothing him but allowing the process to unfold. His pain was palpable, and his commitment to not recreate his family of origin was a theme that was tangible in the therapy room. It was very tender to witness their love, pain, and grief on the past, their ambiguity of how to manage the present, and their struggles on how to move forward in a meaningful way.

Figure 21.4 Fairly Dysfunctional.

Figure 21.5 Dan's Family Drawing—a Resilient Family.

One of the last drawings completed by Dan was a family drawing. The family has shifted from being in close proximity, to being in the same proximity, but more independent (see Figure 21.5). New challenges emerged, which seemed connected to the behaviors related to the attachment challenges, but the family remained committed toward addressing the challenges and moving forward.

Despite the challenges (i.e., early attachment issues) that this family faced, they were resilient; their numerous strengths bonded and held them together as a family.

Conclusion

As family art therapists, entering into a family system is similar to starting to read a book from the middle. We investigate the previous chapters of the family's lives to make sense of the current chapter, while keeping in mind the theoretical and historical blueprints that we work from as art therapists. Our challenge is that we may never know how the book ends, and how future chapters will be written as we terminate therapy.

"The journey of family therapy begins with a blind date and ends with an empty nest." (Carl Whitaker, 1988, p. 28)

References

Arrington, D. B. (2001). *Home is where the art is.* Springfield, IL: Charles C. Thomas.

Goldner, L., & Scharf, M. (2011). Children's family drawings: A study of attachment, personality, and adjustment. *Art Therapy: Journal of the American Art Therapy Association, 28*(1), 11–18.

Holt, E. S., & Kaiser, D. H. (2001). Indicators of familial alcoholism in children's kinetic family drawings. *Art Therapy: Journal of the American Art Therapy Association, 18*(2), 89–95.

Hoshino, J. (2003). Multicultural issues in family art therapy. In C. Malchiodi (Ed.), *The clinical handbook of art therapy.* New York, NY: Guilford Press.

Im, Y. H., Oh, S. G., Chung, M. J., Yu, J. H., Lee, H. S., Chang, J. K., & Park, D. H. (2010). A KFD web database system with an object-based image retrieval for family art therapy assessments. *The Arts in Psychotherapy, 37*, 163–171.

Junge, M. B. (2008). *Mourning, memory and life itself.* Springfield, IL: Charles C. Thomas.

Kaplan, F. (Ed.). (2006). *Art therapy and social action.* London: Jessica Kingsley Publishers.

Kerr, M. (1981). Family systems theory and therapy. In A.S. Gurman & D.P. Knishern (eds.), *Handbook of Family Therapy* (pp. 226–265). New York NY: Brunner/Mazel.

Kerr, C., Hoshino, J., Sutherland, J., Parashak, S. T., & McCarley, L. L. (2008). *Family art therapy: Foundations of theory and practice.* New York, NY: Routledge.

Kim, J. B., Kirchoff, M., & Whitsett, S. (2011). Expressive arts group therapy with middle-school aged children from military families. *The Arts in Psychotherapy, 38*, 356–362.

Kohut, M. (2011). Making art from memories: Honoring deceased loved ones through a scrapbooking bereavement group. *Art Therapy: Journal of the American Art Therapy Association, 29*(3), 123–131.

Kwiatkowska, H. Y. (1978). *Family therapy and evaluation through art.* Springfield, IL: Charles C. Thomas.

Leon, K., Wallace, T., & Rudy, D. (2007). Representations of parent–child alliances in children's family drawings. *Social Development, 16*(3), 440–459.

McGoldrick, M. (2011). *The genogram journey.* New York, NY: W. W. Norton & Co.

Nichols, M. P. (2010). *Family therapy: Concepts and methods.* Boston, M.A.: Allyn & Bacon.

Pifalo, T. (2009). Mapping the maze: An art therapy intervention following disclosure of sexual abuse. *Art Therapy: Journal of the American Art Therapy Association, 26*(1), 12–18.

Riley, S., & Malchiodi, C. A. (2003). Solution-focused and narrative approaches. In C. A. Malchiodi (Ed.), *Handbook of art therapy.* New York, NY: Guilford Press.

Saneei, A., & Haghayegh, S. A. (2011). Family drawings of Iranian children with autism and their family members. *The Arts in Psychotherapy, 38*, 333–339.

Shafer, M. (2008). Talking pictures in family therapy. *Australian & New Zealand Journal of Family Therapy, 29*(3), 156–168.

Snir, S., & Hazut, T. (2012). Observing the relationship: Couple patterns reflected in joint paintings. *The Arts in Psychotherapy, 39*, 11–18.

Sutherland, J. (2011). Art therapy with families. *The Journal of Individual Psychology, 67*(3), 292–304.

Termini, K., Golden, J. A., Lyndon, A. E., & Sheaffer, B. L. (2009). Reactive attachment disorder and cognitive, affective and behavioral dimensions of moral development. *Behavioral Development Bulletin, 15,* 18–28.

Whitaker, C. (1988). *Dancing with the family: A symbolic experiential approach.* Levittown, PA: Brunner/Mazel.

Zilberstein, K. (2006). Clarifying core characteristics of attachment disorders: A review of current research and theory. *American Journal of Orthopsychiatry, 76*(1), 55–64.

22

A Treatment Model for Marital Art Therapy: Combining Gottman's Sound Relationship House Theory with Art Therapy Techniques

Dina L. Ricco

Dramatic changes have occurred in the past hundred years in our culture that have a profound effect on the nature of marriage and committed relationships. As a result, marriages must sustain a longer life and require a new model or evolution (Miles & Miles, 2000). Marriage is no longer an economic necessity. This changes expectations about romantic love and rituals regarding choosing a marriage partner. Adjustment to these changes as well as the evolution of the more equal roles of marriage partners have lead to approximately 55% of today's marriages ending in divorce, with second marriages at an even higher rate (Gottman, 1999; Miles & Miles, 2000). The literature pertaining to the negative effects of divorce and high marital conflict strongly validates the need for research on effective marital therapy techniques. It is important to examine what has been successful in helping couples, what has failed, and to explore new approaches (Gottman & Notorious, 2002).

This chapter will introduce an approach to working with couples that combines art therapy techniques within the Gottman Sound Relationship House Model (Gottman, 1999). The Sound Relationships House Model was chosen because of the extensive long-term research that validates its effectiveness. The marriage and family therapeutic community initially resisted the model because it challenged the long-standing active listening and prevention model. Instead of active listening, which Gottman (1999, p. 10) compared to "emotional gymnastics," the Gottman Model proposes increased softness and gentleness in the start-up in discussions by the wife, de-escalating, changing of balance of power in favor of the husband's increased acceptance of influence of his wife, and increasing physiological soothing by self and partner (Gottman, Coan, Carrere, & Swanson, 1998).

The Wiley Handbook of Art Therapy, First Edition. Edited by David E. Gussak and Marcia L. Rosal.
© 2016 John Wiley & Sons, Ltd. Published 2016 by John Wiley & Sons, Ltd.

This combined approach was developed first through the research affiliated with this writer's dissertation study, *Evaluating the Use of Art Therapy with Couples in Counseling* (Ricco, 2007), and further refined through 5 years in private practice working with couples and individuals with relationship issues. A brief review of the Gottman Model will be followed by a discussion of the advantages of using art therapy with couples. Finally, a treatment model for marital art therapy will be discussed.

The Gottman Sound Relationship House Model

The Gottman model of marital therapy is based on long-term research, which specifically examines what makes a marriage successful and what behaviors eventually lead to its dissolution. It emphasizes the building of a *Sound Relationship House*, which begins with a foundation of friendship or creating a positive affect in nonconflictual contexts (Gottman, 1999). This marital friendship allows for more *Positive Sentiment Override*, which essentially means that there is enough positive regard between the couple that these feelings *override* or buffer the effects of negativity. Positive sentiment also involves the perceptions that the spouses have of each other during repair attempts. Alternatively, if the opposite, *Negative Sentiment Override*, is present, there is not enough fondness and admiration to buffer negative effects and perceptions, and repair attempts are seen as manipulations and may not be received in the spirit in which they are intended.

Regulating conflict is the next step in building *The Sound Relationship House* (Gottman, 1999), referring to a couple's ability to succeed at repair attempts. It does not necessarily mean the conflict is resolved, but rather that the discussion around the conflict during a repair attempt relies on mutual fondness and admiration, and that the couple "knows how to negotiate the terrain of both resolvable and unresolvable problems" (Gottman, 1999, p. 108). The third step in building *The Sound Relationship House* is creating shared meaning. This involves creating a unique culture and compilation of meaning with its own symbols, metaphors, and narratives while focusing on the degree to which a marriage enables both partners to feel supported in their life dreams.

Gottman (1999) also identified what behaviors/patterns to avoid in a marriage such as a harsh start-up, which may cause problems. When a discussion leads off with criticism and/or sarcasm as a form of contempt, it has begun with a harsh start-up and is doomed to failure. He also discussed what he identified as the *Four Horsemen of the Apocalypse; Criticism, Contempt, Defensiveness, and Stonewalling* (p. 41).

Criticism is common in relationships; however, when it becomes pervasive, it evolves to other more serious problems. Contempt involves continuous criticism; sarcasm, cynicism, name-calling, eye-rolling, sneering, mockery, and hostile humor are all forms of contempt. Defensiveness occurs when a complaint is expressed and the recipient does not take responsibility for the behavior. Defensiveness escalates the conflict; it can eventually lead to stonewalling, which is when a partner becomes so flooded with the conflict that they tune out or ignore their partners' criticism, contempt, and defensiveness.

In a recent study, Madhyastha, Hamaker, and Gottman (2011) explored the extent to which one spouse influences the other during conflict over an observed time period. The results suggested an increase in the positivity of the affect with which each person approaches conflict, and a decrease of each person's *emotional inertia* (extent to which one can regulate his or her own emotions) is what keeps a relationship working. Essentially, this study indicated that spousal influence might not be important as one's ability to soothe oneself during conflict and remain positive.

Therapists using this model help couples move from gridlock to dialogue on perpetual problems. Solvable problems are more easily approached by strengthening the marital friendship and using the Five Fundamental Skills—*softened start-up*, *accepting influence, repair and de-escalation, compromise*, and *physiological soothing* (Gottman, 1999, p. 105).

Advantages of Using Art Therapy Techniques

Therapists working with couples need to access many of the nonverbal communications that can affect dyadic relations (Weeks, 1989). Art as communication provides a device for clients who are unable or unwilling to speak about their issues. The art production is less guarded and is done with less inhibition or guilt arousal than spoken words. A single-session of art therapy will often reveal a number of aspects of a couple's relationship for the first time, despite much previous traditional verbal therapeutic work (Barth & Kinder, 1985).

There are five advantages of using art in couples' counseling sessions (Wadeson, 1980): (1) the immediacy of doing a task together; (2) the genuineness of unexpected material revealed in pictures (which may challenge old assumptions or beliefs that the couple holds onto firmly); (3) the spatial expression of pictures (which can symbolically reveal the couple's life space); (4) the permanence encountered whereby the drawing provides a concrete object to study, react to, use for clarification, and review; and (5) the shared pleasure that picture-making can provide for a couple who have stopped experiencing fun together. Immediacy in art therapy is being engaged in the direct immediate task of making pictures. The couple is able to look at their approach to the task, particularly how they relate to each other when they collaborate on a picture together. This experience of working together is not often seen in conventional verbal therapy. Genuineness may occur because picture-making is a less familiar mode of expression than talking, undercutting over-rehearsed assumptions and patterns of communication (Wadeson, 1973).

Verbal expression is sequential and not necessarily the clearest way to describe complex relationships. Visual expression illuminates many facets of the relationship at the same time and with more clarity. As a tangible record, the picture provides permanence. When something as complex and evanescent as a marital relationship is being explored, studying and reacting to a concrete object that represents many facets of the relationship may be crucial to achieving treatment goals. The pictures also can be used as an important way to review the progression of marital therapy over time. They are impervious to the distortions of memory, providing both the couple and the therapist with a permanent record of change. By reviewing art works, trends in relationship development are easily discerned.

Combing Art therapy Techniques with the Gottman Model

Art therapy techniques from several prominent art therapists in the field were adapted to address the goals for Gottman's Sound Relationship House Theory (see Ricco, 2007). Art directives/interventions were originally to be used in sequence. Based on experience, I found the sequence of art interventions to be less important than introducing an art intervention that was most useful to the couple at any given moment in treatment.

Genogram

The genogram has many clinical benefits, including: organizing data in a graphical way, engaging the couple in sessions, teaching systemic ideas; and clarifying family patterns/characteristics while developing an intellectual understanding of issues (Mauzey & Erdman, 1995). The objectives are to provide an art intervention for couples to identify their history, link their family-of-origin history, and make connections to their current situation/dilemma. The genogram intervention may raise awareness that the two people in the couple have a choice of whether they wish to perpetrate the patterns they observe from previous generations or whether new resolutions to relationship issues can be found. The couple may also decide to identify the new cultural norms through creating shared meanings and honoring life dreams.

The art directive is stated as:

> *Make a family map of three generations; the map may include representations of the emotional climate of your family; be sure to include important connections and separations such as marriages, births, miscarriages, separations, divorces, and deaths.*

The therapist demonstrates how to use circles and squares for male and female and other symbols/colors to represent closeness, distance, conflict, etc. Processing the image might include a discussion of the family history, identification of strengths and weaknesses as well as the traditions/rituals that have been passed down through generations. The therapist asks specific questions regarding the history of the couples' parents' marriages, what it was like, and how it reflects or differs from their own marriage.

Marital Landscape

The Marital Landscape may be used as part of Gottman's Oral History Assessment (Gottman, 1999). The therapist may chose to use this in combination with or instead of the genogram. The objective is to help the two individuals express their history as a couple from the time they met through their decision to marry and through the development of the marriage relationship.

The directive for the Marital Landscape is:

> *Create an emotional landscape of your marriage; it may be abstract, using color, line, and form, or may be representational using manmade or natural structures to symbolically represent how you experience the progression of your relationship.*

Discussions about the art pieces begin by having each person explain their image in front of the other. The therapist guides the process with specific questions such as: How and when did you decide to get married? Were you ever in love? Was it a difficult decision to get married? What memories do you have of your wedding? How did you navigate transitions such as becoming parents? What stands out as really happy times? What stands out as difficult times? How did you get through difficult times? Why did you stay together? What is your philosophy for getting through difficult times? How is the marriage different from when you first got together? The therapist also identifies connections between the images and the stories told by the couple.

Lifeline

The Lifeline is to be used as part of Gottman's Meta-Emotional Interview and is conducted separately with each partner, processed individually, and then later together (Gottman, 1999). It is important to use a lifeline or similar directive as it fosters a discussion of difficult issues from the past that impact the individual's current relationship.

The objectives are to (1) establish rapport with each client as an individual; (2) identify personally significant life events; and (3) provide a catalyst for processing and working through unresolved emotion and conflict. Additionally, the therapist aims to provide an opportunity for the couples to begin to recognize each other's "love maps"—including fears and dreams of the future—and begin the process of building shared meaning.

The directive is:

> *Draw a line that represents your life from birth to present* (Tracz & Gerhart-Brooks, 1999). *Then draw a picture (symbol or image) of your birth and continue by indicating other life events along the line. Each mark along the lifeline is accompanied with the drawing of an event (developmental events such as walking for the first time, important life events such as divorce or death of family members).*

A discussion of each event, and identification of unresolved emotion or conflict contributing to present-day interactions in relationships is conducted. Once both individuals have completed this task, the therapist brings the couple together to discuss each other's lifeline. Having partners explain their lifeline to the other provides a rare view into past events that shaped each individual, provides cathartic release, and promotes empathy.

Have/Need Collage

The Have/Need Collage is used within the Gottman Model to focus on *turning toward* instead of *turning away* and avoiding the *Four Horsemen of the Apocalypse* (Gottman, 1999, p. 105). The objectives are to (1) provide an art intervention that will reveal areas of needs and wants; (2) identify and express these needs through images; and (3) make connections to meanings and dreams.

The directive is:

Make a collage using images and words from magazines to express the things that your spouse provides for you that you need and enjoy; on the other side of the paper, create a collage in the same way, expressing the things that you need more of, but which your spouse is not providing for you. (see Figure 22.1).

The discussion begins with the positive aspects of the relationship, what is enjoyable, and continues with a discussion of creating an emotional bank account of positive encounters to be drawn upon when facing negative feelings. Before processing the needs that are not being met, the therapist discusses the *Four Horseman of the Apocalypse* (criticism, contempt, defensiveness, and stonewalling). Examining how to avoid these behaviors and how to prevent them from "taking up residence" (p. 107) in the marital house is vital. Also, advise on how to circumvent them by using softened start-up, self-soothing, regulating conflict, accepting influence, and avoiding flooding is needed. The second collage is explored, emphasizing turning toward each other rather than turning away from each other to get needs met. The processing of these images may take several sessions.

The image in Figure 22.1 is the *Need* side of the Have/Need Collage, completed by the wife in a couple. While discussing this image with her husband, a pivotal moment occurred when the husband was able to truly "see" what was missing for the wife in the relationship. The image of the man with a hand on his mouth symbolized the wife's disappointment with her husband's lack of frequent expression in the marriage. In subsequent sessions, the husband reported that this image alerted him to be more expressive in the relationship (Ricco, 2007).

Figure 22.1   Have/ Need Collage.

Joint Picture

The Joint Picture is to be used with the Gottman's goal of accepting influence. The objectives are: to (1) provide an art intervention that will uncover covert patterns of interaction and communication; and (2) create insight/awareness regarding ingrained patterns of relating. The art directive is, *develop a well-integrated picture together without verbal communication.*

During discussion, the therapist explores (1) how each partner felt during the creation of the image; (2) how nonverbal communication was or was not recognized; (3) how space was allocated between the couple; and (4) how the couple negotiated leading, following, ignoring, accepting influence, domination, retaliation, isolation, or integration. Some discussion questions might be: (1) How effective do you think you were at influencing each other?; (2) Did either of you try to dominate the other, or were you competitive with each other?; (3) Did either of you sulk or withdraw?; (4) Did you have fun?; (5) Did you work as a team?; (6) How much irritability or anger did either of you feel?; and (7) Did you both feel included?

Solvable Problems Collage

Compromising and accepting influence may be addressed with the Solvable Problems Collage. The objectives are to (1) provide an art intervention that will create an opportunity for the couple to visually and verbally express their feelings, needs, and wants in regard to a specific problem that they are facing; (2) challenge the couple to together come up with a creative compromise that will address the needs of each in regard to this specific issue; and (3) practice using a softened start-up, learning to make and receive repair attempts, soothing themselves, and compromising and being tolerant of each other's faults.

The directive is:

> *Think of a specific problem/issue that frequently comes up in your marriage, agree on one issue to focus on for this art activity, chose one or more of the stencils of people in various poses that express how you feel regarding this issue, and trace the stencil and then tear and cut paper to further express your feelings* (see Figure 22.2). After the first image is completed and discussed, the couple is asked to *make a new image together that represents how you will each compromise to solve this issue, use part or all of each of the original images that you each created to make one image that represents the resolution.* Couples are informed that they may add to this second image as well (see Figure 22.3).

The images created independently should be processed first. Include a discussion of what each partner needs and what each is willing to compromise. Give the second directive for the couple to create an image together. Once the second image is completed, the therapist may comment on how the couple worked together. Other points of discussion may be about each person's feelings about the art process. The therapist might also help the couple explore how altering their original images to create the integrated image relate to compromising and accepting influence.

Figures 22.2 and 22.3 illustrate how an image can communicate the depth and breadth of feelings associated with an issue. This couple was very different in their

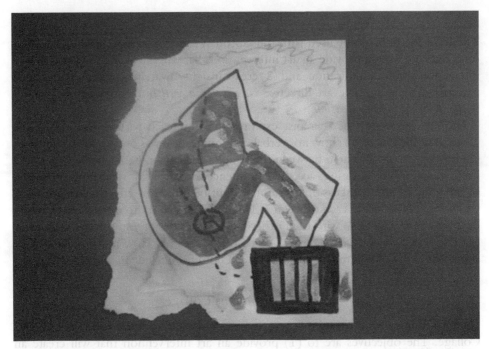

Figure 22.2 Solvable problems collage/front

Figure 22.3 Solvable problems collage/back

approach to life; the wife was carefree and unstructured by nature, and the husband was observant to detail and highly structured. Discussion often centered on this problem, and the couple agreed to soften the terms from "messy" to "carefree" and from "compulsive" to "observant." The images in Figures 22.2 and 22.3 depict the wife's feeling of being stifled by the husband. The image in Figure 22.2 depicts her being forced into a box, and the image in Figure 22.3 reflects her concern that her husband's criticism is "killing her spirit." After the discussing these images, the husband was able to understand the pain that his wife was experiencing and was more open to expressing his needs in a less critical way. Both were able to work toward recognizing what Gottman called the "dream within the conflict" (1999, p. 234), or the dreams that underlie each person's entrenchment in an uncompromising position.

House of the Future

The House of the Future is used to overcome the gridlock that can immobilize a couple and help them create a shared meaning. Gottman defined *shared meaning* as the "degree to which a marriage enables both partners to feel their life dreams are supported" (1999, p. 108). The objectives are: to (1) provide an art intervention that will communicate the goals/dreams of each partner; (2) provide an opportunity to symbolically express these dreams along with the history and meaning that surrounds them; and (3) to learn to approach gridlock from a perspective of acceptance and honor rather than trying to change or take away a dream. The art directive is stated as: *using whatever materials you wish, create an image of your ideal house of the future.*

It is recommended that images be discussed separately, giving attention to each person. Other therapist interventions might be to: (1) encourage listening and observation of each individual's goals, hopes, ideals, and meaning as potentials to still be actualized; (2) identify and discuss goals that are shared by both parties; (3) uncover mutual hopes for the future; (4) help each party accept, honor, and support each other's goals; and (5) discover the symbols that emerge, which represent the couple's shared meaning.

The review of artwork/Bridge Drawing

The Bridge Drawing is to be used to review the artwork, reflect on the progress that has been made by the couple, to assess how far the couple has come, and to discern whether therapy should continue or commence. The objectives are to (1) provide an opportunity to review the images as tangible representations of progress; (2) offer an art intervention that evokes insight and awareness of where the couple is in their journey; and (3) assess the need for further assistance required to continue on a successful path.

The art directive is:

Individually, draw a picture of the two of you crossing a bridge from where you are now to where you want to be; place yourself and your spouse on the bridge where you think you are and indicate the direction in which you are traveling.

During the discussion, have the couple comment on the strength and support of the bridges or lack thereof, the images in the place they are coming from and going to, what is below and above the bridge, where each is on the bridge, and the affect depicted on the faces. Ask the couple to discuss each drawing separately, and encourage each spouse to make comments and ask questions to the other. Help the couple make connections regarding their placement on the bridge to where they are in their marriage, and ask them to decide if they think they need more guidance/therapy or if they think they are ready to continue on their own with a follow-up closure session.

Conclusion

A treatment plan for marital art therapy was the result of combining the Gottman Sound Relationship House Model with art therapy techniques. The Sound Relationship House Model was chosen to pair with art therapy due to its practical application and effectiveness. The Gottman Model is validated by long-term outcome research that explored marital interaction processes that are predictive of divorce or marital stability and processes that further discriminate between happily and unhappily married stable couples (Gottman et al., 1998).

The chapter began with an identification of the need to develop unique successful approaches to marriage therapy. Art therapy as part of couples' counseling helps make complex, sensitive relationship interactions and patterns of behavior visible. Eight art therapy interventions useful in couples' therapy were presented. Images from art therapy case studies provided an example of the clinical applications of art therapy in this treatment model. Art therapy is one method for helping couples resolve difficult issues and find meaning in their marriage.

References

Barth, R. J., & Kinder, B. N. (1985). The use of art therapy in marital and sex therapy. *Journal of Sex & Marital Therapy, 11*(3), 192–198.

Gottman, J. M. (1999). *The marriage clinic: A scientifically based marital therapy.* New York, NY: W.W. Norton & Company.

Gottman, J. M., Coan, J., Carrere, S., & Swanson, C. (1998). Predicting marital happiness and stability from newlywed interactions. *Journal of Marriage and the Family, 60*(1), 5–22.

Gottman, J. M., & Notarious, C. I. (2002). Marital research in the 20th century and a research agenda for the 21st century. *Family Process, 41,* 159–197.

Madhyastha, T. M., Hamaker, E. L., & Gottman, J. M. (2011). Investigating spousal influence using moment-to-moment affect data from marital conflict. *Journal of Family Psychology, 25*(2), 292–300.

Mauzey, E., & Erdman, P. (1995). Let the Genogram speak: Curiosity, circularity, and creativity in family history. *Journal of Family Psychotherapy, 6*(2), 1–11.

Miles, L., & Miles, R. (2000). *The New Marriage: Transcending the happily-ever-after myth.* Fort Bragg, CA: Cypress House.

Ricco, D. (2007). *Evaluating the Use of Art Therapy with Couples in Counseling; A Combined Qualitative and Quantitative Approach (Doctoral Dissertation).* Retrieved from: Florida State University Electronic Theses, Treatises, and Dissertations. ETD 04052007-131105.

Tracz, S. M., & Gerhart-Brooks, D. R. (1999). The lifeline: Using art to illustrate history. *Journal of Family Psychotherapy, 10*(3), 61–63.

Wadeson, H. (1973). Art techniques used in conjoint marital therapy. *Art Therapy, 12*(3), 147–164.

Wadeson, H. (1980). *Art psychotherapy.* New York, NY: John Wiley & Sons.

Weeks, G. R. (1989). *Treating couples: The intersystem model of the marriage council of Philadelphia.* New York, NY: Brunner/Mazel publishers.

23

Rethinking and Reframing Group Art Therapy: An Amalgamation of British and US Models

Marcia L. Rosal

Art therapists easily adapt art therapy into group work. Similar to settling into a cozy armchair, art therapists comfortably conduct groups in a wide variety of settings and with many different client groups. Over the years, several art therapists have offered ideas about the incorporation of art therapy into group work (Hume & Hiti, 1988; Kramer, 1979; Landgarten, 1981; McNeilly, 1983, 1990, 2006; McNiff, 1973; Moon, 2010; Naumburg, 1966; Riley, 2001; Rubin, 1984, 1998; Skaife & Huet, 1998; Tur, 2007; Wadeson, 1980, 1987, 2010), while other art therapists discussed running art therapy groups with certain clients or in specific settings (Allen, 1985; Coholic, 2011; Collie, Bottorff, & Long, 2006; Cooper & Milton, 2003; Dick, 2001; Dorr, 2007; Erickson & Young, 2010; Feen-Calligan, 1995; Hagood, 1991; Isaacs, 1977; Jacobson, 1993; Johns & Karterud, 2004; Pretorius & Pfeifer, 2010; Stone, 1982; Vogt & Vogt, 1983).

From the literature, art therapists learn that the incorporation of art in groups provides members with enriching experiences. Art therapists are aware of the therapeutic power of images produced in group work. Yet, after over 60 years of practice, art therapists may have only skimmed the surface or just begun to explore the depths and intricacies of how art therapy process and group process are intertwined. In this chapter, I hope to add to the discussion about group art therapy by reviewing both US and British models of art therapy, providing strong evidence for the use of art in group work, and offering suggestions of how to do so for maximum effectiveness. Finally, a contemporary model of group will be proposed to provoke future reflections about art in group work.

US and British Group Approaches to Group Art Therapy

The aftermath of World War II had great influence on group therapy. Multitudes of returning veterans of the war needed assistance, and with so many, veterans hospitals in both the United States and Britain needed to use the group method to address

---

"shell shock" or, as we know it today, posttraumatic stress disorder (Aveline & Dryden, 1988). I wrote about these influences in 2007 and will not duplicate that information here, except to report that the United States approached the reincorporation of veterans into mainstream society differently than did the British. These differences led to opposing views of group work: the British model was psychoanalytically based and long-term, whereas the US model was psycho-educationally based and short-term (Rosal, 2007).

Learning from US art therapists

As noted in the introduction to this chapter, many US art therapists have written about the integration of art into group work. Group therapy is, at its core, about the therapeutic power of the relationships formed in the group. The same is true of group art therapy. Both Naumburg (1966) and Rubin (1978, 1984) found that art created in groups can induce increased interaction and communication among group members. Kramer (1979) added that, when therapy is conducted in groups, there is an increase in "creative fervor," which can add to the members' interest in each other and in the group itself.

According to Wadeson (1980), the images created can lead to the "sharing of images" (p. 239), to members getting to know each other better, and to a decrease in isolation, both in the group and socially. Finally, Landgarten (1981) found that art making adds to a sense of group identity. Moon (2010) reiterated this construct when he wrote about how the art created in a group could enhance the development of community among its members. From the writings of group art therapy authors, it is clear that the premise behind using art in group work is the power of art to engender relationships through increased interpersonal interactions, viewing each other's artwork, and uncovering connections with others through the artwork.

Not all art created in groups is positive. Both Kramer (1979) and Landgarten (1981) realized that art produced in groups sometimes contains frightening material. Landgarten added that the art product may "reveal ideas, feelings, and perceptions about the self and significant others" (p. 106); these may or may not be positive experiences. Yet, as McNIff (1973) noted, the artwork, when viewed and discussed by other group members, can help an individual gain perspective and objectivity about his or her personal anxieties. Thus, art therapists know that art in groups can have a deeper purpose than solely facilitating communication among members.

In fact, Rubin (1978, 1984) theorized that the power of art to affect group issues had yet to be explored and was concerned that art therapists had not yet taken "advantage of the potency of both art and the group" (1978, p. 172). Thompson, in a paper presented at the 1993 annual conference of the American Art Therapy Association, echoed this same sentiment and began to explore the British model of group art therapy as a means of mining the group process benefits of art therapy.

Learning from British art therapists

I, too, have been impressed with the work that British art therapists have done in understanding group art therapy and on the use of art as part of group process. McNeilly (1983) challenged my thinking on group art therapy at an important junction as I worked on my doctoral dissertation. He compared a directive, theme-based approach to group art therapy with a non-directive approach on several points including relations among members, relationships with the group leader, and relationships with the art. In his critical analysis, McNeilly uncovered numerous problems with how art therapists think about group work, particularly if they come from a theme-based approach: (1) members battle for the attention of the leader, and this can limit transference themes; (2) the leader avoids anxiety and chaos, which are important factors in groups; and (3) the possibility of transferences among members is decreased as universal themes and resonance in the group is deflated (1983).

Based on his experiences with group art therapy, McNeilly (2006) proposed that non-directive or non-theme-based groups hold more therapeutic power than directive groups. He based his ideas on Foulkes, McDougall, and Bion (as cited in McNeilly, 2006), and termed his approach *group analytic art therapy* (McNeilly, 1990). Translating these authors' group therapy theories for art therapy, McNeilly used the illustration of a drum to represent important aspects of this approach. This illustration proposes the bottom skin of the drum as the foundation of the group and the top portion of the drum skin representing Foulke's understanding of group dynamics (2006). The members of the group are lined around the top of the drum along with their artwork. The drum image elucidates the forces created by the group, including *tensions* (the idea that, when you put various people in a group together, unique pressures will be evoked), and *resonances* (the phenomenon that explains that similar themes and colors emerge in the art of the members) that occur in groups. McNeilly argued that, when the group is open and non-directed, tensions and resonances will emanate from the members and will produce a truer and more honest picture of what is happening in the group, more so than when members are directed to create art with a specific theme.

Another British art therapist, Dalley (1993), paid particular attention to the use of art as a way for the children to cope with the stresses of a group in ways that had not been discussed in the US literature. For example, she talked about the possible refuge that art-making offers to some children. By focusing on their own art, members can be separate from the group, and still be part of the group process. This separation and immersion phenomenon parallels relationships outside of group and can offer insights into how children move in and out of connection with others.

Another construct that Dalley put forth was how artworks created in the group hold the history of the group and can be used to preserve the timeline of the work done in the group and illuminate the relationships in the group and how they have changed over time. Each piece of artwork is a statement on how a member feels about being in the group at that moment in time, and this feeling is concretized in that artwork. According to Dalley, each piece of art is laden with meaning from several perspectives: longitudinal, intrapersonal, and interpersonal.

Taking the best from each side of the Atlantic

The knowledge generated about group art therapy from each side of the Atlantic provides a strong rationale for the use of art in group therapy. There is no doubt that making art in groups ignites a spark that is exciting *and* therapeutic. First and foremost, the art has the power to connect the members in ways that words alone may not be able to do. Even individual art, when placed together in the center of a table, suddenly becomes a part of a whole—a Gestalt concept that Rhyne (1984) put forth when discussing her Gestalt art groups. Dalley (1993) termed the concept of seeing one's art in a field of others' art "an *interpictorial phenomenon*," and noted that, even if a member does not want to speak about his or her art, it is a *speaking picture* because the other members "hear" what the artist is stating nonverbally. Thus, the power of the art moves the members toward group intimacy (Dalley, 1993).

A picture created by a young, aggressive boy caused quite a stir in his small group when that session's artwork was put in the center of the table. Known for this hostility, "Chris" created a battle scene between a tree and an alien (see Figure 23.1). Chris did not want to discuss the drawing, but the other members immediately understood that this drawing was about his impulsivity and how dangerous it was to get in his way.

Working on interpersonal issues is not the only reason for putting a client into group art therapy. Although improved social skills and interpersonal relationships are often a goal in group art therapy, members may want to work on other concerns. Yet, it may be difficult for members to identify or define a personal goal. The artwork can often give clues to therapy goals (Rosal, 2007).

Using art to help group members identify therapy goals When working with adults, I open the group by asking members to develop a collage illustrating his or her reason for being in the group and a goal they would like to work on. The collage can serve

Figure 23.1 Chris' drawing of a battle between a tree and an alien.

as the member's contract to work on a specific issue or concern. Collages are revealing to the group leader, even if some meaning is still not clear to the artist. For example, in an adult group, one female member created a simple collage even though her group-mates were busy with very intricate and colorful collages. She selected one image and glued it to an index card (see Figure 23.2). The yield sign of two adults, with the male holding a woman's arm, held multiple meanings: (1) perhaps the artist felt she could assist the group members; (2) the yield sign could represent her hesitancy about the group; and/or (3) she may yield to others to do the work of the group. Indeed, this member made this realization several sessions later.

Leadership style   Based on cautions from both Wadeson (1980, 2010) and McNeilly (2006), art therapists might examine their leadership style. Although many art therapists in the United States work in short-term, goal-based settings, presenting a theme or a directive in each session may not be warranted. If a theme is not a good fit for that particular session, being open to a change of direction or allowing for ideas to be generated from the members is important and therapeutic. Being mindful of power and control issues as a group leader is important for fostering the therapeutic culture of the group.

Using the art to understand relationships in the group   The art itself holds multiple meanings, and art therapists can mine the artwork for clues about relationships between the art and the artist, between the artist and the group, and between the artist and the therapist; this is what is called *group process*. Yalom (2005) described group process as

Figure 23.2   Contract collage.

the "power cell of the group" (p. 150); it is the therapeutic mechanism by which group members evolve and mature. The art created in groups provides clues into the group process. McNeilly (2006), Dalley (1993), Waller (1993), and Riley (2001) found that art does not merely activate member connection and relationship, but that the images illuminate process. As members create, art therapists can observe how the artwork is created. Are members examining each other's work? Is there a struggle over who has what art materials? Are there shape, color, or theme similarities in the artwork? As the members complete artworks, which images are the members drawn toward? When discussing artworks, art therapists may want to pay attention to both the content of the image and how the group examines the piece; in other words, study the process by which art is deliberated. Some ways to do this may include noticing who talks or does not talk about his or her piece, who pays attention to when a member speaks, and to whom the speaker looks at when presenting the image.

An example of this comes from a pre-adolescent male student with aggressive and depressive symptoms, placed in a small group. The other members were curious about his artwork, more so when he used clay to build cameras (see Figure 23.3). The other five members were excited about the cameras and asked for his help to construct them. Cohesion developed over the crafting of the cameras. The creative fervor that Kramer (1979) spoke of was evident in this group. Cameras are an interesting symbol that evokes multiple meanings, including wanting to examine an incident closely or documenting a moment in time. Once the cameras were completed and fired, members used them to take pictures of their art and of each other, signifying the importance of both the art and the group.

Cooperative group art projects Group art projects can be a catalyst for group process. In my experience, novice art therapists mistakenly direct a group to create murals or group sculptures too soon (Rosal, 2007). Group members often experience anxiety about the group and their role in this novel therapeutic format. Cooperative art projects can raise anxiety and be unproductive in the early stages of a group. Instead,

Figure 23.3 Cameras created in a group setting.

cooperative projects should emanate from the needs and goals of the group. There are instances when groups begin to describe themselves in symbolic or metaphorical terms, and these abstract images can be used to introduce group cooperative projects. For example, one group lamented that they were not as cohesive as they had hoped, but more like the connected cars of a train. This image led to the development of a group project where each member created their unique "train car" and then the group connected the cars to form the train itself. The idea for this cooperative art experience not only came from the members, they also then used the metaphor and the art piece for evaluating its progress from that moment in their treatment until termination.

Safe keeping of group artwork   Keep group artwork safely in the group room for the duration of the group. As Dalley (1993) noted, art holds the history of the group. New art is added to the life and history of the group each week or each session. When it is kept in the art room, members can refer back to these previously created pieces. Members often use art to remember important milestones in the group's history. At the time of termination, either when a single member leaves the group or when the entire group disbands, the art is available for review and evaluation.

Finding meaning in the group experience was a challenge for a struggling adult group until they were asked to use a large box to represent *what they are willing to work on* (the outside of the box) and *what they did not want to deal with* (the inside of the box). The members painted the closed box with a reddish-pink color, which was acknowledged as representing the rawness they felt when in the group. After a suggestion from one of the members, they used yellow paint to put their handprints on the outside of the box. Another member asked the others if it was ok to form a chain to keep people out of the box. Next, it was discovered that artwork from the previous week was in the room (each member had made a hat representing their role in the group), and they decided that these hats signified issues that were difficult for them to discuss, so they put the hats inside the box. They then decided to put the art from all previous sessions into the box. Finally, they realized that they might want to have a few openings to see into the box to see their art, if needed, and then they used graphics imprinted on the box to create openings that could be either opened or closed (see Figure 23.4).

After a flurry of activity, the members were physically tired yet mentally impassioned. They found a way to deal with the personal information held in the art created up to that date. There was now a way to exercise control over difficult material, and they uncovered their power to "let it out" only if and when they wanted. Since the art from all previous sessions was kept in the box, it was available for the group to use when needed.

Toward a Model of Group Art Therapy

In working with student art therapists, I found that models are useful. I wanted to develop a model of group art therapy that took into account the complexities of the group process and the intricacies of the art. I wanted the model to be interactive to

Figure 23.4 Box project created by an adult group.

illustrate that the group informs the art interventions, and that, subsequently, the art informs the group (see Figure 23.5).

Rather than ideas for art experiences coming from a book or a set of conventional interventions, art therapy ideas originate from the needs of the members, the group themes, and group tensions. Once art is created, it offers clues to where the group might go and how to use additional art experiences to address two main objectives of group work: (1) improve group formation, identity, and cohesions; and (2) deepen individual and group meaning. The two-way arrow between "ideas for group art" and "art productions from the group" implies a strong reciprocal relationship. Once a group is working well, the therapist can go back and forth between these two concepts to develop art interventions that best serve the needs of the group.

The adult group that used the box to tackle group and member issues discussed in the preceding text is an example of how this model can be used. The relationship among members was tense, and individual member issues kept the group from addressing group-as-a-whole issues. The idea to use the box was generated from the groups' apprehensions. The completed box project was, in turn, used to help the group revisit these anxieties, and assisted the group to identify problematic relationships and

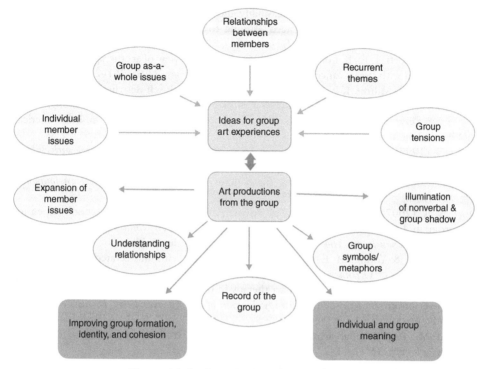

Figure 23.5 A model for group art therapy.

illuminate nonverbal problems. The box was a symbol and a record of the group's fears. Finally, the box project improved group identity as well as the meaning of the group for individual members and for the group as a whole.

Conclusion

Art process and group process, when implemented well, enhance the group therapy experience. Each art creation holds multiple meanings for the artist, but, perhaps more importantly, art pieces illuminate the group process and can signify how the members are responding to each other, to the leader, and to the group itself. Harnessing the power of art is the job of the group art therapy leader. Using observations of member concerns, relationships between members, group tensions, and recurrent themes for the development of therapeutic art interventions is the job of the group art therapist. Carefully conceived art interventions push the group into the process and into dealing with the anxieties of the group experience.

References

Allen, P. (1985). Integrating art therapy into an alcoholism treatment program. *American Journal of Art Therapy*, 24(1), 10–12.

Aveline, M., & Dryden, W. (Eds.) (1988). *Group therapy in Britain*. Philadelphia, PA: Open University Press.

Coholic, D. A. (2011). Exploring the feasibility and benefits of arts-based mindfulness-based practices with young people in need: Aiming to improve aspects of self-awareness and resilience. *Child and Youth Care Forum, 40*(4), 303–317.

Collie, K., Bottorff, J. L., & Long, B. C. (2006). A narrative view of art therapy and art making by women with breast cancer. *Journal of Health Psychology, 11*(5), 761–775.

Cooper, B. F., & Milton, I. B. (2003). Group art therapy with self-destructive young women. In D. J. Wiener & L. K. Oxford (Eds.), *Action therapy with families and groups: Using creative arts improvisation in clinical practice* (pp. 163–196). Washington, DC: American Psychological Association.

Dalley, T. (1993). Art psychotherapy groups. In K. N. Dwivedi (Ed.), *Group work with children and adolescents: A handbook* (pp. 136–158). London: Jessica Kingsley Press.

Dick, T. (2001). Brief group art therapy for acute psychiatric inpatients. *American Journal of Art Therapy, 39*(4), 108–112.

Dorr, A. R. (2007). Collaboration and creativity: Art therapy groups in a school suspension program. In Vanessa A. Camilleri (Ed.), *Healing the inner city child: Creative arts therapies with at-risk youth* (pp. 164–179). London: Jessica Kingsley Publishers.

Erickson, B. J., & Young, M. E. (2010). Group art therapy with incarcerated women. *Journal of Addictions & Offender Counseling, 31*(1), 38–51.

Feen-Calligan, H. (1995). The use of art therapy in treatment programs to Promote spiritual recovery from addiction. *Art Therapy: Journal of the American Art Therapy Association, 12*(1), 46–50.

Hagood, M. (1991). Group art therapy with mothers of sexually abused children. *The Arts in Psychotherapy, 18*(1), 17–27.

Hume, S., & Hiti, J. (1988). A rationale and model for group art therapy with mentally retarded adolescents. *American Journal of Art Therapy, 27*(1), 2–12.

Isaacs, L. (1977). Art-therapy group for latency age children. *Social Work, 22*(1), 57–59.

Jacobson, M. L. (1993). Group art therapy with multiple personality disorder patients: A viable alternative to isolation. In E. S. Kluft (Ed.), *Expressive and functional therapies in the treatment of multiple personality disorder* (pp. 101–123). Springfield, IL: Charles C. Thomas, Publisher.

Johns, S., & Karterud, S. (2004). Guidelines for art group therapy as part of a day treatment program for patients with personality disorders. *Group Analysis, 37*(3), 419–432.

Kramer, E. (1979). *Childhood and art therapy: Notes on theory and application.* New York, NY: Schocken Books.

Landgarten, H. (1981). *Clinical art therapy: A comprehensive guide.* New York, NY: Brunner/ Mazel.

McNeilly, G. (1983). Directive and non-directive approaches in art therapy. *The Arts in Psychotherapy, 10*(4), 211–219.

McNeilly, G. (1990). Group analysis and art therapy: A personal perspective. *Group Analysis, 23*(3), 215–224.

McNeilly, G. (2006). *Group analytic art therapy.* London: Jessica Kingsley Press.

McNiff, S. (1973). A new perspective in group art therapy. *The Arts in Psychotherapy, 1*(3–4), 243–245.

Moon, B. L. (2010). *Art-based group therapy: Theory and practice.* Springfield, IL: Charles C. Thomas.

Naumburg, M. (1966). *Dynamically oriented art therapy: Its principles and practice.* New York, NY: Grune & Stratton.

Pretorius, G., & Pfeifer, N. (2010). Group art therapy with sexually abused girls. *South African Journal of Psychology, 40*(1), 63–73.

Rhyne, J. (1984). *The gestalt art experience: Creative process and expressive therapy*. Chicago: Magnolia Street Publishers.

Riley, S. (2001). *Group process made visible: Group art therapy*. Philadelphia, PA: Brunner-Routledge.

Rosal, M. L. (2007). A comparative analysis of British and US group art therapy styles. In D. Spring (Ed.), *Art in treatment: A transatlantic dialogue* (pp. 35–51). Springfield, IL: Charles C. Thomas.

Rubin, J. (1978). *Child art therapy* (2nd ed.). New York, NY: Van Norstrand Reinhold.

Rubin, J. (1984). *The art of art therapy*. New York, NY: Brunner/Mazel.

Rubin, J. A. (1998). *Introduction to art therapy*. New York, NY: Routledge.

Skaife, S., & Huet, V. (1998). *Art psychotherapy groups: Between pictures and words*. London: Routledge.

Stone, B. (1982). Group art therapy with mothers of autistic children. *The Arts In Psychotherapy, 9*(1), 31–48.

Thompson, L. (1993). *Group art therapy: Towards and articulation of theoretical principles*. Paper presented at the 24th Annual Conference of the American Art therapy Association, Atlanta.

Tur, G. P. (2007). From art to group psychotherapy. *International Gestalt Journal, 30*, 139–151.

Vogt, J., & Vogt, G. (1983). Group art therapy: An eclectic approach. *American Journal of Art Therapy, 22*(4), 129–135.

Wadeson, H. (1980). *Art psychotherapy*. New York, NY: John Wiley & Sons.

Wadeson, H. (1987). *The dynamics of art psychotherapy*. New York, NY: John Wiley & Sons.

Wadeson, H. (2010). *Art psychotherapy* (2nd ed.). New York, NY: John Wiley & Sons.

Waller, D. (1993). *Group interactive art therapy: Its use in training and treatment*. London: Routledge.

Yalom, I. D. (2005). *The theory and practice of group psychotherapy*. New York, NY: Basic Books.

24

Art Therapy with Children
Tracy Councill

Creating art is a uniquely human activity that translates experience into representation. Unlike play or dance or music, visual art is an enduring, visible record. Art created in the therapeutic process forms a bridge between the client's experience and the outside world, allowing the therapist and client to meet on common ground and bring inner and outer experiences closer together. For children, the creative process is empowering: imagination flows through paint onto paper, and the product is something others can see.

The most important difference between adults and children is power: adults are bigger, stronger, they know more, and are generally in charge. Children are hardwired to observe, admire, and emulate the adults in their lives, and unequipped to realistically judge the adults who belong to them. Children long for freedom from school, rules, and chores, and having to follow orders; yet, the structure of society allows them the opportunity to learn and flourish. When society works well, education is compulsory, and children's time is protected to allow them to learn and grow before assuming the burdens of adult responsibility.

Through most of history, human cultures and traditions developed in relative isolation—there was a discernible difference between "them" and "us" in most parts of the world. To be from a particular, distinct place and culture meant that a child had been taught their culture's consensus about what is good or bad. The individual's identity was formed in concert with the community in which they lived. The sheer availability of information in contemporary society allows children unprecedented access to information about cultures outside their own. In the contemporary environment, the traditions of culture are subject to question and comparison.

Art Therapy in Contemporary Culture

The growth of literacy, industrialization, and the World Wars set the stage for the global culture we experience today. Individual identity is no longer dictated by one's origins, but rather by one's gifts, talents, and life experiences. Today, as young people ponder who they are, the click of a computer mouse can bring into awareness images and ideas from every imaginable kind of human experience, and caring adults must help young people make sense of an overwhelming amount of information. Just as today's young people teach their parents how to use new technologies, adults can help children understand the context of what they discover.

People imagine that children have childish feelings, but the fact is that children have access to the full range of human emotions—it is in their thinking that they differ from adults. Children reason at their level of cognitive development, but at any point they may feel anger, grief, despair, or joy (Van Eys, 1981). Many parents, teachers, and caregivers imagine that children are protected from the emotional impact of problems in the family, traumatic events, over-stimulating content in the media, and dysfunction in the community. Children take in a tremendous amount of emotional information, and they may not have the words to express what they know and how they feel. Integrating art therapy into unconventional settings such as schools, communities, and hospitals, in addition to psychiatric treatment programs, creates opportunities to help young people express their feelings and reflect on their experiences.

Technology, Childhood, and Art

The ubiquity of electronic media creates a democratization of the art form. Anyone can make a film, record music, and edit photographs. Using digital media in art therapy is an important growing edge for the field (Malchiodi, 2011).

Gaining facility with technology is important but working with traditional art materials also helps develop essential life skills. Building images, structures, and symbols in paint, clay, and stone, by their physical presence, is different from creating electronic images. Creating a sculpture that must stand upright or enclose an open space, using paint to depict a place remembered or a person in front of us—these are very direct challenges. The artist working in traditional media must cope with gravity, texture, viscosity, volume, and the mechanics of perception, and all these things occur outside the self. The capacity of art to externalize our experience is one of the keys to its therapeutic power.

Project Zero, a research program at the Harvard Graduate School of Education (Hetland, Winner, Veenema, & Sheridan, 2007, p. 6), whose mission is to understand and enhance learning, thinking, and creativity in the arts, identifies eight "habits of mind" that can be learned from working in the visual arts:

1. *Develop craft*: learning to use and care for tools
2. *Engage and persist*: learning to embrace problems ... to develop focus and other mental states conducive to working and persevering at art tasks
3. *Envision*: learning to picture mentally what cannot be directly observed, and to imagine the possible next steps in making a piece
4. *Express*: learning to create works that convey an idea, feeling, or personal meaning
5. *Observe*: learning to attend to visual context more closely than ordinary "looking" requires, and thereby to see things that otherwise might not be seen

6. *Reflect*: learning to think and talk with others about an aspect of one's work or working process
7. *Stretch and explore*: learning to reach beyond one's capacities, to explore playfully without a preconceived plan, and to embrace the opportunity to learn from mistakes and accidents
8. *Understand the art world*: learning to interact as an artist with other artists (i.e., in classrooms, in local arts organizations, and across the art field) and within the broader society

Art therapists will recognize the resonance between the habits of mind and therapeutic goals in art therapy: building frustration tolerance, focus, and executive functioning; expressing feelings in a safe and contained way; interacting with others—these are aspects of the art-making process on which art therapy goals are built. Making art itself can bring about healing and personal growth, and this potential is not exclusive to art therapy. But the profession of art therapy brings practitioners with special skills in facilitating self-discovery and integration through art to those who need them most. Children without specific problems might work with an art therapist in an open studio in their community and develop confidence and self-awareness in the process. The same art therapist working with children with special needs in a school setting would design an art-making experience focused on addressing treatment goals, and guide the clients through the experience in a way that provided the extra measure of emotional safety and support those clients' needs. Art therapy is a truly hybrid profession, blending fine art, art education and psychotherapy to create a new and special art therapy experience.

The History of Art Therapy with Children

Edith Kramer (1971, 1979) is among those who pioneered the use of art therapy with children. A student of psychoanalysis, Kramer developed a rigorous theoretical framework for using art therapy with young people with severe psychopathology. Her intensive, non-directive approach allowed children with severe mental and physical disabilities to unlock their creative potential and achieve milestones in personality development. Her work created a conceptual framework for many art therapists who came after her. She famously describes five ways in which art materials may be used, delineating a progression from experimentation to artistic expression: (1) precursory activities, such as scribbling and smearing; (2) chaotic discharge—kinetic activities such as spilling, splashing, and pounding; (3) stereotypes—copying, tracing, and stereotypical repetition; (4) pictographs—pictorial communication that replaces or supplements words; and (5) formed expression—art that achieves both self-expression and communication (Kramer, 1971).

Kramer also wrote of the special obligations of those who work with children: "Because we work with children, our responsibility is absolute, residing in the adult status which makes us the guardian of any unprotected child who comes into our orbit" (Kramer, 1979, p. 5). Of the relationship between children and adults, she indicated that,

> no child can grow himself up unaided, and the great menace of childhood is failure to mature. ... Indeed, the same children who would reduce the art room to a shambles and the art therapist to a nervous wreck will return again and again to the room where art materials and a person who knows how to use them are available, return in the dogged expectation that somehow something good will come of it. (1979, pp. 6–7)

Foreshadowing current developments in neuro-psychobiology (van der Kolk, Hopper, & Osterman, 2001), art therapist Judy Rubin (1984) underscored the relationship between art therapy and learning:

> As we begin to understand more fully the functioning and flexibility of the human brain, it is likely that a treatment such as art therapy might be useful, not only because it deals with psychological conflict, but also because the very nature of the modality involves the activation of different parts of the human mind. Given the need for integration and synthesis in organized thought and action, a visual and verbal modality, which involves translation from one mode into the other, has tremendous potential for the promotion of higher and healthier mental functioning. (p. 38)

Her vision, similar to Kramer's, emphasized a strength-based approach anchored in cognitive and emotional development.

The Practice of Art Therapy

Art therapists work with children in psychiatric treatment centers, medical facilities, schools, community-based programs, and in private practice. They may specialize in working with children with special needs such as autism (Martin, 2011), attention deficit hyperactivity disorder (ADHD; Safran, 2011), trauma resolution (Gerteisen, 2008), disaster relief (Chilcote, 2004), medical illness (Councill, 2011), and other challenges.

The therapeutic process

Cathy Malchiodi (2011) advocated a phenomenological approach to art therapy with children, emphasizing the therapeutic process over interpretation. "This means looking at their art expressions for a variety of meanings, the context in which they were created, and the child's way of viewing the world" (p. 142). She explained that:

> For children, art making is a process that brings together many different experiences to create something new, personal, and unique. ... Because so many different elements and experiences come together in children's drawings, simple explanations and interpretations of their creative work are not always possible. (1998, p. 19)

Curative factors My own work has been mainly with pediatric oncology patients and their families. Though art therapy in medicine may seem like a highly specialized form of practice, medical illness touches young people and families from every imaginable walk of life. For any of these children and their families, art therapy opens the door to a creative process that can be grounding and engaging in a time of profound loss and turmoil.

Any serious illness is an experience of loss as those diagnosed with any serious ailment must contend not only with the illness itself, but also with the loss of potential achievement, future plans, relationships, and a sense of security. Because they have never been of a particular age before, children do not have a fixed idea of what to expect, so in some ways they are more resilient than adults. Given the opportunity to interact with caring adults, children can be extremely flexible. Through personal clinical experience and the work of other art therapists, the following list of curative factors in art therapy was developed. Although initially conceived as two separate lists—one for those with medical illness and one for those with mental illness—it became clear that the two lists are essentially the same.

1. *Art therapy promotes internal locus of control*: Control is the first thing that is taken away when a diagnosis is made. Life must be re-organized around the demands of the illness and treatment. And the ultimate question—will I regain my health?—is impossible to answer at the beginning of treatment, and is ultimately outside the patient's control. The patient who follows her treatment plan and does all that is asked of her stands a very good chance of recovery. While it cannot cure an illness, working creatively in the treatment space allows patients to experience themselves as creators—active participants in the work of getting well, and not just passive patients—and that is an empowering stance.

2. *Art therapy assists in creating a personal narrative*: Telling one's story is central to integrating traumatic experiences, developing a sense of identity, and helping others understand and relate. Because art making occurs within the realm of the imagination, it opens the door to the story, and to remembering important events that may have been forgotten, or whose significance is unknown.

3. *Displacement into art allows emotional safety to process difficult content*: This is an important dimension of art therapy, especially for children. A monster made of clay or poured out in paint upon paper may embody the rage a child feels, but it cannot really hurt anybody. Children may fear the power of their strong emotions, but art therapy can provide the emotional safety to unleash them without fear of reprisal or of overwhelming their caregivers with strong feelings.

4. *Problem-solving through art therapy supports mastery and cognitive development*: Normal children long to do things for themselves—to learn how to do everything and practice the skills to get it right. Children with serious illness may face cognitive, behavioral, and physical limitations, but they are still driven to develop. Art therapy can provide an environment for problem-solving and accomplishment that gives the child a sense of mastery, both over important developmental tasks and, through self-expression, over troubling events in their lives.

5. *Art therapy allows for nonverbal expression when words fail*: Children may have difficulty expressing themselves in words, especially when there are frightening experiences that need to be expressed. Who has the words to say how they feel

when faced with a diagnosis of cancer? Who can explain what it is like to be the victim of abuse? Not knowing what to say, or the fear of repercussions of telling their story, can leave a child stuck and uncommunicative. Non-verbal expression opens the door to communication.

6. *Using metaphors connects individuals to universal themes.* Isolation is a tremendous problem for ill children. Young people desperately want to fit it, to belong, to be like everybody else, but illness sets them apart. Self-expression through metaphor can give an individual's story the power to resonate with universal cultural themes. The individual's experience is his or her own, but when it relates to a theme or metaphor that others also experience, it transcends the personal and belongs to the whole. Others can see the image and relate to its meaning, even if they do not have the same illness as the artist.

7. *Visual expression levels the playing field for those with stronger verbal defenses.* Children are not in charge. While they may know what the problems are, especially in their families, the adults have bigger voices and more practice in denial, rationalization, and self-justification. Drawing and painting amplify the child's capacity for intuitive expression through art, just as they may provide a way around an adult's pathological defenses.

8. *Provides clients safe access to nonverbal memories.* This quality is especially important when working with clients who have endured traumatic experiences. By their very nature, traumatic memories are non-verbal, so they must often be first accessed through non-verbal means. Art therapy has a natural facility with non-verbal material, and so it offers great promise in healing trauma. The process of bringing traumatic memories from inchoate, scary "stuff" into conscious awareness, and allowing those stories to be safely told, understood, labeled, and put away as memories, not living events, is a powerful dimension of art therapy.

9. *The creative process need not be judged* (Cassou, 2004): Art therapists meet people where they are: no artistic skill or experience is expected or required. Art therapy can create an oasis of creative experimentation and curiosity in a treatment environment that is focused on defining problems and creating measurable goals.

- In order to begin the creative process, one must, to some extent, suspend judgment. If one's inner critic censors every brushstroke, it is difficult to make anything, for the child and the professional artist alike.
- Patients must be given permission to allow the creative process to work: not everything need be kept for posterity, but whatever emerges can be allowed to have its life in the creative moment.
- The art therapist's skill in identifying media and processes suited to the child's needs maximizes the creative potential of the artistic process.
- When working with parents and caregivers alongside children, it is often important to teach the adults that they need not judge, interpret, or celebrate every mark the child makes. It is tempting for adults to ask a lot of questions or give a "play-by-play" narrative about the child's process, but this kind of commentary is generally a way to manage the parent's anxiety, and it often interferes. I say to parents, "I bet Johnny will tell us about this picture when he is done, but for now let's just let him work."

Case Example

The following case example illustrates the use of art therapy with an 8-year old boy who developed anxiety symptoms around the 1-year anniversary of his cancer diagnosis. He had completed a successful course of cancer treatment 6 months before his anxiety symptoms developed.

His fears related to situations where he might be trapped in confined spaces, such as elevators, restrooms and stairwells; getting lost while driving home from the hospital; and being left behind in a store. Immediately following his cancer diagnosis, the patient was unconscious and in the intensive care unit (ICU) for about a week. Though his parents were with him around the clock during the time, he was unconscious and had no awareness of those days in the ICU.

Trauma occurs when an event is so overwhelming that it cannot be fully assimilated into long-term memory (van der Kolk et al., 2001). Though there may be no conscious memory of the troubling event, it is stored as a non-verbal, sensory experience that may be re-experienced out of context. He was evaluated by a psychiatrist and diagnosed with post-traumatic stress disorder (PTSD). Individual art therapy was chosen as the primary mode of treatment.

Adapting the art therapy trauma resolution protocol developed by art therapist Savneet Talwar (2007), I introduced him to the concept of bi-lateral art. He drew first with his dominant hand, then with his non-dominant hand, continuing to draw, alternating hands, until he felt he was done. We used this technique to begin each of his individual art therapy sessions.

In bi-lateral art, troubling material is passed back and forth between the two hemispheres of the brain, being processed first through the lens of verbal dominance and then from the non-verbal, sensory perspective, and back again. Troubling material emerges in a non-threatening way and is gradually brought into awareness.

The process led the patient to create a superhero who could help with his worries. "Worry Free Man" (see Figure 24.1) had special powers to protect him from danger—teeth similar to a shark, a special hat to sense danger, built-in GPS so he could not get lost, and light-up shoes to show him where to go. One of the character's special powers was symbolized by an ocean wave. His psychiatrist had taught him to think of his anxiety as washing over him and then dissipating like a wave. He practiced using this technique to stay calm in anxiety-provoking situations, and in his art he gave this power to Worry Free Man.

In a later session, he created a character who was afraid to go out in the world because he "was born with holes all over his body" (see Figure 24.2). He said this character was "the opposite of Worry Free Man," and seemed to embody the patient's feeling of vulnerability. In the bottom half of the figure, he drew a large "heart" to symbolize that he was a very caring person. Within the heart, there was a small circle outlined in red, which represented the character's "bravery," which he said was "small when he goes outside because of all the holes."

Figure 24.1   Worry Free Man.

Toward the end of our work together, the patient created a "Bathroom Box" (see Figure 24.3). One of his specific fears involved entering the restroom at the clinic—a small, enclosed space within the hospital—a fear that seemed directly related to his time in the ICU. He covered the inside of a small wooden box with collage pictures representing his fears: a scary dragon, a dog (he was very afraid of dogs), and wiggly eyes in the ceiling. He placed a wire figure in the center to represent himself, holding a blue bead to symbolize a shark—his favorite animal and a symbol of strength and power. He also included the emergency call button found in the hospital bathroom. In the "Bathroom Box," the patient brought together many scary symbols, but he placed himself in the midst of the scary situation, equipped with tools to help him cope—the bravery and power of the shark, and the call button to connect him to help from outside.

Figure 24.2 Man with holes all over his body.

Figure 24.3 Bathroom box.

Art therapy helped this young man better understand what happened to him in the beginning of his treatment, bring nameless fears into conscious awareness, and practice strategies for coping with his fears.

Conclusion

In a short chapter, it is impossible to discuss all the dimensions of art therapy with children, but I have tried to lay the groundwork for further exploration by building a case for the importance of the profession to young people in contemporary culture. Art therapy promotes self-discovery; supports cognitive development, integration, and control; and allows young people to discover their strengths. In a world dominated by passive entertainment and virtual reality, art therapy allows young people a safe arena to acquire and practice skills that can help them confront and transcend life's challenges.

References

Cassou, M. (2004). *Kids' play: Igniting children's creativity.* New York, NY: Penguin.

Chilcote, R. (2004). Art therapy with child Tsunami survivors in Sri Lanka. *Art Therapy: Journal of the American Art Therapy Association, 24*(4), 156–162.

Councill, T. (2011). Medical art therapy with children. In C. Malchiodi (Ed.), *Handbook of art therapy* (2nd ed., pp. 222–240). New York, NY: Guilford Press.

Gerteisen, J. (2008). Monsters, monkeys and mandalas: Art therapy with children experiencing the effects of trauma and fetal alcoholism spectrum disorder. *Art Therapy: Journal of the American Art Therapy Association, 25*(2), 90–93.

Hetland, L., Winner, E., Veenema, S., & Sheridan, K. (2007). *Studio thinking: the real benefits of visual arts education.* New York, NY: Columbia University Press.

Kramer, E. (1971). *Art as therapy with children.* New York, NY: Schocken Books.

Kramer, E. (1979). *Childhood and art therapy: Notes on theory and practice.* New York, NY: Schocken Books.

Malchiodi, C. (1998). *Understanding children's drawings.* New York, NY: Guilford.

Malchiodi, C. (2011). Art therapy materials, media and methods. In C. Malchiodi (Ed.), *Handbook of art therapy* (2nd ed., pp. 33–39). New York, NY: Guilford Press.

Martin, N. (2011). Art therapy and autism: Overview and recommendations. *Art Therapy: Journal of the American Art Therapy Association, 26*(4), 187–190.

Rubin, J. (1984). *The art of art therapy.* New York, NY: Brunner Mazel.

Safran, D. (2011). An art therapy approach to attention deficit/hyperactivity disorder. In C. Malchiodi (Ed.), *Handbook of Art Therapy* (2nd ed., pp. 192–204). New York, NY: Guilford Press.

Talwar, S. (2007). Accessing traumatic memory through art making: An art therapy trauma protocol (ATTP). *The Arts in Psychotherapy, 34*(2), 22–35.

van der Kolk, B. A., Hopper, J., & Osterman, J. (2001). Exploring the nature of traumatic memory: Combining clinical knowledge with laboratory methods. In B. A. van der Kolk, J. W. Hopper, J. F. Freyd, & A. P. DePrince (Eds.), *Trauma and cognitive science* (pp. 9–31). Binghamton, NY: Haworth Press.

Van Eys, J. (1981). The truly cured child. In J. Spinetta & P. Spinetta (Eds.), *Living with Childhood Cancer* (pp. 30–40). St. Louis: Mosby.

25
Art Therapy with Adolescents
Debra Linesch

The invitation to write this chapter offers me the opportunity to reconsider my book, *Adolescent Art Therapy*, written in 1988, near the beginning of my art therapy career. At the time, my understandings of psychotherapy were not as well formed as today, and the field's theoretical understandings of adolescence were less complicated by cultural constructs of race, ethnicity, and gender. In this chapter, I extend the traditional psychosocial understandings of adolescent development that informed my early art psychotherapy work, and I include contemporary sociological and postmodern ideas to investigate and understand current and culturally complicated clinical work.

Having considered and reconsidered adolescent developmental theory for over 30 years, I have expanded my understandings of the specific ways in which art therapy can be particularly valuable for teenagers—*engaging* them at the very tender places of their developmental challenges, providing them with *empowering* activities that support their progress, and assisting them in finding answers to the kinds of *identity* questions that our culture makes complex and sometimes irresolvable. By briefly exploring updated theories as context for a discussion of three clinical examples of vulnerable youth, contemporary understandings of art therapy approaches with adolescents can be developed.

Theoretical Understandings

Traditional developmental theories

Erikson's immeasurable contributions to adolescent developmental theory focused particularly around identity as a developmental concept. His work brought to light important ideas about adolescence as a psychosocial moratorium and about the problems of foreclosed identity, in which an individual commits to a life direction without experimenting with alternatives. Needless to say, there have been substantive cultural and social changes for young people since Erikson formulated his ideas about identity, particularly in the areas of globalization and technology. The consequent changes in the world in which adolescents need to navigate their transitions offer new

The Wiley Handbook of Art Therapy, First Edition. Edited by David E. Gussak and Marcia L. Rosal.
© 2016 John Wiley & Sons, Ltd. Published 2016 by John Wiley & Sons, Ltd.

possibilities but are fraught with danger and fragmentation. It is necessary to rethink traditional developmental theory and its delineation of adolescent tasks in light of increasingly complex understandings of the contemporary world. In his useful text on clinical work with contemporary youth, Briggs (2008) pointed out how the teenagers he encounters are very aware of the complexities of the adult world they see:

> Adolescents do not simply have to deal with the problem of leaving childhood certainties and dependencies but they also have to gain a way of relating to adult postmodern society. This means encountering turbulence in the socio-cultural context and the fluctuating, shifting, rapidly changing and uncertain adult world. It means moving into an adult world, which is extremely diverse and definable in many different ways. (Briggs, 2008, p. 15)

Contemporary contributions to developmental theories

Vygotsky (1978), the Russian developmental theorist, articulated ideas about collaborative learning processes contributing to psychological development. These notions augmented the prevailing understanding of development to be more broadly seen as an inherently relationship-based process, a system of interconnectivity by which the individual mind develops. By placing emphasis on the ways in which culture shapes development, by placing emphasis on the ways in which social factors contribute to development, and by placing emphasis on the role of language in development, Vigotsky's theories inform a more contemporary understanding of adolescent experiences than did the earlier and less contextualized theories of Erikson.

Vygotsky's model helps contemporize traditional theories, which minimally addressed the contributions of context to adolescent development and rarely included the ways in which the adult world changes and interacts simultaneously with the youth's development as it progresses.

Feminist thinkers

Beginning with the early work of Carol Gilligan (1982), the feminist theorists contributed to a contemporary understanding of adolescence by comprehensively attending to the social construction of gender identity that is culturally requisite for a transition into adulthood. Based on this pioneering work, many theorists have expanded the understanding of societal and biological pressures and complexities that both boys and girls, heterosexual and homosexual, experience as they move through the process of developing a gender identity.

Postmodern culture

Similarly, adolescents in our society struggle with the complexity of developing a racial and/or ethnic identity. It is crucial to consider what Nakkula and Toshalis (2006) describe as "the impact of racial hierarchies, the legacy of racial and ethnic oppression, and the ongoing challenge of constructing a cohesive yet multifaceted identity in contexts that privilege some as they oppress others" (p. 119). Adolescent development occurs within contexts that are laden with racial meaning, and the developmental process is often complicated by divisive and injurious racial categorizations.

Adolescents and Mental Health

It is useful to look at the mental health difficulties that adolescents experience in the context of the expanded developmental theories discussed in the preceding text. It is beyond the scope of this chapter to enumerate mental health diagnoses that are typical access points for adolescents to seek psychotherapeutic help. Instead, this chapter explores case material to illustrate the three points articulated in the introduction to this chapter: *engagement*, *empowerment*, and *identity* as important clinical constructs that are manifest in the art therapy process. Three art therapy cases, embedded in university research, service, and teaching projects, are closely examined to distill the ways in which the process of making, discussing, and finding meaning in imagery is particularly well suited to adolescents, especially when understood in the expanded conceptualization of developmental theory discussed earlier.

Case I

Immigrating and Acculturating Adolescents

In a 2012 research project (Linesch, Aceves, Quezada, Trochez, & Zuniga, 2012) that investigated the acculturation and assimilation experiences of adolescents whose families had recently immigrated to the United States from Mexico and Central American countries, the data collection process illustrated several ways in which art therapy can be an excellent opportunity for facilitating integration and identity with adolescents. A group of adolescents was brought together to explore and express their ideas about being bilingual, bicultural members of families who were struggling with their undocumented status, their families' legal insecurities, and their economic/occupational hardships.

Right from the beginning, it was easy to see how issues of gender, race, religion, language, socio-economic status, and family made the adjustment to the adult world very complicated for these young people. Just as the teenage girls struggled between the pulls of their traditionally and modestly raised mothers and the pulls of the much-less-modest culture to which they were acculturating, the teenage boys struggled to understand the meanings of "machismo" in the complicated tensions between their family loyalties, their family's pressures to succeed in the new culture, and the culture's own mixed messages about success. Figure 25.1, created by a 15-year-old boy, represents the way that a creative process helped this young person give voice to his concerns and experientially develop a preliminary template for a complex but evolving identity.

Figure 25.1 Adolescent identity puzzle.

Engagement

The exercise of creating a self-representational puzzle was an ego-syntonic opportunity for the adolescent to explore the idea that a whole (identity) could be created out of pieces (different, even fragmented, interests and attachments). When an art therapy activity is conceptualized as a chance to explore and play with the concretized symbols of a psychological process, it invites engagement, a sense that the process suits the expressive needs. As this boy cut into fragments the pieces of both the Mexican and the American flag, he was able to feel engaged in deconstruction and reconstruction of his own life and, in particular, his own journey from immigration to acculturation and assimilation.

Empowerment

Empowerment goes hand in hand with engagement. Just as this youth found himself comfortable expressing his experiences in symbolic and concretized form, he was able to feel that the issues that potentially overwhelmed him were less intimidating, more in his control, and even, perhaps, that he could become the orchestrator of their cacophony. It is interesting to note that, in the completed puzzle, the only fragment that actually has people depicted is the piece entitled "Family." This isolated depiction suggests the central importance that family of origin plays in the complicated navigation that the bilingual youngster forges between the culture from which his family immigrated and the culture into which he is helping them assimilate.

Identity

The engagement in the art process (and the subsequent potential engagement in the expression of self) was certainly empowering, but perhaps its greatest impact was the way it supported the articulation of an identity. Fragments of the puzzle representing soccer and high school are the two pieces that seem to create a whole that cohesively arranges itself around the center piece of family and the contextualizing puzzle pieces that represent the two nations that come together as this adolescent's bicultural identity. This project stands as an illustrative representation of using art processes to construct and arrange oneself as a multi-faceted and complicated human being. This challenge is no doubt the challenge that is faced by every contemporary adolescent but is most poignantly viewed in the experiences of the acculturating teenager.

Case II

Gang Affiliating Adolescents

In a 2004 service project at the Los Angeles Museum of Tolerance, a group of middle school students who had been selected because of their vulnerability to gang affiliation was lead through a week-long experience of learning about diversity and making collaborative art. Figure 25.2 depicts the final step in the collaborative process as the youngsters placed their self-representational

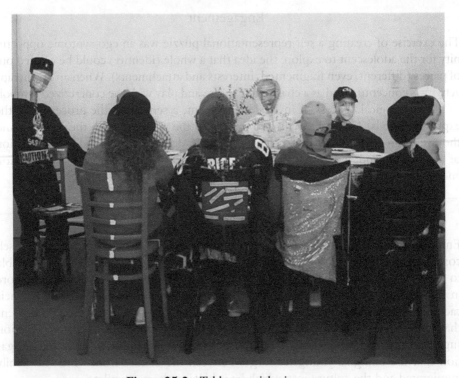

Figure 25.2 Table as social microcosm.

life-size figures on chairs (decorated to represent their individual cultural backgrounds) that were gathered around a table designed to suggest common ground. Several aspects and details of this art piece can be examined for the ways in which they illustrate engagement, empowerment, and identity.

Engagement

Although all the adolescents who participated in this project were initially reluctant (a word carefully chosen as more compassionate than "resistant") to make art in traditional ways, it was not difficult to engage them in building, assembling, and constructing the pieces that were the core of this project. Over the 5 days of the experience, the teens were lead through a series of sequenced projects: designing chairs, setting a table, creating self-representations, and (symbolically) building a community by sitting down at the table together. Although the scope of this chapter does not allow for a detailed discussion of the individual steps of the project, the endeavor is well documented (Linesch, 2004). Again, as discussed in the preceding text, the engagement of reluctant youngsters is often facilitated by ensuring that the art tasks are conceptualized as meeting the participant in ways that allow for the exploration of the very issues that trouble him or her, utilizing processes that in and of themselves symbolically address those issues—that is, construction of self, creation of "seat" in the world, etc.

It is interesting to observe in Figure 25.2 that the most constrained participant, perhaps the one who found the engagement the most threatening, was able to express his ambivalence about joining the project by having his self-representational figure standing on the far side of the table, behind his chair, which had originally been wrapped in yellow police caution tape, with slogans ("grace under pressure" and "A life not ordinary") collaged over his eyes and mouth. What better way to begin to support the development of a silent adolescent's voice than by providing him or her with the symbolic opportunity to depict his/her silence?

Empowerment

Over the week of participation, as each of the teenagers constructed a self-representation, they were able to select, de-select, and re-select the aspects of themselves that they wanted to include. This assembly process seemed reflective of the contemporary adolescent psychological process initially identified by Erikson as establishing an identity. Concurrently the art process seemed to be enriched with cultural understandings as per the work of Vygotsky and the feminist, culturally responsive theorists who augmented the knowledge of adolescent identity development as a dialogue with the environment. By using images from contemporary magazines and artifacts from contemporary culture (sweatshirts, bandanas, police tape, baseball caps) as art materials, the participants were able to immediately see opportunities for self-expression in the project. As they began assembling a self-representation, a chair, and ultimately a table where they could all meet each other, they symbolically took steps toward self-empowerment, taking control over their interactions in the metaphoric arena that this project created. It was a chance to find a different intrapersonal voice and a different interpersonal role and perhaps learn that risk taking and change could restart or reshape a stalled foreclosure.

Identity

Each of the participants was able to find unique and self-expressive opportunities to experiment with their identity, which is a core dimension of Erikson's adolescent tasks. By including in the art materials aspects of the adolescent's world (as noted earlier), the facilitators were able to provide participants with symbolic ways to acknowledge the complicated issues of race, culture, ethnicity, gender, and marginalization. Having the adolescents address these roadblocks, they were able to move forward in the process of acquiring an identity that served as a pathway toward adult maturity.

It is interesting to look more closely at the self-representational figure made by the boy identified in the preceding text as the "most constrained participant." Although reluctant to share much about himself, he dressed his figure in black, suggesting both specific kinds of affiliation and anonymity, but used blue masking tape to completely cover his face, allowing only the words pasted on the surface to give the figure a voice. The words he chose—"grace under pressure" and "A life not ordinary"—may possibly suggest that the teen is trying to individuate, identify, and create a unique self within a challenging and pressured context.

Case III

Incarcerated Adolescents

In a 2012 course project, first-year art therapy graduate students engaged in fieldwork at the Los Angeles Juvenile Hall. Each of the students met one on one with an incarcerated minor who had a history in the foster care system. These youngsters had multiple challenges—poverty, family histories of addiction, racism, inadequate education, etc. By engaging with these teens, the art therapy students were able to examine extreme experiences of the contextual impact of cultural constructs on adolescent development and mental health needs. By integrating this case material into this chapter, the conversation is deepened to incorporate the real worlds in which adolescents live that lie at the margins of our society. The imagery that is included here (Figure 25.3) is a recreated, re-rendered composite of the art that was collected at juvenile hall.

The words that frame the piece express the ambivalence about exposure that was either explicit or implicit in all the imagery. The collage images represent the frequently observed expressions of isolation, yearning for connection, and imminence of disaster. Interestingly, the images simultaneously suggest irrepressible hope for the future. The compartmentalization of the images surrounded by negative space, typical of the incarcerated adolescents' work, reflects both the internal void and the defensive blunting often observed as survival strategies.

Figure 25.3 Adolescent voices from prisoners.
Thanks to Taklai Melissa Li for creating Figure 25.3.

Engagement

It was interesting to observe how stimulated the minors were when they were engaged by the art therapy students; they seemed to physically expand and uncurl within the attentive listening provided, suggesting, as Vygotsky pointed out, that their developing sense of self was dependent on a contextual relationship in which there was dialogue. One of the tragedies of adolescent incarceration is that the experience is often isolating and diminishes interaction. It was also interesting to notice how attracted the minors were to the very simple art materials that the art therapy students made available— limited drawing implements and simple collage items. Importantly, an open-ended prompt to use the art materials for self-expression was all that was offered and, in fact, was all that was needed. The materials and the encouragement increased the minors' willingness to participate in self-disclosure and allowed each teenager to determine how much control they wanted and/or needed.

Empowerment

The art therapy students who engaged with the incarcerated youth acknowledged that their encouragement to the minors to express themselves was "like opening a dam." Despite the very limited materials, the short amount of time, and the unfortunate lack of quiet privacy, the adolescents turned the art-making experience into an act of seizing control, establishing a voice, and (often) imagining an alternative future. It was observed that the minors had a difficult time getting started. Yet, the imagery, and the art therapy students' comments about the deepening of the process as the adolescents become engaged, suggested that this limited experience of creativity within an identity-depriving institution is of enormous importance. The art therapy literature about incarcerated adolescents (Hanes, 2005; Hartz & Thick, 2005; Prescott, Sekendur, Bailey, & Hoshino, 2008) proposes that creativity in general and the art process specifically harness the impulses of incarcerated youth toward self-expression in safe and appropriate manners. Much of the imagery in Figure 25.3 illustrates the deepest concerns about the self, the experience of despair, and the possibility of repair.

Identity

Figure 25.3 also illustrates the ways in which the art process facilitates the exploration of identity issues. The available materials allowed the minors to challenge the stigmatization of their incarceration, to acknowledge the premature foreclosures of their lives (addictions, pregnancy, gang affiliation etc.), to struggle with the feasibility of their future aspirations, and to engage in conversations about gender, culture, and society with personal narratives from their lived experiences.

Concluding Thoughts

It has been a privilege to reconsider my earliest professional thinking about the particular values of art psychotherapy with adolescents in light of current research and contemporary understandings about youth development. With the inclusion of sociological and cultural issues, the conversation about adolescents becomes deeper and is better able to coherently inform clinical conversations. Enriching my earliest clinical ideas about internal psychological processes and external familial processes are the broadly contextual and current theoretical ideas about interactional development that occurs within our complex society.

The three cases that are discussed in this chapter were specifically chosen to explore the experiences of adolescents who struggle at the marginalized edges of our communities. Their responses to the art therapy process poignantly illustrate the suitability of image-based psychotherapy for these youth whose complex clinical issues can best be understood when psychological development is contextualized in the broadest way possible.

References

Briggs, S. (2008). *Working with adolescents and young adults*. New York, NY: Palgrave MacMillan.

Gilligan, C. (1982). *In a different voice*. Cambridge, MA: Harvard University Press.

Hanes, M. J. (2005). Behind steel door: Images from the walls of a county jail. *Art Therapy: Journal of the American Art Therapy Association, 22*(1), 44–48.

Hartz, L., & Thick, L. (2005). Art therapy strategies to raise self-esteem in female juvenile offenders: A comparison of art psychotherapy and art as therapy approaches. *Art Therapy: Journal of the American Art Therapy Association, 22*(2), 70–80.

Linesch, D. (1988). *Adolescent art therapy.* New York, NY: Brunner Mazel.

Linesch, D. (2004). Art therapy at the Museum of Tolerance. *The Arts in Psychotherapy, 31?*(2), 57–66.

Linesch, D., Aceves, H., Quezada, P., Trochez, M., & Zuniga, E. (2012). An art therapy exploration of immigration with Latino families. *Art Therapy, 29*(3), 120–126.

Nakkula, M., & Toshalis, E. (2006). *Understanding youth.* Cambridge, MA: Harvard Education Press.

Prescott, M. V., Sekendur, B., Bailey, B., & Hoshino, J. (2008). Art making as a component and facilitator of resiliency with homeless youth. *Art Therapy: Journal of the American Art Therapy Association, 25*(4), 156–163.

Vygotsky, L. S. (1978). *Mind in society: The development of higher psychological processes.* Cambridge, MA: Harvard University Press.

26

Adult Art Therapy: Four Decades, Ages 20–60 Years

Deborah A. Good

Why Art Making Is Therapeutic for Adults

Adults talk; they verbalize. One of the most important reasons why art therapy is a very effective treatment for adults is because adults verbally have learned how to avoid dealing with issues in their lives. By adulthood, people have learned to get what they want and manipulate their world by talking their way in and out of situations. Adults learn to avoid talking about the real issues in their lives.

Art therapy provides a venue for adults to identify, work on, and resolve life stressors in a metaphoric, imagistic, and safe manner. Although some adults keep a journal, many have not picked up art materials since childhood. "Most adults are unaware of their creative potentialities ... and the self-respect which would make artistic activity constructive in the growth of his personality" (Schaefer-Simmern, 1948, pp. 5–6). Schaefer-Simmern's major contribution to creative development was his approach to "ageless" stages of growth. He felt that, with proper environment and stimulation, people of all ages could release inborn creative abilities in a natural unfolding manner.

Erikson (*New York Times*, 1994) compared the way people interact with each other to watching an artist paint a picture. Early in his career, Erikson took up painting as a way of becoming more involved in the world. His psychosocial theories are founded on a person's need for relationship and how that develops during their lifetime. The stages that relate to this chapter are: Intimacy vs Isolation (18–35 years), and Generativity vs Stagnation (36–60 years). These stages emphasize the need to focus on a career and develop their own family, nurture relationships in a positive and productive manner, become involved in their community, and develop passions and a desire to be useful to others and in the world. Erikson believed that depression often results when a person does not develop loving, healthy relationships, creating a negative self-image that leads to isolation and loneliness. Most of Erikson's theory came from his observations of how people interact and what causes them to have a fruitful or self-destructive life. Creativity is a function of a healthy life. It provides options, which adjusts decision-making, thus affecting one's world view (Erikson, 1994).

The Wiley Handbook of Art Therapy, First Edition. Edited by David E. Gussak and Marcia L. Rosal.
© 2016 John Wiley & Sons, Ltd. Published 2016 by John Wiley & Sons, Ltd.

Culturally, the world is based on analytical thinking—a left-brain world. In comparison, the right brain hemisphere focuses on creativity and imagination. When we engage both the right and left hemispheres of the brain, creative solutions are born to solve issues and questions (Edwards, 1979). Art therapy requires that we use our whole brain. When a pressing issue is presented, thoughts and words combine with images to explain the situation. Art therapy is a safe way for adults to come in contact with their creativity and use their right and left brains to solve problems through images as well as words.

The Therapy Relationship

Working with adults is one of the most rewarding and challenging experiences of a therapist's career. Often, we see ourselves in our clients. As adult therapists, we personally know their struggles, joys, and hopes for the future. We can relate to their unresolved issues, unmet goals and dreams, grief over the loss of loved ones, and struggles with family and friends. Adult clients challenge therapists to continue to improve their own lives in order best to serve them and to maintain clear boundaries in all therapeutic relationships.

Life stages force us to confront challenges that previously may not have been important. Adults have lived through several stages of life, repeated lessons until learned and experienced deep loss, despair, comfort, and love more than any other age group of clients. Many adult clients are going through issues regarding career, relationships, deciding whether to have children and/or how to be a parent, taking care of parents, or developing an adult relationship with their parents (Erikson, 1950, 1975). These clients challenge the therapist to maintain clear boundaries, especially when the issues presented relate closely to the therapist's personal life.

Clear boundaries are increasingly necessary as the client and therapist become deeply engaged in a trusting therapeutic relationship. Most importantly, the therapy relationship is one of trust. Trust must be maintained to keep the client safe in all aspects of the relationship: to allow the therapist to make decisions that are in the best interest of the client, to respect the boundaries set by the client, and to maintain personal boundaries within the professional, therapeutic relationship.

Introducing Art Therapy

Human beings think in images and then put words to those images (Jung, 1964). When it comes to putting thoughts down on paper, adults are more comfortable with words. It is critical self-judgment that keeps adults from freely drawing out their thoughts. Yet, most adults doodle while on the telephone, in a lecture, or mindlessly to relax. Reminding an adult client that they do draw when they doodle normalizes art therapy in a safe, familiar way.

It is likely that many adults have not used art materials since their childhood. Introducing art materials to adults creates a range of responses, everything from inquisitive to no interest at all. It is helpful to ask the adult client a series of questions, such as:

1. What made you choose to enter into art therapy as a course of treatment?
2. Would you be willing to work with art materials to help facilitate your therapy experience?
3. When was the last time you used art materials?
4. Do you have art supplies at home, and what are they?
5. Do you sketch while writing notes, or doodle?
6. Do you keep a personal journal?

These questions may be addressed during an intake inventory session or the first art therapy session. The answers will help the therapist to understand the client's anxiety and/or willingness to express himself/herself through creativity.

Loosening exercises are helpful to re-familiarize the client with using art materials. A simple scribble drawing allows the client to experience the freedom of not having to represent a specific image, but rather to use the art material in a playful manner. Florence Cane (1983) first introduced the "scribble technique." Hanes (1995) gave a thorough review of the history of the "scribble technique," including techniques and materials used by art therapists to elicit conversation or additional drawings. Usually, water-based markers, crayons, oil pastels, or colored pencils are used for this art therapy exercise. These art materials give the client more control over the media, and, therefore, a sense of being in control in the session. After the scribble drawing is completed, the client is directed to see if he or she recognizes any known images and to embellish this part of the drawing. Another way to use the scribble technique is as a warm up to the therapy session—a way in which the client sheds tension from the day while focusing on the therapy session (Landgarten, 1981; Landgarten & Lubbers, 1991; Kerr & Hoshino, 2008).

Assessing the Client's Needs and Goal Setting

Some art therapists begin with a standard battery of art therapy assessments, while others are more informal in evaluating the client's needs and goals. Clients always come into therapy with an expected end result in mind—even if they cannot identify the problem. Therapists must listen closely to the client's story and formulate questions to help areas that are not fully expressed. Also, it is very important to observe if the client's body language matches their words. Body language demonstrates what is being avoided, what the client wants you to hear, and what personal situations cause the client to feel a variety of emotions, including stress. An immediate goal of therapy must be to deal with reducing the client's stress and to identify the client's strengths. Ideally, therapeutic goals should be set with the client in the first session, as well as a discussion held about how to achieve those goals.

In a beginning session, it is helpful to introduce a small variety of 2D art materials from which the client may choose. One way to start is by asking the client to use art

Figure 26.1 This is me, I am. Self-portrait.

materials to tell you something about himself/herself. Encourage them to think about what makes them different from everyone else, or what is important in their lives. A more structured way of approaching this information is provided by Spring (1992) in her work with adults who have experienced trauma. She introduced a five-part drawing series, which begins with an initial drawing, titled (1) "This is me, I am." The client creates a self-portrait that describes for the therapist who they are and what they value in life. From this initial drawing, the therapist and client begin to dialogue about what the client hopes to achieve in therapy. This drawing is followed by drawings depicting (2) "My space," (3) "My life's road," (4) "My family and me," and a second drawing of "This is me, I am" is the fifth in the series. Spring used Gestalt (Perls, Hefferline, & Goodman, 1951) orientation in her art directives in order to keep the client focused on himself/herself. This five-part drawing series works well for most issues that bring adults into therapy.

The drawing in Figure 26.1 is an example of "This is me, I am." The client, Sarah, a 57-year-old woman, was an artist suffering from multiple sclerosis (MS). In this picture made with chalk pastels, Sarah depicted her feelings about longing to find a partner with whom she could share her life. She feared this would never happen and mourned her loneliness in the world and the loss of her physical health. Her grief was evident in this self-portrait. She chose to draw a picture of only her head, and to cover the page in the color green. On considering this picture, it is easy to see that Sarah was disconnected from her body, which had brought her many problems and discomfort. She chose to draw out her facial features in full make-up and verbally expressed that she took pride in the way she looked. The majority of her artwork included the fine, wavy lines, as seen on the right side of the page. She related this to being a 5-year-old Jewish child leaving Europe during World War II, and interpreted the lines as representing the barbed wire that imprisoned many Jews. The black and white forms depicted her thought processing of seeing most things in black and white, later identifying them as specific issues.

Working with an artist in art therapy has its challenges. It was helpful to provide a creative media that Sarah did not use as an art form in her professional work. This allowed her to produce a therapeutic art piece rather than feel pressured to produce an aesthetically pleasing work of art.

Sarah's goals in therapy were to work through her childhood fears, learn to deal with her aloneness and loneliness, and come to a resolution about her physical condition and how it would affect her life in the future. These three goals are represented by the black-and-white symbols in her self-portrait. Sarah also depicted her "life's road" through collage and photographs of her family and friends. By beginning therapy with these two art directives, she was able to become aware of family and friends in her life. She then felt more supported in her struggles, which set a foundation for her to work in therapy to deal with the goals described.

Choosing Art Media and Case Examples

The choice of art materials used in an art therapy session with adults depends on the most appropriate therapeutic goals for the client. As the therapeutic goals change during therapy, so do the creative needs of the client. The client's "artwork ... demonstrates the effectiveness of clinical art therapy for gaining awareness, reality-testing, problem-solving, revealing unconscious material, catharsis, working through conflicts, integration and/or individuation" (Landgarten, 1981, p. 3). The art therapist may guide the session by offering structured art material for a client who is feeling as if his or her life is out of control, or a more fluid art material for a client who wants to look at life choices. The choice of art material also helps to pace the progression of therapy and provides a framework for therapy to occur.

Collage provides a safe way for clients to make art without feeling that they must create all the images themselves (Landgarten, 1993). The mere act of cutting out images from magazines can be relaxing, allowing the clients freely to verbalize their thoughts and feelings. Sensitive issues can be addressed from a distance as images that represent them are placed on a piece of paper. Clients often are amazed at the evolution of the collage and find that verbally processing the end product with the therapist brings them self-insight, and, often, conflict resolution. Using collage in art therapy can be both a formal diagnostic technique (Landgarten, 1993) and a therapeutic intervention.

Oil pastels and chalk pastels are commonly chosen by adult art therapy clients. Pastels provide a means of fluidity, softness, and an ability to blend images and colors together. Oil pastels provide the feeling of crayons with a more sophisticated usage.

Clay is a powerful 3D art material that allows the client to directly manipulate the art image. There is a different emotional impact that occurs when the client is actually making direct contact with the art material. Ceramic clay is wet and earth-like in touch, resulting in an organic sensation that may immediately engage the emotions of the client. Red ceramic clay with grout added works best when the therapeutic intention is to assist the client in regressing to an emotional state to access their feelings, while white smooth clay sets an intellectual tone. A substantive medium, such as ceramic clay, often provides the support needed to work through the client's emotionally charged issues.

A 26-year-old male client, who was working through anger over his chemical addiction, made a snake out of white ceramic clay. He described his addiction as "creeping up on him like a coiled snake ready to pounce at any moment." When this image was photographed from above, it looked more like a question mark. The client felt that this was a fair explanation for his addiction recovery—in the future, he always would have to question his decisions and intentions in relationship to his addictive tendencies. As a young adult, his future life depended on his ability to have a career and surround himself with healthy friends and family, but all these desires hinged on maintaining sobriety.

Mask making often is used in art therapy sessions. Masks can be made out of a variety of materials, from paper to plaster gauze (Sivin, 1986). Using plaster gauze directly on a client's face is one way to create a mask. Masks can be decorated on the inside and/or the outside, depending on the goals of the therapy project. Clay can be pressed into the inside of the plaster mask to produce an exact replica of the client's face. Decorating the inside and the outside of masks to represent what the client allows others to see of them and what they personally feel inside provides a greater opportunity for clients to see what parts of their personality they hide and who they present to the world. This dual concept of self can be applied to feelings of grief and loss, past and present or future, choices to be made in life, or shedding of old memories and behaviors.

Meg, a 38-year-old woman, decorated the heart-shaped mixed-media box shown in Figure 26.2 as a way to honor her mother, who had recently died. Meg covered the outside of the box with tissue paper and decoupage. After it dried, glitter glue was added to outline the designs made by the tissue-paper-collaged shapes. Glass beads were glued on the lid for decoration. Meg lined the inside of the box and lid with red velvet, satin, and pearl beads. She placed items that had belonged to her mother—silk rose and small trinkets—inside the box. Some of the items were glued in permanently, while others could be removed. In some ways, the box seemed to represent a shrine for her mother's memory. In many ways, it helped to contain Meg's grief over the loss of her mother.

Susan, a 43-year-old woman, made the three clay images shown in Figure 26.3. She suffered from severe depression and anxiety, crippling diabetes, rheumatoid arthritis, and numerous other physical aliments. The ceramic form on the left is a depiction of her spine. To Susan, her spine felt as if it had scales that constantly pinched her back.

Figure 26.2 Remembrance box.

Figure 26.3 Three clay pieces—"My pain," "emotional emptiness," and "brain."

She had difficulty lying down to sleep and spent her nights sleeping in a chair. The top middle square box is a small open container. She described this as feeling empty, small, and insignificant. Jung (1964) talked about the container representing the feminine. In many ways, this client felt cheated out of her femininity and mourned her inability to do things that she used to enjoy.

The image on the right is a depiction of her brain. She felt that her intellectual capacity was limited due to her pain medications. Her cognitive functioning had diminished, and she struggled daily to make sense of her life. In processing these images, Susan was encouraged to put them in a place of honor in her home—a place where she could see that her spine and brain were safe. Therapy focused on her developing a sense of compassion with her self and acceptance of her increasing disabilities. She placed a glass heart in her empty container, which she described as a means of filling it up with a sense of love and a reminder that her heart remained unaffected.

Fifty-five year old Mary was a talented artist, minister by profession, abuse survivor, and recovering alcoholic. Mary was single when she entered art therapy and created her first collage (not shown). She made cloth pouches and attached them to the left side of the art piece. Inside the pouches, she placed memories from her past—notes, messages, and symbolic small treasures. Each bag was hand-sewn and decorated. A velvet boundary line separated the left and right sides of the collage. In the center was a plain plaster gauze mask that was made on Mary's face. A mirror was placed behind the mask to allow the viewer to see the inside. It was adorned with a cascading veil of green velvet and ribbon. One cloth pouch was tucked in at the base of the veil. Words of encouragement and affirmations were scattered around the collage. This art piece represented Mary at a point in her therapy when she was looking for change in her life, growing into a new creative person, and expecting adventure. This project took 4 months for Mary to complete and continued to evolve for another 3 months.

Two years later, Mary fell in love and married. A year into her marriage, Mary was diagnosed with breast cancer. After chemotherapy treatments and radiation, Mary had a mastectomy, another year of chemotherapy, and a second round of cancer. When she was first diagnosed, she started the mixed-media collage represented in Figure 26.4. Mary took apart her first collage, painted the mask, separated several of the images, softened the boundary lines that were in the first collage, and changed

Figure 26.4 Life journey collage.

the contents in the memory pouches. The second plaster gauze 3D image that is painted blue in the bottom left hand corner represents the breast that she had removed. The color of the background is different, the images are more separated, and the whole art piece seems to work well as a storyboard of Mary's experience with cancer. This project took many months to complete. Mary worked on it at home between art therapy sessions. The completed art piece was displayed at the cancer center along with the artwork of other cancer survivors. Mary felt that her art expression greatly enriched her recovery.

There are many more examples of the effectiveness of art therapy with adults. The case studies discussed in this chapter present good examples of how creative expression enhances personal growth, stimulates resiliency, and brings healing into dark problematic situations.

Conclusion

Art therapy with adults is as varied as the individuals who walk through a therapist's office door. It is important to listen to the clients' needs and guide them to the creative expression that will best facilitate the goals of therapy. Introducing art to adults stimulates a means of self-expression that is safe in breaking down barriers that prevent issue resolution. Art provides a non-threatening way for clients to deal with their problems in a safe and distanced manner. Different art materials and techniques elicit a variety of emotional responses in the art maker. Hopefully, the client's art therapy experience will bring him or her a new self-insight and understanding so that he or she can make the necessary choices to live a more productive, stress-free life.

References

Cane, F. (1983). *The artist in each of us* (rev. ed.). Craftbury Common, VT: Art Therapy Publications.

Edwards, B. (1979). *Drawing on the right side of the brain.* New York, NY: Jeremy P. Tarcher/Putnam, Inc.

Erikson, E. H. (1950). *Childhood and society.* New York, NY: Norton.

Erikson, E. H. (1975). *Life History and the Historical Moment.* New York, NY: Norton.

Erikson, E. H. (1994). *Identity and the life cycle.* New York, NY: Norton.

Hanes, M. (1995). Clinical application of the "scribble technique" with adults in an acute inpatient psychiatric hospital. *American Art Therapy Association, 12*(2), 111–117.

Jung, C. G. (1964). *Man and his symbols.* Garden City, NY: Doubleday & Company, Inc.

Kerr, C., & Hoshino, J. (2008). *Family art therapy: Foundations of theory and practice.* New York, NY: Routledge, Taylor & Francis Group.

Landgarten, H. B. (1981). *Clinical art therapy: A comprehensive guide.* New York, NY: Brunner/Mazel, Inc.

Langarten, H. B. (1993). *Magazine photo collage: A multicultural assessment and treatment technique.* New York, NY: Brunner-Routledge.

Landgarten, H. B., & Lubbers, D. (1991). *Adult art psychotherapy: Issues and applications.* New York, NY: Brunner/Mazel, Inc.

The New York Times. (1994). Erik Erikson, 91, psychoanalyst who reshaped views of human growth, dies. *The New York Times* (May 13).

Perls, F., Hefferline, R. F., & Goodman, P. (1951). *Gestalt therapy.* New York, NY: Bantam Books.

Schaefer-Simmern, H. (1948). *Unfolding of artistic activity.* Berkeley, CA: University of California Press.

Sivin, C. (1986). *Maskmaking.* Worchester, MA: Davis Publications. Inc.

Spring, D. (1992). *Shattered images: The phenomenological language of sexual abuse.* Chicago, IL: Magnolia Street.

27
Art Therapy with Older Adults: A Focus on Cognition and Expressivity
Amanda Alders Pike

The goal of this chapter is to provide practical, theory-building foundations for art therapy with older adults. For the purpose of this chapter, individuals who are 55 years of age and older will constitute "older adults." The age was chosen (rather than 65 years and older) based on research showing that many older adults who are designated as part of a minority suffer age-related impairments with an earlier onset (National Institute on Aging, 2005). As demographic shifts continue, art therapists may find that they will work with an increasing quantity of minority older adults. The older adult population of a minority group is growing faster than the older adult population as a whole, at a 2:3 ratio (American Psychological Association, 2010; Minckler, 2008).

Many older adults, especially of ethnically diverse backgrounds, have little or no experience in using art materials or in expressing themselves visually. Regardless of past artistic experience, art therapy is an effective means of providing therapeutic care to older adults (Alders, 2009, 2012; Stewart, 2004). In an overview of non-pharmacological approaches to dementia, art therapy is described as a treatment expected to improve the cognitive functioning of older adults by stabilizing emotions (Masazumi, Yuko, & Shin, 2004). The benefits of art therapy are in the expressive components, not in the visual motor act of art-making; copying images (which do not hold emotional significance for the older adult) do not provide the same benefits as creative art-making (De Petrillo & Winner, 2005). Drawing and painting provide individuals with the opportunity for self-expression, decision-making, and other cognitive skills (Harlan, 1993; Kaplan, 2000; Serrano, Allegri, Martelli, Taragano, & Rinalli, 2005; Silvia, 2005). In a qualitative study by Woolhiser-Stallings (2010), art therapy interventions aided older adults in feeling a much-needed sense of dignity and control in life. Art therapy sessions are said to bring a sense of emotional comfort to modern healthcare settings (Pratt, 2004).

The Wiley Handbook of Art Therapy, First Edition. Edited by David E. Gussak and Marcia L. Rosal.
© 2016 John Wiley & Sons, Ltd. Published 2016 by John Wiley & Sons, Ltd.

Cognitive Impairment, Art Therapy Theories and Approaches

Research demonstrates that art therapy is successfully used as a treatment for many of the factors affecting older adults, such as depression, isolation, cognitive impairment, dementia, and Alzheimer's disease (AD). Cognitive impairment will be the primary focus of this chapter, since depression and social isolation negatively affect cognition, and cognitive impairment can lead to AD. Studies show that individuals with untreated cognitive impairment are 2.8 times more at-risk for AD (Manly et al., 2008).

The term "cognitive impairment" in this chapter will reference mild cognitive impairment (MCI) of the amnestic type. In other words, this chapter will deal with language deficiencies (e.g., difficulty with sentence formation), attentional deficit (e.g., difficulty following conversations), and problems with visuospatial skills (e.g., disorientation and an inability to appropriately utilize fine/gross motor skills; Gauthier et al., 2006). To address cognitive impairment, art therapists may benefit from understanding art therapy theory with cognitive training research.

Two art therapy theorists are presented in this chapter as a result of their influence on art therapy methods with older adults: Vija Lusebrink and Noah Hass-Cohen. Lusebrink developed the Expressive Therapies Continuum (ETC), which is based on the idea that information is processed by the brain on three hierarchical levels of knowledge: (a) kinesthetic/sensory; (b) perceptual/affective; and (c) cognitive/symbolic, made visible by graphic indicators in the artwork (Hinz, 2009; Kagin & Lusebrink, 1978). Noah Hass-Cohen developed the Art Therapy Relational Neuroscience Principles (ATR-N), which is a system of six principles that present art therapists with knowledge on the neurobiology of emotion, cognition, and behavior occurring during the art-making process. Both of these theoretical frameworks may benefit art therapists who work with older adults and are seen as complementary (Table 27.1).

An art therapist using a framework provided by ETC may chart art products created by older adult clients in order to track progress and better understand client levels of functioning. From this framework, an art therapist working with older adults may plan art-making for the art therapy sessions along a continuum of increased levels of complexity over a period of time, thereby increasing stimulation systematically (Lusebrink, 2004). Lusebrink's theory may also facilitate art therapists' clinical decision-making, and help art therapists to pre-plan future sessions, while also helping

Table 27.1 Use of theories for art therapy with older adults (Alders, 2014)

Theorist	Theory	Use with Older Adults	Central Tenet
Lusebrink	ETC	Art may be created with an increased level of complexity	Systematically stimulate brain structures and functions
Hass-Cohen	ATR-N	Art-making may assist automatic responses of the autonomous nervous system being placed under conscious control	Fine-tune art-making interventions to enable synchronization of bodily functions

art therapists explain to administrators and stakeholders why older adults may benefit cognitively from art therapy (Hinz, 2009; Kagin & Lusebrink, 1978).

An art therapist using a framework provided by ATR-N may work with clients during the session to help them become conscious of how automatic responses of the autonomous nervous system can be placed under conscious control (Farah & Feinberg, 2000). Using this framework, an art therapist may come to understand the neurological underpinnings that occur during a given session in order to fine-tune art-making interventions in the moment (Hass-Cohen & Carr, 2008). Through ATR-N, art therapists can teach clients to synchronize bodily functions (e.g., breathing and eye movements) with activities during art-making to enhance the therapeutic effect of the session (Hass-Cohen & Carr, 2008). For instance, an art therapist may direct a client to listen to music and create a scribble drawing while breathing in rhythm to the beat.

Training Interventions

Outside of the field of art therapy, cognitive training (CT) is increasingly used to address cognitive performance among the elderly; clinicians have developed techniques for cognitive training such as puzzles, reading and verbal drills, and reasoning exercises (Elias & Wagster, 2007; Sitzer, Twamley, & Jeste, 2006). CT has proven capable of enhancing cognitive performance (e.g., improved memory and a sense of personal control) for up to 5 years following the initial training intervention, with up to 40% of individuals returning to normal cognitive functioning (Willis et al., 2006; Wolinsky et al., 2009).

Art therapy may naturally incorporate CT strategies. CT targets key skills such as episodic memory for language deficiencies, inductive reasoning for attention deficits, and visual search and identification for problems with visual-spatial skills; art therapy does too (Alders, 2012). However, to the older adults' benefit, art therapists often go beyond cognitive goals to address emotional goals as well; emotion is not typically a factor in CT sessions (Table 27.2). Emotion is a critical component in cognitive functioning since factors such as depression directly impact memory, coordination, and other cognitive abilities (Hendrie et al., 2006).

Art therapy provides an opportunity for components of the artwork to be identified, named, and defined in terms of their placement and relationships (Hass-Cohen & Carr, 2008; Rubin, 2001). Thus, artwork discussed in the therapy sessions exercises verbal episodic memory. Likewise, art therapy is said to engage inductive and other reasoning skills through higher cortical thinking, such as planning, focused attention, and problem-solving during art-making tasks (Hass-Cohen & Carr, 2008). Furthermore, art therapy often incorporates exercises of choice, interpretation, and meaning construction to cultivate visual search and identification skills in a practical and straightforward manner (Malchiodi, 2006). A participant may be asked to scan an artistic representation for objects that are recognizable and personally meaningful; for instance, during collage-making, the participant may be asked to select autobiographical images, make unique visual connections between these images, and select complementary shapes or colors.

Table 27.2 Overview of parallels between cognitive training and art therapy (Alders, 2014)

Stimulated Area	Cognitive Training	Art Therapy
Episodic memory	Remembering details of stories	Discussing details of life experiences as related to artwork
Inductive reasoning	Solving problems in a serial pattern	Deriving meaning from images through interpretation, and meaning construction
Visual search and identification	Locating visual information	Deciphering, choosing, and creating images that include visual self-references

Art Therapy and Neuroscience

Understanding the aging process is helpful when working with older adults, and the findings from neuroscience are relevant to today's art therapists. Researchers have realized that the brain is "plastic" and able to undergo neurogenesis through a "sprouting" of new connections between brain cells, particularly within the hippocampus (Stern, 2009). This plasticity occurs as a result of exposure to an enriched environment— which includes the promotion of physical activity, socialization, and problem-solving (Studenski et al., 2006). An enriched environment leads to an increase in new neurons, or neurogenesis, and a substantial improvement in cognitive performance (Kempermann, Gast, & Gage, 2002; Studenski et al., 2006). Physical activity (e.g., manually creating art), problem solving (e.g., deciding on color), and socialization (e.g., describing artwork made) are all naturally incorporated into art therapy sessions, equating to an enriched environment, which may increase the likelihood of neurogenesis (Alders, 2009; Diamond, 2000; Guillot et al., 2009; Riley, 2004).

Socialization is especially important during the art therapy session as it simultaneously addresses risk factors for cognitive impairment: depression and isolation. The increase in socialization resulting from art therapy can be explained as follows (Alders, 2012): (a) art objects aid in communication and provide a point of reference during socializing (Abraham, 2004; Malchiodi, 2006; Østergaard, 2008); (b) older adult art therapy participants can show friends and family their artwork, increasing discussions that may in turn increase interest and motivation for continued socialization (Thoman, Sansone, & Pasupathi, 2007); and (c) social interaction engages diverse cognitive resources and distinct brain areas, facilitating improved cognitive functioning and future art-making (Glei et al., 2005; Ybarra et al., 2008).

Where Art Therapists Serve Older Adults

Art therapists working with older adults are effective in a variety of locations. In this chapter, three types of locations will be described: community centers, day care centers, and skilled nursing/assisted living facilities. Research suggests that many ethnically diverse older adults prefer community-based care (Connell, Roberts, & McLaughlin, 2007), so day care centers and community centers may host more ethnically diverse older adults than skilled nursing or assisted living facilities. Some research suggests that older adults perceived "nursing homes" as a form of

Table 27.3 Facilities where art therapists work with older adults (Alders, 2014)

Type of Facility	Pros	Cons
Adult day care	Structured, non-institutional, high ratio of staff to older adults, higher family involvement	Older adults may not have guardianship of self, older adults vary in functioning
Community center	Informal setting, more opportunities for social relationships, higher functioning/independent older adults	Less structure, lesser funding, higher attrition based on transportation, etc.
Assisted living/ skilled nursing	Well-funded, director position opportunities for art therapists	Lower functioning, higher attrition based on health problems/death, older adults may not have guardianship of self

abandonment and betrayal (Connell et al., 2007). Generally speaking, non-residential options are preferred among minority older adults (Table 27.3).

Adult day care is said to provide a protective setting that is as non-institutional as possible. Based on therapist reports in previous art therapy research, adult day care centers have offered art therapists a structured atmosphere and facilitated predictable start and stop times for art therapy sessions with minimal distractions or interruptions (Alders, 2012). Assisted living facilities/skilled nursing homes also provide structured settings. However, older adults in these facilities may be functioning at a lower level and be experiencing more severe cognitive impairments.

In previous art therapy research, attendance to art therapy sessions in assisted living facilities/skilled nursing homes was limited by the other activities offered by the facility, as well as the cognitive deficits characteristic of the population (Alders, 2012). Art therapists were competing for attendance with such programs as yoga, gardening, bingo, etc. However, at these sites, art therapists were employed in director/administrator positions, suggesting that funding and perceived capacities of art therapists may be good (Alders, 2012).

Art therapists may also provide services in community centers. Such settings may provide a more casual and informal atmosphere for art therapists. However, in contrast to day care centers, previous research showed that a lot of advocacy on the part of the art therapists was required at the community centers to maintain attendance (Alders, 2012). Older adults attended the center irregularly or experienced transportation issues (Alders, 2009, 2012).

Art Therapy Session Goals

When addressing cognitive performance in session, art therapists will find that older adults may be more sensitive to stress than younger clients; older adults experience age-related stressors and depression due to changes in lifestyle and financial status after retirement; death of relatives, loved ones, or close friends; and worries concerning dependence (Miller & O'Callaghan, 2005; Rothman & Mattson, 2010; Silver, 1999). Art therapists may find that encouraging confidence in cognitive abilities while allowing stress relief through reminiscence may be beneficial. Reports on art therapy interventions in the United States and abroad indicate that participants from a variety of ethnicities showed significantly reduced depression following participation in art therapy (Doric-Henry, 1997; Jonas-Simpson & Mitchell, 2005).

Art therapists may be well advised to assess (e.g., through drawing directives) a participant's cognitive functioning before establishing sessions in order to evaluate the likelihood that the prospective participant will benefit from the format of art therapy planned. Some older adults may have poor eyesight or hearing and struggle to engage in group sessions. Several may have more severe cognitive impairment than others and may struggle to stay attentive. In such cases, 1:1 art therapy may be more appropriate than group formats (Alders, 2012). Deciding on the appropriate format for therapy is important for older adult progress. Older adults placed in group formats should have the physical, mental, and emotional faculties to be able to benefit from the social interaction. Otherwise, the group format may create an additional stressor for the older adult and should be avoided.

Although a diverse art therapy group may provide rich opportunities for cultural exchange, obvious differences among participants may prevent enthusiasm for the sessions. If homogeneous groups are not a possibility, art therapists may benefit from establishing "rules" at the beginning of the group's establishment and explicitly stating firm boundaries for participation. Older adult behavior/impulse control varies due to damage that occurs to the limbic system throughout the progression of cognitive impairment. Cursing, violence, and sexual acting-out can and does occur with older adults. In previous art therapy research with older adults, the beginning of romantic relationships, blatant racism, and socio-economic class discrimination could all be observed and required regular redirects (Alders, 2012).

Planning Ahead: Protocols and Duration of Sessions

As part of the normal aging process, some cognitive abilities decline with age— information processing speed, learning rate, the ability to filter out irrelevant information through selective attention, and word-finding (American Psychological Association, 2010). Additionally, studies show that depression can lead to even more slowed functioning, such as decreased executive ability, processing speed, and effortful attention (Gilley, Wilson, Bienias, Bennett, & Evans, 2004). Art therapists may find that older adults require longer sessions; 45-minute sessions may prove to be insufficient, especially in group sessions. In groups, older adults may require sessions closer to 90 minutes (Alders, 2012).

By including additional time, art therapists in recent research were able to provide a range of stimulation and opportunities to optimize cognitive performance (Alders, 2012). Additionally, by using graphic indicators as an opportunity to adjust the remaining session dynamics, those clients who were experiencing symptoms of cognitive impairment could be targeted for increased stimulation (Alders, 2012).

Art therapists may also find that structuring sessions, deciding therapeutic goals before beginning sessions, and lengthening sessions beyond 45 minutes (e.g., 90 minutes) may promote regular attendance to sessions; clients will know what to

Table 27.4 Example session plans

Length	Directive	Goal	Format
90 min	Make a collage of gratitude. Use images to represent experiences and aspects of your life that you are grateful for. Show group members and describe your images.	Visual search and identification, socialization, promote positive mood	Group
90 min	Get to know your neighbor: Visual conversation activity (Liebmann, 1986). In groups of two, select a colored marker. Without talking, create an image. Respond in silence to your partner's drawing. Discuss the experience.	Increase socialization, practice creative decision-making	Group
60 min	Using plastilene, create a representation of at least one of your family members. Include as many details of your family member as possible. Why did you include the details you did?	Inductive reasoning, exercise motor skills, verbal/episodic memory	Individual
60 min	Referencing a word bank of emotions, and while viewing a copy of an expressionistic painting, name all of the emotions that are associated with the painting. Pick colors to represent those emotions. Create a response painting to the image, using those colors.	Verbal/episodic memory, exercise cognitive skills through multi-step instructions	Individual

expect, understand the purpose of the sessions, and be able to anticipate upcoming sessions. This process may also aid in marketing the value of art therapy to administration beyond recreation or arts-and-crafts. In previous studies, the very administrators who hired art therapists to work with older adults did not actually understand what occurred in art therapy sessions—this, mixed with economy recessions and time management constraints, contributed to attrition among the art therapists in employment settings (Alders, 2012). Table 27.4 provides examples of structured session plans, corresponding therapeutic goals, session lengths, and formats (Alders, 2012).

Conclusion

Older adults benefit from art therapy, and art therapists work in a variety of settings when serving older adults. Regardless of location, art therapists will benefit from preparing clearly defined goals and pre-planning sessions in order to highlight the benefits of art therapy sessions to administrators, older adults, and other stakeholders such as family members. Art therapists are at an advantage when working with older adults, in that art therapy techniques may simultaneously stimulate cognitive functioning while also addressing contributing factors to cognitive impairment, such as depression and social isolation. However, older adults may require longer art therapy sessions in order to fully gain from the creative process. Additionally, older adults may require a combination of art-as-therapy and art–psychotherapy techniques and theoretical perspectives in order to make cognitive and emotional progress.

References

Abraham, R. (2004). *When words have lost their meaning: Alzheimer's patients communicate through art.* Westport, CT: Praeger.

Alders, A. (2009). Using creative arts therapy to enhance cognitive performance in Hispanic elderly (Unpublished master's thesis). Nazareth College.

Alders, A. (2012). The effect of art therapy on cognitive performance among ethnically diverse older adults (Unpublished doctoral dissertation). Florida State University.

Alders Pike, A. (2014). *Improving memory through creativity: A professional's guide to culturally-sensitive cognitive training with older adults.* Philadelphia, PA: Jessica Kingsley, Publishers.

American Psychological Association. (2010). Guidelines for psychological practice with older adults. Retrieved from http://www.apa.org/practice/adult.pdf

Connell, C. M., Scott Roberts, J., & McLaughlin, S. J. (2007). Public opinion about Alzheimer's disease among Blacks, Hispanics, and Whites: Results from a national survey. *Alzheimer disease and Associated Disorders, 21*(3), 232–240.

De Petrillo, L., & Winner, E. (2005). Does art improve mood? A test of a key assumption underlying art therapy. *American Journal of Art Therapy, 22*(4), 28–56.

Diamond, K. (2000). *Older brains and new connections.* San Luis Obispo, CA: Davidson Publications.

Doric-Henry, L. (1997). Pottery as art therapy with elderly nursing home residents. *Art Therapy: Journal of the American Art Therapy Association, 14*(3), 163–171.

Elias, J. W., & Wagster, M. V. (2007). Developing context and background underlying cognitive intervention/training studies in older populations. *The Journals of Gerontology Series B: Psychological Sciences and Social Sciences, 62*(Special Issue 1), 5–10.

Farah, M., & Feinberg, T. (2000). A historical perspective on cognitive neuroscience. In T. Feinberg & M. Farah (Eds.), *Patient-based approaches to cognitive neuroscience* (pp. 3–19). Cambridge, MA: The MIT Press.

Gauthier, S., Reisberg, B., Zaudig, M., Petersen, R. C., Ritchie, K., Broich, K., … International Psychogeriatric Association Expert Conference on Mild Cognitive Impairment. (2006). Mild cognitive impairment. *Lancet, 367*(9518), 1262–1270.

Gilley, W., Wilson, L., Bienias, L., Bennett, A., & Evans, A. (2004). Predictors of depression symptoms in persons with Alzheimer's disease. *Journal of Gerontology: Psychological Sciences, 59*(2), 75–83.

Glei, D. A., Landau, D. A., Goldman, N., Chuang, Y.-L., Rodriguez, G., & Weinstein, M. (2005). Participating in social activities helps preserve cognitive function: An analysis of a longitudinal, population-based study of the elderly. *International Journal of Epidemiology, 34*(4), 864–871.

Guillot, A., Collet, C., Nguyen, V. A., Malouin, F., Richards, C., & Doyon, J. (2009). Brain activity during visual versus kinesthetic imagery: An fMRI study. *Human Brain Mapping, 30*(7), 2157–2172.

Harlan, J. (1993). The therapeutic value of art for persons with Alzheimer's disease and related disorders. *Loss, Grief and Care: A Journal of Professional Practice, 6*(4), 99–106.

Hass-Cohen, N., & Carr, R. (Eds.). (2008). *Art therapy and clinical neuroscience.* London, England: Jessica Kingsley.

Hendrie, H. C., Albert, M. S., Butters, M. A., Gao, S., Knopman, D. S., Launer, L. J., ... Wagster, M. V. (2006). The NIH cognitive and emotional health project. Report of the critical evaluation study committee. *Alzheimer's & Dementia: The Journal of the Alzheimer's Association, 2*(1), 12–32.

Hinz, L. (2009). *Expressive therapies continuum: A framework for using art therapy.* New York, NY: Routledge.

Jonas-Simpson, C. J., & Mitchell, G. J. (2005). Giving voice to expressions of quality of life for persons with dementia through story, music, and art. *Alzheimer's Care Quarterly, 6,* 52–61.

Kagin, S. L., & Lusebrink, V. B. (1978). The expressive therapies continuum. *Art Psychotherapy, 5*(4), 171–180.

Kaplan, F. (2000). *Art, science and art therapy.* Philadelphia, PA: Jessica Kingsley.

Kempermann, G., Gast, D., & Gage, F. H. (2002). Neuroplasticity in old age: Sustained fivefold induction of hippocampal neurogenesis by long-term environmental enrichment. *Annals of Neurology, 52*(2), 135–143.

Lusebrink, V. B. (2004). Art therapy and the brain: An attempt to understand the underlying processes of art expression in therapy. *Art Therapy: Journal of the American Art Therapy Association, 21*(3), 125–135.

Malchiodi, C. (2006). *The art therapy sourcebook.* Lincolnwood, IL: Lowell House.

Manly, J. J., Tang, M. X., Schupf, N., Stern, Y., Vonsattel, J. P., & Mayeux, R. (2008). Frequency and course of mild cognitive impairment in a multiethnic community. *Annals of Neurology, 63*(4), 494–506.

Masazumi, T., Yuko, T., & Shin, K. (2004). Basis of dementia treatment; Nonpharmacological approaches (environmental improvement, rehabilitation, recollection methods, art therapy). *Science Links Japan, 24*(10), 2443–2448.

Miller, D. B., & O'Callaghan, J. (2005). Aging, stress and the hippocampus. *Aging Research Reviews, 4*(2), 123–140.

Minckler, D. (2008). U.S. minority population continues to grow. Retrieved from http://www.america.gov/st/peopleplace-english/2008/May/20080513175840zjsredna0.1815607.html

National Institute on Aging. (2005). Progress report on Alzheimer's disease. NIH Publication No. 05-5724. Bethesda, MD: Author. Retrieved from http://www.alzheimers.org/pr04-05/index.asp

Østergaard, S. (2008). Art and cognition. *Cognitive Semiotics, 2008*(3), 114–133.

Pratt, R. (2004). Art, dance, and music therapy. *Physical Medicine and Rehabilitation Clinics of North America, 15*(4), 827–841.

Riley, S. (2004). The creative mind. *Art Therapy, 21*(4), 184–190.

Rhoads, L. (2009). Museums, meaning making, and memories: The need for museum programs for people with dementia and their caregivers. *Curator: The Museum Journal, 52*(3), 229–240.

Rothman, S. M., & Mattson, M. P. (2010). Adverse stress, hippocampal networks, and Alzheimer's disease. *NeuroMolecular Medicine, 12*(1), 56–70.

Rubin, J. (2001). *Approaches to art therapy: Theory and technique.* New York, NY: University Press.

Serrano, C., Allegri, R. F., Martelli, M., Taragano, F., & Rinalli, P. (2005). Visual art, creativity and dementia. *Vertex (Buenos Aires, Argentina), 16*(64), 418–429.

Silver, R. (1999). Differences among aging and young adults in attitudes and cognition. *Art Therapy: Journal of the American Art Therapy Association, 16*(3), 133–139.

Silvia, P. (2005). Emotional responses to art: From collation and arousal to cognition and emotion. *Review of General Psychology, 1*(4), 342–357.

Sitzer, D. I., Twamley, E. W., & Jeste, D. V. (2006). Cognitive training in Alzheimer's disease: A meta-analysis of the literature. *Acta Psychiatrica Scandinavica, 114*(2), 75–90.

Stewart, E. G. (2004). Art therapy and neuroscience blend: Working with patients who have dementia. *Art Therapy: Journal of the American Art Therapy Association, 21*(3), 148–155.

Stern, Y. (2009). Cognitive reserve. *Neuropsychologia, 47*(10), 2015–2028.

Studenski, S., Carlson, M. C., Fillit, H., Greenough, W. T., Kramer, A., & Rebok, G. W. (2006). From bedside to bench: Does mental and physical activity promote cognitive vitality in late life? *Science of Aging Knowledge Environment, 2006*(10), 21.

Thoman, D., Sansone, C., & Pasupathi, M. (2007). Talking about interests: Exploring the role of social interaction for regulating motivation and the interest experience. *Journal of Happiness Studies, 8*(3), 335–370.

Willis, S. L., Tennstedt, S. L., Marsiske, M., Ball, K., Elias, J., Koepke, K. M., … Wright, E. (2006). Long-term effects of cognitive training on everyday functional outcomes in older adults. *JAMA, 296*(23), 2805–2814.

Wolinsky, F. D., Vander Weg, M. W., Martin, R., Unverzagt, F. W., Willis, S. L., Marsiske, M., … Tennstedt, S. L. (2009). Does cognitive training improve internal locus of control among older adults? *The Journals of Gerontology Series B: Psychological Sciences and Social Sciences, 65*(5), 591–598.

Woolhiser-Stallings, J. (2010). Collage as a therapeutic modality for reminiscence in patients with dementia. *Art Therapy: Journal of the American Art Therapy Association, 27*(3), 136–140.

Ybarra, O., Burnstein, E., Winkielman, P., Keller, M. C., Manis, M., Chan, E., & Rodriguez, J. (2008). Mental exercising through simple socializing: Social interaction promotes general cognitive functioning. *Personality and Social Psychology Bulletin, 34*(2), 248–259.

28

Art Therapy and Thanatology: A Unified Approach

Katy Barrington

Death is universal, yet no one experiences it in the same way. Questions and issues arise when confronting death and dying; thanatology examines these issues. Thanatologists possess advanced levels of competency in helping individuals with end-of-life issues. Art therapists are uniquely equipped to work in this area because they understand that engaging in the creative process is a powerful source for personal exploration and expression. Thus, combining art therapy and thanatology encourages individuals to explore and clarify ambiguities while augmenting personal authenticity using the creative process. Individuals are able to find their own pathways toward resolution and restoration in the midst of experiencing loss.

The focus of this chapter is on the intersection of art therapy and thanatology through the stories of Stephanie (a pseudonym), an older adult in hospice; and is told using paradigms rooted in existentialism, constructivism, and the hospice philosophies. Existentialism posits that an individual exists before he or she has essence (Sartre, 1957). A central concept of existentialism is the quest for an individual to search for meaning and purpose. This search involves the recognition that individuals have the freedom and will to make choices. According to Sartre (1957), an individual is what he or she makes of himself/herself. Constructivism focuses on the concept that reality is created and constructed by the individual (Mahoney, 2006). It asserts that "human beings are active participants in shaping their own experiences" (Mahoney, 2006, p. 32). The hospice philosophy focuses on "fully utilizing the life that remains to dying patients" (Beresford, 1993, p. 8). Beresford also noted that, when individuals are in hospice, they are encouraged to make choices and find meaning. He noted that "people who are terminally ill can still be active participants in life" (1993, p. 7).

From the existential and constructivist paradigms, individuals are able to make meaning about their own existence through context, choice, and reflection. This ultimately helps an individual identify reality for herself/himself as well as create meaning and purpose. Stephanie, the individual portrayed in this chapter, told stories about her life, reminisced, and created images representing her recollections. Through her stories and images, she clarified thoughts, beliefs, and values, which led her to recognize the deeper meaning, value, and purpose of her life.

The Wiley Handbook of Art Therapy, First Edition. Edited by David E. Gussak and Marcia L. Rosal.
© 2016 John Wiley & Sons, Ltd. Published 2016 by John Wiley & Sons, Ltd.

Underlying Theories and Principles

Existentialism, constructivism, and the hospice philosophies all emphasize that individuals can find or *construct* meaning and purpose for one's own life (Mahoney, 2006; Sartre, 1957; Saunders, 1976). In constructivism, Mahoney (2006) noted that "human beings are active participants in organizing and making sense (meaning) of their own lives" (p. 53). According to Neimeyer (2001), the understanding that an individual has about his or her world shapes the meaning about an experience. Jean Paul Sartre (1957), an existentialist, said, "man is what he makes of himself" (p. 15).

The hospice philosophy affirms life not death, and focuses on maximizing the overall quality of life for an individual" (DeSpelder & Strickland, 2010, p. 178). The hospice philosophy affirms life, not death" (Corr, Nabe, & Corr, 2006, p. 180) and focuses on maximizing the overall quality of life for an individual. The founder of modern-day hospice, Dame Cicely Saunders (1976), stated that, even though a person is dying, that person still matters. She said, "You matter because of who you are. You matter to the last moment of your life and we will do all we can not only to help you die peacefully, but also to live until you die" (Saunders, 1976, p. 1003). Dying people want their wishes, values, and attitudes respected and honored regarding how to live until death (Egnew, 2004).

Existentialism

Existentialism is based on the concept that a human exists first before any understanding about the world is known. According to Lavine (1984, pp. 330–332), there are six basic principles in existentialism:

- Existence precedes essence. This means that a human exists before one's human essence exists.
- Anxiety is a universal condition. This means that fear is common to everyone.
- The universe is composed of absurdity. The purpose of existence is unclear.
- There is nothingness to the world. A person exists in a world that is ambiguous and lacks structure.
- Death is a universal condition.
- Alienation is a universal condition.

These basic principles point to the necessity for individuals to create purpose and meaning for oneself. Sartre (1957) asserted that the newly born individual *exists* before the individual has *essence*, distinguishing physical existence from the perceived universal conditions of anxiety, fear, and alienation, which occur in varying degrees in all humans, respectively. He asserted that each individual finds meaning and purpose for his/her own life as a result of these universal conditions being presented. Individuals have the ability to construct their existence (Sartre, 1957). This concept of existentialism proposed ways to manage and overcome these universal human conditions. The resultant knowledge about oneself is a dynamic composite, depicting the authentic understandings about oneself and the world.

Authentic understanding or personal authenticity compels individuals to be open, and to confront life with honesty and integrity, resulting in a harmonious relationship with oneself and others (Sartre, 1957). Existentialists May (1975) and Frankl (1984, 1988) supported this by asserting that an individual needs courage to be open and honest with the self. Courage leads to the acknowledgment of personal strengths and weaknesses (May, 1975). Frankl (1984) added that having the ability to transform or *construct* hardships and struggles into opportunities is the way in which individuals will find meaning and purpose.

Constructivism

Constructivism is based on the concept that individuals are "active participants in their own lives" (Mahoney, 2006, pp. 5–7), of which there are five main principles:

- Active agency: humans are active participants in their own lives;
- Ordering processes: humans need order to make meaning;
- Personal identity: what people experience is related to how they have learned to create an orderly reference point;
- Social symbolic processes: much of the order we seek and the meaning we create emerges out of our what we feel and how we interact with one another;
- Dynamic dialectical development: complex tension between the self and social relationships lead to new insight.

In constructivism, multiple realities can exist, but the individual's reality is the one most valued (Charmaz, 2000; Mahoney, 2006). Mahoney (2006) noted, "people can facilitate their own change by actively experimenting with new ways of being and by selectively practicing (strengthening) new patterns that serve them well" (p. 35).

Finding purpose and meaning involves going beyond the self (Sartre, 1957) and includes reaching out to others. Sartre (1957) wrote, "not only is man responsible for himself, he is also responsible for others" (p. 15). Being responsible involves personal knowing, honoring, and responsibility of the self, and it includes helping others. By doing so, the individual becomes authentically stronger as an individual while strengthening her/his community.

Social responsibility

Art therapists who engage in social responsibility do so by reaching out to marginalized individuals. Individuals who are dying are stigmatized and marginalized (Otis-Green & Rutland, 2004). As the body dies, functioning slows, and it becomes increasingly more difficult for the individual to have his/her needs met. Therefore, it is imperative for socially responsible art therapists to reach out to those who are disenfranchised either on an individual basis or through community programming (Kaplan, 2007), so that appropriate resources can be allocated to individuals confronting death (Kuhl, 2002). Dying individuals need reassurance that their needs will be addressed during this vulnerable time (Berzoff & Silverman, 2004).

Additionally, socially responsible art therapists can understand and recognize the need and desire for individuals to freely and authentically express emotions, clarify meaning and purpose, and communicate their wishes to loved ones. It stands to reason, therefore, that socially responsible art therapists also know what it means to be fully present with an individual who has experienced extreme loss and/or who is confronting death. Being fully present means willing to focus on the needs and wants of an individual, allowing him or her to freely express thoughts and feelings in an environment that is respectful, free from judgment, and where illness is not their identity. Heath (2005) explained:

> Presence is entering into an ill person's room and respecting where they are and trying to bring them what they need in the way they need it. Presence is being grounded and breathing and being fully with the patient, not thinking about anything or anyone else or trying to "fix" them. Presence is acting as if we had all the time in the world to be with this person. It is a gift that is so rarely given. (pp. 199–120)

Being "present" provides the individual with the "space" to explore and process new insights.

Death and dying

Though dying is universal, it is also uniquely individual (Heath, 2005). It happens to everyone, but no one dies the same way (Kuhl, 2002). It may seem obvious that there is uncertainty in facing death and that it is difficult for the dying to imminently confront it. As one patient wrote, "dying is hard work—not the physical part, but the part which is inside me, the work about who I am, who I have been, and I will be" (Kuhl, 2002, p. xvii).

Confronting death is a time when numerous issues may arise. For the individual who is dying, unresolved issues may surface. This individual may need to process conflicts so that a form of resolution may occur. Therefore, the art therapist working with this individual must be prepared to help by not only being present, but also by being ready to hear and treat with reverence that which the individual communicates. Yalom (1980) indicated, "some therapists state that death concerns are simply not voiced by their patients [… but …] the real issue is that the therapist is not prepared to hear them" (p. 57). A therapist who is receptive in knowing the concerns will "encounter death continuously in his/her everyday work" (p. 57). Lair (1996) said, "what is best is known only to the individual [and the purpose of the therapist is] to allow that to open up" (p. 153). Being fully present helps the individual work through issues that he or she needs to address (Neimeyer, 2012; Yalom, 1980), and within the timeframe that he or she needs (Zilberfein & Hurwitz, 2004).

Art expression and meaning making

Individuals addressing their needs often face anxiety in doing so. May (1977) indicated that anxiety can prevent or propel individuals into exploring difficult issues, and that it takes courage to face mortality; "courage is necessary to make *being* and *becoming* possible" (p. 13). He noted different kinds of courage, such as the physical, moral, social, and creative, but emphasized that it was creative courage that is "the most important kind of courage of all" (p. 21). By engaging in the creative act, "we *are* able to reach beyond our own death" (May, 1975, p. 25). Otis-Green and Rutland (2004) said, "the dying have many lessons to teach about living. [They] remind us of the importance of living authentically, mindful of our priorities, and of the importance of our relationships" (p. 478).

Individuals confronting death experience an array of mixed feelings (Bolton, 2008), and can swing from sheer terror of the unknown to acceptance that death will happen (Lair, 1996). Jeeves, Blennerhassett, and Petrone (2008) advocated for those confronting death to engage in the creative process. When language becomes difficult, "images become particularly significant both as a means to communicate emotional material and as a means to heal" (Abraham, 2005, p. 9). Thus, it is beneficial to help those confronting death to engage in the creative process.

The creative process provides more opportunity for expressing a wide range of emotions; yet, it can also provide a sense of self-control (Cox, 2000). Creative expression can be a way to solve problems, and/or transform and reconstruct skills and knowledge, and acquire new understandings (Barrington, 2010). Art therapists are able to help individuals sort out a range of emotions by providing a safe environment, so that an individual can engage in the creative process.

Stephanie

The following case emerged from a study on the nature and meaning of art therapy with an older adult in hospice (Barrington, 2010). The woman portrayed, Stephanie, was 96 years old and lived in an assisted living facility.

Stephanie was a tiny woman who had a big laugh. She sat in a recliner where she could view all the pictures on the walls in her room. There was a window overlooking a playground outside, and she often watched children play on the playground equipment. Next to her large recliner was a voluminous stack of letters and cards bound together with a rubber band, which she often read. The chair faced the television, and she kept the remote close to the packet of letters. She was a passionate woman who challenged herself to be the best person she could be; this included being able to laugh at herself when she made, what she called, "mistakes." When the study began, she was 96 years old and lived in an assisted living facility in Wisconsin. She possessed a frail frame and was in constant pain. She was diagnosed with cancer, and had recently become part of the local hospice program. Now approaching death, she gained deeper insight by reflecting on her life's experiences and the ways she coped with them.

Stephanie was an avid football fan and spoke passionately about the Green Bay Packers. She talked about the current quarterback, named linebackers and defensemen with much fervor, and was quite informed about the history of the team, its statistics, and players. She discussed the upcoming season and said that she watched "the game" every week. Stephanie declared her disappointment with last season's team performance, offered several plausible explanations as to why it occurred and then made her predictions for the upcoming season.

After several football stories, she told stories about her childhood. She said that she was frequently mocked, teased, and ridiculed for being overweight. She was told that her clothes were unflattering and unstylish. She noted this was because she could not fit into "store-bought" clothes. She admitted yielding to those who ridiculed her by deciding to make her own clothes. But she also said that, by making her own clothes, she found freedom of expression to design and wear exactly what she wanted. Over time, the mocking stopped. Stephanie perceived anxiety and alienation, and found purpose and meaning by constructing her own existence.

As Stephanie grew older, she recognized it was her determination that helped her become a successful businessperson. Stephanie proactively chose to create her own experiences, which became a representation of herself and her relationship to the world around her.

Stephanie told many other stories about family, working, helping others, travel, fun, and creative outlets. She paged through a picture album describing the people, places, and activities that she made over the years. She proudly showed sets of mittens and scarves that she recently knitted and said she planned on donating them.

The mocking that she endured as a child made an impression on her as an adult, and she told the story of a man who frequently drank to relieve the pain of his problems. She said this man was not well thought of and that people were mean to him. He was ridiculed for his problems. But Stephanie remembered being teased and mocked as child and promised herself she would help others who were in a similar situation. Stephanie recognized the meaning of suffering, based on her own experiences, and bridged the experience to bring meaning to her life. She was compassionate and held the belief that individuals need to help one another, especially those who are outcast and/or suffering. She said:

> There used to be an elderly man and he'd get drunk. And whenever I would see him walking on the road, I'd stop and pick him up and take him home. And he would say to people at the grocery store, "She's the only one who would pick me up when I'm drunk."

Stephanie told several stories that day, more than expected. She appeared to enjoy telling these stories as well as her realizations.

Stephanie was asked if she wanted to expand on her stories by creating an image depicting a story that was a highlight in her life. Stephanie agreed enthusiastically. Several different kinds of materials were offered, such as paper, paints, markers, colored pencils, crayons, and more. The image could be representational or abstract. Stephanie focused on:

> Seeing the first Packer game. They used to play behind a high school. They became so popular that it didn't have enough capacity. So they had to build a bigger field. We had season tickets. We went to every single game. But, after my dad died, my mother was in a wheel chair and I couldn't go to games because I couldn't pawn her off on anybody because she had to have help to go to the bathroom. But, I couldn't do that to my mother.

She chose paper and pencils, and she drew a picture of the first Packer game she saw in 1914 (see Figure 28.1).

Figure 28.1 First Packer game.

Figure 28.2 "Major," the cat.

The person on the left with the ball is a Green Bay Packer; the other player is a "Chicago Bear." Stephanie giggled and commented that she was having fun, asking to "do another drawing."

She was asked to think of another story that was a highlight in her life. Her second story was about her cat named "Major." She said that she owned several cats throughout her life, but there has never been a cat like her first cat, "Major." Major was her good friend, who was always there "through thick and thin," and "someone she still loves." She took another piece of paper and made a drawing of "Major" (see Figure 28.2).

Stephanie was proud of her creations and indicated that she enjoyed sharing the stories and making the drawings. She said she rarely gets visitors and asked if she could tell stories and draw again on another day.

Discussion

The stories Stephanie told reflected her satisfaction in knowing that she lived her life to the best of her ability even in the face of adversity. She was proud that she helped people as often as possible, and was grateful for the opportunities that were afforded her. She also placed value on her own ingenuity and integrity for designing and sewing her own clothes and her determination in achieving her goals. Stephanie indicated that she found meaning in helping others, caring for others, and said her life was filled with both struggles and opportunities. She said she tried to stay connected to friends, which is why she kept the letters close to her, and engaged in several social activities at the facility.

People who ridiculed her in her childhood were mean. But, somehow she overcame the struggles and then transformed that pain by learning how to sew and create stylish clothes for herself. Other pains continued. The memory of being mocked stayed with her. Her way of healing was to reach out to others in a genuine, caring, and thoughtful manner, as she did for the man who frequently drank.

Stephanie created meanings about her life that were unique and meaningful to her from the new insights she gained in the life review and creative processes. Her reflections about the football game and Major depicted the different kinds of courage that May (1975) referenced and transformed her life into meaning. Through this process, she recognized how much she valued caring for others as well as her belief in being the best person possible, whether it was reaching out to a person who needed help or witnessing athletic talents on the football field. She reaffirmed how important it was to be authentic and to care for others. Moreover, she maintained her sense of self as she constructed it by always being authentic to herself and others.

Consistent with the concepts of existentialism and constructivism, Stephanie recalled struggles, and said that she always tried to do the right thing. Her actions aligned with her values and morals. As she articulated thoughts, beliefs, and values, she came to recognize a deeper meaning and purpose about her life. She said that if she could tell young people three things that she learned in her lifetime, they would be: (1) "do good things for people"; (2) "do not snub anybody"; and (3) "do not laugh at anyone."

These words of wisdom communicated important concepts about her worldview. As an art therapist working with her, the overall emphasis was placed on being present and allowing her to discover and construct her own reality and meaning. She was encouraged to explore stories and detail her highlighted stories in an atmosphere of respect and acceptance. This enabled her to explore and recall the highlighted events, which helped her to identify, clarify, and solidify meanings.

Conclusion

Through her struggles, she learned how hurtful others can be and was able to transform those struggles into opportunities, especially hoping to help others. As Sartre (1957) purported, individuals have freedom and the facility of choice, and each individual is able to create his or her own meaning. Additionally, as Sartre (1957) noted, individuals need to be responsible for their own self and reach out to others and help in the way(s) in which he or she is able.

The stories that Stephanie told conveyed that, as one confronts death, the search for meaning and purpose remains important to understanding events. From the existentialist paradigm, Stephanie asked questions and found meaning in her intentions and actions. She made choices about her actions that helped her, such as her own thoughts and feelings when she was bullied. Moreover, she actively chose to help others, such as when she helped the man who was being shunned by the community.

From the constructivist paradigm, Stephanie was an active participant in her own life and all of her choices reflected her reality. Through expression and communication, the creative process helped Stephanie organize thoughts and feelings. She was also able to clarify and solidify meaning and purpose through the stories that were especially meaningful to her. Being authentic is knowing, honoring, and being responsible for one's self through the choices and actions that an individual makes, as well as taking responsibility to help others use their abilities and potentials. The world is comprised of individuals who exist in communities, and each person is unique and important.

Art therapy and thanatology complement one another, and together they can be an impetus for social action to help those confronting death by providing opportunities for expression as individuals explore meaning and purpose. Art therapy continues to expand in hospices not only in communities throughout the United States, but internationally. Most importantly, there is recognition that individuals who are confronting death need to reflect, clarify, and process their life experiences. As such, it is time for art therapists and thanatologists to unite, so that individuals can have opportunities for creative expression and communication as they face end-of-life issues. Engaging in the creative process raises awareness, so that life can be lived more fully (Barrington, 2010).

References

Abraham, R. (2005). *When words have lost their meaning: Alzheimer's patients communicate through art.* Westport, CT: Praeger Publishers.

Barrington, K. (2010). Creative expression for social justice with older adults. In T. Anderson, D. Gussak, K. K. Hallmark, & A. Paul (Eds.), *Art education for social justice* (pp. 92–96). Reston, VA: National Art Education Association.

Beresford, L. (1993). *The hospice handbook: A complete guide.* Boston, MA: Little, Brown and Company.

Berzoff, J., & Silverman, P. (2004). Introduction. In J. Berzoff & P. R. Silverman (Eds.), *Living with dying: A handbook for end-of-life healthcare practitioners* (pp. 1–17). New York, NY: Columbia University Press.

Bolton, G. (2008). Introduction: Dying, bereavement and the healing arts. In G. Bolton (Ed.), *Dying, bereavement and the healing arts* (pp. 13–21). Philadelphia, PA: Jessica Kingsley.

Charmaz, K. (2000). Grounded theory: Objectivist and constructivist methods. In N. K. Denzin & Y. S. Lincoln (Eds.), *Handbook of qualitative research* (2nd ed., pp. 509–535). Thousand Oaks, CA: Sage Publications, Inc.

Corr, C., Nabe, C., & Corr, D. (2006). *Death & dying: Life & living* (5th ed.). Belmont, CA: Thomson Wadsworth.

Cox, G. (2000). The use of humor, art, and music with the dying and bereaved. In J. D. Morgan (Ed.), *Meeting the needs of our clients creatively: The impact of art and culture on caregiving* (pp. 167–178). Amityville, NY: Baywood Publishing Company, Inc.

DeSpelder, L. A., & Strickland, A. L. (2010). *The last dance: Encountering death and dying* (9th ed.). Boston, MA: McGraw Hill.

Egnew, T. (2004). Forward. In J. Berzoff & P. R. Silverman (Eds.), *Living with dying: A handbook for end-of-life healthcare practitioners* (pp. xix–xxviii). New York, NY: Columbia University Press.

Frankl, V. E. (1984). *Man's search for meaning.* New York, NY: Pocket Books.

Frankl, V. E. (1988). *The will to meaning: Foundations and applications of logotherapy.* New York, NY: Meridian.

Heath, W. (2005). The spark of creativity. In C. L. Le Navanec & L. Bridges (Eds.), *Creating connections between nursing care and the creative art therapies: Expanding the concept of holistic care* (pp. 116–128). Springfield, IL: Charles C. Thomas, Publisher.

Jeeves, T., Blennerhassett, M., & Petrone, M. A. (2008). Artists: Survivors. In G. Bolton (Ed.), *Dying, bereavement and the healing arts* (pp. 156–163). Philadelphia, PA: Jessica Kingsley.

Kaplan, F. (2007). Introduction. In F. Kaplan (Ed.), *Art therapy and social action* (pp. 11–17). Philadelphia, PA: Jessica Kingsley.

Kuhl, D. (2002). *What dying people want: Practical wisdom for the end of life.* New York, NY: PublicAffairs.

Lair, G. S. (1996). *Counseling the terminally ill: Sharing the journey.* Washington DC: Taylor Francis.

Lavine, T. Z. (1984). *From Socrates to Sartre: The philosophical quest.* New York, NY: Bantam Books.

Mahoney, M. (2006). *Constructive psychotherapy: Theory and practice.* New York, NY: Guilford Press.

May, R. (1975). *The courage to create.* New York, NY: W.W. Norton & Company.

May, R. (1977). *The meaning of anxiety.* New York, NY: W.W. Norton & Company.

Neimeyer, R. (Ed.) (2001). *Meaning reconstruction and the experience of loss.* Washington, DC: American Psychological Association.

Neimeyer, R. (Ed.) (2012). *Techniques of grief therapy: Creative practices for counseling the bereaved.* New York, NY: Routledge.

Otis-Green, S., & Rutland, S. (2004). Marginalization at the end of life. In J. Berzoff & P. R. Silverman (Eds.), *Living with dying: A handbook for end-of-life healthcare practitioners* (pp. 462–481). New York, NY: Columbia University Press.

Sartre, J. P. (1957). *Existentialism and human emotions.* New York, NY: The Wisdom Library.

Saunders, C. (1976). Care of the dying: The problem of euthanasia. *Nursing Times, 72*(26), 1003–1005.

Yalom, I. (1980). *Existential psychotherapy.* New York, NY: Basic Books.

Zilberfein, F., & Hurwitz, E. (2004). Clinical social work practice at the end of life. In J. Berzoff & P. R. Silverman (Eds.), *Living with dying: A handbook for end of life healthcare practitioners* (pp. 297–317). New York, NY: Columbia University Press.

Part IV

Art Therapy with Various Populations

Introduction

This section is the largest in the handbook, illustrating that art therapists engage with an extensive number and variety of populations. It is important to note that the section is not comprehensive, as there are too many types of clients to address in one book. These 12 chapters in this section offer a glimpse into the types of clients most typically treated by art therapists.

Anderson's introductory chapter, *"Special Needs:" Federal Mandates and Opportunities for Art Therapy*, provides an overview of how art therapy addresses children with a spectrum of disabilities, as defined by federal statutes. Next, Richardson's chapter examines art therapy work with individuals diagnosed with autism, in *Art Therapy on the Autism Spectrum: Engaging the Mind, Brain, and Senses*. She argues that a holistic approach, which includes art therapy, is beneficial for children on the autism spectrum as it builds upon the individuals' strengths to improve communication and socialization skills, as well as sensory challenges. In his chapter *Art Therapy and Developmental Disabilities*, Bailey explores how art therapy provides adaptive and alternative methods to address neurological and intellectual disabilities. He argues that art therapy "provides supportive and safe opportunities for environmental exploration, sensory stimulation, independence and choice, while promoting growth and self-awareness through an empowering 'voice.'"

In the chapter titled *Aggression and Art Therapy: A Social Interactionist Perspective*, Gussak outlines how "the art therapist has unique tools to create new interactions that re-label people, validate and reinforce new behaviors and identities, and redirect the actions associated with aggressive and hostile tendencies." In *Perspectives of Recovery/ Reversing the Stigma: Art Therapy and Severe Mental Illness*, McAlevey stresses how art and art therapy can nullify the negative stigma associated with major mental illnesses and replace it with hope for recovery and health. In her chapter titled *On Considering the Role of Art Therapy in Treating Depression*, Wise discusses the effectiveness of art therapy in one of the more pervasive mental illnesses, depression. While recognizing that there is no single art therapy approach for people with depression, Wise convincingly presents the basic components of art therapy that can be used to support clients with depression.

The Wiley Handbook of Art Therapy, First Edition. Edited by David E. Gussak and Marcia L. Rosal.
© 2016 John Wiley & Sons, Ltd. Published 2016 by John Wiley & Sons, Ltd.

In the chapter *Art therapy and Substance Abuse*, Schmanke examines the benefits of art therapy with those with substance abuse problems. In so doing, she examines the "interface of spirituality, creativity and recovery" through case vignettes and illustrations, ultimately concluding that "The benefits of art therapy ... include bypassing resistance, finding a creative outlet for the expression of difficult feelings, and finding deeper understanding of creative and spiritual meaning of the addiction and of life."

In the chapter titled *Art Therapy with Trauma*, Howie addresses a population currently receiving a great deal of attention from the mental health profession and the media. Illustrating how art therapy can facilitate "trauma processing," Howie clarifies how art therapy "allow[s] the individual to put the traumatic event in the past, and ... to interact in the present with more confidence and more assurance than what is occurring internally..." Hunter argues that "[t]herapists working within a framework of positive thinking and creative expression have a distinct advantage in treatment." In her chapter titled *Art Therapy and Eating Disorders*, Hunter concludes that, by promoting self-acceptance, connection, and trust, art therapy is effective in breaking down the despair that may result in eating disorders.

In *Art Therapy, Homelessness, and Poverty*, Feen-Calligan demonstrates how art therapy is an effective tool in combating the limitations and issues faced by those who live in poverty. A study of an art therapy program in a soup kitchen illustrates her hypotheses. She concludes that "[a]rt therapy can fill a special need by helping people ... strengthen their inner resources, necessary to develop self-determination to take action on their own behalf."

Through examining theoretical perspectives and discussing case examples, Anand investigates art therapy for people with various chronic medical conditions. Her chapter, *Dimensions of Art Therapy in Medical Illness*, delineates the benefits and challenges of practicing art therapy with this population group.

The final chapter in this section is Thompson's *A Complicated Life: Intermodality within Dissociative Identity Disorder*. In this piece, Thompson demonstrates how the application of the creative arts therapies—not just art therapy—mitigates dissociation by addressing, mirroring, and containing the traumatic experience. This chapter provides a smooth transition from this section to the following one, *Practicing Art Therapy in Interdisplinary Settings*.

As a whole, these chapters represent countless years of experience by skilled and sensitive art therapists. Perhaps McAlevey, who offered this thought, captured what each author understands:

> ... art therapists can use their tools to (1) dispel preconceived notions that severe mental illness is a life-long "sentence," (2) educate the public about stigma against people ... (3) acknowledge that recovery ... needs to be defined by the person with the lived experience and not the medical establishment, and (4) foster hope in every artist-client that recovery is achievable.

While the preceding paragraph is specific to mental illness, the overall intent of this section underscores that the benefits that McAlevey espouses can be applied to all populations. This collection of writings offers a glimpse into the complex work that art therapists undertake each day.

29

"Special Needs" Federal Mandates and Opportunities for Art Therapy

Frances E. Anderson

The term "special needs" generally and traditionally has indicated individuals with physical and intellectual disabilities. This chapter will address individuals with disabilities from the perspective of the mandated federal laws to serve and, whenever possible, place them in regular public school classrooms. It is through these laws that art therapists have been funded to serve children with disabilities in pubic schools. The reader should note that two disability categories (children with autism and those with intellectual disabilities) are not included here, because they are discussed in separate chapters in this book.

The Federal Mandates and Art Therapy

The reauthorization of the Individuals with Disabilities Education Act (IDEA) of 2004, PL 108-446 Regulations 34 (October 30, 2007) cited 13 categories of disabilities:

1. Autism
2. Deaf-blindness
3. Deafness
4. Emotional disturbance (ED)
5. Hearing impairment (HI)
6. Intellectual disability (ID)
7. Multiple disabilities (MD)
8. Orthopedic impairment (OI)
9. Other health impairment (OHI)
10. Specific learning disability (SLD)
11. Speech or language impairment (SLI)
12. Traumatic brain injury (TBI)
13. Visual impairment including blindness

The Wiley Handbook of Art Therapy, First Edition. Edited by David E. Gussak and Marcia L. Rosal.
© 2016 John Wiley & Sons, Ltd. Published 2016 by John Wiley & Sons, Ltd.

The definitions and descriptions are made in the education context. Children for whom English is not their first language and those children who are behind in instruction in reading and math are not considered disabled. The law covers children aged 0–21, and there are provisions for earlier interventions if the individual is identified as having autism, deaf-blindness, deafness, or multiple disabilities.

What follows is a discussion of 11 of these categories. For information about individuals with autism and intellectual disabilities, the reader is referred to Chapter 30 by Jane Richardson and Chapter 31 by Kevin Bailey in this handbook, and to the article titled "Understanding and interpreting the ASD 'Puzzle'" by Susan D. Loesl (2010).

Literature Review

A review of the published articles in *Art Therapy, Journal of the American Art Therapy Association*, and *The Arts in Psychotherapy* from 2002 to 2013 was conducted. Students with emotional disturbance, specific learning disabilities, other health impairments, orthopedic handicaps, and autism were the topics reflected frequently in the articles in the review of art therapy literature, particularly when examining the focus of children with disabilities. To be sure, the review only focused on clients up to 21 years of age and articles that covered only art therapy, not arts therapies or other expressive media.

The review identified 76 articles: 60 that fell under the broad category of ED as defined by PL 108-446. Many of these articles did not use the term ED, but warranted inclusion under this category. Therefore, clients who were termed "at risk," who were dealing with grief over loss due to man-made and natural disasters, those who were sexually abused, had attachment disorders, emotional/academic adjustment, juvenile offenses, traumatized or suffered from post-traumatic stress disorders, were included. This long list of descriptors for ED suggests clearly that art therapists could provide services for these clients under the federal IDEA mandate (PL 108-446).

The second largest topic of focus was students with other health impairments. The six articles grouped under OHI included students with ADD/ADHD, as reflected in the federal law. Bone marrow transplant and pediatric surgery were also placed in the OHI grouping. The third largest topic included five articles on children with autism. The remaining articles included three on clients with specific learning disabilities (SLD), and two on Down's syndrome and cognitive disabilities (grouped under ID). One article focused on orthopedic impairment (OI).

There were also five articles that primarily focused on art therapy in public schools. These five were *not* included anywhere else, but many noted work with students with ED. Eighteen of the total 60 articles were in school settings or involved teachers of the clients (Anderson, 2013). The review did not include published literature or research reviews.

Federal Definitions and Adaptations

Emotional disturbance (ED)

ED is defined as:

i. ... a condition exhibiting one or more of the following characteristics over a long period of time and to a marked degree that adversely affects a child's educational performance:

(a) An inability to learn that cannot be explained by intellectual, sensory, or health factors

(b) An inability to build or maintain satisfactory interpersonal relationships with peers and teachers

(c) Inappropriate types of behavior or feelings under normal circumstances

(d) A general pervasive mood of unhappiness or depression

(e) A tendency to develop physical symptoms or fears associated with personal or school problems

ii. Emotional disturbance includes schizophrenia. The term does not apply to children who are socially maladjusted, unless it is determined that they have an emotional disturbance under paragraph (c) (1) (I) of this section. [34 Code of Federal Regulations §300.7(c) (4)], as amended at 72 FR 61306, October 30, 2007]

The following categories are included in ED: eating disorders, obsessive–compulsive behaviors, depression and bipolar disorders, anxiety disorders, conduct disorders, and psychotic disorders (Emotional Disturbance [n.d.]; retrieved December, 15, 2012, from http://nichcy.org/disability/specific/emotionaldisturbance#def).

Children with ED may be passive aggressive, destructive, and/or withdrawn. Children with school phobia, aggressive or acting out behaviors, and with extreme anxiety fall into this category. Such students, those with a pattern of truancy who have violated school rules or broken the law, are placed in an "interim alternate education" setting. Both a "functional behavior assessment (FBA)" and a "behavior intervention plan (BIP)" must be provided to assist students in learning appropriate behaviors and providing support to enable them to be successful in their learning community (Section 504 and IDEA comparison chart [n.d.]); retrieved January 24, 2013, from http://www.ncld.org/disability-advocacy/learn-ld-laws/adaaa-section-504/section-504-idea-comparison-chart). The FBA and the BIP may include art therapy.

Students who have ED are often stigmatized, so confidentiality is important (Moriya, (2006). The IDEA Regulations have addressed how to maintain confidentiality under the section: "Procedural Safeguards Notice"; the emphasis is on maintaining anonymity. Parental consent is paramount prior to any evaluation or developing an individualized education program (IEP) (Emotional Disturbance, n.d.; retrieved December, 15, 2012, from http://nichcy.org/disability/specific/emotionaldisturbance#def).

Art can become an acceptable way of expressing anxious, aggressive, angry, or depressed behaviors. Cognitive behavioral art therapy (Rosal, 2001) is one of the most successful approaches in working with students with ED (Pifalo, 2007; Rosal, 1995, 2001).

Specific learning disability (SLD)

SLD is defined as:

> ... a disorder in one or more of the basic psychological processes involved in understanding or in using language—spoken or written—that may manifest itself in an imperfect ability to listen, think, speak, read, write, spell, or do mathematical calculations. The term includes such conditions as perceptual disabilities, brain injury, minimal brain dysfunction, dyslexia, and developmental aphasia. The term does not include learning problems that are primarily the result of visual, hearing, or motor disabilities; of mental retardation; of emotional disturbance; or of environmental, cultural, or economic disadvantage. (IDEA [34 Code of Federal Regulations §300.7(c) (10)] as amended at 72 FR 61306, October 30, 2007)

Art interventions may be especially helpful with those with an SLD. Individuals with SLD are often very creative and are drawn to artistic activities. Because creating art engages more than one sense, it can help the child to focus and foster better problem-solving strategies. Art uses other mental paths to complete tasks, and art interventions can provide different ways of learning. Using a step-by-step approach can be very important. Using multi-sensory approach demonstrations (verbal, olfactory, kinesthetic, and visual) will assist the child with SLD engage in art activities. Art can offer the child a sense of being highly successful, which may counteract any education failures experienced elsewhere (Anderson, 1992, 1994; Stepney, 2001).

Other health impairment (OHI)

OHI is defined as:

> ... a severe orthopedic impairment that adversely affects a child's educational performance. The term includes impairments caused by congenital anomaly (e.g., clubfoot, absence of some member, etc.), impairments caused by disease (e.g., poliomyelitis, bone tuberculosis, etc.), and impairments from other causes (e.g., cerebral palsy, amputations, and fractures or burns that cause contractures). (IDEA [34 Code of Federal Regulations §300.7(c) (8)] as amended at 72 FR 61306, October 30, 2007)

Children with attention-deficit hyperactivity disorders (ADHD) and attention-deficit disorder (ADD) make up a large part of OHIs. Because art is multisensory, engaging in artistic activities may help with both ADD and ADHD. The use of clay and scented markers provide additional sensory stimulation and, as a result, help children focus on the art making, although it is important to set specific boundaries in the use of art materials, such as having the child draw or paint in a tray with raised edges. Taking care not to present too many choices of art media at the same time and reducing visual stimuli in the art space may also be helpful. It is beneficial to plan art interventions that do not require a long time to master (Anderson, 1992, 1994; Hallahan, Kauffman, & Pullen, 2009).

Orthopedic impairment (OI)

OI is defined as:

> … a severe orthopedic impairment that adversely affects a child's educational performance. The term includes impairments caused by congenital anomaly (e.g., clubfoot, absence of some member, etc.), impairments caused by disease (e.g., poliomyelitis, bone tuberculosis, etc.), and impairments from other causes (e.g., cerebral palsy, amputations, and fractures or burns that cause contractures). (IDEA [34 Code of Federal Regulations §300.7(c) (8)] as amended at 72 FR 61306, October 30, 2007)

The art therapist must be especially aware of safety issues and be knowledgeable about the strengths and limitations that each child with OI may have. Such children often will need special adaptive art materials, including thick or short-handled paintbrushes. Changing the child's physical workspace may be necessary if medically permitted, such as lower tables, working on the floor, or using a thick piece of cardboard taped to the arms of a child's wheelchair. Of course, some art materials and tools may not be easy to use, such as scissors and staplers. Other art activities that require fine motor skills may not be easy to use as sometimes the child may have only a small range of movement; at times, a child may need to be moved so he or she can work on other parts of a painting or drawing. This may also be made easier if the paper is taped down. There are a number of technological advances that can help individuals with OI communicate and express themselves (Hallahan et al., 2009). There are several commercially available products that can be useful, such as special tops for glue bottles, and containers for thick paint that have a small opening at the top that can be held and used, instead of a brush, with one hand (Anderson, 1992, 1994; Loesl, 2008).

The remaining categories of disabilities will be grouped as follows: speech or language impairment, hearing impairments, deafness, blindness and visual impairment, deafblindness, multiple disabilities, and traumatic brain injury.

Speech or language impairment (SLI)

SLI is defined as:

> … a communication disorder, such as stuttering, impaired articulation, a language impairment, or a voice impairment, that adversely affects a child's educational performance. (IDEA [34 Code of Federal Regulations §300.7(c) (10)] as amended at 72 FR 61306, October 30, 2007)

A student with a disorder in articulation may omit, change, or distort certain sounds, making it difficult to understand when he or she speaks. This excludes young children who are just learning to speak.

A child who stutters will have difficulty with the flow of speech, as his or her speech will have repetitions or interrupted words. Stuttering may result in visible tensions in the face, shoulders, neck, or hands. Students with voice problems may sound nasal, may speak too loudly, or too softly. They may lose their voices or experience pain when speaking.

A student may have difficulty with language and not be understood, or may use words in the wrong context. Language problems may result in difficulty in understanding what is said (receptive problems), or in talking or explaining something (expressive problems).

Art can be extremely helpful in providing a nonverbal means of expression for a child with communication disorders. It may be easier for this child to draw what is meant or tell a story using pictures. Often, children who are engaged in the artistic process may become relaxed enough to decrease his or her stuttering. Following verbal directions may be very difficult. Using pictures and actual demonstrations of art media use to explain a task along with words can be very helpful.

Hearing impairment (HI)

HI is defined as:

> ... an impairment in hearing, whether permanent or fluctuating, that adversely affects a child's educational performance but is not included under the definition of "deafness." (IDEA [34 Code of Federal Regulations §300.7(c) (10)] as amended at 72 FR 61306, October 30, 2007)

Hearing impairment means a range of loss of hearing that may be mild, moderate, severe, or profound. Some children can manage by using a hearing aid or amplification system, while others may only hear certain frequencies, making amplification less helpful. Sign language and total communication—using both sign language and lip reading—are the most frequent means of communicating with a child with a hearing impairment that is more than mild. Sometimes an interpreter may accompany the child and communicate what is going on in a classroom using sign language.

Having a hearing loss that is more than mild, or being deaf, can result in social isolation. To understand this, imagine you are in a foreign country and do not speak the language. How would you find your way, use public transport, order food at a restaurant? Because verbal communication is our major means of relating to others, hearing loss and deafness may cause problems with relating to those who are non-hearing-impaired or deaf.

Deafness

Deafness is defined as:

> ... a hearing impairment so severe that a child is impaired in processing linguistic information through hearing, with or without amplification, that adversely affects a child's educational performance. (IDEA [34 Code of Federal Regulations §300.7(c) (10)] as amended at 72 FR 61306, October 30, 2007)

Early intervention (before 3 years of age) is essential to facilitate both children with hearing impairments and those who are deaf. Sign language will be an important means of communication.

If one thinks of a continuum that ranges from mild hearing loss to total deafness, some of the adaptations may apply to both ends of the spectrum. Using pictures, written words, and sign language or total communication may be one means of communication with a student who is deaf or hard of hearing.

Vocabulary development is essential, and the art therapist may often reinforce words that are being taught in the child's classroom. Modeling behaviors and demonstrations using a combination of many kinds of communication will be essential. There is a tendency to copy artwork because copying is one means of learning; however, if a child is copying, it may mean that he or she does not understand what task or action is to be accomplished.

Concrete vocabulary is easier to understand; for example, simply mixing the color in front of the child can demonstrate what the color orange is. Demonstrating how different kinds art media are used will also be important.

Learning the words for specific emotions will be important for the child as he or she will need to know and understand the difference between feeling states such as "mad," "sad," "scared," and "glad." One approach may be to begin with pictures of faces and gestures that reflect each of these words.

Encouraging a child to draw a picture of what happened, or what one wants, will be an important means of communication. Sometimes three-dimensional media is more effective in communicating the meaning of words. The reader is referred to the work of art therapists Rawley Silver and Ellen Horowitz, who have worked extensively with children with these two disabilities (Horowitz, 2007; Silver, 2007).

Visual impairment, including blindness (VI)

VI is defined as:

> … an impairment in vision that, even with correction, adversely affects a child's educational performance. The term includes both partial sight and blindness. (IDEA [34 Code of Federal Regulations §300.7(c) (10)] as amended at 72 FR 61306, October 30, 2007)

Many consider blindness as one of the worst possible disabilities to have. However, this is incorrect, as being visually impaired or blind is less likely to socially cut one off from others, since verbal communication is intact. Of course, art materials would need to be adapted, as would the physical environment.

Three-dimensional materials such as small wood shapes or clay are especially useful. Small card or matt board shapes can be used if slots are cut in them so they can be attached.

Often, providing a hand-sized example of a completed art piece can be helpful for the person with blindness to explore using his or her hands. This idea is similar to showing completed visual examples of art to individuals with hearing impairments in order to communicate how to use the art materials.

In interacting with individuals with visual impairments, it will be helpful to orient them to their workspace. This can be done by taping down art paper and then adding a tactile "cue," such as putting some tape on one corner of the page. Then, with the individual's permission, one can move his or her hand so that it touches the corner cue, while explaining, "This is the lower left corner of the page." Next, the student's hands could be moved all around the edges of the page, so that the size of the paper can be understood. The paper can even be taped all around its edges to provide reference points, with extra tape placed on one corner. Art materials and the specific workspace should remain constant, so that the student can easily learn and remember where things are.

Deaf-blindness (DB)

DB is defined as:

> ... concomitant [simultaneous] hearing and visual impairments, the combination of which causes such severe communication and other developmental and educational needs that they cannot be accommodated in special education programs solely for children with deafness or children with blindness. (IDEA [34 Code of Federal Regulations §300.7(c) (10)] as amended at 72 FR 61306, October 30, 2007)

Perhaps the most challenging work is with someone who is deaf-blind. Special one-on-one interaction will be important. It will be important to consider a focus on the other senses (touch, smell, and movement). Fingerspelling in the palm of the hand is a major communication method.

Using sensory properties of art media can help the student gain a concept. For example, hand over hand in working with clay can facilitate learning how to connect pieces of clay. Using clay with different stages of softness might help the student understand "hard" and "soft" if these words are fingerspelled in the hand after touching the clay.

Those who work with individuals who are deaf and blind will need a willingness to experiment—to be willing to fail, as well as succeed.

Multiple disabilities (MD)

MD is defined as:

> ... concomitant [simultaneous] impairments (such as mental retardation–blindness[1], mental retardation–orthopedic impairment, etc.), the combination of which causes such severe educational needs that they cannot be accommodated in a special education program solely for one of the impairments. The term does not include deaf-blindness. (IDEA [34 Code of Federal Regulations §300.7(c) (10)] as amended at 72 FR 61306, October 30, 2007)

Working with students who have simultaneous impairments is as challenging as working with those who are deaf-blind. It would be important for the student and the therapist to be a team. Selecting specific art media for a student with multiple disabilities will require feedback from that student, making creative adaptations in the media or the artwork space when necessary. Another consideration must be selecting art media that are both appropriate to the individual's specific needs and that are (mental) age appropriate. It will sometimes be necessary to pre-prepare art materials. For example, in case of a child who has orthopedic disabilities and mental retardation, working with shapes to create a picture would involve pre-cutting the shapes. It might be beneficial to have contact paper on which the shapes can be easily placed and adhered to. Planning art experiences that have a high success factor will be very important, with a focus on the art-as-therapy approach.

Traumatic brain injury (TBI)

TBI is defined as:

> … an acquired injury to the brain caused by an external physical force, resulting in total or partial functional disability or psychosocial impairment, or both, that adversely affects a child's educational performance. The term applies to open or closed head injuries resulting in impairments in one or more areas, such as cognition; language; memory; attention; reasoning; abstract thinking; judgment; problem-solving; sensory, perceptual and motor abilities; psychosocial behavior; physical functions; information processing; and speech. The term does not apply to brain injuries that are congenital or degenerative, or brain injuries induced by birth trauma (IDEA [34 Code of Federal Regulations §300.7(c)(10)] as amended at 72 FR 61306, October 30, 2007). As with autism, traumatic brain injury (TBI) was added as a separate category of disability in 1990 under PL 101-476.

Individuals with TBI present multiple challenges. Each impairment that an individual has may necessitate multiple art adaptations, with, again, a focus on art as therapy. Art experiences that result in age-appropriate and highly successful outcomes will be priorities and challenges.

Initially, it will be important to determine what abilities each student has. This might mean doing an art interview using only one or two kinds of art materials at a time, and then assessing what the student with TBI can do with them, and what he or she prefers.

The therapist will likely be part of a team with the child who has TBI. This might mean using hand over hand to facilitate painting and preparing clay that can be easily manipulated. It might mean becoming the hands of the client, and having him or her tell you what they want you to paint or draw, or where to attach a wood shape.

Students with TBI will be dealing with considerable frustration, especially if that student remembers what he or she was able to do before the accident that caused the brain injury. Expressing frustration and anger may be important goals, and can easily be addressed using the art medium.

It may be important to review the specific characteristics discussed under each category of impairment that pertains to the specific student with TBI. For example, if the child has both language difficulty and motor problems, then researching issues and adaptations for individuals with orthopedic impairments and individuals with communication disabilities may help.

Conclusion

This chapter has focused on 11 categories of individuals with special needs, as defined in PL 94-142 and its reauthorizations (PL 99-497, 1990; PL 105-17, 1997; PL 108-446, 2004 and 2007; as the Individuals with Disabilities Education Act [IDEA]).

It is these laws that have enabled art therapists to work in public schools. It is hoped that the information and examples provided may encourage art therapists to gain additional footholds with their students with disabilities. It is also hoped that more quantitative research on the benefits of art therapy will be conducted. This concern was expressed in many of the articles in the literature review noted in the preceding text (Anderson, 2013). Both research and more opportunities for work in the schools are essential to the future of art therapy.

Endnote

1 In 2010, Rosa's Law mandated the use of the term "intellectual disability" instead of "mental retardation" (MR), because of the stigma attached to MR (Pub.P L. 111–256).

References

Anderson, F. E. (1992). *Art for all the children: Approaches to art therapy for children with disabilities.* Springfield, IL: Charles C. Thomas.

Anderson, F. E. (1994). *Art centered education and therapy for children with disabilities.* Springfield, IL: Charles C. Thomas.

Anderson, F. E. (2013). A review of the published literature on individuals with disabilities appearing in *Art Therapy: Journal of the American Art Therapy Association and The Arts in Psychotherapy from 2010–2013.* Unpublished paper. Charleston, SC.

Emotional Disturbance. (n.d.). Retrieved December 15, 2012 from National Dissemination Center for Children with Disabilities web site http://nichcy.org/disability/specific/emotionaldisturbance-def

Hallahan, D. P., Kauffman, J. M., & Pullen, P. C. (2009). *Exceptional learners: An introduction to special education* (11 ed.). Upper Saddle River, NJ: Pearson Education.

Horowitz, E. (Ed.) (2007). *Visually speaking: art therapy and the deaf.* Springfield, IL: Charles C. Thomas.

Loesl, S. (2008). Students with physical disabilities. In B. J. Gerber & D. R. Quay (Eds.), *Reaching and teaching students with special needs through art.* Reston, VA: National Art Education Association.

Loesl, S. (2010). Understanding and interpreting the ASD "Puzzle." In B. J. Gerber & J. Kellman (Eds.), *Understanding students with autism through Art* (pp. 71–82). Reston, VA: National Art Education Association.

Pifalo, T. (2007). Jogging the cogs: Trauma-focused art therapy and cognitive behavioral therapy with sexually abused children. *Art Therapy: Journal of the American Art Therapy Association, 24* (4), 170–175.

Rosal, M. (1995). *Approaches to art therapy with children.* Bloomington, IL: Abbeygate Press.

Rosal, M. (2001). Cognitive-behavioral art therapy. In J. A. Rubin (Ed.), *Approaches to art therapy: Theory & technique. Second edition.* Philadelphia, PA: Brunner-Routledge.

Section 504 and IDEA comparison chart. (n.d.). Retrieved January 24, 2013, from National Center for Learning Disabilities http://www.ncld.org/disability-advocacy/learn-ld-laws/adaaa-section-504/section-504-idea-comparison-chart.

Silver, R. (2007). *The Silver drawing test and draw a story: Assessing depression, aggression, and cognitive skills.* New York, NY: Routledge, Taylor and Francis Group.

Stepney, S. A. (2001). *Art therapy with students at risk: Introducing art therapy into an alternative learning environment for adolescents.* Springfield, IL: Charles C. Thomas.

Public Laws

Public Law 94-142, The Education for All Handicapped Children Act, 1978.

Public Law 99-497, 1990.

Public Law 105-17, 1997.

Public Law 108-446, The Individuals with Disabilities Act 2004.

Public Law 108-446, The Individuals with Disabilities Act 2004, Reauthorization, October 30, 2007.

Public Law 111-256, 2010.

Rosa's Law.

30

Art Therapy on the Autism Spectrum: Engaging the Mind, Brain, and Senses

Jane Ferris Richardson

A person on the autism spectrum (AS) is as individualistic as the autistic symptoms that he or she may exhibit. Yet, the communication and social and sensory challenges experienced by people on the AS remains constant, regardless of the prevailing diagnostic criteria or label. Autism impacts the mind, brain, and senses. Thus, a holistic, individualized approach to understanding it, based on awareness of an individual's sensory needs and neurological makeup, and understanding the potential behaviors and emotions that emerge in therapy, is essential.

Herbert (2010), in her holistic view of diagnosis and treatment, suggested, "just as autism is not simply a genetics problem, it is not simply a brain problem, either"; "autism involves the whole body" (p. 7). Art therapists are in a unique position to engage the mind, brain, and senses through art making, and to support communication through the art product (Malchiodi, 2003).

Research on autism, together with the experiences and advocacy of accomplished artists who are on the spectrum, enable art therapists to integrate multiple perspectives into their work and to understand the minds, brains, and individuality of clients on the AS (Grandin, 2006; Hosseini, 2012; Shore, 2006b; Williams, 2006). Lara and Bowers (2013) noted that, "for many individuals on the spectrum who have difficulties connecting, art can be an integral, valid part of therapy—a tool to show us who they are and what they are made of" (p. 1). Grandin stressed the importance of "thinking in pictures" both in her own early development and in her professional work (Richardson, 2009). Stephen Shore (2006a, 2006b) noted the importance of considering the interplay of all the senses in working with people on the AS. Thus, using sensory approaches should play a central role in art therapy; exploring the kinesthetic and sensory aspects of art materials along with the visual aspects of art making is valuable.

Art therapy goals for a person diagnosed with autism might include building on the individual's strengths and enabling creativity. The development of effective coping strategies, enhanced expression, and broader avenues of communication, as well as recognition and representation of affect, are all worthy art therapy goals. Repetitive or restrictive behaviors and sensory challenges might be addressed through the art materials and creative processes.

The Wiley Handbook of Art Therapy, First Edition. Edited by David E. Gussak and Marcia L. Rosal.
© 2016 John Wiley & Sons, Ltd. Published 2016 by John Wiley & Sons, Ltd.

Building a therapeutic relationship within a flexible, creative environment allows the art to become a focus of shared attention and interest. The artwork provides a welcome mediation in the relationship between the client and the therapist (Henley, 1992; Martin, 2009). Creative approaches support progress in therapy for children and adolescents (Bromfield, 2010), and enable "better emotional and communicative expression" for clients of all ages on the spectrum (Moat, 2013, p. 27).

There have been many changes since the word *autism* became part of the psychiatric lexicon in 1943 (Grandin & Panek, 2013), and the number of cases diagnosed of autism annually is increasing (Shore, 2006a). The reason behind this increase remains the focus of research and of controversy. Advances in understanding autism spectrum disorder (ASD), based on biological and psychological knowledge, is essential for more effective support, education, and treatment. To further understand the potential of art therapy in addressing autism, a brief history of the disorder is necessary.

A Brief History of ASD

The very meaning of being "on the spectrum" has itself changed over the years (Baron-Cohen as cited in Grandin & Panek, 2013). Kanner's initial description of the diagnosis in 1943 identified autism's communication and relationship challenges for the first time, but conceptualized these challenges as being psychologically based. Kanner (1943) described children with autism disorders requiring consistency and solitude. For example, one child, "disregarded the people, and instantly went for objects, preferably those that could be spun" (Kanner, 1943, p. 220).

Wing (1997) noted how Kanner first recognized autism as an early form of childhood schizophrenia. Kanner provided the possibility of improvement for children with autism, as seen through increased contact with the environment and relationships to others. He also noted that "there were very few really warmhearted fathers and mothers" (1943, p. 250) among the parents of the children in his sample, which called into question the role that the dynamics of primary relationships has for children with autism.

ASD, Asperger's syndrome, and pervasive developmental disorder differed in severity and presentation of symptoms in *DSM-IV-TR* (American Psychiatric Association [APA], 2000). When *DSM-5* (APA, 2013) was published, a continuum of these diagnoses was proposed based on the level of severity of the symptoms; under *DSM-5*, as each individual improves, the severity of the diagnosis diminishes Thus, the present version of the diagnosis in *DSM-5* compresses the range of autism spectrum diagnoses into a single diagnosis of ASD. The current diagnosis of ASD encompasses two core criteria: (i) communication and social deficits, and (ii) fixed or repetitive behaviors. While communication style and problematic behaviors certainly affect relationships, they are no longer seen as caused by the quality of primary relationships, as Kanner first considered.

For clinicians working with clients on the AS, it is more current and appropriate to conceptualize that "autism (is) more of an umbrella term covering a range of possibilities, rather than a useful diagnosis in itself" (Moat, 2013, p. 10). Clinicians now view the individual on the AS holistically and work on both nonverbal and verbal communication.

Current perspectives of ASD recognize the biologically and neurologically based connections between the brain and the "behaviors that make up the diagnosis of autism" (Grandin & Panek, 2013, p. 47). Currently, in marked contrast to Kanner's psychodynamic etiology of autism, autism research (Grandin & Panek, 2013; Herbert, 2010) and research on the neurobiology of relationships have established that empathic relationships require neurological integration (Badenoch, 2008; Cozolino, 2010; Porges, 2011; Siegel, 2012). Synchrony between mothers and infants has an impact on the health, learning, and development of infants: "In a baby with significant risk factors for autism, developing this connectedness may take extra effort" (Herbert, 2010, p. 236). Interventions aim to target "early core deficits (that) may lead to a cascading effect on neurodevelopment that arises from impoverished social interaction" (Wetherby, 2007, symposium presentation). The relational information that neurotypical children readily acquire, synthesize, and process must be painstakingly assembled for children on the AS (Badenoch & Bogdan, 2012). This process of integration is part of the work of therapy.

Using Art in Therapy

Creating art facilitates the neurological integration process. Beatrice Leprouste, a photographer on the spectrum, described how her photographs represented the way "I see the world through little details … I must add each of these details, one after another, to have a general view of things" (as cited in Hosseini, 2012, p. 10). While not art therapists, Badenoch (2008) and Badenoch and Bogdan (2012) pointed out how using visual art in therapy parallels other integrative meta-verbal approaches, such as Sandtray/Worldplay, in providing neurological integration for clients (Schadler & De Domenico, 2013). The rationale for using art therapy with individuals on the AS is supported by its contribution to neurological integration as well as its impact on the mind and the body. Thus, art therapists can build on the foundation of clinical neuroscience to "enhance the therapeutic advantages of arts in action" (Hass-Cohen, 2008, p. 21). Australian artist Nekea Blagoev (2013) wrote, "I believe art is the answer and 'cures' my Asperger's." She indicated that her art career was built on the foundation of giving her mind "what it thrives on"—the freedom of visual expression and a rich range of materials for expression.

Challenges and Goals for the Art Therapist

Descriptions of the therapeutic treatment and art-making for people on the spectrum suggest differences in the manner of neurological processing. However, Herbert's (2010) studies of brain anatomy of school-age children with autism did not find "broken brain regions" in these children (p. 10). Instead, Herbert found what Just and Keller (2013) termed "underconnectivity" among the different regions of the brain—when the brain regions are not efficiently connected, communication and emotional regulation are impacted, and flexible behavior becomes a challenge.

Porges' (2011) research indicated that, while the social engagement system is "neuroanatomically and neurophysiologically intact" in children on the AS (p. 18), they do not engage socially without support. He suggested that both stimulation of neural pathways and facilitation of the "neuroception" of safety in environments and relationships "will allow the social engagement system to function" in children with autism (p. 19). Creating an environment for therapy that clients perceive as both engaging and safe is essential to building this connection, in turn supporting social communication.

The core challenges for the children, adolescents, and young adults on the AS include difficulties with social communication, emotional regulation, sensory challenges, and a need for support in understanding the world of others (Greenspan & Shanker, 2004; Greenspan & Wieder, 2006; McAfee, 2002; Wetherby & Prizant, 2000). Individualized approaches through art that address sensory needs, needs for emotional regulation, and communicative styles are useful in assessing and conceptualizing a client's life within the broader contexts of family, community, and educational settings.[1]

The child or adolescent with Asperger's Syndrome typically "has a clinically significant difficulty with the understanding, expression, and regulation of emotion" (Attwood, 2006, p. 29), and is at risk for anxiety and depression (Kim, Szatmari, Bryson, & Wilson, 2000). Cozolino (2010) noted that support for emotional regulation and targeting stress "should always be an aspect of healing relationships" (p. 350). Attwood (2006) indicated that a paintbrush makes an effective stress reduction tool and helps to address clinical challenges. Using paints is essential for art therapy practice, where painting tools are used to help clients relax and self-regulate as well as to create expressive imagery.

In art therapy, reducing stress and supporting emotional regulation occurs through the choice of materials with various sensory qualities, the images created, and the energetic presence of the work itself. These elements evoke responses in both the creator and the observer on the emotional and sensory levels. "Due to an intense desire to cut, to tear, to blend colors, to put sticks and other materials into their works, individuals on the autism spectrum are naturally drawn to their unique, preferred, art form" (Hosseini, 2012, p. 7).

One adolescent client recognized the significance of using the different materials and making art for self-regulation, and explained how using a pencil made her "hold on, very hard" (Richardson, 2009, p. 103). Painting enabled the same teen to tap into sensations of flow and relaxation—"I like painting ... it makes me feel relaxed." As the paint flowed, she breathed more deeply and appeared more comfortable. As Kapitan (2013) indicated, young people on the AS who are engaged in the shared creative process are poised in "art therapy's sweet spot between art, anxiety, and the flow experience" (p. 54).

In witnessing individual choices of images and themes, the therapist acknowledges the significance of those particular interests, images, and themes to the child or adolescent (Richardson, 2009, p. 20). Acknowledging individual interests allows the child to feel "special" in a positive sense rather than vulnerable to criticism or disinterest (Bromfield, 2010, p. 92). Such interests provide a point of connection. Moving toward reciprocal or shared interests begins with receptivity from the therapist and demands flexibility of the artist–client.

For example, one young boy repeatedly jumped up from my art table to track the path of ambulances or police cars he heard through the window (see Figure 30.1).

He was made to feel comfortable and was often asked to return to drawing. Sometimes, the baskets of stress balls and other "fidgets" on the art table aided with this work, helping him either to focus on his drawing or to communicate his curiosity to the therapist. Together, we wondered about what might be going on outside the window, such as "were the helpers keeping people, including us, safe?" Noting his interest in trucks, he was told the story of a hook and ladder truck parked partly on the sidewalk across the street. He was informed that I wished he were there that day to see this unusual event. After listening carefully to this story, he asked questions and began to show an increased interest in a relationship with me. He realized that my thinking about his interests, and about him when he was not present, meant that I cared about him, and he began to be more engaged.

Art therapy helps to move individuals from a fixated interest toward reciprocity, social communication, and understanding of greater empathy. Art therapy provides a "communicative scaffold ... onto which further development, including the use of verbal language, can hang" (Evans & Dubkowski, 2001, p. 101). The connection between verbal language and the images created is a significant one. For children on the AS, "the symbols a child chooses reflect (their) emotional experience" (Weider, 2012, p. xiv).

The aforementioned client was able to discuss his repetitious imagery and narrow focus and move toward a greater understanding of affect. While similar therapeutic changes can be made through other expressive modalities, such as play (Badenoch & Bogdan, 2012; Gallo-Lopez & Rubin, 2012; Richardson, 2012; Schadler & De Domenico, 2013), art-making may allow for fuller reflection and communication.

Figure 30.1   Vehicles outside the therapy office window.

Figure 30.2 T-rex with a smile.

Art, Reflection, and Communication

One young client resisted drawing, painting, and clay. His play involved battles between dinosaurs and dragons. As he became fascinated by the sandtray, his play began to shift, creating vivid and increasingly detailed worlds full of animals; he eventually chose to draw as well. The sandtray provided an environment that was rich in sensory experience and visual imagery (De Domenico, 2000; Richardson, 2012). As he began to search for helpers, for fairness, and for a sense of safety in his sand "world," he explored the relationships between the animals and creatures. He recreated an image of a struggling dragon from his sandtray into a drawing, portraying it with a big smile. He then added a thought bubble with the words, "thank you" (see Figure 30.2).

This drawing explored cooperation, even as he struggled with self-control at school. Over time, his patience increased. The images in the sandtray helped him to create order, and, through art therapy sessions, a shared narrative emerged out of what had been chaotic play. The act of drawing seemed to help him to focus on and share his feelings.

Meta-Verbal Processes in Art Therapy

Moon (2008) indicated that art therapy was "meta-verbal," or beyond words. Meta-representations facilitate a fuller range of expression for those on the AS, and may contain a complexity that might surpass verbal communicative abilities (Martin, 2009). Art therapy can build on the cognitive strengths seen in individuals on the AS when therapists "partner to develop symbols and better communicate ideas" through "shared creative experience" (Goucher, 2012, p. 296).

Lusebrink's (1990) expressive therapies continuum is a model of how physical, sensory, and emotional interactions with art materials and processes promote information processing on a number of levels—from the sensory and kinesthetic preverbal level to the integrative creative level (1990). Art-making experiences at a sensory/kinesthetic level of the continuum, such as finger-painting or rolling clay, can take on meaning for the artist and can be a pleasurable, shared, and calming activity. Art is "an interesting crossroads for children on the spectrum because it is an activity in which strengths (visual learners, sensory interests) and deficits (imagination, need for sensory control) merge" (Martin, 2009, p. 28).

In my own experience, an essential element of supporting the art-making experience is the careful use of what Kramer (2000) termed the art therapist's "third hand" to rescue work that would otherwise fall victim to the perfectionism or frustrated sensory overload of the creator. Grandin cautioned that some individuals on the AS would get frustrated with visual expression, "because they can't get it absolutely perfect" (Richardson, 2009, p. 110). Herein is the value of the third hand—to support the expression, communication, and relationship enabled by the shared art experience. I move quickly to first rescue and then reflect on the image. A strong therapeutic relationship provides trust, tolerance for imperfection, and openness.

While it is satisfying for children to experiment with materials, such as squeezing, rolling, or pounding clay, an encouraging invitation from the therapist can help move the art-making from a sensory and visual activity to a shared emotional narrative and process. This "invitation" need not be a directive from the therapist, but can be a subtle shift as the therapist engages with both the child and with the materials.

For example, I often create a simple, changeable "face" from clay, transformed into a stick puppet that can portray different, exaggerated emotions. One 7-year-old child was fascinated by clay as he enjoyed its tactile qualities. He carefully observed what was around him, similar to the scientist or the artist, to help him make sense of the world and his experiences. He made models of his own hand and of his favorite animal, a cat. He was interested in the clay faces, as well, and began to create expressions on his own clay characters, either real or fantastical creatures.

One day, we sat in the sun and created tiny clay eggs together; I followed his lead. He then made a bird, then a cat. He smiled broadly; cats and birds are not notable for their friendship. He created additional props, including a large, intricate nest for the bird and eggs, and allowed the cat to come and visit. This relational story took place through shared art-making with very little talking.

Creativity and Coping through Art Therapy

Older children and adolescents are able to talk about their own creative process, which is important to them. For one adolescent client on the AS, who also had a diagnosis of depression, art therapy provided materials and a means to cope with strong emotions, which at times were overwhelming.

One client, Leanne, spoke about her "inspiration" to create a picture, a story, or a song. She said, "When you can't take your eyes or your mind off that thing, that's inspiration!" After carefully choosing art materials, she would begin painting or

Figure 30.3   The blue rose.

drawing. Leanne was responsive to color and used color to explore and understand the range of her feelings; these feelings were often connected her color choices, her movement, and the intensity of the colors. In her rainbow of feeling colors, she said, "yellow is happiness," while moving into yellow–orange showed how she "began to be upset"; red represented "frustrated and angry" (Richardson, 2009, p. 115).

Leanne also used drawing to comfort her from "feeling bad about myself." She used art-making to move beyond coping toward a greater self-understanding. As she drew a blue rose with concentric petals, methodically filling up a large sheet of paper, she relaxed (see Figure 30.3). As the blue rose with a mandala form emerged on the paper, the concentric and centering nature of the image resonated for Leanne. She explained that creating this drawing "felt very peaceful … like a wonderful sleep." One of the strengths that Leanne was beginning to develop was recognizing her creativity as a source of insight. A positive sense of self was acquired as she mastered challenges in her art and in her life.

Conclusion

Autism is a disorder that involves the brain, mind, and senses. The impact of this disorder can be profound, affecting communication, comfort, and relationships with others. Art can build on the interests and strengths of individuals with autism and address their challenges. Hosseini (2012), in her work with the Art of Autism Collaborative, noted how "people with autism have learned to work with their strengths and have used their unique perspective on the world to create their art" (p. 6). Individuals with autism have "hidden gifts … even if they are blocked by lots of confusion and difficulties ... people with autism are capable of creativity and insight" (Herbert, 2010, p. 245). Art therapists use a holistic, individualized approach when working with those on the AS. Involvement in art processes increases coping skills, emotional regulation, communication, and creativity for the clients.

Endnote

1 Two such programs are: (1) DIRFloortime, developed by Greenspan and his colleagues, which is developmentally and relationship-based, and always individualized (Greenspan & Weider, 2006); and (2) the Social Communication, Emotional Regulation, and Transactional Support (SCERTS) Method (Wetherby & Prizant, 2000).

References

American Psychiatric Association. (2000). *Diagnostic and statistical manual of mental disorders* (4th ed., text rev.). Washington, DC: Author.

American Psychiatric Association. (2013). *Diagnostic and statistical manual of mental disorders* (5th ed.). Arlington, VA: American Psychiatric Publishing.

Attwood, T. (2006). Asperger's syndrome and problems related to stress. In G. Baron, J. Groden, G. Groden, & G. Lipsitt (Eds.), *Stress and coping in autism* (pp. 351–371). Oxford: Oxford University Press.

Badenoch, B. (2008). *Being a brain-wise therapist: A practical guide to interpersonal neurobiology.* New York, NY: W.W. Norton and Company.

Badenoch, B., & Bogdan, N. (2012). Safety and connection the neurobiology of play. In L. Gallo-Lopez & L. Rubin (Eds.), *Play-based interventions for children and adolescents with autism spectrum disorders* (pp. 3–18). New York, NY: Routledge.

Blagoev, N. (2013). *The magical world of Nekea Blagoev.* Retrieved on September 19, 2013 from: the-art-of-autism.com/the-magical-world-of-nekea-blagoev/

Bromfield, R. (2010). *Doing therapy with children and adolescents with Asperger's syndrome.* New York, NY: John Wiley and Sons.

Brooke, S. (Ed.) (2009). *The use of the creative therapies in Autism Spectrum Disorders.* Springfield, IL: Charles C. Thomas.

Cozolino, L. (2010). *The neuroscience of psychotherapy.* New York, NY: W.W. Norton.

De Domenico, G. (2000). *Comprehensive guide to the use of sandtray in psychotherapy and transformational setting.* Oakland, CA: Vision Quest Images.

Evans, K., & Dubowski, J. (2001). *Art therapy with children on the autistic spectrum: Beyond words.* London: Jessica Kingsley.

Gallo-Lopez, L., & Rubin, L. (Eds.). 2012. *Play-based interventions for children and adolescents with autism spectrum disorders.* New York, NY: Routledge.

Goucher, C. (2012). Art therapy: Connecting and communicating. In L. Gallo-Lopez & L. Rubin (Eds.), *Play-based interventions for children and adolescents with autism spectrum disorders* (pp. 295–316). New York, NY: Routledge.

Grandin, T. (2006, March). *Keynote address: Bold steps.* Presented at the VSA International Conference, Washington, D.C.

Grandin, T., & Panek, R. (2013). *The autistic brain: Thinking across the spectrum.* Boston: Houghton Mifflin Harcourt.

Greenspan, S., & Shanker, S. (2004). *The first idea: How symbols, language, and intelligence evolved from our primate ancestors to modern humans.* Cambridge, MA: Da Capo Press.

Greenspan, S., & Weider, S. (2006). *Engaging autism: Using the Floortime approach to help children relate, communicate, and think.* Cambridge, MA: Da Capo. Press.

Hass-Cohen, N. (2008). Partnering art therapy and clinical neuroscience. In R. Carr & N. Hass-Cohen (Eds.), *Art therapy and clinical neuroscience* (pp. 21–42). London: Jessica Kingsley Publishers.

Henley, D. (1992). *Exceptional children exceptional art: Teaching art to children with special needs.* Worcester, MA: Davis Publications.

Herbert, M. (2010). *The Autism Revolution.* New York, NY: Harvard Medical School, Ballantine Books.

Hosseini, D. (2012). *The art of autism: Shifting perceptions.* Carpinteria, CA: The Art of Autism.

Just, M., & Keller, T. (2013). *Is "underconnectivity" in autism specific to frontal cortex?* Retrieved on September 17, 2013 from: http://sfari.org/news-and-opinion/specials/2013/connectivity/is-underconnectivity-in-autism-specific-to-frontal-cortex.

Kanner, L. (1943). Autistic disturbances of affective contact. *Nervous Child, 2,* 217–250.

Kapitan, L. (2013). Art therapy's sweet spot between art, anxiety, and the flow experience. *Art Therapy: Journal of the American Art Therapy Association, 30*(2), 54–55.

Kim, J. A., Szatmari, P., Bryson, S. E., & Wilson, F. J. (2000). The prevalence of anxiety and mood problems among children with autism and Asperger syndrome. *Autism, 4*(2), 117 132.

Kramer, E. (2000). *Art as therapy: Collected papers.* London: Jessica Kingsley.

Lara, J., & Bowers, K. (2013). Expressive arts: Learning, growing, and expressing. *Autism Asperger's Digest,* September/October 2013. Retrieved: http://autismdigest.com/expressive-arts-learning-growing-and-expressing

Lusebrink, V. (1990). *Imagery and visual expression in therapy.* New York, NY: Plenum Press.

McAfee, J. (2002). *Navigating the social world: A curriculum for individuals with asperger's syndrome, high functioning autism, and related disorders.* Arlington, TX: Future Horizons Publishing.

Malchiodi, C. (2003). Art therapy and the brain. In C. Malchiodi (Ed.), *Handbook of art therapy.* New York, NY: Guilford Press.

Martin, N. (2009). *Art as an early intervention tool for children with autism.* London: Jessica Kingsley Publishers.

Moat, D. (2013). *Integrative psychotherapeutic approaches to autism spectrum conditions.* London: Jessica Kingsley Publishers.

Moon, B. (2008). *Introduction to art therapy: Faith in the process.* Springfield, IL: Charles C. Thomas.

Porges, S. (2011). *The polyvagal theory.* New York, NY: W.W. Norton.

Richardson, J. (2009). Creating a safe space for adolescents on the autism spectrum. In S. Brooke (Ed.), *The use of creative therapies with autism spectrum disorders* (pp. 103–122). Springfield, IL: Charles C. Thomas.

Richardson, J. (2012). The world of the sand tray and the child on the autism spectrum. In L. Gallo-Lopez & L. Rubin (Eds.), *Play-based interventions for children and adolescents with autism spectrum disorders* (pp. 209–230). New York, NY: Routledge.

Schadler, G., & De Domenico, G. (2013). Sandtray-worldplay for people who experience chronic mental illness. *International Journal of Play Therapy, 21*(2), 87–99.

Shore, S. (2006a). *Understanding autism for dummies.* New York, NY: John Wiley and Sons.

Shore, S. (2006b). *Beyond the wall: Personal experiences with autism and Asperger syndrome.* Shawnee Mission, KS: Autism Asperger Publishing Company.

Siegel, D. (2012). *The developing mind.* New York, NY: Guilford Press.

Weider, S. (2012). Forward. In L. Gallo-Lopez & L. Rubin (Eds.), *Play-based interventions for children and adolescents with autism spectrum disorders* (pp. xi–xiv). New York, NY: Routledge.

Wetherby, A. (presenter) (2007). Red flags of autism spectrum disorders in the second year of life. *Autism spectrum disorder: Recent advances in infantile origins, early childhood detection, & intervention*. Providence Rhode Island: Brown University.

Wetherby, A., & Prizant, B. (Eds.) (2000). *Autism spectrum disorders: A transactional developmental perspective*. Baltimore, MD: Brookes Publishing.

Williams, D. (2006). *Donna Williams the artist*. Retrieved on January 28, 2009, from http://www.donnawilliams.net/artist.0.html

Wing, L. (1997). The history of ideas on autism. Legends, myths, and reality. *Autism: The International Journal of Research and Practice, 1*(1), 13–23.

31

Art Therapy and Developmental Disabilities

Kevin Bailey

A recent study by the Centers for Disease Control and Prevention (CDC) found that one in six children in the United States had been diagnosed with some form of developmental disability (DD), an increase of over 17% since 1997 (Boyle et al., 2011). The expanded prevalence of DDs, combined with the current trend for early intervention, inclusion, least restrictive living environment, and improvements in quality of life (QOL), make it apparent that this is a population with a need for more effective specialized treatments and services. Art therapy is a specialized treatment that has received recent attention due to its focus on using art as an alternative way to communicate and as self-expression (Lister & Rosales, 2009; Murray, 2003; Sormanti & Ballan, 2011; Wilk et al., 2010). Art therapy enriches the lives of those with DD by providing creative and sensory opportunities for environmental exploration, socialization, validation, self-identification, and empowerment.

Developmental Disabilities

According to the Developmental Disabilities Assistance and Bill of Rights Act (2000), DD is a severe and chronic condition characterized by mental and physical impairments that occurred before adulthood. The disability limits self-care, learning, mobility, language, and self-direction, and may require lifelong, specialized individual services and support.

As an umbrella term, DD describes a large number of syndromes and disorders with diverse symptoms and qualities. Simultaneously, individuals with DD have many commonalities such as overcoming social stigmas; undergoing numerous medical appointments and evaluations; utilizing adaptive accommodations; and managing mental, physical, and emotional stressors. This chapter will focus primarily on these common characteristics and the challenges that art therapists' experience. Thus, intellectual and neurological disabilities will be referred throughout as DDs.

Significantly, no two persons with DD are alike, and each person has his or her own unique challenges, qualities, passions, and abilities. The focus should be on the individual and not on the disability. DDs are generally associated with limited cognitive

The Wiley Handbook of Art Therapy, First Edition. Edited by David E. Gussak and Marcia L. Rosal.
© 2016 John Wiley & Sons, Ltd. Published 2016 by John Wiley & Sons, Ltd.

skills, but many individuals diagnosed with autistic spectrum disorder, cerebral palsy, Prader–Willi syndrome, spina bifida, and Williams syndrome present with average to above-average intelligence. Special care should be taken to conduct thorough assessments and collect accurate data before finalizing any assessment of the patient's abilities, interests, and treatment goals.

Neurological disabilities

Neurological disabilities are a group of disorders that affect the central nervous system, which consists of the brain and spinal cord. They are primarily characterized by physical limitations such as muscle weakness, poor coordination, and impairments in motor skills (Langtree, n.d.). Sometimes referred to as "physical disorders" or "motor disorders," they include, but are not limited to, autistic spectrum disorders, cerebral palsy, muscular dystrophy, Prader–Willi syndrome, Sanfilippo syndrome, spina bifida, and Williams syndrome.

According to the National Institute of Neurological Disorders and Stroke (2013), cerebral palsy is defined as a group of neurological disorders that occur prenatally or in infancy and permanently affect movement and muscle coordination. With many subtypes, it is caused by abnormalities in or damage to the brain that disrupts movement and posture. Symptoms vary widely, and some people may require minimal to no special assistance. General symptoms include lack of muscle coordination, poor balance, difficulty swallowing, stiff or tight muscles, and variations in muscle tone that can lead to the inability to independently ambulate, speak, or control muscle movements. Additional mental and medical conditions may include: dysphagia, seizures, mental retardation, constipation, impaired vision and speech, sensory processing issues, and psychiatric disorders.

Autistic spectrum disorders (ASDs) are a group of neurological disabilities related to complex issues of brain development. They include autism, Asperger's syndrome, childhood disintegrative disorder, and Rett's syndrome. Symptoms vary and are often characterized by repetitive behaviors, maladaptive behaviors, sensory processing issues, social impairments, and difficulties with verbal and non-verbal communication. ASDs can be associated with intellectual disabilities, health conditions, limitations with motor coordination, and other psychiatric illnesses. Some individuals with ASD can be exceptionally gifted in music, math, and the visual arts (Autism Speaks, 2013).

Intellectual disabilities

Intellectual disabilities (formerly "mental retardation") include, but are not limited to, other disabilities such as Down syndrome, fetal alcohol syndrome, and fragile X syndrome. They are characterized by significant limitations in intellectual and adaptive functioning that are evident in early childhood and may have been caused by genetic conditions, injury, disease, birth defects, or a neurological abnormality. Levels of intellectual disabilities can vary greatly from mild to severe and may reflect intellectual deficits, including one's ability to learn, reason, think, and solve problems. These are generally measured through an IQ test. A score below 75 is characterized as a limitation, but recent trends focus more on social and environmental issues, combined with IQ scores. Limitations in adaptive functioning affect conceptual, social, and practical skills, such as activities of daily living. Other areas of poor functioning include a lower capacity to process information, achieve tasks, adapt to new situations, function in social settings, and regulate self-control (American Association on Intellectual and Developmental Disabilities, 2010).

Treatment Issues

People with DD are at a greater risk for developing emotional, psychological, and behavioral issues (Mazzucchelli & Sanders, 2011). One of the psychologically damaging, yet addressable, issues for those with DD is societal stigmatization. Those with DD have been given many unfortunate labels: "slow," "spazz," "pinheads," "cripples," "gimps," "idiots," "morons," "feebleminded," and "the mental defective," including the most common clinical term today, "mentally retarded." Beyond the stigma of a label lie the even more dehumanizing encounters with society—ranging from staring, ridicule, baby talk, and blatant rejection, to physical and sexual abuse (Dudley, 1997).

Due to their developmental, cognitive, and communication delays, children with DD have an increased risk of physical, emotional, and sexual abuse and neglect (Murray, 2003; Paschos & Bouras, 2007). Neglect can range from the lack of opportunity to make choices to the denial of basic rights and ordinary freedoms. Exposure to childhood neglect and trauma can result in self-harm behaviors, increased feelings of loss (Murray, 2003), and may lead to PTSD and depression.

Maladaptive behaviors

Maladaptive behaviors, such as physical and verbal assault, property destruction, and self-injury, can affect the lives of many children and adults with DDs, their primary caregivers, and the support system. Children with DD are more likely than their typical peers to use maladaptive behaviors, including self-injurious behaviors (SIB), as coping strategies for physical, emotional, or psychological stress (Sormanti & Ballan, 2011).

Such behaviors may result from medical or psychiatric issues, or an under- or over-stimulating environment (Paschos & Bouras, 2007). Kahng, Iwata, and Lewin (2002) stated that the most common explanation for SIB may be to escape a stressful situation or to avoid undesirable demands. SIB may also result from misinterpreted or poorly received communication attempts, from attempts to gain social reinforcements (Halliday & Mackrell, 1998), as well as due to medical issues such as seizures, thyroid disorders, blocked shunt, constipation, urinary tract infections, ear infections, or headaches.

Grief and loss

The grief of those with DD is often ignored or misinterpreted as a maladaptive behavior. In addition to the normal losses that the general population may experience, individuals with DD may also experience secondary losses such as the loss of identity, opportunity, accessibility, independence, and the ability to understand or express their feelings associated with trauma or grief (Read, 2000). Research has shown that the failure to acknowledge such issues can lead to additional developmental and emotional problems (Clements, 2004).

Co-morbidity with mental illness

Review of the literature reveals that the prevalence of psychiatric disorders in individuals with DD is two to four times greater than that of the general population, and over a quarter of this population presents with behavioral problems that may require mental health services (Fletcher, Loschen, Stavrakak, & First, 2007). Unfortunately, assessing and diagnosing such disorders is difficult. Maladaptive behaviors have long been considered to be part of the disability rather than due to possible mental health issues. This population is often left out of psychotherapeutic mental heath services due to the limited cognitive and verbal functioning and the inability or unwillingness of the service providers to assume responsibility (Demanchick, Cochran, & Cochran, 2003; Paschos & Bouras, 2007).

Art Therapy with DDs

The limited verbal, physical, and cognitive functioning of people with DD is challenging for mental health professionals and service providers. These limitations create additional roadblocks for inclusion and integration into the community. Those with DD may receive few opportunities for self-expression, normalization, and personal and social growth. The lack of opportunities may lead to problem behaviors, isolation, depression, and low self-identity; these issues were described by Paschos and Bouras (2007) as "secondary handicaps." The ability to safely address these secondary handicaps can have a positive effect on the lives of individuals with DD. Art therapy can provide one avenue of overcoming personal and developmental barriers through adaptive and alternative methods of communication (Lister & Rosales, 2009).

The daily routine of those with moderate to severe DD is filled with intensive therapy and training developed and implemented by treatment teams and caregivers. These highly structured daily agendas can leave the person void of choices and opportunities for self-expression, which in turn can escalate maladaptive behaviors and cause a lack of motivation (Demanchick et al., 2003). In contrast to their regular interventions and activities of daily living, creative activities can provide an alternate means for gaining control, making choices, and expressing one's "voice" (Reynolds, 2002).

Art therapy and nonverbal communication

Limitations in communication can pose an insurmountable challenge to effective mental health services, which can lead to frustration, self-injurious behaviors, and the avoidance of social activities. Art can bypass limitations in the intellectual and verbal ability to assist with assessments, help build a trusting therapeutic relationship, and provide a starting point for future interventions and support (Chong, Mackey, Stott, & Broadbent, 2013; Lister & Rosales, 2009).

Art interventions can assist those with language skill impairments by providing them with a form of communication and creative self-expression to help individuals with DD feel empowered, helping to promote personal and social development (Epp, 2008; Silver, 1977). Chong et al. (2013) found that asking people with cerebral palsy to draw their illness helped assess their perception of their disability and provided them with a means for self-expression. Those with DD may find emotional release by engaging with various art materials:

> The advantage of art therapy for patients with speech and language disturbances, including dysarthria, is that it provides them an opportunity and motivation to speak, to express themselves without the self-consciousness caused by conscious participation in speech therapy per se. (Wilk et al., 2010, p. 229)

Art therapy treatment issues

A key component of art therapy is its ability to use the visual arts to assist in engaging healthy emotional expression as an alternative to expressing feelings in a destructive way (Saunders & Saunders, 2000). In addition, maladaptive behaviors should not be seen as the primary issue, but rather as a symptom or sign of what is being communicated (Putnam, 2009). Research outcomes have verified that art can be used as a way to assist people with DD in expressing themselves nonverbally and in validating their feelings associated with grief, loss, and trauma (Cooke, 2003; Webb, 2011).

Art therapy and socialization   Social relationships are often difficult. Children with DD may avoid group or social activities due to a lack of confidence. They may be excluded from activities with their peers, and therefore rely on their family or caregivers for social relationships. They may develop a sense of isolation and poor self-identity, which could affect the development of appropriate social and coping skills, and possibly lead to SIB (Darrow, Follette, Maragakis, & Dykstra, 2011). Chadsey (2007) found that positive social relationships are important predictors for happiness and QOL.

Art therapy can assist in building social relationships, create opportunities for community integration, and promote social acceptance. Community-based projects, such as art shows, joint community art festivals, and group art projects, can help sensitize the general population to people with DD by creating dialogue and providing a glimpse of their unique challenges and talents (Lister, Tanguay, Snow, & D'Amico, 2009). Social opportunities can provide a sense of normalization, belonging, and a more positive self-identity.

Art therapy and QOL   One of the main goals when working with individuals with DD is to increase their independence and improve their QOL. QOL is described as an individual's overall satisfaction with their life, and can be based on one's availability to resources, opportunities, and choices (D'Amico, Miodrag, & Dinolfo, 2009). This may be difficult to assess with DD, but is simple to implement by providing a safe environment that empowers and enriches their lives.

Freedom of choice is important to human development and to QOL, as it can motivate participation. Lamore and Nelson (1993) found that adults interacted significantly more with art media when provided choices through a variety of art materials and alternate communication choices, fostering self-esteem and promoting independence.

Art therapy considerations

Art therapy with people with DD involves more than meeting treatment goals. It requires an understanding of, and special consideration to, the disability, including the individual's physical and mental limitations, medical risks, and environmental implications (Anderson, 1992). Many people with DD present medical complications along with their challenging behaviors and impairments. Art therapists need to be aware of environmental conditions, and how sensory tools and art materials may complicate such medical issues.

A total team approach is necessary for the safest, least restrictive, and most effective treatment with DD. Working with the physician, rehabilitative (physical, occupational, speech) therapists, psychologists, and behavioral specialists, art therapists can incorporate their recommendations to develop a plan that meets the individual's emotional, behavioral, and physical needs. Input from the team members may provide the necessary information on allergies, side effects of medication, behavioral modifications, proper positioning, duration of physical activity, and hand preference. Many of the art therapy goals I use involve art interventions and materials to complement physical, behavioral, occupational, and speech outcomes. These include directives that improve fine motor skills and increase range of motion, encourage eye contact and head movement toward the midline, and increase nonverbal communication. Sensory art materials are used to achieve desensitization and increase motivation, interaction, and independence.

Understanding specific disabilities, limitations, and risk factors is essential to developing safe and effective treatment plans. But to be able to fully enter their world and help provide a voice for their expression, hope, and development, an art therapist must focus on the person and his or her abilities rather than disabilities. Anderson (1992) described four main categories for adapting art therapy to meet the individualized needs of those with DDs: (1) adaptations in the physical environment; (2) adaptations in the art materials, including use of sensory materials; (3) adaptations in the instructional sequence; and (4) adaptations in technology. All of these rely on communicating with the treatment team, and are individualized to meet the specific needs and abilities of each person.

Art therapy environment The art therapy environment should be one that involves exploring sensory and art materials while promoting a sense of safety and appropriate behavior. Adaptations may include: adequate space and equipment for wheelchairs; limited distractions on the tables or walls of the room for those with attention and focus deficits; a clean and safe work area for individuals at risk for self-harm; open spaces surrounding individuals with uncontrollable movements; and music or sensory items to increase relaxation, participation, and focus. It is important to be consistent with classroom routines and treatment sessions to build trust and create a safer, therapeutic environment.

Adaptive art materials and interventions The art process is often more important that the final product due to its ability to offer choices, control, and opportunities for socialization. If the art process is not adapted for individual success, then it can produce heightened anxiety, and may lead to frustration or maladaptive behaviors. All art materials are capable of being adapted to fit the specific needs of an individual. Some of the adaptive techniques I have used include:

- Taping paper to the table or walls for individuals with limitations in motor control or motor skills
- Providing thick and long-handled brushes for easier grip and control
- Using pre-cut shapes to increase motivation and success
- Using lockable plastic bags filled with paint and paper to shake and engage in the art process
- Using toy trucks or balls dipped in paint to roll across the paper
- Using torn paper collages
- Using materials that can be easily manipulated and materials that engage and evoke the various senses.

When choosing art materials to use or adapt, it is always important to remember safety, weight, and stability.

Adaptive art interventions should focus on independence through mastery. There is a tendency for professionals to want to help or rescue the people working on a task. Art therapists should provide just enough assistance for individuals to feel empowered and achieve a level of independence. "Hand over hand" techniques are useful for helping those with severe physical limitations, but it is important to make sure that they always have choices and are actively involved in as many aspects of the experience as possible. Self-interaction with the art, no matter how limited, is crucial for acquiring new skills that can lead to a higher self-esteem and greater independence (Anderson, 1992).

Intellectual and social impairments can lead to difficulties in processing sensory information (Ayers, 1972; Kwok, To, & Sung, 2003). This "sensory processing disorder" (Ayers, 1972) can lead to maladaptive behaviors and avoidance of daily and social activities. Art and play can assist with safely exploring and integrating the senses through what is known as "sensory stimulation" (Malchiodi, 2003). Sensory stimulation can facilitate interaction, relaxation, and empowerment by providing safe opportunities to engage with art materials that aid in the exploration of their senses and environments. Materials to address sensory stimulation include: sand, rice, Model Magic, textured objects, gel pads, bubble wrap, music, water, aromas, and objects that light up or vibrate. The art therapist can act as a support system during the sensory exploration, yet should always be aware of the potential risks involved with using these materials. See Figures 31.1 and 31.2 for examples of various materials explored in artwork.

Instructional sequences Skill acquisition program (SAP), or task analysis, describes an instructional sequencing of learning where all the steps necessary for achieving a specific behavioral objective are isolated, described, and sequenced.

Figure 31.1 Acrylic paint on canvas, masking tape stencils, paint applied by hands.

Figure 31.2 Acrylic paint on canvas, colored tissue paper, plastic toy car wheels rolled in paint.

The focus should always be on the behavior and skill to be mastered and not on the specific disability of the individual. The sequenced steps need to be individualized, be observable, should rely on the skills of the individual, and be demonstrated by the therapist to decrease anxiety and increase success. Art therapy goals that allow individual choices and promote skills that can be mastered can result in increased control and a sense of empowerment. Some examples include object manipulation, choice-making, activity engagement, and desensitization to touch.

Some things to consider when developing an SAP include: age-appropriate materials, level of staff assistance, using activities grounded in the real world, and developing objectives that are specific to learning and which aid in the development of survival skills (Anderson, 1992). Some SAPs are developed to act as an alternative or replacement behavior to the current maladaptive behavior. Interactions with preferred stimuli, such as art and sensory materials, can serve as replacement behavior, and current research has found their use to increase the likelihood of effective interventions (Fava & Strauss, 2010).

Technology

With the advancement of augmentative communication devices and more practical and affordable technology, such as the Apple iPad and Nintendo Wii, those with DD have increased opportunities for social interactions, normalization, and validation. Historically, art therapists have been reluctant to embrace high-tech media (Austin, 2009; Williams, Kramer, Henley, & Gerity, 1997). However, as Anderson (1994) stated, technology "can become the hands of those with limited hand use" (p. 82). It is important to allow the individuals to make aesthetic choices without the frustration of creating art that requires fine motor skills. In my experience, the hand and machine can work together to increase attention span, fine and gross motor use, independence, motivation, and object engagement, to create art that empowers and promotes personal development and happiness. Technological benefits may lead to reducing problem behaviors and can lead to an increase in social opportunities and a healthy self-esteem. Computer technology is an ever-expanding adaptive tool that could aid art therapists in offering a wider range of individualized creative outlets for bridging the gap between self-expression and personal limitations.

Conclusion

Art therapy is based on the principle that all persons are capable of exploring, creating, and growing through interactions with art. It is this idea that verifies art therapy as a key component to any multidisciplinary team approach to providing people with DDs the least restrictive and most effective means to addressing their emotional, behavioral, and physical needs.

Art therapy provides adaptive and alternative methods to traditional verbal language that provide people with DD the opportunity to safely express their feelings through a normalizing experience. Once a safe outlet for communication and expression is established, the art can then provide choices and a sense of control that can lead to self-confidence, positive social interactions, and an increase in their QOL (Got & Cheng, 2008).

Art therapists rely on their education, knowledge, and creativity to adapt and develop effective individualized treatment plans that can safely address the personal needs and goals of people with DD. The current trends toward inclusion and community integration stress the importance for art therapists to increase research, network with other disciplines, and become knowledgeable of technology in order to provide the most effective services. Art therapy offers a promising treatment approach for people with DD and their caregivers. It provides supportive and safe opportunities for environmental exploration, sensory stimulation, independence, and choice, while promoting growth and self-awareness through an empowering "voice."

References

American Association on Intellectual and Developmental Disabilities. (2010). *Intellectual disability: Definition, classification, and systems of supports* (11th ed.). Washington, DC: American Association on Intellectual and Developmental Disabilities.

Anderson, F. E. (1992). *Art for all the children: Approaches to art therapy for children with disabilities.* Springfield, IL: Charles C. Thomas.

Anderson, F. E. (1994). *Art centered education and therapy for children with disabilities.* Springfield, IL: Charles C. Thomas.

Austin, B. A. (2009). Evaluating the effectiveness of art therapy through a quantitative, outcome-focused therapy. *Art Therapy, 26*(2), 83–85.

Autism Speaks Inc. (2013). Autism speaks. Retrieved from http://www.autismspeaks.org/what-autism

Ayers, A. J. (1972). *Sensory integration and learning disorders.* Los Angeles, CA: Western Psychological Services.

Boyle, C. A., Boulet, S., Schieve, L., Cohen, R. A., Blumberg, S. J., Yeargin-Allsopp, M., Visser S., & Kogan, M. D. (2011). Trends in the prevalence of developmental disabilities in US children, 1997–2008. *Pediatrics, 127*(6), 1034–1042.

Chadsey, J. (2007). Adult social relationships. In S. L. Odom, R. H. Horner, M. E. Snell, & J. Blancher (Eds.), *Handbook of developmental disabilities* (pp. 449–466). New York, NY: Guilford Press.

Chong, J., Mackey, A. H., Stott, N. S., & Broadbent, E. (2013). Walking drawings and walking ability in children with Cerebral Palsy. *Health Psychology, 32*(6), 710–713.

Clements, P. T. (2004). Making sense of the senseless. *The Journal of Psychosocial Nursing, 42*(1), 6–7.

Cooke, L. B. (2003). Treating the sequelae of abuse in adults with learning disabilities. *The British Journal of Developmental Disabilities, 49*(1), 23–28.

D'Amico, M., Miodrag, N., & Dinolfo, F. (2009). Assessing the effects of creative art therapies on the quality of life of individuals with developmental disabilities. In S. Snow & M. D'Amico. *Assessment in the creative arts therapies: Designing and adapting assessment tools for adults with developmental disabilities* (pp. 257–294). Springfield, IL: Charles C. Thomas.

Darrow, S. M., Follette, W. C., Maragakis, A., & Dykstra, T. (2011). Reviewing risk for individuals with developmental disabilities. *Clinical Psychology Review, 31*, 472–477.

Demanchick, S. P., Cochran, N. H., & Cochran, J. L. (2003). Person-centered play therapy for adults with developmental disabilities, *International Journal of Play Therapy, 12*(1), 47–65.

Developmental Disabilities Assistance and Bill of Rights Act of 2000. Public Law 106–402, (2000).

Dudley, J. R. (1997). *Confronting the stigma in their lives: Helping people with a mental retardation label.* Springfield, IL: Charles C. Thomas.

Epp, K. M. (2008). Outcome based evaluation of a social skills program sing art therapy and group therapy for children on the autistic spectrum. *Children and Schools, 30*(1), 27–36.

Fava, L., & Strauss, K. (2010). Multi-sensory rooms: Comparing effects of the Snoezelen and the stimulus preference environment on the behavior of adults with profound mental retardation. *Research in Developmental Disabilities, 31*, 160–171.

Fletcher, R., Loschen, E., Stavrakak, C., & First, M. (2007). Introduction. In R. Fletcher, E. Loschen, C. Stavrakak, & M. First (Eds.), *Diagnostic Manual—Intellectual disability: A clinical guide for diagnosis of mental disorders in persons with intellectual disability* (pp. 1–7). Kingston, NY: NADD Press.

Got, I. L. S., & Cheng, S. T. (2008). The effects of art facilitation on the social functioning of people with developmental disability. *Art Therapy, 25*(1), 32–37.

Halliday, S., & Mackrell, K. (1998). Psychological interventions in self-injurious behavior. *British Journal of Psychiatry, 10*, 164–173.

Kahng, S., Iwata, B. A., & Lewin, B. (2002). The impact of functional assessment on the treatment of self-injurious behavior. In S. R. Schroeder, M. L. Oster-Granite, & T. Thompson (Eds.), *Self injurious behavior: Gene-brain-behavior relationships* (pp. 119–131). Washington, DC: American Psychological Association.

Kwok, H. W. M., To, Y. F., & Sung, H. F. (2003). The application of a multisensory Snoezelen room for people with learning disabilities—Hong Kong experience. *Hong Kong Medical Journal, 9*(2), 122–126.

Lamore, K. L., & Nelson, D. L. (1993). The effects of options on performance of an art project in adults with developmental disabilities. *American Journal of Occupational Therapy, 47*(5), 397–401.

Langtree, I. (n.d.). Disability: Definition, types and models. Retrieved on November 12, 2012 from http:/www.disabled-world.com/disability/types/

Lister, S., & Rosales, A. (2009). The kinetic-house-tree-person adapted to adults with developmental disabilities. In S. Snow & M. D'Amico (Eds.), *Assessment in the creative arts therapies: Designing and adapting assessment tools for adults with developmental disabilities* (pp. 29–45). Springfield, IL: Charles C. Thomas.

Lister, S., Tanguay, D., Snow, S., & D'Amico, M. (2009). Development of a creative arts therapies center for people with developmental disabilities. *Art Therapy, 26*(1), 34–37.

Malchiodi, C. A. (Ed.) (2003). *The handbook of art therapy.* New York, NY: Guilford Press.

Mazzucchelli, T. G., & Sanders, M. R. (2011). Preventing behavioural and emotional problems in children who have a developmental disability: A public health approach. *Research in Developmental Disabilities, 32*, 2148–2156.

Murray, B. L. (2003). Self-harm among adolescents with developmental disabilities, *Journal of Psychosocial Nursing, 41*(11), 37–45.

National Institute of Neurological Disorders and Stroke. (2013). *Cerebral palsy: Hope through research* (NIH Publication No. 13-1059). Bethesda, MD: Office of Communications and Public Liaison.

Paschos, D., & Bouras, N. (2007). Mental health supports in developmental disabilities. In S. L. Odom, R. H. Horner, M. E. Snell, & J. Blancher (Eds.), *Handbook of developmental disabilities* (pp. 483–499). New York, NY: Guilford Press.

Putnam, C. (Ed.) (2009). *Guidelines for understanding and serving people with intellectual disabilities and mental, emotional and behavioral disorders.* Tallahassee, FL: Florida Developmental Disabilities Council.

Read, S. (2000). Bereavement and people with learning disabilities. *Nursing & Residential Care, 2*(5), 230–234.

Reynolds, F. (2002). An exploratory survey of opportunities and barriers to creative leisure activity for people with learning disabilities. *British Journal of Learning Disabilities, 30,* 63–67.

Saunders, E. J., & Saunders, J. A. (2000). Evaluating the effectiveness of art therapy through a quantitative, outcome-focused therapy. *The Arts in Psychotherapy, 27*(2), 99–106.

Silver, R. A. (1977). The role of art in developing and evaluating cognitive skills. *Journal of Learning Disabilities, 10*(7), 27–35.

Snow, S., & D'Amico, M. (2009). *Assessment in the creative arts therapies: Designing and adapting assessment tools for adults with developmental disabilities.* Springfield, IL: Charles C. Thomas.

Sormanti, M., & Ballan, M. (2011). Strengthening grief support for children with developmental disabilities. *School Psychology International, 32*(2), 179–193.

Webb, N. B. (2011). Play therapy for bereaved children: Adapting strategies to community, school, and home settings. *School Psychology International, 32*(2), 132–143.

Wilk, M., Pachalska, M., Lipowska, M., Herman-Sucharska, I., Makarowski, R., Mirski, A., & Jastrzebowska, G. (2010). Speech intelligibility in Cerebral Palsy children attending an art therapy program. *Med Sci Monit, 16*(5), 222–231.

Williams, K., Kramer, E., Henley, D., & Gerity, L. (1997). Art, art therapy and the seductive environment. *American Journal of Art Therapy, 35,* 106–117.

Aggression and Art Therapy:
A Social Interactionist Perspective[1]

David E. Gussak

While working as a "behavioral specialist" in a Southern California psychiatric hospital in 1987, a diminutive 15-year-old Hispanic boy, Rick (a pseudonym), was admitted to the locked unit for adolescents. Despite his small stature, Rick acted tough and seemed quite strong. He had difficulty in school for "acting out," and was in trouble with the law for gang activities. His family admitted him because of his violent tendencies. He believed himself "tougher" than all others in the unit, including the staff. Rarely a day went by when he did not try to attack a peer or a staff member for what he perceived to be disrespect. He would often end up in restraints.

Proud of the gang to which he belonged, Rick constantly "tagged" his gang moniker on the walls of the unit. As there was a rule against displaying gang insignias and writing on the walls, he was often in trouble with the staff of the hospital. He became angry when the graffiti was removed from the walls and, at times, physically attacked those who washed off the drawings. It was obvious that he identified himself with his gang. By removing the graffiti from the walls, he believed the staff was letting him know he was unacceptable; the perceived disrespect resulted in anger.

After several such incidents, with permission from the unit administrator, I made a deal with Rick. If he agreed to work with me, he could do his gang markings on paper and keep them in his desk drawer. He had to promise he would not display the drawings. He agreed to the stipulations, and he spent several afternoons drawing quietly with pencils on white paper. Each drawing was meticulously realized. After completing several gang tag drawings, I suggested he create a drawing of the name his gang called him. Eventually, the drawings evolved into an embellishment of his real name. These he would proudly show to others, and because they depicted his name, they could be hung on the wall in his room. By the time he left the unit, he was more responsive with staff directives and decidedly less aggressive. Working with Rick, I realized the importance of how interactions demonstrated acceptance and validation of Rick's identity. His behavior aligned with healthy, socially acceptable expressions, and his self-concept was strengthened. He eventually saw himself as part of society, and his aggressive tendencies were altered.

From this experience, I learned first hand the benefits of art with aggressive and violent clients. It provided an avenue for Rick to feel valued, a means for acceptable

The Wiley Handbook of Art Therapy, First Edition. Edited by David E. Gussak and Marcia L. Rosal.
© 2016 John Wiley & Sons, Ltd. Published 2016 by John Wiley & Sons, Ltd.

interaction, and paved a way for him to develop and maintain a new identity. In future job settings, I would encounter many aggressive and violent people. However, it was Rick who taught me the value of art as a means to divert and redirect anger and aggression.

Various Theoretical Perspectives on Aggression

Psychological perspectives

There are numerous psychological explanations about what causes a person to act aggressively. Freud believed that aggression was an "energy," a drive that resulted in the clash of the life force (Eros) and the death force (Thanatos) (Freud, 1990). Lorenz found similarities between the aggressive reactions of people to those experienced by animals. Aggressive actions come from the release of accumulated energy. If this energy is not released gradually, it is released in an explosive manner—a result illustrated in what Lorenz termed the "hydraulic model" (Lorenz, 1967).

Horney theorized that aggression was a response to narcissistic injuries. According to Horney (1945/1992), compensatory grandiosity and pathological rage come from the pain of not being loved and accepted by parental figures, causing the individual to develop a false self, one that is idealized yet vulnerable. This results in the person pushing others away, which causes further anger about not being loved or accepted. These problematic interactions create a never-ending cycle of poor social interactions leading to feelings of betrayal and further rage. This rage is expressed through hostility or violence. Horney also speculated that aggression could result from a neurotic need for power, social recognition, personal admiration, and achievement.

The cognitive approach to understanding violent and hostile behavior challenges the original view that anger is an initial response to feeling wronged (Beck, 1999). Beck's cognitive perspective hypothesized that a chain reaction of violence begins when a person is in distress. It is this feeling of distress that triggers the "I have been wronged" response, which then leads to retaliation and violence. Understanding that stress is part of the equation offers therapists clues for interrupting the cycle of violent behavior.

> We take the role of the protagonist and other players are our supporters and antagonists. … Our egocentrism also leads us to believe that other people interpret the situation as we do; they seem even more culpable because they "know" that they are hurting us but persist in their noxious behavior anyhow. In "hot" conflicts, the offender also has an egocentric perspective, and it sets the stage for a vicious cycle of hurt, anger and retaliation. (p. 27)

These major psychological views have been used to dissect aggressive and violent responses. Significantly, aside from Freud's perspective, the majority of psychological theories postulate that interaction with others trigger and perpetuate aggressive responses. In other words, it is social interactions, and the interpretation of these interactions, that contribute to and maintain aggressive and violent propensities. While a psychological theory may be enough to explain aggressive tendencies, the sociological perspective of social interactionism can be used to clarify and make sense of aggressive actions, and can inform how to alleviate aggressive tendencies.

Social interactions

Aggression and violent tendencies emerge from social interactions. While a person may *feel* angry, they *act* aggressively or violently toward others or themselves. In order to make sense of social actions, researchers, specifically sociologists, focus on the *inter*action that occurs between individuals. James (1890/1918) believed that the social self is the result of the interaction between the individual and social groups. Cooley (1964) indicated that a mutual interdependence between the social environment and individuals exists. Mead (1964) understood that the self developed from the "... process of social experience and activity... [which] develops in the given individual as a result of his relations to that process as a whole and to other individuals within that process" (p. 199).

Meaning emerges from the interaction between people (Blumer, 1969). It is through continuous interpretations, redefining each other's acts, that societal contexts, and the roles of humans within these contexts, are defined. "By making indications to himself and by interpreting what he indicates, the human being has to forge or piece together a line of action" (Blumer, 1969, p. 64). Ultimately, people are defined through interactions. Therefore, meanings and interpretations are social products. Aggression and violent responses can emerge from interpretations of unsatisfactory or misperceived interactions.

According to the theories explored in the preceding text, an unacceptable interaction with someone can result in an aggressive response; aggression can also emerge from a desire to coerce someone to bring about a "desired social and self identit[y]" (Anderson & Bushman, 2002, p. 31). Similar to Horney's and Beck's models of aggression, the social interactionist perspective maintains that "aggression is often the result of threats to high self-esteem, especially to unwarranted self-esteem" (p. 31).

Aggression is perpetuated through continuous social interactions. By its very nature, aggressive and violent acts are deemed unacceptable by society, and those who engage in aggressive and violent acts are labeled deviants (Becker, 1963/1991; Sagarin, 1975). Since aggression is created and defined through social interaction, a person becomes identified with aggressive acts. Once a person is labeled "aggressive" or "violent," this moniker is maintained by future social interactions. Unless this characterization is lifted and identity changed, the aggression may continue. Bartusch and Matsueda (1996) believed that the mechanisms of role-taking and labeling was a major influence on delinquency in adolescent boys and girls. Labels provided by parents and teachers perpetuated the delinquent identity. Rick's aggressive tendencies were maintained and supported by his gang. The staff at the hospital reinforced his identity by their strong reaction to his reputation and behavior.

Zimbardo, Haney, Banks, and Jaffe (1973) also recognized that people may develop aggressive and dominating characteristics after roles and labels are assigned and accepted. In their study, a Stanford University class was divided into two groups (one group role-played prison guards and the other group played the inmates) to:

> ... understand more about the process by which people called "prisoners" lose their liberty, civil rights, independence, and privacy, while those called "guards" gain social power by accepting the responsibility for controlling and managing the lives of their dependent charges. (p. 38)

The guards locked up and watched over the inmates in the basement of the psychology building. The study had to be terminated earlier than originally planned because both groups inhabited their roles more seriously than anticipated. The original identities of the students were quickly transformed. The guards became aggressive toward their "wards," and the "inmates" became docile and cunningly resistive. The researchers soon realized that aggressive actions or reactions emerged from role-taking and labeled identities.

Social Interaction, Aggression, and Art (Therapy)

It is through social interaction that aggression is defined, propagated, and maintained. Conversely, it is through social interaction that aggression can be redirected or alleviated.

It is through re-labeling of people (or removing the detrimental labels), validating new behaviors and identities, and redefining the actions of those seen as aggressive and violent that such tendencies can be halted and perhaps reversed. The art therapist uses the art-making process to aid in developing appropriate interactions and decrease aggressive tendencies.

Blumer (1969) indicated that interaction can occur between people and objects as well as between two people; meaning is "... not intrinsic to the object but arises from how the person is initially prepared to act toward it ... objects—all objects—are social products in that they are formed and transformed by the defining process that takes place in social interaction" (pp. 68–69). It is through using, sharing, and interpreting the use of objects that action and interaction are defined. Introducing an aggressive client to art materials creates a scenario whereby a new interactional pattern begins to occur. By interacting with the art materials and the art product, a person begins to redefine himself or herself.

Also, a relationship is established between the artist and the therapist. Both belong to the same socially acceptable art world, constructed and maintained through the shared conventions of the media (Becker, 1982). Teaching a client how to use art materials for self-expression creates a new mode of interaction. Mastery of art materials promotes a new sense of self-worth apart from previously established hostile identities.

In summary, the art therapeutic process provides a means to interrupt the cycle of violence and the reinforcement of aggressive identity by: (1) strengthening a sense of self; (2) providing an avenue to express negative emotions such as distress and sadness, which can result in anger and aggression; (3) creating new meanings; and (4) tapping into empathic responses (Gussak, 1997, 2004; Gussak, Chapman, Van Duinan, & Rosal, 2003). While it is common to believe that the client creates an art piece with little thought to the viewer, all artists take into account what the viewer may think of the result.

> [I]t is crucial that, by and large, people act with the anticipated reactions of others in mind. This implies that artists create their work, at least in part, by anticipating how other people will respond, emotionally and cognitively, to what they do. (Becker, 1982, p. 200)

Even when the artist creates an image with hostile content, he or she may be doing it as a means to "attack" the viewer. However, art is an acceptable way to express hostility. The therapist can use pictures to promote a culture of acceptance and success. Over time, clients begin to understand that they and their art images are accepted. Once a client feels validated, the images evolve into more complex and thought-inducing products.

Case Vignette—Eric

Eric (a pseudonym) was an 11-year-old boy seen in private practice. He was referred to art therapy because he needed someone who could address his anger, and he was not willing to talk with a counselor or therapist. He was a slight-in-stature Caucasian boy, dressed with sagging slacks and oversized baggy shirts. He spoke with a "rapper's" lingo. His parents were divorced. He lived with his mother, and saw his father inconsistently once every several weeks. He was under medical care and on medication for attention-deficit disorder.

He talked about his admiration for rapper artists, and would often recite some of the more aggressive lyrics. The presenting problems included having trouble in school due to difficulty in following directions, being in trouble with his mother for "acting out," and getting into further trouble for inappropriate outbursts—his school problems resulted in further belligerence from Eric, resulting in Eric getting in trouble with his mother; the cycle was continuous.

In the first session, his affect was flat and blunted. He was controlled in both his behavioral presentation and in his drawing style. When he spoke, he told fantastical and exaggerated stories. Eric required constant redirection. After several sessions and as he became more comfortable with therapeutic interactions, he began to exhibit more aggressive and resistive tendencies. During one session, he spent the entire time alternating between loud outbursts while attempting to rip up the paper, to sitting sullenly with his face toward the wall.

When he was in a good mood, he exhibited a sense of humor, and once came to the session with yellow "caution" tape, which he had found at a construction site, wrapped around his forehead and arms. Even when in a good mood, he had difficulty focusing and needed several prompts to stay on task. Regardless of his mood or behavior, Eric was provided consistent direction on what was expected and was responded to patiently but with firm redirection. He began each session by a description of what happened during the week, followed by a quick check-in drawing. After a few rapid, energetic drawings, which were generally superficial and schematic, he was able to sit and address the tasks at hand.

He enjoyed using clay and used it to create three-dimensional images. During one session, Eric was given Styrofoam blocks (used for packing material), large Popsicle sticks, and paint, and was asked to create a sculpture with the provided materials. He worked diligently on the project. At first, it was difficult to ascertain what he was creating, but eventually he indicated that it was a torture chamber (see Figure 32.1), and that he got the idea from a program he saw on the Discovery Channel the night before. The image is quite graphic.

Figure 32.1   Eric's torture chamber made of Styrofoam blocks and Popsicle sticks.

The poorly developed human form lies on top of what appears to be a torture platform. Jutting out and through the form are sticks, painted in red, which highlight the places where they emerge from the figure. He knew the sculpture was graphic, and he was surprised when it was placed carefully on a shelf, not to be disturbed for the remaining weeks Eric was in therapy.

After this pivotal session, Eric talked more in sessions. Although he would have periodic episodes of aggressive outbursts, he disclosed more about the incidents that made him angry at school and at home. He spoke about the way he responded to his mother and considered various ways in which he could handle difficult situations with his parents.

In one session, he described his anger as a separate animal. He was asked to sculpt what his anger beast would look like. Using Model Magic© sculpting compound and paint, he created a "Rastafarian-scorpion anger beast" (see Figure 32.2).

This sculpture was completed with a large "E" on his chest (his own initial). Different from the torture chamber, he took his time with this piece, and it was meticulously constructed and painted. He immediately started working on the piece upon arriving at the session. After the sculpture was finished, he proudly showed it to his mother and explained to her what it was. He used the piece to verbalize his frustrated and aggressive feelings. Essentially, this final art piece reflected the "self" presented in an acceptable fashion. It was a side of him that he took pride in, albeit, still a reflection of his aggressive nature. Unfortunately, therapy had to end due to scheduling conflicts, and further development of an acceptable self-image had to be put on hold.

Figure 32.2 Eric's Rastafarian-Scorpion Anger Beast made from Model Magic©.

Conclusion

Although there are many psychological beliefs about the manifestation of aggression in people, the social interactionist perspective offers a means to clarify aggressive actions and informs therapists on how such tendencies can be alleviated. Through interaction, aggression is defined and maintained. Equally, it is through interaction that aggression can be assuaged. The art therapist has unique tools to create new interactions that re-label people, validate and reinforce new behaviors and identities, and redirect the actions associated with aggressive and hostile tendencies. Rick and Eric, although different, exhibited aggressive tendencies. Yet, both reacted positively to art and demonstrated marked improvement in their behaviors. The art therapy process interrupted the cycle of aggressive identity reinforcement by strengthening their sense of self, creating new interaction patterns, and forming new ways to interpret interactions.

Endnote

1   This chapter has been adapted with permission from the author's chapter titled "Symbolic interactionism, aggression, and art therapy" in the book *Art therapy and social action* (see Gussak, 2006). The author would like to thank Frances Kaplan and Jessica Kingsley Publishers for this permission.

References

Anderson, C. A. & Bushman, B. J. (2002). Human aggression. *Annual Review of Psychology*, *53*, 27–51.

Bartusch, D. J., & Matsueda, R. L. (1996). Gender, reflected appraisals, and labeling: A cross-group test of an interactionist theory of delinquency. *Social Forces*, *75*, 145–176.

Beck, A. T. (1999). *Prisoners of hate: The cognitive basis of anger, hostility, and violence.* New York, NY: Harper Collins, Publishers.

Becker, H. S. (1963/1991). *Outsiders: Studies in the sociology of deviance.* New York, NY: The Free Press.

Becker, H. S. (1982). *Art worlds.* Berkeley, CA: University of California Press.

Blumer, H. (1969). *Symbolic interactionism: Perspective and method.* Berkeley, CA: University of California Press.

Cooley, C. H. (1964). *Human nature and the social order.* New York, NY: Schocken Books.

Freud, S. (1990). *Beyond the pleasure principle* [The standard edition]. New York, NY: W.W. Norton & Company, Inc.

Gussak, D. (1997). Breaking through barriers: Art therapy in prisons. In D. Gussak & E. Virshup (Eds.), *Drawing time: Art therapy in prisons and other correctional settings* (pp. 1–11). Chicago, IL: Magnolia Street Publishers.

Gussak, D. (2004). A pilot research study on the efficacy of art therapy with prison inmates. *The Arts in Psychotherapy*, *31*(4), 245–259.

Gussak, D., Chapman, L., Van Duinan, T., & Rosal, M. (2003). *Plenary session: Witnessing Aggression and Violence—Responding Creatively.* Paper presented at the annual conference of The American Art Therapy Association, Chicago, IL.

Gussak, D. (2006). Symbolic interactionism, aggression, and art therapy. In F. Kaplan (Ed.). *Art therapy and social action* (pp. 142–156). London; Philadelphia, PA: Jessica Kingsley Publishers.

Horney, K. (1945/1992). *Our inner conflicts: A constructive theory of neurosis* (Reissue ed.). New York, NY: W.W. Norton & Company.

James, W. (1890/1918). *The principles of psychology, Vol. 1 and Vol. 2.* New York, NY: Henry Holt and Company.

Lorenz, K. (1967). *On aggression.* New York, NY: Bantam Books.

Mead, G. H. (1964). *On social psychology.* Chicago, IL: University of Chicago Press.

Sagarin, E. (1975). *Deviants and deviance: An introduction to the study of disvalued people and behavior.* New York, NY: Praeger Publishers.

Zimbardo, P. G., Haney, C., Banks, W. C., & Jaffe, D. (1973, April 8). The mind is a formidable jailer: A Pirandellian prison. *The New York Times Magazine, Section 6*, pp. 38, ff.

33

Perspectives of Recovery/ Reversing the Stigma: Art Therapy and Severe Mental Illness

Mary Ellen McAlevey

Introduction

People with severe mental illness (SMI) live with serious psychological symptoms, side effects from medications, psychosocial stressors, and medical issues (APA, 2013). As they strive toward recovery, they struggle with stigmatization, not only from the general public but also from staff members at treatment facilities (Wadeson, 2010) and other health and mental health professionals (Garey, 2013). According to the US president's New Freedom Commission on Mental Health's *Interim Report* (2003), the mental health system has not been "oriented to the single most important goal of the people it serves—the hope of recovery" (p. 5).

The definition of SMI:

> "… used in the President's New Freedom Commission on Mental Health requires that three criteria be met: (1) the person has a mental, behavioral, or emotional disorder; (2) of sufficient duration to meet diagnostic criteria specified within current *DSM*; and (3) which has resulted in functional impairment that substantially interferes with or limits one or more major life activities (Section 1912[c] of the Public Health Services Act, as amended by Public Law 102/321)". (Dickey, 2005, p. 4)

In this chapter, SMI will be addressed, including symptomology, pertinent literature, and case examples. This chapter will conclude by illustrating how art therapy can be used as a tool to educate the public about mental illness, and to mitigate its stigma.

Language and Stigmatization

Throughout this chapter, people with SMI will be referred to as just that: people with SMI. This nomenclature is in accordance with person-first language, which stresses that a person is not his or her diagnosis, meaning that they are not schizophrenics or

The Wiley Handbook of Art Therapy, First Edition. Edited by David E. Gussak and Marcia L. Rosal.
© 2016 John Wiley & Sons, Ltd. Published 2016 by John Wiley & Sons, Ltd.

bipolars; they are people with an illness (Research and Training Center on Independent Living, 2013). Spaniol (2005) wrote about the importance of "a language of wellness" (p. 88) in order to support commonalities rather than segregating people with SMI. In Great Britain, the term "service user," instead of "client" or "patient" is used (Woods & Springham, 2011). The New Jersey State Assembly recently passed a law that deleted, from all statutes, language considered pejorative against people with mental illness (Politicker NJ, 2013).

The artists who contributed artwork to this chapter will be presented in terms of their commonalities with the general public first, followed by information about their diagnosis. This is to depict people with SMI with compassion rather than categorize them by diagnosis. Saks, a law professor, in speaking about destigmatizing mental illness, implored the public to remember that "these people may be your spouse, they may be your child, they may be your neighbor, they may be your friend, they may be your co-worker" (TEDGlobal, 2012). Furthermore, Saks stated that "the humanity we all share is more important than the mental illness we may not" (TEDGlobal, 2012).

New recommendations for journalism may also improve public perceptions of mental illness and increase treatment for people so diagnosed. The Associated Press (AP) added an entry to its stylebook on how reporters should cover mental illness. One of the additions to the AP stylebook instructs the media to avoid describing people as "mentally ill" unless mental health is clearly pertinent to the story, and the diagnosis has been properly determined through a reliable source (Blinderman, 2013). In June 2013, the White House sponsored the National Conference on Mental Health, a daylong event with service providers, experts, and administration officials. The intent of the conference was to frame a national conversation about mental health in the United States (White House Blog, 2013).

Recovery and Psychiatric Rehabilitation

The field of psychiatric rehabilitation, which has been around for about 30 years, countered the belief that people with SMI face inevitable deterioration. Rather, psychiatric rehabilitation seeks to educate consumers, family members, service providers, and the general public that recovery from SMI "is possible and not a rare or unusual event" (Farkas, 2008, p. 16). Recovery from SMI is one of the most important goals of psychiatric rehabilitation (Pratt, Gill, Barrett, & Roberts, 2007). Service providers for people with SMI adopt a recovery vision that promotes listening to the client (Farkas, Ashcraft, & Anthony, 2008).

Spaniol, Wewiorski, Gagne, and Anthony (2002) theorized that recovery occurs in a series of stages, and not in a linear process. These phases are as follows:

1. Being overwhelmed by the disability
2. Struggling with the disability
3. Living with the disability
4. Living beyond the disability

Boundaries between the phases are diffuse, and movement within and beyond the boundaries exists.

In the first phase, *being overwhelmed by the disability*, the person tries to understand and control what is happening, feels confused, is disconnected from self and others, and feels out of control and powerless to control his or her life. In the second phase, *struggling with the disability*, the person understands what is occurring, recognizes the need for coping with the disability in order to maintain quality of life, faces fear of failure, and is cautious or reluctant to take risks. The person utilizes coping mechanisms and might be struggling with addictions or serious health conditions. The third phase, *living with the disability*, is characterized by confidence in managing the disability and control over his or her life, utilization of effective coping skills, assuming meaningful roles, and finding a "niche in the world" (p. 331). In the fourth phase, *living beyond the disability*, the disability is seen as playing a minor role in the life of the person diagnosed, and the person is seen as connected to self, others, and the environment; he or she experiences a sense of meaning. Spaniol et al. (2002) theorized that persons recovering from SMI would ideally accomplish the following tasks of recovery:

1. Developing a framework for understanding the experience of the diagnosis
2. Getting control over the illness
3. Moving into roles that are meaningful, productive, and valued by society

This concept of recovery is different from McGlashan, Levy, and Carpenter's 1975 concept of recovery (as cited in Wadeson, 2010). They classify recovery as either integration or "sealing over" for people with acute schizophrenia (Wadeson, 2010). An observer, rather than the person with the lived experience of the illness, assesses for integration or sealing over. The McGlashan, Levy, and Carpenter approach can be seen as a form of "medicalizing" (a term borrowed from Dyer & Hunter, 2009) the client rather than eliciting the recovery vision of the individual with SMI.

Spaniol (2003) dispelled such ideas of mental illness and debated the accuracy of the term "chronic" as terminology to describe people diagnosed with SMI. She cited a study conducted on adults living with SMI in Vermont who were deinstitutionalized decades after their hospitalization. Many of these adults (62–68%) demonstrated no signs of schizophrenia upon discharge (Harding, Brooks, Ashikaga, Strauss, & Breier, 1987 as cited in Spaniol, 2003).

Art Therapy and Recovery: A Research Review

Art therapy has been used with measured and anecdotal success in programs with persons with SMI. Interestingly, the success with people with SMI has had more than a merely moderate impact on psychiatric symptoms. For example, art therapy programs, which included mentored weekly art workshops in a community setting, have also had a positive impact on community engagement and financial independence. Other art therapy sessions in psychosocial rehabilitation settings focused on the consumers' ability to reflect on where they would like to be in recovery and an opportunity to connect with others as artists, not consumers, in a non-stigmatizing manner. Still other studies featured 90-minute weekly art therapy sessions utilizing an interactive group approach and/or open studio approach; regardless of the art therapy approach, most participants in these studies benefitted on many levels.

Creative Recovery, an Australian arts-in-health program for Indigenous people with a mental health diagnosis, aimed to improve quality of life by capacity-building, reducing stigma and promoting social inclusion, building on talent, providing a sense of belonging within community, and gaining economic independence (Dyer & Hunter, 2009). In this program, weekly art workshops were held for individuals with SMI at a pre-existing art center, which lead to regular access to the art center outside of the scheduled workshop time, and subsequent exhibition of their artwork. Some outcomes of the program included participant recognition as artists in the community, participants seeking appropriate medical care, and participants accessing other training opportunities (Australasian Centre for Rural & Remote Mental Health, 2012).

To uncover how people with SMI perceived how art therapy experiences assist with recovery, Van Lith, Fenner, and Schofield (2011) interviewed 18 participants from an art-based psychosocial rehabilitation program. Three overarching themes that emerged from the interviews on how art therapy aids the recovery process were:

1. That art-making was seen as helping in the recovery process through the release of tensions and other emotions
2. That insight is gained through the development of the image
3. That images are motivating for the individual and provide a means of connecting with others.

All interviewees were attending psychosocial rehabilitation programs that were strong in the visual arts, including painting, drawing, sculpture, ceramics, and textiles. Some participants indicated that they relied on art-making when they were symptomatic because it fostered relaxation and groundedness, the image reflected back to them their level of wellness, and the image provided a message about where they would like to be in their lives. It also offered an opportunity to connect with others that was neither mental-health-related nor stigmatizing (Van Lith, Fenner, and Schofield (2011). The authors suggested that there was a need to include the views and experiences of the consumer of mental health services to ensure optimal recovery services.

Richardson, Jones, Evans, Stevens, and Rowe (2007) hypothesized that art therapy would decrease the negative symptoms of schizophrenia. Negative symptoms reflect a lessening of functioning—such as restricted affect, reduced productivity of thought, lack of motivation, and inability to experience pleasure (APA, 2013; Pratt, Gill, Barrett, & Roberts, 2007). In the Richardson et al. study, mental health service users with schizophrenia participated in a 12-session art therapy group and demonstrated a statistically significant decrease of negative symptoms than people with SMI who did not participate in this therapy. Sessions were conducted using British art therapist Diane Waller's interactive approach, and the 12 group sessions lasted 90 minutes each.

Qualitative studies of art therapy and SMI

Cochrane Reviews are recognized internationally as the highest standard of systematic reviews of healthcare-related, evidence-based programs (Cochrane Collaboration, 2014). The authors of the Cochrane Collaboration research report, which explored the effects of art therapy as an adjunct to treatment for people with schizophrenia and schizophrenia-like illnesses, found only two randomized control trials of art therapy that met their criteria for inclusion in their review. Therefore, further evaluation of the use of art therapy for SMI is needed to determine its effectiveness (Ruddy & Milnes, 2005).

The MATISSE (Multi-centre study of Art Therapy in Schizophrenia—Systematic Evaluation) study (Crawford et al., 2010), from the United Kingdom, had 417 participants. The participants were from 15 mental health facilities across the United Kingdom. The authors set out to demonstrate that participation in 90-minute weekly group art therapy sessions over 1 year—described as supportive, not psychotherapeutic—would result in long-term improvement in global functioning. Unfortunately the results did not demonstrate that art therapy improved global functioning, symptoms of schizophrenia, or other health-related outcomes for those participants receiving services as compared to participants in a control group of activities (Crawford et al., 2012). These findings challenged the British National Institute for Health and Care Excellence (NICE), which recommended that creative arts therapies be offered to all people with schizophrenia to alleviate negative symptoms (NICE, 2009). The researchers of the MATISSE study explained that the arts therapies might result in improved outcomes when used in combination with other interventions such as music therapy and movement therapy (Crawford et al., 2012). In their subsequent trial, the authors examined the outcomes of 12 additional weekly art therapy sessions but group attendance was low (3.5 sessions) and fewer than half of participants had follow-up. They recommended studying the impact of art therapy with consumers in inpatient treatment settings (Crawford et al., 2012).

Caddy, Crawford, and Page (2012) studied the effectiveness of creative arts with people hospitalized for affective, anxiety, and thought disorders. The researchers assessed 403 inpatients who participated in "art, craft, or expressive art-based activit[ies]"; these included painting, beading, sewing, clay work, paper craft, and more, over a 5-year period (p. 327). Subjects in the experimental creative arts group showed improvements in depression and anxiety levels, quality of life, subjective experiences of mental illness, and domains of functioning. These participants described "flow" states—perception of time was altered during the creativity period, enabling clients to forget about their symptoms and stressors.

Art therapy is considered an optimal choice for people with schizophrenia because it involves engagement with another individual in a way that verbal therapeutic modalities do not (Patterson, Crawford, Ainsworth, & Walter, 2011). Art therapy in the United Kingdom is viewed as a method to liberate people with schizophrenia from the "systematized" nature of mental healthcare (p. 76). Furthermore, art therapists interviewed by Patterson et al. described art therapy as being conducive to people with schizophrenia adopting the identity of an artist, which is "perceived as preferable to that of a person with mental illness" (p. 77).

The benefits of art therapy to people with SMI ranged from reduction in symptoms to adoption of a new identity as an artist. As Ruddy and Milnes (2005) recommended, more randomized controlled trials should be facilitated to prove the effectiveness of art therapy in people with SMI. One of the studies related poor follow-up in aftercare groups (Crawford et al., 2012). Perhaps more opportunities for follow-up can be facilitated in community settings such as homeless shelters and soup kitchens (Allen, 2007), since there is a high correlation between SMI and homelessness. Also, art therapy may be utilized with other treatments that have already been determined as "evidence-based" (NREPP, 2013) in order to reach people with SMI in a multitude of settings and to make an effort to quantify the success of art therapy.

Examples of Artwork

The stigma of mental illness has been theorized as a public health issue (Pescosolido, Medina, Martin, & Long, 2013). Persons in recovery are concerned with how the media has focused on a minority of people with psychiatric diagnoses acting in a threatening or dangerous manner.

For example, Tom, a 52-year-old single man, wanted people to know that people with mental illness "are harmless. We don't hurt people and just try to get through the day ... there are a lot of people with mental illness who you would never believe had it."

Some themes in the artwork and accompanying artist's statements include commonalities that people with and without mental illness share. These commonalities include anything from hobbies, talents, and music preferences to a desire for safety.

Tee shirt projects

Tee shirt and "clothesline" projects have been conducted for a variety of groups, including survivors of domestic violence (Campbell-Mapp, 2010; Louisville Clothesline Project, 2005), survivors of military sexual trauma (Fatigues Clothesline, 2012), children affected by natural disasters and their care providers (Anderson, Arrington, & Wolf Bordonaro, 2012; Hurlburt & Wolf Bordonaro, 2010), and people with mental illness and their care providers (Florida State University, 2013), to name a few examples. In clothesline projects, tee shirts are designed by clients and hung for display in order to educate the viewer about societal issues. In settings where purchasing a tee shirt is prohibitive for budgetary reasons, outlines of tee shirts on paper can be substituted. The tee shirts can then be cut out and displayed with clothespins on a clothesline. This project is ideal because of its portability.

Gina   Gina (a pseudonym), a 60-year-old divorced woman who was an award-winning schoolteacher, drew the picture shown in Figure 33.1. She has spoken regretfully about the manner in which she pressured her students to excel when she was in the throes of mania, despite the fact that the projects they completed had placed competitively in various competitions against other school programs. Gina stated that she might not have forced them to strive so much, had it not been for her mania and the feelings of inadequacy cultivated by her mother who told her "you're not smart, you're ugly, and you'll never amount to much." Gina is in recovery from bipolar disorder, substance abuse, self-mutilating behavior, and binge eating. During art therapy groups, Gina worked on changing her mantra to "I'm beautiful, I'm intelligent, and I can eat wisely." Gina has walked up to strangers in the parking lot of the institution that hosts the program that she attends to tell them that she would pray for them. On one occasion, a stranger responded that he did not want her to pray for him. Gina later recounted in the group, "Well, I'm going to pray for him anyway."

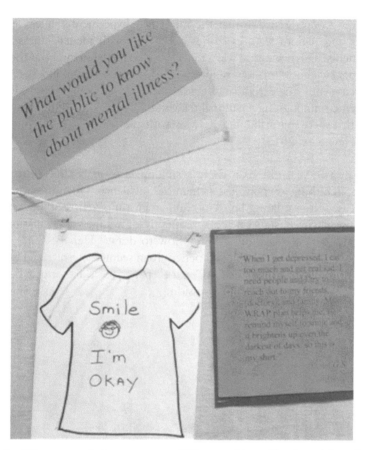

Figure 33.1   Client art made in response to: "What would you like the public to know about mental illness?" The tee shirt designs were displayed on a bulletin board in a hallway in a common area of an outpatient behavioral health center.

Gina's tee shirt reads, "Smile. I'm okay." She wrote, in part: "When I get depressed, I eat too much and get real sad. I need people and I try to reach out to my friends, [doctors], and family. My WRAP [Wellness Recovery Action Plan] (Copeland, 2000) plan helps me. I remind myself to smile and it brightens up even the darkest of days, so this is my shirt."

Steve   Steve, a 49-year-old man, takes care of his aging mother and takes medical transportation to the program because he does not want to financially burden his brother who generously pays for Steve's gasoline. He has jokingly been referred to at his program as the "spokesperson for distress tolerance," a principle of dialectical behavior therapy (Linehan, 1993), because he uses it on a daily basis to deal with his paranoia and delusions. Steve indicated that he would not watch the movie *The Truman Show* because that is one of his delusions. Another delusion he experiences from time to time is that there is "poison" in his veins.

Steve designed a tee shirt that proclaims "No, I'm Not Dangerous" in his effort "to dispel the false belief that people with mental illness are dangerous." His artwork was created after a group discussion that the media can hype mental illness as a cause of criminal acts and seldom features stories of persons with mental illness for positive accomplishments. This discussion was a follow-up to a media story about the AP adding an entry to its stylebook on how reporters should cover mental illness (Blinderman, 2013). More recently, the executive director of the National Alliance on Mental Illness issued a statement impugning a national television news anchor and well-known media mental health expert for maligning persons with mental illness and contributing to stigma (PR Newswire, 2013).

Joan Twenty-two-year-old Joan drew a smiling face on her tee shirt and wrote, "There's no such thing as crazy, just a chemical imbalance." Joan uses art as a coping skill to decrease self-mutilating behaviors and as a form of self-soothing when she has an urge to use illicit substances. Joan frequently draws images of marijuana leaves, stating that it is "the only thing I know how to draw." Her tee shirt, depicted in Figure 33.2, was completed in colored pencil. Joan seemed mesmerized by the repetitive actions of coloring this large, 18" x 24" paper tee shirt, and it occupied her attention for nearly the entire 2-hour session.

Figure 33.2 "There's no such thing as crazy—just a chemical imbalance!" by a 22-year-old woman who advised that she made art to divert herself from self-mutilating behaviors. She used colored pencils to create this 18" x 24" paper tee shirt design.

Despite her young age, Joan had had several rounds of electroconvulsive therapy, which caused severe memory impairment. She has been diagnosed with bipolar disorder, schizoaffective disorder with and without psychotic features, and oppositional defiant disorder. Joan had minimized behaviors that included walking up to people, barking at them, and giggling as she walked away.

Bev Bev's jersey-style tee shirt reads, "I'm a survivor!!"; this despite her adding the numbers "00" on the jersey. Fifty-year-old Bev worked 3 days a week at a volunteer job at a local hospital. She enjoyed going to the beach, reading, and visiting with her aging father. She had not had an episode of disordered eating in years. She wrote about her art: "From my point of view—we're all the same—we're all one. I have found my identity—I'm a survivor. Now I'm not just looking in—I'm now living life.—Connection."

Visions of recovery

Jay, a 67-year-old man who requested Thorazine, a medication that has been discontinued because of the disabling side effect of tardive dyskinesia, wrote, "I'm not Jesus Chrisit [sic]" on his tee shirt (Figure 33.3). The circles and arrows that embellish the design seemed to resemble eyes with angry eyebrows. Jay broke down in tears when he

Figure 33.3 "I'm Not Jesus Chrisit" This tee shirt response was made during a period of loneliness for a 67-year-old man. It was drawn after his experience of sitting in a park and watching people who were nearby moving away from him after his arrival.

described people in the park moving away from him when he sat nearby. He thought that their expectations of him were too high, and he defended his behavior in writing: "Never been on (1) alcohol, (2) smokeing [sic], (3) drugs (meds) 'most of my life'." In another "recovery drawing" not depicted here, Jay drew himself on an altar near a cross, depicted as an altar boy. He saw himself going to "high mass" and later asked the art therapist if there is such a thing as a "low mass."

About her recovery, Kim, a 44-year-old mother of one, wrote: "Just like a tree w/ the proper sunlight, rain, evaporation & condensation it's able to grow and give back—as will I with the proper tools, love, structure and support become a productive member and give back by helping seniors in need." Kim had not had an illicit substance in over 30 days.

Collaborative Hopefulness

British art therapist Ami Woods (Woods & Springham, 2011) wrote about her voluntary psychiatric hospitalization for treatment of depression and anxiety: "The stigma and fear that often surrounds a mental health diagnosis can greatly affect a [service user's] sense of self and can create a feeling of hopelessness and helplessness..." (p. 66). She urged art therapists to be genuine in their work with people with SMI and to offer hope.

Some of the tee shirt examples reflected that the artist, in spite of being aware of stigma, has neither internalized the stigma nor has decreased self-esteem. Rather, some clients are "energized by prejudice," and others disregard the effects of stigma (Corrigan, Mueser, Bond, Drake, & Solomon, 2008, p. 43). Some of the tee shirt examples also reflected a recovery definition that "refers to a person's right and ability to live a safe, dignified, and meaningful life in the community of his or her choice despite continuing disability associated with the illness" (Davidson, Harding, & Spaniol, 2005, p. xxi).

It is important that people with SMI embody their own definition of recovery. To quote Kyle, a client with SMI, "I use my mental illness as a tool to make myself better." He added that his enjoyment in life comes from the projects he works on: art; expanding the selling of plants that he grows, from seeds provided by staff members at his program, to the general public; and striving to get his poetry published.

Only a minority of those I worked with defined their recovery by focusing on "no more meds" or "no more symptoms." The majority focused on growth, resuming roles as parents, returning to work, having peace of mind, enjoying nature, abstaining from substances, and financial independence. The recovery images of these people are no different from those without a psychiatric diagnosis.

Conclusion

According to the World Health Organization (2011), one in four people in the world will be affected by mental illness at some point in their lives (National Institute of Mental Health, no date). Publicly funded mental health, substance abuse treatment, and substance abuse prevention programs include consumers of these services as staff members because they have the "lived experience" of seeking treatment and can offer comfort and advice unlike any professional who has not been in recovery from SMI.

Recovering activist, academic, and keynote speaker Patricia Deegan wrote about a "conspiracy of hope" (1987) in encouraging people with SMI and service providers to refuse to allow people with mental illness be reduced to nothing but their diagnoses. To borrow this phrase, art therapists can help people with SMI strive toward collaborative hopefulness. To this end, art therapists can use their tools to (1) dispel preconceived notions that SMI is a life-long "sentence"; (2) educate the public about stigma against people with SMI; (3) acknowledge that recovery from SMI needs to be defined by the person with the lived experience and not the medical establishment; and (4) foster hope in every artist–client that recovery is achievable.

References

Allen, P. B. (2007). Facing homelessness: A community mask making project. In F. F. Kaplan (Ed.), *Art therapy and social action* (pp. 59–71). Philadelphia, PA: Jessica Kingsley.

American Psychiatric Association. (2013). *Diagnostic and statistical manual of mental disorders* (5th ed.). Washington, DC: Author.

Anderson, F. E., Arrington, D., & Wolf Bordonaro, G. P. (2012, July). *Weaving the global tapestry of art.* Panel presented at the 43rd Annual American Art Therapy Association conference, Savannah, GA.

Australasian Centre for Rural & Remote Mental Health. (2012). From Creative Recovery to creative livelihoods: "It's not just art … it's a healing thing." The benefits of an arts based health initiative in remote Indigenous communities. *Evaluation Report 2011.* Retrieved from www.acrrmh.com.au/assets/Uploads/Creative-Recovery-Livelihoods-Report-Web3.pdf

Blinderman, I. (2013, March 8). Associated Press changes guidelines on mental illness. *New York Daily News.* Retrieved from www.nydailynews.com/blogs/pageviews/2013/03/associated-press-changes-guidelines-on-mental-illness

Caddy, L., Crawford, F., & Page, A. C. (2012). "Painting a path to wellness": Correlations between participating in a creative activity group and improved measured mental health outcome. *Journal of Psychiatric and Mental Health Nursing, 19*(4), 327–333.

Campbell-Mapp, R. (2010, May). Hope clothesline project benefits women. *Jefferson County Public Schools Global Connections, 4*(4). Retrieved from: http://www.jefferson.kyschools.us/Programs/mcconnections/GlobalConnect/News.html

Cochrane Collaboration. (2014). *Cochrane Reviews.* Retrieved from www.cochrane.org/cochrane-reviews

Copeland, M. E. (2000). *Wellness recovery action plan.* Dummerston, VT: Peach Press.

Corrigan, P. W., Mueser, K. T., Bond, G. R., Drake, R. E., & Solomon, P. (2008). *Principles and practice of psychiatric rehabilitation: An empirical approach.* New York: NY: Guilford.

Crawford, M. J., Killaspy, H., Barnes, T. R., Barrett, B., Byford, S., Clayton, K., Dinsmore, J., Floyd, S., Hoadley, A., Johnson, T., Kalaitzaki, E., King, M., Leurent, B., Maratos, A., O'Neill, F. A., Osborn, D. P., Patterson, S., Soteriou, T., Tyrer, P., & Waller, D. (2012). Group art therapy as an adjunctive treatment for people with schizophrenia: Multicentre pragmatic randomized trial. *British Medical Journal.* Retrieved from: http://www.bmj.com/content/bmj/344/bmj.e846.full.pdf, doi: 10.1136/bmj.e846 (Published 28 February 2012).

Crawford, M. J., Killaspy, H., Kalaitzaki, E., Barrett, B., Byford, S., Patterson, S., Soteriou, T., O'Neill, F. A., Clayton, K., Maratos, A., Barnes, T. R., Osborn, D., Johnson, T., King, M., Tyrer, P., & Waller, D. (2010). The MATISSE study: A randomized trial of group art therapy for people with schizophrenia. *BMC Psychiatry, 10*(65), 1–9.

Davidson, L., Harding, C., & Spaniol, L. (Eds.). (2005). *Recovery from severe mental illness: Research evidence and implications for practice.* Boston, MA: Center for Psychiatric Rehabilitation.

Deegan, P. E. (1987). Recovery, rehabilitation, and the conspiracy of hope. Retrieved from https://www.patdeegan.com/sites/default/files/files/conspiracy_of_hope.pdf

Dickey, B. (2005). What is severe mental illness? In R. E. Drake, M. R. Merrens, & D. W. Lynde (Eds.), *Evidence-based mental health practice: A textbook.* New York, NY: W.W. Norton.

Dyer, G., & Hunter, E. (2009). Creative recovery: Art for mental health's sake. *Australasian Psychiatry, 17*(Supplement). Doi: 10.1080/10398560902948431

Farkas, M. (2008). Rehabilitation in the 21st century: Partnership not prescription. *Research Insights, 5*(3), 16–19.

Farkas, M., Ashcraft, L., & Anthony, W. A. (2008). The 3 Cs for recovery services. *Behavioral Healthcare, 23*(2), 24–27.

Fatigues Clothesline. (2012). *Home.* Retrieved from http://www.semperfidelishealthandwellness. org

Florida State University, WFSU. (Producer). (2013, June 19). *Art therapy on combating mental illness* [Audio broadcast]. Retrieved from www.arted.fsu.edu/News/FSU-Art-Therapy-on-Combating-Mental-Illness

Garey, J. (2013, August 10). When doctors discriminate. *The New York Times,* Sunday Review, The Opinion Pages. Retrieved from http://www.nytimes.com/2013/08/11/opinion/sunday/when-doctors-discriminate-html

Harding, C., Brooks, G., Ashikaga, T., Strauss, J., & Breier, A. (1987). The Vermont Longitudinal study of persons with severe mental illness, I: Methodology, study sample, and overall status 32 years later. *American Journal of Psychiatry, 144*(6), 718–735.

Hurlburt, G., & Wolf Bordonaro, G. P. (2010). *Introducing expressive therapy constructs and applications to medical professionals following a national disaster.* Paper session presented at Kings Hospital Symposium, Port au Prince, Haiti.

Linehan, M. (1993). *Cognitive-behavioral treatment of borderline personality disorder.* New York: NY: Guilford Press.

Louisville Clothesline Project. (2005). *Mission and history.* Retrieved from www.louisvilleclothesline. org

McGlashan, T., Levy, S., & Carpenter, W. (1975). Integration and sealing-over: Clinically distinct recovery styles from schizophrenia. *Archives of General Psychiatry, 32,* 1265–1272.

National Institute for Health and Care Excellence. (2009). *Core interventions in the treatment and management of schizophrenia in primary and secondary care.* Retrieved from http://publications.nice.org.uk/schizophrenia-cg82

National Institute of Mental Health. (no date). *The numbers count: Mental disorders in America.* [website]. Retrieved from http://www.nimh.nih.gov/health/publications/the-numbers-count-mental-disorders-in-america/index.shtml

National Registry of Evidence-based Programs and Practices, U. S. Department of Health and Human Services, Substance Abuse and Mental Health Services Administration. (2013). *NREPP: SAMHSA's National Registry of Evidence-based Programs and Practices.* Retrieved from http://www.nrepp.samhsa.gov/ViewAll.aspx

PR Newswire. (2013). *Dr. Phil and Brian Williams: You can do better; Listen to President Obama about ending stigma.* Retrieved from http://www.prnewswire.com/news-releases/dr-phil-and-brian-williams-you-can-do-better-listen-to-president-obama-about-ending-stigma-218160431.html

Patterson, S., Crawford, M. J., Ainsworth, E., & Walter, D. (2011). Art therapy for people diagnosed with schizophrenia: Therapists' views about what changes, how and for whom. *International Journal of Art Therapy, 16*(2), 70–80.

Pescosolido, B. A., Medina, T. R., Martin, J. K., & Long, J. S. (2013). The "backbone" of stigma: Identifying the global core of public prejudice associated with mental illness. *American Journal of Public Health, 103*(5), 853–860.

Politicker, NJ. (2013, August 8). *Angelini bill that updates NJ Statues regarding Individuals with mental health conditions.* Retrieved from http://www.politickernj.com/67603/angelini-bill-updates-nj-statues-regarding-individuals-mental-health-conditions-now-law#ixzz2c8swhw02

Pratt, C. W., Gill, K. J., Barrett, N. M., & Roberts, M. M. (2007). *Psychiatric rehabilitation* (2nd ed.). Burlington, MA: Elsevier Academic Press.

President's New Freedom Commission on Mental Health, U. S. Department of Health and Human Services. (2003). *Achieving the promise: Transforming mental health care in America, final report.* Rockville, MD: Author.

Research and Training Center on Independent Living, University of Kansas. (2013). *Guidelines: How to write and report about people with disabilities* (8th ed.). Lawrence, KS: Author.

Richardson, P., Jones, K., Evans, C., Stevens, P., & Rowe, A. (2007). Exploratory RCT of art therapy as an adjunctive treatment in schizophrenia. *Journal of Mental Health, 16*(4), 483–491.

Ruddy, R., & Milnes, D. (2005). Art therapy for schizophrenia or schizophrenia-like illnesses. *Cochrane Database of Systematic Reviews* 2005, (4). Art. No.: CD003728. doi:10.1002/14651858CD003728.pub2

Spaniol, L., Wewiorski, N. J., Gagne, C., & Anthony, W. A. (2002). The process of recovery from schizophrenia. *International Review of Psychiatry, 14*(4), 327–336.

Spaniol, S. (2003). Art therapy with adults with severe mental illness. In C. Malchiodi (Ed.), *Handbook of art therapy* (pp. 268–280). New York, NY: Guilford.

Spaniol, S. (2005). "Learned hopefulness": An arts-based approach to participatory action research. *Art Therapy: Journal of the American Art Therapy Association, 22*(2), 86–91.

TEDGlobal. (2012). *Elyn Saks: A tale of mental illness—from the inside* [video]. Retrieved from http://www.ted.com/talks/elyn_saks_seeing_mental_illness.html

Van Lith, T., Fenner, P., & Schofield, M. (2011). The lived experience of art making as a companion to the mental health recovery process. *Disability and Rehabilitation, 33*(8), 652–660.

Wadeson, H. (2010). *Art psychotherapy* (2nd ed.). Hoboken, NJ: Wiley & Sons.

White House Blog. (2013). *The National Conference on Mental Health.* Retrieved from http://www.whitehouse.gov/blog/2013/06/03/national-conference-mental-health

Woods, A., & Springham, N. (2011). On learning from being the in-patient. *International Journal of Art Therapy, 16*(2), 60–68.

World Health Organization. (2001). *Mental disorders affects one in four people.* Geneva, Switzerland: Author. Retrieved from http://www.who.int/whr/2001/media_centre/press_release/en/

34

On Considering the Role of Art Therapy in Treating Depression

Stephanie Wise

"… the despair beyond the despair."
William Styron (*Darkness Visible: A Memoir of Madness*)

Treating depression can leave even the most seasoned therapists with feelings of trepidation and ineptitude. Depression is paradoxically specific and generally common. It can be the major symptom of a mental illness or a partial component of a person's emotional life. Oftentimes, depression may be the presenting complaint for those seeking treatment where other underlying issues may be at the core, including trauma. Depression is ubiquitous and often normalized as part of the human condition. It may be multifaceted to ascertain cause and effect, leaving professionals questioning their professional skills and intuition. Depression can leave even the experienced therapist in a quandary—knowing there may be causal relationships that factor in to the depressive episodes and yet finding appropriate treatment elusive because the source of the condition may not be readily apparent. Art therapy process and product offer an opportunity to express and externalize inner emotional experiences so that patient and therapist are able to begin to work to bring light into the darkness.

This chapter will provide an evaluation of the literature about depression and will offer an understanding of how depression is reflected in the art of those suffering from this disease. It will next provide a brief summation of how art therapy may be effective in addressing it. A case study of "Robert" provides a narrative on how art therapy was used to address the needs of one client who suffered from depression.

An Overview

Depression encompasses a wide range of symptoms from mild to severe and may or may not include psychotic features with recurrent and non-recurrent episodes. This illness spans the entire developmental spectrum, and the degree to which someone suffers from depression will likely vary over the course of the person's life. Author

Andrew Solomon (2001), who has spent his life battling major depression, described it thus:

> If one imagines a soul of iron that weathers with grief and rusts with mild depression, then major depression is the startling collapse of a whole structure. … It is a long time from the first rain to the point when rust has eaten through an iron girder. Sometimes the rusting is at such key points that the collapse seems total, but more often it is partial: this section collapses, knocks that section, shifts the balances in a dramatic way. (p. 17)

The newly published *Diagnostic and Statistical Manual of Mental Disorders—Fifth Edition* (DSM-5) of the American Psychiatric Association (APA) includes significant structural changes about depression from its predecessor, DSM IV-TR. The "Mood Disorders" section has been eliminated in favor of a new section titled "Depressive Disorders." The complicated process of identifying one of the depressive diagnoses within the mood disorders category seems to be a less labyrinthine endeavor now, although most of the current specifiers used to determine clinical episodes remain the same.

DSM IV-TR included Major Depressive Episode (both single and recurrent), Dysthymic Disorder (both early onset and late onset), and Depressive Disorder Not Otherwise Specified (NOS). DSM-5 categorizes the depressive disorders as Disruptive Mood Dysregulation Disorder; Major Depressive Disorder (both single and recurrent); Dysthymic Disorder; Premenstrual Dysphoric Disorder; Substance-Induced Depressive Disorder; Depressive Disorder Associated with Another Medical Condition; and Depressive Disorder Not Elsewhere Classified (NEC). This last category seems to be the most innovative. Replacing Depressive Disorder (NOS) with Depressive Disorder (NEC) will likely capture more people who are experiencing depression but whom heretofore would not have met the criteria for the more dramatic depressive diagnoses. This new category includes Recurrent Brief Depression; Mixed Subsyndromal Anxiety and Depression; Short Duration (4–13 days) Depressive Episode; Subthreshold Depressive Episode with Insufficient Symptoms; and Uncertain Depressive Disorder (including Depressive Disorder of Unknown Etiology, Uncertain Depressive Condition Observed in a Clinical Examination, and Uncertain Depressive Condition in a Medical Record).

Most symptoms of depression are familiar to both laypeople and mental health clinicians: exhaustion, poor self-esteem, feelings of guilt, worthlessness, inability to focus or concentrate, sleep problems, changes in appetite, tearfulness, as well as thoughts of suicide and self-annihilation. While there are a number of causes, depression may commonly be triggered by some kinds of loss, grief, or bereavement. Typical treatments include medication, electroconvulsive therapy (for intractable severe depression), and various types of psychotherapy, including art therapy.

Silver (2011) analyzed data collected for her Stimulus Drawing Task assessment procedure, from which she was able to demonstrate that, "Among children, symptoms of depression may be masked by anger …" (p. 174). This provided additional insight into the potential treatment for depressed children who might otherwise be construed as simply defiant.

Over time, Silver observed that some adolescents created images displaying suicidal fantasies, thus prompting her to develop the Draw a Story (DAS) assessment in 1988 to specifically screen for depression. This has proved to be an invaluable diagnostic tool as suicide stemming from depression is the third leading cause of death of adolescents between the ages of 12 and 19 in the United States (Miniño, 2010).

Slayton, D-Archer, and Kaplan (2010) compared quantitative analytic studies and the efficacy of art therapy as a form of treatment for "a variety of symptoms, age groups and disorders" (p. 108). They recognized studies that reflected significant improvement with art therapy for depression in two particular populations. Adult cancer patients utilized "weekly individual art therapy with an anthroposophic philosophy: water color painting" (Bar-Sela, Atid, Danos, Gabay, & Epelbaum, 2007, p. 113). Incarcerated adult men participated in group art therapy (Gussak, 2006). In the first study, depression and fatigue demonstrated measurable improvement, although anxiety levels remained the same. Gussak's study revealed "significant improvement in symptoms of depression as a result of the group work" (Slayton et al., 2010, p. 114).

Field and Kruger (2008) analyzed the efficacy of "creative expression" as a positive factor in reducing depression as well as in the reduction of an "external HLOC (health locus of control) orientation in black women living with HIV ..." (p. 467). Improved locus of control was deemed important as it can "manifest as better self-care, better adherence to medications regimes and decreased high-risk behavior," which carry important implications for people experiencing serious depression and potential risk to life (Field and Kruger, 2008, p. 467). They used a Psychocybernetic Model of Art Therapy—a "systemic perspective" whereby a "visually created art product (a doll) is verbally examined, engaged and concretized in therapy" (p. 471). This model has four phases: "unfreezing," "doing," "dialoguing," and "ending and integrating" (p. 472). These were designed to move clients from intuitive right-brain expression toward discursive left-brain engagement with the doll products. The integration between right-brain and left-brain engagement appeared to lead to more future orientation in the participants—a state of mind that depressed persons often have difficulty achieving. The study results indicated that the art psychotherapy intervention appreciably and immediately lowered levels of depression among participants, as HLOC appeared to show significant improvement after a few weeks.

Pretorius and Pfeifer (2010) developed an "existential-humanistic, Gestalt, client-centered and abuse focused" group art therapy program with sexually abused girls aged 8–11 years (p. 63). The group art therapy sessions included mural making, box decorating for holding feelings, symbolic images of their perpetrators, role playing, storytelling, reflection on the experience, and continual discussion throughout the entire time to assess for depression symptom changes. According to the reported analysis, their results suggested that this group art therapy program might ameliorate symptoms of depression and anxiety (Pretorius & Pfeifer, 2010).

Wadeson's contributions

When Harriet Wadeson (2010) worked with depressed patients early in her career, she felt challenged by the findings—or lack thereof—in the literature. The absence of adequate analyses compelled her to "undertake a systematic study of characteristics of art expression in depression" (Wadeson, 2010, p. 148). Her research relied on the graphic indicators revealed in the art images of each individual patient.

> To test characteristics of depression in art expression, pictures produced during increased depression were compared with pictures made when depression was diminished. The sample comprised pairs of pictures made by 10 different patients (five male and five female). One picture was produced on a day when the patient was highly depressed and one picture from a day when depression was low ... each patient serve[d] as his or her own control. (p. 148)

The patients were rated separately for daily levels of depression using a 15-point scale by a psychiatric nursing team. Then, after both the highest and lowest days of depression were recorded, five psychiatrists independently rated pairs of drawings that had been made on those days by each of the 10 patients. Overall, the following characteristics (p. 149) were present in each patient's artwork on their most depressive day:

- Less color
- More empty space
- More constriction
- Less investment of effort or less completeness
- Less meaningfulness
- More depressive affect or less affect

Wadeson found that:

> This paucity in picture-making is congruent with the total image presented by the severely depressed individual: psychomotor retardation, general inhibition of expressiveness (e.g., flattened affect), lack of productivity and impoverished interpersonal communications, sometimes to the extent of being mute. The total impact of depressed patients' picture is frequently one of pervading emptiness. (p. 154)

Such information was vital in recognizing depression in clients' graphic work and has substantially provided the scaffolding for future assessment procedures, including Gantt and Tabones' Formal Element's Art Therapy Scale (1998).

While depression is ubiquitous, Wadeson (2010) encouraged the distinction between "ordinary sadness and grief on the one hand, and the diagnosis of depression as psychopathology, on the other" (p. 131). She stressed the need to encourage the creative endeavors of the person who is suffering and to underscore that all artistic expressions will be valued by the art therapist. Wadeson additionally cautioned that the "projective expectation [is] that my judgment of the patient will be as harsh as the patient's judgment of him- or herself" (p. 134), and thus art therapists should be vigilant in continually attending to and nurturing the therapeutic alliance. To that end, art therapists working with the severely depressed should be acutely aware of the potential for self-harm even when the patient appears to be improving.

Robert—A Case Example

Robert was a 40-year-old psychiatric nurse of slight build, working fulltime in an inner-city hospital. Having been born in Trinidad, he, his mother, and younger brother moved to the United States when he was an adolescent; his father remained behind. As a child, Robert experienced his father as overly stern, and occasionally physically abusive and emotionally withholding. According to Robert, this contributed to his lifelong, intermittent, low-level depression. Robert, who is Catholic, identified his faith and mother as his main supports. He also enjoyed art making, from time to time, as a means of relaxation. The "call" to become a nurse came to Robert in response to a desire to be of service to humankind, wanting to help those in need. His 20-year career in nursing was stellar, and he derived great dignity and positive self-worth from being in the nursing profession.

Six months before Robert was referred to art therapy services, a male patient on the psychiatric unit in the hospital where he worked physically assaulted him. The taller patient came up behind him, and lifted him by his head from the floor. The patient then grabbed Robert in his arms while the staff was trying to encircle and subdue him. He eventually dropped Robert who landed on his back and neck on the cement floor.

The injuries he sustained to his neck and spine left Robert permanently disabled and in pervasive pain. In addition to the trauma of the assault, he felt that the hospital's response was not supportive. He stated that he felt isolated and betrayed. Robert found himself struggling in an effort to get medical assistance, pain management, and disability status. There was also collateral damage, as he was no longer employed by the hospital. As a result, his housing, which was tied to the institution, was in jeopardy. Most significant for Robert was that he could no longer physically practice nursing again. As a psychiatric nurse, Robert recognized that he was slipping into a deep depression. Robert's legal counselor knew of my trauma work as an art therapist and Robert's interest in art, and therefore suggested that he contact me. After consulting with his psychiatrist, Robert decided to come for art therapy on a weekly basis.

In his first session, Robert indicated that he was overwhelmed by all the work he needed to do to get his paperwork ready to apply for disability status. He spoke about the constant pain he was in and of his frustration with the hospital to get even the simplest documents to him. He discussed how he was emotionally; as a psychiatric nurse, he was able to be precise in describing his depression, knowing it was categorically more "serious" than the depression he had lived with most of his life. He was asked to make an image of what the feeling looked like. In response, he drew an impoverished faint single horizontal line on a sheet of white paper. He interpreted his own mark by stating it resembled the "flat line" the heart monitor shows when someone has died. He then spoke at length about "not being alive" any longer, yet stressed that this did not mean he felt suicidal.

Understanding that the combination of the recent trauma, his history of depression, and the reality he now found himself in might cause him to feel desperate, he was questioned more about his current state to determine if his psychiatrist should be contacted with concerns of suicidality. Robert reassured that he was not suicidal and that such self-harm was contrary to his religious beliefs. At the end of the session, Robert indicated that the simple drawing "brightened" him. He said he loved art and was moved when given the pad he had been drawing on to take home. He was encouraged to create any time he wanted and was invited to bring his artwork to the sessions. This connection between sessions became an important means for developing and maintaining the therapeutic alliance. Sometimes he would complete a drawing in session, which was started at home, while at other times he would bring in ideas for projects, and begin them in session, completing them on his own during the week.

A few weeks into the treatment, Robert despondency grew as he struggled to get medical appointments; his legal situation was progressing poorly. His physical impairments rendered him unable to do more than what was minimally necessary for his self-care. The reality that nursing was not going to be his profession left him with a profound sense of loss. Robert actively questioned whether life was worth living. What compounded the difficulties was that he did not want to burden his mother with his doubts and no longer felt connected to his faith. His psychiatrists and I continuously monitored Robert to ascertain if he needed to be hospitalized, although this was not preferred as it was clear that such a drastic step might re-traumatize him.

Two weeks later, Robert brought in the artwork shown in Figure 34.1, which seemed to clearly embody the despair he felt. He stated that he felt alone, and that life held little meaning for him anymore. Concerns were great, so focus was placed on what resources he could rely on to help him through this dark time.

He had painted the black spiral at home without the human figure. As the session progressed, he took out a tiny bottle of Wite-Out® and painted the ghost-like person with arms raised standing near the mouth of the all-consuming spiral. The physical stance of the invisible man made it appear as if he was walking away from the doom. The sense was that what he wanted most in that moment was to be truly seen, since he felt so invisible to the "system." Much time was spent sitting in meaningful silence staring at this powerful image. I measured my breathing to match his. He was told that his struggles were clear and how much it was appreciated that he clearly trusted me with the depth of his emotional sufferings. In it together, in that room, in that moment, the alliance that was formed helped push back his death wish. He indicated "the invisible man could leave the spiral if he walked carefully and took his time." He was reminded the real work does take time and that those working with him would be sure to walk carefully beside him.

Over the following months, Robert began to discover, explore, and appreciate his artist within. His disabilities left him unable to complete average daily tasks so being

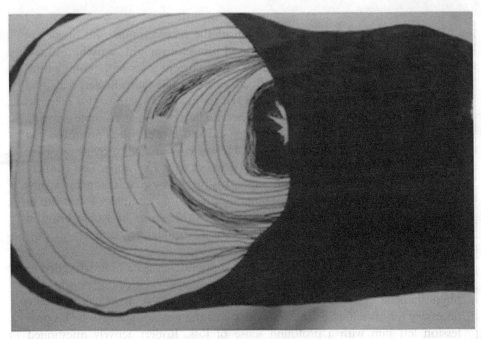

Figure 34.1 Invisible man.

able to create art whenever he wanted was quite empowering. He developed a system for holding the paper horizontally at an angle that was comfortable for his back, neck, and hands in the bed-chair in which he slept. This left him with a feeling of competency and accomplishment. He talked of Frida Kahlo, and he was shown photographs of her painting from her bed. His images deeply explored his hopelessness, loss of identity, and confrontations with fears about the future. He described feeling moments of joy and hope while he was engaged in art making, in spite of the heaviness of the imagery he created. Robert brought ideas for new drawings and art images from books that inspired him into the sessions. Our times together were rich with dialogue about art techniques, the history of art, and art making.

Two months after his sessions began, he completed the artwork shown in Figure 34.2, which was inspired by a dream he had. Robert wrote, "A person was being locked in a freezer. I was an observer and could stop them. Woke up terrified." The coffin-like freezer had been chained closed with the little person inside. However, it was opened by the "observer," whom we do not see, with the chain and lock left alone on the floor. After externalizing his dream through his art, he was able to talk about this image, capturing the paradox of being both the victim and hero in his own life. As alarming as the image was, Robert imbued the "observer–self" with the power to put a stop to the death act. The observer–self demonstrated to the victim–self that he had the capacity to save himself.

A large part of Robert's duties as a psychiatric nurse involved observing the patients. When discussing the piece, Robert was able understand that he could use the skills he had as a nurse to help himself. As a clinician, this is an example where the context of the image is crucial to fully understanding the artistic intent; otherwise, this

Figure 34.2   Just a dream.

dichotomous split might be construed simply as a form of dissociation. The safety of the therapeutic alliance helped open possibilities for gaining such insight. At this point in the therapy, the shift toward a lightening of the depression became evident in his demeanor and self-reporting.

As the therapy continued, Robert developed many strategies for emotional healing. He created lists, assigned himself tasks, and continued to make art daily. His artwork consistently contained blood, surgical stitches, and images, which at times could be unsettling. It was important for the therapist to be able to sit with difficult imagery—to be the "observer–therapist."

One person in the artwork shown in Figure 34.3 is bleeding in a hospital bed, with another person, faintly drawn, standing at the bedside. This other figure is a replication of the "invisible" person who walked out of the spiral in the artwork in Figure 34.1. The words hovering around the rest of the page are Robert's self-prescribed "nursing orders," delineating emotional, cognitive, and spiritual assignments for him to work on. In the section for therapy, he wrote, "Don't set unrealistic goals ... this is a process ... it will take time. Don't be overly rushed to finish, take time and consider." Robert understood that he needed an orderly process for managing his emotional

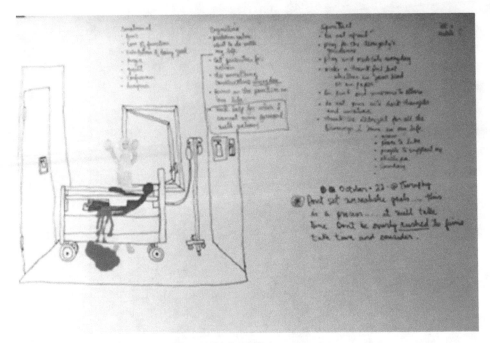

Figure 34.3 Life is a process.

Figure 34.4 This is not depression.

healing. The art making and the lists became common ways for him to move forward to regain a sense of safety in his world. According to Robert, he derived pleasure in visually capturing the difficult feelings while verbally while the lists were reassuring reminders of the tasks before him.

In the final weeks of treatment 3 months later, Robert wanted to explore what "not being depressed" might mean for him. He recollected earlier times in Trinidad as being carefree and relatively happy and wanted to create a picture that portrayed how he wanted his life to look.

Figure 34.4 depicts him standing with his beloved dog outside his childhood home in Trinidad. While it is clear that the family home was highly defended against perceived outside forces, he was a fully formed person, walking his dog outside. He used a stick as an aid to help him walk. He was no longer invisible, confined to the spiral, locked in the deep freezer, or alongside the hospital bed. The cow appeared ready to deliver her milk, and, although the landscape remains sparse, there was a sense of warmth about this composition. Work remained, but the crisis had passed.

Summary

Robert experienced classic symptoms of depression, including feelings of worthlessness, the inability to focus, sleep problems, changes in appetite, tearfulness, and thoughts of suicide and self-annihilation. In his early artwork, "Invisible man," Robert demonstrated the depth of his sense of overwhelming depression and loss. The tiny white figure stood in defiance at the mouth of the enormous, life-devouring spiral. Through his creative work, Robert worked through the journey of this invisible being, along with the little figure, from the deep freezer to the bedside in the hospital to finally a place where he became a full person within his own life. Over time, the earlier desolation frequently expressed in his artwork was transformed into depictions that were less severe and nihilistic. As Robert both created and witnessed his own art in the presence of a caring person, the art-making process began taking on new meaning for him. In essence, Robert became more interested in himself—he mattered, and this, in turn, added meaning to his life.

There is no single art therapy technique for people suffering from depression. The complexities of emotional strata within depression make formulating a typical method unlikely. There are, however, certain basic components that increase the odds of being able to help. A truly compassionate therapeutic alliance, including the therapist having the capacity to sit with very difficult emotions, a belief on the part of the patient in the healing potential of art making, and allowance for enough time for our patients to process the art properly, represent some necessary elements. It remains essential to embrace a way of being with patients, in which the therapeutic alliance optimizes interweaving conditions of safety and creative engagement to enhance possibilities for reducing deep depression. The steps away from the precipice of despair may be incrementally slow—at times almost imperceptible. To know there is real movement, we must truly know the person with whom we are working, and persistently, delicately, and compassionately assist in pushing back the dark.

References

American Psychiatric Association. (2013). *Diagnostic and statistical manual of mental disorders* (5th ed.; *DSM-5*). Retrieved from:
http://www.dsm5.org/ProposedRevision/Pages/proposedrevision.aspx?rid=47
http://www.dsm5.org/ProposedRevision/Pages/proposedrevision.aspx?rid=46
http://www.dsm5.org/ProposedRevision/Pages/proposedrevision.aspx?rid=160
http://www.dsm5.org/ProposedRevision/Pages/proposedrevision.aspx?rid=584

Bar-Sela, G., Atid, L., Danos, S., Gabay, N., & Epelbaum, R. (2007). Art therapy improved depression and influenced fatigue levels in cancer patients on chemotherapy. *Psycho-Oncology, 16*, 980–984. doi: 10.1002/pon.1175

Field, W., & Kruger, C. (2008). The effect of an art psychotherapy intervention on levels of depression and health Locus of Control orientations experienced by black women living with HIV. *South African Journal of Psychology, 38*(3), 467–478.

Gantt, L., & Tabone, C. (1998). *The formal elements art therapy scale: The rating manual.* Morgantown, WV: Gargoyle Press.

Gussak, D. (2006). The effects of art therapy with prison inmates: A follow-up study. *The Arts in Psychotherapy, 33*, 188–198.

Miniño, A. M. (2010). Mortality among teenagers aged 12–19 years: United States 1999–2006. NCHS Data Brief, No. 37. National Center for Health Statistics, Hyattsville, MD.

Pretorius, G., & Pfeifer, N. (2010). Group art therapy with sexually abused girls. *South African Journal of Psychology, 40*(1), 63–73.

Silver, R. (2011). Identifying children and adolescents with depression: Review of the stimulus drawing task and draw a story research. *Art Therapy: Journal of the American Art Therapy Association, 26*(4), 174–180.

Slayton, S. C., D'Archer, J., & Kaplan, F. (2010). Outcome studies in the efficacy of art therapy: A review of the findings. *Art Therapy: Journal of the American Art Therapy Association, 27*(3), 108–118.

Solomon, A. (2001). *The noonday demon: An atlas of depression.* New York, NY: Scribner Simon & Shuster.

Wadeson, H. (2010). *Art psychotherapy* (2nd ed.). Hoboken, NJ: John Wiley & Sons.

35

Art Therapy and Substance Abuse
Libby Schmanke

Art therapists are uniquely equipped to provide alternative and complementary services for people with substance use problems. This chapter will examine the benefits and uses of art therapy with the population; review assessment and characteristics of the art; examine the interface of spirituality, creativity, and recovery; explore the special importance of group work; and explain the usefulness of directives. Case vignettes and illustrations illuminate the treatment issues presented in this chapter.

Approaches and Benefits

The use of art therapy with people with substance use problems has been documented since the early 1950s (Moore, 1983). In earlier years, particularly in Great Britain, a psychoanalytic approach was favored. Albert-Puleo (1980) invited patients to paint whatever came to mind, allowing impulses to be expressed safely. Kaufman (1981) noted that more structured art assignments could enhance structuring of the ego. Luzzatto (1989) explored symbols of attachment issues using an object relations framework in brief therapy.

Work on feeling states is important in substance abuse treatment. Forrest (1975) described how art-making stimulated a client's ability to discuss feelings verbally. By externalizing feelings into imagery, Foulke and Keller (1976) found that it may be easier for clients to tie emotions to cognitions and verbal expressions. Devine (1970) observed that client artwork became looser as recovery progressed, indicating an increased comfort level when dealing with feelings. Groterath (1999) noted that individuals with addictions may feel uncomfortable using verbal communication, or what she termed the "stage of words" (p. 21). The discomfort with verbal language may be a reminder of failure in a classroom or courtroom. Arts therapies may provide a more permissive "stage" for communicating feelings.

Motivational interviewing (MI) and the stages of change (SOC) models have been widely incorporated into modern substance abuse treatment. These methods uncover and enhance the motivation to change and guide treatment in a nonconfrontational manner (Center for Substance Abuse Treatment, 1999). Holt and Kaiser (2009)

The Wiley Handbook of Art Therapy, First Edition. Edited by David E. Gussak and Marcia L. Rosal.

devised a protocol of five art therapy directives that coordinate with MI/SOC models, particularly in assisting clients to normalize ambivalence toward treatment. Horay (2006) used specific directives to explore a client's ambivalence and discourage rigid thinking. Diehls (2008) used an SOC scoring instrument with a group of clients receiving art therapy and found improvement.

Harm reduction is a pragmatic approach used to decrease negative consequences of drug abuse. Wise (2009) described an open art studio in an inner-city harm reduction center whose primary goal was to reduce the spread of HIV in substance abusers. Matto, Corcoran, and Fassler (2003) paired harm reduction and solution-focused therapy, which builds on strengths and past successes, with art therapy in substance abuse treatment through the use of specific directives and a verbal processing protocol.

Hinz (2009) created a model for assessing and treating substance abuse clients that was built on Kagin and Lusebrink's Expressive Therapies Continuum (1978). Her model linked functions associated with levels of the continuum to addiction-specific characteristics and needs, and provides corresponding interventions and directives. Moschini (2005) described a model wherein phases of therapy paralleled phases of development into a more mature identity; art interventions were designed to complement Eriksonian stages of development.

Several art therapists have described incorporating art therapy into existing programs. Allen (1985) observed that treatment agencies may require a more directive approach than might be desired by the art therapist. Matto (2002) described the integration of art therapy into a brief inpatient setting. Dickson (2007) used patient questionnaires to evaluate art therapy in a residential program and found that 66% of the 53 participants found both psychological and art therapy aspects of the treatment to be useful, and that 8% found art therapy only to be effective.

Mahony (1999) reviewed the use of art in substance abuse treatment programs in Great Britain and identified three models: educative, healing, and psychotherapeutic. An art-as-therapy approach in a studio setting was preferred by Wittenberg (1975) for adolescents receiving substance abuse treatment in a residential setting. Wadeson (2000) described working on substance abuse issues with persons receiving psychiatric inpatient care, women with sexual abuse histories, and child abuse survivors.

Clearly, the use of art therapy in the treatment of addictions has numerous benefits. Waller and Mahony (1999, pp. 9–11) summarized these as follows: facilitating expression of repressed or complicated emotions; protecting as well as uncovering defenses and denial; providing containment of shame and anger; enabling feelings of control through distancing; identifying strengths to counteract feelings of inadequacy; and addressing isolation through improved verbal communication and symbolic expression. Additionally, art therapy can assist in the assessment of individuals with substance use issues. In the next section, an overview of how art therapy can be used in the assessment of individuals with substance use issues will be provided.

Assessing and Characterizing the Art of Substance Abusers

Whether formal or informal, art therapy assessments can offer clues to the issues and concerns of individuals with substance use problems. In this section, a short overview of the assessments found in the literature is presented.

Research on assessments

Rockwell and Dunham (2006) used the Formal Elements Art Therapy Scale (FEATS) to compare drawings by people with substance use disorder diagnoses against those by a control group. Scores on three of the 12 FEATS elements reached significance: realism, developmental, and person scales and were found to be predictors of those in the substance use group. Using the Bird's Nest Drawing, Francis, Kaiser, and Deaver (2003) found that a treatment group had greater likelihood of insecure attachment and used less color than the comparison group. Holt and Kaiser (2001) analyzed Kinetic Family Drawings of two groups of children, one with parents identified with alcoholism. Scores indicating isolation of self and of family members were significantly higher in the treatment group.

Informal evaluation

Art therapists have described ways in which certain drawing directives provide informal assessment value in addition to therapeutic value in substance abuse treatment. For example, Hrenko and Willis (1996) found that the amusement park technique elicited discussions of powerlessness. Hanes (1995) asked clients to create a road drawing. One client with a heroin addiction realized that his road resembled a heart-shaped syringe; he then made the connection that heroin was his "love" and that it had replaced intimate relationships.

Characteristics of the art

Ault (n.d.) reflected that the sensation-seeking of illicit drug users is echoed in qualities of their art: incorporation of graffiti or poetry, elements that create a sense of movement, and content chosen for shock value. Wadeson (2010) noted themes of loss, a sense of passing time, ambivalence, and incident-type drawings. Gantt and Howie (as cited in Moore, 1983) listed pictorial content of art by persons with alcoholism: depression, jobs, ambivalence, symbols including boats and water, denial, and grief. Devine (1970) found that men with alcoholism rarely painted people, but that boats, water, and crosses were frequently depicted.

Spring (1985) observed that a "dual symbolic language" of eye and wedge forms, in conjunction with a set of symbols including red flowers, was common in the early drawings of women in treatment for chemical dependency who also had experienced sexual abuse. As treatment progressed, these elements were less prominently incorporated into the artwork. Hanes (2007) observed ways that spontaneously produced self-portraits signified a readiness to come "face to face" with the addiction.

Springham (1999) found a high volume of "paradise pictures," especially "a tropical island basking under a beneficent sun" (p. 153), which may represent unrealistic expectations of life in sobriety. Schmanke (2006) noted a predominance of images of luxury or wealth when asking clients to make a collage about the future.

Red flags

Kaufman (1981) theorized that drawings could provide diagnostic impressions and identify patients who were experiencing potentially destructive impulses such as getting high or leaving treatment. Dickman, Dunn, and Wolf (1996) performed a 5-year retrospective study and found that three of 11 indicators reached statistical significance in the drawings of patients who relapsed within 3 months of treatment: drugs or drug paraphernalia, lack of a detailed self or other articulated figure, and predominant use of an abstract or geometric drawing style.

To explore the use of a bridge drawing, Schmanke (2005) examined 71 drawings of treatment dropouts and treatment completers. She found no indication of particular markers for treatment success or failure using the bridge drawing. She cautioned that red flags may be projections of the therapist or may have benign meaning. Therapists may overreact to a phenomenological norm (i.e., drawing drugs may be a natural reflection on the predominant part of a client's life).

When a therapist is working clinically with an individual rather than conducting research, it is undesirable to predict the treatment outcome based on drawings. Red flags might be explored by checking with the client. Therapists can make ongoing treatment observations and provide appropriate interventions as needed. Often a review of several drawings may seem indicative of treatment dropout, and appropriate actions can be taken to intervene. At times, clients literally "paint a picture" of intent to drop out of treatment with no advance warning.

Case Example: Brandon

Aged barely 18 years, Brandon was referred by his parents to an intensive outpatient adolescent program for his drug abuse and "bad attitude," which had resulted in difficulty completing high school. During the initial individual session, Brandon was asked about his alleged bad attitude and he sneered in reply, "Lady, you can't *touch* my bad attitude." Attempting to move beyond Brandon's defensive swagger, he was asked to do a kinetic–house–tree–person drawing (see Figure 35.1). Judging from the detail depicting a bong, he was capable of drawing a more complete person than the stick figure, as was asked. The house was drawn in the same schema he used later that day to depict the treatment agency building and his school.

On a symbolic level, this drawing reflected Brandon's desire to distance himself from home, treatment, and school—and his perceptions of authority. The primary function of the tree seemed to be to hide Brandon's behavior from the building. Certain branches resemble human limbs, one kicking the building with a foot, while simultaneously appearing to be firmly stuck to the building. The tree evinces agitation and anger, as well as a lack of coherent direction; the dearth of twigs and leaves prohibit healthy growth; and the inadequate stick person seems subsumed by the detailed addictive behavior. Brandon stopped attending treatment after the first day. The other adolescents indicated that, during bathroom break from group, he had run behind the Laundromat next door to smoke marijuana. The parents decided he would "grow out of it," and rejected a referral to inpatient treatment. In essence, Brandon's drawing was a perfect snapshot of his world.

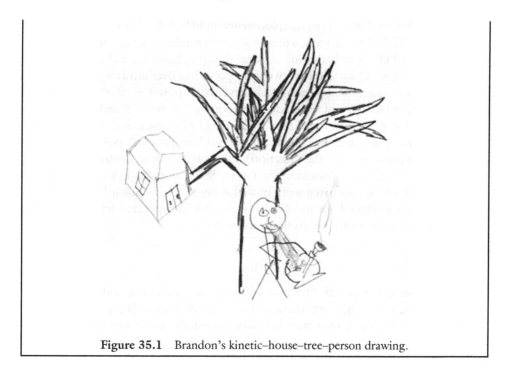

Figure 35.1 Brandon's kinetic–house–tree–person drawing.

Creativity, Spirituality, and Addiction

Addiction is viewed by many in the field as a bio-psycho-social disease; spiritual aspects are often added to the original tripartite model and have particular relevance to creativity and art therapy. In the early 1960s, "Bill W." (Wilson, 1963), co-founder of Alcoholics Anonymous in 1935, and Carl Jung (1963) exchanged letters in which they reflected on the spiritual nature of alcoholism. Since then, many writers (Cameron, 2002; Grof, 1993; Leonard, 1990; Maisel & Raeburn, 2008) theorized that the creative person is one with a "thirst … for wholeness" (Jung, 1963, p. 1), which may be subverted through substance abuse. An addiction may block creative energy, and thus a spiritual quest may become a search for the perfect high—or, failing that, an escape from the real world. One way to transform the dilemma of addiction may be to "bring the mystical vision back to earth by embodying it in creative life" (Leonard, 1990, p. 69). Involvement in art therapy may facilitate this process.

Feen-Calligan (1995) explored the shared qualities of spirituality, art, and recovery, and reported positive gains from a meditative "Doing by Not Doing" studio group in an inpatient setting. This grounded theory research study identified enlightenment as a key concept describing the effects of art therapy in substance abuse treatment (Feen-Calligan, 1999).

The Twelve Steps

David Read Johnson (1990) advocated for arts therapies to be more specifically helpful for this population by aligning with the Twelve Steps, a spiritual and self-improvement model for recovery originally developed by the founders of Alcoholics

Anonymous (Wilson, 1963). For example, clients could be helped to avoid stereotypical interpretations of God by imaging a personally meaningful understanding of a higher power. Krebs (2008) described using collage, drawing, painting, and clay to explore the first three steps: (1) we admitted we were powerless over alcohol—that our lives had become unmanageable; (2) came to believe that a power greater than ourselves could restore us to sanity; and (3) made a decision to turn our will and our lives over to the care of God *as we understood Him*. Julliard's (1995) research protocol using art therapy and role play increased chemically dependent patients' belief in step one (admitting powerlessness over the addiction). His work culminated into a monograph, which provided a helpful discussion of the Twelve Steps, and ways in which art therapy and group work can support step work in a treatment setting (Julliard, 1999). Nobis (2009) created a workbook for the Twelve Steps that incorporated art directives and stimulus questions for written reflections on the art.

Shame

The issue of shame is closely tied to spirituality and addiction, and may be more readily addressed through art therapy than verbal means (L. Johnson, 1990; M. Wilson, 2012). *Guilt* over past behaviors is usually an appropriate and useful human response. *Shame* may be compounded by personal behaviors, but involves feelings of a defective identity as well; this existential aspect is tied to the broken spirituality. Substance abusers typically feel that they are "not good enough" or are flawed at a core level. Often, this experience of shame is barely repressed, and as the protective factors of substance use and denial give way in treatment, painful feelings are exposed. When shame is left unacknowledged and untreated, relapse is likely.

Lynn Johnson (1990) described shame or exposure of the inadequate self as an obstacle to spiritual rebirth and recovery, but observed that "creativity is an antidote to shame" (p. 307), in that it connects a person to a higher creative power and to his or her true self. Marie Wilson (2012) proposed a helpful art therapy protocol to enhance shame reduction in substance abusers by exploring family-of-origin messages, addressing perfectionism and the need for control, and affirming a positive self-image. Shame is frequently compounded by characteristics or experiences beyond a client's control, such as being from a rural area, physical unattractiveness, poverty, incest, etc. Horovitz (2009) described working with a woman on shame that involved substance abuse, sexual abuse, and hearing impairment.

Group Work

Special advantages of group therapy for this population include positive peer support and morale, reduction in the sense of isolation, and observation of peer models of recovery (Center for Substance Abuse Treatment, 2005). Individuals with substance use issues often feel that no one but another addict or recovering addict can understand them; hence, the experience of universality is particularly important. The concept of universality is an underlying therapeutic factor in group work (Yalom, 1995). Riley (2001) explored how imagery in group therapy intensifies universality and other therapeutic factors and helps to keep process in the here-and-now. The here-and-now focus is important for a population that may otherwise use group time to tell "war stories" or blame past circumstances for their addiction.

Winship (1999) remarked that individuals with addiction issues typically do not want to be with others in an intimate sense; making art during group provides the needed "space." Similarly, Springham (1998) noted that these clients engage on a "false self" level rather than a true emotional level. Group work is positively impacted by individual art-making, which allows for withdrawal into a "narcissistic reverie" (p. 151) before coming back into a verbal group processing phase. Liebmann (2004) described a group in a hospital alcohol unit that used a more directive approach to address the problem of the false self by having members paint the masks that they perceived each other wearing.

Group treatment formats

A typical model for formatting art therapy groups was described by Scaife and Huet (1998) as the "sonata-form." The three-part session opens with group exposition of a theme, moves to working individually on developments of the theme through the artwork, and comes back into group process for verbal recapitulation. This format is adaptable in settings where the art therapist is required to provide themes or directives that enhance the psycho-educational curriculum.

Unique designs for group art therapy with substance abusers appear in the literature. Adelman and Castricone (1986) described an Expressive Arts Model that integrated psychodrama, art therapy, and music therapy to aid clients in self-expression and the development of empathy. Virshup (1985) found that a weekly workshop that elicited sharing of art products and journaling enabled methadone clinic clients to develop social skills and gain insight. Working with a group of minority women, Feen-Calligan, Washington, and Moxley (2008) described the use of fine art reproductions specifically chosen to enable access to emotions and stimulate recall of repressed areas. Fernandez (2009) used a comic drawing procedure and commented on the pitfalls and benefits of humor in therapy groups. For families with substance-abusing adolescents, Perkoulidis (2009) proposed a multifamily group protocol using family sculptures and body drawings in conjunction with health education.

Resonance and the group image

Springham (1998) explored the "group image," which may emerge as the one art work in a session to which all members strongly relate. He explored one group's "magpie's eye" (p. 141), which revealed initial mistrustful attitudes of the group toward the therapist and provoked in-depth discussion. Canty (2009) explored a similar "key image" in a group doing free drawings; one member realistically articulated an issue about which the other members had created more abstract, subconscious versions. Similar to the group image is the experience of having several group members incorporate the same symbol or content into a drawing, without having consciously done so. This is referred to as "resonance," or unconscious linkage between group members, as applied to images produced in art therapy groups (McNeilly, 2006).

Art therapists working with groups will experience resonance in the art and should be alert to its emergence (McNeilly, 2006). At times, clients may suspect that group members are surreptitiously "copying" another's work. The therapist can acknowledge that, while sometimes this may be the case, it is still valuable information when more than one group member creates the same image or symbol: it is as if the group is telling itself where to go in order to process important issues. The therapist can guide discussion by asking for emotional responses or brainstorming about meanings. By keeping the tone light and curious, rigid interpretations are avoided and freer thinking encouraged, which is of particular value to this population.

In some instances, the creation of similar drawings by group members may not be indicative of resonance. When a preponderance of members regularly produce defensive symbols such as rainbows or hearts, the therapist may decide to take a more active role and guide the group toward exploring those defenses.

The directive approach

Although a nondirective or studio approach is a boon for this population, many art therapists working in substance abuse settings are required to match services to specific treatment plan goals, adhere to a curriculum, and document outcomes. Directives may be described more readily in terms of outcomes and are more congruent with cognitive behavioral approaches. Use of directives should be undertaken with a sense of particular client needs. It is preferable to assess a group or individual at the beginning of a session and respond to presenting issues, rather than adhere to a preplanned calendar of directives.

Use of treatment themes   Internalizing treatment teachings through a visual modality reinforces learning. Clients can be asked to use art materials to depict personal examples of "continued use despite adverse consequences" (a simple definition of addiction); "remembering your last drunk or high" (the event that was the last straw, rather than euphoric recall of fun times); or "a time you did something you wouldn't have, if you had been sober" (breaking through denial and acknowledging harm to self or others). Asking clients to simply "depict your problem" can be revealing in the amount of personal responsibility shown, that is, whether they depict themselves; their drug of choice; or a probation officer, boss, or family member. When this is done in a group, participants will more clearly understand the various ways in which problems can be interpreted and responsibility assumed. Cox and Price (1990) asked adolescents in substance abuse treatment to "draw about an incident that occurred during the time you were drinking/drugging" (p. 335). "Incident drawings," particularly when shared in group, help break down denial, allow participants to express feelings, and explore values and alternative behaviors.

Incorporating ritual into the group process is often valuable. "Check-in drawings" can be used in place of the traditional verbal check-in at the beginning of substance abuse treatment groups. These free drawings encourage more honest self-revelation and enliven the process. Rituals that acknowledge treatment completion are affirming and provide closure. Clients can be asked to create a drawing with words that sends an encouraging message to future clients. In one facility, the drawings were pinned to colorful paper backgrounds on the group room wall to create a giant paper quilt of inspiration.

Bridge drawings The bridge drawing, developed by Hays and Lyons (1981), is a powerful metaphor for persons in treatment for addictions. The original directive was to "draw a picture of a bridge going from someplace to someplace"; when done, the person was asked to place a dot showing "where you are in the picture" and an arrow to indicate direction of travel (p. 208). A version used by Holt and Kaiser (2009) in an SOC protocol revealed the metaphor by instructing clients to "Complete a bridge depicting where you have been, where you are now, and where you want to be in relation to your recovery" (p. 247).

Case Examples

Darleen

New in an outpatient treatment group, Darleen understood the bridge metaphor immediately and personalized it (see Figure 35.2). Having received a citation for DUI, her future in a beloved job depended not only on completing treatment but also on the decision of her work supervisor. She felt shame, despair, and panic. Creating and processing this image allowed Darleen to express her feelings to an extent she had been hesitant to do before. This in turn led to increased empathy from other group members and an enhanced sense of group cohesiveness. Darleen was able to relax into the supportive atmosphere, which enabled successful treatment.

Figure 35.2 Darleen's bridge drawing.

In my group work with clients who have addiction issues, I ask them to "Draw a picture that has a bridge and a person in it. You can add anything else that you want." When clients are done drawing, they are asked to write a one-paragraph story about the picture. The addition of the person and the story provides a richer basis for interpretation and discussion. The nature and placement of the person (self); bridge (treatment); and content on the left (past/addicted self or environment) and right (future/recovering self or environment) are the primary elements for consideration.

I believe that if a specific meaning about recovery is given in the directive, clients will be more likely to create a false-self drawing to please the therapist. Eventually, clients understand the metaphor (or it is revealed in group discussion), but it is their own discovery. By claiming ownership, the clients seem to ensure greater interest, and in turn greater investment in the drawing, story, and ensuing discussion.

Rhonda Rhonda's bridge drawing (see Figure 35.3) demonstrates how the art speaks louder than words. Her written story was an innocuous tale about a woman relaxing on a bridge and enjoying the nice day. Yet, the voided eyes, clownish false-self smile, and sliding attitude of the body in the drawing depict someone who may be exiting treatment/ the bridge, which is revealed as a chancy structure over a swift-flowing river. Rhonda's alternative to this inpatient treatment program was to serve a prison sentence.

Group members were instructed to make observations of each other's drawings when invited to do so and during the processing phase of the session. Rhonda invited

Figure 35.3 Rhonda's bridge drawing.

group comments. The group picked up on the puns with the comments she made about her drawing: being "sent up the river" (to prison) or being "sold down the river" (betraying herself, by sitting on her hands rather than holding on tight to the treatment bridge). They noted the "behind bars" appearance created by part of the bridge. Initially, Rhonda insisted that the figure was happy and relaxed; after additional group processing, she began to see her drawing differently. She admitted to being scared that she would not be able to remain sober. As she began to process the comments made by others as well as her own feelings, she realized that she might relapse or "slip" from the bridge. Her bridge drawing, combined with the power of group work, marked a turning point in Rhonda's ability to make use of treatment.

Conclusion

Working with people who have substance use issues can be exasperating, disappointing, and also intensely rewarding. Although frequently resistant in the beginning, clients often respond well to creative treatment interventions. The benefits of art therapy treatment for people with substance use disorders and addictions are numerous and important, and include bypassing resistance, finding a creative outlet for the expression of difficult feelings, and finding deeper understanding of creative and spiritual meaning of the addiction and of life.

Art therapists working in addiction treatment settings may be required to provide themes that fit within a substance abuse treatment curriculum. Yet, with a creative mindset, art therapists can devise and facilitate art therapy interventions to enable recovery.

References

Adelman, E., & Castricone, L. (1986). An expressive arts model for substance abuse group training and treatment. *The Arts in Psychotherapy, 13*, 53–59.

Albert-Puleo, N. (1980). Modern psychoanalytic art therapy and its application to drug abuse. *The Arts in Psychotherapy, 7*(1), 43–52.

Allen, P. (1985). Integrating art therapy into an alcoholism treatment program. *American Journal of Art Therapy, 24*, 10–12.

Ault, R. E. (n.d.). Paper on drugs-hippy culture (Unpublished manuscript notes).

Cameron, J. (2002). *The artist's way: A spiritual path to higher creativity* (10th anniversary ed.). New York, NY: Tarcher/Putnam.

Canty, J. (2009). The key to being in the right mind. *International Journal of Art Therapy, 14*(1), 11–16. doi:10.1080/17454830903006083

Center for Substance Abuse Treatment. (1999). *Treatment Improvement Protocol (TIP) series, 35: Enhancing motivation for change in substance abuse treatment.* Rockville, MD: Substance Abuse and Mental Health Services Administration.

Center for Substance Abuse Treatment. (2005). *Treatment Improvement Protocol (TIP) series, 41: Substance abuse treatment: Group therapy.* Rockville, MD: Substance Abuse and Mental Health Services Administration.

Cox, K. L., & Price, K. (1990). Breaking through: Incident drawings with adolescent substance abusers. *The Arts in Psychotherapy, 17*, 333–337.

Devine, D. (1970). A preliminary investigation of paintings by alcoholic men. *American Journal of Art Therapy, 9*(3), 115–128.

Dickman, S. B., Dunn, J. E., & Wolf, A. (1996). The use of art therapy as a predictor of relapse in chemical dependency treatment. *Art Therapy, 13*(4), 232–237.

Dickson, C. (2007). An evaluation study of art therapy provision in a residential Addiction Treatment Programme (ATP). *International Journal of Art Therapy, 12*(1), 17–27. doi:10.1080/17454830701265220

Diehls, V. A. (2008). *Art therapy, substance abuse, and the Stages of Change* (Unpublished master's thesis). Emporia State University, Emporia, KS.

Feen-Calligan, H. (1995). The use of art therapy in treatment programs to promote spiritual recovery from addiction. *Art Therapy, 12*(1), 46–50.

Feen-Calligan, H. (1999). Enlightenment in chemical dependency treatment programs: A grounded theory. In C. A. Malchiodi (Ed.), *Medical art therapy with adults* (pp. 137–162). London, England: Jessica Kingsley.

Feen-Calligan, H., Washington, O. G. M., & Moxley, D. P. (2008). Use of artwork as a visual processing modality in group treatment of chemically dependent minority women. *The Arts in Psychotherapy, 35*(4), 287–295. doi:10.1016/j.aip.2008.05.002

Fernandez, K. M. (2009). Comic addict: A qualitative study of the benefits of addressing ambivalence through comic/cartoon drawing with clients in in-patient treatment for chemical dependency. In S. L. Brooke (Ed.), *The use of creative therapies with chemical dependency issues* (pp. 80–105). Springfield, IL: Charles C. Thomas.

Forrest, G. (1975). The problems of dependency and the value of art therapy as a means of treating alcoholism. *Art Psychotherapy, 2*(1), 15–43.

Foulke, W., & Keller, T. (1976). The art experience in addict rehabilitation. *American Journal of Art Therapy, 15*(3), 75–80.

Francis, D., Kaiser, D., & Deaver, S. (2003). Representations of attachment security in the Bird's Nest Drawings of clients with substance abuse disorders. *Art Therapy, 20*(3), 125–137. doi:10.1080/07421656.2003.10129571

Grof, C. (1993). *The thirst for wholeness: Attachment, addiction, and the spiritual path.* New York, NY: HarperCollins.

Groterath, A. (1999). Conceptions of addiction and implications for treatment approaches. In D. Waller & J. Mahony (Eds.), *Treatment of addiction: Current issues for arts therapies* (pp. 14–22). London, England: Routledge.

Hanes, M. (1995). Utilizing road drawings as a therapeutic metaphor in art therapy. *American Journal of Art Therapy, 34*(1), 19–23.

Hanes, M. J. (2007). "Face-to-face" with addiction: The spontaneous production of self-portraits in art therapy. *Art Therapy, 24*(1), 33–36. doi:10.1080/07421656.2007.10129365

Hays, R. E., & Lyons, S. (1981). The Bridge Drawing: A projective technique for assessment in art therapy. *The Arts in Psychotherapy, 8*, 207–217.

Hinz, L. D. (2009). Order out of chaos: The Expressive Therapies Continuum as a framework for art therapy interventions in substance abuse treatment. In S. L. Brooke (Ed.), *The use of creative therapies with chemical dependency issues* (pp. 51–68). Springfield, IL: Charles C. Thomas.

Holt, E., & Kaiser, D. H. (2001). Indicators of familial alcoholism in children's Kinetic Family Drawings. *Art Therapy, 18*(2), 89–95. doi:10.1080/07421656.2001.10129751

Holt, E., & Kaiser, D. H. (2009). The First Step Series: Art therapy for early substance abuse treatment. *The Arts in Psychotherapy, 36*(4), 245–250. doi:10.1016/j.aip.2009.05.004

Horay, B. J. (2006). Moving towards gray: Art therapy and ambivalence in substance abuse treatment. *Art Therapy, 23*(1), 14–22. doi:10.1080/07421656.2006.10129528

Horovitz, E. G. (2009). Combating shame and pathogenic belief systems: Theoretical and art therapy applications for chemical/substance abusive Deaf clients. In S. L. Brooke (Ed.),

The use of creative therapies with chemical dependency issues (pp. 11–36). Springfield, IL: Charles C. Thomas.

Hrenko, K. D., & Willis, R. (1996). The amusement park technique in the treatment of dually diagnosed, psychiatric inpatients. *Art Therapy, 13*(4), 261–264.

Johnson, D. R. (1990). Introduction to the special issue on creative arts therapies in the treatment of substance abuse. *The Arts in Psychotherapy, 17,* 295–298.

Johnson, L. (1990). Creative therapies in the treatment of addictions: The art of transforming shame. *The Arts in Psychotherapy, 17,* 299–308.

Julliard, K. (1995). Increasing chemically dependent patients' belief in Step One through expressive therapy. *American Journal of Art Therapy, 33*(4), 110–119.

Julliard, K. (1999). *The Twelve Steps and art therapy* (Monograph). Mundelein, IL: American Art Therapy Association.

Jung, C. G. (1963, January). Dr. C. G. Jung's reply to Bill W.'s letter. (Publication of personal letter written 1961). *The Grapevine.* Retrieved from http://www.silkworth.net/grapevine/cgjungtobw.html

Kaufman, G. H. (1981). Art therapy with the addicted. *Journal of Psychoactive Drugs, 13*(4), 353–360.

Krebs, K. A. (2008). Art therapy used to enhance Steps One, Two, and Three of a Twelve-Step recovery program for addictions treatment (Master's thesis). Ursuline College, Pepper Pike, OH. Retrieved from http://etd.ohiolink.edu/view.cgi/Krebs%20Kathleen%20A.pdf?urs1210866880

Leonard, L. S. (1990). *Witness to the fire: Creativity and the veil of addiction.* Boston: Shambhala.

Liebmann, M. (2004). *Art therapy for groups: A handbook of themes and exercises* (2nd ed.). New York, NY: Routledge.

Luzzatto, P. (1989). Drinking problems and short-term art therapy: Working with images of withdrawal and clinging. In A. Gilroy & T. Dalley (Eds.), *Pictures at an exhibition: Selected essays on art and art therapy* (pp. 207–219). London, England: Routledge.

Mahony, J. (1999). Art therapy and art activities in alcohol services: A research project. In D. Waller & J. Mahony (Eds.), *Treatment of addiction: Current issues for arts therapies* (pp. 117–140). London, England: Routledge.

Maisel, E., & Raeburn, S. (2008). *Creative recovery: A complete addiction treatment program that uses your natural creativity.* Boston, MA: Shambhala.

Matto, H. C. (2002). Integrating art therapy methodology in brief inpatient substance abuse treatment for adults. *Journal of Social Work Practice in the Addictions, 2*(2), 69–83. doi:10.1300/J160v02n02_07

Matto, H., Corcoran, J., & Fassler, A. (2003). Integrating solution-focused and art therapies for substance abuse treatment: Guidelines for practice. *The Arts in Psychotherapy, 30,* 265–272. doi:10.1016/j.aip.2003.08.003

McNeilly, G. (2006). *Group analytic art therapy.* London, England: Jessica Kingsley.

Moore, R. W. (1983). Art therapy with substance abusers: A review of the literature. *The Arts in Psychotherapy, 10,* 251–260.

Moschini, L. B. (2005). *Drawing the line: Art therapy with the difficult client.* Hoboken, NJ: John Wiley & Sons.

Nobis, W. (2009). *The art of recovery: A reflective and creative path through the twelve steps.* Mustang, OK: Tate.

Perkoulidis, S. A. (2009). Multifamily group art therapy for adolescent substance abuse: Time for creative repair and relief in family relationships and adolescent self care. In S. L. Brooke (Ed.), *The use of creative therapies with chemical dependency issues* (pp. 69–79). Springfield, IL: Charles C. Thomas.

Riley, S. (2001). The language of art in group therapy. In S. Riley (Ed.), *Group process made visible: Group art therapy* (pp. 1–33). Philadelphia, PA: Brunner-Routledge.

Rockwell, P., & Dunham, M. (2006). The utility of the Formal Elements Art Therapy Scale in assessment for substance use disorder. *Art Therapy, 23*(3), 104–111. doi:10.1080/07421656.2006.10129625

Schmanke, L. (2005, November). Women in substance abuse treatment: Bridges to recovery. Paper presented at the 36th annual conference of the American Art Therapy Association, Atlanta, GA.

Schmanke, L. (2006, November). Harnessing the power of imagery to rebuild women's lives. Paper presented at the 37th annual conference of the American Art Therapy Association, New Orleans, LA.

Spring, D. (1985). Sexually abused, chemically dependent women. *American Journal of Art Therapy, 24,* 13–21.

Springham, N. (1998). The magpie's eye: Patients' resistance to engagement in an art therapy group for drug and alcohol patients. In S. Skaife & V. Huet (Eds.), *Art psychotherapy groups: Between pictures and words* (pp. 133–155). London, England: Routledge.

Springham, N. (1999). "All things very lovely": Art therapy in a drug and alcohol treatment programme. In D. Waller & J. Mahony (Eds.), *Treatment of addiction: Current issues for arts therapies* (pp. 141–166). London, England: Routledge.

Virshup, E. (1985). Group art therapy in a methodone clinic lobby. *Journal of Substance Abuse Treatment, 2,* 153–158. doi:10.1016/0740-5472(85)90045-5

Wadeson, H. (2000). *Art therapy practice: Innovative approaches with diverse populations.* New York, NY: John Wiley & Sons.

Wadeson, H. (2010). *Art psychotherapy* (2nd ed.). Hoboken, NJ: John Wiley & Sons.

Waller, D., & Mahony, J. (1999). Introduction. In D. Waller & J. Mahony (Eds.), *Treatment of addiction: Current issues for arts therapies* (pp. 1–13). London, England: Routledge.

Wilson, M. (2012). Art therapy in addictions treatment: Creativity and shame reduction. In C. A. Malchiodi (Ed.), *Handbook of art therapy* (2nd ed.; pp. 302–319). New York, NY: Guilford.

Wilson, W. G. (1963, January). Bill W.'s letter to Dr. C. G. Jung. (Publication of personal letter written 1961). *The Grapevine.* Retrieved from http://www.silkworth.net/grapevine/bwtocgjung.html

Winship, G. (1999). Group therapy in the treatment of drug addiction. In D. Waller & J. Mahony (Eds.), *Treatment of addiction: Current issues for arts therapies* (pp. 46–58). London, England: Routledge.

Wise, S. (2009). Extending a hand: Open studio art therapy in a harm reduction center. In S. L. Brooke (Ed.), *The use of creative therapies with chemical dependency issues* (pp. 37–50). Springfield, IL: Charles C. Thomas.

Wittenberg, D. (1975). Art therapy for adolescent substance abusers. In E. Ulman & P. Dachinger (Eds.), *Art therapy in theory and practice* (pp. 150–158). New York, NY: Schocken Books.

Yalom, I. (1995). *The theory and practice of group psychotherapy (4th ed).* New York, NY: Basic Books.

36

Art Therapy with Trauma

Paula Howie

Trauma is defined as "exposure to actual or threatened death, serious injury or sexual violation. The exposure must result from one or more of the following scenarios, in which the individual directly experiences the traumatic event; witnesses the traumatic event in person; learns that the traumatic event occurred to a close family member or close friend (with the actual or threatened death being either violent or accidental); or experiences first-hand repeated or extreme exposure to aversive details of the traumatic event (not through media, pictures, television, or movies unless work-related)" (American Psychiatric Association [APA], 2013, p. 143). Posttraumatic stress disorder (PTSD) is distinguished by four clusters of symptoms: (1) intrusion re-experiencing, (2) avoidance of reminders and triggers, (3) negative alterations in cognitions and mood (numbing), and (4) alterations in arousal and reactivity, including exaggerated startle response (APA, 2013, p. 144, 145). It is caused in part by the nature of traumatic memories, which often exist as dissociated emotional, perceptual, or sensory fragments. This impedes the creation of a coherent trauma narrative and makes PTSD difficult to treat.

Dissociated and fragmented information occurs in the implicit memory system. These memories lack temporal, causal, or logical connections; therefore, intrusive traumatic memories are experienced as occurring in the present (Schacter, 1987). Declarative memories of an event can become disconnected during the trauma, making it difficult to describe the occurrence in words or to integrate it as part of one's life history (Van der Kolk & Fisler, 1995).

Standard treatments for PTSD include eye-movement desensitization and reprocessing (EMDR), emotion-focused therapy (EFT), and cognitive behavioral therapy (CBT). EMDR has been extensively researched and, along with EFT, has proved to be an effective way of reconsolidating memories to treat the symptoms of PTSD (Ecker, Ticic, & Hulley, 2012). CBT includes prolonged exposure therapy (PE) and stress inoculation therapy (SIT) (Friedman, 2006). During prolonged exposure therapy, the individual experiences detailed and repeated imagining of the trauma in a safe, controlled context to desensitize him/her to the fear and distress of the trauma (Foa, Hembree, & Rothbaum, 2007; Foa, Keane, & Friedman, 2000). Although good results have been achieved with this and other forms of CBT, these

The Wiley Handbook of Art Therapy, First Edition. Edited by David E. Gussak and Marcia L. Rosal.
© 2016 John Wiley & Sons, Ltd. Published 2016 by John Wiley & Sons, Ltd.

particular treatments may require specialized equipment; clients may refuse or drop out of treatment, and run the risk of re-traumatization (Shapiro, 2010). Alternative treatments such as art therapy address such symptoms as avoidance and emotional numbing and, in most cases, do not entail a reliving of the trauma and reemergence of symptoms (Collie, Backos, Malchiodi, & Spiegel, 2006).

Traumatic memories can be organized and their emotional charge reduced through the development of a coherent trauma narrative, which shifts traumatic memories to declarative memory so they can be reinterpreted and integrated into the person's life history. By their nature, traumatic memories are difficult to express in words alone because they are not in the verbal, declarative memory system (Collie et al., 2006).

This chapter will introduce the reader to an art therapy trauma intervention, and the rationale for using this approach in the treatment of PTSD. The technique described was developed by Gantt and Tinnin (2013) in their Morgantown West Virginia Intensive Trauma Treatment clinic, and has been used for decades to treat clients diagnosed with PTSD, DID, and related disorders.

Art Therapy's Special Role in Trauma Treatment

As early as 1995, Morgan and Johnson researched the use of a drawing task for treating nightmares in war veterans with combat-related PTSD. Participants who used art versus writing to express their nightmares reported fewer and less intense nightmares. The authors reported that those who used art also had an improved ability to return to sleep and a reduction in startle response upon awakening. They wondered if the use of art for expressing the emotional states of trauma maybe useful as it affords visual symbolization, since trauma symptoms may occur as visual memory.

Ford, Courtois, Steele, Van der Hart, and Nijenhuis (2005) proposed that trauma treatment consist of three stages: symptom reduction and stabilization, processing of traumatic memories and emotions, and life integration and rehabilitation after trauma processing. Marr (personal communication, 2012) further refined the categories of universal trauma treatment to include safety, stabilization, assessment, and therapy, which include re-narration and working with victim mythology, or the parts arising in response to the traumatic event. Safety includes a holding environment; stabilization includes helping the person regulate affect and disassociation; and trauma assessment includes considering the degree of dissociation and using a trauma list. Trauma re-narration and addressing victim mythology are the final phases of treatment.

Outcomes from art therapy work with victims of trauma, including traumatized children, sexual abuse survivors, veterans of war, and survivors of major disasters, have been reported (Kaiser et al., 2005; Spinner, 2007). Art interventions endeavor to reduce symptoms of depression, increase emotional expression, reduce emotional numbing, and facilitate the creation of a coherent trauma narrative. The goal of narrative trauma processing (Gantt & Tinnin, 2007) is to eliminate intrusive and arousal symptoms and diminish numbing symptoms. This is accomplished by processing traumatic memories in order to achieve narrative closure. The objective is to integrate all of the dissociated images into a graphic narrative that depicts the entire traumatic experience as a historical event. The artist reviews the pictured event, puts it into words, and it becomes part of one's personal history. This transforms the images from unfinished (seemingly present) experience to past history. Once narrative closure and verbal coding is achieved, the images are no longer dissociated (Gantt & Tinnin, 2007).

As a treatment for PTSD, art therapy operates on multiple levels simultaneously, addressing immediate symptoms as well as underlying conditions that cause symptoms to persist. The American Art Therapy Association identified four major contributions of art therapy to the treatment of PTSD, which include reducing anxiety and mood disorders; reducing behaviors that interfere with emotional and cognitive functioning; externalizing, verbalizing, and resolving memories of traumatic events; and reactivating positive emotions, self-worth, and self-esteem (American Art Therapy Association [AATA], 2012). Art therapy can assist in gaining access to traumatic images and memories. If, as stated earlier, the encoding of traumatic memories involves a visual process, then it would follow that a visual media offers a unique means by which these memories may more easily become conscious.

In addition to the preceding text, descriptions by art therapists of the benefits of art therapy with several traumatized populations point to its effectiveness. These include the following—in the area of sexual abuse (Anderson, 1995; Gil, 2006; Powell & Faherty, 1990) and in the area of trauma resulting from war and natural disasters (Byers, 1996; Howie, Burch, Conrad, & Shambaugh, 2002; Roje, 1995).

Intensive Trauma Therapy Approach and the Graphic Narrative

Gantt and Tinnin (2000, 2007, 2013) have devised the *graphic narrative*, a uniquely art-based approach for treating simple and complex PTSD. It is structured such that the trauma narrative can be pictorial rather than verbal. Indeed, visual imagery is vital for the symbolic processing involved in constructing a trauma narrative. The graphic narrative format adheres to that of instinctive trauma response (Tinnin & Gantt, 2000) and includes the following nine pictures:

- A before picture
- The *startle*, a predictable alarm response to perceived danger
- *Thwarted intention*, when the urge to escape is foiled
- The *freeze* with its instinctual physiological components of immobility, analgesia, and emotional numbing
- The *altered state of consciousness* manifested by altered time sense, depersonalization, and derealization
- The *body sensations*, which are the nonverbal bodily perceptions during the altered state that tends to return later as physical symptoms such as pain, gagging, or gasping for air
- The state of *automatic obedience* in which the person may show a form of obedient catatonia or automaton-like behavior

- The phase of *self-repair*—when pain returns, wound care and self-repair ensue, along with the aftermath of grief and anger
- The after picture when the event is finally relegated to the past (Gantt & Tinnin, 2013).

According to Gantt and Tinnin (2007), the major difficulty in achieving narrative closure is that the conscious mind has its own verbal memory of the trauma that usually does not admit the existence of other images, and hence seals over any gaps of recall. Even when the verbal mind has forgotten the event or has only a repressed memory of it, the dissociated images in the non-verbal memory remain inaccessible. The repressed memory might be recalled by verbal questioning but the dissociated memory will not be accessed this way. Because it is not verbally coded, the memory remains unconscious, in parallel within the repressed memory. The problem for the therapist becomes how to bypass the verbal mind with all of its conscious and repressed content, to gain access to dissociated nonverbal memory (Gantt & Tinnin, 2013). The graphic narrative gains access by drawing. While the verbal mind claims total ownership of the body and its actions, it fools itself about drawing. According to Gantt and Tinnin, during the process of drawing, the person's hand obeys nonverbal commands on par with the verbal. This will be important in the following case study, as the client literally does not know consciously what her hand has drawn. It is only after the therapist points this out that the client consciously "sees" what she has drawn. Because both verbal and nonverbal aspects of the brain have input into the motor commands for each hand, nonverbal motor control can trump verbal motor control. Therefore, a person's drawing may be as influenced by unconscious, nonverbal intention as much as by conscious, verbal will; in other words, "the hand remembers what the mind forgets" (2013, p. 59).

Although the subject runs a risk of emotional reenactment when drawing dissociated images, the risk greatly diminishes when the point of narrative closure is reached (Gantt & Tinnin, 2013). Fortunately, the nature of the drawing task creates some emotional distance from the event since the pictures can be viewed at a physical distance and as "out there" (Gantt & Tinnin, 2007). There are other ways to help the artist avoid being drawn into the trauma scenes, such as using a floor plan of the area where the trauma occurred.

It helps to maintain emotional distance if the entire graphic narrative is drawn in the "observer mode." The artist draws himself or herself in every picture and avoids drawing a scene "as seen" at the time of the trauma. Both "before" and "after" pictures help the artist view the narrative as historical (Gantt & Tinnin, 2013).

When the artist successfully completes the graphic narrative and avows it as personal history, then any intrusive symptoms that were due to this trauma should cease within a few days (Gantt & Tinnin, 2007). If this is not the case, then either the processing was incomplete or the symptoms most likely relate to another trauma. Once narrative closure and verbal coding is achieved, the images are no longer dissociated. The traumatized individual is then freer to interact with others in a more open way, to allow more of his/her inner world to emerge, and to perceive the environment as less threatening and frightening (Gantt & Tinnin, 2013).

Case Study Using the Intensive Trauma Therapy (ITT) Method

The author has been using the ITT method to treat individuals with a trauma history for a decade in her outpatient art therapy practice.

Debra (pseudonym), a 40-year-old woman, entered treatment because each day she had to drive by the house where she was molested when she was 14 years old. At the time, she worked for a large, inter-denominational company where she was the assistant to the CEO. She was also going to night school in the graphic arts.

Early history

Debra's early memories included her mother and father fighting while she was left in her bedroom alone. Debra had significant losses, which included her sister dying of SIDS when Debra was aged 3 years and the sister was 6 months old. After the death of her sister, her father pressured her mother to have an abortion rather than have a third child. She remembered pornography being shown in her house from the time she was aged 5 years.

Not surprisingly, Debra's mother and father were divorced when she reached age 7. After the divorce, she visited her father every other weekend, but was often taken care of by her father's girlfriends and sometimes saw her father very little during these "visits." When she was aged around 7 years, Debra remembered sexual play (touching) with her dad's girlfriend's son. Debra's father remarried when she was 13; her mother never remarried. At 14, Debra's 20-year-old boyfriend's father molested her. Debra and her father were estranged, although she had recently made contact with him and considered seeing him at some point in the future. Debra's feeling was that her father always wanted a boy and was disappointed that she was a girl.

Debra felt that she had only one significant relationship with a man during her early adulthood from the ages of 18 to 21 years. She described this young man as her best friend, and fully expected to marry him someday. She became pregnant with this man's child at age 19. With Debra's mother's urging, her boyfriend talked Debra into having an abortion. [Debra has since had two subsequent abortions from pregnancies with different men since her relationship ended with this man]. After Debra and her boyfriend broke up, he was diagnosed with HIV from someone he was seeing after their relationship ended.

Debra described herself as having been promiscuous and a heavy alcohol user. In her early 30s, her home was repossessed, and she was fired from her job due to her unreliable work performance. She had been alcohol-free for the last couple of years, and her promiscuity had decreased. The impetus for change, according to her, was that she saw herself being treated badly, and felt she did not deserve this. Her promiscuity also decreased as a result of giving up alcohol. Her abstinence coincided with making three serious suicide attempts where she took 300 pills over the course of 1 week. She decided suicide was another thing at which she had failed. In 2002, she became a born-again Christian and no longer considered suicide as an escape. She was on no medication. She had uterine cancer in her 30s, which resulted in a radical hysterectomy. The resulting inability to have children was another loss, although she felt that she would be ill-prepared to nurture a child, given her background.

Treatment

One of the earliest discussions with Debra was to help her figure a way to reach her work without going by the house, which required her to take a longer route and added time to her commute. This was done to assist her in the short term until she was able to process this trauma. At the time of treatment, she did not drive by this area, as she had a new job and had moved since the first meeting.

Part of the preparation for trauma treatment entailed several self-report scales, such as the Dissociative events scale, Impact of events scale, Symptom checklist-45 (see Tinnin & Gantt, 2000, for a complete listing of scales), before undergoing treatment to assess her ability to utilize this approach. Debra's testing indicated that she was ready to process her traumas, and that she had good resources to cope with what would emerge. Trauma treatment was indicated.

As another aspect of preparation for trauma processing, each client is shown a video that explains the ITT approach (Gantt & Tinnin, 1999). After watching it, Debra identified most with the "altered state of consciousness" and "automatic obedience" portions of the trauma response. Debra said that, at one point, she thought she was schizophrenic as she could see herself doing things that she did not want to do. She also described zoning out, part of the out-of-body experience. Debra let people tell her what to do, which may be a sign that she was stuck in the automatic obedience stage. When she discussed her behavior, she was relieved to find that much of what she described was due to her trauma, which was treatable.

Each client was asked to make a "safe place" picture in order to assist with grounding, should that become necessary. The client is told to look at the safe place when he or she becomes disassociated. This can be a drawing, or some other form of expression such as a sand tray, which is then photographed. The safe place picture is displayed each time the person attends a therapy session. Debra's safe place picture was a balcony from four or five stories up, from which she could see the ocean. She said that she could be alone and contemplative in this safe place.

Debra's trauma list was three typed pages long. Some of the traumas she listed are considered "small t" traumas, or the times she was embarrassed and stressed. Out of this list, she highlighted the traumas that were to be addressed by processing with the ITT method.

When Debra described her mother, she talked about someone whose fear of being alone was so great that she could never tell anyone "no." Debra gave an example of when she was a teenager, asking her mother if she could bring a 26-year-old into her room, and her mother agreed to let this happen. Debra believed this was a major problem for her as well. She felt that if she said "no" or asserted herself, she would be alone. This was both automatic obedience and related to her feeling of being unworthy and damaged; she equated loneliness with being bad. These were issues with which she had struggled her entire life, remembering her early memory of being alone in her room.

Figure 36.1 Graphic narrative—safe place.

In order to demonstrate the process and give the client a template for subsequent processing, it is suggested that the client complete a graphic narrative of a preverbal crib trauma or a baby in distress. The client is first asked to relax, and then asked to assume the position of the hidden observer (Hilgard, 1977), so that she will have some distance from and not relive the trauma. Debra showed an ability to relax and to utilize the hidden observer mode, which Gantt and Tinnin (2013) assert occurs around 90% of the time. She was asked to recall the house where she lived when she was aged 1 or 1½ years. She was able to visualize the kitchen in this home, but found nobody home when she was asked to look around. The hidden observer was instructed to go outside the house and wait until later in the year to go back; she went back to the house when she was 5 years of age and her parents were watching porn movies.

These were movies they were showing on a large movie projector in the living room with other couples. Her before picture occurred when she and her cousin were playing upstairs and wanted to go downstairs to be with their parents. Her cousin hung back but Debra started to creep down the stairs. She saw a big projection screen and people seeming upset and they seemed afraid. She was frightened by the images on the screen (her freeze), and was seen by her father, who yelled at her to return to the bedroom or he would beat her. Debra was worried that she might have been "turned on" by the movies as a child, but after discussing this, it was more likely that she was confused and frightened by what she saw. She states that she was aroused by pornography as an adult.

After her freeze, Debra and her cousin ran back upstairs. An 18-year-old male cousin was sent upstairs to help settle the girls and to get them to return to their beds. This cousin came in and began playing with them on the bed. This was shown in Debra's self-repair picture.

In processing this trauma, Debra's hand had indeed remembered what her mind had forgotten. Her 18-year-old cousin had been downstairs watching pornography and had

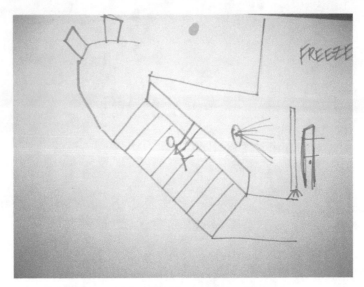

Figure 36.2   Graphic narrative—the freeze.

Figure 36.3   Graphic narrative—self repair.

been aroused by these movies. In her self-repair picture, Debra shows him with an erect penis. It was clear that Debra had depicted something of vital importance. She had learned at the tender age of 5 to associate comfort and self-repair with a man who was sexually aroused. She had no conscious memory of what she had shown. Her promiscuous behavior seemed to make sense. Arousing men was her attempt to receive comfort and caring from her environment. In fact, she was not aware of this when I re-presented the trauma, as I retold it just as Debra had. I did not point out the difference in how she had drawn her 18-year-old cousin and other figures. It was also apparent that, in her after picture, the cousin still had genitalia but was no longer aroused.

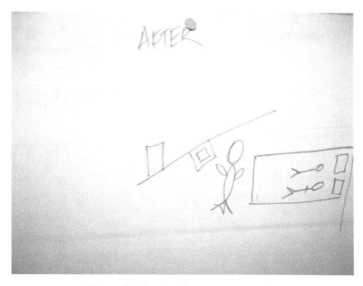

Figure 36.4 Graphic narrative—after.

At the beginning of the next session, Debra said she had "spaced out" when she left the previous session, and that she was distracted while at school that evening. Since she had disassociated, we talked about grounding. She took a grounding stone with her, which she carried at all times.

During this session, her graphic narrative was considered. It became clear that she was not going to recognize what she had drawn, so it was pointed out to her. She seemed surprised and interested, and I made the connection that she had talked about promiscuity, and that it would make sense that an aroused man would mean that she was attempting to soothe that little part of herself when she was frightened and lonely. The distinction was stressed that the little girl would be looking for comfort and love, and would not be able to deal with what followed in an adult male's body. If this were an attempt at self-repair, she would look for someone thinking that they would hold and contain her fears, only to have their adult bodies become aroused so that she would be required to have sex in order not to be abandoned and shamed. She acknowledged that this made sense to her, and that this might be an aspect of her feeling that men were taking advantage of, and that she could not say no to them.

The next part of ITT trauma processing is a video or written externalized dialogue. The written dialogue was used, since video equipment was not available in the office. The client was asked to write to the traumatized self with her dominant hand and answer as the child part with her non-dominant hand. Debra did not want to use her non-dominant hand, but elected to use orange for her adult part and red for her child part. The externalized dialogue is a method that enables the client to acknowledge the part, and to soothe and reintegrate the feelings and disavowed emotions associated with the trauma. Debra wrote to this little 5-year-old part of her, asking that she talk to her so she could get to know her better. At one point, she wrote "I love you" to the child and then scribbled over it. When discussing this dialogue, Debra said it was not something that she would say to that little part. She could not remember her father saying this to her, and her mother had only said it to her a couple of times. She

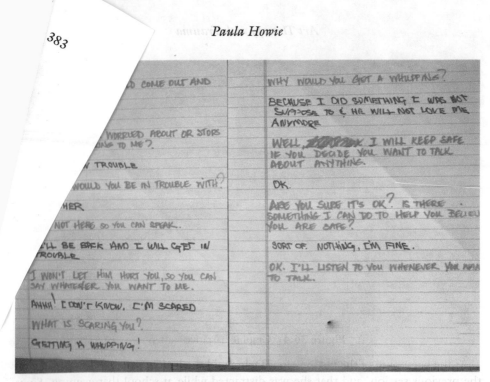

COME OUT AND	WHY WOULD YOU GET A WHUPPASS?
	BECAUSE I DID SOMETHING I WAS NOT SUPPOSE TO & HE WILL NOT LOVE ME ANYMORE
WORRIED ABOUT OR STOPS ... TO ME ?	WELL, ~~XXXXX~~ I WILL KEEP SAFE IF YOU DECIDE YOU WANT TO TALK ABOUT ANYTHING.
TROUBLE	
WOULD YOU BE IN TROUBLE WITH?	OK.
HER	ARE YOU SURE IT'S OK? IS THERE SOMETHING I CAN DO TO HELP YOU BELIEV YOU ARE SAFE?
NOT HERE SO YOU CAN SPEAK.	
'LL BE BACK AND I WILL GET IN TROUBLE	SORT OF. NOTHING, I'M FINE.
I WON'T LET HIM HURT YOU, SO YOU CAN SAY WHATEVER YOU WANT TO ME.	OK. I'LL LISTEN TO YOU WHENEVER YOU ARE TO TALK.
AHHH! I DON'T KNOW. I'M SCARED	
WHAT IS SCARING YOU?	
GETTING A WHUPPING!	

Figure 36.5 Externalized dialogue.

said she had never loved herself. The dialogue is supportive, but there was still a lack of trust between the adult and child parts, which would need to be addressed in future sessions.

A week after this meeting, Debra emailed to say she was quitting treatment due to her finances. Even though she did have major monetary difficulties, the timing of this break was a concern, and I thought it might have to do with her discovery of the traumatized child part of herself by processing the trauma.

During the termination meeting, she talked about her work and how she was doing. I clarified that the child part really was attempting to secure closeness and not adult sex. Debra did say that she wanted to come back when finances would allow it, and she wanted to leave her pictures until she was able to return to treatment.

Conclusion

Although there were many reasons to think she would not return to treatment, Debra called about a year later and wanted to continue her trauma processing. She said she was especially interested in further treatment as she had gotten married to someone whom she really loved, and she wanted to see if the trauma processing would improve her life further. We talked about how the prior trauma processing had freed her up to be with someone who was interested in being with her as a person and not only as a sex object. She had been freed up for a different kind of relationship. To date, Debra and I have processed three of her "big T" traumas using the ITT approach, and she continues to benefit from these interventions.

As Gantt and Tinnin (2013) have written, trauma processing can allow the individual to put the traumatic event in the past, and to interact in the present with more confidence and with more assurance that what is occurring internally is reflected more accurately in their lives. Debra continues to benefit from the ITT approach, in that she is able to make different choices for herself and to embrace the possibility that she may live in the present without being compelled to re-experience her traumatic past.

References

Anderson, F. (1995). Catharsis and empowerment through group clay work with incest survivors. *The Arts in Psychotherapy, 22*(5), 413–427.

American Psychiatric Association. (2013). American Psychiatric Association: Desk Reference to the Diagnostic Criteria From DSM-5. Arlington, VA: American Psychiatric Association.

American Art Therapy Association, Inc. (2013). Art therapy, posttraumatic stress disorder, and service members [Electronic Version]. Retrieved August 30, 2012 from www.arttherapy.org/upload/file/RMveteransPTSD.pdf

Byers, J. (1996). Children of the stones: Art therapy interventions in the West Bank. *Art Therapy: Journal of the American Art Therapy Association, 13*, 238–243.

Collie, K., Backos, A., Malchiodi, C., & Spiegel, D. (2006). Art therapy for combat related PTSD: recommendations for research and practice. *Art Therapy: Journal of the American Art Therapy Association, 23*(4), 157–164.

Ecker, B., Ticic, R., & Hulley, L. (2012). *Unlocking the emotional brain: Eliminating symptoms at their roots uing memory reconsolidation.* New York: Routledge.

Foa, E. B., Hembree, E. A., & Rothbaum, B. O. (2007). *Prolonged exposure therapy for PTSD: Emotional processing of traumatic experiences, therapist guide.* New York, NY: Oxford University Press.

Foa, E. B., Keane, T. M., & Friedman, M. J. (2000). *Effective treatment for PTSD.* New York, NY: Guilford.

Ford, J. D., Courtois, C. A., Steele, K., Van der Hart, O., & Nijenhuis, E. R. S. (2005). Treatment of complex posttraumatic self-dysregulation. *Journal of Traumatic Stress, 18*(5), 437–447.

Friedman, M. J. (2006). Posttraumatic stress disorder among military returnees from Afghanistan and Iraq. *American Journal of Psychiatry, 163*(4), 586–593.Gantt, L., & Tinnin, L. W. (2000). *The trauma recovery institute treatment manual.* Morgantown, WV: Gargoyle Press.

Gantt, L., & Tinnin, L. W. (2007). Intensive trauma therapy of PTSD and dissociation: An outcome study. *The Arts in Psychotherapy, 34*(1), 69–80.

Gantt, L., & Tinnin, L. W. (2013). *The instinctual trauma response dual-brain dynamics: A guide for trauma therapy.* Intensive Trauma Therapy, Inc.:Morgantown, VW.

Gil, E. (2006). *Helping abused and traumatized children: integrating directive and nondirective approaches.* New York, NY: Guilford Press.

Hilgard, E. (1977). *Divided consciousness: Multiple controls in human thought and action.* New York, NY: Wiley.

Howie, P., Burch, B., Conrad, S., & Shambaugh, S. (2002). Releasing trapped images: Children grapple with the reality of the September 11 attacks. *Art Therapy: Journal of the American Art Therapy Association, 19*, 100–104.

Kaiser, D., Dunne, M., Malchiodi, C., Feen, H., Howie, P., Cutcher, D., & Ault, R. (2005). Call for art therapy research on treatment for PTSD. *American Art Therapy Association website* (www.arttherapy.org).

Morgan, C. A., & Johnson, D. R. (1995). Use of a drawing task in the treatment of nightmares in combat-related post-traumatic stress disorder. *Art Therapy: Journal of the American Art Therapy Association, 12,* 244–247.

Powell, L., & Faherty, S. L. (1990). Treating sexually abused latency aged girls: A 20 session treatment plan utilizing group process and the creative arts therapies. *The Arts in Psychotherapy, 17,* 35–47.

Roje, J. (1995). LA '94 earthquake in the eyes of children: Art therapy with elementary school children who were victims of disaster. *Art Therapy: Journal of the American Art Therapy Association, 12,* 237–243.

Schacter, D. L. (1987). Implicit memory: history and current status. *Journal of Experimental Psychology: Learning, Memory, and Cognition, 13,* 501–518.

Shapiro, R. (2010). *The trauma treatment handbook: Protocols across the spectrum.* New York, NY: W.W. Norton.

Spinner, J. (2007). War's pain, softened with a brush stroke. *The Washington Post.* Sunday, April 15, 2007.

Tinnin, L., & Gantt, L. (2000). *Manual of trauma therapy.* Morgantown, WV: Gargoyle Press.

Van der Kolk, B. A., & Fisler, R. (1995). Dissociation and the fragmentary nature of traumatic memories: Overview and exploratory study. *Journal of Traumatic Stress, 8*(4), 505–525.

37

Art Therapy and Eating Disorders
Margaret Hunter

Therapists working within a framework of positive thinking and creative expression have a distinct advantage in the treatment of eating disorders. By the time a person experiencing symptoms seeks therapy, he or she may have been stereotyped and judged by people and systems they have interacted with. They may not trust others to see them for who they really are. Above all, they may not trust their own perception of self. The inability to see beyond a narrow and skewed definition of self has been established and reinforced by an internal eating disorder voice. People who enter art therapy treatment benefit from the art therapist's ability to recognize and appreciate the unique qualities of each individual. Reindl (2002), author of *Sensing the Self: Women's Recovery from Bulimia*, has discussed Kadison's (1993) findings that a client's preparedness to join with the therapist in working toward recovery occurs in an ephemeral state, so the possibility for intervention must be maximized while willingness to seek help exists. Thus, it is during the first session that the therapist must able to capitalize on the process of joining with the client in a creative atmosphere that promotes trust and hope.

The first art therapy session is one of the most important aspects of treatment for individuals with eating disorders. The initial session introduces the client to the style of the art therapist and the general feel of how art is used therapeutically. The artistic development of positive affirmation statements and imagery establishes the foundation necessary to reduce fear and sustain hope in the healing process. In this chapter, I will explore the aspects of art therapy that best assist the individual with recovery from an eating disorder. The focus will be on the initial session of art therapy and the perceptions of art therapy based on interviews with three participants, each diagnosed with an eating disorder.

The Multidisciplinary Team

In order to address the complex, multi-faceted aspects of eating disorders, art therapists must join with other members of a multidisciplinary team to determine appropriate levels of treatment and treatment goals. According to Zerbe (1993), there is a continuum of eating pathologies; a spectrum that contains common concerns about weight

The Wiley Handbook of Art Therapy, First Edition. Edited by David E. Gussak and Marcia L. Rosal.
© 2016 John Wiley & Sons, Ltd. Published 2016 by John Wiley & Sons, Ltd.

and dieting, as well as entrenched thoughts and behaviors that indicate the diagnosis of an eating disorder. Therefore, a team of professionals, each with a specific role, is needed to monitor a client's status. Zerbe (2008) found another significant benefit of working with other professionals: "Being part of a multi-disciplinary team helps the clinician avoid burnout and the tendency to fall into the all too common clinical trap of trying to become the patient's rescuer or savior" (p. 36).

The treatment team, which typically consists of a physician, registered dietician, and a psychotherapist, observes the client's medical, nutritional, and psychological status. The team may also include a psychiatrist and a family therapist. The art therapist joins with the client to explore the inner world where the eating disorder has assumed a position of influence and/or control.

The Voice of the Eating Disorder

Individuals presenting for treatment of an eating disorder commonly report feeling fearful that the therapist has an underlying agenda. An internal eating disorder voice may convince the client that the therapist will form judgments based on appearance, particularly weight. Clients often suspect that the therapist's goal is to force changes in body size or to try to control product use and/or amount of exercise. Maisel, Epston, and Bordon (2004) stressed the importance of understanding the stronghold that the eating disorder has on the client by means of an anorexic/bulimic (a/b) voice. This internal voice is persuasive and affects the way a person perceives the self and the world.

According to Maisel et al. (2004), "… a/b seeks, covertly, to knock a person to her knees so that, in desperation and despair, she will be inclined to invest her hopes in its promises and reassurance" (p. 22). Consequently therapy may be viewed as an invasive process that has the potential to bring protected thoughts, beliefs, and behaviors into light for judgment and extinction. The fear of loss of control and the potential for increased shame leads to heightened anxiety. Use of art in the first session helps to reduce anxiety and resistance to the therapeutic process.

The Importance of the Initial Art Therapy Session

During the course of an eating disorder, a client's capacity for meaningful hope may be diminished. The hope that becomes familiar is superficial and dependent on body size and overall appearance. Negative beliefs that a client develops are reinforced by the immediate environment and/or society at large. Many clients come to counseling because a friend, family member, or health provider insisted they do so, rather than from a strong belief that they can get better. The belief that change is *unlikely* fuels a sense of hopelessness in the recovery process. The act of engaging in an art process to develop a positive affirmation may help to create a shift in the way that a client conceptualizes the possibility for improvement in quality of life and recovery. Buchalter (2009) described the benefits of developing affirmations in the art process: "Creating a tangible piece of art that reflects the feeling of the chosen affirmation can enhance its effectiveness and increase self-esteem" (p. 200). People affected by eating disorders often forget about their own creative nature. The eating disorder voice demands constant accountability relating to numbers: weight, calories, measurements of food, clothing sizes, and amount of exercise are common preoccupations. Frequently, people report that they have given up drawing or painting or no longer play the instrument that brought them joy, release, and a sense of accomplishment. The initial art therapy session has the potential to reawaken a person's association with art and emotions. Hass-Cohen (2008) stated, "Many clients report that the sense of well-being, pleasure and reward felt during and after the creation of art is profound and fundamental to their change processes" (p. 298). Development of positive affirmations in the form of written word and imagery helps to instill the hope necessary for transformation and healing.

For the initial art therapy session, a wide variety of positive affirmation cards are provided. Affirmation cards are available to clinicians and the general public and may be found online and in most bookstores. They are cards with images, often symbolic in nature, with encouraging words and/or statements. The use of an affirmation card during an art therapy session has the potential to create sustainable change. If the client decides not to return for additional treatment, he or she leaves with a reminder that beauty and hope exist and may be found within the creative process.

Perceptions of Art Therapy

To underscore the importance of the first session in art therapy for individuals with an eating disorder, I interviewed three participants. Each participant was diagnosed with an eating disorder. The purpose of the interviews was to gather perceptions of the introductory process used in treatment.

Before I met with each participant, client information and consent forms were completed, and an appropriate level of treatment was determined. Each woman participating in this process was diagnosed with an eating disorder by a healthcare professional, and all were new to art therapy. For the purpose of this chapter, I asked the women specific questions about their experience of this art process. The art therapy session lasted approximately 1 hour.

I met with each woman individually for this initial art therapy session. Upon entrance into the room, the women were invited to choose a place at a 6' table. Art materials were set up in the center of the table, with two pieces of 12" x 18" papers positioned next to each other. A chair was placed in front of each paper. The table setting appeared similar to the setting for a meal (see Figure 37.1). Makin (2000) has described the work of British art therapist Schaverian. She said Schevarian discussed the "physical presence" of food and art materials. Makin says, "as a mother provides her child with food, an art therapist offers art materials to her patient" (p. 44). The table with art supplies becomes a metaphor for the table set with food, both providing a kind of nourishment.

After choosing a seat, participants were encouraged to take a few moments to explore the art materials and affirmation cards. The art supplies were positioned strategically, based on qualities of structure/control associated with each material.

Figure 37.1   The table setting.

Colored pencils were placed in the direct center where they could be easily seen and accessed. Hinz (2006) described the benefits of colored pencils: "Some people find great pleasure working with them because of the feeling of control that this more restrictive medium offers" (p. 17). Hinz encouraged use of two types of pastels, oil and chalk, because of the differences in qualities, including how they blend. Both types of pastels were placed on one side of the colored pencils. Hinz found that fluid materials, such as watercolor paints, have the potential to evoke emotion. Watercolor paints and watercolor pencils were on the other side of the colored pencils. Instrumental music, combined with sounds of nature, played softly in the background.

Sitting directly next to each participant, I described the benefits of positive statements and imagery to help develop new ways of conceptualizing the self and the world. I explained that the words on the cards may counter negative messages asserted by the eating disorder voice, and that many of the statements reflect how we would *like* to think and feel rather than how we actually feel. The directive given was: "Select any art materials you would like to use to develop the message of the affirmation card/s you choose." I worked on development of my own affirmation card during the art-making process (this was addressed in the comments made by the women). While creating a simple design on my own paper, I frequently glanced over at the client to maintain a sense of interest and connection. The drawing process for each person took approximately 30 minutes. The interviews and completed drawings for each participant are discussed in the following text.

Becky

Becky, a 23-year-old graduate student, was referred to art therapy by her primary therapist. She had received treatment for anorexia for several years, and had made some progress. Because Becky was very creative, her therapist thought that she may benefit from art therapy treatment.

When Becky first came into the art room, she appeared hesitant and guarded. She quickly chose her seat, and avoided eye contact for several moments. She looked at the items on the table while I described the purpose of using affirmation cards. During the interview, which occurred after the session, she said that she began to relax when she saw the art materials and colorful cards on the table. She said she felt "very relieved" when she discovered that she could work in silence during the art process if she wanted to. She said, "I felt like I could spend time, sit down, and have a moment."

She reported that the directive felt too broad at first; however, she was able to conceptualize what she wanted to do when I provided examples of developed affirmation cards. She looked through the cards on the table carefully and selected one with the theme of *loving the self.*

Becky quickly chose watercolors to work with, a medium she had used before. She said she felt comfortable with the materials and was glad that she had several types available to her. She stated, "I felt I could be as creative as I wanted to be, I was not restrained." She found that she was aware of the potential to express her feelings with the paints, and commented that "the watercolors would let me become emotional if I wanted to."

Becky described what she referred to as her "need for perfection." She said that the free-flowing images on the affirmation cards helped her to "let go" of her desire to create a perfect image. Becky addressed how she felt about having me sit next to her while working on my own card: "I felt like I wasn't alone, like I had company." She remarked, "it was cool having someone work with me."

Becky discussed the subject matter in her drawing and commented that the wolf, the bird, and the cat do not typically get along with each other (see Figure 37.2). In fact, they are often enemies who cause harm to each other. She noted that they "coexist" on the paper, and this gave her hope that different parts of her can live together without doing harm to each other. She thought that human beings can learn more about loving themselves from the "loving, innocent world of animals." She articulated that it was important to have the words "I am loved" at the *center* of the paper because the center is "where everything begins inside of us." Becky described frequent, negative thoughts about herself, and she expressed surprise that she was able to give "voice" to her ideas so clearly today. She expressed a desire to continue working with positive affirmations.

Vanessa

Vanessa, a 34-year-old married professional woman, was self-referred to art therapy because of her desire to "work on body and mental health issues through art." Vanessa had been told by medical providers that a recent miscarriage was likely caused by overeating and excessive body weight. Vanessa began to cry as she sat down at the table; she described feeling like a "failure ... [who] harmed my baby."

Figure 37.2 I am loved.

Vanessa expressed her desire to live a "healthy life," which would include feeling at peace with her body. She revealed that "hatred" of her body caused her to overeat and then experience overwhelming feelings of shame and disgust. She was diagnosed with binge eating disorder.

After several moments of general discussion, the items on the table seemed to capture Vanessa's attention. She looked at the art materials and cards with considerable interest, and asked if these things were for kids who came to art therapy. She seemed surprised when I told her that we would be using the materials in the art therapy session.

She took several moments to look through the positive affirmation cards and seemed to have trouble finding one to work with because, as she disclosed, "I don't feel the way any of these say." It was clarified that she could choose a card that contained a thought or feeling that she would *like* to have. She asked to make a brief list of things that she wanted and needed in her life, and then selected a card based on those needs. The theme of the card she chose was *love and appreciation of body*.

Once Vanessa selected her affirmation card, she touched the different art materials and selected colored pencils and oil pastels. She reported that she had become insecure about art in college because her work was critiqued. She found that she felt at ease using colored pencils for the basic structure of her drawing, and oil pastels, which would allow for more expression of emotion.

Vanessa stated that she felt comfortable sitting next to me at the table. She said that my participation validated the importance of the art process. She verbalized that this helped her to feel "accepted." She said that, if I had sat across from her in the process, she may have felt very self-conscious, fearful that I would be watching and judging, and added that the music helped create a calm environment.

Vanessa said that the art therapy session today felt very different from talk therapy sessions because she was able to "create evidence of what is in my head." She

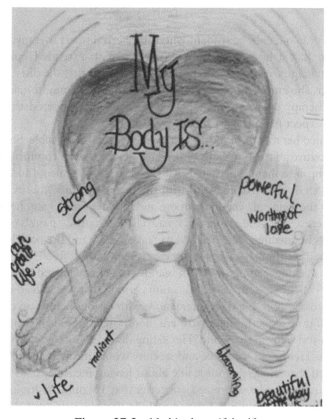

Figure 37.3 My big, beautiful self.

revealed that she felt like she had used her heart and mind to help create her drawing. She expressed that she appreciated having a "witness" to her drawing process today.

Vanessa was tearful as she described her anger regarding the stereotypes that she had dealt with "because of my large body" (see Figure 37.3). She reported that she also heard negative comments about her body in her own mind. She depicted herself naked in her drawing in an attempt to appreciate her body, perhaps even love her body one day. She described things that her body allows her to do: walk, run, work, and *possibly* create life. She carefully selected a gold pastel for her skin because "that color is beautiful and radiant." She ignored the negative talk of the eating disorder voice, and allowed herself to appreciate her body and hope for a future of peace within herself.

Vanessa described her plans to continue to work with affirmations in anticipation that she might love and accept herself in the moment she is in, rather than wait to love herself at a lower weight. Vanessa noticed that the negative voice was fairly quiet during the art process today. The positive statements she said out loud strengthened her resolve to work toward the life of her dreams. During this first session, she experienced *hope*. The affirmation and drawing will help her to remember that hope.

Terri

Terri was a 28-year-old college student who was referred to art therapy by her primary therapist. Terri had a history of bulimia nervosa with extended episodes of food restriction to manage weight. Terri repeatedly mentioned that she did not have artistic talent; however, she enjoyed being creative and thought she might gain some benefit from the art therapy process. She appeared nervous and reported that she did not know what to expect from the art therapy session.

Terri was invited her to look at the art materials and cards on the table. She reported that she had used positive affirmation cards earlier, and seemed to gain comfort and confidence as she looked through them. She stated that she liked the statements and images on the cards. Terri selected an affirmation card with the theme of *inner serenity and peace*. She commented on the music playing in the room and found it was helping her relax.

She was interested in the materials I had chosen to use (pastels) and expressed curiosity about the medium. She decided to "take a risk" and use pastels in part of her drawing, and said, "I think it's ok to get messy if I am having fun." Terri used the pencils to develop a bridge leading out to an island. She acknowledged this current period of her life (as a college student) as a "transition period" that would lead to an uncertain future. She discussed both the daily interactions with various people on campus and the long periods of time alone in her apartment, and how both led to contemplations on her worthiness and value in the world. Her eating disorder voice was very strong during the alone times. Her hopes for peace and serenity would mean a quieting of this voice.

Terri revealed that she felt comfortable about having me sit next to her, as she was not being "stared at." She expressed concerns that I would be looking at her and judging her weight; she thought I may conclude that she was "not thin enough" to seek treatment for an eating disorder. She described her experience with providers who did not think she had a problem because she maintained average weight.

Terri disclosed that her drawing depicted an actual place that she had discovered on campus (see Figure 37.4). She said the place had a large pond with a small island in the middle, and that she went there whenever she could to "focus on quiet when life is chaotic." She found that this place gave her hope for learning how to relax and "not think negatively." She revealed that the negative eating disorder voice in her mind was hard to silence at times because of all the mistakes she had made. She described a general sense of feeling "unworthy" in most environments and in relationships she encountered in life.

Terri concurred that she would like to continue to work with positive affirmations. She agreed to challenge herself to create artistic images to go with her affirmations. The process helped her to realize that, similar to the turtle in her image, she could go to the pond or island in her imagination if she became anxious or fearful of the world. She paralleled the process of the turtle moving inward and isolating itself from the world to her own process of retreating to her apartment in order to "shut out" the world around her. She acknowledged her potential to stay present with the world and agreed that taking brief moments to recall the place of serenity and peace would be helpful.

The art therapy environment created the structure needed for freedom of expression in the art process. The seating arrangement at the table and the participation of the art therapist reduced fears of being watched or judged. The women agreed that the positive affirmation images developed in the art process could continue to inspire and instill hope throughout the recovery process.

Figure 37.1 Standing, still.

Conclusion

There is a significant amount of work and research being done to increase the understanding of how art therapy may be used most effectively in the treatment of eating disorders. In this short chapter, it was not possible to cover all the contemporary treatment issues. For example, there is much discussion about how symptoms transfer into the art process itself. The unique therapeutic qualities of art therapy will become evident if art therapists carefully attend to each client.

When clients are invited to the art therapy table, the promise of self-acceptance and recovery is served. A sense of connection and trust is developed when meals of creativity are shared. For each client, from the initial session and throughout the therapeutic process, the aim of art therapy is to uncover the light that exists within the darkness of despair.

References

Buchalter, S. I. (2009). *Art therapy techniques and applications.* London: Jessica Kingsley Publishers.

Hass-Cohen, N. (2008). CREATE: Art therapy relational neuroscience principles (ATR-N). In N. Hass-Cohen & R. Carr (Eds.), *Art therapy and clinical neuroscience* (p. 283). London: Jessica Kingsley Publishers.

Hinz, L. D. (2006). *Drawing from within: Using art to treat eating disorders.* London: Jessica Kingsley Publishers.

Kadison, R. D. (May, 1993). Square peg in a round hole: Eating disorders and managed care. Presented at *Eating Disorders: A Multidimensional Focus,* sponsored by Anorexia Bulimia Care, Inc. Boston, MA.

Maisel, R., Epston, D., & Borden, A. (2004). *Biting the hand that starves you: Inspiring resistance to anorexia/bulimia.* New York, NY: W.W. Norton & Company.

Makin, S. R. (2000). *More than just a meal: The art of eating disorders.* London: Jessica Kingsley Publishers.

Reindl, S. R. (2002). *Sensing the self: Women's recovery from bulimia.* Cambridge: Harvard University Press.

Zerbe, K. (1993). *The body betrayed: Women, eating disorders and treatment.* Washington DC: American Psychiatric Press.

Zerbe, K. (2008). *Integrated treatment of eating disorders: Beyond the body betrayed.* New York, NY: W.W. Norton & Company, Inc.

38

Art Therapy, Homelessness, and Poverty

Holly Feen-Calligan

A veteran soldier is discharged from an inpatient facility and given a bus ticket. She is homeless.

Children report they cannot do their homework at home. There is no electricity, and they are hungry.

Responding to poverty and homelessness is becoming integral to the practice of art therapy. Inspired by students' internship and service-learning experiences, I have found the need to assist students as they encounter people who have been affected by these two key societal problems. The scope of this chapter encompasses: (1) current issues on poverty and homelessness; (2) a discussion of service-learning (Howard, 2001) and self-determination theory (SDT) (Ryan & Deci, 2000) as frameworks for understanding and addressing these problems; (3) art therapy interventions for people living in poverty or experiencing homelessness; and (4) examples of art therapy at a soup kitchen. Finally, a conversation is presented about compassion and self-care as significant components of professional practice for professionals whose work addresses poverty and homelessness.

Poverty and Homelessness

In 2010, 15.1% of all persons in the United States were living in poverty, the highest percentage since 1993 (National Poverty Center, n.d.)—and more than one in five were children (Macartney, 2011). Two measures are used to define poverty in the United States. The *poverty threshold* represents the annual amount of cash income minimally required to support families of various sizes, and it is calculated annually by the US Bureau of the Census (2012). For example, in 2011, a family of four was considered to be living in poverty if their annual income was less than US$23,021. Poverty thresholds are used for statistical purposes such as preparing estimates of the number of Americans living in poverty. *Poverty guidelines* are issued each year in the Federal Register by the US Department of Health and Human Services (2012). A simplification of the poverty thresholds, the *guidelines* are used for administrative

The Wiley Handbook of Art Therapy, First Edition. Edited by David E. Gussak and Marcia L. Rosal.
© 2016 John Wiley & Sons, Ltd. Published 2016 by John Wiley & Sons, Ltd.

purposes, such as determining financial eligibility for certain federal programs. An annual income of US$23,050 is the poverty guideline for a family of four (in the 48 states) to be eligible for assistance.

People living in poverty are at risk of becoming homeless. Between April 2008 and April 2009, the National Coalition for the Homeless (2009) found a 32% jump in the number of foreclosures, and since the start of the recession, a loss of 6 million jobs. The National Low Housing Coalition estimates that 7 million households living on very low incomes are at risk of foreclosure (National Coalition for the Homeless, 2009). In the past 20–25 years, the rise in homelessness has been attributed to the shortage of affordable rental housing and a simultaneous increase in poverty. These statistics suggest the likelihood that art therapists will encounter poor and homeless people in their practices.

A homeless person is defined in the 1994 Stewart B. McKinney Act as someone who "lacks a fixed regular and adequate night-time residence" (National Coalition for the Homeless, 2009, para. 1). Similar to poverty, homelessness is difficult to measure. *Point-in-time counts* estimate the number of people in shelters and on the streets on any given day or week. This measure misses many people, including those who may be residing temporarily with friends or relatives, or those living in their vehicles, and therefore might underrepresent the number of people who experience homelessness. However, because some people leave homelessness and others become homeless, the point-in-time counts may overestimate the number of chronically homeless people. *Period prevalence counts* attempt to measure chronic homelessness (National Coalition for the Homeless, 2009).

Homelessness can occur with a single unexpected crisis or expense. Factors contributing to homelessness include unemployment, underemployment, decreases in public safety net programs, rising housing costs, substance abuse, and lack of medical care (National Coalition for the Homeless, 2009). Poor and homeless people experience physical deprivation (malnutrition, exposure to health risks, lack of healthcare, and suitable housing) and psychosocial deprivation (knowledge, social participation, self-esteem, and competence; Sen cited in Daher & Haz, 2011). In addition, the external indicators of poverty, such as using food stamps, living in projects, and lacking material possessions, are stigmatizing, demoralizing, and humiliating (Camilleri, 2007).

Poverty adversely affects the health of adults, including contributing to anxiety and affective disorders (Daher & Haz, 2011). Homeless adults may also be at risk for substance abuse, mental illness, and/or domestic violence (Camilleri, 2007; Siddiqui, Astone-Twerell, & Hernitche, 2009). Chronically poor people are never secure about food or being able to take care of their health needs (Braun, 1997; Jyoti, Frongillo, & Jones, 2005).

Children growing up in poverty experience multiple stressors such as exposure to drugs, violence, overcrowded homes, trauma, depression, alienation, and increased risks of abuse that can impact their development (Anthony, King, & Austin, 2011; Cameron, 1996; Camilleri, 2007). Some mothers cannot recognize the needs of their children because they themselves are in crisis (Wadeson, 2000). Lack of proper nutrition affects brain development and can result in cognitive deficiencies and diminished academic progress (Anthony et al., 2011). Academic achievement is also affected by missing school due to poor health, lack of transportation to medical appointments, or access to healthcare (J. Haussler, personal communication, February, 7, 2012). Furthermore, the stress of living in unsafe environments produces fatigue, affecting children's abilities to focus (Anthony et al., 2011).

Programs addressing poverty and homelessness

Many government programs established to address poverty are successful in achieving their short-term objectives (e.g., reducing hunger), but fail to lessen the effects of poverty (e.g., affect food insecurity or long-term health). The emphasis of many programs is on the externally provided resources believed to reduce deficiencies or to stimulate positive change (Straub, 2011). Human agency, or the capacity to develop inner resources, receives far less attention, but developing inner resources is essential for people to be able to take full advantage of such programs (Straub, 2011). For example, many homeless people who have had the opportunity to participate in vocational or educational programs have difficulty finishing them due to unresolved and unaddressed post-traumatic stress disorder (PTSD; Cameron, 1996). They may be "crippled by institutional violence, and may have developed coping attitudes and behavior that prevent them from taking constructive steps" (Cameron, 1996, p. 183).

Helping poor and homeless people to develop their inner resources and strengths is essential for alleviating poverty over the long term and effectively augmenting the social programs or other external efforts to reduce deficits (Daher & Haz, 2011; Hopson & Lee, 2011). Strengthening capabilities such as imagination, thought, personal awareness, expression of emotions (Noltemeyer, Bush, Patton, & Bergen, 2012), motivation, and agency (Straub, 2011) can be accomplished regardless of financial, economic, or other external resources. Moreover, these capabilities can be fostered through art therapy.

Theoretical Underpinnings of Working with Homelessness and Poverty

SDT and service-learning provide a conceptual framework for understanding and responding to the needs of people living with poverty and homelessness. SDT (Ryan & Deci, 2000) is a theory of motivation about how the environment and a person's inner resources impact the desire and ability to satisfy needs for well-being. Service-learning (Howard, 2001) is a pedagogy with potential to facilitate self-determination skills among art therapy students grappling with questions on how to offer service to the population.

SDT

SDT proposes a continuum from least motivation (amotivation) to most motivation (intrinsic motivation or self-regulation). Motivation is related to mental health and well-being because it affects behaviors such as seeking assistance, taking medication, and following an aftercare plan. Human development ideally progresses toward intrinsic motivation and self-regulation, and this is facilitated through the process of developing the inner resources and basic needs of competence, autonomy, and the ability to relate to others. Furthermore, intrinsic motivation is facilitated when the social environment supports autonomy, competence, and relatedness. An environment or culture *not* conducive to meeting these basic needs, such as in cases of poverty and homelessness, often results in motivational deficits (Chirkov, Ryan, Kim, & Kaplan, 2003; Kane, 1987). People may fail to act on their own behalf if they have learned through repeated experience that they have no control over their environment (Kane, 1987).

Judging from their experiences in internships, art therapy students may also feel helpless in provide relevant service to people living in conditions of poverty and homelessness. A feeling of helplessness may be engendered by an environment or work setting that does not value art, or graduate art therapy programs that fail to teach students how to work for social justice (Junge, Finn Alvarez, Kellogg, & Volker, 1993).

Service-learning theory

Service-learning can assist students with developing advocacy skills through its emphasis on social responsibility learning. Service-learning refers to the integration of community service into academic curricula, where students offer their talents and abilities to meet a community need (often via a social service agency), and where the agency, its constituents, *and* the students work together to achieve goals agreed upon mutually (Howard, 2001). In this way, both the service recipients *and* providers receive from and give to one another, fostering solidarity and community (Daynes & Longo, 2004; Howard, 2001), and building relationships conducive to developing competence and autonomy. Franklin, Rothaus, and Schpok (2007) describe how, in service-learning, "an inner alchemy unfolds transforming one who sincerely offers his or her service" (p. 215).

Service-learning requires students to critically engage with problems and difficulties and to reflect on how they might contribute to solutions. Rather than following prescribed techniques, in service-learning, providers (students) and recipients work together to imagine strategies and co-create techniques for addressing problems. For students, autonomy, competence, and interpersonal skills are fostered in large part through their written and artistic reflections (Moon, 1999) throughout the service-learning assignment.

Art Therapy with Homelessness and Poverty

A number of publications describe art and art therapy interventions for people who are homeless (Allen, 2007; Arrington & Yorgin, 2001; Braun, 1997; Cameron, 1996; Davis, 1997; Feen-Calligan, 2008; Prescott, Sekendur, Bailey, & Hoshino, 2008; Prugh, 1987; Stokrocki, Sutton Andrews, & Saemundsdottir, 2004; Timm-Bottos, 2006). Wadeson (2000) documented the programs of several art therapists working with homeless individuals (Juliana Van der Ent-Zgoda, Anne Morrill, Suzanne Canby, Sarah Frahm, and Jean Durkin), and the problems growing out of poverty and drug culture, such as prostitution (Beth Black and Ximena Saloman). Art therapy with youth who are at risk because of poverty and related conditions are described by Camilleri (2007), Nelson (2010), and Wallace-DiGarbo and Hill (2006).

Wadeson (2000) explained that those using homeless shelters may be people who have lost their homes due to poverty; they may be immigrants or refugees, and/or people escaping violence and trauma. She found that adults living in shelters benefit from art therapy to help them adjust to their changing circumstances, and for relief, support, and understanding. Timm-Bottos (2006) determined that people who were homeless appreciated opportunities for art-making with others, because it validated their creative abilities and provided a sense of community (relatedness). Cameron (1996) used art therapy with families escaping domestic violence for healing the after-effects of violence, for improving insight, and for developing creative problem-solving skills. Because art-making may be conducive to peacemaking (Kapitan, 1997), cultivating imagination (Jenkins, 2007), and promoting resilience (Prescott et al., 2008), art therapy may also help children to develop coping and conflict-resolution skills (Gibbons, 2010).

Various art materials and techniques have been mentioned in the literature. Allen (2007) made masks on the faces of homeless and non-homeless people and exhibited them together, as an educational and awareness-raising project about homelessness. Morrill (cited in Wadeson, 2000) also made masks with child residents of a domestic violence shelter to represent feelings, and then the masks were used in role-plays to express and understand feelings. She encouraged children to draw of the times they felt angry and to explore aggression through drawing the often-confusing situations in violent families. Self-esteem was promoted through books about themselves and life-size drawings.

Van der Ent-Zgoda encouraged children to draw where they used to live in order to help them adjust to living at a community crisis center. Black used doll making (cited by Wadeson, 2000) with women who were leaving prostitution to help them examine aspects of identity and self-care. Moxley, Feen-Calligan, Washington, and Garriott (2011) used quilting with women leaving homelessness to facilitate community and support. Similarly, art was found by Stokrocki et al. (2004) to facilitate communication, healing, and social bonding. They offered an art program with a computer and Internet component to help homeless women and victims of domestic violence set up their own websites to feature the arts in their everyday lives and art made for sale in order to survive. The authors found that "homeless women may be without a permanent home, but they, like other people can express or display their cherished ideas and their images of protection" (p. 73).

Murals were cited by several authors as ways to develop self-esteem in adolescents (Wallace-DiGarbo & Hill, 2006), as well as self-determination (Durkin, cited in Wadeson, 2000), and to advocate for public awareness about homelessness and related social problems (Allen, 2007). Durkin worked with homeless women (cited in Wadeson, 2000) to paint a mural outside their shelter. She found that the mural was "a public, self-determining, willful, self-identifiable image that will last a long time" (p. 276). Joseph (2006), working with young to middle-aged African-American and Latino/a day hospital patients, found that painting murals helped provide relief from their stressful neighborhood environment. As the participants became acquainted with each other, collective concerns about their oppression—specifically how their underserved neighborhoods contributed to their own psychiatric problems—began to emerge in the content of the murals. While painting the murals, the participants became aware of a public protest about the quality of emergency and inpatient services at the hospital. They realized the objectives of the protests were exemplified in their murals, and asked (and were given permission) to take part in the planning meetings and join the protests. Their efforts to bring about positive changes in their community were a therapeutic achievement for them, and serve as an example of developing self-determination.

Service-Learning at Capuchin Soup Kitchen

A ministry of the Capuchin Province of St. Joseph, the Capuchin Soup Kitchen (CSK) has tended to people's basic needs, especially the need for food, since 1929. The CSK also attempts to address root causes of social injustice (CSK website, n.d.). Located on the east side of Detroit, Capuchin's program is primarily attended by "the working poor." When money is limited, the meals provided by CSK make it possible for families not to have to choose between paying bills or buying groceries.

Because of the needs of the children, in 1999, the CSK started a program called the Rosa Parks Art Studio and Children's Library, under the direction of Sr. Nancyann Turner, ATR-BC. It began as a tutoring program designed "to help break the cycle of poverty by giving children an outlet to express themselves in a constructive and creative way and at the same time expose them to different arts and cultures" ("Our Story," 2001, para 1). The program evolved to include art therapy groups, a lending library, a peace education program to strengthen children's skills in handing conflicts without escalation into violence, teen support groups, and music sessions. A 3-week peace camp is offered in the summers focusing on inner peace for the children, the children's families, communities (see Figures 38.1–38.3), and the world.

The philosophy of CSK is that exposure to creativity, beauty, respect, affirmation, art, imagination, education, and gardening are effective antidotes to the violence that permeates the city's east side. Capuchin's programs provide the social context for developing competence, autonomy, and relatedness (Jenkins, 2007; Noltemeyer et al., 2012). Art therapy groups help children to utilize creative expression as a way of processing conflicts, expressing feelings, and becoming empowered through awareness and strengthening of their inner resources and capacities.

In one example observed during the December holiday season, children in an art therapy group made at least four holiday greeting cards. For the card covers, children cut pieces from African-designed batiks that they had learned about and made during a previous art session. Writing the greeting was a thoughtful process. Children worked with service-learners to answer questions about people who were helpful to them and people who they knew needed help, and, from their answers, developed poetry for the greetings. Two cards were to be given to family members or friends, and two cards were to be given to individuals they met or observed having meals in the CSK dining room.

In addition to assisting in the art therapy sessions and working individually with children, service-learners have contributed to Capuchin's programs in various ways. They have researched and developed original art therapy experientials consistent with CSK's peace curriculum; they have served as tutors or guest artists facilitating special media-based sessions (e.g., the African batik session); and they have helped to develop

Figure 38.1　Figure 38.1 shows a child experimenting with "rocking" a paper boat by tossing small rocks into the water. Children role-played themselves as boats, describing how it feels to be tossed and turned. They also role-played as the rocks, thinking of the rocks as representing feelings that would have the effect of rocking the boat. Children wrote feelings on rocks and took turns dropping the rocks near the boat, causing the boat to be upset or to sink. Children then made paper boats. Once they identified at least two strengths or strategies for keeping themselves at peace, they were given weighted anchors to insert, illustrating how they could right themselves, and remain steady. Children brainstormed ideas for keeping themselves at peace when in troubled waters, or when they feel not at peace (photo and experiential by Jonathan Hale).

girls' and boys' support groups. When students see that their efforts produce results, their sense of autonomy and competence increases, as well as their ability to relate to others different from themselves. In their reflections, students have written:

> I feel like I have more power to shape things in the community. ... I always seem to think I can't do things ... working ... like this shows me I can.
>
> I have learned a ... more about ... my own personal perspectives as well as accepting and engaging different perspectives.
>
> Everyone thinking the same way is of little use to progress. It takes many different minds and thoughts to make up the world.

Figure 38.2 Paper boats made by children and staff (photo and experiential by Jonathan Hale).

Figure 38.3 To explore peace within the family, children experimented with balance using weights and a fulcrum. Children took turns taping pictures representing different family members and how family balance is affected by individual members. Children thought about what they can do to create balance, or what others do for them to create balance/peace in their lives. The exercise was followed by drawings of the family as trapeze artists who could balance on a tight rope and get across safely (photo and experiential by Jonathan Hale).

Students learn to be social activists through examples set at Capuchin. When Turner observed that, in addition to the children, the mothers also needed support, she initiated a weekly mothers' group. This group is structured similar to a traditional support group, but the women are encouraged to take action for changing the unjust or unfair treatment that they experience. One example was when the principal of an elementary school attended by many of the neighborhood children was laid off. The mothers suspected her dismissal was based on the school's poor test scores. This principal was beloved because she knew the names of all the children and was a positive influence in their lives. To protest the lay-off, as well as the closing of other public schools and the library in the neighborhood, the mothers organized a letter-writing campaign to the School Board and City Hall. Those for whom writing was difficult were assisted by more experienced writers in the group. The bond between the mothers contributed to a sense of relatedness while competence and autonomy were enhanced. Self-determination evolved as the recipients of CSK's social services became active participants in social justice and in addressing their own problems.

The Rhythm of Compassion

The final section of this chapter deals with the self-care required of art therapists working with serious social problems such as poverty and homelessness. In her books, *The Rhythm of Compassion: Caring for Self, Connecting with Society* (2000) and *Circle of Compassion: Meditations for Caring for Self and the World* (2001), Gail Straub wrote about the responsibility of helping professionals to balance caring for others with caring for themselves. Straub found that people deeply committed to social change may ignore their basic needs, allowing exhaustion and lack of self-compassion to limit their effectiveness in the world. The best way to become a better helper (teacher/therapist) is to become a better person. According to Straub (2000), this can be done through finding one's rhythm of compassion. Straub uses the metaphor of breathing: *Breathing in care for self, and breathing out care for others.* Both are necessary to sustain life on all levels.

> Without the in-breath of self-care and reflection we can't sustain our involvement with the suffering of the world, nor do we have the clarity of heart and mind required for the complex challenges we face. On the other hand, without the out-breath of compassionate engagement with society our inner work implodes upon itself leading to the dead end of narcissism and spiritual emptiness. (Straub, 2000, p. 5)

Straub found that the *in-breath of self-care* requires reflection on one's own pain. Unearthing heartbreaks is a way for connecting with the suffering of the world. It is necessary to reflect on *in-breath* (*and out-breath*) activities that can nourish and sustain (Straub, 2000). In addition, activities that drain and keep one feeling empty are important to identify. Showing compassion toward oneself will support caregivers in their care for others.

Straub (2001) identified four qualities of mature compassion: a quiet mind, an open heart, presence (all you have to be is yourself), and radical simplicity—meaning that, in the "immense complexity of the world's suffering, my service is radically simple. I do whatever small thing is needed in a given moment with a loving heart" (p. 113).

Leah, an art therapy student, exemplified "presence" with regard to an adolescent client whose adoptive mother no longer wanted her. Leah felt helpless to offer any comfort or hope to the client, who was distraught and angry. She found herself practicing "presence," and found guidance in Straub's (2001) meditation: "Today when I encounter the pain of my child, partner, colleague or friend, I pause, I breathe in, I quiet my mind ... I am a still lake for them" (p. 108).

Conclusion

Art therapy can fill a special need by helping people who are homeless or who live in poverty to strengthen their inner resources, necessary to develop self-determination to take action on their own behalf. Critical inquiry into how a person's social environment supports or detracts from well-being, guarding against unintended encouragement of a client's adaptation to a destructive environment (Junge et al., 1993), and helping people to be advocates for themselves and for social change (Joseph, 2006) can and should be among the functions of art therapists working with people living in poverty and experiencing homelessness (Kaplan, 2007).

Service-learning helps students to develop understanding about serious social problems for which there are no easy solutions. Service-learning offers opportunities for students to learn from people often different from themselves, and to imagine and co-facilitate solutions to social problems.

Art therapists and other helping professionals assisting those living in poverty and homelessness must practice self-care and show compassion toward themselves in order to be supported in their care of others. Reflection, meditation, and quiet contemplation are essential to develop compassion toward the suffering of others and awareness of the actions we can take to foster solidarity and community.

References

Allen, P. (2007). Facing homelessness: A community mask making project. In. F. Kaplan (Ed.), *Art therapy and social action* (pp. 59–71). Philadelphia, PA: Jessica Kingsley Publishers.

Anthony, E. K., King, B., & Austin, M. J. (2011). Reducing child poverty by promoting child well being: Identifying best practices n a time of great need. *Children and Youth Services Review, 33,* 1999–2009. doi: 10.1016/j.childyouth.2011.05.029

Arrington, D., & Yorgin, P. D. (2001). *Art therapy as a cross-cultural means to assess psychosocial health in homeless and orphaned children in Kiev, 18*(2), 80–88.

Braun, L. N. (1997). In from the cold: Art therapy with homeless men. *Art Therapy: Journal of the American Art Therapy Association, 14*(2), 118–122.

Our Story. (2001, Fall/Winter). *Breaking bread: A newsletter of the Capuchin Soup Kitchen.* Detroit, MI: Self-published.

Cameron, D. F. (1996). Conflict resolution through art with homeless people (pp. 176–206). In M. Liebman (Ed.). *Arts approaches to conflict.* London, England: Jessica Kingsley Publishers.

Camilleri, V. A. (Ed.). (2007). *Healing the inner city child: Creative arts therapies with at-risk youth.* London, England: Jessica Kingsley Publishers.

Capuchin Soup Kitchen Website. (n.d.) Accessed July 27, 2012, from http://cskdetroit.org/

Chirkov, V., Ryan, R. M., Kim, Y., & Kaplan, U. (2003). Differentiating autonomy from individualism and independence: A self-determination theory perspective on internalization of cultural orientations and well-being. *Journal of Personality and Social Psychology, 84*(1), 97–110. doi: 10:1037/0022-3514.84.97

Daher, M., & Haz, A. M. (2011). Changing meanings through art: A systemization of a psychosocial intervention with Chilean women in urban poverty situation. *American Journal of Community Psychology, 47*, 322–334. doi: 10.1007/s10464-010-9400-3

Daynes, G., & Longo, N. V. (2004, Fall). Jane Addams and the origins of service-learning practice in the United States. *Michigan Journal of Community Service-Learning, 11*(1), 5–13.

Davis, J. (1997). Building from scraps: Art therapy within a homeless community. *Art Therapy: Journal of the American Art Therapy Association, 14*(3), 210–213.

Feen-Calligan, H. (2008). Service-learning and art therapy in a homeless shelter. *The Arts in Psychotherapy, 35*, 20–33.

Franklin, M., Rothaus, M. E., & Schpok, K. (2007). Unity in diversity: Communal pluralism in the art studio and in the classroom. In F. Kaplan (Ed.), *Art therapy and social action* (pp. 213–230). Philadelphia, PA: Jessica Kingsley Publishers.

Gibbons, K. (2010). Circle justice: A creative arts approach to conflict resolution in the classroom. *Art Therapy: Journal of the American Art Therapy Association, 27*(2), 84–89.

Hopson, L. M., & Lee, E. (2011). Mitigating the effect of family poverty on academic, and behavioral outcomes: The role of school climate in middle and high school. *Children and Youth Services Review, 33*, 2221–2229. doi: 10.1016/j.childyouth.2011.07.006

Howard, J. (2001). *Service-learning course design workbook.* Ann Arbor, MI: OCSL Press.

Jenkins, T. (2007). Rethinking the unimaginable: The need for teacher education in peace education. *Harvard Educational Review, 77*(3), 366–369.

Joseph, C. (2006). Creative alliance: The healing power of art therapy. *Art Therapy: Journal of the American Art Therapy Association, 23*(1), 30–33.

Jyoti, D. F., Frongillo, E. A., & Jones, S. J. (2005, December). Food insecurity affects school children's academic performance, weight gain and social skills. *The Journal of Nutrition, 135*, 2831–2839.

Junge, M., Finn Alvarez, J., Kellogg, A., & Volker, C. (1993). The art therapist as social activist: Reflections and visions. *Art Therapy: Journal of the American Art Therapy Association, 10*(3), 148–155.

Kane, T. J. (1987). Long-term poverty and motivation. *Social Service Review, 61*(3), 405–419.

Kapitan, L. (1997). Making or breaking: Art therapy in the shifting tides of a violent culture. *Art Therapy: Journal of the American Art Therapy Association, 14*(4), 255–260.

Kaplan, F. (Ed.). (2007). *Art therapy and social action.* Philadelphia, PA: Jessica Kingsley Publishers.

Macartney, S. (2011, November). Child poverty in the United States 2009 and 2010: Selected race groups and Hispanic origin. American Community Survey Briefs. *United States Census Bureau.* Accessed June 13, 2012 from www.census.gov

Moon, B. (1999). The tears make me paint: The role of responsive artmaking in adolescent art therapy. *Art Therapy: Journal of the American Art Therapy Association, 16*(2), 78–82.

Moxley, D., Feen-Calligan, H., Washington, O. G. M., & Garriott, L. (2011). The quilting workshop as self-efficacy group work with older African American women transitioning out of homelessness. *Art Therapy: Journal of the American Art Therapy Association, 28*(3), 113–122.

National Coalition for the Homeless. (2009, July). Fact sheets. Accessed July 20, 2012 from http://www.nationalhomeless.org/factsheets/

National Poverty Center. (n.d.). Poverty in the United States: Frequently asked questions. University of Michigan. Gerald R. Ford School of Public Policy. Accessed June 13, 2012 from http://www.npc.umich.edu/poverty/

Nelson, C. L. (2010). Meeting the needs of urban students: Creative arts therapy in New Jersey City Public Schools. *Art Therapy: Journal of the American Art Therapy Association, 27*(2), 62–68.

Noltemeyer, A., Bush, K., Patton, J., & Bergen, D. (2012). The relationship among deficiency needs and growth needs: An empirical investigation of Maslow's theory. *Children and Youth Services Review, 34,* 1862–1867. doi: 10.1016/j.childyouth.2012.05.021

Prescott, M. V., Sekendur, B., Bailey, B., & Hoshino, J. (2008). Art making as a component and facilitator of resiliency with homeless youth. *Art Therapy: Journal of the American Art Therapy Association, 25*(4), 156–163.

Prugh, P. (1987, November). *Ladies of the eighties: Outreach to homeless women.* Paper presented at the annual conference of the American Art Therapy Association, Bal Harbor, Florida.

Ryan, R. M., & Deci, E. L. (2000). Self-determination theory and the facilitation of intrinsic motivation, social development, and well-being. *American Psychologist, 55*(1), 68–78. doi: 10.1037/0003-066X.55.1.68

Siddiqui, N., Astone-Twerell, J., & Hernitche, T. (2009). Staff perspectives on modified therapeutic community services for homeless dually diagnosed clients: An exploratory study. *Journal of Psychoactive Drugs, 41*(4), 355–361.

Stokrocki, M., Sutton Andrews, S., & Saemundsdottir, S. (2004). The role of art for homeless women and survivors of domestic violence. *Visual Arts Research, 58,* 73–82.

Straub, G. (2000). *The rhythm of compassion: Caring for self, connecting with society.* Boston, MA: Tuttle Publishing.

Straub, G. (2001). *Circle of compassion: Meditations for caring for the self and for the world.* Boston, MA: Journey Editions.

Straub, G. (2011). The missing piece in the empowerment equation: A strategy for delivering personal agency to women in the developing world. *Imagine: A global initiative for the empowerment of women: A program of Empowerment Institute.* Accessed May 1, 2012 from http://www.imagineprogram.net/

Timm-Bottos, J. (2006). Constructing creative community: Reviving health and justice through community arts. *The Canadian Art Therapy Association Journal, 19*(2), 12–26.

US Bureau of the Census. (2012, September 12). *Poverty: Poverty Thresholds.* Accessed December 1, 2012 from http://www.census.gov/hhes/www/poverty/data/threshld/

US Department of Health and Human Services. (2012). *The 2012 HHS Poverty Guidelines.* Accessed July 25, 2012 from http://aspe.hhs.gov/poverty/12poverty.shtml#guidelines

Wadeson, H. (2000). *Art therapy practice: innovative approaches with diverse populations.* New York, NY: John Wiley and Sons.

Wallace-DiGarbo, A., & Hill, D. C. (2006). Art as agency: Exploring empowerment of a-risk youth. *Art Therapy: Journal of the American Art Therapy Association, 23*(3), 119–125.

39

Dimensions of Art Therapy in Medical Illness

Susan Ainlay Anand

"Medicine and art have a common goal: to complete what nature cannot bring to a finish"—M. T. Southgate

Medical illness affects nearly everyone. The psychological effects of medical illness are known to include depression, anxiety, and post-traumatic stress disorder (PTSD), and require appropriate evaluation and management. Since the medically ill are seen in a variety of treatment settings, art therapists will inevitably encounter these patients in their practice and therefore need to be cognizant of the principles of medical art therapy (MAT).

Although the roots of art therapy are linked to psychiatric illness, it is interesting that the first person usually given credit for using the term "art therapy" was Adrian Hill, a patient recovering from tuberculosis. Hill, a professional artist, found that art making was an integral part of his rehabilitation, and that it contributed to his and other patients' recovery (1945, 1951). Almost two decades after Hill documented his findings, art therapists began publishing accounts of their work in medical settings, emphasizing the treatment of psychosocial issues resulting from illness and the use of patient drawings for assessment purposes (Junge & Asawa, 1994; Rubin, 1999). Since the mid 1970s, there has been a growing body of evidence that supports art therapy as a beneficial treatment for medically ill populations (Reynolds, Nabors, & Quinlan, 2000; Slayton, D'Archer, & Kaplan, 2010). Recent studies suggest that the use of the arts in healthcare helps to reduce cost and prevent disease (Christenson, 2011).

Medical art therapy (MAT) refers to art therapy with the medically ill, and is "the specific use of art therapy with individuals who are physically ill, experiencing trauma to the body, or undergoing aggressive medical treatment such as surgery or chemotherapy" (Malchiodi, 1993, p. 66). Medical art therapists provide a range of services to hospitals, outpatient clinics, rehabilitation centers, home health agencies, hospice centers, geriatric treatment facilities, etc. As a member of a treatment team, they work closely with physicians, nurses, psychologists, social workers, child life specialists, and other healthcare professionals. Art therapists also work with the medically ill in private practice, or in hospitals and agencies as consultants.

The Wiley Handbook of Art Therapy, First Edition. Edited by David E. Gussak and Marcia L. Rosal.
© 2016 John Wiley & Sons, Ltd. Published 2016 by John Wiley & Sons, Ltd.

Classification of Medical Illnesses

Patients seek medical attention due to acute or chronic disease, non-intentional or intentional trauma, accidents, or the need for end-of-life care. The nature of each of these medical conditions is different, and the use of art therapy will vary depending on the type and stage of illness being treated, the patient's age, and treatment setting. Knowledge of medical conditions, including specific treatment protocols, is relevant to the development of effective and appropriate art therapy interventions.

Medically ill patients can be grouped into four broad treatment categories: medical, surgical, neurological, and palliative care. Published accounts from each of these groups form a substantial base of knowledge for art therapists working with the medical ill:

1. *Art therapy with specific medical conditions.* These include HIV/AIDS (Rao et al., 2009; Rosner-David & Sageman, 1987), tuberculosis (Rosner-David & Ilusorio, 1995), asthma (Beebe, Gelfand, & Bender, 2010), arthritis (Lusebrink, Turner-Schikler, & Schikler, 1992), burns (Appleton, 2001; Russell, 1995), diabetes (Stuckey & Tisdell, 2010), obesity (Anzules, Haenni, & Golay, 2007), hemodialysis (Weldt, 2003), heart failure (Sela et al., 2011), and cystic fibrosis (Fenton, 2000).
2. *Art therapy with neurological conditions.* These include stroke (Kim, Kim, Lee, & Chun, 2008), dementia (Stewart, 2004), Alzheimer's disease (Safar & Press, 2011), Parkinson's disease (Elkis-Abuhoff, Goldblatt, Gaydos, & Corrato, 2008), migraine (Vick, Sexton-Radek, & Kaplan, 2009), and epilepsy (Anschel, Dolce, Schwartzman, & Fisher, 2005).
3. *Art therapy in surgical patients.* These include renal transplant (Wallace et al., 2004), bone marrow transplant (Gabriel et al., 2001), and laryngectomy (Anand & Anand, 1999).
4. *Art therapy as palliative care* for patients struggling with chronic or life-threatening illness (Luzzatto & Pratt, 1998; Nainis, 2008; Pratt & Wood, 1998; Thomas, 1995).

The needs of the patients in each of the aforementioned classifications are quite distinct and varied. For example, a patient with poor prognosis will have different needs than a patient recovering from surgery. For those in immuno-suppressed states, it is usually necessary to isolate or avoid direct contact. Art therapists must take appropriate measures and modify the therapeutic intervention in these cases. Cancer patients who need support and would benefit from social interaction may gain more from group therapy over individual sessions.

Cancer patients encompass any or all of the four listed medical categories based on type of disease, stage of illness, and treatment. In the field of oncology, art therapy is often referred to as a complementary therapy, and is increasingly being used to treat children and adults. This is partly due to improved awareness and recognition of the field, along with evidence-based research. For example, studies have shown that cancer patients who participate in art therapy experience decreased symptoms of pain, anxiety, and tiredness (Nainis et al., 2006). Additional benefits include increased relaxation and communication, heightened feelings of self-control, improved self-esteem, and expression of emotions (Reynolds & Lim, 2007). A recent study by Forzoni, Perez, Martgnetti, and Crispino (2010) found that individuals undergoing chemotherapy treatment were able to relax, engage in self-narrative, and find new meaning through expressed emotions in art. Research from the field of psychoneuro-immunology and investigations of mind–body connections to healing provides support for therapies that strengthen the immune system and reduce stress in cancer patients (Kelly, 1997; Koch & Fuchs, 2011).

Goals of MAT

Goals will differ depending on the patient, illness, treatment setting, and circumstances. Several may include:

- Decrease isolation and improve socialization
- Increase self-confidence through mastery of art materials and processes
- Express feelings associated with illness or medical condition
- Decrease symptoms of anxiety and depression
- Increase independent functioning
- Explore issues related to body image
- Identify personal strengths to support resilience

In chronic or life-threatening illness, art therapy can assist patients in dealing with thoughts of mortality and fears about their future. In general, MAT helps medically ill patients maintain their integrity while finding meaning in their lives.

MAT with Children

MAT with children differs from adults for a variety of reasons, but mainly because of developmental factors. Ideally, the approaches and materials used in art therapy need to be tailored to meet the child's personality, developmental level, artistic level of development, adjustment to illness, and personal strengths. One way to help determine these is by using art-based assessments. With proper administration and accurate interpretation, assessments for use in MAT with children can be invaluable to members of the medical team in meeting patient needs (Councill, 2003).

The child's level of cognitive development affects how he or she comprehends illness. Psychosocial factors such as access to medical care and level of family involvement will also influence a child's emotional response and ability to cope with illness and treatment interventions (Councill, 1993). Additionally, children may experience exacerbation of difficulties related to preexisting psychiatric or medical conditions if surgical or other invasive medical procedures are experienced as traumatic. By incorporating MAT into patient care, art therapists can help children manage their symptoms of distress and contribute to an overall sense of well-being; develop and maintain hope; identify and assist with changes in body image; increase mastery and self-confidence; aid in compliance with medical procedures; and reduce symptoms of anxiety and depression (Chapman, Morabito, Ladakakos, Schreier, & Knudson, 2001; Councill, 2003; Malchiodi, 1999).

With medically ill children, it is important to consider the family, as they will most likely be present during treatment and/or hospitalization. Consequently, there may be times in the pediatric setting when there is less privacy for art therapy sessions. Parents and family members typically experience a range of emotions regarding illness, as it becomes part of family life. Their ability to cope will affect the child's adjustment and response to treatment. Families may benefit from additional support or therapy, especially in chronic or life threatening illness. In certain situations, medical art therapists provide family art therapy or encourage participation of siblings and/or parents in art therapy sessions.

Figure 39.1 is an example of an 8-year-old patient's use of puppets and a house made during art therapy. Diagnosed with leukemia at the age of 2, she responded well to treatment and is now in remission for the disease. This child was referred to individual outpatient art therapy to help her express emotions and reduce anxiety related to situations she viewed as potentially harmful. Through the creation and use of puppets and stories, she identified personal strengths; made cognitive connections that assisted in conflict resolution; and expressed thoughts and feelings previously avoided. Family sessions and art therapy sessions with her sister were scheduled as needed to address conflicts at home and bring about behavioral change in the family.

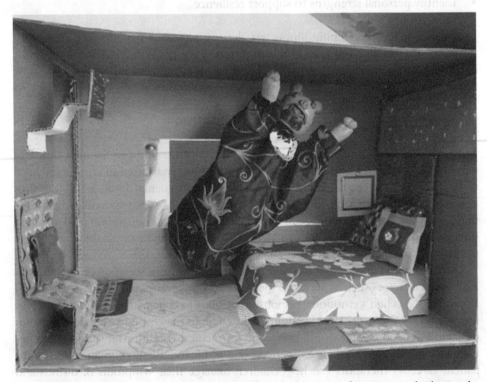

Figure 39.1 An 8-year-old child in remission from leukemia used puppets and a house she made in art therapy to develop stories related to her illness.

Considerations for Art Therapy with the Medically Ill

Responses to medical diagnosis and treatment cover a broad range of psychological and emotional distress, many times not evident to even family members or the patient's support network. Assessment and intervention methods used by art therapists require sensitivity and comprehension of even the subtlest nuances of the underlying condition and psychological response in the individual patient.

Psychological Aspects of Illness

People diagnosed with an illness respond in different ways. Some may find ways to reconstruct their personal and social identities following illness and emerge feeling stronger and more positive. Others have difficulty moving beyond their illness and become preoccupied with loss (Crossley, 2000). Preexisting psychosocial conditions will affect one's ability to cope with illness. Psychological distress can result from these factors and the additional challenges medically ill patients face such as access to care, financial hardships resulting from unemployment or lack of insurance coverage, and limited family or social support. In a recent study of chronically ill adult patients, elevated psychological distress was found in all age groups, and included symptoms of anxiety, depression, hostility, and somatization (Goulia et al., 2012).

Psychological distress manifests through changes in behavior, such as regression, withdrawal, or hostility. A medical diagnosis can exacerbate psychiatric symptoms. In chronic or life-threatening illness, a patient is often forced to confront his or her mortality. For some patients with general medical conditions, this can lead to thoughts of self-harm and suicide. Druss and Pincus (2000) found a significant association between medical conditions and suicidality. Their findings support the need to incorporate additional screening tools for suicide risk in general medical settings. Art therapists can help by administering art-based assessments, and document observations of art therapy sessions.

Self-Identity and Illness

Reynolds (2003) described the interface of self-identity and illness and the role of art-making as a way to maintain or reconstruct positive identity in patients. Diagnosis of a medical condition often results in dramatic changes in a person's life and can include numerous physical challenges along with adaptation to a new lifestyle. Identity loss and reconstruction then become key challenges for ill patients, particularly those with chronic disease (Charmaz, 1983). A phenomenon referred to as "biological disruption" can occur with these changes (Bury, 1982). Thoughts and stories about one's past, present, and future life are disrupted due to uncertainty about the future. When this occurs, it is important to assist the patient in retaining aspects of their core identity while identifying personal strengths to help them adapt to illness.

Through art therapy, resilience is supported as patients utilize their strengths in meaningful activities that restore identity and contribute to reconstruction of the self.

For example, a young woman diagnosed with sickle cell anemia found that creating artwork in an outpatient group provided her with opportunities to develop her art skills and express feelings associated with both positive and negative relationships in her life. She was able to identify strengths she had utilized in coping with her illness (such as tenacity and patience), and how she could use these assets in dealing with current marital problems. During the course of her involvement in art therapy, she often described a growing sense of courage and commitment to her family values that she had lost track of since her mother's death.

Since the self seems to be partially grounded in bodily experience, physical changes brought about by medical illness and treatment will also have an effect on self-identity (Corbin & Strauss, 1987; Leventhal, Idler, & Leventhal, 1999). Medical illness can bring significant alterations in weight and growth patterns affecting posture and appearance. Surgical interventions can cause disfigurement, and certain medications such as chemotherapy will lead to hair loss. Radiation, often used as a treatment in oncology, might affect normal bodily function. As a result, the physical self may feel unfamiliar (Reynolds, 2003). Patients need opportunities to express the emotional aspects of these changes, and with the potential to acquire new skills through art making, the focus can shift from loss to autonomy and hope.

The case below is an example of the multifaceted process of clinical work with the medically ill. While attending art therapy groups, the patient suffered from a chronic medical condition that required inpatient and outpatient medical procedures, changes in medication and diet, and disruption in work and family life. She encountered personal and family psychological distress amidst a deepening awareness of her mortality. Group art therapy provided the patient with an opportunity to reclaim her creative self that she said was crucial to her identity, and allowed her to express an array of difficult emotions.

Case Example

The following is an example of a patient who was able to reconstruct her self-identity through involvement in art therapy and creative work. J. S. was a surgical nurse, daughter, wife, mother, and grandmother—all of these roles helped to form her personal identity. However, following a diagnosis of stomach cancer, her life was consumed with treatments that included surgery, chemotherapy, and radiation. J. S. began attending weekly outpatient art therapy groups for cancer patients 7 months after her diagnosis. She also painted at home between sessions as she rediscovered her love of creative work. Before her death at the age of 47, J. S.'s paintings were featured in an art exhibit. One of her paintings depicts two musicians holding guitars above an absent lower body (Figure 39.2). J. S. described art making as a way to express her feelings about illness, spirituality, and mortality, and said that "Each piece is a work of love and is prayerfully done with the knowledge that I don't have to be an artist to create ... this is God's way of allowing me to leave a part of me with those I love."

Figure 39.2 Following treatment for stomach cancer, J. S. completed this acrylic painting of two guitar players.

Materials

Art therapists who work with the medically ill must be mindful of appropriate materials and media for patient age or developmental level, medical condition being treated, and type of treatment situation. Typically, there are strict guidelines for the use of art supplies in hospital settings, and art therapists are usually required to submit an inventory of all materials and substances used. Perhaps the single most important factor concerning art media is infection control and avoiding disease transmission (Moon, 2010). With some medical conditions, new materials must be used with every patient unless media and equipment can be sterilized after each use.

Art supplies that might exacerbate a medical condition or those that contain fungus or bacteria, such as certain clays, should be avoided. Art therapists also need to pay particular attention to features of materials such as smell that may cause discomfort in some patients (Nainis, 2008). Providing the same materials during each session can give hospitalized patients a sense of continuity when they experience depersonalization, disorientation, and loss of self-identity (Appleton, 1993). Computers are useful in medical settings where art therapists work with patients who have physical or cognitive deficits, or need to avoid exposure to certain substances.

Therapy Space

The space and time set aside for MAT differs from other art therapy settings and presents unique challenges, especially with inpatients. Medical team meetings and patient rounds provide opportunities for art therapists to educate the staff on the benefits of art therapy and can lead to increased patient referral. However, since the focus of treatment is typically on the medical condition, other treatment interventions often take precedence over art therapy.

In hospital settings, sessions may take place at bedside, in public spaces, or with family present. In these cases, the medical art therapist needs to be flexible in scheduling art therapy and be willing to compromise privacy and confidentiality. The time period for each session will depend on the circumstances, such as patient condition and location. Patients in crisis with their illness or experiencing negative side effects from treatments require adjustments in scheduling, approach, and goals. Some medical conditions require routine monitoring by staff. In these cases, the patient is usually seen in the hospital room with the possibility of interruptions by healthcare staff or visitors. With some patients, art therapists need to wear a mask, gown, and gloves to avert the spread of infection. Basically, the inpatient environment must be as psychologically safe as possible while meeting the medical needs of patients.

Case Example

C. F. was 50 years old when he suffered a major stroke and was hospitalized. Prior to his stroke, he was on faculty at a small college where he taught vocal pedagogy, and was an accomplished pianist and artist. C. F. was transferred to a private rehabilitation facility in another state to be closer to family. He immediately began treatment for several medical problems, including right hemiplegia and expressive aphasia. Unable to communicate and walk, he appeared to lose interest in life and exhibited symptoms of depression.

Initially, C. F. was reluctant to participate in therapies. During the first few weeks of treatment, staff observed that he was easily frustrated when unable to complete tasks and often refused involvement in subsequent therapeutic interventions. Because of his previous interest in art, the family requested that art therapy be added to the rehabilitation regimen to provide an outlet for self-expression. Though difficult to engage during the first session, C. F. slowly became interested in the art materials offered to him and selected oil pastels to draw a Cezanne landscape from a postcard reproduction. He was able to work from his wheelchair at a floor easel placed at a comfortable height and position. Following the first session, he was given a sketchbook and drawing materials to use between sessions. Prior to the next session, he completed two ink drawings— one was of a grand piano drawn from memory. The piano was well proportioned and detailed, as seen in Figure 39.3, yet the strings are noticeably jumbled and resemble the shape of a brain. While C. F. was unable to describe this drawing, it is suggestive of a self-portrait and feelings he had about his neurological deficits.

Figure 39.3 Stroke patient, C. F., completed this drawing of a grand piano from memory shortly after his first art therapy session.

C. F. participated in weekly individual art therapy sessions for 5 months of his rehabilitation. His sessions took place in his room. He also attended speech therapy, but never regained his ability to effectively communicate through words. Instead, he relied on the use of gesture and visual cues. During sessions, he continued to create oil pastel paintings of seated figures from selected reproductions of Cezanne and William Merritt Chase. C. F. appeared to struggle with a changing self-identity, perhaps best seen through the difficulty he had in adding facial features to his figures. Interactions with hospital staff changed as they became curious about his artistic abilities and routinely praised him for his work; the attention and notoriety he received in the rehabilitation center for his artistic abilities continued in the nursing home where he was eventually placed. Through art therapy, C. F. found an outlet for his emotions and worked through feelings of loss and grief by utilizing the therapeutic relationship, selected imagery for reproduction in his artwork, and the art process itself.

Conclusion

MAT is a rapidly growing subspecialty within the field of art therapy. Increasing numbers of art therapists are working with medically ill patients both in medical and non-medical settings to assess and treat a variety of medical conditions. Innovative programs have been developed along with treatment protocols for the use of art therapy with specific illnesses in children and adult patients. There is potential for art therapy to be more solidly integrated into medical treatment to help patients with psychological, physiological, spiritual, and social needs.

Challenges exist for art therapists who work with the medically ill, regardless of treatment settings. Further evidence-based research to demonstrate the efficacy of art therapy in medical illness would facilitate the expanded role of MAT. Education of various healthcare professionals to increase awareness of the benefits of art therapy is needed and paramount for developing referrals. Insurance coverage and payment for art therapy services is dependent on favorable state and federal licensure and government laws. Despite the many challenges for art therapists working with the medically ill, there are unique opportunities both for the profession and individual practitioners. Perhaps the most important aspect of this work is in the realm of the creative and therapeutic space where art therapists honor patient experiences by listening to stories, witnessing creative work, supporting resilience, and helping people find meaning in illness.

References

Anand, S., & Anand, V. (1999). Art therapy with laryngectomy patients. *Art Therapy: Journal of the American Art Therapy Association, 14*(2), 109–117.

Anschel, D. J., Dolce, S., Schwartzman, A., & Fisher, R. S. (2005). A blinded pilot study of artwork in a comprehensive epilepsy center population. *Epilepsy and Behavior, 6*(2), 196–202.

Anzules, C., Haenni, C., & Golay, A. (2007). An experience of art therapy for patients suffering from obesity. *European Diabetes Nursing, 4*(2), 72–76.

Appleton, V. (1993). An art therapy protocol for the medical trauma setting. *Art Therapy: Journal of the American Art Therapy Association, 10*(2), 71–77.

Appleton, V. (2001). Avenues of hope: Art therapy and the resolution of trauma. *Art Therapy: Journal of the American Art Therapy Association, 18*(1), 6–13.

Beebe, A., Gelfand, E. W., & Bender, B. (2010). A randomized trial to test the effectiveness of art therapy with children with asthma. *The Journal of Allergy and Clinical Immunology.* Published online 12 May 2010, Corrected Proof.

Bury, M. (1982). Chronic illness as biographical disruption. *Sociology of Health and Illness, 4*, 167–182.

Chapman, L., Morabito, D., Ladakakos, C., Schreier, H., & Knudson, M. M. (2001). The effectiveness of art therapy intervention in reducing posttraumatic stress disorder (PTSD) symptoms in pediatric trauma patients. *Art Therapy: Journal of the American Art Therapy Association, 18*(2), 100–104.

Charmaz, K. (1983). Loss of self: A fundamental form of suffering in the chronologically ill. *Sociology of Health and Illness, 5*, 168–195.

Christenson, G. (2011). Why we need the arts in medicine. *Minnesota Medicine*, July. Retrieved from http://www.minnesotamedicine.com

Corbin, J., & Strauss, A. (1987). Accompaniments of chronic illness: Changes in body, self, biography, and biographical time. *Research in the Sociology of Health Care, 6*, 249–281.

Councill, T. (1993). Art therapy with pediatric cancer patients: Helping normal children cope with abnormal circumstances. *Art Therapy: Journal of the American Art Therapy Association, 10*(2), 78–87.

Councill, T. (2003). Medical art therapy with children. In C. A. Malchiodi (Ed), *Handbook of Art Therapy* (pp. 207–219). New York, NY: Guilford Press.

Crossley, M. (2000). *Introducing narrative psychology: Self, trauma, and the construction of meaning.* Buckingham, UK: Open University Press.

Elkis-Abuhoff, D. L., Goldblatt, R., Gaydos, M., & Corrato, S. (2008). Effects of clay manipulation on somatic dysfunction and emotional distress in patients with Parkinson's disease. *Art Therapy: Journal of the American Art Therapy Association, 25*(3), 122–128.

Druss, P., & Pincus, H. (2000). Suicidal ideation and suicide attempts in general medical illnesses. *Archives of Internal Medicine, 160,* 1522–1526.

Fenton, J. F. (2000). Cystic fibrosis and art therapy. *The Arts in Psychotherapy, 27*(1), 15–25.

Forzoni, S., Perez, M., Martignetti, A., & Crispino, S. (2010). Art therapy with cancer patients during chemotherapy sessions: An analysis of the patients' perception of helpfulness. *Palliative and Supportive Care, 8*(1), 41–48.

Gabriel, B., Bromberg, E., Vandenhovenkamp, J., Walka, P., Kornblith, A., & Luzzatto, P. (2001). Art therapy with adult bone marrow transplant patients in isolation: A pilot study. *Journal of Psycho-Oncology, 10,* 114–123.

Goulia, P., Papdimitriou, I., Machado, M. O., Mantas, C., Pappa, C. Tsianos, E., & Hyphantis, T. (2012). Does psychological distress vary between younger and older adults in health and disease? *Journal of Psychosomatic Research, 72*(2), 120–128.

Hill, A. (1945). *Art versus illness.* London: George Allen & Unwin.

Hill, A. (1951). *Painting out illness.* London: Williams & Norgate.

Junge, M. B. (with Asawa, P. P.). (1994). *A history of art therapy in the United States.* Mundelein, IL: American Art Therapy Association.

Kelly, J. (1997). Revealing and healing illness with art therapy. *Alternative and Complementary Therapies, 3*(2), 107–114.

Kim, S.-K., Kim, M.-Y., Lee, J.-H., & Chun, S.-I. (2008). Art therapy outcomes in the rehabilitation treatment of a stroke patient: A case report. *Art Therapy: Journal of the American Art Therapy Association, 25*(3), 129–133.

Koch, S. C., & Fuchs, T. (2011). Embodied arts therapies. *Arts in Psychotherapy, 38*(4), 276–280.

Leventhal, H., Idler, E., & Leventhal, E. (1999). The impact of chronic illness on the self system. In R. Contrada & R. Ashmore (Eds.), *Self, social identity and physical health* (pp. 185–208). Oxford, UK: Oxford University Press.

Lusebrink, V., Turner-Schikler, L., & Schikler, K. (1992). Art therapy with Juvenile Rheumatoid Arthritis patients. *Proceedings of the 23rd Annual Conference of the American Art Therapy Association* (p. 82). Mundelein, IL: AATA.

Luzzatto, P., & Pratt, A. (Eds.). (1998). *Art therapy in palliative care: The creative response.* London: Routledge.

Malchiodi, C. A. (1993). Introduction to special issue: Art and medicine. *Art Therapy: Journal of the American Art Therapy Association, 10*(2), 66–69.

Malchiodi, C. A. (1999). *Medical art therapy with children.* London: Jessica Kingsley.

Moon, C. H. (2010). *Materials and media in art therapy: Critical understandings of diverse artistic vocabularies.* London: Routledge.

Nainis, N. A. (2008). Approaches to art therapy for cancer inpatients: Research and practice considerations. *Art Therapy: Journal of the American Art Therapy Association, 25*(3), 115–121.

Nainis, N., Paice, J., Ratner, J., Wirth, J., Lai, J., & Shott, S. (2006). Relieving symptoms in cancer: Innovative use of art therapy. *Journal of Pain and Symptom Management, 31*(2), 162–169.

Pratt, M., & Wood, M. (Eds.). (1998). *Art therapy in palliative care: The creative response.* London: Routledge.

Rao, D., Nainis, N., Williams, L., Langner, D., Eisin, A., & Paice, J. (2009). Art therapy for relief of symptoms associated with HIV/AIDS. *AIDS Care, 21*(1), 64–69.

Reynolds, F. (2003). Reclaiming a positive identity in chronic illness through artistic occupation. *OTJR: Occupation, Participation and Health, 23*(3), 118–127.

Reynolds, F., & Lim, K. H. (2007). Contribution of visual art-making to the subjective well-being of women living with cancer: A qualitative study. *The Arts in Psychotherapy, 34*(1), 1–10.

Reynolds, M. W., Nabors, L., & Quinlan, A. (2000). The effectiveness of art therapy: Does it work? *Art Therapy: Journal of the American Art Therapy Association, 17*(3), 207–213.

Rosner-David, I., & Ilusorio, S. (1995). Tuberculosis: Art therapy with patients in isolation. *Art Therapy: Journal of the American Art Therapy Association, 12*(1), 24–31.

Rosner David, I., & Sageman, S. (1987). Psychological aspects of AIDS as seen in art therapy. *American Journal of Art Therapy, 26*(1), 3–10.

Rubin, J. (1999). *Art therapy: An introduction.* Philadelphia, PA: Brunner/Mazel.

Russell, J. (1995). Art therapy on a hospital burn unit: A step towards healing and recovery. *Art Therapy: Journal of the American Art Therapy Association, 12*(1), 39–45.

Safar, L. T., & Press, D. T. (2011), Art and the brain: Effects of dementia on art production in art therapy. *Art Therapy: Journal of the American Art Therapy Association, 28*(2), 96–103.

Sela, N., Baruch, N., Assali, A., Vaturi, M., Battler, A., & Ben Gal, T. (2011). The influence of medical art therapy on quality of life and compliance of medical treatment of patients with advanced heart failure. *Harefuah, 150*(2), 79–83.

Slayton, S. C., D'Archer, J., & Kaplan, R. (2010). Outcome studies on the efficacy of art therapy: A review of the findings. *Art Therapy: Journal of the American Art Therapy Association, 27*(3), 108–119.

Stewart, E. G. (2004). Art therapy and neuroscience blend: Working with patients who have dementia. *Art Therapy: Journal of the American Art Therapy Association, 21*(3), 148–155.

Stuckey, H., & Tisdell, E. (2010). The role of creative expression in diabetes: An exploration into the meaning-making process. *Qualitative Health Research, 20*(1), 42–56.

Thomas, G. (1995). Art therapy and practice in palliative care. *European Journal of Palliative Care, 2*(3), 120–123.

Vick, R., Sexton-Radek, K., & Kaplan, F. (2009). Art and migraine: Researching the relationship between art-making and pain experience. *Art Therapy: Journal of the American Art Therapy Association, 26*(3), 114–123.

Wallace, J., Yorgin, P. D., Carolan, R., Moore, H., Sanchez, J., Belson, A., Yorgin, L., Major, C., Granucci, L., Alexander, S., & Arrington, D. (2004). The use of art therapy to detect depression and post-traumatic stress disorder in pediatric and young adult renal transplant recipients. *Pediatric Transplant, 8*(1), 52–59.

Weldt, C. (2003). Patients' responses to a drawing experience in a hemodialysis unit: A step towards healing. *Art Therapy: Journal of the American Art Therapy Association, 20*(2), 92–99.

40

A Complicated Life: Intermodality within Dissociative Identity Disorder

Laurel Thompson

I first met Kate 14 years ago at a treatment center for eating disorders, when she was soon to turn 40 years of age. She was a compulsive eater, but came seeking help for "body image." She had been a compulsive overeater for most of her life and vehemently hated her body, which led her at times to cut herself. She had had much therapy experience and was quite sophisticated in her verbal insights about family influences, intrapsychic dynamics, and her own strengths and limitations. She felt however, that her tortuous thoughts about her body were the last thing keeping her from recovery from her eating disorder.

She had a very successful career as an educator, which brought her much professional satisfaction. Yet, her professional life was the only area in which she could feel competent and sure of herself. She had a circle of friends, but could easily be thrown into inner confusion and terror, often triggered by seemingly innocuous surprises in social interactions. "At the speed of light," she was pitched into this state, desperate to find some safety until it passed, ruminating about her weight, her choice of clothes, and her entire worth as a person, all the while managing to carry on a conversation. While she appeared normal to the outside world, she was mercilessly tormented by her inner experience.

After many courses of treatment with various individual therapists, using verbal therapy alone, she intuitively felt that nonverbal work would be a realm in which significant changes could be made. As will be explored, over the years that Kate has been in treatment, we found that using multiple art forms were useful; this has been the backbone of her treatment and her significant evolution. Visual art and dance movement were the primary art forms used. Their use in a creative arts therapy and expressive arts therapy context, utilizing an arts-based methodology, will be the backbone through which intermodality is explored in telling Kate's story.

The Wiley Handbook of Art Therapy, First Edition. Edited by David E. Gussak and Marcia L. Rosal.
© 2016 John Wiley & Sons, Ltd. Published 2016 by John Wiley & Sons, Ltd.

Creative Arts Therapy and Expressive Arts Therapy

As discussed previously, creative arts therapists and expressive arts therapists have explored the use of different art forms in tandem, or guided by the inherent issues that arise in a session (Thompson, 2010, 2012). Within creative arts therapy, there is a history of integrating differential art forms in treatment. Especially relevant to this chapter's focus, several studies have specifically addressed the collective use of dance/movement and art (Avstreih & Brown, 1979; Cane, 1983; Hammond-Meiers, 2005, as cited in Thompson, 2010). Best (2003) described the combined use of movement, visual art—specifically sculpture—and role-play. She based the order and reasoning of these within social constructionist or systemic ideas, not exclusively on the properties of the art forms themselves, which she called *interactional shaping*. Kaslow and Eicher (1988) found that, in work with individuals with eating disorders specific to body image, art work in the form of gestural and squiggle drawings functioned as projective drawings, and movement improvisations served as a direct link to unconscious material. Lett (1993), using a phenomenological model, avoided transference and countertransference in using the arts, instead centering attention on the sensory qualities of art forms and their progression into images, emotions, and meaning. Expressive arts therapists, who focus on using all art forms in treatment, are considered specialists in the considered use of multiple art forms. They do not necessarily see themselves as specialists in the use and execution of all art forms individually but often base their work on a particular art form that they have had extensive training in or gravitate to (Knill, Barba, & Levine, 2004; McNiff, 2009; Rea, 2013). Regardless of the particular theories and consequent definitions employed, the general use of intertwining art forms is commonly referred to as *intermodal* or *multimodal*.

Artistic inquiry

Artistic inquiry, as seen by creative arts therapists, is research that employs artistic means to collect, examine, and impart data, based on a range of creative practices and driven by the researcher's aesthetic beliefs and framework (Hervey, 2000; McNiff, 1998). Eisner (1991/1998), relying on his educational perspective, proposed that artists could offer new perspectives and knowledge of the world. Emmison (2004) referred to "image-based visual enquiry" situated in a critical inquiry context. He acknowledged the centrality of the viewer in making the meaning, not those who make the images, with the researchers either making imagery themselves or examining pre-existing images and representations (p. 249). He focused on what the images conveyed beyond the concrete image, and the subsequent study of the "seen and observable." Finley (2005) perceived artistic inquiry from a post-modern activist lens, within a moral and political, arts-based context. She also, following Eisner, viewed artists of many persuasions as having the inherent ability to offer knowledge of the world in particular, often unique, ways.

Kate's Story

Initial exploration of art forms

It became clear that so much of Kate's treatment was predicated upon telling her story, in a relational way, based on an authentic relationship (Stark, 2000). Consequently, her therapeutic process will be presented in the same form, that is, telling her evolving story in therapy sessions, and sharing her artwork and writing.

When Kate first entered creative arts therapy, she committed to only five sessions. She was asked in her first session to pay attention to her body experience, structured by techniques from Gendlin's book titled *Focusing* (Gendlin, 1981, 1997; Weiser Cornell, 1996). Kate's attempts to attend to her bodily felt experience resulted in heart-wrenching and prolonged sobbing. She repeatedly succumbed to a "black hole," with the exception of bodily cues from her head, which remained intact.

In order to introduce more distance and safety within Kate's art experience and production, I suggested that Kate incorporate visual art. Kate selected Plasticine, intuitively selecting an art material that could include her body experience, facilitated by the clay's mobility. She worked quickly, still sobbing intermittently. She created five separate objects, which were placed in a straight sequential line (see Figure 40.1).

As we talked, she realized that each piece represented what she thought was a separate part of her body.

The first was of her head, done in orange and yellow Plasticine. The head had a wide-eyed expression with traces of wonder, deadness, invitation, and aliveness simultaneously, reinforced by fiery vibrant hair. The piece felt animated to her, both in content and color, and reflected the great pleasure she took in her thoughts, as she identified with thinking as a very creative part of herself. The second piece was a heart, created in warm shades of red. She reflected that she had the capacity to have a range of feelings, including warmth and loving feelings, although she could not always apply them. To her, this was her still partially unformed use of heartfelt feelings, although

Figure 40.1 So much thinking, no answers.

with a clear presence. The third piece was a red ball-like shape, covered by blue. The blue felt as if it was threatening to take over the red. Kate recognized that her sexuality was reflected in the red, but regretted that she was not in a relationship at the moment. The fourth shape was the largest. It was practically an unworked lump of clay, standing as an imposing, monolithic structure in comparison to the rest; Kate could not speak about it. The fifth and last piece was a small rounded ball that Kate felt was comforting to hold and represented her feet. She described them as "too big and ugly."

As she looked at her sculptures, she felt calmer and hopeful. She could differentiate disparate parts of her body experience; she was able to recognize parts that she liked, parts that she knew, and parts that she did not know at all. Because she did not usually experience painful feelings as having limits and endings, this helped find and organize her feelings in context of the actual details of her life. The lack of a container called for the use of visual art, thereby utilizing the boundaries afforded by the inherent structure of this art form, transforming the diffuseness that she experienced in the primeval nature of her body. Consequently, she could experience the difference between creative engagement and becoming lost in an experience without boundaries, thereby delving into the improvisational, restorative aspects of the creative process.

During the next few sessions, Kate repeatedly began with the same bodily felt image, that is, the black hole that she had discovered in *Focusing*, although at this juncture it was diminished in size and intensity and located in the center of her body, instead of her entire body. She was willing and able to progress to a series of dance/movement improvisations, stemming from a kinesthetic image of torturous but unspecified experience, reinforcing a theme of becoming immobilized, and then ending with finding a way to resolve this in some way.

She initially moved across the floor as if she was the "Michelin Man," that is, a large, bloated, clumsy person with unarticulated movement. She suddenly became very angry, hit the table a number of times, and then became powerless. I asked her what place in her body she *could* move, referring to the unknown parts of her body that could be mobilized, literally and metaphorically. She found that she could use her feet, the part of her body she could accept, to inch out of her position and center herself.

Several more sessions in dance/movement evolved according to this theme, of immobilization transformed into recovery. In the third session, she started with a discussion about living with relatives who were very ill in her childhood, who suffered significant mental deterioration and body disfigurement. As she moved, she found herself impaled on the floor. Initial attempts to use her feet, stemming from the previous session, were to no avail. After much excruciating and wasted effort to climb to a standing position, she sadly realized that the only way she knew to center herself was to brace against the world. The body disintegration she absorbed as a child via her relatives' bodies became the prototype for her frequent body fragmentation. For each step forward, she experienced regret and sadness alongside.

During the week following this session, the feeling that she did not have a center troubled her. Her eating had been affected, and she found herself binging. We again used visual art, specifically Plasticine. Kate created three sculptures. The first was a curved shape that felt protective and reminded her of a shell. The second was of two boats, which she envisioned gently moving backward and forward in the water. The third was a set of squares that were satisfying; she liked that they were not perfect, and they reminded her of blocks that she had as a young child, again incorporating a soothing memory from childhood. She created a second level of blocks that she felt were trying to find a balance with the original set. She saw them as cobblestones, which were both ground and earth images. At the end of this session, Kate committed to five more sessions. Kate began an extensive series of collages that filled my office walls. They were not accessible to verbalization, until later upon an extensive review that reflected on all aspects of her history, including family experiences and trauma.

Trauma

As treatment progressed, it became clear that Kate relied on outside cues to help her navigate troubling situations. When faced with a situation that she could not immediately encode, she was thrown into feelings of bewilderment, terror, and fragmentation. It later became clear that this originated from trauma, internal narcissistic and moralistic demands, and emotional abandonment within the family. In creating corporal-like shapes that were not perfect, she could begin to embody, in a safe way, the reality of her body. This countered her previous reliance on her considerable intellect as her mind could consciously monitor the external details of an event. This solution, however, created conflicts when her mind and somatic responses were vastly different. As decisions cannot be made without affect (Damasio, 1994), she was left with a black hole, incomprehension and dread. Emotional eating helped to fill the gaping pit.

Kate steadily used movement, visual art, and kinesthetic imagery to discover a self and form new responses. She used artwork outside of the sessions to contain stressful situations and was able to incorporate body experience to monitor eating in some ways. In movement sessions, she explored qualities of directness and indirectness in movement (Bartenieff, 2002; Laban, 2011). This led to the understanding that she was narrowly focused in her interactions and actions; indirectness led to her familiar sense of becoming inundated with formlessness. She could feel and recognize her limited ability to take in the world, as her lack of ability to balance spatial dualities did not support this attitude (North, 1975). Concurrently, she committed to ongoing weekly sessions and terminated with her verbal therapist. She felt that non-verbal processing in conjunction with verbal processing, which creative arts therapy could provide, was most helpful to her. She eventually committed to two sessions a week, reflecting that her inner experience was not as frightening, and that she was willing and able to tolerate and explore the increased intimacy that it brought. She experimented with new kinds of contact with people in her life, she could monitor her eating to a greater degree, and she could allow more relatedness and openness with me.

Awareness of a system

One day, Kate silently handed me a letter. It said "I know her better than you do." My understanding deepened as I realized there was a possibility that Kate was an individual with dissociative identity disorder (DID).

DID is a "complex process of change in a person's consciousness that causes a disturbance or alteration in the normally integrative functions of identity, memory, thought, feeling, and experience" (Cohen & Cox, 1995, p. 296). It is often brought about by trauma, such as a severe accident or ongoing child abuse. The DID is often accompanied by "the presence of two or more distinct identities or personality states (each with its own relatively enduring pattern of perceiving, relating to, and thinking about the environment and self)" (American Psychiatric Association, 2000, p. 519). These distinct, alternate personalities or states (often referred to as "alters") demonstrate marked change in affect, cognition, behavior, and memory (American Psychiatric Association, 2013). Kate revealed these tendencies.

As our work continued over time, we discovered that Kate had 15 alters, each performing a different function that could be called into action when needed. It became clear that they were formed in response to a need for separate circumscribed containers within her overall psyche. As Kate described the central organization of the system:

> Each alter has tremendous strength, conviction, clarity, and expertise. Though certain behaviors or points of view initially seemed counterintuitive and/or contradictory, Dr. Thompson and I realized that all decisions were always in service to the system, and to the Wounded Part in particular. The Wounded Part holds crushing trauma, shame, anguish, torment, fear, and humiliation. The Boy's ability to express anger and to "swagger" through experiences have helped her when she has been overwhelmed and immobilized, and, as alters, they are two sides of the same coin.

Kate continued to make art. Figure 40.2 is a cardboard handmade journal that explores life and death, as well as gender.

Figure 40.2 Life, death, androgyny, and decay.

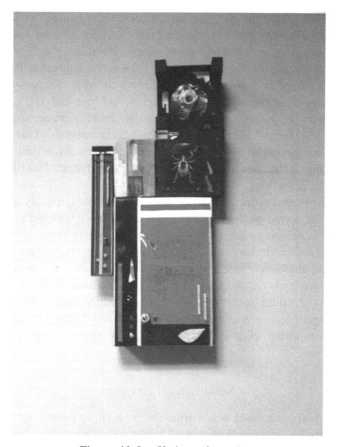

Figure 40.3   Clarity and scrutiny.

Figure 40.3 depicts the process of becoming a system. Most of the alters are included in the sculptural piece and the figure incorporates mixed media.

Differential use of art forms

The following section describes two sessions that concentrated on the employment of dance/movement and visual art, but also incorporated bodily felt experience and verbal processing. Kate had been going through a very distressing and anxiety-provoking situation at work, which provoked strong transferences and was linked to issues surrounding eating, which had lain quiescent for some time. During these sessions, Kate was able to use art forms in a clear sequence of bodily felt imagery, dance/movement, and visual art. This allowed her to utilize art forms that tapped into a circumscribed image embedded in the body that evoked very primal and direct contact with feeling, as well as provided an opportunity to gain perspective from the feelings.

In the first session, Kate started by speaking about the pain in her back that she was working on with her chiropractor. In *Focusing*, this localized pain switched to a bodily felt sense located in her entire body, which was "black, dense, weighty." She felt rooted to the floor. As she moved to the dance floor, she became a cat stalking its prey, low to the ground, freezing so she could be still, waiting. A lizard emerged, tongue ready to snare an insect, very fast and still. In exploring this in dance/movement, her movement took the form of an active stance of not moving, ready to pounce. Her head eventually moved as it dropped, embodying a coiled bodily posture. Her hands opened and closed, as she contacted feelings of holding and trying to let go of enormous tension, both from work and from her family, feeling boxed in. As she continued, the transference she felt for a child in her classroom, and his mother whose actions were incomprehensively cruel and controlling, surfaced. Although many alters were contributing to the conversation, they were in agreement about the student, and concerned about his welfare.

Beginning the next session, Kate lay on the floor, puzzled, initially wondering why she was there. She stayed on the floor, lying on her stomach with her arms spread out. She again had the fantasy of becoming a large cat, ready to pounce; this tapped into a fantasy of being a fierce fighter, a predator, ready to propel herself if needed.

After a while, the development of her process changed, as she sat back on her knees and pronounced that she had had enough of trauma, it didn't have "a draw" anymore, and she could protect herself. To our amazement, the corresponding bodily felt imagery she sensed was dissolved. She had found her rage, and it was significantly diminished. She felt hopeful and she smiled, with some delighted self-consciousness.

Solidifying the system

Kate's last art piece (to date) was a triptych, with three panels, set in mat board, covered by white house paint (Figure 40.4). The panels were intended to make links among the content of the three. Although she planned the piece, she was surprised with the result.

The second panel was the centerpiece, consisting of a photo of body piercings she had had done many years earlier. The photo served as a metaphor for the pain, grief, and distress she bore, as a result of her family's trauma and PTSD, the family's extreme religiosity, and fractured relationships, all of which were internalized via her own body image. At the bottom of this middle panel is the Scrabble piece, M worth 3 points; this represented M3. Instead of the emergence of a new alter in the system, M3 was the system itself, thriving and intact, making decisions as a unit, with decreased splintering, due to our work, and the help of the Integrator's efforts. The Integrator was the one to do this, "as he was an advocate for the system, always working behind the scenes to keep things moving in the right direction." What had started in movement a few weeks earlier was further solidified, in visual art.

The left panel echoed feelings of home, feeling connected and safe. She did not know where such a home would be in the world. The panel elicited sturdiness and strength to her, but it was not a "literal home or psychic home" as there was a "chasm" between the two. At the bottom of this panel was a map that included San Francisco, which referenced dressing in leather and engaging in sado-masochist behaviors. This was a contribution from the Libertine, who is "fun-loving, open-minded, loves a party, and has a 'say yes to everything' outlook on life."

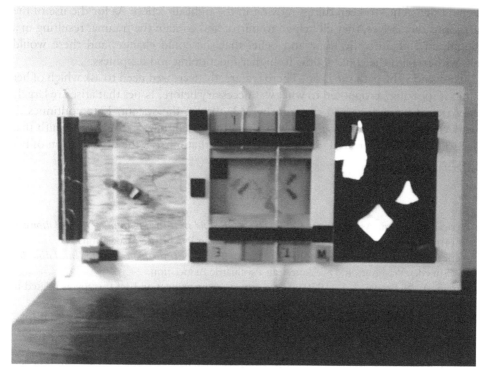

Figure 40.4 A dark and dangerous journey.

The right panel contained small pieces of a broken mirror, the pieces of which signified the newness of the system functioning more as a unit. The largest piece, in particular, was cracked, not splintered, held together by a backing. Several small rocks at the farthest left in the panel had a link to prior pieces that were weighted down, hard to move, perhaps containing feelings of how difficult it was to process this material.

Conclusion

Making art, in various forms, was a central part of Kate's treatment. This was evidenced by the centrality that art bore, and the role that it acquired in her overall progress. Several features attest to this. Her more sophisticated art provided her with the opportunity to articulate meaning, where it had been inaccessible previously. She was able to achieve greater insight where there had been confusion and chaos before, eventually making peace with the family members and others who contributed to or were the origin of her internalized trauma. She could look at this trauma, without becoming it. She had insight into generational trauma, and how it applied to her. Her initial symptoms were not increased; in fact, they were decreased or dormant. Importantly, the system became a working unit, with all alters eventually working in support of each other. The Integrator especially was a system advocate, always working behind the scenes to keep things moving in the right direction. As for the use of the art forms themselves, they all helped to mirror and contain the trauma, resulting in a significant shift into the hope and belief that she could change, and there would always be a path she could follow to higher functioning and happiness.

This is now the path she is on. There is a greatly decreased need to ask which of her alters is speaking, as opposed to what was necessary before. Issues that arise are largely approached by and worked through by M3, that is, the system. Kate continues to work on questions that arise, but with a new approach, new strength, and faith that she will find a way through. She has a directness that mirrors the organization of her psyche and spirit.

References

American Psychiatric Association. (2000). *Diagnostic and statistical manual of mental disorders* (4th ed.—text revised). Washington, DC: American Psychiatric Association.

American Psychiatric Association. (2013). *Diagnostic and statistical manual of mental disorders* (5th ed.). Washington, DC: American Psychiatric Association.

Avstreih, A., & Brown, J. J. (1979). Some aspects of movement and art therapy as related to the analytic situation. *The Psychoanalytic Review, 66*(1), 49–68.

Bartenieff, I. (2002). *Body movement: Coping with the environment.* New York, NY: Routledge.

Best, P. A. (2003). Interactional shaping within therapeutic encounters: Three dimensional dialogues. *The USA Body Psychotherapy Association Journal, 2*(1), 26–44.

Cane, F. (1983). *The artist in each of us* (Rev. ed.). Craftsbury Common, VT: Art Therapy Publications.

Cohen, B., & Cox, C. (1995). *Telling without talking: Art as a window into the world of Multiple Personality.* New York, NY: WW. Norton and Company.

Damasio, A. (1994). *Descartes' error: Emotion, reason, and the human brain.* New York, NY: Putnam and Sons.

Eisner, E. (1991/1998). *The enlightened eye: Qualitative inquiry and the enhancement of educational practice.* Upper Saddle River, NJ: Prentice Hall.

Emmison, M. (2004). The conceptualization of and analysis of visual data. In D. Silverman (Ed.), *Qualitative research: Theory, method and practice* (2nd ed.). Thousand Oaks, CA: Sage.

Finley, S. (2005). Arts-based inquiry: Performing revolutionary pedagogy. In N. K. Denzin & Y. S. Lincoln (Eds.), *The sage handbook of qualitative research* (3rd ed., pp. 681–694). Thousand Oaks, CA: Sage.

Gendlin, E. T. (1981). *Focusing* (2nd Rev. ed.). New York, NY: Bantam Books.

Hammond-Meiers, J. (2005). *A phenomenological study in art and dance/movement therapy: The experiences of women in a group* (Unpublished master's thesis). Vancouver, Canada: Vancouver Art Therapy Institute.

Hervey, L. (2000). *Artistic inquiry in dance/movement therapy: Creative research alternatives.* Springfield, IL: Charles C. Thomas.

Kaslow N. J., & Eicher, V.W. (1988). Body image therapy: A combined creative arts therapy and verbal psychotherapy approach. *The Arts in Psychotherapy, 15*(3), 177–188.

Knill, P. J., Barba, H. N., & Fuchs, M. N. (2004). *Minstrels of soul: Intermodal expressive therapy* (2nd ed.). Toronto, Canada: EGS Press.

Laban, R. (2011). *The mastery of movement.* London, England: MacDonald and Evans.

Lett, W. (1993). Therapist creativity: The arts of supervision. *Arts in Psychotherapy, 20*(5), 371–386.

McNiff, S. (1998). *Art-based research.* Philadelphia, PA: Jessica Kingsley.

McNiff, S. (2009). *Integrating the arts in psychotherapy: History, theory and practice.* Springfield, IL: Charles C. Thomas.

North, N. (1975). *Personality assessment through movement.* Boston, MA: Plays.

Rea, K. (2013). *The healing dance: The life and practice of an expressive arts therapist.* Springfield, IL: Charles C Thomas.

Stark, M. (2000). *Modes of therapeutic action: Enhancement of knowledge, provision of experience, and engagement in relationship.* Northvale, NJ: Jason Aronson.

Thompson, L. (2010). Integration of art, movement and verbal processing with women in an eating disorders program. In S. Riley (Ed.), *Group process made visible; Group art therapy* (pp. 209–220). Philadelphia, PA: Brunner-Routledge.

Thompson, L. (2012). *Artistic choices in therapeutic practice: The use of art forms in creative arts therapy.* Doctoral dissertation, Union Institute and University, 2010.

Weiser Cornell, A. (1996). *The power of focusing.* New York, NY: MJF Books.

Part V

Practicing Art Therapy in Interdisciplinary Settings

Introduction

The staff members who are a part of a work team strive toward an agreed-upon goal; for a clinical team, the common goal is the treatment of clients. The settings that employ art therapists are likely to be interdisciplinary in nature. Relationships between art therapists and the other professional members of a team have evolved over the years, such that they have become integral to a team. Today, art therapists are an integral part of numerous educational, medical, and clinical systems. While the previous section focused on art therapy work with specific populations, the seven chapters included in this section investigate the *settings* in which art therapists may find themselves.

In *School Art Therapy*, Siegel offers an overview of art therapy in one of the first settings where art therapists were employed. Recognizing that art therapy is effective in this setting because "this is where the children are," Siegel draws upon his own experiences as the director of one of the largest school-based art therapy programs in the United States, the Miami-Dade Unified School District in South Florida. He focuses on the role of the art therapist to facilitate healthy development for students in this setting.

Rosner-David's chapter, *Art Therapy in Medical Settings*, explores the personal, professional, and environmental struggles that art therapists encounter in medical settings. The chapter also includes strategies for art therapists to effectively integrate themselves with the medical team. The next chapter is written by an occupational therapist. As a long-time practitioner providing rehabilitative care for people who have suffered traumatic physical ailments, Cox, in her chapter titled *Art Therapy in Rehabilitation Centers*, describes her learning experiences supervising art therapy practicum students. She not only defines the role of the occupational therapist as part of a rehabilitation team, but also reports on her involvement in helping art therapists integrate into this milieu. Specifying the challenges and triumphs, Cox illustrates how art therapy can complement and supplement the continuum of care available in rehabilitation settings.

Carolan addresses the many ways art therapists deliver services in substance abuse settings in his chapter, *Addiction and Art Therapy: Interdisciplinary Considerations*.

The Wiley Handbook of Art Therapy, First Edition. Edited by David E. Gussak and Marcia L. Rosal.
© 2016 John Wiley & Sons, Ltd. Published 2016 by John Wiley & Sons, Ltd.

Art therapy in forensic settings is the topic of Cohen-Liebman's chapter, *Forensic Art Therapy: Epistemological and Ontological Underpinnings*. She examines the unique ontological and epistemological foundations of art therapy in the forensic arena. She espouses a "pragmatic investigative approach" to using art therapy in the court system. Gussak offers an overview of his work in forensic settings. In *Art Therapy in the Prison Milieu,* he outlines the theoretical perspectives and research outcomes that demonstrate the practice as well as the efficacy of art therapy in prisons and other correctional settings.

The final chapter in this section, *Bringing Art Therapy into Museums*, explores the use of art therapy in a relatively new setting, the art museum. Drawing upon her exploratory work with colleague Marcia Rosal, Brown-Treadon examines the various functions that an art therapist may afford an art museum. Unlocking this site as an agent of therapeutic change is outlined in her chapter.

Each chapter in this section paints a picture of how art therapists integrate into these settings. Together, a collage is created of the exciting and far-reaching strides that art therapists have taken to integrate into numerous professional settings. In the near future, the reach of the art therapist may stretch further into other settings yet to be discovered.

41

School Art Therapy

Craig A. Siegel

Legend has it that when Willie Sutton was asked why he robbed banks, he responded by saying, "That's where the money is." It is important to understand the need for art therapy in schools because "that's where the children are." Schools are playing an increasing role in identifying and treating mental health problems. Current research on the mental health status of children and youth points to public schools as major providers of such services for children and adolescents (SAMHSA, 2010), and reports such as the US president's New Freedom Commission on Mental Health identify the key role that schools can play in continuing these services (Foster et al., 2005). Whereas an emphasis of the research focuses on therapeutic interventions as it relates to emotional and behavioral disorders, it is rather limited in regard to addressing the unique needs of children and adolescents with varying abilities in the school system.

Much has been written about art therapy as it relates to artistic development (Kellogg, 1969; Lowenfeld & Brittain, 1975; Rubin, 1978) and the use of art therapy with children and adolescents (Kramer, 1977; Landgarten, 1981; Levick, 1983; Linesch, 1988; Rubin, 1978). However, the emphasis of this chapter is not to rehash the theories and approaches to art therapy practice with this specific age population. Instead, this chapter will address the role and scope of practice of the art therapist in the school milieu, and will identify how to provide therapeutic support within a system that was not originally established to do so.

The Decline of Mental Services for US Youth

Over the last 25 years, there has been a steady decline in the availability of mental health services for children and adolescents. From 1986 to 2004, the number of mental health organizations within the United States decreased by 17.7%, from 3,512 to 2,819; this has lead to a decline of 20.7% in available beds, from 267,613 to 212,231. Due to the decrease in available programs and space, admissions during that same time period dropped by 43.3%, from 324,966 to 184,301 (SAMHSA, 2010). The overall impact of this trend has been that more individuals are waiting to seek treatment, and when they do, they tend to seek assistance from an emergency room. This leaves numerous children

The Wiley Handbook of Art Therapy, First Edition. Edited by David E. Gussak and Marcia L. Rosal.
© 2016 John Wiley & Sons, Ltd. Published 2016 by John Wiley & Sons, Ltd.

and adolescents without access to services, both preventative and ongoing. It is within the school setting that concerns are identified and intervention is initially provided.

Historic and Contemporary Issues in School Art Therapy

School art therapy has its roots in the pioneering efforts of art educators—for example, Cole (1941, 1966), Cane (1951), and Lowenfeld (1957)—who introduced the therapeutic aspects of art making with school children. With the 1975 passing of the Individuals with Disabilities Education Act (IDEA), also known as Public Law 94-142, children of varying abilities were guaranteed a free, appropriate public education. This paved the way for school systems to provide the necessary accommodations and related services to help children learn.

As children entered public schools, it became clear that the schools were not prepared to meet the array of individualized needs. School systems throughout the country were faced with the challenge of meeting the needs of students who were frequently ignored in the past. This time period spawned the outgrowth of special education. Whereas school systems were researching on means of helping students of varying abilities participate in core curriculum classes, there was limited focus on how to integrate these students into other educational areas such as art and music. The field was ripe for the introduction of art therapy.

The same year that IDEA passed, Felice Cohen, in her article *Introducing art therapy into a school system: Some problems,* discussed her experience in utilizing art therapy within a Texas school district to explore its use as a diagnostic and therapeutic tool (1974, pp. 121–135). Shortly thereafter, Virginia Minar (1978) completed a 3-year pilot study of the benefits of art therapy in the West Allis public school system. In 1979, Janet Bush introduced a pilot art therapy program within Miami-Dade County Public Schools to address challenges that art educators and others were experiencing in working with students identified with autism and physical impairments, or those who were considered emotionally or profoundly mentally handicapped. It was the success of this program that paved the way for art therapists to enter the school setting. Ms. Bush's program expanded from a single art therapist to four to eventually employing over 20 art therapists.

As Ms. Bush's clinical art therapy department expanded, new challenges arose for art therapists providing school-based intervention. It became necessary for art therapists who were trained in a medical model to adapt their skills and language to assimilate into the educational system framework. As Ms. Bush and the early pioneers of school art therapy made further inroads, it was evident that school art therapy was, in itself, a distinct subset of art therapy training.

The goal of school art therapy has been to assist the student to manage social, emotional, cognitive, and behavioral barriers, which impede the ability to successfully access educational opportunities. These goals may be established through the development of a behavior intervention plan (BIP) or listed on a student's individual education plan (IEP). However, to qualify and quantify objective and observable goals, the goals must be based on the art therapist's clinical findings. It was determined that the most logical way to accomplish this task was to utilize an art therapy assessment tool.

Assessment

A major emphasis of training to become a school art therapist is a profound under-standing of art therapy assessments and diagnostic tools. The art therapy assessment serves as the initial step to understanding a student's needs and being able to report on those needs within cognitive and emotional constructs. The assessment results provide information on the student's ability to perform in the classroom, understand concepts, and make learning gains. IEPs are developed based on such data that high-light a student's strengths and weaknesses. The assessment tools used, such as the Levick Emotional and Cognitive Art Therapy Assessment (LECATA; 2009), are those designed to identify certain developmental milestones, and the skills, if any, that fall above or below normative expectations. This initial step then serves as the overall roadmap for the development of treatment goals within art therapy.

Often, art therapy assessments are implemented with students who have already experienced difficulties within the general education setting and/or those students who have not demonstrated progress with traditional forms of therapy offered by the school. It is therefore recommended that schools consider using art therapy assess-ments as an early intervention tool. As of this writing, many school districts have adopted a multi-tiered system of success (MTSS) approach to addressing students' social, emotional, behavioral, and cognitive needs for academic success.

MTSS is a three-tiered system that categorizes students based on the levels of inter-ventions needed. An art therapy assessment could provide significant data to schools related to those students who are typically overlooked. Myra Levick addressed this same conclusion upon completion of her normative research on the LECATA[1]:

> It is inconceivable to me to consider art therapy tasks for someone, child or adult, without assessing that individual's strengths, weaknesses, as well as levels of functioning cognitively and emotionally. After completing this study, I am more convinced than ever of the efficiency and efficacy of art as an assessment not only in the area of establishing treatment goals, but in identifying children and adolescents at risk before symptoms erupt in the environment. (Levick, 2009, p. 131)

The following list includes the types of information that an art therapy assessment may be able to provide regarding a student's current functioning, all of which are essential for a student to perform successfully in the classroom:

1. Cognitive development
    (a) Ability to perform fine and gross motor skills
    (b) Ability to copy or transfer
    (c) Ability to comprehend, retain, and follow single-step directions
    (d) Ability to comprehend, retain, and follow multiple-step directions
    (e) Ability to sequence
    (f) Ability to understand spatial relationships
    (g) Ability to use abstract thinking
    (h) Ability to combine
    (i) Ability to focus
    (j) Ability to demonstrate problem-solving skills

2. Emotional development
    (a) Ability to recognize and express feelings
    (b) Ability to control impulses
    (c) Ability to cope with frustration
    (d) Ability to delay gratification
    (e) Ability to maintain reality orientation
    (f) Ability to accept consequences

3. Social development
    (a) Ability to cope with environmental stressors
    (b) Ability to communicate thoughts, ideas, and needs
    (c) Ability to interact with peers
    (d) Ability to interact with adults/authority figures
    (e) Ability to empathize
    (f) Ability to cooperate

Once an art therapy assessment is completed and the results shared with all involved parties, the next focus can be on intervention. Interventions can be provided through many different models based on the recommendations from the art therapy assessment and can be provided through consultation, collaboration, individual, and/or group design. The first two—consultation and collaboration—may be used when accommodating students' needs within the classroom setting. They may be as simple as preferential seating to more involved strategies based on the needs of the student.

Engagement

Art therapy intervention is derived from the understanding that the focus is on assisting the student to gain the skills necessary to be a successful learner. Often, other school personnel determine the need for treatment, and, as a result, many students receiving such services are "placed" in therapy, creating a challenge that must be addressed before an art therapist can proceed. Therefore, significant time must be allotted for developing a therapeutic relationship with the student to break through any initial resistance and to assist the student to become a "willing partner" in the therapeutic journey.

This chapter does not present any particular art therapy intervention techniques, as there are as many unique needs within the school environment as there are art therapists bringing their own style and approach to meet those needs. Instead, emphasis is placed on the need for interventions that enhance student engagement. Art material availability and selection is paramount to the level of student investment. Whereas a school art therapist must adjust to the situation—such as having one's own classroom/studio space; having to work from a cart and provide interventions in the corner of the room; or having to work under a tree in a courtyard—media choice must not be a barrier to engagement and self-expression. Materials must be inviting, well maintained, and aligned with the therapeutic goals in mind.

Many materials available to the school art therapist are similar to those that the student has been exposed to in the classroom or art room, such as crayons, markers, and pencils. Although there may be some level of comfort and security derived from familiarity, it may also serve to stunt creativity in lieu of stereotypic imagery. These materials may also create a perceived lack of distinct separation between the classroom/ art room and the art therapy setting, thus indirectly reinforcing resistance and avoidance. A school art therapist would benefit from using materials that entice the student to want to participate, which may include found objects, photography, and computers.

Collaboration, consultation, and communication

Once a school art therapist has established an ongoing therapeutic relationship with the student and they are working toward treatment goals, it is vital for him or her to also maintain communication with all concerned parties. This involves participating in and/or establishing weekly team meetings with teachers and other mental health professionals within the school to discuss student progress, challenges, and necessary changes to the overall treatment plan. If the student is receiving services from an outside resource, then collaboration is necessary to assist in the continuum of care. Regular contact with the parent or guardian can improve parental involvement and consistency as it relates to behavioral intervention strategies.

It is incumbent upon the school art therapist to use these forums to educate others about the benefits of art therapy for each particular student. Through formal and informal in-service presentations, school art therapists can enhance their recognition and value.

Establishing a School Art Therapy Program

Whether one is trying to start an art therapy program within a school setting or hired into an existing program, there are strategies that may help ensure success. First, an art therapist must find the money. As in many settings, art therapy is looked upon favorably, but many institutions still have difficulty finding the financial resources to hire an art therapist. In the United States, this will hopefully change as healthcare reform progresses, the change in classification of the profession within the US Department of Labor occurs, and the number of US states seeking and/or achieving licensure increases.

As an art therapist approaches a particular school or school system, he or she would benefit from conducting preliminary research and formulating a plan that focuses on which department/population has the best opportunity for success. This may vary based on particular needs and or events. Art therapists have found success within the art education, special education, counseling, or student services departments.

School systems are managed by administrators trained in educational administration, curriculum, law, and other aspects of school governance (Bush, 1997). Often minimized in their training is learning how to work with students with varying abilities and needs. An art therapist can educate these administrators on the benefits of art therapy with school-based populations, particularly timely topics. These may include bullying prevention, dropout prevention, reducing in-school violence, decreasing suspension rates, and reducing absenteeism. If successfully addressed, all these issues can reduce costs, which is an added benefit for budget-minded administrators.

When it comes to funding an art therapist, one should be prepared to discuss a plethora of options. One option available to all public schools is the federal funds attached to IDEA. These monies are specifically designated for the support and services necessary for an individual to access a free and appropriate public education. Another option is obtaining funds from general revenue structures, for which an administrator may hire service providers at their discretion. Other strategies may include grants for pilot studies and/or research, request for proposals (RFPs) to provide contracted services, or volunteering services for a period of time to demonstrate the benefits of school art therapy.

Once an art therapist gains entry into the school milieu, the ability to maintain that foothold becomes an ongoing challenge. As federal, state, and local municipalities continue to struggle with maintaining a steady revenue source, school administrators are constantly looking to find ways to cut what they deem to be unnecessary expenditures. School art therapists must continuously demonstrate their value through in-service presentations, exhibits, parent workshops, and community out reach. Such demonstrations include research illustrating its effectiveness.

Research

As institutions focus more on evidence-based intervention strategies, it is important for ongoing research to strengthen the efficacy of art therapy within the school milieu. There are a multitude of opportunities for both qualitative and quantitative research, including longitudinal studies addressing emotional growth and learning gains. Ms. Bush stated that, "research could spur … a concerted effort to have art therapy included in school programs for all children" (1997, p. 126). Since her comments, there have been numerous research studies conducted, focusing on an array of topics related to school art therapy.

Studies targeting at-risk populations (Rosal, McCullouch-Vislisel, & Neece, 1997; Wallace-DiGarbo & Hill, 2006), those identified with learning disabilities (Freilich & Schechtman, 2010; Silver & Lavin, 1997), and autism spectrum disorders (Kearns, 2004) have been conducted. Other areas of inquiry that directly impact child and adolescent development are being entertained by a new breed of professionals who understand the importance of research to validate the efficacy of art therapy. School art therapists working in conjunction with students conducting research as part of graduate study can forge an alliance to identify future research topics. In turn, knowledge and benefits of art therapy within educational settings will not only be expanded, but will also assist in future employment opportunities.

Conclusion

School art therapy programs differ greatly from each other based on the framework of the school and the orientation of the art therapist. What remains constant is that the school setting has increasingly become the "catch-all" for a child's healthy development. State comprehensive test scores demonstrate a trend that today's youth appear considerably regressed in terms of their ability to communicate and express themselves appropriately through verbal and written means. This, coupled with societal challenges, has created a significant need for therapeutic support in the educational arena. Therefore, it is in the schools that an art therapist can assist in both the identification and intervention of children and adolescents in need. Armed with a unique skill set, art therapists are in the schools to intervene because "that's where the children are."

Endnote

1   Please refer to Chapter 51 in this book, by Myra Levick and Craig Siegel, on the LECATA.

References

Bush, J. (1997). *The handbook of school art therapy.* Springfield, IL: Charles C. Thomas.

Cane, F. (1951). *The artist in each of us.* Craftsbury Common, VT: Art Therapy Publications.

Cohen, F. (1974). Introducing art therapy into a school system: Some problems. *Art psychotherapy, 2,* 121–136.

Cole, N. (1941). *The arts in the classroom.* New York, NY: John Day.

Cole, N. (1966). *Children's arts from deep down inside.* New York, NY: The John Day Company.

Foster, S., Rollefson, M., Doksum, T., Noonan, D., Robinson, G., & Teich, J. (2005). *School mental health services in the United States, 2002–2003.* HHS Pub. No. (SMA) 05-4068. Rockville, MD: Center for Mental Health Services, Substance Abuse and Mental Health Services Administration.

Freilich, R., & Shechtman, Z. (2010). The contribution of art therapy to the social, emotional, and academic adjustment of children with learning disabilities. *The Arts in Psychotherapy, 37*(1), 8–12

Kearns, D. (2004). Art therapy with a child experiencing sensory integration difficulty. *Art Therapy: Journal of the American Art Therapy Association, 21*(2), 95–101.

Kellogg, R. (1969). *Analyzing children's art.* Palo Alto, CA: National Press Books.

Kramer, E. (1977). *Art as therapy with children.* New York, NY: Schocken Books.

Landgarten, H. (1981). *Clinical art therapy.* New York, NY: Brunner/Mazel.

Levick, M. F. (1983). *They could not talk and so they drew: Children's styles of coping and thinking.* Springfield, IL: Charles C. Thomas.

Levick, M. F. (2009). *Levick emotional and cognitive art therapy assessment: A normative study.* IN: AuthorHouse.

Linesch, D. (1988). *Adolescent art therapy.* New York, NY: Brunner/Mazel.

Lowenfeld, V. (1957). *Creative and mental growth* (3rd ed.). New York, NY: MacMillan.

Lowenfeld, V., & Brittain, W. L. (1975). *Creative and mental growth* (6th ed.). New York, NY: MacMillan.

Minar, V. (1978). Report on a pilot study: Art therapy in public schools. In R. Shoemaker & S. Gonick-Barris (Eds.), *The dynamics of creativity: Proceedings of the Seventh Annual Conference.* American Art Therapy Association, Baltimore, MD.

Rosal, M., McCulloch-Vislisel, S., & Neese, S. (1997). Keeping students in school: An art therapy program to benefit ninth grade students. *Art Therapy: Journal of the American Art Therapy Association, 14*(2), 30–36.

Rubin, J. A. (1978). *Child art therapy: Understanding and helping children grow through art.* New York, NY: Van Nostrand Reinhold.

Silver, R. A., & Lavin, C. (1997). The role of art in developing and evaluating cognitive skills. *Journal of Learning Disabilities, 10*(7), 416–424.

Substance Abuse and Mental Health Services Administration. (2010). *Mental Health, United States, 2008.* HHS Publication No. (SMA) 10-4590, Rockville, MD: Center for Mental Health Services, Substance Abuse and Mental Health Services Administration.

Wallace-DiGarbo, A., & Hill, D. C. (2006). Art as agency: Exploring empowerment of at-risk youth. *Art Therapy: Journal of the American Art Therapy Association, 23*(3), 119–125.

42

Art Therapy in Medical Settings

Irene Rosner David

The benefits of art therapy in medical settings are to alleviate emotional intensity, instill mastery, cultivate self-esteem, contribute to effective adaptation and enhanced coping with diagnoses and prognoses, as well as to provide diagnostic insights. However, the practical application of art therapy is somewhat hampered in a medical setting, due to environmental elements. Unlike other settings that have art rooms, community venues, and able-bodied ambulatory clients, the medical setting is by definition one of active medical intervention. The medical environment is designed for treatment and is, therefore, laden with challenges for the art therapist. Patients are primarily, and understandably, focused on their medical conditions, and challenged by disease or disability-related psychological issues. Art therapists must embrace these clinical aspects, as well as work within the design and activity of a healthcare facility space, be aware of uncertain periods for treatment, and be cognizant of a narrowed repertoire of media.

Primarily, patients' physical status will be apparent to the art therapist in such a setting. Psychological and emotional aspects related to physical status and hospitalization will form the therapist's clinical goals and dictate direction in the art process. Mental health or illness, pre-existing psychological issues, or psychiatric treatment may not be known to the art therapist or other medical caregivers. As Prager (1995) noted, the patient's mental health is important, but medical procedures have precedence over psychosocial treatments such as art therapy. Clearly, the broader concept of mental status integrates pre-existing coping styles as reaction to diagnoses, prognoses, and medical interventions.

The underlying psychological structures merged with the overlay of medically related psychological issues are reflected in the artistic process and products. For example, a mature insight-oriented woman lost her leg in an auto accident and endured a period of reactive depression followed by successful integration of her prosthesis and, ultimately, life adjustment. She was immediately receptive to engaging in art therapy, and used the resource to externalize initial emotions, depict phases of mourning for the lost limb and its function, and finally affirmed her reformed sense of self.

In contrast, a young student was similarly impaired, but was spared amputation after a subway accident. Her resultant nerve damage left her less able to ambulate effectively than if she had a prosthetic leg. Early on, she was reluctant to draw, but

The Wiley Handbook of Art Therapy, First Edition. Edited by David E. Gussak and Marcia L. Rosal.
© 2016 John Wiley & Sons, Ltd. Published 2016 by John Wiley & Sons, Ltd.

engaged upon coaxing and created aesthetic renderings of which she was self-critical, and dismissed them for any merit—artistic or personal. The artwork reflected her interest in design, which was validating, but lacked meaningful content. The absence of emotional association seemed more to do with her lack of self-confidence and inner resources prior to the accident, than as a defense against dealing with the trauma. From intensive care, to rehabilitation, to outpatient sessions, her artwork remained beautiful but disconnected from her experience. These examples illustrate different inherent levels of self-awareness, and capacities for expression, insight, and reflection. The art therapist needs to extrapolate what a patient is bringing to the medical experience, and then interface with the underlying psychological issues that would most likely be elicited by the condition.

The environment of a medical setting is rarely conducive to art-making. The art therapist working in such a setting should expect to do a great deal of one-to-one bedside work and, therefore, would have to modify the existent environment into an art-making space. With regard to the challenges of physical space, Moon (2002) referred to unalterable "givens," leaving the art therapist to shape the space into one that is "conducive to therapeutic work" (p. 69). This can mean working around medical devices in proximity and connected to patients, as well as the level of the patient's physical pain. The patient's ability to sit up, level of verbal communication, limited use of hands, diminished dexterity, and any missing limbs must be taken in consideration. Ambient sound emanating from equipment, breathing tubes, cardiac monitors, suctions, and overhead pages will also cause distraction. Invariably, there are interruptions by other caregivers to tend to an apparatus, as well as disruptions of sessions due to tests, procedures, or emergent situations. Therefore, a common feature in a medical setting is inconsistency in scheduling and unpredictable duration of sessions, given the distractions and interruptions. To the extent possible, reviewing medical records for anticipated tests or procedures and checking with nurses, doctors, and technicians may forestall or minimize truncated or cancelled art sessions.

Furthermore, people are hospitalized for varying lengths of stay. While most medical procedures have projected average periods of care associated with them, there may be individual variations or unforeseen situations. This makes the duration of art therapy treatment virtually impossible to determine. It also makes goal setting difficult, creating a need for short-term art therapy. Some clinicians, anticipating a condensed opportunity, consider a single-session focus the most viable approach (Hughes, 2012).

Art therapists generally have a broad range of materials in their armamentarium, and offer media that would best facilitate clinical goals. Such clinicians are familiar with the different responses elicited by different materials matched to a patient's presentation and need. However, in a medical setting, the options are reduced, in consideration of lack of space and hygienic concerns. For example, one would not offer wet media to someone with insufficiently healed incisions, lacerations, or intravenous lines. Positional aspects may dictate media choice as well (e.g., not being able to use fluid media for those in a prone position).

All of the aforementioned elements require significant flexibility and creativity of the art therapist working in a medical setting. Although the healthcare environment cannot be changed, the art therapist can modify an area into a metaphoric non-clinical corner. Clearing off a tray table and/or using boards mounted on cushions or pillows can make art-making possible. Repositioning one's self in unorthodox ways may be necessary as well. One might lean into the bedside, maneuver among poles and equipment, hold pads upright, guide in a hand-over-hand manner, tape paper down—all in the spirit of finding the patient's ability vs disability (Rosner, 1982).

Multidisciplinary vs Interdisciplinary

For clinicians who do not fill a traditional role as a healthcare professional, there is an inherent challenge to weave oneself into the commonly known fabric of caregiving. Patients and their families know to expect physicians, nurses, technicians, and social workers to provide services, but rarely do they expect art therapists. Moreover, at the time of this writing, there is inconsistency as to the prevalence of art therapy in medical settings, variation as to how such a service is perceived by staff, and the increasing presence of artists in such facilities. British music therapist Nigel Hartley described the need to introduce the arts in inpatient palliative care programs so that it fits within "their world and the healthcare experience" (2008, p. 46). Although there is yet to be such a standard in the United States, as a psychological discipline, art therapists must strive to have this discipline integrated into patients' clinical goals and care plans.

There is much to consider as to how art therapists can fold themselves into the medical team. Full integration is the result of exposing other professionals to the substantive nature of the work and clinical benefits to patients. This includes the ability to articulate objectives, processes, and outcomes that are relevant to the population served. The art therapist in a medical setting would be wise to learn as much as possible about the disabilities and disease entities confronting their patients, along with the commonly associated psychological reactions. Such knowledge will help art therapists contribute to patient care in significant ways and in relation to other treatment services. Art therapists in medical settings should also develop an understanding of the role and lexicon of other disciplines. These can be very specific in the medical world, and everyone on a team should be able to find a common ground for communication.

Numerous professionals treat medically compromised patients, including art therapists. Engaging patients in art processes and guiding patients toward enhanced coping through artistic expression make for a strong contribution in itself, but this should be conveyed to other members of the treatment team. Different disciplines or modalities may have different profession-specific purposes, but all team members work in the spirit of patients' health maintenance and overall improvement. For example, an art therapist may support a patient's reactive depression or anxiety after an ominous prognosis or decline, while respiratory or physical therapists have defined physical goals. This reflects discipline-specific work, but the progress made by each discipline is enhanced by communicating respective goals, encouraging the patient to participate in other forms of treatment, and finding ways to co-treat.

However respectable and successful an intervention may be, it is not always fully collaborative. The optimal manner of working is an interdisciplinary one. Interdisciplinary collaboration is created when different healthcare perspectives culminate in harmonious clinical goals. For example, an art therapist may have a patient work with a malleable medium for dissipating anxiety, while there is the secondary gain of strengthening the musculature of the hand. An occupational therapist may give the same patient the same material for the converse reason—primarily to strengthen the musculature of the hand, and secondarily to dissipate anxiety. The interdisciplinary dynamic is that the two therapists collaborate on and discuss the goals established for the patient. Similarly, a speech therapist and an art therapist may effectively co-treat by conceptualizing complementary goals and then implementing treatment sessions together, creating true teamwork. An example might be an art therapist's use of a visual image to encourage and reinforce a phonating technique used by a speech therapist. This interdisciplinary approach to patient care is not only immensely gratifying, but makes for more efficient attainment of the established clinical goals.

The team should strive for ongoing discourse about patients' status in an exchange of information about each patient's involvement in a range of disciplines. Ongoing communication, sharing observations and ideas, and reinforcement of one another's goals often make for more efficient overall goal attainment. Interdisciplinary work reflects a greater degree of coordination as opposed to working with a collection of professionals (Ozer, Payton, & Nelson, 1990), and "implies a degree of blurring of professional roles whilst still preserving the separate identity and expertise of individual professions. Multidisciplinary is a term that simply describes a number of different disciplines working with the same disabled person" (Barnes & Ward, 2000, p. 26). Hence, interdisciplinarity reflects the true coordination of professional approaches and serves to elevate the art therapist from ancillary to integral.

The difference between multidisciplinarity and interdisciplinarity should be kept in mind by the art therapist working with other caregivers in a medical setting. As simply a member of the team, the work may be perceived as beneficial yet tangential. It is far more desirable to work collaboratively and, more important, in the best interest of the patient. When the art therapist's goals and interventions are interfaced with those of others and related to the patient's ability to adjust, true interdisciplinarity is achieved.

Promoting Art Therapy in a Medical Setting

The way art therapy is perceived is inevitably in response to the way it is conveyed. In a medical setting, where the arts are more likely to be seen as diversional, it is crucial to ensure that art therapy is thought of as strong and equitable with other healthcare services. The aforementioned team communication includes various forms of participation. Having a voice in team meetings is one way to convey the nature of interventions, especially in relation to patients' medical conditions and psychological issues. It is also important to ensure ongoing notations in medical records and case reports. The old healthcare adage "if you didn't write it, you didn't do it" (Anonymous) holds true even more today when art therapy has been elevated but still needs to raise its bar. Clear communication is important on a broader scale as the profession advocates for recognition and insurance reimbursement. It is critical to consistently articulate and document the salient points of art therapy treatment and goal attainment.

Art therapists in medical settings and elsewhere should concern themselves with relevance and effectiveness. Conducting research is a natural extension of uncovering the effectiveness of art therapy methods. The medical art therapist is in the fortunate position to collaborate with a range of team members. Partnering with healthcare professionals can assist in conceptualizing ways to demonstrate efficacy. For example, a neuropsychologist may utilize cognitive evaluation tools, a radiologist may utilize neurologic imaging, and medical personnel may assess thermal or blood pressure variations in relation to art-making. Such collaborations, in themselves, convey functional and sophisticated professional relationships, while eliciting the endorsement of the better known disciplines. Art therapists, typically challenged to develop quantitative methodologies, would do well to dip into the realm of medical barometers and technology to measure the effects of an art experience.

Fostering interdisciplinary relationships and engaging in collaborative work provides opportunities to publish in medical and healthcare publications. Similarly, an art therapist may present at relevant medical forums as a means of broadening exposure within the healthcare professional community. From several perspectives, the art therapist in a medical setting is able to promote the substance of the work by identifying advantageous elements inherent in the milieu.

Exhibiting patient artwork may promote the benefits of and shape viewers' understanding of art therapy and how it fits into medical treatment. When planning an exhibit, numerous features should be carefully considered. The universal tendency in viewing art products is to react to quality. Indeed, artwork produced by medially ill and disabled people may be aesthetic, which is validating for the artist and pleasing to the viewer. Yet, art therapists emphasize art process over product, which takes on more importance as part of the larger course of medical treatment. Despite the myriad aspects that affect creating art, such as the restrictive environment (e.g., presence of equipment, ergonomic limitations, and diminished capacity due to disease or disability), sensitive and meaningful artwork is often created. The goals of exhibiting the work should be clear; displaying artwork may provide validation of the patient and enhance self-esteem at a time when one is vulnerable. Exhibiting is also an opportunity to raise staff awareness about art therapy and its role in patient care.

The essence of therapeutic gain is better conveyed by using supplementary descriptors, fliers, and postings. Providing informative but succinct specifics about the goals of art therapy with medical populations, personal goals for the artist–patient, emotions elicited, and insights derived creates a full "picture" of the role of art therapy. Direct quotes that reflect how the experience was perceived as well as insights achieved can be displayed. A viewer should come away with awareness of how art therapy fits into treatment, how the art was created, and what it meant to the creator. Examples of artwork may be a means of sensitizing viewers to the patients' experience of medical challenges and simultaneously informing caregivers about medical art therapy.

Patient art exhibits in a medical setting should be handsomely installed, as the presentation also reflects the seriousness of the field. Given likely budgetary limitations, the art therapist must be creative in aiming to balance practical aspects with the goals of exhibiting. Simplicity of installation may result in an appealing setup—for example, using temporary mounting adhesives and/or easel displays are economical yet attractive.

As artwork created in a medical setting is part of treatment, it should be considered a confidential aspect of care. Therefore, informed consent forms should be signed by the patient with clear indication that the consent allows for the showing of his or her artwork within the healthcare facility. Other aspects of the consent form, such as specific health information, artwork reproduction, media, or use for training purposes should also be in the consent document. Most medical settings have an institutional generic consent used for patient releases; however, an art therapist may wish to request that a consent form be modified or specifically created. Such documents should be reviewed and approved by administrative levels and legal departments. Despite careful use of written informed consent documents, it is still prudent to camouflage signatures for anonymity. In instances where a patient expresses a preference to have his or her identity known, this may be written into the consent to ensure an airtight document. It should be noted that utilizing informed consent represents compliance with national standards delineated by the Health Insurance Portability and Accountability Act (HIPAA) and the Privacy Rule, which "addresses the use and disclosure of individuals' health information" (US Department of Health and Human Services, 2012). Further, it ensures compliance with Section 4.6 of the *Ethics Principles for Art Therapists* developed by the American Art Therapy Association, requiring that "Art therapists obtain written, informed consent from the client before displaying client art in any public place" (American Art Therapy Association, 2011).

Care for the Caregiver

Self-care for clinicians cannot be overstated. The ability to recognize one's own emotions, associations, and responses to those in treatment is a cornerstone of successful service to the client and for the well-being of the caregiver. In medical art therapy, there is an additional dimension that must be built into the provision of care for the patient and care for one's self as patients decline. In some healthcare settings, art therapists may be faced with the death of their clients. Sadness can be pervasive, and the art therapist must be prepared for this. Commonly, team members are supportive of one another, but it is up to the individual professional to process feelings of loss and grief.

Early in the AIDS epidemic, Winiarski (1991) emphasized the importance of coming to terms with the reality that, as therapists, we may not always make a difference as our efforts are "thwarted by the client's illness" (p. 136). This calls for modifying expectations and deriving sufficient gratification by supporting patients via art and the quality of the relationship. Being attentive to and processing one's feelings can be achieved in several ways. He suggested clinical supervision that focuses on the therapist's emotional responses and likens the supervisor–supervisee relationship to that of the therapist–client as one seeks "attentiveness, acceptance, regard, and direction" (p. 138). It is natural to become immersed in the intensity of the environment and practice of art therapy in a medical setting, and it can be overwhelming if not balanced by the intentional inclusion of life-enhancing activities.

Art therapists are fortunate to have a natural means of nurturing themselves and restoring personal balance in their own art-making. Art guides patients in the expression of the "inexpressible" (Bardot, 2008), and art also allows the art therapist to deal with issues of grief and to feel renewed. Unless emotions are dealt with, the art therapist in a medical setting is likely to encounter repeated loss and cumulative unprocessed grief. Artistic engagement is therefore a beneficial self-care activity that allows one to remain effective. Those who care for dying patients are at risk for both burnout and compassion fatigue. Kearney, Weininger, Vachon, Harrison, and Mount (2009) made the distinction that "burnout results from stresses that arise from the clinician's interaction with the work environment while compassion fatigue evolves specifically from the relationship between the clinician and the patient" (p. 1156).

Art therapists working in such complex and energetic environments must be introspective and self-nurturing. The clinician giving care to patients who are physically compromised is constantly made aware of the inevitability of illness and death. The reality of the finiteness of health and life is ever-present, but can be gently redirected so as to enrich one's own life. As eloquently stated by Shapiro (2008), "the heart must first pump blood to itself."

Conclusion

The complexity inherent in working within a medical setting—environmental, professional, and personal—are readily manageable, and in fact appealing for those attracted to it. There are numerous obstacles not faced by art therapists in other settings, but they are part and parcel of this exacting treatment milieu and constitute a particular vibrancy. In this chapter, a number of challenges have been delineated along with strategies for integrating them into a successful art therapy approach. With all its challenges and despite the obstacles, the rewards of practicing art therapy in a medical setting can be deeply meaningful.

References

American Art Therapy Association. (2011). *Ethical principles for art therapists*. Retrieved from http://www.americanarttherapyassociation.org/upload/ethicalprinciples.pdf

Bardot, H. (2008). Expressing the inexpressible: The resilient healing of client and art therapist. *Art Therapy: Journal of the American Art Therapy Association, 25*(4), 183–186.

Barnes, M. P., & Ward, A. B. (2000). The rehabilitation team. In M. P. Barnes & A. B. Ward (Eds.), *Textbook of Rehabilitation* (pp. 25–31). New York, NY: Oxford University Press.

Hartley, N. (2008). The palliative care community—using the arts in different settings. In N. Hartley & M. Payne (Eds.), *The creative arts in palliative care* (pp. 40–51). London and Philadelphia, PA: Jessica Kingsley.

Hughes, J. (2012). *Developing a therapeutic atmosphere in single art therapy sessions on adult medical unit*. (Unpublished master's thesis), Department of Art Therapy, School of Visual Arts, New York, NY.

Kearney, M. K., Weininger, R. B., Vachon, M. L. S., Harrison, R. L., & Mount, B. M. (2009). Self-care of physicians caring for patients at the end of life: "Being connected … a key to my survival." *Journal of the American Medical Association, 301*(11), 1155–1164.

Moon, C. H. (2002). *Studio art therapy: Cultivating the artist identity in the art therapist*. Philadelphia, PA: Jessica Kingsley.

Ozer, M. N., Payton, O. D., & Nelson, C. E. (1990). Coordinated planning. In M. N. Ozer, O. D. Payton, & C. E. Nelson (Eds.), *Treatment planning for rehabilitation: A patient-centered approach* (p. 77). New York, NY: McGraw-Hill.

Prager, A. (1995). Pediatric art therapy: Strategies and applications. *Art Therapy: Journal of the American Art Therapy Association, 12*(1), 32–38.

Rosner, I. (1982). Art therapy with two quadriplegic patients. *American Journal of Art Therapy, 21*(4), 115–120.

Shapiro, S. L. (2008). The art and science of meditation. Paper presented at Cassidy Seminars; June 27, 2008; Skirball Cultural Center, Los Angeles, CA.

US Department of Health and Human Services. (2012). *The health insurance portability and accountability act of 1996 (HIPAA) privacy and security rules.* Retrieved from http://www.hhs.gov/ocr/privacy

Winiarski, M. (1991). Caring for ourselves. In M. Winiarski (Ed.), *AIDS-related psychotherapy* (pp. 134–143). New York, NY: Pergamon Press.

43

Art Therapy in Rehabilitation Centers

Cynthia Cox

It has been a privilege and a challenge to help establish and supervise a fieldwork site for art therapy practicum students from the nearby state university's graduate art therapy program at a regional rehabilitation hospital in North Florida. When first approached by the program's clinical coordinator, I was both excited and stymied. As an occupational therapist, I had never been exposed to art therapy in any setting. Although I understood the importance of addressing the psychological needs of our patients and was sure there was a niche for art therapy in our hospital, inpatient rehabilitation is not a traditional setting for art therapy. However, it became clear that the skills and creativity that the art therapists have are a perfect fit for the needs of this rehabilitation population. This chapter will introduce a comprehensive medical rehabilitation center and how art therapy has been integrated into its rehabilitation program for the inpatient adult population.

Rehabilitation

Stedman's Medical Dictionary (2012) defined "rehabilitation" as "the therapeutic restoration, after disease, illness, or injury, of the ability to function in a normal or near normal manner" (p. 1443). Rehabilitation is a continuum of care in a multitude of settings, including home health and inpatient and outpatient services. Inpatient rehabilitation occurs in four settings: an acute care hospital rehab unit, a freestanding rehab hospital, a long-term care hospital or long-term acute care facility (LTAC), and a sub-acute unit in a skilled nursing facility (SNF). The process is driven by the standards set by the accrediting bodies for each facility and payer sources. Accrediting bodies include state and federal agencies such as The Joint Commission (TJC) and the Commission on Accrediting Rehabilitation Facilities (CARF). TJC and CARF are nonprofit organizations dedicated to improving the quality of life of patients served in accredited rehab programs. Both organizations support an integrated interdisciplinary team approach to the rehabilitation of individuals with a disability (2012 Medical). The setting in this chapter is a freestanding rehabilitation facility.

The Wiley Handbook of Art Therapy, First Edition. Edited by David E. Gussak and Marcia L. Rosal.
© 2016 John Wiley & Sons, Ltd. Published 2016 by John Wiley & Sons, Ltd.

Typically, the team consists of core disciplines including a physician, nurse, case manager, physical therapist, occupational therapist, and speech therapist. There are also many consultative disciplines included in the team, based on individual patient needs. These can include, but are not limited to, dieticians, respiratory therapists, psychologists, neuropsychologists, and various specialty physicians, such as neurologists, pulmonologists, and orthopedists. In SNFs, the core team typically includes the activities director, a position that is unique to this medical setting. This position can be held by an art therapist.

Definition of Roles

Each team member has a unique role in the functioning of the rehabilitation center:

- The *physician* leads the team, and is typically either a physiatrist, a specialist in physical medicine and rehabilitation (PM+R), a neurologist, or an internist. The physician oversees the team's activities, and directs the medical care of the patient.
- The *nurse* provides the medical care as directed by the physician, with special emphasis on personal hygiene, and bladder and bowel control. The nurse assists the patient in reaching his therapy goals when in the nursing unit. Nurses can specialize in rehabilitation through a course of study and certification exam.
- The *physical therapist* (PT) focuses on motor function and ability. Goals in the PT arena concentrate on ambulation (walking), balance, posture, strength, and endurance.
- The *occupational therapist* (OT) addresses activities of daily living (ADLs)—from self-feeding, bathing, and dressing to home management, driving, and child care. Component skills needed to perform ADLs addressed by OT include strength, coordination, vision, perception, and cognition.
- The *speech–language pathologist*, more commonly referred to as a speech therapist (ST), deals with language, cognition, and dysphagia/swallowing issues. Components of language include verbal expression and visual and auditory comprehension. Cognition includes memory, attention, social interaction, and executive function.
- The *case manager* serves as liaison between the various team members, including patient and family and coordinates care, and is responsible for ensuring that all team members are cognizant of all aspects of a patient's issues. They are also responsible for implementing a safe, smooth discharge for each patient.
- *Psychologists and neuropsychologists* address the mental health of each patient. Particular areas of concern during rehab are depression, posttraumatic stress disorder (PTSD), and adjustment to disability. They are pivotal in identifying and addressing behavioral problems and cognitive deficits. They often guide the team in treating these issues.

In rehabilitation facilities, the team meets formally at least once a week to discuss each patient's progress, goals, and barriers to progress. Each team member gives input and insight into each area of concern. A treatment plan is developed with clear, common goals for the team to address when working with the patient. At meetings, discharge plans are discussed at length, including recommendations for equipment and community resources that will be needed to make a safe transition to home successful. The patient and/or family members may or may not be present at the meeting. The case manager will communicate the outcome of the meeting with the patient and his or her family if they were not in attendance to give input.

Informally, interdisciplinary collaboration occurs daily. The team members interact throughout the day and communicate issues, needs, and progress as warranted. The facility has multiple therapy gyms that are not discipline specific. PTs and OTs provide care throughout the clinic. Patient treatment occurs in the gyms, in the nursing units, and on the facility's grounds outside. A speech therapist may provide treatment in the "ADL kitchen." An OT will provide ADL training in the patient's room. A PT may take the patient outside to maneuver on grass or up-and-down curbs. Nursing may report to the gym to administer medications. Case managers seeking patients will often find them in the gyms during treatment time. This provides multiple opportunities to observe a patient performing functional tasks or receiving treatment from another discipline and may encourage informal communication between disciplines. By the time the team meets formally, most team members may already be aware of any issues and have made adjustments to the plan of care.

The Balanced Budget Act (BBA) of 1997 significantly changed the course of the rehabilitation system (Cotterill & Gage, 2002). The new payment system led to clinical changes in inpatient rehabilitation care. Prior to the BBA, such facilities typically had full-time psychology and neuropsychology staff. These crucial disciplines provided treatment for the psychological issues faced by the patient population and guided the rest of the team in meeting the challenges that these issues presented.

Recreation therapists were also a critical component of the rehab team. They addressed leisure skill training and community re-entry. In the early 1990s, the facility on which this chapter was based employed multiple full-time recreation therapists, one neuropsychologist, one psychologist, and two to three psychology students. Prior to the BBA, patients with any kind of neurological insult (stroke, traumatic brain injury, or spinal cord injury) typically remained in rehabilitation at least 3–4 months, sometimes up to 1 year. Even someone with a simple hip fracture or joint replacement received inpatient services up to 8 weeks.

With the implementation of the BBA, recreation therapists have become a rarity in rehabilitation. Psychology and neuropsychology services have been significantly reduced, often to a consultative service. According to the Centers for Medicare and Medicaid Service (CMS), expected length of stay (LOS), based on diagnosis, age, and level of motor and cognitive function upon admission to rehab, is around 7–18 days for lower-extremity joint replacement and 10–52 days for a traumatic spinal cord injury (Centers for Medicare & Medicaid Services, 2012). A stroke patient's LOS is expected to be in the range of 8–33 days. All other diagnoses fall somewhere within this range. The intensity, pace, and LOS described in this chapter are reflective of an acute care hospital unit and a freestanding hospital. The SNF or LTAC setting, which was created to serve a more frail elderly population, provides less daily therapy intensity and a longer LOS. Those settings provide a greater opportunity for more extensive psychotherapy than our setting.

Recent changes created a significant reduction in LOS time and services for our patients. Yet, their needs have not significantly changed. There is ample evidence of depression in survivors of stroke, heart attack, cancer, and other traumatic injuries and illnesses that needs to be addressed (Thombs et al., 2006). Adjustments to loss of independence and loss of family roles are difficult and take time. With the loss of consistent daily therapy to address these issues, progress can be hampered. Patients can be less motivated to participate in rehab and/or they may fear being discharged home back to their "real" lives, while struggling with major life-changing issues. With the loss of recreation therapy and shorter lengths of stay, leisure skills are often neglected or barely addressed. As these two disciplines were significantly reduced or eliminated, a void was left that art therapy eventually filled.

Incorporating Art Therapy

Many logistical obstacles arose once the decision to incorporate art therapy into our program was made. First, space was an issue. Ultimately, it was decided to place art therapy students with the PTs and OTs in the gym. This allowed them to observe the patients during therapeutic activities and discuss their issues with the other disciplines. It afforded routine opportunities to identify patients who would benefit from art therapy services. This also helped with a second issue—how to screen patients and determine appropriate referrals to art therapy. As the average length of stay is 14 days, there is an entirely new caseload every 2 weeks. No one person could possibly screen all 50 patients and then provide treatment to those in need. Thus, it was determined that the art therapy students would take part in the weekly team conference meetings. This forum allowed identification of the patients who could benefit from art therapy.

It was also a challenge to fit art therapy into the patients' schedules. Since art therapy is not currently reimbursable, it could not be included in the "minimum 3 hours of therapy 5 days per week" required. It was initially thought that art therapy could only be offered when patients were not scheduled for PT, OT, or ST. Since 3 hours does not seem like much, it was assumed that this could easily be accomplished. This is simply not the case.

Starting as early as 7 AM, the patients use the toilet, bathe, dress, eat breakfast, have their wounds cared for, attend nutrition counseling, and receive their medication. They then have lunch, use the bathroom again, and take necessary rest. Of course, there are unexpected conditions that impede or prevent the patients from attending all of these activities, such as low blood pressure, nausea, and symptoms related to an acute illness. If any of these interfere with the required schedule, then the therapy and structured activities get rescheduled, taking into account priorities. At 4 PM, families visit, and supper follows. It became clear that fitting art therapy into such a tight schedule would be rather difficult. However, before we could come up with a solution, our first art therapy student arrived.

Beginnings

The art therapy student's first days were spent becoming oriented to our facility and introducing our staff to art therapy. She was assigned to shadow the OTs, since, for our purposes, these two disciplines are very closely aligned in both philosophy and education. There were some initial challenges. Her first attempts to approach patients with her services were not met positively. Patients declined, not understanding their own needs, or what art therapy could do for them; just the word "art" seemed to intimidate most of our geriatric population.

However, the art therapy student was determined and creative. For example, the OTs run "standing groups" every day with the goal to increase a patient's ability to stand while he or she performs functional tasks to improve balance and standing endurance. The patients often need a distraction as they are in pain and/or may have a fear of falling. While the OT attended to the patients' tolerance for standing, one art therapist created origami birds as she casually talked with individuals in the group. Eventually, one patient asked how to make a bird, and soon the entire group joined in (see Figure 43.1). Someone started talking about birds, and the art therapy student steered the conversation to flight and freedom of movement. This evolved into a discussion on how difficult it was for many patients to experience freedom due to their current medical issues, loss of movement, and independence. The patients were so involved in the discussion that they forgot to focus on their pain or fear of falling.

Figure 43.1 Origami Birds.

While the OT monitored progress, cued for posture, and provided close supervision for those who needed it, the art therapy student provided interventions that diverted focus from uncomfortable physical symptoms toward positive, prosocial alternatives.

Because this standing group was held in the middle of the gym, multiple disciplines were able to hear and observe what happened that day. Suddenly, more and more PTs, OTs, and STs approached the art therapist with requests to work with particular patients. As staff came to understand what art therapy could accomplish, the issue of how to find appropriate art therapy patients diminished significantly. With an "ah-ha" moment for all those involved and a pivotal moment for the program, there was a dawning realization of the value of art therapy with this population. Since then, art therapy has been applied in many different capacities.

Examples of Art Therapy Interventions

The facility cares for many victims of assault with varying medical issues. These patients in particular suffer from PTSD. Since its inception, these patients were referred to art therapy to help address anxiety issues. Because trust is needed between the patient and staff in order to engage in the rehabilitation activities, initial treatment is focused on alleviating this anxiety. Art therapy interventions have been particularly successful in this capacity, such as name embellishments; anxiety boxes that are filled with a list of the patient's stressors and then put away; and building "recovery ships" that are filled with a list of tools or behaviors that will aid in the patient's recovery.

Those suffering from cardiopulmonary issues are often anxious about their difficulties with breathing; therefore, asking them to use watercolors, paint, or markers to create marks or brush strokes as they breath has been effective. This allows them to see how they are breathing, which can, in turn, alleviate their anxiety.

Art therapy has also been able to assist patients in pain through guided imagery and progressive body relaxation followed by creating a mandala depicting the patient's response to the relaxation technique used. Patients can create a body map or a "coping collage," illustrating what pain looks like in their body and then surrounding those spots with images representing coping strategies. These depictions become tools that patients can take home and use as they continue to experience chronic pain.

Many rehabilitation patients have neurological deficits including physical and cognitive impairments. Art therapy can address any of the goals set by the team based on the medium they choose. Patients can be oriented to time and place, with calendar drawings reflecting seasons, significant events, or celebrations on the monthly headings of blank calendar pages, memory journals, or name plates with time-of-year decorations. Hands can be strengthened by using clay to create items such as coil pots. Range of motion or increased use of an affected arm/hand can be facilitated through watercolor painting or merely by asking the patients to sketch lines. Fine motor coordination can be improved through jewelry making or beadwork.

Poor motivation is another obstacle in rehabilitation settings. Elderly patients who have recently experienced trauma or illness have poor endurance, physical pain, and are facing a life-changing crossroad that impedes engagement in their rehabilitation program. Art therapy can help by giving them the opportunity to self-reflect and learn coping strategies through past/present/future collages, coping skills collages, goal commitment boxes, goal books, goal cards for the self, bridge drawings, strength sculptures, and goal sculptures.

There have been several incidences that remain particularly memorable. An art therapy student was asked to work with a young patient, a 20-something-year-old woman diagnosed with a traumatic brain injury (TBI) following a motor vehicle accident. The patient was deficient in all functioning areas including speech, ambulation, and memory. She was quiet and rarely initiated interaction with anyone. The team knew she was depressed; they became frustrated in trying to get her to engage in therapeutic activities. The patient was asked to create an inside–outside mask as the art therapy student made one herself. Although her outer mask was bright and embellished, much like the art therapy student's mask, her inner mask was painted black and without embellishments, revealing her fear that she would never be "normal." This was communicated to the treatment team, who then focused a portion of each treatment session on education addressing her recovery, making sure each session ended with successful performance of a real-life task. This encouraged the patient to become more engaged in the exercises and activities in therapy, which ultimately led to a positive treatment outcome.

Another case involved an older woman who suffered a stroke, consequently losing the use of her left arm and her ability to communicate. However, she did have the tendency to repeatedly yell "RE-HA-BIL-I-TATION" over and over, no matter the circumstances, making it difficult to engage her in therapeutic or functional tasks. The art therapy student discovered that the patient enjoyed coloring, doing so for hours without shouting. As a result, the art therapy student collaborated with the speech therapist, and soon the patient was able to name each color when asked. A coloring activity was incorporated into all of the sessions, and the patient made prominent gains. Art therapy was the critical component of treatment that lead the patient to make significant gains in functioning and to return home to her family.

Group projects are often successful as they help patients motivate each other through peer support. Art therapy activities engaged patients in creating banners that are displayed throughout the facility. During one Rehabilitation Week celebration, an art therapy student had patients do a "wheelchair painting." She taped the word REHAB on a bed sheet and laid it on the ground outside the gym. Patients rolled their wheelchairs in different color paints and then rolled over the sheet. After the paint dried, the tape was pulled off, leaving large white letters. The patients hung it up on a hallway wall and added notes on what rehabilitation meant to them on the banner. At a party the next day, the patients reflected on their progress and goals for the future.

Setting realistic goals is a significant objective with patients in a rehabilitation setting. Total recovery for most illnesses is rarely accomplished in the time they spend in the facility, as it may take months or even years for full recuperation. On admission, patients are asked to identify their goals for the time they are in our care with the intention of helping them maintain and prepare for the long recovery. Recently, an art therapy student worked with the other members of the treatment team and developed a directive that helped patients focus on immediate goals. The intern outlined a large tree on one wall in the gym. Everyone wanted to help her paint it, including the staff.

Figure 43.2   The Goal Tree.

Once the tree was ready, the art therapy student helped patients make leaves on which they wrote a realistic goal to be accomplished during their hospitalization. PT or OT would then assist them in placing their leaf on the tree, effectively becoming a visible reminder of what they needed to work toward (see Figure 43.2).

Once goals were accomplished, patients could keep the leaf to remind themselves of their progress. Since this project was initiated, it continues to evolve, particularly for different holidays and events. For example, instead of leaves, patients created hearts for Valentine's Day and eggs for Easter. Although still a work in progress, it continues to be effective in helping patients visualize and achieve reachable goals during their stay.

Conclusion

Although not the norm for comprehensive medical rehabilitation, art therapy has been demonstrably effective with our program. We have been fortunate to have the opportunity to incorporate art therapy into our services. Consequently, I would challenge art therapists to continue to reach out and establish art therapy's place in this arena as well as in other rehabilitation programs to incorporate this discipline into their programs. The patients' needs are great, and their time in rehabilitation care is short. Art therapy can make a critical difference in their success.

References

Medical Rehabilitation Program Descriptions. (2012). [Brochure]. Carf International.

Centers for Medicare & Medicaid Services. (2012). *Case-mix groups, relative weights, and average length of stay values for the notice (75 FR 42836)* (Version 2012) [Data file]. Retrieved from http://www.cms.gov/Medicare/Medicare-Fee-for-Service-Payment/InpatientRehabFacPPS/Data-Files.html

Cotterill, P. G., & Gage, B. J. (2002). Overview: Medicare post-acute care since the balanced budget act of 1997. *Health Care Financing Review, 24*(2), 1–6.

Stedman's Medical Dictionary for the Health Professions and Nursing (7th ed.). (2012). Philadelphia: Wolters Kluwer. (Original work published 1987)

Thombs, B. D., Bass, E. B., Ford, D. E., Stewart, K. J., Tsilidis, K. K., Patel, U., Fauerbach, J. A., Bush, D. E., & Ziegelstein, R. C. (2006). Prevalence of depression in survivors of acute myocardial infarction. *Journal of General Internal Medicine, 21*(1). Abstract obtained from *Wiley Online Library.*

44

Addiction and Art Therapy: Interdisciplinary Considerations

Richard Carolan

Behavioral patterns conditioned to achieve rewards have been part of the human experience throughout history. The survival and subsequent evolution of the human system has been dependent on the rigor of these reward-seeking behaviors. The brain, the conductor of the human system, in its early form is primarily encoded with survival strategies, and later developed the ability to integrate contextual variables in decision-making. When we are in an environment that offers opportunities to prosper, we have the freedom to access the complexity of the brain to function as an integrated orchestra; when we are in survival mode, the brain focuses on core instruments. Addiction is the brain and the human system operating in survival mode, and the addict is locked in destructive patterns, suffering and feeling unable to change. Perspectives on how this can be reversed vary, and there is a preponderance of literature that presents various interdisciplinary options on how to treat addictions.

Art has served an important evolutionary factor in the human experience (Dissanayake, 1992), and art therapy can play a significant role in counteracting addictive patterns and facilitating more developed and integrated responses, supporting not only survival but prospering. This chapter is about the role the art therapist has among the interdisciplinary perspectives prevalent in the substance abuse treatment literature, and how the art therapist can work within already existing theories.

Definition of Addiction

Addiction is defined as a cluster of symptoms that include behavioral, cognitive, and physiological symptoms, and historically has included consideration of a "spiritual" component. One area that has had some controversy is the inclusion of the term "disease" in the definition of addiction. A more current definition by the American Society of Addiction Medicine defines addiction as a chronic brain disorder (American Society of Addiction Medicine, 2012). The *Diagnostic and Statistics Manual of Mental Disorders* (American Psychiatric Association; DSM-IV-TR, 2000) separates the definitions of substance abuse from substance dependence. Both definitions include emphasis on individuals being unable to control the use of the addictive substance despite multiple negative

The Wiley Handbook of Art Therapy, First Edition. Edited by David E. Gussak and Marcia L. Rosal.
© 2016 John Wiley & Sons, Ltd. Published 2016 by John Wiley & Sons, Ltd.

consequences. The distinction between abuse and dependence is primarily that addiction also involves tolerance and withdrawal (DSM-IV-TR, 2000).

Prevalence of Addiction

The Center for Substance Abuse and Mental Health Services Administration (SAMHSA, 2011) conducted a survey on drug use in 2010. The results of this survey show that more than 50% of Americans drink alcohol, and more than 25% of the population of individuals over 12 years of age are "binge" drinkers; among young adults aged 18–25, the rate of binge drinking was 40.6% (binge drinking in this survey is defined as having five or more drinks on the same occasion on at least 1 day in the 30 days prior to the survey). In 2010, an estimated 22.1 million persons (8.7% of the population aged 12 or older) were classified with substance dependence or abuse in the past year. Continued research into a definition of addiction is critical in determining risk factors and treatment options. Difficulty is perhaps enhanced when we attempt to narrow to a "cause." It is important to note that the use of mind-altering substances have been part of the human behavior pattern throughout history.

Addiction, as an issue that compromises the human experience and causes tremendous cost and suffering, is not limited to substance abuse. There are other significant addictions, including areas related to food (National Eating Disorder Association, 2012) and gambling (Ko et al., 2009). However, for the sake of this chapter, the focus will primarily be on the treatment of substance abuse. The following sections will begin with an overview of the neurobiological condition that those who abuse substances find themselves in and how an art therapist can benefit from such understanding. This will follow with an examination of four specific treatment agendas—*stages of change, motivational enhancement therapy, harm reduction therapy*, and *the ubiquitous 12-step program*—and explore the art therapists' potential role in each.

Neurobiological Considerations

Drugs alter the brain communication system and result in the brain operating in a disintegrated manner. A popular description of this is that drugs "hijack" the brain (Volkow, 2013). Drugs cause some areas of the brain to "overact," and other areas of the brain to function less. Primarily, drugs affect the brain by impacting its neurotransmitters as these nerve cells use electrical signals to relay information from one part of the neuron to the other. The neuron then converts the electrical signal to a chemical signal. The chemical transports the information across the synaptic space (space between neurons) to another neuron where it is converted back into an electrical signal. Neurotransmitters are the chemical message carriers between brain cells, which are the basis of individuals' thinking, feeling, moving, and maintaining homeostasis.

Drugs of abuse interfere with the homeostasis and disrupt neurotransmission in multiple ways: drugs can increase the release of neurotransmitters, they can impact the ability to "receive" neurotransmitters, and they can impact the removal of the neurotransmitter from the synaptic space. Primarily, drugs disrupt the brain's homeostasis through its limbic system and the reward component of the brain system. When drugs of abuse are taken, they release a greatly increased amount of neurotransmitters (primarily dopamine) into the synaptic space. Dopamine is a natural chemical produced by the body and is a critical component of human survival; it is experienced as a sense of pleasure.

Taking drugs over a period of time has multiple effects on the brain, two of which are critical in addiction—the first is that, as a result of the drugs increasing the release of neurotransmitters and the stimulation of the reward center, the brain's normal system ceases to function as a means of stimulating the reward system consequently without the drug's lethargic results; secondly, since drugs of abuse greatly increase the release of neurotransmitters, nerve cells grow many additional "receptors" to take the neurotransmitters into the receptor cell. When the drug is not in the system, there are many receptors cells seeking matching neurotransmitters that are not in the synaptic space, this is experienced as "craving."

This increased release of neurotransmitters through drug abuse over time creates an altered homeostasis. The brain is then driven to maintain this new homeostasis. When this new homeostasis is threatened, the brain moves into survival mode, dominated more by the old brain, and, as a result, the limbic system drives decision-making with less integration with the pre-frontal cortex. When the addict says, "I just was not thinking," he may be neurologically accurate. This "hijacked" brain results in patterns of thinking and behaving by individuals in which they are making decisions driven by the need to stimulate the reward system, and consequently return to the new homeostasis. The brain is acting on its perceived survival need, and, as a result, makes choices that are harmful to the individual's relations, responsibilities, and health.

What is needed is a therapeutic approach that can alter the drug-induced neurological homeostasis. The individual must be supported in developing new patterns where the reward system is stimulated in a manner that integrates the thinking and feeling modules of the brain. The plasticity of the brain, its ability to grow new neuron transmission patterns, must be stimulated and supported. Art therapy can play an important role in this recovery process.

It is arguable that there is an innate human drive toward alternative experiences of being. While this drive manifests itself in the attraction to mind-altering substances, it may also be a component of a spiritual "quest." I would propose that this is a significant component of the evolutionary role of art in human experience, as Dissanayake (1992) wrote when she identified art as critical for human evolution.

Art has served as a means of going beyond ordinary patterns of experiencing and knowing. Engaging the creativity within an individual and facilitating his or her engagement in the art process is a means of developing the plasticity of the brain. An important component of enhancing plasticity is participation and practice of novel experiences; creating art is an intrinsically novel experience. Creativity is a process of expanding neurological networks. D. Siegel (2007) defined critical variables in new patterns of neural activity as including openness to novelty, an alertness to distinctions, having context sensitivity, being able to have multiple perspectives, and having a present orientation. Each of these attributes is a core element of the art process.

Dealing with control and maintaining homeostasis in the human experience for the addict is not just a factor when they are under the direct influence of the addictive substance, it becomes the pervasive factor in their daily life. For example, binging and purging was one of the most addictive patterns of a particular client. Although there was strong therapeutic contact and positive motivation for change on her part, she lost focus during one session and began imagining a plan for her next binge and how and where she might purge afterward. She drifted from clear contact; the "hijacking" was in operation.

The art therapist has a significant role with the individual struggling with addiction, through supporting him or her in externalizing the internal struggle (Waller & Mahoney, 1999). Creating art provides the novel practice of being present and intentional in response to triggers that stimulate the "hijacked" reward system, and offering images as a means of stimulating the reward system through integration of the limbic system and the pre-frontal cortex. The awakened artist in an individual can serve what the 12-step approach refers to as a "higher power." While there are various treatment approaches currently practiced in working with addiction, all of them deal with the neurological component of addiction.

Treatment Approaches

For many years in the United States, treatment for addiction was primarily based on the 12-step model and an insistence on abstinence. The addiction counselor used confrontation of denial as a primary recovery strategy, and it was often believed that the best addiction counselors were individuals who themselves were in recovery from addiction. There has been significant development in the last several decades in recognizing the prevalence of dual diagnosis issues in working with individuals with addiction and in integrating alternative approaches, including motivational enhancement therapy, harm reduction therapy, and pharmaceutical interventions. Art therapy is an important treatment approach in working with addiction; it has been used as a component of the 12-step approach for many years (Holt & Kaiser, 2009; Julliard, 1999). Art has also served as a valuable approach in working with motivational enhancement therapy (Miller & Rollnick, 2002) and harm reduction (Denning & Little, 2012). Prochaska and DiClemente (1986) contributed greatly to the broadening of approaches in working with addiction in their research about the stages of change.

Stages of Change

The stages of change concept was one of the primary approaches to understanding recovery and change in working with individuals suffering from addiction, and more broadly with the concept of change in the human experience. The concept involves a sequence of stages through which people typically progress as they think about, initiate, and maintain new behaviors, both within and outside of the therapeutic environment. There are five primary stages in this model.

Pre-contemplation

This stage involves individuals who do not think they have problems, and have no intent to change as they see their problem behavior as having more pros than cons. He or she may be more surprised than resistant when told that he or she has a problem. Individuals in the pre-contemplation stage rarely seek treatment unless compelled.

What is recommended in therapy with individuals in this stage includes encouraging, establishing rapport, and building trust. This is accomplished through eliciting the client's perceptions of the problem, providing non-confrontational feedback, and expressing concern while keeping "the door open."

The use of art as a therapeutic process can play an important role in this stage. It can serve as a means of self-exploration, bypassing the automatic defensive reactions to threats that may be associated with having an addiction. This may create much more possibility for self-exploration. Active engagement with art materials introduces a means of expression and understanding other than repetitive cognitive verbal patterns that "lock" in limited verbal exploration. The use of materials creates opportunity for novel experience and expressiveness.

Contemplation

This stage involves the individual's struggles with ambiguity about a "problem" with substance use. They are not in denial but are not certain. Individuals at this time are experiencing ambivalence, which comes about with growing awareness of risks and problems associated with substance use. They both consider and reject change. It is common for people to come to treatment in this stage.

The therapeutic process at this stage involves normalizing the ambivalence and helping to "tip the decisional balance scales" by eliciting pros and cons of use while also emphasizing client choice and responsibility. The therapist can also elicit self-motivational statements from the client and reflect them back to him or her. The client is thinking about changing and seeking information about the problem. He or she is evaluating, but probably not prepared to change yet.

Art therapy is useful at this stage, relying on the image as a means of understanding and reflecting on the cost/benefits of use. Art can be used as a type of graphic organizer, externalizing the internal dialogue, and as a way of bringing the ambivalence to the foreground. In addition, the process of engaging the artist within oneself offers the individual a more opportunistic means of finding form in ambiguity. The work of the artist is often that of finding form in ambiguity.

Preparation

Once the individual moves to the "preparation stage," the process of change has already begun. They are ready to change in attitude and behavior, have likely begun to increase self-regulation, and are prepared to make commitments and develop strategies.

Art therapy can be used at this stage to engage creativity, identifying with the artist in them as an agent of change. Images can be used as a means of identifying and externalizing critical variables in the process of change, such as barriers to the change process, image of support systems, image of higher power, images to serve as supports, and guides along the path. Images can be used as a means of dialogue with self/others concerning plan and support.

Action

It is in this stage that the individual must demonstrate a firm commitment to change, and motivation must be engaged and supported; the artist in the individual must be activated and supported. Alternative means of viewing oneself and one's experience are critical to beginning and following through on new and creative action plans. The use of the imagination is critical in this process. The individual must be supported in seeing beyond their patterned reactivity. Modifying the problem behavior is the first component of this stage, followed by learning skills to prevent relapse.

This stage also requires exercising the creative imaginative self. Art therapy can be used to provide concrete form to the internal experience as well as to the vision of moving forward. Directives include creating diagrams of action plan, images of triggers, images of celebrating progress, and developing art making as an outlet and a means of support.

Maintenance

This is a critical stage in the process of change; one has to develop practices that allow alternative rewarding experiences while maintaining pathways that avoid reactive patterns in relation to triggers. The emphasis is on sustaining changes that have been accomplished, which requires an emphasis and effort on avoiding "slips." Fear and anxiety over relapse may be experienced and can be addressed through intentional expression of emotions in the art form, which can result in reflection and the opportunity to develop maintenance strategies. Intense triggering of desire to use substances may be experienced.

Art therapy can be used in this stage both as a means of maintaining engagement with the artist in the process and as a means of focusing on critical content areas. The use of images for insight and motivation is very valuable in this stage. It is also important to maintain the practice of engagement and dialogue with the images and to maintain the practice of art making for outlet and support.

Motivational Enhancement Therapy

Motivational enhancement therapy (Miller & Rollnick, 2002) is an intervention based on the understanding that people are most likely to change when the motivation comes from themselves, rather than being imposed by a therapist. It is based on the understanding that motivation is viewed as dynamic, and not static. It is a strength-based approach that is client-centered. The steps in this process are: express empathy, develop discrepancy, avoid argumentation, roll with resistance, and support self-efficacy.

Substance abuse treatment can be facilitated through the development of therapeutic relationships supporting client autonomy and the development of a partnership between the client and the therapist. Motivation for change is a key component. The responsibility for motivation is shared between the client and the therapist. The therapist focuses on the client's strengths rather that weaknesses, and does not de-personalize the client by using terms such as "addict" or "alcoholic." Those who subscribe to this approach are more open to recognizing that substance abuse disorders exist along a continuum, recognizing that clients may have co-existing disorders that impact stages of change, and that treatment goals should involve interim, incremental, and even temporary steps toward goals (SAMHSA, 1999; Miller & Rollnick, 2002).

Art therapy can be a significant contributor to the steps in motivational enhancement therapy. Art and images can serve as powerful motivators that prompt toward intended responses. Art can be a means of reflecting without activating defense systems that can be triggered by verbal processes. Engaging the artist within the individual can play a valuable role in supporting self-efficacy. The stages in motivational enhancement therapy can each be effectively facilitated through the use of the art therapy process. The steps in this process, as identified earlier, are: express empathy, develop discrepancy, avoid argumentation, roll with resistance, and support self-efficacy.

Expressing empathy can be facilitated through the art therapist's support of the client's engagement in the art process. In addition, collaborative drawing exercises such as mirror drawing can increase a sense of empathy. Developing discrepancy can be facilitated through the use of images as representing the different perspectives with which the client is struggling. The art therapy process supports the individual in exploring different perspectives without activating the defense mechanisms that the verbal process may often limit. Art can serve as a means of depicting the *resistance*, which in turn allows hesitancy and uncertainty to have a voice. Empowerment facilitates less resistive movement toward change. The created images can serve as reinforcement tools and can provide recognition of both progress and future vision.

Harm Reduction Therapy

Harm reduction therapy has been a prevalent treatment approach in European countries for many years (Denning & Little, 2012). The primary principle of this approach is to *Do No Harm*. Harm reduction recognizes that drug addiction is a biopsychosocial phenomenon. It posits that there is no single cause for addiction, and that a person must have several different forces acting on him or her to create the conditions necessary for a serious and persistent drug problem. The approach recognizes that drug use is initially adaptive and often seen as beneficial. This approach asserts that there is no inevitable progression from use to dependence. Treatment is tailored toward goals of the individual and is respectful of his or her assessment of problems and needs. It is believed that expectations such as abstinence can negatively impact treatment. Success is related to self-efficacy and is a function of the client's belief in his or her own power to effect change. According to Denning and Little (2012), this approach recognizes that any reduction in drug-related harm is a step in the right direction.

The harm reduction approach is an invitation to the artist to play a leading role in recovery. The artist within the individual allows the potential of the client's belief in their ability to create change. Art allows a healthy adaptive pattern that can serve as a means of reward. Art can be used as a means of externalizing the internal, exploring the relationship with substances, and uncovering avenues for reducing harm. Art can serve a significant role in the different phases of harm reduction work. Art can help individuals complete their own assessment of the problems and needs through externalizing their concepts and feelings of the benefits and harm related to his or her use. Art can also serve as a means of exploring the perceived benefits that may have been the initial basis of their beginning addiction, as well as of exploring alternative means of experiencing those perceived benefits.

Conclusion

Ronald Siegel (2005) wrote that the human pursuit of intoxication from mind-altering substances constitutes the fourth drive in the human process, along with food/sleep/sex, and that its roots may be based on the human drive for survival. There is also a parallel notion that art has played a substantial role in the human drive for survival. Art therapy can contribute to alleviating the suffering of addiction and support the individual in achieving a more peaceful and productive homeostasis. Siegel's work suggests that there is a human need for experiences that are other than the routine, other than what the individual's day-to-day experiences and sense of self provide. Individuals are driven toward other experiences; they may suffer in their inability to encounter these mind-altering occurrences. Consequently, and throughout time, many individuals, driven by survival instincts, have turned to substances as a means of having mind-altering experiences. These practices of altering the day-to-day patterns of experience often have turned into addictive practices that result in suffering for the individual and society. Art has served throughout time as a means of altering day-to-day experiences and ways of knowing. Art should serve as a primary means of working with addiction.

References

American Psychiatric Association. (2000). *Diagnostic and statistics manual of mental disorders* (4th ed., text rev.) Washington, DC: Author.

American Society of Addiction Medicine. (2012). Retrieved June 15, 2012, http://www.asam.org/for-the-public/definition-of-addiction

Center for Substance Abuse Treatment. Substance Abuse and Mental Health Services Administration. (1999). *Enhancing motivation for change in substance abuse treatment.* Treatment Improvement Protocol Series (TIPS), Series Number 35 (DHHS Pub. No. SMA 99-3354).

Center for Substance Abuse and Mental Health Services Administration. (2011). *Results from the 2010 national survey on drug use and health: Summary of national findings* (NSDUH Series H-41, HHS Publication No. SMA 11-4658).

Denning, P., & Little, J. (2012). *Practicing harm reduction therapy.* New York, NY: Guilford Press.

Dissanayake, E. (1992). *Homo aestheticus: Where art comes from and why.* New York, NY: Free Press.

Holt, E., & Kaiser, D. (2009). The first step series: Art therapy for early substance abuse treatment. *The Arts in Psychotherapy, 36*(4), 245–250.

Julliard, K. (1999). *The twelve steps and art therapy*. Mundelein, IL: American Art Therapy Association.

Ko, C., Liu, G., Hsiao, S., Yen, J., Yang, M., Lin, W., Yen, C., & Chen, C. (2009). Brain activities associated with gaming urge of online gaming addiction. *Journal of Psychiatric Research*, 43(7), 739–747.

Miller, W. R., & Rollnick, S. (2002). *Motivational interviewing: Preparing people to change addictive behavior* (2nd ed.). New York, NY: Guilford Press.

National Eating Disorder Association. (2012). http://www.nationaleatingdisorders.org/in-the-news/in-the-spotlight.php?year=2012

Prochaska, J. O., & DiClemente, C. C. (1983). Stages and process of self-change of smoking: Toward an integrative model of change. *Journal of Clinical and Counseling Psychology*, 51(3), 390–395.

Siegel, D. (2007). *The mindful brain*. New York, NY: W.W. Norton & Company Inc.

Siegel, R. (2005). *The "fourth drive" intoxication: The universal drive for mind altering substances*. Rochester, VT: Park Street Press.

Volkow, N. (2013). How Drug Addiction Hijacks the Brain—YouTube. www.youtube.com/watch?v=cL97QKupu1g

Waller, D., & Mahoney, J. (1999). *Treatment of addiction: Current issues for art therapists*. London: Routledge.

45

Forensic Art Therapy: Epistemological and Ontological Underpinnings

Marcia Sue Cohen-Liebman

Forensic art therapy is a unique application of art therapy that blends forensic and social science. Forensic art therapy is a fact-finding method of investigation used to help in the resolution of legal matters in dispute. The epistemological and ontological underpinnings of forensic art therapy will be explored in the context of child sexual abuse investigations. A brief review of the literature pertaining to the use of drawings in investigative interviews will be presented. The need for research regarding drawing within the relational context of investigative interviews will be considered.

Comparison of Forensic and Social Science Epistemology and Ontology

Epistemological underpinnings of the legal system contrast with those of the social sciences. The former is based in scientific objectivity, while the latter is considered more subjective (Milchman, 2011). In the most basic sense, scientific knowledge is construed as objectively valid, while subjectivity is often associated with clinical applications. In order to best meet the expectations of the legal system, there needs to be a balance between the two (Milchman, 2011).

Ontologically, there are very different realities between the legal system and the social sciences. Reconciliation of these different approaches is contingent upon a melding of different philosophies and theoretical frameworks. Integration of the ontological foundations of forensic and social science results in a comprehensive fact-finding approach (Gould & Stahl, 2009).

The legal system adheres to a conceptual framework in which truth, veracity, and validity are underlying precepts. The epistemology of law is, "a mode of inquiry with the purported goals of discovering truth and avoiding errors" (Ward, 2006, p. 350). Facts and evidence are central to legal findings. The establishment of burden of proof is paramount to the legal system. Standards range from "beyond reasonable doubt"

The Wiley Handbook of Art Therapy, First Edition. Edited by David E. Gussak and Marcia L. Rosal.
© 2016 John Wiley & Sons, Ltd. Published 2016 by John Wiley & Sons, Ltd.

to "a preponderance of evidence," depending upon the nature of the judicial process. In deference to this judicial process, the issue the court faces is deciding whether or not the proof before them has been determined true or false. In the social sciences, the aim is to evaluate through observation, interaction, and clinical procedures (Gould & Stahl, 2009). The objective is to address the needs of the client. The establishment of burden of proof is not the goal, and absolutes are not the priority. Fact-finding is construed as information gathering.

Judicial decision-making often relies on the translation of social science. Educating the court about individual and group behavior is the province of the social sciences. This information assists the judicial system in its decision-making role. Experts from the social sciences educate the trier of fact (judge or jury) by organizing, integrating, and interpreting data from empirical studies (Gould & Stahl, 2009). Observations or information singularly and in combination with other pieces of data yield meaning or lend a basis for inference or interpretation that guides conclusions and recommendations (Gould & Stahl, 2009). These efforts contribute to the resolution of legal matters in dispute.

Comparison of Forensic and Clinical Interview Methods

The goals and objectives of forensic interviews contrast with clinical interviews. There are inherent differences between approaches to interviewing children. Differences exist with regard to the interviewer; the intent and the context of the interview; and data collection and question format (Cohen-Liebman, 1999; Steinmetz, 1997). According to the American Professional Society on the Abuse of Children (APSAC), the purpose of a forensic interview is to "elicit as complete and accurate a report from the alleged child or adolescent victim as possible in order to determine whether the child or adolescent has been abused (or is in imminent risk of abuse) and, if so, by whom" (APSAC, 2002, p. 2). Sexual abuse is described as a complex event that children are ill prepared to describe (Everson & Boat, 2002). There is a lack of objective scientific standards for the determination of child sexual abuse (Brooks & Milchman, 1991). Investigation often hinges upon information elicited during an investigative interview in combination with other factors.

Forensic interviews require the acquisition of accurate information, while mental health processes promote expression of thoughts and feelings (Carnes, 2000). The task of the forensic interviewer is to identify "the most effective means of getting an accurate, complete report" (Everson & Boat, 2002, p. 383). The task of the clinical interviewer is to "match the interview with the individual client in order to maximize the child's ability to convey significant information" (Salmon, Roncolato, & Gleitzman, 2002, p. 65). The clinical process addresses the safety and well-being of the child, including protective, medical, and emotional needs. According to the guidelines of the American Academy of Child and Adolescent Psychiatry (AACAP, 1990), determining whether abuse has occurred is the premise. The goal is to gather information in a nonthreatening manner while minimizing secondary trauma.

Forensic interviews are conducted for fact-finding purposes. They adhere to rules of evidence in accordance with judicial standards. These processes are directed at facilitating a child's recall of experienced events. Additional objectives are the protection and safety of children, the conviction of perpetrators (Cronch, Viljoen, & Hansen, 2006), and avoidance of wrongful convictions (Salmon, Pipe, Malloy, & Mackay, 2012). Forensic interviewers maintain objectivity and neutrality in an effort to obtain reliable and accurate information. Assessment of competency and credibility are factors that distinguish a forensic interview from a clinical interview. Alternative hypotheses are considered in an effort to demonstrate reliability and validity within a reasonable degree of scientific certainty in order to meet standards of admissibility (Gould & Stahl, 2009).

Forensic interviews are designed to adhere to scientific thinking and method. The systematic collection of data into observations, inferences, and hypotheses grounds the process in scientific thinking (Gould & Stahl, 2009). Scientific methods and procedures enhance reliability and validity since the scientific method is forensically sound and legally defensible (Gould & Stahl, 2009). Current trends in forensic mental health assessments support adherence to scientific principles and practices while also recognizing the validity of clinical methodologies. Elements delineated from both scientific and clinical epistemologies combine to strengthen expert opinion (Gould & Stahl, 2009).

Forensic Art Therapy

Forensic art therapy emerged from the integration of standard art therapy principles and practices with forensic applications. This juxtaposition constituted an innovative and unique mode of practice that extends the parameters of the field of art therapy beyond evaluation/diagnoses and intervention/treatment (Cohen-Liebman, 1997, 2002). Forensic art therapy is a fact-finding endeavor, assisting in the resolution of legal matters in dispute. It is investigative in nature, rather than interventive or evaluative (Cohen-Liebman, 1997, 2002, 2003; Gussak & Cohen-Liebman, 2001).

Forensic art therapy is a specialized field of art therapy requiring modification of standard art therapy practice to meet the needs of the legal system. It commingles social science and forensic science tenets with art therapy conventions. This dialectical confluence is pragmatically oriented. Pragmatism is problem-centered and real-world-oriented (Greene & Hall, 2010). The pragmatic use of art is congruent with the pragmatic nature of the interview process. Interviews happen in an intersubjective matrix that has a corresponding influence on the process. A meaning-making experience rather than an aesthetic one is fostered. The child assists in the fact-finding process in a developmentally congruent manner through drawing. Enabling a child to find the images and the words to communicate his or her experience is the pragmatic piece of the process.

Investigative Method

Art therapy is predicated upon a relationship and the process of art making. When combined with forensic protocols, it yields a distinct and complex investigative method. Forensic art therapy is sensitive to the parameters of clinical interviewing; however, it adheres to forensic interviewing principles. This is necessary for the process to be acceptable within a court of law. Investigative interviews that derive from forensic art therapy are based on a scientific framework, while subscribing to an art therapy paradigm. Gould (1998) stated, "The use of a standard forensic interview protocol provides a more systematic means of data gathering in a manner that is consistent with the evidentiary needs of scientific information" (p. 400).

Forensic art therapy incorporates non-directed or free drawings within the investigative interview format. The use of free drawing provides a method of obtaining information in an investigative interview with a child (Cohen-Liebman, 1999, 2003). In this context, drawings function in the capacity of open-ended prompts to facilitate recall of traumatic events. Telling or fact-finding is facilitated via drawing. Drawing often stimulates verbal disclosure, enabling a child to provide details and information that may not otherwise be disclosed. The child's associations are critical to the process. Drawing as an open-ended prompt may assist a child in uncovering material related to the traumatic event previously unknown. Through the use of drawing, a child may provide collateral information, including situational and contextual material. Drawing enables information to be provided via a spatial matrix. Without the constraints of formal language, a child may depict his or her experience in a more tangible way. Drawing may encompass elements of the event and sensory details that may have occurred simultaneously and might be difficult to describe linearly. As Wadeson (2010) stated, "Sometimes this form of expression more nearly duplicates experience" (p. 13).

Drawing to disclose provides a child with a means of conveying and communicating experience including details related to the event as well as the sensorial nature of the experience. It enables a child to depict the experience and provide salient information because drawing allows for the concurrence of temporal, spatial, and sensory material. A child experiences and encodes a multiplicity of information that can only be linguistically explained one element at a time. Drawing as an open-ended prompt provides the means for disclosure of the various sensorial as well as logistical aspects in a manner that is congruent with real-time experience. Idiosyncratic details that emerge lend credence to a child's disclosure and assist in facilitating additional fact-finding.

Blending of Forensic and Clinical Epistemologies

Forensic art therapy juxtaposes basic art therapy tenets with forensic and clinical methodologies, including clinical understanding and scientific thinking, thorough observation, and judicial procedure. The convergence of behavioral science and legal standards of admissibility underlie the foundation (Gould & Stahl, 2009). The synthesis results in a supportive process that meets the standards of the legal system. The process is predicated upon creative methods of expression procured within a relational context. Art therapy is not a part of the legal system in a traditional sense; however, it offers a child victim of sexual abuse a way to relate his or her experience in a nonthreatening way. Within the forensic interview process, the use of drawing promotes elicitation of information that may otherwise not be communicated due to the encoding of traumatic material.

Forensic art therapy has the capacity to meet the respective goals of the law, while protecting the rights of the child. It can help provide the trier of fact with information needed to make a decision. Forensic art therapy enables the interviewer to place the child's experience in context for the court (Cohen-Liebman, 1999, 2003). Drawings may provide evidentiary information that may contribute to charge enhancements (Cohen-Liebman, 2003). Free drawings may provide corroboratory information and serve as judiciary aids in court (Cohen-Liebman, 1995, 1999, 2003).

Epistemology of Forensic Art Therapy

Forensic art therapy integrates clinical and forensic processes with basic art therapy tenets. Preverbal cognition encompasses different ways of knowing (Leclerc, 2006, 2011), which is intrinsic to the process of information gathering. Acquisition of information at a preverbal level is derived through kinesthetic, sensory, and imaginal means. An intersubjective relationship in which information, comprehension, and understanding occur at a nonverbal or an unconscious level is the platform for the creation of meaning (Leclerc, 2006, 2011). The relationship component within a forensic art therapy process is critical to the procurement of fact-finding. Interviewer and child are co-investigators working together to explore allegations. Information is uncovered through imagery created in a dialogical process in which verbalization is concomitant. In forensic art therapy, a free drawing is used as an open-ended prompt within a relational context to facilitate disclosure. Disclosure in this context is identified as a "fundamentally dialogical process" (Jensen, Gulbrandsen, Mossige, Reichelt, & Tjersland, 2005) in which evidence about the alleged abuse is described within the interview relationship. Within the investigative interview format, drawing supports the dialogical process between the interviewer and the child. Fact-finding is emergent as information is disclosed in the artwork, often precipitating verbal elaboration. Associations often lend authenticity as well as credibility to a child's graphic productions.

Philosophy of Forensic Art Therapy

Sexual abuse is a sensory-based crime. Children often suppress the sensorial nature of their experience, which is often encoded in images. In order to disclose information, drawing may mediate the re-experiencing through a safer and protected manner. The risks associated with revealing a traumatic event may be lessened through the use of drawing. Drawing allows for empowerment, enabling a child to take a risk in order to be understood. Children are able to express their experiences both indirectly and directly. Fact-finding is facilitated via drawing; externalization of internalized facts and details may occur. Images rather than words may expose new information, leading to enhanced verbal disclosure. The creative process facilitates recall, enabling a child to express his or her experience in an ego-syntonic manner. Evidentiary disclosure is concretized through drawing.

Drawing and Investigative Interviews

There are a host of factors that can contribute to a child's lack of disclosure within a verbal format (Melinder et al., 2010). Literature and studies pertaining to forensic interviews advocate the use of open-ended prompts and questions to enhance accuracy. Research studies directed at assessing children's responses to open-ended prompts as well as focused prompts reveal that open-ended prompts elicit enhanced information (Lamb, Hershkowitz, Orbach, & Esplin, 2008). Free recall appears to augment information (Lyon, Ahern, & Scurich, 2012).

Research on best practice offers contradictory information regarding the use of drawings within investigative interviews (Lyon, Lamb, & Myers, 2009). Caution against the use of drawings in these processes has been raised by some authors and researchers (Lyon et al., 2009), while others advocate for drawings in the investigative interview format (Faller, 2003). In some studies where drawings are used, researchers, depending on the study design, are reporting conflicting findings (Wesson & Salmon, 2001). Still others encourage weighing the benefits of interviewing techniques against the risks (Salmon et al., 2012).

In some studies, drawings support accurate recall (Butler, Gross, & Hayne, 1995; Gross & Hayne, 1998, 1999; Salmon et al., 2002; Wesson & Salmon, 2001). In other studies, drawings have been associated with a decrease in accuracy (Salmon & Pipe, 2000). Some studies suggest that memory retrieval may be facilitated through drawing. Other research provides that, without the addition of a drawing strategy, a child's capability to fully describe an experience may be inhibited due to communicative or expressive abilities (Butler et al., 1995; Salmon et al., 2002).

Drawings have been identified as a means to facilitate disclosure of emotionally laden material among child victims of sexual abuse (Burgess & Hartman, 1993; Cohen-Liebman, 1999; Gross & Hayne, 1998). Salmon et al. (2002) concluded that, when eliciting information pertaining to emotionally laden experiences, "drawing appears to be a relatively robust interview strategy" (p. 77). They found that more verbal information was elicited through drawing than through telling or re-enactment (Salmon et al., 2002). Findings from this research indicated that children who drew reported more information than children who were not provided with the drawing strategy (Salmon et al., 2002). These researchers offered that drawing allows children to be removed from the nature of the interview context. This finding was similar to findings reached in other studies (Thomas & Jolley, 1998). According to these researchers, distancing allowed for a narrative account of an event, given the child's perception of the process (Salmon et al., 2002). The ameliorating effect of drawing, including distancing, which promotes externalization of internalized material, within the investigative interview process has been examined with regard to forensic art therapy (Cohen-Liebman, 1999, 2002).

Drawings have been studied as a secondary retrieval strategy within forensic interviews. As such, drawings are introduced after children describe abusive events in response to open-ended questions (Katz & Herskowitz, 2010). Salmon et al. (2012) reported no support for the addition of drawings as a secondary retrieval strategy: "Clearly, when and how the opportunity to draw an experienced event affects children's accounts of that event is determined by multiple variables" (p. 375).

A consensus has still not been reached about the implementation of drawings within investigative interviews. Advantages and disadvantages associated with the use of drawings in stimulating memory recall in a forensic context with children have been identified. According to some researchers, children provide more information about actual experiences when given the opportunity to draw and verbalize simultaneously. These findings are consistent regardless of age and type of abuse (Gross & Hayne,

1998, 1999; Katz & Herskowitz, 2010). Fact-finding, which is the primary objective of an investigative interview, improves when approached within a format that is commensurate with a child's developmental level and interactive patterns (Cohen-Liebman, 1999; Melinder et al., 2010).

The Need for Research

Increasingly, research studies have identified the need for empirical evaluation of drawings within best practice guidelines of investigative interviews (Salmon et al., 2012). Research that is empirically sound and forensically relevant is advocated (Everson & Boat, 2002; Faller, 1993, 2007; Lamb et al., 2008).

Literature in the forensic interview field does not consider the creative process. There is a lack of analysis regarding active engagement in art making and why children often draw what they cannot say in an investigative interview. Interview research often centers on verbal cues, prompts, and responses, as well as interactive patterns of behavior between interviewers and children. Research pertaining to the utility of free drawings within investigative interviews as a means of facilitating evidentiary disclosure is warranted in an effort to explore and explain the impact of the creative process on a child's ability to draw and tell.

Conclusion

The epistemological and ontological underpinnings of forensic art therapy, a pragmatic investigative approach, were explored. An overview of forensic art therapy, a fact-finding method that is informative yet supportive, and legally compliant yet clinically responsive, was provided. The philosophy of this non-traditional art therapy practice was considered, including how drawing may influence evidentiary disclosure within investigative interviews of alleged child victims of sexual abuse. A brief review of the literature and research selected for this chapter demonstrated contradictions regarding the use of drawings in investigative interviews of alleged child victims of sexual abuse. The need for empirical research on the use of free drawings as open-ended prompts within a relational context and the corresponding influence on disclosure, identified as a "fundamentally dialogical process" (Jensen et al., 2005), merits study. The integrity of forensic art therapy as a viable investigative interview practice is contingent upon systematic investigation.

References

American Academy of Child and Adolescent Psychiatry. (1990). *Guidelines for the evaluation of child and adolescent sexual abuse*. Washington, DC: Author.

American Professional Society on the Abuse of Children. (2002). *Practical guidelines: Investigative interviewing in cases of alleged child abuse*. Chicago, IL: Author.

Brooks, C. M., & Milchman, M. S. (1991). Child sexual abuse allegations during custody litigation: Conflicts between mental health expert witnesses and the law. *Behavioral Sciences and the Law, 9*, 21–32.

Burgess, A. W., & Hartman, C. R. (1993). Children's drawings. *Child Abuse & Neglect, 17,* 161–168.

Butler, S., Gross, J., & Hayne, H. (1995). The effect of drawing on memory performance in young children. *Developmental Psychology, 31,* 597–608.

Carnes, C. (2000). *Forensic evaluation of children when sexual abuse is suspected.* National Children's Advocacy Center, Huntsville, AL.

Cohen-Liebman, M. S. (1995). Drawings as judiciary aids in child sexual abuse litigations: A composite list of indicators. *The Arts in Psychotherapy, 22*(5), 475–483.

Cohen-Liebman, M. S. (1997, November). *Forensic art therapy.* Preconference full day course presented at the annual conference of the American Art Therapy Association, Milwaukee, WI.

Cohen-Liebman, M. S. (1999). Draw and tell: Drawings within the context of child sexual abuse investigations. *The Arts in Psychotherapy, 26*(3), 185–194.

Cohen-Liebman, M. S. (2002). Intro to art therapy. In A. P. Giardino & E. R. Giardino (Eds.), *Recognition of Child Abuse for the Mandated Reporter* (3rd ed.). St. Louis, MO: G. W. Medical Publishing.

Cohen-Liebman, M. S. (2003). Drawings in forensic investigations of child sexual abuse. In C. Malchiodi (Ed.), *Handbook of Art Therapy* (pp. 167–179). New York, NY: Guildford Press.

Cronch, L., Viljoen, J., & Hansen, D. (2006). Forensic interviewing in child sexual abuse cases: Current techniques and future directions. *Aggression and Violent Behavior, 11*(3), 195–207.

Everson, M. D., & Boat, B. W. (2002). The utility of anatomical dolls and drawings in child forensic interviews. In M. L. Eisen, J. A. Quas, & G. S. Goodman (Eds.), *Memory and Suggestibility in the Forensic Interview* (pp. 383–408). Hillsdale, NJ: Lawrence Erlbaum Associates.

Faller, K. (1993). *Child sexual abuse: Intervention and treatment issues.* Washington, D.C.: Department of Health and Human Services.

Faller, K. C. (2003). *Understanding and assessing child sexual maltreatment.* Thousand Oaks, CA: Sage.

Faller, K. C. (2007). *Interviewing children about sexual abuse: Controversies and best practice.* New York, NY: Oxford University Press.

Gould, J. W. (1998). *Conducting scientifically crafted child custody evaluations.* Thousand Oaks, CA: Sage.

Gould, J. W., & Stahl, P. M. (2009). The art and science of child custody evaluations. *Family and Conciliation Courts Review, 38*(3), 392–414.

Greene, J., & Hall, J. (2010). Dialectics and pragmatism: Being of consequence. In A. Tashakkori & C. Teddlie (Eds.), *Handbook of mixed methods in social & behavioral research* (pp. 119–144). Thousand Oaks, CA: Sage.

Gross, J., & Hayne, H. (1998). Drawing facilitates children's verbal reports of emotionally laden events. *Journal of Experimental Psychology: Applied, 14,* 163–179.

Gross, J., & Hayne, H. (1999). Drawing facilitates children's verbal reports after long delays. *Journal of Experimental Psychology: Applied, 5,* 265–283.

Gussak, D., & Cohen-Liebman, M. S. (2001). Investigation vs. intervention: Forensic art therapy and art therapy in forensic settings. *American Journal of Art Therapy, 40,* 123–135.

Jensen, T. K., Gulbrandsen, W., Mossige, S., Reichelt, S., & Tjersland, O. A. (2005). Reporting possible sexual abuse: A qualitative study on children's perspectives and the context for disclosure. *Child Abuse & Neglect, 29*(12), 1395–1413.

Katz, C., & Hershkowitz, I. (2010). The effects of drawing on children's accounts of sexual abuse. *Child Maltreatment, 15*(2), 171–179.

Lamb, M. E., Hershkowitz, I., Orbach, Y., & Esplin, P. W. (2008). *Tell me what happened: Structured investigative interviews of child victims and witnesses* (Vol. 36). Hoboken, NJ: Wiley.

Leclerc, J. (2006). The unconscious as paradox: Impact on the epistemological stance of the art psychotherapist. *The Arts in Psychotherapy, 33,* 130–134.

Leclerc, J. (2011). When the image strikes: Postmodern thinking and epistemology in art therapy. In H. Burt (Ed.), *Art therapy and postmodernism: Creative healing through a prism* (pp. 367–378). London, UK: Jessica Kingsley.

Lyon, T. D., Ahern, E. C., & Scurich, N. (2012). Interviewing children versus tossing coins: Accurately assessing the diagnosticity of children's disclosures of abuse. *Journal of Child Sexual Abuse, 21*(1), 19–44.

Lyon, T. D., Lamb, M. E., & Myers, J. (2009). Legal and psychological support for the NICHD interviewing protocol. *Child Abuse & Neglect, 33,* 71–74.

Melinder, A., Alexander, K., Cho, Y. I., Goodman, G., Thoresen, C., Lonnum, K., & Magnussen, S. (2010). Children's eyewitness memory: A comparison of two interviewing strategies as realized by forensic professionals. *Journal of Experimental Child Psychology, 105,* 156–177.

Milchman, M. (2011). The roles of scientific and clinical epistemologies in forensic mental health assessments. *Psychological Injuries and Law, 4,* 127–139.

Salmon, K., & Pipe, M. E. (2000). Recalling an event one year later: The impact of props, Drawing and a prior interview. *Applied Cognitive Psychology, 14,* 261–292.

Salmon, K., Pipe, M. E., Malloy, A., & Mackay, K. (2012). Do non-verbal aids increase the effectiveness of "best practice" verbal interview techniques? An experimental study. *Applied Cognitive Psychology, 26,* 370–380.

Salmon, K., Roncolato, W., & Gleitzman, M. (2002). Children's report of emotionally laden events: Adapting the interview to the child. *Applied Cognitive Psychology, 17,* 65–80.

Steinmetz, M. (1997). *Interviewing for child sexual abuse: Strategies for balancing forensic and therapeutic factors.* Notre Dame, IN: Jalice.

Thomas, G. V., & Jolley, R. P. (1998). Drawing conclusions: A re-examination of empirical and conceptual bases for psychological evaluation of children from their drawings. *British Journal of Clinical Psychology, 37,* 127–139.

Wadeson, H. (2010). *Art Psychotherapy* (2nd ed.). Hoboken, NJ: John Wiley & Sons, Inc.

Ward, T. (2006). English law's epistemology of expert testimony. *Journal of Law and Society, 33*(4), 572–595.

Wesson, M., & Salmon, K. (2001). Drawing and showing: Helping children to report emotionally laden events. *Applied Cognitive Psychology, 15,* 301–320.

46

Art Therapy in the Prison Milieu
David E. Gussak

Where art therapists work vary greatly in their focus and mission, and often they must learn to adapt to a particular environment, almost acting as a visiting ambassador to a foreign subculture. Such settings may maintain their own set of rules and mores; some might even be antithetical to a clinician's expectations, with additional challenges to therapeutic care. This is the experience of art therapists in prison, which can be considered "among the few blatantly anti-therapeutic places resistive to psychological well-being" (Gussak, 2013, p. 328). Some correctional staff may consider clinical care adverse to their own mission—to punish the guilty and protect the public.

Compounding these difficulties is the interference posed by the inmates' tendency to "build rigid defenses and put on 'masks', which ensure survival" (Gussak, 1997a, p. 1). Hesitant to admit to weaknesses and vulnerabilities, inmates may avoid therapy programs that expect them to divulge personal issues. Thus, difficulties traverse both ends of the correctional continua, from staff to inmates. While experiences vary in intensity from state to state and setting to setting, based on institutional and political policies, the overall dynamics remain somewhat consistent. Yet, art therapy has overcome these limitations, providing an avenue for therapeutic change within this milieu.

This chapter examines how and why art therapy can be effective in a correctional system, and attempts to demonstrate how an art therapist can use the inmates' creativity and libidinal drives to provide services while still maintaining safety and security. Toward this, it begins with a review of some of the challenges that a therapist might face in working in these environments; following this will be an overview of the history of the arts in prisons, with a summation of how and why the arts are prevalent; and next, a brief summary of the benefits of art therapy along with a synopsis of some recent studies that support this will be presented.[1]

Therapeutic Challenges in Prison

This primitive milieu of a prison maintains its own values and morals; if an art therapist violates its tacit "policies," he or she may find his or her attempts to access its inner workings and relationships thwarted. Adding to these difficulties is the fact

The Wiley Handbook of Art Therapy, First Edition. Edited by David E. Gussak and Marcia L. Rosal.

that correctional facilities are environments where survival of the fittest is the rule; weakness and vulnerabilities may be taken advantage of for personal gain, retribution, or to assert one's power and dominance. In this environment, it may be deemed unhealthy, even dangerous, for an inmate to disclose personal issues. "Admitting to a mental illness, sadness of one's circumstances, or an inability to adjust to the setting may be seen as a weakness" (Gussak, 2013, p. 330). The inmate who expresses personal or emotional issues may fear retaliation, be reviled, or experience domination by others. "There is an inherent mistrust for such verbal disclosure, and a well-grounded fear of prisoners taking advantage of others' voiced vulnerabilities; rigid defenses are built to achieve basic survival" (Fenner & Gussak, 2006, p. 414). As inmates learn not to trust anyone, they may develop a resistance to therapy, or limit honesty within the helping relationship.

> If a therapist tries to break through necessary barriers, the inmate/patient may become dangerous even if initially charming and cooperative. The inmate's defenses take over, making him anxious and angry, perhaps even violent, to a much greater extent ... than clinicians are accustomed to with the general population. (Gussak, 1997a, p. 1)

To compensate, a therapist must be prepared to work with inmates in a way that does not raise suspicion or increase vulnerability. While this might be a challenge in talk therapy, art therapists have tools at their disposal that allow them to work around these limitations—the art (Gussak, 1997b).

Art in Prison: An Overview

Although illogical and anti-intuitive given the desolate environment of a prison, history demonstrates that inmates have a drive to create. In fact, the ability to create tangible art is a status builder among peers and correctional officers (Gussak, 1997a; Kornfeld, 1997). For example, works of art, prolifically displayed "through prison craft shops, inmate-painted wall murals, decorative envelopes that inmates can 'buy' from each other to send letters to loved ones, and intricate tattoos" (Gussak & Ploumis-Devick, 2004), are highly valued.

As Ursprung (1997) surmised, prison art is probably as old as the institution of prison itself. Rojcewicz (1997) recognized that the writings of Plato and Socrates were inspired by their respective incarcerations, and Kornfeld (1997) pointed out that, in the first century AD, gladiators enslaved in the Pompeii arena scratched graffiti onto the walls of their imprisoning barracks. While excavating a Pennsylvania prison built in 1829, workers discovered inmate-produced handicrafts including carved wooden toys and figurines (Ursprung, 1997). It was not just the visual arts; many writers wrote some of their greatest works while imprisoned, including Oscar Wilde and François Villon, both of whom composed poems about their experiences (Rojcewicz, 1997). Indeed, there have been many correctional programs that recognize the benefits of the arts in prison settings (Alexander, 2003; Bruna, 2007; Tannenbaum, 2000; Williams, 2003).

Why?

Creative expression in the prison subculture is not surprising since the act of creating art has been directly linked to aggression, sexuality, and escape. Primitive instinctual impulses are prevalent but institutionally controlled in correctional settings (Fox, 1997). Generally, impulses require release, but to do so within this subculture may have dire consequences for those who express these impulses and for those around them. Creating art may provide a safer outlet for the expression of these libidinal urges.

Art and sex are "each primal behaviors that have become elaborated in the essential service of affiliation and bonding" (Dissanayake, 1992, p. 193), and "the impulses that drive some people to create are perhaps alike primarily in the fact that both can be considered expressions and agents of feelings" (Dissanayake, 1988, p. 140). Creative expression can be a socially acceptable byproduct of sublimating aggressive and libidinal impulses (Kramer, 1993; Rank, 1932; Rubin, 1984). The act of creating also allows the inmate to "escape" (if only for a few moments or hours) into his or her created world; it provides a diversion from this primitive subculture (Gussak, 1997b; Gussak & Cohen-Liebman, 2001; Hall, 1997).

Understandably, members of the correctional milieu resists these impulses if expressed in their pure form (Fox, 1997); thus, redirecting these instincts into creative, artistic expression is more acceptable to the institution, even if members of the institution are not aware of the motivation of these creative expressions. In other words, members from both inside and outside the prison subculture accept the inmates' creative expressions.

An additional challenge for art therapists who work in prisons is the limited number and types of tools allowed in the institution. This is due to safety and security concerns. More confusing is that regulations about art tools may seem arbitrary; they may vary from setting to setting, or even from week to week within a single institution. Determining what tools can be used and how to work with established regulations is an ongoing challenge.

The Benefits of Art Therapy in Prison

The advantages of art therapy for the prison population, particularly the men's prison, have been widely documented (Gussak, 1997a; Gussak & Cohen-Liebman, 2001). The underlying benefit is that art making and art therapy meets the therapeutic needs of inmates without the need for vulnerable, verbal self-disclosure. Art therapy mitigates instinctual, libidinal impulses, and diminishes pathological symptoms without verbal interpretation. Creating art provides the environment for the reemergence of the self and the development of personal identity. This can occur in an environment where control is maintained by objectifying the inmate, identifying them by number, and requiring him or her to wear a uniform.

Art making and art therapy may be an easier way for inmates to express themselves. Often, illiteracy or diminished capacity, which runs rampant in the correctional system, limits the inmate's capacity to clearly articulate himself or herself. The art provides a means of communication that may otherwise be hindered by such limitations.

Art therapy can bypass conscious and unconscious defenses, including the tendency to lie. While an inmate may or may not tell the truth—deliberately or inadvertently due to a defense mechanism that allows them to reconstruct their own reality—the art does not lie, and provides the therapist much needed information about the inmate that may not otherwise be available.

Finally, art making provides diversion and allows for emotional escape, which is certainly necessary in an environment where confinement can activate mental illness and aggravate personality or psychiatric symptoms. While the benefits of art therapy in the prison environment are clear, it has only been within the past 10 years that research has been conducted to determine if art therapy is indeed an effective approach to meeting any needs or to promoting wellness with prison inmates.

Studies of Art Therapy in Prisons[2]

My research on the benefits of art therapy within correctional institutions began in the summer of 2003 with the help of art therapy practicum students and graduate assistants. These studies were conducted at various North Florida prisons in partnership with the Department of Corrections. Initially, these studies were conducted in a men's moderate–maximum-security prison, and later expanded to a second men's minimum–moderate-security prison and a woman's minimum–moderate-security prison.

The treatment protocol for each outcome study was standardized throughout the studies. The length of treatment of these three studies ranged from 4 weeks to 15 weeks, with 8–15 sessions offered. The directives began simply and became increasingly more complicated; early sessions focused on the individual, but became progressively more group-focused. For example, an early art therapy directive asked participants to complete a name embellishment by writing their name on a piece of paper and then adorning the name in a way that would tell the other members of the group something new about themselves (i.e., a hobby or occupation). A later directive focused on frustration tolerance and problem-solving. For example, the participants were asked to construct three-dimensional forms, such as a white paper sculpture, with few supplies (paper, glue, and safety scissors).

As the sessions became more group-focused, the inmates participated in the draw-and-pass directive—each participant drew an image within a set period of time, after which he or she passed the drawing to the person sitting next to him or her, who worked on it by drawing for a few more minutes. This continued until all of the participants added something to each drawing.

The sessions often culminated in a large, more complicated group task. For example, the participants would be asked, as a group, to design and construct a large three-dimensional form, such as their ideal or dream environment or a bridge construction. This project often took several sessions to complete.

Pilot Study

A quasi-experimental, single-group, pretest–posttest design pilot study was conducted to examine the effects of art therapy with male prison inmates in a moderate–maximum-security prison. The hypothesis was that inmates receiving art therapy services would demonstrate marked change (Gussak, 2004). Art therapy group sessions were conducted in the prison's mental health unit by the researcher and four art therapy practicum interns. Forty-four participants, chosen by the facility's mental health counselor, attended eight 1-hour group art therapy sessions. There were no more than eight inmates assigned to a single group. These men embodied various demographic criteria (age, race, marital status, education, socio-economic status, and crimes).

Two measurement tools were used: (1) a survey developed by the prison's mental health staff, and (2) an established, standardized art therapy assessment, the Formal Elements Art Therapy Scale (FEATS; Gantt & Tabone, 1998). The survey collected data on compliance with medication, compliance with unit rules, and improved social interaction. The art-based assessment was a person picking an apple from a tree [PPAT] (Gantt & Tabone, 1998), and the drawings were evaluated using FEATS.[3] Both the survey and the PPAT were administered pretest and posttest. The correctional and mental health counseling staff completed the surveys, whereas the drawings were administered and evaluated by the art therapy personnel.

The results indicated a decrease in depression and an increase in problem-solving and socialization. It was also noted by the staff that the inmates who participated in the art therapy program followed directions better, were more compliant with the prison rules, and were less impulsive (Gussak, 2004). The scores of FEATS drawings also indicated an elevation of mood and an increase in energy and problem-solving abilities. The hypothesis was supported: inmates who participated in art therapy sessions demonstrated a measureable change in behavior and mood.

The Follow-Up Study

Based on the results of the pilot, a follow-up outcome study was conducted a year later at the same facility. The hypothesis was that art therapy would help reduce depression in prison populations (Gussak, 2006, 2007). Again, FEATS was used, and the Beck Depression Inventor-Short Form (BDI-II; Beck, Rial, & Rickets, 1974; Beck & Steer, 1993) was added to determine if art therapy would impact significant changes in mood. The BDI-II had been used effectively in previous studies with correctional inmates to assess for depression (Boothby & Durham, 1999).

The participants were randomly assigned to either the control group or the experimental group. A schedule of the art therapy directives similar to that used for the pilot study (simple to complex, individual to group-focused) was used for those in the experimental group. The control group did not receive treatment, but completed the pretest–posttest assessments. Control group inmates were assured that they would receive art therapy after the study was completed.

The BDI-II and other evaluations indicated that art therapy produced positive and statistically significant changes in the inmates' mood and problem-solving and socialization abilities. FEATS did not exhibit any substantial statistical change in all but one of the scales (rotation), and therefore the overall results were mixed (for complete study statistics, please refer to Gussak, 2006).

Studies Comparing Male and Female Inmates

Next, the study was expanded to include another men's minimum–moderate-security correctional institution and a woman's minimum–moderate-security correctional institution (Gussak, 2009a). The focus of the study was to demonstrate an improvement in mood, socialization, and problem-solving, as well as to assess changes in locus of control (LOC) as measured by the Adult Nowicki-Strickland Locus of Control Scale (ANS; Nowicki & Duke, 1974). Two hypotheses were developed:

(a)   Male inmates receiving art therapy services will exhibit marked improvement in mood, socialization, problem-solving abilities, and internal LOC within the correctional environment.
(b)   Female inmates receiving art therapy services will exhibit marked improvement in mood, socialization, problem-solving abilities, and internal LOC within the correctional environment.

The participants in the experimental group received 15 weeks of sessions, and another assessment tool was introduced to measure change of LOC. The ANS had, in the past, specifically been used to ascertain whether or not the participants had primarily internal or external locus of control (LOC).

Over the next 2 years, one to two art therapy graduate interns were placed in each facility. The art therapy treatment over 15 weeks was similar to that of the previous studies (simple to complex, and individually focused to increased group-focused art therapy interventions). The control groups received the assessments during the same 15-week period as those placed in the experimental group. The studies demonstrated a significant improvement in mood and internal LOC. However, women inmates demonstrated greater improvement in mood and internal LOC than the men. To further explore this, a third hypothesis was formulated:

(c)   Although both male and female inmates will exhibit marked improvement, the male inmates will exhibit different responses to the art therapy services in mood and locus of control than female inmates within their respective correctional environments.

This final hypothesis was supported: the female inmate population demonstrated a change in LOC and mood and made significantly greater changes than the male inmate population. After closed examination of the data, it was concluded that, while the posttest scores of both men and women were similar, the women exhibited pretest scores that reflected greater depression and external LOC than their male counterparts *prior* to receiving treatment. Therefore, their change scores were more significant (Gussak, 2009b). This provided valuable information to future art therapy interns on how to approach the male and female inmate populations, and how to develop art therapy programs to best meet their needs. For example, art directives with female inmates may focus more on strengthening self-identity and mood, whereas directives for male inmates may focus more on socialization and anger management.

Conclusion

Prisons are a unique and, at times, difficult environment to practice art therapy services. While counterintuitive, in actuality many prison inmates have a natural need to create or respect those who do. Art therapists can capitalize on this desire to involve inmates in treatment. Also, art therapists can engage other inmates who have strong, primitive impulses to create art. Involvement in the creative process provides prisoners with a means to express their weaknesses and difficulties without leaving them vulnerable. As the research demonstrated, art therapy is beneficial in improving the mood, internal locus of control, problem-solving skills, and positive socialization within the inmate population. The changes that art therapy generates may lead to a safer, more productive environment.

Postscript

For several years now, I have led the master supervision session on forensic art therapy for the annual conference of the American Art Therapy Association. In past years, between 20 and 25 people would attend. However, something remarkable happened at the conference in 2013. While prepared for 25 attendees, more than 70 art therapists arrived; many worked in various correctional settings and were anxious to meet others who worked in similar venues. It was impressive that many of the participants had extensive experience; I found their work to be significant. The increased number of participants may reflect a broader awareness of the role that art therapists can play in these settings. The discussion was enlightening and inspired a great deal of hope for future investigation of the role of art therapy in prisons.

The session ended with a call to arms for increased research. The participants were implored to write about their experiences, conduct research, and participate in public relations to educate others about the value of art therapy services in the prisons. This chapter will conclude with the same plea—I can only imagine that the attendees of the 2013 master supervision session were only a small percentage of those art therapists who work in prisons. It is important that more research be conducted and more theoretical papers be published that explore the benefits and challenges that art therapists have in these environments. Please encourage others to heed the call to publish their much-needed work.

Endnotes

1　Please note that this chapter relies on a number of previously published chapters and articles on art therapy in prisons, most recently, Gussak (2013).

2　These studies are available for download from www.arttherapyinprison.com

3　For a comprehensive description of this assessment, please refer to the FEATS rating manual (Gantt & Tabone, 1998) and the chapter in this Handbook that covers this assessment.

References

Alexander, B. (2003). Smitty, prayer, astronomy, "Y2K and the wicked stepmother," and Asia Romero: Dimensions in the work of the prison creative arts project. In R. M. C. Williams (Ed.), *Teaching the art behind bars* (pp. 125–137). Boston, MA: Northeastern University Press.

Beck, A. T., Rial, W. Y., & Rickets, K. (1974). Short form of depression inventory: Cross-validation. *Psychological-Reports, 34*(3), 1184–1186.

Beck, A. T., & Steer, R. A. (1993). *Beck Depression Inventory Manual.* New York, NY: Harcourt Brace.

Boothby, J. L., & Durham, T. W. (1999). Screening for depression in prisoners using the Beck Depression Inventory. *Criminal Justice and Behavior, 26*(1), 107–124.

Bruna, K. (2007). *Creating behind the razor wire: An Overview of arts in corrections in the U.S.,* January 2007. Retrieved from: http://www.communityarts.net/readingroom/archivefiles/2007/01/creating_behind.php#_ftnref4

Dissanayake, E. (1988). *What is art for?* Seattle, WA: University of Washington Press.

Dissanayake, E. (1992). *Homoaestheticus: Where art comes from and why.* New York, NY: The Free Press.

Fenner, L., & Gussak, D. (2006). Therapeutic boundaries in a prison setting: A dialogue between an intern and her supervisor. *The Arts in Psychotherapy, 33,* 414–421.

Fox, W. M. (1997). The hidden weapon: Psychodynamics of forensic institutions. In D. Gussak & E. Virshup (Eds.), *Drawing time: Art therapy in prisons and other correctional settings* (pp. 43–55). Chicago, IL: Magnolia Street Publishers.

Gantt, L., & Tabone, C. (1998). *The formal elements art therapy scale: The rating manual.* Morgantown, WV: Gargoyle Press.

Gussak, D. (1997a). The ultimate hidden weapon: Art therapy and the compromise option. In D. Gussak & E. Virshup (Eds.), *Drawing time: Art therapy in prisons and other correctional settings* (pp. 59–74). Chicago, IL: Magnolia Street Publishers.

Gussak, D. (1997b). Breaking through barriers: Advantages of art therapy in prison. In D. Gussak & E. Virshup (Eds.), *Drawing time: Art therapy in prisons and other correctional settings* (pp. 1–12). Chicago, IL: Magnolia Street Publishers.

Gussak, D. (2004). Art therapy with prison inmates: A pilot study. *The Arts in Psychotherapy, 31*(4), 245–259.

Gussak, D. (2006). The effects of art therapy with prison inmates: A follow-up study. *The Arts in Psychotherapy, 33,* 188–198.

Gussak, D. (2007). The effectiveness of art therapy in reducing depression in prison populations. *International Journal of Offender Therapy and Comparative Criminology, 5*(4), 444–460.

Gussak, D. (2009a). Comparing the effectiveness of art therapy on depression and locus of control of male and female inmates. *The Arts in Psychotherapy, 36*(4), 202–207.

Gussak, D. (2009b). The effects of art therapy on male and female inmates: Advancing the research base. *The Arts in Psychotherapy, 36*(1), 5–12.

Gussak, D. (2013). Art therapy in the prison subculture: Maintaining boundaries while breaking barriers. In P. Howie, S. Prasad, & J. Kristel (Eds.), *Using art therapy with diverse populations: Crossing cultures and abilities.* (pp. 328–337). London: Jessica Kingsley, Publishers.

Gussak, D., & Cohen-Liebman, M. S. (2001). Investigation vs. intervention: Forensic art therapy and art therapy in forensic settings. *The American Journal of Art Therapy, 40*(2), 123–135.

Gussak, D., & Ploumis-Devick, E. (2004). Creating wellness in forensic populations through the arts: A proposed interdisciplinary model. *Visual Arts Research, 29*(1), 35–43.

Hall, N. (1997). Creativity and Incarceration: The purpose of art in a prison culture. In D. Gussak & E. Virshup (Eds.), *Drawing time: Art therapy in prisons and other correctional settings* (pp. 25–41). Chicago, IL: Magnolia Street Publishers.

Kornfeld, P. (1997). *Cellblock visions: Prison art in America.* Princeton, NJ: Princeton University Press.

Kramer, E. (1993). *Art as therapy with children* (2nd ed.). Chicago, IL: Magnolia Street Publishers.

Nowicki S., & Duke, M. (1974). A locus of control scale for noncollege as well as college adults. *Journal of Personality Assessment, 38,* 136–137.

Rank, O. (1932). *Art and artist.* New York, NY: W.W. Norton.

Rojcewicz, S. (1997). No artist rants and raves when he creates: Creative arts therapists and psychiatry in forensic settings. In D. Gussak & E. Virshup (Eds.), *Drawing time: Art therapy in prisons and other correctional settings* (pp. 75–86). Chicago, IL: Magnolia Street Publishers.

Rubin, J. A. (1984). *The art of art therapy.* New York, NY: Brunner/Mazel Publishing.

Tannenbaum, J. (2000). *Disguised as a poem: My years teaching poetry at San Quentin.* Boston, MA: Northeastern University Press.

Ursprung, W. (1997). Insider art: The creative ingenuity of the incarcerated artist. In D. Gussak & E. Virshup (Eds.), *Drawing time: Art therapy in prisons and other correctional settings* (pp. 13–24). Chicago, IL: Magnolia Street Publishers.

Williams, R. M. C. (2003). Introduction. In R. M. C. Williams (Ed.), *Teaching the art behind bars* (pp. 3–13). Boston, MA: Northeastern University Press.

47

Bringing Art Therapy into Museums

Carolyn Brown Treadon

I believe in the power of images—their ability to put us in touch with the creative impulse, to yield insights about human experience in other times and places, and to move us spiritually and emotionally. (Ray Williams)

The inherent benefit of museums is not a new concept; however, it was not until recently that they began to appear in the research literature as a therapeutic resource. Throughout history, museums have been established to protect and preserve items for the edification and entertainment of individuals (Hein, 1998). Early museums held private collections and were only enjoyed by a select few, primarily in the upper classes. The eighteenth century saw the evolution of the museum as an institution for the display of objects for the enjoyment of the public. The major expansion of museums into significant public institutions occurred in the nineteenth century. Following the Great Depression, museums were seen as a means to educate the masses in order to improve overall well-being. The following brief history highlights the purpose of museums as agents of social change (Silverman, 2010).

Museums as Agents of Social Change

Historical shifts in the focus of museum education from disseminating information on the preservation and value of artifacts to engaging patrons in meaningful experiences has led to a change in practitioners', policy makers', and the general public's belief in the power of museums to better the world through healing and improving lives (Hein, 1998; Silverman, 2010). At their core, "museums have always been institutions of social service" (Silverman, 2010, p. 13). Throughout history, museums have "both intentionally and unintentionally facilitated the expression and transformation of individuals" (p. 13) by helping with identity formation, forging friendships with individuals and improving social bonds between families and cultures.

Eisner and Dobbs (1988) stated that works of art cannot speak for themselves; rather, they are understood by those who have learned how to listen to what they have to say. Museums, museum educators, and other facilitators such as therapists can

---

The Wiley Handbook of Art Therapy, First Edition. Edited by David E. Gussak and Marcia L. Rosal.

provide a museum visitor with some assistance in bridging the barrier between the artworks and himself or herself, which may facilitate a meaning-making experience. This dialogue between a work of art and the viewer has occurred throughout history. However, in order for visitors to reap the greatest benefit from a museum visit, it is necessary for museum educators, and other facilitators such as therapists, to understand the dynamics involved (Hein, 1998).

Meaningful museum experiences can also transcend beyond an isolated visit. Using a constructivist approach, Hein (1998) considered several factors. Of primary importance is the consideration of what an individual already knows—their life experiences. The physical space of a museum is also important, and a museum professional must also consider the associations that an individual has to the built environment. Comfort in a physical space is essential to learning. Orientation—both to the physical space and the contents of the exhibit—has significant impact on an individual's ability to feel comfortable and relaxed. Hein's final consideration is an individual's intellectual comfort, which is the ability to associate the current exhibit with what is already known. Since visitors bring with them their life experiences, it is not difficult for them to make some connection or self-reflection to the museum environment. The success of a museum visit can be measured by the strength of an individual's connection between old and new ideas (Hein, 1998; Silverman, 2010).

Therapeutic uses of Museums

Williams (1994) and Mayer (1998) noted that the focus of education in art museums has changed over the years from passive learning to active engagement. This shift created a dilemma on how to meet the needs of existing patrons while increasing the general public's involvement (Mayer, 1998). To increase it, two changes have been identified. First, museums must be seen as more than institutions for preserving and displaying objects. Museum educators have realized the power of art objects "to elicit feelings and meaning in addition to stimulating appreciation" (Treadon, Rosal, & Wylder, 2006, p. 290). Second, the profile of a museum attendee must be redefined to include individuals from varying socio-economic, cultural, and ability levels. Subsequently, museum educators have been charged with increasing participation of diverse audiences (Treadon et al., 2006). This new vision has resulted in increased collaborations between art therapists and museum educators, as well as created possible employment opportunities for individuals who understand the varying needs of potential attendees.

There are several elements inherent to museums that make them useful settings for therapy: artistic diversity, architectural boundaries, the collective nature of the images and artifacts, interpersonal relationships that occur between patrons, and the change in personal routine that occurs when visiting a museum (Salom, 2008, 2011). Several factors must be taken into account when utilizing the museum for therapeutic purposes. Similar to the constructivist approach put forth by Hein (1998) relating to museum curation and education, Salom (2011) addressed the need for logistical awareness relating to space, artifacts, and the duration of group meetings when using the museum as a resource. Decisions must be made based on the needs of the clientele.

Including museums as a resource for art therapists "honors the origins and evolution of our field" (p. 81).

Several experimental museum programs have emerged to test the power of the art museum to encourage meaning-making (Silverman, 1989, 2010; Treadon et al., 2006). Williams (1994) explored the use of museums for increasing personal reflection and enhancing meaningful connections. He sent small groups into the art museum to find an art object and to use it to answer incisive, thoughtful questions. Once each person completed this task, the group went on a *personal highlights tour* to discuss this object from a personal perspective.

Silverman (2010) used various museum resources over the last 25 years to create opportunities for families and groups to improve relationships. Through these opportunities, decision-making, communication, discipline, and many other patterns of interaction occur. Museums can serve as institutions for addressing dysfunctional patterns, thus allowing for new means of interaction to occur. Through task assignment, focus areas can be addressed by clientele between therapy sessions. For example, the museum holds unlimited therapeutic possibilities for adults with dementia using a museum visit to reminisce or a disenfranchised family that needs a non-threatening activity to do together.

Poulter (2010) created opportunities for individuals with diverse beliefs and backgrounds to dialogue and debate in order to explore the contemporary relevance of museum objects. The Talking Objects project, which spanned 3 years, connected individuals to historical museum objects. On the first day of the process that spans four half-days, the curator provided an oral history and context for the selected object. On the following 2 days, participants created personal responses to the object. On the final day, individuals discussed their ideas and feelings toward the object. This process was especially successful in helping to increase self-confidence and spark interest in museum objects for disadvantaged youth.

Creating art may be another means to engage diverse populations. By broadening the scope of an art museum from just viewing art to including art-making can promote self-reflection and meaning-making during the museum experience. Winn (2001) employed a gallery-based art therapy program to assist individuals with chronic illness to explore how their lifestyle affects health, as well as to increase self-awareness and esteem. The *Arts for Health* program held eight 4-hour weekly sessions. During the sessions, participants created art in the gallery to reflect on their past week, followed by looking at art within the gallery that related to their earlier art making.

Alter Muri (1996) found that her clients with chronic mental health and cognitive deficits displayed increases in self-esteem, ability to express emotion through their artwork, socialization skills, introspection, and creativity after she encouraged them to explore works of artists with similar styles as their own, as well as to visit galleries and museums, which led to increased identity formation in them as artists. Working on art in the museum space also helped foster this new identity and required clients to use socially appropriate behaviors. Stiles and Mermer-Welly (1998) similarly explored the role of poor self-esteem in early teen pregnancy and found that the art museum, as a component of art therapy, could assist in increasing self-esteem and decreasing problematic symptoms in teens aged 13–15 years with mild and moderate intellectual disabilities.

Linesch (2004), in collaboration with the Museum of Tolerance in Los Angeles, used art therapy to transform visitors from passive observers to active participants. In both her 1-day workshops for adults and 5-day camps for children, creating art in the museum space allowed participants to become "actively connected to an exhibit through experimental art processes [and] experience a deeper sense of involvement with the museum" (p. 66).

Understanding that empathy is a leading factor in facilitating social change, Betts and Potash (2012) explored how touring the permanent collection at the United States Holocaust Memorial Museum affected adult participants' levels of empathy. Further research sought to determine if participating in an art therapy experiential following the visit led to a sustained change (2-, 7-, and 12-month follow-up) in empathy as well as in the desire to effect social change. Experimental group participants who had engaged in art making, reflective writing, and group discussion had sustained increased empathy while control participants had not changed (Betts, Potash, Luke, & Kelso, 2015).

A Pilot Museum Art Therapy Program

In 2004, the groundwork began for a pilot project involving collaboration between the art therapy program at Florida State University, the Florida State University Museum of Fine Art, and a local school for youth with emotional and behavioral disabilities (Treadon et al., 2006). The project opened the university art museum to diverse populations and helped it to reach out to community organizations that served the needs of those with special needs. The project also led to the establishment of an art therapy student practicum internship at the museum and prompted its use to educate art therapy students about disabilities.

The pilot program was part of a 3-year initiative that culminated in an exhibition titled *The Family Experience: Deconstruction and Reconstruction*. In addition to developing therapy goals, the art therapists and the museum's curator of education (henceforth referred to as "curator") identified art objects to help students identify family concerns, roles, and feelings associated with being a member of a family group. The strength of this partnership rested in the curator's ability to introduce the art objects, and the art therapists' ability to facilitate discussions about emotional reactions to the selected pieces. The curator addressed the aesthetics of the art while the art therapists tended to the sensitive issues of the vulnerable population. The art therapists also prepared the students to visit the museum—a new and possibly threatening environment. The curator of education led the tours.

The group consisted of six boys and one girl, between 12 and 14 years of age, who were enrolled in the fifth to seventh grade levels. The group members had poor social skills, poor impulse control, were manipulative and attention-seeking, had a history of making inappropriate comments, and were argumentative. They also presented with depression, obsessive-compulsive tendencies, and hyperactivity. Over the course of 8 weeks, seven sessions were held, including two museum visits.

In the first session, following a discussion on the meaning of family, students were asked to create a collage using a list they developed about who was a part of their family. Shapes cut from colorful construction paper were provided. While some students only listed immediate family members, others had large extended families exceeding 30 people. In the second session, students were asked to select images chosen from magazine pictures to symbolize the family members identified in the collage. Care taking and support emerged as two prominent themes; one student stated that he could not open up to anyone else but his mother.

The curator joined the art therapists in visiting the school for the third session. She brought two of William Walmsley's self portraits, Bill Pericola's *The Silent Woman*, and Paul Travis' *Lumbwa Young Man, Kenya* from the museum. These art pieces were selected because they depicted strong emotion and related to the students' discussions in previous sessions. The curator discussed the artists and their use of portraiture to convey emotion. Students formed smaller groups, each of which discussed a selected image with one of the art therapists. Following the discussion, students were asked to create a portrait of themselves or someone in their family. To assist them, the art therapists provided pre-outlined shapes (see Figure 47.1). One student drew an image of a person, based on Pericola's image, which he described as someone who had gone through pain. He stated the person in the drawing "feels bad and sad … this person has not done much with their life … the scar was from some mistake the person had made" (Treadon et al., 2006, p. 294).

To familiarize students with the museum, the fourth session was held in the museum conference room. Three works were selected by the curator that echoed themes of the

Figure 47.1 Final exhibition.

students' artworks: Erich Hackel's *Head of a Young Woman,* Alexander Calder's *Balloons,* and Ynez Johnson's *Tribal Coast.* Again, the curator led the discussion about the artworks; this discussion culminated in a discussion on how *Tribal Coast* represented family and community. Students were asked to complete an action drawing of two members of their family or community doing something together. They were provided figure cutouts for tracing if they so desired. The only female student explained that her image of two figures were friends who were playing together, and "they were just people." She did not include family members nor did she address their sad expressions.

For the fifth session, students were asked to create a mono-print using watercolor paint on Plexiglas. Students were able to see how their emotions were reflected in the colors they selected and the images they drew. One student discussed that, in his prints, each color represented a different feeling; red was between happy and sad, pink was on the verge of being mad, brown was mad, green was not wanting to be bothered, and blue was enjoyment.

Prior to the final museum visit, the art therapists and the curator carefully selected art objects that reflected family or relationship issues for a final discussion. Using Ray Williams (1994) approach, students were asked to study the objects and then select one that they felt connected to, and then discuss their choice with the group. All of the students engaged in and demonstrated an investment in the process. Following this student-led tour, the group went to an area where they could sit and again view four artworks from the permanent collection: Art Werger's *Pursued by Conscience,* William Walmsley's *Study of Gloria,* an anonymous piece titled *Plaster Relief,* and David Bungay's *Wright and Walmsley.* The students were invited to discuss what they felt the art represented. For them, strong feelings were a central theme in all of the images.

At the conclusion of the discussion, *Plastic Shirt* was displayed, and the students were asked to think about a shirt logo that would represent their family. Each student was given two cutouts in the shape of a shirt. Once each was decorated, the pieces were stapled together and stuffed with newspaper (see Figure 47.1) to form the front and the back of the shirt.

At the end of this session, since it was the final one, students were asked to select four pieces of their art for inclusion in an exhibit featuring their work along with the pieces from the permanent collection (see Figure 47.1). Students were paired to discuss their selected works. This was to incorporate social skills into the experience, a deficit recognized during the formation of this group. One student, who had explored Walmsley's work in session three, drew a portrait without a mouth. The student stated that he liked the image because it looked like him when he was little. After selecting the piece, he asked for a pencil to draw a mouth, returning the drawing to the art therapists stating that it was now finished and ready for exhibition (see Figure 47.2).

The teacher, support staff, art therapists, and curator noted changes in the students over the 8 weeks. The female student, who typically did not participate in class, engaged not only in art-making but also in group discussions. Each session provided an unexpected lack of resistance, reduction of negative behaviors, and eagerness to engage and talk about their work.

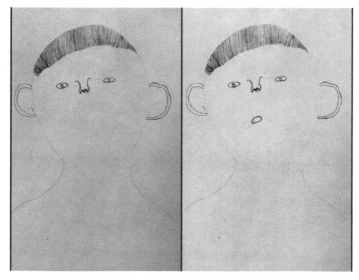

Figure 47.2 Student work from pilot project.

Development of a Student Practicum Placement

Due to the success of the pilot project, the art therapy program and the curator discussed about expanding the museum's outreach into the community. To implement such a program, an art therapy practicum program was developed at the museum, where an intern would liaise between agencies that served special-needs populations and the museum. Since its development in the spring semester of 2006, various agencies are asked to participate each year. In addition to the school that participated in the pilot program, a developmental preschool, GED program for adults, two different day centers for adults with developmental disabilities, and senior residential centers have participated.

For the practicum experience, the art therapy practicum students work closely with the curator; together, they develop a theme for the art therapy interventions and tailor the interventions to the theme of the exhibit at the museum during scheduled visits. Over the course of a 15-week semester, the art therapy students facilitate weekly sessions at various agencies. The students also work closely with the curator to select pieces from the permanent collection to take to each site as preparation for museum visits.

The intern is charged with developing a therapeutic theme with a current exhibit. For example, in response to the exhibition by Jim Roche, an art professor from Florida State University, the art therapy student had her groups create a three-dimensional bridge. Using mixed media, one box was to represent a goal or aspiration, and the other for how life may be different if that goal were attained. The bridge between the two represented the journey to reaching the goal.

One exhibit entitled *Threads of Life* featured quilting artists such as Faith Ringold. The art therapy student developed the theme *Interwoven: A Community Exhibition of Textiles and Relationships*. Throughout the semester, groups worked on creating art that reflected their self-identity and relationships using various textiles and media.

Figure 47.3 Art exhibit from student practicum experience.

While some created sewn self-symbols, others created a group-woven wall hanging or sculpture. At the end of the semester, the art therapy student organized an exhibit of the participants' work (see Figure 47.3). The local community college has partnered with the university museum of fine arts to provide exhibition space.

The success of the students utilizing the museum space with clients lent itself for further exploration on the benefits and uses of the museum space. Because art therapy education is by its nature experiential and constructivist, it was a natural progression to include the museum in the student's educational opportunities for learning.

Utilizing the Museum to Enhance Classroom Learning

Students enrolled in the Florida State University graduate art therapy course, titled *Art Therapy for Special Populations*, spend the semester learning about various disabling conditions and how to adapt the art-making process and materials to meet the needs of diverse populations. However, many have never experienced a disabling condition. To assist them in gaining such understanding, the art therapists collaborated again with the museum curator of education for a class tour of the museum.

Prior to leaving the classroom for the museum, students were assigned a "disabling condition." They had to navigate to the museum, participate in an experiential-based tour, return to the classroom, and create response art while maintaining the disability (see Figures 47.4 and 47.5). Student journal writings indicated that this encounter

Figure 47.4   Students at the university art museum tour.

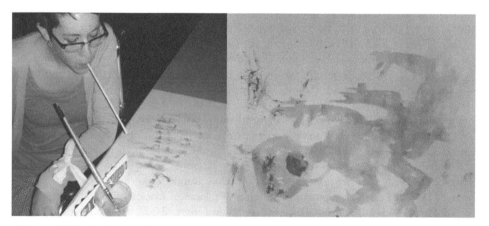

Figure 47.5   Student making response artwork to museum tour with disabling conditions.

with a disabling condition taught them more about living with a disability than classroom discussions or other art experiences.

One student who experienced a motor restriction stated that:

> The walk to the museum and the tour were so exciting. My experience was enhanced by helping [another student] experience the world without sight. I found that the duality of the art products of my right and left hand paralleled the theme of the piece I discussed.

Another student expressed, I have never been "blind" for such a long period of time. It was amazing to experience that transformation from terror/anxiety ("I'm going to do WHAT?!!") to slowly allowing myself adjustment (senses became heightened) and final acceptance. I realized that it's not just textures which are important in art making to the visually impaired—the sounds, smells and even temperatures of the materials make a difference as well.

Conclusion

Understanding the function of museums to enhance the human condition is a recent and ongoing process (Silverman, 2010). The shift from thinking about museums as places for taking care of valued objects to places that include active participation from visitors is novel and exciting. This paradigm change opens the doors of museums as places where lives are enriched (Hein, 1998).

The art museum is a powerful tool for art therapists, as it can serve to reinforce the strength of art in therapy (Salom, 2011). Traditionally, art museums have been places where individuals have gone throughout history to find solace and self-improvement. Art therapy has an innate connection to the use of such spaces to foster creativity and increase an individual's well-being. While exploring such connections is still in its early stages, there are many possibilities yet to be discovered.

References

Alter Muri, S. (1996). Dali to Beuys: Incorporating art history into art therapy treatment plans. *Art Therapy*, 13(2), 102–107.

Betts, D. J., & Potash, J. (2012, July). *An art therapy study of visitor reactions to the United States Holocaust Memorial Museum experience.* Paper presented at the meeting of the American Art Therapy Association, Savannah, GA.

Betts, D. J., Potash, J. S., Luke, J. J. & Kelso, M. (2015). An art therapy study of visitor reactions to the United States Holocaust Memorial Museum DOI:10.1080/09647775.2 015.1008388 . *Museum Management and Curatorship*, 30(1), 21–43.

Eisner, E. W., & Dobbs, S. M. (1988). Silent pedagogy: How museums help visitors experience exhibitions. *Art Education*, 41(4), 6–15.

Hein, G. E. (1998). *Learning in the museum.* London: Routledge.

Linesch, D. (2004). Art therapy at the museum of tolerance: Responses to the life and work of Friedl Dicker-Brandeis. *The Arts in Psychotherapy*, 31(2), 57–66. doi:10.1016/j.aip.2004.02.004

Mayer, M. M. (1998). Can philosophical change take hold in the American art museum? *Art Education*, 51(2), 15–19.

Poulter, E. (2010). Engaging objects: The talking objects programme at the British Museum. *The International Journal of the Arts in Society*, 4(5), 341–349.

Silverman, L. H. (1989). Johnny showed us butterflies: The museum as a family therapy tool. *Marriage & Family Review*, 13(3–4), 131–150.

Silverman, L. H. (2010). *The social work of museums.* London: Routledge.

Salom, A. (2008). The therapeutic potentials of a museum visit. *International Journal of Transpersonal Studies*, 27, 98–103.

Salom, A. (2011). Reinventing the setting: Art therapy in museums. *The Arts in Psychotherapy*, 38(2), 81–85. doi:10.1016/j.aip.2010.12.004

Stiles, G. J., & Mermer-Welly, M. J. (1998). Children having children: Art therapy in a community-based early adolescent pregnancy program. *Art Therapy: Journal of the American Art Therapy Association*, 15(3), 165–176.

Treadon, C. B., Rosal, M. L., & Wylder, V. D. T. (2006). Opening doors of art museums for therapeutic processes. *Arts in Psychotherapy*, 33(4), 288–301. doi:10.1016/j.aip.2006.03.003

Williams, R. (1994). Honoring the museum visitors' personal associations and emotional responses to art: work towards a model for educators. Unpublished paper presented to the faculty at Harvard University. Cambridge, Massachusetts.

Winn, P. (2001). The National Gallery of Australia, Art Therapy and Health Country Communities. 6th National Rural Health Conference, Canberra, Australian Capital Territory, 4–7 March 2001.

Part VI

Art Therapy Assessments

Introduction

Emerging from psychologically developed projective assessments, art-based assessments have become a fundamental aspect of art therapy practice. While some argue that standardized art-based assessments yield rich and valuable data using simple art materials that are easy to use, are quickly administered, belie illiteracy, and are able to withstand deliberate manipulation by clients, other art therapists find them ineffective, invalid, unreliable, and countertherapeutic. Regardless of the argument, many can agree that a single drawing holds a great deal of information about the artist; this is the core of art-based assessments. It is this notion upon which projective and art-based assessment development began.

While there are numerous art-based assessments that have developed over the years, the instruments identified in the 10 chapters in this section were selected to report on the most-practiced assessment tools developed thus far by art therapists. The introductory chapter by Betts, *Art Therapy Assessments: An Overview*, provides a comprehensive history as well as a summary of these tools. Next is Kaiser's *Assessing Attachment with the Bird's Nest Drawing*. This chapter introduces the theory and application of a one-drawing directive used to ascertain psychological attachment issues. The chapter by Asawa and Haber, *Family Art Assessment*, offers an overview of the history and use of art-based assessments employed in family art therapy. In Chapter 51, Levick and Siegel outline the development and application of the school-based art therapy assessment, *The Levick Emotional and Cognitive Art Therapy Assessment (LECATA)*.

In Chapter 52, Earwood and Fedorko reintroduce *The Silver Drawing Test* and *The Draw a Story*, two tools developed by Rawley Silver to assess cognitive, developmental, and emotional functioning in school age children through various drawing procedures. *The Diagnostic Drawing Series at Thirty: Art Therapy Assessment and Research* by Cohen and Mills presents the use of one of the most researched and oldest art-based assessment tools. The authors review numerous studies that support the integrity of this assessment. Gantt's chapter on *The Formal Elements Art Therapy Scale* provides a detailed account of this assessment tool and its uses. Gantt's assessment

The Wiley Handbook of Art Therapy, First Edition. Edited by David E. Gussak and Marcia L. Rosal.
© 2016 John Wiley & Sons, Ltd. Published 2016 by John Wiley & Sons, Ltd.

scale uses the formal elements found in artistic works and assesses these quantifiable elements to provide a clear diagnostic conclusion. It is considered by some to be one of the more reliable and valid art-based instruments available today.

Computers are becoming increasingly important in psychological assessment. Art therapists are also using technology to aid in assessing drawings. The chapter by Mattson and Betts on *The Face Stimulus Assessment (FSA)* introduces a unique tool that was designed to understand the developmental, cognitive, and creative potential of children and adults with communication difficulties. This assessment drawing can be evaluated by an art therapist or with computer assistance. In the chapter titled *Assessments and Computer Technology*, Kim maintains that computers provide an easy and quick way to gather data from drawings. He posits that computer assessment can be more reliable and effective than when done by people, who may be prone to human error and bias.

To conclude this section, we asked Deaver to present her proposal for a more robust and careful examination of art-based assessments through large normative samples. In her chapter, *The Need for Norms in Formal Art Therapy Assessment*, she reports her initial findings. Her call for larger studies is of utmost importance for the continued development of valid and reliable assessment art therapy instruments.

Although not exhaustive, this section emphasizes the research that has been done and is continuing to be done to develop robust, valid, and reliable art-based assessments. Gaining an understanding of the effectiveness and applicability of these tools enhances art therapy practice and assists the practitioner in using art-based assessments for treatment planning and for gauging a client's progress in therapy.

48

Art Therapy Assessments: An Overview

Donna Betts

Introduction

The manner in which art therapy is practiced depends upon the clinician's theoretical orientation and the institution's specifications, and this certainly applies to the use of assessments. In this book, art as therapy is conceived as a profession that concentrates on the process of art making and psychotherapy, focusing on the finished created product and relying on the triangulated relationship between the therapist, the client, and the artwork. These premises are reflected in the art therapy assessment literature, as is described in the present chapter. In an effort to provide breadth and depth of information on art therapy assessments, this handbook includes a compendium of information and research on Rawley Silver's Assessments (SDT; DAS; Silver, 1983, 1988), the Levick Emotional and Cognitive Art Therapy Assessment (LECATA; Levick, 2001), the Face Stimulus Assessment (FSA; Betts, 2003), the Bird's Nest Drawing (BND; Kaiser, 1993), the Diagnostic Drawing Series (DDS; Cohen, Hammer, & Singer, 1988), the Formal Elements Art Therapy Scale: The Rating Manual (FEATS; Gantt & Tabone, 1998), assessments and computer technology, normative data on development in drawings, and family assessments. These instruments are preceded in time by the pioneering researchers who planted the seeds from which the roots of art therapy assessment sprang forth.

Historical Overview

Understanding the history of projective drawing tests is conducive to appreciating the development of art therapy assessments (Gantt, 1992). Furthermore, knowing the history can help us continually improve art therapy assessments and rating scales for clinical and research purposes. Anthropologists, educators, psychologists, and psychiatrists have used artwork in therapy, evaluation, and research for over a century (see Betts, 2006). From 1885 to 1920, educators collected and classified children's art (D. Harris, 1963). In 1887, Corrado Ricci, an art critic with interests in psychology, published the first known book of

The Wiley Handbook of Art Therapy, First Edition. Edited by David E. Gussak and Marcia L. Rosal.
© 2016 John Wiley & Sons, Ltd. Published 2016 by John Wiley & Sons, Ltd.

children's art, in which drawings were presented as potential psychodiagnostic tools (J. Harris, 1996). In 1931, Eng published an extensive bibliography of the literature on children's art. This review covered English, German, French, and Norwegian publications from 1892 to 1930, citing early developmental and descriptive studies.

Prior to 1900, a number of scientific articles describing the spontaneous artwork of mental patients were published in the United States and Europe (Hrdlicka, 1899; Lombroso, 1888; Simon, 1888; Tardieu, 1886). These papers were mostly impressionistic. Several studies related to the psychodiagnostic potential of art followed (Klepsch & Logie, 1982), including Fritz Mohr's (1906) work in establishing standardized procedures and methods using drawing tests with psychiatric patients (Gantt, 1992). Mohr (1906) reviewed the nineteenth-century literature and dismissed the earlier contributions as "merely descriptive" (MacGregor, 1989, p. 189). The structural elements of an artwork were of particular concern to Mohr, because, in his experience, they revealed information about the artist's mental processes. He found that, the more fragmentary the picture, the more fragmentary was the thought process. Mohr's work influenced the development of psychological projective instruments such as the House-Tree-Person (HTP) test (Buck, 1948), and the Thematic Apperception Test (TAT; Murray, 1943), as well as some procedures used by art therapists.

Hermann Rorschach published his inkblot projective test in 1921, and it is widely used even today (Walsh & Betz, 2001). In 1926, another popular tool was developed: the Goodenough Draw-A-Man technique. Draw-A-Man was the first systematized arts-based assessment method for estimating intelligence. Currently known as the Goodenough-Harris Draw-A-Man Test (D. Harris & Roberts, 1972), this instrument is the earliest example of a class of open-ended drawing tasks known as human figure drawings (HFDs). Other work also led to the use of drawings in nonverbal intelligence tests, including Lowenfeld's (1947) research demonstrating that children pass through a sequence of orderly developmental stages in their drawings (Gantt, 1992).

Roback (1968) examined 18 years (1949–1967) of findings on the Draw-A-Person (DAP) test. Overall, the studies cited failed to support Machover's (1949) hypothesis, that drawing a person is a natural vehicle for the expression of one's body needs and conflicts, and that the figure drawn is related to the individual artist. It was concluded that there is a great need for validated and standardized scales for the use of figure drawings in estimating personality adjustment.

In contrast to Roback (1968), Swensen (1968) found support for the use of HFDs in assessment. Swensen reviewed HFD studies published since 1957 and found that the quality of the research had improved considerably. The evidence suggested that the reliability of a specific aspect of a drawing is directly related to its validity: global ratings were found to be more valid and reliable than individual signs. It was also found that the presence of certain signs was related to the overall quality of the drawings, and, as such, it was suggested that future research should control for the quality of the drawings. Similarly, Suinn and Oskamp (1969) identified the potential of artistic skill as a likely moderating influence on drawing outcomes. In their 15-year review of the personality test literature, they found only a paucity of evidence relating to the validity of tests such as the DAP and the HTP.

Klopfer and Taulbee (1976) reviewed more than 500 journal articles pertaining to projective techniques from 1971 to 1974, and determined that "if projective techniques are dead, some people don't seem to have gotten the message" (p. 543). They explored problems of validation, especially relating to the three most widely used projective tests, the TAT, the Rorschach, and HFDs. They accurately concluded that psychologists would continue to develop, use, and rely upon projective instruments as long as they maintain an interest in the inner person and on probing the depths of the psyche. Contrary to Klopfer and Taulbee's prediction, the Rorschach has not become "a blot on the history of clinical psychology" (p. 543)—quite the contrary, it has been revitalized and regained popularity.

A few other studies conducted in the 1970s and 1980s reveal mixed results. Russell-Lacy, Robinson, Benson, and Cranage (1979) studied the validity of assessing art productions made by 30 subjects with acute schizophrenia as a differential diagnosis technique. They concluded that the use of art in differential psychiatric diagnosis is questionable. In 1984, Dawson investigated differences between the drawings of depressed and nondepressed adults. A discriminant function analysis of the variables did not discriminate between the drawings of the depressed and nondepressed subjects above a chance level. It was suggested that future research should include the exploration of other measures of depression as criteria for identifying the groups used to analyze drawing variables, and the investigation of the structural variables—*Empty Space, Size, Color, Extra Details*, and *Missing Details*—in the drawings of other clinical groups.

Kahill (1984) examined the quantitative literature published between 1967 and 1982 on the validity and reliability of HFDs used as projectives with adults. Focusing on the assertions of Machover (1949) and E. Hammer (1958), Kahill discussed reliability estimates and evidence pertaining to the body–image hypothesis. Validity of structural and formal drawing variables (e.g., size, placement, perspective, and omission) and the content of figure drawings (e.g., face, mouth and teeth, anatomy indicators, and gender of first-drawn figures) were addressed, and the performance of global measures and the influence of confounding factors were described. It was concluded that establishing the meaning of figure drawings with any predictability or precision is difficult due to the inadequacies of the research.

So, during the 1970s and 1980s, the use of projective tools declined due to decreased belief in psychoanalytic theory, greater emphasis on situational determinants of behavior, questions regarding the cost-effectiveness of these tools, and poor reviews about their validity (Betts, 2006; Groth-Marnat, 1990). The scientific value of projective tests has been widely questioned for decades, resulting in Groth-Marnat's (2003) exclusion of the chapter on projective drawing tests from his *Handbook of Psychological Assessment*. Nonetheless, clinicians continue to find merit in the ability of these tools to augment the assessment process. The existence of these instruments paved the way for the development of assessments in the field of art therapy. In the 1950s, art therapists began exploring a need for standardized methods that could provide clients with an enriched assessment experience.

General Overview

Foundational art therapy assessments

Some of earliest art therapy instruments that influenced the development of subsequent art therapy tools include the Ulman Personality Assessment Procedure (UPAP; Ulman, 1965), the Family Art Evaluation (Kwiatkowska, 1978), and Rawley Silver's tests

(1983, 1988). The UPAP was the first standardized drawing series (Ulman, 1965). Using gray bogus paper and a set of 12 hard chalk pastels, the patient is asked to complete four consecutive drawings in one session, each with a specific directive. Ulman's success in using art to derive diagnostic information was attributed to her "exquisite sensitivity and broad experience" (Kwiatkowska, 1978, p. 86). Hanna Yaxa Kwiatkowska (1978) developed a structured evaluation procedure for use with families at the National Institute of Mental Health (see Asawa and Haber in the chapter on Family Assessments). Rawley Silver developed the Silver Drawing Test of Cognition and Emotion (SDT; 1983) and the Draw-A-Story (DAS; 1988) interview technique. The SDT includes three tasks: predictive drawing, drawing from imagination, and drawing from observation. The DAS is a semi-structured interview technique using stimulus drawings to elicit response drawings. As is further described by Earwood and Fedorko in Chapter 52, Silver's work represents a valuable contribution to the field.

Art therapy assessments today

Many formal assessments have since been developed. A recent survey of professional members of the American Art Therapy Association indicated that 85% of respondents assess their clients, although only 397 art therapists participated, yielding a response rate of 11.7% (Petersen, 2012). Nonetheless, some of the data derived from this study warrant consideration. Of those who responded, 37.9% reported using an informal assessment method; 33.6%, a modified version of a formal assessment; 14.6%, a formal assessment; and 13.9%, a self-designed method. A list of eight common art therapy assessments was provided, and participants were asked to indicate which tools they use most often. Of the respondents, 74% indicated that they used a formal assessment "other" than those listed. The next two top rankings were attributed to the PPAT (29%) and the DDS (26%). For the "other" category, respondents were asked to indicate which other tools they used, and the two most commonly included were the HTP test (28.2%), and the Kinetic Family Drawings (16%). These data provide information about the commonly used tools in the field.

Domains of art therapy assessment

The profession has lacked clarity on what tools should be used and when. Assessments should be selected for specific reasons, and there is no single assessment that is best for all clients in all settings (see Betts, 2013a). The most important factor to determine the appropriateness of test choice should be based on an instrument's ability to address the referral question (Groth-Marnat, 2009). Thus, to aid in appropriate assessment selection, and to help make sense of the range of tools available, Betts (2013a) organized and described the domains of art therapy assessments in a table, which has been updated and presented here (see Table 48.1). Betts consulted different sources to develop this classification system: Feder and Feder (1998), Groth-Marnat (2009), and the Buros Institute of Mental Measurements (Buros, n. d.). The resulting domains are organized as follows: (1) clinical interview; (2) assessment of relationship dynamics; (3) cognitive/neuropsychological and developmental evaluation; and (4) tools that address various realms of treatment (Table 48.1). These four categories reflect a shift

Table 48.1 Art therapy assessment domains (not an exhaustive list, and subject to change).

Art Therapy Assessment Instruments	Corresponding Rating System
(1) Clinical Interview	
Art Therapy-Projective Imagery Assessment (AT-PIA; Raymond et al., 1998/2010)	No scoring manual: interpretations are made both impressionistically and through matching and research-based methods.
Diagnostic Drawing Series (DDS; Cohen et al., 1988)	Drawing Analysis Form; Content Checklist (Cohen, 1985, 1994, 2012)
Ulman Personality Assessment Procedure (UPAP; Ulman, 1965)	A checklist
(2) Assessment of Relationship Dynamics	
Art Therapy Evaluation for Couples (Wadeson, 1980)	
Bird's Nest Drawing (BND; Kaiser, 1993)	Manual for Kaiser's Bird's Nest Drawing checklist (Kaiser, 2009)
Kinetic Family Drawings (Holt & Kaiser, 2001)	FADS training manual
Kwiatkowska System (Kwiatkowska, 1978)	Scoring system
Landgarten's Family Art Psychotherapy Assessment (Landgarten, 1987)	17 observational points; interactional information
(3) Cognitive/Neuropsychological and Developmental Evaluation	
Brief Art Therapy Screening Evaluation (BATSE; Gerber, 1996)	
Cognitive Art Therapy Assessment (CATA; Horovitz-Darby, 1988)	Observational guidelines
Expressive Therapies Continuum (ETC; Kagin & Lusebrink, 1978; Lusebrink, 2010)	
Face Stimulus Assessment (FSA; Betts, 2003)	FSA Rating Manual, 1st ed. (Betts, 2013b)
House-Tree-Person (HTP; Buck, 1948; Lopez & Carolan, 2001)	51 formal element indicators (Lopez & Carolan, 2001)
Human Figure Drawing (HFD; Deaver, 2009; Golomb, 1974; D. Harris, 1963; Koppitz, 1968; Naglieri, 1988)	Five modified FEATS scales (Deaver, 2009)
Kramer Art Therapy Evaluation (Kramer & Schehr, 1983)	Observational considerations
Levick Emotional and Cognitive Art Therapy Assessment (LECATA; Levick, 2001)	Scoring manual
Person Picking an Apple from a Tree (PPAT; Gantt, 1990)	Formal Elements Art Therapy Scale (FEATS; Gantt & Tabone, 1998)
Silver Drawing Test (SDT; Silver, 1983)	Scoring manual
(4) Tools that Address Various Realms of Treatment	
Arrington Visual Preference Test (AVPT; Arrington, 1986)	Interpretation manual
Art Therapy Dream Assessment (ADTA; Horovitz, 1999)	

(continued)

Table 48.1 *(continued)*

Art Therapy Assessment Instruments	Corresponding Rating System
Belief Art Therapy Assessment (BATA; Horovitz, 2002)	
Bridge Drawing (Hays & Lyons, 1981)	*The Bridge Drawing Rating Manual 2nd ed.* (Martin & Betts, 2012)
Favorite Kind of Day (Manning Rauch, 1987)	Aggression depicted in the AFKD Rating Instrument (three-item checklist)
Mandala drawing technique (Elkis-Abuhoff, Gaydos, Goldblatt, Chen, & Rose, 2009)	Formal elements (color checklist, etc.)
Mandala Assessment Research Instrument (MARI) Card Test (Kellogg, 2002)	Interpretation manual
Pictured Feelings Instrument: A nonverbal vocabulary of feelings (Stone, 2004)	Rating manual
Road Drawings (Hanes, 1995)	

http://donnabettsphd.wordpress.com/assessment/©Donna Betts.

in the purpose and applications of art therapy assessments in the past couple of decades, and are in keeping with Groth-Marnat's (2009) observation that the number of traditional approaches to assessment have declined due to an expansion in the definition of assessment.

Domain (1): Clinical Interview

A broader approach to assessment goes beyond the test, and includes a well-rounded assessment of a client, which is likened to a clinical interview process. Assessments categorized in Domain (1) are considered to be clinical interviews because they require obtaining information about a client from multiple sources. Such sources include: collection of more than one artwork as part of the standardized process (i.e., a series of images), behavioral observations of the assessment session, the client's verbal associations to the artwork, and derivation of quantitative scores of formal elements of the artwork, to name a few key components (Betts, 2012). The Ulman Personality Assessment Procedure (UPAP; Ulman, 1965) is included in Domain (1) as a four-drawing interview-format series. The Diagnostic Drawing Series (DDS; Cohen et al., 1988) is conducted in an interview format and consists of three drawings, as described by Barry Cohen in Chapter 53.

The Art Therapy-Projective Imagery Assessment (AT-PIA; Raymond et al., 1998/2010) is also included in Domain (1). The AT-PIA is one of the best examples of an integrative approach to assessment in art therapy. It is a systematic clinical interview based on the use of interview procedures, drawing tasks, and administrators' observations. Ron Hays, a former student of Myra Levick's at Hahnemann/Drexel, is responsible for the inception of the AT-PIA (Raymond et al., 1998/2010). In 1973, Hays and his colleagues developed the EVMS Art Therapy Assessment. Since that time, variations of the AT-PIA have been used by the faculty, students, and alumni of the EVMS Graduate Art Therapy and Counseling Program. In 1990, the EVMS Assessment was named the "Psycho-Imagery Assessment," and its administration guidelines were established by Matthew Bernier, Jim Consoli, and Trudy Manning. In 1998, the name was changed to "Art Therapy-Projective Imagery Assessment" (AT-PIA) in order to promote its acceptance in a variety of settings. An extensive literature review supported selection of the six consecutive drawing tasks that comprise the standardized tool. The AT-PIA of today consists of (1) Projective Scribble; (2) Favorite Weather Drawing; (3) Human Figure Drawing; (4) Kinetic Family Drawing; (5) Reason for Being Here Drawing; and (6) Free Choice. The AT-PIA is compatible with psychiatric evaluations and psychological tests (see Deaver & Bernier, 2014). The assessment is intended for use by art therapists in mental health settings with children, adolescents, and adults to identify developmental level, diagnoses, problem areas, strengths, defenses, and potential for engaging productively in a therapeutic relationship. Assessments such as the AT-PIA that foster the client–therapist relationship are advantageous, since the success of an intervention is largely dependent upon the quality of this relationship (Martin, Garske, & Davis, 2000). One way this relationship is enhanced through the AT-PIA includes how the artwork, verbal associations, and behavior are interpreted impressionistically (Lally, 2001; Scribner & Handler, 1987), and through matching and research-based approaches (Gantt, 2001, 2004; Groth-Marnat, 1999).

The clinical interview format of the Domain (1) assessments results in a more accurate, nuanced, and comprehensive evaluation of the client (Betts & Groth-Marnat, 2014). These procedures take time to administer, which is possible in some treatment settings. However, in other settings, when time does not permit such thorough approaches to assessment, or when a more specific need for an assessment is called for, alternatives are available.

Domain (2): Assessment of Relationship Dynamics

Tools for examining couples, family, and group dynamics are included in this domain. The Bird's Nest Drawing (BND; Kaiser, 1993) is included here, as its primary purpose is to assess attachment, a function of interpersonal relationships. Donna Kaiser elucidates the BND in Chapter 49. Family assessments include Kinetic Family Drawings (Holt & Kaiser, 2001), the Kwiatkowska System (Kwiatkowska, 1978), Landgarten's Family Art Psychotherapy Assessment (Landgarten, 1987), and the Art Therapy Evaluation for Couples (Wadeson, 1980). As is presented by Asawa and Haber in Chapter 50, some of these assessments incorporate a series of drawings and follow a clinical interview format.

Domain (3) Cognitive/neuropsychological and developmental evaluation

Instruments included in this domain are: the Brief Art Therapy Screening Evaluation (BATSE; Gerber, 1996); the Cognitive Art Therapy Assessment (CATA; Horovitz-Darby, 1988); the Face Stimulus Assessment (FSA; Betts, 2003; Mattson and Betts, Chapter 55); Human Figure Drawings (HFD; Deaver, 2009; Deaver, Chapter 57); the Levick Emotional and Cognitive Art Therapy Assessment (LECATA; Levick, 2001; Levick and Siegel, Chapter 51); the Kramer Art Therapy Evaluation (Kramer & Schehr, 1983); the House-Tree-Person (HTP; Buck, 1948); the Person Picking an Apple from a Tree (PPAT; Gantt, 1990; Gantt, Chapter 54); and the Silver Drawing Test (SDT; Silver, 1983; Earwood and Fedorko, Chapter 52).

Assessments included in this domain may have multiple applications, and are conducive to identifying cognitive/neuropsychological and developmental indicators. The LECATA (Levick, 2001) and the Kramer (Kramer & Schehr, 1983) both employ series of drawing tasks, and are also clinical interviews. They are included in Domain (3) because of their focus on development. Procedures designed to measure cognitive skills or intelligence tend to overlap with those that measure developmental levels, as a developmental evaluation generally produces a global judgment about clients' emotional, cognitive, and/or physical abilities.

As a theoretical model for art therapy assessments and media use, the Expressive Therapies Continuum (ETC; Kagin & Lusebrink, 1978) focuses on clients' strengths and challenges with information processing on each of the ETC levels, as opposed to symptoms of psychopathology (Lusebrink, 2010). The ETC's value in examining media use and how media stimulate brain structures and functions supports its inclusion in Domain (3). Hinz (2009) encouraged the use of the ETC model to guide materials and directives to address issues and treatment goals in therapy.

Domain (4): Tools that Address Various Realms of Treatment

Assessments and techniques included in this domain can be used for treatment planning, to address the presenting problem, goals of therapy, and other aspects of the clinical process. Several are listed in Table 48.1. Both formal and informal (non-standardized) tools, including portfolio review, can be considered part of this domain.

Artwork scoring and interpretation Table 48.1 also includes information about rating systems that correspond to the various assessments. These systems range from qualitative, observational, and interpretive methods of evaluation, to quantitative rating of formal elements. Characteristics of artwork that can distinguish between patient groups and/or normal controls have been identified by researchers with varying results, all of which were influential in the development of the FEATS manual (Gantt & Tabone, 1998) and its application of global characteristics. Art therapists have used the FEATS in a variety of contexts to assess a range of client populations, with some success in differentiating between groups. Gantt discusses this further in Chapter 54. Scoring specific formal element scales using a computer has shown promise, as discussed by Seong-in Kim in Chapter 56.

Two texts describe comprehensive evaluation methods for clinical use. The primer, *A Clinical Guide to Writing Assessments, Diagnosis, and Treatment*, is a practical guide for writing clinical reports based on results of art therapy assessments conducted with a client, and integrating these with treatment goals, summaries, and termination reports (Horovitz & Eksten, 2009). This evaluation process results in a thorough review of a patient's presenting problem, and increases the treatment plan's accuracy. Vass (2012) approaches art-based assessment from a holistic systems approach with his Seven-Step Configuration Analysis (SCCA) method. Vass' text provides a comprehensive overview of the psychological aspects of artwork, which includes references to some art therapy assessments, and has interesting implications for their use.

Art Therapy Assessment in the Years to Come

Recommendations for improvements to psychological assessment research point the way for improvements to art therapy methods. Many psychologists today consider their drawing-based assessments (e.g., the HTP, HFDs) as part of a battery of tests that one would use to evaluate a client, in a triangulation approach. This is in keeping with the concept of the integrative approach to assessment, part of the clinical interview format. To improve assessment research and accuracy in approaches, more studies combining drawing variables with other information about the client (Riethmiller & Handler, 1997) have been encouraged. Furthermore, "the most crucial task in demonstrating the validity of projective drawing approaches is to place drawing variables within idiographic contexts" (Riethmiller & Handler, 1997, p. 471). In other words, to be beneficial, assessments need to be relevant to the individual.

Many art therapy researchers work on a rather small scale, without the benefit of funding from large grants. Over 25 years ago, Gantt (1986) identified the need for "a file of pictures done by members of particular social, national, or diagnostic groups, with comments from the artists and the art therapist and pertinent demographic and diagnostic data" (p. 114). Gantt wanted to take advantage of the growing capacities of the Internet to amass data that a single researcher could not. So, Betts and Lorance launched the International Art Therapy Research Database (IATRD; www.arttherapyresearch.com). Databases such as the IATRD are promising resources for facilitating larger-scale assessment research than previously possible, and will help keep art therapy relevant in the future.

References

Arrington, D. (1986). *The Arrington Visual Preference Test (AVPT) and Manual.* Belmont, CA: Abbeygate Press.

Betts, D. J. (2003). Developing a projective drawing test: Experiences with the Face Stimulus Assessment (FSA). *Art Therapy: Journal of the American Art Therapy Association, 20*(2), 77–82.

Betts, D. J. (2006). Art therapy assessments and rating instruments: Do they measure up? *The Arts in Psychotherapy: An International Journal, 33*(5), 371–472.

Betts, D. J. (2012). Positive art therapy assessment: Looking towards positive psychology for new directions in the art therapy evaluation process. In A. Gilroy, R. Tipple, & C. Brown (Eds.), *Assessment in art therapy* (pp. 203–218). New York, NY: Routledge.

Betts, D. J. (2013a). Art therapy assessment and evaluation. In R. Flaum Cruz & B. Feder (Eds.), *Feders' the art and science of evaluation in the arts therapies: How do you know what's working?* (2nd ed., pp. 266–306). Springfield, IL: Charles C. Thomas.

Betts, D. J. (2013b). *The Face Stimulus Assessment (FSA) Rating Manual* (2nd ed.). Department of Art Therapy, George Washington University, Washington, DC.

Betts, D. J., & Groth-Marnat, G. (2014). The intersection of art therapy and psychological assessment: Unified approaches to the use of drawings and artistic processes. In L. Handler & A. Thomas (Eds.), *Figure drawings in assessment and psychotherapy: Research and application* (pp. 268–285). New York, NY: Routledge.

Buck, J. N. (1948). The H-T-P technique, a qualitative and quantitative scoring manual. *Journal of Clinical Psychology Monograph Supplement, 4,* 1–120.

Buros. (n.d.). *The Buros Institute of Mental Measurements: About* http://buros.unl.edu/buros/jsp/search.jsp

Cohen, B. M. (1985/1994/2012). *The Diagnostic Drawing Series Rating Guide.* Self-published manual, Alexandria, VA.

Cohen, B. M., Hammer, J. S., & Singer, S. (1988). The diagnostic drawing series: A systematic approach to art therapy evaluation and research. *Arts in Psychotherapy: Special Research in the creative arts therapies, 15*(1), 11–21.

Dawson, C. F. S. (1984). *A study of selected style and content variables in the drawings of depressed and nondepressed adults.* Unpublished dissertation, University of North Dakota, Grand Forks, ND.

Deaver, S. P. (2009). A normative study of children's drawings: Preliminary research findings. *Art Therapy: Journal of the American Art Therapy Association, 26*(1), 4–11.

Deaver, S. P., & Bernier, M. (2014). The Art Therapy-Projective Imagery Assessment (AT-PIA). In L. Handler & A. Thomas (Eds.), *Figure drawings in assessment and psychotherapy: Research and application* (pp. 131–147). New York, NY: Routledge.

Elkis-Abuhoff, D., Gaydos, M., Goldblatt, R., Chen, M., & Rose, S. (2009). Mandala drawings as an assessment tool for women with breast cancer. *The Arts in Psychotherapy: An International Journal, 36,* 231–238.

Eng, H. (1931). *The psychology of children's drawings: From the first stroke to the color drawing.* London: Kegan Paul, Trench, Trubner & Co.

Feder, B., & Feder, E. (1998). *The art and science of evaluation in the arts therapies: How do you know what's working?* Springfield, IL: Charles C. Thomas.

Gantt, L. (1986). Systematic investigation of art works: Some research models drawn from neighboring fields. *American Journal of Art Therapy, 24*(4), 111–118.

Gantt, L. (1990). *A validity study of the Formal Elements Art Therapy Scale (FEATS) for diagnostic information in patients' drawings.* Unpublished doctoral dissertation, University of Pittsburgh, Pittsburgh, PA.

Gantt, L. (1992). A description and history of art therapy assessment research. In H. Wadeson (Ed.), *A guide to conducting art therapy research* (pp. 119–139). Mundelein, IL: The American Art Therapy Association.

Gantt, L. M. (2001). The Formal Elements Art Therapy Scale: A measurement system for global variables in art. *Art Therapy: Journal of the American Art Therapy Association, 18*(1), 50–55.

Gantt, L. (2004). The case for formal art therapy assessments. *Art Therapy: Journal of the American Art Therapy Association, 21*(1), 18–29.

Gantt, L., & Tabone, C. (1998). *The formal elements art therapy scale: The rating manual.* Morgantown, WV: Gargoyle Press.

Gerber, N. (1996). The Brief Art Therapy Screening Evaluation (BATSE). Unpublished manual, PhD Program in Creative Arts Therapies, Drexel University, Philadelphia, PA.

Goodenough, F. (1926). *Measurement of intelligence by drawings.* New York, NY: World Book Co.

Groth-Marnat, G. (1990). *Handbook of psychological assessment* (2nd ed.). New York, NY: John Wiley & Sons, Inc.

Groth-Marnat, G. (1999). *Handbook of psychological assessment* (3rd ed.). New York, NY: John Wiley & Sons, Inc.

Groth-Marnat, G. (2003). *Handbook of psychological assessment* (4th ed.). New York, NY: John Wiley & Sons, Inc.

Groth-Marnat, G. (2009). *Handbook of psychological assessment* (5th ed.). New York, NY: John Wiley & Sons, Inc.

Hammer, E. F. (1958). *The clinical application of projective drawings.* Springfield, IL: Charles C. Thomas.

Hanes, M. J. (1995). Utilizing road drawings as a therapeutic metaphor in art therapy. *American Journal of Art Therapy, 34*(1), 19–23.

Harris, D. B. (1963). *Children's drawings as measures of intellectual maturity*. New York, NY: Harcourt, Brace, & World.

Harris, J. B. (1996). *Children's drawings as psychological assessment tools*. Retrieved April 19, 2003, from http://www.iste.org/jrte/28/5/harris/article/introduction.cfm.

Harris, D. B., & Roberts, J. (1972). Intellectual maturity of children: Demographic and socioeconomic factors. *Vital & Health Statistics, Series 2*, 1–74.

Hays, R. E., & Lyons, S. J. (1981). The Bridge Drawing: A projective technique for assessment in art therapy. *Arts in Psychotherapy, 8*(3-sup-4), 207–217.

Hinz, L. D. (2009). *The expressive therapies continuum: A framework for using art in therapy*. New York, NY: Routledge.

Holt, E. S., & Kaiser, D. H. (2001). Indicators of familial alcoholism in children's Kinetic Family Drawings. *Art Therapy: Journal of the American Art Therapy Association, 18*(2), 89–95.

Horovitz, E. G. (1999). *A Leap of faith: The call to art*. Springfield, IL: Charles C. Thomas.

Horovitz, E. G. (2002). *Spiritual art therapy: An alternate path* (2nd ed.). Springfield, IL: Charles C. Thomas.

Horovitz, E. G., & Eksten, S. (Eds.) (2009). *The art therapists' primer: A clinical guide to writing assessments, diagnosis, and treatment*. Springfield, IL: Charles C. Thomas.

Horovitz-Darby, E. G. (1988). Art therapy assessment of a minimally language skilled deaf child. Proceedings from the 1988 University of California's Center on Deafness Conference: *Mental Health Assessment of Deaf Clients: Special Conditions*, Little Rock, AK: ADARA.

Hrdlicka, A. (1899). Art and literature in the mentally abnormal. *American Journal of Insanity, 55*, 385–404.

Kagin, S. L., & Lusebrink, V. B. (1978). The expressive therapies continuum. *The Arts in Psychotherapy: An International Journal, 5*, 171–180.

Kahill, S. (1984). Human figure drawing in adults: An update of the empirical evidence, 1967–1982. *Canadian Psychology, 25*(4), 269–292.

Kaiser, D. (1993). *Attachment organization as manifested in a drawing task*. Unpublished master's thesis, Eastern Virginia Medical School, Norfolk, VA.

Kaiser, D. H. (2009). *Manual for Kaiser's Bird's Nest Drawing Checklist*. Self-published manual, Creative Arts Therapies Department, Drexel University, Philadelphia, PA.

Kellogg, J. (2002). *Mandala: Path of beauty* (3rd ed.). Belleair, FL: ATMA, Inc.

Klepsch, M., & Logie, L. (1982). *Children draw and tell: An introduction to the projective uses of children's human figure drawings*. New York, NY: Brunner/Mazel.

Klopfer, W. G., & Taulbee, E. S. (1976). Projective tests. *Annual Review of Psychology, 27*(54), 3–567.

Kramer, E., & Schehr, J. (1983). An art therapy evaluation session for children. *American Journal of Art Therapy, 23*, 3–11.

Kwiatkowska, H. Y. (1978). *Family therapy and evaluation through art*. Springfield, IL: Charles C. Thomas.

Lally, S. (2001). Should human figure drawings be admitted to court? *Journal of Personality Assessment, 76*(1), 135–149.

Landgarten, H. B. (1987). *Family art psychotherapy: A clinical guide and casebook*. New York, NY: Brunner/Mazel, Inc.

Levick, M. F. (2001). *The Levick Emotional and Cognitive Art Therapy Assessment. (LECATA)*. Boca Raton, FL: The South Florida Art Psychotherapy Institute.

Lombroso, C. (1888). *The man of genius*. London: Walter Scott.

Lopez, J. R., & Carolan, R. (2001). House-Tree-Person drawings and sex offenders: A pilot study. *Art Therapy: Journal of the American Art Therapy Association, 18*(3), 158–165.

Lowenfeld, V. (1947). *Creative and mental growth*. New York, NY: Macmillan.

Lusebrink, V. B. (2010). Assessment and therapeutic application of the Expressive Therapies Continuum: Implications for brain structures and functions. *Art Therapy: Journal of the American Art Therapy Association, 27*(4), 168–177.

MacGregor, J. M. (1989). *The discovery of the art of the insane*. Princeton, NJ: Princeton University Press.

Machover, K. (1949). *Personality projection in the drawing of the human figure*. Oxford, England: Charles C. Thomas.

Manning Rauch, T. (1987). Aggression depicted in abused children's drawings. *The Arts in Psychotherapy: An International Journal, 14*, 15–24.

Martin, K., & Betts, D. (2012). *The Bridge Drawing Rating Manual* (2nd ed.). Department of Art Therapy, George Washington University, Washington, DC.

Martin, D. J., Garske, J. P., & Davis, M. K. (2000). Relation of the therapeutic alliance with outcome and other variables: A meta-analytic review. *Journal of Consulting and Clinical Psychology, 68*(3), 438–450.

Mohr, F. (1906). Über Zeichnungen von Geisteskranker und ihre diagnostische Verwertbarkeit. *Journal für Psychologie und Neurologie, 8*, 99–140.

Murray, H. A. (1943). *Thematic apperception test*. Cambridge, MA: Harvard University Press.

Petersen, K. L. (2012). *American art therapists' use of and opinion regarding art therapy assessments: A survey study*. Unpublished master's thesis, Drexel University, Philadelphia, PA.

Raymond, L., Bernier, M., Rauch, T., Stovall, K., Deaver, S., & Sanderson, T. (1998/2010). *The Art Therapy-Projective Imagery Assessment*. Unpublished manual, Eastern Virginia Medical School, Norfolk, VA.

Riethmiller, R. J., & Handler, L. (1997). Problematic methods and unwarranted conclusions in DAP research: Suggestions for improved research procedures. *Journal of Personality Assessment, 69*(3), 459–475.

Roback, H. B. (1968). Human figure drawings: Their utility in the clinical psychologist's armamentarium for personality assessment. *Psychological Bulletin, 70*(1), 1–19.

Rorschach, H. (1921). *Psychodiagnostics: A diagnostic test based on perception*. Oxford, England: Grune & Stratton.

Russell-Lacy, S., Robinson, V., Benson, J., & Cranage, J. (1979). An experimental study of pictures produced by acute schizophrenic subjects. *British Journal of Psychiatry, 134*, 195–200.

Scribner, C., & Handler, L. (1987). The interpreter's personality in Draw-a-Person interpretation: A study of interpersonal style. *Journal of Personality Assessment, 51*, 112–122.

Silver, R. A. (1983). *Silver drawing test of cognitive and creative skills*. Seattle, WA: Special Child Publications.

Silver, R. A. (1988). *Draw a story, screening for depression and emotional needs*. New York, NY: Ablin Press.

Simon, P. M. (1888). Les écrits et les dessins des aliénés. *Archivio di Antropologia Criminelle, Psichiatria e Medicina Legale, 3*, 318–355.

Stone, B. A. (2004). *Pictured feelings instrument, a nonverbal vocabulary of feelings*. Melbourne, AU: Australian Council for Educational Research (ACER).

Suinn, R. M., & Oskamp, S. (1969). *The predictive validity of projective measures: A fifteen-year evaluative review of research*. Springfield, IL: Charles C. Thomas.

Swensen, C. H. (1968). Empirical evaluations of human figure drawings: 1957–1966. *Psychological Bulletin, 70*(1), 20–44.

Tardieu, A. (1886). *Etudes médico-légales sur la folie*. Paris: JB Baillière.

Ulman, E. (1965). A new use of art in psychiatric diagnosis. *Bulletin of Art Therapy, 4*, 91–116.

Wadeson, H. (1980). *Art psychotherapy*. New York, NY: Wiley.

Vass, Z. (2012). *A psychological interpretation of drawings and paintings: The SCCA Method: A systems analysis approach*. Pécs, Hungary: Pécsi Direkt, Ltd.

Walsh, B., & Betz, N. (2001). *Tests and assessment* (4th ed.). Upper Saddle River, NJ: Prentice Hall.

49

Assessing Attachment with the Bird's Nest Drawing (BND)

Donna H. Kaiser

Since the Bird's Nest Drawing (BND; see Kaiser, 1996) was developed over 20 years ago for assessing attachment security, there has been growing interest in attachment theory in art therapy. I developed the BND because I was interested in an art therapy measure of attachment that would be easy to administer; would access unconscious dimensions of a person's mental models informing feelings and expectations about family and intimate relationships; and would circumvent defenses that tend to arise when a person is asked to complete a family drawing. The BND was also attractive for its potential ability to evoke attachment concerns that could be addressed therapeutically.

Before undertaking research on the BND, I introduced it in clinical work. With a colleague, I used the BND in a family art therapy assessment with a 7-year-old boy whose parents were divorced. They were referred for evaluation because of his disruptive behaviors in school, suggestive of attention-deficit hyperactivity disorder (ADHD)—his therapist wanted an evaluation of the family dynamics to gauge whether this situation might have also been affecting him. Joe (a pseudonym) was living part of the week with his father, who had remarried, and part of the week with his mother and her new partner. Joe was first evaluated with his father and stepmother, and then with his mother and her partner, as there was tension among the family members— the tension could have potentially been exacerbated if everyone was together in the first session. The family members were asked to draw BNDs instead of family drawings. This was also to avoid more anxiety than what already existed about their current situation, and to capture information about the family dynamics and Joe's possible attachment concerns, given the parental conflict. They also completed a joint family drawing together as a group in each individual family session. Joe, his father, and stepmother were seen first; each family member drew two individual drawings, one of which was the BND, and then a joint drawing. Joe titled his BND *The Lonely Nest*.

The same drawings were done with Joe, his mother, and her partner. When the three were asked to complete the joint drawing, Joe immediately suggested they depict a bird's nest together as a family—they titled it *The Family Nest*, and this image seemed to dramatically communicate Joe's concerns about family and his feelings of insecurity. When viewing all the drawings as a group, dramatic differences were noted

The Wiley Handbook of Art Therapy, First Edition. Edited by David E. Gussak and Marcia L. Rosal.
© 2016 John Wiley & Sons, Ltd. Published 2016 by John Wiley & Sons, Ltd.

between the father's and the mother's BNDs. None of the BNDs appeared secure (as research since then has suggested), nor did they appear pathological. The primary impression was that there was an absence of life or of anything happening in any of the drawings. The father's drawing was the most colorful and included a tree that held the nest in a strong and secure manner while the mother's image was done lightly in pencil. Her drawing included a tree with spindly branches and with the nest placed precariously on the end of a limb, giving an impression of vulnerability.

The nest images along with the family's associations to them suggested Joe's apprehension about his family situation metaphorically, and that he did not have a sense of a secure base in his life. The BND seemed to symbolically capture his unconscious attachment concerns and aspects of the family dynamics, which the referring therapist was able to use in subsequent family sessions to help Joe's parents alter his living situation in a way that would give him an increased feeling of security. One of the most helpful outcomes was that his behavioral problems were determined as arising from attachment anxiety instead of from ADHD. Joe was able to communicate his experiences, needs, and preoccupations in his drawing, titled *The Lonely Nest*, and in his request to his mother to make their family drawing about a nest.

This assessment occurred before what has now grown to 25 years of research on the BND. Beginning with several small thesis studies, attempts to improve validity and reliability continue to accrue. Procedures for administration have been standardized while the methods for assessing the drawing remain in development (Kaiser & Deaver, 2009). Numerous iterations of the rating system, which began as a sign-based approach examining individual indicators, has now evolved to a scale to determine secure or insecure attachment based on a more global approach.

Attachment Theory, Working Models, and Attachment Security

John Bowlby made important contributions to modern psychoanalytic theory with insights he generated while synthesizing constructs from ethology, object relations, cybernetics, and cognitive developmental theory (Mikulincer & Shaver, 2007). From 1940 to 1990, he developed an attachment theory to explain the significance of early childhood relationships on personality throughout life. His theory inspired Mary Ainsworth's research on the behavioral manifestations of attachment seen in the separation and reunion sequences between infants and their caregivers in the procedure titled the Strange Situation. The Strange Situation is a formal laboratory procedure that identifies four categories of attachment security—one secure and three insecure. This important research laid the groundwork for the burgeoning study of attachment theory that exists today.

One of the constructs of attachment theory pertinent to art therapy is Bowlby's working model of attachment, also referred to as a *representational model* (George & West, 2001; Mikulincer & Shaver, 2007). A person's internal working model (IWM) of attachment is explained by the fact that interactions over time, beginning in infancy, are stored in the form of long-term associative memory that informs the person's expectations about relationships. This construct is similar to cognitive scripts or social schemas in social psychology. They not only hold expectations about behavior in close relationships but also connect these with the emotional and autobiographical aspects of a person's attachment experiences as they influence the regulations of emotions in attachment-relevant encounters. From childhood onward, people construct these schemas to guide behavior, thoughts, feelings, and emotions related to attachment relationships. Family drawings and the BND are viewed as graphic representations of aspects of this IWM.

Secure or insecure IWMs of adults are classified by developmental psychologists as secure/autonomous, dismissing, preoccupied, or unresolved/disorganized attachment (Holmes, 2001). These terms diverge from categories designating attachment status in children (secure, avoidant, resistant/ambivalent, and disorganized). These are in contrast to social psychologists' designations of attachment *styles* (secure, dismissing-avoidant, preoccupied, fearful-avoidant), which have evolved out of a separate line of research that uses self-reports to determine a person's perceptions and attitudes rather than IWMs (Mikulincer & Shaver, 2007). These alternative designations can confuse clinicians who read the literature to better understand the categories. The first set of terms will be used here because they are more congruent with how art therapists conceptualize attachment as primarily unconscious IWMs. A brief explanation of the adult attachment categories will enhance understanding of how the categories might be manifested in treatment and represented graphically.

Adult Attachment Categories

Individuals who are secure/autonomous are comfortable with intimacy and with solitude, can reflect on their emotions, and are able to seek help from others when stressed (Holmes, 2001). Those with dismissing attachment tend to deactivate attachment concerns and deny feelings. This latter behavior is found in children whose caregiver is averse to physical contact or dependency and the child learns to play quietly and suppress need for contact in order to keep the attachment figure as close by as possible.

Those with preoccupied attachment become overwhelmed with emotions when confronted with attachment concerns and often feel both excessive neediness and anger about not getting their needs met (Karen, 1998). Individuals with unresolved/ disorganized attachment have no organized strategy for managing emotions or gaining help from others when distressed. In childhood, the caregiver was experienced as frightening by either being abusive and invoking fear in the child, or having expressed other frightening behaviors such as dissociation, which also alarms the child. The reader interested in a more in-depth understanding of these individual differences in attachment is encouraged to read one of the many resources available.

Attachment Theory in Art Therapy

In art therapy, it is useful to assess attachment status and also use the BND as a way to open the therapeutic dialogue to explore relational problems that are tied to the presenting problem. If the client has secure attachment, then it is expected that developing the therapeutic alliance will take less time and effort than if the person has insecure attachment. It would also be anticipated that, unless there were some kind of severe trauma or loss that precipitated treatment, the amount of time needed for treatment would be shorter. Figure 49.1 shows a painting that was done by a woman who scored high on an attachment scale—it shows a peaceful and serene environment with a bird family (Kaiser, 1996). She gave her drawing a whimsical title, as had others in the higher attachment group—titles such as *Saturday morning in the nest* and *Little nest in the big woods,* which were in sharp contrast to the titles by women with lower attachment scores: *Messy nest, Waiting,* and *The Lonely Nest.*

Clients assessed with insecure dismissing attachment have a tendency to avoid feelings and rely on intellect and cognitive function—they are dismissive of attachment needs. This is helpful to the therapist, who must recognize the need to establish rapport in manner that allows trust to develop, so that feelings can be explored. This might involve joining on a thinking level before introducing, perhaps, a psycho-educational plan for teaching the importance of emotional identification and expression. An example of a drawing from an adolescent indicative of dismissing attachment (Figure 49.2) is from a thesis by Trewartha (2004)—there is no environment, little color, and the nest is drawn with the bottom missing, suggesting a denial of the containing function of the nest. Also of note is the use of the paper space with so much white space left blank. These features suggest avoidance of affect and tendency to dismiss needs for connection.

When a person has preoccupied attachment, the therapeutic plan will need to account for the person's intensity of emotional expression and for the proclivity to not trust that their needs will be met by the therapist. The development of the therapeutic alliance will be critical to treatment success, along with treatment strategies that are designed to engage clients cognitively while helping then contain strong affect. In another thesis, a participant judged to have preoccupied attachment focused her attention not on the nest or what it usually contains but on the application of thick marker strokes to the tree, knothole, and sky, and extensive cross-hatched lines on the nest (see Figure 49.3; Pigg, 2010). There are no signs of life, no birds, eggs, or

Figure 49.1   Secure attachment.

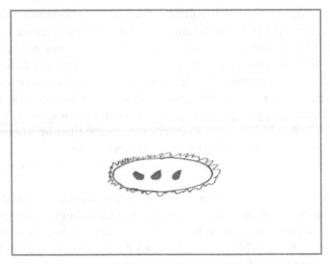

Figure 49.2 Dismissing attachment.

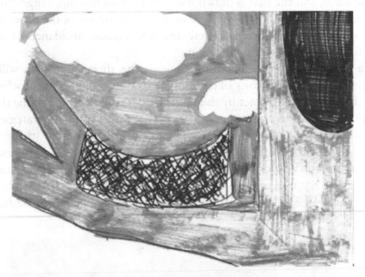

Figure 49.3 Preoccupied attachment.

vegetation. The kinesthetic energy needed to draw this suggests behavioral dysregulation that the person is working hard to contain.

If a client has unresolved/disorganized attachment, the therapist should recognize that the individual most likely has a history of trauma or traumatic loss that calls for specialized attention. This individual will require the most care and time in order to develop trust in the therapeutic relationship, build safety into daily functioning, and gradually explore difficult material while judiciously helping the client sustain and reinforce internal feelings of safety. The IWM of someone with disorganized attachment is difficult to change, and the goal is to, in the end, help him or her alter the disorganized model to one of the other IWMs. Disorganized attachment is

Figure 49.4 Disorganized attachment.

manifested graphically by bizarre or incoherent images, such as the drawing in Figure 49.4 done by an elementary-school-aged child. Here, it is hard to discern the nest, which is presumably the circle, within which are two smaller circles that may represent eggs. This drawing is quite odd in its organization, the addition of smiley faces across the top, and the words across the top. The image has a remarkably unsettling quality.

Insecure attachment is amenable to change with attachment-informed treatment that aims to use the therapeutic relationship as a secure base from which a client can explore past experiences and its meaning. Treatment involves an approach that is tailored to the client's attachment but always involves establishing security in the therapy relationship as the foundation for moving forward.

Administration of the BND

The materials needed to administer the BND include an eight-pack of Crayola © fine-line, classic color markers, 9 × 12-inch drawing paper, and a sharpened pencil with eraser. Extra 8.5 × 11-inch unlined copy paper may be used for the story. Also, extra drawing paper should be provided if the artist wants to restart—keep the old attempt and note the restart. To administer the BND, a person is directed to

"Draw a picture of a bird's nest." If the person asks what to include or any similar questions, reply that "You can do your drawing any way you want." After it is completed, ask the person to "Give the drawing a title other than '*Bird's Nest*'—make the title personal to your drawing. Please write this on the second piece of paper." Then ask the person to "please use this second piece of paper to write a story about your drawing that includes at least two–three sentences." If the person cannot or does not want to write the story, especially if it is a young child, ask him or her to dictate it and then read it back for accuracy.

The scale for determining secure or insecure attachment incorporates graphic signs that have been found in research and clinical work, and they are used in a global manner—it also now includes themes and coherence of the story. Fourteen items are rated using a Likert scale to determine the extent to which they are evident:

1. One of more birds are depicted.
2. A bird family is included.
3. An environment is included.
4. Four or more colors are used in the drawing.
5. Green is the dominant color in the drawing.
6. The BND story is coherent AND contains mostly positive themes.
7. Brown is the dominant color in the drawing.
8. The nest is tilted 45 degrees or more, such that it appears the contents might fall out.
9. The nest lacks a bottom, such that it appears the contents might fall out.
10. The nest is depicted in a vulnerable position.
11. Line quality suggests excessive energy and fills most of the paper space.
12. There are restarts, erasures, or areas crossed out.
13. There are unusual, bizarre, incoherent, or disorganized elements or approaches to the drawing.
14. The BND story is either incoherent OR includes mostly negative themes, or BOTH. (Kaiser, 2012)

The first six items are related to secure attachment; research data from previous studies point to the validity of items one through five (Kaiser & Deaver, 2009). The sixth item relates to the coherence and themes of the story. Items 7–14 have been found to be associated with insecure attachment, except for item 11 (which is about line quality) and item 14 (this item is about the story, but this time it is in reference to incoherence and negative themes).

All but one of the items have been described previously (Kaiser & Deaver, 2009). Item 11 relates to line quality and is included because many BNDs by insecure individuals have been drawn with excessive energy, filling most of the page space, suggesting anxiety. This is similar to Gantt and Tabone's (1998) *Formal Elements Art Therapy Scale*, which includes a scale for implied energy. Raters are asked to speculate about the amount of energy involved in making a drawing and rate it from "least amount of energy possible" to "done with excessive amount of energy" (p. 6); including this item would help capture an aspect of insecurity in drawing that had not yet been accessible.

Scoring

Scoring is accomplished by (1) adding the first six items and averaging them, and (2) adding the remaining eight and averaging them. If the first average is greater than the second, the drawing is determined to represent secure attachment; if the second average is greater, it is determined to represent insecure attachment. If both are the same, the default classification is insecure, because there are a sufficient number of insecure items present to justify this designation. The present scoring has been piloted with a small sample of individuals in treatment for eating disorders, and it appears promising (Kellerher, 2012). The present scoring system does not yield information about the categories of insecure attachment that are of interest to clinicians. More research with larger samples is needed to achieve this.

The BND Story

This section explains how the story's congruence and negative-versus-positive themes are rated. The Adult Attachment Interview (AAI) by Main and colleagues was used as the basis for how to incorporate the story component of the BND. The AAI uses a narrative interview to determine attachment security; the authors reasoned that discourse about attachment concerns reflects representational aspects of attachment (Mikulincer & Shaver, 2007). The AAI asks the individual about early experiences with parental figures, and then responses are coded for access to—and reports of—childhood memories and descriptions of attachment-relevant experiences. Interview transcripts are also coded for coherence, consistency, and organization.

The Adult Attachment Projective (AAP; George & West, 2001), which similarly theorizes narrative as representative of attachment, was also studied. George and West (2001) also code the respondent's language in the AAP for the stories' coherence that a person provides to stimulus pictures designed to evoke attachment themes. Accordingly, for the BND, a story was coherent if: (1) it made sense in relation to the drawing; (2) it was about the drawing and not some other topic; and (3) it was appropriate in length, being neither too long nor too short. In addition, based on the research on themes generated in several BND studies, the story had to express mostly positive themes to be considered secure. Thus, secure stories had to be both coherent and contain mostly positive themes, and insecure BND stories were either incoherent or contained mostly negative themes, or had both of these elements.

The following is an example of a story that is coherent and has positive themes:

> It was a beautiful spring day, and the mother bird set out to gather twigs and soft feathers for her nest. She worked on the nest all day with help from the father bird, and then settled in to lay three small blue eggs. The eggs soon hatched, and she kept the chicks warm while the father bird gathered worms for their first meal.

In contrast, incoherence is reflected in inappropriate length or if a story is not about the nest but instead is a description of the person's drawing ability or a description of the nest itself. For example, "The nest is brown and made of sticks," is too short and describes the drawing instead of giving a story. The same is true for the following: "I cannot draw but here is the best I can do. A messy nest."—this is also too short, and, instead of telling a story, notes the artist's inability to draw, and contains negative themes "messy" and "cannot draw." Incoherence is sometimes seen when the story is too long or tangential.

Positive themes are generally self-evident and relate to the function or purpose of the nest in terms of safety, security, holding, protecting, nurturing, or feeding, as is seen by the themes of the first story cited earlier. In this sense, they are also coherent. Negative themes include words or phrases that are indicative of the following: loneliness, abandonment, waiting for food or for the parent bird to return, being left behind, or some kind of danger. An example of danger is seen in this story: "The purple birds were having a nice time frolicking on the spring day but knew there wasn't much time to hatch eggs before the snakes made their way up the tree in hopes of devouring their future."

These examples illustrate how narrative adds to the ability to judge the security or insecurity of a BND. There is evidence from the image and the narrative related to the image that provides triangulation of evidence within the scale.

Conclusion

A bird's nest is a familiar image in most of the world. Those of us in North America usually encounter our first bird's nest in our preschool years when an attachment figure leads us to view this tiny miracle of nature and joins us in expressing a sense of awe and wonder at the sight. A nest is a carefully crafted structure that provides safety, warmth, and caring—it is a home in which to nurture the growth of baby birds. Children often spontaneously draw bird's nests; sometimes clients do too. After using the BND for over 20 years, and assisting with thesis projects on the BND, I continue to be surprised at the varied ways in which individuals approach these portrayals and their stories, and how they often poignantly, as with Joe and his family, point to ways to approach therapy informed by attachment theory.

The iteration of the BND described here is offered for art therapists who wish to use it in their work. It is a step along the way to developing a more valid and discriminating measure that will require a great deal of research with large samples. In the meantime, the BND is useful in art therapy for providing powerful clinical information—personal expression that reflects the inner world relevant to attachment security.

References

Gantt, L., & Tabone, C. (1998). *The formal elements art therapy scale: The rating manual.* Morgantown, WV: Gargoyle Press.

George, C., & West, M. (2001). The development and preliminary validation of a new measure of adult attachment: The Adult Attachment Projective. *Attachment and Human Development, 3,* 30–61.

Holmes, J. (2001). *The search for the secure base: Attachment theory and psychotherapy.* Philadelphia, PA: Brunner-Routledge.

Kaiser, D. H. (1996). Indications of attachment theory in a drawing task. *The Arts in Psychotherapy, 23,* 333–340.

Kaiser, D. H. (2012). *Kaiser's Bird's Nest Drawing rating scale.* Unpublished Manuscript.

Kaiser, D., & Deaver, S. (2009). Assessing attachment with the Bird's Nest Drawing: A review of the research. *Art Therapy: Journal of the American Art Therapy Association, 26,* 26–33.

Karen, R. (1998). *Becoming attached: First relationships and how they shape our capacity to love.* New York, NY: Oxford University Press.

Kellerher, M. (2012). *A correlational study of the BND and the ECR-R.* Unpublished master's thesis, Eastern Virginia Medical School, Norfolk, VA.

Mikulincer, M., & Shaver, P. S. (2007). *Attachment in adulthood: Structure, dynamics, and Change.* New York, NY: Guilford.

Pigg, S. M. (2010). *Using the Bird's Nest Drawing to assess attachment style and caregiving behaviors in adults.* Unpublished master's thesis, Albertus Magnus College, New Haven, CT.

Trewartha, S. (2004). *Attachment strategies of adolescents in foster care: Indicators and implications.* Unpublished master's thesis, Eastern Virginia Medical School, Norfolk, VA.

50

Family Art Assessment

Paige Asawa and Meirav Haber

Introduction

Family art therapy is often described as the most challenging and rewarding work in the field of art therapy. As Paige Asawa, one of the co-authors of this chapter, indicated: "After teaching and providing family art therapy for over two decades, it is a great honor and privilege to co-author this chapter on family art assessment. I have had the great pleasure of working with some of the leading pioneers in family art therapy, which influenced my own work in private practice." The groundwork for this chapter came from a pilot project—and then research project—that provided family art assessments as a consultation service for agencies that provide family therapy.

There are many controversies in the field of art therapy, and questions concerning family art assessment continue to stimulate much discussion. The discourse of these controversies has motivated an exchange of perspectives resulting in integration and creative insight. One such debate is the differentiation between formal and informal assessments and issues of reliability and validity. For the purposes of this chapter, *formal assessments* are defined as standardized procedures that provide comparison to peer performance, typically with the intention of diagnostic determinations. *Informal assessments* can be structured; however, they are primarily focused on gathering information on a specific family or individual client. Most of the family art therapy assessments, while consisting of set procedures, are considered informal. These assessments emerged from work in both research and clinical settings as a means to further understand family structures and dynamics without primary concern for comparison, reliability, or validity. Historically, art therapists have argued that current art therapy assessments, including family art assessments, do not require scientific standardization or validity to be considered as valuable sources of information about client dynamics.

This chapter is a comprehensive overview of family art assessments developed and authored by art therapists. The chapter begins with a brief background of its history, and then reviews each major assessment chronologically with commentary from various art therapy authors. Next are additional family art assessment tools, highlighted by many authors. The controversies regarding family art therapy

The Wiley Handbook of Art Therapy, First Edition. Edited by David E. Gussak and Marcia L. Rosal.
© 2016 John Wiley & Sons, Ltd. Published 2016 by John Wiley & Sons, Ltd.

assessment are then revisited, followed by a conclusion. While there are many family assessments that include art processes developed by psychologists and family therapists, they have been consciously excluded in order to focus on the tools established by art therapists.

Background

During the 1930s, roughly one decade before the emergence of the field of art therapy, psychologists and psychiatrists began experimenting with the use of drawing tests to find more effective ways of diagnosing individuals (Deacon & Piercey, 2001; Feder & Feder, 1998; Jenkins & Donnelly, 1983; Junge & Asawa, 1994). As family therapy grew in popularity, the use of drawing tests in family assessment was brought into question. Family assessment is grounded in family systems theory, in which the family unit is the focus and context of interactional and behavioral issues (Arrington, 1991; Wadeson, 1980). Most of these tools were designed for the individual client and were therefore ill-equipped to assess the family system, yet family therapists continued to rely on projective drawing tests that do not easily "translate" to work with families (Deacon & Piercey, 2001).

In the late 1970s, art therapists endeavored to create a series of art tasks specifically tailored for family art assessment (Kwiatkowska, 1978; Landgarten, 1981; Wadeson, 1980). Kwiatkowska developed the family art evaluation (FAE) as part of her research at the National Institute of Mental Health (NIMH) with patients and their families. She found the procedure to be a quick and effective way to uncover family dynamics and relational patterns that contribute to problems in the family. Wadeson (1980), who worked closely with Kwiatkowska at NIMH, adapted and modified the FAE in her own art evaluation of couples. Kwiatkowska and Wadeson both conducted formal studies using their art assessment techniques and consistently applied the assessments in their practice.

It was during this time that Landgarten (1981, 1987) published work on her procedure for family art assessment, citing case studies from years of experience using this approach. Although Landgarten did not conduct a formal research study on the use of her assessment in family therapy, Landgarten's family art assessment has captured the interest of many clinicians who find it to be a powerful visual reflection of family dynamics (Riley, 2004). Landgarten's family art assessment continues to be useful to art therapists without the need for formal validation.

Kwiatkowska's Family Art Evaluation (FAE)

The first family art assessment, Kwiatkowska's (1978) FAE developed at NIMH, is composed of a sequence of six drawings:

1. A free drawing
2. A family portrait
3. An abstract family portrait

4. A scribble drawing
5. A joint family scribble
6. A free drawing

Kwiatkowska stressed the importance of this sequence in managing the family's anxiety levels throughout the procedure. With the exception of the joint family scribble, each drawing was to be completed individually by family members in the same room. For the free-drawing tasks, Kwiatkowska instructed each member to "draw whatever comes to mind" (p. 87). She suggested that this first drawing often provides a diagnostic impression of each family member. The abstract family portrait allows therapists to assess clients' capacities for abstract thinking based on how they interpret the task. Interestingly, Kwiatkowska noted that this task is difficult even for high-functioning children, individuals, and families, but nevertheless found it valuable in assessment. She asserted that the joint scribble encourages lively family interaction, is less threatening to clients, and allows for expression of subconscious feelings. She believed that the selection process of one joint family scribble provides insight into passive and dominant roles in the family.

After the completion of each art task, the family is instructed to title and sign their work. Kwiatkowska (1978) wrote that the FAE reflected the uninhibited representations of the complex relational dynamics, which oftentimes differed from the way they verbally presented in the family sessions.

Kwiatkowska (1978) conducted a research study in collaboration with James K. Dent (known as the Dent–Kwiatkowska Study) in which over 1,500 pictures from family art evaluations were collected and rated. Kwiatkowska provided clients with semi-hard pastels for these tasks. She allotted 90–120 minutes for conducting the evaluation within a single session, but emphasized that there should be no strict time limit as even the length of time taken may provide clues about the family's functioning. Kwiatkowska used a numerical rating scale to assess over 60 variables in family art evaluation, including meaningfulness of title, emotional feeling, movement or action, color descriptors, use of space, fragmentation, distortion, closeness, isolation, prominence, and compartmentalization. Assessment of the joint drawing task included the therapist's subjective response, quality of behavioral interaction, involvement, indicators of individuation, and ability to focus on the joint task. Although she felt that her pilot study demonstrated the potential for a standardized, reliable method of assessment and scoring, she wrote that a larger sample might help confirm her findings.

Kramer and Iager (1984) cited Kwiatkowska's study of family art evaluation as one of the most systematic studies ever conducted, involving "an elaborate and generally well-defined rating manual ... [and] a consistent art assessment procedure" (p. 200). Sobol and Williams (2001) asserted that the FAE requires family members to work cooperatively in close proximity, which raises the anxiety level of the family in a way that safely exposes family dynamics. They also noted that a careful reading of an FAE, involving subjective and objective analyses of both the symbolic content and the interaction, will uncover "a deep, but usually unarticulated truth about the relationships within the family" (p. 264). They stressed that the FAE can assist art therapists plan a course of treatment targeting deep insight or behavioral change.

Wadeson's Couple Art Evaluation

Wadeson (1980), working alongside Kwiatkowska at NIMH, developed a modified version of Kwiatkowska's family art evaluation for couples. Wadeson offered thick pastels for her evaluation and allotted a single 2-hour session for evaluation. Her art evaluation procedure consisted of four tasks:

1. A family portrait
2. An abstract portrait of the marital relationship
3. A joint scribble
4. A self-portrait given to and altered by a spouse

All drawings except for the joint scribble were to be completed by each partner "simultaneously but separately" (p. 290).

The first task required the couple to "draw a picture of the family, making full figures of all individuals, including oneself, and no stick figures" (p. 301). Wadeson (1980) asserted that the relative size, arrangement, similarities, differences, and level of detail of the figures correspond to inclusion, alliances, identifications, and other aspects of relationships within the family.

The second task involved asking the couple to draw an abstract portrait of their marital relationship. Personal associations to color and symbolic content in the abstract art enabled couples to express less conscious yet highly substantial truths about their marital dynamics, perceptions, or themes of their relationship as a whole.

The third task was an adaptation of Kwiatkowska's family scribble directive with additional instructions to "tell a story about the picture once it is completed" (p. 299) to encourage greater projection. Wadeson believed that observing the joint scribble while it is created helps therapists learn valuable information about deeply ingrained response patterns, decision-making, cooperation or sabotage, dominance, and interpersonal involvement.

The final task asked the couple to create a realistic, figurative portrait each, exchange portraits with their spouse, and add whatever they wished to each other's portraits. According to Wadeson, this task allows couples to symbolically offer themselves to their spouse and identify what they would like to change about their spouse, thereby providing valuable clinical information about relationship dynamics.

Landgarten's Family Art Assessment

The family art assessment, developed by Landgarten in 1981, is comprised of three tasks completed by the family in the first session:

1. Nonverbal team art task
2. Nonverbal family art task
3. Verbal family art task

Each member is asked to select one color marker to be used for the entire session. This "color rule" allows the art therapist to observe more clearly each member's level of participation and interaction (Landgarten, 1987, p. 14). It also provides information on who breaks the rules or challenges the rules in the process. During the first team art task, members are asked to select their partner(s) and work together on a single piece of paper without speaking, gesturing, or writing to each other. Landgarten proposed that the team art task provided the art therapist with valuable information regarding family alliances and power dynamics. During the second task, all family members are instructed to work together on a single sheet of paper, again without speaking or gesturing. For the third task, family members are instructed again to work together on a single sheet of paper, but this time they may speak to each other while working. After each task, the art therapist informs members that they can speak to come up with a title together. Although Landgarten did not specify a length of time, she intended for the assessment to be completed within a single therapy session.

Analysis of the family art assessment consisted primarily of observing the family's interaction during the process. Landgarten outlined 17 points of observation for art therapists to note, such as who initiated the picture, who followed and who reacted, in what order members participated, and which members' suggestions were utilized or ignored (p. 15). She also urged art therapists to pay careful attention to the family's style of interaction, each member's level of involvement, use of space and boundaries, and whether members were cooperative, individualistic, or discordant with the rest of the family. Although most of the observations were behavioral and process-oriented, she also encouraged examination of symbolic content in each person's drawings.

Landgarten (1987) emphasized the importance of engaging the family in discussing their perceptions and observations, asking guiding questions, and offering limited observations of the interactions. Landgarten believed that observing family interactions, including verbal and nonverbal communication, were keys to understanding the family system. Analysis of content and examination of suggested titles also added to knowledge of family dynamics: "Every gesture and mark provides a clue to the family system" (p. 15). Using case examples, Landgarten illustrated how observations during the evaluation help to directly identify target symptoms and behaviors for treatment planning.

Johnson (1991) maintained that Landgarten's assessment was an immense contribution to the study of families among art therapists, especially in work with reluctant families. Riley (2004) recommended using Landgarten's dyadic and joint family drawings as an immediate opportunity to observe behavioral enactment, define the problem, and formulate future art interventions to restructure family interaction. Riley also noted that, "How the family paired, who was the leader, who was the scapegoat, and what kinds of resistance were observable were valuable pieces of information gleaned" (Riley, 2004, p. 158).

Additional Family Art Assessments

Many art therapists have written about the use of family sculpture as an assessment tool. Several authors deemed family sculpture as highly valuable (Arrington, 1991; Keyes, 1984; Kwiatkowska, 1967, 1978; Landgarten, 1981, 1987). Family sculpture requires the family to create a three-dimensional form. There is flexibility with the media used to assemble the structure, although clay is typically used.

Keyes (1984) stressed that the family sculpture reveals four levels of information: the history of the family of origin, projections onto family members, introjections and current perceptions, and identification of treatment goals. Power distribution, family alliances, values, distortions, and avoidances are also enacted through placement of the clay forms. Insights can emerge by examining the use of space, design comparisons, relative size, proximity, and prominence of figures (Arrington, 1991; Keyes, 1984). Kwiatkowska (1978) noted that clients' underlying psychopathologies usually become "evident through a more primitive, less controlled mode of expression" (p. 136) with clay. However, Kwiatkowska warned of the inherent difficulties in handling loose media with clients, and Landgarten (1987) stressed the need to thoughtfully consider the level of structure provided by the media.

Many of the major family art assessments also include a joint family drawing. Although the origins of the joint picture are unclear, it is most commonly described as a task in which a family engages in a spontaneous drawing together (Kwiatkowska, 1967; Landgarten, 1981, 1987; Wadeson, 1980). Wadeson's (1980) work with couples in therapeutic settings often involved a joint picture with instructions to "develop one well-integrated picture together without verbal communication" (p. 285). Landgarten (1981, 1987) similarly instructed families to draw a picture together without speaking, but did not instruct the families to integrate their drawing. Landgarten (1987) claimed that greater ambiguity of instructions presented the opportunity for families to make more projective decisions during this process.

Family Art Assessment Controversy

The controversy regarding family art assessment has provided an opportunity for contrasting perspectives to be explored. The challenge to push beyond the comfort of consensus seeking has benefited the field in immeasurable ways as it has propelled and motivated art therapists to discuss and debate important concerns. With regard to family art assessment, some of the main opposing ideas focus on issues of validity and reliability, as well as objectivity and subjectivity in analysis. All of these factors are considered as they impact the role of the art therapist in family art assessment. The field of art therapy has evolved multiple views and approaches in family art assessment, which is an unintended benefit of this historical debate.

Validity and reliability

Art therapists have debated the validity and reliability of current art assessment tools and argued that further research on these tools must be undertaken (Betts, 2006; Brooke, 2004; Cox, Agell, Cohen, & Gantt, 2000; Gantt, 2004; Gantt & Tabone, 1998; Kaplan, 2011; McNiff, 1998). McNiff (1998) stated that many art assessments lack the psychological theory and data to make claims regarding reliability or validity. He also argued that correlations between art expressions and character traits need to be developed, measured, and agreed upon. However, art therapists have argued that current art assessments do not require scientific standardization or validity and reliability measures to be considered rich and valuable sources of information about client dynamics (Anderson, 2001; Brooke, 2004; Cox et al., 2000; Kwiatkowska, 1978; Wadeson, 1980). Cox et al. (2000) warned that therapists' attempts to emulate psychological standards in art assessment can be problematic, as many psychological tests lack reliability. Wadeson (1980) added that there is no "systematic procedure sufficiently refined to diagnose a patient simply on the basis of art expression" (p. 197); rather, art may be used in the context of other information to arrive at diagnosis or assessment (Cox et al., 2000; Wadeson, 1980). Anderson (2001), Kwiatkowska (1978), and Wadeson suggested standardizing the structure of the art assessment session instead by consistently using the same art media, procedures, instructions, and setting with a sufficiently large sample.

Objectivity and subjectivity in analysis

Art therapists have also noted a lack of satisfactory rating methods for quantifying art elements in existing art assessments, and have asserted that analysis of art assessments should involve clear, objective, quantifiable rating systems with a focus on form over content (e.g., Betts, 2006; Gantt, 2004; Gantt & Tabone, 1998; Kramer & Iager, 1984). Brooke (2004) and Cox et al. (2000) recommended development of descriptive yet easy-to-read manuals with case examples; images for comparison; and information on design, administration, scoring, and interpretation. Gantt and Tabone (1998) developed the Formal Elements Art Therapy Scale, better known as FEATS, in order to analyze how a drawing was made, rather than what was drawn. Gantt (2001) proposed that the FEATS can be applied to any art assessment for greater generalizability, but cautioned that ratings may vary with raters' clinical experience and art therapy training, as well as with clients' artistic skill levels.

Other art therapists challenged the necessity to standardize rating scales, and argued that more subjective analysis preserves the rich and meaningful content of the art assessment (Brooke, 2004; Kwiatkowska, 1978; McNiff, 1998; Wadeson, 1980). McNiff (1998) supported assessment research that is attentive to the context, process, and nature of art expression as subjective experience. He warned against quantifying and categorizing nonobjective data in art assessments and claiming it to be anything more than speculative. Brooke (2004) and Klorer (2000) similarly cautioned against a cookbook approach to interpreting client's art. Gantt (2004) agreed that finding meaning from individual symbols or characteristics is flawed: "If one plucks a part out of the whole, it becomes devoid of meaning. Context is the key to understanding how the symbol functions" (p. 22). For a better scoring system, art therapists suggested looking for a pattern, connection, or theme among characteristics (Cox et al., 2000; Gantt, 2004). Many art therapists stressed that a client's subjective interpretations and free associations are crucial to effective art assessment analysis (Betts, 2006; Brooke, 2004; Gantt, 2004; Riley, 1993; Wadeson, 1980). Wadeson (1980) argued that the substance of a client's subjective vision would be lost through adherence to a "strictly scientific procedure that would require quantification and a statistical analysis" (p. 319). Some art therapists have acknowledged the possibility that more objective, standardized art assessments may compromise the role of the art therapist (Anderson, 2001; Gantt, 2004; McNiff, 1998). McNiff (1998) noted that perhaps some of the resistance to art assessment research stems from fear of transforming art therapy assessment into "a diagnostic adjunct to primary therapy" (p. 122). The question of who is qualified to administer and score art assessments has also been debated (Gantt, 2004). Anderson (2001) observed that the specialized training that art therapists receive contributes to a rich understanding of the many subtleties within art assessment.

Multiple approaches

Art therapy researchers agreed that family assessment should include multiple approaches (e.g., Anderson, 2001; Betts, 2006; Bruscia, 1988; Gantt, 2004; Gantt & Tabone, 1998; McNiff, 1998). Betts (2006) stated that the most effective assessment approaches include standardized formal assessments, behavioral checklists, and portfolio evaluation, as well as subjective approaches that elicit the client's personal art and interpretations. Several authors suggested thoughtfully combining several art directives in assessment to maximize the amount of information obtained, to create an opportunity for observing recurring themes, and to better evaluate clients (e.g., Brooke, 2004; Cox et al., 2000; Gantt, 2004; Gantt & Tabone, 1998; Kramer & Iager, 1984). Brooke (2004) and Cox et al. (2000) recommended making informed choices between different art assessments to harness the strengths that each one has to offer. Anderson (2001) suggested that further research should address which combination of art-based assessments will best suit clients with certain disorders.

Conclusion

Family art assessments have been an integral part of the field for decades, yet there is controversy regarding the direction of family art assessment research. Some authors believe that researchers should work to standardize art assessments, develop extensive norms, conduct large-scale validity studies, and include easy-to-use quantitative guidelines for interpretation and scoring (e.g., Anderson, 2001; Brooke, 2004; Gantt, 2004, Gantt & Tabone, 1998; Kaplan, 2011). Others believe that art assessments are valuable with or without scientific validity and reliability measures and suggest standardizing through consistent procedures, instructions, and settings with sufficiently large samples (e.g., Aiken & Groth-Marnat, 2006; Deacon & Piercey, 2001; Feder & Feder, 1998; Kwiatkowska, 1978; Wadeson, 1980).

Despite considerations regarding the best practice for family art assessments, art therapists generally agree that family art assessments contribute valuable data in family assessment. Art directives are easy to administer, lend structure to assessment, and provide information that may be equivalent to many hours of verbal interviews. Family art assessments can overcome linguistic and communication barriers with diverse cultural and ethnic groups. Family art assessments have been described as interventions that strengthen or alter the structure of a family, stimulate involvement, and provide greater therapist–client collaboration. Hence, in spite of the ongoing debate and controversy, art therapists continue to utilize family art assessments as valuable assets in deepening their understanding of the family structure and dynamics and as key diagnostic and therapeutic tools in their clinical work.

References

Aiken, L. R., & Groth-Marnat, G. (2006). *Psychological testing and assessment*. Boston, MA: Pearson Education Group.

Anderson, F. E. (2001). Needed: A major collaborative effort. *Journal of the American Art Therapy Association, 18*, 74–78. doi:10.1080/07421656.2001.10129755.

Arrington, D. (1991). Thinking systems-seeing systems: An integrative model for systematically oriented art therapy. *The Arts in Psychotherapy, 18*, 201–211. doi:10.1016/0197-4556(91)90114-P.

Betts, D. J. (2006). Art therapy assessments and rating instruments: Do they measure up? *The Arts in Psychotherapy, 33*, 422–434. Retrieved from http://www.sciencedirect.com/science/journal/01974556.

Brooke, S. L. (2004). *Tools of the trade: A therapist's guide to art therapy assessments*. Springfield, IL: Charles C. Thomas.

Bruscia, K. (1988). Standards for clinical assessment in the arts therapies. *The Arts in Psychotherapy, 15*, 5–10. doi:10.1016/0197-4556(88)90047-0.

Cox, C. T., Agell, G., Cohen, B. M., & Gantt, L. (2000). Are you assessing what I am assessing? Let's take a look! *American Journal of Art Therapy, 39*, 48–68. Retrieved from www.ebscohost.com.linus.lmu.edu.

Deacon, S. A., & Piercy, F. P. (2001). Qualitative methods in family evaluation: Creative assessment techniques. *The American Journal of Family Therapy, 29*, 355–373. doi:10.1080/01926180127627.

Feder, B., & Feder, E. (1998). *The art and science of evaluation in the art therapies: How do you know what's working?* Springfield, IL: Charles C. Thomas.

Gantt, L. M. (2001). The formal elements art therapy scale: A measurement system for global variables in art. *Art Therapy: Journal of Art Therapy association, 18*, 50–55. doi: 10.1080/07421656.2001.10129453.

Gantt, L. (2004). The case for formal art therapy assessments. *Art Therapy: Journal of Art Therapy association, 21*, 18–29. Retrieved from http://www.arttherapy.org/.

Gantt, L., & Tabone, C. (1998). *The formal elements art therapy scale: The rating manual*. Morgantown, WV: Gargoyle Press.

Jenkins, H., & Donnelly, M. (1983). The therapist's responsibility: A systemic approach to mobilizing family creativity. *Journal of Family Therapy, 5*, 199–218. doi:10.1046/j..1983.00616.x

Johnson, D. R. (1991). Introduction to the special issue on the creative arts therapies and the family. *The Arts in Psychotherapy, 18*, 187–189. doi: 10.1016/0197-4556(91)90111-M.

Junge, M., & Asawa, P. (1994). *A history of art therapy in the United States*. Mundelein, IL: AATA Inc.

Kaplan, F. F. (2011). Areas of inquiry for art therapy research. *Art Therapy: Journal of the American Art Therapy Association, 18*, 142–147. doi:10.1080/07421656.2001.10129734

Keyes, M. F. (1984). The family clay sculpture. *The Arts in Psychotherapy, 11*, 25–28. doi: 0197-4556 84 53.00-.00

Klorer, P. G. (2000). *Expressive therapy with troubled children*. Lanham, MD: Jason Aronson, Inc.

Kramer, E. S., & Iager, A. C. (1984). The use of art in assessment of psychotic disorders: Changing perspectives. *The Arts in Psychotherapy, 11*, 197–201. doi:0197-4556 84 53.00-.00.

Kwiatkowska, H. (1967). Family art therapy. *Family Process, 6*, 37–55. doi:10.1111/j.1545-5300.1967.00037.x.

Kwiatkowska, H. Y. (1978). *Family therapy and evaluation through art*. Springfield, IL: Thomas.

Landgarten, H. B. (1981). *Clinical art therapy*. New York, NY: Brunner-Mazel.

Landgarten, H. B. (1987). *Family art psychotherapy: A clinical guide and casebook*. New York, NY: Brunner/ Mazel.

McNiff, S. (1998). *Art-based research*. Philadelphia, PA: Jessica Kingsley, Publishers.

Riley, S. (1993). Illustrating the family story: art therapy, a lens for viewing the family's reality. *The Arts in Psychotherapy, 20*, 253–264. doi:10.1016/0197-4556(93)90020-3.

Riley, S. (2004). *Integrative approaches to family art therapy*. Chicago, IL: Magnolia Street Publishers.

Sobol, B., & Williams, K. (2001). Family and group art therapy. In J. A. Rubin (Ed.), *Approaches to art therapy: Theory and technique* (pp. 261–280). New York, NY: Brunner-Routledge.

Wadeson, H. (1980). *Art psychotherapy*. New York, NY: John Wiley & Sons.

The Levick Emotional and Cognitive Art Therapy Assessment (LECATA)

Myra F. Levick and Craig A. Siegel

The Levick Emotional and Cognitive Art Therapy Assessment (LECATA) was developed as a school-based tool to evaluate the therapeutic needs of special-needs children in the Miami-Dade County Public Schools (M-DCPS; Levick, 2009). The value of this assessment is that it is comprehensive in nature and allows for both a means of dialoguing with other mental health professionals within the school system and in the community as well as measuring the progress of a child over time. In this chapter, an overview of the LECATA will be provided, along with some data to support its validity and reliability as an important art therapy assessment.

The Beginnings

The LECATA was heavily influenced by the tenets of psychoanalytic thinking. Psychoanalytic theory served as a guide toward a greater understanding of defense mechanisms. As interest grew in the study and teaching of Sigmund and Anna Freud's work on defenses (S. Freud, 1959; A. Freud, 1966), Levick found that their work might be the basis for understanding drawings. Halsey (1977) discussed S. Freud's views on art productions as he wrote that S. Freud "freely admitted that he had approached the psychological insights of artists with the primary intention of confirming the findings he had made in examining unpoetic, neurotic human beings" (p. 99). Halsey believed that Freud's:

> greatest service to the understanding of art is his convincing reminder to us that works of art cannot be comprehended without an awareness of the dynamic role psychological factors play in both their creation and assimilation (p. 101).

Levick also began to question the efficacy of focusing only on dysfunctional behaviors, which generally indicated pathology. An affiliation between Hahnemann University and Anna Freud's Hampstead Clinic in England was developed, and offered an opportunity for Levick to seek permission to illustrate Ms. Freud's book (1966; mentioned earlier). Work in Anna Freud's clinic during a sabbatical leave provided the basis for

The Wiley Handbook of Art Therapy, First Edition. Edited by David E. Gussak and Marcia L. Rosal.
© 2016 John Wiley & Sons, Ltd. Published 2016 by John Wiley & Sons, Ltd.

Levick's doctoral dissertation (Levick), which later became a text for art therapy students and practicing art therapists (Levick, 1983). Soon thereafter, students and colleagues began to utilize the criteria designed for recognizing defenses in drawings in their clinical work with child and adult patients, and the data began to be disseminated among art therapists (Levick, 2009).

In 1986, Janet Bush, a graduate of the art therapy program at Hahnemann and the then director of the Clinical Art Therapy Department at M-DCPS, spearheaded the development of the LECATA. Her objective was to develop a single art therapy assessment that would bridge the communication gap between the art therapists, school counselors, and psychologists. Her motivation was based on the fact that, among the 11 art therapists under her supervision, there were at least five different assessments being used to determine the diagnoses, treatment plans, and progress of the special needs population for which she was responsible. With permission from the school administration, Levick met with Bush's staff to develop a school-based art therapy assessment based on her book (1983). The basis of the assessment was to meet Bush's requirements, and what was planned as a 1-year project extended beyond a 3-year period (Levick, 1989, 2009).

The relationship between normal emotional and natural cognitive development shaped the basis for the creation of the LECATA. This assessment was designed to be given at the first meeting with a student/patient, and to provide information on both strengths vs weaknesses and pathology vs normality, in order to develop a treatment plan. It was copyrighted in 1989 and soon became an integral part of the Miami-Dade school program for children with special needs. Over the years, Bush, Levick, and, later, Craig Siegel (an art therapist in the M-DCPS and current chairperson of the Clinical Art Therapy Department there) continued to conduct training seminars and supervision for professionals interested in utilizing this instrument for adults and children identified as having a broad range of cognitive and/or emotional problems. The assessment was also based on both published literature and years of experience looking at drawings from an emotional and cognitive developmental perspective.

Kellogg and O'Dell (1967) reported the influence of age and level of maturation on children's drawings. Hardiman and Zernick (1980) described a relationship between Piaget's cognitive theory and the artistic development of children's drawings. Lowenfeld (1969) looked at the nature of creativity on a developmental hierarchy. Koppitz (1968) based her psychological evaluation of children's human figure drawings (HFDs), on the earlier works of Goodenough (1926) and Machover (1949, 1953, 1960). Koppitz, more than other investigators, identified emotional indicators manifested in children's drawings in relation to symptoms and behavior. In addition to the pros and cons of the reliability and validity of projective techniques as a diagnostic instrument (see Hammer, 1978), there was little in the literature supporting psychoanalytic theory and, particularly, defense mechanisms of the ego as the basis for a drawing assessment. Thus, the evolving goal was to merge the theories of cognitive and emotional development as viewed through a single art-based assessment. It was also an opportunity to create an art assessment that incorporated the principles of Anna Freud's Diagnostic Profile:

> ... [which] is intended to draw the diagnostician's concentration away from the child's pathology and to return it instead to an assessment of his developmental status and the picture of his total personality. (1971, p. 184)

Defining Test Criteria

To record the presence of defenses in drawings, it was required for the criteria to be defined for identifying each defense. To simplify the process, only the original 19 defenses outlined by A. Freud (1966) were selected.

The relationship between emotional and cognitive development, as seen in the artwork of children, is defined in Table 51.1 (see Levick, 1983). The cognitive criteria are based on Piaget's cognitive stages of development (see Rosen, 1977); artistic lines are based primarily on the work of Kellogg and O'Dell (1967). Psychosexual sequences of development are based on S. Freud's theories (1959), and the hierarchal scale of ego mechanisms of defenses is listed as defined by A. Freud (1966).

According to the literature, children do not normally begin to scribble until at least 18 months of age, and shapes making recognizable images do not normally appear until around 2½–3 years of age (Kellogg, 1969, 1970). While defenses are described from infancy up through the years, obviously they cannot be identified in graphic images until a child begins to draw. Therefore, Table 51.1 begins with the early pre-operational stage and parallels the progression from random scribbles to shapes and from the anal the Oedipal stages. Investigators in these domains also agree that, by

Table 51.1A Correlation of developmental lines of cognitive, artistic, psychosexual sequences, and defense mechanisms of the ego appropriate for those periods of development. Age group: 2½–5 years. Criteria: author—Myra Levick (1983, 1992)

Cognitive	Artistic	Psychosexual	Defenses
Early Preoperational	**Period of Progression from Random Scribbles to Shapes**	**Anal Stage to Oedipal Stage**	**Early Anal** (2½–3 years)
Thinking is centered	Shapes become combined	Issues:	Regression
			Incorporation
		Self-assertion	
Only one aspect of	Forms become		Reversal
something is attended to	balanced	Control	Undoing
at a time			Denial
	Beginning of spatial	Regulation of	
Thought is	organization	body functions	**Late Anal**
representational			(3–4½ years)
			Avoidance
	Emergence of		
Symbolization present	recognizable objects		Projection
			Symbolism
Differentiation between			**Oedipal**
self and others present			(3½–5 years)
			Imitation
Animism, realism,			
artificialism in thought			
still present			

Table 51.1B   Correlation of developmental lines of cognitive, artistic, psychosexual sequences, and defense mechanisms of the ego appropriate for those periods of development. Age group: 5–7 years. Criteria: author—Myra Levick (1983, 1992)

Cognitive	Artistic	Psychosexual	Defenses
Animism, realism, artificalism may appear in the form of magical thinking	Period of greatest quantitative difference within sequences	*Post-Oedipal Stage*	Identification
			Reaction formation
			Isolation
Early development of logical consistency	Period of greatest qualitative differences between sequences	Major task is process toward resolution of Oedipal conflict and identification	Isolation of affect
			Displacement
Early development of capacity to understand concepts of classification and conservation	Images reflect movement from a single aspect to an object or form to pictorial drawing	Positive identification with same-sex parent	Simple rationalization
More than one aspect of something can be attended to at the same time	Several objects may be related in one drawing	Negative identification with parent of opposite sex	Earlier defenses are available and used appropriately
	Pictorial images begin to tell stories		**Note: defenses may develop in any sequence between 5–7 years of age.**

around age 11 years, all normally functioning children have progressed through the concrete operational stage; are now able to realistically represent familiar objects; and are moving from the post-Oedipal stage through latency into the pre-adolescent stage. By around 11 years of age, all normal individuals have acquired the cognitive skills and ego mechanisms of defense to progress from adolescence to adulthood. (Levick, 1983, 2009)

Designing the Tasks

This designing of the five drawings tasks of the LECATA began by reviewing the assignments in the family art therapy evaluation by Kwiatkowska (1978). The first task of the LECATA, a free drawing, is intended to create a sense of freedom and was adopted as a logical beginning. The request for a story about the image was

Table 51.1C Correlation of developmental lines of cognitive, artistic, psychosexual sequences, and defense mechanisms of the ego appropriate for those periods of development. Age group: 7–11 years. Criteria: author—Myra Levick (1983, 1992)

Cognitive	Artistic	Psychosexual	Defenses
Concrete Operational Period	**Period of Realistic Representation of Familiar Objects**	*Latency Period*	Repression Reaction formation
Thinking moves away from centration and irreversibility	Relationships are drawn in more orderly fashion	Infantile past closed off	Simple rationalization Introjection
Cognitive reversibility emerges	Elevated base lines and ground lines appear	Parental attitudes and values internalized	Denial Identification
Advancement to a higher stage of equilibrium occurs	Horizon line Human figures move from static to action	Child's attention directed primarily toward learning and peer relationships	Identification with the aggressor* Intellectualization
Reasoning can move from the beginning to the end of a process	More frontal and profile views of people and objects appear Houses and people take on a more proportional relationship	New role models perceived in teachers, movie and television stars, and sports heroes	**Notes: Earlier defenses are available and used appropriately. Defenses may develop in any sequence during 7–11+ years of age.**

*This defense may appear at any age.

added. This task also serves as a baseline in identifying defenses most frequently used by the individual being tested. A picture of the self was selected for the second task of the LECATA, and the direction is to *draw a picture of your whole self at the age you are now*.

Doing a scribble and making a picture from it was first described by Naumburg (1947). This initially became the third and fourth tasks, but was later numbered the third task with two parts. The second part, making something from the scribble, was seen as providing an estimation of the degree to which an individual was capable of cognitive abstraction. Piaget's theory maintains that abstraction is a higher level of cognitive functioning that generally appears in formal operations at around 11 years of age.

The first three tasks selected seemed satisfactory in providing the direction for imaging the developmental indicators being sought, with the exception of Introjection. This defense is very important in the identification process as an individual begins to carry out the demands of the caretaker (parent) as if they were his/her own, even when parents are not present. Thus, an underlying assumption of the test is that the values or mores of the person(s) that the artist is in the process of identifying with are also in the process of being internalized by the artist. Therefore, the fourth task was a request to draw a place that is important and explain why that place was chosen. In preliminary testing, it was found that children under the age of 5 years were not sure what the word *important* meant. It was agreed that, for children aged 3–5 years, the task would be to *draw a place where you would like to be*; and for ages 6 years and up, the task would be to *draw a place that is important*. For both age groups, the subject was asked to speak about why that place was chosen.

The family drawing was deemed an essential aspect of comprehensive assessment and is the fifth and last task. The test taker is asked to draw a picture of a family— if possible, his or her own family. The objective of this task is to make it as open a request for a family picture as possible.

It must be noted here that creating an art assessment that required five tasks is in keeping with Levick's and Bush's philosophy. They felt strongly that no conclusion or treatment goals should be based on a single drawing.

Developing the LECATA Manual

A manual was designed to assist practitioners in using the LECATA and has been revised twice, most recently in 2001. It includes a specific, structured format to ensure consistency in administration; a scoring procedure; a script for presentation of each of the five tasks; a score sheet for each task; and a scoring worksheet. In addition, there is a sample report form, a sample case, and blank score sheets that may be copied. This manual, previously available directly through this author, is now appended to the publication of the normative study and may be copied as needed (see Levick, 2009). What follows are examples of the five tasks produced by normal children from kindergarten through sixth grade.

Task one

The examples used for task one (Figures 51.1 and 51.2) represent images that are similar in terms of meeting identified cognitive criteria, while at the same time differing in regard to emotional criteria. The image on the left does not include Identification, which in this example is age-appropriate, and prevents the individual from scoring higher in terms of emotional functioning. The image on the right is indicative of clearly defined Identification, as observed through the inclusion of different bodily features, most notably the variation in hair length for the artist and her brother.

Figure 51.1

Five year, four month old female	
Cognitive score	9 years
Emotional score	5 years

Figure 51.2

Seven year, eight month old female	
Cognitive score	9 years
Emotional score	9 years

Task two

The directive for task two is a self-portrait. The examples (Figures 51.3 and 51.4) included for this task are from children who differ in age by 4 months, but demonstrate a larger disparity in relation to both the cognitive and emotional functioning. Whereas the artist on the left appears to be emerging from earlier stages of artistic development as he begins to demonstrate elaboration of detail, the image on the right is representative of a more realistic, mature representation of a figure.

Figure 51.3

Ten year, eleven month old male	
Cognitive score	9 years
Emotional score	9 years

Figure 51.4

Eleven year, three month old female	
Cognitive score	11 years
Emotional score	11 years

Task three

Task three is a scribble drawing followed by the artist's development of the scribble. The examples (Figures 51.5 and 51.6) included for this task represent children who differ in age by approximately 3½ years; however, cognitively, they approach the directive in a similar fashion. Whereas abstract thinking is not expected to have emerged by age 7, it should be more visible by age 11. We are aware that this task often fosters regression in both domains. The 7-year-old child did regress in the emotional domain, while the 11-year-old child indicates regression cognitively. However, the older child is using a more mature defense seen in Figure 51.6, the right hand image of Task 3.

Figure 51.5	Seven year, eight month old female	
	Cognitive score	7 years
	Emotional score	5 years

Figure 51.6	Eleven year, three month old female	
	Cognitive score	7 years
	Emotional score	8 years

Task four

Task four (Figures 51.7 and 51.8) focuses on an individual's ability to master the developmental task of internalizing values from parents/caretakers. Both children, 1 year apart, indicate that they have mastered this task. Their verbal associations to their images (not reported here) documented that they understood the meaning of the word "important." The difference in the scoring is based on the elaboration of detail seen in the drawing on the right. The emotional defense of introjection, once acquired, is scored at the same level of the cognitive domain.

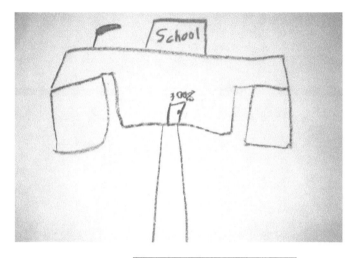

Figure 51.7	Nine year, one month old male	
	Cognitive score	8 years
	Emotional score	8 years

Figure 51.8	Ten year old female	
	Cognitive score	9 years
	Emotional score	9 years

Task five

The directive for task five is to draw a family. The examples (Figures 51.9 and 51.10) included for this task range from a stereotypic image of figures arranged in a line, floating on the page, to one that provides relevant information for what is excluded as much as for what is included. The image on the right provides rich information about the individual's perception of family through the omission of the self in the drawing. This highlights a point—that one must focus equally on the message being conveyed in the image, as well as on the scoring criteria. In both images, the cognitive domain and emotional domain are scored on the same developmental level.

Figure 51.9	Eight year, one month old female	
	Cognitive score	7 years
	Emotional score	7 years

Figure 51.10	Ten year old female	
	Cognitive score	9 years
	Emotional score	9 years

Implementation within Miami-Dade County Public Schools

The development of the LECATA for initial use in the M-DCPS has been ideal for providing clinically rich information while being easily translated into terms understandable, not only by other art therapists, but by other professionals in the clinical arena. The ability to provide age-equivalency scores based on cognitive and emotional development allows the school art therapist to communicate across professional language barriers, which helps strengthen the value of their existence within the school setting. Prior to the use of this assessment tool, educators had a difficult time understanding how art therapy benefitted a student in making academic gains.

The administration of the LECATA is one of the first procedural steps prior to a student receiving clinical art therapy services within M-DCPS. The process of administering the assessment helps the school art therapist glean important information, such as the student's willingness to comply with directives, comfort level working with art media, ability to maintain focus on the task presented, and ability to communicate both graphically and verbally. Upon completion of the administration, a structured assessment report is written that includes the following sections: the student's clinical history, clinical observations, assessment results, discussion, summary, and recommendations.

The results of the assessment are then shared with the student, his parents, teachers, and other clinical and/or administrative staff in attendance at the student's individualized education plan (IEP) meeting. The school art therapist utilizes this forum to present the scores of both the cognitive and emotional domains, and to explain how the scores correlate to both individual strengths and areas of concern. The results of the cognitive domain are discussed in correlation with previous intellectual and academic testing, highlighting how current functioning can impact the ability to meet grade-level academic tasks. It also serves as an identifier for academic challenges.

The review and scoring of the graphic representations can provide data as to whether particular visual learning milestones have been achieved. A child's ability to move from recognizable shapes to recognizable objects to sequencing recognizable objects is a determining factor in whether the same child will be able to move from recognizing a letter, to recognizing multiple letters to form words, to recognizing multiple words to form sentences. It is the role and responsibility of the school art therapist to help translate the results into a language that parents and educators can understand. Student artistic development is further discussed in relationship to potential academic challenges. Results of the emotional domain are discussed in correlation with previous psychological testing and in relation to current behaviors of concern. Emphasis is placed on how identified defenses are adaptive or maladaptive in relation to the cognitive score and the ability to successfully access educational opportunities.

The LECATA serves as the foundation for determining the appropriateness of art therapy services and assisting in the development of priority educational needs (PENs), goals, and benchmarks to be included on a student's IEP. This portion of the IEP then serves as the foundation for the school art therapist's treatment plan. The school art therapist administers task one of the LECATA on an annual basis, prior to the IEP meeting, to serve as a progress summary, and completes a full reassessment every 3 years. The progress summary drawing is reviewed in comparison to the previous task one to determine both cognitive and emotional growth, as well as to determine updated goals and benchmarks.

As students transfer from school to school or matriculate from an elementary program to a secondary program, the assessment is shared with the receiving school art therapist. Due to the common language of the assessment within the district, school art therapists within M-DCPS can easily review the assessment and have a firm grasp of the assessment results, allowing for a smooth transition for the student.

The use of the LECATA (for over 20 years by school art therapists within M-DCPS) has helped the department reach the original goal of having a formalized tool that provides significant data about a student's current cognitive and emotional functioning, and this data can be easily shared among colleagues and other professionals within the clinical and educational arenas. The LECATA has been a cornerstone within the structure of the M-DCPS Clinical Art Therapy Department and has had a significant influence on its long-term stability.

Normative Study

The many years of positive feedback and data from art therapists working with children and adults from many different populations necessitated that Levick and her colleagues develop a normative study. The LECATA results, although consistent with the literature identifying emotional and cognitive development, raised important questions. As the study was in process and data was being accumulated, it was presented to different groups of mental health professionals, including art therapists, psychologists, and school counselors. Many concurred that a new norm was emerging, and every professional group agreed that data anomalies seemed to be emanating, in part, from what we have come to call the "latch key child"—a child whose parents are either both working, separated, or divorced, and who comes home to an empty house after school (US Department of Commerce Economics and Statistics Administration, 1994). The latch key phenomenon is due to the growing divorce rate over the past 20 years. In addition to being home alone, the LECATA researchers began to consider the impact that technology (iPods, computers, and computer games) has on traditional teaching methods and learning behaviors.

The data, which revealed an obvious slowing down of development, necessitated a return to the literature that informed the basis for this assessment (Levick, 2009). Piaget concurred with S. Freud (1959)—that there is neither a "purely affective state" nor a "purely cognitive state"—and believed that they are parallel (p. 30). Piaget also regarded "affective operation" equal to cognitive operations in the concrete operational stage (Rosen, 1977, p 26). Defining developmental lines in the process of assessing normality vs pathology, A. Freud (1965) emphasized that, in normality, the cognitive and emotional domains will develop in a parallel process. With this in mind, a Pearson correlation was performed on the relationship between emotional and cognitive scores for each grade. Results of the analysis indicated that the correlation was significant for each grade, at either $p \leq 0.01$ or $p \leq 0.05$ levels.

Table 51.2 Correlation of average cognitive and average emotional means for each grade—Pearson.

Grade	Mean Age	Mean Cognitive Score	Mean Emotional Score	Pearson r
Kindergarten	5.9000	6.4941	5.8084	0.371**
First	7.0200	7.3234	6.1921	0.635**
Second	7.8614	7.7641	6.6714	0.606**
Third	9.1646	7.9118	6.9703	0.574**
Fourth	9.9641	8.5257	7.1396	0.654**
Fifth	10.7495	8.5638	7.3593	0.370*
Sixth	11.8932	8.7302	7.5129	0.573**

*Correlation is significant at the 0.05 level.
**Correlation is significant at the 0.01 level (two-tailed).

This data (Table 51.2) suggests that new norms reflect a decline in the norm postulated and accepted in the past. It must, however, also be acknowledged that, when past norms were defined, there were no televisions or computers, more families were intact, and fewer mothers were in the work force. There is obviously a great need for more research to examine the relationship between the critical changes in our society and cognitive and emotional development in normal children.

No children included in the study gave any indication of learning or emotional problems in their classroom performance. However, of the 330 children tested, the results of the LECATA, as predicted, indicated problems in four children. A brief description of the results of two assessments might demonstrate the efficiency of the LECATA in identifying children at risk.

One child, in kindergarten, produced drawings that suggested there may be some minimal brain dysfunction. This child's teacher reported that she was beginning to suspect this type of deficit. Armed with the results of the LECATA, the teacher was more prepared to follow this child's progress. The drawings of a third-grade child were age-appropriate for all tasks. However, the figure drawings in task two and task five, while complete, were strange and suggested a medical problem. When Levick discussed the LECATA images and her analysis of the drawings with the child's teacher, she, too, revealed concerns about the child; she reported that the suspected medical "condition" might be familial, and that she saw signs of it in the classroom. As revealed by the LECATA and other art therapy assessment, it is not unusual to see manifestations of medical problems and/or physical impairment in drawings.

Summary

Since its inception in 1989, the LECATA has moved beyond the confines of the Miami-Dade County Public Schools, for which it was originally developed. The LECATA has been taught and utilized around the world. Continued implementation will not only provide rich data on the current cognitive and emotional functioning of individuals, but also a plethora of data for future studies. Further research using the LECATA is needed to examine shifts in normative data and inter-rater reliability, and to research the effectiveness of this assessment tool in other art therapy treatment programs and mental health facilities.

References

Freud, A. (1965). *Normality and Pathology in Childhood: Assessments of Development* (Vol. 6.). New York, NY: International Universities Press.

Freud, A. (1966). *Ego and mechanisms of defense* (rev. ed.). New York, NY: International Universities Press.

Freud, A. (1971). *Problems of psychoanalytic training, diagnosis, and the technique of therapy.* New York, NY: International Universities Press.

Freud, S. (1959). Inhibitions, symptoms, and anxiety. In J. Strachey (Ed. and Trans.). *The standard edition of the complete works of Sigmund Freud* (Vol. 20, pp. 77–174). London: Hogarth Press. (Original work published 1936)

Goodenough, F. L. (1926). *Measurement of intelligence by drawings.* New York, NY: World Book Co.

Halsey, B. (1977). Freud on the nature of art. *The American Journal of Art Therapy, 16,* 99–104.

Hammer, E. F. (1978). *The clinical application of projective drawings.* Springfield, IL: Charles C. Thomas.

Hardiman, C. W., & Zernich, T. (1980). Some considerations of Piaget's cognitive-structuralist theory and children's artistic development. *Studies in Art Education, 21*(3), 12–19.

Kellogg, R. (1969). *Analyzing children's art.* Palo Alto, CA: Mayfield Publishing Co.

Kellogg, R. (1970). *Analyzing children's art.* Palo Alto, CA: Mayfield Publishing Co.

Kellogg, R., with S. O'Dell. (1967). *The psychology of children's art.* New York, NY: CRM-Random House Publication.

Koppitz, E. M. (1968). *Psychological evaluation of children's human figure drawings.* New York, NY: Grone and Stratton.

Kwiatkowska, H. (1978). *Family therapy and evaluation through art.* Springfield, IL: Charles C. Thomas.

Levick, M. F. (1983). *They could not talk and so they drew.* Springfield, IL: Charles C. Thomas.

Levick, M. F. (1989). On the road to educating the creative art therapist. *The Arts in Psychotherapy, 16*(1), 57–60.

Levick, M. F. (2009) *Levick emotional and cognitive art therapy Assessment: A normative study.* Bloomington, IN: Author House.

Lowenfeld, V. (1969). The nature of creative activity. In R. Alschuler & L. W. Hattwick (Eds.), *Painting and personality* (p. 118). Chicago and London: The University of Chicago Press.

Machover, K. (1949). *Personality projection in the drawing of the human figure.* Springfield, IL: Charles C. Thomas.

Machover, K. (1953). Human figure drawings of children. *Journal of Projective Techniques, 17,* 85–91.

Machover, K. (1960). Sex differences in the developmental pattern of children as seen in human figure drawings. In A. I. Rabin & M. Haworth (Eds.), *Projective techniques with children.* New York, NY: Grune and Stratton.

Naumburg, M. (1947). *Studies of free art expression in behavior of children as a means of diagnosis and therapy.* New York, NY: Coolidge Foundation.

Rosen, H. (1977). *Pathway to Piaget.* Cherry Hill, NJ: Postgraduate International.

US Department of Commerce Economics and Statistics Administration. (1994). *Who's minding the kids?* by Lynne M. Casper, Mary Hawkins, and Martin O'Connell. Current Population Reports, P70 36. [Washington, DC]: US Department of Commerce, Economics and Statistics Administration.

52

Silver Drawing Test/The Draw-A-Story (SDT/DAS): Assessment Procedures

Cheryl Earwood and Melinda Fedorko

The art assessments presented here evolved from a belief that we tend to underestimate the intelligence of inarticulate children and adults. (Silver, 2002, p. 1)

While teaching art classes in a school for students with language and hearing impairments in the early 1960s, Rawley Silver was inspired by a student who could not respond to traditional tests of intelligence. "Charlie," age 11, quickly learned art techniques from observation. When Silver administered the *Torrance Test of Creative Thinking*, he scored in the upper ½% in Originality, the upper 3% in Fluency, and the upper 10% in Flexibility. E. Paul Torrance, who scored Charlie's responses, wrote that Charlie's score in Elaboration was "truly outstanding" and "almost unexcelled," reflecting "a high order of ability to acquire information, form relationships and in general, to think" (Silver, 2002, p. 2).

After discussing this with Charlie's school psychologist, Silver was told that Charlie's scores "change nothing, because language comes first, and there's a limit to what you can do without language" (Silver, 2002, p. 3). As a response, the Silver Drawing Test (SDT) and Draw-A-Story (DAS) were designed to assess cognitive, developmental, and emotional functioning, bypassing the spoken or written word through drawings. This ensures fairness, equity, and access to the assessment from the individual's area of strength, allowing an accurate look at the whole person's functioning.

The SDT and the DAS

The SDT measures cognitive abilities, emotional content, and the self-concept, and assesses three concepts said to be fundamental for math, reading, and everyday life: the concepts of space, sequential order, and class, or category. It connects the drawing responses of individuals to cognitive skills related to math, reading, and writing, through drawings that predict sequences and concepts of horizontality and verticality. Drawings depicting depth, left–right order, and height relate to the individual's

---

The Wiley Handbook of Art Therapy, First Edition. Edited by David E. Gussak and Marcia L. Rosal.
© 2016 John Wiley & Sons, Ltd. Published 2016 by John Wiley & Sons, Ltd.

mastery of skills necessary for reading and science. Drawings from imagination relate to the ability to select, combine and represent thoughts and ideas, abilities inherent in reading and writing skills. These concepts were based on the research of Bannatyne (1971), Rugel (1974), Piaget (1970), and Bruner, Oliver, and Greenfield (1966; Silver, 2002, p. 14), who adhered to the premise that art can be a language parallel to the spoken or written word. The SDT includes three subtests.

In the *predictive drawing* subtest, the respondent is asked to predict changes in the appearance of objects by adding lines to outlined drawings. The ability to recognize that an object remains the same in spite of changes in appearance is part of logical thinking. The ability to conserve, or to place objects in systematic order, usually develops after the age of 7 years. The concepts inherent in this ability to predict correlate strongly to mathematics.

The *drawing from observation* subtest measures mastery of the concepts of straight lines, parallels, and angles. These include horizontal relationships, (left/right), vertical relationships (above/below), and relationships in depth. In this task, four simple objects are arranged in a predetermined way on a sheet of paper below eye level. The surface of the paper is viewed as a flat plane rather than a line. Subjects are asked to draw the arrangement as they see it.

The *drawing from imagination* subtest is more directly related to writing and reading comprehension. In this task, the respondent is asked to select stimulus drawings, imagine something happening between the figures, and then draw what is imagined. When the drawing is finished, a title or a story is added. This task is scored for the "ability to select." This is a measure of the respondent's ability for conceptual grouping based on abstract, invisible attributes, such as concepts of class inclusion. The "ability to combine" is a measure of the mastery of spatial relationships based on proximity. The "ability to represent" measures originality, independence, and the ability to manipulate ideas (Torrance, 1980).

The *drawing from imagination* subtest includes creativity and a non-verbal measure of intelligence. The emotional content component of this task reflects feelings and conflicts, as well as inner resources such as resilience and humor.

The rating scale ranges from 5 to 1; those who choose powerful and effective subjects score a maximum score of 5 points, and those who identify with subjects they portray as sad, isolated, or in mortal danger receive a minimum score of 1 point. Because the emotional projection scale does not distinguish between self-images and fantasies about others, which may conflict, a self-image scale is also included in the assessment.

The DAS, developed as an attempt to screen for depression, assesses the level of emotional functioning and self-concept through metaphors. It is based on the premise that children who draw morbid pictures, unpleasant fantasies, and stories of sadness may need further evaluation. Silver used the DAS as a follow-up to students whom she felt were depressed. The DAS was validated and administered to 1,028 people throughout the United States (Silver, 2005, p. 23). It was found to be an excellent indicator for aggression and depression, to identify children at risk.

The DAS findings provide incentives for further research with a variety of populations. The populations included in Silver's research include children, adolescents, younger adults, and senior adults, as well as subjects from Australia, Brazil, China, Russia, and Thailand (Silver, 2010).

In *Identifying Risks for Aggression and Depression Through Metaphors: The Mouse, the Bride, and the Use of Humor* (2010), Silver analyzed the themes and implications for treatment behind her most commonly used stimulus drawings. The book examines self-esteem, emotional content, and humor through the use of metaphors. Metaphoric dialogues also provide opportunities to introduce healthier adaptations or alternate solutions, rather than predatory or reactive aggression. Predatory aggression is when a person initiates aggression without provocation; reactive aggression is a response to an aggressive act upon him or her. The results of a study conducted in 2005 indicated that aggressive children and adolescents have distinctive characteristics that can be quantified and scored to identify those who are at risk.

In the same book, Silver documented an in-depth exploration of the use of humor. A succinct review of her findings and observations concludes with the discovery that:

> "the examples of responses by children, adolescents and adults, and the studies reviewed seem to indicate that responses tend to be metaphors that can identify respondents who may be at risk for depression and/or aggressive behavior." (Silver, 2010, p. 78)

This book updated SDT and DAS, and included outcome studies which found that those who took part in art therapy programs scored higher, more positive scores in emotional content and self-image on post-tests. Silver concluded the text by raising questions on the difference between violent fantasies and violent behaviors, and of how the drawing of these fantasies might prevent and predict the occurrence of violent behavior.

The following case studies are examples of the preventative nature of art therapy and use of the DAS in clarifying students' levels of emotional functioning and self-concept, leading to the formulation of specific treatment goals.

Nicky

Nicky was a 9-years-4-month-old boy in the second grade when he entered the art therapy program. He was held back a grade due to excessive absence. His developmental milestones were delayed, and he had hearing loss in his left ear. His previous school in another county had placed him in classes for emotional and intellectual disability. Nicky was the oldest of four children. He and his younger brother were living with his maternal aunt, uncle, and cousins. A younger sister was living with another relative. The children had just been removed from the custody of their mother, who had a history of alcohol abuse, suicide attempt, and incarceration. The children had been neglected, and, at age 8, Nicky was the caretaker of the family. A 10-month-old brother drowned accidentally while Nicky was watching him; his mother held him responsible. Nicky was asked to complete the SDT and the DAS (see figures 52.1a-e).

In the *predictive drawing* subtest of the SDT (figure 52.1a), Nicky scored an 8, which is close to the norm for a third grader. In *predicting a sequence*, he scored a 5, the highest score possible, as the drawing had evenly spaced increments and no corrections. In *predicting horizontality*, he scored 2 points, because the line almost parallels the tilted bottle. His house on the hill is perpendicular to the slope, which scored 1 point.

In *drawing from observation* (figure 52.1b), Nicky scored 13 out of a possible 15 points, several points above the norm for his age, because he was able to place the

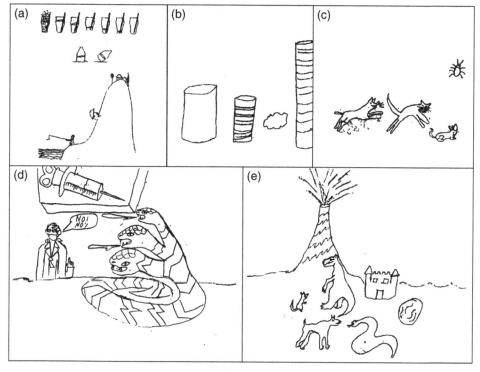

Figure 52.1   Nicky's SDT and DAS.

objects in left–right order, and all four objects were the correct height. The paper towel roll was too far forward, which scored a 3.

In *drawing from imagination*, he scored 12 of the maximum 15 points; in the *ability to select, combine, and represent*, he scored several points above the norm for his age. He copied the stimulus drawings and drew "The dog chasing the cat, a cat chasing the mouse. The mouse can't get the bug because it climbed up" (figure 52.1c). Therefore, in two of the three cognitive tests, he scored above the norm. The dog, cat, and mouse were smiling, so it is unclear if they were being playful or assaultive. His emotional score and self-image score were both 3 points. The cognitive score indicates that Nicky was intellectually functioning in the average–above-average range for his age, and was not disabled. His *drawing from imagination* was ambiguous, and therefore did not affect the planning of treatment goals.

He was artistic and enjoyed attending art therapy sessions, often drawing super-heroes in class and in therapy. His early work in art therapy was guarded and revealed little about him. However, at the time of his yearly reassessment, he was told that his mother was not complying with treatment, and that his two younger surviving siblings were moving 250 miles away. Nick appeared sad, but would not discuss it. When he was 10, he completed the DAS assessment. He drew a picture of a three-headed snake with fangs, of which, he indicated, two of the snake heads had venom (figure 52.1d). He also drew a large syringe and a man with a surgical mask saying, "No! No!" The drawing's accompanying story was: "A three-headed snake going on a doctor's appointment to take away the two heads. The snake is in pain by the two extra heads.

The two extra heads attack and the doctor says, 'No! No!'" When asked what will happen next, he wrote, "The shot will calm the snake down, then the Doctor will take the two heads off. The sleeping head won't feel a thing." This story possibly revealed Nicky's denial and devastation at losing his brother and sister through the move. His score in emotional content was 2, a moderately negative score, and his self-image score was 3.5, an ambiguous outcome.

From this point in treatment, Nick's behavior regressed. He was irritable, boastful, and impatient with his peers. However, he was able to use art therapy to express his frustration, and to build self-esteem. Nick began to learn that he was only a young boy and was not responsible for keeping his family together, nor was the death of his brother his fault. At the end of 2½ years, he exhibited more control over his feelings.

In his final DAS, which he completed at the end of the school year, he chose and drew a volcano erupting, a castle, four animals, and a large rock (figure 52.1e). His story was: "A volcano is erupting. The castle did not know. All the animals gathered on top of the rock so they could save the castle and themselves." Symbolically, it seemed that Nick did not trust that the castle, which may have represented his mother, will know when there is mortal danger. This earned 1 point for *emotional content*. However, the drawing may also indicate that, while Nick still had concerns about going home, he demonstrated an improvement by having all the animals, which may have represented his siblings, gather together to save themselves. Consequently, Nick was no longer the caretaker, which earned him a self-image score of 5 points. While Nick and his family had more healing to do, they were reunited.

Clifford

Upon entering the primary (K-3) classroom to meet and evaluate a new student, several of the children called out "He doesn't speak!" Thus began my work with Clifford, a 9-year-old third grader, who is selectively mute and is repeating second grade. Clifford spoke very little at home; when he did, it was only in Spanish to his mother, father, and younger brother. His parents were divorced, and his father had a girlfriend with three children. He did not speak to them. Parents reported that he had tubes in his ears at 9 months of age. They felt that an emotional trauma occurred at age 3—when his brother was born, when his grandfather died, and there were two hurricanes—indicating, "Weather terrifies him." At the time of the interview, there was evident animosity between the parents in the way they spoke and behaved.

Clifford did not make eye contact, but hesitantly walked to the art therapy room where the SDT would be administered. Clifford walked on his tiptoes, moving awkwardly and slowly. He seemed anxious, but relaxed when it was explained to him what an art therapist does and that he did not need to speak. He was compliant during the assessment procedure, pantomiming or writing down questions if there was a directive he did not understand. He needed to be asked if he was finished at the end of each subtest. He scored 7 points on the *predictive drawing* test, below the norm for his age. Despite his ability to make recognizable shapes for the *drawing from observation* portion, his score of 4 was well below the norm, as his placement, height, and depth of the four objects were incorrect. Both of these scores indicate that Clifford's cognitive functioning is below the norm.

Some of the more emotionally evocative stimulus drawings were used with Cliff. When it came to the *drawing from imagination* test, he scored a 14 out of a possible 15 points for the abilities to select, combine, and represent, above the norm for his age. He chose to use a dragon and a volcano to tell his story. In emotional content, his score was 1, because the dragon in his drawing was in mortal danger from the erupting volcano. In self-image, he scored a 5 as he was able to achieve his goal and protect himself.

There is a faintly drawn volcano in the background of the picture, a wall in the middle ground, and a dragon and some trees in the foreground. The dragon is drawn in a darker shade, with more attention to detail. Also, he drew the dragon first. During the post-interview, it appeared that he saw himself as the dragon. His story was, "One day there was a dragon and the volcano erupted. Then the volcano stopped. Then there was lava and the dragon builds a wall and the lava couldn't get through." Metaphorically, the volcano and lava could reflect events in his life that Cliff saw as "dangerous," such as his grandparent's death, birth of his brother, or the divorce of his parents. The wall could represent a wall of silence that he built for himself, so he would not have to address his feelings or explain what was bothering him. He included the wall as an attempt to cope with the problem.

All the students in his class had accepted Clifford's mutism, as did his teachers. He worked well in class, but would infrequently exhibit some frustration when he could not communicate his point. At other times, when his teacher gave him an opportunity to choose a reward he earned, Clifford did not make eye contact and did not choose, subsequently losing the reward.

The therapy sessions focused on several themes to encourage trust building: puppet making, a photograph album of family members, and a book about himself. The book was very revealing, as it was about a robot that would not talk and consequently had no friends to play with. With encouragement, he created a "fairy" who served as his helper. The robot was drawn relatively; after he drew the fairy, he indicated that the robot was able to speak, indicating that he wanted "to turn back" to his regular size: "Then the fairy turned him big again and then the robot 'talk,talk,talk,talk,talk,talk!'—the end!" Although Clifford never made progress in speaking, he was eager to attend art therapy; his artwork became more animated, and he smiled more frequently.

For his post-assessment, he drew a large superhero that turns into a dinosaur. The superhero appeared aggressive, but the angry dinosaur, with small arms and legs, did not appear stronger than the superhero. Therefore, Clifford's emotional score went from 1 to 5 points as he, represented by the superhero, was no longer in mortal danger. His overall score was 15 points, with a score of 3 for both emotional and self-image. Despite the progress, it was believed that, until he reconciled his anger and anxiety, it would have been difficult for him to trust himself enough to speak.

Joey

Joey was a small, verbally aggressive sixth grader in a public middle school who was identified as having a conduct disorder. He was in a self-contained program for children with externalized emotional/behavioral disabilities. He lived with his mother and four sisters in an urban neighborhood, with extended family nearby. Several of his family members had suffered from mental illnesses or had been incarcerated. His presenting problems included inability to stay in his seat or in the classroom, refusal to follow adult directives, and verbal aggression toward peers and teachers. His teachers, however, repeatedly described him as "having a good heart" and caring about the welfare of others.

In Joey's first response to the DAS task, he drew a mouse with a knife going through its body, and added a man who appeared to be startled. He described the drawing as "a mouse that had stabbed itself and the guy saw it and started screaming." When asked what might happen next, he quietly drew a mouse surrounded by blood and covered with drops, indicating, "He dies." Joey was exceptionally small for his age and frequently acted out with the apparent purpose of shocking others; therefore, it appeared that he identified with the mouse in his drawing. The configuration of a strongly negative emotional score with a strongly negative self-concept with lethal fantasy is considered a red flag, suggesting depression and possible thoughts of suicide.

As the school year progressed, Joey became invested in the art therapy process, using his sessions to express his frustrations, to problem-solve, and to increase his feelings of self-worth as he experienced success with the art. However, his behavior remained unstable and defiant, resulting in his suspension from school several times. The concerns about possible depression were communicated to his mother, but she was reluctant to consider medication, since he had experienced a negative reaction with ADHD medication in the past. His response in the follow-up assessment procedure at the end of his first year fell into another high-risk category, with a strongly negative emotional content paired with a powerful self-concept. The combination of scores indicated risk for aggression, with an emotional content score of 1 and a self-concept score of 5. He subsequently was suspended for the last 2 weeks of school for fighting.

During the summer, with his mother's capitulation, Joey was placed on medication. He entered the seventh grade with improved behavior, but he began to deteriorate within the first 2 weeks when he found himself in a classroom with aggressive students. Eventually, relying on the results of the assessments conducted during the previous year, he was moved to a classroom of students with more internalized emotional disabilities, which had more structure and less aggression; his behavior improved.

In response to the subsequent DAS task, he drew a mouse watching two people on TV, with a door in the right foreground of the picture. When the mouse was done watching TV, it "leaves and goes home." His response indicated a higher, more positive score, earning a 3.5 in emotional content for ambivalent emotional content, suggesting pleasant outcome, and a 3.5 in self-image for an ambivalent, somewhat positive response.

In a more recent DAS, completed at the end of his second year of middle school, when his mother was no longer regularly giving him medication, he drew a "dog barking at a cat." When asked what might happen next, he replied that the cat ran away. Consequently, he earned 2 points in emotional content, for it being moderately negative. He earned 3 points in self-mage as it was considered ambiguous, with the cat escaping from a threat. While Joey was still involved in fights, he would do so in front of an administrator's office or security guards, which ensured a quick intervention, suggesting that he was seeking the safety of adult assistance and attention rather than impulsively placing himself in danger of physical harm. He was able to stay in the classroom most of the time and was more respectful toward his teachers. At the end of his seventh grade school year, he was able to identify "learning to handle it when people try me" as the most important goal that he wanted to achieve in his next school year.

It is not uncommon for scores to fluctuate over time with the student's developmental tasks, medication changes, and/or life events. Although Joey's final score in self-concept was lower than the previous one, the configuration of scores is not in a high-risk category, and is thus suggestive that both his emotional content and self-concept scores were more within a normal range for his age, with less risk for depression or aggression than earlier scores indicated.

Conclusion

The SDT and DAS assessments provide us with valuable information about the effectiveness of the art therapy intervention. In the case studies provided in this chapter, most scores increased to levels that were more positive after participation.

The assessments inform the trajectory of treatment of the students, and ultimately the goal is to increase the scores in the emotional and self-concept areas. They also seek to ascertain the students' improvement in the ability to select, combine, represent, and draw horizontal and depth relationships, reflecting an improvement in reading, writing, and math. In turn, the art therapist may meet with math and language arts teachers to discuss the assessment findings and how they relate to students' individualized education plans (IEPs) and contribute to goals, benchmarks, and directives for art therapy treatment that may also relate to their academics.

References

Banatyne, A. D. (1971). *Language, reading and learning disabilities.* Springfield, IL: Charles C. Thomas.

Bruner, J. S., Oliver, R. R., & Greenfield, P. M. (1966). *Studies in cognitive growth.* Oxford, UK: Wiley.

Piaget, J. (1970). *General epistemology.* New York, NY: Columbia University Press.

Rugel, R. P. (1974). WISC subtests scores of disabled readers: A review with respect to Bannatyne's recategorization. *Journal of Learning Disabilities, 7*(1), 48–55.

Silver, R. A. (2002). *Three art assessments: The Silver drawing test of cognition and emotion, draw a story, screening for depression, and stimulus drawings and techniques.* New York, NY: Brunner-Routledge.

Silver, R. A. (2005). *Aggression and depression assessed through art; Using Draw-A-Story to identify children and adolescents at risk.* New York, NY: Brunner Routledge.

Silver, R. A. (2010). *Identifying risks for aggression and depression through metaphors: The mouse, the bride, and the use of humor.* Dewitt, NY: Purple Finch Press.

Torrance, E. P. (1980). Creative intelligence and an agenda for the 80s. *Art Education, 33*(7), 8–14.

53

The Diagnostic Drawing Series (DDS) at Thirty: Art Therapy Assessment and Research

Barry M. Cohen and Anne Mills

Developed by art therapists in 1982, the Diagnostic Drawing Series (DDS) is a standardized three-picture art interview for use with adolescents and adults. By 2012, more than 60 DDS studies had been completed by students at the masters and doctoral levels. This included 48 studies from norm groups sharing a psychiatric diagnosis or another commonality, or that replicated earlier normative research.[1] Fifteen DDS studies had been published in peer-reviewed journals, and several studies had been published as book chapters. By 2012, the DDS Archive contained about 4,000 drawings by adults and adolescents from around the world. We are not aware of any other repository of art that was collected in such a standardized way, which is comparable in size, or any art therapy assessment that has been studied to a similar extent. According to Fowler and Ardon (2002), the DDS may be the most researched assessment in the field, while Mills (2003) indicated that it is the most widely taught.

The DDS did not grow out of any particular theoretical model or theme. It offers a relatively neutral structure that a clinician can use for psychological assessment, diagnostic clarification, or treatment planning. Administered on a tabletop, each of the three pictures in the series has its own piece of paper and specific directive. It is designed to be completed in a 50-minute session with people 13 years and older; most finish in 20 minutes. This allows time to discuss the pictures with the artist/subject afterward.

Materials and Tasks

The DDS is created with a 12-color pack of square, soft chalk pastels (Alphacolor or Blick brands in North America; Faber-Castell or Jaxell elsewhere). A single box is used for many administrations. DDSs are drawn on 18" × 24" (45 × 60 cm outside the United States), 60–70 lb. white drawing paper that has a tooth or slightly "fuzzy" surface. At the time of this writing, the per-administration cost of materials is about US$1.

The Wiley Handbook of Art Therapy, First Edition. Edited by David E. Gussak and Marcia L. Rosal.
© 2016 John Wiley & Sons, Ltd. Published 2016 by John Wiley & Sons, Ltd.

Chalk pastels were chosen for their versatility. Precisely made drawings, regardless of artistic skill, reflect the capacity to control. Excessive chalk dust, smears, and fingerprints on a drawing reveal a client who is unable or unwilling to control the medium. Additionally, chalk pastels are congruent with art therapy treatment for adults, can be found in most art therapy studios, and are not associated with child- or school-quality materials. The large-size and good-quality white drawing paper replicates the artist's confrontation with the blank canvas. Those without formal art training find that working on a tabletop, as directed by *The Diagnostic Drawing Series handbook* (Cohen, 1985), is more comfortable than working on an easel. Tabletops are the typical working space at home, on the job, and for most inpatient art therapy sessions.

One of the essential strengths of the DDS is its standardization, not just in materials, but in tasks and administration as well. Every DDS is completed in the following order, with the specified materials, and with the directions unchanged: "Make a picture using these materials" (Figure 53.1) is the directive for the first picture. This is the unstructured task of the series, and is often referred to as the *free picture*. This drawing typically results in a manifestation of the client's defenses. The free picture reflects what a maker consciously or unconsciously wants known, depending on him or her defensive or emotional style, skill, intelligence, and psychopathology. These drawings range from concrete to abstract, from vague or impoverished to direct and boldly expressive.

Figure 53.1 Free picture by a 33-year-old man diagnosed with schizoaffective disorder. Source: Mucci (2011). Photo: Mucci.

The directive for the second picture (Figure 53.2) is "Draw a picture of a tree." In the literature of projective drawing tests, tree drawings have been thought to provide the deepest tapping of the psyche (Bolander, 1977; Koch, 1952). With the inclusion of the tree, the DDS incorporates a traditional projective drawing task that connects it to decades of earlier drawing assessments and research (Buck, 1948; Hammer, 1980). Viewed as a symbolic self-portrait, Jung (1967) likened a tree drawing to "the self depicted as a process of growth." The basic tree gestalt is familiar to most people from childhood, and is considered easy to draw.

This task, immediately following the open-ended first picture, allows for a relaxing of defenses. It facilitates an outpouring of psychopathological indicators that previously might have been withheld by the client. In the trunk, branches, crown, and leaves, symbolic manifestations of the artist's sense of ego or body integrity may emerge, or disconnections that could be graphic indicators of a trauma history. Even if a client draws a tree in the first picture, the second (tree) picture must still be administered. When a tree has been drawn in the first picture, the differences between the two drawings are often substantive.

Figure 53.2 Tree picture by a 40-year-old woman diagnosed with dissociative identity disorder. Source: Heijtmajer and Cohen (1993). Photo: Heijtmajer.

Figure 53.3 Feeling picture by a 31-year-old woman diagnosed with schizophrenia. Source: Louisiana. Photo: D'Alessandro.

The third picture (Figure 53.3) is referred to as the *feeling picture* because its directive is to "Make a picture of how you're feeling, using lines, shapes, and colors." The words ask the clients to identify and express their moods, while at the same time specifically prompting them to think about how they will do so. Thus, the directive invites both emotion and cognition to be utilized, which may decrease spontaneity. This may be heard as a request for an abstract picture—which it is—but some subjects will not comprehend that. Others will readily grasp that all drawings are made up of lines, shapes, and colors. In response to the feeling picture directions, clients make images ranging from abstract to representational, from stereotypic to idiosyncratically personal.

Although an uncommon response for most diagnostic groups, a client's refusal or inability to complete any single picture in the series is valuable data as part of that person's assessment. When that does occur, the blank page is always kept in its appropriate place, as an integral part of that client's series.[2]

Art therapists are cautioned that assessments or diagnoses should be based on more than a single sign or drawing. Taken as a whole, the varied task structure of the DDS elicits valuable cognitive, symbolic, affective, content-based, structural, and process information that can inform the clinician as to the strengths and psychopathology of the subject. Thus, the DDS facilitates a rich resource for treatment planning.

Assessment and Research

From the inception of the DDS assessment, samples were collected, archived, and studied in a multicenter research project that is still active after three decades and continues to grow in its scope and reach. Over the years, this has caused some to think of the DDS as a research tool more than as a clinical tool. It is both.

Prior to the start of the DDS research project, not more than one aspect of conventional social sciences research appeared in art therapy research designs. DDS research design employs 11 such criteria (American Educational Research Association, 1999). They include: standardization of art materials and directives; standardization of instructions for administration and collection; two independent agreeing diagnosticians; objective criteria for rating; blind rating; use of a control group; and centrally coordinated collection. In 1983, the AATA granted a research award to the DDS for its collaborative multicenter design.

Arnheim's theory of isomorphism (1974) could be considered a foundational principle of the expressive therapies. It suggests that a relationship exists between emotive mental states, perception, and behaviors, including art-making. Accordingly, a single DDS will reflect the psyche of its maker. Successive DDSs by one subject will show the variability of content, while the structural level does not change appreciably (personal communication, A. Mills and K. Johnson, November 19, 2011), and DDSs by a group of subjects diagnosed with the same psychiatric disorder will share a cluster of structural elements, as reflected by their graphic profiles. This is seen clinically and in DDS research. Therefore, the DDS seems to measure trait (in structure) and state (in content), and provide conditions under which the principle of isomorphism holds true.

Perhaps the most significant misperception about DDS research is that the art therapist administering it is responsible for making the diagnosis. In fact, DDSs in the archive are collected along with the participants' DSM diagnoses—or occupation, for a control subject—as established by two agreeing diagnoses, usually by psychiatrists, and demographic information.

A partial list of normative studies, a number of which have been replicated, includes: non-hospitalized adolescents, adults, and seniors; major depressive disorder in children, adolescents, and adults; post-traumatic stress disorder in adults and adolescents; dysthymic disorder; bipolar disorder (manic phase); schizophrenia; schizoaffective disorder; dementia; eating disorders; borderline personality disorder; and dissociative identity disorder.

The DDS has also been used for outcome studies, studies on color use, and collected from groups that do not have a psychiatric diagnosis (e.g., atomic bomb survivors, former terrorists). Six studies with children have been done, and two versions of the DDS have been created for use with children (Neale, 1994; Sobol & Cox, 1991/2004).[3] Those using the DDS are asked to submit samples to the archive and are invited to do research and apply for the annual DDS Research Award.[4]

Tests of Validity and Reliability

In general, some rating systems for projective drawing tests developed by psychologists have not always been found reliable and valid (Kaplan, 2003). The DDS rating system, on the other hand, is considered both reliable and valid for its current purposes (Mills, Cohen, & Meneses, 1993). Evidence continues to accrue as trained raters demonstrate strong inter-rater reliability in each new study, such as the results achieved by Johnson (2004; $\alpha = 0.74–1.0$ in intra-class correlations). *The Diagnostic Drawing Series rating guide* is the most tested and appropriate tool to use with DDS drawings, but it can also be used experimentally with other clinical art. In regards to reliability and validity, the scope of the DDS is defined as distinguishing between mental health and illness in adults, using DSM diagnoses; contributing to a diagnostic process; and supporting or confirming a diagnosis.

Although the DDS was originally created for use by art therapists, any mental health professional can administer a DDS. To go further, however, requires knowing how to use *The Diagnostic Drawing Series rating guide* (Cohen, 1986/1994/2012) and learning to identify the graphic profiles that derive from research studies.

Creating a Reliable Rating System

Prior to the introduction of the DDS rating system, there was no common language for describing therapeutic artwork, and the generally accepted approach to the image was content-based and theory-driven. To create one, the first author and his colleagues had to identify the primary qualities and elements that might occur in an infinite array of unique drawings, and name and define them, which resulted in the development of *The Diagnostic Drawing Series rating guide* (1986) and Drawing Analysis Form (DAF; 1985). In them, 23 characteristics—related primarily to the structure or formal components of a drawing—were identified that could describe an unpredictable variety of potential graphic responses. Most were designated with a simple yes/no; the characteristics were either there, or not. This structural approach introduced a finite number of specific terms to describe art that were simple and clearly defined.

In 1994, diagrams were added to the rating guide, and, in 2012, some criteria and wording were added or changed. This was done for clarity, and to reflect the advances in our understanding about which data were most useful clinically and in research.

Because the rating guide got updated, so did the DAF (now known as the DAF II; Cohen, 2012). It is expected that there will be little to no change between ratings made with these two versions of the DAF (Mills, 2012). Cohen also devised the *tri-level model*, a holistic approach to analyzing a DDS or other clinical art. Cohen's tri-level model looks at DDS using an anatomical metaphor: skeleton, muscle, skin. The *skeleton level* refers to the structural elements of the pictures, especially those items on the DAF. These are the qualities of a picture that are *looked at* and consciously noted as present. The *muscle level* consists of the latent content (including metaphors and symbols) that emerges from narrative, art historical and cultural contexts. These are the qualities that clinicians *looked for* in light of their personal associations, theoretical orientation, and professional experience. The *skin level* is the manifest content, the process of making the picture, including the artist's physical behavior, verbalizations, associations, and the title given to the picture. Using the tri-level model, the clinician integrates the DDS findings; the symbolic, metaphoric, and other approaches to the image she favors; and her observations of the client's behavior. This leads to a "three-dimensional" clinical understanding of the client's strengths and treatment issues.

International/Multicultural Studies

The basic DDS directions have been translated into Arabic, Dutch, French, German, Japanese, Latvian, and Spanish. The DDS has been used clinically worldwide since the 1980s. Overseas research studies have been conducted primarily in Japan, Canada, and the Netherlands. DDS results have been replicated (Heijtmajer & Cohen, 1993) and meaningfully compared to local samples (Yamashita, 1989).

Ichiki, Naito, and Kanai (2005) examined whether, owing to socio-cultural traditions, the large size of DDS drawing paper might cause Japanese subjects to regress or become anxious. They found that there was no statistically significant difference in the formal elements of DDSs administered on "original size" paper (45 × 60 cm) as compared to the paper typically used by Japanese art therapists (27 × 38 cm). Ichiki (2009) reported that using different media (i.e., the DDS's chalk pastels versus pencils) evoked different subjective reactions from Japanese subjects.

In Latvia, Dakse (2013) examined the DDSs of adults diagnosed with depression, and concluded that the results corresponded to previous DDS findings. Also in Latvia, Dzene (2013) confirmed that DDSs by people diagnosed with schizophrenia differed on a structural level from DDSs of a control or "well" group.

The first major article about the DDS was published in the Dutch magazine *Psychologie* in 1986. Several DDS study groups were subsequently established in the Netherlands. In the early 2000s, a Dutch DDS Archive and website were established. The DDS is taught at both the undergraduate and graduate levels to Dutch art therapists, and there are many studies conducted by students who use the DDS with various populations (e.g., autism, refugees, learning disorders). In 2008, official Dutch governmental directives for providing art therapy treatment to adults with depression and borderline personality disorder were published, both of which specified the use of the DDS because of its extensive research base (Landelijke Stuurgroep Multidisciplinaire Richtlijnontwikkeling in de GGZ, 2008; Nederlandse Vereniging voor Psychiatrie et al., 2009).

Benefits of Using the DDS

The terminology of *The Diagnostic Drawing Series rating guide* is a common language that can be used by any art therapist to describe clinical art work. This, together with the standardized art interview, provides continuity with all other DDS research, so that each study can contribute to a central core of knowledge.

The DDS project has explored how "normal" adults draw (Cohen, Hammer, & Singer, 1988; Mills & Cohen, 2001). In addition, graphic profiles of a dozen diagnostic groups show the likelihood of belonging to a particular group or groups.

There are many of advantages to using the DDS when the situation calls for an assessment or drawing stimulus. In addition to being a multi-picture art-based interview tool that features standardized artist-quality materials and administration, the DDS features varied task structures, including a familiar theme and art-therapy-style activity, which can be done in a simple, single session. It has been found to be a reliable and valid instrument and is supported by multicenter systematic research. There is an available tested rating system, established norms for controls, and numerous psychiatric diagnostic groups. It offers users a centralized clearing house for information, training, research, and publication support, as well as international networking. The cost of administration is extremely low, compared with the normed tests associated with commercial publishers.

For art therapists working within multidisciplinary treatment teams, the DDS can serve as an aid in educating staff in case conferences, in-service presentations, and treatment-planning meetings. Familiarizing colleagues with its standardized format and basic research findings allows non–art therapists to recognize the patterns and variations among DDSs of clients of different diagnostic groups. Clinicians who regularly use the DDS indicate that they notice increased interest in, respect for, and sophistication about art therapy services among their co-workers. Having data from decades of DDS research available to substantiate clinical or diagnostic observations enhances an art therapist's value as a member of the treatment team.

Each of the three DDS tasks taps a different capacity: cognitive, symbolic, and affective. This helps the art therapist to assess the client's issues, defenses, and strengths. While created for individual use, the DDS can also be used in group art therapy sessions. It can be administered repeatedly over the course of treatment (Cohen, Mills, & Kijak, 1994). The drawings can be approached clinically in any manner, including an imaginative dialogue that amplifies, rather than reduces, the meaning of the images for the patient. Thus, the DDS is well placed for use in both inpatient and outpatient treatment.

Training

Art therapy students can administer DDSs and work with the pictures and the patients' process in a clinical setting. However, there are no "cookbooks" for the DDS, and students need thorough DDS training to begin to get the most from the tool. It takes knowledge of the DDS research to use it fully, and familiarity with the tool across time to use it most effectively. Unfortunately, complete training in the DDS and its associated research is usually beyond the scope of what students learn in school.

In 2-day trainings, the clinical applications of the tool and its most up-to-date research are presented. Attendees learn to become consciously aware of one's very quick but not necessarily accurate judgments of art (i.e., intuition), and to balance that with the slow "close noticing" that is fostered by learning how to rate a DDS. Such training is considered essential for responsible practice—a relatively small investment of time in exchange for essential professional knowledge and skills that can protect and enhance one's career.

The Challenges Ahead

A challenge to the proper consolidation and progress of this longstanding work are the students and others who attempt to launch novel assessments. Typically, these tasks employ a thematic metaphor embedded within a directive in order to "covertly" evaluate something of interest to the investigator. As the profession's theories and clinicians' areas of interest change, more assessments will be proposed. This dissipates investigative energy while failing to contribute to ethically sound and responsible assessment of patients. We understand that researchers need to follow questions of personal interest, and they should be encouraged to consider how they can do so creatively while using the DDS and drawing upon the DDS Archive.

This chapter is written at a time when a broken health insurance system continues to compromise mental health treatment in the United States. Often, inpatient admissions require one or more diagnoses be given from a handful of "reimbursable" diagnoses, so that the patient's hospital stay is covered by insurance. These diagnoses are made without regard for clinical accuracy or the natural history of mental illness. Accurate diagnoses can change the lives of people in psychiatric treatment, and save countless healthcare dollars. Familiarity with the DDS can help art therapists be respected voices in understanding the patient and planning his or her treatment.

After 20 years as director of the DDS Network, Cohen wrote:

> Little did I realize back in the early eighties that the creation of a valid art-based assessment, especially if it is correlated with psychiatric diagnostic nomenclature, is ultimately a lifetime's work. And it is not just one person's lifetime work. Like other things of importance in this world, it definitely takes a communal effort. (in Brooke, 2004, p. viii)

In this communal effort, some art therapists collect DDSs for donation to the archive, some start study groups or provide supervision, some perform research, and some teach the results. A relatively small group is putting forth a lot of effort on behalf of the field of art therapy as a whole, from which all benefit.

This three-picture art interview can be administered for assessment and effective treatment with clients from any country or culture. For all these reasons, art therapists around the world are strongly encouraged to continue to collect DDSs and to contribute to the substantial body of collaborative DDS studies undertaken over the past three decades. Art therapists trained in the use of the DDS can contribute competently and responsibly to the art and science of planning psychotherapy.

Endnotes

1   A lengthy list of citations is beyond the space limitations of this chapter. Please see the DDS Resource List, compiled by Mills, for references: http://www.diagnosticdrawingseries. com/resource.html.

2   Complete instructions for administering the DDS are described in *The Diagnostic Drawing Series handbook* (Cohen, 1985), which is included in the DDS ePacket, available for purchase via the DDS website www.diagnosticdrawingseries.com.

3   For a complete list of DDS studies and citations, please refer to the resource list at www. diagnosticdrawingseries.com.

4   Those who want to apply for the annual DDS Research Award should contact the first author at landmarc@cox.net; the deadline for submission is October 15 each year.

References

American Educational Research Association. (1999). *Standards for educational and psychological testing*. Washington, DC: AERA.

Arnheim, R. (1974). *Art and visual perception*. Berkeley, CA: University of California Press (original work published 1954),

Bolander, K. (1977). *Assessing personality through tree drawings*. New York, NY: Basic Books.

Buck, J. N. (1948). The H-T-P test. *Journal of Clinical Psychology, 4*, 151–159.

Cohen, B. M. (1985/2012). *Drawing analysis form.* (All documents available from Barry M. Cohen via landmarc@cox.net (preferred), or PO Box 9853, Alexandria, Virginia, USA 22304.)

Cohen, B. M. (Ed.). (1985). *The Diagnostic Drawing Series handbook.* (All documents available from Barry M. Cohen via landmarc@cox.net (preferred), or PO Box 9853, Alexandria, Virginia, USA 22304.)

Cohen, B. M. (Ed.). (1986). *The Diagnostic Drawing Series rating guide.* (All documents available from Barry M. Cohen via landmarc@cox.net (preferred), or PO Box 9853, Alexandria, Virginia, USA 22304.)

Cohen, B. M. (1986/1994/2012). *The Diagnostic Drawing Series rating guide.* (All documents available from Barry M. Cohen via landmarc@cox.net (preferred), or PO Box 9853, Alexandria, Virginia, USA 22304.)

Cohen, B. M. (Ed.). (1994). *The Diagnostic Drawing Series revised rating guide.* (All documents available from Barry M. Cohen via landmarc@cox.net (preferred), or PO Box 9853, Alexandria, Virginia, USA 22304.)

Cohen, B. M. (2012). *Drawing analysis form II.* (All documents available from Barry M. Cohen via landmarc@cox.net (preferred), or PO Box 9853, Alexandria, Virginia, USA 22304.)

Cohen, B. M. (2004) in S. Brooke, *A therapist's guide to art therapy assessments: Tools of the trade* (2nd ed.). Springfield, IL: Charles C. Thomas.

Cohen, B. M., Hammer, J. S., & Singer, S. (1988). The Diagnostic Drawing Series: A systematic approach to art therapy evaluation and research. *The Arts in Psychotherapy, 15*(1), 11–21.

Cohen, B. M., Mills, A., & Kijak, A. K. (1994). An introduction to the Diagnostic Drawing Series: A standardized tool for diagnostic and clinical use. *Art Therapy, 11*(2), 105–110.

Dakse, E. (2013). *The Diagnostic Drawing Series adaptation in Latvia and its application in art therapy according to BDA-II criteria for adult Major Depression.* [Latvian]. Prepared for Rigas Stradina Universitaté, Riga, Latvia.

Dzene, D. (2013). *Diagnostic Drawing Series (DDS) test adaptation in Latvia and its specific characteristic marks in the structure of drawings of schizophrenia patients* [Latvian]. Prepared for Rigas Stradina Universitaté, Riga, Latvia.

Fowler, J. P., & Ardon, A. M. (2002). The Diagnostic Drawing Series and dissociative disorders: A Dutch study. *The Arts in Psychotherapy, 29*(4), 221–230.

Hammer, E. F. (1980). *Clinical application of projective drawings.* Springfield, IL: Charles C. Thomas, Ltd.

Heijtmajer, O. A., & Cohen, B. M. (Speakers). (1993). MPD and the DDS: A Dutch replication study. In B. G. Braun (Ed.), *Proceedings of the 10th International Conference on Multiple Personality/ Dissociative States.* Chicago: Rush Hospital. Audiotape: Audio Transcripts, Alexandria, VA.

Ichiki, Y. (2009). *The research of the art-making process in assessment influenced by different drawing materials* [Japanese]. Bulletin of Koshien University, No. 37.

Ichiki, Y., Naito, A., & Kanai, N. (2005). The Diagnostic Drawing Series—Drawing in different paper size: The future application of the Diagnostic Drawing Series in Japan [Japanese with English summary]. *Japanese Bulletin of Art Therapy, 36*(1, 2), 65–72.

Johnson, K. M. (2004). *The use of the Diagnostic Drawing Series in the diagnosis of bipolar disorder* (Doctoral dissertation, Seattle Pacific University).

Jung, C. G. (1967). The philosophical tree. In H. Read et al., Vol. XIII, *The collected works of C. G. Jung: Alchemical studies.* Bollingen Series XX. New Jersey: Princeton University Press.

Kaplan, F. F. (2003). Art-based assessments. In C. A. Malchiodi (Ed.), *Handbook of Art Therapy.* New York, NY: Guilford.

Koch, K. (1952). *The tree test: The tree-drawing test as an aid in psychodiagnosis* (2nd ed., Eng. Trans.). Berne: H. Huber.

Landelijke Stuurgroep Multidisciplinaire Richtlijnontwikkeling in de GGZ [National Steering Committee on Multidisciplinary Guideline Development in Mental Health]. (2008). *Multidisciplinaire richtlijn persoonlijkheidsstoornissen. Richtlijn voor de diagnostiek en behandeling van volwassen patiënten met een persoonlijkheidsstoornis [Multidisciplinary Directive personality disorders. Guideline for the diagnosis and treatment of adult patients with personality disorders].* Utrecht, The Netherlands: Trimbos Instituut. [Dutch]

Mills, A. (2003). The Diagnostic Drawing Series. In C. Malchiodi (Ed.), *Handbook of Art Therapy* (pp. 401–409). New York, NY: Guilford.

Mills, A. (2012). *Crosswalk between Diagnostic Drawing Series Revised Rating Guides 1994 and 2012.* (Available from Barry M. Cohen via landmarc@cox.net (preferred), or PO Box 9853, Alexandria, Virginia 22304.)

Mills, A., & Cohen, B. M. (2001). *How do normal people draw?* Paper presented at the meeting of the American Art Therapy Association, Albuquerque, NM.

Mills, A., Cohen, B. M., & Meneses, J. Z. (1993). Reliability and validity tests of the Diagnostic Drawing Series. *The Arts in Psychotherapy, 20*(1), 83–88.

Mucci, N. B. (2011). *Use of the Diagnostic Drawing Series in identifying Schizoaffective Disorder: A pilot study* (Unpublished master's thesis). Antioch University, Seattle.

Neale, E. L. (1994). The children's Diagnostic Drawing Series. *Art Therapy, 11*(2), 119–126.

Nederlandse Vereniging voor Psychiatrie et al. (2009, Eerste revisie). Richtlijnherziening van de Multidisciplinaire richtlijn: Depressie. Richlijn voor de diagnostiek, behandeling en begeleiding van volwassen patiënten met een depressieve stoornis. [*Dutch National Multidisciplinary Guidelines for Mental Health Diagnosis and Treatment: Directives Review of the Multidisciplinary Approach. Depression (1st ed.) Directive for the diagnosis, treatment, and support of adult patients with a depressive disorder.*] Utrecht, The Netherlands: Trimbos Instituut.

Sobol, B., & Cox, C. T. (1991/2004). *Child Diagnostic Drawing Series rating guide.* Unpublished manuscript.

Yamashita, Y. (Speaker) (1989). Analysis of Japanese general psychiatric population, in *The Diagnostic Drawing Series: Its use in clinical practice.* Unpublished paper presented as part of preconference course, American Art Therapy Association national conference. Taught by B. M. Cohen, A. Mills, C. T. Cox, J. N. Creekmore, C. Leavitt, & Y. Yamashita. San Francisco, CA.E

54

The Formal Elements Art Therapy Scale (FEATS)

Linda Gantt

The Formal Elements Art Therapy Scale (FEATS) is a rating system designed to measure global variables in a specific drawing. Elsewhere, I have described the development and application of the FEATS (Gantt, 2001; Gantt & Tabone, 1998) and the patterns for four major diagnostic groups (Gantt, 1993, 2012). In this chapter, I provide an overview of the FEATS and its key principles and describe some recent projects.

Answering a Challenge

One of the greatest challenges to art therapy is making it a scientific discipline (Gantt, 1998). An important piece of this effort is putting numbers to art in order to conduct quantitative studies. Looking now at the FEATS rating manual (Gantt & Tabone, 1998), one might think its development was relatively straightforward. However, the early days involved starts and stops, blind alleys, and a re-thinking of what the enterprise of art therapy was all about. It also required looking at many drawings over several decades.

Some 30 years ago, my co-researcher Carmello Tabone and I began building on the work of our professors Elinor Ulman, Bernard Levy, and Hanna Yaxa Kwiatkowska at the George Washington University. We wanted to see what diagnostic information drawings conveyed *without any additional information from or about the artist*. We attempted to study spontaneous art using a decision tree modeled on those in the *Diagnostic and Statistical Manual of Mental Disorders* (DSM-III; American Psychiatric Association, 1980). We were stymied at the very first fork on that tree. We could not go beyond that point when we could not reliably separate attempts at realism from abstract or nonobjective ones. Therefore, we narrowed our study to drawings in which the content was held constant, so we could see *how* people from different groups drew without having to deal with *what* they drew.

The Wiley Handbook of Art Therapy, First Edition. Edited by David E. Gussak and Marcia L. Rosal.
© 2016 John Wiley & Sons, Ltd. Published 2016 by John Wiley & Sons, Ltd.

An Overview of the FEATS

The FEATS has 14 equal-appearing interval scales for rating a Person Picking an Apple from a Tree (PPAT; "Draw a person picking an apple from a tree"). The materials required are white drawing paper (12" × 18") and "Mr. Sketch"™ wide-tipped markers (12 colors in a set). (For more information on collecting PPATs, see the FEATS Rating Manual [Gantt & Tabone, 1998].)

The scales measure global variables, some of which can be applied to other drawings, and several that are specific to the PPAT. The scales are shown in Table 54.1.

Other variables can be measured on nominal scales such as colors used for particular elements, clothing of the person, and action of the person (such as sitting, standing, jumping, or climbing the tree) (as recorded by "The Content Tally Sheet" in the FEATS manual).

An advantage of the PPAT is that it incorporates a person and a tree and the problem of getting the apple. Unexpectedly, problem-solving distinguished each of the four diagnostic groups and a control group from each of the other groups (Gantt, 1990). The origin of this drawing was traced to studies by art educator Viktor Lowenfeld (1939, 1947).

Key Principles of the FEATS

A set of key principles form the core of the FEATS approach. These principles are not exclusive to the FEATS but are shared at least in part by rating systems such as the Diagnostic Drawing Series (DDS; Cohen, Hammer, & Singer, 1988). In general, the assumptions behind the FEATS contrast with those behind projective drawings. The FEATS is an attempt to take salient aspects from both approaches. (For a chart comparing the two, see Gantt, 2012.)

The key principles of FEATS are discussed in the following text.

Numbers can be applied to drawings with considerable precision

Raters can achieve acceptable inter-rater reliability for the majority of the FEATS scales (Gantt, 1990; Williams, Agell, Gantt, & Goodman, 1996). Furthermore, the 14 global variables can be assigned numbers on *equal-appearing interval* scales. This makes it possible to use more powerful statistical tests than those for nominal or ordinal scales. The FEATS rating sheet also permits using half-point intervals for a more finely gauged instrument.

Table 54.1 FEATS scales.

#1—Prominence of Color	#6—Logic	#11—Line Quality
#2—Color Fit	#7—Realism	#12—Person
#3—Implied Energy	#8—Problem-solving	#13—Rotation
#4—Space	#9—Developmental Level	#14—Perseveration
#5—Integration	#10—Details of Objects and Environment	

Art tracks psychological states

It is assumed that drawings reflect changes in psychological states. Considerable differences were seen if drawings were collected before and after a person received psychotropic medication. Therefore, drawings needed to be obtained as close to hospital admission as possible. Drawings cannot reveal through structure what was experienced in the past; once psychotic symptoms subsided, they would be absent from the drawings.

Information is obtained from structure

Ulman and Levy (1968) suggested that form might yield more diagnostic information than content. Therefore, the scales were constructed to apply to art in general without needing to know what the artist said about it. The focus is on "expressions given off" rather than "expressions given" (content and the artist's associations; Goffman, 1969).

Some areas studied include substance abuse (Rockwell & Dunham, 2006), attention deficit disorder (Munley, 2002), and epilepsy (Anschel, Dolce, Schwartzman, & Fisher, 2005). Other studies looked at depression in prisoners (Gussak, 2004, 2006) and in children and adolescents with renal transplants (Wallace et al., 2004). Lande, Howie, and Chang (1997) compared the PPATs of prisoners with those of patients in a psychiatric hospital.

Global variables are the "graphic equivalent of symptoms"

After initially sorting several hundred PPATs we realized we were making instantaneous decisions to put them into specific diagnostic groups. We were puzzled about how we could do this until we hit upon the concept of *pattern matching* (Gantt & Tabone, 1998, Chapter 6). This explained how our professors recognized diagnostic information without needing words to describe the process. In the pattern-matching process, several variables are taken together as a whole.

It became clear the elements to which we responded should be considered as *the graphic equivalent of symptoms* and could be lined up with the clusters of symptoms in the DSM. This liberated it from the atomistic approach of projective drawings wherein small details were presumed to carry diagnostic material. The FEATS scales—with the exception of Problem-Solving (#8) and Developmental Level (#9)—correlate with (but are not necessarily the exact equivalent of) the cardinal symptoms of four important diagnoses: major depression, schizophrenia, organic mental disorder, and bipolar disorder.

Recent Developments in FEATS Research

The International Art Therapy Research Database

At the 2011 American Art Therapy Association conference, Donna Betts, John Lorance, and I announced the International Art Therapy Research Database (IATRD), a dream of mine since I discovered two important databases during my doctoral studies. The Human Relations Area Files (HRAF) and the Archives for Research in Archetypal Symbolism (ARAS) were established before personal computers were widely used and before digitized images were common. The HRAF consists of ethnographic studies. The ARAS has photographs and images of religious symbols and art from around the world. Both are available online. Over 25 years ago, I urged art therapists to develop a comparable resource (Gantt, 1986). At that time, I had no idea of the relative ease with which researchers in the twenty-first century would be able to do so.

Realizing that many art therapy researchers work on a rather small scale, I wanted to take advantage of the Internet to amass data that a single researcher could not. Through the George Washington University, Betts was instrumental in getting funds for the first stage. Lorance, a computer engineer turned art therapist, built the basic structure of an expandable database with sufficient capacity to investigate a number of artist variables.

The basic structure for the database is in three parts, with each part or level being accessible to approved "subscribers" with specific qualifications. The first level is for those wanting general information about collecting PPATs and the use of the FEATS. This level is the public face of the IATRD. The second level is open to art therapists, art therapy students, and other qualified researchers. These individuals can access an online training session and compare their FEATS ratings to a sample of PPATs rated by experts. There will be immediate feedback as individuals score sample drawings. Successful navigation of the second level will give passage to the third level, where researchers can upload data to add to the collection.

Focusing on normative samples first will relieve researchers of finding their own control groups. The normative samples can yield drawings from controls closely matched to the sample under study with respect to demographic variables such as age, gender, socio-economic status, and education. Some of the technical aspects are being worked out with a sample of 100 PPATs gathered from college students (Bucciarelli, 2011).

The George Washington University (GWU) Institutional Review Board (IRB) granted approval for the database, and the university houses the server on which it is stored. The GWU IRB also approved a protocol for prospective contributing researchers. The protocol provides all templates necessary to ethically collect PPATs for publication in the database, such as a site permission letter, informed consent and assent forms (with approval for waiver of documentation of consent), and so forth. Contributing researchers from outside the university are responsible for their own IRB approvals, but the owner of the database is responsible for data integrity.

The structure of the database permits collecting drawings other than PPATs. The Face Stimulus Assessment (Betts, 2003) will be the second assessment added. As the components of the IATRD are refined and tested, the web site (www.arttherapyresearch. com) will be continually updated.

The FEATS in the emergency room

The capacity of art to track significant changes in psychological states makes it possible to use the FEATS as part of a crisis intervention process in a hospital emergency room. Art therapist Joseph Jaworek has been piloting such a procedure in a large

Mid-Atlantic regional healthcare facility. In a typical 24-hour period, there can be some 250 people of all ages seen for medical and psychological emergencies. If a person is held for psychological observation for more than 6 hours, the facility requires services to be provided within the emergency department. Current shortages for psychiatric beds in the region mean that many people wait well over 6 hours before being admitted to an inpatient unit. During the lengthy waiting periods, Jaworek administers the PPAT, scores it with the FEATS, and collects other pertinent clinical information. He then presents his findings to the attending physician and the psychiatrist. He also helps develop a treatment plan with the patient.

In this setting, the PPAT and the FEATS scoring system have both advantages and disadvantages. Perhaps the greatest advantage is that information is captured even if a person has trouble with traditional verbal interviews. What may be most apparent are psychotic symptoms and organic disorders. In this regard, the FEATS may reveal more than the Mini-Mental Status Exam (MMSE).

A person who is acutely psychotic may have lower FEATS scores on Color Fit (#2), Integration (#5), Logic (#6), Realism (#7), and Person (#12). On the other hand, a person who has an organic disorder would likely have a PPAT that cannot be scored more than a "1" on many, if not most, of the scales. Some people with the beginning stages of Alzheimer's disease may still be fairly verbal but unable to draw a PPAT with recognizable constituent parts. With more research, it might be possible to devise a post-drawing interview and to find some associated patterns of FEATS scores to identify certain types of apraxia or agnosia.

A score less than a 4 on Rotation (#13) or Perseveration (#14) should be a red flag. PPATs with either of these variables are rare in our archives of thousands of drawings. While either may appear in the PPATs of young children of around 4 years of age, or in those of some people with schizophrenia, art therapists will more likely see them in the PPATs of people with some type of organic disorder.

One disadvantage is the lack of ability to make finer distinctions *within* the range of certain disorders. In general, the pattern in PPATs of people who are depressed shows lower scores on Prominence of Color (#1), Implied Energy (#3), Space (#4), and Details of Objects and Environment (#10); mid-range scores on Realism (#7), Problem-solving (#8), and Person (#12); and higher scores on Integration (#5) and Logic (#6). However, making any distinctions within this range using the FEATS may not be possible at this time.

Mood disorders cover a wide territory in terms of severity, occurrence, course, and associated features (such as rapid cycling, catatonia, and seasonal pattern). On the dimension of severity, depressive disorders range from mild, moderate, or severe, to severe with psychotic features. There are also variables related to history that cannot be captured in PPAT.

Simplifying scoring and using computers

When rating 14 scales and 13 categories of nominal variables on the Content Tally Sheet, judges can easily succumb to rater fatigue. It may be possible to omit some scales by using factor analysis to decide which ones give the greatest amount of information. Also, an investigator might discard certain scales when studying specific populations. Rotation (#13) and Perseveration (#14) are rarely found except in the PPATs of people with organic mental disorders. Developmental Level (#9) might be less useful in studies of certain adult populations.

Kim and colleagues are using computers in various art therapy assessments (Kim, 2008; Kim, Bae, & Lee, 2007; Kim & Hameed, 2009).[1] FEATS scales such as Prominence of Color (#1) and Line Quality (#11) may lend themselves to computerized scoring. Space (#4) can certainly yield far more precise information if measured using computers.

Mattson (2011) demonstrated that people could measure Rotation (#13) more accurately by using a computer than otherwise. However, some variables, most notably Problem-solving (#8), require human judgment. A computer-assisted measurement that could augment the FEATS is the ratio of tree to person (possibly useful in studies of children and the developmentally delayed).

Tabone collected PPATs before, during, and after electroconvulsive therapy (ECT; Gantt & Tabone, 2003). Using computer ratings on just a few variables, such as placement of person and tree (Kim, Kang, & Kim, 2008), use of space, and rotation, could yield statistical support for clinical decisions as to whether the PPAT was improved, worse, or unchanged.

An Outcome Study in Process

A vexing complication is that of co-morbid disorders. Many people treated in Intensive Trauma Therapy, Inc., a trauma clinic for post-traumatic stress disorder (PTSD), have also been given a diagnosis of major depression. Teasing out the effects of these two conditions is a significant challenge. To this end, PPATs are collected at admission and discharge. The facility's marathon treatment varies from 5 to 10 days of individual sessions (30 or more hours per week). Clients are also administered a battery of paper-and-pencil assessments before and after treatment at 1 week, 3 months, and 6 months. By correlating scores on the assessments with the FEATS, we hope to see what the drawings contain in the way of trauma-related features versus depressive ones.

Two sets of PPATs show how the drawings can change during intensive therapy. A woman in her late 40s with a history of depression and anxiety drew the images shown Figure 54.1 (first day of treatment) and Figure 54.2 (5 days later, on the last day of treatment). She had a number of traumas, including childhood physical and sexual abuse, a serious car accident as a teenager, and an emotionally abusive first marriage. A woman in her mid-20s created the images shown in Figure 54.3 (first day of treatment) and Figure 54.4 (done at discharge after 10 days of therapy). She had multiple traumas in childhood (physical injuries, surgery, sexual harassment) and had been treated for anxiety and depression.

Both admission PPATs show a pattern that accords with that of moderate depression. The discharge PPATs show measurable improvement. In fact, Figure 54.4 is similar to the non-patient sample. Did the changes show a reversal of depressive symptoms or an elimination of trauma symptoms? Does trauma mimic depression but not require medication? Clearly, more research is needed.

Figure 54.1 PPAT of woman with depression and anxiety—first day of treatment.

Figure 54.2 PPAT of woman with depression and anxiety—last day of treatment.

Figure 54.3 PPAT of woman suffering multiple childhood traumas—first day of treatment.

Figure 54.4 PPAT of woman suffering multiple childhood traumas—upon discharge.

The Future

Research across the age span and large-scale normative studies using the FEATS are only two of the major types of potential projects. Joseph Jaworek's project is in its infancy but shows promise. This screening process could be duplicated in other crisis settings, and the findings pooled for a multi-site study, as could the ECT studies. Since art therapists are gathering PPATs in other countries, we should be able to sort out cultural variables from psychological ones. For example, a number of red suns have turned up in a Japanese sample (whereas many PPATs from the East Coast of the United States have yellow suns, sometimes accented with orange). This is not surprising, given that the national symbol on the Japanese flag is a red rising sun. By focusing on form, we could more easily research developmental stages in children's art and drawings from different subcultures, as well as special populations. The possibilities for future research are exciting indeed.

Endnote

1   *Editors' note:* See Chapter 56, by Seong-in Kim, in this book.

References

American Psychiatric Association. (1980). *Diagnostic and statistical manual for mental disorders* (3rd ed.). Washington, DC: Author.

Anschel, D. J., Dolce, S., Schwartzman, A., & Fisher, R. S. (2005). A blinded pilot study of artwork in a comprehensive epilepsy center population. *Epilepsy & Behavior, 6*(2), 196–202.

Betts, D. (2003). Developing a projective drawing test: Experiences with the Face Stimulus Test (FAS). *Art Therapy: Journal of the American Art Therapy Association, 20*(2), 77–82.

Bucciarelli, A. (2011). A normative study of the Person Picking an Apple from a Tree (PPAT) assessment. *Art Therapy: Journal of the American Art Therapy Association, 28*(1), 31–36.

Cohen, B., Hammer, J., & Singer, S. (1988). The Diagnostic Drawing Series: A systematic approach to art therapy evaluation and research. *The Arts in Psychotherapy, 15*(1), 11–21.

Gantt, L. (1986). Systematic investigations of art works: Some research models drawn from neighboring fields. *American Journal of Art Therapy, 24*(4), 111–118.

Gantt, L. (1990). *A validity study of the Formal Elements Art Therapy Scale (FEATS) for diagnostic information in patients' drawings.* Unpublished doctoral dissertation, University of Pittsburgh, Pittsburgh, PA.

Gantt, L. (1993). Correlation of psychiatric diagnosis and formal elements in art work (Chapter 16). In F. Bejjani (Ed.), *Current research in arts medicine.* Pennington, NJ: A Cappella Books.

Gantt, L. (1998). A discussion of art therapy as a science. *Art Therapy: Journal of the American Art Therapy Association, 15*(1), 3–12.

Gantt, L. (2001). The Formal Elements Art Therapy Scale: A measurement system for global variables in art. *Art Therapy: Journal of the American Art Therapy Association, 18*(1), 51–56.

Gantt, L. (2012). Tending to the "art" in art therapy assessment. In A. Gilroy, R. Tipple, & C. Brown (Eds.), *Assessment in art therapy.* London: Routledge.

Gantt, L., & Tabone, C. (1998). *The Formal Elements Art Therapy Scale: The rating manual.* Morgantown, WV: Gargoyle Press.

Gantt, L., & Tabone, C. (2003). The Formal Elements Art Therapy Scale and "Draw a Person Picking an Apple from a Tree." In C. Malchiodi (Ed.), *Handbook of Art Therapy.* New York, NY: Guilford.

Goffman, E. (1969). *Strategic interaction.* Philadelphia, PA: University of Pennsylvania Press.

Gussak, D. (2004). Art therapy with prison inmates: A pilot study. *The Arts in Psychotherapy, 33,* 188–198.

Gussak, D. (2006). The effects of art therapy with prison inmates: A follow-up study. *The Arts in Psychotherapy, 31,* 245–259.

Kim, S. (2008). Computer judgment of main color in a drawing for art psychotherapy assessment. *The Arts in Psychotherapy, 35*(1), 140–150.

Kim, S., & Hameed, I. (2009). A computer system to rate the variety of color in drawings. *Art Therapy: Journal of the American Art Therapy Association, 26*(2), 73–79.

Kim, S., Bae, J., & Lee, Y. (2007). A computer system to rate the color-related formal elements in art therapy assessments. *The Arts in Psychotherapy, 34*(3), 223–237.

Kim, S., Kang, H., & Kim, K. (2008). Computer determination of placement in a drawing for art therapy assessments. *The Arts in Psychotherapy, 35*(1), 49–59.

Lande, R., Howie, P., & Chang, A. (1997). The art of crime. *American Journal of Art Therapy, 36*(1), 2–10.

Lowenfeld, V. (1939). *The nature of creative activity.* New York, NY: Harcourt, Brace.

Lowenfeld, V. (1947). *Creative and mental growth.* New York, NY: Macmillan.

Mattson, D. (2011). Standardizing the Formal Elements Art Therapy Scale (FEATS) rotation scale with computerized technology: A pilot study. *The Arts in Psychotherapy, 38*(2), 120–124.

Munley, M. (2002). Comparing the PPAT drawings of boys with AD/HD and age-matched controls using the Formal Elements Art Therapy Scale. *Art Therapy: Journal of the American Art Therapy Association, 19*(2), 69–76.

Rockwell, P., & Dunham, M. (2006). The utility of the Formal Elements Art Therapy Scale in assessment for substance use disorder. *Art Therapy: Journal of the American Art Therapy Association, 23*(3), 104–111.

Ulman, E., & Levy, B. (1968). An experimental approach to the judgment of psychopathology from paintings. *Bulletin of Art Therapy, 8*, 3–12.

Wallace, J., Yorgin, P. D., Carolan, R., Moore, H., Sanchez, J., Belson, A., et al. (2004). The use of art therapy to detect depression and post traumatic stress disorder in pediatric and young adult renal transplant recipients. *Pediatric Transplantation, 8*(1), 52–59.

Williams, K., Agell, G., Gantt, L., & Goodman, R. (1996). Art-based diagnosis: Fact or fantasy? *American Journal of Art Therapy, 35*, 9–31.

55

The Face Stimulus Assessment (FSA)

Donald C. Mattson and Donna Betts

The Face Stimulus Assessment (FSA) is an art-based instrument designed to facilitate the production of artwork in individuals presenting with communication disorders (Betts, 2003, 2009, 2013c). Betts noticed that children with autism, intellectual disability, and general communication disorders often experienced difficulty in beginning a drawing. However, when given a stimulus drawing of a face, these children more readily completed the image, which also served to provide rich psychological information.

The FSA is similar to many other art therapy instruments, in that it is a projective art instrument (Cohen, 1985; Gantt & Tabone, 1998; Silver, 1983). As such, it offers a format in which a respondent can project psychological information onto it in an unrestricted manner (Hersen, 2004). The multidimensional aspect of the FSA permits a wide range of responses from subjects. The FSA's format allows the respondent to freely associate with art media, which often uncovers unconscious material that may be explored further by the administrator (Plotnik & Kouyoumdjian, 2011).

The projective nature of the FSA offers several unique qualities in contrast with structured psychological testing (Groth-Marnat, 2009; Hersen, 2004). Because there generally is no right or wrong answer with projective instruments, it is difficult for a respondent to introduce bias or to fake answers. Since projective art instruments reveal uniquely personal information, there is an increasing interest in standardizing them to instill measures of reliability and validity in scoring (Butcher, 2009). Offering a stimulus within the FSA was a step toward achieving some measure of standardization among projective art assessments (Betts, 2003).

Purpose of the FSA

The main purpose of the FSA is to provide the clinician with a tool for better understanding the cognitive, developmental, and creative potential of children, adolescents, and adults (Betts, 2003; Brooke, 2004). It reveals the client's capacity for retaining visual information and ability to arrange elements of the human face through successive drawings, and examines the client's capacity for understanding and

The Wiley Handbook of Art Therapy, First Edition. Edited by David E. Gussak and Marcia L. Rosal.
© 2016 John Wiley & Sons, Ltd. Published 2016 by John Wiley & Sons, Ltd.

organizing the human face. Furthermore, it is a tool to gauge the client's strengths, and was designed to be a culturally sensitive instrument for use with cross-cultural and multicultural populations (Betts, 2013a). Children, adolescents, and adults with developmental disabilities and communication difficulties are the intended population for the FSA, although it is open to further normative studies on various populations (Betts, 2003). Robb (2002) applied the FSA to a group of children in a 6-week day camp for Russian immigrants as a means to record the progress of art therapy in reducing symptoms of trauma. Due to insufficient sample size, the researcher could not conclude that the FSA worked as a progress marker, although she did find that, overall, the act of making art with the FSA reduced anxieties that the children had regarding immigration.

History and Development of the FSA

The FSA was developed largely to expand on gaps in art-based assessment research. In a critical review of projective human figure drawing instruments, Golomb (1992) discovered inconsistent results, far-reaching conclusions, and poor reliability measures. Additionally, few established art-based projective instruments addressed developmental and communication disabilities. With its stimulus and projective capacity, the FSA proved suitable in working with such individuals (Betts, 2003; Robb, 2002).

Research on the significance of depicting the human face prompted the FSA's development. For instance, the human face is a proven source of information and emotional expression (Cacioppo & Petty, 1983; Kemp et al., 2007). Face recognition is crucial to the development of infants, and adults actively search for cues on others' faces to assist in fostering communication and forming relationships (Morton & Johnson, 1991). Furthermore, recent work in neurological imaging revealed differences in how those with affective disorders encode information about the face in contrast to normal subjects (Dickstein et al., 2006).

Lowenfeld and Brittain (1947/1970) noted that the human face is among one of the first recognizable objects drawn by children, and that no early artistic expression occurred without some component of self-identification within an art piece. Previous research exists in using a face drawing as a means of extracting psychological information. Gair (1975) used self-portraits to gauge psychological change. Golomb (1992) used drawing directives that included filling in blank face templates as a form of assessment. Early versions of face-oriented assessment instruments include the Draw-A-Face test (DAF; Burns & Zweig, 1980), and also the Franck Drawing Completion Test (FDCT; Franck, 1976), which included a manual of stimulus drawings for participants to use.

The theoretical basis of stimulus drawings relies heavily on *behavioral fading* (Martin & Pear, 2010), in which a participant receives fewer cues with each successive drawing. The participant then responds to the final stimulus without referring to the previous drawings, with the intention that the participant learned the faded cues. Theory and past work contributed to the overall design of the FSA.

FSA Design

One of the most significant contributors to the stimulus underpinning of the FSA was Rawley Silver (1983), who developed the Silver Drawing Test (SDT), which is a stimulus drawing series. The FSA is a series of three 8.5" x 11" stimulus drawing templates. The first contains a pre-drawn face; the second has an outline of the face; and the third is a blank sheet of paper. Using several drawings in an assessment tool tends to elicit more information than if just one is used (Cohen, 1985).

Through a series of trials with cognitively impaired students, the standard shape of the FSA face emerged. The image is gender-neutral and race-neutral (Betts, 2003). The neck, ears, and nose underwent considerable revision to match them as closely as possible to a face that embodied a wide range of cultures. After additional edits, Betts decided that there should be space above the forehead to allow for the expression of hair configurations.

All three pictures in the FSA series are vertically oriented; perception of the face is most significant to humans when presented in this manner (Alley, 1998; Golomb, 1992). Ultimately, Betts maintained the three-drawing format because it could help determine clients' memory level, visual retention, and perceptual organization. These areas are potentially useful for assessing clients' developmental level and cognitive abilities (Betts, 2003). In addition, this format permits multiple opportunities for the client with a disability to communicate information onto the paper.

Administration

Materials

The FSA uses the following materials: one pack of eight Crayola® Classic Markers, one pack of eight Crayola® Multicultural Markers; picture #1: one 8.5" x 11" sheet of white copy paper with the complete face image, picture #2: one 8.5" x 11" sheet of white copy paper with face and neck outline only, and picture #3: one 8.5" x 11" sheet of blank white copy paper.

Procedure

The FSA may be administered individually, or in small groups. The administrator issuing the instrument should arrange all 16 markers randomly on the table to the side of the drawing space. The time allotted is 50 minutes to 1 hour. After 20 minutes, the administrator reminds the client of the time remaining. The procedure for administering the FSA does not require direct observation, freeing the administrator from the duties of monitoring its use. However, as with any thorough assessment of clients, particularly children, behavioral observations should be noted and integrated into the assessment report (Betts, 2012). A clinician may also use the FSA as an informal drawing procedure (Brooke, 2004).

The client is asked to "Use the markers and this piece of paper." If a participant asks a question, the administrator repeats the directions, and informs him or her that questions may be asked following the activity. The administrator removes each drawing upon its completion. On the reverse side of the page, in the bottom left-hand corner of each drawing, the administrator records the client name, date, and picture number. The administrator then keeps the original drawings as assessment data, providing the client with photocopies if needed.

Rating and Interpretation

The rating system for the FSA is an integrated approach, combining both a quantitative data gathering method in the form of rating scales, and a qualitative interpretation guide. The quantitative portion is discussed in *The Face Stimulus Assessment (FSA) Rating Manual* (2nd ed.) (Betts, 2013d). This manual is based upon, with permission, the *Formal Elements Art Therapy Scale: The Rating Manual* (*FEATS©*;[1] Gantt & Tabone, 1998), adapting nine of the original 14 FEATS scales for rating the FSA drawings: Prominence of Color; Color Fit; Implied Energy; Logic; Realism; Developmental Level; Details of Objects and Environment; Line Quality; and Perseveration. *The Face Stimulus Assessment (FSA) Rating Manual* is used to rate drawing 2 of the FSA series (Betts, 2003), although some scales may be applicable for drawings 1 and 3, at the rater's discretion. These scales appeared most relevant for rating the second FSA drawing, as this drawing provides minimal stimulus (just the outline of the face), thereby leaving space for the client to "project" his or her imagery onto the stimulus, and determining the client's developmental level and cognitive skills.

The qualitative interpretation guide for the FSA aids the clinician in determining:

*   Whether or not the client possesses the motor ability to color within the lines
*   The client's ability to use realistic colors, and determine the general configuration of the human face
*   Addition of details
*   Adjusting face to look like self and what this indicates for self-perception (with race and gender consideration)
*   Use of space within picture, background, or in color differentiation between face and background

For the second picture, if the client scribbles or draws over the prompt, the rater should determine whether the client is aware of or interested in the face. If the drawing does not represent a face, the rater references details in the first drawing to make a comparison. If the client does not draw one, the rater assesses line, color, or other relevant formal elements within the drawing.

For the third picture, the rater determines if the client draws a face out of compliance with the first drawings, or the possible creative reasons for the client not drawing a face. The rater should make comparisons between the third picture and the previous two, and then determine the overall page orientation, line, and color usage. The rater then assesses all the drawings holistically, and records the results.

Reliability and Validity

Normative data for the FSA have yet to be well-established. However, Hamilton (2008) conducted her master's thesis research with a convenience sample of 30 normative participants enrolled at a Midwestern University in Illinois, United States. This sample contributed to establishing norms for further validity and reliability studies of the FSA rating system. The participants were 19–28 years of age; six participants were men and 24 were women. The study investigated the use of the modified FEATS as a formal rating guide for the FSA (Gantt & Tabone, 1998). The findings identified statistically significant results supporting the use of the modified FEATS with drawing 2 of the FSA. Findings from this study served as the foundation for *The Face Stimulus Assessment (FSA) Rating Manual* (Betts, 2013d), and will ultimately aid in supporting the use of the FSA as an assessment to measure clients' developmental level and cognitive abilities.

Betts (2013b) collected FSA drawings from approximately 200 normative participants in South Korea. Preliminary results demonstrated the validity of the adapted FEATS rating scales in identifying normative features of the artwork. Raters are now evaluating the FSA drawings, computing reliabilities, and coding survey themes. The survey questions help control for the mediating variables of artistic skill and ethnic background. There are also other research findings that tentatively support the ability of the FSA to determine developmental level and cognitive abilities.

For instance, in an effort to develop and validate an evaluation method for the FSA, S. R. Kim (2010) conducted a large-scale study in South Korea. Among 921 potential participants identified from the elementary school system, 296 non-normative and 240 normative student drawings were analyzed. The non-normative sample was comprised of 152 students with a hearing impairment and 144 students with a developmental disorder. The FSA evaluation method developed in this study was able to discriminate between the non-normative and normative groups. The FSA evaluation method demonstrated success in evaluating the cognitive abilities of the children with developmental disabilities and hearing impairment.

Betts, Schmulevich, Hu, Kelly, and Choi (2013, April) implemented the FSA in a study on the medication responsiveness of individuals with autism in the United States. FSA drawing data derived from 57 participants validate the ability of many of the FSA rating scales to reflect the developmental level and cognitive abilities of individuals with autism.

The FSA-R

Recently, the FSA underwent computerization in an effort to examine formal elements. Researchers developed a computer system that evaluated 54 drawings of those with dementia and 20 drawings from undergraduate students (S. Kim, Kim, & Hong, 2012). The system divided the FSA drawings into several areas of color and compared them for measurement. The quadratic weighted kappa of two human raters yielded inter-rater reliability values between 0.94 and 0.98, while raters operating the computer system produced reliability values in the range of 0.85–0.96, indicating the effectiveness of the system.

Similarly, Mattson (2009) discovered that image analysis software was able to detect the FSA formal elements of color and line. Subsequent studies led to the development of a computer-rated version of the FSA instrument, known as the Face Stimulus Assessment—Revised (FSA-R; Mattson, 2011). The construction of the FSA-R resulted from an extensive literature review on major depressive disorder (MDD) and art in efforts to establish an instrument with some measure of reliability and validity. The FSA-R differs from the FSA in that it includes more free space for easier examination by a computer, and has additional stimulus objects built from previous research on differentiating MDD from healthy controls. The FSA-R was standardized on 20 individuals with MDD and 20 individuals without MDD. The results of an adjusted t-test of these samples revealed that those with MDD drew less purple than controls ($t(38)$ = –2.95, p = 0.05, d = –0.96), which indicated a difference in color usage between groups. As a result, further work will commence on computerized image analysis of the FSA, so that it can obtain additional measures of reliability and validity (Mattson, 2009, 2011).

Future Directions

Further research using *The Face Stimulus Assessment (FSA) Rating Manual* (Betts, 2013d) will likely increase the tools' reliability and validity. Further work on the FSA and other art therapy assessments claiming to measure developmental level and cognitive ability should include the use of norm groups for children, and those with developmental delays, so as to determine changes in graphic language over a series of face drawings (Golomb, 1992). Research with matched groups should incorporate parallel instruments to study self-esteem, behavior, and mood (Betts, 2003; Mattson, 2011). Submitting collections of FSA samples to the International Art Therapy Research Database (IATRD; www.arttherapyresearch.com) will make it easier for future researchers to access the material for their own studies. Art therapists should continue to explore the development of the FSA in order to substantiate its psychometric properties.[2]

Endnotes

1   The FEATS is explained more fully in Chapter 54 of this book.
2   For information on ordering the FSA, contact dbetts@gwu.edu.

References

Alley, T. R. (1988). Social and applied aspects of face perception: An introduction. In T. R. Alley (Ed.), *Social and applied aspects of perceiving faces* (pp. 1–8). Hillsdale, NJ: Lawrence Erlbaum.
Betts, D. J. (2003). Developing a projective drawing test: Experiences with the Face Stimulus Assessment (FSA). *Art Therapy: Journal of the American Art Therapy Association, 20*, 77–82.

Betts, D. J. (2009). Introduction to the Face Stimulus Assessment (FSA). In E. G. Horovitz & S. Eksten (Eds.), *The art therapists' primer: A clinical guide to writing assessments, diagnosis, and treatment*. Springfield, IL: Charles C. Thomas.

Betts, D. J. (2013a). A review of the principles for culturally appropriate art therapy assessment tools. *Art Therapy: Journal of the American Art Therapy Association, 30*(3), 98–106. doi: 10.1080/07421656.2013.819280

Betts, D. J. (2013b). Art therapy assessments with diverse populations. In P. Howie, S. Prasad, & J. Kristel (Eds.), *Using art therapy with diverse populations: Crossing cultures and abilities* (pp. 41–55). London, UK: Jessica Kingsley.

Betts, D. J. (2013c). *The Face Stimulus Assessment (FSA) E-packet*. Department of Art Therapy, George Washington University, Washington, DC.

Betts, D. J. (2013d). *The Face Stimulus Assessment (FSA) Rating Manual* (2nd ed.). Department of Art Therapy, George Washington University, Washington, DC.

Betts, D. J., Schmulevich, G., Hu, V., Kelly, B., & Choi, J. (2013, April). *Diagnostic criteria for autism reflected in graphic features of artwork*. Poster session presented at George Washington University Research Days, Washington, DC.

Brooke, S. L. (2004). *Tools of the trade: A therapist's guide to art therapy assessments* (2nd ed.). Springfield, IL: Charles C. Thomas.

Burns, W. J., & Zweig, A. R. (1978). An investigation of the Goodenough-Harris Drawing Test and the Coopersmith Self-Esteem Inventory. *Educational and Psychological Measurement, 38*, 1229–1232. doi: 10.1177/001316447803800448

Butcher, J. N. (2009). *Oxford handbook of personality assessment*. New York, NY: Oxford University Press.

Cacioppo, J. T., & Petty, R. E. (Eds.) (1983). *Social psychophysiology: A sourcebook*. New York, NY: Guilford Press.

Cohen, B. M. (Ed.). (1985). *The Diagnostic Drawing Series handbook*. Alexandria, VA: Author.

Dickstein, D. P., Rich, B. A., Roberson-Nay, R., Berghorst, L., Vinton, D., Pine, D. S., & Leibenluft, E. (2006). Neural activation during encoding of emotional faces in pediatric bipolar disorder. *Bipolar Disorders, 7*, 679–692. doi: 10.1111/j.1399-5618.2007.00418.x

Franck, K. (1976). *Franck Drawing Completion Test*. Victoria, New South Wales: Australian Council for Educational Research.

Gair, S. B. (1975). An art-based remediation program for children with learning disabilities. *Studies in Art Education, 17*, 55–67.

Gantt, L., & Tabone, C. (1998). *The Formal Elements Art Therapy Scale: The Rating Manual*. Morgantown, WV: Gargoyle Press.

Golomb, C. (1992). *The child's creation of a pictorial world*. Berkeley: University of California.

Groth-Marnat, G. (2009). *Handbook of psychological assessment* (5th ed.). Hoboken, NJ: John Wiley & Sons Press.

Hamilton, M. (2008). *Developing a standardized rating system for the Face Stimulus Assessment (FSA) using 12 scales adapted from the Formal Elements Art Therapy Scale (FEATS)* (Unpublished master's thesis). Avila University, Kansas City, MO.

Hersen, M. (2004). *Comprehensive handbook of psychological assessment: Personality assessment* (Vol. 2). Hoboken, NJ: John Wiley & Sons.

Kemp, A. H., Felmingham, K., Das, P., Hughes, G., Peduto, A. S., Bryant, R. A., & Williams, L. M. (2007). Influence of comorbid depression on fear in posttraumatic stress disorder: An fMRI study. *Psychiatry Research: Neuroimaging, 155*, 265–269. doi: 10.1002/hbm.20415

Kim, S. R. (2010). *A study on development of FSA evaluation standard and its validation (Unpublished doctoral dissertation)*. Yeungnam University, Daegu, South Korea.

Kim, S., Kim, J. H., & Hong, E. (2012). *A computer system for the Face Stimulus Assessment*. Manuscript submitted for publication.

Lowenfeld, V., & Brittain, L. W. (1947/1970). *Creative mental growth* (5th ed.). London, UK: The Macmillan Company.

Martin, G., & Pear, J. (2010). *Behavior modification: What it is and how to do it* (9th ed.). Boston, MA: Pearson.

Mattson, D. C. (2009). Accessible image analysis for art assessment. *The Arts in Psychotherapy*, *36*, 208–213. doi: 10.1016/j.aip.2009.03.003

Mattson, D. C. (2011). Constructing the computer-rated face stimulus assessment–revised (FSA-R) to assess formal elements of major depressive disorder (MDD). *The Arts in Psychotherapy*, *39*, 31–37. doi: 10.1016/j.aip.2011.11.003

Morton, J., & Johnson, M. H. (1991). CONSPEC and CONLERN: A two-process theory of infant face recognition. *Psychological Review*, *2*, 164–181. doi: 10.1037/0033-295X. 98.2.164

Plotnik, R., & Kouyoumdjian, H. (2011). *Introduction to psychology* (9th ed.). Belmont, CA: Wadsworth.

Robb, M. (2002). Beyond the orphanages: Art therapy with Russian children. *Art Therapy: Journal of the American Art Therapy Association*, *19*, 146–150.

Silver, R. A. (1983). *Silver Drawing Test of cognitive and creative skills*. Seattle, WA: Special Child Publications.

56

Assessments and Computer Technology

Seong-in Kim

Since its advent in 1946, computer science has progressed remarkably and at a fantastic rate, and the computer is now a huge influence on society. There are various fields that leverage this technology, including manufacturing, design, education, and law. However, the art therapy field has been relatively slow in adopting these new tools. Art therapists use personal computers and email, and some use remote sessions to improve the quality of art therapy practices (Hartwich & Brandecker, 1997; Orr, 2006). Thong (2007) used a combination of traditional art therapy techniques and computer software. Im et al. (2010) developed a computer module that allowed the client to draw online and the art therapist to save and review the whole sketching process. To date, most of art therapy research has been confined to computer-assisted art therapy (McLeod, 1999), using the computer as a tool for art-making and as a medium for remote communication with clients (Malchiodi, 2000).

Only a few studies have ventured beyond the aforementioned scope, including using a computer system for evaluating drawings (S. I. Kim, 2010; Mattson, 2012) and decision-making (S. I. Kim, Ryu, Hwang, & M. S. H. Kim, 2006). This may be due to art therapists' lack of knowledge about computer technology and because some art therapists are skeptical about the effectiveness of such tools (Fryrear & Corbit, 1992; Hartwich & Brandecker, 1997). Asawa (2009) reported that art therapists' typical response to the use of technology is mostly rooted in anxiety and fear.

However, the following examples demonstrate that this trend is reversing. In 1999, *Art Therapy: The Journal of the American Art Therapy Association* (AATA) published a special issue on "Digital Art Therapy." In 2007, Kapitan (2007) emphasized the advantages of using computers for managing and practicing art therapy, and stressed on the importance of multidisciplinary research for new media. The theme of the 2008 AATA conference held in Cleveland, in Ohio, United States, was "Art Therapy on the Cutting Edge: Invention and Innovation." In 2009, the AATA published another special issue on "Art Therapy's Response to Techno-Digital Culture."

One obstacle to adopting technology may be that knowledge in art therapy can be heuristic, subjective, inconsistent, and even contradictory, relying on the art therapist's professional expertise and experience. Contrarily, solving problems with computers requires scientific methods based on quantification. Since it is difficult to quantify the process of art therapy, practitioners may not have used computers to their fullest extent, and many art therapists still claim that their evaluations are complex and difficult to quantify. This can soon change. Computer algorithms such as color analysis and edge extraction can provide basic building blocks for quantifying the evaluations of drawings.

Furthermore, recent progress in artificial intelligence research allows computers to solve problems where quantification is difficult or even impossible. Conventionally, computers were only able to solve problems where a sequence of instructions (i.e., an algorithm) could be written and applied. However, computers may now be able to solve problems with uncertain or imperfect specifications. S. I. Kim (2008b) asserted that art therapists might adopt artificial intelligence techniques to assist them.

In this chapter, *computational art therapy* (CAT) is defined as art therapy that actively uses computer technology. It is different from the limited use of computers as a tool for generating drawings or as a communication method for remote sessions. It applies computer technology such as artificial intelligence to evaluate and interpret drawings and assess clients. This chapter will include how and what computer technologies are relevant to art therapy as applied to a *computational art therapy system* (CATS). Some of the art evaluation and interpretation results from CATS, using common art therapy assessments for comparison and examples, will be discussed. This chapter will conclude with a discussion on how progress in art therapy can be made through CAT.

Computer Technology Relevant to Art Therapy

Computers assimilate a drawing by splitting it into pixels of an enormous number of shades and colors. There are a number of software tools available for drawing—for example, Corel Painter, Tux Paint, InkScape, CADian, and, of course, Adobe Photoshop (Adobe Creative Team, 2004), which is possibly the most well-known program. Such advances in computer graphics software provide a novel way to generate drawings and to create a finer scale of information, in turn computerizing traditional art therapy assessments and facilitating new ones for improving the reliability and validity of current assessments. This is done through several means, most specifically pattern recognition, expert systems, and the Bayesian network.

Pattern recognition, a subfield of cognitive science, serves to automatically recognize characters or shapes using computational machines. Figure 56.1 shows how the computer recognizes colors and extracts boundaries between colors. A computer algorithm refers to a sequence of instructions or computational methods to solve a given problem.

Artificial intelligence is a field that seeks to make machines (e.g., computers or robots) adapt to new situations, learn from past experiences, and recognize things unique to human intelligence. Expert systems, subfields of artificial intelligence, focus on capturing the human expert knowledge for making computers reason and make decisions. Some expert systems are capable of learning, automatically accumulating and improving knowledge; such information is stored into a knowledge base for

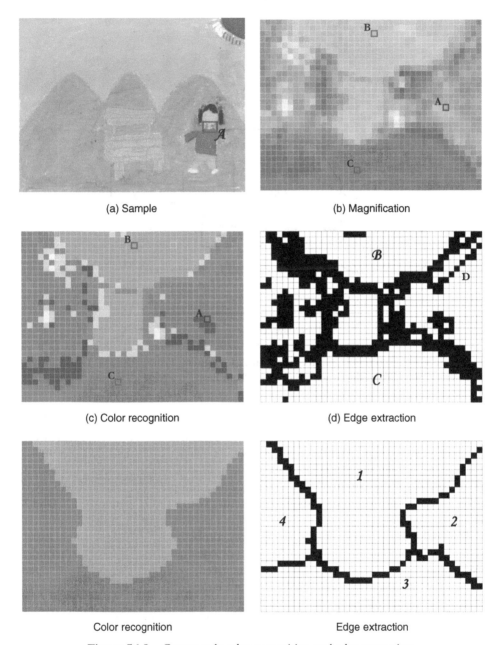

(a) Sample

(b) Magnification

(c) Color recognition

(d) Edge extraction

Color recognition

Edge extraction

Figure 56.1 Computer's color recognition and edge extraction.

continuous accumulation and updating. For example, newly discovered knowledge on the relation between psychological states and the drawing for art therapy assessments can be stored and updated in a knowledge base as shown in Figure 56.2.

The Bayesian network graphically represents the probabilistic cause-and-effect relationship using a set of random variables as nodes and their conditional probabilities as edges in a directed acyclic graph (Charniak, 1991). It allows a user

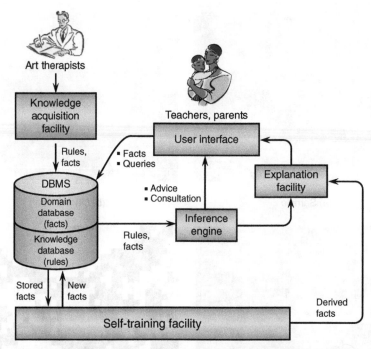

Figure 56.2   The common architecture of an expert system. From S. I. Kim, Y. H. Kim, and E. J. Kim (2008). Reproduced with permission from Elsevier.

to encode knowledge that is not deterministic. For example, the traditional deterministic interpretation of art is that "children suffering from attention-deficit and hyperactivity disorder (ADHD) tend to draw a full picture using more than 90% of the paper." Using the Bayesian network, a more quantitative expression can be made, such as, "the children with ADHD draw a full picture with a probability of 0.75, whereas normal children draw such picture with a probability of 0.1" (Ghil & Kim, 2010).

The computer can perform art evaluations by combining pattern recognition, expert systems, and computer algorithms to measure or rate drawing elements. Furthermore, existing art therapy assessments can be computerized, and new ones can be developed. The expert systems in artificial intelligence and Bayesian network can also be used to interpret drawings inferring the information on the patient's psychological state from the formal and generic elements of the drawing. Applying this technology can make the art therapist's knowledge more structured and systematic.

CATS for Art Evaluation

This section introduces some representative art therapy assessments, such as the Diagnostic Drawing Series (DDS; Cohen, 1986/1994), Formal Elements Art Therapy Scale (FEATS; Gantt & Tabone, 2003), and how several CATS, including the Computer Color-Related Elements Art Therapy Evaluation System (C_CREATES;

Kim, 2010; S. I. Kim, Bae, & Lee, 2007), can classify their evaluation elements and examine their interrater reliabilities.

Classification of elements in art evaluation

The DDS (Cohen, 1986/1994) was designed to gather clinical information about a client in a single session. The FEATS (Gantt & Tabone, 2003) provides a method for understanding and examining the non-symbolic aspects of art, and for demonstrating how structural characteristics of a drawing furnish information on a person's clinical state and his or her diagnosis. These assessments focus on formal elements rather than the contents of a drawing. These are used as examples here because of the supposition that, if there are differences between two or more groups, these differences will result from *how* the group members drew rather than *what* they drew, as it would be difficult to measure differences in content (Gantt & Tabone, 2003).

A combination of the elements assessed in both the DDS and FEATS totals 37. Several are listed in both the DDS and FEATS, such as "integration," "line quality," and "space usage," and some elements use different names such as "idiosyncratic color" in the DDS and "color fit" in the FEATS. Thus, there are really only 30 elements between the two. Meanwhile, C_CREATES evaluates only 19 elements. For example, the "number of colors" in the image is determined by counting the number of pixels for each, which yields more detail as both the existence and the area of each color are given. In another example, "space usage" is evaluated not by only the number of colored areas but also in their grade, rank, and percentile.

Many of the assessment elements are concerned directly or indirectly with color. The C_CREATES classifies the color elements into four categories:

1. *Basic color-related elements.* This category is analyzed by digital image-processing techniques and computer algorithms such as color recognition and edge extraction. It includes (a) number of colors used, (b) color list, (c) number of clusters, (d) length of the color edges, (e) area colored, (f) number of grids colored, and (g) area of colored convex hull. Among them, Figure 56.3 shows the computer technology and its mechanism to evaluate elements (f) and (g).
2. *Explicitly color-related elements.* This category is identified by constructing an appropriate knowledge base, centered on the basic color-related elements. It includes (a) primary and secondary colors, (b) warm and cool colors, and (c) complementary colors.
3. *Implicitly color-related elements.* This category can be determined by applying regression models to the basic color-related elements. It includes (a) unusual placement, (b) variety of colors, (c) main and subsidiary colors, (d) prominence of colors, (e) details of objects and environment, and (f) space.
   Pattern color-related elements. This category is rated by the computer algorithm, expert system, and statistical method (S. I. Kim, Kang, & Y. H. Kim, 2009). It includes (a) completeness, (b) accuracy, and (c) degree of concentration. For example, the Structured Mandala Coloring (SMC; Curry & Kasser, 2005) and the first picture of the Face Stimulus Assessment (FSA; Betts, 2003) were given patterns of clusters lines. It involves only coloring work, not drawing.

Figure 56.3 Number of grids and area of convex hull. From S. I. Kim, Han, and Oh (2012). Reproduced with permission from Elsevier.

Reliability

All ratings of elements in the DDS and FEATS are more or less subjective, and their rating results may differ depending on the reviewers. Even when raters were provided with concrete descriptors for rating all levels for each scale, they likely rated aspects of drawings differently, simply because they may have preferred certain drawings over others (White, Wallace, & Huffman, 2004). Some rating methods of elements may be time consuming, such as rulers or grids made of tracing paper marked off in millimeters, and they may still be inaccurate. Thus, the problem of low interrater reliability emerges.

Although interrater reliability in a DDS study was reported to be 95.7% (Mills, Cohen, & Meneses, 1993), Fowler and Ardon (2002) found the rating to be unsatisfactory as they felt it was too heavily dependent on experience. Although they agreed that the handbook and training were clear and precise, their work suggested that clarification and precision were insufficient in practice. Brooke (2004) reported that the reliability of the FEATS yielded results of 0.74 and higher for various scales, except for perseveration, which yielded various scores.

To overcome the problems of subjective rating and low interrater reliability, several CATS for art evaluations have been developed. In many cases, CATS, including C_CREATES, can automatically provide more accurate and detailed information than human raters. For several elements, CATS can provide perfectly accurate measurements, such as: (a) number of colors and color list; (b) area colored; (c) number of clusters; (d) area of colored convex hull; and (e) length of edges. Also, CATS can provide not only the measurement but also the grade, rank, or percentile. Moreover, there are elements that can be provided only by CATS, but cannot be provided by human raters, such as the "area colored."

For certain elements, reliabilities between human raters and CATS, as well as the reliabilities among human raters, were rated. For example, CATS of S. I. Kim and Hameed (2009) rated the variety of color so that the drawing with the largest number of colors was ranked the highest. When two drawings were found to have the same number of colors, the one with the longest color edges was ranked the highest. S. I. Kim and Hameed (2009) reported high reliability between the two human raters and moderate reliability between the raters and CATS: the rank correlation coefficient (RCC; Walpole & Myers, 2006) between the raters was 0.825. The RCC between CATS and rater 1 ($r = 0.759$) was found to be higher than between CATS and rater 2 ($r = 0.662$).

The CATS of S. I. Kim (2008a) judged the main color by computer algorithm. The CATS of Kim, Kang, et al. (2008) determined the types of placement by computer algorithm. The CATS of S. I. Kim, Y. H. Kim, & E. J. Kim (2008) evaluated space usage by computer algorithm and statistical model. The CATS of S. I. Kim (2010) measured color prominence and details quantitatively by computer algorithm and statistical model. The CATS of S. I. Kim, J. H. Kim, and Hong (2013) rated five elements in the FSA (Betts, 2003) in grades. Mattson (2011) standardized, although did not automate, the "rotation" of the FEATS using computerized angle tools. The reliabilities between human raters and these CATS showed high consistencies between them.

The relative merits of CATS as compared to conventional art therapy assessments are as follows: objective, consistent, quantitative, detail, automatic, and instantaneous. Further studies on using this computer approach are expected to form the basis for the quantification and objectification of the currently subjective decisions made by expert raters based on individual experience. This does not imply that the computer system can replace human experts. Rather, the system can free human experts from the mundane task of gathering mechanical information about the drawings, so that they may concentrate on the more nuanced aspects of evaluation that require professional judgments by humans. In doing this, CATS never avoids its duty, is never fatigued with its responsibility, and never makes a mistake of omission.

CATS for Art Interpretation

Traditional interpretations and CATS

The purpose of the DDS and FEATS is to gather clinical information on a person's clinical state and psychiatric diagnosis. The validity of the DDS and FEATS has been tested on various psychiatric symptoms. It is difficult for computers to interpret a free drawing with vast subjects because the present computer technology cannot identify its forms. However, the C_CREATES can interpret a free drawing as far as its colors are concerned. The SMC involves coloring work only, so there are no needs to identify forms. The SMC (S. I. Kim, Betts, H. M. Kim, & Kang, 2009) is a typical example of assessment to which the C_CREATES can be fully applied. Kim, Betts et al. (2009) reported that the elements "brown," "light-green," "green," "the number of clusters," and "accuracy" were selected as important elements for estimating the

Mini-Mental State Examination (MMSE) score (Folstein, Folstein, & McHugh, 1975). They also estimated the probability of severe dementia by stepwise regression.

S. I. Kim, Y. H. Kim, and E. J. Kim (2008) developed an expert system for interpreting the SMC based on the color preference of family members. The usefulness of the system depends on the validity of the information and the size of the knowledge base. S. I. Kim, Han, Y. H. Kim, and Oh (2011) developed a CATS for Kinetic Family Drawings (KFDs; Burns, & Kaufman, 1972), where various images of the family members and backgrounds were given, and the client selected a few among them, expanded or contracted, moved, and colored them. There is even an app for CATS for the free drawing, SMC, and KFD, developed by the AAA (stands for artificial intelligence, applied statistics, art therapy) Lab at Korea University, South Korea (Malchiodi, 2012).

S. I. Kim, Yoo, K. E. Kim, and Lee (2007) and S. I. Kim, K. E. Kim, Y. Lee, S. K. Lee, and Yoo (2006) expressed the relationship between elements of the human figure drawing (HFD; Koppitz, 1968) and the social backgrounds and environment, culture, and the psychiatric symptoms, into knowledge. The knowledge is systematically classified into: (a) themes of drawings; (b) diagnosis mechanisms; (c) characteristics of drawings; (d) psychological symptoms; (e) cause–effect relationships; (f) clinics in art psychotherapy; (g) psychology; and (h) research in the field of art. This information is accumulated in the knowledge base. The level of evidence (appropriateness) of each is evaluated. The feedback processes considering various backgrounds make the interpretation of art different from the one-to-one equivalence interpretation. The knowledge classified systematically is accumulated, updated, or discarded according to the appropriateness of the data.

S. I. Kim, Kang, Chung, and Hong (2012) proposed a statistical approach to comparing the effectiveness of several art therapy assessments. They applied the approach to the FEATS, FSA, and SMC in estimating dementia. Choosing an effective assessment and analyzing the relationship between the test scores and its estimated values may aid art therapists seeking evidence to support their observations and impressions. The approach is a generalized one, and thus can be used to compare the effectiveness of any special art therapy assessment in estimating the levels of various psychological states.

Validity

There is still debate among a number of art therapists about whether art interpretation can be objectively measured (Gantt, 1998). Difficulty with such interpretations lies in the fact that a client's personal and cultural backgrounds influence the choice of shapes, colors, and styles in drawings. This implies that even seemingly identical drawings may be subjected to diverse, inconsistent, and sometimes even contradictory interpretations. For example, one study found that the human figures drawn by people who were depressed were smaller than the figures drawn by those who were not depressed (Lewinsohn, 1964), whereas another study reported no relationship between depression and the size of figure drawings (Salzman & Harway, 1967). Machover's hypotheses dealing with the "placement" variable (element) was not supported by later studies, and, according to Roback (1968), it was not "generally" supported. Swensen (1968) reported nine studies supporting the hypotheses and six negatives; he concluded that such findings should be accepted with caution.

One-to-one equivalency of specific drawing details (signs and symbols) with particular clinical features was doomed from the start (Gantt, 2004). Before interpreting the meaning of the signs and symbols, the context is the key to understanding how they function (Gantt, 2004). The interpretation methodology developed by Kim, Ryu et al. (2006) is not based on the one-to-one equivalence. Rather, it is on a process of comprehensive decision-making that considers the client's various circumstances, including the social and cultural background in which the individual grew up, and with a view to diversity and uncertainty.

For another solution for diversity and uncertainty in the interpretation of art, Ghil and Kim (2010) adopted the concept of probability. They applied the Bayesian network, which visually represented the cause-and-effect relationships among a set of random variables (elements), and their conditional independencies via a directed acyclic graph (Charniak, 1991). The Bayesian network was useful in systemizing and materializing the knowledge in the fields where it was not organized. In addition, the Bayesian network enabled art therapists to comprehend the cause-and-effect relationships between mental diseases, psychological symptoms, the environment, and art elements, and to integrate individual knowledge into a shared one. Moreover, the Bayesian network helped make a more objective and logical decision by reasoning interactions of variables based on the probability value. In summary, one of the major advantages of the Bayesian network is that it enables art therapists to more clearly communicate their theories and results by demonstrating probabilistic values along with the cause-and-effect relationship in a graph (Uusitalo, 2007).

Discussion and Conclusion

The rapid advancement of computer technology has brought about remarkable progress in many fields and has made a great contribution to human welfare. Austin (2009) stressed that art therapy professionals should adopt computers as an innovative therapeutic medium, and become proficient in using them. Kapitan (2009) asserted that this new trend might renew the art therapy profession by exposing it to global ideas and practices, infusing it with knowledge from outside the field, cultivating grass-roots affiliations, and moving the field beyond its traditional boundaries. A number of art therapists have already realized that a scientific approach is essential to resolving implicit ambiguity and uncertainty in art therapy, and stressed that the academic sustainability of art therapy depends on science (Kaplan, 2000). Expert systems, computer algorithms, and statistical models are emerging as useful methods to overcome the limitations of art therapy. Computer technology is changing the way art therapists practice their profession (Peterson, Stovall, Elkins, & Parker-Bell, 2005).

The art therapy assessments presented in this chapter can be easily adapted and implemented as computer programs. There are a number of possible extensions, for example, applying CATS with a battery of assessments using the SMC, KFD, and

Kinetic School Drawing (KSD): after having children fill out questionnaires on their color preferences, ask them to color the SMC, and then complete the patterned KFD and KSD. Art therapists can then obtain information on the children's status in their primary living spaces such as home and school.

Although a reliable approach to evaluating art emphasizes the global aspects of form rather than content, sign, or interpretation (Kaplan, 2003), the major challenge for computer technology for art therapy assessments is that it is in a preliminary stage of development for understanding arbitrary drawings. However, although there are a few software packages that only recognize characters or scenes in photos, progress is being made in recognizing and understanding pictures and drawings. Thus, we are getting closer to an automatic art therapy assessment.

Recently, projective tools have encountered a number of serious challenges. Their reliability and validity have been questioned (Betts, 2005; L. J. Chapman & J. P. Chapman, 1967), and many psychologists are no longer using most of them. Given that questions have arisen about the lack of reliability and validity of projection techniques and picture interpretations, the method proposed in this chapter can contribute to making art therapy and its assessments more structured and principled through scientific methods.

There have been numerous efforts to build the foundation of art therapy as a discipline (Gantt & Tabone 2003; Kaiser, John, & Ball, 2006; Kapitan, 2010; McNiff, 1998; Tibbetts, 1995). CATS can provide a way to overcome the limitations of conventional art therapy assessments such as subjective evaluation, contradictory interpretation, and dictionary type of one-to-one interpretation by building a structured and systematic knowledge of art therapy. Artificial intelligence techniques including expert systems and Bayesian networks can be valuable approaches for converting art therapy into a scientific discipline.

In order to advance CAT, time and effort is needed from multiple disciplines such as psychology, psychiatry, art education, art therapy, and computer science. Ethical issues, such as security and privacy, need to be addressed. Art therapist educators and associations need to understand the importance of CAT and prepare personnel for using cutting-edge technologies. In conclusion, CAT as an interdisciplinary approach, applying computer science to art evaluation and interpretation, can significantly expand the potential and value of art therapy by overcoming the limitations of the existing art therapy assessments.

References

Adobe Creative Team. (2004). *Adobe Photoshop 7.0 classroom in a book*. San Diego, CA: Adobe Press.

Asawa, P. (2009). Art therapists' emotional reactions to the demands of technology. *Art Therapy: Journal of the American Art Therapy Association, 26*(2), 58–65.

Austin, B. D. (2009). Renewing the debate: Digital technology in art therapy and the creative process. *Art Therapy: Journal of the American Art Therapy Association, 26*(2), 83–85.

Betts, D. J. (2003). Developing projective drawing test: Experience with the Face Stimulus Assessment (FSA). *Art Therapy: Journal of the American Art Therapy Association, 20*(2), 77–82.

Betts, D. J. (2005). *A systematic analysis of art therapy assessment and rating instrument literature*. Dissertation. Florida State University, Tallahassee, FL. Published online at http://www.art-therapy.us/images/Donna Betts.pdf.

Brooke, S. L. (2004). *Tools of the trade: A therapist's guide to art therapy assessments*. Springfield, IL: Charles C. Thomas.

Burns, R. C., & Kaufman, S. H. (1972). *Actions, styles, and symbols in Kinetic Family Drawings (KFD): An interpretive manual*. New York, NY: Brunner/Mazel.

Chapman, L. J., & Chapman, J. P. (1967). Genesis of popular but erroneous psychodiagnostic observations. *Journal of Abnormal Psychology, 72*(3), 193–204.

Charniak, E. (1991). Bayesian networks without tears. *AI Magazine, 12*, 50–63.

Cohen, B. M. (Ed.) (1986/1994). *The diagnostic drawing series rating guide*. Unpublished guidebook.

Curry, N. A., & Kasser, T. (2005). Can coloring mandalas reduce anxiety? *Art Therapy: Journal of the American Art Therapy Association, 22*(2), 81–85.

Folstein, M. F., Folstein, S. E., & McHugh, P. R. (1975). Mini-mental state: A practical method for grading the cognitive state of patients for the clinician. *Journal of Psychiatric Research, 12*, 189–198.

Fowler, J. P., & Ardon, A. M. (2002). Diagnostic Drawing Series and disassociate disorders: A Dutch study. *The Arts in Psychotherapy, 29*(4), 221–230.

Fryrear, J. L., & Corbit, I. E. (1992). *Photo art therapy. A Jungian perspective*. Springfield, IL: Charles C. Thomas.

Gantt, L. (1998). A discussion of art therapy as a science. *Art Therapy: Journal of the American Art Therapy Association, 15*(1), 3–12.

Gantt, L. (2004). The case for formal art therapy assessments. *Art Therapy: Journal of the AATA, 21*(1), 18–29.

Gantt, L., & Tabone, C. (2003). The formal elements art therapy scale and "Draw a Person Picking an Apple from a Tree." In C. A. Malchiodi (Ed.), *Handbook of art therapy* (pp. 420–427). New York, NY: The Guilford Press.

Ghil, J. H., & Kim, S. I. (2010). *Probabilistic interpretation of arts using the Bayesian network of artificial intelligence technique*. Paper to be presented at the 41st Annual American Art Therapy Association Conference, Sacramento, California.

Hartwich, P., & Brandecker, R. (1997). Computer-based art therapy with inpatients: Acute and chronic schizophrenics and borderline cases. *The Arts in Psychotherapy, 24*, 367–375.

Im, Y. H., Oh, S. G., Yu, J. H., Lee, H. S., Chang, J. K., & Park, D. H. (2010). A KFD web database system with an object-based image retrieval for family art therapy assessments. *The Arts in Psychotherapy, 37*, 163–171.

Kaiser, D. H., St. John, P., & Ball, B. (2006). Teaching art therapy research: A brief report. *Art Therapy: Journal of the American Art Therapy Association, 23*(4), 186–190.

Kapitan, L. (2007). Will art therapy cross the digital culture divide? *Art Therapy: Journal of the American Art Therapy Association, 24*(2), 50–51.

Kapitan, L. (2009). Introduction to the special issue on art therapy's response to techno-digital culture. *Art therapy: Journal of the American Art Therapy Association, 26*(2), 50–51.

Kapitan, L. (2010). *Introduction to art therapy research*. New York, NY: Routledge.

Kaplan, F. F. (2000). *Art, science and art therapy: Repainting the picture*. London: Jessica Kingsley.

Kaplan, F. F. (2003). Art-based assessments. In C. A. Malchiodi (Ed.), *Handbook of art therapy* (pp. 25–35). New York, NY: The Guilford Press.

Kim, S. I. (2008a). Computer judgment of main color in a drawing for art psychotherapy assessment. *The Arts in Psychotherapy, 35*(2), 140–150.

Kim, S. I. (2008b). Commentaries, to the editor. *Art Therapy: Journal of the American Art Therapy Association, 25*(1), 41.

Kim, S. I. (2010). A computer system for the analysis of color-related elements in art therapy assessment: Computer Color-Related Elements Art Therapy Evaluation System (C CRE-ATES). *The Arts in Psychotherapy, 37*(5), 378–386.

Kim, S. I., Bae, J., & Lee, Y. (2007). A computer system to rate the color-related formal elements in art therapy assessments. *The Arts in Psychotherapy, 34*(3), 223–237.

Kim, S. I., Betts, D. J., Kim, H. M., & Kang, H. S. (2009). The statistical models to estimate level of psychological disorder based on a computer rating system: An application to dementia using structured mandala drawings. *The Arts in Psychotherapy, 36*(4), 214–221.

Kim, S. I., & Hameed, A. I. (2009). A computer system to rate the variety of color in drawings. *Art Therapy: Journal of the American Art Therapy Association, 26*(2), 73–79.

Kim, S. I., Han, J., Kim, Y. H., & Oh, Y. J. (2011). A computer art therapy system for Kinetic Family Drawing (CATS KFD), *The Arts in Psychotherapy, 38*(1), 17–28.

Kim, S. I., Han, J., & Oh, Y. J. (2012). A computer art assessment system for the evaluation of space usage in drawings with application to the analysis of its relationship to level of dementia. *New Ideas in Psychology, 30*(5), 300–307.

Kim, S. I., Kang, H. S., Chung, S., & Hong, E. J. (2012). A statistical approach to comparing the effectiveness of several art therapy tools in estimating the level of a psychological state. *The Arts in Psychotherapy, 39*(5), 397–403.

Kim, S. I., Kang, H. S., & Kim, K. E. (2008). Computer determination of placement in a drawing in art therapy assessment. *The Arts in Psychotherapy, 35*(1), 49–59.

Kim, S. I., Kang, H. S., & Kim, Y. H. (2009). A computer system for art therapy assessment of elements in structured mandala. *The Arts in Psychotherapy, 36*(1), 19–28.

Kim, S. I., Kim, J. H., & Hong, E. (2013). *A computer system for the face stimulus assessment with application to the analysis of dementia. The Arts in Psychotherapy, 40*(2), 245–249.

Kim, S. I., Kim, Y. H., & Kim, E. J. (2008). An expert system for interpretation of structured mandala. *The Arts in Psychotherapy, 35*(5), 320–328.

Kim, S. I., Kim, K. E., Lee, Y., Lee, S. K., & Yoo, S. (2006). How to make a machine think in art psychotherapy: An expert system's reasoning process. *The Arts in Psychotherapy, 33*(5), 383–394.

Kim, S. I., Ryu, H. J., Hwang, J. O., & Kim, M. S. H. (2006). An expert system approach to art psychotherapy. *The Arts in Psychotherapy, 33*(5), 59–75.

Kim, S. I., Yoo, S., Kim, K. E., & Lee, Y. (2007b). A framework for expert system knowledge base in art psychotherapy. In A. R. Tyler (Ed.), *Expert systems research trends* (pp. 181–206). Haupauge, NY: Nova Science Publishers.

Koppitz, E. M. (1968). *Psychological evaluation of Children's Human Figure Drawings.* New York, NY: Grune & Stratton.

Lewinsohn, P. M. (1964). Relationship between height of figure drawings and depression in psychotic patients. *Journal of Consulting Psychology, 28*, 380–381.

Malchiodi, C. A. (2000). *Art therapy & computer technology: A virtual studio of possibilities.* London: Jessica Kingsley.

Malchiodi, C. (2012, February 29). Re: Art therapy: There's an app for that [Web blog message]. Retrieved from http://www.psychologytoday.com/blog/the-healing-arts/201202/art-therapy-there-s-app-1

Mattson, D. C. (2011). Standardizing the Formal Elements Art Therapy Scale (FEATS) rotation scale with computerized technology: A pilot study. *The Arts in Psychotherapy, 38*, 120–124.

Mattson, D. C. (2012). An introduction to the computerized assessment of art-based instruments. *Art Therapy: Journal of the American Art Therapy Association, 29*(1), 27–32.

McLeod, C. (1999). Empowering creative with computer-assisted art therapy: An introduction to available programs and techniques. *Art Therapy: Journal of the American Art Therapy Association, 16*(4), 201–205.

McNiff, S. (1998). Enlarging the vision of art therapy research. *Art Therapy: Journal of the American Art Therapy Association, 15*(2), 86–92.

Mills, A., Cohen, B. M., & Meneses, J. Z. (1993). Reliability and validity tests of the diagnostic drawing series. *The Arts in Psychotherapy, 20,* 83–88.

Orr, P. P. (2006). A documentary film project with first-year art therapy students. *The Arts in Psychotherapy, 33,* 281–287.

Peterson, B. C., Stovall, K., Elkins, D. E., & Parker-Bell, B. (2005). Art therapists and computer technology. *Art Therapy: Journal of the American Art Therapy Association, 22*(3), 139–149.

Roback, H. B. (1968). Human figure drawings: Their utility in the clinical psychologist's armamentarium for personality assessment. *Psychological Bulletin, 70*(1), 1–19.

Salzman, L., & Harway, N. (1967). Size of figure drawings of psychotically depressed patients. *Journal of Abnormal Psychology, 72,* 205–207.

Swensen, C. H. (1957). Empirical evaluations of human figure drawings. *Psychological Bulletin, 54,* 431–466.

Swenson, C. H. (1968). Empirical evaluation of human figure drawings: 1957–1966. *Psychological Bulletin, 70,* 20–24.

Thong, S. A. (2007). Redefining the tools of art therapy. *Art Therapy: Journal of the American Art Therapy Association, 24*(2), 52–58.

Tibbetts, T. J. (1995). Art therapy at the crossroads: Art and science. *Art Therapy: Journal of the American Art Therapy Association, 12*(4), 257–259.

Uusitalo, L. (2007). Advantages and challenges of Bayesian networks in environmental modeling. *Ecological Modelling, 203,* 312–318.

Walpole, R. E., & Myers, R. H. (2006). *Probability and statistics for engineers and scientists* (8th ed.). New York, NY: Macmillan.

White, C. R., Wallace, J., & Huffman, L. C. (2004). Use of drawings to identify impairment among students with emotional and behavioral disorders: An exploratory study. *Art Therapy: Journal of the American Art Therapy Association, 21,* 210–218.

57

The Need for Norms in Formal Art Therapy Assessment

Sarah P. Deaver

Art therapy assessment may take the form of an art-based clinical interview (Deaver & Bernier, 2014) or an observational session such as described by Kramer and Schehr (1983) or Rubin (1984). These approaches to assessment, which typically occur in the art therapy studio, involve offering clients a variety of directives and both two- and three-dimensional media. Inferences about client functioning are drawn through a combination of the art therapist's impressionistic sense of the artwork, observations of the client's behavior and approach to the art media, knowledge of projective drawing literature, comparison to many previous clients' responses, and the art therapist's appraisal of the client–therapist interaction.

On the other hand, there are structured, formal art therapy assessments that include those in our field currently under research. Contemporary examples include the Face Stimulus Assessment (FSA; Betts, 2003), the Bird's Nest Drawing (BND; Kaiser, 1996; Kaiser & Deaver, 2009), the Human Figure Drawing (HFD; Deaver, 2009), the Diagnostic Drawing Series (DDS; Cohen, Hammer, & Singer, 1988), and the Formal Elements Art Therapy Scale (FEATS; Gantt, 2001; Gantt & Tabone, 1998). As opposed to clinical interviews or observational sessions, formal art therapy assessments generally involve from one to three drawings, standardized art materials, standardized and consistent procedures or directives, and a rating or scoring system. A standardized scheme for rating the artwork produced in formal art therapy assessments quantifies elements in the drawings by producing a score on one or several different variables seen in the assessment artwork. Of critical importance, however, is that there is no way to make sense of the scores unless we have accrued a large sample of normative assessment drawings against which to compare our clients' assessment (Bucciarelli, 2011; Cicchetti, 1994; Deaver, 2009; Gantt, 2004). Normative samples of art therapy assessments provide descriptions of non-clinical populations' drawings, or of subgroups of clinical populations' drawings. Normative samples provide descriptions in the form of numerical scores, and involve "empirically establishing a standardized reference point from which to judge individual ... scores" (Nelson, 1994). In other words, they allow art therapists to understand their clients, based on their assessment scores, as similar to or varying from others who have executed the same assessment. Based on assessment scores, judgments or decisions may be made about treatment planning, media choices, referrals for further testing or for medication evaluation, placement in a special education classroom, progress in treatment, and so on. Unfortunately, the absence of large normative samples of art therapy assessments hinders our ability to make valid inferences and useful decisions based on our assessments.

A Promising Beginning

Important steps have been taken toward establishing norms for several assessments. In fact, efforts have been made to establish and enlarge normative samples for every art therapy assessment in this section. For example, Silver (2002) reported creating normative samples for the Silver Drawing Test (SDT) of cognition and emotion from hundreds of drawings by children and adults from several areas of the United States. Mills (2003, 2008) and Cohen and Mills (1998) reported having acquired over 1,000 DDS drawings, and that norms have been established for over 21 groups of research interest. Levick (2009) undertook an ambitious 3-year normative study, collecting 330 sets of LECATA drawings from children who were functioning at an average level in their elementary school.

Bucciarelli (2011) conducted a carefully designed normative study of the Person Picking an Apple from a Tree (PPAT) drawing as assessed by the FEATS (Gantt, 2001) scales. The participants, 100 college students aged 18–24 years, were ethnicity and gender matched so that they represented contemporary US census data on college students. Bucciarelli was able to establish means on all 14 of the FEATS scales that describe a typical or "normal" young adult's PPAT. Hamilton (2008) undertook a similar study of the FSA (Betts, 2003). She adapted nine of the FEATS scales for use with FSA drawings, and collected 30 drawings from college students aged 19–28 years. Hamilton, too, was able to establish means on the adapted FEATS scales that would describe an FSA drawing done by a typical young adult in her university.

As promising as these initial steps toward establishing normative samples of art therapy assessments are, problems clearly exist, and art therapy researchers have many more steps to take in support of the scientific basis for our assessment methods. In addition to the relatively small size of the normative samples described earlier, most of them suffer from lack of geographic, age, and ethnic diversity, and thus are not generalizable to many of the groups of people with whom art therapists work. Furthermore, the US population is changing rapidly, and few of the existing small normative samples represent these changes. For example, in the 10 years from 2000 to 2010, the Hispanic or Latino population in the United States grew 43% and the Asian population grew 43.3%, whereas the African American population grew only 12.3% and Whites only 5.7% (2010 Census Results). In clinical psychology assessment, the problems of rapidly changing US populations and using psychological assessments in locales outside of the United States are being addressed mainly by translating existing psychological tests into multiple languages and making adaptations to test instruments to ensure appropriate cultural sensitivity while preserving their psychometric integrity (Geisinger, 1994).

Persistent and Emerging Problems

When considering the applicability of art therapy assessment in diverse populations of people, there are even more aspects of assessment to consider than in psychology, including the impact of cultural, educational, and artistic traditions upon the way people draw. Three examples of my own students' research illustrate some of the challenges that we face in developing art therapy assessments and establishing norms for them. The database of 467 children's HFDs at Eastern Virginia Medical School (EVMS; Deaver, 2009) has served as a comparison group for several students who have examined the HFDs drawn by special populations of children from diverse cultures. The FEATS scales that were modified and standardized for use with HFDs in the original 2009 study include Prominence of Color, Color Fit, Space, Developmental Level (congruence with Lowenfeld's stage theory), and Details of Objects and Environment. In all of the student research described here, HFDs were administered using standardized procedures and art materials to "normal," non-clinical experimental subjects whose drawings were then age- and gender-matched to drawings in the database. Raters were trained to score the drawings, and, in each study, acceptable interrater reliability that matched or exceeded that described in the original study was attained. Statistical analyses compared experimental drawings to database drawings along age, gender, group, and the scores on the five modified FEATS scales used in the original study. In every case, the drawings under research differed significantly from the database drawings in ways that suggest important implications for art therapy assessment.

Elizabeth Dukes' (Smead, 2004) research compared HFDs drawn by 148 children in the West African country of Benin to age- and gender-matched HFDs from the database. The statistical differences between the two groups of children's HFDs were significant on all five of the modified FEATS scales ($p < .000$). The American children's HFDs' higher scores indicated greater use of color, more realistic color, more space used, greater congruence with Lowenfeld's stages (Lowenfeld & Brittain, 1987), and more environmental details. Although our assessment approach provided information about formal elements in the Beninese children's HFDs, it failed to capture the intense richness of their drawings, including depictions of fabric details indicative of family identity and suggestive of culture-specific appliqué tapestries, culture-bound scarification of faces, and the influence of artistic and academic traditions upon absence of perspective and environmental details (Smead, 2004). Similarly, Ashy Palliparambil (2011) compared HFDs drawn by 50 children from Kerala, India, to 50 age- and gender-matched drawings in the EVMS database. Statistical analysis revealed significant differences between the two groups. The Indian children used more realistic color and less space, and drew fewer details. Their HFDs were not congruent with Lowenfeld's stages as the American children's drawings were; the Indian children drew only the human figure and did not include baselines or environmental details. Furthermore, the Indian children used more color, but this difference was not statistically significant. Based upon the implications noted in Smead's study, Palliparambil's methodology differed from other similar student studies, in that, to evaluate the cultural elements in their drawings, the Indian children were asked to draw an additional picture of a topic of their own choice. The contents of these free-choice drawings were assessed by completing the content tally sheets for each one. In contrast to the HFDs, these drawings were more colorful, took up more space on the page, and contained numerous environmental elements and details such as birds and animals. Some culture-specific content was included, such as huts, traditional clothing, and a canoe.

Finally, Suhyun Tess Lee (2011) compared 23 HFDs collected from school children in Gyeonggi-do, South Korea, to 23 age- and gender-matched HFDs from the EVMS database. Data analysis revealed that differences between the two groups on the amount of space used and on environmental details were significant; the Korean children used less space ($p < .005$) and fewer details ($p < .003$). The differences between the two groups on two additional scales could be conceptualized as approaching significance; the Korean children used less color ($p < .071$) and less realistic color ($p < .080$) than did the American children. Once again, the analysis provided information about the characteristic use of formal elements in the Korean children's drawings but did not capture culturally relevant aspects, such as the prominence of manga-style HFDs typically depicted in warm, bright hues.

Since all of the comparisons in these examples were between groups of normal, typically developing children, it is obvious through using the EVMS database of American children's drawings that there is a different norm for the African and Asian children's drawings in these studies: single figures, filling 25% or less of the paper space, few baselines or horizons, with little or no depiction of perspective or an environment. Although Lowenfeld's (Lowenfeld & Brittain, 1987) stage theory of artistic development may be applicable across Western cultures (Alter-Muri, 2002), it is clearly not directly transferable to the African and Asian cultures studied. The student researchers examined the culture, educational systems, and artistic traditions of their research subjects, and attributed the differences seen in the drawings to these factors. For example, in both India and Korea, elementary education is less experiential than in the United States, and involves strict adherence to teachers' directives (Shin & Koh, 2005; Shukla, 1983). Perhaps this explains the literal interpretation of the directive to draw a person—the children drew only a person, floating (without a ground line) in the center of the page. Furthermore, all three researchers were able to see the influence of artistic traditions in the drawings, traditions that do not appear to incorporate depiction of perspective as the endpoint (Wolf & Perry, 1988).

Summary and Implications

The lack of large normative samples of art therapy assessments is a significant deficit in the field, because, without them, we are unable to make empirically based inferences and treatment decisions about our clients based upon their assessments. There are a number of dimensions of this deficit, among them several ethical ones: Is it ethical to make decisions about client care based upon assessments that do not have sufficiently sound psychometric properties? Are we placing our clients and even our profession at risk by doing so? Is it ethical to apply assessments based in Eurocentric psychology and art therapy traditions to populations of people who are culturally diverse? Fortunately, there are some approaches to remedying the deficit.

First, based on several cross-cultural studies completed by EVMS students and found in hundreds of pages of literature devoted to the tenets of cultural sensitivity and competence, it is clear that, despite the belief in art as a universal language, culture-specific factors may prevent the transferability of art therapy assessments across cultures. As art therapy grows across the planet (see Section VIII of this handbook), there is an obvious need for establishing normative samples for art therapy assessment use that would reflect the culture-specific aspects of particular countries.

One obvious solution to the deficit represented by the lack of assessment norms would be to obtain large amounts of grant funding to support development of normative samples. Costs covered would include art materials, paying data collectors and raters, paying research assistants to scan all drawings, and statistical support. Collaboration among art therapy assessment researchers and educational programs would be crucial for the success of any multi-site effort of this nature. Although institutional review board processes are slow and arduous, it is possible to get large, multi-site research studies approved. With several individuals and programs cooperating, it would be possible to gather large amounts of assessment drawings from populations that are geographically, racially, and ethnically diverse, and which range in age from young children through adults. This collaborative approach would present many opportunities for students to incorporate development of normative samples in their thesis work, while accruing large numbers of assessment drawings. Both the finished theses and the drawings would add valuable data to the research underpinnings of the profession.

Conceived by Linda Gantt and overseen currently by Donna Betts at George Washington University, the International Art Therapy Research Database (IATRD, www.arttherapyresearch.com) is the logical repository for all normative art therapy assessment samples. Although licensing and contractual matters, complicated by laws and regulations governing institutional review board in the United States, are thorny, it is my view that the IATRD represents the greatest hope for establishing the necessary normative databases for art therapy assessment. The collaborative nature of IATRD is ideally suited for the field as it grows and develops throughout the world.

References

2010 Census Results. Available from http://2010.census.gov/2010census/data.

Alter-Muri, S. (2002). Viktor Lowenfeld revisited: A review of Lowenfeld's preschematic, schematic, and gang age stages. *American Journal of Art Therapy*, 40(3), 170–192.

Betts, D. (2003). Developing a projective drawing test: Experiences with the Face Stimulus Assessment (FSA). *Art Therapy: Journal of the American Art Therapy Association*, 20(2), 77–82.

Bucciarelli, A. (2011). A normative study of the Person Picking an Apple from a Tree (PPAT) assessment. *Art Therapy: Journal of the American Art Therapy Association*, 28(1), 31–36.

Cicchetti, D. (1994). Guidelines, criteria, and rules of thumb for evaluating normed and standardized assessment instruments in psychology. *Psychological Assessment*, 6(4), 284–290.

Cohen, B., Hammer, J., & Singer, S. (1988). The Diagnostic Drawing Series: A systematic approach to art therapy evaluation and research. *Art Therapy: Journal of the American Art Therapy Association*, 15(1), 11–21.

Cohen, B., & Mills, A. (1998). *The Diagnostic Drawing Series handbook* (rev. ed.). Available from the DDS Project, PO Box 9853, Alexandria, VA 22304.

Deaver, S. (2009). A normative study of children's drawings: Preliminary research findings. *Art Therapy: Journal of the American Art Therapy Association, 26*(1), 4–11.

Deaver, S., & Bernier, M. (2014). The Art Therapy-Projective Imagery Assessment. In L. Handler & A. Thomas (Eds.), *Drawings in assessment and psychotherapy: Research and application* (pp. 131–147). New York, NY: Routledge.

Gantt, L. (2001). The Formal Elements Art Therapy Scale: A measurement system for global variables in art. *Art Therapy: Journal of the American Art Therapy Association, 18*(1), 50–55.

Gantt, L. (2004). The case for formal art therapy assessments. *Art Therapy: Journal of the American Art Therapy Association, 21*(1), 18–29.

Gantt, L., & Tabone, C. (1998). *Formal Elements Art Therapy Scale: The rating manual.* Morgantown, WV: Gargoyle Press.

Geisinger, K. (1994). Cross-cultural normative assessment: Translation and adaptation issues influencing the normative interpretation of assessment instruments. *Psychological Assessment, 6*(4), 304–312.

Hamilton, M. (2008). *Developing a standardized rating system for the Face Stimulus Assessment (FSA) using 9 scales adapted from the Formal Elements Art Therapy Scale (FEATS).* Unpublished master's thesis, Avila University, Kansas City, MO.

Kaiser, D. (1996). Indications of attachment security in a drawing task. *The Arts in Psychotherapy, 23*(4), 333–340.

Kaiser, D., & Deaver, S. (2009). Assessing attachment with the Bird's Nest Drawing: A review of the research. *Art Therapy: Journal of the American Art Therapy Association, 26*(1), 26–33.

Kramer, E., & Schehr, J. (1983). An art therapy evaluation session for children. *American Journal of Art Therapy, 23*(1), 3–12.

Lee, S. T. (2011). *A cross-cultural study of Korean and American children's Human Figure Drawings.* Unpublished master's thesis, Eastern Virginia Medical School, Norfolk, VA.

Levick, M. (2009). *The Levick Emotional and Cognitive Art Therapy Assessment: A normative study.* Bloomington, IN: AuthorHouse.

Lowenfeld, V., & Brittain, L. (1987). *Creative and mental growth* (8th ed.). New York, NY: Macmillan.

Mills, A. (2003). The Diagnostic Drawings Series. In C. Malchiodi (Ed.), *Handbook of art therapy* (pp. 401–409). New York, NY: Guilford.

Mills, A. (2008). *Diagnostic Drawing Series resource list.* Available from the DDS Project, PO Box 9853, Alexandria, VA 22304.

Nelson, L. (1994). Introduction to the special section on normative assessment. *Psychological Assessment, 6*(4), 283.

Palliparambil, A. (2011). *Culture's impact on drawing styles: A comparison of Indian, Indian-American, and American children's Human Figure Drawings.* Unpublished master's thesis, Eastern Virginia Medical School, Norfolk, VA.

Rubin, J. (1984). A diagnostic art interview. In *Child art therapy* (pp. 51–76). New York, NY: Van Nostrand Reinhold.

Shin, S., & Koh, M. (2005, Summer). Korean education in cultural context. *Essays in Education, 14.* Available from http://www.usca.edu/essays/vol14summer2005.html.

Shukla, S. (1983). Public educational systems in a colonial context: The case of India's transition from indigenous to modern ideas and institutions in the nineteenth century. *Journal of Education, 165*(4), 399–406.

Silver, R. (2002). *Three art assessments.* New York, NY: Brunner-Routledge.

Smead, E. (2004). *A cross-cultural study of children's development as reflected in their artwork: An investigation of children's drawings from the African country of Benin.* Unpublished master's thesis, Eastern Virginia Medical School, Norfolk, VA.

Wolf, D., & Perry, M. (1988). From endpoints to repertoires: Some new conclusions about drawing development. *Journal of Aesthetic Education, 22*(1), 17–34.

Part VII

Research Models in Art Therapy

Introduction

One challenge that the field of art therapy faces is the lack of *robust* research about the profession. Originally, narrative case studies were the research method of choice by art therapists and were based in psychoanalytic practice. Until recently, there has been little, albeit much needed, empirical evidence–based research to support the efficacy of art therapy. As the field matured, so did knowledge of how to use and conduct research. Today, art therapists recognize the importance of vigorous, quantitatively based empirical research. Yet, there is also an understanding of the importance of in-depth, thoughtful explorations using qualitative methods. Mixed methods are also being embraced by art therapists who realize that the nuanced combination of both quantitative and qualitative methods may offer a far-reaching means of enquiry.

The seven chapters that make up this section offer a range of research methodologies, from qualitative to quantitative and beyond. For the introductory chapter, *Research: An Overview of Historical and Contemporary Perspectives in Art Therapy Research in America*, Robb interviewed a number of art therapy educators and researchers in North America to explore the contemporary views of art therapy research. She did this within the context of the profession's historical roots. Robb reported that, although many art therapists were adverse to research initially, scientific enquiry is now seen as a valuable and necessary means of advancing the field.

While early art therapy research began through anecdotal narratives labeled as "case studies," Gussak points out, in his chapter titled *A Case for Case Studies: More than Telling a Story*, that a well-crafted, correctly applied case study methodology can provide rich, valuable exploratory results that focus solely on human element experiences and interactions with the environment.

In *Social Action Research Methods and Art Therapy*, Potash and Kalmonowitz argue that observing people in their natural environment, during sessions, and at other events, "allow[s] researchers to use their theoretical knowledge and practical skills in collaboration with participants in order to promote political, social, and economic reforms." The authors delineate the theoretical and philosophical tenets of social action research. They also offer ways to use this method in art therapy research.

The Wiley Handbook of Art Therapy, First Edition. Edited by David E. Gussak and Marcia L. Rosal.
© 2016 John Wiley & Sons, Ltd. Published 2016 by John Wiley & Sons, Ltd.

In the chapter titled *Quantitative Investigations: Alternative Choices*, Elkis-Abuhoff provides a concise overview of the various quantitative methods that an art therapist may use. Next, Patricia St John's chapter, *Experimental and Control Group Research Designs*, provides further explorations of the designs that lead to uncovering therapeutic efficacy. St John deconstructs these complicated research methods into understandable steps.

Gerber combines the valuable components of both qualitative and quantitative approaches in her chapter on *Mixed Methods Research and Art Therapy*. More than simply adding hard data to qualitative narrative, Gerber introduces the rich and complex melding of two very distinct research designs to provide a rich tapestry of empirical support with detailed qualitative depth. More than merely defining this approach, Gerber contends that there is a natural synergy between mixed-methods approaches and art therapy.

This section concludes with the Kaiser and Kay chapter titled *Arts-based Research: The Basics for Art Therapists*. In art-based research methods, the art is not merely a variable to be studied but rather the data-gathering mechanism itself. As the authors posited, "what better tool can an art therapist use to rigorously explore and make sense of the world?"

Although only seven chapters comprise this important section, together they deliver a thought-provoking array of methods by which to research the intricacies of the art therapy field. The intent of this section is for readers to ponder on the importance of conducting research. Although not all art therapists will be inspired to conduct research, reading, evaluating, and incorporating research findings in treatment is critical to effective practice of art therapy.

58

An Overview of Historical and Contemporary Perspectives in Art Therapy Research in America

Megan Robb[1]

Understanding the intricacies and value of art therapy has long been an issue for art therapists and professionals in related fields. Since the inception of the American Art Therapy Association (AATA) in 1969, art therapists have investigated numerous theories about clinical practice and examined the phenomenon of helping others through art. Over that same timeframe, art therapy research, which started with case histories and theory building, evolved into the publication of peer-reviewed studies in alignment with the research standards of other disciplines. Art therapists are now using a variety of research approaches in attempting to investigate how art therapy helps clients.

As the field matured, the number of researchers increased from a relatively small and contained group of people to widespread involvement in research enquiry. The scope of research has broadened as well, from beyond finding one truth, as in positivism, toward embracing a post-modern spectrum of research methods. As it evolved, there has been considerable debate within AATA about how and what to research.

This chapter will review the history of research in art therapy in the United States. In addition, through interviews with several art therapists, researchers, and educators, a contemporary view of art therapy research is described, which includes addressing current trends in education, evidence-based research, and research methods. A thorough look at the history of educating art therapists about research is included.

Historical View of Art Therapy Research in America

Art therapy research has a longer lineage than is commonly understood, and it is rooted in the worlds of both psychology and art. Junge and Linesch (1993) studied early mental health research methods and stated that, "during [the] nineteenth century, psychiatrists and psychologists interacted with their patients to develop comprehensive case histories that sought to illuminate human behavior, psychopathology and the subjective human experience" (p. 61). One early research method was to look at art

---

The Wiley Handbook of Art Therapy, First Edition. Edited by David E. Gussak and Marcia L. Rosal.
© 2016 John Wiley & Sons, Ltd. Published 2016 by John Wiley & Sons, Ltd.

made by individuals with mental illness. In 1922, Hans Prinzhorn, a German psychiatrist and art historian, published *Artistry of the Mentally Ill: A Contribution to the Psychology and Psychopathology of Configuration*. This text focused on art phenomena as "universal conditions such as the tendencies towards order, ornamentation, and repetition that he observed in patient artwork" (McNiff, 1998, p. 99).

Jung developed his psychological theories through art-making as documented in *Red Book*, published in 2009. Another early theorist, Rudolf Arnheim (1966), studied the aesthetic qualities of art as perceived by the artist and the viewer. Pioneers in art therapy built upon the work of Prinzhorn, Jung, Arnheim, and others, combining the arts, psychology, anthropology, literature, and mythology, among other fields.

One early example of a formalized research relationship occurred with art therapists at the National Institutes of Health, a federally funded research facility in the United States that began functioning in the 1970s. Hanna Kwiatkowska, Harriet Wadeson, and Sadie Fishman established art therapy protocols that sought to clarify the specific role played by art therapy in practice, as well as to answer arts' role in mental health diagnosis, symptomology, and treatment (Robb, 2012). During the 1980s, Arthur Robbins analyzed the intersection of aesthetics and psychodynamic theory, particularly the inner thoughts of the therapist and the client–therapist relationship, establishing the still-relevant concept of intersubjectivity (Gerber et al., 2012; Robbins, 1986).

These early research efforts were highlighted through the *Bulletin of Art Therapy* (started in 1968 and eventually renamed the *American Journal of Art Therapy*) and *Art Therapy: Journal of the American Art Therapy Association* (Kapitan, 2010). *The Arts in Psychotherapy*, which began publication in 1973, provided the first platform for tracking research on an international level (Kapitan, 2010). On an organizational level, AATA sought ways through which to promote research. The association established a research committee in 1978, chaired by Kwiatkowska. The research committee sought to increase awareness about research by creating a research project competition that same year, which granted a monetary award (Wadeson, 1992).

While AATA demonstrated commitment to research, it was difficult to garner support from its membership. During the mid-1980s, AATA chose to suspend the research award (Wadeson, 1992). At that point, few research projects were being submitted, and many of those submitted had poor research designs (M. Rosal, personal communication, April 25, 2012). Research still was not a primary focus for most art therapists, who remained focused on their clinical work.

Kapitan (2010) reported that art therapists lacked a common research language during the 1980s. Perhaps to address this problem, the journal *Art Therapy* shifted to peer-reviewed publications with a focus on research reports in 1983 (Kapitan, 2010). By the end of the 1980s, there was a widespread desire to create a guide for art therapists to increase knowledge and skills about research, which led eventually to the publication of *A Guide to Conducting Art Therapy Research* (Wadeson, 1992).

One of the difficulties in finding common ground for conducting research in art therapy was the lack of consensus about the best goals and purposes for research. Early on, there was a public debate, evident in publications as well as at professional meetings, about research fundamentals such as how to conduct research and which research methods were appropriate for the field. The push among some for qualitative research was resisted by those who favored empiricism, in an effort to "legitimize art therapy" (Junge & Linesch, 1993, p. 61). Favoring empirical research came with a consequence. Linesch (1995), in a study examining the experience of art therapy researchers, found several obstacles to conducting empirical research (such as the weak research designs selected). There was a perception that there was a lack of rigor in art-based research, which led to feelings of "intimidation, alienation, and ambivalence" (p. 265). This lack of agreement about directions and methods led to a period of conflict within the field. Metzl (2008) purported that the debate was a "reflection of this young field's struggle to maintain its unique identity while obtaining validation within at least three communities (scientific, clinical, and artistic)" (p. 62).

In 1999, AATA created a research task force that "developed short papers on conducting research, and organized panels on research for conferences and assisted in the re-development and management of research awards" (Betts & Laloge, 2000, p. 292). One successful effort was to create a revised *Guide to Conducting Art Therapy Research* as two special sections published in *Art Therapy* in 2001–2002 (Vick, 2001). The intention was to put to rest the longstanding debate about the merits of qualitative versus quantitative research by presenting instruction across this whole spectrum of approaches (Anderson, 2001; Carolan, 2001; Deaver, 2002; Kaplan, 2001). Today, art therapists find value in both methodologies and often used a mixed-methods approach in art therapy research. The evolution of research opinions within art therapy can be seen in two membership surveys, the first in 2000 (Betts & Laloge, 2000) and the other in 2009 (AATA, 2009), where membership involvement in research-related activity increased from 5% to 20%, regardless of the method of choice.

Trends in Research Education

As educational standards in master's-level programs "matured and aligned themselves with the research requirements of psychology and other established methods of conducting mental health research" (McNiff, 1998, p. 86), research was included in the AATA's Educational Standards as a required content area in July 2002 (Vick, 2001).

In an effort to meet this required content area, the research competencies expected from graduate students included the "ability to read critically and to understand published research" (Kaiser, St. John, & Ball, 2004), but not necessarily to be ready to conduct research. This is in line with the focus of clinician training programs on producing *research practitioners* (Kapitan, 2006). Research practitioners are "consumers of research findings about assessment and treatment, evaluators of their own interventions" (Haring-Hidore & Vacc, 1988, p. 286), with an emphasis on evidence-based practice (Brennan, 2011). Yet, opportunities to conduct original research while learning might prepare students to be better researchers once they are in the field, which some hold as a long-term goal for the field (L. Gantt, personal communication, April 4, 2012; J. Potash, personal communication, May 10, 2012; E. Warson, personal communication, April 18, 2012).

Some believe that art therapy students may need exposure to research that is more qualitative in its approach, such as using art-based enquiry as a way of developing clinical skills. One method is Goebl-Parker's (2012) use of art documentation in practice and in research. Another is Mount Mary College's art therapy thesis research project, which provides an opportunity to explore aspects of art therapy by making art and disseminating the research through art as well (B. Moon, personal communication, July 17, 2012).

Educators, many of whom have only completed master's level training, may not be well-prepared to teach rigorous research methodologies (Junge, 2010). Malchiodi (1995) reported that only a minority of art therapy educators conduct research. Anderson (2001) found that a minority of art therapists write the majority of research. In addition, as the majority of the membership is women with master's degrees, they are less likely to be supported, groomed, and accepted into a medical model research arena (Metzl, 2008).

Today, there is a surge in the number of art therapy faculty with doctorates; these faculty members may increase the amount of research conducted. Faculty members with research experience are improving the research education of art therapy students. For example, rather than simply being exposed to a general research survey course, students are now exposed to the methodologies that are the specific focus of art therapy faculty members (S. Talwar, personal communication, March 21, 2012).

With the advent of the twenty-first century, there is a push to create more doctoral programs in art therapy. Gerber stated that doctoral and post-doctoral programs have a profound effect on defining the practice of art therapy and the shape of research conducted within the field (2006, p. 99). Gerber found that many doctoral programs maintain an emphasis on positivism, just as Junge and Linesch reported in the early 1990s. Doctoral programs, in Gerber's view, need to perform a wider function, "embracing existing research traditions, as well as [cultivating] new research paradigms" (p. 106) beyond the framework of positivism.

Trends in Evidence-Based Research

The arch of art therapy research has been influenced by many factors, including evidence-based research and its relationship with managed care and licensure requirements. Gleaned from randomized-controlled trials, evidence-based practice (EBP) dictates appropriate and proscribed treatment. American researchers may look to the United Kingdom, where the national health care system resulted in art therapy's collective effort to produce evidence-based practice (Gilroy, 2006). In *Art Therapy, Research, and Evidence-based Practice*, Gilroy supported seeking evidence-based research that informs our discipline with our "own kind of evidence" (p. 5), rather than disadvantaging art therapy for not adhering to the EBP model of research (Kaplan, 2000).

Such studies not only help to inform clinical work, but also aid in licensure efforts. In many states, providing evidence that someone without art therapy skills and training can harm clients is essential for title protection (P. Howie, personal communication, March 23, 2012; Springham, 2008). EBP can aid in licensure but it is not the only way to demonstrate efficacy (B. Moon, personal communication July 18, 2012). Gilroy (2006) proposed using a cycle of implementing best practices and then auditing these practices to ensure quality of service and positive treatment outcomes; this information can inform policy-makers, managers, or the public.

Art therapists are attempting to position research to fit within outcome studies (Julliard, 1998; Kapitan, 2010). Currently, there are collaborations with federal programs such as Complementary and Alternatives Medicine and other working groups within the National Institutes of Health (M. Rosal, personal communication, April 25, 2012; N. Gerber, personal communication, May 5, 2012). The AATA research committee attempted to create a congressional line item—a governmental source of earmarked spending—to fund the first national clinical outcomes study (Kapitan, 2010). The committee sought a congressional sponsor for this effort to fund large-scale art therapy protocol-based research, but did not succeed (P. Howie, personal communication, March 23, 2012). In pursuit of outcomes studies, there is an identified need for multi-site, large-scale research projects, which has been stressed by Deaver, Gantt, and Howie.

Trends in Methods of Research

Collaboration is the key to future research, in which "art therapists work collectively" with allied health professionals (Gilroy, 2006, p. 35; Robb, 2012). Funders are looking for diverse teams of experts (D. Betts, personal communication, May 7, 2012). Collaboration also provides the opportunity to conduct larger-scale studies, as well as possible multi-site studies. However, collaboration must be based on equal partnerships (B. Moon, personal communication, July 17, 2012). Rather than using psychological measures as a sole data collection mechanism, art therapy can find equal footing with art-based data collection. Research partners that only perceive art therapists in an adjunctive role miss the opportunity to explore the power of art therapy as a primary mode of therapy and to uncover how art informs clinicians about the concerns and needs of the client (N. Gerber, personal communication, May 4, 2012; S. McNiff, personal communication, April 19, 2012; J. Potash, personal communication, May 10, 2012).

Kaiser and Deaver (2012) found that the use of a mixed-method approach to research was one of the top five research methodologies cited by art therapists as important and timely; the others were experimental, multi-site studies, assessment-oriented, and cross-cultural methods. The authors realized that, by supporting a multiplicity of techniques to collect and interpret data, art therapists may have a better chance of becoming equal partners within research teams. Kaiser and Deaver (2012) also discovered that art therapists think that outcome and efficacy studies are of utmost importance, and that there is a strong contingent of art therapy researchers who are attempting to create and replicate systemic, rigorous art-based research methods. One outcome of their research was the development of a research agenda for art therapists. Included in the agenda were both topics to address and populations to study (see Table 58.1).

Yet, the survey of art therapists interviewed for this chapter generated a very different set of issues for an art therapy research agenda than what Kaiser and Deaver found (see Table 58.2). In fact, McNiff asked, "If we believe art is an intelligence, a core way of knowing, and that is our rationale in our profession, then why don't we practice that in our research?" (personal communication, April 19, 2012). Several art therapists stated that researching *art as a way of knowing* through art-enquiry methods is key to understanding the mechanisms of art therapy that is supported in other fields (e.g., Knowles and Cole's *Handbook of the Arts in Qualitative Research*, 2008; J. Potash, personal

Table 58.1 Results from Kaiser and Deaver's Delphi Study (2012).

Important areas to study	1. Outcome/efficacy/evidence-based research
	2. Art therapy and neuroscience
	3. Research on the processes and mechanisms in art therapy
	4. Art therapy assessment validity and reliability
	5. Cross-cultural/multicultural approaches to art therapy assessment and practice
	6. Establishment of a database of normative artwork across the lifespan
Populations to be studied	1. Trauma/complex trauma/trauma in inner city, vets
	2. Psychiatric major mental illness (includes eating and attachment disorders)
	3. Autism/Autism Spectrum Disorder (ASD)
	4. Medical/Cancer (CA)
	5. At-risk youth in schools (includes learning disorders)
	6. Geriatric (includes Parkinson's disease)

Table 58.2 Potential questions for art therapy research (various personal communications).

Some of the fundamental questions being asked or researched are:

- What does art therapy do differently from other mental health professions?
- If someone is not trained and he/she conducts art therapy, could someone be hurt?
- What does it mean to include art in therapy?
- Is there a difference between doing self-immersion reflection in art and art-based research?
- What makes it art therapy and not art?
- What are the factors in art making that contribute to healing?
- Is art therapy safe?
- What is the difference between doing art by yourself and with others?
- Answer questions what, why, and how is art therapy useful?
- What is the aesthetic and psychological significance of creative objects?
- What qualities of mind and therapist behaviors are unique, not unique, essential, compatible, or prescribed to the practice of art therapy?

communication, May 10, 2012; B. Moon, personal communication, July 17, 2012; McNiff, 2011). Linesch called for investigating art therapy with a wider set of methods that embrace the arts and its processes (personal communication, April 4, 2012). Gerber encouraged using our language, but in a way that scientists understand (N. Gerber, personal communication, May 4, 2012). Goebl-Parker (2012) found that aesthetic listening described one process of combining clinical practice and research.

Conclusion

Since the beginning of the profession, research has played a major role in the development of art therapy. The profession has moved beyond being divisive about conducting and publishing research toward an understanding that research is of upmost importance. Today, research is supported by a majority of art therapists, many of whom are developing novel and various ways of thinking, researching, and critically analyzing art therapy. Educators who are knowledgeable about research have improved the learning outcomes of art therapy research courses. For students, understanding how to read and become better consumers of research is furthering the field by producing more thoughtful and knowledgeable clinicians. As support for research increases, more rigorously designed, funded, and treatment-oriented art therapy research will be conducted. With an improvement in the quality as well as a burgeoning in the quantity of art therapy research, the inclusion of art therapy in healthcare initiatives is possible. The ongoing work of art therapy researchers could drastically shape and change our profession for the better.

Endnote

1 *Author's note*: In order to investigate historical and contemporary landscapes of art therapy research, I interviewed several art therapists, educators, and researchers in the United States, as well as one in Canada. I started with the authors of primary research texts and asked them for further referrals. In response to questions about the state of art therapy research, many themes emerged from the interviews. When an idea has been shared, no individual is cited; however, when an idea came from an individual, personal communication is referenced. I want to thank the following professionals for their contributions to our field and for their candor during the interview process: Donna Betts, Kate Collie, Sarah Deaver, Linda Gantt, Nancy Gerber, Shelly Goebl-Parker, Paula Howie, Lynn Kapitan, Debra Linesch, Shaun McNiff, Bruce Moon, Jordan Potash, Marcia Rosal, Savneet Talwar, and Elizabeth Warson.

References

American Art Therapy Association. (2009). *2009 Membership Survey*. Retrieved from http://www.americanarttherapyassociation.org/upload/2009membershipsurvey.pdf

Anderson, F. E. (2001). Benefits of conducting research. *Art Therapy: Journal of the American Art Therapy Association, 18*(3), 134–141.

Arnheim, R. (1966). *Art and visual perception: A psychology of the creative eye*. Berkeley, CA: University of California Press.

Betts, D., & Laloge, L. (2000). Art therapist and research: A survey conducted by the American Art Therapy Association. *Art Therapy: Journal of the American Art Therapy Association, 17*(4), 291–295.

Brennan, C. (2011). The role of research in art therapy master's degree programs. *Art Therapy: Journal of the American Art Therapy Association, 28*(3), 140–144.

Carolan, R. (2001). Models and paradigms of art therapy research. *Journal of American Art Therapy Association, 18*(4), 190–206. doi:10.1080/07421656.2001.10129537

Deaver, S. P. (2002). What constitutes art therapy research? *Art Therapy: Journal of the American Art Therapy Association, 19*(1), 23–27. doi: 10.1080/07421656.2002.10129721

Gerber, N. (2006). The essential components of doctoral-level education for art therapists. *The Arts in Psychotherapy, 33*, 98–112. doi: 10.1016/j.aip.2005.08.002

Gerber, N., Templeton, N., Chilton, G., Liebman, M. C., Manders, E., & Shim, M. (2012). Art-based research as a pedagogical approach to studying intersubjectivity in the creative arts therapies. *Journal of Applied Arts and Health, 3*(1), 39–48. doi: 10.1386/jaah.3.1.39_1

Gilroy, A. (2006). *Art therapy, research and evidence-based practice*. London: Sage Publications.

Goebl-Parker, E. M. (2012). Aesthetic listening: A Reggio-inspired studio research paradigm for art therapy. In H. Burt (Ed.), *Art therapy and postmodernism* (pp. 325–343). London: Jessica Kingsley Publishers.

Haring-Hidore, M., & Vacc, N. (1988). The scientist-practitioner model in training entry-level counselors. *Journal of Counseling and Development, 66,* 286–288.

Julliard, K. (1998). Outcomes research in health care: implications for art therapy. *Art Therapy: Journal of the American Art Therapy Association, 15*(1), 13–21.

Jung, C. G. (2009). *The red book.* New York, NY: W.W. Norton & Company.

Junge, M. B. (2010). *The modern history of art therapy in the United States.* Springfield, IL: Charles C. Thomas.

Junge, M. B., & Linesch, D. (1993). Our own voices: New paradigms for art therapy research. *The Arts in Psychotherapy, 20,* 61–67.

Kaiser, D., & Deaver, S. P. (2012, July). *Generating a research agenda for art therapy using the Delphi Method. The American Art Therapy Association's 43rd annual conference,* Savannah, GA.

Kaiser, D., St. John, P., & Ball, B. (2004). Teaching art therapy research: A brief report. *Art Therapy: Journal of the American Art Therapy Association, 23*(4), 186–190. doi: 10.1080/07421656.2006.10129331

Kapitan, L. (2006). The "Multiplier Effect": Art therapy research that benefits all. *Art Therapy: Journal of the American Art Therapy Association, 23*(4), 154–155.

Kapitan, L. (2010). *Introduction to art therapy research.* New York, NY: Routledge.

Kaplan, F. F. (2000). *Art, science and art therapy.* London: Jessica Kingsley Publishers.

Kaplan, F. F. (2001). Areas of inquiry for art therapy research. *Art Therapy: Journal of the American Art Therapy Association, 18*(3), 142–147. doi 10.1080/07421656.2001.10129734

Knowles, J. G., & Cole, A. L. (Eds.) (2008). *Handbook of the arts in qualitative research.* Los Angeles, CA: Sage Publications.

Linesch, D. (1995). Art therapy research: Learning from experience. *Art Therapy: Journal of the American Art Therapy Association, 12*(4), 261–265.

McNiff, S. (1998). *Art-based research.* London: Jessica Kingsley Publishers.

McNiff, S. (2011). Artistic expressions as primary modes of inquiry. *British Journal of Guidance and Counseling, 39*(5), 385–396. doi: 10.1080/03069885.2011.621526

Malchiodi, C. (1995). Does a lack of art therapy research hold us back? *Art Therapy: Journal of the American Art Therapy Association, 12*(4), 218–219.

Metzl, E. S. (2008). Systemic analysis of the art therapy research published in *Art Therapy: Journal of the AATA* between 1987 and 2004. *The Arts in Psychotherapy, 35,* 60–73. doi:10.1016/j.aip.2007.09.003

Prinzhorn, H. (1922). *Bildnerei der geisteskranken: Ein beitrag zur psychologie und psychopathologie der gestaltung* [Artistry of the mentally ill]. Germany: Springer.

Robb, M.A. (2012). The history of art therapy at the National Institutes of Health. *Art Therapy: Journal of American Art Therapy Association, 29*(1), 33–37. doi: 10.1080/07421656.2012.648097

Robbins, A. (1986). *Expressive therapy: A creative arts approach to depth-oriented treatment.* New York, NY: Human Sciences Press.

Springham, N. (2008). Through the eyes of the law: What is it about art that can harm people? *International Journal of Art Therapy, 13*(2), 65–73. doi: 10.1080/17454830802489141

Vick, R. M. (2001). Introduction to the special section on research in art therapy: When does an idea begin? *Art Therapy: Journal of American Art Therapy Association, 18*(3), 132–133. doi: 10.1080/07421656.2001.10129732

Wadeson, H. (Ed.). (1992). *A guide to conducting art therapy research.* Mundelein, IL: American Art Therapy Association, Inc.

59

A Case for Case Studies:
More than Telling a Story
David E. Gussak

A *case study* is an in-depth analysis or examination of a single case to obtain information pertaining to a specific situation. It is a methodology "in which a single individual, group, or important example is studied extensively and varied data are collected and used to formulate interpretations applicable to the specific case ... or to provide useful generalizations" (Fraenkel & Wallen, 2009, p. 13). Historically, there has been a paradoxical acceptance/rejection of the case study methodology. Gerring (2004) argued that, after considerable consideration of the ambiguous nature of this methodology, and the numerous types of studies labeled "case studies," a single definition is apt: a case study is "an intensive study of a single unit for the purpose of understanding a larger class of (similar) units" (p. 342). What is clear is that there exists a distinction, often blurred, between effectual case study research and those labeled as such, but may in fact be otherwise.

The case study permeates many fields and professions, most notably those involved with the social sciences; this includes clinical fields such as art therapy. Many early art therapy publications relied on case studies and presentations to investigate art therapy in many settings, with various clinical and medical populations. In these instances, as Kapitan (2010) pointed out, the researcher was "... interested in discovering what can be learned from a particular encounter or encounters in the field that have bearing on art therapy practice" (p. 103). Often questioned for their validity as a form of scientific enquiry, case studies can be effective, provided that the focus is on people and their interactions (Gordon & Shontz, 1990; Kapitan, 2010).

Research in the field of art therapy has since developed to include many methodological approaches. However, despite some perspectives that case studies may no longer be rigorous enough with the ongoing focus on empirical research (Woodside, 2010), they have greatly evolved. Some argue that they remain a valuable methodological tool: "[T]he case study method retains considerable appeal ... [and] is solidly ensconced, and, perhaps, even thriving" (Gerring, 2004, p. 341). Of course, case studies, similar to any methodological approach, are subject to incorrect application, or merely not a well justified methodology for a given research question. Some may be misled about what it really is, appearing to some to be a comparatively easy approach, such as telling a story. Clearly, it is much more than that, and careful

The Wiley Handbook of Art Therapy, First Edition. Edited by David E. Gussak and Marcia L. Rosal.
© 2016 John Wiley & Sons, Ltd. Published 2016 by John Wiley & Sons, Ltd.

consideration must be made prior to its use. Gerring argued that several characteristics must be considered in order to effectively apply a case study:

- When inferences are descriptive rather than causal
- When propositional depth is prized over breadth and boundedness
- When (internal) case comparability is given precedence over (external) case representativeness
- When the insight into causal mechanisms is more important than insight into … effects
- When the causal proposition is at issue is invariant rather than probabilistic
- When the strategy of research is exploratory, rather than confirmatory
- When useful variance is available for only a single unit or a small number of units. (p. 352)

While not all of these considerations seem to fit all case studies, and not all may resonate with members of the art therapy field, they underscore the need to carefully consider and justify the rationale before this approach is used.

If done correctly, case studies can be sufficient on their own or can contribute to a variety of other methodological approaches. Since case studies have been widely used, a complete examination of all of the ways in which it has been considered, applied, and argued about would fill its own volume. Consequently, this chapter is able to only provide a glimpse of the issues.

This chapter will explore the ambiguities that the term "case study" may imply, provide robust examples, and examine the various types of case studies. Because of the numerous ways that case studies have been used, examples will be drawn from various fields, not just art therapy, to best illustrate them. This chapter will then provide an example of an art therapy case study that became a full-length manuscript, ultimately concluding that case studies continue to have its place among the research pantheon.

Different Considerations

Study or storytelling? Does it matter?

How a case study is used or how something is deemed to even be a case study may be somewhat ambiguous. In some situations, a narrative is deemed to be a case study if it demonstrates a singular example of an overall premise. However, case study narratives differ from case vignettes, which are simply anecdotal accounts to illustrate conclusions or theories obtained through other methodological approaches. For example, these descriptions can often be used in conjunction with quantitative data to flesh out the numbers and statistical results, and, in fact, can make the conclusions seem more real. For example, in my own empirical studies of the effectiveness of art therapy in prison settings, I relied on such narratives to provide the picture of what the statistics were indicating. Narratives, called "case examples," of Devin and Mark were provided to compare and contrast how art therapy affected two prison inmates (Gussak, 2004). Although not necessary for the article, these case vignettes helped make sense of the numbers.

Such examples are not restricted to research. Many theoretical presentations and publications rely on such vignettes to illustrate the point that an author is trying to make. The art therapy literature is filled with such examples, dating back to some of the earliest texts in the field (Kramer, 1971; Landgarten, 1981; Ulman & Dachinger, 1975; Wadeson, 1980). A number of chapters included in this volume rely on case vignettes to illustrate various theoretical positions.

In some publications, certain explorations were labeled "case studies," yet it is not clear if the authors started with an intention toward research or if they simply relied on narrating experiences to inform already developed theories, and then called them "case studies." While such articles may be valid explorations and important contributions, labeling them as such may be imprecise. Broecher's (2012) article on how children use drawings to cope with surgery explored a particular child's response through information provided by his father in a parenting class. While titled a "case study," there was no clearly articulated methodology and no research question. It was unclear if the author intended for this interaction to become a "study," or if he simply used the story to illustrate the positive outcome. Regardless, the outcome and information was sound, and it provided valuable information from which future explorations can be drawn. In an article simply entitled "Case Study," in the journal *Sexual Addiction and Compulsivity: The Journal of Treatment and Prevention*, Manley told the story of Bill, a man in treatment for sexual addiction (1998). With no preamble such as a rationale for the study, established research question, or justification of the methodology, Manley concluded that this illustration "is an excellent example of the three stages of recovery ... [from such compulsions]" (p. 138). In "A Professor's Experience with Loss," Comerchero (2012) used her own story, an "autobiographical case study," to illustrate "obstacles faced in dealing with anticipatory grief ... demonstrates how clinicians and research may use adverse life circumstances to develop research and applied programs ..." (para 1). The paper, presented in a first-person account, evaluated the author's own experiences with grief, similar to how Victor Frankl examined his own experiences in a death camp in *Man's Search for Meaning* (1959). Although the author recognized that conclusions from this examination cannot be generalized to larger populations, she did reflect on its ability to "provide a starting point" for others who suffer grief themselves or for researchers examining effects of bereaved individuals. While valuable contributions to their respective fields, these examples nevertheless demonstrate how loosely the term "case study" may be applied.

When only a case study will do

A successful case study is both robust and comprehensive, and, as the only effective method of enquiry, may be quite time-consuming. Sunde Peterson's 15-year longitudinal study on an "exceptional female" (2012), although not an art therapy study, is a remarkable example of the detail and attention necessary for an effectual case study. The study required a great deal of planning and organization; the researcher began corresponding with the participant when she was only 15 years old. She gathered data from the participant through e-mails, letters, and face-to-face unstructured interviews, and recorded the gathered information through handwritten notes and occasional audiotapes. Eight years into the study, the researcher gathered additional interview data from the participants' "mother, a gifted-education teacher, a former employer, her husband, and three university peers, usually posing only one question to each" (p. 247). Her mother also provided the researcher the participant's journals, school records, and projects. As the study progressed, literature was gathered from various resources. Sunde Peterson used the literature to triangulate the interview data. Upon reaching saturation, she was able to construct a comprehensive review of how a person's giftedness can be simultaneously a burden and an asset.

Overall, this single case provided an exhaustive understanding of what a gifted individual may experience: "[w]hether she is typical of gifted individuals struggling with difficult circumstances is unknown. However, the study offers a rare and credible glimpse of the subjective experience of giftedness in various contexts ..." (p. 258). It can be argued that such comprehensive information would not have been readily available had she not conducted a case study. From this, other mental health professionals and educators can understand similar experiences, and use this as a basis for conducting their own research.

Often, a single-case study may be combined with other methodologies. More than simply providing a vignette to support the overriding conclusion, a researcher may conduct several qualitative studies simultaneously to create a possibly richer reflection of human experiences (Kincheloe, 2005; Van Lith, 2008). For example, Van Lith (2008), in examining how art therapy may aid a client's transition from inpatient care to a residential setting, combined "a single-case study framework and an art-based research approach. This format allowed for in-depth, client-centered exploration of verbal and non-verbal phenomena, as part of the therapeutic process of transition" (p. 25). Her data collection consisted of the client's visual journal, her artwork, the researcher's own session notes and reflections to the client's artwork. Observations of the clients' interaction with the art during the sessions, her behaviors, and notes from the verbal discussions about each of the images were recorded to support the case study. While she recognized that the study may have been stronger had she elicited responses from the client's family, friends, other residents, and the professionals who were simultaneously working with the client, Van Lith was ultimately able to arrive at a much more substantial conclusion with the combination of methodological approaches.

Can a Case Study be Quantitative?

While oftentimes associated with qualitative research, in which the data is gathered through observations in the single subject's natural setting and his or her interactions with surrounding phenomena, it can be used as a quantitative examination. Data and findings can be obtained through controlling variables and establishing particular measures for a subject of one ($N = 1$). Known as a single-case design, Behling and Merves (1984) recognized it as a systematic observation of a specific behavior, and thus could be operationalized to accommodate an empirical means of measure, specific to clinical research.

> The pattern created by these observations [of a specific behavior or set of behaviors] is analyzed for change through time and in relation to an introduced (intervention) or experimental variable. Single-case designs include the major features of time series analysis

... the experimental dimension is added when an intervening (experimental or treatment) variable "X" is introduced after the establishment of baseline behavior ... this will be followed by a period of continued observation and data collection of the target behavior or set of behaviors. (p. 3)

To strengthen the validity of such a model, additional steps are added, and often a return to the baseline, with additional evaluations of the interventions. Known as an A-B-A model, "... confidence in this hypothesis is further increased ... if the pattern of response in the second intervention condition (B) replicates the change of the early intervention (B) condition" (Carolan, 2001, p. 195). In this case, the A-B could be repeated until saturation is reached.

Several single cases can be combined to strengthen an overall hypothesis, by adding participants, or changing behaviors or settings. It is for this reason that Carolan (2001) argued that such a design should not be confused with a qualitative case study, as it is often used "primarily with a small number of subjects (i.e., 6–12) at the same time, not with one subject. ... The 'single' refers to the fact that the same individual serves both as the experimental and control samples" (p. 195). However, while in the spirit of conducting robust and valid research, this may be true, it can be argued that this is simply semantics. The empirical approach may be taken with a single participant, and hence focus on a single case. While perhaps not as strong as multiple baselines, such enquiry may provide a basis or scaffolding for future studies.

For example, Hoffmann (2011), in her thesis examining how art therapy may address the cognitive symptoms in a patient with Parkinson's disease, used an A-B-A single-subject research design with multiple baselines. Overall, she determined that, after 6 weeks of intervention, art therapy was effective in reducing the patient's depression and stabilizing her at her current level of dementia. In examining the effectiveness of art therapy in increasing the self-esteem of an imprisoned sex-offender, Ackerman (1992) used a single-case study A-B-A design, in which the B was the art intervention used. The outcome was then measured through changes between pretest and posttest measures in this one individual. Howard's study on the benefits of using art therapy in treating a client with posttraumatic stress disorder relied on a single-case A-B-A design with pretest and posttest instruments to determine that art therapy was indeed effective with this client (1990). Although Carolan might argue otherwise, I would stress that these examples are indeed case studies, even though they use single-case designs that could be applied to numerous cases or participants. As Woodside and Wilson (2003) indicated, not all "... case study research is limited to samples of $n = 1$" (p. 493). Rather, to reiterate Gerring's definition from the beginning of this chapter, case study research relies on the in-depth examination of single units—empirically or otherwise.

In addition, the case may not be of a single individual, but may comprise a single unit made up of two to many members, such as a dyad, group, or even city. For example, in Oyinlade and Haden's quantitative case study to examine the "perceived influence of business power on local government" (2004), Lincoln, Nebraska, served as the single subject of examination. Similarly, Deitrick and Ellis (2004) used Pittsburgh, Pennsylvania, as the single subject in their article on examining how "new Urbanism" contributes to community development; and Callahan (2000) used a not-for-profit organization to determine how members of this group managed their emotional experiences. Frame (2006) used a couple for her case study to demonstrate the benefits of mandala drawings on their relationship and the effectiveness of the Couple Compatibility Assessment as a tool to inform the clinician.

As already noted, a particular focus or a unique situation an art therapist may find him or herself in may best be explored more in-depth through a case study. Despite personal experience in conducting research through a variety of quantitative to qualitative methodologies, I believed that a case study was most advantageous in exploring how art therapy assessment was used for a murder trial defense.

Art on Trial—An Extensive Example

In 2006, I was asked to provide expert witness testimony for a man who was arrested for murdering one of his children and attempting to murder the other. The prosecution sought the death penalty, whereas the defense suspected that serious mental illness was the driving force behind the crime. During the course of his life, the defendant had completed many art pieces, and the defense wanted to use the art as evidence to support their case. The defense had collected well over 100 pieces of work to evaluate.

The evaluative process took 3 years, resulting in a court hearing at which I testified how the art revealed a schizoaffective disorder, a conclusion supported by the other expert witnesses. Although the defendant received a sentence of 95 years, he was not placed on death row, and the judge determined that the defense had demonstrated that the defendant indeed had a mental illness. During the proceedings (which included evaluating the images, assessing the defendant on two separate occasions, being deposed by the prosecutor, meeting with the defense team on several occasions, and providing court testimony), it was concluded that this particular case may be worth studying to determine two outcomes: (1) the effectiveness of art as evidence in court proceedings, and (2) its reception within this forensic system. Thus, during the case study process, notes were kept and discussions noted, with an eye toward documenting this case. Even after the judge issued a decision and my role as expert witness was completed, data was collected via researching court documents and interviewing various people who were part of (and could inform) the case. Initially intended to be an article, the abundance of data resulted in a full-length manuscript, *Art on Trial: Art Therapy in Capital Murder Cases* (Gussak, 2013). In this book, an extensive account of the trial is carefully documented, wherein the artwork became as much a participant in the story as the person on trial.

This is an example of where there were several sources of data beyond the story. Along with notes taken during the experience of the interactions with the defendant, the defense team, and the prosecuting attorney, follow-up interviews were conducted with members of the defense team, the prosecuting attorney, and the presiding judge. Each interview was recorded and transcribed for reference. The transcriptions of the deposition and the testimony were obtained to supplement notes taken of the experiences. Notes of the original evaluations of the art, and of all further examinations, were also used.

To strengthen the case, information about similar experiences of other art therapists were obtained to cross-reference, compare, and contrast with similar court cases—in particular, three art therapists who had served as expert witnesses for murder cases. Myra Levick, Maxine Junge, and Sandra Graves[1] provided court transcripts of their testimonies, case notes, and copies of the art. In addition, each art therapist agreed to be interviewed, and this data was recorded and transcribed for review. All data was coded for similar patterns from which conclusions were drawn. This case demonstrated that: (1) the art was a reliable method to assess for the presence of a mental illness despite the amount of time that had passed and after the defendant was no longer a reliable source; (2) the process was deemed a valuable contribution by the defense and valued as evidence; (3) the prosecution learned of and respected the process of art as assessable material; and (4) the judge recognized how such information could corroborate traditional testimonial procedures. This examination also provided an opportunity to explore and deconstruct the ethical and moral considerations in such situations.

Ultimately, because of the structure of the experience, the data that was obtained, and the uniqueness of the situation, the case study method was deemed to be the best method in which to examine the circumstances. As stated in the preface of the book:

> ... this book relies on a qualitative approach. Similar to what Stake (2004) termed an "intrinsic case study approach," this case was pre-determined; therefore, without choosing this particular situation, what could be learned from it? The desire for deeper inquiry arose during the process, and it became clear that information could be gleaned from this single event that could then be provided to those "... who share commonalities of experience" (Kapitan, 2010, p. 103). The purpose of this approach was to learn something important from a singular experience. That is precisely what evolved—the amount of information gathered from this single event has yielded a great deal of information, which in turn can be communicated to a number of people who may benefit. (Gussak, 2013, p. xiii)

Conclusion

If used correctly, a properly implemented case study can provide valuable, in-depth, exploratory results; such information can provide the scaffolding for future investigations. This is especially true when only one or few units/subjects are available for investigation. Alone, this method simplifies and streamlines longitudinal exploration. When supplementing other research methods, a case study can provide anecdotal illustrations that may humanize the statistics or generalizations. Even though a case study is more than just a story, such narratives can be appealing to many readers, allowing the conclusions to reach a wider, more heterogeneous audience. Although this topic is much too complicated and convoluted to disentangle in one brief chapter, it is important to remember that this methodology permeates and resonates successfully in the social sciences, such as art therapy, because these fields rely on the illumination and examination of human interactions through observation and analysis of individuals within their environment. Ultimately, the case study is an adaptable approach that centers on the human element when numbers may not be enough.

Endnote

1 Although already done so in the book, I would like to again extend my warmest appreciation to Myra Levick, Sandra Graves, and Maxine Junge for their help, support, and contributions to *Art on Trial*.

References

Ackerman, J. (1992). Art therapy intervention designed to increase self-esteem of an incarcerated pedophile. *American Journal of Art Therapy, 30*(4), 143–149.

Behling, J. H., & Merves, E. S. (1984). *The practice of clinical research: The single case method.* Lanham, MD: University Press of America.

Broecher, J. (2012). Children coping with surgery through drawings: A case study from a Parenting class. *Art Therapy: Journal of the American Art Therapy Association, 29*(1), 38–43.

Callahan, J. L. (2000). Emotion management and organizational studies: A case study of patterns in a not-for-profit organization. *Human Resource Development Quarterly, 11*(3), 245–267.

Carolan, R. (2001). Models and paradigms of art therapy research. *Art Therapy: Journal of the American Art Therapy Association, 18*(4), 190–206.

Comerchero, V. (2012). A professor's experience with loss: An autobiographical case study. *Journal of Loss and Trauma: International Perspectives on Stress and Coping.* doi: 10.1080/15325024.2012.737645

Deitrick, S., & Ellis, C. (2004). New urbanism in the inner city: A case study of Pittsburgh. *Journal of the American Planning Association, 70*(4), 426–442.

Frame, P. G. (2006). Assessing a couple's relationship and compatibility using the MARI Card test and mandala drawings. *Art Therapy: Journal of the American Art Therapy Association, 23*(1), 23–29.

Fraenkel, J. R., & Wallen, N. E. (2009). *How to design and evaluate research in education* (7th ed.). New York, NY: McGraw-Hill.

Frankl, V. (1959). *Man's search for meaning.* Boston, MA: Beacon Press.

Gerring, J. (2004). What is a case study and what is it good for? *American Political Science Review, 98*(2), 341–354.

Gordon, J., & Shontz, F. (1990). Representative case research: A way of knowing. *Journal of Counseling and Development, 69,* 62–66.

Gussak, D. (2004). A pilot research study on the efficacy of art therapy with prison inmates. *Arts in Psychotherapy, 31*(4), 245–259.

Gussak, D. (2013). *Art on trial: Art therapy with capital murder cases.* New York, NY: Columbia University Press.

Hoffmann, N. C. (2011). Using art therapy to address cognitive symptoms of Parkinson's Disease. *Electronic Theses, Treatises and Dissertations.* Paper 3986. Retrieved from http://diginole.fsu.edu/etd/3986

Howard, R. (1990). Art therapy as an isomorphic intervention in the treatment of a client with Post-traumatic stress disorder. *American Journal of Art Therapy, 28*(3), 79–86.

Kapitan, L. (2010). *An introduction to art therapy research.* New York, NY: Routledge.

Kincheloe, J. L. (2005). Onto the next level: Continuing the conceptualization of the bricolage. *Qualitative Inquiry, 11*(3), 323–350.

Kramer, E. (1971). *Art as therapy with children.* New York, NY: Schocken Books.

Landgarten, H. (1981). *Clinical art therapy.* New York, NY: Brunner/Mazel.

Manley, G. (1998). Case study. *Sexual Addiction & Compulsivity: The Journal of Treatment & Prevention, 5*(2), 133–139.

Oyinlade, A. O., & Haden, M. (2004). Business power and community governance: A quantitative case study of perceived influence of business power on local government in Lincoln, Nebraska. *Sociological Spectrum: Mid-South Sociological Association, 24*(1), 71–91.

Peterson, J. S. (2012). The asset-burden paradox of giftedness: A 15-year phenomenological, longitudinal case study. *Roeper Review, 34*(4), 244–260.

Stake, R. (2000). Case studies. In N. Denzin & Y. Lincoln (Eds.), *The handbook of qualitative research* (2nd ed.) (pp. 435–454). Thousand Oaks, CA: Sage.

Ulman, E., & Dachinger, P. (Eds.) (1975). *Art therapy in theory and practice*. New York, NY: Schocken Books.

Van Lith, T. (2008). A phenomenological investigation of art therapy to assist transition to a psychosocial residential setting. *Art Therapy: Journal of the American Art Therapy Association, 25*(1), 24–31

Wadeson, H. (1980). *Art psychotherapy*. New York, NY: John Wiley & Sons.

Woodside, A. G., & Wilson, E. J. (2003). Case study research methods in theory building. *The Journal of Business and Industrial Marketing, 18*(6/7), 493–508.

Woodside, A. J. (2010). *Case study research: Theory, methods and practice*. Bingly, UK: Emerald Group Publishing, Ltd.

60

Social Action Research Methods and Art Therapy

Jordan S. Potash and Debra Kalmanowitz

Introduction

Research is not only the systematic process of generating new knowledge, but an opportunity to *re-search*—that is, look again (OED, 2011). Considering art therapy research as a chance to look again, to re-examine the way in which art therapists understand and perceive their work, creates a path to utilize research not only for demonstrating evidence-based practice, but also for pursuing social justice. In this sense, the systematic pursuit of knowledge involves studying particular situations or problems in society with the intent to take steps toward a desirable change. Art therapy practices can illuminate, investigate, present, and stimulate such change in order to further the goals of social science.

Social action research methods are derived from the traditions of action research and participatory action research, which allow researchers to use their theoretical knowledge and practical skills in collaboration with participants in order to promote political, social, and economic reforms (Brydon-Miller, 1997; Fals Borda, 2001). This type of research is not limited to traditional mental health issues or the interest area of the researcher, but rather may be "concerned with the problems of everyday living" caused by inequality and which may be in need of change (Antel & Regehr, 2003; Borshuk & Cherry, 2000, p. 199). It is a "method of research in which creating a positive social change is the predominant force driving the investigator and the research" (Berg, 2004, p. 196).

In this chapter, we first discuss the philosophical and theoretical underpinnings of this research method. Then we will discuss ideas for how to pursue social action research methods in art therapy. By highlighting various art therapy studies, we compare the processes of social action research with the processes of art therapy. We do not advocate that all art therapy research should be geared toward social action, as there is a place for all types of research in our profession, including methods that demonstrate efficacy and evidence-based practice. However, even these approaches, when properly positioned, can be directed toward the goals of social action by bringing an increased awareness and informed attitude toward research.

The Wiley Handbook of Art Therapy, First Edition. Edited by David E. Gussak and Marcia L. Rosal.
© 2016 John Wiley & Sons, Ltd. Published 2016 by John Wiley & Sons, Ltd.

Philosophical Underpinnings

The inclusion of the arts in research confronts us with the notion of aesthetics—the philosophy of art, beauty, and perception. Just as social action research methods reject distant objectivity, we adopt Levine's (2009) approach to the relationship in aesthetics. The making of art demands the "relationship with the participation and involvement that the experience of art brings" in contrast with "traditional aesthetics ... which places an emphasis on the 'disinterestedness' of the viewer" (p. 165). Art therapists cannot remain detached, but must authentically engage in the effective reality of the work.

According to Knill, Barba, and Fuchs (1995), an "aesthetic response" occurs within the artist, or the individual who engages in the artistic/creative process, and the viewers or observers of the art made. "The aesthetic response describes characteristic ways of being in the presence of a creative act or work of art—ways that touch the soul, evoke imagination, engage emotions and thought" (p. 71). Art's potential to engage us and society points to the significance in integrating art therapy and social action research that allows for the authentic expression of an experience, its documentation, and most importantly the transmission of findings. The arts allow not only for an immediate and experiential understanding, but also appeals to the emotions and the senses in a way that communicates experiences that are consistent with that which is lived, heard, felt, or seen.

Theoretical Framework

Social activist Thich Nhât Hanh (2003) wrote, "There is no walk for peace; peace must be the walk" (p. 65). Similarly, we may consider that research geared toward social action must make use of social action methods. In general, the steps involved with a participatory action research project include the researcher and participants mutually identifying the problem to be investigated, gathering the information needed, analyzing and interpreting the data, and sharing the results with the participants (Berg, 2004).

Brydon-Miller (1997) identified three important steps that separate action research from other forms of research: (1) the work should be centered on a community that has traditionally been exploited or marginalized; (2) the research should address community concerns and causes of oppression; and (3) the process should be considered educational, in which all participants are able to contribute and learn. Through this method, traditional structures may be undermined, and/or ways to bring about change may be identified.

This subversive quality contained in research is also evident in art therapy:

> The ultimate subversive activity occurs when the issues society seeks to deny are overturned, the invisible transformed into the visible. In effect, art empowers clients to claim and refine the self that has been denied. The process of self-definition is a political act. (Moon, 2002, p. 296)

What makes art subversive is that it makes known what is unknown or denied. While in a clinical context this may refer to unconscious impulses, unforeseen archetypes, or unintentional patterns, in a societal context it may relate to the forces of discrimination, racism, sexism, homophobia, xenophobia, or classism that maintains certain members of society in perpetual despair. Similarly, social action research can uncover destructive forces that may explain why certain clients or groups are more prone to illness, victimization, or poverty. It is for all of these reasons that Huss (2011) wrote, "'Showing', rather than 'telling', this through visual means can be understood as a form of indirect resistance" (p. 95).

This research method offers new ways of studying human behavior, attitudes, circumstances, and environments. The aim is to affect change, and to uncover the best way of illuminating and understanding what obstacles to change exist. Lincoln and Denzin (2000) referred to this type of research as the *Seventh Moment*, and defined it as a method that "breaks from the past, a focus on previously silenced voices, a turn to performance texts, and an abiding concern with moral discourse, with conversations about democracy, politics, race, gender, class, nation, freedom and community" (p. 1048). Further, "there is a pressing demand to show how the practices of critical, interpretive qualitative research can help change the world in positive ways" (Denzin, 2002, pp. 26–27).

This form of enquiry is interactive as it challenges institutional norms of correctness that marginalizes people through abuses of power. It also serves to straddle the academic world of external reasoning with the world of internal experience. "It helps persons imagine how things could be different. It imagines new forms of human transformation and emancipation. It enacts these transformations through dialogue" (Denzin, 2002, p. 31). To this aim, Seventh Moment researchers use a variety of research tools, including poetry, drawing, documentary, and ethnographic writing. In addition to documenting experiences and promoting sustained social engagement, community arts initiatives lead to transformative processes well beyond documenting the results through traditional quantitative means (Froggett, Little, Roy, & Whitaker, 2011).

Art therapy, as an element of social action research, can be used to challenge institutional norms by empowering a community to ask questions, uncover answers, and disseminate findings in order to better their situation. This process of mutual respect in searching for shared truths for the betterment of society is rooted in Gandhi's methods of creative nonviolence (Fals Borda, 2001). As embodied in his term *satyagraha*, or "truth seeking," researchers and participants engage each other in a search for dialogue and social change (Gandhi 1928/1956). Social action research allows for the maintenance and repair of mutual and authentic relationships, which may result in Buber's ideal of a society as a learning community (Kramer & Gawlick, 2003). By using art-making for social engagement and understanding, we honor Allen's (2005) vision of creating image communities—art- infused meeting opportunities that provoke questions in order to foster and sustain peace. Reason (1994) described the work of human inquiry as:

> an approach to living based on experience and engagement, on love and respect for the integrity of persons; and on willingness to rise above presuppositions, to look and look again, to risk security in the search for understanding and action that opens possibilities of creative living. (p. 9)

This definition underscores the underlying feeling of respect for others that is necessary for social action researchers. Researchers engaged in these pursuits generally believe that, in order to be an agent of change, one must participate and not disengage, thereby expanding the engaged stance in the arts (Knill et al., 1995; Levine, 2009) to the world as a whole.

Framing Research Questions

The ongoing search for answers establishes the researcher as an activist and conscientious objector who maintains persistent presence "that is charged with unspoken truth and giving it form through the image" (Allen, 2007, pp. 73–74). Research questions, from a social action viewpoint, are intended to provoke the status quo, raise awareness, and lead to change—even at the expense of finding absolute answers. The focus of art therapy social action inquiry is on "the broader social and cultural conditions" and "may actually work to individualize social and economic disadvantage by focusing the persons' problems at the level of her personal biography and personality" (Lupton, 1997, p. 1).

As an example of a research question framed within the context of social action, Huss (2011) set out to understand how impoverished Bedouin women in Israel portrayed space in art therapy. By focusing her research question on observations of space usage in art, she hoped to understand the social factors that restricted the women. Creating art about their struggles revealed the theme of their inability to access the natural outdoors, which led to discussion on the women's limited mobility as a result of socio-economic and cultural barriers. The act of creating such natural spaces in art was viewed as an act of defiance as art therapy promoted experimentation with image as political voice.

Participants, Collaborators, and Partners

In social action research methods, participants are not passive; they are co-collaborators (Argyris & Schön, 1991) in the process to uncover information. This method empowers the average individual to be part of a community (Berg, 2004). Participants may advocate for new policies (O'Neill, Woods, & Webster, 2005), and recommend changes in practice (Hall, 2006). Marecek, Fine, and Kidder (1997) offered a *revisioning* of the roles of both participants and researchers:

> When researchers listen to participants, we learn new things. Participants become more than transmitters of raw data to be refined by statistical procedures. They become active agents, the creators of the worlds they inhabit and the interpreters of their experiences. At the same time, researchers come to be witnesses, a word whose root means knowledge. In bringing their knowledge—of theory, of interpretive methods, and of their own intellectual, political, and personal commitments—to participants' stories, researchers become active agents as well. (p. 637)

Therefore, the researcher is fully engaged with his or her participants, while maintaining professional ethics (Brydon-Miller & Tolman, 1997; Fine, 2006; Morawski, 1997; Munford & Sanders with Andrew, 2003). While engaging in social action research, it is impossible, and at times ineffective, for a researcher to maintain objectivity or for practitioners to be removed from the world of research (McNiff & Whitehead, 2006; Whyte, Greenwood, & Lazes, 1991). To be successful, social action researchers remain actively aware of how to "decolonize" their actions, which means that both the researcher and the participants benefit from the research process and outcomes (Fals Borda, 2001, p. 29).

These ideas are not foreign or new to art therapists. Their clients are active participants in the selection, creation, refinement, and interpretation of their images. Extending one's professional skills for the benefit of another, whether in the therapeutic process or in research, upholds social action research principles (Hall, 2006). Just as the art created in therapy represents a dimension of the client–artist's experience that may be explored for future change, so too, the stories and images of participant/co-collaborators present themselves as messengers for societal change.

Members of a community are encouraged to act with intention and creative inquisitiveness by conducting the literature review, designing the research project, administering the program, evaluating the data, presenting the results, and determining new courses of action (Whyte et al., 1991). Co-collaborators are often recognized for their contributions and are engaged subjectively in a relational manner (I-Thou), rather than in the interest area of an objective researcher (I-It) (Buber, 1923/1970). Here again, there are parallels between the tenants of social action research and the studio approach to art therapy (whereby art therapists often create art alongside their clients). As artists, art therapists recognize the struggles of creating forms that best express themselves and how to bring these creations to fruition (Moon, 2009). Art therapists appreciate how images affect clients and understand that client images influence us. When art therapy is practiced as a collaboration among art therapists, artist/clients, and art products, it parallels participatory action research methods. Therefore, it is a natural framework for conducting research in art therapy (Carolan, 2001).

For example, Spaniol (2005) developed a study in which art therapists and clients living with mental illness came together to uncover pressing needs and potential solutions for improving mental health services. Instead of adopting a top-down inquiry, the "Creative Partnerships" program integrated participatory action research with the creative arts. Through creating art collaboratively, the participants discovered a role for flexible boundaries as shared humanity was integrated into traditional role distinctions, and shared power as mental illness was viewed on a spectrum of wellness, rather than a narrowly defined category.

Similarly, Kapitan, Little, and Torres (2011) demonstrated how art therapy practices could be used to assess community needs in Nicaragua. By joining with community members and providing opportunities for art making, the art therapists facilitated the community toward rejuvenation and increased empowerment by successfully "creating capacity for communities to effect change by strengthening and transforming the critical consciousness of their members" (p. 72)

For both projects, the result was a dynamic engagement among participants and facilitators, who functioned as participant–collaborators and researcher–collaborators. The unique arts-based form of engagement allowed art-making itself to function as the conduit of understanding. Art was not just a form of data to collect, but a process of inquiry and knowledge production. Art making was a common ground to discover unchallenged assumptions and to point to sustainable results.

Identifying participant–collaborators is not limited to those who are members of a marginalized group. Other sectors of society can be considered. Those in a dominant or power role can be engaged as participants in social action research to uncover how they contribute to and maintain inequality. In a research project to raise awareness about mental illness, Potash and Ho (2011) invited mental health professionals and members of the community to an exhibit created by people living with mental illness. They reflected on the exhibit pieces by writing, creating art, and discussion. Participants indicated having an expanded awareness of mental illnesses, appreciated art as a process of understanding, and expressed desire to help and invite others to view the exhibit. From an aware stance that unintentionally maintained marginalization, participants became partners in social change.

Engaging in Analysis

McNiff and Whitehead (2006) recommended an action–reflection cycle during the data collection phase of social action research. The cyclical process entails: (1) observation (what needs to change); (2) reflection (developing strategies); (3) action (initiating); (4) evaluation (checking action in light of data); and (5) modifying. These steps may lead to new research directions. Participant–collaborators are as involved in the data analysis as they choose to be, thereby making them active partners in discovering patterns and building theories to explain and describe their situations (Heron & Reason, 2001).

One of the goals of social action research is to ascertain how and why communities cope with calamities (Whyte et al., 1991). In their work in former Yugoslavia, Kalmanowitz and Lloyd (1997) engaged in social action research. They were there to provide training in working with the arts—and trauma, individual, and community support through the arts—when they received repeated appeals from organizations, mental health professionals, and individuals for training, information, clinical help, and financial help. The impetus for the research was in response to the temporary fragmentation of family, community, and society. This impacted on social services, education, and health services, all of which were overwhelmed and ceased to function in a meaningful way. In addition, the lack of centralized information led to a repetition of services from international organizations coming in to help. Seeking to know what, why, and how services were being provided, the researchers engaged in extensive interviews and observations of on-site pilot art therapy projects and fieldwork. The goal of the study was to seek insight into how to assist this community, and the approach was geared toward practical problem-solving. Participants included local and international humanitarian workers, service providers, and people receiving services, all of whom were active in defining the problems and searching for solutions. Data collection even extended to the researchers sharing the same living conditions (for a period of time) as the individuals, so as to understand better the condition and needs of the communities. The information gathered was collaboratively collected, collated, and assessed. The result was a report of the services existing at that time, but also a model for safe arts-based interventions. To ensure accessibility, it was written in everyday language and disseminated to humanitarian agencies, along with a list of existing arts-based programs.

Due to the subjective nature of action research, internal and external validity is a concern, and it needs to be attended to in order to produce meaningful research. Social action research validity is assessed differently than in quantitative studies;

validity and credibility are related to how the theories generated through the research are applied in practice with the specific group or focus (Greenwood & Levin, 1998). *Critical subjectivity* is used in social action research, which includes: (1) a balance between enmeshed subjectivity and distant objectivity (Reason, 1994); (2) through instituting triangulation (Fals Borda, 2001); or (3) appointing co-researchers to challenge the assumptions of the researcher (Heron & Reason, 2001).

Presenting Findings

Results of social action research studies are often personal images and stories, which can be used to transform communities. Although the publication of social action research studies in scholarly journals will disseminate information to other researchers, the information may not reach practitioners and other individuals, particularly those in marginalized communities. In order to display narratives and stories, alternative forms of distribution might be considered, including galleries, exhibitions, press conferences, and documentary films and videos. Cahnmann-Taylor and Siegesmund (2008) offered examples of social action research in which findings were depicted through the arts: visual art, drama, poetry, or music. The benefits of presenting results in these alternative ways include reaching a wider audience, making use of symbols and metaphors, and initiating more questions. The resulting arts products may vary in quality, but the audience response can be powerful, nonetheless. Knill et al.'s (1995) concept of the aesthetic response, as that which moves us emotionally, can lead to action. In addition, we can consider crafting data findings into social policy. The presentation format is based on what might best lead to action and social change, either direct changes or via ripple effect from audiences dialoguing with others.

Given the sensitive nature of the social action research, special consideration needs to be given to how images are displayed and whether or not participant–collaborators or their families will be put at risk. Protecting the participants is of utmost importance. Allen (2007) stated, "Having the image process provides a shield that must be used with discernment both to mirror and protect" (p. 84). The image can also mirror the lived experience. By displaying images, rather than people, personal stories are made public, and yet privacy is maintained—whether by personal choice or political necessity.

Stepakoff et al. (2011) argued that art created in a therapeutic space can be displayed for therapeutic benefit and for social action. As poetry therapists, they found that when poems created in the therapy were read publicly both the clients and the community were empowered. Tan (2012) demonstrated how art created in art therapy could simultaneously function as therapy while also informing larger patterns of experience. Women who were survivors of sex trafficking in Cambodia engaged in storytelling and art-making in an art therapy setting. The art images discussed in the group were exhibited. In one situation, the women gave permission for the art images to be used for advocacy and even prosecution of traffickers.

Conclusion

"Social change is always about bringing flexibility into the dominant" (Marcow-Speiser, personal communication, February 9, 2012). As such, thinking about research as an opportunity to *re-search* creates opportunities for discovering meaning, uncovering injustice, and becoming partners in building socially just communities. The arts serve as a potent element in social action research and can be used to investigate community processes and to advocate for social change. Understanding the influential roles that art images and art therapy have to offer may encourage art therapists to undertake social action research projects. Using this type of research methodology may lead to art therapists taking active and prominent roles in asking complex, provocative social questions and working toward solutions.

References

Allen, P. B. (2005). *Art is a spiritual path*. Boston, MA: Shambhala.

Allen, P. B. (2007). Wielding the shield: The art therapist as conscious witness in the realm of social action. In F. F. Kaplan (Ed.), *Art therapy and social action* (pp. 72–85). Philadelphia, PA: Jessica Kingsley.

Antel, B. J., & Regehr, C. (2003). Beyond individual rights and freedoms: Metaethics in social work research. *Social Work, 48*(1), 135–144.

Argyris, C., & Schön, D. A. (1991). Participatory action research and action science compared: A commentary. In W. F. Whyte (Ed.), *Participatory action research* (pp. 85–96). Newbury Park, CA: Sage.

Berg, B. L. (2004). *Qualitative research methods* (5th ed.). Boston, MA: Pearson.

Borshuk, C., & Cherry, F. (2004). Keep the tool-box open for social justice: Comment on Kitzinger and Wilkinson. *Analyses of Social Issues and Public Policy, 4*(1), 195–202.

Brydon-Miller, M. (1997). Participatory action research: Psychology and social change. *Journal of Social Issues, 53*(4), 657–666.

Brydon-Miller, M., & Tolman, D. L. (Eds.) (1997). Transforming psychology: Interpretive and participatory research methods. *Journal of Social Issues, 53*(4), 597–603.

Buber, M. (1970). *I and thou*. (W. Kaufman, Trans.) New York, NY: Charles Scribner's Son. (Original work published 1923.)

Cahnmann-Taylor, M., & Siegesmund, R. (Eds.). (2008). *Arts-based research in education: Foundations for practice*. New York, NY: Routledge.

Carolan, R. (2001). Models and paradigms of art therapy research. *Art Therapy: Journal of the American Art Therapy Association, 18*(4), 190–206.

Denzin, N. K. (2002). Social work in the seventh moment. *Qualitative Social Work, 1*(1), 25–38. doi: 10.1177/147332500200100102

Fals Borda, O. (2001). Participatory (action) research in social theory: Origins and challenges. In P. Reason & H. Bradbury (Eds.), *Handbook of action research: Participative inquiry and practice* (pp. 27–37). London, UK: Sage.

Fine, M. (2006). Bearing witness: Methods for researching oppression and resistance— a textbook for critical research. *Social Justice Research, 19*(1), 83–108.

Froggett, L., Little, R., Roy, A., & Whitaker, L. (2011). New model visual arts organisations and social engagement. University of Central Lancashire, Psychosocial Research Unit. Accessed 4 May 2012, available http://www.uclan.ac.uk/schools/school_of_social_work/research/pru/files/wzw_nmi_report.pdf

Gandhi, M. K. (1956). *Satyagraha in South Africa*. In H. A. Jack (Ed.), *The Gandhi reader: A sourcebook of his life and writings* (pp. 59–66). New York, NY: Grove. (Reprinted from *Satyagraha in South Africa*, pp. 161–173, by M. K. Gandhi, 1928, Madras, India.)

Greenwood, D. J., & Levin, M. (1998). *Introduction to action research*. Thousand Oaks, CA: Sage.

Heron, J., & Reason, P. (2001). The practice of co-operative inquiry: Research "with" rather than "on" people. In P. Reason & H. Bradbury (Eds.), *Handbook of action research: Participative inquiry and practice* (pp. 179–188). London, UK: Sage.

Hall, J. E. (2006). Professionalizing action research—a meaningful strategy for modernizing services? *Journal of Nursing Management, 14*, 195–200.

Huss, E. (2011). A social-critical reading of indigenous women's art: The use of visual data to "show," rather than "tell," of the intersection of different layers of oppression. In E. G. Levine & S. K. Levine (Eds.), *Art in action: Expressive arts therapy and social change* (pp. 95–103). London, UK: Jessica Kingsley.

Kalmanowitz, D., & Lloyd, B. (1997). *The portable studio. Art therapy and political conflict: Initiatives in the former Yugoslavia and South Africa*. London, UK: Health Education Authority.

Kapitan, L., Litell, M., & Torres, A. (2011). Creative art therapy in a community's participatory research and social transformation. *Art Therapy: Journal of the American Art Therapy Association, 28*(2), 64–73.

Knill, P. J., Barba, H. N., & Fuchs, M. N. (1995). *Minstrels of soul. Intermodal Expressive therapy*. Toronto, Canada: Palmerton Press.

Kramer, K. P. with Gawlick, M. (2003). *Martin Buber's I and Thou: Practicing living dialogue*. New York, NY: Paulist Press.

Levine, S. K. (2009). *Trauma, tragedy, therapy. The arts and human suffering*. London, UK: Jessica Kingsley.

Lincoln, Y. S., & Denzin, N. K. (2000). The seventh moment: Out of the past. In N. K. Denzin and Y. S. Lincoln (Eds.), *Handbook of qualitative research* (2nd ed., pp. 1047–1065). Thousand Oaks, CA: Sage.

Lupton, D. (1997). Foreward. In S. Hogan (Ed.), *Feminist approaches to art therapy* (pp. 1–9). London: Routledge.

Marecek, J., Fine, M., & Kidder, L. (1997). Working between worlds: Qualitative methods and social psychology. *Journal of Social Issues, 53*(4), 631–644.

McNiff, J., & Whitehead, J. (2006). *All you need to know about action research*. London: Sage.

Moon, B. L. (2009). *Existential art therapy: The canvas mirror* (3rd ed.). Springfield, IL: Charles C. Thomas.

Moon, C. H. (2002). *Studio art therapy: Cultivating the artist identity in the art therapist*. Philadelphia, PA: Jessica Kingsley.

Morawski, J. (1997). The science behind feminist research methods. *Journal of Social Issues, 53*(4), 667–681.

Munford, R., & Sanders, J. with Andrew, A. (2003). Community development—action research in community settings. *Social Work Education, 22*(1), 93–104.

Nhât Hanh, T. (2003). *Creating true peace: Ending violence in yourself, your family, your community and the World*. New York, NY: Free Press.

O'Neill, M., Woods, P. A., & Webster, M. (2005). New arrivals: Participatory action research, imagined communities, and "visions" of social justice. *Social Justice, 32*(1), 75–88.

Oxford English Dictionary. (2011). Online version. <http://www.oed.com/view/Entry/163435>; accessed 21 February 2012.

Potash, J. S., & Ho, R. T. H. (2011). Drawing involves caring: Fostering relationship building through art therapy for social change. *Art Therapy: Journal of the American Art Therapy Association, 28*(2), 74–81.

Reason, P. (Ed.). (1994). *Participation in human inquiry*. London, UK: Sage.

Spaniol, S. (2005). "Learned hopefulness": An arts-based approach to participatory action research. *Art Therapy: Journal of the American Art Therapy Association, 22*(2), 86–91.

Stepakoff, S., Hussein, S., Al-Salahat, M., Musa, I., Asfoor, M., Al-Houdali, E., & Al-Hmouz, M. (2011). From private pain toward public speech: Poetry therapy with Iraqi survivors of torture and war. In E. G. Levine & S. K. Levine (Eds.), *Art in action: Expressive arts therapy and social change* (pp. 128–144). Philadelphia, PA: Jessica Kingsley.

Tan, L. (2012). Surviving shame: Engaging art therapy with trafficked survivors in South East Asia. In D. Kalmanowitz, J. S. Potash, & S. M. Chan (Eds.), *Art Therapy in Asia: To the Bone or Wrapped in Silk* (pp. 283–296). London, UK: Jessica Kingsley.

Whyte, W. F., Greenwood, D. J., & Lazes, P. (1991). Participatory action research: Through practice to science in social science research. In W. F. Whyte (Ed.), *Participatory action research* (pp. 19–55). Newbury Park, CA: Sage.

61

Quantitative Investigations:
Alternative Choices
Deborah Elkis-Abuhoff

Jamie is an art therapist at a state psychiatric facility. Since she arrived 5 months ago, she has noticed that her patients with a history of alcohol abuse and/or addiction consistently include water in their drawings. She wants to find out whether water is a standard element for those struggling with alcohol abuse and/or addiction. She decides this would be a good project to investigate; she needs to decide her methodological approach. She understands she will employ a non-experimental design and will explore which specific approach would work best.

Non-experimental research encompasses a variety of different levels of inquiry and designs for this type of investigation. The main difference from an experimental design is that a non-experimental design does not manipulate the participants' situations, circumstances, or the experiences, examining populations in as natural an environment as possible. It ultimately describes behavior—it does not focus on or address the reasons for that behavior (Kumar, 2011).

There are several different research designs for Jamie to consider that fall under the definition of non-experimental research—descriptive, quasi-experimental, longitudinal, correlational, and historical research. The following sections examine each approach and explore how they have been applied to research in art therapy (see Table 61.1 for a summary of these research models). This chapter will conclude with a summary on which approach would be best suited for Jamie's research project.

Quasi-Experimental

Quasi-experimental research design is often referred to as *causal* or *comparative research*. The focus is to describe and compare existing differences, and to attempt to identify potential causes for any discovered differences. Where true experimental design uses random assignment for both the participant to group and the group to treatment, quasi-experimental design uses preexisting, intact groups and randomly assigns treatment conditions (Lapan & Quartaroli, 2009). This type of design compares the outcome of one group before and after the group's involvement in a program (also known as a pre-test/post-test design). Quasi-experimental studies help to enhance

The Wiley Handbook of Art Therapy, First Edition. Edited by David E. Gussak and Marcia L. Rosal.
© 2016 John Wiley & Sons, Ltd. Published 2016 by John Wiley & Sons, Ltd.

Table 61.1 Overview of non-experimental research design.

Design	Type	Purpose	Approach
Quasi-experimental	Causal or comparative	Identify differences and explore possible causes	Pre-test/post-test design
Descriptive	Relationships without explanation or assumption	Gain generalizations of problems, situations, attitudes, and/or opinions	Survey and/or observations
Correlational	Associations between two or more variables	Compares relationships between variables and be able to predict variable performance	Survey and/or observations
Longitudinal	Observe the same subjects over time, or similar groups at different points (age/education)	Explore how, over time, situations, perceptions, attitudes, and/or behaviors change	Pre-test/post-test Survey, and/or observations
Historical	Examine existing data. Also known as *archival research*.	Review past information and apply it to present-day situations to test research hypotheses	Collect and review literature and artifacts

information that can lead to potential cause and effect, but is not able to definitively establish a link or cause (Lapan & Quartaroli, 2009).

For example, Goldblatt, Elkis-Abuhoff, Gaydos, and Napoli (2010) examined the potential effects of using modeling clay to reduce the negative symptomology of patients diagnosed with Parkinson's disease. Through a quasi-experimental design, they used a pre- and post-assessment to explore if there was a change in obsessive-compulsive thinking, phobia, and depression after the modeling clay engagement, as compared to before the experience occurred. What they found was that those patients diagnosed with Parkinson's disease ($n = 22$) who engaged in the modeling clay experience had a decrease in their symptomology after the engagement in all three areas measured (obsessive-compulsive thinking, phobia, and depression) from before engaging in the modeling clay. They were able to report that modeling clay could have influenced that change, and that it might have the potential to decrease these symptoms for Parkinson's patients. However, because of the nature of the design, they were not able to conclude that the modeling clay actually affected the symptoms. As another example, Hartz and Thick (2005) compared the impact of two art therapy approaches on the self-esteem of 27 female juvenile offenders. The researchers provided either an art psychotherapy or art as therapy group intervention to the participants of the study. A pre- and post-intervention assessment was applied to explore if self-worth changed from before the intervention to afterward, and then compared both groups' outcomes to assess if one group had a larger impact than the other. The researchers found that participants in the art as therapy group reported an increase in feeling a sense of mastery, connection, and self-approval, whereas the art psychotherapy group showed an increase in areas of close friendships and behavioral conduct. Although there was a positive outcome for both groups, the researchers could only conclude that engagement in either art therapy approach, art as therapy or art psychotherapy, may potentially increase the participant's self-esteem, but it may not necessarily be the cause.

The pre-test provided a baseline understanding of the participants, and the posttest revealed possible changes that might have occurred during the studied experience. These quasi-experimental art therapy research examples indicated positive outcomes of change, which supported the subsequent research question. This, in turn, can lead to the development of a hypothesis and further investigation.

Descriptive

The descriptive research design approach simply describes a relationship between variables or situations that provide an explanation or assumption for what has been observed. It is most appropriate when the researcher is first starting an investigation, but is not quite sure what he or she will find. The potential outcome of this approach is to generalize from observations (Bordens & Abbott, 2008); it "attempts to describe systematically a situation, problem, phenomenon, service or programme, or provides information about, say the living conditions of a community, or describes attitudes toward issues" (Kumar, 2011, p. 10). It is an important first step to consider when developing new research in an area that has not been previously explored, and can bring insights to issues that can then be addressed or further explored.

Since the focus of a descriptive design is to gain overall general attitudes, opinions, and behaviors, collecting data for this approach is usually conducted through surveys or direct observation that focuses on the question at hand. For example, the researcher might ask the participant: *how many times over the past month have you attended group art therapy, how often are you fearful in a crowd, or do you prefer to work with watercolors, oil pastels, or colored pencils?*

In 1998, Manheim explored how creativity plays a role in personal growth by examining the connection between the artistic process and self-actualization. The researcher investigated probable parallels between creativity, self-actualization, and an administered art experience based on the 65 participants included in the study.

The researchers distributed a questionnaire to students in a continuing education art class. The questions examined the student's perception regarding the impact that the art studio experience had on their daily lives. The researchers sought to find if the students' perception of the impact of the continuing education class had a positive effect on their day-to-day living, which in turn enhanced their quality of life. What they discovered was that 98.4% of the participants reported that they believed that engaging in the continuing education art studio class did indeed enhance their lives. Further outcomes also indicated an increased sense of openness and self-acceptance. Findings also suggested that those who were most motivated found a more globally enriching experience outside the studio (Manheim, 1998).

Another example of descriptive research is the work conducted by Goldblatt, Elkis-Abuhoff, Gaydos, Rose, and Casey (2010) that looked at participants' perceived visual perception of conflict. The researchers gave participants a list of words from Alan K. Cooper's "Conflict Ladder," a 14-rung ladder with words ranging from the first-rung "peace" up to the highest-rung "kill" (Goldblatt et al., 2010). Participants ($n = 98$) were asked to draw a line related to their perception of each listed word. After they completed this task, they were asked to create a line drawing related to a relationship they had experienced, either positive or negative, with either a person or institution.

The results of this study indicated that the participants were able to express and communicate their conflict through visual communication, as evidenced by the high inter-rater reliability. This supported a consistency between the Conflict Ladder and the perceived visual understanding of conflict by the participants. As an outcome of this study, and through further investigation, the Conflict Ladder and the developed assessment scoring may become a viable addition to the tools that art therapists could use to help clients/patients connect through visual communication with their present perceived situations (Goldblatt et al., 2010).

The focus of both of these descriptive design studies was to extrapolate consistent information that could provide general outcomes of the specific area of research. For Manheim (1998), the experience of a continuing art education program and its overall benefits in increasing self-actualization gave insights to its effect on the participants. In Goldblatt et al. (2010), the focus was to understand a potential relationship between visual communication and conflict. Both of these art-therapy-related research projects provide a good indication of how descriptive research design can be applied to gather information for further investigations.

Correlational

The focus of correlational research design is to determine if two or more variables have an association to each other. There is no attempt to manipulate variables, but simply to observe them and compare how a change in one might affect the other. By establishing a correlational relationship between variables, the outcome or change of one helps to make it possible to predict how the other variable(s) will perform (Bordens & Abbott, 2008).

When a correlational relationship is employed for prediction, one variable, or the *predictor variable*, is used to calculate the value of another variable, or the *criterion variable* (Bordens & Abbott, 2008). Although the analysis of the variables might present a strong link or correlation between the two variables, it cannot definitively conclude that the two variables are relationally causal.

Prescott, Sekendur, Bailey, and Hoshino (2008) investigated the correlation between involvement in art therapy and resiliency in homeless youth. The study evaluated the attendance of $N = 212$ homeless youth who attended a drop-in art center. The researchers reviewed the art center logs for attendance and progress over a period of 5 years. The information obtained included frequency of attendance, daily activities, behaviors, and personal information communicated during each session.

The life achievements that were of interest were secure housing, substance cessation, returning to school, employment, positive social skills, taking initiative, and the ability to sell their artwork. The analysis of the data produced a Pearson *r* score (a statistical outcome that expresses the strength of a correlation) of 0.92. This is impressive, as the closer the score is to 1.00, the stronger the relationship. This supported that there was a correlation between homeless youth attendance and life achievement. The researcher concluded that the more frequent the attendance to the drop-in art center, the greater the incidence of life achievements.

Correlational studies can also be significant in evaluating and developing assessments tools (Kapitan, 2010). In order to support a new assessment, it is important to have a comparison with an already established tool. The goal is to have the newly developed tool support the standardized assessment to which it is being compared. The higher the correlation, the stronger the assessment tool is in identifying the same information as the original tool.

One example would be the development of the Formal Elements Art Therapy Scale (FEATS). The researchers looked at specific characteristics presented in art with specific diagnoses in the *Diagnostic and Statistical Manual of Mental Disorders* (3rd ed., *DSM-III;* American Psychiatric Association, 1980) to investigate if there was a correlation between visual elements and DSM-III diagnoses (Gantt, 2009). Using the "Draw a Person Picking an Apple from a Tree" (PPAT) assessment pictures, collected from both psychiatric patients and non-patients, they sought to determine if there was a relationship between the patient's art and their differential diagnosis. From this information, they devised a 14-scale assessment procedure (please refer to the manual and Chapter 54 in this book on the FEATS for a complete description). Presently, their archive includes over 5,000 drawings.

They have since concluded that the FEATS can measure variables in "free" art, as well as the PPAT. This finding supports the use of the FEATS as a standardized assessment for a wide variety of applications, for both clinical and non-clinical uses (Gantt, 2009).

Longitudinal

A longitudinal research approach observes how situations, perceptions, attitudes, and/or behaviors change for a specific subject or group over an extended period of time, or similar groups at different times. This type of study is also called a *developmental study* and is used to identify or predict trends (Kapitan, 2010).

In this type of study, participants are visited at different times, at different intervals, usually over a long period. There is no definitive interval that all longitudinal studies follow, but it is set based on the particular study. Data studies can be as short as a week, or longer than a year (Kumar, 2011). An example would be following an art therapy group monthly to understand how it the different phases of group process effects the level of engagement, or it could be following school children once a year from kindergarten through high school graduation to observe changes in levels of creativity.

An example of an art-therapy-based longitudinal study completed by Schreier, Ladakakos, Morabito, Chapman, and Knudson (2005) explored posttraumatic stress symptoms in children after their experience with a pediatric trauma. The researcher followed *N* = 83 children/adolescents and their caregivers from within 24 hours of the child/adolescent's hospital admission, and then again at 1 month, 6 months, and 18 months to gather data related to their posttraumatic stress disorder (PTSD) symptomology. After the initial interview and determining that there was at least mild symptomology present, researchers randomized the child/adolescent participants to either an art theory intervention or standard level of services only.

The outcome of this study found that 69% of the children/adolescents presented with at least mild PTSD at the first interview (or baseline) and 57% at 1 month, 59% at 6 months, and 38% at 18 months. They also concluded that parents initially under-reported their child's symptomology, but over time the parents' results converged to match the child/adolescents' reported symptomology (Schreier et al., 2005). The significance of this study was that symptomology appears to continue post-discharge and, although somewhat reduced, is still apparent 18 months later. This may indicate a need for continued support for children and adolescents who experience pediatric trauma.

Another example of a longitudinal study was conducted by Lee (2011). This study gathered data from Canadian art therapists in 2005, and then again in 2010. In this study, the researcher evaluated demographic information from the national surveys of art therapists and compared them to reveal current trends and changes relating to the art therapy profession job market in Canada. The outcome information from this study could then be used to bring important insights into the development of the profession over time, and how situations, attitudes, perceptions, and behaviors have an impact on art therapy in Canada as it continues to move forward.

Historical

An investigation that examines existing data to test a hypothesis is known as a *historical* or *archival approach* to research. This approach does not seek to collect new information, but collects information related to past events to define the experience and investigate what could be learned. Data can be collected through any type of past work—literature, texts, films, videos, slides, audio recordings, photos, and of course artwork are all examples of types of historical data utilized by researchers (Gilroy, 2006).

In an illustration of just such an approach, Reynolds, Nabor, and Quinlan (2000) reviewed art therapy literature to identify studies that gave evidence to the effectiveness of art therapy. They reviewed 17 published studies on the positive effects of art therapy, each of which applied one of three types of research designs—single group with no control, controlled clinical trial and randomized clinical trials. They found that there was only a small amount of quantifiable data available to explore the outcomes of art therapy treatment, concluding that there is a need for more studies to gain further insight and information that could support the level of effectiveness of art therapy as a modality of treatment.

An updated study was published in 2010 by Slayton, D'Archer, and Kaplan, with a historical review of published research from 1999 to 2007 of clinical and non-clinical populations that also explored the effectiveness of art therapy treatment.

The researchers supported the conclusion of Reynolds, Nabors, and Quinlan that art therapy is effective for treating a variety of symptoms, age groups, and disorders. Simply put, historical or archival research provides informative evidence that may help guide the future.

Jamie Revisited

Using the information in the preceding text, Jamie can now decide which research design to use in answering her question, on whether or not water is a common element in the artwork of those diagnosed with alcohol abuse or addiction. A quasi-experimental design focuses on the differences and possible causes of a variable, utilizing a pre-test/post-test design approach. Since Jamie is not creating an intervention, and it is too early in her investigation to explore possible causes, a quasi-experimental design would not fit her research question.

A descriptive design would help her identify generalizations as to the prevalence of water in the artwork of those diagnosed with alcohol abuse and/or addiction, as compared to the artwork of patients not diagnosed with alcohol abuse/or addiction. Through a descriptive design, Jamie can gain valuable information that can support her observations and research question. Therefore, a descriptive approach could be a viable design for Jamie to use.

A correlational approach would assist Jamie in finding out if her variable (the visual of water in patients' artwork) has a relationship with alcohol abuse and/or addiction. It would be easy enough for her to collect artwork from her patients with this diagnosis and see how many incorporate water into their artwork. Even if Jamie found a correlation between the two, she would not be able to support her research question unless she also collected artwork from those not diagnosed with alcohol abuse and/or addiction. If Jamie chose this design, she would have to create two correlational studies and then make a comparison between the two outcomes (the correlation outcome of those with an alcohol diagnosis to the correlation of those not diagnosed).

Jamie could develop a longitudinal study, but would have to collect artwork for an extended amount of time at specific intervals from both patients with an alcohol diagnosis and those without the diagnosis. Her analysis would not be looking for change over time, but for consistent representation within the artwork. This is an extended process and probably not the most efficient approach.

Finally, a historical design would not be feasible in this case. Since the artwork that Jamie is observing is being created in her group, there is a very good chance that there is not an archive of artwork for her to review. However, this would be information she would look for in her initial step of literature review as she develops her research proposal.

In the end, it looks like a descriptive research design would be the best approach for Jamie to follow. This would be a good choice since a descriptive design is the most appropriate when the researcher is first starting an investigation, but is not quite sure what he/she will find. The outcome of this study could then lead to further investigations in this area.

Conclusion

Approaching research from either a quasi-experimental, descriptive, correlational, longitudinal, or historical approach puts the researcher in the role of a detective, searching out the answers to specific enquiries. As with any investigation, the methodology used should best fit the question at hand. The important thing is to fully define and understand what you are investigating, so that you can properly choose the correct approach. Only after the correct methodology has been chosen and data collected can the answers be found.

References

American Psychiatric Association. (1980). *Diagnostic and statistical manual of mental disorders* (3rd ed.). Washington, DC: Author.

Bordens, K. S., & Abbott, B. B. (2008). *Research design and methods: A process approach* (7th ed.). New York, NY: McGraw Hill.

Gantt, L. (2009). The formal elements art therapy scale: A measurement system for global variables in art. *Art Therapy: Journal of the American Art Therapy Association, 26*(3), 124–129.

Gilroy, A. (2006). *Art therapy, research and evidence-based practice*. London: Sage.

Goldblatt, R., Elkis-Abuhoff, D., Gaydos, M., & Napoli, A. (2010). Understanding the clinical benefits of modeling clay exploration with patients diagnosed with Parkinson's disease. *Arts & Health, 2*(2), 140–148.

Goldblatt, R., Elkis-Abuhoff, D., Gaydos, M., Rose, S., & Casey, S. (2010). Unlocking conflict through creative expression. *Arts in Psychotherapy, 38*(2), 104–108.

Hartz, L., & Thick, L. (2005). Art therapy strategies to raise self-esteem in female juvenile offenders: A comparison of art psychotherapy and art as therapy approaches. *Art Therapy: Journal of the American Art Therapy Association, 22*(2), 70–80.

Kapitan, L. (2010). *Introduction to art therapy research*. New York, NY: Routledge.

Kumar, R. (2011). *Research methodology: A step-by-step guide for beginners* (3rd ed). London: Sage Publications Ltd.

Lapan, S., & Quartaroli, M. T. (Eds.) (2009). *Research essentials: An introduction to designs and practices*. San Francisco, CA: John Wiley/ Jossey Bass.

Lee, A. C. Y. (2011). Art therapy in Canada, now and then—A comparison between the national surveys of art therapists in Canada 2005 and 2010. *Canadian Art Therapy Association Journal, 24*(2), 20–29.

Manheim, A. R. (1998). The relationship between the artistic process and self-actualization. *Art Therapy: Journal of the American Art Therapy Association, 15*(2), 99–106.

Prescott, M. V., Sekendur, B., Bailey, B., & Hoshino, J. (2011). Art making as a component and facilitator of resiliency with homeless youth. *Art Therapy: Journal of the American Art Therapy Association, 25*(4), 156–163.

Reynolds, M. W., Nabors, L., & Quinlan, A. (2000). The effectiveness of art therapy: Does it work? *Art Therapy: Journal of American Art Therapy Association, 17*(3), 207–213.

Schreier, H., Ladakakos, C., Morabito, D., Chapman, L., & Knudson, M. M. (2005). Posttraumatic stress symptoms in children after mild to moderate pediatric trauma: A longitudinal examination of symptom prevalence, correlates, and parent-child symptom reporting. *Journal of Trauma-Injury Infection & Critical Care, 58*(2), 353–363.

Slayton, S. C., D'Archer, J., & Kaplan, F. (2010). Outcome studies on the efficacy of art therapy: A review of findings. *Art Therapy: Journal of the American Art Therapy Association, 27*(3), 108–118.

62

Experimental and Control Group Research Designs

Patricia St John

When I ask students to come up with an idea for a thesis research project, many say, "I want to prove that art therapy works!" This is one wish that we can all applaud. Yet, in the field, few research studies demonstrate that "art therapy works." Such studies are difficult to conduct and are time consuming and expensive. Studies that demonstrate the effectiveness of art therapy use experimental and control group research designs. Experimental research is about cause-and-effect relationships; a change in behavior or improvement (the effect) is caused by the therapy or treatment. In this chapter, the following questions will be addressed: (1) how does this research look in a clinical setting; (2) how might art therapists apply these designs in their clinical or academic setting; and (3) how can you demonstrate that "art therapy works"?

It has only been within the past 20 years that the field of art therapy has actively supported research. Therapy effectiveness research, including experimental and control group studies, is relatively new in the profession. Although the first effectiveness study was published in the mid-1970s, only recently have art therapists conducted randomized controlled trials (RCTs) (e.g., Chandraiah, Anand, & Avent, 2012; Kimport, & Robbins, 2012; Lyshak-Stelzer, Singer, St John, & Chemtob, 2007; Sandmire, Gorham, Rankin, & Grimm, 2012). Experimental and RCT designs are the "gold standard" in research and are used to establish cause-and-effect relationships. RCTs are at the pinnacle of the research design hierarchy. Research using these designs contributes to the growing body of literature which demonstrates that art therapy is an effective treatment modality, and thus adds credence to the fact that "art therapy works."

Changes in response to treatment are the basis for an experimental study. Experimental research designs and control group designs are similar and often overlap, but are not always the same. Gay, Mills, and Airasian (2011) broadly define experimental research as follows: "In *experimental research* the researcher manipulates at least one independent variable, controls relevant variables, and observes the effect on one or more dependent variables" (p. 249). *Variables* are, as my students often say, "things that vary,"—that is, self-esteem, depression, anxiety, aggression, or trauma symptoms. Experimental designs are used to study one group (the treatment group)

The Wiley Handbook of Art Therapy, First Edition. Edited by David E. Gussak and Marcia L. Rosal.

or two groups: an experimental group, which receives the treatment being studied, and a control group, which does not receive the treatment being researched. Control groups can receive treatment-as-usual, that is, the usual treatment available from a psychiatric unit, another treatment modality (e.g., music therapy), or even no treatment at all (oftentimes called placebo groups).

Setting Up an Experimental Study

Experimental research is a natural extension of good clinical practice. Based on practice, therapists begin by asking a question. The research question is transformed into a hypothesis, which states what might occur as the result of art therapy treatment. For example, the research question, "Does art therapy decrease aggressive behaviors in middle-school children who are identified as belligerent," becomes a hypothesis that reads, "art therapy treatment will decrease aggressive behaviors in middle-school children identified as belligerent." The next step in experimental research is to identify a group of clients who consent to participate in the study. Participants for the study might be from an existing treatment group or may be newly identified intakes. In this example, all participants would be middle-school children identified as bellicose. After participants are identified, parental consent is required before children can participate in the study. Child participants should agree to participate in the study by signing an assent form.

Next, because treatment or behavioral change must be measurable, one or more standardized or non-standardized assessments to measure the variable (e.g., aggression) are selected. For example, the *Silver Draw-A-Story* (DAS; Silver, 2007) can be used as to test the children for aggression levels before and after the treatment. In addition, staff members can be asked to keep aggression incident reports before, during, and after the treatment period. If there is a large enough decrease in aggression in the treatment group, as indicated by a statistical test (i.e., the *t*-test for matched samples), then the hypothesis is supported, and there is evidence that the treatment *works* or is effective and might be suitable for similar groups.

A control group experimental study can be created by comparing scores from the treatment (experimental) group with a control group who receives art-therapy-as-usual, or is on a treatment wait list. Control group research designs, a subgroup of experimental designs, are more robust than the one-group designs; for example, the aggression-reduction study as discussed earlier is strengthened by comparing the art therapy treatment for aggression to a control group. Both groups take the DAS (Silver, 2007) before and after treatment, and incident reports are maintained. A statistical analysis of pretest–posttest differences (e.g., *t*-test for non-matched samples) reveals the degree of pretest–posttest differences between groups and whether the degree of difference was *statistically significant* (i.e., caused by the treatment and not some other factor). A comparison of the two treatments provides stronger evidence that one treatment more effectively reduces aggression in aggressive middle-school children. In other words, you will have demonstrated that "art therapy (aggression-focused-art therapy) works."

Internal and External Validity

There are several formats used in experimental and control group studies; some are stronger or more valid than others. To demonstrate that art therapy is effective without a shadow of a doubt, researchers employ the strongest possible research design, one that has greatest *validity*.

> Any uncontrolled extraneous variables that affect performance on the dependent variable [e.g., aggressive behavior] are threats to the validity of an experiment. An experiment is valid if results obtained are due only to the manipulated independent variable [e.g., Aggression-Focused-Art-Therapy] and if they are generalizable to situations outside the experimental setting. (Gay et al., 2011, p. 275)

According to Best and Kahn (2003), there are two types of validity: internal and external. Internal validity is "the extent that factors that have been manipulated (independent variables) [e.g., aggression-focused-art-therapy and art-therapy-as-usual] actually have a genuine effect on the observed consequences (dependent variables) [e.g., aggressive behavior] in the experimental setting" (p. 166). External validity is "the extent to which the variable relationships can be generalized to other settings, other treatment variables, other measurement variables, and other populations" (p. 166).

The validity of an experimental study depends on the degree of control that the research has over factors that affect results. Researchers try to control as many internal and external factors as possible to ensure that the results after studying a treatment are caused by the treatment and not something else (i.e., such as the researcher's bias toward a new treatment or using subjectively interpreted measurement instruments to gather data). Variables in a study that are not controlled are called "threats."

Threats are outside variables that a researcher cannot control. For example, if the researcher is conducting treatment in both the experimental and control groups, his or her bias toward the *aggression-focused treatment* compared to *art-therapy-as-usual* will affect results. Nor should positive results occur because the researcher decides to test the treatment on previously formed groups that are not equal in severity of aggression symptoms. When selecting an experimental research design, the art therapist chooses the strongest possible design to control threats to the study's validity as possible.

A full discussion of threats is beyond the scope of this chapter. However, any good research text examines this problem in depth. Threats that apply to each type of experimental and control group design, discussed in the text that follows, are given in the corresponding tables. Notice that the stronger the experimental design, the fewer the threats to the study's validity.

Two types of experimental designs have been discussed in Gay et al. (2011): a *one-group design* and a *control-group design*. Yet, many more subgroupings of experimental designs are available. Some are stronger than others to demonstrate a cause-and-effect relationship. The selection of a research design is based on the research question and available resources: setting, finances, time, and statistical support.

Single-Variable and Factorial Designs

Under the umbrella of experimental and control group designs, there are two major research design groups: *single-variable* and *factorial designs*. Single-variable designs are used when one variable is under study. Factorial designs are used when more than two variables are under study and results will be compared.

Single-variable experimental formats

Experimental study designs are organized on three levels: pre-experimental, quasi-experimental, and true experimental. As stated previously, the gold standard, true experimental research, or RCT, is the gold standard for experimental research. It is the only design that requires *random* assignment of participants to either an experimental or a control group. Random assignment means that all participants have an equal chance of being assigned to either the experimental or control group. Random assignment may be done by flipping a coin, by drawing participants' names or code numbers from a hat, or by using the table of random numbers. (For more about how to use the table of random numbers, see any good research textbook.)

Although researchers strive for the gold standard, few art therapy researchers have the means to carry out such extensive studies. Undoubtedly, a lot of good research is conducted by graduate (master's and doctoral) students for thesis or dissertation requirements, but few reach publication. Such studies often use formats other than those used in RCT studies. Some experimental and control group studies are conducted using already-formed groups, or only one group. The form of experimental or control group design selected depends on the research question. Keep in mind, however, that the other two subgroups of experimental designs (pre-experimental and quasi-experimental) are characterized by weaker validity.

A trauma study (Lyshak-Stelzer et al., 2007) described below under true experimental designs (pretest–posttest control group design) tested at least one independent variable (trauma symptoms) and controlled as many relevant variables as possible to "observe the effect" of the two treatments on the dependent variable (degree of trauma symptom reduction). However, not everyone has the resources needed to conduct a true experimental study, so other designs are used.

Pre-experimental designs   The least robust of the experimental designs is the pre-experimental design, and it is selected when there can be no distinct control group, because withholding treatment is not possible nor appropriate when studying a pre-existing group. This design is used when testing for differences in the dependent variable (e.g., degree of trauma symptoms) before and after treatment. One group or two previously formed groups may be used. One group is used when there are a limited number of potential participants; two groups are utilized when pre-existing groups must remain intact, as often is the case in art therapy settings.

Pre-experimental designs are further sub-grouped, also in terms of study strength or validity: *one-shot case study*, *one-group pretest–posttest design*, and *static-group comparison* (Gay et al., 2011). Participants are *not* randomly assigned to groups. The *one-shot case study* is simply designed. A single group of subjects is treated and then tested on a treatment variable (e.g., trauma, anxiety, depression). One problem with this design is that the level of functioning before treatment is unknown; thus, the actual effect of the treatment can be questioned.

The *one-group pretest–posttest* design is used when the group is pretested for functioning level on a variable (e.g., anxiety, depression). After participating in the experimental treatment, the group members are retested. The pretest and posttest results are compared to establish the degree of change after treatment. This is a stronger design than the one-shot case study, but there is no way of knowing whether results were caused by the treatment or other extraneous variables (e.g., another treatment, medication changes).

In a *static-group comparison* design, two pre-existing groups participate. One group, the experimental group, receives the experimental treatment; the other group, the control group, engages in treatment-as-usual, or other activities. Each group completes a posttest. Test data from each group is compared for differences. Results indicate whether there are significant differences between the two groups; if so, then it can be concluded that the treatment was the cause of the increased changes to the treatment variable (e.g., trauma, anxiety, depression). This design is appropriate for exploratory studies on a small scale prior to launching a study with many participants.

The organization of a *one-group pretest–posttest design* is shown in Table 62.1. A hypothetical study is used to present the research question, the conversion to a hypothesis, the variables under study, selected participants (the sample), the treatment, the data collection tools or measurement instrument, and the data analysis procedures. Threats to the design's validity are included.

Pre-experimental designs are used to conduct preliminary tests of the effects of an experimental treatment on pre-existing groups of clients whose assessed variables

Table 62.1 A pre-experimental research design.

One-Group, Pretest–Posttest Design	
Research question	What are the pretest–posttest differences in trauma symptom reduction for one group that is given art therapy trauma treatment?
Hypothesis	There will be significant differences in trauma symptoms after one pre-existing group of inpatient youth participate in art therapy trauma treatment.
Variables	Dependent variable: trauma symptoms Independent variable: trauma-focused art therapy
Sample	Inpatient, psychiatric youth who meet the threshold for trauma symptoms One group pretested, given the experimental treatment, and posttested using measures of trauma symptoms
Measurement instrument(s)	UCLA PTSD Reaction Index (Steinberg, Brymer, Decker, & Pynoos, 2004)
Statistical analysis	t-test for matched samples
Threats to validity	History, maturation, testing, instrumentation, statistical regression, pretest–posttest interaction (Cook & Campbell, 1979, cited in Gay et al., 2011, pp. 254–262)

(trauma symptoms) require treatment. These designs control for some threats to validity, but the many "holes" in the research design raise legitimate questions about results, positive or negative. Results of such studies typically cannot be generalized to similar patient or client groups. When resources allow, researchers prefer to use stronger designs such as quasi-experimental or true experimental designs.

Quasi-experimental designs   Quasi-experimental designs have greater validity than pre-experimental studies because they have fewer threats. As a result, they test the hypothesis more rigorously. Similar to the pre-experimental studies, this design is used when it is not possible to randomly assign participants to groups. As with pre-experimental designs, there are three quasi-experimental subgroups: *non-equivalent control group design*, *time-series design*, and *counterbalanced design*.

The *non-equivalent control group design* requires two intact, pre-existing groups. A coin flip determines which whole group receives the new treatment. Both groups are tested before and after the treatment. The control group receives traditional treatment, an alternative treatment, or no treatment. Results of pretest and posttest differences on the variable in question (e.g., trauma symptoms, aggressive behaviors) determine which treatment causes greater benefits to the participants. This design is problematic because the two groups might not be equivalent on the variable prior to treatments. However, a statistical maneuver, analysis of covariance (ANCOVA), is used to equate groups. An example of a quasi-experimental study using the non-equivalent control group design is shown in Table 62.2.

The *time-series design* requires only one group. The group is tested at multiple points before the onset of treatment until scores are unchanging. Throughout the experimental treatment and again after the completion of the treatment, the group is

Table 62.2   A quasi-experimental research design.

Non-Equivalent Control Group Design	
Research question	What is the effect of an art therapy trauma treatment versus traditional art therapy on trauma symptoms in inpatient, psychiatric youth in pre-existing treatment groups?
Hypothesis	There is a significant difference in trauma symptoms between inpatient youth who participate in art therapy trauma treatment and youth in arts-and-crafts.
Variables	Dependent variable: trauma symptoms
	Independent variable: trauma-focused art therapy treatment or arts-and-crafts
Sample	Inpatient, psychiatric youth who meet the threshold for trauma symptoms
	Two or more pre-existing groups are pretested, receive either an experimental or traditional treatment, and are posttested
Measurement instruments	UCLA PTSD Reaction Index (Steinberg et al., 2004)
Data analysis	*t*-test for independent samples
Threats	Statistical regression, selection interactions, and pretest– treatment interactions (Cook & Campbell, 1979, cited in Gay et al., 2011, pp. 254–262)

tested repetitively. Scores might rise, fall, or remain relatively stable, providing evidence of an initial treatment effect as well as the lasting or long-term effects of the treatment.

The *counterbalanced design* is used when several treatments are under study. Any number of intact groups can participate, but there must be as many groups as treatments. Treatments are given in different sequences in order to counter the effects of one treatment on another. For example, using four groups (A, B, C, D) and four treatments (1, 2, 3, 4), the sequence of treatments might be: group A: 1, 2, 3, 4; group B: 2, 3, 4, 1; group C: 4, 2, 1, 3; and group D: 4, 3, 2, 1. All groups are given a test at pretest and posttest. According to Gay et al. (2011), "a counterbalanced design should be used only when the treatments are such that exposure to one will not affect the effectiveness of another" (p. 272). It is challenging to design such a study.

Some early art therapy studies used quasi-experimental designs. However, a growing number of recent studies use true experimental designs, especially RCT studies. These are also categorized into three types.

True experimental designs To be called a *true experimental design*, the random assignment of participants to either an experimental or control group is a must. In other words, pre-existing groups are not used. Subgroups of true experimental designs are the *pretest–posttest control group design, posttest-only control group design*, and the *Solomon four-group design*. Whether you select a true experimental or another design depends on your research question and the feasibility of conducting the study given your financial, staffing, and time-availability resources.

To set up a *pretest–posttest control group design*, two distinct treatment groups (e.g., trauma-focused art therapy treatment and arts-and-crafts treatment) are developed and measured. As patients are admitted for treatment, they are randomly assigned to the experimental or control group using a coin flip or the table of random numbers. Both groups receive a pretest, participate in the treatment, and are given a posttest. A comparison of pretest–posttest change is calculated to determine whether a significant difference exists between the two treatments. An example of this design is shown in Table 62.3.

The *posttest-only control group design* does not utilize a pretest, and only posttest is given to the two randomly assigned groups; this controls for one of the threats to validity, the effect of pretesting, or learning the test on the results. The *Solomon four-group design* uses four groups. Participants are randomly assigned to one of the four groups. Other aspects of this design include: only two of the four groups are given the pretest (one experimental group and one control group), two groups receive the experimental treatment, two groups receive the control treatment, and all groups are posttested. This design has no threats to validity but requires considerable resources to conduct. An example is given in Table 62.4.

Factorial designs

So far, the discussion has been on *single-variable designs*. For more complex studies, *factorial designs* are used. By comparison, a study using a single-variable design is easier to create and conduct, but the factorial design produces more information.

Table 62.3 A true experimental design

Pretest, Posttest Control Group Design	
Research question	When randomly assigned inpatient youth are pretested, then participate in art therapy trauma treatment or arts-and-crafts, then posttested, which group has significantly greater reduction in trauma symptoms?
Hypothesis	Randomly assigned inpatient youth who are pretested, then participate in art therapy trauma treatment, and then posttested have significantly less trauma symptoms than those who participate in an arts-and-crafts group, and then are posttested.
Variables	Dependent variable: trauma symptoms Independent variable: trauma-focused art therapy treatment or arts-and-crafts
Sample	Inpatient, psychiatric youth who meet the threshold for trauma symptoms Participants are randomly assigned to either the experimental or control group, pretested, undergo treatment, and are posttested
Measurement instruments	UCLA PTSD Reaction Index (Steinberg et al., 2004)
Data analysis	*t*-test for independent samples
Threats	Pretest interaction (Cook & Campbell, 1979, cited in Gay et al., 2011, pp. 254–262)

Table 62.4 Solomon four-group design.

Groups and Testing	*Experimental Group*	*Control Group*
Pretest and posttest	Pretest and posttest with experimental treatment	Pretest and posttest with control treatment
Posttest only	Posttest-only with experimental treatment	Posttest only with control treatment

"When more than one independent variable is included in a study, whether a true experiment or a quasi-experiment, a factorial design is necessary" (Best & Kahn, 2003, p. 187).

The purpose of a factorial design is to test whether there is a relationship between or among multiple variables. This design is used because single-variable designs cannot test the effects of interactions between or among variables. According to Gay et al. (2011), "… a variable found not to be effective in a single-variable study may interact significantly with another variable" (p. 264). Factorial designs take two forms: the *2 x 2 factorial design* and the *2 x more-than-2 design*. More complex multiples are also typical of factorial designs (e.g., 3 × 3; 3 × 3 × 3, and so forth). Only the 2 × 2 design is discussed in the following text as an example of factorial designs.

The 2 x 2 factorial design   Envision that you have two groups that are different in some way—in this case, age grouping—but manifest the same symptoms and trauma

Table 62.5 2 × 2 Factorial design.

Groups by Age	Treatments	
	Art Therapy Trauma Treatment	Arts-and-Crafts Treatment
Adolescents	Group 1	Group 2
Adults	Group 3	Group 4

(see Table 62.5). You want to find out which of two treatments is more effective in trauma-symptom-reduction based on age differences. Your research questions might include: "does an art therapy trauma-symptom treatment more effectively reduce trauma symptoms in adolescents or adults," and "does an arts-and-crafts treatment more effectively reduce trauma symptoms in adolescents or adults."

Your participants are pre-existing groups of adolescents and adults, but they are *randomly* assigned to either the art therapy trauma treatment or the arts-and-crafts treatment. All groups receive the pretest and the posttest. Group differences are analyzed to determine which treatment was more effective for each age group. Results provide support for either continuing the current treatment or changing it to one that more effectively reduces trauma symptoms.

Conclusion

Creating, conducting, and publishing experimental and control group research is critical to establishing art therapy as a viable, valid, and effective treatment. There needs to be a critical mass of experimental research about the populations served by art therapists and about the specific symptoms and diagnoses that art therapists address. The challenge is to move art therapy to the forefront of preferred interventions and to earn the prominence and the respect it deserves. To accomplish this, art therapists will need to engage in experimental and control group research.

Two broad types of experimental and control group research strategies—*single-variable* and *factorial*—are considered to be the most robust research designs in terms of evaluating treatment and assessing behavior and emotional change. The various experimental designs were reviewed herein for the purpose of introducing the research possibilities available to the art therapy clinician. In addition, support and mentoring is essential for practicing art therapists to collaborate, create, and conduct experimental and control design studies.

The field of art therapy is poised to empirically demonstrate that "art therapy works." To move forward, an assertive campaign is required on several levels to establish this assertion: (1) training students at the master's and doctoral levels to conduct experimental and control group studies; (2) publishing master's and doctoral experimental research studies; (3) mentoring practicing art therapists to learn how to conduct experimental research through involvement in multi-site studies; (4) collaborating on such studies with colleagues in related fields; and (5) identifying funding for experimental and control group studies, while simultaneously training art therapists to successfully obtain grant funding. This initiative will yield new, exciting experimental design studies that join the meritorious, albeit small, body of research that demonstrates the power of art therapy. It is our responsibility to establish that *art therapy works*. Attaining this goal might lead to licensure and insurance reimbursement for art therapists across the United States. Experimental research by art therapists is critical to uncovering the capability of art therapy to heal.

References

Best, J. W., & Kahn, J. V. (2003). *Research in education* (9th ed.). Boston, MA: Allyn and Bacon: A Pearson Education Company.

Chandraiah, S., Anand, S. A., & Avent, L. C. (2012). Efficacy of group art therapy on depressive symptoms in adult heterogeneous psychiatric outpatients. *Art Therapy: Journal of the American Art Therapy Association, 29*(2), 80–86.

Cook, T. D., & Campbell, D. T. (1979). *Quasi-experimentation: Design and analysis for field settings.* Chicago, IL: Rand McNally.

Gay, L. R., Mills, G. E., & Airasian, P. (2011). *Educational research: Competencies for analysis and applications* (10th ed.). Upper Saddle River, NJ: Pearson Education, Inc.

Kimport, E. R., & Robbins, S. J. (2012). Efficacy of creative clay work on reducing negative mood: A randomized controlled trial. *Art Therapy: Journal of the American Art Therapy Association, 29*(2), 74–79.

Lyshak-Stelzer, F., Singer, P., St John, P., & Chemtob, C. (2007). Art therapy for adolescents with Posttraumatic Stress Disorder symptoms: A pilot study. *Art Therapy: Journal of the American Art Therapy Association, 24*(4), 163–169.

Sandmire, R., Gorham, S. R., Rankin, N. E., & Grimm, D. R. (2012). The influence of art making on anxiety: A pilot study. *Art Therapy: Journal of the American Art Therapy Association, 29*(2), 68–73.

Silver, R. (2007). *The Silver Drawing Test and Draw A Story: Assessing depression, aggression, and cognitive skills.* New York, NY: Routledge.

Steinberg, A. M., Brymer, M. J., Decker, K. B., & Pynoos, R. S. (2004). The University of California at Los Angeles Post-traumatic Stress Disorder Reaction Index. *Current Psychiatry Reports, 6*(2), 96–100.

63

Mixed Methods Research and Art Therapy

Nancy Gerber

Introduction

The field of art therapy is at a crucial point in its evolution where clinical wisdom is not enough to sustain and grow the profession. It is well acknowledged that research is required to evaluate and build theory, test the outcomes of assessment and treatment approaches, and compile evidence that legitimizes the practices in the field (Deaver, 2002; Deaver & Kaiser, 2013; Kapitan, 2010). As the field embarks on this phase of professional development, the challenge is to find research approaches that possess the necessary validity, trustworthiness, rigor, and creativity to satisfy the dominant culture while simultaneously preserving the philosophical and theoretical integrity of the field (Deaver, 2002; Deaver & Kaiser, 2013; Junge & Linesch, 1993; Kapitan, 2010; McNiff, 1998). *Mixed methods research* provides viable options for advancing the art therapy research agenda while preserving the essential meaning of the field.

One approach to addressing the challenges in art therapy research is to begin by identifying the foundational philosophical assumptions or worldviews of art therapy that contribute decisions about research phenomena, questions, methods, and future directions. *Worldview* is a construct that defines the world according to a particular set of philosophical assumptions and system of beliefs about the truth, reality, knowledge, and values of a particular domain or field (Creswell & Plano Clark, 2011; Mertens, 2005). The declaration of a worldview, often used interchangeably with the term *paradigm* or *mental model* (Greene, 2007), is essential to critical decisions regarding the phenomena, questions, methods, and interpretations that position a field or domain relative to a research perspective.

The primary purpose of this chapter is to discuss the philosophical assumptions and synergistic compatibility between art therapy and mixed methods research. The worldview in art therapy, which might be called *dialectical aesthetic intersubjectivity*, includes multiple intrapsychic and interpsychic intersubjective realities from which aesthetic knowledge emerges, informs, acquires meaning, and transforms through a dynamic, creative, dialectic process. The dynamic aesthetic, intersubjective, and dialectical nature of art therapy parallels the philosophical assumptions and methodologies of mixed methods research, which embraces creativity, pluralism, eclecticism,

The Wiley Handbook of Art Therapy, First Edition. Edited by David E. Gussak and Marcia L. Rosal.
© 2016 John Wiley & Sons, Ltd. Published 2016 by John Wiley & Sons, Ltd.

dynamism, dialogism, and dialecticism in pursuit of truth and knowledge (Greene, 2007; Johnson, 2012; Tashakkori & Teddlie, 2010).

The philosophical and methodological constructs in mixed methods research provide a framework by which art therapy researchers can reflectively and critically assess the philosophical and methodological decisions that drive their art therapy research agenda, questions, methods, and interpretations, while simultaneously conducting critical conversations that position art therapy within the dominant culture. A mindful approach to research advocates for art therapists to purposefully and thoughtfully re-envision and establish the criteria that defines evidence and efficacy for the field while preserving the meaning and mission of art therapy (Gerber, in press a).

In this chapter, a brief contextual overview of the sociocultural and sociopolitical influences on research is presented, followed by a more detailed discussion of the philosophical assumptions or worldview of art therapy. Subsequently, a brief introduction to mixed methods philosophies, typologies, and designs is presented, after which a summary about the synergy between art therapy and mixed methods research concludes the chapter.

Contextual and Cultural Influences

In considering research in the field of art therapy, art therapists need to become mindful of several variables that influence the choices we make in deciding upon research approaches. These variables include, but may not be limited to, sociocultural and sociopolitical contexts; the research hegemonies of the dominant culture; the economic dynamics of research; the healthcare culture; and the essential nature and curative factors of art therapy that form our research agenda and contribute to the sustenance of the field. Within the broad context of our sociopolitical culture, which influences the more specific healthcare culture, the dominant accepted forms of research, and therefore the research that is most often funded, adheres to particular philosophical assumptions. Historically, and, for the most part, currently, these philosophical assumptions belong to a worldview called *positivism* or *post-positivism*, which posits that the universe is of one singular reality in which knowledge manifests as observable, causal, and linear variables of natural and social phenomena, the correlation and/or measurement of which prove or disprove an existing theory (Creswell & Plano Clark, 2011). The positivist/post-positivist approach, although effective for studying observable natural and social phenomena, is not necessarily generalizable to the study of all human phenomena. Investigations of phenomena in the social sciences require pluralistic, eclectic, and dialectical research perspectives and approaches to answer questions related to multiple intersubjective realities and multi-dimensional knowledge of the mind (Greene, 2007; Guba & Lincoln, 1998; Johnson, 2012; Johnson & Gray, 2010; Paul, Graffam, & Fowler, 2005).

Philosophically positioning art therapy within the dominant culture requires critical evaluation of our research agenda relative to the philosophical assumptions that will best support the advancement of knowledge in the field consistent with those assumptions. Mixed methods research provides a viable alternative to the dilemma of selecting one paradigmatic or methodological tradition to address multifactorial research phenomena and questions often central to art therapy research. Mixed methods research is an emergent approach, gaining acceptance in the dominant culture, the philosophical assumptions of which embrace diverse paradigms, theories, and methods emphasizing the creative and improbable dialectical dialogues between multiple worldviews essential to generating new innovative knowledge while sustaining rigor, authenticity, and credibility (Greene, 2007; Johnson, 2008; Johnson & Gray, 2010).

Philosophical Assumptions in Art Therapy

Defining the *philosophical assumptions* that contribute to a *worldview* or paradigmatic stance of the research, the researcher, and the discipline is essential to critically evaluating research directions and decisions. More specifically, these philosophical assumptions provide the constructs by which we formulate research problems, questions, designs, methods, and results (Mertens, 2005; Paul et al., 2005). One way of identifying the philosophical assumptions and constructing a worldview in research is by systematically examining (1) the *ontology* or the nature of truth or reality; (2) the *epistemology*, referring to types of knowledge and ways of knowing; (3) the *axiology*, relating to the aesthetics and values guiding the research; and (4) the *methodology*, which is the way of investigating these assumptions.

Although the field of art therapy has not explicitly stated its worldview, there are several constructs from which we can infer the underlying philosophical assumptions that contribute to the worldview of, and theory development in, art therapy. The worldview in art therapy originates in its interdisciplinary heritage, positioning the philosophical assumptions within multiple interactive divergent and convergent realities and bodies of knowledge such as the arts and humanities; medicine and biology; psychoanalysis and psychology; and semiotics and anthropology (Gerber, 2006, in press b; McNiff, 1986).

Emergent from the interdisciplinary heritage of the field, the *ontology* for art therapy might be considered pluralistic, meaning that multiple *intersubjective* realities best represent an understanding of our view of being, reality, and truth. The nature of intersubjectivity includes the acknowledgement that we live in a socially and interpersonally constructed world where our perceptions, thoughts, and emotions converge in co-constructing shared realities (Greene, 2007; Johnson, 2012; Johnson & Gray, 2010). Defined as both a meta-social and relational construct, intersubjectvity is a "jointly constructed narrative … [which] ascribes meaning to experience for which no language previously existed" (Brown, 2011, p. 1). Intersubjectivity is also considered to represent a joining on an unconscious preverbal level where "communication and meaning making between two intra psychic worlds … results in changes within each member…" (p. 109). Johnson and Gray (2010) have called the co-existence of multiple intersubjective realities "ontological pluralism" or "multiple realism" (Johnson & Gray, 2010, p. 72). The dynamic and dialectic interactive process between these multiple intrapsychic/interpsychic and intersubjective realities contributes to the development of a creative philosophical frame foundational for both an art therapy theory as well as a research mentality and methodology, the purpose of which is the generation of new knowledge (Johnson, 2008; Johnson & Gray, 2010).

The knowledge that inhabits and co-constructs these intersubjective realities is multidimensional aesthetic knowledge, which comprises the epistemology of art therapy and represents an epistemological eclecticism. Aesthetic knowledge, operationally defined as "sense-based awareness" (Harris Williams, 2010) or perceptual knowledge (Cooper, 1997), actually and symbolically expresses the preverbal experiences of our earliest and developing human relationships (Dissanayake, 2009; Gerber, in press a; Hagman, 2011; Harris Willliams, 2010). The multiple dimensions of aesthetic knowledge represent the perceptual language of the preverbal intersubjective experiences encoded in sensorial, imaginal, symbolic, nonsensical, spatial, timeless, and paradoxical forms of cognition. The meaning of aesthetic knowledge emerges when exposed to the intersubjective context wherein dialectical dialogic processes occur between self and other, internal and external, intrapsychic and interpsychic, past and present, conscious and unconscious, subjective and objective, linear and spatial, and logic and chaos, resulting in the construction of new intersubjective realities and the emergence of meaning, insight, and transformation (Gerber, in press a; Johnson, 2008, 2012; Johnson & Gray, 2010).

In art therapy, the philosophical assumptions of pluralistic intersubjective realities, eclectic forms of aesthetic knowledge, and the dialectic dialogues between these multiple realities and ways of knowing are considered to have moral and ethical value. These values are embedded in the *axiology* of art therapy since they contribute to self-knowledge, knowledge of the other, and the acquisition of meaning that contributes to personal freedom, creativity, and the individual and collective health of the culture or society.

One *method* for investigating these philosophical assumptions, which might be called *dialectic aesthetic intersubjectivity*, is the dialectical approach. The dialectic relates to the positioning of and conversation between dynamic, improbable, conflicting realities and ways of knowing, the purpose of which is generating new knowledge (Greene, 2007). The dialectical approach is one that has been advocated in mixed methods research and seems compatible with the fundamental nature and characteristics of creativity and psychotherapy inherent in art therapy.

Summarily, central to the dialectical aesthetic intersubjective worldview of art therapy are the philosophical assumptions of pluralistic intersubjective realities, eclectic forms of aesthetic knowledge, and the dialectic dialogues between these multiple realities and ways of knowing that contribute to the creation of new knowledge, the construction of new self/other realities, insights, and transformation. The articulation of this worldview contributes to the purposeful and mindful assessment and construction of a research agenda for art therapy that includes compatible research paradigms, strategies, and interpretations.

Definitions and Worldviews of Mixed Method Research

Definition

The generally accepted definition of mixed methods research includes a philosophical position that drives the "… direction of the collection and analysis and mixture of qualitative and quantitative approaches in many phases of the research process"

(Creswell & Plano Clark, 2011, p. 5), and a methodological approach "… in which the investigator collects and analyzes data, integrates the findings, and draws inferences using both qualitative and quantitative approaches in a single study or program of inquiry" (Tashakkori & Creswell, as cited in Creswell & Plano Clark, 2011, p. 4). Essential to mixed methods research is that "… the use of quantitative and qualitative approaches, in combination provides a better understanding of research problems than either approach alone" (Creswell & Plano Clark, 2011, p. 5).

Philosophical assumptions or worldviews

In mixed methods research, philosophical assumptions, paradigms, or worldviews directly influence all phases and mixing configurations of the research (Creswell & Plano Clark, 2011, p. 5). Although an exhaustive review of the paradigms associated with mixed methods research is beyond the scope of this chapter, an overview of some of these worldviews will help to situate the methods within the philosophical contexts and to establish their relevance to—and synergy with—art therapy philosophical assumptions and methodologies.

The philosophical essence of mixed methods is what Greene (2007) called the embracing of "divergence and dissonance" for the purpose of generating "puzzles and paradoxes, clashes and conflict" that result in "… new perspectives and understandings, insights not previously imagined, knowledge with originality and artistry" (p. 24). She asserted that mixed methods research accommodates for the shortcomings of causal, linear, positivist, and post-positivist perspectives that exclude the narrative, contextual, spatial, multi-dimensional, "iterative," and particular interactional and intersubjective aspects of the human experience in a social world (p. 19). These revolutionary ways of conceptualizing research have contributed to the development of innovative perspectives and creative methods that can answer multidimensional questions extending beyond the limitations of one dominant perspective (Creswell & Plano-Clark, 2011; Greene, 2007; Johnson, 2008, 2012; Johnson & Gray, 2010).

As a manifestation of this perspective, mixed methods research embraces one or more traditional or innovative worldviews that can be used singularly or interactively. For instance, Creswell and Plano-Clark (2011) suggested four worldviews that represent a general compatibility with mixed methods—positivism/post-positivism, constructivism, participatory/transformative, and pragmatism. Adding to and elaborating on these paradigms, Greene (2007) introduced the "dialectical stance," which is used "to engage meaningfully with difference and, through the tensions created by juxtaposing different paradigms, to achieve dialectical discovery of enhanced, reframed or new understandings" (p. 69). Johnson (2012), acknowledging the work of Greene (2007), developed a new "meta paradigm" that he called "dialectical pluralism" (p. 752), which also places the emphasis and value on a pluralistic ontology of divergent and paradoxical realities, knowledge, values, methods, and the creation of new knowledge through attuning to differences. The "dialectical stance" (Greene, 2007) and "dialectical pluralism" (Johnson, 2012) capture and mirror the complexity, fluidity, and multi-dimensionality of social and human phenomena and best represent the values, assumptions, and researchable phenomena in the domains of creativity, psychotherapy, and art therapy.

Methods

A brief introduction to the rationales, typologies, and designs in mixed methods research is warranted to demonstrate the transferability of these philosophies to research practice. The methodologies provide thoughtful constructs by which these realities and forms of knowledge can be systematically studied with rigor, comprehensiveness, and creativity by a reflective, philosophically positioned, and skilled researcher or a team of researchers.

Conducting mixed methods research begins by identifying the contextual worldview of the research, researcher, and theory/discipline. In mixed methods research, reflection and assessment of the worldview and skills of the researcher is an essential part of designing the study. Since both quantitative and qualitative research methods are used in mixed methods, skill in both is necessary. If a single researcher does not possess proficiency in both skill sets, then recruiting a partner or research team to complement research skill sets is recommended (Creswell & Plano-Clark, 2011; Greene, 2007).

Rationale

The decisions for conducting mixed methods research require a very purposeful, reflective, and systematic evaluation of the reasons for electing to use mixed methods. Once the worldview of the research, the discipline, and the researcher has been identified, the following reasons for choosing mixed methods research should be considered: (1) supplementing insufficient results; (2) adding description, elaboration, corroboration, or explanation to existing or emergent results; (3) generalizing qualitative results; (4) understanding or enhancing preliminary data by embedding a second method during the research; (5) exploring a theory; and (6) evoking "paradox, contradiction, divergence … in the service of fresh insights, new perspectives and original understandings"(Greene, 2007, pp. 102–103) as well as integrating multi-phase research (Creswell & Plano-Clark, 2011; Greene, 2007).

Additionally, the reason why mixed methods research is both philosophically and methodologically appropriate in comparison to other research approaches is essential to designing a mixed methods study: (1) what is the purpose of the research; (2) what are the philosophical and methodological dimensions of the research that require mixing; (3) what are the implications of mixing methods or paradigms; and (4) what are the projected or desired outcomes (Greene, 2007)?

Typologies and designs

With this rationale in mind, the next step is to explore the different typologies and designs used to implement these strategies. Typology in mixed methods research refers to a systematic classification of "useful mixed methods designs and the selection and adaptation of a particular design to a study's purpose and questions" (Creswell & Plano-Clark, 2011, p. 55).

Situated within the worldview and rationale, selection of mixed methods research types and designs focuses on research phenomena, problems and questions, and strategic decisions about mixing during all or any of the phases of data collection, analysis, and interpretation. One approach to this process is to use a typology. According to Creswell and Plano-Clark (2011), types of mixed methods design include four major components that exist in various combinations and relationships in all designs and throughout all phases of the research: (1) positioning/timing; (2) interactive relationship; (3) priority; and (4) points of mixing relative to the qualitative (QUAL) and quantitative (QUAN) strands (p. 63).

The positioning or timing of the strands refers to convergent, parallel, concurrent, or sequential design types (Creswell & Plano-Clark, 2011; Greene, 2007; Tashakkori & Teddlie, 2010). Concurrent, parallel, and convergent are similar, in that they represent the use of the QUAN and QUAL methods simultaneously throughout the data collection and analysis phases of the study. Sequential types of designs are those in which either the QUAL or QUAN methods are used first, while the other method is used secondarily to explore or explain the result of the first strand. The *interactive relationship* describes the degree of independence, inter-relationship, and interaction of the quantitative and qualitative strands during one or more phases of the research (Creswell & Plano-Clark, 2011; Greene, 2007).

The *priority or status* refers to the weight or prominence of the QUAL and QUAN strands within the study—the two strands have equal status, the QUAN strand has dominance or the QUAL strand has dominance (Creswell & Plano-Clark, 2011). The last consideration is the procedure for *integration* or "*mixing of the strands*" (Creswell & Plano-Clark, 2011, p. 64; Greene, 2007). Mixing refers to the strategic points in the research where the QUAL and QUAN strands are integrated for purposes of corroboration, information, elaboration, elucidation, or interpretation about the phenomena under investigation (Creswell & Plano-Clark, 2011; Greene, 2007).

The components of the mixed methods types described in the preceding text are used to evaluate and formulate research design decisions. The mixed methods literature is replete with examples of numerous designs, some of which represent the same general constructs but include different descriptors. For the purpose and scope of this chapter, only a few designs can be identified; however, these designs exemplify the nature and spirit of the majority of designs. Creswell and Plano-Clark (2011) proposed six major mixed methods designs that are situated within the typological frameworks described in the preceding text, thereby representing variations on timing and positioning, interactive relationship, priority, and mixing. The six major designs are: (1) the convergent parallel design; (2) the explanatory sequential design; (3) the exploratory sequential design; (4) the embedded design; (5) the transformative design; and (6) the multiphase design. Further elaboration about these designs exceeds the limitations and overall purpose of this chapter, but readers are encouraged to learn more if they are interested.

Mixed methods research thus provides structures and opportunities for creative and innovative research at every decisive phase from philosophy to design, implementation, and interpretation. Most notably for the field of art therapy, these research approaches allow for the dynamic and dialectic interactions and investigations between the multiple realities and forms of knowledge to inform the theory and practice of art therapy. In a recent Delphi study by Deaver and Kaiser (2013), key informants in the field of art therapy were surveyed in an attempt to identify an art therapy research agenda. The results included a prioritized listing of topics, including outcome research, art therapy and neuroscience, art therapy assessments, processes and mechanisms of art therapy, cross-cultural approaches, and a database of normative lifespan artwork (p. 115). The diversity inherent in the philosophical perspectives of these topics, and consequently in the projected research strategies, makes a strong case for the consideration of mixed methods research approaches to begin to address these rich, multi-factorial research phenomena and problems.

Conclusions

Art therapy is at a critical and opportunistic point in its professional development when decisions about a research agenda can contribute to clarifying the essential nature or worldview of art therapy, identifying phenomena and/or variables requiring research, mindfully selecting the most compatible and rigorous methodologies resulting in increased efficacy and growth in the field. A brief examination and comparison of the worldviews in art therapy and mixed methods research accentuate the possibilities and provide the essential structures for the systematic investigation of multidimensional intersubjective realities and aesthetic forms of knowledge without apology, compromise, reductionism, or distortion of the philosophical assumptions or worldview in our field.

Central to the worldview of art therapy are the philosophical assumptions of pluralistic intersubjective realities, eclectic forms of aesthetic knowledge, and the dialectic dialogues between these multiple realities and ways of knowing that contribute to the creation of new knowledge, the construction of new self/other realities, insights, and transformation—the dialectical intersubjective aesthetic art therapy paradigm or worldview. Ontological and dialectical pluralism are worldviews in mixed methods research that mirror the philosophical assumptions embedded in the dialectic intersubjective aesthetic paradigm in art therapy (Johnson, 2012; Johnson & Gray, 2010), which assign credibility, value, and meaning to creativity in research. Methodologically mixed methods research presents systems by which art therapists can distinguish measurable phenomena from narrative, visual, relational, or contextual phenomena, and position or juxtapose them in various relationships with one another, resulting in a more holistic understanding of essential research questions in art therapy. The multiplicity and dialectical stances of mixed methods research, as art therapy, celebrate and commit to humanity and creativity—the belief that the inclusiveness of and dialectical tension between diverse, paradoxical, conflicting forms of knowledge within multiple intersubjective realities yield new knowledge essential to understanding the emergent symbolic meaning, depth, and dimensionality specific to the human relationship and the human condition.

References

Brown, L. J. (2011). *Intersubjective processes and the unconscious.* New York, NY: Routledge.

Cooper, D. E. (Ed.) (1997). *Aesthetics: The Classic readings.* Malden, MA: Blackwell Publishing.

Creswell, J. W., & Plano Clark, V. L. (2011). *Designing and conducting mixed methods research* (2nd ed.). Thousand Oaks, CA: Sage Publications, Inc.

Deaver, S. P. (2002). What constitutes art therapy research. *Art Therapy: Journal of the American Art Therapy Association, 19*(1), 23–27. doi: 10.1080/07421656.2002.10129721

Deaver, S. P., & Kaiser, D. (2013). Establishing a research agenda for art therapy: A Delphi study. *Art Therapy: Journal of the American Art Therapy Association, 30*(3), 114–121. doi: 10.1080/07421656.2013.819281

Dissanayake, E. (2009). The artification hypothesis and its relevance to cognitive science, evolutionary aesthetics and neuroaesthetics. *Cognitive Semiotics, 5,* 148–173.

Gerber, N. (2006). The essential components of doctoral education. *The Arts in Psychotherapy, 33*(2), 98–112.

Gerber, N. (in press a). The therapist artist: An individual and collective worldview. In M. B. Junge (Ed.), *Identity and the art therapist.* Springfield, IL: Charles C. Thomas.

Gerber, N. (in press b). *Art therapy education: A creative dialectical intersubjective approach.* In D. E. Gussak & M. L. Rosal (Ed.), *The Wiley-Blackwell handbook of art therapy.* London: Wiley-Blackwell.

Greene, J. (2007). *Mixed methods in social inquiry.* San Francisco, CA: Jossey-Bass.

Guba, E. G., & Lincoln, Y. S. (1998). Competing paradigms in qualitative research. In N. K. Denzin & Y. S. Lincoln (Ed.), *The landscape of qualitative research* (pp. 195–220). Thousand Oaks, CA: Sage Publications, Inc.

Hagman, G. (2011). *Aesthetic experience: Beauty, creativity and the search for the ideal.* New York, NY: Rodopi.

Harris Willliams, M. (2010). *The aesthetic development: The poetic spirit of psychoanalysis.* London, UK: Karnac Books.

Johnson, B. (2008). Editorial: Living with tensions: The dialectic approach. *Journal of Mixed Methods Research, 2*(3), 203–207. doi: 10.1177/1558689808318043

Johnson, B. (2012). Dialectical pluralism and mxed methods research. *American Behavioral Scientist, 56*(6), 751–754. doi: 10.1177/0002764212442494

Johnson, B., & Gray, R. (2010). A history of philosophical and theoretical issues for mixed methods research. In A. Tashakkori & C. Teddlie (Ed.), *Sage handbook of mixed methods in social & behavioral research* (pp. 69–94). Thousand Oaks, CA: Sage Publications.

Junge, M. B., & Linesch, D. (1993). Our own voices: new paradigms for art therapy research. *The Arts in Psychotherapy, 20*(1), 61–67. doi: 10.1016/0197-4556(93)90032-W

Kapitan, L. (2010). *Introduction to art therapy research.* New York, NY: Routledge.

McNiff, S. (1986). *Educating the creative arts therapist.* Springfield, IL: Charles C. Thomas.

McNiff, S. (1998). Enlarging the vision of art therapy research. *Art Therapy: Journal of the American Art Therapy Association, 15*(2), 86–92. doi: 10.1080/07421656.1989.10758718

Mertens, D. M. (2005). *Research and evaluation in education and psychology: Integrating diversity with quantitative, qualitative, and mixed methods* (2nd ed.). Thousand Oaks, CA: Sage Publications, Inc.

Paul, J. L., Graffam, B., & Fowler, K. (2005). Perspectivism and critique of research. In J. L. Paul (Ed.), *Introduction to the philosophies of research and criticism in education and the social sciences* (pp. 43–65). Upper Saddle River, NJ: Pearson Prentice Hall.

Tashakkori, A., & Teddlie, C. (Eds.) (2010). *Sage handbook of mixed methods in social & behavioral research* (2nd ed.). Thousand Oaks, CA: Sage Publications.

64

Arts-based Research: The Basics for Art Therapists

Donna H. Kaiser and Lisa Kay

Is there a role for art in the research process? Art in the performance of research is a compelling province for discovering new and powerful means for understanding the practice of art therapy and the creative process itself (Kapitan, 2010; McNiff, 1998). Art—because of its power to evoke, to engage, and particularly to enhance under-standing—has been used in the fields of education, anthropology, sociology, and other social sciences in various phases of the research process (Cahnmann-Taylor & Siegesmund, 2008; Collier & Collier, 1986; Leavy, 2009; Prosser, 1996). Not only has data collection involved art created by research participants, it has been brought into play in data analysis, interpretation, and even in the representation of research findings. This chapter will present the value of art in research, address epistemology and ontology of this approach, provide examples in art therapy and art education to clarify the ways in which this can be accomplished, and discuss the judgment of quality.

Many terms have been used to refer to the various uses of the arts in the research process—"art-based" (McNiff, 1998), "arts-based," "arts-informed" (Cole & Knowles, 2001), "artistic enquiry" (Kapitan, 2010), and "artistically crafted enquiry" (Eisner, 1995). The term "arts-based research" (ABR) is the most widely accepted, and we prefer using this to inclusively refer to the many ways in which art can enrich the research process. This chapter will concentrate primarily on the use of visual art; however, please note that many researchers also use other arts, such as poetry, literary forms, music, dance, and drama.

ABR, a relatively new approach in qualitative research (Leavy, 2009), systematically uses the artistic process in all its forms as a primary means for better understanding the experiences of researchers and research participants (McNiff, 1998). Art making, by its very nature, is a creative method through which the researcher can both generate data and examine and clarify multiple relationships, patterns, and meanings in the data (Sullivan, 2004). Since the late 1900s, the turn to the arts in social science research has been associated with the shift toward postpositivist and constructivist paradigms that have challenged the traditional positivist worldview (Paul, 2005). Eisner's (1995) work on artistically crafted research and the American Educational Research Association's special interest group on arts-based educational research

The Wiley Handbook of Art Therapy, First Edition. Edited by David E. Gussak and Marcia L. Rosal.
© 2016 John Wiley & Sons, Ltd. Published 2016 by John Wiley & Sons, Ltd.

(Knowles and Cole, 2008) continue this tradition, and have exerted much influence on the growth of ABR in education as well as in other fields.

McNiff (1998) called for the use of what he termed *art-based* research by art therapists. He has continued to write about the importance of the creative process in research for our profession (see, e.g., McNiff, 2008), yet little seems to have emerged into art therapy literature, education, or research practice—a notable exception is a chapter in Kapitan's (2010) text on art therapy research. McNiff pointed out that his view of art-based research is not the same as research that uses art as data in the more traditional sense—his focus is not on art therapy assessments, or on imagery created by participants making art to be interpreted by the researcher. Rather, he defined art-based research as "a method of inquiry which uses the elements of the creative arts therapy experience, including the making of art by the researcher, as a means of understanding the significance of what we do within our practice" (1998, p. 12). Thus, he advocated for the use of art making as a way to comprehend what is studied, and for devising research that is congruent with the artistic process. This seems to be in line with what art therapists do, and seems a fitting way to conduct research for informing our practice.

Educational researchers such as Eisner (1991, 1995) have long recognized the power of art for constructing knowledge. Barone and Eisner (2011) emphasized that ABR allows for the expression of meanings that are difficult, if not impossible, to express verbally. ABR advances understanding because it can more readily speak to multifaceted and understated aspects of phenomena in ways that encourage new perspectives of researchers and audiences alike. Thus, it can deepen and broaden knowledge in an especially illuminating manner.

In addition to being consistent with the way in which art therapists practice, and the way it can be used to enhance knowledge construction, ABR has the potential to be activist in nature (Kapitan, 2010; Leavy, 2009). Leavy (2009) called attention to the fact that the social justice movements of the 1960s and 1970s were influential in affecting change in academic research when these movements highlighted the voices of marginalized people and led researchers to turn to the arts for empowering them, and for conducting research on difference, diversity, and the confrontation of stereotypes. When art is used to present findings, it can challenge viewers' assumptions and perspectives and potentially shift their beliefs about a topic. This potential for social change is related to the epistemology and ontology of ABR that inform how art is incorporated into methodology.

Epistemology and Ontology Inform Method

Researchers' beliefs about how knowledge may be acquired or constructed represent their epistemology; their assumptions and values about the nature of reality represent their ontology (Butler-Kisber, 2010). All research is grounded in the researcher's philosophical worldview, based in his or her epistemology and ontology (Paul, 2005)—this is the foundation upon which the researcher's methods are situated. In quantitative research, knowledge is seen as existing apart from the researcher, as "out there," to be observed and measured in order to arrive at some certainty about what is true about the world. While quantitative research may be viewed as one end of the enquiry continuum, qualitative research is at the other, with knowledge viewed as constructed by participants and researchers; such knowledge emerges from interactions between them, and is dependent on context and history (Butler-Kisber, 2010). In qualitative terms, there is no fixed truth; instead, truth is ever changing and dependent on humans who endeavor to express their construction of what is true.[1]

According to Barone and Eisner (2011), epistemology is taken a step further in ABR. They explained that ABR should promote uncertainty about how a phenomenon of interest is viewed—the viewer should be moved to see with fresh eyes—researchers should be surprised with new perspectives of the world that the research evokes. In ABR, knowledge can be represented through art work that can engage the researcher or the audience in reflection on its meaning. Leavy (2009) similarly affirmed that ABR should engage the audience by perturbing their current understandings, shift perspectives in some significant way, and ideally lead to some kind of social change. In ABR, reality may be interpreted via contemplating visual forms, and this can lead the viewer to question events, issues, or settings that are the topic of enquiry. Rather than seeking the final truth then, the personal judgment of the researcher or viewer is privileged.

The following section describes specific ways to infuse visual art into art therapy research: data elicitation, data collection and analysis, interpretation, documenting the research process, and representation of research findings.

Imagery as Data Elicitation

Imagery used to elicit data has origins in photo elicitation, a strategy traditionally used by researchers in sociology and ethnography (Harper, 2002; Prosser, 1996). Harper (2002) deemed photo elicitation an ideal model for research because it can access deeper aspects of human awareness than "words-alone interviews" (p. 23), and provides greater potential for expanding on participants' meanings through discussion of the photos. Photo-elicitation may use photographs taken by the researcher, but, more typically, participants are asked to take their own photographs related to the topic of study. Expanding on this, visual or graphic elicitation uses participant-created art or other forms of visual images to heighten memory during interviews and to express complex and multiple meanings while often also empowering participants (Leavy, 2009).

Jung (2011) used photo and graphic elicitation in her thesis research to generate interview material in her study of individuals who were identified as "trans-cultural kids"—that is, individuals who have spent their developmental years outside their home culture. Jung asked participants to collect photographs and pictorial images from various sources—such as the Internet or family albums—that represented their experiences, and then to write about the images prior to an interview. The imagery sparked their memories and thoughts, which ultimately generated themes of identity fragmentation, loss, and the specific coping resources they used. One participant, talking about her images, stated movingly: "Actually, deep inside me, I don't know where I am from. I felt rootless without a sense of home." In this and other instances, using images seemed to both allow for more emotional content to surface than would have been possible in a verbal interview alone, and this encouraged participants to express these feelings in a way that was empowering for them.

Imagery as Data

Data can be gathered in the form of visual representations—drawings, photos, and video—a practice that is becoming more acceptable among scholars (Richards, 2005). In an arts-based heuristic thesis study, Schlegel (2012) explored her experiences as an intern in an oncology setting by making paintings or sculptures about weekly events and encounters with patients and staff. Data was generated in the art forms and in journaling about the art. The most prevalent theme that emerged from the artwork was related to depictions of bodies in one form or another; this theme was repeated in the journals. She was perplexed about what this meant until she got to the creative synthesis phase of the analysis, when she realized that this theme represented the visceral experiences she had relating to patients with bodily impairment. She described the painting she made of a young girl whose health was deteriorating quickly:

> I attempted to honor the little girl's bravery in her fight, but quickly became frustrated with the painting, as it was not turning out the way that I wanted it to. I wanted to paint the silhouette of a girl, with lots of texture and different shades of gray, but I was becoming more and more agitated. The colors seemed wrong and the girl's features were not right. After quite some time struggling with the piece, I decided to take a new direction. I took linseed oil to the oil painting and watched as the girl's features slowly blurred and deteriorated. It was not until after the piece was finished that I realized I had used the destruction of the painting as a metaphor for the decline in her health that I was witnessing on a weekly basis. This week's art making process allowed me to address the emotions that I was repressing, which ranged from anxiety to grief, regarding the young girl's illness (Schlegel, 2012, pp. 51–52).

Barone and Eisner explained how ABR can serve as a catalyst for action, in that it illuminates complex aspects that might not otherwise be explicit.

Imagery for Documenting the Research Process

Leavy (2009) indicated that the visual diary could be used to document one's research experiences, much like research field notes or journals. Kay (2008) used visual field notes to document observations in her study of art teachers' practice and interactions with students with special needs. She recorded and documented in written form and through visual imagery as an ongoing record of the process of research with 84 small mixed-media collages. Figure 64.1 is an example of a visual field note that she created after visiting and observing the two art classrooms she studied. The area of loose blue paint contrasts dramatically with the brown diagonal zigzag line, an aspect of the image that was helpful for recognizing how the different structure and approach at each school impacted students' and teachers' approaches to making art.

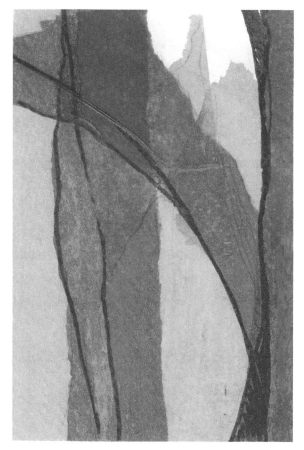

Figure 64.1　Image created by Kay.

Some students have drawn upon their skills as artists to document their thesis research—this later helped them to visually construct the meaning of the research experience. Kay's student, Flynn (2010), created cartoon storyboards (Figure 64.2) as visual field notes to document his affective experiences while collecting data from children battling cancer. The storyboards also documented the children's experiences, as he perceived them, during the course of the study.

Imagery for Data Analysis and Interpretation

The use of imagery for data analysis has been discussed by scholars in art education and found to be useful in the interrogation, triangulation, and alternative readings of the data (Eisner, 1991, 1995; Irwin, 2004; Sullivan, 2004). Jahns (2010), for her thesis research, created embroideries that visually diagrammed the foci of her study, staff open-studio sessions, to observationally capture the research process. This also served as an audit trail; the series she made was eventually helpful for illuminating emerging themes. Her final creation, shown in Figure 64.3, is a "visual representation

Figure 64.2 Image created by Flynn.

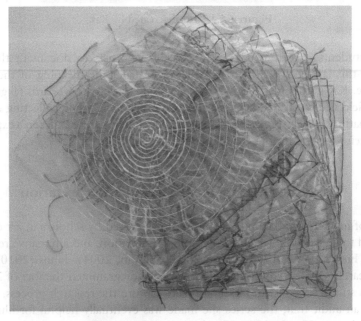

Figure 64.3 Image created by Jahns.

of data which open[ed] up a space for multiple interpretations and perspectives" (Leavy, 2009, p. 231), and represented a holistic portrait of the research findings. By incorporating arts-based research methods, Jahns artistically crafted (Eisner, 1995) her findings, which allowed her to gain insight, triangulate the data, and then synthesize findings to construct knowledge in an especially informative way.

Kay's (2010) play, *T...O...R...N...*, represented another form of data interpretation, in literary rather than visual form. She integrated and synthesized interactions that she observed between teachers and students into subjects that became scenes for a one-act play. Each of the nine scenes illuminated specific themes (such as life issues, individual needs, taboos, and violence), and the play served as a way to synthesize the data. It presented participants' stories in their own words, and the researcher's narrative voice provided both a description and interpretation of the data.

Judging Quality

Standards for judging the quality of a scholarly qualitative study are highly variable, and have been debated by several authors from the stances of different epistemologies (Creswell, 1994; Denzin & Lincoln, 1998). Denzin and Lincoln (1998) described the legitimization crisis in qualitative research as the re-theorizing of the traditional positivist evaluation criteria of validity, reliability, and generalizability. They contended that the postpositivist, constructivist, and critical theory perspectives require criteria unique to their respective aims and worldviews. Lincoln and Guba (1985) discussed quality criteria in terms of the designations of trustworthiness and authenticity as opposed to validity and reliability, terms associated with quantitative research. Trustworthiness and authenticity hinge on the accuracy of the account; the credibility of the data collection and analysis relies on its accuracy and its degree of fit with the participants' situations (Creswell, 1994).

Barone and Eisner (2011) stressed that ABR is not "an anything goes process" (p. 162). ABR researchers should instead seek credibility with structural corroboration and referential adequacy. *Structural corroboration* relates to the coherence and persuasiveness—the findings are gathered together to make sense holistically. Researchers must ask: "Does the evidence presented lead us to believe the conclusions?" *Referential adequacy* is a term that Barone and Eisner use to deem a study consistent and convincing—the data analysis is rigorous, rational, and leads to conclusions that are well argued and sound, both credible and cogent. Barone (2005) further asked: "Does the study raise new questions, does it compel the viewer to be engaged, does it enlighten and empower?"

According to Creswell (1994), strategies for ensuring trustworthiness and authenticity include the following: prolonged engagement with participants; triangulation using multiple data collection methods, sources, investigators, or theoretical perspectives; clarification of researcher bias through reflection on one's own subjectivity; and establishing means for monitoring it during the research process.

Monitoring researcher bias can take several forms: member checking; peer review and debriefing to augment the researcher's viewpoint with external input; alternative case analysis by consciously searching for disconfirming evidence to refine the researcher's emergent assertions; member checking by sharing interview transcripts, analyses, or drafts of results with participants to ensure accurate representation of their ideas, thoughts, and feelings; rich, in-depth description; and external audit by people outside the research process.

When publishing ABR studies, it is particularly important to describe the methods employed, as well as to clearly explain when and why certain strategies were used. Too often, there is insufficient transparency to allow readers to discern how findings were arrived at and what conclusions were based on. One area quite often neglected is elucidation of data analysis procedures. Here again, it is important to maintain rigor if ABR is to be taken seriously.

Summary

This chapter presented just a few of the ways that art therapists can begin to think about using visual imagery to deepen comprehension of what they study; it intended to reveal ABR's value in understanding and constructing knowledge in our field. Various forms of evidence contribute to the knowledge base in art therapy, and ABR can be used to study some of the "why" and "how" questions, including how the distinctive nature of the therapeutic relationship provides benefit in art therapy, how the creative process operates in art therapy, and why art making is a healing process.

An area of great importance that remains neglected is studying the perspectives of people who use art therapy services. We wonder: how can art therapists use art in the design of research that foregrounds their voices while revealing what it is about art therapy that is beneficial?

This chapter proposes that ABR is a viable research approach that resonates with the worldviews of most art therapists. To foster the inclusion of the visual into art therapy research, art therapists must carefully examine their own epistemology and ontology as art therapy researchers; explore how other disciplines have successfully engaged in ABR; work together to ascertain the best research questions to address, and use creativity to design ABR studies to address them. Dialogue is needed on how to connect important art therapy research questions that tap what visual art forms can offer in ABR, in ways that the profession has not yet considered.

This chapter has offered a basic introduction to ABR. We encourage art therapists to apply time and energy to understand this important approach to enquiry for several reasons, but especially because it matches how art therapists practice and understand clinical work. Learning to do any kind of research is arduous, and ABR is no less challenging and demanding than any other approach. Much study should be applied to reading examples from art therapy and from other fields while reflecting on one's beliefs about what counts as knowledge and how knowledge can be constructed. ABR requires researchers to employ rigorous systematic methods, and to have adequate grounding in understanding epistemology and ontology and the ways in which visual art can be used to create new knowledge in art therapy.

Endnote

1 This explanation of epistemology and ontology is necessarily brief, and the reader is encouraged to explore these topics further to prepare for engaging in ABR, since methodology should be informed thoughtfully and carefully by the researcher's thoughts, beliefs, values, and assumptions about the world.

References

Barone, T. (2005). "Arts based educational research." In J. Paul (ed.), *Introduction to the philosophies of research and criticism in education and the social sciences* (pp. 68–72). Upper Saddle River, NJ: Pearson.

Barone, T., & Eisner, E. (2011). *Arts based research.* Thousand Oaks, CA: Sage.

Butler-Kisber, L. (2010). *Qualitative inquiry: Thematic, narrative and arts-informed approaches.* London: Sage.

Cahnmann-Taylor, M., & Siegesmund, R. (Eds.) (2008). *Arts-based research in education: Foundations for practice.* New York, NY: Routledge.

Cole, A., & Knowles, G. J. (Eds.) (2001). *Lives in context: The art of life history research.* Walnut Creek, CA: Alta Mira Press.

Collier, J., & Collier, M. (1986). *Visual anthropology: Photography as research.* Albuquerque, NM: University of New Mexico Press.

Creswell, J. (1994). *Research design: Qualitative and quantitative approaches.* London: Sage.

Denzin, N., & Lincoln, Y. (1998). *The handbook of qualitative research.* Newbury Park, CA: Sage.

Eisner, E. (1991). *The enlightened eye: Qualitative inquiry and the enhancement of educational practice.* New York, NY: Macmillan.

Eisner, E. (1995). What artistically crafted research can help us understand about schools. *Educational Researcher, 45,* 1–5.

Flynn, R. (2010). *Story: Tales of the art of critically ill children.* Unpublished masters thesis, School of the Art Institute of Chicago, Chicago, IL.

Harper, D. (2002). Talking about pictures: A case for photo elicitation. *Visual Studies, 17,* 13–26.

Irwin, R. (2004). A/r/tography: A metonymic metissage. In R. Irwin & A. de Cosson (Eds.), *A/r/tography: Rendering self through arts-based living inquiry* (pp. 27–38). Vancouver, BC: Pacific Educational Press.

Jahns, L. (2010). *Creating space: Making art together to support non-clinical staff and build community at a residential therapeutic center for children.* Unpublished masters thesis, School of the Art Institute of Chicago, Chicago, IL.

Jung, S. Y. (2011). *Trans-cultural kids: A qualitative inquiry.* Unpublished masters thesis, Albertus Magnus College, Yale, CT.

Kapitan, L. (2010). *Introduction to art therapy research.* New York, NY: Routledge.

Kay, L. (2008). *Art education pedagogy and practice with adolescent students at-risk in alternative high schools.* Unpublished dissertation, Northern Illinois University, DeKalb, IL.

Kay, L. (2010). T...O...R...N... Research findings as performance art. *Liminalities: A Performance Studies Journal, 6*(1), 1–40.

Knowles, J. G., & Col, A. (Eds.) (2008). *Handbook of the arts in qualitative research: Perspectives, methodologies, examples, and issues.* Thousand Oaks, CA: Sage Publications.

Leavy, P. (2009). *Method meets art: Arts-based research practice.* New York, NY: Guilford Press.

Lincoln, Y. S., & Guba, E. G. (1985). *Naturalistic inquiry.* Newbury Park, CA: Sage.

McNiff, S. (1998). *Art-based research*. London: Jessica Kingsley.

McNiff, S. (2008). Art-based research. In J. G. Knowles & A. Cole (Eds.), *Handbook of the arts in qualitative research: Perspectives, methodologies, examples, and issues* (pp. 29–40). Thousand Oaks, CA: Sage.

Paul, J. L. (2005). *Introduction to the philosophies of research and criticism in education and the social sciences*. Upper Saddle River, NJ: Pearson/Merrill/Prentice Hall.

Prosser, J. (1996). What constitutes an image-based qualitative methodology? *Visual Sociology*, *11*, 25–34.

Richards, L. (2005). *Handling qualitative data: A practical guide*. London: Sage.

Schlegel, D. M. (2012). *The experience of working on an oncology unit as explored through an art therapy student's practice of artistic expression: An artistic heuristic study*. Unpublished masters thesis, Drexel University, Philadelphia, PA.

Sullivan, G. (2004). *Art practice as research: Inquiry in the visual arts*. New York, NY: Teachers College.

Part VIII
Art Therapy Around the World

Introduction

While the profession of art therapy may have had its roots in the United States and Great Britain, the practice has now expanded to all corners of the globe. Art therapists from around the world have submitted chapters for this book, describing the development, challenges, and practice issues in their respective countries or regions of the world. The scope of these chapters is immense, from the multiple European and Asian locales to the tiny islands of the Caribbean. This collection of essays demonstrates the global impact of this field. As Wolf-Bordonaro state in this section's introductory chapter, *International Art Therapy*, "the development of national art therapy organizations in North America, South America, Europe, Scandinavia, the Middle East, Asia, and Australia/New Zealand epitomizes the global growth of the field of art therapy."

Each of these chapters represents a different region or country, written by art therapists who are native of, or a witness to, art therapy development in their respective countries. For example, in *Art Therapy in Great Britain*, Westwood thoroughly explores the development of art therapy in Great Britain, her home country, whereas Timm-Bottos, a recent emigrant to Canada, presents her historical research on the development of art therapy in Canada in her chapter titled *Art Therapy in Canada: A Place-based Métissage*. Luxembourg-based art therapist d'Elia tackles the difficult task of reporting on art therapy throughout the vast expanse of Europe, and includes an appendix with websites and contact information for over 30 European countries.

Coulter writes about art therapy in her own home country in the chapter titled *Art Therapy "Down Under": Perspectives on the Profession from Australia and New Zealand*. Coss, with the help of art therapist Wong, reports on the *Cultural Context and the Practice of Art Therapy in Asia*. Regev and Lev-Wiesel discuss the development of art therapy in Israel in the chapter titled *Art Therapy in Israel: Current Status and Future Directions of the Profession*.

Kuwaiti art therapist Behbehani writes about researches in art therapy throughout the Arab nations in *A Portrait of a Nation: Culturally Sensitive Art Therapy in the Arab World*. Linesch, Metzl, and Treviño draw from the relationship that emerged

The Wiley Handbook of Art Therapy, First Edition. Edited by David E. Gussak and Marcia L. Rosal.
© 2016 John Wiley & Sons, Ltd. Published 2016 by John Wiley & Sons, Ltd.

between California art therapists and psychologists in Mexico to inform the chapter titled *Various Aspects of Art Therapy in Mexico/Algunos Aspectos de la Terapia de Arte en México*. In this chapter, the authors report on the development of an art therapy program south of the border, and the collaboration that made it happen. Further south, art therapists Cornai and Ruiz provide a complete overview of art therapy throughout Central and South America in *Latin American Art Therapy: Collective Dreams and Horizons of Hope*. Finally, in their chapter titled *Art Therapy in the Caribbean*, Belnavis and Soo Hon introduce us to one of the newest areas of the world where art therapy is developing—the Caribbean.

While these 11 chapters do not represent all nations where art therapy is flourishing, the intention of this section is for the reader to understand the expanding influence of art therapy worldwide. Collectively, they offer a global perspective on the struggles and triumphs experienced by each region in gaining recognition of art therapy as a profession.

65

International Art Therapy

Gaelynn P. Wolf Bordonaro

The words "international art therapy" have evolved to represent two separate constructs within the discipline of art therapy. The first is the growing global practice of art therapy and the formalization of the field in countries around the world, including educational criteria and standards of practice. The second is the cross-cultural application or introduction of art therapy in international and cross-cultural contexts by international practitioners. These distinct constructs are presented in the following sections.

Global Growth of Art Therapy

International growth of the profession

The development of national art therapy organizations in North America, South America, Europe, Scandinavia, the Middle East, Asia, and Australia/New Zealand epitomizes the global growth of the field of art therapy (Rosal & Wolf Bordonaro, 2007). More than three dozen countries have established multi-disciplinary expressive arts associations; more than two dozen countries boast of established art therapy associations; and art therapists are actively organizing in at least a dozen more (Rosal & Wolf Bordonaro, 2007; Stoll, 2005). The primary functions of national organizations include providing professional, educational, and ethical standards; promoting efficacy and governmental recognition; providing communication among members; disseminating research and best practice information; and hosting professional conferences.

Few countries have successfully established formal governmental recognition of art therapy; however, professional organizations in some countries have effectively worked within the parameters of governmental structures to gain such recognition (Rosal & Wolf Bordonaro, 2007). For example, in 2004, the Taiwan Art Therapy Association's (TATA) application for governmental recognition was approved; this was required for the establishment of their association. Additionally, since 1988, art therapy has been recognized in Israel as a paramedical profession overseen by the Ministry of Health. Furthermore, in the United Kingdom, practitioners may only call

The Wiley Handbook of Art Therapy, First Edition. Edited by David E. Gussak and Marcia L. Rosal.
© 2016 John Wiley & Sons, Ltd. Published 2016 by John Wiley & Sons, Ltd.

themselves art therapists or art psychotherapists if they are qualified and registered by the Health Professions Council; professional membership in the British Art Therapy Association (BAAT), the oldest art therapy association in the world, is only open to clinicians qualified and regulated by the government.

Cross-border organizations—such as the European Advisory Body of National Art Therapy Associations, the European Consortium for Arts Therapies Education (ECArTE), the International Society for the Psychopathology of Expression & Art Therapy (SIPE), and the International Association for Art, Creativity, and Therapy (IAACT)—foster international alliances in the promotion of professional opportunities and recognition of the field, support of ethical and training standards, and recognition of professional qualifications (Rosal & Wolf Bordonaro, 2007). Acknowledging that there is political strength in numbers, Cruz (2005) wrote, "information on the international scope of professional practice of arts therapists never fails to gain the attention of other professionals and law makers" (p. 167).

A growing body of literature and research

As the profession and practice of art therapy grow around the globe, so too does awareness that best practices, as well as professional recognition, require the support of efficacy studies. International journals, including *The Arts in Psychotherapy*, *Art Therapy Online*, and the *International Journal of Art Therapy: Inscape*, regularly feature qualitative and quantitative art therapy research articles. Additionally, art therapy authors and researchers (Mueller, Alie, Jonas, Brown, & Sherr, 2011; Pretorius & Pfeifer, 2010; Schmidt & Wolf Bordonaro, 2012; Schmidt, Pimple, & Wolf Bordonaro, 2011; Svensk et al., 2009) contribute to the literature through peer-reviewed publications in mental and medical health journals specific to particular fields or populations; for example, art therapists publish in journals dedicated to tropical medicine, international health, psychology, cancer, nursing, and end-of-life care.

In a unique multi-country enquiry, Silver (2012) summarized art therapy studies conducted in the United States (Silver, 2002), Brazil (Allessandrini, Duarte, Dupas, & Bianco, 1998), Russia and Estonia (Kopytin, 2002a, 2002b), Thailand (Dhanachitsiriphong, 1999), and Australia (Hunter, 1992) in an effort to begin to understand "whether cultural differences and similarities in scores on the Silver Drawing Test (SDT) can illuminate cultural preferences and contribute to cultural practices" (p. 16), including therapeutic and educational practices. One of the implications, Silver suggested, was that art therapy and specific drawing tasks such as the SDT could be used to better understand the metaphors of children who have experienced trauma in regional disasters. Furthermore, she suggested that differences in cognitive and creativity scores could help us understand cultural differences in educational systems and values, or "what children should learn and how they should be taught" (Silver, 2012, p. 19).

Betts, Gantt, and Lorance (2011) announced an exciting addition to the realm of international art therapy research, the International Art Therapy Research Database. Betts (2012) reported that the database will allow contributors and subscribers to (1) access broad collections of data to facilitate large-scale research, as well as inform client evaluation and treatment plans; (2) build a vast foundation of empirical data regarding normative standardized drawings to inform a better understanding of deviations and exceptions; and (3) address or determine cultural variables in normative and psychological data. According to Betts (2012), "Once copious amounts of data have been added, the International Art Therapy Research Database will also facilitate comparative studies like Silver's" (2012).

Information exchanges and communication networks

Opportunities for art therapists to communicate and share information are more readily accessible than ever. Kapitan (2012) wrote, "Due to the ubiquitous reach of the Internet, art therapy is now global" (p. 2). With the click of a mouse, the global breadth of art therapy reaches our laptops, iPads, and smartphones. The International Art Therapy Organization (www.internationalarttherapy.org), Art Therapy Alliance (www.arttherapyalliance.org), Art Therapy without Borders (www.atwb.org), the Global Art Therapy Network (http://arttherapynetwork.wordpress.com), and Communities Healing through Art (CHART) (www.chartaid.org) offer websites, blogs, Facebook pages, Twitter feeds, and other platforms for art therapists to post ideas, projects, exhibits, experiences, programs, trainings, and practices.

Cross-Cultural Training and Practice

For decades, trained art therapists from countries with recognized credentialing and educational standards have traveled the globe, primarily providing services to special populations or in response to political, social, or environmental crisis. In this context, the service(s) provided by international art therapists can be described as (1) clinical endeavors; (2) cross-cultural training, primarily for professionals and paraprofessionals from related fields; or (3) a combination of clinical work and trainings.

Clearly, "art does not exclusively belong to art therapists" (Kalmanowitz & Potash, 2010). Non–art therapists, such as Keeling and Neilson (2005), have published research on the therapeutic uses of art; others (Kollontai, 2010; Yohani, 2008; Zelizer, 2003) have published articles supporting both theory and practice of creative art making in a therapeutic context. Authors from related fields acknowledge a need for culturally sensitive therapies that can be used in cross-cultural contexts (Keeling & Neilson, 2005), and professionally and personally identify with the belief that the arts "provide a non-linguistic form through which the unspeakable events, good or bad, in people's lives are articulated and can challenge our values and the way we view each other" (Kollontai, 2010, p. 263). Zelizer (2003) clearly understood the constructs that define the profession of art therapy when he described peace-building following violent political conflicts. Art can, he wrote,

> ... provide a safe space where people can come together to explore their experiences and emotions, can be used as a tool in conflict resolving, help those badly traumatized to have a mechanism through which to express and confront their experiences and fears, and help build empathy and understanding amongst outsiders. (p. 68)

With such thoughtful, sympathetic, and even academic reports on how art is used around the globe in service to the human condition, what is special about what art therapists offer? In particular, if we acknowledge that art therapy is a Western construct (Anderson, Arrington, & Wolf Bordonaro, 2012; Chu, 2010; Hocoy, 2002; Kalmanowitz & Potash, 2010; Kapitan, Litell, & Torres, 2011; Talwar, Iyer, & Doby-Copeland, 2004), how may we purport that services and trainings exported around the globe are appropriate, valuable, and ethical? One of the most salient contributions to the contemporary literature on the ethical considerations, critiques, and challenges of international art therapy was Kalmanowitz's and Potash's (2010) *Ethical Considerations in the Global Teaching and Promotion of Art Therapy to Non-Art Therapists.* Similar to Kalmanowitz and Potash (2010), I believe that the answers are grounded in comprehensive training and ethical foundations. Art therapists who work internationally must demonstrate (1) thorough academic and practical art therapy experience; (2) multicultural competence and curiosity, including reverence for local perceptions, customs, and rituals; (3) willingness to study local and national historical, cultural, and aesthetic perspectives; (4) acute recognition of health and safety issues; (5) knowledge of the skill sets of prospective participants (Anderson, Arrington, & Wolf Bordonaro, 2012; Gómez Carlier & Salom, 2012; Kalmanowitz & Potash, 2010); (6) understanding of art therapy, therapeutic arts, and/or studio art practices in the identified community; (7) maintenance of an "education stance" (Kalmanowitz & Potash, 2010, p. 25); (8) careful consideration of the construct of interpretation; (9) capacity to seek "culturally equivalent concepts" (Kalmanowitz & Potash, 2010, p. 24) or "dimensional identity" (Duijker & Frijda, 1960, p. 23); (10) broad theoretical and functional knowledge of art media, as well as ethical consideration of how images and artwork are treated; (11) commitment to sustainability and continuity; and (12) decisive preparation and planning skills coupled with Zen-like nonattachment to expectations.

Use of art media and directives

As clinicians interested in serving the human condition, art therapists have long responded to catastrophic global events by offering their unique skills in the provision of psychosocial support (Arrington, 2005; Atlas, 2009; Stoll, 1991). Paramount to their skill set is the ethical and psychologically appropriate use of art media and materials. The materials we provide, encourage, or find, are not value-free (Gómez Carlier & Salom, 2012; Moon, 2010). Traditional and contemporary media, and even household, personal, recycled, scavenged, and found objects, carry embedded values, applications, social significance, and historical contexts that are both personal and cultural. For art therapists working internationally, ethical provision of art media requires not just knowledge of the psychological, developmental, adaptive, and practical functions of diverse media, but also careful consideration of the cultural and personal associations that the materials hold. The complex intersections of local resources, weather, infrastructure, geography, and politics further complicate ethical and practical decision-making regarding art media.

Chu (2010) thoughtfully explored the cross-cultural use of specific art media and directives in her work with survivors of genocide in Rwanda. Drawing on Hocoy's (2002) discussion of "dimensional identity" (Duijker & Frijda, 1960, p. 23) within the context of cross-cultural art therapy, Chu determined that Rwandan culture had parallels with a frequently utilized art therapy intervention. Chu introduced the art form of box making after she determined that it held a "functional equivalence in Rwandan culture. The simple attribute of the box as a container connects with the larger, important role of [physical and psychological] containers within Rwandan culture" (p. 5).

In work in Port au Prince, Haiti, after the 2010 earthquake (Wolf Bordonaro & Hurlbut, 2011), art material choices were informed by the country's detrimental dependence on non-governmental organizations (NGO) and charities for goods and services, widespread poverty, vast numbers of the population living in tent cities, political turbulence, and even the humidity. Service work and trainings in Haiti have drawn upon the use of recycled materials, including fabric from discarded tee-shirts, while cross-cultural art making with members of the hill tribes in Thailand required art therapy ingenuity, flexibility, and resourcefulness. Anderson, Arrington, and Wolf Bordonaro found that sturdy sticks made functional drawing tools in the damp dirt (2008).

Sustainability and continuity

Art therapists utilize psychological approaches, interventions, and techniques that normalize human experiences and provide relief from traumatic situations. Nonetheless, a primary criticism of international art therapy has been that the unique psychosocial support we can offer quickly evaporates when the art therapist(s) return home. To avoid *causing harm*, sustainable programming is paramount. Kalmanowitz and Potash (2010) argue that "in all cases, we believe that the most appropriate response is that which will be sustainable and outlive the duration of the training" (p. 21); this holds true for direct contact work as well.

Examples can be found in the work of art therapists working internationally. Communities Healing through Art (CHART), a small international art therapy non-profit organization, works to provide art therapy responses in areas of the globe impacted by human-created and natural disasters. Sustainable efforts focus on networking with and supporting local and regional art therapists; if this is not possible, CHART utilizes a "train-the-trainers" model to support direct care providers. Art therapy responses also include working with children and families who survive disasters, in which case relation-ships with local agencies and organizations facilitate continuity and return visits. Utilizing this model, CHART participated in eight service missions to Haiti in the 2-year period following the 2010 earthquake.

Summary

Cruz (2005) argued that "the fact that arts therapies have penetrated so many areas of the globe" was evidence that they had "officially come of age" (p. 167). As an international profession, and in international efforts to provide cross-cultural psychosocial support, art therapy is indeed growing. National associations, cross-border alliances, a growing literature base, the outreach of multiple international art therapy organizations on the Internet, and art therapy support and trainings in international service to the human condition, all symbolize and buttress this progression. Nonetheless, Gómez Carlier and Salom (2012) wrote, "with the forces of globalization contributing ever-more to art therapy's migration, its identity faces further challenges as it acculturates to different countries" (p. 8). Confronted with this challenge, art therapists can draw upon our critical thinking, assessment, and imaginative skills to facilitate growth that is appropriate, ethical, and valuable.

> In each new culture, the profession of art therapy must develop coping skills and inter-cultural competence ... for the profession to accomplish a successful adaptation to new cultures, art therapy needs to know itself, to be open and interested in getting to understand the host culture, and to gradually learn to compromise through empathetic communication. (Gómez Carlier & Salom, 2012, p. 8)

References

Allessandrini, C. D., Duarte, J. L., Dupas, M. A., & Bianco, M. F. (1998). SDT: The Brazil-ian standardization of the Silver Drawing Test of Cognition and Emotion. *Art Therapy: Journal of the American Art Therapy Association*, 15(2), 107–115.

Anderson, F. E., Arrington, D., & Wolf Bordonaro, G. P. (2008). *Art and Thai hill tribes*. Paper presented at the 39th Annual American Art Therapy Association Conference. Cleveland, OH.

Anderson, F. E., Arrington, D., & Wolf Bordonaro, G. P. (2012). Weaving the global tapestry of art. Panel presented at the 43rd Annual American Art Therapy Association Conference, Savannah, GA.

Arrington, D. B. (2005). Global art therapy training—Now and before. *The Arts in Psychotherapy*, 32(3), 193–203.

Atlas, M. (2009). Experiencing displacement: Using art therapy to address xenophobia in South Africa. *Development*, 52(4), 531–536.

Betts, D. (2012). Personal communication at the Consortium of Art Therapy Educators (CATE). Meeting at the 43rd Annual American Art Therapy Association Conference, Savannah, GA.

Betts, D., Gantt, L., & Lorance, J. (2011). The international art therapy research database: Introducing an innovative and essential resource. Paper presented at the 42nd Annual American Art Therapy Association Conference, Washington, DC.

Chu, V. (2010). Within the box: Cross-cultural art therapy with the survivors of the Rwanda genocide. *Art Therapy: Journal of the American Art Therapy Association*, 27(1), 4–10.

Cruz, R. F. (2005). Introduction to special issue: The international scope of arts therapists. *The Arts in Psychotherapy*, 32, 167–169.

Dhanachitsiriphong, P. (1999). *The effects of art therapy and rational art therapy on cognition and emotion development of male adolescents in Barn Karuna Training School of the Central Observation and Protection Center*. Unpublished thesis, Burapha University, Thailand.

Duijker, H. C. J., & Frijda, N. H. (1960). *National character and national stereotypes*. Amster-dam: Noord-Hollandse.

Gómez Carlier, N., & Salom, A. (2012). When art therapy migrates: The acculturation challenge of sojourner art therapists. *Art Therapy: Journal of the American Art Therapy Association*, 29(1), 4–10.

Hocoy, D. (2002). Cross-cultural issues in art therapy. *Art Therapy: Journal of the American Art Therapy Association*, 19(4), 141–145.

Hunter, G. (1992). *An examination of some individual differences in information processing, personality, and motivation with respect to some dimensions of special thinking or problem solving in TAFE students*. Unpublished thesis, The University of New England, School of Professional Studies, Armidale, Australia.

Kalmanowitz, D., & Potash, J. S. (2010). Ethical consideration in the global teaching and promotion of art therapy to non-art therapists. *The Arts in Psychotherapy, 37*, 20–26.

Kapitan, L. (2012). Checking the source: Critical evaluation of art therapy claims to knowledge. *Art Therapy: Journal of the American Art Therapy Association, 29*(1), 2–3.

Kapitan, L., Litell, M., & Torres, A. (2011). Creative art therapy in a community's participatory research and social transformation. *Art Therapy: Journal of the American Art Therapy Association, 28*(2), 64–73.

Keeling, M. L., & Nielson, R. (2005). Indian women's experience of a narrative therapy intervention using art and writing. *Contemporary Family Therapy, 27*(3), 435–452.

Kollontai, P. (2010). Healing the heart in Bosia-Herzegovina: Art, children, and peacemaking. *International Journal of Children's Spirituality, 15*(3), 261–271.

Kopytin, A. (2002a). The Silver Drawing Test of cognition and emotion: Standardization in Russia. *American Journal of Art Therapy, 40*, 223–237.

Kopytin, A. (2002b). *Using the Silver Drawing Test for assessing normal and traumatized children and adolescents living in the area affected by the Chernobyl nuclear accident.* Presentation at the Conference on Trauma and Creativity, Salzburg, October 4–6, 2002.

Moon, C. H. (2010). *Materials & media in art therapy: Critical understandings of diverse artistic vocabularies.* New York, NY: Routledge.

Mueller, J., Alie, C., Jonas, B., Brown, E., & Sherr, L. (2011). A quasi-experimental evaluation of a community-based art therapy intervention exploring the psychosocial health of children affected by HIV in South America. *Tropical Medicine and International Health, 16*(1), 57–66.

Pretorius, G., & Pfeifer, N. (2010). Group art therapy with sexually abused girls. *South African Journal of Psychology, 40*(1), 63–73.

Rosal, M. L., & Wolf Bordonaro, G. P. (2007). *The status of national art therapy associations: A global perspective.* Presentation at the national conference of the American Art Therapy Association. Albuquerque, NM.

Schmidt, L., & Wolf Bordonaro, G. P. (2012). Inner-outer boxes: An arts-based self-reflection experience about death and dying. *Journal of Hospice and Palliative Nursing, 14*(8), 559–662.

Schmidt, L., Pimple, C., & Wolf Bordonaro, G. P. (2011). Palliative care for children: Preparing undergraduate nursing students. *Nurse Educator, 34*(4), 162–165.

Silver, R. (2002). *Three art assessments—The Silver Drawing Test of cognition and emotion; Draw A Story screening for depression; and Stimulus Drawings and Techniques.* New York, NY: Brunner-Routledge.

Silver, R. (2012). Cultural differences and similarities in responses to the Silver Drawing Test in the USA, Brazil, Russia, Estonia, Thailand, and Australia. *Art Therapy: Journal of the American Art Therapy Association, 20*(1), 16–20.

Stoll, B. (1991). Art therapy: From isolation to international visibility. *International Journal of Arts Medicine, 1*(1), 27–32.

Stoll, B. (2005). Growing pains: The international development of art therapy. *The Arts in Psychotherapy, 32*, 171–191.

Svensk, A. C., Öster, I., Thyme, K. E., Magnusson, E., Sjödin, M., Eisemann, M., Åstrom, S., & Lindh, J. (2009). Art therapy improves experienced quality of life among women undergoing treatment for breast cancer: A randomized controlled study. *European Journal of Cancer Care, 18*, 69–77.

Talwar, S., Iyer, J., & Doby-Copeland, C. (2004). The invisible veil: Changing paradigms in the art therapy profession. *Art Therapy: Journal of the American Art Therapy Association, 21*(1), 44–48. doi: 10.1080/07421656.2004.10129325

Wolf Bordonaro, G. P., & Hurlbut, G. (2011). Art for Haiti: A collaborative service learning project. *American Art Therapy Association Newsletter, XLIV*(2), 8–11.

Yohani, S. C. (2008). Creating an ecology of hope: Arts-based interventions with refugee children. *Child & Adolescent Social Work Journal, 25*(4), 309–323.

Zelizer, C. (2003). The role of artistic processes in peacebuilding in Bosnia-Herzegovina. *Peace and Conflict Studies, 10*(2), 62–75.

66

Art Therapy in Great Britain

Jill Westwood

Introduction and Background Context

Great Britain (GB) is a complex nation with various long-charted histories of conflict and cooperation between peoples, empires, and countries. It stretches from prehistoric and Roman times through many centuries of war and peace, the rise and fall of imperial power, the Industrial Revolution, and the growth of multiculturalism. Known as the British Isles and described by Shakespeare as "this sceptred isle," it is geographically located on the edge of North Western Europe, and is a relatively small, productive land with many resources (coal, oil, natural gas, and iron ore, among others). It has varied terrain, featuring mainly lowlands of rolling green pastures, some highlands, and interesting coastline. It has a temperate climate, known for grey skies, plentiful rain, and distinct seasons. It is a sovereign nation, governed by a constitutional monarchy, and comprised of four countries—England, Northern Ireland, Scotland, and Wales. These different countries all have distinctive identities, but are held together within this alliance.

GB is one of the most densely inhabited countries in the world, with a culturally diverse population of approximately 64 million people. This diversity has arisen from the history of the British Empire and its colonial past, which has brought together a wide range of people from the former colonies and other places across the world. The historical wealth of this nation, while built upon contentious colonial exploits, has also enabled freedom for the individual, providing conditions for a great variety of innovation in a wide range of fields. GB is known for its highly developed welfare and health care systems and progressive psychological approaches, and is considered to be one of the most important centers for creative practices. While small in size, it remains a powerful economic force, which is the seventh largest in the world and the second largest in Europe. It has close links to Europe through the European Union (EU), to which art therapy in GB is becoming more connected through the EU directives on free movement of professionals. From this thickly layered context, the profession of art therapy in GB has emerged with its own particular character. As an artist and art therapist, I turned to art to help me think about this topic. Figure 66.1 is a visual portrait to capture the spirit of art therapy in GB and to accompany this account.

The Wiley Handbook of Art Therapy, First Edition. Edited by David E. Gussak and Marcia L. Rosal.
© 2016 John Wiley & Sons, Ltd. Published 2016 by John Wiley & Sons, Ltd.

Figure 66.1 Art therapy in Great Britain, 2012, Jill Westwood, 85 × 60 cm. History of art therapy in Great Britain © Jill Westwood.

Art therapy as a discipline in GB could be described as emerging out of the rubble of World War II. This history has been researched and discussed by several authors (Edwards, 2004; Hogan, 2001; Karkou & Sanderson, 2006; Waller, 1991; Wood, 1997, 2011). These histories suggest that art therapy evolved from a context where particular conditions came together to facilitate its emergence. These conditions were connected to artistic, cultural, and social movements, people, and events.

Waller (1991) provided one of the first accounts of the history of the development of the profession in GB during the period 1940–1982. She charted the process and struggle involved in its becoming a profession and highlighted the influences of psychoanalysis, child art education, and the anti-psychiatry movement. Wood (1997) built upon this study, focusing on the treatment of psychosis. Hogan (2001) is also notable for her historical and cultural analysis of the ideas that led up to the formation of art therapy in GB from 1790 through to the founding of the profession in 1966. Wood (1997) identified three overlapping periods of development. The first is identified as a time where the use of art as therapy in hospital settings began to emerge in a variety of ways (around 1930–1959). The second phase is when the professional association named the British Association of Art Therapists (BAAT) was formed, creating a ground swell allied to the anti-psychiatry movement and to humanistic schools of thought (around 1960–1979). Following this, the third phase saw professional practice become more established in the public sector, and psychoanalytic and group systems theory become more dominant (around 1980–1999). Since then, Wood (2011) has added a fourth contemporary phase where a variety of approaches and adaptations of practice have evolved toward a social view in a market-driven context (approximately since 2000). The work of these authors is integral to this chapter, and I have loosely followed Wood's phases in order to weave this overview.

First Period (1930–1959): Art as Therapy in Hospitals

In this era, one of the most significant factors enabling the emergence of art therapy as a discipline was the establishment of the social welfare system. A progressive Labour government founded the National Health Service (NHS) in 1948. This created an overarching health care system for the country with access to free health care at the point of delivery. At the same time, innovative approaches were being developed in health and education. The work of child educationalist Franz Cizek encouraged individual creative expression. In the field of trauma and mental health, the work of Foulkes and Bion pioneered group therapy (the Northfield Experiments) and the establishment of the Tavistock Institute (1946), which took forward ideas and practices from psychoanalysis (Waller, 1991).

Within this context, the first art therapists in GB emerged; they were artists (Hill, Adamson, Simon), therapists (Champernowne, Milner), and teachers who began to flourish in the fields of health, education, and the arts, working in a variety of diverse yet linked ways. The expression *art therapy* as it arose in GB can be traced back to the 1940s when Adrian Hill introduced the term. Hill, an artist, contracted tuberculosis during World War II. While recuperating, he began using art making as part of a recovery process and experienced positive effects. Hill was concerned with the inherent capacity of art to foster well-being (1948). While this is considered the beginnings of art therapy in Britain, other pioneers were developing similar practices (Edwards, 2004; Hogan, 2001; Waller, 1991).

Edward Adamson (1990), also an artist, initially worked with Hill, and then went on to work in Netherne Psychiatric Hospital, assisting with some image-making research for diagnostic purposes led by psychiatrists Cunningham Dax (1953) and Reitman (1950). This involved facilitating an art studio where patients were encouraged to make images with minimal instruction and intervention. The psychiatrists were interested to see if they could gain insight into the artist's state of mind from viewing the images. Adamson's calm and consistent presence was seen to have a positive impact and became a beneficial part of patients' experience. Several other art therapy pioneers with art backgrounds were inspired by Hill and worked in psychiatric hospitals during the 1950s as well. They published their work and became founder members of the profession, including: Jan Glass, at Warlingham Park Hospital in Surrey; Joyce Laing, based in the prison sector in Scotland; and Rita Simon, who worked in social psychiatry settings and went on to establish the Northern Ireland Group for Art Therapists. Simon was influenced by Jung and developed her own approach based on an interest in pictorial styles (Simon, 1992, 1997).

Psychoanalysts, such as Irene Champernowne and Marion Milner, also became involved. Champernowne, a Jungian analyst, set up the Withymeade Centre in Devon (1942–late 1960s) with her husband Gilbert. This was a Jungian-based therapeutic community where the arts were a primary mode of communication. Several influential figures worked at or visited Withymeade Centre during this time, including Hill, Adamson, and the psychiatrist R. D. Laing, who was part of the anti-psychiatry movement that challenged the dehumanizing practices in the treatment of mental illness (Laing, 1959). Champernowne became a champion of art therapy, and was also influenced by the work of Naumburg (1958), who had begun publishing her work in the United States around this time.

E. M. Lyddiatt (1971), a friend and colleague of Champernowne, was also influenced by the ideas of Jung, and published the first book in GB on art therapy, titled *Spontaneous painting and modelling*. Milner (1950), a psychoanalyst, wrote about her experiences of free-association drawings during her own analysis. Her seminal book, titled *On not being able to paint*, reflected on her own image-making experiences and the struggle of trusting the imagination to transform unconscious material through art. Milner became an honorary president of the British professional association until her death in 1998. During this early era, a variety of ideas and practices developed in the use of art as therapy, based on a belief in the power of expression led by these key figures.

Second Period (1960–1979): Social Change and the Formation of the Profession

The 1960s were a time of radical change in British society. Art therapy was part of a wave of left-wing social action that aimed to challenge the psychiatric mainstream. At the time, people with mental health conditions were separated from the rest of the community in large psychiatric hospitals. As the anti-psychiatry movement developed, government policy shifted toward care in the community. This saw the closure of the large asylums where art therapy studios had first been set up, and a change in thinking about people and mental health. In the midst of this change and growth, the BAAT was formed in 1964 with the aims of establishing art therapy as a profession within the NHS and training in the public sector (Waller, 1991). Close links were forged with the Union movement, with allegiances to both the teaching and health sectors.

Significantly, during this period, art therapy training programs also began to be set up. Withymeade Centre, in existence since 1942, is considered one of the first informal training programs in art therapy, where several founder members of BAAT has worked and visited. One such member was Michael Edwards, who set up the first formal training course in art therapy at the Birmingham School of Art in 1969. This was an option on the postgraduate course for art education. Other courses followed; a Certificate in Remedial Art was offered at St Albans School of Art (now Hertfordshire University) in 1970. This was aligned to the health sector, and later developed into the Diploma in Art Therapy in 1975. Then, the program at Goldsmiths College, University of London, commenced in 1974, led by Diane Waller. This was part of an Art Teachers Certificate course, which became a Postgraduate Diploma in Art Therapy in 1978. Initially, art therapy education grew out of an experiential process, the programs at Birmingham and Goldsmiths being influenced by art education, open studio, and theme-centered approaches. These trainings were at the postgraduate diploma level, of 1-year duration, and established a career path for those coming from an art degree background. In 1977, the BAAT produced the core course requirements that set out the content of the training programs; the option at Birmingham did not meet these criteria, and it closed.

There was very little literature on art therapy at the time; a few texts were available from the United States (Kramer, 1971; Naumburg, 1958; Ulman & Dachinger, 1975) and from the United Kingdom (Lyddiatt, 1971). These represented different approaches that focused either on art making or on the analysis of images. In 1979, a defining moment for the profession was BAAT's decision to ally itself with a broadly clinical orientation rather than continue its alignment with art education.

Third Period (1980–1999): Professional Recognition and Psychotherapeutic Influences

This third period saw significant developments in the profession, training programs, and the literature. After much campaigning by BAAT, and with their trade union (the Association of Scientific, Technical and Managerial Staff—ASTMS), the Department of Health and Social Security memorandum issued a definition in 1992 that supported the recognition of the profession, and set in place salaries and conditions of employment. This was a major step forward. Positions became established within the NHS, and employment opportunities were carved out in the community and education sectors.

In 1981, another training program began at Sheffield University, and, during the 1990s, others emerged in Edinburgh and Belfast. The next major shift in education was in 1992, when 1-year postgraduate diplomas became 2-year diplomas that were eventually recognized as MAs, and personal therapy became a mandatory requirement. This made a significant difference in the training process in containing and working with the emotional process for students, deepening the learning in alignment with psychotherapy, and increasing the status of the training with employers (Westwood, 2010).

During the 1980s–1990s, more art therapy literature emerged from GB, which promoted a psychoanalytic and object relations perspective (Case & Dalley, 1992; Dalley et al., 1987). These authors drew on the work of Freud, Klein, and Winnicott. Theoretical advances were developed by Schaverien (1992, 1994) from an analytic (Jungian) perspective, conceptualizing the triangular relationship, and notions of diagrammatic and embodied images and the scapegoat transference. Also, Simon (1992, 1997) developed an art-based theory of the symbolism of styles. Other authors developed thinking about art therapy groups (Liebmann, 1986; McNeilly, 1983; Skaife & Huet, 1998; Waller, 1993); art therapy with different client populations (Case & Dalley, 1990; Killick & Schaverien, 1997); feminist perspectives (Hogan, 1997); and research (Gilroy & Lee, 1995; Payne, 1993). Toward the end of this period in 1997, another campaign led to the state registration of art therapists with the Council for Professions Supplementary to Medicine (CPSM).

Fourth Period (2000 onward): Contemporary Adaptations

During this period, the CPSM became the Health Professions Council (now known as the Health Care Professions Council—HCPC), responsible for the registration of arts therapists and ensuring that art therapy became a protected title. This led to positive developments in terms of recognition, and further defined the training requirements and the regulatory processes around the education of art therapists. It also separated registration from the professional association.

During this contemporary period, there has been a sustained growth in the literature and more consideration of social and cultural issues (Kalmanowitz & Lloyd, 2005); the materiality of art (Maclagan, 2001); the diversity of approaches (Hogan, 2009); and research (Gilroy, 2006, 2011; Karkou & Sanderson, 2006). There have also been significant changes and reform in the NHS, which is the largest employer in the country and a major employer of art therapists. In 2007, an "Agenda for Change" process began, which involved a review and harmonizing of pay and conditions in the NHS, resulting in art therapists being more highly graded. While this was positive, it also resulted in significant job losses due to the expense of employing an art therapist.

Economic issues have become more dominant, and the National Institute for Clinical Excellence (NICE) has been established to assess the evidence-base for treatments and recommend what will be funded. This has put pressure on the profession to develop research and evidence within the medical paradigm, which, as Gilroy (2006) points out, produces particular kinds of evidence that may not always fit with art therapy practices. Evidence-based practice is now a fundamental part of the health context, and art therapy interventions need to meet these requirements in order to survive and be recognized and funded. There is now an imperative for the development of research and clinical guidelines to ensure art therapy's place in the NHS.

Current Position and Horizons

GB is one of the places in the world where art therapy is most well recognized and organized as a profession. The social and cultural conditions and driving figures have enabled it to achieve state recognition as a health care profession and for its training to be at advanced postgraduate levels. In 2012, there were 2,914 registered arts therapists, of which 1,590 were art therapists (HCPC, 2012), and membership of BAAT numbered approximately 1,456 (BAAT, 2012). Ten qualifying master's-level art therapy programs exist across the country, representing a diversity of theoretical views. Several special interest groups have formed within BAAT, based on client populations and other specialties. There is also a peer-reviewed international journal (*International Journal of Art Therapy* [formerly *Inscape*]) published twice yearly, and an online journal (*Art Therapy OnLine*—ATOL).

Art therapy has developed significantly, and is now practiced in a variety of settings, and from many different theoretical perspectives. This was discussed by Karkou and Sanderson (2006) as reflective of general sociological trends toward accepting diversity, influenced by the development of post-modern perspectives. The distinguishing character of art therapy in GB was discussed by Woddis (1986) as individualistic and phenomenological, reflecting a propensity for "continuing questions" rather than answers (Woddis, 1986, p. 148). The predominance of artists as art therapists in GB could partly account for this position, suggesting that artists are more likely to be at ease with uncertainty and less likely to take a prescriptive position.

State registration has created both positive and negative effects. There is increased status, but also greater regulation. The evolving relationship between the various bodies (HCPC, BAAT, educational institutions/educators) around power, control, and consensus are areas of on-going dynamic tension. The rise of evidence-based practice and market-driven approaches are shaping adaptations to practice more toward a cognitive base. This presents a tension that threatens to undermine the complexity of the work of art therapy and limit the possibilities in differences of thinking and is reflective of neo-liberal agendas.

The impact of the economic downturn and climate of austerity across Britain and Europe is increasing a drive toward generic practice and de-professionalization of specialists in order to reduce costs. Employment opportunities are retracting in the health sector, and are only likely to advance through evidence-based research on art therapy interventions for treatment of specific conditions, such as the MATISSE project (Imperial College, 2012) or other particular focused, short-term models. Meanwhile, opportunities seem to be shifting toward the education and community sectors, as these agencies have greater freedom to employ people. This is reflected in the increasing presence of discourses on arts and wellness.

The spaces between community arts, arts and health, and art therapy seem to be the fruitful places for art therapists to focus with an entrepreneurial spirit. Revisiting the areas of practice where art therapy first emerged, but returning with a theoretical eye that was not developed at the time, may inform and open up possibilities (Gilroy in Westwood, 2010). Karkou and Sanderson (2006) identified a neglect of art theory in art therapy. Further reflection on the art side of the "uneasy partnership" (Champernowne, 1971) and consideration of the social and cultural issues at the interface of contemporary art may be relevant, timely, and yield valuable employment opportunities.

Art therapy is firmly established as a discreet discipline in GB, but it remains in dynamic evolution, shaped by the prevailing social, cultural, and economic conditions. Its challenge will be to sustain its multifaceted and questioning character as it braves the current climate.

References

Adamson, E. (1990). *Art as healing.* London: Coventure.

British Association of Art Therapists. (2012). Number of members. Accessed July 30, http://www.baat.org.

Case, C., & Dalley, T. (1990). *Working with children in art therapy.* London: Tavistock Routledge.

Case, C., & Dalley, T. (Eds.) (1992). *The handbook of art therapy.* London, UK: Routledge.

Champernowne, I. (1971). "Art and therapy: An uneasy partnership." *American Journal of Art Therapy, 10*(3), 131–143.

Cunningham Dax, E. (1953). *Experimental studies in psychiatric art.* London: Faber & Faber.

Dalley, T., Case, C., Schaverien, J., Weir, F., Halliday, D., Nowell-Hall, P., & Waller, D. (Eds.) (1987). *Images of art therapy.* London: Routledge.

Edwards, D. (2004). *Art therapy.* London, UK: Sage.

Gilroy, S. (2006). *Art therapy, research and evidence-based practice.* London, UK: Sage.

Gilroy, A. (Ed.) (2011). *Art therapy research in practice.* Bern, Switzerland: Peter Lang.

Gilroy, A., & Colin L. (Eds.) (1995). *Art and music: Therapy and research.* London: Routledge.

Health Professions Care Council. (2012). *Number of registered arts therapists.* Accessed 30 July, www.hcpc-uk.org/aboutregistration/theregister/stats.

Hill, A. (1948). *Art versus illness.* London, UK: Allen & Unwin.

Hogan, S. (Ed.) (1997). *Feminist approaches to art therapy.* London: Routledge.

Hogan, S. (2001). *Healing arts: The history of art therapy.* London, UK: Jessica Kingsley Publishers.

Hogan, S. (2009). The art therapy continuum: A useful tool for envisaging the diversity of practice in British art therapy. *International Journal of Art Therapy: Inscape, 14*(1), 29–37.

Imperial College. (2012). *Matisse project BMJ article. Group art therapy as an adjunctive treatment for people with schizophrenia: Multicentre pragmatic randomised trial.* Accessed 10 August, www.bmj.com/content/344/bmj.e846

Kalmanowitz, D., & Lloyd, B. (Eds.) (2005). *Art therapy and political violence: With art, without illusion.* London, UK: Routledge.

Karkou, V., & Sanderson, P. (2006). *Arts therapies: A research based map of the field.* UK: Elsevier, Churchill, Livingstone.

Killick, K., & Schaverien, J. (Eds.) (1997). *Art, psychotherapy, and psychosis.* London: Routledge.

Kramer, E. (1971). *Art as therapy with children.* New York, NY: Schocken Books.

Laing, R. D. (1959). *The divided self.* London, UK: Penguin Books.

Liebmann, M. (1986). *Art therapy for groups: A handbook of themes, games and exercises.* London: Routledge.

Lyddiatt, E. M. (1971). *Spontaneous painting and modelling: A practical approach in therapy.* London, UK: Constable.

Maclagan, D. (2001). *Psychological aesthetics.* London, UK: Jessica Kingsley Publishers.

McNeilly, G. (1983). Directive and non-directive approaches in art therapy. *The Arts in Psychotherapy, 10*(4), 211–219.

Milner, M. (1950). *On not being able to paint.* London: Heinemann.

Naumburg, M. (1958). *Dynamically oriented art therapy.* New York, NY: Grune & Stratton.

Payne, H. (Ed.) (1993). *Handbook of inquiry into the arts therapies: One river, many currents.* London: Jessica Kingsley.

Reitman, F. (1950). *Psychotic art.* London: Routledge and Kegan Paul.

Schaverien, J. (1992). *The revealing image: Analytic art psychotherapy in theory and practice.* London: Routledge.

Schaverien, J. (1994). Analytical art psychotherapy: Further reflections on theory and practice. *Inscape, 2,* 41–49

Simon, R. (1992). *The symbolism of style: Art as therapy.* London, UK: Routledge.

Simon, R. (1997). Symbolic images in art as therapy. London, UK: Routledge.

Skaife, S., & Huet, V. (Eds.) (1998). *Art psychotherapy groups: Between pictures and words.* London, UK: Routledge.

Ulman, E., & Dachinger, P. (Eds.) (1975). *Art therapy: In theory and practice.* New York, NY: Schocken.

Waller, D. (1991). *Becoming a profession: The history of art therapy in Britain 1940–1982.* London, UK: Tavistock/Routledge.

Waller, D. (1993). *Group interactive art therapy: It's use in training and treatment.* London, UK: Routledge.

Westwood, J. (2010). *Hybrid creatures: Mapping art therapy education in Australia.* PhD thesis. University of Western Sydney, Australia.

Woddis, J. (1986). Judging by appearances. *The Arts in Psychotherapy, 13,* 147–149.

Wood, C. (1997). The history of art therapy and psychosis (1938–1995). In K. Killick and J. Schaverien (Eds.), *Art, psychotherapy and psychosis.* London, UK: Routledge.

Wood, C. (2011). The evolution of art therapy in relation to psychosis and poverty. In A. Gilroy (Ed.), *Art therapy research in practice.* Bern, Switzerland: Peter Lang.

67

Art Therapy in Canada: A Place-based *Métissage*

Janis Timm-Bottos[1]

> "*Nous connaîtrions-nous seulement un peu nous-mêmes, sans les arts?*" ("Could we ever know each other in the slightest without the arts?") (Roy, 1961/1962)

The preceding quote, by francophone novelist Gabrielle Roy, was juxtaposed on the bilingual C\$20 bill with two images of modern aboriginal sculptures—*The Spirit of Haida Gwaii* and *Raven and the First Men*, both by British Columbia Haida artist Bill Reid. It proudly remained on the bill for almost a decade, "remind[ing] us that arts and culture define who we are, as well as the system of beliefs, values, and customs we share as Canadians" (Bank of Canada, n.d.). The braiding of distinct, diverse cultural threads creates a new way of seeing something, such as Roy's quote together with Reid's art, and aptly provides an example of cultural *métissage*, "the weaving of a cloth from different fibres" (Hasebe-Ludt, Chambers, & Leggo, 2009, p. 35). This melded image serves as a place to fabricate a viewpoint of what is unique, vital, and also challenging about art therapy in Canada.

Music therapist Hyun Ju Chong (2010) referred to the investigation of national uniqueness as "internationalization" or "what occurs among the countries through the exchange of what is 'theirs' to the other parts of the world" (p. 1). Identifying special qualities, such as the qualities of art therapy in Canada, begins, according to Chong, through recognition of the country's art identity and heritage in order to answer the question "What has Canada contributed to art therapy that enriches and diversifies the profession?"

To respond to this question, a perspective and context for art therapy in Canada will be offered in this chapter. To do this, the intertwining and overlapping nature of the documentation on the history, places, people, and differing standpoints uncovered about art therapy in Canada will be explored. This *métissage* will be sensitively investigated, and will contribute to the complex plait started many years ago in the skillful hands of many dedicated and passionate Canadian art therapist–authors with the hope that many more threads will be located, pulled forward, and continued onward.

The Wiley Handbook of Art Therapy, First Edition. Edited by David E. Gussak and Marcia L. Rosal.
© 2016 John Wiley & Sons, Ltd. Published 2016 by John Wiley & Sons, Ltd.

An Initial Knot Held in Place

For well over 400 years, art making skills and "minutely detailed environmental knowledge" (Basso, 1996, p. 43) of the First Nations secured the survival of French and English colonists in this rustic new world landscape. For example, immediately upon arrival, the handcrafted canoe replaced the European wheel in importance for travel and moving freight. Arthur Lismer, one of the Canadian landscape painters from the *Group of Seven*, eloquently stated, "When the art impulses of a nation are stirred then something vital moves into a responsive rhythm" (Lismer, in McKay, 2002, p. 50). The daily involvement over several centuries with particular materials and tools for the construction of handmade objects has had an enormous and continuous role in reinforcing the Canadian citizen's identity.

Canada was built on three pillars—First Nations, French, and English—forming a complex triangular foundation (Saul, 2009). Even through the changing tides of polarizing federalist governments and regretful examples of misuse of power, Canada maintains a particular cultural humility toward its citizens. By actively fostering diversity and supporting social determinants of health through welcoming new immigrants, providing universal health care (Mann, 2012), social housing, new parent support, subsidized post-secondary education, etc., Canada is known for caring for its people.

Geographical and climatic elements contribute to the need for government care, and these factors have also affected the way art therapy has evolved in Canada. Most of the country's 34.5 million inhabitants (one-tenth the population of the United States) live within a 100-mile southern band of land bordering the United States (2010 Data from Statistics Canada, www.nrcan.gc.ca). Extensive natural landscapes surround relatively small outcroppings of people within abundant forests and glacier peaks, on vast stretches of prairie lands, among diverse wild life, and along the world's longest coastlines. Most importantly, this vast beauty lies within its people, who have learned to prosper in a land of extreme temperatures. The country's cold temperatures and the great distances between cities, towns, and villages have historically deterred an ease of national collaboration; this is no less true between its 600 or so art therapists. For these reasons, "Art therapy in Canada, like the nation itself, developed along provincial lines" (Edwards, 2004, p. 130).

Colorful Pioneering Threads

It was within particular geographical landscapes that the seeds of the profession now known as art therapy took root. As aptly phrased by French Nobel Prize–winning author Albert Camus, "Sense of place is not just something that people know and feel, it is something people do" (Camus as cited in Basso, 1996, p. 143). In the words of Irene Dewdney, a pioneering Canadian art therapist, "Our relative isolation from other art therapy practitioners allowed us to make our own discoveries; evaluate our own approaches and techniques; and create our own picture of an art therapist" (I. Dewdney & Nichols, 2011, p. 47).

Selwyn Dewdney (1909–1979), an accomplished artist, art educator, author, and aboriginal rock art scholar, conveyed a strong sense of place through his writings (S. Dewdney, 1975). In one of his books titled *They Shared to Survive: Native Peoples of Canada*, S. Dewdney articulated how the "impact of aboriginal values and attitudes has shaped us more than we know" (1975, p. 4). As a child, his imagination was captivated by the marshlands of Northern Ontario's waterways, which he later canoed extensively with friends and family. Serving as a future testament of their professional partnership, he and his wife, Irene Dewdney, traveled by canoe for their 500-mile honeymoon trip in 1937 (A. K. Dewdney, 1997). This distinctively Canadian mode of travel seemed to have prepared and nurtured the couple's fervor for bringing forward a piece of a profession that highly values the watery meandering through the swamps and waterways of the unconscious.

Art therapy in Canada, as in other nations, was birthed during the age of modernism, a time when the imagination and the unconscious came into its own as the harbingers of human potential. Canadian art therapist Helene Burt (2012), in her edited book *Art Therapy and Postmodernism*, discussed how, after generations of a lack of individualism due to dominating political and religious systems, Sigmund Freud brought forward a popular notion of the "self." In response, many writers and artists began to investigate the "individual psyche" (Burt, 2012, p. 18) through their work that then served to "revitalize art as an instrument for the creative empowerment of the human spirit" (Haslem, 2005, p. 20). In his fascinations with these new ways of thinking, Lismer, influenced by the American art therapist Florence Cane (Grigor, 2002), said, "Art unfolds the purpose of humanity [and] the art of a nation is the expression of the nation's presence on the path that leads towards things of the spirit" (Lismer as cited in McKay, 2002, p. 50).

It was no wonder that Martin Fischer (1914–1992), a charismatic Vienna-based medical professional who had studied with Freud (Burt, personal communication, January 4, 2013), quickly had a following of students who agreed to view art as a way of gathering insights and information from the unconscious. Leaving Europe, along with many others under duress, Fischer immigrated to Canada and immediately began working as a psychiatrist at Toronto's Lakeshore Psychiatric Hospital in the late 1940s (Woolf, 2003). Edwards, in describing the impact of psychoanalysis on the origins of art therapy, indicated:

> Psychoanalysis has exercised such a strong influence on art therapy mainly because it offers a ready-made language through which art therapists can both think about and articulate aspects of their work. Without this language, art therapy could not have developed in the way it has. (2004, p. 69)

Fischer exemplified the medical expert who practiced and taught his psychoanalytic art therapy approach, which differed from the Dewdneys' interdisciplinary approaches. Edwards (2004) continued:

> In some respects, however, as Skaife (2001, p. 41) suggests, "art therapy may be being held back by some of the language of psychoanalysis." While this may in some ways be true, in common with developments in related disciplines like counseling and psychotherapy, art therapists have tended to "assemble concepts and techniques into their own personal *bricolage*, thereby creating a set of interlocking local knowledges rather than a 'universal' theory." (p. 69)

Ten years earlier in London, Ontario, only 100 kilometers away from where Fischer set up shop, S. Dewdney taught painting, and led mural projects and geology expositions in order to provide for his growing family. In 1938, S. Dewdney had an interesting opportunity to collaborate with Lionel Penrose on developing the first projective art therapy test for "shell-shocked" veterans, referred to as the "M test" (I. Dewdney & Nicholas, 2011). A decade later, about the time Fischer started at Lakeshore, he accepted a job at Westminster Hospital in London, Ontario, teaching art to psychiatric patients (A. K. Dewdney, 1997). This led to S. Dewdney becoming the first government-appointed art therapist in Canada (I. Dewdney & Nicholas, 2011), seeking "to make the process of art therapy understandable to his patients" (I. Dewdney & Nicholas, 2011, p. 24). In his wife's words:

> Selwyn was not interested in following the medical model of diagnosis and labeling but quite the opposite, in fact; he preferred to dissect and demystify the processes that seemed to help mental patients, and to give the voice of authority to the patient when it came to his or her own art productions. (I. Dewdney & Nicholas, 2011, p. 24)

Gathering to Organize a Profession

Meanwhile, Fischer was teaching image-making as a tool of therapy to his psychiatric residents (Woolf, 2003) and developing a national vision for the profession of art therapy. He was untethered from provincial constraints and had the personal and professional authority to extend a wide reach. He founded two private clinical training institutes: one in the east (Toronto Art Therapy Institute) and one in the west (Vancouver Art Therapy Institute). His training also influenced a third training institute, Kutenai Art Therapy Institute, located in the interior of British Columbia. In 1977, Fischer also initiated a national association, the Canadian Art Therapy Association (CATA), offering governance, registration, conferences, and later a professional journal for qualified art therapists. The control of the association remained under Fischer's influence and leadership until his sudden death in 1992 (Gilroy & Hanna, 1998; Woolf, 2003).

Fischer's enthusiasm was often met with strong reactions, and it was quickly pointed out that the CATA did not represent all Canadian art therapists. The British Columbia Art Therapy Association (BCATR) and the Ontario Art Therapy Association (OATA), both established in 1978, were developed in response to Fischer's "national" umbrella. In 1981, the Association des Arts-therapeutes du Quebec/Association of Art Therapists of Quebec (AATQ) followed suit, established by Nancy Humbar, Rachel Garber, and Sandy Cooke. The 16 enthusiastic members donated C$1 each to start this organization (Woolf, 2003). The AATQ continues to produce an informative communiqué twice a year for its members.

In 1982, a governing body was established out of the BCATA, called the Victoria Institute of Art Therapy Association (VIATA). The Alberta Art Therapy Association (AATA) was formed in 1983, but did not initially stabilize because members joined the BCATA. Around this same time, an alternate national effort was put forth when the four provincial associations founded the National Art Therapy Council of Canada

(NATCC) and invited CATA to join. The purpose of the council was to act as a national forum in conjunction with the existing provincial associations to develop and standardize criteria for training, ethics, and provincial registration. The council disbanded in 1998 (Collis, 1998). However, in 2012, a promising effort was launched between BCATA and CATA, and a formal agreement of collaboration was signed. "The goal of the Alliance has always been to find a way to weave art therapists across our nation together; to build our profession as a strong entity that can be looked as a positive model" (Oucharek-Deo, 2012, p. 2). Another national-level organization is the Creative Arts in Counseling chapter within the Canadian Counseling and Psychotherapy Association (CCPA), which requires an MA in a related field. Currently, it has 190 members. From the CCPA's January 2010 survey, it appears that art therapists are the majority of its members, with almost all provinces and territories represented (Lu, 2010).

Women Leaders

While it was men who were first acknowledged for developing and disseminating art therapy in Canada, it was a larger-by-far group of women who stayed close to the work, often without the recognition they deserved. By the 1950s, I. Dewdney (1914–1999) began working with her husband, Selwyn, at the Westminster Hospital (I. Dewdney & Nicolas, 2011). As S. Dewdney increasingly traveled to document aboriginal rock art, the Dewdneys worked together over the next 20 years to set up and deliver services in art therapy clinics at Westminster Hospital, St. Joseph Hospital, and London Psychiatric Hospital (I. Dewdney & Nicholas, 2011, p. 41). Over many years, I. Dewdney developed the "objective approach" to art therapy. An informal training program led to the establishment of the Graduate Diploma Program in Art Therapy at the University of Western Ontario in 1986. Unfortunately, it closed 20 years later, mostly due to economic reasons.

One of the proposed titles for the book outlining I. Dewdney's seminal approach to art therapy, edited by her friend and former student, Linda Nicholas, exemplified her imagination and creativity. The book was originally called *A Nest of Dolls*, to illustrate how the inner child lives within each client, along with "the smaller selves," such as in Russian nesting dolls (I. Dewdney & Nicholas, 2011). However, the title of this online book was eventually changed to *Drawing out the Self: The Objective Approach in Art Therapy* (please see the Ontario Art Therapy Association website). Nicholas stated, "Irene was one of the last of a vanishing breed: the untrained, highly skilled, broadly experienced pioneer art therapist" (Woolf, 2003, p. 4). In her article titled "Art Therapy in Canada: Origins and Expectations," art therapist Lois Woolf eloquently wrote about the Dewdneys:

> The Dewdneys were political activists and through their work they brought together their political principles and art. Seeing psychiatric patients as dispossessed and needing recognition as people, they encouraged the use of art as a vehicle for social empowerment; a way to resist the undermining of their social status and to gain personal acceptance (Woolf, 2003, p. 4).

In Montreal, Quebec, another art therapy visionary was working independently and experimenting with ways to engage psychiatric patients in art-making. Marie Revai (1911–1997) an artist with a teaching diploma from Budapest, and had trained with Arthur Lismer, the *Group of Seven* artist and progressive art educator, at the Montreal Museum of Fine Art. Revai then worked extensively in surrounding community centers, introducing art to children and adults. This experience helped Revai formulate her ideas about how art could provide a particular "solace, and a new perception of the world" (Lamy, 2006, p. 67). In 1957, she was hired by a psychiatrist to work as an arts specialist in the occupational therapy department at the Allan Memorial Institute. She was thrilled with the large, windowed studio space offered to her, which overlooked a grove of trees, because inner as well as outer natural worlds were important to Revai's methods. She stated, "I tried to make the art room as inspiring as possible. Plants, aquarium, turtles, budgie birds and drift woods of interesting shapes were decorating the room" (Lamy, 2006, p. 66). It was reported over time that, as patients attended the studio and moved around the space, spontaneous things happened to help foster healing (Schwartz, 1994). Revi's noninterventionist open studio stayed as such until the mid-1970s. She also developed "very structured" closed groups, which addressed different ways of being, including: "the Opinion group, the Perceptual group, the Training group and the Projective Art group" (Lamy, 2006, p. 66). Marie Revai also organized art exhibits at the hospital to educate and demonstrate the links between modern art and the art made by her patients in the hospital.

It was one of these art exhibits that inspired Leah Sherman, the director of fine arts at Concordia University, to invite Michael Edwards (2010), a Jungian art therapist from England, to teach a survey class in art therapy in 1978 at Concordia University. This led to the development of the first art therapy master's program in Canada. Julia Byers, a Canadian, was later hired from the United States to support expansion of the program within the Art Education Department. Today, a 60-credit psychodynamically oriented art therapy option, approved by CATA as well as the American Art Therapy Association, is offered within the Fine Arts Department of Creative Arts Therapies (Leclerc, 2011).

Across the country, especially in the west, other schools were evolving, driven by passionate, professional, and extremely dedicated women. The Vancouver Art Therapy Institute was founded in 1982 by Lois Woolf, Fischer's former student. The British Columbia School of Art Therapy in Victoria was founded by Kay Collis in 1985. Collis was befriended by the American art therapy pioneer Robert Ault, and was invited to attend the inaugural meeting of the American Art Therapy Association in 1969. Collis was responsible for establishing important north–south links. In 1995, Monica Carpendale, another former student of Fischer, founded the Kutenai Art Therapy Institute, situated in one of Canada's "best small art towns," Nelson, BC (Villani, 1998, 22–25).

The art therapy program at St. Stephen's College, within the University of Alberta in Edmonton, evolved as a progressive response to spiritual development within an innovative theological college. "It began with transpersonal art therapy elective courses taught by Madeline Rugh, an art therapist from the US." Her efforts, combined with those of Straja Linder-King, inspired a critical mass of students to request the formation of a formal art therapy specialization within the master's degree in 2004. More recently in Sherbrooke, Quebec, two independent art therapy initiatives merged to form a Jungian oriented 45-credit MA program at the Universite du Quebec en Abitibi-

Temiscamingue (UQAT). Initiated by Louise Poirer-Magassouba and joined by Johanne Hamel and Lorraine Dumont this Canadian program represents, "The first and only university to offer masters level art therapy study in French" (Labreche, 2011, p. 37).

Current Issues and Trends

The latest CATA survey, which went out to the four art therapy associations representing Canadian art therapists, indicated that there were a total of 609 members in these associations. With almost a third of Canada's population located in three major cities, Montreal, Toronto, and Vancouver, it is not surprising that the majority of the 281 responses from the 2009 survey came from these metropolitan centers. Only 29% of the art therapy respondents resided in rural Canada. According to the survey, while these therapists may enjoy a lack of competition for jobs, they also experience a sense of isolation, a lack of professional identity, limited supervision options, and a lack of continuing education opportunities (Lee, 2010). "Considering these challenges, Canadian art therapists have been quick to embrace local collaborations with other professions, distance supervision, online continuing education, and enthusiasm for gathering for conferences" (Zip, 2013, personal communication, February 24, 2013).

In her 2011 follow-up article, Lee noted trends that emerged in art therapy in Canada over the 5-year period since the last survey (Burt, 2005). Lee noted a 25% increase in the number of art therapists responding to the survey, and she reported the following trends: older age, income concerns, part-time versus full-time workers, necessity of multiple titles, art therapy research, and MA versus diploma options.

Art therapists responding to the survey included recent MA graduates who were making significantly more income than post-graduate-level diploma holders: C$41,000–C$45,000 starting incomes in the first 2–5 years, compared to C$26,000–C$30,000 for diploma holders. This reflected the economic value of graduate-level degree programs. Most professionals (65% of respondents) were operating under several job titles. Concerns that emerged from this comparison report used Statistics Canada's low-income cut-offs (2010), and showed that, on average, 22% of art therapists were earning below the poverty levels, earning less than C$20,000 annually (inclusive of all jobs). This is in contrast to the wage scale that the Quebec Minister of Health and Services provides on the ministry's website, which indicates an 18-scale pay range for art therapists with the starting scale in 2012 for 35 hours per week from C$39,494 (C$21.70 per hour) to C$72,709 (C$39.95/per hour; data from "Sante´ et services sociaux—professionnels, 2012": http://www.tresor.gouv.qc.ca/fileadmin/PDF/echelles_salariales/sss_prof.pdf).

While there is commensurable value in post-baccalaureate certificates in Canada, with which you can hold the title of "Registered Canadian Art Therapist" and office in CATA, there is a trend toward master's-level art therapy education due to increasing push for credentialing. The art therapy institutes have responded by developing MA degrees through established universities. For example, the Vancouver Art Therapy Institute is now in partnership with Athabasca University and their Graduate Centre for Applied Psychology. Other institutes have been less successful in securing master's programs and have instead opted to develop extension programs. Christine Lummis, president of the Kutenai Art Therapy Institute, described their efforts of developing a

Halifax, Nova Scotia, extension from their institute in BC: "In some ways this is due to the need to remain accessible to students and the mandate to reduce obstacles to people interested in learning about art therapy" (personal communication, July, 25, 2012).

Credentialing pressures come primarily from the United States because increasing numbers of art therapists are attempting to find a foothold in the workforce through title protection. In Quebec, Law 21 currently prevents art therapists from using the term "psychotherapy" to describe their work, while in Ontario, "it is projected that by the summer of 2012, the new College of Registered Psychotherapists and Registered Mental Health Therapists regulating the practice of psychotherapy will be opening its doors to registrants" (OATA website). The fact that this has not yet happened may indicate that the process for title recognition will move quite slowly, and will face many obstacles.

The other trends are in the areas of eco-psychology, expressive arts therapies, community arts studio methods, and research innovation, including aboriginal research methods, arts-based research, creative arts research, as well as in inspiring new locations for service delivery. For example, the St. Stephen's "Arts-based Research Studio" is "an accessible and inclusive space" that espouses, "We know more than we think" (St. Stephen's University website, www.ssu.edu, 2013).

Art therapists in Canada work in a wide range of settings—including hospitals, clinics, schools, private practice; senior, community, and transitional housing venues; and universities, employment offices, and family and youth programs. The weaving of these practices and places is the work of current and future art therapists. Each represents creative diversity based on mutual regard and important partnerships.

It is with consideration of the value and complexity of this diversity, across such a huge expanse of land, that a place-based art therapy *métissage* is woven. A long braid is formed across Canada, which is a respectful mixture of its many different ways of practicing, learning, organizing, and working in the dynamic field of art therapy.

> "(T)hink about our unbroken past here and those tens of thousands of experiences of *métissage* and their influence on what we have become. And beyond those physical experiences is the long history of Aboriginal ideas and ways of life mixing in with those who arrived from the sixteenth century on." (Saul, 2009, p. 20)

From this heritage, where "art is the language that cuts across the existing boundaries and obstacles that stand in the way of human communication" (Fischer, 1990), art therapy in Canada proudly sits in many expansive places.

Endnote

1   The author would like to thank the following Canadian art therapists for their contribution to this chapter: Theresa Zip, Sarah Tevyaw, Josee Leclerc, Irene Gericke, Christine Lummis, Mehdi Naimi, Linda Nicholas, and Yvon Lamy. And thank you, Leo Bottos my Canadian husband.

References

Bank of Canada. (nd). *Gabrielle Roy: Canadian author of the quotation on the back of the new $20 note*. Retrieved from: http://www.bankofcanada.ca/banknotes/bank-note-series/canadian-journey/gabrielle-roy-canadian-author-of-the-quotation-on-the-back-of-the-new-20-note.

Basso, K. H. (1996). *Wisdom sits in places: Landscape and language among the western apache.* Albuquerque: University of New Mexico Press.

Burt, H. (2005). The 2004–2005 National survey of members of the national and provincial art therapy associations in Canada. *Journal of Canadian Art Therapy Association, 18*(1), 2–8.

Burt, H. (Ed.) (2012). *Art therapy and postmodernism: Creative healing through a prism.* London: Jessica Kingsley.

Chong, H. J. (2010). Internationalization vs. Globalization of Music Therapy. *Voices: A world forum for music therapy.* Retrieved June 25, 2012, from http://testvoices.uib. no/?q=colchong030510.

Collis, K. (1998). A message from the president. *Newsletter of the BC Art Therapy Association, 20*(3), 1, 3, 9.

Dewdney, A. K. (Ed.) (1997). *Daylight in the swamp: Memoirs of Selwyn Dewdney.* Toronto-Oxford: Dundurn Press.

Dewdney, S. (1975). *They shared to survive: Native peoples of Canada.* Toronto: Macmillan.

Dewdney, I., & Nicholas, L. (2011). *Drawing out the self: The objective approach in Art Therapy.* London, ON: The Ontario Art Therapy Association.

Edwards, D. (2004). *Art therapy.* London: Sage.

Edwards, E. (2010). *A Jungian circumambulation of art & therapy: Ornithology for the birds.* UK: Insider Art.

Fischer, M. (1990). Vancouver Art Therapy Institute graduation ceremony. VATI website.

Gilroy, A., & Hanna, M. (1998). Conflict and culture in art therapy: An Australian perspective. In A. R. Hiscox & A. C. Calisch (Eds.), *Tapestry of cultural issues in art therapy* (pp. 249–275). London, UK: Jessica Kingsley Publishers.

Grigor, A. N. (2002). *Arthur Lismer: Visionary art educator.* Montreal & Kingston: McGill-Queens University Press.

Hasebe-Ludt, E., Chambers, C., & Leggo, C. (2009). *Life writing and literary métissage as an ethos for our times.* New York, NY: Peter Lang.

Haslem, M. (2005). Modernism and art therapy. *Canadian Art Therapy Association Journal, 18,* 1.

Labreche, J. (2011). The history of art therapy at UQAT: A Long road towards the master's in Art Therapy. *AATQ Communique, 29*(2), 36–37.

Lamy, Y. (2006). *Marie Revai: Pioneer of art-therapy in Quebec .* Montreal: Self published.

Leclerc, J. (2011). History of development of Creative Arts Therapies Programs: Concordia University. *AATQ Communique, 29*(2), 32, 35.

Lee, A. (2010). 2009–2010 National survey of art therapists in Canada. *Journal of Canadian Art Therapy Association, 23*(2), 35–49.

Lee, A. (2011). Art therapy in Canada, then and now: A comparison between the national surveys in Canada 2005 and 2010. *Journal of Canadian Art Therapy Association, 24*(2), 20–29.

Lu, L. (2010). Creative arts in counselling chapter survey results. *Newsletter for the Creative Arts in counseling chapter in CCPA,* Winter, 5–8.

Mann, B. (2012). Canada's single-payer health care system turns 50. http://www.marketwatch. com/story/canadas-single-payer-health-plan-turns-50-2012-07-03.

McKay, M. (2002). *A national soul: Canadian mural painting, 1860s–1930s.* Montreal & Kingston: McGill- Queens University Press.

Oucharek-Deo, M. (2012). A message from the president. *Newsletter of the BC Art Therapy Association, 32*(4), 1–2.

Roy, G. (1962). *The hidden mountain* (Trans. Harry L. Binsse). New York, NY: Harcourt, Brace & World (original work published in 1961).

Saul, J. R. (2009). *A fair country: Telling truths about Canada.* Toronto: Viking Canada/ Penguin Group.

Schwartz, C. L. (1994). Art therapy: Opening doors, video and organizational manual. *Unpublished masters thesis*. Concordia University, Montreal, QC.

Skaife, S. (2001). Making visible: Art therapy and intersubjectivity. *Inscape, 6*(2), 40–50.

Statistics Canada. (June 2010). Low income Lines. 2008–2009. *Statistics Canada catalogue no.* 755F002M, no. 005 ISSN 1707-2840, 22–23.

Villani, J. (1998). *100 Best small art towns in America: Discover creative communities, fresh air, and affordable living*. Santa Fe, NM: John Muir Publications.

Woolf, L. (2003). Art therapy in Canada: Origins and explorations. *Canadian Art Therapy Association Journal, 16*(2), 2–9.

68

Art Therapy in Europe
Maria d'Elia

With subtle irony, artist Jimmie Durham captured the difficulties of grasping Europe as a fixed geographical, political, or cultural concept in his multimedia installation titled "The History of Europe," exhibited at the 2012 dOCUMENTA (13)[1] in Germany:

> Where and what is Europe? It is a fat-looking peninsular protrusion on the west end of the continent of Eurasia. There is much confusion among the Europeans about their identity. One reason for this is that they were conquered by a small group from Rome who came to refer to the East as Asia. For some reason that made the group from Moscow call the lands east of the Ural Mountains Asia also. This makes Europeans believe that Europe is a continent. An additional problem is that Christianity, and later Communism, made more East/West divisions.

A look at the maps of the European continent from different time periods reveals continuously shifting frontiers. The twentieth century alone has been marked by two World Wars, leading to the formation of NATO and Warsaw pact territories. With the termination of the Cold War at the end of the last century, Europe has entered yet another transformational phase.

Today, Europe counts 45 sovereign national and five city-states. Before the fall of the Berlin Wall in 1989, many of these now independent countries were part of the Soviet Union or Yugoslavia. Currently, 28 eastern and western European states have integrated the economic entity of the European Union (EU); however, national diversities still constitute a major challenge for defining and realizing common goals and policies.

Europe is not only characterized by a multitude of ethnicities with distinct cultures, mentalities, and historical and political traditions, but also by more than 100 different spoken languages and local dialects, not to mention several alphabets. Since the enabling of the free movement of professionals between EU member states in 1988 and the opening of the borders of the former Warsaw-pact countries, inner-continental migration and mobility have been on a steady rise, as is the immigration of economic, political, and war refugees from Asia and Africa. This has recreated the Southwestern sphere as a melting pot of races, nationalities, religions, and socio-cultural backgrounds.

The Wiley Handbook of Art Therapy, First Edition. Edited by David E. Gussak and Marcia L. Rosal.
© 2016 John Wiley & Sons, Ltd. Published 2016 by John Wiley & Sons, Ltd.

Based on these premises, it is impossible to give a brief yet comprehensive account of the historical, current, and actual situation of art therapy in Europe. Due to rapid changes, Stoll's statement that "information about art therapy in various nations, whether sparse or abundant, is now often outdated, incomplete or unreliable" (2005, p. 172) ironically applies just as much to her own article as to those to whom she was referring. More accurate information can be retrieved from papers by many different European authors compiled by Kossolapow, Scoble, and Waller (2003, 2005) and from the "Directory of European Education & Training Progammes" of the European Consortium for Arts Therapies Education (ECArTE, 2015), which can be found online. Actual developments can also be monitored through the various art therapy associations (see Appendix A).

Waller's book, *Towards a European art therapy* (1998), remains a valuable reference with regard to accurate analysis and evaluation of problems of definition and professional socialization and identity. Her work was as much a presentation of the results of her investigations as a stipulation of the need for a common European vision. However, while it is correct to state that art therapy exists almost everywhere in Europe, there is still no such thing as *the* European art therapy.

Linguistic Obstacles

As people travel, so do their ideas. This has largely contributed to the spreading of art therapy in recent years, especially to countries formerly under the Soviet reign. An Internet search reveals traces of art therapy activities as far as Moldova, Belarus, Azerbaijan, and Georgia, and a growing number of professional associations, such as in the Ukraine. Virtual mobility via social and professional Internet networks has added visibility and given a strong impetus to the accessibility and exchange of information. Still, language often remains a barrier and contributes to a somewhat lopsided development. Because English is the prevalent vehicular language, the European art therapy scene has always been strongly influenced by British and American models. Europeans, especially from countries where no formal training is available (e.g., Cyprus, Malta, Ukraine), keep seeking art therapy training mainly in the United Kingdom and the United States, as so many others have done in the past, often importing the new information to their home countries. Co-operations between British and American universities and European schools and numerous franchising programs have shaped the transfer of knowledge to other countries, but, over time, the curricula continue to evolve autonomously to adapt to cultural particularities and needs.

Whereas Anglo-American literature is widely studied and some classics have been translated into several European languages, the reverse does not necessarily apply. Upon closer inspection, intensive publication activities abound, especially within the larger nations such as Germany and France, where there is a critical mass of like-minded people to exchange, develop, and cultivate their ideas, allowing for a relatively independent evolution. Unfortunately, these writings remain inaccessible to a wider audience. In French-speaking areas, this is reinforced by the reluctance to use English or other foreign languages. This is particularly evident in Belgium, where art therapy in the Walloon area is closely linked to France, whereas in the Dutch-speaking Flemish area, the situation strongly resembles that in the neighboring Netherlands (another country with a long and rather independent history in the creative therapies). Even though the lack of "contamination" fosters autonomous thinking, it can also create a tendency to reinvent the wheel and slow down the process of innovation. Kossolapow and Mannzmann (2005) made a plea for publishing in both the native language *and* in English: because of the "vital importance that the diversity of expression of the linguistic cultures … be preserved … bilingual or even multilingual expression should be one of the distinguishing features of European art therapy" (p. vii).

Therefore, it is important to note the ambitious joint research project by German universities (University of Applied Sciences, Nürtingen; University of Applied Sciences and Arts, Ottersberg; and the Witten/Herdecke University), which has created a scientific art therapy literature database (see www.arthedata.de). This marks a clear shift from the pioneering stage of the art therapy profession to the establishment of the field as an academic discipline with a specific body of knowledge. Since 2008, all relevant publications are being digitally referenced. They began with German literature from the turn of the nineteenth/twentieth century, but have already extended to books and articles in English, French, and Dutch. Further expansion (to other European languages) could contribute enormously to historical and scientific research.

Problems of Definition

Language is not only a technical communication tool but also an expressive device that bears and reflects emotions, mindsets, and social and cultural concepts. Both the terms "art" and "therapy" have various connotations in many European languages, from which multiple conceptions and practices of art therapy have been derived. Mechler-Schönach (2005) identified 47 different denominations for diverse art therapy practices in the German language alone. "*Kunsttherapie*" is often perceived as being too ambiguous and fraught with associations. "*Kunst*" (art) oscillates from a cultural concept of aesthetic values, or technical qualities embracing all artistic modalities, to a synonym for the visual arts. It can either relate to the creative process or to an aesthetic product, and may evoke specific ideas of form or content, techniques, or genres, often vibrating with several or all of these connotations. In Romanic and Slavic languages, "*art(e)*" generally implies all modalities of creative expression (visual, music, drama, and dance). Consequently, the arts therapies are often taught under a common theoretical body (e.g., France, Portugal), albeit not necessarily as a multimodal approach. Contrarily, the Swedish term "*bildterapi*" ("picture" or "image"-therapy) has its roots in a strong cultural tradition in painting.

Likewise, the meanings of "therapy" range from "healing" to supportive measures; from medical treatment, and curative and re-educational/rehabilitative interventions, to counseling and psychotherapy; and from a narrow clinical understanding to a wider social dimension. The resulting plurality creates a major obstacle for the definition of art therapy, and hence in its recognition as a profession. For example, despite the efforts of the Fédération francaise des art-thérapeutes (Ffat) in France to increase constructive dialogue, the debate among competing factions bears a strong resemblance to the former art-as-therapy (*art-thérapie*) versus art-in-psychotherapy (*psychothérapie médiatisée*) controversy in the United States.

History

A comprehensive and comparative history of the evolution of art therapy in Europe has yet to be written, as the necessary in-depth multilinguistic research constitutes a major challenge. While historical accounts can often be found in art therapy handbooks or on association websites, they appear to be rather general, incomplete, even biased versions of uncritically adopted material from other sources. The omission of concurrent views or parallel developments sometimes is simply due to a lack of thorough research, <u>or because of an author's biases and preferences</u>. Few extensive historical enquiries have been conducted and published. Among the better-documented historiographies are Hogan (2001) for the United Kingdom, Menzen (2000) for the theoretical foundations, and Dunkel and Rech (1990) for the emergence of the profession in Germany. De Bruyn, Haeyen, Husken, Rutten-Saris, and Visser (2009) provided ample information about the Netherlands and Klein (2010) on France.

Pre– and post–World War sources for art therapy as an *idea* can be found in European philosophy, (art) psychology, psychiatry, and pedagogy/education, as well as in social movements and the arts. More precisely, the widespread "moral treatment" approach and occupational therapy in psychiatry, as well as different psychotherapeutic theories, have contributed to the professional development of art therapy. Reform pedagogy, anthroposophy, and artistic theories in the wake of Joseph Beuys's concept of art as "social sculpture"[2] have also played a role, especially in Germany.

Although the creation of specialist associations is no clear-cut indicator for the emergence of art therapy as a *profession*, it proves the existence of a professional self-image and its accompanying political interests. This is often paralleled by the establishment of art therapy education.

In 1959, the International Society for the Psychopathology of Expression (SIPE) was founded as a learned society in France. Its French section, created in 1964, explicitly included a focus on art therapy, becoming SFPE-*AT* in the 1980s. However, the Dutch art therapy association, founded in 1962, has to be considered the oldest professional body, closely followed by the British association, established in 1964. Beginning in the 1970s, associations were constituted mainly in Northern Europe; and throughout the 1980s and early 1990s, associations were founded in Central and South/Southwest Europe. In the late 1990s, and from 2000 on, an expansion to the former Warsaw-pact countries was observed, leading to the creation of the East European Arts Therapy Association in 2011. Recently, smaller states such as Luxembourg, Belgium, and Malta have developed associations (see Appendix A).

Professional Recognition

British art therapists are often envied for having achieved full statutory recognition.[3] With the exception of Switzerland, there is no official regulation in other parts of Europe, although Finnish art therapists were eligible for registration as psychotherapists from 1995 to 2007 when a new psychotherapy law was adopted; unfortunately, non-mental-health professionals such as artists are now excluded from training, registering, and exercising as art psychotherapists. The Swiss model is quite exceptional; since 2011, a national diploma is conferred after passing a state exam to which all arts therapists are subjected, regardless of their prior training. A consensus about the required professional competencies was achieved after many years of negotiations between all concerned parties (Stitelman, 2010).

Ironically, it is the current lack of regulations that guarantees the free exercise of the profession and the unhindered movement of art therapists in most parts of Europe. The real challenge, therefore, lies in the harmonization of definitions, qualifications, and training standards of *future national* regulations, so that art therapists may be granted registration everywhere. Aside from the difficulties in reaching the necessary consensus, differing national legal and educational frameworks complicate reciprocity. The longed-for recognition (social and political) and regulations (educational/ professional standards, quality assurances, and ethics) are expected to help create further job opportunities and adequate remuneration. Of course, the main argument remains the protection of the client.

The Training Landscape

The Bologna accords from 1999[4] for the reformation of university education have had the biggest impact on art therapy training throughout Europe. Forty-seven European countries are currently involved in this ongoing process. The goal of the reform is to ensure mutual recognition and comparability of standards of higher education qualifications to increase the mobility of students and professionals. Generally, studies are now to be divided into three cycles with a modular course structure: bachelor's (3–4 years), master's (1–2 years), and doctorate studies.

Before the 1980s, private art therapy education was the rule, and many of those currently teaching at universities and who received prior training did so privately. Now, more university art therapy training courses are being established. This trend began in the late 1980s and early 1990s in the Netherlands, France, Germany, Scandinavia, and Spain. In some Eastern countries that were formerly behind the iron curtain, there have been a series of recent and dynamic start-up programs (i.e., the Baltic States and Hungary). At the same time, existing programs have adapted to the new requirements, such as the training at Sorbonne/Descartes in Paris, which has become France's first MA program. All Dutch programs have undergone scrutiny by state-certified agencies for academic accreditation.

The growing attractiveness of university qualifications has created new market pressures for the competing private institutions. Academic titles are granted protection and clearly distinguish the trained professional from the self-declared provider, leaving the owners of private training certificates to prove their worth. In 2011, an initial cooperation between the over 30-year-old, well-established German private training institution, the Deutscher Arbeitskreis für Gestaltungstherapie, and the Katholische Hochschule für Sozialwesen, in Berlin, eventually led to a merger and the creation of a baccalaureate program.

Nevertheless, the training situation in Europe is still heterogeneous and confusing, making Waller's statement, that "there are many different levels and astonishingly varied syllabuses even within the same country" (1998, p. 114), ring as true today as when it was written. This statement applies just as much to the academic world as to private training. Art therapy can be studied full-time or part-time as a separate course at art academies, universities, polytechnical schools, or universities of applied sciences. Art therapy can also be studied as a specialization within another discipline, such as curative pedagogy or social work, as in Finland, Germany, Slovakia, Slovenia, and Croatia. Bachelor's degrees are bestowed for part-time further education courses for experienced health professionals, as well as for 3–4 year fulltime graduate foundation courses such as in Germany, the Netherlands, Finland, Belgium, and Estonia; the latter integrate both the artistic training as well as the relevant psychological foundations plus methodological therapy training and supervised placements. Full-time-equivalent programs of 1–2-year duration, catering to artists, art educators, pedagogues, psychologists, and other psycho-social professionals, confer a certificate, a "university diploma," or a master's degree. Other, so-called consecutive master's degree programs, often with an emphasis on research, are tailored to trained art therapists.

Although academic art therapy education has gained momentum, private education is still the prevalent model in the European South (Italy), Southwest (Portugal), Southeast (Greece), and the Centre-East, such as in Austria, Poland, Bulgaria, and the Czech Republic.

A primary academic degree in the fine arts, education, psychology, or in the social or medical field is usually an entry requirement for art therapy training, but universities may validate professional experience to grant access to a program. Some private institutions also recruit their students from among nonacademic health workers with proven professional experience. This, too, is bound to change, because many such health professions are in the process of developing academic curricula (e.g., nursing or occupational therapy in Germany).

Without venturing into a discussion of the diverse (psycho)therapeutic orientations and the related coursework content, extreme variations in scale and scope can be noted. In France, a continuing education university diploma may be awarded for as little as 60 hours of coursework. Stepped models also exist, mostly but not exclusively in private offerings: one can book a "basics" course; begin as an "*animateur d'ateliers d'expression*"; go on to "practitioner," "médiateur," or "art-therapy interventions specialist"; and then proceed to become a "full" art therapist. All graduates of these programs seek their good fortune in a market where the differences are so often ignored.

Professional Identity and Ownership

The professional socialization processes of art therapists clearly differ greatly within single countries and across Europe. Therefore, the construction of a professional identity remains a conceptual as well as a structural problem. Officially, claims to the field are motivated on the grounds of specialist knowledge, but a closer look often reveals interests aligned to the preservation of status. In many countries, psychotherapy regulations are still missing, such as in Luxembourg, or registration is restricted to doctors or psychologists, such as in Italy, Hungary, and Bulgaria. Therefore, the initial qualification of the art therapist often impacts the profession to the effect of creating different "classes" of art therapists, even when their actual art therapy training does not distinguish between these levels.

The identity confusion is mirrored by the existence of different types of associations active in the field: there are learned societies (such as the SIPE and its various regional sections), registered associations for the purpose of offering private training, and professional bodies that defend political interests or define and promote standards for the safeguarding of the quality of education and the exercise of the profession. They sometimes have overlapping objectives; some specialize on visual art therapy, while others embrace all modalities, especially in smaller states. In a number of countries, rivalry between several groups claiming supremacy can be observed.

Unlike music, dance, and drama therapy, art therapy is still lacking a European association. No actual evidence can be found of the European Advisory Board of National Art Therapy Associations (EABONATA) initiative from 1991. ECArTE currently represents only 32 academic bodies from 14 countries. Moreover, it is not restricted to visual art therapy. However, its biannual conferences generally draw ample attendance from a wide audience and provide opportunity for exchange. The growing number of international conferences and student conventions (see www.association4arts.wix.com/4arts) testify to the increasing openness and mutual interest among art therapists.

Conclusion

Europe's diversity is at the same time a challenge and a chance for its art therapists. European art therapists have much to gain from conceiving of themselves as a professional and scientific community. Constructive dialogue and the willingness to openly tackle the problems of definition and training standards could actually bring new incentives to the field and thus create favorable conditions for innovative developments. Both the shift toward academic programs and the strong European tradition in theoretical substantiation are leading to increased research activities, and will guarantee the art therapy profession in Europe a promising future.

Appendix A

Homepages of art(s) therapy associations in Europe (with emphasis on professional organizations), and year of establishment (where known) © Maria d'Elia. (No associations have been found for: Bosnia-Herzegovina, Macedonia, Montenegro (all former Yugoslavia), Albania, Armenia, Azerbaijan, Belarus, Cyprus, Georgia, Kazakhstan, Moldova, and the five city states: San Marino, Vatican City, Liechtenstein, Andorra, and Monaco.)

Austria: www.kunsttherapie-fachverband.org; *founded as a society (ÖGKT) in 1992 and reorganized as a professional organization (ÖFKG) in 1997*; http://f-mgt.at *2003*; www.anthroposophische-kunsttherapien.at *2010*; www.ikt.or.at/ *(ÖBKT) 2013*

Belgium: www.bvct-abat.be *2010*; www.art-therapeutes.be; www.art-the.be; www.artesana.be

Bulgaria: http://arttherapy-bulgaria.org *2006*

Croatia: www.savez-spuh.hr/vijesti/modaliteti/art-terapija *1998*

Czech Republic: www.arteterapie.cz *1994*; www.expresivniterapie.org *(umbrella organization arts therapies)*

Denmark: www.kunstterapeuter.dk *1994*

East European Arts Therapy Association: www.eeata.net *2011*

Estonia: www.loovteraapiad.ee *(umbrella organization arts therapies) 2004*

European Academy for Anthroposophic Art Therapy Trainings (EAAAT): www.eaaat.org

European Consortium for Arts Therapies Education (ECArTE): www.ecarte.info

Finland: www.suomentaideterapiayhdistys.fi *1974*; www.kuvataideterapia.fi *1979*

France: www.sfpe-art-therapie.fr, *founded as SFPE in 1964; changed to SFPE-AT when art therapy was incorporated in the 1980s*; www.inecat.org/L-association-art-therapie.html *1981*; http://ffat-federation.org *1988*; *refounded 2000*; http://artherapie.levillage.org

Germany: http://bvakt.de *1978*; http://dagtp.de *1979*; www.dgkt.de *1981*; http://vdkt.de *1981*; www.bkmt.de *1986*; www.dfkgt.de *1992*; www.bag-kuenstlerische-therapien.de *(federal arts therapies work group) 2008*

Greece: www.art-therapy.gr *1989*; http://arttherapists.gr *2005*

Hungary: www.mmszke.hu *2003*; www.muvterapia.hu, www.facebook.com/MagyarMuveszetterapiasTarsasag *2009*

Iceland: www.listmedferd.com *1998*

Ireland: www.iacat.ie *1986*—**Northern Ireland**: www.nigat.org *1976*

Italy: www.arttherapyit.org *1982*; http://digilander.libero.it/apiart/home.html *(arts therapies umbrella organization) www.apiart.eu, 1999*; www.artiterapie-italia.it *2011*

Latvia: http://arttherapy.lv *2005*

Lithuania: www.ldtta.org *1997*; www.menuterapija.lt *2010*

Luxembourg: www.alatd.lu *2008*

Malta: www.catsmalta.org *2005*

The Netherlands: www.beeldendetherapie.org *1962*; www.kunstzinnigetherapie.nl *1970*; www.vaktherapie.nl *(umbrella organization creative therapies) 2006*

Norway: www.angelfire.com/nf/billedterapi/tidligere-index.html *1978/2001*; www.kunstterapi.org *2002*; www.kunst-uttrykksterapi.no *2006*

Poland: www.kajros.pl *2003*; www.arteterapia.pl *2007*

Portugal: www.arte-terapia.com *1996*

Romania: http://expresive.ro; *2009*

Russia: http://rusata.ru *1997*; www.art-therapy.ru *1998*

Serbia: www.iap.org.rs *1999*

Slovakia: www.terratherapeutica.sk *2000*

Slovenia: www.szut.si *2004*

Spain: www.arteterapia.org.es *2003*; www.grefart.es *2006*; http://www.asociacion-ath.org *2008*; http://www.murartt.org *2009*; http://feapa.es *(AT associations federation) 2010*; http://www.andart-andalucia-arteterapia.blogspot.com.es *2011*; http://www.arts7.es *2012*

Sweden: www.bildterapi.se *1997*; *reorganized 2006*; www.konstterapi.se

Switzerland: www.fiac.ch *1987*; http://araet.ch *1993*; www.svakt.ch *1994*; www.art-therapeute.ch *2000*; www.gpk-verband.net *2001*; www.kskv-casat.ch *(federal arts therapies umbrella) 2002*

Turkey: http://www.sanatpsikoterapileridernegi.org *2012*

UK: www.baat.org *1964*; www.aata-uk.org

Ukraine: www.art-therapy.org.ua *2003*

Endnotes

1 Curated international exhibition of modern and contemporary art that takes place every 5 years in Kassel, Germany. In 2012, it was centered on forms of artistic research and the investigation of the social and therapeutic functions of art in a broad sense.
2 See http://en.wikipedia.org/wiki/Joseph_Beuys.
3 See Chapter 66 on art therapy in the United Kingdom, by Jill Westwood.
4 The official Bologna Process website: www.ehea.info.

References

de Bruyn, J., Haeyen, S., Husken, B., Rutten-Saris, M., & Visser, H. (2009). *Handboek beeldende therapie: Uit de verf* (pp. 25–77). Houten: Bohn Stafleu van Loghum.

Dunkel, J., & Rech, P. (1990). Zur Entwicklung und inhaltlichen Bestimmung des Begriffes "Kunsttherapie" und verwandter Begrifflichkeiten. In H. Petzold & I. Orth (Eds.), *Die neuen Kreativitätstherapien: Handbuch der Kunsttherapie, Band I* (pp. 73–89). Paderborn: Junfermann Verlag.

ECArTE. (2015). Directory of European Education & Training Progammes. Accessed August 8th 2015 at http://www.ecarte.info/membership/directory

Hogan, S. (2001). *Healing arts: The history of art therapy*. London and Philadelphia: Jessica Kingsley Publishers.

Klein, J. -P. (2010). *L'art-thérapie* (7th ed., pp. 5–45). Paris: P.U.F. "Que sais-je?."

Kossolapow, L., & Mannzmann, A. (2005). Introduction. In L. Kossolapow, S. Scoble, & D. Waller (Eds.), *Arts—Therapies—Communications, Vol. III: European arts therapy—Different approaches to a unique discipline—Opening regional portals* (pp. iv–xxi). Münster: LIT Verlag.

Kossolapow, L., Scoble, S., & Waller, D. (Eds.) (2003). *Arts—Therapies—Communications, Vol. II: On the way to a regional European arts therapy*. Münster: LIT Verlag.

Kossolapow, L., Scoble, S., & Waller, D. (Eds.) (2005). *Arts—Therapies—Communications, Vol. III: European arts therapy—Different approaches to a unique discipline—Opening regional portals*. Münster: LIT Verlag.

Mechler-Schönach, C. (2005). InSzene Kunsttherapie. In F. von Spreti, P. Martius, & H. Förstl (Eds.), *Kunsttherapie bei psychischen Störungen* (pp. 9–22). München, Jena: Elsevier Urban & Fischer.

Menzen, K. H. (2000). *Eine kleine illustrierte Geschichte der Kunsttherapie*. Butzbach-Griedel: Afra-Verlag.

Stitelman, J. (2010). L'art-thérapie, lorsque la création est au service du développement humain: une nouvelle profession. In *L'art-thérapie, une profession à part entière* (pp. 87–94). *Proceedings of the Ffat (Fédération francaise des art-thérapeutes) 10ième weekend d'échanges*.

Stoll, B. (2005). Growing pains: The international development of art therapy. *The Arts in Psychotherapy, 23*, 171–191.

Waller, D. (1998). *Towards a European art therapy*. London: Open University Press.

69

Art Therapy "Down Under": Perspectives on the Profession from Australia and New Zealand

Annette M. Coulter

The growth and development of art therapy in Australia and New Zealand is a tale of collaborative necessity, integrative orientation, and adaptation to local culture, as art therapists promote, expand, and apply their art therapy knowledge to local networks, systems, and culture. It is also a tale of often working in professional isolation or in small groups, of being unappreciated in terms of financial remuneration, and of choosing to work extra hours to profile and promote what art therapy has to offer at forums, conferences, and professional events. Until recently, there has been little published about Australian and New Zealand art therapy activities, despite its establishment in Australia in the early 1980s (Coulter, 2006) and in New Zealand in the early 1990s (Woodcock, 2007). From 1988, the most accurate accounts of art therapy development in Australia and New Zealand are found in the regular newsletters of the Australian and New Zealand Arts Therapy Association (ANZATA), and the recent launch of the *Australian and New Zealand Journal of Art Therapy* (ANZJAT), an annual publication promoting research, education, and clinical practice from perspectives that include Southeast Asia.

ANZATA

ANZATA is the current professional association for the two countries, and there are strong links with Southeast Asian representation from Singapore. From its inception, the art therapy association had intentions to join with New Zealand to form ANZATA (Edwards, 1990, 1991). To this end, New Zealand representation was encouraged and contributions to committees and conferences supported. However, this union was only recently implemented officially as ANZATA in 2006.

The Wiley Handbook of Art Therapy, First Edition. Edited by David E. Gussak and Marcia L. Rosal.
© 2016 John Wiley & Sons, Ltd. Published 2016 by John Wiley & Sons, Ltd.

Literature Review

Internationally, the only *known* documented comments about Australian and New Zealand art therapy were impressionistic accounts "written by visiting European and North American art therapists" (Edwards, 2004, p. 134). Significant contributors include North American art therapists such as Franklin (1996), Campanelli (1996), and Campanelli and Kaplan (1996); and Canadian and British art therapists such as Gilroy and Hanna (1998). Campanelli and Kaplan wrote a personal account of their Australian teaching experiences in Perth, referring to the influence of indigenous culture, the geographic proximity to Southeast Asian cultures, and the work of Australian art therapy pioneer Jo Allison (Campanelli & Kaplan, 1996). Gilroy and Hanna (1998) shared a collaborative experience in Sydney, where they researched their combined interest in issues of conflict in cultures in Australia, similar issues to when art therapy was pioneered throughout North America, Canada, and Britain.

The Development of Art Therapy in Australia and New Zealand

Australia is a vast country, largely uninhabited due to extensive regions of predominantly dry desert and sparse scrubland. Most of the 23 million inhabitants live around the coastal fringes, and the capital cities of each of the seven states have densely populated urban sprawl. By comparison, New Zealand is significantly smaller, a vegetation-rich moist land of significant rainfall, tall mountains, deep rivers, pine forests, and ferns. In Australia, training programs were established in the 1990s, and ANZATA has ensured that regular conferences and symposiums have taken place on either side of what is colloquially termed "the ditch" (the expanse of water that lies between Australia and New Zealand).

In both Australia and New Zealand, art therapists from different training backgrounds were destined to gravitate together motivated by professional isolation and curiosity of "otherness." In art therapy development, Australia and New Zealand was always destined to be a meeting place for European and North American concepts (Coulter, 2006; Hogan & Coulter, 2014; Woodcock, 2007). Over time, the sense of mutual respect is most evident in the development of art therapy in Australia (Coulter, 2006) and New Zealand (Woodcock, 2007).

In New Zealand, a similar partnership built on a shared interest to promote art therapy was established between Sedgewick (1991) and Jones (1991). This trend is also reflected in the recent development of art therapy in Asia (Kalmanowitz, Potash, & Chan, 2012), and will continue as art therapists meet outside their countries of origin, migrate to new locations, or work collaborative on a jointly funded project such as disaster relief. It is only where European and North American trained art therapist are establishing art therapy and working cooperatively that mutual respect can be promoted and built upon.

Training: integrating difference

In Australia, there are currently three master's training programs recognized by ANZATA as meeting art therapy training standards: these are from the University of Western Sydney (UWS), LaTrobe University, and, most recently, the University of

Queensland. The UWS has the longest running program, established in 1993. Although originally modeled more as training in art psychotherapy, this has recently changed to be allied more with a generalist counseling training course. For some, this is disappointing; however, it can be argued that this curriculum change is advantageous for art therapists seeking employment. The LaTrobe program is the only recognized program in the state of Victoria, and it attracts students from New Zealand and Asia. The program at the University of Queensland is one of several programs for allied health in the Health Sciences and is more closely linked to art psychotherapy.

Australian and New Zealand art therapy education includes aspects of British and North American models, adopted into a unique set of training standards that respect differences, and bridge both European and North America origins. At the inception of training, lecturers were generally appointed from overseas; however, more recently, training programs have begun to employ Australian art therapists. This trend to assume that something from overseas is better than something "home-grown" is not confined to the profession of art therapy, and is sometimes linked to the "cultural inferiority complex" of a relatively young country. This might be unheard of in Britain or North America, but importing overseas expertise is more easily accepted in younger countries with colonial histories.

In New Zealand, art therapy development took place in the 1990s, including the establishment of the first post-graduate arts therapy training program (Woodcock, 2007). One of the earliest accounts of New Zealand art therapy are the impressions shared by Franklin after a 3-month sabbatical (Franklin, 1996). The training program at Whitecliffe College, Auckland, provides a research master's in the creative arts therapies.

It is interesting to note that, in both New Zealand and Australia, a creative arts therapies interest group laid the foundation for membership and networking. In Australia, this organization was the Network for Creativity in Therapy through the Arts (NECTA) (Coulter, 2006). In New Zealand, the Creative Therapies Association of Aotearoa (CTAA) brought like-minded creative therapists together for an inaugural conference (Miller, 2007).

Employment issues

It is not easy to find work in a designated "art therapist" position in either Australia or New Zealand. Although some graduates manage to negotiate an art therapy position from successful internships, practicums, or placements, it is more often than not a poorly paid and under-utilized position that exploits the expertise of the new art therapy graduate. In Australia, salary awards vary from state to state, depending on the job title and band under which the position is established. More often than not, successful employment is achieved by accepting a position titled under another profession or a more generic title such as "child therapist," "activities coordinator," "art specialist educator/consultant," "clinical coordinator," or a generalist counselor or therapist position that often only requires a graduate degree. Employment difficulties have caused a significant number of disillusioned art therapists to leave the profession. This is reflected in the number of registered professional art therapists in ANZATA, which has remained stagnant for some years despite the fact that, each year, there is a new cohort of graduating art therapists. As people leave the profession, new graduates join, but the consequent number of registered professionals remains the same.

The fact that until recently many students were trained by art therapists who had never worked as Australian clinicians must impact in some way on the generally poor attrition rates of the profession, possibly contributing to the problem of establishing post-training employment for graduates. On British and North American programs, this situation would be likely regarded as unethical and unfeasible.

Working with indigenous cultures

Adapting the use of art therapy to indigenous cultures has been at the forefront of art therapy development in Australia and New Zealand. Before training programs were established, art therapists were working with disadvantaged populations, including Australian Aboriginals and the native Maori communities of New Zealand. Art therapy is a particularly effective way to work with indigenous cultures because it respects the role of the traditional arts as part of its identity (Ault, 1988; Campanelli, Stuhr, & Barger-Cottrill, 1990; Franklin, 1996; Kalmanowitz et al., 2012; Westrich, 1994).

Australia and New Zealand have significant indigenous populations that appreciate the arts. Specifically, art is important to community life and cultural identity, and they appreciate its healing potential for inner spiritual well-being. Culturally specific contributions that are unique to the practice of art therapy are promoted in clinical placements and alternative employment options, such as working in remote communities or Aboriginal detention centers.

In 2011, *Relationships Australia* incorporated art therapy into the teaching methodology for its Aboriginal counselors training program. Aboriginal counselors requested more visual input into their course content, and found that input from art therapists made the rigorous training more accessible.

Therapists have been working with indigenous populations in both Australia and New Zealand, appreciating the added visual component to their work. Art therapy has been used effectively with various Aboriginal communities and populations in Australia. Although this work is largely undocumented, it has included: an Aboriginal women's circle; individual work with an Aboriginal artist; male Aboriginal adolescents in detention; and work with remote Aboriginal communities and clinical placements with Aboriginal populations, particularly in Western Australia (Campanelli, 1996).

In 1991, Australian and New Zealand family therapists invited an Aboriginal woman to address the family therapy conference, and another Aboriginal woman was asked "to create a painting that would help family therapists understand the plight of many of her generation." This painting was displayed at the conference, and the Aboriginal woman "told ... the meaning of its symbols, of her agonizing struggle for a sense of family and Aboriginal identity" (Brown & Larner, 1991, p. 175).

Australian and New Zealand Models of Practice

Narrative therapy

White and Epston developed their theory of "narrative therapy" through their trans-Tasman connections, and this model has significantly influenced art therapy. In Australia, the narrative therapy movement has produced some models of "home grown" art therapy. Such notions as "re-authoring lives" and "externalizing conversations" particularly suit art therapy (Linnell, 2009; White & Epston, 1989). Working with adolescents with an integration model of narrative therapy through a solution-focused approach was used successfully with resistant clients and transient youth (Coulter, 2012). Both groups of clients were not keen to commit to long-term art therapy. The solution-focused model provided a positive experience for a single-session contact; "it is recommended to assume this may be a one-off session … that their experience is positive, so that they feel inclined to attend in the future" (p. 90). The narrative approach focuses on the client's story and provides opportunities to consider an alternate story, thus re-authoring their life experiences. Through this narrative approach, art is used therapeutically to separate the person from the problem, and "finding an alternate solution" and "to imagine an alternate story" through visual means are encouraged (p. 85).

Linnell (2009) described a narrative model of art therapy in working with Aboriginal children. Rather than focusing on case content and the client/therapist dichotomy, therapy becomes "moments in the emerging shape of a post-colonial politics of poetics of art therapy [and concludes that] art therapy can contribute to effective acts of reconciliation" (p. 25).

Interactive drawing therapy (IDT)

IDT is a uniquely successful application of therapeutic drawing interventions that was developed in New Zealand in the 1990s (Withers, 2006). Training in the IDT method began in New Zealand and Australia, and is now expanding to Asia. It is particularly popular with school counselors and non–art therapy informed therapists who wish to use drawing interventions more effectively in their work without completing a master's degree in art therapy. The underlying principles of IDT practice are successful because they are indirectly built on similar foundations as art therapy. For example, IDT upholds that the client manages content while the therapist manages process, a principle reminiscent of Kramer's notion that the therapist "wants neither to impose his ideas not to elicit any specific information, but that the therapist is there to help him in any way he can to achieve what he wants to do" (Kramer, 1971, p. 44). The difference is that IDT is restricted to using only wax crayons. For this reason, some art therapists do not regard IDT as "art therapy"; however, it is interesting to note that, in the recent cohort of IDT teachers, three of the four were art therapists from Australia and New Zealand (Hogan & Coulter, 2014).

Similarities and differences between IDT and art therapy are not being examined here, but it can be argued that the structure of IDT practice offers a set of practice-based principles that are packaged in a 4-day foundation training that best practice in art therapy would easily consider. These guiding principles take the therapeutic use of drawing into a marketable realm as an effective "tool" that can be mastered in a short amount of time by allied health professionals. It could be argued that IDT's success is because it upholds principles that are closely linked to particular aspects of art therapy, but the uniqueness of the IDT method is in its succinct and practical effectiveness that, if followed explicitly, offers guaranteed success that is easy to grasp. The growing popularity and general influence of the IDT method in Australian and

New Zealand therapy practice is assisting the ongoing appreciation, promotion, and acceptance of art therapy.

Both art therapy and IDT promote the integration of unconscious processes by bridging the client's internal and external worlds as viewed through an image-making process that sits external to the client. In the IDT method, this viewing of what is "on the page" is an important part of the therapeutic process (Withers, 2009). Similarities and differences between the IDT method and art therapy practice are examined elsewhere (Hogan & Coulter, 2014), but what IDT offers is a tangible structure for the delivery of more accessible principles of art therapy. It could be argued that IDT is the scaffolding upon which art therapy can hang. Initially, IDT seems related to but different from art therapy; however, the richness that IDT brings to the importance of mark-making and "working the page" becomes increasingly important as one's understanding of the IDT method develops. IDT originally stated that it was quite different from art therapy; however, owing to a request from ANZATA, this statement has been withdrawn from the training manual.

Promoting "Difference"

Maintaining an international perspective (Hogan & Coulter, 2014) is the most promising future for art therapy in Australia and New Zealand, and the ASEAN region. Australia and New Zealand are multi-cultural societies that embrace differences and are flexible to change. Art therapists who have been invited from overseas have stimulated thinking and helped educate other professional groups in promoting published professional expertise. Harriet Wadeson first visited Australia in 1982, presenting at one of the first conferences; Bobbi Stoll and John Henzell were keynote speakers at the inaugural conference in 1989; Marcia Rosal conducted the first Australian doctoral research in art therapy at Queensland University (Rosal, 1985); Shirley Riley promoted a recent publication in 1995; Andrea Gilroy and Michael Campanelli lectured; Nancy Slater stimulated the promotion of the LaTrobe art therapy program; and Margarete Hanna, Frances Kaplan, Edith Kramer, Lucia Cappacione, and others have also contributed to Australian art therapy over the years as university lecturers and visiting lecturers.

In this joining that continues today (Potash, Bardot, & Ho, 2012), the agenda is always to accommodate, celebrate, and promote differences. The over-riding goal to establish the art therapy profession in a new country is that the integration of differences is tolerated and encouraged. This has been observed by visiting overseas art therapists (Campanelli & Kaplan, 1996; Gilroy & Hanna, 1998; Slater, 1999). Increasingly, Australian and New Zealand art therapists are commenting on their cross-cultural experiences (Brownlow in Woodcock, 2007; Coulter, 2006; Jones, 1991; Sedgewick, 1991), and, as the profession grows throughout the world, there is a broader discourse that is taking place about the challenge of harnessing differences (Gilroy, Tipple, & Brown, 2012; Potash et al., 2012). For too long, the offshore development of art therapy has looked to UK and US origins for confirmation and direction, support and validation (Hogan & Coulter, 2014). The realization that art therapy must adapt to the culture, beliefs, and politics of the geographic location in which it finds itself is gaining momentum as local art therapists, regardless of their training origins, work together to promote the local development of the profession.

References

Ault, R. E. (1988). Social application of the arts. *Art Therapy, Journal of the American Art Therapy Association, 5*(1), 10.

Brown, C., & Larner, G. (1991). Every dot has a meaning. *Australian and New Zealand Journal of Family Therapy, 12*(3), 127–132.

Campanelli, M. (1996). Pioneering in Perth: Art therapy in Western Australia. *Art Therapy, Journal of the American Art Therapy Association, 13*(2), 131–135.

Campanelli, M., & Kaplan, F. F. (1996). Art therapy in Oz: Report from Australia. *The Arts in Psychotherapy, 23*(1), 61–67.

Campanelli, M., Stuhr, P., & Barger-Cottrill, S. (1990). Trails—a drug and alcohol prevention program which utilizes traditional Indian culture and artistic production. *The Journal of Multi-cultural and Cross-cultural Research in Art Education, 8*(1), 18–28

Coulter, A. (2006). Art therapy in Australia: The extended family. *Australian and New Zealand Journal of Art Therapy, 1*(1), 8–18.

Coulter, A. (2012). Contemporary art therapy with transient youth. In H. Burt (ed.), *Art Therapy and Postmodernism: Creative Healing through a Prism* (pp. 83–93). London, UK: Jessica Kingsley Publishers.

Edwards, C. (1990). Editorial. *Newsletter of Australian National Art Therapy Association, 2*(2), 1.

Edwards, C. (1991). Editorial. *Newsletter of Australian National Art Therapy Association, 3*(1), 1–4.

Edwards, D. (2004). Art therapy in Australia. *Art Therapy* (pp. 134–138). London, Thousand Oaks, New Delhi: Sage Publications.

Franklin, M. (1996). A place to stand: Maori culture-tradition in a contemporary art studio. *Art Therapy, Journal of the American Art Therapy Association, 13*(2), 126–130.

Gilroy, A., & Hanna, M. (1998). Conflict and culture in art therapy: An Australian perspective. In A. R. Hiscox & A. C. Calisch (Eds.), *Tapestry of cultural issues in art therapy* (pp. 249–275). London, UK: Jessica Kingsley Publishers.

Gilroy, A., Tipple, R., & Brown, C. (2012). *Assessment in art therapy.* London, UK: Routledge.

Hogan, S., & Coulter, A. (2014). *The introductory guide to art therapy: Experiential teaching and learning for students and practitioners.* New York, NY: Routledge.

Jones, M. (1991). Letters to the editor. *Newsletter of the Australian National Art Therapy Association, 3*(1), 3–4.

Kalmanowitz, D., Potash, J. S., & Chan, S. M. (2012). *Art therapy in Asia: To the bone or wrapped in silk.* London, UK: Jessica Kingsley Publishers.

Kramer, E. (1971). *Art as therapy with children.* New York, NY: Schocken Books, Inc.

Linnell, S. (2009). Becoming "otherwise": A story of a collaborative and narrative approach to art therapy with indigenous kids "in care." *Australian and New Zealand Journal of Art Therapy, 4*(1), 15–26.

Miller, C. (2007). Development of the arts therapies professions within Aotearoa/New Zealand. *Australian and New Zealand Journal of Art Therapy, 2*, 21–27.

Potash, J. S., Bardot, H., & Ho, R. (2012). Conceptualizing international art therapy education standards. *The Arts in Psychotherapy, 39*(2), 143–150.

Rosal, M. (1985). *The use of art therapy to modify the locus of control and adaptive behaviour of behaviour disordered students.* Doctoral dissertation, Schonell Education Research Centre, University of Queensland, Brisbane.

Sedgewick, C. (1991). Letters to the editor. *Newsletter of the Australian National Art Therapy Association, 3*(1), 2–3.

Slater, N. (1999). *Keynote address.* Tenth Annual Conference of the Australian National Art Therapy Association, Brisbane, September.

Westrich, C. A. (1994). Art therapy with culturally different clients. *Art Therapy, Journal of the American Art Therapy Association, 11*(3), 187–190.

White, M., & Epston, D. (1989). *Literate means to therapeutic ends.* Adelaide, SA: Dulwich Centre Publication.

Withers, R. (2006). Interactive drawing therapy: Working with therapeutic imagery. *New Zealand Journal of Counseling, 26*(4), 1–14.

Withers, R. (2009). The therapeutic process of interactive drawing therapy. *New Zealand Journal of Counseling, 29*(2), 73–90.

Woodcock, M. (2007). A viewpoint and reflections on the development of art therapy in New Zealand. *Australian and New Zealand Journal of Art Therapy, 2*, 8–20.

70

Cultural Context and the Practice of Art Therapy in Asia
Elizabeth Coss[1] with John Wong

The term "Asia" is a bit of a misnomer, and is believed to be a Western construct. Asia is the largest and most populous continent in the world, and is incredibly diverse. This chapter covers the cultural context and practice of art therapy in the three traditional regions of Asia—East Asia (EA), South Asia (SA), and Southeast Asia (SEA). Another chapter in this book (Chapter 72, by Amar Abdulla Behbehani) addresses the Middle East, currently known as Western Asia (WA), as a separate section. Although Russia is considered part of Europe and Asia, its most populous part is currently in Europe, and hence it is included in the section on Europe (Chapter 68, by Maria d'Elia). Akrotiri and Dhekelia and British Indian Ocean Territories are British overseas territories, which are also not considered here.

The research for this chapter examined the cultural context and models of practice that have developed in Asia. Approximately 27 people—clinicians or others deemed as significant in the development of the field in Asia—were interviewed: 19 were resident Asian art or expressive (arts) therapists, three were art therapists trained in Asia but of European or South African descent, two were expressive (arts) therapists of Asian descent currently living in the United States but with strong ties to the East, one was a resident Asian university professor and his staff member, and one assisted this professor with work done in Southeast Asia. While it is understood that there are significant art therapy contributions by expatriates in the region, this chapter will focus on the work of resident Asian art therapists.

The first section of this chapter focuses on the historical development of mental health, issues of cultural context and relevance, settings, ethics, regulations, challenges, and limitations of practice in the field of art and expressive (art) therapies. The second section consists of key country reports that includes a sampling of the work and challenges from resident Asian art therapists who are practicing in the three regions.

The Wiley Handbook of Art Therapy, First Edition. Edited by David E. Gussak and Marcia L. Rosal.
© 2016 John Wiley & Sons, Ltd. Published 2016 by John Wiley & Sons, Ltd.

Historical Context: Mental Health in Asia

Art and expressive arts therapists of Asian descent who were interviewed indicated that countries such as China and Japan have an ancient practice of using art as a form of therapy that would be useful to Western practitioners to understand and incorporate into their work. From brush painting and calligraphy to the art of bonsai and bokei, the region is rich with practice that has been used for thousands of years to express and sublimate feelings. This was supported by feedback from graduates of the master's program in Singapore. They felt that the training and support they received from their local lecturers and supervisors helped them in working cross-culturally even after they left Singapore.

Initially, many resident Asian art therapists received their training in Western countries, which can be as diverse and varied in practice as the East. Many countries have a contingent of artists who are doing therapeutic work. Some of these local therapeutic art practices may be considered a precursor to a professionally developed field. As training programs have developed in the region, the location of training is quickly changing. Korea, Singapore, and Taiwan are all strong in college and university training. Institutes that provide expressive arts therapy training are emerging in China and Japan, and more culturally appropriate training and practice is developing.

Cultural Context

There was strong desire from the art therapists who were interviewed to have Asian art therapists speak for themselves and about the way the field is developing in their own countries. Since the field initially drew from Western education and therapeutic practices, and in some cases Western practitioners, there was frustration expressed by resident Asian art therapists about the lack of understanding of their own cultural norms both in theory and in practice. The contributors clarified differences in Eastern and Western philosophies, which included that the Eastern perspective tends to focus more on family than on self, adheres sometimes to controversial views on gender roles, and believes more in gathering measurable data regarding practice rather than relying on qualitative methods. Korea has been at the forefront of realizing the need for the creative arts in therapy to be more suitable to the Asian psyche than traditional Western models.

Key Cultural Norms and Beliefs

Yalom (2005) emphasized the need for affinity and recognition of cultural norms in the dynamics of group process as important in the therapeutic healing process. This is important for Western readers and therapists to remember with regard to the Asian psyche. Overall, those who were interviewed were somewhat reluctant to discuss diversity, gender, and other issues considered controversial, and their impact on therapy, a practice that is still not fully accepted in some Asian cultures. Openness is not always seen as a virtue in Asia, where one often finds other ways to get the needed outcomes. This is viewed as normal behavior and corresponds to a philosophy of "saving face" in a culture with collectivist values (Foo, Merrick, & Kazantzis, 2006). The respondents reinforced this notion, stressing that issues such as filial piety, family hierarchy, moderation, and protecting others from embarrassment can greatly influence the therapeutic dynamic, especially with parents. However, it was also recognized that some Asian values are changing, as some indicated a desire for more open, public debate about diversity, racism, and sexual harassment in order to address these issues in both the public and private spheres.

Settings, Ethics, and the Challenges and Limitations of Practices

Art therapists in Asia often find themselves working in schools, hospitals, special needs facilities, prisons, and private practice. In Southeast Asia, there have been positive outcomes with its use with former combatants in rehabilitation centers. Some Asian countries, such as Korea, Singapore, and Taiwan, have more developed mental health support systems. In the developing countries, art therapists are working toward local supervision guidelines, specified reporting procedures, and referral resources.

There was a feeling among the practitioners that *ethics, licensing, and/or credentials* are important as the field grows. Korea and Taiwan now have the required credentials to practice. Singapore currently aligns itself with the arts therapy credentials in Asia Pacific, but is expected to have a credentialing process established through its own Ministry of Health soon. In Japan and Hong Kong, where the foundation of the field is still developing, credentialing was recognized as an important need. In countries where the mental health structure is very limited, such as Pakistan, there is a sense of urgency. A need for clarification and regulation between trained clinicians, artists doing therapeutic work, and others who claim to be art therapists after taking a workshop or short course was voiced by many resident Asian art therapists. For those who trained overseas and returned to their own country, they found limited local supervision and a lack of malpractice insurance. Many of those interviewed emphasized the importance of being multilingual or having collaborators who (1) can accurately translate, and (2) are aware of the confidentiality and therapeutic processes, given the vast array of languages and dialects in any one country in Asia.

The extensive ethnic diversity and geography of Asia makes it, at times, very complicated to implement generalized standards that address challenges that may be important or unique for a specific culture or area. However, it makes for interesting possibilities for cross-cultural practice, training, and research in culture-specific practice.

Key Country Reports

The following regional, key country reports provide some insight into the development and challenges of the field of art therapy in each region of Asia. In most instances, the content is from resident local or regional Asian art or expressive arts therapists. The field is evolving quickly; therefore, it is not possible to cover all developing practice. This is a small but relevant sampling. (Please note that many of our contributors chose to have their family name written first, as is traditional in many Asian cultures.)

East Asia

East Asia consists of China, Hong Kong, Japan, Korea, Macau, and Taiwan. Art or expressive art therapy is the most developed in this large and economically growing part of the world.

China and Taiwan   China has seen many visiting practitioners regionally and internationally, whether in response to the 2008 earthquake or to work in special needs, schools, or medical settings. Gong Shu is an expressive arts therapist, social worker, and a teacher of Chinese philosophy and painting. She is an adjunct professor at Soochow University who has been teaching *Yi Shu*, an integration of Traditional Chinese Medicine (TCM) and expressive arts therapy in China, since 1993. The 3-year program, taught in Mandarin, requires 800 training hours plus supervision. After the first year of training, students need to apply to continue, and are required to have at least an MA in psychology or a related field. The coursework is all experiential. Gong feels that art therapy was practiced in China thousands of years ago. "Music has been used as a healing art since the time of Fu Xi. The spontaneous expression of poetry and painting by the founder of the Southern School of painting, Wang Wei, introduced the concept of Chinese brush stroke that can be considered as a form of art therapy, meditation, and concentration" (S. Gong, personal communication, May 10, 11, 2012).

Since 2004, University of Tapei (formerly the Taipei Municipal University of Education) has the only graduate art therapy program approved by Taiwan's Ministry of Education. It was the first to be developed in Chinese, and has 2-year and 3-year programs. The 3-year pathway enables graduates to sit for Taiwan's counseling and clinical psychologist exams. This highly competitive program requires fluency in Mandarin and English. Taiwan now has the required credential of Taiwan Registered Art Therapist (TRAT; Lu, 2009), according to Liona Lu, who has helped to pioneer the field in Taiwan.

Korea   Lim, Sela, the ambassador for art therapy from Nungin University of Buddhism in Korea, indicated that "Curricula in art therapy were first established at Daegue University Graduate School in 1999 by Professor Dong Yeon Kim and later at Wonkwang University Graduate School in 2000 by Dong Hun Chung," (personal communication, May 17, 2012) a rehabilitation psychologist and ceramicist, respectively. The two universities offer the only art therapy master's degrees in Korea; however, there are other programs that offer graduation certificates or diplomas.

The field has grown rapidly over the past 10 years, and there are at least 17 graduate schools with art therapy training. There is a code of ethics and a formulation for consistency of curricula agreed upon by the Coalition of Korean Arts Therapy Associations, the umbrella organization for the arts and psychology associations in Korea. Recent research has pointed out the need for additional hours of clinical practice for those trained in the United States, since the Korean collective conscious-ness is so different from the Western individual focus. Adopting foreign models without considering the culture where it is being introduced has proved to be inad-equate, and it is clear that art therapy training should focus on this (S. L. Lim, personal communication, May 17, 2012).

Japan In Japan, expressive arts therapy is taught through institutes and associa-tions by expressive arts therapists such as Kyoko Ono, who has been training stu-dents at her Expressive Arts Therapy Institute for the past 10 years. She also provides training at other local universities (K. Ono, personal communication, May 11, 12, 13, 15, 2012).

Japanese clinical psychologist Tomatsu Sakaki, who specializes in art therapy at Ube Frontier University, uses the term *expressive psychotherapy*, which he says tends to be more individually focused. It "has been developed as nonverbal therapy initially through the connections between basic psychology and art, and then along with the development of clinical psychology ... these developments have been largely influ-enced by Japanese culture, particularly by Bonkei and Bonsai" (T. Sakaki, personal communication, May 17, 21, 2012). Despite Western influences, "Japanese original techniques in clinical psychology such as Naikan Therapy and Morita Therapy have been recognized worldwide. These days, we have our own art therapy, for example, a collage technique, alternate coloring method, and color blotting technique. ... Even if art therapy is not used as the main approach, it would be applied in therapy by using drawings and images in many cases" (T. Sakaki, personal communication, May 17, 21, 2012).

Hong Kong Hong Kong has its roots in the arts in therapy located in the rehabilita-tion and special needs sector, spearheaded by Fang Sum-Suk Marian in the 1980s. Through a fusion of artists, art therapists, social workers, and psychiatrists, the field of expressive arts therapy has emerged. Workshops, conferences, and other types of trainings over the past few decades have evolved into the need for more structured education (M. Y. F. Chang, personal communication, May 17, 2012). Chang M. Y. Fiona, an expressive arts therapist who has been intrinsically involved in the field's development, indicated that the integration of expressive arts in therapy works well in Hong Kong.

> The enhancement of our whole system is in line with the holistic concept of the body–mind–spirit connection in traditional Chinese medicine. For social harmony, our ances-tors used arts as socially acceptable ways to manage buried emotions and express their views about social policy. Expressive arts are safe alternatives of authentic expression for communication, self-healing, and advocacy. (M. Y. F. Chang, personal communication, May 17, 2012)

In 2011, the first expressive arts therapy training program was started at the Centre for Behavioral Health (CBH) at the University of Hong Kong (HKU). It is a 3-year program taught in Cantonese and English to professionals in social work, healthcare, and psychology.

Southeast Asia

Southeast Asia consists of Brunei, Burma (Myanmar), Cambodia, Indonesia, Laos, Malaysia, Philippines, Singapore, Thailand, and Vietnam. Southeast Asia is another quickly developing part of the world, as is the field of art therapy.

Indonesia Indonesia has the largest Muslim population in the world, and approximately 300 different ethnicities. It is considered to be prone to disaster and social conflict. Art therapy has been included in the master's program in clinical psychology at Tarumanagara University since 2006. It was established by Monty P. Satiadarma, who started as a clinical psychologist, with additional educational training as a musician and artist, and then trained as an art therapist. He worked for many years as the only trained art therapist in Indonesia where there are still relatively few art therapists practicing (P. Rusly, personal communication, May 13, 2012; M. P. Satiadarma, personal communication, April 25, 27, 28, June 8, 2012).

> In Indonesia, extended families are an important variable in therapy, and various customs, such as nonverbal gestures, are crucial to be taken into account in a therapeutic relationship; for example, with physical touch—there is a certain belief in some of the population that a handshake between an adult male and an adult female who is not his wife is inappropriate. Harmony and conformity in a social relationship is valued. This indirectly would affect self-expression and how a person developed (P. Rusly, personal communication, May 13, 2012).

The art therapy training program in Singapore has seen a recent influx of Indonesian students who are interested in returning to their home country to help pioneer the field's development in schools and hospitals.

Singapore The field of mental health has grown rapidly over the last 30 years in Singapore. This is largely due to the contributions of Kua Ee Heok, an influential and well-published figure in the field of Asian psychiatry, who has actively supported the arts in therapy and the development of the master's program at LASALLE College of the Arts in Singapore. One of the first Singaporean art therapists, Koh Jessica, has supervised the multidisciplinary unit in a special school for several years. She emphasized the need for more training in family art therapy, believing that what the West refers to as "co-dependency" is a valuable part of being Asian. She feels the emphasis on "self" is a complicated concept for Asians, who prefer sharing, and not making one person too powerful. However, she does believe that it is possible to increase the sense of the agency to make one's life better (J. Koh, personal communication, May 13, 15, 2012).

Other art therapists in Singapore indicated the need for more community service, as private practice has become popular and lucrative in the current successful Singaporean economy. This was stressed within the contexts of the need for improved salaries for those who choose more community-minded work, and the need for affordable tuition.

Contributors also said that the successful economy had increased the social and academic pressures for men, women, and schoolchildren who could benefit from art therapy. On a positive note, the government encourages programming that promotes bonding between fathers and their children, and many recent art therapy graduates are interested in implementing art therapy in the schools to provide some balance to the intense academic pressures.

South Asia

South Asia consists of Bangladesh, Bhutan, India, Nepal, Maldives, Pakistan, and Sri Lanka.

India   Joyce Tan is an art therapist in Singapore who, since 2009, has spent several weeks a year training counselors in South India with a leading NGO.

> Because there are so many main languages in South India, mainly Kannada, Konkani, Malayalam, Tamil, and Telugu, it was critical to have cross-cultural bridges through the NGO faculty leaders who translated the teaching content and the art directives into the language(s) best understood by the participants. Art therapy, as a mental health discipline among others such as psychiatric social work, clinical psychology, and counseling psychology, does not appear to be present or available in South India. Hence, my hosts were very open and welcoming of my contributions in the develop ment and implementation of art therapy. (S. Y. J. Tan, personal communication, May 14, 2012)

Some of the feedback that Joyce received from her peers included how useful art therapy was in exploring and understanding the participants' different cultures.

Pakistan   Shazia Mohamed is the first trained art therapist to practice in Karachi, Pakistan, and has managed to do so despite a limited mental health support structure. Shazia's comments shed light on the reality of developing a new field:

> Establishing trust and boundaries, setting up referrals, and defining and enabling access to crisis measures are all left to the therapists and their adherence to an internally defined ethical framework and standard of practice. And even amidst this chaos, people are getting help; they find qualified, professional therapists; and they do get better, improve their lives, and live more fully. (S. Mohamed, personal communication, April 25, 2012)

Shazia does have access to supervision and is happy to report that she now has another art therapy colleague in Karachi. One of her other frustrations is that she cannot qualify to be a "registered" art therapist with the association in Canada (where she trained) because the lack of precedence in Pakistan makes indemnity insurance unaffordable there.

Sri Lanka   Sri Lanka has suffered from a brutal civil war for nearly three decades. The conflict ended in 2009, and approximately 12,000 former combatants have participated in rehabilitation. Both art making and art therapy were used in the rehabilitation process. Rohan Gunaratna, who is of Sri Lankan descent, heads the Nanyang Technology University International Centre for Political Violence and Terrorism Research (ICPVTR) in Singapore. The organization has become a strong proponent of using the creative arts in the rehabilitation of former combatants, beginning with the combatants in the north of the country (R. Gunaratna, personal communication, May 17, 18, 2012). The clients reported feeling a sense of safety, an increase in both verbal and nonverbal expression, and increased insight and optimism for their future goals (C. N. Wickramasinha, personal communication, June 11, 2012).

The work in Sri Lanka demonstrates potential alternative uses for art therapy as well as a collaborative spirit between art therapists and artists working therapeutically. This collaborative approach may be thought of as illustrating the collective consciousness in Asia that can be very different in both theory and practice from the more boundary-conscious Western therapeutic psyche.

The practice and development of the creative arts in therapy is occurring in other countries in Asia too, such as Cambodia, Nepal, and Thailand. One can assume that the interest in the field, combined with the possibilities in countries as vast as China, India, and Indonesia, that art therapy training and practice will continue to flourish.

Conclusion

Asia is a large region with many unique and different cultures contained within its boundaries. Each country is developing its own version of art therapy that integrates collectivist, Asian values. Issues of local supervision and regulation as well as credentialing are paramount. There seems to be a reinvigoration of traditional artistic and medical practices combined with clinical mental health models that enhances the uniqueness of art therapy in Asia. This region has rich cross-cultural versions of art and expressive (arts) therapy that are transforming and influencing practice globally.

Endnote

1   The author would like to give special thanks to Wong C. M. John, Department Head, associate professor and senior consultant psychiatrist, Department of Psychological Medicine, Yong Loo Lin School of Medicine, National University of Singapore, and National University Hospital, for his invaluable help with reviewing the text with regard to the Asian cultural perspective.

   She would also like to profusely thank the researchers, clinicians, and contributors, listed in the following text, who made this chapter possible. It is from their work that we know more about the cultural nuances of art therapy taking place in Asia. The dates following the names on this list refers to when the authors communicated with each person.

Chan, Y. W. J., May, 16, 2012. Singapore
Chan, N. C., June 8, 2012. Hong Kong
Chang, M. Y. F., May 17, 2012. Hong Kong
Chung, D. H., April 25, 2012. Iksan, South Korea
Durrani, H., April 26, 2012. Singapore/Pakistan
Gong, S., May 10, 11, 2012. MO, United States/China
Gunaratna, R., May 17, 18, 2012. Singapore/Sri Lanka

Handayani, D., April 22, 2012. Singapore/Indonesia

Hassan, M. F. B. M., May 18, 2012. Singapore

Khoo, G. A., May 14, 2012. Singapore

Koh, J., May 13, 15, 2012. Singapore

Lim, S. L., May 17, 2012. Iksan, South Korea

Lu, L., April 23, May 1, 8, 2012. Taipei, Taiwan

Lourier, N., May 14, 2012. Singapore/Holland

Mohamed, S., April 25, 2012. Karachi, Pakistan

Ono, K., May 11, 12, 13, 15, 2012. Tokyo, Japan

Orphanudaki, P., May 15, 2012. Hong Kong/Greece

Rusly, P., May 13, 2012. Singapore/Indonesia

Sakaki, T. and Yoshinaka, S., May 17, 21, 2012. Ube,Yamaguchi, Japan

Satiadarma, M. P., April 25, 27, 28, June 8, 2012. Jakarta, Indonesia

Tan, S. Y. J., May 14, 2012. Singapore/India

Siow, T. T., May 14, 2012. Singapore

Unambuwe, M., May 25, 2012. Colombo, Sri Lanka

Vandoros, R., May 13, 2012. Sydney, Australia/South Africa

Wan, J. L., April 18, 2012. Singapore

Wickramasinha, C. N., May 9, June 11, 2012, Singapore/Sri Lanka

References

Foo, K. H., Merrick, P. L., & Kazantzis, N. (2006). Counselling/psychotherapy with Chinese Singaporean clients. *Asian Journal of Counselling, 13*(2), 271–293.

Lu, L. (2009). *Introduction to art therapy graduate program in TMUE*, proceedings from: *The Asian Art Therapy Symposium*, March 19–21, Hong Kong.

Yalom, I. (2005). *The theory and practice of group psychotherapy*. New York, NY: Basic Books.

71

Art Therapy in Israel: Current Status and Future Directions of the Profession

Dafna Regev and Rachel Lev-Wiesel

Each profession tends to be molded and shaped in accordance with the uniqueness of the society and culture in which it is embedded. The purpose of this chapter is to portray the art therapy profession in Israel and how it is influenced by Israeli society and culture.

To understand Israeli society and culture, there must be an understanding of the history of the country. On May 14, 1948, Israel declared independence, and the modern state of Israel has fought seven major wars since that time with its neighboring Arab countries, and has experienced seven violent terror confrontations. The modern state has rarely experienced a period of prolonged peace, and this has had a profound effect on the society of Israel in terms of psychosocial and cognitive life perspectives.

Additionally, since the founding of the state, profound demographic changes have taken place in Israeli society as a result of successive waves of immigration. Each immigrant group, with its own unique characteristics, has had to contend with the difficulties of integrating into an emerging society that is in a constant state of flux. Over the years, Israel's social–cultural–political discourse has changed. Gradually, the "melting pot" policy that sought to establish a uniform and unified Israeli collective faded, and a more pluralistic approach evolved, one that stresses individualization and accepts the existence of a multicultural identity. Consequently, each of the major immigrant waves was received by the Israeli society in a different way, with the manner of its acceptance affecting its assimilation into the society.

In accordance with the uniqueness of the Israeli society, Israeli creative arts therapies (CAT) as a profession have a set of principles that are put into practice, and to which its members are committed. They hold a strong belief in the strength of the human spirit to overcome adversities and strive to develop. The main goal is therefore to improve the personal well-being and quality of life through creativity (found to contribute to coping), creation (associated with growth and vitality), and holism (an integration between mind and body). Using different artistic expressions, whether art

The Wiley Handbook of Art Therapy, First Edition. Edited by David E. Gussak and Marcia L. Rosal.
© 2016 John Wiley & Sons, Ltd. Published 2016 by John Wiley & Sons, Ltd.

or drama, movement or music, enables clients to better express their emotions and inner difficulties, bypass dissociative mechanisms, strengthen dialogue with the external and internal worlds, and encourage verbalization.

Undoubtedly, the uniqueness of Israel's history and the characteristics of its society have influenced the development of the art therapy profession. The need to acknowledge, assist, and treat different populations, which include those who came from different cultural backgrounds, Holocaust survivors, and combat veterans and their families, led art therapists to develop new models of interventions and techniques to meet a variety of clients' needs. Drawing from all of this information, this chapter will focus on the historical development and current situation of art therapy in Israel, including a comprehensive review of research conducted in Israel on various aspects of the benefits and effectiveness of art therapy.

Historical Overview

Similar to how the art therapy profession developed in the United States and United Kingdom during the 1960s, art therapists who immigrated to Israel brought the profession to hospitals and educational systems. The first educational program for art therapy in Israel was opened in the University of Haifa in 1981, under the supervision of Perez Hesse. During the following 10 years, additional training programs were opened in several academic and non-academic institutions such as Lesley College, Tel Chai Academic College, Seminar Hakibuzim, Beit Berl College, and David Yellin Academic College. While most of the practitioners were women during the start of the profession, it became more popular among men during the 1990s. Nowadays, art therapy is an integral part of the human services provided in Israel's medical and educational domains (Hazut, 1998).

The Israeli Association of Creative and Expressive Therapies (ICET) was established in 1971 as a non-profit organization. It is the professional organization for Israel's art therapists, dance and movement therapists, bibliotherapists, music therapists, drama therapists, and psychodramatists. The organization is the only one in Israel that represents creative arts therapists, and it has the authority to negotiate with the authorities for all those who work in the field.

Current Situation: Regulation and Legal Status

As of 2004, there were 2,000 art therapists practicing in Israel. That year, the Supreme Court ordered the authorities to stop issuing certificates recognizing paramedical professions that were not regulated by law, including art therapy. Since then, the profession has been unsupervised. The process of regulating paramedical professions has been going on since the Supreme Court ruling in 2005. In March 2011, a law was enacted that regulated the fields of physical, occupational, speech, and nutrition therapies. Other health-related practices were later added to the law, including chiropractic, clinical criminology, podiatry, and surgical podiatry. Once the practices were regulated, anyone presenting himself or herself as a creative art therapist but lacking the proper education and training is considered to be committing a criminal offense.

The field of creative arts therapies is expected to receive official regulations soon based on recommendations by a Higher Education Council panel and the Ministry of Health. The Higher Education Council has recommended that only master's degree graduates be recognized as creative arts therapists, which will include graduate studies in music, visual art, movement and dance, bibliotherapy, psychodrama, and drama therapy. Students with bachelor's degrees in other subjects who apply for the CAT master's degree need to complete therapeutic prerequisite studies such as basic psychology courses and courses in their preferable therapeutic art modality. The supplementary art courses include 300 hours of formal art training at an academic or professional institution and 200 hours of field experience. Students could receive an exemption by submitting a relevant portfolio of works. The 2-year master's in art (MA) graduate program includes 600 hours of practical training. In order to receive a ministry license to practice, graduates will have to complete an additional 960 hours of internship for a year after the completion of their MA, and also pass a Ministry of Health exam. These training programs will enable the Ministry of Health to supervise the practice of CAT and control how many people may enter the field of CAT.

Innovative Research Directions

In general, efforts to systematically assess the efficacy of art therapy and its unique opportunities have been indicated to promote field development. In 2000, Reynolds, Nabors, and Quinlan conducted a literature review of studies that examined the effectiveness of therapy using plastic arts. Despite the difficulties in assessing these studies (due to small samples and a variety of methodologies), their conclusion was that art therapy was effective and comparable to other kinds of emotional therapy. Many additional researchers from around the world (e.g., Eaton, Doherty, & Widrick, 2007; Gussak, 2007; Slayton, D'Archer, & Kaplan, 2010) and also in Israel (Freilich & Shechtman, 2010; Regev & Guttmann, 2005; Regev & Reiter, 2011) have since increased our understanding of the therapeutic effects of art therapy on different populations.

Although clinical evidence shows that art therapy is effective, there is still limited research in the field. Based on the need to increase and broaden its research, the Emili Sagol Research Center for CAT was established within the Graduate School of CAT at the University of Haifa. The main objective of the research center is to investigate the following questions:

- Why is CAT effective?
- How is CAT effective?
- What parts of the body are affected by CAT?
- What is the connection between the brain, the body, and the arts?
- Which populations benefit from CAT?
- Which problems and difficult situations benefit from CAT?

The following are some examples of the research conducted in Israel.

Adaptation of Theoretical Models in Art Therapy

Art materials constitute the basis for art therapy interventions (Moon, 2010). It is essential for therapists to be cognizant of the qualities of the different materials they offer to clients and the potential responses that engagement with the materials may evoke. Snir and Regev (2013b) studied the responses to art materials by means of reflections written by 120 students after they worked with five different types of art materials. The findings highlight the importance of understanding the significance of using different materials in clinical settings.

Bar-On (2007) focused arts-based qualitative research on the interaction between non-artist creators and a specific art material—clay—and the meaning they make from this interface. Results of the research included a typology of *thinking and doing* strategies, seen as two interdependent aspects of the creative process. These "dialogues" between creator and material exemplify an individual's way of "making sense" in the interaction between sensing, feeling, thinking, and doing with the material, in which structure, process, content, and meaning intertwine.

Bat-Or (2010) also focused on clay sculpting and explored the processes of mentalization as unfolded during a sculpting task administered to mothers of 2–4-year olds. Twenty-four first-time mothers created clay sculptures of themselves with their child and were then interviewed. Four characteristics of the specific task (visual reflectiveness, wondering, transformation, and implicit memories) were identified as enabling, enhancing, and even triggering parental mentalization.

In the Israeli clinical field, Miriam Ben Aaron and her colleagues (Harel, Kaplan, Avimeir-Patt, & Ben-Aaron, 2006) developed the parent–child psychotherapy model. This model is based on a unique psychoanalytically oriented model for treating relational disturbances in childhood. It has been adapted to art therapy (Gavron, 2010) and other modalities (Regev, Kedem, & Guttmann, 2012).

Markman Zinemanas (2011) tried to conceptualize the additional value of art psychotherapy on a philosophical, psychoanalytic, and neurological foundation. She found that, through visual symbolization, concrete realization of inter-subjective processes can occur, and its implicit components can become explicit for mentalization. These processes—visual symbol formation and inter-subjectivity—are like the warp and woof of the same fabric of consciousness: if a therapeutic change has occurred, it would present in future visual symbolization and can be used for the patient's evaluation throughout treatment.

Another interesting clinical model is in Steinhardt's book (Steinhardt, 2012) regarding a Jungian sandplay model. Her book discusses the deep inner process of becoming a sandplay therapist and addresses important creative aspects of understanding and practicing sandplay. This book integrates the Jungian foundations of sandplay with an art-therapy-based understanding of the inherent properties of the materials that are part of Israel's natural Mediterranean coastline, including sand and water.

Models of Interventions with Specific Populations in Israel

Due to Israel's uniqueness, creative art professionals in Israel developed several intervention models, such as using thematic drawings to encourage verbalization among incest survivors (Lev-Wiesel, 1998) and art materials in a group setting to create reconciliation between people who hold different political attitudes (Lev-Wiesel, 2000). Israeli practitioners have also invested in developing specific interventions for people with special needs. For example, Regev and Snir (2013) focused on a systematic qualitative analysis of perceptions of art therapists on the unique contribution of working with art materials in treating children diagnosed with autism spectrum disorders (ASD).

Evaluation and Assessment Measures

The field of validated measures in CAT is relatively limited. The diversity of the Israeli society demands valid tools and measures that may help evaluate the state of either individuals or groups in distress. This need has already been underscored by other well-known art therapists, such as Kapitan (2010) and Rubin (1984). Several researchers in Israel responded to this challenge. Consequently, Israeli researchers have examined pictorial indicators of: childhood sexual abuse within self-figure drawings of children and adults who were abused as children (Lev-Wiesel, 1999); dissociative identity disorder in self-figure drawings of children and adults (Lev-Wiesel, 2005); violent aggressive behavior within self-figure drawings (Lev-Wiesel & Hershkovitz, 2000); mental illnesses such as schizophrenia within self-figure drawings (Lev-Wiesel & Shvero, 2003); and pedophilia (Lev-Wiesel & Wiztum, 2006) and physical impairments such as deafness and stuttering in self-figure drawings (Lev-Wiesel, Shabat, & Tsur, 2005; Lev-Wiesel & Yosipov-Kaziav, 2005).

Bat-Or has conducted research in Israel to validate the use of the Person Picking an Apple from a Tree (PPAT) drawing assessment directive (Gantt, 1990). In addition to scoring the PPAT according the Formal Element Art Therapy Scale (FEATS; Gantt & Tabone, 1998), the PPATs are rated by an innovative tool that measures the symbolic visual features of object-relation, the Relational Representations in PPAT (RR-PPAT; Bat-Or, Ishai, & Levi, 2011). These studies are being conducted in Israel and Greece. In addition, Bat-Or is involved in validating other art-based assessment tools such as the Bridge drawings (Hays & Lyons, 1981) and Bird Nest Drawings (Kaiser, 1996) with specific groups.

In the context of dyadic parent–child psychotherapy, Gavron evaluated the relationship between parents and children using the Joint Painting Assessment Procedure (JPP; Gavron, 2013). The JPP emerged from a necessity to assess the needs, strengths, and weaknesses of each parent–child dyad seeking therapy. The JPP is analyzed through a manual that describes six scales of the parent–child relationship in middle childhood. The results of the study indicate high reliability and strong correlations between the JPP measures and verbal questionnaires.

Snir and colleagues have been investigating the effectiveness of joint paintings in assessing interpersonal themes in romantic couples' relationships. Based on a qualitative analysis of these paintings, 13 categories of pictorial phenomena were identified as potentially significant for understanding a couple's relationship (Snir & Hazut, 2012). Further analysis identified three distinct styles in these couple paintings—specifically, *balanced, enmeshed*, and *disengaged* (Snir & Wiseman, 2013).

Goldner and Scharf (2011, 2012) concentrated on children's family drawings as a tool to evaluate the adjustment of middle-school children, using an empirically based attachment paradigm to code children's drawings (Kaplan & Main, 1986). The results demonstrated the better adjustment of children classified as secure. Poor adjustment of children was evident among children whose drawings were classified as ambivalent or disorganized, while avoidant children functioned relatively well (Goldner & Scharf, 2011). In another study, researchers focused on the indicators in children's drawings that detected internalizing problems. Their study revealed a moderation of children's gender on the associations between specific indicators and children's internalizing problems (Goldner & Scharf, 2012).

Finally, the Art-Based Intervention Questionnaire (ABI; Snir & Regev, 2013a) was developed in Israel as part of the broader effort to create valid and reliable tools for assessment in the field of visual art therapy. The ABI comprises of 41 items, which were formulated based on the responses of 120 students who reflected on their experiences of using art materials. Factor analysis indicated 10 subscales, as shown in the following list:

- Feelings and thoughts preceding the artistic process
    (1)   Excitement in anticipation of the artistic process
    (2)   Sense of confidence
    (3)   Avoidance

- Reactions during the artistic process
    (4)   Pleasantness and therapeutic value
    (5)   Capability–confidence
    (6)   Difficulty carrying out the artistic task
    (7)   Playfulness

- Attitude towards the artistic product
    (8)   Emotional response to the product

- Approaches to the various materials
    (9)   Expressive material
    (10) Pleasant material

Conclusion

Art therapy as a profession in Israel is rapidly changing into a legalized evidence-based practice, acquiring prestige and appreciation from other professions such as social work, psychology, and education. Many art therapists who are employed in health, welfare, and educational institutions prefer to identify themselves as art therapists following the completion of their master's degree in art therapy. Due to the profession's strengthened prestige, many academic institutions in Israel have begun to submit proposals for master's degree programs in creative art therapy to The Council for Higher Education for approval. Recently, the *Academic Journal of Creative Arts Therapies* (English–Hebrew–Spanish) was launched in the Graduate School of Creative Arts Therapies at the University of Haifa, which publishes research articles in the field of creative arts therapies. This journal combines articles from researchers and clinicians, representing a new generation of art therapy in Israel, where research, theory, and practice can co-exist.

References

Bar-On, T. (2007). A meeting with clay: Individual narratives, self-reflection, and action. *The Psychology of Aesthetics, Creativity, and the Arts, 1*(4), 225–236.

Bat-Or, M. (2010). Clay sculpting of mother and child figures encourages mentalization. *The Arts in Psychotherapy, 37*(4), 319–327.

Bat-Or, M., Ishai, R., & Levi, N. (2011). RR-PPAT: Relational representations in PPAT. Unpublished Manuscript, University of Haifa.

Eaton, L. G., Doherty, K. L., & Widrick, R. M. (2007). A review of research and methods used to establish art therapy as an effective treatment method for traumatized children. *The Arts in Psychotherapy, 34*(3), 256–262.

Freilich, R., & Shechtman, Z. (2010). The contribution of art therapy to the social, emotional, and academic adjustment of children with learning disabilities. *The Arts in Psychotherapy, 37*(2), 97–105.

Gantt, L. (1990). *A validity study of the Formal Elements Art Therapy Scale (FEATS) for diagnostic information in patients' drawings.* Unpublished dissertation, University of Pittsburgh, Pittsburgh, PA.

Gantt, L., & Tabone, C. (1998). *The formal elements art therapy scale: The rating manual.* Morgantown, WV: Gargoyle Press.

Gavron, T. (2010). Psychotherapy and assessment of parent–child relationship through joint painting. In J. Harel, R. Pat-Avimeir, & H. Kaplan (Eds.), *Parent–child psychotherapy.* Haifa: The University of Haifa. (In Hebrew)

Gavron, T. (2013). Meeting on common ground: Assessing parent-child relationships through a Joint Painting Procedure. *Art Therapy: Journal of the American Art Therapy Association, 30*(1), 12–19.

Goldner, L., & Scharf, M. (2011). Children's family drawings: A study of attachment, personality, and adjustment. *Art Therapy: Journal of the American Association of Art Therapy, 28*(1), 11–18.

Goldner, L., & Scharf, M. (2012). Children's family drawings and internalizing problems. *The Arts in the Psychotherapy, 39*(4), 262–271.

Gussak, D. (2007). The effectiveness of art therapy in reducing depression in prison populations. *International Journal of Offender Therapy and Comparative Criminology, 51*(4), 444–460.

Harel, J., Kaplan, H., Avimeir-Patt, R., & Ben-Aaron, M. (2006). The child's active role in mother-child, father-child psychotherapy: A psychodynamic approach to the treatment of relational disturbances. *The British Psychological Society, Psychology and Psychotherapy: Theory, Research and Practice, 79*(1), 23–36.

Hays, R., & Lyons, S. (1981). The Bridge Drawing: A projective technique for assessment in art therapy. *Arts in Psychotherapy, 8,* 207–217.

Hazut, T. (1998). Art therapy in Israel: Towards 2000, A portrait of a profession. *ISER, 13*(2), 7–16. (In Hebrew)

Kaiser, D. H. (1996). Indications of attachment security in a drawing task. *The Arts in Psychotherapy, 23*(4), 333–340.

Kapitan, L. (2010). *An introduction to art therapy research.* New York and London: Routledge.

Kaplan, N., & Main, M. (1986). *Instructions for the classification of children's family drawings in terms of representation of attachment.* Berkley: University of California.

Lev-Wiesel, R. (1998). Use of drawing technique to encourage verbalization in adult survivor of sexual abuse. *The Arts in Psychotherapy, 25*(4), 257–262.

Lev-Wiesel, R. (1999). The use of the Machover Draw-A-Person test in detecting adult survivors of sexual abuse: A pilot study. *American Journal of Art Therapy, 37*(4), 106–112. Also appeared in Russian language in *Art Therapy, 3*(1), 19–31.

Lev-Wiesel, R. (2000). Group intervention model for dealing with members holding different political attitudes. *Mikbaz, Journal of the Israeli Association of Group Psychotherapy, 5*(2), 22–33. (Hebrew)

Lev-Wiesel, R. (2005). Dissociative identity disorder as reflected in drawings of sexually abused survivors. *The Arts in Psychotherapy, 32*(5), 372–381.

Lev-Wiesel, R., & Hershkovitz, D. (2000). Detecting violent aggressive behavior among male prisoners through the Machover Draw-A-Person test. *The Arts in Psychotherapy, 27*(3), 171–177.

Lev-Wiesel, R., Shabat, A., & Tsur, A., (2005). Stuttering as reflected in adults' self-figure drawings. *Journal of Developmental and Physical Disabilities, 17*(1), 99–105. Also published in: *Mifgash* (2003), *18*, 41–52 (Hebrew).

Lev-Wiesel, R., & Shvero, T. (2003). An exploratory study of self-figure drawings of individuals diagnosed with schizophrenia. *The Arts in psychotherapy, 30*(1), 13–16.

Lev-Wiesel, R., & Wiztum, E. (2006). Child molesters vs. rapists as reflected in their self-figure drawings: A pilot study. *Journal of Child Sexual Abuse, 15*(1), 105–117.

Lev-Wiesel, R., & Yosipov-Kaziav, J. (2005). Deafness as reflected in self-figure drawings of deaf people. *Journal of Developmental and Physical Disabilities, 17*(2), 203–212.

Markman Zinemanas, D. (2011). The additional value of art-psychotherapy—Visual symbolization. *Academic Journal of Creative Arts Therapies, 2*, 131–139.

Moon, C. H. (2010). *Materials and media in art therapy: critical understandings of diverse artistic vocabularies.* New York, NY: Routledge.

Regev, D., & Guttmann, J. (2005). The psychological benefits of artwork: The case of children with learning disorders. *The Arts in Psychotherapy, 32*(4), 302–312.

Regev. D., Kedem, D., & Guttmann, J. (2012). The effects of mothers' participation in movement therapy on the emotional functioning of their school-age children in Israel. *The Arts in Psychotherapy, 39*(5), 479–488.

Regev, D., & Reiter, S. (2011). Occupational, speech and emotional therapy with students attending booster classes. *International Journal of Adolescent Medicine and Health, 23*(3), 245–250.

Regev, D., & Snir, S. (2013). Art therapy for treating children with Autism Spectrum Disorders (ASD): The unique contribution of art materials. *The Academic Journal of Creative Arts Therapies, 3*(2), 251–260.

Reynolds, M. W., Nabors, L., & Quinlan, A. (2000). The effectiveness of art therapy: Does it work? *Art Therapy: Journal of the American Art Therapy Association, 17*(3), 207–213.

Rubin, J. A. (1984). *The art of art therapy.* New York, NY: Brunner/Mazel, Inc.

Slayton, S. C., D'Archer, J., & Kaplan, F. (2010). Outcome studies on the efficacy of art therapy: A review of findings. *Art Therapy: Journal of the American Art Therapy Association, 27*(3), 108–118.

Snir, S., & Hazut, T. (2012). Observing the relationship: Couple patterns reflected in joint paintings. *The Arts in Psychotherapy, 39*, 11–18.

Snir, S., & Regev, D. (2013a). ABI: Art-based intervention questionnaire. *The Arts in Psychotherapy, 40*(3), 347–351.

Snir, S., & Regev, D. (2013b). A dialogue with materials: Creators share their experiences. *The Arts in Psychotherapy, 40*(1), 94–100.

Snir, S., & Wiseman, H., (2013). Relationship patterns of connectedness and individuality in the couple joint drawing method. *The Arts in Psychotherapy, 40*(5), 501–508.

Steinhardt, L. F. (2012). *On becoming a Jungian Sandplay Therapist.* London: Jessica Kingsley Publishers.

72

A Portrait of a Nation: Culturally Sensitive Art Therapy in the Arab World

Amar Abdulla Behbehani

The Arab world is an immense part of the Middle Eastern region. It is a combination of 22 countries that share a central location in the old world; its borders stretch from the Atlantic Ocean to the Persian/Arabian Gulf (United Nations Development Programme [UNDP], 2013). It is also the cradle of the oldest civilizations in the world, where Babylon was built, and the pharaohs flourished. These countries share a mother tongue, deep-rooted traditions, geographic location, and historical emphases. However, they are drastically different when it comes to local traditions and sociocultural perspectives of modern life, especially inventive practices such as art and therapy—or both.

To examine a Western-based profession such as art therapy in the Arab world, a cultural interpretation of the profession is required. As a recent art therapist in Kuwait, a small Arab country on the Persian/Arabian Gulf, I found that the social construct within each country is significantly influenced by multiple sociocultural and political factors caused by interrelated yet complicated fusions. However, when examining this region, many tend to generalize or stereotype the differences of cultural perceptions that Arabs have toward mental health services. Al-Krenawi and Graham (2000) indicated that a deeper understanding of local cultures and nuanced differences within these cultures are needed to obtain "international translations" (p. 9) of mental health services in culturally sensitive practices.

This investigative process allows for questioning, enquiry, and phenomenological experiences in portraying the development of art therapy in the Middle East. How can one tackle such a complex profession in a context where free artistic expression and therapy are still considered taboo? How common is it to use art as a different therapeutic modality here? How would an Arab-based art therapy practice serve this complex society in the midst of economic and political upheaval? Basically, how can art therapy develop in the Arab world?

The Wiley Handbook of Art Therapy, First Edition. Edited by David E. Gussak and Marcia L. Rosal.

Careful consideration was given to the sociocultural nature of the region to define, assess, and reflect the possible nature of art therapy in the Arab world. Thus, this chapter will discuss the following topics:

1. A visual scan of the Arab world
2. Art as expression: controversial perspectives
3. The Arab world: the hidden dimensions
4. Art therapy in Kuwait: removing the stigmatization of therapy
5. The faces of art therapy in the Arab world

A Visual Scan of the Arab World: Visual Culture Perspectives

The power of the visual language starts before the art therapy session. The visual culture in the Arab world is complex because it ties the old to the new, the East to the West, and the classic to the modern. Visually, it is similar to moving from one movie set to another, each shooting a different culture and era. In the Arab world, the art and architectural patterns vary from one place to another. Some societies stick to the old, some modernize, some city-states tear down the old and build the new, others urbanize their old and new, and some are just satisfied with how things are. Some Arab nations do not have the privilege of creating or producing architectural solutions or aesthetical developments owing to political and economic complications. These visual variations reflect the intensity of differences that these nations have in aesthetics, political influences, and economic development. Hall and Hall (1969/1990) called this investigative route "the hidden dimension," because of the depth of cultural concepts of space and environment. It is valuable for art therapists to bear in mind that working in the Arab world requires enculturation, anthropological investigation, religious examination, psycho-social understanding, and an appreciation of each country's visual expression and identity.

Art as Expression: Controversial Perspectives

The cultural diversity, various religious beliefs, and strict traditions of the different Arab communities affect their qualities and levels of expression. As with therapy, art is also a controversial tool of expression, especially for those who are not familiar with its value. In many Arab societies, art is considered a contradiction to religious ideology, despite the fact that Islam has a deep-rooted connection with art, as seen through their massive architectural façades, calligraphy, geometric arts, abstract arts, and "reciting," a form of tuned music. The Islamic call of prayer (*adhān*) is performed through reciting certain tuned phrases five times a day. It is distinctively based on pitch, melody, and rhythm. It is also recited from the highest points of the mosques (minaret). These mosques too are a creative product of the great legacy of Islamic architecture that is based on a cultural identity related to expression. So, with all of this artistic influence, why do so many radicals believe, from their religious perspective, that art is so controversial?

Creative expression also flourishes in academia, personal studios, and private galleries. Artists can freely express their thoughts and experiences. However, once this expression reaches the public, communication about the arts is not encouraged, and, as a result, the definition and message of art are often jeopardized. The concept of honor is a prevalent value in Arab society. Cultural beliefs regarding honorable practices impose important barriers on free expression. An example of such honor in this society is noted by Kinoti (2008), who indicated that the male's honor (*sharaf*) encompasses family reputation, chivalry, honesty, generosity, and socioeconomic and political power, while images that depict nudity, female bodies, sex, eroticism, body sculptures, and erotic expressions are considered taboo.

Because of the confidential nature of art therapy, trust is developed between clients and their therapists as visual expression flourishes. Discussing feelings and thoughts with others is considered taboo and is discouraged in the Arab world, especially among women, who experience more cultural limitations than their male counterparts. The creative process of art therapy can be used to help Arabs visually explore their problems rather than talk about them, allowing expression without violating cultural expectations.

The Arab World: The Hidden Dimensions

A deeper understanding of the centuries-old traditions, ideological shifts, and taboos can help art therapists identify contextual issues regarding their practices and stigma while engaging in therapy with this culture. Therefore, it is important to provide working definitions as used for the purpose of this chapter.

Traditions are the customs passed down through generations, emerging as the beliefs, historical emphases, and cultural values in a society. Traditions in the Arab world are an immeasurable part of the heritage, social formation, and personality development (El Saadawi, 2007). Arabs value traditions such as kinship, the formation of large families, patrilineality, marriage, and parent–child relationships (Beitin & Aprahamian, 2014). Yet, the modern culture of the Arab world is striving to unmask traditions that cause the decline of individual and social well-being, especially for women (El Saadawi, 2007).

Rapid ideological shifts are repetitive phenomena in the Arab world. Ideologies, similar to traditions, are a set of beliefs or rules. However, they are influenced by politics and philosophy, rather than beliefs or habits (Kimmerling, 1992). The region experienced multiple civilizations, wars, invasions, and political movements that affected the ideological quality among the Arabs. The rise of Islam, intermarriage and kinship, trade, and invasions have helped solidify the recent dynamics of the Arab world (El Saadawi, 2007). The Arab states are in constant ideological shift, perhaps faster than many other regions in the world because of their exposure to local and foreign political changes (Abu-Lughod, 1989). For example, some Arab countries are greatly affected by economic change, such as Egypt. Other countries, such as Iraq and Lebanon, are in constant struggle with sectarian conflicts. The Arabian Gulf also suffers from tribal involvement and sectarian concerns, preventing the formation of a unifying social and ideological structure (Haber & Menaldo, 2010).

A deeper understanding of these issues is needed to serve those who are suffering from political instabilities.

Taboo is the term that emphasizes behaviors considered improper from a cultural perspective. From the Arabic perspective, many situations in the Western world could be perceived as taboo. For example, a Western art therapist could view drinking alcohol, eating pork, and premarital sex as typical behavior, whereas a legal ban of these activities is normal in many parts of the Arab world due to Islamic and Arabic traditions' general expectations of behavior. Rebelling against a taboo may result in creating social aversion due to what are considered irregular behaviors. A deeper understanding of both content and context of a taboo is essential in therapy, since an accidental violation may lead to therapeutic rejection or fear.

Despite the increased presence of psychotherapy in the Arab world, it is still not integrated into most Arab communities (El-Islam, 2006). Arabs, especially tribal ones, are expected to rely on one another to solve issues. Fortunately for art therapy, with the rise of the nuclear family and individuality in the modern Arab urban life, the use of psychotherapy and alternative treatments has increased, especially for children with disabilities. However, regardless of the progress, there is still a stigma associated with visiting a therapist to talk about issues such as religious beliefs, sex, gender identities, rape, domestic violence, and women issues. Clients, especially women, are fearful of discussing private matters. The concept of confidentiality is not fully realized, and thus fear of social humiliation and strict observance of Arabic traditions and religious values prevent them from discussing sensitive issues, particularly women's issues, such as loss of virginity, honor, rape, and domestic violence (Hamid & Furnham, 2013).

Art Therapy in Kuwait: Removing the Stigmatization of Therapy

Until recently, there were no art therapy associations in Arab nations, and the region lacks art therapy education programs that can train interested candidates to join the field. While there is limited access to art therapy practices in the Arab world, many psychotherapy, educational, and nonprofit institutes use art as expressive and therapeutic outlets. As a result, Arabs tend to obtain the necessary qualifications and credentials from other parts of the world, especially Europe and the United States. Some non-Arab art therapists have joined the different agencies that serve various local and international programs in the region. As an Arab-born citizen, I chose to reflect on what I perceived through my experiences in Kuwait, my homeland.

The Soor experience

The Kuwaiti art therapy practice started in November 2013 at the Soor Center for Cognitive Behavioral Psychotherapy. The term "Soor" is Arabic for "gate" or "protective wall." My late uncle Jaafar Behbehani was a well-known psychologist in the region. He was known for innovative pro bono therapy. His dream was to remove the stigma associated with mental health treatment and therapeutic services (J. Behbehani, personal communications, March 9, 2009). My uncle did not live to see his dream, the Soor Center, prosper and develop; however, Naif Al-Mutawa, the director of the Soor

Center's clinical operations, shared my uncle's vision, and is still building the blocks of a holistic practice in Kuwait, where innovative therapy is progressing. His aim is to change the focus of psychology in Kuwait to client-centered, striving for excellence in policy and practice (S. Schuilenberg, personal communication, April 8, 2014).

The Soor Center offers art therapy services to children, adolescents, and adults. I started my practice wanting to focus on art therapy at Soor, to offer a creative gate that leads to alternative therapeutic paths where the creative intelligences of both therapist and client are used to strengthen the channels of communication, develop therapy goals, and increase well-being.

The goals of art therapy differ according to clients' needs and therapeutic modalities. Art therapy services address many needs such as depression, anxiety, trauma-related issues, self-harm, self-medication, and learning disabilities. While working in this community, I found that clients in Kuwait seek alternative modalities and new ways of expression.

Art is an international visual language, and great attention and respect is necessary when addressing religious needs, traditions, and social constructs through art therapy interventions and assessments. Many traditional art therapy interventions are redesigned to use abstract art and less figure drawing in an effort to respect religious beliefs and accommodate cultural mores. An example of just such an accommodation can be considered when assessing figure drawings; because of the lack of attention given to the figure in this society, cultural considerations are accounted for when considering the "self" in images. Another example is the Person Picking an Apple from a Tree assessment (Gantt & Tabone, 1998). In the Arab world, there are no apple trees, so the directive is adapted to include palm trees instead. These considerations do not restrict the use of media and art as an expressive element; in fact, they allow therapeutic interventions to flourish within the cultural parameters.

Gender and therapy

Gender plays a significant role in the development of the therapeutic relationship and the initial efficacy of art therapy. It has been found that female clients require additional time and effort to build the bridge of trust in individual and group art therapy. Abu-Khalil (1997) indicated that male supremacy in the Middle East was socially, culturally, economically, politically, and legally manifested. This phenomenon is still present. In the Soor Center, group art therapy started with men before women when it was realized that male clients accepted the exchange of group therapeutic experiences and did not feel "shame" when sharing them. Women feel shame from the pressures of society and often refrain from discussing their emotional and sexual problems. Gender inequality and the expectations for women affect their openness to group therapy. Due to social restrictions, Kuwaiti women rarely have opportunities to express emotional distress because of the harsh consequences for discussing issues such as abuse and rape.

Abu-Khalil (1997) indicated that male dominance remained a feature of Arab societies, and that many women were emotionally suppressed because of this phenomenon. Most psychological practices in Kuwait chose to ignore sexuality and gender issues, deferring instead to the clients' religious faith and spirituality. Abu-Khalil called for independent research in social and sexual issues to "approach this subject with an open mind, and free of the taboos of religion and of the state" (p. 102).

The concept of honor in Arab society is one of the important barriers in therapy. Kinoti (2008) indicated that male honor (*sharaf*) encompasses family reputation, chivalry, honesty, generosity, and socioeconomic and political power. Female honor (*ardh*) encompasses the preceding factors as well as female sexuality and the sexual use of their bodies. A woman is expected to maintain her virginity until marriage; in some rural areas, men have the right to sentence women to death if they lose their honor. Because of these ramifications and others, women prefer to suffer in silence if exposed to physical or sexual abuse, so that their families do not suffer the indignities of such consequences. Through art therapy, the women found an alternative means of expression. Painting, photography, ceramic making, narration, and journaling were different media experiences that allowed the women of Kuwait to slowly unmask their emotions without violating their sociocultural needs of privacy within groups.

Women and art therapy

Women are the pillars of the Kuwaiti family. The art therapy practice at Soor Center encourages female clients to explore therapy, recognizing that they are the gateways to Kuwaiti families. By encouraging the female family members to come, it is believed that they will in turn persuade the rest of the family—especially children—to attend (J. Behbehani, personal communications, March 9, 2009).

The cultural formation of Kuwait's physical urban development reflects the history of women and the effects of its society's influential perceptions. Metaphorically speaking, Arab women jumped the high walls of the old Kuwaiti fortress, tore down its walls, and unveiled their female within. This social development has changed the definition of the Kuwaiti family, and, as a result, has improved women's marriage processes and their defined role within the family. Despite all these developments, J. Behbehani mentioned that families still hesitate to come to therapy because of certain cultural issues that women face (personal communication, March 9, 2009); clearly, overcoming taboo is not easy. El-Islam (2006) indicated that "sociocultural heritage of beliefs, attitudes and traditions are involved in the recognition, pattern, management and outcome of mental ill health problems in Kuwait" (p. 145). Hoshino and Cameron's (2007) narrative technique addresses this. It was integrated with the Arabic feminine narration to evoke women's feelings, needs, and problems.

It was challenging to establish such an unorthodox therapeutic context in a culture that still fears the stigma of being in therapy. However, the visual language, empathy, patience, and determination of both client and therapist are creating multiple gates for art therapy to expand.

The Faces of Art Therapy in the Arab World

Art as communication

Kuwaiti Society for the Handicapped (KSH), established in 1971, is the first charity-based, and the only inpatient, disability center in Kuwait. Hashim Taqi, who is the regional chair of the Arab world and the head of the educational committee for Rehabilitation International (RI), administrates the society and is the founder of its psychology-based creative programs. The society is funded by a number of local families who are interested in providing inpatient services for those who suffer from severe mental and physical disabilities. Their aim is to help families provide better care for their loved ones and provide social, psychological, and health care for children under the age of 18.

KSH has been a pioneer in providing creative therapy for their clients in this region. They use play, music, drama, writing, and art to meet various therapeutic goals. In 1995, it became the home of Very Special Arts (VSA) in Kuwait.

VSA's mission is to provide opportunities for children with disabilities to engage with the local and international communities through the process of art making. They believe that art helps children with disabilities strengthen their identities as individuals. The children's art has been exhibited at the *World Bank Exhibition*, *Children Beyond Borders*, *ArtLink*, and *MusicLink*, and many of the children have earned international awards. Although the VSA center does not have art therapists, the art program has been administrated by psychotherapists, activity specialists, and certified creative directors (H. Taqi, personal communication, May 11, 2013).

Art as medicine

There is, however, an art therapy program located in the Kingdom of Saudi Arabia (KSA), one of the most conservative countries in the Arabian Gulf. Despite its conservative politics and religion, KSA has been a pioneer in creative innovation and development. In 2005, a medical-based art therapy program was established in a clinical rehabilitation program at King Fahad Medical City (KFMC) in Riyadh. It is the first official practice in the Arab world, and the founder of the program, Awad Alyami, is one of the first Arab art therapists in the region. The goals of the program are to: practice medical art therapy as a creative alternative for patients who experienced medical trauma; raise art therapy awareness on regional and international levels; establish an art therapy education program to serve the region; and to expand art therapy services to other settings when needed (A. Alyami, personal communication, January 2, 2013).

Alyami's latest project is *From Jihad to Rehab*, an art therapy and religious re-education project to reform former Saudi terrorists. The program is funded by the government of KSA to help these former terrorists shift their ideology toward the real message of Jihad, which is related to defending one's own honor, family, land, and country. In the video documentary "Art Therapy Helps Reform Terrorists," Alyami recognized the use of cognitive-behavioral approach as an effective tool in helping his clients modify their outlook on religion, their responsibilities as human beings, and becoming effective citizens (International Art Therapy Organization, Inc., 2009). He recognized that art is an effective vehicle to expose an individual's inner thoughts and feelings about his or her self and ideologies.

Art as political expression

The Arab world is an active war zone and a region of intense political conflicts. There are many casualties of war, and children are particularly vulnerable. Children who experience such conflicts are also victims of crime, emotional distress, sense of detachment,

PTSD, poverty, and lack of nutrition. The Middle East Children's Alliance (MECA) is a US-based nonprofit organization that defends the rights of Arab children in Lebanon, Iraq, and Palestine. This organization concentrates on funding humanitarian aid projects and on providing awareness in the United States about the effects of US foreign policy on children in the region. Since 1988, they have been generating projects to solve problems regarding shelter, food, clean water, education, and cultural exchange.

One of MECA's ongoing projects is *Art by Palestinian Children in the Gaza Strip*. They encourage children in Gaza to express their thoughts and feelings regarding their personal and community issues through visual narration (Veronese, Castiglioni, & Said, 2010). They believe in the healing power of producing a tangible creative product that reflects the children's suffering. The project helps children boost their sense of self. Art educators, psychotherapists, local artists, and social workers are all assisting in this project. MECA has been displaying the children's creative expressions around the world; one of the difficulties they face is that certain museums refuse to exhibit the artistic, personal, and political perspectives of the Arab children. Regardless of this limitation, the art of MECA reaches beyond boarders as an example of cross-cultural collaboration between the East and the West (a link to this organization can be found at https://www.mecaforpeace.org).

Art for healing violence

In 2005, the Queen Rania Family and Child Center (QRFCC), a non-government organization, opened its doors in East Jordan to protect women and children from violence, bullying, and domestic abuse. Their goals are to: increase awareness of people against these phenomena; involve the society and promote their cause; create programs that help both women and children survive; and enable women and children to protect themselves on societal and personal levels. One of their most effective methods of outreach is creative therapy, believing that art helps children unleash their feelings, trauma experiences, and various other problems they face every day. They also believe that the creative process empowers children to become effective individuals and, in turn, effective members of society. The program they created embraces the sociocultural sensitivities of the Arab world, yet follows international standards of psychotherapy and rehabilitation. The children engage in art-, drama-, play-, and music-based therapeutic experiences. They also have interactive therapy where children are exposed to multi-media and technology-based interventions that encourage them to speak, write, discuss, and represent their feelings (a link to this organization can be found at http://www.jordanriver.jo/?q=content/jrcsp/queen-rania-family-and-child-center).

Art for survival

The rate of autistic spectrum disorders (ASD) in the Arab world is lower than in the West (Taha & Hussein, 2014), but being a child with ASD is still difficult. Furthermore, there is a shortage of childhood specialists capable of diagnosing ASD, and of offering parental and family assistance. Egypt established a government-based association in 1999 to serve children and families who are coping with ASD, The Egyptian Autistic [Autism] Society. One of their projects includes learning the art of weaving to help underprivileged children who suffer from ASD learn a skill, increase their sense of worth, develop a work ethic, and earn an income. The repetition and precision of weaving is also found to be soothing and comforting. As one of the native arts in the Arab world, this activity is considered a culturally sensitive form of expression, making it easier to integrate into the program.

Conclusion

The Arab world is new territory for the creative therapies. The increased recognition of mental illness has led many foundations and specialized programs to use the arts as means of expression inclusive of many forms of media. There is a limited number of Arab art therapists, and there is a need for expanding the innovative art therapy services in this region. According to my own humble experience in living here, I sense the newer generation's willingness to seek help and experience alternative modalities such as art therapy. There are many settings and populations to serve in the Arab world; however, activism and raising awareness are necessary precursors. To conduct art therapy, therapists must bear in mind the sociocultural factors that might be very different from the international concepts of art and/or therapy. Therapists need to understand the nature of the culture and how to weave Western and Eastern approaches to art therapy in the Arab world.

The Arab world addresses medicine and psychotherapy differently from the Western world. As a collectivist society, such services address the individual but also his or her family, extended family, community, and/or tribal background. For example, in most of the Western world, children leave their homes by the age of 18 and begin the process of individualism. Arabs are not encouraged to individualize. Even if Arabs leave home for education or employment, they are still part of the larger family system. Women do not leave their family homes until they marry. This familial clanship serves as a support system, but, at times, this support comes at a price. Individuality is usually compromised, and, at times, confidentiality is jeopardized. As a result, art therapists must bear in mind the collectivist ideologies that build the Arab individuals, and thus their social construct.

Therapy is a phenomenological experience. The rise of art therapy in the Arab world is unlike any other journey that art therapists have gone through to carve their identities as mental health professionals, educators, volunteers, and/or healers. This part of the world is in deep need of alternative care, especially in the recent circumstances of political and philosophic shifts where alternative communication may facilitate peace and self-worth. The Arabs may have sociocultural factors that seem difficult to overcome; however, they are hospitable by nature and will accept change and new ideas if they fit into their rich heritage. These nations have suffered from intense negative media regarding their system of beliefs and traditional values. Extremism, as in any culture, exists. However, these extremists do not represent the whole and do not define a large populace such as the Arab world. There is a wish in every Arab child's heart for peace, and art therapy may address this wish through the universal language of art.

References

Abu-Khalil, A. (1997). Gender boundaries and sexual categories in the Arab world. *Feminist Issues, 15*(2), 91–104.

Abu-Lughod, L. (1989). Zones of theory in the anthropology of the Arab World. *Annual Review of Anthropology, 18*(1), 267–306.

Al-Krenawi, A., & Graham, J. R. (2000). Culturally sensitive social work practice with Arab clients in mental health settings. *Health & Social Work, 25*(1), 9–22.

Beitin, B. K., & Aprahamian, M. (2014). Family values and traditions. In S. C. Nassar-McMillan, K. J. Ajrouch, & J. Hakim-Larson (Eds.), *Biopsychosocial perspectives on Arab Americans* (pp. 67–88). New York, NY: Springer.

El-Islam, M. (2006). The sociocultural boundaries of mental health: Experience in two Arabian Gulf countries. *World Cultural Psychiatry Research Review, 1*(3/4), 143–146.

El Saadawi, N. (2007). The hidden face of Eve: Women in the Arab world. London, UK: Zed Books.

Gantt, L., & Tabone, C. (1998). *The formal elements art therapy scale: The rating manual.* Morgantown, WV: Gargoyle Press.

Haber, S., & Menaldo, V. A. (2010). Rainfall, human capital, and democracy [unpublished white paper].

Hall, E. T., & Hall, E. T. (1969/1990). *The hidden dimension.* New York, NY: Anchor Books.

Hamid, A., & Furnham, A. (2013). Factors affecting attitude towards seeking professional help for mental illness: A UK Arab perspective. *Mental Health, Religion & Culture, 16*(7), 741–758.

Hoshino, J., & Cameron, D. (2007). Narrative art therapy within a multicultural framework. In C. Kerr, J. Hoshino, J. Sutherland & S. T. Parashak (Eds.), *Family art therapy: Foundations of theory and practice* (pp. 193–219). London, UK and New York, NY: Routledge.

International Art Therapy Organization, Inc. (Producer). (2009). *Art therapy helps reforms terrorists* [Video webcast]. Retrieved from http://www.internationalarttherapy.org/films.html.

Kimmerling, B. (1992). Sociology, ideology, and nation-building: The Palestinians and their meaning in Israeli sociology. *American sociological review, 57,* 446–460.

Kinoti, K. (2008). *Women for women's human rights—new ways: Gender, sexuality and the criminal laws in the Middle East and North Africa.* Istanbul: WWHR.

Taha, G. R., & Hussein, H. (2014). Autism spectrum disorders in developing countries: Lessons from the Arab world. In *Comprehensive Guide to Autism* (pp. 2509–2531). New York, NY: Springer.

United Nations Development Programme. (2013). *Human development report 2013—The rise of the South: Human progress in a diverse world.* New York, NY: United Nations Development Programme.

Veronese, G., Castiglioni, M., & Said, M. (2010). The use of narrative-experiential instruments in contexts of military violence: the case of Palestinian children in the West Bank. *Counseling Psychology Quarterly, 23*(4), 411–423.

73

Various Aspects of Art Therapy in Mexico/*Algunos Aspectos de la Terapia de Arte en México*

Debra Linesch, Einat Metzl, and Ana Laura Treviño

Introduction

The story of art therapy in Mexico is inherently multilayered, combining contextual meanings of art within Mexican culture with understandings of psychotherapy and with experiences of art therapy as a specific profession that has transplanted itself in Mexican soil. This discussion focuses on art therapy that grew out of the connections between Californian art therapists and psychoanalytically trained psychologists from Mexico City. It is written in three parts: (1) an overview of the context that provided fertile ground for the development of art therapy in Mexico; (2) the development of art therapy in Mexico; and (3) the specific story of the American/Mexican collaboration that lead to the Instituto Mexicano de Psicoterapia de Arte. The third-person voice of the first two sections shifts to a first-person voice as the story becomes the lived experiences of the authors, the Canadian/American art therapist who initially envisioned the program, the Mexican art therapist who understood how to transplant it, and the Israeli/American art therapist who re-engaged in cultural–social–political work after experiencing the program as both a student and faculty member.

Historical Cultural and Political Context

Mexico is a country where art can be found everywhere and is a natural place for art therapy to thrive. Its history is abundant with unique forms of self-expression—pyramids, frescos, ceramics, and textiles were created by individuals, groups, cultures, and regions. The country's artistic expression illustrates how the understanding of everyday life was expressed in carving, painting, and sculpture, where rituals created a space for transitions and life cycles as well as communication with the gods. From the frescos in Bonampack to the murals of Diego Rivera, from the pots of the Aztecs to

The Wiley Handbook of Art Therapy, First Edition. Edited by David E. Gussak and Marcia L. Rosal.
© 2016 John Wiley & Sons, Ltd. Published 2016 by John Wiley & Sons, Ltd.

the art making of Orinalá, from the expression of Frida Kahlo to Mexican modern art, the Mexican people have evolved within a culture embedded with art.

Indigenous cultures used art to express their understanding of life events as well as their internal world. Art throughout the centuries was used as a way to "make special," and find physical, psychological, and cultural meanings (Dissanayake, 1990, 1992).

One of the first manifestations of art in Mexico was ceramics. Over time, ceramics, textiles, woodcarving, music instruments, calendars, murals, jewelry, etc., became symbols of the stories and emotional content of each civilization. When the Spanish arrived in Mexico, art was transformed. European theology, ideas, and ways of under-standing the world were incorporated into the indigenous paintings, sculpture, music, and ceramics. Rituals have always been part of Mexican culture, and the Day of the Dead is one of the clearest examples of how art has provided symbolic ways to process transitions and losses. Its rituals represent the layering of pre-Hispanic and Spanish beliefs and values.

The Mexican Revolution created a mural renaissance, making art more accessible to the public and developing a visual dialogue with the Mexican people. The muralists played a central role in the culture and social life of Mexico following the revolution (Collin, 2006). Frida Kahlo, the famous Mexican painter, was one of the first artists to incorporate symbols of her personal experiences of pain and sorrow. She said, "I never painted dreams, I painted my own reality" (Cerro, 2007). It could be said the Kahlo was the first art therapist in Mexico.

This rich tradition of art within Mexican culture exists alongside a complex history of mental health informed by both indigenous cultural understandings of healing and transplanted Western perspectives on psychotherapy. Traditional psychotherapy in Mexico has its roots in psychoanalytic and psychodynamic approaches that are still predominant—as distinguished from the United States, where cognitive, brief, and evidence-based therapies currently predominate. Frequently, psychotherapeutic training in Mexico occurs in institutions that provide certificates, and most psycho-therapists work in private practice or schools since there are fewer community mental health clinics. The current political context in Mexico and the United States, and the complicated dynamics between the two countries, create challenges due to issues such as migration (Linesch, Aceves, Quezada, Trochez, & Zuniga, 2012; Mauro, 1998) and illegal activities (Nieri, Hoffman, Marsiglia, & Stephen, 2012). These issues, among others, impact the integration of art therapy in Mexico. The enthusiasm for art therapy in Mexico is strong (Tucker & Trevino, 2011), but so is the need to examine US practices from a critical perspective that supports culturally relevant practices.

Preliminary Development of Art Therapy in Mexico

Although the beginnings of art therapy in Mexico are not well documented, it is evi-dent (Junge & Asawa, 1994) that it began in ways that were similar to art therapy's beginnings in the United States and England, facilitated by informal interactions rather than through formal training (Williams, 2010). Art therapy started in Mexico with several introductory presentations, the establishment of certificate programs, and, eventually (looking to the future), the development of master's degree programs

(Junge, 2010). It was clear that the people behind these institutions understood the fertile ground for art therapy and the connection that the country had with art and its psychological processes.

Early on, many Mexican individuals who gravitated to art therapy had traveled abroad for training but initially did not establish distinct organizations. In 1987, El Centro Integral de Terapia de Arte (CITA) was established as a working group, with different agendas and connections to various national and international organizations related to art therapy. CITA was created by Glenda Nosovsky, who received her PhD in clinical psychology from the National Autonomous University of Mexico (UNAM). CITA continued developing a specialty in brief therapy (personas), and a specialty in couples therapy (AMETEP), with studies and supervision by the New England Art Therapy Institute. Nosovky articulates that art therapy allows clients to make their problems visible through art, find alternatives for their solutions, and make the problem concrete and the solution tangible. This process is very adaptable to Mexican culture, due to the fact that Mexican people are very creative and inclined to engage in imagery. In 1996, CITA began offering courses and workshops in art therapy, as well as facilitating conferences in different educational and health institutions in Mexico. In 1998, an art therapy program was offered by CITA including supervision using a Gesell chamber. In 2002, CITA began an on-site certificate program in art therapy (Diplomado) at the UNAM, and later developed a distance-learning component for the program. Today, CITA is an art therapy center that offers certificate programs, supervision, workshops, seminars, and conferences in public and private institutions.[1]

Another pioneer who studied in Spain is Ana Bonilla, the creator of *Taller Mexicano de Arte Terapia*. Bonilla studied visual arts as an undergraduate at the UNAM, and received a certificate in social exclusion and confinement. Subsequently, she started to use art with a social action focus. In 2000, she completed a master's program in art therapy in the Universidad Complutense in Madrid, Spain. She was part of the first generation of art therapists in Madrid who founded an association called Foro Iberoamericano de Arteterapia. Bonilla returned to Mexico and, in 2003, founded Taller Mexicano de Arteterapia, where art therapy is practiced with children, adolescents, and adults, also offering workshops in prisons, shelters for battered women, hospitals, etc. Taller Mexicano de Arteterapie also offers courses and certificate programs to specialized professionals in the field. Bonilla has taught at the Master Oficial Interuniversitario en Arteterapia y Educación Artística for Social Inclusion at the Universidad Autonoma in Madrid, the Universidad Complutense de Madrid, and in various art therapy certificate programs organized by Mexican institutions such as Consejo Nacional para la Cultura y las Artes (CONACULTA), Consejo para la Cultura y las Artes (CONARTE), UNAM, and Universidad Autónoma de San Luis Potosí.[2]

Art Psychotherapy in Mexico: Intercultural Dialogue in the Making

The story shifts here to the personal voice of the facilitators of a clinical art psychotherapy program in Mexico, focusing on the development of summer courses in San Miguel de Allende as the original core, interweaving experiences, intentions, and hopes for this program—as it was created—in dialogue. Three authors narrate: Ana Laura's voice grounds the story in Mexico, while Debra and Einat reflect on the consequences of intercultural explorations.

Voice 1: Ana Laura

As a psychoanalytically trained psychologist, I—Ana Laura Trevino—had 10 years of clinical experience in Mexico. I worked in the United States for 3 years, developed an art practice, and discovered the therapeutic power of art in my personal and professional life. I was motivated to learn about art therapy in the United States.

When I returned to Mexico, I looked for clinically based art therapy training but found none. Eager to expand my knowledge and understandings, I was excited when I found Loyola Marymount University's (LMU) summer program in San Miguel de Allende, a mere 40-minute drive from my home in Queretaro. In 2004, I took three courses in the LMU summer program. My interest grew, and after having several conversations with Debra Linesch, I embarked on an online art therapy curriculum. Because I had a master's degree in psychoanalysis and years of clinical work, my LMU study focused specifically on the theories and practices of art psychotherapy.

Ongoing supervision with professors and clinicians at LMU enhanced my understanding of the process and the art. Working as a volunteer in different settings, with homeless children, pregnant adolescents, and immigrating families, while being supervised by registered and experienced art therapists helped me learn about multiculturalism and deepened my understanding about clinical art therapy.

As I gained confidence in the art therapy world, I started to organize and offer workshops in Mexico to help people understand the practice. Surprisingly, many had not even heard about art therapy, but the interest was strong.

In 2005, we forged connections between Universidad Iberoamericana in Mexico City and LMU in Los Angeles, both Jesuit Universities. In 2006, within a complicated collaboration, we offered training in the modality of art therapy to Mexican psychotherapists who wished to utilize art therapy in their work with clients. It became clear that the American students in the summer art therapy courses in Mexico very much benefited from the inclusion of Mexican students in the classrooms and in the conversations.

Since 2006, this coursework has been offered every summer in 3-week increments at the Instituto Allende in San Miguel de Allende, Guanajuato, Mexico. For 3 years, upon completing three consecutive summers of this course work, Mexican psychotherapists were able to receive a certificate in art therapy awarded by the LMU/UIA alliance. Since 2009, the alliance between UIA and LMU shifted, for a variety of reasons, to a partnership between LMU and Instituto Mexicana de Psicoterapia de Arte (an organization I was in the process of establishing).

My art therapy experience continued to grow when I was fortunate to attend the American Art Therapy Conference in San Diego in 2004, and in Albuquerque in 2006. I was invited to be a visiting professor at LMU for the 2009–2010 academic year, where I expanded my knowledge and clinical practice in art therapy. Because of LMU's emphasis on multiculturalism, I taught with department faculty engaging in deeper methodologies about teaching, supervising, and practicing art therapy.

In 2010, I moved back from Los Angeles to Mexico City and formally established *Instituto Mexicano de Psicoterapia de Arte*, where clinical art therapy is practiced, taught, and supervised. This program was conceptualized to be different from the existing art therapy institutions in Mexico, and I found the interest in Mexico for art therapy expansive enough to embrace a variety of approaches.

There have been four complete certificate cycles at the IMPA, each one lasting 10 months, exploring different points of view: clinical, developmental, artistic, and emotional, among others. There have been many challenges to starting a program in Mexico, and in aligning it into an ethical, professional, and culturally relevant practice.

It is not surprising that art therapy in Mexico has found fertile ground. The interest has grown, and people have started to become more curious about art therapy. I am proud to say that my own contribution to art therapy has been to add another voice to the growing chorus of voices about art therapy in Mexico. There are many opportunities to grow the field in this country and to create a community of art therapists to share and support each other's practices. Important progress is being made in extending art therapy into other regions of Mexico (Chiapas in the south and Hermosillo in the north), and holding international workshops and speaker opportunities.

Voice II: Debra

The reciprocal nature of this intercultural relationship is, in many ways, a reminder of all we have to gain, as art therapists, educators, and human beings, from consciously engaging in intercultural exploration. It is important to recognize that there are similarities and differences between the cultures which informs the projective material expressed in therapy. It is crucial to examine what each culture identifies as problematic and non-existent culturally, and it is valuable to recognize the beauty and challenges of communicating in a place that is far from home, where neither English nor Spanish is the shared dominate language. The importance of multicultural considerations regarding language, therapy, and identity are well documented in current literature regarding psychotherapy training (e.g., Sue & Sue, 1998; Tatum, 1998). Over the last few decades, it has become clear that cultural gaps directly translate to micro-aggressions (Sue et al., 2007), crucial misunderstanding and mismanagement, in medical (Fadiman, 1997) and mental health services in California (Morrell & Metzl, 2005). Also, it has been illustrated over and over again that cultural considerations are crucial for sound art therapy treatment (e.g., Acton, 2001; Junge, Alvarez, Kellogg, & Volker, 1993; Linesch & Carney, 2005; Mauro, 1998).

As I have proudly watched our program in Mexico grow and been witness to the consequent development of art psychotherapy in Mexico, I am humbly aware of something so much bigger than anything I imagined or initiated. As of result of these developments, our training program in California is immeasurably better, and opportunities for training in Mexico are enhanced. As reflected by my connecting role in this chapter, the work we have done stands across both sides of the border where as of yet, the unimagined potential to deepen the dialogue about the relationships between culture, art, and art psychotherapy is only now becoming realized.

Voice III: Einat

Year after year, art therapy students are transformed by the profound collaboration between LMU and IMPA, between new and seasoned therapists, and between Mexican and US residents. My experiences as a student in the first year of the LMU prógram in Mexico highlighted a part of myself that I desperately tried to push away; I was an Israeli in self-exile, a burned-out peace activist who fled Israel for graduate school in the heat of the post-Oslo days. Frequent bombings and loss from all sides made it intolerable for me to stay in touch with what I knew was my life's work as a facilitator of Jewish–Arab conflict-resolution groups. In Mexico, I had to ask myself what I still could do, needed to do, as an Israeli *and* US citizen. This dialogue—verbally in class, and through my own writing and art making, had a profound impact. Returning to the United States, the faculty and students at LMU created art workshops in local schools addressing tolerance and overcoming borders as part of the "10,000 kites" international project. I was reminded that I had a responsibility to engage in this important work, and, after my doctorate was completed, I came back to LMU to teach— first and foremost—the multicultural class, at LMU, and later in San Miguel de Allende as well.

As an instructor and director of the summer program in Mexico, I have witnessed American students explore their identity, examine their biases, and engage in new understandings of who they are. While teaching the multicultural class in San Miguel with both American and Mexican students present, I witnessed LMU students revisit their perceptions of Latino culture, both in Mexico and in their clinical experiences. Some come to terms with the layered aspects of their identities—a language that was spoken only at home or that they refused to learn and speak, or a grandparent whose immigration story suddenly made more sense. I have also seen LMU students who had not traveled out of the United States previously come to terms with the complicated identity of "being from the United States." Additionally, I have observed how Mexican students benefit immensely from our dialogue. Cultural norms and taboos are discussed in a different way when a foreigner initiates the topic. Language proficiency and differing abilities in English and Spanish bring up personal insecurities and ideas about socioeconomic and educational status. The articulation of American assumptions about art therapy bring up questions about cultural relevancy and allow seasoned and new therapists in Mexico to add the creative and expressive art modality to their practice. Students in both groups reexamine their perception of art making, how the product is understood and cared for in therapy, as well as how to discuss and respond to art. Additionally, in the fieldwork component of the program, we are able to provide services to the community, demonstrating a model of intercultural collaboration and dialogue.

It is essential to stay in dialogue as we develop, maintaining a link to who we are and the circumstances that have shaped us, so that we can understand and learn to welcome the similarities and differences we can expect in our clients. This kind of collaboration benefits our communities in the most profound ways and enhances the field of art therapy.

Vision for the Future

There are many things that need to happen in the development of the field of art therapy in Mexico; the establishment of a master's program, the development of a professional organization that can sustain the diverse voices of art therapy in Mexico, and the articulation of coherent professional and ethical parameters for the field.

Also needing further exploration are the liaisons with other Spanish-speaking countries, creating an enlarged view of how Latin American culture can contribute to the art therapy field. Sensitivity to cultural differences and the creation of unique approaches to the field will contribute to more attuned therapeutic interventions within the specific cultures of Latin America.

Endnotes

1   More information about CITA can be found at their website: www.terapia-de-arte.com.
2   More information about TMAT can be found on their website: www.arteterapia.com.mx.

References

Acton, D. (2001). The "color blind" therapist. *Art Therapy, 18*(2), 109–112.

Cerro, S. (2007). *El legado manuscrito de Frida Kahlo.* México DF: www.sandracerro.com.

Collin, H. (2006). *Mito e Historia del Muralismo Mexicano.* Buenos Aires, Argentina: Red Scripta Etnológica.

Dissanayake, E. (1990). *What is art for?* Seattle, WA: Washington University Press.

Dissanayake, E. (1992). *Homo aestheticus: Where art comes from and why.* New York, NY: Free Press.

Fadiman, A. (1997). *The spirit catches you and you fall down.* New York, NY: Farrar, Straus and Giroux.

Junge, M., (2010). *The modern history of art therapy in the United States.* Springfield, IL: Charles C. Thomas.

Junge, M., Alvarez, J., Kellogg, A., & Volker, C. (1993). The art therapist as social activist: Reflections and visions. *Art Therapy, 10*(3), 148–155.

Linesch, D., & Carnay, J. (2005). Supporting cultural competency in art therapy training. *The Arts in Psychotherapy, 32*(5), 382–394.

Linesch, D., Aceves, H., Quezada, P., Trochez, M., & Zuniga, E. (2012). An art therapy exploration of immigration. *Art Therapy, 29*(3), 120–126.

Mauro, M. (1998). The use of art therapy in identity formation: A Latino case study. In A. Hiscox & A. Calish (Eds.), *Tapestry of cultural issues in art therapy* (pp. 134–151). New York, NY: Jessica Kingsley.

Morrell, M., & Metzl, E. (2005). Seeking treatment in California: Motivators, barriers. Perceptions. The Therapist: CAMFT Magazine. www.camft.org/PressRoom/Articles_Pub/SeekingTreatment.pdf.

Nieri, T., Hoffman, S., Marsiglia, F., & Stephen, K. (2012). Interpersonal violence and its association with US migration desires and plans among youths in Guanajuato, Mexico. *Journal of International Migration and Integration, 13*(3), 365–381.

Sue, D. W., & Suc, D. (1998). *Counseling the culturally diverse: Theory and practice, overcoming our racism, and understanding abnormal behavior.* New York, NY: Wiley.

Sue, D. W., Capodilupo, C. M., Torino, G., Bucceri, J. M., Holder, A., Nadal, K., & Esquilin, M. (2007). Racial micro-aggressions in everyday Life. *American Psychologist, 62*(4), 271–286.

Tatum, B. (1998). *Why are all the Black kids sitting together in the cafeteria?* New York, NY: Basic Books.

Tucker, N., & Treviño, A. L. (2011). An art therapy domestic violence prevention group in Mexico. *Journal of Clinical Art Therapy, 1*(1), 16–24.

Williams, C. (2010). *Postgraduate art therapy in Mexico.* Unpublished masters research project. Loyola Marymount University, Los Angeles CA.

74

Latin American Art Therapy: Collective Dreams and Horizons of Hope

Selma Ciornai and Maria Cristina Ruiz

The scope of the current practice and field of art therapy in Latin America is traversed by the historical, economic, cultural, and social conditions in which the profession has developed in the region. This is evident in the responses of art therapists from Argentina, Uruguay, Brazil, Chile, Peru, Colombia, and El Salvador who replied to a common questionnaire, provided at the end of this text, to inform this chapter.[1] Thus, all references are through personal communications. The information from these interviews has been organized into four parts: first, an overview of the common trends in Latin American history, and Latin America's socioeconomic standing in the world, which provides consistency for art therapists in this region; second, a description of the influence of some pioneers, which has led to some training programs; third, a discussion concerning some of the main trends of current practice; and last, a reflection about our current horizons of action.

Latin America's Sociopolitical Context

The 1960s and the 1970s were characterized by dictatorships in Latin America supported and stimulated by the US government. The phantom of Cold War turned decent people—such as some artists who aimed for social change to combat major inequalities that characterized these countries—into dangerous "threats," often labeled as "communists." Torture and massive imprisonment were used, inducing censorship and a total lack of freedom.

In the following years, Latin American countries have lived with the contradictory, and sometimes painful, impact of becoming "modern" through established standards that did not always suit the needs of the local populations. Hence, internal wars, dictatorships, and other oppressive conditions caused large segments of the populations to live in the extremely harsh conditions of poverty, marginalization, and inequity, such as in Colombia and El Salvador.

The Wiley Handbook of Art Therapy, First Edition. Edited by David E. Gussak and Marcia L. Rosal.
© 2016 John Wiley & Sons, Ltd. Published 2016 by John Wiley & Sons, Ltd.

Despite these conditions, grassroots movements fostered by the theology of liberation and through social activism grew throughout the region. Such activism was rooted in the expressive and communicative arts, creating avenues of hope, solidarity, and conditions for a dignified means to earn one's livelihood. Such major influences included Paulo Freire and Augusto Boal, who were "signposts for the path" in creating a society with social justice and recognition of the *oppressed* (Boal, 1993; Freire, Ramos, & Macedo, 2000). Musicians, poets, theater players, and fine arts creators who defied the oppressive system developed other social activism initiatives. Using such art-based interventions, protestors and grassroots activists guided others toward raising people's consciousness and courage to act in defense of a more just society. These ideals and preoccupations became the foundation of Latin American art therapy. As Martin Zavala, a colleague from Peru, indicated: "it is important to highlight the importance of the arts as a response, also political, to the injustice and marginalization conditions that life nowadays imposes on us" (Zavala, personal communication, 2012).

Later, facing the struggles of vulnerable groups of people, it became clear that art therapy offered many avenues for action. Today, in these varied countries, art therapy's focus on psychosocial problems is evident. Art therapists work in clinics, institutions, and all kind of health and social programs, either dealing with populations diagnosed with pathologies, or with those who need individual and community support to build the capacities to cope and respond to the harsh conditions they face.

Early Encounters and Pioneers of Latin American Art Therapy: From Psychiatric Clinics to Training Schools

As in the United States, the immigration of refugees from World War II affected the early development of art-based interventions in clinical settings. Countries from the south, such as Argentina, Chile, and Brazil, developed art therapy earlier. Experiences in psychiatric hospitals occurred around the 1940s and 1950s due to the dissemination of psychoanalytical and Jungian approaches, brought by refugees from the war, or by those who traveled and had interacted with those who used these approaches.

For example, Hanna Yaxa Kwiatowska, a pioneer in family art therapy, at the time a sculptor, lived in Brazil for a while as a refugee. She then moved to the United States, where she trained as an art therapist, and later returned to Brazil in the 1960s to give art therapy courses and workshops. It is clear that she was the one who really planted the first seed of art therapy in Brazil. Maria Margarida de Carvalho, psychologist and professor, attended one of these courses, and was probably the first Brazilian psychotherapist who used art therapy resources explicitly.

However, prior to this, in 1923, Osório César began studying the artistic expressions of patients at the Psychiatric Hospital of Juqueri, in Sao Paulo, Brazil. He corresponded with Freud, organized several expositions, and published several books.

Later, in 1946, Nise da Silveira did similar work at the Psychiatric Hospital of Engenho de Dentro, Rio de Janeiro. Using art as treatment with psychiatric patients instead of electric shocks, she created the "Museum of the Unconscious" in 1952, a collection of patient's artworks that focused on Jungian archetypes. Silveira later visited Carl Jung and showed him the work she was developing. The book she published remains essential reading on the Jungian approach to art therapy.

Argentina's art therapy history was clearly influenced by the early psychoanalytical developments. By 1943, the Asociación Argentina de Psicoanálisis was created with the help of pioneer Matilde Ravscovski, who also trained as an artist, and integrated art in her work with children. Arminda Aberastury and her husband Enrique Pichon Riviere advocated the Kleinian approach to children's psychotherapy.

In other countries, such as Salvador, Colombia, Peru, and Uruguay, there was a growing number of art therapists who had trained abroad since the 1970s, studying psychoanalytical, Jungian, Gestalt, humanistic, systemic, and transpersonal approaches. At this time, a few foreign art therapists too were visiting and bringing their expertise to these Latin American countries, including Judith Rubin, Bobby Stoll, Frances Anderson, and Michael Franklin.

In Brazil, Argentina, and Chile, some of the aforementioned initiatives in the psychiatric milieu allowed for the research and onsite training needed to create formal training programs. Still, art therapists who trained in the United States, Israel, Switzerland, and Spain started other programs between the late 1980s and the early 2000s.

Argentina

"A relevant precedent in Argentina was the development of the music therapy program in 1968, crucial for building awareness of the healing power of the arts. In this country, art therapy experiences originally received strong influence from psychoanalytical currents. Later, Gestalt, psychodrama, and Jungian trends came to play a role in training new professionals" (excerpt from Alejandro Reisin's written survey, 2012).

In 1995, the Superior School of Fine Arts Ernesto de la Cárcova started an art therapy seminar. While in this class, graduate students worked at the women's psychiatric hospital's day program, followed by a series of seminars concerning art therapy. This eventually led to the creation of Instituto Universitario Nacional del Arte (IUNA), a graduate program in art therapy in Buenos Aires. This program, coordinated by Adriana Farias, a psychopedagogist (who also held a degree in art), and Marcelo Magnasco, a psychologist, was the first Latin American graduate program given in Spanish at a university. The program was officially approved in 2000, and partnered with diverse psychiatric hospitals, schools, geriatric institutions, women's jail, and other government organizations for health and educational services, having already graduated more than 200 professionals (Farias & Magnassco, personal communication, 2014). Frances Anderson, a guest teacher, was an important contributor to its development.

In 1996, Alejandro Reisin and Alicia Boljat founded and coordinated Escuela Argentina de Arteterapia, also in Buenos Aires. Both are psychologists and artists, and offer multimodal training with a humanistic approach. They emphasize health promotion with a clinical perspective in clinical, educational, and community settings, and have a staff of teachers with different specialties. Lately, other institutes have started offering shorter training, such as Asociación de Psiquiatras Argentinos, which promotes panels, forums, and training.

Other Argentinian institutions also offer shorter courses, such as Inter-American Space for Art Therapy and Music Therapy in Buenos Aires, coordinated by Hector Fiorini and Estela Garber. Over the last 10 years, two new spaces have opened in Cordoba: Arteterapia Cordoba, coordinated by Verónica Corna and Lia Ana Romero, and Chez Nous, coordinated by Javier Larrecochea and Viviana Ripoll. Both offer seminars, introductory courses, and workshops.

Chile

Art therapy arose in Chile in the 1950s when psychiatry and mental health were being incorporated into general health institutions, and psychodynamic psychotherapies were common. In 1955, Mimi Marinovic, considered the pioneer of art therapy in Chile, started working in the recently founded Servicio de Medicina Psicosomática y Psiquiatría Social, in Hospital del Salvador, in Santiago. Through Marinovic's initiatives, the principles and techniques of art therapy were applied to wide array of people through individual and group sessions. This work was also applied at the community level, and taught to students at Universidad de Chile. Likewise, she carried out therapeutic activities through music, performing arts, and psychodrama. This alliance of arts with an anthropological view of medicine meant putting into action arts therapies through creative, interpretative, and receptive processes in the prevention, treatment, rehabilitation, and recovery of health.

In 1957, she was invited to initiate the course of "Psychology on Art" at Universidad Católica de Chile. This work continued uninterrupted until 1980, when she had to leave the hospital and universities because of her nation's political situation. The American Art Therapy Association granted her professional member status in 1983. Currently, she is vice president of the Société Internationale de Psychopathologie de l'Expression et d' Art Thérapie.

When Marinovic eventually returned to academic life at the University of Chile, she founded the first graduate program in arts therapies in 1999 (from Marinovic's written survey). The program's coordination passed in 2004 to Pamela Reyes, a psychologist and art therapist who had trained in the master's program in art therapy at the Universidad de Barcelona, Spain.

Since 2007, Chile has offered continuing-education and graduate programs that examined art therapy through a larger scope, including expressive art therapy and body-based art interventions. Daniela Gloger and Eduardo Torres started a master's degree course in art therapy at the Universidad del Desarrollo's Espaciocrea Centro de Arte Terapia y Psicodrama (from Eduardo Torres' written survey, 2012). These two programs included visiting teachers from abroad and, recently, collaborative agreements between local universities and universities from other countries.

Training at Universidad de Chile emphasized research in art therapy, especially concerns with the relationship between art, health, and community. The recently developed master's degree course at the Universidad del Desarrollo is psychodynamically oriented. There is also a Jungian-oriented graduate program in expressive therapies at Universidad Católica, a fellowship course in expressive therapies at Universidad Adolfo Ibañez, and an art-body, humanistic-oriented course at Universidad Andrés Bello. However, overall, there is more weight on psychodynamically oriented training in Chile (from Pamela Reyes' written survey, 2012).

However, as in all Latin America, there is still concern with the recognition of art therapy as a profession in Chile.

> The fact that Universidad de Chile is accredited and is widely recognized as a public university for its academic excellence has contributed to the goodwill regarding the professional performance and expertise of our alumni. Even though there is acknowledgment of the contribution of art therapy to areas of health, community and education, it is

very difficult to find specific work spaces and job offers for art therapists. In this regard, the Chilean Association of Art Therapy (ACAT), founded in 2006, has been making some efforts, especially with the Ministry of Health. An important issue to consider which limits their actions is that Chile is a country whose dictatorial government does not recognize the political influence of professional associations. In this regard, the association is more effective in the dissemination of art therapy than in a legal recognition of the profession (excerpt from Pamela Reyes' written survey, 2012)

Brazil[2]

Maria Margarida de Carvalho and Joya Eliezer offered short, introductory, and extension courses in the 1970s in São Paulo, Brazil. But it was not until the 1980s that training programs really developed. Clinica Pomar offered one of the two initial training programs. Since 1982, Jungian psychologist Ângela Philippini opened a study group that years later became a training program. Philippini had contact with Nise da Silveira and was part of a group that invited Diane Rode and Bobby Stoll to Rio de Janeiro to provide training. Philippini later studied in Paris with Jackes Klein and his team at Institut National d'Expression, de Création, d'Art et Thérapie (INECAT), and completed a master's degree in Barcelona. She also created new groups in Minas Gerais, Recife, and Goiânia.

The other Brazilian art therapy training program was housed at the Instituto Sedes Sapientiae in São Paulo. It was founded in 1989 by Gestalt therapist Selma Ciornai, who studied art therapy in Israel in the early 1970s with Peretz Hesse and, later, with art therapists in the United States, including Janie Rhyne, Vija Lusebrink, and Cay Drachnik. She received her MA in art therapy through California State University and became a credentialed member of the American Art Therapy Association. Upon returning to Brazil in 1984, she led workshops, study groups, and introductory courses in Rio de Janeiro and São Paulo. The extension course that she created at Sedes turned into a training program in 1989. Later, a branch was started in Porto Alegre.

For more than two decades, São Paulo and Rio de Janeiro were the only states to offer art therapy training. However, from 1986 to 1990, Marise Zimmerman led an art therapy study group in Porto Alegre, south of Brazil, with professionals who worked with her in a psychiatric clinic. New training programs have since started in these and other cities in Brazil in the late 1990s and early 2000s.

A group of art therapy teachers from several cities became important references in Brazil. This pioneer generation harbors mostly Jungian, Gestalt, transpersonal, and systemic approaches. Too numerous to mention, these professionals attended national and international congresses, founding União Brasileira de Associações de Arteterapia (UBAAT) in 2006—a union of 11 regional art therapy associations. "Today there are more or less 120 training programs all over Brazil connected to UBAAT's criteria" (Angelica Shigihara, personal communication, 2014).

Peru

In 1996, a team led by José Bárcenas, a psychologist and musician, formed the Centro para el Desarrollo de las Terapias de Arte in Peru, and began their work displaying a large body of art produced by patients from the psychiatric hospital Víctor Larco

Herrera. In 2001, this team began a long-term program in art therapy with the Universidad Mayor de San Marcos and, since 2004, with the Women's University of the Sacred Heart.

In 2004, Martin Zavala formed Terapia de Artes Expresivas (TAE) in Peru, and began working with the intermodal methodology of expressive arts therapy in association with the European Graduate School in Switzerland, and with support from several educators, including Paolo Knill, Steve Levine, and Ellen Levine. Its intention was to integrate the value of ancestral knowledge and the healing power of traditional Peruvian and Latino-American arts with art therapy.

Colombia

Sasana Colombia, a transpersonal-oriented organization, integrated a short workshop in its training on contemplative art therapy in Colombia in 2001. By 2003, a program of about 150 hours oriented toward teaching how to approach the art therapist–client relationship was established. Andree Salom and María Cristina Ruiz, alumni from Pratt Institute and Naropa University, respectively, taught for the initial program. AR.TE, the Colombian Art Therapy Association founded in 2009,[3] offers bimonthly lectures in an art gallery in Bogotá and has an art therapy exhibit every year. AR.TE's art therapists in Bogotá work in private practice, support art development at schools, and work with children at *Sanar* and other medical institutions; a core group from the association provides peer supervision. However, there is no formal university training yet, and only very few courses available.

There are also initiatives in Medellin, led by Luces Montoya and other artists, psychologists, anthropologists, occupational therapists, and communication experts who are interested in the connection between arts and healing and the psychosocial impact of art practices. Among these artists is Carlos Gutierrez, who worked in a therapeutic community that supports people confronting substance abuse. His work integrates puppetry, costume design, and performance as an avenue for expression, and has been presented in several art therapy conferences in Latin America.

El Salvador

Ruth Guttfreund has been an active member of the nascent art therapy network in El Salvador. After training at the University of Hertfordshire, England, she established her practice in El Salvador in 2002.

> In El Salvador, art therapy is not yet recognized as a profession, even though governmental institutions have required my services in crisis intervention due to natural disasters, prevention of violence projects, and a seminar/training to mental health professionals who work in the public sector of the Mental Health Program of the Health Ministry. We live a very difficult reality, which entails poverty, violence, delinquency, domestic violence, and gang activity. In a natural disaster intervention, for example, we have to improvise and see where our clients could sit and paint … not knowing in advance whether the following week the same people will be there, or if they will have been moved to a different place. Many of the emergency situations demand flexibility, and an engagement in the here and now far more intense than the usual session you give in a studio in normal circumstances. You may have only that day to touch souls with your client, give some hope, give space to

express and contain an unimaginable pain. ... Is it possible? Yes, they did not teach me about this in my training, but I have experienced this, and know that it is possible. (excerpt from Guttfreund's written survey in 2012)

Uruguay

While art therapy has not yet developed as a standalone area of study, Jungian psychologist Ana Carolina Berta Hernández has begun offering study groups and a training program in Montevidéo.

> The mental health professionals who work with art are mostly trained solely in verbal psychotherapy. The image is generally seen as a way to clarify, underline, or amplify what words say, and in need to be further elaborated with words. This state of affairs certainly has to do with the impact of a long-term tradition where classic psychoanalysis—and its emphasis in secondary elaboration—played a very important role. I have been witnessing a change in this paradigm in the last few years, thanks to the growing impact of Jungian analysis and Gestalt therapy in Uruguay. Both Jungian and Gestalt therapists are still working—most of the time—with arts in therapy, not yet as therapy, but with a comprehension of the value of the image "per se" that is not present in other anthropological models. (excerpt written from Hernández's written survey in 2012)

Common Trends, Problems, and Developments

In sum, several of these countries have developed alliances and knowledge to support practice and formal training programs. In other countries, this is starting to happen. Some of these programs' students had further trainings in countries abroad and opened avenues for art therapy from diverse schools of thought. This has allowed further understandings of the specificity of art therapists' work.

However, there continues to be a need for wider dissemination of this knowledge among mental health professionals and within the general public. It is necessary to establish a distinguishable identity that supports development of careers and respect for the way the art therapist approaches the art product, content, and process of their clients. The boundaries between professional art therapists' work and other uses of art in the clinical milieu are not always clear, and the term *art therapy* is used without proper distinction. To exemplify, the Uruguayan art therapist Ana Carolina Berta Hernández described a situation that is also common in other countries:

> The Spanish term for art therapy, "arteterapia," is starting to be used among mental health professionals, yet the meaning of the word is not fully understood and is often misused. Art was first introduced in our psychiatric hospitals in the early 1960s, as a way to provide patients with a productive activity. Over time, ateliers in hospitals worked as occupational therapy spaces, or recreational ones, but the therapeutic value was relegated and the importance of the whole process revolved around the product. What was created needed to be useful or to be adaptive. Despite that, there was an understanding that art was able to provide some structure and relief for those who suffered from severe mental health disorders. Nowadays, art in psychiatric or nursery settings is still misunderstood as crafting—sometimes even trivialized. (excerpt from Hernández's written survey in 2012)

Currently, the practice of art therapy in the region has expanded to include many trends in how professional art therapists approach their work. Some implement Jungian, Gestalt, phenomenological, or transpersonal approaches, while others cultivate psychoanalytic and psychodynamic perspectives.

Art therapy was included in the Brazilian Classification of Occupations in 2013. Work is being done to extend this achievement by recognizing art therapy as a profession by Brazil's Health Ministry. A big step in this direction is that art therapy is included in the basic health care modalities (integrative practices) in many states. The neighboring countries will certainly follow this path of recognition.

Additional resources include a large bibliography of art therapy books and journals published in Brazil and Argentina. "Brazil alone has well over 200 books on art therapy or books that contain chapters on art therapy" (Angelica Shigihara, personal communication, 2012). Brazil also has a number of publications from a few American authors, translated to Portuguese. "Doubtless, Brazil is the country that offers the higher amount of art therapy publications" (Alejandro Reisin, personal communication, 2012).

Art therapy books, chapters, and journal articles have been published in Argentina. In Chile, following the last congress, an art therapy journal was edited and compiled that contained all of the main presentations. In addition, there are books edited in Spain for the Spanish-speaking countries.

The second decade of the twenty-first century has begun with diverse circumstances. Countries such as Chile, Brazil, and Argentina have gained some recognition for art therapy, while countries such as Colombia, Peru, Uruguay, and El Salvador still have work to do, particularly in areas such as professional identity and careers opportunities.

Congresses and Associations

In all of the countries that participated in the survey that informs this chapter, a significant group of professionals trained abroad in various universities' graduate programs,[4] and returned to their countries of origin to create new training programs. In some of these countries, these professionals established and joined national associations that developed standards for training programs, requirements for teaching and supervision in art therapy, a common code of ethics, and guidelines for research. These associations evaluate training programs and bring information to new students and to the public. In some cases, they support supervision.

The challenges faced and the lessons learned about the practice of art therapy in each of these seven countries became the spark to initiate a series of regional congresses. Initially, all of these countries worked directly with North American and European schools of art therapy, and virtually knew nothing about each other.

The idea of a congress that could promote contact and exchange of experiences among South American countries had its first seed at the 1999 American Art Therapy Association (AATA) conference in Orlando, Florida,[5] and later at the European Consortium for Arts Therapies in Education's (ECARTE) Madrid conference (2003), in which a few representatives from Brazil and Argentina met for the first time. Later, in 2003, in a meeting in Goiania, at a Brazilian National Congress to which Adriana Farias and Marcelo Magnasco from Buenos Aires and Mimi Marinovic from Chile were invited, the idea for the congress was born. From then on, art therapists started to invite each other to regional and national art therapy conferences.

First held in 2005 in Rio de Janeiro, Brazil, the Mercosul Congress brought together art therapists from Brazil, Chile, Argentina, and Uruguay. The second Mercosur Congress and the First Art Therapy Latin American Congress were held in 2007, in Buenos Aires. Later, art therapists from Peru, Colombia, and El Salvador became active in the network formed at these congresses. Since then, art therapists and people interested in the field gather every 2 years: 2009 in Santiago, Chile; 2011 in Ouro Preto, Brazil; and 2013 and again in 2015 in Buenos Aires. These meetings have fostered the exchange of work experiences, as well as discussions and networking opportunities toward common projects.

Current Challenges and Hopes

Although the challenges are many, Latin American art therapists seek to respond to and address the needs of people through building initiatives from regional perspectives. Collective disasters, such as floods, mudslides, and earthquakes, have captured the attention of these art therapists. The same attention has been given to community work.

There are many undiscovered needs for the professional art therapist in Latin America, but there is, as well, an extremely rich environment to work in, cooperate, and grow together. In considering the many issues and complex realities of this continent, there seems to be a need and an urgency to write and publish more books and articles, and present more in congresses to other professions.

As Chilean art therapist Pamela Reyes indicated:

Latin American art therapists face a twofold process: on the one hand, we have previous and present currents of practice articulating the problems of art and social or psychological health; these currents are rooted in the traditions of popular education—as it is widely seen on cultural practices around music creation, collective theater, and other art related to grassroots movements. One the other hand, the professional development in the field of art therapy in European and North American countries have defined a tradition according to their standards. Thus, Latin American art therapy development is traversed by the effort to find the basis of our work on the boundaries between these two processes—by studying, valuing, and understanding the relevance of our work and local experiences, and by taking on critically what is already a canon for the art therapists abroad. (from Pamela Reyes' written excerpt, 2012)

Similarly:

Among the different theoretical currents that guide the formation [of] graduate programs, [we] can frame ours as critical regionalism; that is to say, a position that, without denying the internationalization or globalization of scientific thought, seeks a differentiated production from the region. (excerpt from Adriana Farias and Marcelo Magnasco's written survey, 2012)

This has been the path until now. In our congresses, it is clear that, although we live in a global world, and have much to learn from all experiences and countries where art therapy has been long developed, we need to look for our own identity and develop our own way. And, in our congresses, we realize that we have many rich contributions to offer and share with the global art therapy community.

Appendix I   List of Survey Participants

We would like to give special thanks to those who were willing to be interviewed, and lent their words to this chapter:

Adriana Farias y Marcelo Magnasco—Departamento de Artes Audiovisuales. Pos grado en Arteterapia, Inst Universitario nacional del Arte, IUNA, Buenos Aires, Argentina

Alejandro Reisin—Primera Escuela Argentina de Arteterapia, Buenos Aires, Argentina

Ana Carolina Berta Hernández—Montevideo, Uruguay

Angelica Shigihara—Instituto da Familia—INFAPA, Porto Alegre, Brazil

Carlos Gutiérrez—Bogotá, Colombia

Eduardo Torres y Daniela Gloger—Espacio Crea, Santiago, Chile. PosGrado en Arteterapia, Universidad del Desarrollo

Pepe Barcenas y Milagros Meza—Equipo de Terapias de Arte, Diplomado de Terapias de Arte, Universidad Femenina del Sagrado Corazón, Lima, Peru

Javier Larrecochea y Viviana Clarisa Ripol—Espacio Terapéutico "Chez Nous"—Cordoba, Argentina.

Maria Cristina Ruiz—Universidad del Valle, Instituto de Educación y Pedagogía, Cali, Colombia, PhD student at Simon Fraser University

Martin Zavala—TAE (Terapia de Artes Expresivas)—Peru

Mimi Marinovic—Universidad de Chile, Santiago, Chile

Pamela Reyes—Universidad de Chile, Santiago, Chile

Ruth Guttfreund—El Salvador

Selma Ciornai—Art Therapy Department, Instituto Sedes Sapientiae, São Paulo, Brazil/Instituto da Familia—INFAPA, Porto Alegre, Brazil

Verónica Corna & Lia Ana Romero—Arteterapiacordoba, Córdoba, Argentina

Appendix II   Survey Questionnaire

1. Since when did art therapy begin in your country, and who are its main pioneers?
2. Where did the pioneers get their training from? With whom? What type of approaches? What were their main influences?
3. Has art therapy been recognized at a legal level in your country? What kind of certification is required for its practice? Are there any openings for paid positions

in the government or non-governmental fields? Overall, what is the employment situation and legal recognition of the professionals in the field in your country?

4. Traditionally, art therapy practice has two main currents: the ones who concentrate on art as therapy, and those who give more importance to art as psychotherapy. There are also diverse art therapy approaches: analytical, psychoanalytical, Jungian, Gestalt, cognitive, etc. Give some information about the main approaches guiding the current practice in your country, especially the approaches that have been the main influence in the formal and nonformal trainings.

5. Considering the social, cultural, and economic realities of the diverse populations that receive any treatment or art-based intervention, how are the needs and demands of these populations met by art therapists in your country? Is there any specific aspect that you think should be highlighted under the consideration given to these social, cultural, and economic realities? Please give examples to illustrate your answer.

6. Which are the current developments in art therapy in your country that are bringing new light into the field? What do you see as enriching or innovating for the global art therapy community? Please be specific, and give examples.

7. There is some discussion concerning the use of art and other expressive "resources" by psychologists with no specific training in art therapy. In your point of view, which are the psychologists' traits that overlap with the ones of the art therapists (as it may happen with occupational therapists or art educators). How do your country's training programs and art therapists approach these discussions?

8. How many publications concerning art therapy have been published in your country? Please be specific about books and magazines

9. Please list the research initiatives and studies made by local art therapists.

10. How do you see the future of art therapy in your country and in the region? Are there new paths and challenges lying ahead?

Endnotes

1   The authors acknowledge the support given by the art therapists who provided information for this chapter. As we moved to the process of writing, we had to choose a way to organize the information, keeping the time and space limits established by the editors. We also restricted our survey to the colleagues we had personal contacts with and who we came to consider as key persons in the art therapy field in their countries. We hope that our colleagues are well represented in our words.

2   This section on Brazil was partially informed by: S. Ciornai & L. Diniz (2008). Arteterapia en Brasil. In *Arteterapia* (Vol. 3). Universidade Complutense de Madrid.

3   During the early 2000s, art therapy alumni from programs in Argentina, Spain, the United Kingdom, Australia, and the United States, originally from Colombia, returned home.

4   Including the United States, Israel, Spain, United Kingdom, Switzerland, Canada, France, and Germany.

5   At this Congress, Selma Ciornai and Eloisa Fagalli from Brazil met Marcelo Magnasco from Argentina for the first time.

References

Boal, A. (C. A. McBride [trans.]) (1993). *Theatre of the oppressed*. New York, NY: Theatre Communications Group.

Freire, P., Bergman Ramos, M., & Macedo, D. (2000). *Pedagogy of the oppressed: 30th anniversary edition*. New York, NY: Bloomsbury Academic.

75

Art Therapy in the Caribbean
Lesli-Ann M. Belnavis and Sarah A. Soo Hon

Art therapy is practiced in the Caribbean; however, there is little documentation of its impact in the region. The intention of this chapter is to attempt to repair this deficit by highlighting developments in art therapy within the English-speaking Caribbean. This chapter will focus on the experiences of two art therapists who are native to, and practice in, the islands of Jamaica and Trinidad and Tobago. Additionally, it will include the contributions of other art therapists who also practice in the Caribbean, and who have graciously granted interviews. We intend to address issues related to cross-cultural art therapy experiences, including: the cultural approach to art, the perception and response to therapy, and the type of infrastructure required to support an art therapy service.

Perception of Art Therapy

In Jamaica and Trinidad and Tobago, people typically view art as an expression of skilled individuals. It is mostly appreciated through decorative work, or perceived as utilitarian. In many instances, individuals create art as a form of recreation or expression, but stop at a young age. Those who continue to engage in art making through high school and tertiary level usually do so because they are perceived as "skilled." While art forms such as music, dance, and drama have been incorporated into mainstream Caribbean cultures, these forms of expression are generally supported in theatres, schools, or during national celebrations. Oftentimes, the people involved in these art forms are not encouraged to pursue their skills as a career. Artists are often encouraged to pursue other livelihoods that can provide for themselves and their families (Williams, 2010). This may include professions in law or medicine.

Although it seems clear the Caribbean region can benefit from therapies that encourage self-expression, it is also clear that the process of therapy is not always natural for individuals. This is not to imply that people from the Caribbean do not know how to be self-expressive, because they are certainly known to express themselves in various visual and performing art forms. However, many of them have difficulty appropriately expressing emotionally traumatic experiences, and the concept of psychotherapy is not

The Wiley Handbook of Art Therapy, First Edition. Edited by David E. Gussak and Marcia L. Rosal.
© 2016 John Wiley & Sons, Ltd. Published 2016 by John Wiley & Sons, Ltd.

readily accepted or understood among Caribbean populations (Gopaul-McNicol, 1993). Typically, people do not seek psychological treatment when they feel overwhelmed. They do not share with strangers about personal or family matters; however, they rely heavily on their faith and seek counseling from spiritual leaders. Even though therapy may be initiated through guidance counseling, psychological help, and psychiatric services, the typical response to therapy is "Me nuh need therapy because me nuh mad," which translates to "I don't need therapy because I'm not crazy or mentally ill." People often reject therapeutic services because of its stigma[1] and because they do not believe they need therapeutic services to help them cope with difficulties. Nevertheless, it is acknowledged that there is a potential for great benefits for art therapy services in the Caribbean, and we support the growing awareness of the need for established structures to facilitate these services.

In the Caribbean, there are only a handful of practitioners in art therapy and few existing employment opportunities. Owing to the lack of awareness about art therapy, art therapists spearhead the development of new art therapy programs, in addition to providing therapeutic services. Many do not easily receive the benefits of art therapy, and art therapists need to make a conscious effort to market themselves to potential employers.

One of the chapter authors, Lesli-Ann Belnavis, is an art therapist working in Jamaica. She notes that she had to make a conscious effort to network with professionals in mental health and education. This required her to approach psychologists, psychiatrists, educators, government ministries, and professional organizations in order to establish a system of referral. In her experience, some professionals were unwilling to refer cases to her, even though it was recognized that the client might benefit from art therapy interventions. This response may be due to a lack of understanding about the benefits of art therapy, and difficulty with understanding clients' suitability for such services. In addition, other professionals admitted inability to support the service financially, despite acknowledging the usefulness of art therapy for some of their clients. The process of increasing awareness about art therapy is difficult because the concept challenges preconceived ideas about therapy, counseling, and the use of medication. To help dispel this misconception and encourage awareness, Belnavis utilized various forums such as radio and television interviews, newspaper articles, workshops, and guest lectures.

An art therapist[2] based in Grenada affirmed that there is no "support for art therapy in Grenada, but there is interest in its efficacy among the psychiatric population, as well as growing interest in how it can be applied to child and adolescent trauma victims." Kim Bryan, who is based in Barbados, added that there are currently no structures in place to support art therapy in Barbados, such as training and supervision opportunities. She contended that agencies of health, mental health, and childcare are unable to accommodate the practice of art therapy. The therapist is left with limited resources to facilitate art therapy sessions. Even though some professionals are aware of art therapy, Bryan suggested they tend to focus on its use as an assessment tool for children only. This is a sentiment echoed by all the Caribbean-based art therapists we interviewed, who observed that some professionals place value solely on the use of art as an assessment tool. As such, little or no value is given to the creative process and the art materials required to enable art making.

There are also challenges related to the art product—how it is valued, perceived, and what happens to it after the art therapy session. Little value is given to the art product, and this influences what clients do with their artwork after the session. Some throw away the art or give it to the therapist, as they do not value the artwork they created. Additionally, supporting professionals who do not fully understand the creative process may ask clients to create a "pretty" picture rather than respect the symbolic value of the image and the therapeutic process.

Cultural Factors that affect the Art Therapy Process

Key elements that affect the implementation of art therapy in a Caribbean setting include: the existence of subcultures, spiritual beliefs, funding for art therapy, and continued professional development. Art therapists working in a community or with at-risk groups need to consider cultural factors that affect the art therapy process within that subculture. We observed that, in the Caribbean, many only seek professional advice when situations become critical. Individuals may not discuss their problems for fear of looking weak among their peers or of being seen as an "informer."[3] In these instances, persons view self-disclosure as a type of informing, and attempt to guard themselves by remaining silent. For that reason, the establishment of trust and rapport are key cultural aspects of the therapeutic process in the Caribbean (Gopaul-McNicol, 1993). Caribbean-based art therapists also observed that art therapy may bypass such defenses by focusing on the creative process rather than verbal interaction. Furthermore, as art therapy facilitates expression without words, the art therapy process can be useful for children (Malchiodi, 2007). This is especially suitable for children in the Caribbean, who are raised to focus on achievement rather than to be self-reflective.

Many also prefer to rely on spiritual beliefs to aid them through difficult issues (Gopaul-McNicol, 1993). An art therapist based in Grenada reported that religious figures and practices are often used to cope with challenges. Ethnic groups in the Caribbean often identify with religious traditions, which influence their receptiveness to seeking counsel outside of their family unit or religious group. In Trinidad and Tobago, for example, families may prefer to seek counseling from persons with similar family traditions, ethnic backgrounds, and religious beliefs.

Funding also affects the practice of art therapy in the Caribbean. A person may recognize a need for therapy, but may be unable to afford it. Williams (2010) noted that high unemployment and underemployment in the Jamaican economy makes access to therapy difficult. Art therapy in the Caribbean is not as developed as in other regions, and therefore therapeutic services are typically funded through grants from private sector organizations. This affects the therapeutic process, as the duration of services depends on the funding provided.

Belnavis shared her experience of working in a school, where art therapy services were only funded for a year through a grant. She observed that staff and students were unfamiliar with her role as a therapist; they exhibited difficulty with distinguishing between her occupation as an art therapist, as opposed to a guidance counselor or art teacher. Belnavis noted that this experience highlighted the continuous need to spread awareness about art therapy and to provide in-service training for staff. She also became aware of the need for students to become comfortable with expressing themselves through art making.

There also does not seem to be a structure in place for the provision of clinical supervision. Art therapists in the Caribbean seek supervision from registered art therapists who reside outside of the region. Additionally, continued professional development is acquired in other countries, as there is no opportunity for this within the Caribbean. Art therapists in the Caribbean remain registered with the Art Therapy Credentials Board and the British Association of Art Therapists in order to maintain professional identity. It is clear that the development of professional bodies, within the islands, will address issues related to: protection from malpractice; title protection; supervision; continued training; peer support; ethics; and research. Despite establishing the Caribbean Art Therapy Association (CATA), which will be discussed in later sections, there is the ongoing need for formal recognition of art therapy as an allied health profession in the region.

Development of Art Therapy in Jamaica and Trinidad and Tobago

Non-native art therapists have been known to visit the Caribbean to provide therapeutic services, offer workshops, and deliver other brief training sessions in art therapy. While there is some awareness of these services within the local community, there does not seem to be published literature that identifies or explores what has been done. In considering the development of art therapy in the islands of Jamaica and Trinidad and Tobago, the chapter authors provided personal accounts of their experiences. The chapter authors are both qualified in the United States, but have been working in their native islands. Their experiences have been grounded in three key areas: education, community, and public health.

Art Therapy in the Schools

Belnavis conducted art therapy sessions at three schools in Kingston, Jamaica. Her services were sponsored by non-governmental organizations, which heavily impacted the duration of the art therapy program and the amount of time she was able to provide.

The School for Therapy, Education & Parenting Centre (STEP) and Genesis Academy both cater to the needs of students with psychological, physical, and developmental disabilities. Belnavis conducted individual and group art therapy sessions with students at these institutions, encouraging non-verbal communication, while focusing on their developmental needs. She incorporated treatment goals in the students' individual educational plans (IEPs), which included: increasing communication and social interaction among peers; increasing cognitive awareness; promoting self-awareness; improving coping skills related to a disability; encouraging sensory stimulation and integration; encouraging self-expression; and increasing self-esteem.

Based on the students' emotional and developmental needs, such services should be integrated within the educational system, so they can receive art therapy regularly. While Belnavis ensured that her treatment goals were congruent with the students' IEPs, support was not established within the educational system for mandatory therapeutic services. It was evident that staff and parents needed to be educated on the process of art therapy and how it fits within the current educational structure.

Belnavis also organized an art therapy exhibition, entitled "True Expressions—Our Story," to showcase the benefits of art therapy for students with disabilities. Part of the exhibition highlighted the case of Rohan (a pseudonym), a boy who had been receiving services for a year. Diagnosed with cerebral palsy, he had limited mobility in his fingers and communicated non-verbally (gestures). Typically, he engaged in regressive and repetitive behavior, but after 1 year, Rohan was able to initiate the session by requesting to trace the art therapist's hand, before having her trace his. He used gestures to request glue and glitter, which he used to make a circular form in his drawing (see Figure 75.1). When Belnavis acknowledged what he had created, Rohan communicated through gestures that his image depicted "You [the therapist], me, and the school." He indicated that the circular form was his representation of the school. His ability to illustrate this image highlighted the influence of art therapy on his cognitive development. It allowed him to express himself and communicate his feelings and observations through the art, despite his difficulty with verbal interaction.

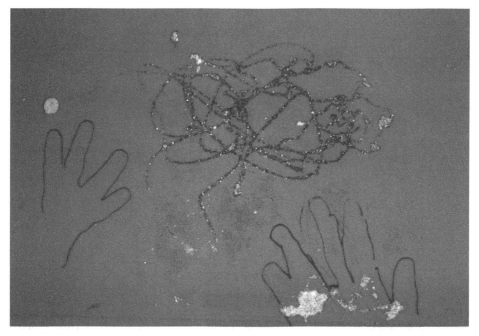

Figure 75.1 You, me, and the school.

Art Therapy in the Community

Sarah Soo Hon worked with the Autistic Society of Trinidad and Tobago to provide group art therapy services in a community setting. Similar to the schools highlighted earlier in the chapter, this non-governmental organization was funded by corporate sponsors. Group art therapy sessions were offered to persons with autism and their families. Parents were educated on the value of making art with their children, and were encouraged to experience the art therapy process. Clients were invited to explore the art process and experiment with materials during art therapy (see Figure 75.2). Soo Hon observed that community-based art therapy helped clients to adapt to new experiences and engage in social interaction. Many parents participated in groups and reported that art therapy was relaxing for them.

Belnavis volunteered with a recreational club known as Blue Hair Purple Hats. This group met once per month, and Belnavis conducted group art therapy sessions with the elderly members, who had lost loved ones or were coping with illness and displayed signs of memory loss or dementia. She observed that group members became more active, and the sessions allowed them to process traumatic memories.

Figure 75.2   Masks from a children's summer camp at the Autistic Society of Trinidad and Tobago.

Art Therapy in Public Health

Sarah Soo Hon provided art therapy at the St. Ann's Hospital, which offers public healthcare for patients with psychiatric illness. She developed an art therapy program that catered to the needs of patients who also received pharmacotherapy. Although most sessions were with individuals, she also conducted group sessions or workshops in both inpatient and outpatient settings.

Patients were often curious about art therapy and how the process functioned as a form of treatment. Adults sometimes insisted that art was only useful with children. Nevertheless, their perspectives usually changed, and they became receptive to art therapy interventions. They learnt to explore the materials; to create; and to address issues in their lives that were internalized for years such as using the art therapy process to address her feelings of loss, owing to the death of of a close family member. The artwork shown below reflects the reality of a mother's absence. In particular, it shows the processing of grief through the symbol of a skeleton, which represents a mother's body. (see Figure 75.3).

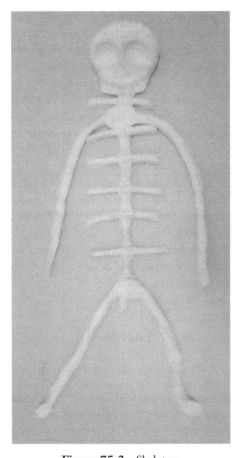

Figure 75.3 Skeleton.

Soo Hon observed that staff education was an effective tool for building awareness and acceptance of art therapy. Education included conference presentations for the benefit of colleagues in the setting, and psycho-education for patients to engage in discussion about art therapy. Soo Hon reflected that the progress of art therapy was encouraging, although challenging. She noted that many professionals were curious about art therapy and recognized the value of a multimodal approach to treatment, while others did not acknowledge the value of interventions other than pharmacotherapy.

Future of Art Therapy in the Caribbean

Overall, the development of art therapy in the Caribbean continues to be a challenging journey. Art therapists have to be flexible and open to networking and educating others about the profession, while conducting services both voluntarily and paid. It can be said that the region has some distance to go in terms of providing support for art therapists. Needless to say, some progress has been made in terms of educating the public and professionals. The Edna Manley College of the Visual and Performing Arts in Jamaica, for example, has established a post-graduate certificate program in art therapy. Students of this program graduate as art therapy assistants, under the supervision of a qualified art therapist. While the need arises for art therapists to be sensitive to cultural issues related to their clients, there is hope that contributions will be made in meaningful research unique to the practice of art therapy in the Caribbean.

Support for art therapists in the Caribbean began July 2011, through the formation of the Caribbean Art Therapy Association (CATA). CATA functions as a support network for art therapists in the Caribbean region and its diaspora. It began with the coming together of art therapists from various islands in the region. Two issues raised during the discussion were: (1) creating awareness of art therapy, and (2) addressing feelings of isolation owing to physical distance from peers. The association was formed based on the perceived need to address art therapy in the context of Caribbean culture. As awareness of this field continues to grow in the Caribbean, and as art therapy professionals return to the region, there is hope that CATA will develop and contribute to the establishment of licensing, which can ensure the ethical practice of art therapy. There is also optimism that art therapists will play an integral role in mental health and education programs within government agencies, and that more institutions will be involved in the education of professionals.

Endnotes

1 The stigma is associated with the belief that one only receives therapy if he or she has a psychotic disorder, and may be viewed as an outcast.
2 This art therapist is Grenadian-born and preferred not to be named.
3 "Informer" in this context is one who may be viewed as a snitch, a person who discloses information about the community or another person (i.e., illegal activities). The typical reaction to one who is deemed an informer is often negative.

References

Gopaul-McNicol, S. A. (1993). *Working with West Indian Families.* New York, NY: Guilford Press.

Malchiodi, C. A. (2007). *The art therapy sourcebook* (2nd ed.). New York, NY: McGraw Hill.

Williams, C. Y. (2010). *Art: A healing tool for children: An introduction to art therapy in the Caribbean.* New York, NY: Barlands Press.

Part IX

Current and Contemporary Issues in Art Therapy

Introduction

The final section of this handbook is dedicated to the issues that art therapists have debated in recent years. The authors address some of the concerns that an art therapist may face in his or her professional lifespan.

Phillips' introductory chapter wrestles with the first and foremost question of the field, *Identity of the Art Therapist*. In her thought-provoking chapter, Philips deconstructs this question. While Phillips recognizes the past 50–60 years as a time of "progress and mapping of the territory of art therapy, the identity issue for art therapists still appears to have twists and turns ahead." How members of the field deal with such ambiguity may be the real concern. In the following chapter, Kaplan discusses *Social Action Art Therapy*. She explores how art therapy can ameliorate social woes that have long been neglected. Kaplan explores the role that an art therapist has in bearing "the responsibility to the larger community." Kaplan concludes:

> Perhaps art cannot save the world, but, combined with therapy, it can have a significant part to play in rescuing some of its citizens. I advocate that social action art therapy can be done most successfully when considering these citizens *in their full context*.

In *Art Therapy Education: A Creative Dialectic Intersubjective Approach*, Gerber reexamines the educational philosophy of the art therapy field and re-envisions a "dialectical paradigm." Calling for "dynamic learning," Gerber emphasizes that the "types of knowledge to be taught and how it is to be taught can be adjusted based upon the learning culture, educational and psychological maturity of the student, and the … student and peer relationships."

In an art therapist's career trajectory, becoming credentialed follows the completion of education. Greenstone agreed to tangle and untangle one of the field's most prevalent and contentious issues in her chapter titled *Issues in Credentialing and Licensing for Art Therapy in the United States: Who Ate My Pie?* Greenstone makes a convincing argument for duality—art therapists practicing with and within other regulated identities such as counseling, social work, or education. Yet, the art therapist

The Wiley Handbook of Art Therapy, First Edition. Edited by David E. Gussak and Marcia L. Rosal.
© 2016 John Wiley & Sons, Ltd. Published 2016 by John Wiley & Sons, Ltd.

would maintain his or her identity and individual practice while working within a broader licensing context.

In the simply titled *Ethics in Art Therapy*, Ballbé ter Maat and Espinola outline the not-so-simple professional ethical and moral guidelines that are specific to the field. In *Art Therapy and Multi-culturalism*, Boston "provides information and guidelines for improving multicultural competency for the art therapist." She argues that, in order to gain multicultural proficiency, art therapists need to thoroughly examine their own identities, biases, and prejudices. While difficult, "[t]he rewards of effective culturally sensitive art therapy service include: heightened self-awareness, better rapport with clients, and improved ability and skill to navigate outside of the comfort zone on related issues with professors, colleagues, multidisciplinary staff, and employers."

As the field evolves, art therapists often find themselves in nontraditional settings. This is the topic of Vick's chapter, *Community-based Disability Studios: Being and Becoming*. While he admits that there really *isn't* a single *community-based disability studio model,* Vick outlines options for art therapists to provide services at creative studio spaces for those with disabilities. While it may not be art therapy per se, it is clear there are therapeutic benefits to providing services in these studios. Talwar, in her chapter titled *Creating Alternative Public Spaces: Community-Based Art Practice, Critical Consciousness, and Social Justice,* explores nontraditional venues even further. Using a single community-based art program as an example, Talwar examines "how social justice and advocacy can become a central part of art therapy services leading to empowerment and instilling agency."

For the final chapter of this handbook, Towne agreed to discuss the future of the profession. In the chapter titled *Looking Forward—Thoughts on the Future of Art Therapy—A Personal Perspective*, Towne explores a myriad of possibilities that may lie ahead for the profession, and concludes by simultaneously sounding an alarm and offering a positive outcome for the future of the profession.

> Taking serious steps to refurbish the way we look at ourselves, and by supporting and nourishing a purposeful membership and collective identity, we can be pioneers prepared to face the challenges of the future we are creating. Let us think of a future where, not just a few, but all Veterans Health Administration Medical Hospitals and Centers provide art therapy services. Let us investigate why only a handful of sites in a large chain of long-term-care facilities offer art therapy services. Let us do this work because we know that art therapy has a bright future.

The goal of this concluding section of the book is to inspire art therapists around the world. However, inspiration is hollow without tackling the difficult issues that come with the maturing of a profession. Using the entirety of our knowledge base, with a global perspective, and with so many great minds, the profession of art therapy is making strides toward a flourishing future. Perhaps the next handbook will be twice the size of this one.

76

Identity of the Art Therapist

Joan Phillips

The identity of art therapists is embedded in the work they do. Who they are is what they do and how they are trained to do it. The simplest way to explain the identity of the art therapist is as "one who practices art therapy." However, this simplistic statement then leads into a multiplicity of practice settings, theoretical approaches, and training models in the art therapy field. All contain therapy and art and imply an integration of these fields into a unique arena and professional identity as an art therapist. As a profession and as individuals practicing art therapy, the path to this integrated identity has been long and winding. Despite much progress and mapping of the territory of art therapy, the identity issue for art therapists still appears to have twists and turns ahead. There is agreement on the importance and primacy of art; art-making and art process are central to the identity. Art therapists are also committed to self-examination, in relation to other fields that art therapists train in and collaborate with.

The United States is a land of immigrants. A study of art therapy reveals a professional territory pioneered and settled by immigrants from many fields. Passion about art and creativity appeared to be one factor motivating individuals to enter and populate the largely uncharted land that became art therapy after World War II. The field was established by "immigrants" from other professions such as art education, psychiatry, art, counseling, education, rehabilitation, nursing, social work, and others. This "melting pot" of professions has been diminished by the professions' attempts to homogenize the field through common training requirements. Yet, the complex diversity that enlivens the field is still honored.

Even today, there are many tourists to the land of art therapy, and their presence accounts for some of the ongoing debate about identity. As other professionals sample or utilize art therapy techniques and ideas, many have chosen not to obtain the training and experience required to be a "citizen" of art therapy (i.e., to attain the credentials developed by the field). This chapter will examine some of the history of such debates and provide a contemporary look at the evolving understanding of the art therapists' identity. Considering both educational paths and credentials, some insight is gained into this identity. However, beyond that lies continued discussion and the ability to embrace an evolving and questioning approach to this field.

The Wiley Handbook of Art Therapy, First Edition. Edited by David E. Gussak and Marcia L. Rosal.
© 2016 John Wiley & Sons, Ltd. Published 2016 by John Wiley & Sons, Ltd.

A History of Reflection on Identity

It often appears that the identity of the art therapist is mired in long-standing debates. In the early years, practitioners wrestled with integration of the interdisciplinary threads that created art therapy. Philosophical and practical divisions arose early in the field's literature; for example, a 1971 article by a Jungian analyst, published in the *American Journal of Art Therapy*, explored the topic "Art and Therapy: An Uneasy Partnership" (Champernowne, 1971). Although the role of art has always been a central focus of the debate, art therapists' relationships to other professions have also been deliberated. For example, pioneering art therapist Elinor Ulman stated that what art therapists do is under an umbrella of activity therapy; "… 'art therapy' is currently used to designate widely varying practices in education, rehabilitation, and psycho-therapy" (1975, p. 3), adding that there was a need to examine the field in relation to occupational therapy.

At the 1974 AATA conference, a learned panel presented a symposium titled "Integration of Divergent points of view in art therapy," and, while the discussion was primarily around theory and practice, there was a subtext about the identity of art therapists—"defining ourselves as what we are NOT more than what we are." According to the panel, art therapists were not activity therapists, nor artists seeking a backdoor entrance to the world of psychotherapy. Such a means of self- definition requires a nametag that says "Hi my name is not _____," and this has never worked well for any profession. The panelists conjectured that saying "I am an art therapist" invited the question, arising from the self as well as from fellow professionals and the public, "so what is that?" or "what do you do?" There was agreement that it is in the practices and education for the professional life that found and affirmed the identity (Levy et al., 1974).

The title for the 1976 (seventh annual) conference of AATA was "Creativity and the Art Therapist's Identity," and this may have been a time when art therapists began trying, in earnest, to define themselves. At the conference, a panel of pioneers spoke about the dilemmas and issues related to identity. These ranged from gender issues in the profession to the "dual professional identity" of artist and art psychotherapist (the latter articulated by panelist Helen Landgarten). Concerns about primary versus adjunctive roles as well as marketplace issues were addressed. These issues continue to be lightning rods for the profession and its identity. Harriet Wadeson moderated this panel and closed with remarks reinforcing the "inter-relatedness of the issues" discussed (Wadeson, McNiff, Free, & Levy, 1976, p. 42).

More evident in the identity discussion than concerns about the relationships to other professions is the role the arts and arts training has for art therapists. Ulman provided an early definition that read, "the materials of the visual arts are used in some attempt to assist integration or reintegration of the personality" (1975, p. 3). Robert Ault, one of the founders of the American Art Therapy Association, posed the question that domi-nated the early debates regarding identity in titling a paper for the 1976 conference— "Are you an artist or a therapist? A professional dilemma of art therapists" (Ault, 1976).

Nearly 30 years later, Ault framed the foundations of the professional identity in this way: "A good art therapist is like a skater. One skate is an understanding of art and the other is an understanding of people, of psychology and counseling. …

Sometimes you push off with one skate, sometimes you push off with the other. And sometimes you glide along on both" (Emporia State University, 2004, p. 2). This analogy for identity remains in question, but not to the degree that it was in the early years. Aults' analogy acknowledged the dual disciplines that came together in art therapy, while also asserting the strength and individual power of each of these disciplines. Rubin (1999), another founder of the field, identified a common definition, which began to emerge and which art therapists began to be comfortable with: "Art therapy is a hybrid, reflected in its name, its origins, and its history" (p. 124).

The early settlers of the profession were trained in various ways (they were often something else and then "became" art therapists). Many, but not all, early art therapists were artists who found in practice the therapeutic value of arts with a variety of clinical and educational populations. As they took on this new identity of being "art therapists," they examined the differences between artists and art therapists.

At the 1978 AATA conference, McNiff, Rhyne, and Ault, all leaders of the emerging profession, discussed the influence of being an art therapist on their practice as artists. It was again noted that many early art therapists were formally trained as artists, holding MFA degrees and/or actively creating and exhibiting art. The focus of the panel was not only on the use of cooperative art-making in sessions but also on how much art therapists did or did not make art outside of their professional art therapy work. The conclusion was that art-making outside of professional art therapy work was essential to the practice of an art therapist (McNiff, Rhyne, & Ault, 1978, p. 103). Today, a studio art background is required before entering an art therapy educational program, and subsequently it is part of the ATR (Art Therapist Registered) credential (ATCB, 2012).

The analogy about which "skate" to push off from has most often dealt with the art part of the identity. Over the years, there has been a strong push for art therapists to strengthen identity through maintaining and developing the artist part of their identity. This thread of "we are artists" is an enduring theme in the identity discussions of the art therapy profession.

As early as 1976, at the AATA conference, there was a presentation entitled "Let's bring the art back into art therapy" (Austin, 1976). Moving forward almost 20 years, members of the field continue to hear the call to reinforce the art in art therapy. In 1989, again at the AATA conference, a panel of art therapy educators addressed "where is the art in art therapy?" focusing on art as the key to identity and also posing it as what makes it unique:

> As art therapists, we are constantly asking ourselves what our identity is, what our expertise is, and what makes us different from other mental health professionals. Art therapy is a treatment modality which utilizes art-making as its core; however, our profession seems to be moving in a direction opposite to that definition and identity which makes us unique. (Malchiodi, Cattaneo, & Allen, 1989, p. 75)

In 1997, Lachman-Chapin et al. stated, "For practical as well as idealistic reasons, it is time now to recommit ourselves to being the artists we are," adding that "perhaps we have become primarily clinicians who use art, rather than artists with clinical insights" (p. 147). These discussions continue the theme of either/or thinking about professional identity.

One aspect of this dilemma is that art therapists have repeatedly asked how they are different from other professionals, seeking uniqueness rather than similarities. Debates frequently posited the issues of identity in an either/or format, holding on to the art as the one core identity that makes the field "unique." The problem has been that even art does not make an art therapist unique. A significant number of counselors, psychologists, and other helping professionals have interest, training, and experience in the arts. To hold onto art as the unique domain has proved problematic. Recently, movements such as arts-in-medicine or community arts programs, or arts-as-healing programs, are seen, at times, as overstepping the art therapists' domain. This causes discomfort despite the credence that all art therapists give to the power of art to heal and help. A broader view, taken by this author, is that the entire fields of arts, medicine, counseling, therapy, education, and others are natural collaborators for the "interdisciplinarily" trained professional that is an art therapist—including collaborations with non-art-therapists interested in using the arts in their professional or community settings. This does not preclude art therapy being an identifiable profession with a strong identity—it just opens doors to collaboration and cross-training, and thus strengthens our place within all the helping and art professions.

Credentials as a Factor in Identity

One way to identify an art therapist is through credentials that can be examined by regulators, other professions and even the public at large. The very nature of creating a credential requires that a field identify the knowledge and tasks that are necessary for competent practice. For art therapists in the United States, this process took place in the 1990s with development of the Art Therapy Credentials Board (ATCB), created as an independent credentialing body by the American Art Therapy Association). One of the first mandates of the ATCB was to conduct a task analysis, which closely scrutinized the practice of art therapy to identify the core knowledge base and the common skills needed to be a competent art therapist. The results formed the basis of the ATCB certification examination, which was first administered in 1994. Not surprisingly, the core areas of the exam included art-therapy-specific knowledge as well as art and psychological foundations. It appears the two skates continue to be art and therapy. The establishment of credentials and standards gave art therapists an identity in a more unified manner, despite some continued debate over what the core knowledge and skills of the profession are. Art therapist Carol Olson (2011) wrote in the ATCB review, "Going for an ATR and then BC (board certification) helped me personally solidify my commitment, bond me with that identity and with others in my field" (p. 4).

Any move toward developing and embracing that other skate—the one gliding into the realm of psychology, counseling, or other profession—can be a threat. The threat and the debate may be rooted in the fear that a bias exists in favor of science over art. The fear that the "art part" of the profession may be in danger is significant. Vying for recognition from the wider mental health culture, while feeling vulnerable to takeover by the scientific/clinical aspects of the work or training, is a challenge for the field.

The seminal work of Pat Allen (1992) regarding the "clinification" of art therapy embodied important parts of this identity debate. Her concerns about what she saw as the waning of art skills and practice among art therapists brought the debate about artist or therapist to the fore. She noted the clinical training that increasingly became a part of the art therapist's journey, and stated: "While clinical understanding is a basic requirement in working with clients in therapy, the emphasis on the clinical over the art has led to a stunting of the development of art therapy as a discipline in its own right" (Allen, 1992, p. 23).

Each individual art therapist has to define himself or herself amidst the ongoing debates of the field. As Carol Olson stated:

> I consider myself an art therapist first, and identify myself as an art therapist, addiction specialist and trauma specialist who is also licensed in my state as an LPC. While I have pursued additional education and certifications to fit the populations I work with, I see those additional specialties as enhancing my work as an art therapist, not subsuming it. (ATCB Review, 2011, p. 5)

Education as a Factor in Identity

Over time, the profession seems to have settled into a more nuanced and non-dichotomous understanding of identity. Art therapists have moved into asking not how they are unique or different but asking how they are similar to and overlap other professions. Just as early art therapists were wary of fields such as occupational therapy or activity therapy, the more recent concerns of art therapists have centered around counseling. Recent debates about "are we counselors" are framed in an either/or stance. Instead of "are we artists or therapists," the new debate is "are we art therapists or counselors" (Feen-Calligan, 2012; Schoenholtz, 2007). The discussions surrounding the relationship of art therapy and counseling have taken place in the last 10 years and focus both on educational standards and credentials. Terms such as "cross-training" have been discussed, and a strong debate emerged as to whether art therapists should seek additional counselor licensure, given that our training parallels in many ways the education of counselors, or whether a single license for art therapy could encompass this training but still give art therapy a license, and, thus, in some views, a stronger identity (Kapitan, 2004a). Gantt, speaking for dual licensure, stated, "I believe we will ultimately benefit from a multiplier effect if we have on our business cards 'Licensed Professional Counselor' and 'Registered (or Board Certified) Art Therapist'" (Gantt, 2004, p. 3). Nonetheless, fears about being swallowed up by other professions continued, and a common thread of the primacy of art therapy remained. As Schoenholtz asserted in 2007, "For me, identity as an art therapist comes first" (2007, p. 2).

Much of the heat in this debate seems to have come from a lack of distinction between the concepts of identity and the more mundane practicalities of state regulations, reimbursement, and administrative issues. This is the same dichotomous thinking that emerged in the artist or therapist debates early on, and which continue in the art therapist or counselor debates. The idea that having credentials in a variety of disciplines might serve to water down or negate our art therapist identity may belie some insecurity that may be related more to the small numbers of practitioners than to any true confusion over role or identity.

Parallels between the training of counselors and art therapists have always existed. In recent years, the Masters' Education Standards of the American Art Therapy Association (2007) have been reviewed and revised to more closely parallel standards in the counseling profession education. The diversity of departments, schools, and programs that art therapy training exists within makes it difficult to follow a rigid set of accreditation standards. Nonetheless, most programs are mindful of the need for graduates to have cross-training and comprehensive backgrounds to facilitate work in a collaborative and larger mental health and social services world. This is not to say that art therapists always qualify for licensure as counselors, although a vast majority do. Educators are aware of the similarities and differences in training that can prepare both art therapists and counselors. Art therapists need to be ready for the current mental health landscape that is focused on credentials, cross-training, and collaboration (Gantt, 2004; Kapitan, 2004b). The educational and credentials landscape, however, still does not completely provide the identity as this is something internalized and developed by each art therapist as part of his or her own professional growth.

Feen-Calligan (1996, 2005) has given thoughtful attention to both the education and identity of art therapists, looking at what can be gleaned from other professions, as well as the benefit of service as a professional guiding ideal. For example, she discussed graduate training that incorporates service learning components, pointing out that, due to the reflective nature of service learning as well as the focus on professional identity within these experiences, students were able to effectively begin development of their own professional identity unique to their art therapy training. She has also addressed the more recent trend of dual-degree preparation, that is, art therapists gaining both a counseling and an art therapy curriculum in a graduate program. Not surprisingly, graduates with such dual preparation also describe their professional identity as "a combination of art therapy, counseling, and teaching" (Feen-Calligan, 2012, p. 152). This finding can be seen through the ongoing debate from our profession's earliest days, and her research also supports the idea that encouraging awareness and willingness to learn from many perspectives and professions is a supportive feature in a students' professional identity development as an art therapist.

Questioning as a Core Value

The reflection on who art therapists are is an integral part of the professional identity. The identity of an art therapist involves being aware that the diversity and shifting nature of this identity is part of what is valued about the profession. Art therapists embrace questioning, adapting and recreating themselves. Gussak reminds the field that "One of the problems is that, as art therapists, what we know and do is often so embedded in practice, that it is only partially available to us" (Giddens, 1979). Also: "We often operate on instinct and faith that, although what we do works, we are not always able to explain *how* and *why* it works" (Gussak, 1999, p. 116). Our self-perceived and perpetuated dichotomies are, at times, at the core of the professional identity. Art therapists do lay claim to a large territory that includes knowledge also held in counseling, marriage and family therapy, art, education, community work, and creative expression. The identity of the art therapist is that of someone who is trained in all these areas and integrates these fields into a unique helping profession. It is not either/or but instead both/and. The vast majority of presentations at art therapy conferences are focused on the work of art therapy—settings, techniques, approaches, and research. Over time, art therapists have been clearly defining themselves through practice. "Flexibility, thus, may be a key factor in how art therapists negotiate complex professional identities" (Kapitan, 2012, p. 149).

Early in the field's development, Robbins (1982) examined his own process in developing an identity as an art therapist, detailing the struggles to integrate theory and practice. He concluded that his identity as an art therapist was "no longer static, but ebbs and flows with each session and patient," adding: "Within this process remains the core of myself who is the artist and has merged with the psychologist to discover a new sense of wholeness and professional mastery" (p. 8).

In another intriguing look at our identity, Bouchard (1998) considered a Jungian perspective on the ways identity personally and professionally plays into how art therapists handle issues as a larger professional community of art therapists. I would like to suggest that art therapy, more than any other helping profession, has found a way to integrate the self into the therapist identity. This is not merely *therapy + art*, nor is it a model that anyone can emulate after one or two art therapy workshops; the identity of the art therapist is embedded in the artistic and in the psychological, integrated through a constant process of self-reflection and practice.

Broadening the Debate

The AATA conference proceedings of 2007 contained many panels and papers on topics such as supervision and research. There were no presentations on the perennial "who are we" focus of early conference proceedings. The scope of presentations was expansive. For example, Rosal and Bordanaro (2007) presented an overview of art therapy associations around the globe and pointed out that one of the universal issues addressed by emerging associations was *who could be considered an art therapist*. Thus, the search for identity is as part of the development of any profession.

Currently, there is a trend for professionals to hold multiple credentials. Each payment source may require a specific credential. These economic stressors have added to art therapists seeking additional credentials because it is important to receive compensation for services in today's economic environment. When art therapists receive additional credentials, they do open their practice to recognition within the larger mental health worlds. Addressing the current climate of credentialing with developing art therapists will help them think critically about their future practice. Credentialing is only one of the future trends that challenge art therapists.

Another challenge that art therapists face now and in the future is how closely they should be aligned with the field of counseling. Counselors continue to show increased interest in the use of creative and expressive methods, yet often do not reference or acknowledge the relevance of the field of art therapy in these pursuits (Van Velsor, 2013; Ziff, Johanson, & Pierce, 2012). While the lack of acknowledgement is often seen as some kind of professional slight, the truth is that any profession can and often does use art, art activities, and art processes in the work they do. With increased collaborative dialogue, as suggested by many leaders in the art therapy field, hopefully the territorial debates will evolve into productive alliances.

While counseling is one of the field's closest sister professions, it is not the only profession with which art therapists collaborate or cross-train. Ronaldson and Hanna (2001) pointed out, in discussing opening borders between art therapy, family therapy, and other mental health professions, that "students can find increased opportunities for professional growth" through collaboration clinically with other disciplines, and in particular in serving disadvantaged populations (p. 152). Marriage and family therapy, education, wellness, arts, social work and social services, psychology, nursing, and many other professions share a comparable knowledge base. Rubin (1999) agreed that there are "… practical advantages of obtaining training—and perhaps certification or licensure—in a related field which is better established, and can therefore open more doors" (p. 328). Whether through cross-training, multiple credentials, or clinical and community collaborations, the identity of the art therapist can encompass a range of experiences while always maintaining the primacy of the art therapist as an identity.

Conclusion

Rubin, reminiscing on the development of our field and the American Art Therapy Association, noted: "As our own identity as art therapists has developed and become more secure, our earlier chameleon-like need to be the same as more established groups has diminished. We are clearer about who we are, how we are similar to and different from other disciplines…" Rubin goes on to note that "we do seem less prone to seeing issues in black-and-white terms … in relation to both our theories and our personal practice as an art therapists" (1988, p. 28).

These comments reflect both the personal and professional identity issues discussed here. However, these remarks were made more than 25 years ago. Over time, has the field made progress on defining its identity? It may not be that clear. Wadeson (2002) advocated for art therapists to put aside disputes over territory and training and again embrace the rich diversity; to work with less polarization to advance the profession; and recognize the rich diversity that is the hallmark of the field's identity.

A consensus is emerging that the art therapist's identity is one that puts the processes of art and creativity as first and foremost. Second, the integration of theory and skills from counseling, psychology, and many other fields make up the amalgamated professional called the *art therapist*. The combined energies of art and therapy create the unique and identifiable profession of art therapy. The field should celebrate its particular "heritage," which includes education, training, and experience. Hopefully, future art therapy practitioners will not be concerned about which "skate" they may be wearing. They may even take their skates off now and then. A future of additional credentials and modes of working may await that ultimately serves to further the profession and practitioners' identity as art therapists.

I see a future where the identity of art therapy does not force us to choose between two or more options; rather, I predict a time when we embrace many possibilities for both our clients and ourselves. The very thing that makes our profession unique is the flexible and creative territory that we claim. This territory includes art, therapy, counseling, community work, wellness, education, creativity, and more. We are not the sum of our credentials, nor are we completely defined by our education. We are neither this nor that; we are art therapists.

References

Allen, P. (1992). Artist in residence: An alternative to "clinification" for art therapists. *Art Therapy: Journal of the American Art Therapy Association, 9*(1), 22–29.

American Art Therapy Association. (2007). *Masters education standards.* Retrieved June 9, 2012, from http://americanarttherapyassociation.org/upload/masterseducationstandards.pdf

Art Therapy Credentials Board. (2011). Credential holder profile. *ATCB Review Summer, 18*(2), 4–5.

ATCB. (2012). *Registered Art Therapist (ATR).* Greensboro, NC: ATCB, Inc.

Ault, B. (1976). Are you an artist or a therapist: A professional dilemma for the art therapist. In R. Shoemaker (Ed.), *Creativity and the art therapist's identity: Proceedings of the seventh annual conference of the American Art Therapy Association* (pp. 55–56).

Austin, V. (1976). Let's bring the art back into art therapy. In R. Schoemaker (Ed.), *Creativity and the art therapist's identity: The proceedings of the seventh annual conference of the American Art Therapy Association* (pp. 28–29).

Bouchard, R. R. (1998). Art therapy and its shadow: A Jungian perspective on professional identity and community. *Art Therapy: Journal of the American Art Therapy Association, 15*(3), 158–164.

Champernowne, H. I. (1971). Art and therapy: An uneasy partnership. *American Journal of Art Therapy, 10*(3), 131–142.

Emporia State University. (2004). *Teachers College Newsletter, 12*(4), 2.

Feen-Calligan, H. R. (1996). Art therapy as a profession: Implications for the education and training of art therapists. *Art Therapy: Journal of the American Art Therapy Association, 13*(3), 166–173.

Feen-Calligan, H. R. (2005). Constructing professional identity in art therapy through service-learning and practice. *Art Therapy: Journal of the American Art Therapy Association, 22*(3), 122–131.

Feen-Calligan, H. R. (2012). Professional identity perceptions of dual-prepared art therapy graduates. *Art Therapy: Journal of the American Art Therapy Association, 29*(4), 150–157.

Gantt, L. (2004). The time has come—Support the cross-training initiative with counseling. *Newsletter—American Art Therapy Association, 37*(4, Fall), 1–3.

Giddens, A. (1979). *Central problems in social theory: Action, structure and contradiction in social analysis.* Berkeley, CA: University of California Press.

Gussak, D. (1999). What are art therapists? Finding a place that makes sense. In *Art Therapy Frameworks: A Sense of Place: Proceedings of the 30th Annual American Art Therapy Association Conference. Art Therapy Frameworks: A Sense of Place* (p. 116).

Kapitan, L. (2004a). Economic realities: Update on the Cross-training inititative. *AATA Newsletter, 37*(3), 4–5.

Kapitan, L. (2004b). Cross-training: The case for creating the next generation of art therapy credentials. *Newsletter—American Art Therapy Association, 37*(2), 1–2.

Kapitan, L. (2012). Editorial: Educating the future practitioner of art therapy. *Art Therapy: Journal of the American Art Therapy Association, 29*(4), 148–149.

Lachman-Chapin, M., Jones, D., Semekoski, S., Fleming, M., Cohen, B., & Sweig, T. (1997). Connecting with the art world: Expanding beyond the mental health world. In *Making our mark: Art therapy and social responsibility: American Art Therapy Association 28th annual conference: Conference proceedings* (p. 147).

Levy, B., Kramer, E., Kwiatkowska, H., Lachman, M., Rhyne, J., & Ulman, E. (1974). Symposium: Integration of divergent points of view in art therapy. *American Journal of Art Therapy, 14*(1), 13–17.

Malchiodi, C., Cattaneo, M., & Allen, P. (1989). Where is the art in art therapy? (Or are we our own worst enemy?) In *Painting portraits: Families, groups and systems: The proceedings of the 20th annual conference of the American Art Therapy Association* (p. 75).

McNiff, S., Rhyne, J., & Ault, B. (1978). The art therapist as artist. In L. Gantt (Ed.), *Art therapy: Expanding horizons: Proceedings of the 9th annual conference of the American Art Therapy* (pp. 103–105).

Robbins, A. (1982). Integrating the personal and theoretical splits in the struggle towards an identity as art therapist. *Arts in Psychotherapy, 9*(1), 1–9.

Ronaldson, C., & Hanna, S. (2001). Opening borders between art therapy, family therapy and other mental health professions. In *Art therapy landscapes: Defining boundaries, opening borders: Proceedings of the 32nd annual conference of the American Art Therapy Association* (p. 152).

Rosal, M., & Bordanero, G. (2007). The status of national art therapy associations: A global perspective. In *The art of connecting from personal to global: 38th annual conference proceedings of the American Art Therapy Association* (p. 156).

Rubin, J. (1988). Coming of age: A subjective perspective. *Art Therapy: Journal of the American Art Therapy Association, 5*(8), 22–29.

Rubin, J. (1999). *Art therapy: An introduction.* Philadelphia: Taylor and Francis/Brunner-Mazel.

Schoenholtz, R. (2007). Art therapy—A counseling profession? *AATA Newsletter, 40*(2), 1–2.

Ulman, E. (1975). Art therapy: Problems of definition. In E. Ulman & P. Dachinger (Eds.), *Art therapy in theory and practice.* New York, NY: Schocken Books.

Van Velsor, P. (2013). Thinking creatively: Expressive arts for counseling youth in the schools. *Counseling Today, 55*(8), 52–54.

Wadeson, H. (2002). Confronting polarization in art therapy. *Art Therapy: Journal of the American Art Therapy Association, 19*(2), 77–84.

Wadeson, H., McNiff, S., Free, K., & Levy, B. I. (1976). Panel: The identity of the art therapist: Professional self concept and public image. In R. Shoemaker (Ed.), *Creativity and the art therapist's identity: Proceedings of the 7th annual conference of the American Art Therapy Association* (pp. 38–42).

Ziff, K., Johanson, S., & Pierce, L. (2012). ArtBreak: Creative counseling for children. *Counseling Today, 55*(3), 46–48.

77

Social Action Art Therapy[1]

Frances F. Kaplan

Why This Topic?

Some people are still waiting to be convinced that *art* and *therapy* go together. Certainly for them—and possibly for some of you who are reading this and who may accept art therapy as a viable modality—*social action art therapy* is something of a contradiction in terms. After all, art therapy endeavors to facilitate inner, individual change, and social action strives to make outer, collective change. But before addressing what social action art therapy is, or might be, the reasons for attempting to combine the two approaches should be addressed. In an attempt to present a holistic view, I will start with some underlying personal motivations and build from there.

Throughout much of my life, I have felt the urge to bring together seemingly disparate entities. This probably began in childhood with my attempt to be the glue for a family that did not quite fit together—with, as one can imagine, only limited success. As an adult, I have responded to this urge in ways both trivial and significant. For example, when I took up cooking, I searched for recipes that combined unusual ingredients, such as the "soup to nuts" cake that uses condensed tomato soup as a major component. When I sought my life's work, I looked for ways to combine my two loves: art and science. In so doing, I thought I had "invented" the concept of art therapy and then discovered that others had gotten there before me (Kaplan, 2000). Finally, in midlife, I became interested in promoting change—not just on an individual level but also on a societal one—and spent many years involved with the peace movement.

Thus began my efforts to apply art therapy to larger issues; as it happened, I found that others had preceded me there as well (e.g., Junge, Alvarez, Kellogg, & Volker, 1993). Knowing that I was not alone in seeing the potential for art therapy to widen its scope encouraged me to put together an edited book on this topic (Kaplan, 2007) that not only represented my own predilections but also presented some of the remarkable work that others had been doing. In this way, art therapists and other members of the helping professions could be offered models for expansion of their fields and could, in the process, quite possibly increase the effectiveness of what they do.

The Wiley Handbook of Art Therapy, First Edition. Edited by David E. Gussak and Marcia L. Rosal.
© 2016 John Wiley & Sons, Ltd. Published 2016 by John Wiley & Sons, Ltd.

What Is Social Action Art Therapy?

During the first half of the twentieth century when art therapy had its beginnings, psychoanalysis was the therapy of choice. Consequently, art therapy started out as a form of psychoanalysis that used visual imagery. Indeed, it has been said that Margaret Naumburg, considered the original "mother" of art therapy in the United States, simply substituted the easel for the couch (Ulman, 1987). Her focus was on exploring the individual's unconscious, and the painting or drawing by the client was the object of free association in a manner similar to the Freudian approach to dreams.

By the 1960s, when I was undergoing my personal therapy, psychoanalysis was beginning to widen its scope. Although many psychoanalysts were against seeing clients in groups, the psychoanalyst I went to had an interpersonal focus and used group therapy in combination with individual therapy. Art therapists, initially more out of necessity than theory (seeing a number of people at a time was cost efficient), were conducting groups as well. However, under the influence of Edith Kramer (the "second mother" of art therapy), the group approach was by and large an art studio approach, with little emphasis on interpersonal interactions. By the time I started my art therapy training in 1974, however, change was evident. Interactional group art therapy based on neo-Freudian psychodynamic theory was being advocated and practiced.

The latter part of the twentieth century and the first part of the twenty-first century have seen additional changes. Art therapy has embraced many psychotherapeutic approaches in addition to psychoanalysis, and it has begun to be sensitive to the diverse cultural backgrounds from which clients originate. This means some art therapists, in addition to becoming more culturally competent, try to assist clients with culture-related problems as well as intrapersonal and interpersonal problems. It also means a few art therapists have approached certain problematic aspects of society as though these were the "clients" they wished to help.

But we are not yet at a point where the question—what is social action art therapy?—can be adequately answered. When I began soliciting authors for the chapters in my edited book, *Art Therapy and Social Action* (2007), I had only a vague idea of how social action art therapy could be defined. When a potential contributor to that volume expressed confusion about what was required, I responded with a succinct yet simplistic definition: in effect, social action art therapy operates outside the usual box of individual illness (mental or physical), and addresses societal problems by providing services to perpetrators, victims (potential or actual), or people who work with members of these groups. However, in the process of editing the book, the contributors educated me by expanding my perspective: *social action art therapy is this and more.*

In the interest of clarification, let us return to the problem of creating an amalgam of the seemingly incompatible elements of art, social action, and therapy. Recall that many artists have used their art to address social issues (for some examples, see O'Brien & Little, 1990). Also recognize that therapists, too, have a certain history of working for the betterment of society—for example, the organizations *Psychologists for Social Responsibility* and *Counselors for Social Justice* (for information about these groups, see www.psysr.org and www.counselorsforsocialjustice.org, respectively).

These realizations could lead to the conclusion that it is primarily individual artist–therapists who undertake social action to address certain social problems. And, indeed, this is part of what social action art therapy is about. It could also mean using art making to help clients deal with environmental calamities and cultural biases or for practicing therapeutic art outside traditional therapy settings—taking art therapy into the streets, as it were. And, again, these are only partial answers.

But, in different ways, practitioners of social action art therapy invite us to look at this brand of art therapy from another angle. What these practitioners suggest is that social action and art therapy cannot—or at least should not—be separated.

Now, how to reconcile these ideas? The solution is both complicated and simple—complicated in practice yet ultimately simple in concept. Therapists cannot separate clients from the cultural settings in which they live and by which they have been influenced. Nobody exists in a social vacuum; each person comprises a unique amalgam of genetic endowment, family upbringing, environmental influences, and collective history.

Therapists have been inclined to think about personality and psychopathology in terms of nature or nurture—often attempting to assign etiology to one or the other. Lately, however, they have begun to understand that the origins of both are an interaction of the two. At the same time, largely due to the multicultural movement, therapists have come to understand that they cannot ignore the contributions of culture, which have sources well beyond the family unit and even beyond ethnicity and race (Lee, 1999). This means that, when therapists treat people, they must take into account the culture that the clients come from and to which they will return. It also means that therapists must honor clients' backgrounds and yet assist them in dealing with aspects of society that have contributed to their suffering. And, given the uniqueness of each individual, it means that, whenever therapists attempt to help someone, they must be aware that they are essentially working cross-culturally. Therefore, they must proceed with all the sensitivity and self-knowledge that they can muster. To do otherwise would run the risk of imposing on clients some of the same injustices they have experienced in the larger social order.

Where Does This Leave Us?

The inescapable conclusion is that whether art therapists take art therapy into the streets or remain secluded in their treatment settings, they would do well to "think" social action. Just as some family therapists have stated that family therapy is a way of conceptualizing treatment as well as a set of treatment techniques, social action art therapy is a state of mind as well as a method of action. A therapist does not necessarily need to have the whole family in the room to treat family problems (Goldenberg & Goldenberg, 1985); the same therapist does not necessarily need to demonstrate in public places to effect social change.

Social Action Art Therapy Techniques

Aside from maintaining a social action perspective, therapists can avail themselves of techniques that have been developed by others to address problems such as violence, prejudice and discrimination, inability to resolve conflict, lack of a sense of community, and so on. For instance, Rachel O'Rourke (2007) developed an art activity that focused on the violent consequences of handgun ownership. Further, Lani Gerity (2007) described an arts camp for marginalized peoples who work together on art projects that reflect aspects of their culture. A stronger sense of community is built through this shared activity, along with increased pride in what a particular culture has to offer. Similarly, Anndy Wiselogle (2007), through community workshops, provided a series of drawing activities relating to conflict—either interpersonal or intergroup—that led to deeper understanding of the conflict situation (so many conflicts arise from misinterpretations) and offered possibilities for successful resolution. As a final example, Susan Berkowitz (2007) created a celebration called *All People's Day*® that uses art, role playing, and cultural festivities to address issues of bias and discrimination, and has conducted training in this for groups of diverse youth.

A Social Action Art Therapy Project for the Future

Social action art techniques and a social action mindset build on one another because they can go a long way toward promoting societal betterment and stimulating awareness that an individual's problems can stem from societal dysfunction as well as from psychological issues. Take the matter of peace versus violence: most would agree that peace is the more desirable state but that it is very difficult to achieve on a worldwide basis. In order to bring something about, it is important to be able to visualize it. It has been my experience that, when asking workshop participants to draw what peace looks like and what violence looks like, the pictures of violence have generally been much more dynamic, colorful, and exciting. This suggests the underlying reason why violence is hard to eradicate and raises the question of what kinds of images would make peace more appealing and violence less so. Working on creating and publicizing reconciliatory images would seem a productive endeavor—one highly suitable to the methods and approaches of art therapy.

In Summary

Trends in treatment have ranged from seeing mental problems largely as the result of internal processes, be they of psychological or biological nature (Freud, 1949; Shuchter, Downs, & Zisook, 1996), to locating the cause in early family relationships (Kernberg, 1976; Kohut, 1971), to placing it within the larger social realm (Laing, 1967), and to initial attempts to give credence to all these sources (Erikson, 1963). Social action art therapy puts the emphasis on societal factors because they have been neglected too often. It has been conceived as working to create social change, elevate awareness of social problems, provide community service, understand the origins of socially unacceptable behavior, offer instruction in socially oriented interventions, and increase sensitivity to the social context of troubled individuals. But none of this means that personal and relationship factors should be neglected. Rather, it means that a third component should be added to these two. Absurdities in thinking can occur when it is not included. For example, individuals can be accused of "inviting" a deplorable cultural practice, such as discrimination against their ethnic group, into their lives.

As the preceding text implies, writings on this topic tend to be quite different in style and content (Kaplan, 2007; Sajnani & Kaplan, 2012). Some are mostly practical, providing techniques that others can adopt or adapt; others are highly personal, offering insight into the type of person the artist–therapist tends to be; and additional writings are conceptual in whole or in part, supplying the groundwork for a theoretical approach. Nevertheless, there is a common thread that runs through all these ideas. Looked at from a broad perspective, the literature examined the degree to which art therapists and other members of the helping professions bear a responsibility to the larger community from which their clients originate. They also provide a variety of creative answers and raise significant questions as to how artists–therapists might proceed in shouldering a rather overwhelming but highly important obligation.

Lunching with an art therapist colleague a while back, I was struck by a comment she made when the conversation inevitably turned to art. "I don't think art can save the world these days," she said with a sad shake of her head. I nodded in dejected agreement. Thinking about this exchange later, I came to a more nuanced conclusion: perhaps art cannot save the world, but, combined with therapy, it can have a significant part to play in rescuing some of its citizens. I advocate that social action art therapy can be done most successfully when considering these citizens *in their full context*.

Finally, the focus here has been on visual art therapy. But it should be kept in mind that much of what has been said can also be applied to other creative approaches—dance/movement therapy, drama therapy, music therapy, poetry therapy—used by helping professionals (Sajnani & Kaplan, 2012).

Post Script

Now, I shall let you in on something else. I almost abandoned working on trying to spread the word about social action art therapy. The reason had a great deal to do with what happened on September 11, 2001. I had barely begun to work on my edited book on the topic (Kaplan, 2007) when the terrorists struck, badly damaging the Pentagon and destroying the World Trade Center in New York. Suddenly, my project seemed trivial—frivolous even—and extremely futile. These judgments were reinforced by the United States government declaring a "War on Terror," which some media pundits also referred to as "the *first* [emphasis added] war of the twenty-first century." I went through a period during which I vacillated between rebuking myself for being grandiose (Who was I to think I had anything to contribute?) and berating humanity for being such a lost cause.

Shortly after the devastating events of 9/11, however, I read an article by John Rockwell, in *The New York Times* (2001), whose message eventually worked its way into the depths of my consciousness and helped to bring me around (along with a reminder to myself that whatever small bit we can do is better than doing nothing at all). Rockwell asked, "What is the role of the arts in the present crisis, and how will the arts change in response to the new circumstances in which we live?" (p. 1). He also conjectured that, on the basis of responses to the crisis from nine artists from different fields, artists in general felt helpless and judged their work "irrelevant, even offensive" (p. 1). He concluded his piece, however, with these memorable words:

In any crisis, there is a risk that the arts will be scorned or dismissed as an irrelevant distraction. Now that the real news, of terror and death and war, has arrived, attention to art with a different agenda might seem out of place.

But art has its own importance; it stakes its own claim. We are told that, in times of crisis, we need to rely on faith. Art can be a faith, too, from which some of us draw the deepest solace. A terrible consequence of this new climate of fear and revenge would be for our enemies, blind and intolerant, to turn us into them. We must retain our values, and those values very much embrace the sometimes messy creativity of the arts.

Art is life itself. If we can sustain our arts in a diversity as rich as our social and political and religious diversity, then our artists can indeed play a most valuable role. They can sustain and inspire us, but they can also lead us—directly or, more likely, indirectly—from darkness to light. (Rockwell, 2001, p. 3, copyright © 2001 by The New York Times Co.; reprinted with permission)

To add to this would be superfluous.

Endnote

1   This chapter is a modified version of the introduction to F. F. Kaplan (Ed.). (2007). *Art therapy and social action*. London, England: Jessica Kingsley.

References

Berkowitz, S. (2007). Art therapy for this multicultural world. In F. F. Kaplan (Ed.), *Art therapy and social action* (pp. 244–262). London, England: Jessica Kingsley.

Erikson, E. H. (1963). *Childhood and society* (2nd ed.). New York, NY: Norton.

Freud, S. (1949). *An outline of psycho-analysis* (rev. ed., J. Strachey, trans.). New York, NY: Norton.

Gerity, L. (2007). Art and community building from the puppet and mask maker's perspective. In F. F. Kaplan (Ed.), *Art therapy and social action* (pp. 231–243). London, England: Jessica Kingsley.

Goldenberg, I., & Goldenberg, H. (1985). *Family therapy: An overview* (2nd ed.). Monterey, CA: Brooks/Cole.

Junge, M. G., Alvarez, J. F., Kellogg, A., & Volker, C. (1993). The art therapist as social activist: Reflections and visions. *Art Therapy: Journal of the American Art Therapy Association*, *10*(3), 148–155.

Kaplan, F. F. (2000). *Art, science, and art therapy: Repainting the picture*. London, England: Jessica Kingsley.

Kaplan, F. F. (2007). *Art therapy and social action*. London, England: Jessica Kingsley.

Kernberg, O. (1976). *Object relations theory and clinical psychoanalysis*. New York, NY: Jason Aronson.

Kohut, H. (1971). *The analysis of the self: A systematic approach to the psychoanalytic treatment of narcissistic personality disorders*. New York, NY: International Universities Press.

Laing, R. D. (1967). *The politics of experience*. New York, NY: Pantheon Books.

Lee, W. M. L. (1999). *Introduction to multicultural counseling*. Philadelphia, PA: Accelerated Development.

O'Brien, M., & Little, C. (Eds.). (1990). *Reimaging America: The arts of social change.* Santa Cruz, CA: New Society.

O'Rourke, R. C. (2007). The Paper People Project on gun violence. In F. F. Kaplan (Ed.), *Art therapy and social action* (pp. 157–172). London, England: Jessica Kingsley.

Rockwell, J. (2001, September 23). Peering into the abyss of the future. *The New York Times.* Retrieved from www.nytimes.com.

Sanjani, N., & Kaplan, F. (2012) [Contributing Co-editors]. The creative arts therapies and social justice: Special Issue. *The Arts in Psychotherapy, 39*(3).

Shuchter, S. R., Downs, N., & Zisook, S. (1996). *Biologically informed psychotherapy for depression.* New York, NY: Guilford Press.

Ulman, E. (1987). Variations on a Freudian theme: Three art therapy theorists. In J. A. Rubin (Ed.), *Approaches to art therapy: Theory and technique* (pp. 277–298). New York, NY: Brunner/Mazel.

Wiselogle, A. (2007). Drawing out conflict. In F. F. Kaplan (Ed.), *Art therapy and social Action* (pp. 103–121). London, England: Jessica Kingsley.

78

Art Therapy Education: A Creative Dialectic Intersubjective Approach

Nancy Gerber

The field of art therapy originated from a tradition of diverse dynamic multidisciplinary ways of knowing and being. These traditions contributed to the formation of the philosophy, curriculum, and pedagogy in art therapy education. Initially emerging from apprenticeship practice and experiential learning in medical and psychiatric hospitals (Feen-Callaghan, 1996; Junge, 1994; Rubin, 1999), art therapy education today boasts of a developing educational tradition reliant upon its cumulative experiential knowledge, while accommodating to current and changing culture, standards, and regulations. The developing educational tradition also includes the expansion of art therapy education beyond the entry-level practitioner master's degree to include undergraduate preparatory programs and doctoral programs, emphasizing the much-needed scholarship and research.

Located within this developing educational tradition in art therapy are numerous challenges. One challenge is preserving the essential constructivist nature of art therapy while adapting to the pragmatics of an ever-changing cultural and political climate. The interaction between these two dominant knowledge traditions—the linearity of pragmatism and the aesthetics of constructivism—require art therapy educators to think creatively and dialectically in creating curricular and pedagogical strategies. To address this and other existing and emerging challenges in art therapy education a creative dialectic intersubjective (CDI) paradigm is proposed that emphasizes the dynamic interaction between constructivist and pragmatic forms of knowledge, intersubjective ways of being, and emergent meaning-making along an educational continuum.

The philosophical assumptions and traditions of this paradigm are borrowed from mixed methods research, a viable arts-therapy-friendly worldview (Greene, 2007; Greene & Hall, 2010; Johnson & Gray, 2010), but are also firmly rooted in the interdisciplinary philosophical traditions shared by our field of art therapy (Gerber, 2004; McNiff, 1986). The ideas in this chapter are not new to art therapy, but are rather to be considered as art therapy education re-envisioned. The hope is that it simultaneously conveys the essential philosophy of all levels of art therapy education; incorporates the diverse multidisciplinary traditions of art therapy knowledge; parallels and preserves the dynamics of the art therapy experience; and provides flexibility relative to the fluid meta intersubjective, professional, and cultural realities.

The Wiley Handbook of Art Therapy, First Edition. Edited by David E. Gussak and Marcia L. Rosal.
© 2016 John Wiley & Sons, Ltd. Published 2016 by John Wiley & Sons, Ltd.

Philosophical Context

A discussion of art therapy education cannot occur without addressing the philosophical assumptions specific to the field of art therapy, which include its interdisciplinary origins. The interdisciplinary heritage of art therapy and its education in the arts and humanities, psychology and psychoanalysis, medicine and biology, and anthropology contribute to a vibrant culture of collective knowledge that is essentially embedded in the philosophy of art therapy (Gerber, 2004; McNiff, 1986). The examination of these interdisciplinary origins contributes to our understanding of the multiple realities, forms of knowledge, and values inherent in art therapy theory, practice, and education. The multiple human realities represent an "ontological pluralism" (Johnson & Gray, 2010, p. 72), and the multiple forms of knowledge represent a dialectic epistemological tension (Greene & Hall, 2010). "Ontological pluralism" and epistemological tension (Greene & Hall, 2010; Johnson & Gray, 2010, p. 72) are philosophical constructs embedded in art therapy and its teachings (Gerber, 2004; McNiff, 1986). These multiple ways of being and knowing are mirrored in the constant professional and cultural dialectic between traditions such as the arts and the sciences (McNiff, 1986), holism and reductionism, rational causality and dialecticism (Burckhardt, 2001; Kavanaugh, 1996b, 1998; Mahoney, 2000), scientific naturalism and humanism (Johnson & Gray, 2010, p. 71), and phenomenology and behaviorism (Johnson & Gray, 2010, p. 83). Considering this philosophical perspective, we might conclude that an art therapy worldview or paradigm is inherently dialectic. Such a worldview acknowledges multiple levels of individual, intersubjective, and cultural realities and consciousness (Johnson & Gray, 2010, p. 72); the co-existence of and creative interaction between levels of consciousness; and the value of emergent symbolic meaning within and to human relationship (Gerber, 2004; McNiff, 1986; Robbins, 1988).

The Dialectical Position

The use of a paradigm provides a lens by which we can re-envision art therapy education. Based upon the interdisciplinary origins of art therapy and its training, a dialectical stance (Greene, 2007; Greene & Hall, 2010; Johnson & Gray, 2010), in which multiple paradigms or philosophical traditions co-exist and dynamically inform each other in the pursuit and creation of knowledge, provides a viable conceptual paradigm for art therapy educational philosophy, curriculum, and pedagogy.

The dialectical stance presented in this chapter includes the juxtaposition of two philosophical traditions—constructivism and pragmatism—on a dialectical continuum as a paradigm for art therapy education. According to Paul, Graffam, and Fowler (2005), constructivism is reality as "constructed through the interaction of the creative and interpretive work of the mind with the physical/temporal world" (p. 46). Constructivism is a philosophical perspective that conceptualizes reality as multiple and dynamic intrapsychic and interpsychic and social constructs—a pluralistic ontology (Johnson & Gray, 2010).

Pragmatism, however, is oriented toward external singular or multiple realities (Creswell & Plano Clark, 2007), based upon "warranted assertions and justified beliefs ... [which] are held until we have evidence that can make them untrustworthy"

(Paul et al., 2005, p. 46). The fundamental principles of pragmatism originate within science and address the linear concepts of cause and effect in theory and practice (Noddings, 2005). Pragmatism does not assert a single or confirmable truth, but rather relies upon what Dewey (as cited in Noddings, 2005, p. 58) called "warranted assertions"— realization that the truth is not absolute.

The concept of the dialectic is prevalent in philosophy, psychoanalysis, creativity, art therapy, and research. The dialectical stance (Greene, 2007) amplifies the conversation between two paradigms such as pragmatism and constructivism, and values the inclusion of multiple perspectives as generators of new knowledge. Within this philosophical construct, the visible realities of the physical world coexist in dynamic interaction with the invisible psychological realities of the individual as emergent within the intersubjective social discourse (Johnson & Gray, 2010, p. 72).

In ancient and contemporary thought, healers, psychotherapists, philosophers, and artists have embraced the dialectic as the primary agent for transformation of the self (Ellenbogen, Goldberg, Roland, & Spotnitz, 1978; Mahoney, 2000; McNiff, 1986; Twemlow, 2001). For instance, in object relations theory and art therapy, Winnicott's transitional or potential space (Ogden, 1990; Robbins, 2000), an early "dialectic constructivist" concept (Israelstam, 2007, p. 593), captures the intersubjective experience essential to human emotional connections, creativity, and psychological well-being. Creativity theory is another domain in which the dialectic is implicit in the dynamic interaction between levels of cognition and consciousness in the generation of new knowledge (Arieti, 1976; Csikszentmihalyi, 1996). Creativity, psychotherapy, and art therapy are thus partners in their reliance upon the dialectic.

CDI Paradigm

The CDI paradigm is a construct that embraces multiple philosophical traditions to describe the process of dynamic, creative, and intersubjective learning in art therapy education. The curriculum and pedagogy in the CDI are conceptualized to parallel the lived experience of the art therapy process in which symbolic and metaphorical knowledge emerges between human beings who are trying to understand their meaning.

The expansion of "CDI" includes terms that require operational definitions. The term *creative* explicitly means dynamic innovative thought and experience that generates new meaningful knowledge, and implicitly references aesthetic ways of knowing. The term *aesthetics* is defined based upon the Greek translation meaning "perception" (Cooper, 1997, p. 1), or "… sense-based awareness" (Harris Williams, 2010, p. xiii), to convey the preverbal sensory and emotional experience as expressed symbolically within a human relationship (Robbins, 2000).

The term *dialectic* has been defined previously, and hence it requires no further explanation here. However, defining the term *intersubjective* is necessary. *Intersubjective* is defined as the relationship within which "jointly constructed narrative … ascribes meaning to experience for which no language previously existed" (Brown, 2011, p. 1). Intersubjectivity is also considered to represent a joining on an unconscious preverbal level where "communication and meaning making between two intrapsychic worlds … results in changes within each member…" (Brown, 2011, p. 109).

Ultimately, intersubjectivity is essential human contact reminiscent of Winnicott's transitional space (as cited in Ogden, 1990), where external and internal human realities meet and creative dialogue results in well-being.

Curricular and Pedagogical Components

The curriculum and the pedagogy represent the actualization of the CDI paradigm. The curricular and pedagogical elements exist along a dynamic continuum and are selected, emphasized, and adjusted predicated on the following contextual variables: the multiple forms of pragmatic and constructivist knowledge; the emotional holding environment or transitional space of the program; faculty/student intersubjective relationships; and the educational and psychological maturity of the individual student and student collective (Gerber, 2004). The identification of these variables on the continuum provides the opportunity for "the creation of a learning environment which is intellectually and emotionally balanced [and] ... that integrates fundamental theory, practice, research, and personal learning ..." (Gerber, 2004, p. 180). The degree to which the pragmatic or constructivist traditions, and the dialectic between them, are emphasized is relative to these contextual variables. The dialectic is initiated along the CDI continuum, facilitated primarily by the pedagogy, as contradictions arise between the pragmatic and the constructivist traditions such as theory and practice, intellect and aesthetic, and self and other knowledge.

The first contextual variable is the multiple forms of pragmatic and constructivist knowledge. The curricular and pedagogical components in this paradigm are conceptualized as belonging to, in varying degrees, a pragmatic or constructivist tradition situated along an educational continuum. The curricular components are also based on but not restricted to the competency areas identified by the American Art Therapy Association (AATA) educational standards (AATA, 2007).

The pragmatic curricular components are those that are primarily associated with extrinsic knowledge, while the constructivist components are conceptualized as intrinsic knowledge. Pragmatic knowledge includes collective wisdom, philosophy and theory, scientific and material realities, and systemic cultural constructs. For art therapy education, the extrinsic forms of knowledge include theoretical/intellectual knowledge, practical applications of theory and technique, cultural diversity, research, standards, and ethics. The approach to knowledge in this category follows the tradition of pragmatism, in that the goal is the presentation and critical evaluation of existing theory and practice.

The constructivist components emphasize the pedagogies more than content. These ways of knowing include aesthetic or preverbal, experiential, intersubjective knowledge, reflective self-knowledge, and cultural self-awareness. The constructivist components may be situated in studio-art-based enquiry (Cahn, 2000), supervision (Fish, 2008), group art therapy or group dynamics (Swan-Foster et al., 2001), methods and media workshops or skills courses (Robbins, 2000), practicum/internship (Elkis-Abuhoff, Gaydos, Rose, & Goldblatt, 2010), and intersubjectivity (Gerber et al., 2012).

The second variable is the emotional holding environment or creative dialectical space where students can experience and explore the theoretical and personal aesthetic realities and meanings within the intersubjective art therapy process (Gerber, 2004; Kavanaugh, 1996a; Symington, 1996). Essential to the holding environment is the clear statement of educational goals and methods, the identification of the educational boundaries, and the simultaneous cultivation of an atmosphere of creative self/other exploration within the boundaries of the learning objectives (Gerber, 2004; Gerber et al., 2012). Within the creative dialectical space, students are encouraged to deconstruct, reconstruct, and synthesize multiple forms of knowledge, be open and receptive to emergent knowledge and the anxiety of not knowing, cultivate curiosity and imagination, develop the capacity to engage in self and self/other exploration, and to develop therapeutic emotional presence (Belfiore & Della Cagnoletta, 1992; Gerber, 2004; Gerber et al., 2012; Kapitan & Newhouse, 2011; McNiff, 1986; Robbins, 1988, 2000; Symington, 1996).

Related to the emotional holding environment is the third variable—the emphasis on attunement to the educational and psychological maturational level of each student and the collective student group. "The considerations regarding both the student's personal maturity and their educational developmental process directly relate to the receptivity to the material being presented..." (Gerber, 2004). *Educational maturity* refers to the academic degree level as well as the progression through the program at that particular degree level. Psychological maturity refers to the receptivity to learning based upon personal and collective development in the context of the educational program. The flexibility and dynamics of the CDI paradigm allow for the adjustment of the pedagogy and content, based upon the educational and psychological maturational levels of the student.

For instance, in undergraduate or beginning master's degree courses, the emphasis is more upon pragmatic knowledge, where theory and intellect predominates, but arts-based methods are introduced to amplify and reflect upon the pragmatic knowledge. Extrinsically driven arts-based learning in response to a theoretical concept introduces the dialectic between extrinsic and intrinsic knowledge in a safe and structured manner. In contrast, the more mature master's or doctoral students can use student-directed intrinsic self/other artistic enquiry to increase therapist self-awareness and to research, test, and develop theory. As learners proceed through their education, they cultivate trust with their cohort, develop psychological resilience and receptivity, and commit to their education the emphasis shifts to constructivist intrinsic learning. Group or individual supervision and studio-based venues provide the opportunity for self/other reflective experiences with varying clinical or research goals using artistic enquiry, journal documentation, contextual case examples, and discussion.

Because the intersubjective art therapy experience is not taught but rather co-constructed within the teacher/student intersubjective matrix, the fourth variable addresses the relational pedagogy that mirrors the emotional communication of the therapeutic relationship. The relational pedagogies exist along and parallel the other variables on the CDI educational continuum. They range from traditional teacher-centered approaches to student-centered structured classrooms, student-directed emergent, and free associative learning (Gerber, 2004; Kavanaugh, 1996b; Mahoney, 2000; Robbins, 2000; Skorczewski, 2002; Symington, 1996). Teacher-centered approaches may be associated with pragmatic knowledge, while student-directed and free associated approaches are more compatible with constructivist knowledge. In this model, the teacher must be receptive, flexible, and responsive to the intellectual, emotional, and aesthetic educational needs of the student.

Parallel to the relational pedagogy, the methods in this continuum range from lecture, discussion, debate, case examples, and arts-based response on the pragmatic end to supervisory and artistic enquiry, journal documentation, self and group reflection, and theory testing on the constructivist end. Approaches that include the creation of art within an intersubjective context are central to art therapy education, and warrant a brief discussion. Arts-based learning and artistic enquiry allows the student to experience how aesthetic knowledge emerges, the metaphorical and symbolic forms of expression, and the assignation of meaning within the intersubjective context. The type *aesthetic pedagogy* ranges from an extrinsically driven arts-based learning approach, used to grapple with the pragmatics of abstract theoretical concepts, to the intrinsically driven artistic enquiry from which meaning is constructed through personal self and self/other reflective practice. Along the CDI continuum, the method of aesthetic learning is dynamic and parallels the type of knowledge being taught (pragmatic or constructivist), respects the emotional holding environment, reflects the developing relational context, and considers the maturational development of the students. The art therapy literature is rich with examples of innovative arts-based pedagogies that reflect those that might be used along the CDI continuum. For instance, Cahn (2000) invoked the studio-based model of art therapy education. Robbins (1988, 2000) and Elkis-Abuhoff et al. (2010) used student reflective art processes to increase self-awareness about patients, professional identity, and institutional systems. Swan-Foster et al. (2001) designed a group educational experience to study the intrinsic nature of the group art therapy situation (p. 161). Gerber et al. (2012) used student-directed self/other artistic enquiry to study intersubjectvity. Deaver (in press) surveyed art therapy program directors about the types and frequencies of arts-based pedagogies. The consensus was that arts-based learning was used to reflect on theory, techniques, group dynamic experiences, and personal reflection.

Conclusion

In this chapter, a creative dialectical paradigm was introduced as a way of re-envisioning art therapy education. Art therapy education includes not only the study of theoretical and intellectual or pragmatic knowledge, but also, and most importantly, the study of aesthetic self/other constructivist knowledge. The transmission and integration of these ways of knowing and being within art therapy is both challenging and creative. The CDI is a paradigm that philosophically represents the ontological pluralism and epistemological tension inherent in art therapy theory and practice. This paradigm situates pragmatic and constructivist knowledge along a creative dialectic continuum that calls for dynamic learning within an intersubjective or transitional space. The emphasis on the types of knowledge to be taught and how it is to be taught can be adjusted based on the learning culture, educational and psychological maturity of the student, and the intersubjective student and peer relationships.

References

AATA. (2007). *Masters Education Standards For Master's Degree programs providing Art Therapy education (effective date: June 30, 2007)*. Alexandria, VA: AATA, Inc.

Arieti, S. (1976). *Creativity: The magic synthesis*. New York, NY: Basic Books, Inc.

Belfiore, M., & Della Cagnoletta, M. (1992). Art therapy training in Italy: Toward a pedagogical model. *The Arts in Psychotherapy, 19*(2), 111–116.

Brown, L. J. (2011). *Intersubjective processes and the unconscious*. New York, NY: Routledge.

Burckhardt, D. M. (2001). *The scientific approach: A dead end? Academy for the Study of Psychoanalysis*. Retrieved on March 26, 2001 from http://www.academyanalyticarts.org/burck.html

Cahn, E. (2000). Proposal for a studio-based art therapy education. *Art Therapy: Journal of the American Art Therapy Association, 17*(3), 177–182.

Cooper, D. E. (Ed.) (1997). *Aesthetics: The classic readings: Introduction*. Malden, MA: Blackwell Publishing.

Creswell, J. W., & Plano Clark, V. (2007). *Designing and conducting mixed methods research*. Thousand Oaks, CA: Sage Publications, Inc.

Csikszentmihalyi, M. (1996). *Creativity: Flow and the psychology of discovery and invention*. New York, NY: Harper Collins.

Deaver, S. (2012). Art-based learning strategies in art therapy graduate education, *Art Therapy: Journal of the American Art Therapy Association, 29*(4), 158–165.

Elkis-Abuhoff, D., Gaydos, M., Rose, S., & Goldblatt, R. (2010). The impact of education and exposure on art therapist identity and perception. *Art Therapy: Journal of the American Art Therapy Association, 27*(3), 119–126.

Ellenbogen, R., Goldberg, J., Roland, A., & Spotnitz, H. (1978). Exploring the parameters of psychoanalytic training: NAAP Conference. *Modern Psychoanalysis, 3*(1), 45–57.

Feen-Calligan, H. (1996). Art therapy as a profession: Implications for the education and training of art therapists. *Art Therapy: Journal of the American Art Therapy Association, 3*(13), 166–173.

Fish, B. (2008). Formative evaluation research of art-based supervision in art therapy training. *Art therapy: Journal of the American Art Therapy Association, 25*(2), 70–77. Accessed on August 4, 2012. http://dx.doi.org/ 10.1080/07421656.2008.10129410

Gerber, N. (2004). The essential components of doctoral level education for art therapists. PhD Dissertation. The Union Institute and University.

Gerber, N., Templeton, E., Chilton, G., Cohen Liebman, M., Manders, E., & Shim, M. (2012). Art based research as a pedagogical approach to studying intersubjectivity in the Creative Arts Therapies. *Journal of Applied Arts and Health, 3*(1), 39–48.

Greene, J. (2007). *Mixed methods in social inquiry*. San Francisco, CA: Jossey-Bass.

Greene, J., & Hall, J. (2010). Dialectics and pragmatism. In A. Tashakkori & C. Teddlie (Eds.), *Mixed methods in social & behavioral research* (pp. 119–143). Thousand Oaks, CA: Sage Publications, Inc.

Harris Williams, M. (2010). *The aesthetic development: The poetic spirit of psychoanalysis*. London, UK: Karnac Books. Ltd.

Israelstam, K. (2007). Creativity and dialectical phenomena: From dialectical edge to dialectical space. *International Journal of Psychoanalysis, 88*, 591–607.

Johnson, B., & Gray, R. (2010). A history of philosophical and theoretical issues for mixed methods research. In A. Tashakkori & C. Teddlie (Eds.), *Mixed methods in social & behavioral research* (pp. 69–94). Thousand Oaks, CA: Sage Publications, Inc.

Junge, M. (1994). *A history of art therapy in the United States*. Mundelein, IL: AATA.

Kapitan, L., & Newhouse, M. C. (2011). Playing chaos into coherence: Educating the postmodern art therapist. *Art Therapy: Journal of the American Art Therapy Association, 17*(2), 111–117.

Kavanaugh, P. (1996a). The impossible patient meets the impossible profession under impossible conditions: Implications for psychoanalytic education. Accessed October 20, 2012. http://www.academyanalyticarts.org/kava4.htm.

Kavanaugh, P. (1996b). Postmodernism, psychoanalysis & philosophy: A world of difference for the future of psychoanalytic education. Accessed on October 20, 2012. www.academyanalyticarts.org/kava3.htm.

Kavanaugh, P. (1998). Rethinking the influence of philosophical premises in the psychoanalytic moment. Accessed on October 21, 2012. www.academyanalyticarts.org/kava8.htm.

Mahoney, M. (2000). Training future psychotherapists. In Rick E. Ingram & C. R. Snyder (Eds.), *Handbook of psychological change: Psychotherapy processes and practices for the 21st century* (pp. 772–735). New York, NY: John Wiley & Sons.

McNiff, S. (1986). *Educating the creative arts therapist*. Springfield, IL: Charles C. Thomas.

Noddings, N. (2005). Pragmatism. In J. L. Paul (Ed.), *Introduction to the philosophies of research and criticism in education and the social sciences* (pp. 57–59). Upper Saddle River, NJ: Pearson Prentice Hall.

Ogden, T. (1990). *The matrix of the mind*. Northvale, NJ: Jason Aronson Inc.

Paul, J. L., Graffam, B., & Fowler, K. (2005). Perspectivism and critique of research: An overview. In J. L. Paul (Ed.), *Introduction to the philosophies of research and criticism in education and the social sciences* (pp. 43–65). Upper Saddle River, NJ: Pearson Prentice Hall.

Robbins, A. (1988). A psychoaesthetic perspective on creative arts therapy and training. *The Arts in Psychotherapy, 15*(2), 95–100.

Robbins, A. (2000). *The artist as therapist* (2nd ed.). London, UK: Jessica Kingsley Publishers, Ltd.

Rubin, J. A. (1999). *Art therapy: An introduction*. New York, NY: Routledge, Inc.

Skorczewski, D. (2002). Whose neighborhood is this?: Intersubjective moments in psychoanalytic education. *PsyArt: An online journal for psychological study of the arts*. Accessed on October 20, 2012. http://www.psyartjournal.com/article/show/skorczewski-whose_neighborhood_is_this_intersubjecti

Swan-Foster, N., Lawlor, M., Scott, L., Angel, D., Ruiz, C. M., & Mana, M. (2001). Inside an art therapy group: The student perspective. *The Arts in Psychotherapy, 28*, 161–174.

Symington, N. (1996). *The making of a psychotherapist*. Madison, CT: International Universities Press.

Twemlow, S. (2001). Training psychotherapists in attributes of "mind" from Zen and psychoanalytic perspectives, Part 1: Core principles, emptiness, impermanence and paradox. *American Journal of Psychotherapy, 5*(1), 1–21.

79

Issues in Credentialing and Licensing for Art Therapy in the United States: Who Ate My Pie?

Laura Greenstone

It is important for art therapists to understand credentials, occupational regulations, and licensure in order to thrive in the broader world of professionals interested in our nation's health and well-being. Much has been discussed in art therapy publications, at conferences, and on the Internet about the status of the field, regulations, and professional identity. This chapter does not attempt to catalog or weigh in on all the details of that dialogue; its intent is to clarify how art therapy is occupationally defined at the state and federal levels.

The goal of this chapter is to navigate the complex web of occupational regulations pertaining to art therapy in simple terms. This topic is critical to understanding the ethical and legal implications of your practice, whether an aspiring art therapist, a student, an academic, or already working in the field. The end portion of this chapter offers some practical suggestions for remaining competitive in the marketplace.

The ABCs of Occupational Regulations

Currently, there is a lack of consistent regulations for art therapy across the United States. Opportunities for gaining a license vary from state to state and are governed by different boards and regulatory philosophies. There is little protection for the consumer about who is qualified to deliver art therapy services. This leaves the practice wide open for interpretation by professionals utilizing techniques from art therapy without the body of training and ethical guidelines about the use of art in therapy.

The only nationwide credential in art therapy is Art Therapy Registration/Board Certification (ATR-BC), granted by the Art Therapy Credentials Board, which is accredited by the National Commission of Certifying Agencies. The ATCB is distinct from the American Art Therapy Association (AATA).

The Wiley Handbook of Art Therapy, First Edition. Edited by David E. Gussak and Marcia L. Rosal.
© 2016 John Wiley & Sons, Ltd. Published 2016 by John Wiley & Sons, Ltd.

A registry or registration establishes recognition that the practitioner has met the minimum standards of education and supervised clinical experience as set by the profession. Certification indicates that the holder has met the standards of the credentialing organization and is entitled to make the public aware of his or her professional competence, but it is distinct from the state laws and regulations that govern practice (American Counseling Association, 2014; McAlevey, 2012).

Historically, only the state has the jurisdiction to regulate a profession. Currently, there is no form of national licensure for professions. Only a handful of states license art therapists specifically (American Counseling Association, 2010). Some states may allow master's-level art therapists equivalency under another licensed profession, but this varies from state to state. Registration and board certification such as the ATR-BC is a voluntary national credential that is granted from an independent professional certification organization and is not regulated by either the federal government or via a state's regulatory process (American Counseling Association, 2014).

The intent of licensure is to protect the public from harm. A licensure or a credentialing law such as a state registry is regulated by a state agency or department. Only licensure restricts or prohibits the title and/or practice of a profession from individuals not meeting the qualification standards set by the regulating body that oversees the license. Occupations are regulated on a state-by-state basis to protect the health, safety, and welfare of its citizens from harm. Violators may be subject to legal sanctions such as fines, loss of license to practice, or imprisonment.

All licensee applicants must prove documented experience and passage of an examination to qualify for a license. Licensure may consist of title protection alone, which regulates who can use the title of the profession, or may also include the scope of practice, which defines the activities of a profession. Licensure alone does not mandate that private insurance or public entitlement programs such as Medicare and TRICARE, the two largest federal governmental health insurance providers in the United States, or state-run federal programs such as Medicaid, reimburse for the services of the profession, unless stated in law. Insurance is only mandated if there is a clause in the law that mandates coverage; otherwise, it is up to the individual discretion of the insurance provider.

A clear example of an insurance mandate at the federal level is within the Affordable Health Care Act for coverage of pre-existing conditions and mental health services. In a state license, this is referred to as a vendorship clause. Insurers want to determine who is qualified to deliver services with a minimum of screening by insurance panels. They look toward the highest form of regulation within a state (licensure) to determine if a provider is qualified.

Lack of licensure for art therapy in most states limits reimbursement potential by third-party payers. Consumers may be limited to paying for services out of pocket if they are denied coverage because the provider does not qualify (Vaccaro, personal communication, July 25, 2012). Healthcare agencies and other organizations may also need to absorb the costs of providing art therapy services through private monies, if insurance coverage is limited. The lack of licensure can make the economics of art therapy practice very difficult for individual art therapists or for nonprofits that provide art therapy services. Accordingly, many art therapists choose to practice under another title or discipline.

The Many Faces of Licensure

"The licenses art therapists hold may carry different titles, such as art therapists, licensed professional counselor–art therapist, clinical psychologist, marriage and family counselor, mental health counselor, creative arts therapist, or others, depending upon state licensing practices and individual qualifications. Some states provide an Art Therapy license using the specific title, such as Maryland, Mississippi, Kentucky, and New Mexico. The Creative Arts Therapy license is offered in New York. In a number of states art therapy licensure is included under a Professional Counselor License" (American Art Therapy Association, 2012; refer to AATA for the most current license titles for art therapists in the United States; these can be found on AATA's website, www.arttherapy.org).

Although the educational training for art therapists is comparable to counselors and marriage/family therapists, this statement is not widely supported by state laws and needs to be considered carefully by those in pursuit of an art therapy education,[1] and who wish to be licensed. While the American Art Therapy Association (AATA) supports state licensing,[2] at the time of this writing, less than 20% of US states have either independent licensure for art therapists or have art therapy specifically included in other mental health regulations. The majority of art therapists are licensed under another profession. AATA has a 30-year history of advocacy at the state and federal levels by many dedicated volunteers, staff, and professional consultants, yet licensing exists in only a handful of states and lacks consistency from place to place (Gantt, 1998).

In 2012, AATA voted on a position statement to be an independent profession and to encourage states to seek standalone licensure. However, the heterogeneity of existing licenses that currently contain some form of art therapy licensing may make it very difficult to develop an art therapy licensing framework that provides a coherent view of the art therapy scope of practice from state to state. For instance, the New York Creative Arts Therapy License is an umbrella license that includes other creative arts disciplines. Since there is no equivalent licensure anywhere else in the United States, the New York Creative Arts Therapy license is not transferable to another state.

Despite recent success in receiving licensure in some states, these states may lack the critical mass of art therapists needed to serve as benchmarks or as models for licensing legislation. We need to be careful that our profession's licensing efforts are not driven by the politics of a particular state and the ease of opportunity at any given moment in time, but instead by our scope and body of practice.

For those entering the art therapy field or thinking of obtaining a license, both the advantages and challenges of obtaining a license as an art therapist or other mental health provider needs to be considered. The advantages of holding a professional license are many; they:

- May add credibility and familiarity to your credentials
- May make you more likely to serve as a primary therapist rather than an adjunctive therapist
- May enable you to practice without having to be supervised by another licensed professional

- May make the licensee more employable
- May help the licensee receive insurance reimbursement and gain access to managed care panels and State Medicaid and Federal Entitlement Programs (i.e., Medicare, TRICARE, CHAMPVA)
- May be the only option if an employer requires a license
- May be the only legal way to practice mental health, depending on the laws in a given state

However, there are significant challenges to the licensee as well:

- Licensing fees can be expensive.
- Licensure does not always guarantee access to third-party payers, such as private insurance or managed care companies; Art Therapy Board Certification alone may gain access to third-party payers in special circumstances.
- Unless stated specifically in the law, licensure in another field does not restrict untrained people from practicing art therapy.
- It may not be feasible to obtain a license as an art therapist or mental health professional if the laws in your state are not open to equivalency with an academic degree in art therapy alone.
- Holding a professional license in a given state does not always carry over to another state.
- An out-of-state license is often not recognized by private insurance companies for reimbursement purposes in another state. (Greenstone, 2000)

Challenges to Achieving Licensure

The main challenge in achieving independent licensure for the art therapy profession is that an increasing number of professions and disciplines are incorporating the creative arts within their own practice areas. At the same time, many professions are also tightening their scopes of practice, making it more difficult for practitioners from other disciplines to practice as unique professions (Boles, Greenstone, & Simpson, 2010).

If independent licensure in art therapy is achieved, it may require some licensees to hold multiple licenses/credentials with limited benefit to the art therapist (i.e., an art therapist in the schools would need to hold an art therapy license as well as teaching credentials; an art therapist who is a marriage and family therapist, social worker, or counselor may also need to hold a license in art therapy if it is not regulated within that license).

Licensure as an independent profession is unlikely in most states due to the lack of numbers of credentialed art therapists across the country, limited financial resources available for advocacy, and overlap in practice with other professions that consider the use of the therapeutic arts as part of their domain. Although there are pockets of success in gaining licensure in the states for art therapy, wide success is unlikely in the current environment of political and economic uncertainty. It is feasible to achieve independent art therapy licensure in some states (even with limited numbers of credentialed art therapists), but this may not always be in the best interest of the art therapy profession for a variety of reasons, as discussed throughout this chapter. The current state of the economy is another major obstacle for achieving independent licensure. State budgets are being cut across the country, making it unlikely that states would create new boards simply to oversee art therapy licensing. Due to limited resource and staff reductions, many state legislatures may be reluctant to add pressure to the work of existing boards and state agencies by adding the licensing review and supervision that would come with licensing for art therapists. The lack of sufficient numbers of art therapists in a state is also an obstacle, as the income generated from licensure fees may not cover the costs to administrate an independent license or may be cost-prohibitive to the licensee.

Other licensed professions may be more inclined to protect their turf and scope of practice in this uncertain environment, especially if they are not included during state lobbying efforts and perceive art therapy licensing efforts as a threat to their practice. In these circumstances, art therapists may need to pursue a hostile amendment to existing laws and potentially meet much opposition.

Licensure pursuits in art therapy unfortunately may create a system that does not allow the easy transfer of licenses across states, as the qualifications have the potential to vary greatly due to differing political environments and different relationships with other professions in each state. Portability with any form of state licensure can be difficult to navigate. Some states and some professions have reciprocal relationships with specific licensure boards, allowing the direct transfer of licenses between these states when their standards are equivalent.

All states in the United States license professional counselors, social workers, psychiatric nurses, and psychologists, allowing, for the most part, the ability to move a license from state to state. Of all the major mental health providers, counseling is the most closely related to the practice of art therapy, and their licensing efforts may yield the most insights into what is necessary to ensure that consumers are protected and the scope and body of the art therapy practice is kept intact. In fact, AATA has worked to ensure that their educational standards for academic program approval are equivalent to the counseling profession.

Who Ate My Pie? Master's-Level Mental Health Professionals by the Numbers

As clearly illustrated in Figure 79.1, the art therapy profession is a very small component of master's-level mental health professionals in the United States[3] (Art Therapy Credentials Board, 2012; Bannister, personal communication, July 24, 2012; American Counseling Association, 2011).

The small number of art therapists nationwide could impact our ability to influence federal issues and to effectively participate in larger organizations' discussions around the creative arts. Credentialed art therapists represent less than 1% of all practicing master's-level mental health professionals in the United States. Adding psychiatric nurses and psychologists makes art therapists' share of the mental health services pie even smaller. The small size of the art therapy profession makes it very difficult for art therapists to achieve the critical mass necessary to make state lobbying efforts for licensure successful, or to be effective at the federal level in gaining inclusion in federal reimbursement programs.

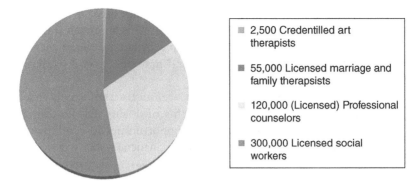

Figure 79.1 Comparison of credentialed/licensed master's-level mental health professionals in the United States.

Lessons Learned by Allied Professions

Lessons learned from the American Counseling Association's (ACA) 30-plus years of successful efforts to achieve licensure can be instructive for the art therapy community. The ACA only recently achieved licensure in their fiftieth state,[4] and their long campaign teaches us that there is a need for a strategic plan that allows for portability, and which avoids the risks of a lack of uniformity in licensure and regulation of the profession (Kaplan & Gladding, 2011; Rollins, 2012; Roudow, 2011).

There may be opportunities for the inclusion of art therapy in national healthcare reform, although this will be extremely competitive and likely restricted to occupations that are already uniformly regulated or fit into one of the existing categories. Unless art therapy can fit into one of these categories, it is unlikely that there will be a significant growth in the number of professionals seeking training solely as art therapists. Given the rapid changes likely to happen in healthcare reform in the United States over the next decade, the art therapy community does not have the luxury of a quarter-century campaign to achieve licensure in all 50 states, even if the number of practicing art therapists supported such an effort.

As the use of the creative arts expands in the practices of counseling, marriage/ family therapy, social work, and psychology, and as the overall use of arts in health grows, creative arts therapists continue to struggle to differentiate arts therapy services. Lack of occupational regulations for art therapy has moved many professionals to define their practice as a specialty or as a duality with another field in order to gain reimbursement (Malchiodi, 2011a).

A Possible Solution: Duality for Reality

Challenges in receiving licensure in many states may lead one to consider art therapy within a duality in which the art therapy scope and body of practice serve as the intellectual framework of an art therapist's practice in counseling, social work, education, or other regulated professions. This would allow individuals who want to offer art therapy services to remain competitive in the marketplace and ensure that they are able to universally practice. This approach should be considered when an art therapist wants a license in a broader, related mental health field along with the art therapy credentials, and may be a useful strategy for the art therapy profession as a whole.

One must question if pursuing independent licensure without reimbursement or guarantee of employability outweighs the benefits of duality. As the cost of higher education continues to rise, and with minimal opportunities to gain an art therapy education at public universities or colleges, issues of financial viability arise (Malchiodi, 2011b, 2011c).

There are many opportunities for art therapy to complement other approaches to health and wellness within the framework of more established and growing fields such as arts in education, health, counseling, psychology, and social work. Many allied groups use the arts in their own disciplines (Americans for the Arts, 2011). These organizations include the Global Alliance for Arts & Health (formerly the Society of the Arts in Healthcare),[5] The Association for Creativity in Counseling,[6] and the National Coalition of Creative Arts Therapies Associations.[7] Given the small numbers of credentialed art therapists, active engagement in coalition-building activities with these and similar organizations may provide a stronger voice for art therapists at the federal and state levels, as well as within much larger professional associations.

"Of all the major mental health providers (psychiatry, psychology, social work, and psychiatric nursing), counseling is the most closely related to the practice of art therapy" (Greenstone, 2000). The most direct way for an art therapist to ensure that he or she is able to receive a license would be to attend a program that prepares the student to be both a counselor and an art therapist with the same degree. (Refer to the AATA website about programs that prepare students for this duality.)

Art therapy is a very small piece of the mental health services pie. Collaboration with other like-minded professions is our best opportunity for survival in the larger context of the rapidly evolving healthcare delivery system. We must carefully consider the history of regulations of other healthcare professions and learn from their successes and challenges.

We should move toward regulating the body of our training and code of practice represented by the ATR-BC, but within a system that will also directly improve consumer protection and access to creative arts modalities, such as recognition of the ATR-BC credential in a state registry while also pursuing inclusion in existing laws, with equivalency. Our goal should be to open access to a wider group of professionals serving more consumers while ensuring that practitioners who use the creative arts are well versed in understanding their implications.

As increasing numbers of professions use the creative arts in their practices, art therapists have an ethical responsibility to ensure that those integrating the arts are aware of the powerful dynamics that the creative arts create for clients. This responsibility should transcend our occupational concerns, and we should continue to seek ways to influence how art is used by practitioners in other disciplines, regardless of how and where the art therapy profession is licensed and regulated.

Art therapists should remain aware that we exist in a continuum with other providers and be conscious of the potential for collaboration or division with our peers. These relationships may either be harmed or strengthened by our pursuits for occupational regulations in the states. Coalition building may be the key. We have more in common with these allied disciplines than we have differences.

The creative arts process is becoming an increasingly significant part of health and wellness services and treatment. This is in line with broader trends in medical and neuroscience research that are uncovering the benefits of mind–body links. We do not own art or therapy, but can be leaders in the dynamic movement of the arts in therapy. We may not be a very big piece of the pie, but we can be a tasty one.

Endnotes

1 Art therapy master's degrees differentiate art therapists from other practitioners. However, state licensing boards do not universally view art therapy master's degree programs as equivalent to master's degree programs in related disciplines, from which graduates may more easily meet state licensure requirements. www.arttherapy.org.

2 "AATA supports federal and state policies, legislation, regulations, judicial actions, and initiatives that encourage, promote, and support efforts to gain a professional art therapy license and licensure of art therapists through a variety of related titles, depending on the state, where it assists individuals to practice as art therapists." www.americanarttherapyassociation.org/upload/licensuretitles.pdf.

3 In early 2012, AATA announced their successful efforts to reclassify art therapy with other master's-level professionals under Code 21 within the Bureau of Labor Statistics (BLS) Job Classification System. The system is used by employers, insurance companies, government agencies, and others to gauge the education and scope of service level of each job title. www.arttherapy.org.

4 Although regulated across the country, counseling created an unintended consequence of varying qualifications for licensed counselors (Erford, *Counseling Today*, January 2012, Volume 54/Number 7). The ACA has a plan in place to bring uniformity to all existing state counseling licenses to achieve portability.

5 Arts in Health is "a diverse, multidisciplinary field dedicated to transforming the healthcare experience by connecting people with the power of the arts at key moments in their lives. This rapidly growing field integrates the arts, including literary, performing, and visual arts and design, into a wide variety of healthcare and community settings for therapeutic, educational, and expressive purposes" (www.artsusa.org/pdf/get_involved/advocacy/congressional_arts_handbook/issue_briefs/2009/healthcare09.pdf).

6 The Association for Creativity in Counseling (ACC) is a division of the American Counseling Association. The ACC was founded to create a forum where counselors and counselor educators could come together to celebrate their passion for the creative; where music, media, art, theater, storytelling, and other creative processes could be explored in the service of increasing self awareness (Thelma Duffy, Founder, *Journal of Creativity in Mental Health*, 2(3), 2006/2007; available online at http://jcmh.haworthpress.com).

7 The National Coalition of Creative Arts Therapies Associations (NCCATA) is an alliance of professional creative arts associations dedicated to the advancement of the arts as therapeutic modalities. www.nccata.org.

Credentialing and Licensure Q&A

Q: *I am planning to attend a graduate art therapy program. How do I ensure that my graduate program is preparing me to gain the credentials needed to practice?*

A: Review the list of AATA-approved universities and programs (http://arttherapy.org/aata-educational-programs.html) to ensure that the program prepares you for ATR-BC certification. Have an idea of the setting you want to work in, and ask if the program prepares you for that work setting. Consider if the program prepares you for the most opportunities for employment, ability to transfer your license to other states, reimbursement outlook, and least occupational restrictions. Each state has varying requirements for licensure.

Q: *I have been practicing as an art therapist for a number of years, and my credentials do not qualify for licensure in my state. What should I do?*

A: Consider if you are willing to seek further education and/or credentials, the length of time you want to continue to practice, and if you can afford the associated costs. Training may include additional coursework or possibly a second master's degree. Determine how much longer you wish to work, and if the benefit of pursuing more training outweighs the costs.

Work with your AATA state chapter to determine the success rate of other art therapists who may have applied for a license. If you feel you have been unjustly denied licensure by a board, you can independently appeal the decision, or hire an attorney to represent you who understands occupational and regulatory law. In some circumstances, it may be helpful to contact your state legislative office to advocate on your behalf. Make sure you have well documented your application and communication process with the licensure board in this circumstance.

Q: *Can I have a private practice as an art therapist without a license?*

A: It is important to understand the laws regulating mental health in your state and how they may impact your practice. As the mental health professions have become more uniformly regulated across the country, much of the scope of practice in these fields has been defined. If your practice does not overlap with another licensed profession in the state, you may legally practice art therapy in private practice without a license. An art therapist in private practice should adhere to the ethical guidelines established by the ATCB and AATA.

Q: *Can I receive insurance reimbursement without a license?*

A: Holding a license does not guarantee third-party reimbursement from private or government insurance programs. Insurers are not mandated to include a licensed professional unless specifically stated in the law. Even with an insurance mandate, private insurers can deny access to their panels if they are full. With some insurers (including state and federal programs), art therapists can bill directly, with proof that their services are necessary. Refer to the AATA website for more specifics on insurance reimbursement.

Note that providers of services are limited to billing according to the contract that they signed with each insurer when they became an in-network provider, and to the insurance plan's contract/coverage of each patient in treatment, regardless of whether the services they provide are in-network or out-of-network.

Q: *Can I bill for art therapy services under another professional's license?*

A: Professions are getting more restrictive about this as licensure has become more universal. An art therapist wishing to bill under another's insurance needs to confirm with all the regulations pertaining to licensed mental health professions in the state in which they practice for specifics. In some states, it is unlawful to bill under another professional's license without a specific supervision plan filed with the board that oversees the license. It may be possible to practice without a clinical license if you are working for fee-for-service or bundled services in a licensed facility. Occasionally, consumers have advocated with a private insurer successfully. Medicare legislation currently indicates that non-clinical-level licensed providers cannot accept any fee directly from a client.

Q: *I work in the schools as an art therapist and have registration/board certification. Do I need more licensing or credentials?*

A: If you want to work in a school setting, in some states you may need to gain teaching credentials as well. As long as your practice does not overlap with another licensed profession in the state, you can work in the school setting as an unlicensed professional. If there is a license for art therapy in the state in which you work, you will need to abide by the laws that govern that profession and hold a license in art therapy or other license with equivalency, unless there is an exemption clause in the law for practice in a school setting by a credentialed art therapist.

Q: *I already hold a master's degree and a license in a mental health profession. How do I gain the credentials to become an art therapist?*

A: Gaining art therapy credentials can be a great way to add to your skills as a mental health professional and specialize your practice in an area of widening public interest. It is important that you follow the ethical guidelines established by the bodies that regulate art therapy, so that you are qualified to deliver services. It is unethical to practice outside your body of knowledge. If you already hold a license in a mental health profession, and art therapy is regulated in your state, it will be necessary for you to obtain the art therapy license in addition, unless there is an exception clause in the licensure law. Refer to AATA and ATCB for information about obtaining the art therapy education and credentials.

References

American Art Therapy Association. (2012). Art therapy licensure by state. *American Art Therapy Association Website*. Retrieved from www.arttherapy.org/upload/licensereqat&mft.pdf; www.arttherapy.org/upload/arttherapylicensurebystate.pdf.

American Counseling Association (2010). *Licensure requirements for Professional Counselors—2010*. Alexandria, VA: American Counseling Association.

American Counseling Association (2011). Statistics on mental health profession, *American Counseling Association Website*, retrieved from www.counseling.org/PublicPolicy/PDF/Mental_Health_Professions%20_Statistics_2011.pdf.

American Counseling Association (2014). Licensure and certification. *American Counseling Association Website*. Retrieved from www.counseling.org; www.counseling.org/knowledge-center/licensure-requirements.

Art Therapy Credentials Board, Inc. (2012). ATR-BC receives accreditation. *Art Therapy Credentials Board, Inc. Review, 19*(2), 1.

Boles, A., Greenstone, L., & Simpson, J. (2010). *Strengthening the arts in healthcare and National Service*, presented at the Arts Advocacy Day Conference, Washington, DC.

Gantt, L. (1998). *Position paper on state licensing*. Unpublished manuscript prepared for Fall 1998 National Coalition of Creative Arts Therapy Associations Meeting.

Greenstone, L (2000). Guidelines for establishing art therapy and counselor equivalency. *American Art Therapy Association Newsletter, Fall*, 2.

Kaplan, D. M., & Gladding, S. T. (2011). A vision for the future of counseling: The 20/20 principles for unifying and strengthening the profession. *Journal of Counseling and Development, 89*(3), 367–372.

Malchiodi, C. (2011a). So you want to be an art therapist, part three: The art therapy credentials maze. *Psychology Today*. Retrieved on February 9, 2011 from www.psychologytoday.com/blog/the-healing-arts/201102/so-you-want-be-art-therapist-part-three-the-art-therapy-credentials-maz.

Malchiodi, C. (2011b). So you want to be an art therapist, part four: Can I get an art therapy job? A counselor in art therapist clothing. *Psychology Today*. Retrieved on February 18, 2011 from www.psychologytoday.com/blog/the-healing-arts/201102/so-you-want-be-art-therapist-part-four-can-i-get-art-therapy-job.

Malchiodi, C. (2011c). So you want to be an art therapist, part five: The tale of two art therapists. *Psychology Today*. Retrieved on March 29, 2011 from www.psychologytoday.com/blog/the-healing-arts/201103/so-you-want-be-art-therapist-part-five-the-tale-two-art-therapists.

McAlevey. M. (2012). "I still don't get It:" The difference between ATCB and AATA. *Art Therapy Credentials Board Inc., Review, 19*(2), 4.

Rollins, J. (2012). Creating a common language: 20/20 delegates reach consensus on licensure, title, continue work on other building blocks to licensure portability. *Counseling Today, 55*(1), 44–46.

Roudow, H. (2011). 20/20 delegates pushing toward licensure portability. *Counseling Today, 54*(5), 42.

Additional Resources

American Art Therapy Association. (2012). "Licensed professional art therapist" license and other licenses held by art therapists. *American Art Therapy Association Website*. Retrieved from www.americanarttherapyassociation.org/upload/licensuretitles.pdf.

American Counseling Association. (2014). Licensure and certification. *American Counseling Association Website*. Retrieved from www.counseling.org; www.counseling.org/knowledge-center/licensure-requirements

Chapin, M. (2000). Is art therapy a profession or idea? *Journal of the American Art Therapy Association, 17*(1), 11–13.

Elkins, E., & Deaver, S. (2010). Art Therapy Association Inc., 2009 Membership Survey Report. *Art Therapy: Journal of the American Art Therapy Association, 27*(13), 141–147. Retrieved from www.tandfonline.com/doi/abs/10.1080/07421656.2010.10129665.

Feen-Calligan, H. (2009). AATA at 40: Reflecting on the past, constructing the future. *Art Therapy: Journal of the American Art Therapy Association, 26*(3), 98–99.

Gantt, L., & Kleinman, S. (1997). *Historical record of recognition of the creative arts therapies*. Unpublished manuscript prepared for the National Coalition of Arts Therapies Associations.

Greenstone, L. (2001). Art therapy in the age of advocacy. *American Art Therapy Association Newsletter, fall*. Cover.

Greenstone, L. (March 2012). *The evolution of the creative arts therapy professions: Past, present and future*. Presented at the New Jersey Creative Arts Therapies Conference, Morristown Medical Center, Morristown, NJ.

Gussak, D. (2000). The invisible college of art therapy: Profession or idea? *Journal of the American Art Therapy Association, 17*(1), 4–6.

Hadzima, J. (no date). How much does an employee really cost? *Boston Business Journal*. Re-print retrieved from http://web.mit.edu/e-club/hadzima/how-much-does-an-employee-cost.html

Kapitan, L. (2010). Art therapists within borders: Grappling with the collective "we" of identity. *Art Therapy: Journal of the American Art Therapy Association, 27*(3), 106–107.

Wadeson, H. (2004). Guest editorial, to be licensed: Is that the question? *Art Therapy: Journal of the American Art Therapy Association, 21*(4), 182–183.

80

Ethics in Art Therapy

Mercedes Ballbéter Maat and Maria Espinola

An ethical foundation in the profession of art therapy has been at the core of educational training programs and clinical practice by members of the American Art Therapy Association (AATA—the national association that sets guidelines for education standards and ethical practice) and the Art Therapy Credentials Board (ATCB). The ethical codes of AATA and ATCB share similarities with the ethical codes held by the American Psychological Association (APA) and the American Counseling Association (ACA).

Some of these similarities include the responsibility that therapists bear toward clients, research participants, supervisees, and students. The ethical guidelines drafted by AATA and ATCB also cover issues that are unique to art therapists. This chapter will briefly review some of these unique issues, including the safety of art materials, cultural sensitivity and harassment through art, confidentiality of artwork, the use of technology in art therapy, consent forms used by art therapists, the ownership of artwork, and professional responsibility.

What Is the Law? What Are Ethics? What Are Morals?

Laws are rules agreed-upon by a society. They set forth the basic principles for living together as a group. Laws can be general or specific regarding what is allowed and what is required of individuals. They are set by elected officials and government entities, typically representing the majority vote.

Ethics and *morals* are philosophical concepts that involve cognitive, emotional, and attitudinal judgments and actions about what is good and bad, right or wrong. They both pertain to the study of human conduct and human relationships, and involve values and worldviews in their decision-making process. Morals are tied to values and attitudes that follow a certain set of beliefs, typically set within cultural or religious contexts. Ethics is a discipline within philosophy that is concerned with governing human conduct. In the case of the art therapy profession, ethics are defined as the standard of conduct or actions, good or right, by which fellow art therapists have agreed to be governed as a professional group. Once consensus is reached, the right behaviors of practice are codified to become ethical standards, guidelines, or principles to which we are expected to adhere in our professional lives. Laws dictate the minimum standards of behavior that society will tolerate. Ethics represent the ideal standards set by the profession. Professionalism strives to combine ethics, the law, and our identity and competence as art therapists in the professional arena.

Principle Ethics, Virtue Ethics, Aspirational Ethics vs Mandatory Ethics

Principle ethics answers the question "How shall I act?" (Corey, Corey, & Callanan, 2011). When faced with a professional dilemma, we may reflect on three tenets under the larger umbrella of ethics. Principle ethics encompass a set of moral principles, assumptions, and beliefs about ideals of conduct shared by members of a profession. The most commonly applied moral principles in decision-making are: (1) autonomy—to foster client self-determination, or the right of clients to choose their own direction; (2) non-maleficence—to do no harm and to avoid actions that will hurt clients; (3) beneficence—to provide services that benefit the client and society; (4) justice—to practice equality, non-discrimination, and equitable treatment of all clients; (5) fidelity—to be loyal and faithful in promises made; and (6) veracity—to be honest with clients. At times, one moral principle may be in competition with another, in which case the art therapist may need to compromise one principle in order to uphold the best decision for the client (Corey et al., 2011).

Virtue ethics answers the question, "Who shall I be?" (Corey et al., 2011). Virtue ethics encompasses principle ethics as well as the therapist's character traits and strengths in ethical decision-making. A therapist's assets may include: (1) integrity—to do things due to the belief that they are right; (2) discernment—to take decisive action in the midst of ambiguity; (3) acceptance of emotions—to inform reason; (4) self-awareness—to know your own assumptions, convictions, and biases, and how these affect your relationships with others; and (5) interdependence with the community—to be aware of how your values are connected with those of your community (Corey et al., 2011).

The practice of aspirational ethics goes beyond mandatory ethics. Art therapists practicing mandatory ethics merely comply with minimal, codified standards. Some of the statements from art therapists practicing mandatory ethics might be: "it isn't unethical if I don't know an ethical standard that prohibits it"; "it can't be unethical if I know other practitioners who do it"; or "it isn't an ethical problem so long as no client has ever complained about it." These statements could endanger client welfare and appear as justifications for either not following ethical guidelines or misinterpreting/ignoring ethical responsibility. Instead, art therapists should aspire to follow a set of higher standards of conduct. Art therapists should not only follow mandatory ethical principles and codes, but also challenge their own thinking and behavior to do what is best for the client. Art therapists practicing aspirational ethics look at the intent and spirit behind applicable codes of conduct to answer questions such as: "Am I doing what is right for the client?" and "What is the true meaning of this ethical standard?" In dealing with ethical dilemmas, art therapists seek supervision and consultation from art therapy educators specializing in ethical issues, colleagues who are leaders in the field, and those who have shown high standards of professionalism and practice. Seeking the advice of a lawyer specializing in ethical and legal issues in mental health professions also is recommended at times.

Ethical Principles for Art Therapists

Ethical principles, guidelines, and codes have multiple parallel goals: (1) to protect and promote the welfare of clients; (2) to educate members about what constitutes sound, ethical conduct; (3) to provide a means to ensure accountability by enforcing standards; (4) to serve as a catalyst for improving practice; (5) to allow the profession to function more autonomously by regulating itself; (6) to help control internal disagreement by providing stability within the profession; and (7) to protect practitioners trying to do the right thing (AATA, 2003, 2011b; ATCB, 2011; Corey et al., 2011). Conduct in line with accepted standards not only protects clients from malpractice but also art therapists from accusations of malpractice. If an ethical complaint were raised, an authority may ask: "What would another art therapist do?" or "How would a reasonable therapist act in the same situation?" The accepted community standard of practice, codified in the Ethical Principles for Art Therapists (AATA, 2011b) and adopted by art therapists, provides a ready answer.

One of AATA's first set of comprehensive ethical guidelines was published in 1995 (AATA, 1995). In 2000, art therapists Haeseler, Deaver, Iyer, Semekoski, Spaniol, and Tibbetts held a panel at the AATA conference in St. Louis, Missouri, to introduce and seek feedback by the membership on possible changes to AATA's existing standards. This led to a comprehensive revision in 2003 that included revisions to the AATA vision, mission, and values statements, and to ethical considerations in multicultural practice and assessment techniques. The AATA principles were revised again in May 2011. Today, AATA is in the process of revising this document again to include, among other things, important ethical considerations in the use of art and

Table 80.1 Sections of the 2011 AATA Ethical Principles for Art Therapists.

1.0	Responsibilities to Clients
2.0	Confidentiality
3.0	Assessment Methods
4.0	Client Artwork
5.0	Professional Competence and Integrity
6.0	Multicultural Awareness
7.0	Responsibility to Students and Supervisees
8.0	Responsibility to Research Participants
9.0	Responsibility to the Profession
10.0	Financial Arrangements
11.0	Advertising
12.0	Independent Practitioner
13.0	Referral and Acceptance Referral
14.0	Art Therapy by Electronic Means
15.0	Abiding by the Ethical Principles for Art Therapists
16.0	Complaints

Table 80.2 Sections of the 2011 ATCB Code of Professional Practice.

1. GENERAL ETHICAL PRINCIPLES: 1.1 Responsibility to Clients; 1.2 Professional Competence and Integrity; 1.3 Responsibility to Students and Supervisees; 1.4 Responsibility to Research Participants; 1.5 Responsibility to the Profession.
2. ELIGIBILITY FOR CREDENTIALS: 2.1 Compliance with ATCB Standards, Policies, and Procedures; 2.2 Complete Application; 2.3 Property of ATCB; 2.4 Pending Litigation; 2.5 Criminal Convictions.
3. STANDARDS OF CONDUCT: 3.1 Confidentiality; 3.2 Public Use and Reproduction of Client Art Expression and Therapy Sessions; 3.3 Professional Relationships; 3.4 Financial Arrangements; 3.5 Advertising; 3.6 Measurement and Evaluation; 3.7 Documentation; 3.8 Termination of Services; 3.9 Electronic Means.
4. STANDARDS OF CONDUCT: DISCIPLINE PROCESS: 4.1 Grounds for Discipline; 4.2 Release of Information; 4.3 Waiver; 4.4 Reconsideration of Eligibility and Reinstatement of Credentials; 4.5 Deadlines.
5. DISCIPLINARY PROCEDURES: 5.1 Appointment of Disciplinary Hearing Panel; 5.2 Submission of Allegations; 5.3 Procedures of the Disciplinary Hearing Panel; 5.4 Appeal Procedures; 5.5 Sanctions; 5.6 Resignation from ATCB; 5.7 Bias, Prejudice, Impartiality.

technology, technology in the practice and supervision of art therapy, exposing and transmitting client art work electronically, and client's rights and confidentiality in digital communication (Table 80.1).

ATCB also drafted a document that sets expectations for art therapists' behavior and conduct. The ATCB Code of Professional Practice created ethical standards for registered art therapists (ATR) and board-certified art therapists (ATR-BC). The latest and most comprehensive version of this document was published in March 2011 (Table 80.2).

Similarities exist among the AATA and ATCB standards. Both guide art therapists in fundamental ethical concepts expected in the practice of art therapy (e.g., the relationship, assessment, and treatment of clients), in client welfare (e.g., confidentiality, respect, and competence), and in the handling of artwork. These documents complement each other, and art therapists should consult both when faced with an ethical dilemma.

One obvious difference among these documents is Section 2 in the ATCB Code of Professional Practice, which outlines credentialing requirements for art therapists. Another important distinction is found in Sections 4 and 5, delineating the ATCB's ability to enforce the code, accept and investigate complaints of ethical violations, and impose disciplinary actions when appropriate. AATA purposely removed its ability to enforce, investigate, and discipline members violating ethical guidelines from its bylaws (AATA, 2012), and relinquished this task to the ATCB. The mission of AATA's Ethics Committee (AATA, 2011c) is now merely to educate, recommend, and endorse ethical principles, and make recommendations for updates to the ethical principles. This change to the AATA bylaws created an unforeseen loophole, in that the ATCB only enforces its Code of Professional Practice (and no other document) on its credentialed members. In other words, neither AATA nor ATCB assumes the authority to enforce ethical codes or investigate alleged ethical violations by master's-level, practicing art therapists who are not credentialed, whether or not they are AATA members. More work is needed by these two organizations to ensure that all art therapists, credentialed or not, members of AATA or not, pledge to the most fundamental ethical principles and standards of art therapy practice so carefully crafted by these two leading entities.

Specific Ethical Considerations for Art Therapists

Among a wide range of ethical considerations in the practice of art therapy, three are of specific importance: responsiveness to multicultural issues, the use of technology in art therapy, and consent.

Becoming self-aware of personal values, biases, and assumptions, and gathering knowledge and developing skills for working in culturally diverse communities, are essential for the development of competence in art therapy. Art therapists must consider their clients' cultural background, socioeconomic situation, gender identity, ethnicity, race, age, country of origin, disability, and language as well as other individual characteristics when selecting appropriate materials and art therapy interventions (AATA, 2011b; ATCB, 2011). AATA addressed the minimum necessary awareness, knowledge, and skills in the ethical practice of art therapy services with diverse clients in a recently published document, titled "Art Therapy Multicultural/Diversity Competencies" (AATA, 2011a). In order to promote cultural sensitivity and a safe environment, art therapists' "multicultural and diversity competency implies a specific and measurable set of deliberate actions and results that increase the ability to serve diverse populations" (AATA, 2011a, p. 1).

The use of technology in the practice of art therapy requires another specific competency. Increasingly, art therapists are choosing to communicate with supervisees, students, colleagues, and clients through email, distance learning platforms, the Internet, social media, texting, and video conferencing. Art therapists use the latest technical devices and programs to interact with clients, including computers and tablets, animation software, digital photography and film, and virtual meeting places such as Second Life (Carlton, Orr, St. John, & Garner, 2012). Results from art therapists surveyed by Orr revealed that their primary concern was the ethical use of digital media in art therapy practice. Orr concluded that art therapy education programs are in dire need to expand curricula to include training in effective and responsible uses of technology in clinical art therapy (Carlton et al., 2012).

The primary challenge arising from the use of electronic media is the protection of client privacy. With the objective of protecting clients' confidentiality, art therapists shall refrain from sending clients' protected health information through the Internet, shall use a pseudo-name instead of the client's real name when transmitting or posting documents with client information, shall cover or delete any identifiable information when disseminating or posting photographs of clients' artwork, and obtain written consent from their clients prior to the digitization or utilization of their artwork or information. Further, art therapists must take precautions such as using passwords or inscriptions to protect electronic documents containing client information from dissemination. Both AATA and ATCB are in the process of updating guidelines to enhance current standards, as the risks of sharing clients' information online are both complex and increasing.

Special attention also should be placed on the type of consent forms that art therapy clients are asked to sign. Frequently, the consent forms used by hospitals and mental health facilities during the admissions process do not stipulate guidelines regarding artwork. As such, art therapists should use supplementary written consent forms that clearly determine the limits of confidentiality, including sharing client information for educational and training purposes and the unique issues of artwork ownership, electronic transmission, exhibition, photography, storage by the therapists or facility, and destruction of the artwork. Of utmost importance is that the ownership of clients' artwork is the clients' (AATA, 2011b, p. 4). In instances in which the artwork is regarded by an institution as part of the clients' medical record, art therapists should make every effort to inform the client of such rules prior to the creation of the art-work and offer, if possible, to include copies of the artwork as part of the medical record. It may be that the artwork has to be kept for a certain period of time where the client was treated. The therapist and the facility must follow state regulations and sound clinical practice when deciding the amount of time for storing clients' records, which shall not be lesser than 7 years after termination, and the method for discarding client's records (AATA, 2011b, p. 3). Art therapists also should obtain written consent from clients or legal guardians before taking photographs or videotaping clients or clients' artwork, before making copies or exhibiting client's artwork, and before using artwork for assessment, research, or educational purposes (AATA, 2011b).

The Ethical Use of Art by Non–Art Therapists

The benefits of using art as a therapeutic technique have been highlighted by practi-tioners in different fields. Professionals from the areas of social work, psychology, recreational therapy, education, mental health counseling, and nursing often demon-strate interest in using techniques that incorporate art. This interest frequently leads them to seek specific training without necessarily pursuing a degree in art therapy (Kalmanowitz & Potash, 2010).

AATA, ACA, and APA have established ethics codes precluding mental health and related professionals from providing services beyond their area of competence. Thus, the training of non–art therapists has generated a discussion regarding the ethical obligations toward trainees, clients, and the field of art therapy. While some authors contain that art therapy should advance as a profession independently (Landgarten & Lubbers, as cited in McNiff, 1997), others claim that art therapists should be open to work from a multidisciplinary perspective by providing and acquiring knowledge from practitioners in different fields (Kalmanowitz & Potash, 2010; McNiff, 1997; Moon, 1997). Offering training on the use of art to non–art therapists can be inter-preted from two opposite ethical perspectives. Those who are against providing this type of education can argue that it violates the ethic codes of "Responsibility to the Profession" (AATA, 2011b, p. 7) and "Professional Competence and Integrity" (AATA, 2011b, p. 5), because the work of the individuals receiving this training would not be regulated by AATA or ATCB, nor would such individuals be fully trained in the complexity of the therapeutic aspects of merging art and psychotherapy techniques. As a result, these trainees might incorrectly use the knowledge gained. On the contrary, those who argue for providing training to non–art therapists may say that art therapists who offer this kind of education are following the AATA ethics code "Responsibility to Clients" by encouraging professionals from other arenas to use art appropriately (AATA, 2011b, p. 2; Kalmanowitz & Potash, 2010; Moon, 1997). It could be further argued that practitioners who have the opportunity to be trained by art therapists may hold the profession of art therapy in higher regard than those who did not have access to such training (Kalmanowitz & Potash, 2010).

While highlighting the ethical considerations of using art in counseling, Hammond and Gantt (1998) stated that all counselors who have been appropriately trained in their profession should have the ability to suggest to clients about using art as a way to express themselves, particularly if the clients have difficulty expressing their feelings verbally, and to engage in a discussion with their clients about the clients' artwork. These authors say that counselors who use art should treat client's artwork in the same manner as they treat everything else that clients share during sessions. Nevertheless, Hammond and Gantt warn against the interpretation of client's artwork by counselors who have not been specifically trained in art therapy.

Because the number of licensed art therapists around the world is relatively small, it would be impossible to reach all the clients who could be helped by the use of art. Olivera (1997) proposed a series of guidelines that other mental health professionals can use to establish their own boundaries when utilizing art in therapy. Moreover, Olivera encouraged these mental health professionals to seek advice from art therapists or to make appropriate referrals. Given that the most fundamental ethical principle for all health professionals involves avoiding causing harm to clients, art therapists should use caution when choosing art materials for their clients that are non-toxic and appropriate for the age and mental health conditions of their clients. Appropriate monitoring of clients who are at risk of harm due to age, mental health disorder, or disability is paramount.

Professional Responsibility

Professional engagement and responsibility is an area that encompasses a wide variety of action and behaviors, including the therapist's commitment to achieve competence and expertise in areas of clinical practice. Responsibility calls for actions as unassuming as being punctual and responding to clients' enquiries within 24–48 hours. It also calls for more cognizant behaviors such as maintaining integrity, advocating for social justice and the best interest of clients, consulting and seeking expert supervision, and practicing self-care. The Ethical Principles for Art Therapists (AATA, 2011b, p. 7) prescribes that "art therapists respect the rights and responsibilities of professional colleagues and participate in activities that advance the goals of art therapy." Sections 5 and 9 of AATA's Ethical Principles for Art Therapists and 1.2 and 1.5 of the ATCB's Code of Professional Practice specifically target concepts of personal responsibility and professionalism (AATA, 2011b; ATCB, 2011). Ethics, morals, values, principles, standards, competence, and client well-being all contribute to purposely doing the right thing.

Moreover, each art therapist must decide the extent to be engaged in giving back to the profession. This could include, for example, membership and service in professional organizations, participation in educational forums, research initiatives, and publications, as well as adhering to educational, credentialing, and licensing requirements.

References

American Art Therapy Association. (1995). *Ethical standards for art therapists*. Mundelein, IL: Author.

American Art Therapy Association. (2003). *Ethical principles for art therapists*. Mundelein, IL: Author.

American Art Therapy Association. (2011a). Art therapy multicultural/diversity competencies. Retrieved from www.americanarttherapyassociation.org/upload/multiculturalcompeten cies2011.pdf.

American Art Therapy Association. (2011b). Ethical principles for art therapists. Retrieved from www.americanarttherapyassociation.org/upload/ethicalprinciples.pdf.

American Art Therapy Association. (2011c). Policy and procedures manual. Retrieved from www.americanarttherapyassociation.org/upload/P&P.pdf.

American Art Therapy Association. (2012). Bylaws of the American Art Therapy Association. Retrieved from www.americanarttherapyassociation.org/upload/bylaws2012.pdf.

Art Therapy Credentials Board. (2011). Code of professional practice. Retrieved from http://atcb.org/export/sites/atcb/_resources/author_files/2011-ATCB-Code-of-Professional-Practice.pdf.

Carlton, N., Orr, P., St. John, P., & Garner, R. (2012). Media arts and technology in art therapy: Research & education panel. *American Art Therapy Association, Inc. 43rd Annual Conference Proceedings*. Retrieved from www.xcdsystem.com/aata2012/proceedings/prof105.html.

Corey, G., Corey, M. S., & Callanan, P. (2011). *Issues and ethics in the helping professions*. US: Brooks/Cole.

Haeseler, M., Deaver, S., Iyer, J., Semekoski, S., Spaniol, S., & Tibbetts, T. (2000). The AATA ethics document, responsive to membership needs. *American Art Therapy Association, Inc. 31st Annual Conference Proceedings* (p. 94). Retrieved from http://www.americanart therapyassociation.org/conferenceproceedings/2000.pdf.

Hammond, L., & Gantt, L. (1998). Using art in counseling: Ethical considerations. *Journal of Counseling and Development, 76*(3), 271–276.

Kalmanowitz, D., & Potash, J. (2010). Ethical considerations in the global teaching and promotion of art therapy to non–art therapists. *Arts in Psychotherapy, 37*, 20–26.

McNiff, S. (1997). Art therapy: A spectrum of partnerships. *The Arts in Psychotherapy, 24*(1), 37–44.

Moon, C. H. (1997). Art therapy: Creating the space we will live in. *The Arts in Psychotherapy, 24*(1), 45–49.

Olivera, B. (1997, Winter). Responding to other disciplines using art therapy. *American Art Therapy Association Newsletter, 30*, 17.

81

Art Therapy and Multiculturalism

Charlotte Boston

This chapter provides information and guidelines for improving multicultural competency for art therapists. Its purpose is to facilitate the efforts of art therapists to explore their identity as cultural beings and to provide a context for culturally sensitive considerations when using art therapy interventions. The development of becoming culturally aware begins with the art therapist. Unless one is willing to honestly examine his or her own prejudices, biases, cultural assumptions, family origins, beliefs, and traditions, cultural roadblocks may lead to ineffective treatment and poor client rapport.

The Problem

The population in the United States has shifted drastically since the early years of the art therapy profession. In 2010, the United States Census Bureau identified five race groups (white, black or African-American, American Indian or Alaska Native, Asian, and Native Hawaiian or Other Pacific Islander), and a sixth category of "some other race" (Humes, Jones, & Ramirez, 2011, p. 2). The 2010 census reported a significant increase in the Hispanic and Asian population due to the increase in immigration. Just over one-third of the respondents in the 2010 census identified themselves as a minority, and this group shows a growth increase of 29% in the last decade. Geographic patterns were also seen in specific areas of the country where the minority population was larger than what previously had been the white majority. Some of the places with "majority-minority" populations included Texas, California, Hawaii, and New Mexico (Humes et al., 2011, p. 19).

Although the composition of the nation has changed, problems still arise on all levels of multicultural issues. The media continues to broadcast the instances of discriminatory practices that reach across race, ethnicity, class, sexuality, and gender. Multicultural issues in society occur in a broad context, often subtle, sometimes seen as microaggressions. *Microaggressions* refer to specific interactions between people of different races, cultures, or genders that are considered non-physical aggression. The term was first coined by American psychiatrist Chester M. Pierce (as cited by DeAngelis, 2009), and described as:

The Wiley Handbook of Art Therapy, First Edition. Edited by David E. Gussak and Marcia L. Rosal.
© 2016 John Wiley & Sons, Ltd. Published 2016 by John Wiley & Sons, Ltd.

... brief and commonplace daily verbal, behavioral, or environmental indignities, whether intentional or unintentional, that communicate hostile, derogatory, or negative racial slights and insults toward people of other races. Some racism is so subtle that neither victim nor perpetrator may entirely understand what is going on—which may be especially toxic for people of color. (p. 42)

While this concern involves African Americans, Asians, and whites, other researchers are beginning to study the impact of racial microaggressions on other groups as well, including people of various ethnic groups, people with disabilities, and gay, lesbian, bisexual, and transgendered individuals. As indicated in DeAngelis' essay "Unmasking Racial Micro Aggressions," Dr. Derald Wing Sue pointed out that, "Microaggressions hold their power because they are invisible, and therefore they don't allow us to see that our actions and attitudes may be discriminatory" (2009, p. 42).

Most often, it seems that many urban, metropolitan areas across the nation find diverse populations in a growing majority. Geography is an important factor to consider as well. Multicultural issues address a broader context, in which responsible art therapists are obligated to be as prepared and as competent as possible. Developing competency in multicultural issues is ongoing, since no one person can know everything related to all multicultural groups or issues.

National Initiatives on Multicultural Competencies

The demographics of the American Art Therapy Association (AATA) in its early years included a small diverse population. Multicultural pioneers included Cliff Joseph, Lucille Venture, Sarah McGee, and Georgette Powell who, in 1973, convened a panel entitled "Art Therapy and the Third World" (Joseph, 1974; Rubin, 2010). This set the stage for the development of a growing multicultural awareness within the art therapy professional organization over the years.[1]

Instituting formal initiatives began slowly. An ad hoc committee was formed in 1978 to investigate how to attract and encourage "minority groups" to enter the field of art therapy; this committee was chaired by Georgette Powell and Lucille Venture. In the late 1980s, the "Special Committee on Recruitment of Third World Groups— Asian, Black, Hispanic Diaspora and Native Americans to Enter and Study the Field of Art Therapy" formally emerged. In 1990, a separate committee to address multicultural issues and awareness, the Mosaic Committee, formed, from which Cultural Awareness Interview Manual and Cross-Cultural Needs Assessment form were developed.

In 1995, the Mosaic Committee's name changed to the Multicultural Committee, and awareness and implementation of increasing such awareness increased. The theme for the 1997 National AATA conference, held in Philadelphia, Pennsylvania, focused on multicultural education. Its title was *Many Paths: Multicultural Perspectives in Art Therapy*. Other tools were developed for the association's members, including a roster of mentors, and a selected bibliography and resource list. The year 1996 also saw the first Multicultural Committee Exchange at the national conference. Curriculum guidelines on multicultural awareness were developed and adopted by the educational institutions, approved by AATA's education committee. In 1997, Marcia Rosal was elected as president, the association's first Hispanic president.

Several notable publications and creative projects ensued. To name just a few: in 1998, Hiscox and Calish published their book *Tapestry of Cultural issues in Art Therapy*. In 2005, the journal *Art Therapy: The Journal of the American Art Therapy Association* published "Lifestory of an Art Therapist of Color" as part of its Lifestories Series. In 2010, the film *Wheels of Diversity: Pioneers of Color* made its debut, and "Multicultural Corner," an online resource site, was added to the AATA website.

Due to the recent emphasis on multiculturalism and the understanding that art therapists work with clients from all races and cultural backgrounds, AATA has taken action to include multicultural issues in its overall mission. In 2009, AATA made it a requirement that multicultural education be included in art therapy program curriculums. In 2011, multicultural/diversity competencies were embedded in AATA's policies and procedures, and a component for awareness was added to the association's ethics document in 2013. The year 2011 also witnessed the most ethnically diverse AATA board of directors in its brief history, which included Meredes ter Maat, the association's second Hispanic president, and three African American directors. Although slow in its development, this demonstrates some of the endeavors the association has undertaken to ensure a growing awareness and proficiency in understanding multiculturalism. This brief synopsis provides a glimmer of the strides and challenges that the field of art therapy has seen in its growing multicultural awareness.

Defining a Culturally Sensitive Art Therapist

This process of preparation begins in the classroom. It is to be embedded in course curriculum, and in relationships between peers, students, and professors, with the purpose that it should continue even after graduation. The multicultural competencies are intended to strengthen the identity of art therapists by advancing multicultural and diversity proficiency as essential to ethical practice. These are considered to be the cornerstone for effective art therapy practice, and are in concert with the AATA's strategic plan priority, to ensure that AATA is an effective, efficient, and sustainable organization.

These competencies include that, first, art therapists need to be aware of the cultural issues brought to the therapist–client relationship. They should examine their own family history, culture, life experiences, cultural development, cultural assumptions, and biases. They need to consider their knowledge base of the client. While it may be natural to make assumptions from appearance or language, one cannot rely on dress, skin color, or physiological appearance to consider a client's cultural issues, though this may be a natural response to initially influence the perception of a client. Has the clinician explored the culture of the population[s] with whom he or she works? What is the clinician's area of skills? Is the clinician aware of their own personal biases and stage of racial identity? How familiar is the art therapist with an employer's policies to address cultural issues?

As it relates to cultural sensitivity, I am able to compare my beginnings in the field to how this has developed currently, given the multicultural components of the art therapy curriculum and the Art Therapy Credentials Board (ATCB) code of ethics for art therapists, as well as related expressive therapies and similar human service organizations and companies.

While some framework has been established as a guide to ensure that art therapists are supplied with the necessary guidance to address cultural issues, there is still too little research in this arena for art therapists to be able to clearly identify "best practice" (Malchiodi, 2011). In the meantime, art therapists may consult the resources of related groups in counseling. They need an ongoing willingness to broaden their understanding of themselves culturally as well as their clients, as this can facilitate competent treatment.

I am reminded of incidents in inpatient wards where I have worked, and I recall awkward moments between staff and patients, and patients and peers. I have had art therapy groups where addressing cultural issues was resisted, and others where cultural issues were discussed frankly and openly; there were learning moments of what to do and not to do. All art therapists have experienced these moments, especially those who have traveled internationally. In this age, art therapists have a very short window of time in which to establish rapport and deliver treatment.

Oftentimes, clinicians are faced with a number of questions: How can I be culturally sensitive when I do not have the materials I need? What resources can I use until I am able to obtain them? How does my organization support efforts to be culturally sensitive? Where have there been infractions, and what was done to address and/or correct it? What supports staff's ability to be culturally aware in their treatment of patients? Discussions and presentations help to build knowledge. Experiential workshops and coursework experiences with other cultures can improve clinical skills. One can never know everything about all cultural issues. Yet, as I talk to students of color and ask of their experiences in art therapy programs, reviews are mixed, and the general agreement is that there is still much work to be done.

The use of specific art directives to address multicultural themes may vary widely. Methods to identify relevant directives can stem from general information one has about the client. Consider translating a theme into one that may reflect cultural issues related to family, traditions one grew up with, rites of passage, or family celebrations and holidays. Consider also how clients may relate to different media. All have traditions that provide rich material. Petersen's *110 Experiences for Multicultural Learning* (2004) is helpful, as many of his ideas can be translated into art therapy directives, to be used either in the clinical setting or for art therapists to explore their own cultural issues.

Becoming a Culturally Sensitive Art Therapist

Just as art therapy multicultural competencies are designed to clarify the types of multicultural awareness, knowledge, and skills that art therapists need to work effectively with persons from diverse groups, so will they require ongoing self-assessment. Art therapists enter the field from various backgrounds and life experiences. Students may come from a privileged background with no exposure to inner-city issues or populations, and be ill equipped to understand such issues without support. Professionals may come from strong ethnic roots and move to an area quite different from where they lived with a different population.

Table 81.1 Racial/cultural identity development (Atkinson et al., 1998).

Stages of Minority Development	Attitude toward Self	Attitude toward Others of the Same Minority	Attitude toward Others of Different Minority	Attitude toward Dominant Group
Stage 1 Conformity	Self-depreciating	Group-depreciating	Discriminatory	Group-appreciating
Stage 2 Dissonance	Conflict between self-depreciating and appreciating	Conflict between group-depreciating and group-appreciating	Conflict between dominant-held views of minority hierarchy and feelings of shared experiences	Conflict between group-depreciating and group-appreciating
Stage 3 Resistance and Immersion	Self-appreciating	Group-appreciating	Conflict between feelings of empathy for other minority experiences and feelings of culturocentrisim	Group-depreciating
Stage 4 Introspection	Concern with basis of self-appreciation	Concern with nature of unequivocal appreciation	Concern with ethnocentric basis for judging others	Concern with the basis of group-depreciating
Stage 5 Integrative Awareness	Self-appreciating	Group-appreciation	Group-appreciating	Selective appreciation

Source: Donald R. Atkinson, George Morten, and Derald Wing Sue. (1998). *Counseling American minorities: A cross-cultural perspective* (5th ed.). Dubuque, IA: William C. Brown.

The following questions may provide a constructive strategy to guide a clinician's preparation:

- How would you learn about the clients with whom you work?
- What would your homework be? What resources would you seek?
- Do you have the right tools and art materials?
- What interventions would you use to address multicultural issues?
- What issues in your cultural identity do you need to come to terms with?
- What is your awareness of your own and your client's stages of racial identity development?
- What stage or racial identity is your client in?
- What is your sensitivity to beliefs and values on time, family traditions/rituals, and spirituality of your client?
- What facilitated sharing among staff/colleagues has there been about their own experiences of racism and prejudice?
- What multicultural exercises have you included that examine similarities and differences in your groups?

All this may, to some extent, be part of the clinician's experience on some level, regardless of origin. An art therapist may recall past experience[s] in their family and/ or education, or they may have witnessed multicultural issues that made their stomach turn or triggered anger/sympathy.

Effective clinicians need be prepared to be flexible. Working with clients of diverse cultures is not a cookbook approach. Just because they may be comfortable with an art therapy intervention that is usually used in a given setting, it does not mean that the client will respond. Good supervision may also help with raising your cultural awareness.

Two models that may enhance an art therapist's knowledge base to improve awareness of racial identity development are (1) Janet Helms' Racial Identity Scale (Helms, 1990; Helms & Carter, 1990) and (2) Atkinson's Racial/Cultural Identity Development Scale (see Table 81.1) (Atkinson, Morten, & Sue, 1998). These models, in particular the one provided in Table 81.1, make clinicians aware of their clients' behavior and how they reflect the particular identity stage they may be on or near. In turn, treatment focusing on identity can then be developed to bring such clients through the stages, until ultimately the clients reach "integrative awareness." Art directives can be offered that focuses on these stages.

Conclusion

In the course of their journey, art therapists should expect to feel uncomfortable. It is actually normal for someone to experience discomfort. This is part of the process of developing improved self-awareness and gaining knowledge and skills. The rewards of effective and culturally sensitive art therapy services include: heightened self-awareness, better rapport with clients, and improved ability and skill to navigate outside of the comfort zone on related issues with professors, colleagues, multidisciplinary staff, and employers.

Endnote

1   The following chronological summary is adapted from *Wheels of Diversity: Pioneers of Color Course Materials for Students of Art Therapy*, printed and distributed by the American Art Therapy Association in 2011.

References

Atkinson, D. R., Morten, G., & Sue, D. W. (1998). *Counseling American minorities: A cross-cultural perspective* (5th ed.). Dubuque, IA: William C. Brown, Pub.

DeAngelis, T. (2009).Unmasking racial micro aggressions. *American Psychological Association, 40*(2), 42.

Helms, J. E. (1990). Black and white racial identity: Theory, research, and practice. *Development of the white racial identity inventory* (pp. 67–80). New York, NY: Greenwood Press.

Helms, J. E., & Carter, R. T. (1990). Development of the white racial identity attitude inventory. In J. E. Helms (Ed.), *Black and white racial identity: Theory, research, and practice* (pp. 67–80). Westport, CT: Greenwood Press.

Hiscox, A. R., & Calisch, A. C. (1998). *Tapestry of cultural issues in art therapy*. London: Jessica Kingsley Publishers.

Humes, K. R., Jones, N. A., & Ramirez, R. R. (2011). Overview of race and Hispanic origin: 2010. Retrieved from http://www.census.gov/prod/cen2010/briefs/c2010br-02.pdf.

Joseph, C. (1974). Art therapy and the third world. *Proceedings of a panel discussion at the meeting of American Art Therapy Association, Inc.*

Malchiodi, C. (2011). Handbook of art therapy (2nd ed.). New York, NY: Guilford Press.

Petersen, P. (2004). *110 experiences for multicultural learning*. Washington, DC: APA Press.

Rubin, J. (2010). Introduction to art therapy (2nd ed.). New York, NY: Routledge.

82

Community-Based Disability Studios: Being and Becoming

Randy M. Vick

There is really no such thing as *the* "community-based disability studio" model. Communities are dynamic entities, and artist studios are idiosyncratic places of creative transformation. They echo the "open studio" approach (see Cathy Moon's chapter on this topic), but with some important distinctions. These studios (also called workshops, centers, or ateliers) will often have a poetically aspirational title with references to vision, ability, growth, or creativity. In the fine print of the signage or mission, one might find some reference to "special needs" or "disability." What these studios often *don't* have is an art therapist or overt therapy orientation per se, and they, in fact, frequently claim an adamant position to the contrary. In this chapter, I will address a specific application of art for people with disabilities where the mission is to create a place where positive changes happen, yet, in many instances, these studios exist beyond the practice and awareness of most art therapists.

The irony of this situation became powerfully clear to me in 2003 when I visited a number of excellent examples of such places across Europe. I admired the quality of the art, innovation of the programs and facilities, and talent and devotion of the staff. The diversity of these studios truly impressed me, as did the clear benefits they brought to their artists and communities. As I toured the sites, saw the art, met the artists, and sat down for conversations with the staff, I was invariably told in some fashion: "This is not art therapy!" Initially, this baffled me. "Wait," I thought, "this is a professionally organized program for a clinical population where art is the central means of intervention with the intent of helping create positive change in the lives of the participants and community—how is this *not* art therapy?"

When I returned home, this question remained with me, and I approached a colleague with an idea for comparing the programs I visited with studio-based art therapy programs in the United States. The results of our research demonstrated far more similarities than differences—but the differences are crucial (Vick & Sexton-Radek, 2008). I have long been interested in the intertwining histories of psychiatric art collections (MacGregor, 1989), "outsider art" (Peiry, 2001), and the profession of art therapy. My subsequent visits to studios in Europe and the United States, my further research for publications (Vick, 2012a) and presentations (Vick,

The Wiley Handbook of Art Therapy, First Edition. Edited by David E. Gussak and Marcia L. Rosal.
© 2016 John Wiley & Sons, Ltd. Published 2016 by John Wiley & Sons, Ltd.

2013), and my involvement as a consultant to a studio for artists with special needs (Vick, 2012b) deepened my understanding of the role that art therapists can play in such studios.

Intersecting Histories

Studios are the birthplaces of art therapy. Pioneers such as Mary Huntoon in the United States (Wix, 2010) and Edward Adamson in England (Adamson, 1984) ran studios for patients in psychiatric hospitals. With shortening hospital stays, art therapists formed workshops in community mental health centers (Lishinsky, 1980). Other studios have been established beyond the mental health model to address physical (McGraw, 1995) and developmental disabilities (Lister, Tanguay, Snow, & D'Amico, 2009), homelessness (Timm-Bottos, 1995), and even the "unidentified patient" (Ault, 1989). Some programs have sprung from healthcare organizations (Lishinsky, 1980; McGraw, 1995), but others were deliberately set up outside the medical world (Allen, 1995; Block, Harris, & Laing, 2005; Franklin, Rothhaus, & Schpok, 2007).

In 1921, psychiatrist Walter Morganthaler (1992) published *Ein Geisteskranker als Künstler* ("A Mental Patient as Artist"), a book-length case study of his patient Adolf Wölfli's life before and during his years in a Swiss psychiatric asylum. Wölfli produced an extraordinary body of art that is still admired today, and, while Morganthaler does not discuss its therapeutic function, he does acknowledge him as an artist whose art making was supported by the hospital and whose work was commissioned, purchased, and exhibited while he was a patient. A year later in 1922, the German psychiatrist and art historian Hans Prinzhorn (1995) published his *Bildnerei der Geisteskranken* ("Artistry of the Mentally Ill"). Prinzhorn was hired to build the University of Heidelberg's psychiatric art collection, yet he came to view these works less as diagnostic material and more as a window into human creativity. Together, these books had far-reaching influence on multiple psychological disciplines, including art therapy (Naumburg, 1950), and fueled generations of modern and contemporary artists, such as French painter Jean Dubuffet, who launched the concept of "art brut," better known in English-speaking countries as "outsider art" (MacGregor, 1989).

Edelson (2011) cited the popularization of "outsider art" as one of the several cultural forces that converged in the mid-1970s, setting the stage for the development of what she refers to as the "Studio Art Movement" in the United States. Early programs such as Gateway Arts (in Boston, Massachusetts), as well as Creative Growth, Creativity Explored (in Oakland, San Francisco) and the National Institute on Art and Disability (in Richmond, California), all began as community studios addressing the needs of deinstitutionalized adults with developmental, physical, or mental disabilities.

During this same period at a psychiatric hospital outside of Vienna, psychiatrist Leo Navratil was developing a live/work space on the hospital grounds for the group of his artistically talented patients. The "Center for Art-Psychotherapy" at Gugging opened in 1981 and later came to be known as the "Haus of Artists" (Feilacher, 2004). While the Gugging artists have long had a strong reputation in the art brut world, this program has become the most fully realized example of what such an organization can become with a studio, living space, sales gallery, museum, permanent collection, gift shop, and an international audience.

There are important parallels between the events that laid the foundation for the Studio Art Movement (to use Edelson's term, 2011) in the United States and Europe and the emergence of art therapy as a profession. Modernism upended the Western art world with the notion that the unique vision of an individual artist supersedes the standards set by the academy. Many artists turned away from art historical sources looking instead to non-Western art and the art of children and psychiatric patients for inspiration. Dubuffet with his championing of art brut was one of a number of modernist artists who embraced the work of untrained individuals working outside the cultural mainstream, thereby creating new definitions of what art is and who artists can be (MacGregor, 1989).

A combination of medical, philosophical, and legal changes reversed the trend of long-term institutionalization of people with developmental and psychiatric disabilities. The communities they were reentering were themselves undergoing sweeping social and political changes in the wake of the civil rights and women's movements. In a similar fashion, legislative protections were extended to this segment of society as well (Junge, 2010). It was in this period of rapid, mid-twentieth-century changes that art therapy and the first disability studios emerged.

Philosophies and Theories

Psychologist Elisas Katz (1994), along with his artist/educator wife Florence Ludins-Katz, founded the three pioneering California programs mentioned earlier. The couple also wrote a manual that is still seen as an important resource by studio facilitators (Ludins-Katz & Katz, 1990). These two publications characterized these studios as operating within a developmental rather than medical model, and cited Rubin (1982) to make this contrast. Curiously, Rubin's two-page article was a reprint of one directed at an art education audience to distinguish the interventions of the then young profession from art used in learning and recreational contexts. While the early practice of art therapy did have a strong medical model orientation, this has never been the exclusive approach, and, since 1982, a far wider range of theoretical positions has emerged. It seems that Katz (1994) established a false dichotomy based in his narrow understanding of art therapy.

Ludins-Katz and Katz (1990) described 17 goals for creative art centers for people with disabilities, which, for the most part, are quite familiar to the vast majority of contemporary art therapists. They mention "artistic development," "enhancement of self-image and self-esteem," "improvement of communication skills," and the "education of the general public" (pp. 15–17), among others. Though Katz (1994) does not deny the therapeutic benefit of such studios, he wrote that the emphasis is on "personal growth rather than on treatment of illness, the environment and the methods are quite different from what one sees in art therapy settings" (p. 33).

In my experience visiting numerous studios, the dread of the medical model is widespread. A facilitator at one Dutch studio that serves people with intellectual disabilities reflected this perspective when she made the trenchant remark, "We do not do therapy here because our artists are not sick." I find that disability studios, if they advocate a "treatment philosophy" at all, are more likely to operate in ways aligned with the paradigms found in developmental, humanistic, rehabilitation, recovery, wellness, vocational, educational, disability studies, and social justice models. Again, these approaches are not foreign to most contemporary art therapists, nor are they brand new. Lishinsky advocated a psychiatric rehabilitation model in 1980, and Spaniol (2000) supported a recovery approach that "contradicts the medical model because it refers to the consequences of the illness rather than its symptoms, and focuses on human potential rather than disease" (p. 79).

A model that combines elements of these approaches is social role valorization (SRV; Wolfensberger, 2000). This theory takes the position that, in addition to the medical circumstances faced by people with various disabilities, they suffer from the stigmatization they experience within their society. Wolfensberger claimed that these negative perceptions inevitably lead to mistreatment of such individuals by their communities; yet, if these perceptions can be shifted, quality of life can improve. SRV is an indirect approach that advocates for the systematic and strategic modification of social perspectives to help bring about enhanced life circumstances for people with disabilities, rather than "curing" the handicapping condition itself. Attending to visual cues is very much a part of this approach, which focuses on how members of socially devalued groups are literally and figuratively "seen" by others. It is this aspect of this model that makes its application to disability studios particularly relevant.

Project Onward: A Program Model

Project Onward is a studio and gallery for artists with mental and developmental disabilities. It was originally launched in 2004 as an offshoot of Gallery 37, the city of Chicago's youth art program. Two Gallery 37 facilitators conceived the new studio as an option for talented artists with special needs to move "onward" as they aged out of the youth program. As the studio evolved, it continued to bring in the occasional Gallery 37 "graduate," but expanded the roster of artists (currently 40) with individuals referred by families, agencies, and themselves. Over time, the program separated administratively from the city, becoming a freestanding not-for-profit. It is my great good fortune to have been serving as the art therapy consultant to Project Onward (n.d.) since its inception.

The mission statement sets three goals: *to create* art in a safe and supportive environment; *to connect* the artists with the larger community through exhibitions and sales; and *to inspire change* by bringing this art out into the world (http://project onward.org/about/mission). Project Onward was established as a professional art studio with a social agenda, rather than as a social service agency. This is a vital distinction. In writing about art brut, Weiss (1992) observed, "art therapy has therapy as its primary goal, and not the creation of art (though, it occasionally inaugurates true art); to the contrary, art workshops have the creation of 'art'—even if at a rudimentary, didactic level—as its primary aim" (p. 67). Any professional art studio, regardless of the health status of the artists, must have as a primary goal the "creation of work of the highest artistic merit" (Ludins-Katz & Katz, 1990, p. 15), and, if it is to be financially self-sustaining, a plan for the "marketing of art" (p. 16). To meet these goals, Project Onward conducts a portfolio review with all artist applicants and has a clear marketing plan regarding the sale of artworks. These are not the strategies of the typical social service agency.

To give a sense of how Project Onward operates, I will introduce one of our artists, Louis DeMarco. To begin, this is *not* a pseudonym; as a professional artist, Louie has a public presence—his name appears on his work, on the organization's website, and in gallery materials. Since Louis and I relate as coworkers, rather than as therapist and client, notions of strict therapeutic confidentiality do not apply. While this may surprise many art therapists, it makes perfect sense when viewed through the SRV lens, where shifting from the notion of "handicapped client" to "talented artist" is central to the larger goal of helping alter social perceptions (Wolfensberger, 2000).

Louie attended Gallery 37 while in high school and became a member of Project Onward in 2005. He is a master of the felt-tipped marker and creates works with images and text that have both humor and poignancy. Ongoing themes in his work include a series of cards that began as helpful self-talk that have become appreciated as words of folk wisdom to his audience (see Figure 82.1), and his "Cloud Charts" (see Figure 82.2) that catalogue the unending array of colored clouds that float over him and convey his emotional state. Louie's talent with words extends beyond visual

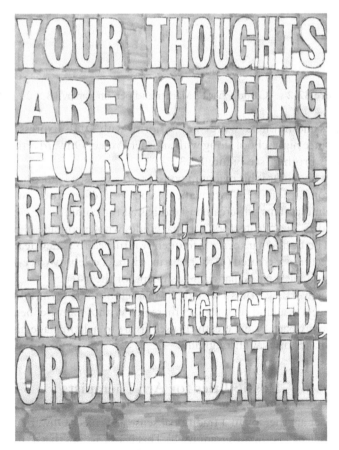

Figure 82.1 "Your thoughts..." Marker and pen on paper; 9 × 12 inch.

Figure 82.2 "Cloud Chart." Marker and pen on paper; 18 × 24 inch.

art to the lyrics and music he writes and performs with DHF Express, a band he has performed in since high school along with another Project Onward artist, their former teacher, and his brother (see Figure 82.3).

Chief among his works is his magnum opus: Loudemar (see Figure 82.4). For Louie, Loudemar (a contraction of his own name) is a place of refuge from a world that is too often overwhelming. This self-created island has all the comforts he could ever desire and is inhabited by the "Protectors," animal guides who encourage him and others to do their best. The Loudemar theme is frequently returned to as new features are added and more Protectors are created (each speaks in a distinct celebrity voice—impersonated by the artist—and has a particular admonishment for the listener).

While each artwork by Louis DeMarco is marvelous in its own right, I have come to view his process as a kind of "auto-art therapy." Without any deliberate art therapy intervention on my part, Louie creatively uses his art to help manage his thoughts and feelings as he makes his way through life.

Possibilities for Art Therapists

I do not conduct art therapy in a traditional sense at Project Onward, and I am clear that my only "client" is the program itself. This is not to say that I am not aware of ongoing and emergent issues with the artists. I discuss these with staff and have been

Figure 82.3 "DHF Express Poster." Marker and pen on paper; 11 × 14 inch.

Figure 82.4 "Loudemar Map." Marker and pen on paper; 18 × 24 inches.

approached by more than one artist with a "You're some kind of therapist, right?" conversation. It is essential that I recognize (as every therapist must) that there are limits to the services my organization can offer. I have come to describe my role (only half-jokingly) as the employee assistance officer at an art factory. If one of our employees is in distress, it is my role to find suitable support or services either within our organization or, when necessary, beyond.

During my weekly visits to Project Onward, I have learned a lot about art, therapy, and art therapy. I have come to recognize that, as with so many of the studios I have visited, Project Onward is "not art therapy"—at least in an orthodox manner. Yet, I am a continual witness to profound personal and social transformations that happen through and around the art in this and other studios of its kind. In one of the earliest and best attempts to define art therapy, Ulman (1961) wrote, "Therapeutic procedures are those designed to assist favorable changes in personality and living that will outlast the session itself" (p. 20). These studios are places where artists with disabilities are deliberately gathered and supplied with the resources for creating, and they become environments where "favorable change" is achieved. It is as though art therapy happens despite the denials to the contrary and (curiously) without art therapists!

Yet, despite this robust and uncultivated form of "feral" art therapy that exists without the involvement of professional art therapists, I would argue that there *are* important contributions we can make with our particular knowledge of both art and working with special-needs populations. However, to do this well, we must adapt, as any therapist must when shifting to work in a new setting with a new population. We must put aside many of the cherished trappings of the psychotherapy model—the client/therapist relationship, the nomenclature, the exploratory dialogues, being the "expert"— as they simply do not apply here, and can be counterproductive. These elements can certainly have their place, but it is not within the context of these studios.

This context demands the reexamination of other aspects of the traditional art therapy ethos as well. When artwork is produced with the expressed purpose of being exhibited and (with luck) sold to others, our traditional paradigms regarding the ethics of privacy and exhibition must be reexamined (Vick, 2011). Additionally, the woefully misguided aphorism "it doesn't matter what it looks like," is anathema in a professional studio, since it certainly *does* matter to both the artist and the audience that the work is the best it can be. Product trumps process. Issues of connoisseurship (critique, technical guidance, quality materials, professional display, and the thoughtful admission of artists to programs) are all strategies for improving the professional level of the artwork. If at first the idea of selecting for talent seems antithetical to art therapy, remember that all kinds of admissions limitations are used by healthcare agencies (catchment area, insurance coverage, age range, sobriety, etc.) as ways of managing resources and directing services. If a studio is viewed as a specialty vocational program, fostering the development of the highest-quality art product is a natural objective.

In the SRV approach, perceptions are reoriented toward socially valued qualities such as capability and dignity rather than familiar stereotypes associated with disability, such as incapacity, infirmity, and pity. In this model, the latter are viewed as having a powerful, regressive pull for all stakeholders (the artists, their families, staff, and the public) that can reinforce rather than reverse stigma (Wolfensberger, 2000).

The visibility and setting for such a program is crucial, and Project Onward's original location in the Chicago Cultural Center and new home in a thriving arts district send a strong message about the artists' place in the cultural life of the city in a way that a basement room in a social service agency cannot. Even the term "disability studio" becomes problematic, as it conveys the notion of incapacity rather than capacity. I use it here with caution for the sake of clarity, but in actual practice, this sort of clinical language is best avoided.

As with any specialty application, the art therapist working in the context of such a studio must think differently and develop new talents. In a hospital, we have colleagues who are doctors, nurses, psychologists, and so on, because a variety of skill sets are necessary to treat patients. With studios, other knowledge is needed for the program to be successful in the commercial art world. One writer observed, "many people who start these kinds of programs come from social work or medical backgrounds ... they're so well intentioned, but they don't really understand the philosophy of art making" (DeCarlo, 2006, p. 39). My colleagues at Project Onward have experience negotiating with galleries, curating shows, and running the business of a financially successful studio and gallery. These are strengths that I do not possess, and which I imagine are rare among art therapists. Yet, I bring an understanding of various developmental and mental health circumstances and services that are outside the expertise of even the most empathic artist facilitator.

Conclusion

The world of the disability studio lies just beyond the current edges of the profession of art therapy, and this is unfortunate, since they are places of enormous potential for not only the artists but for the profession of art therapy. As stated earlier, these studios are creative places shaped by their artists, staff, and context. My colleague pointed out that facilitators "in a manner both ironic and thoroughly apt, are often self-taught: individuals working in professional isolation and with limited resources to create working models from scratch" (Lentz, 2008, p. 13).

"Being and Becoming" is the subtitle for my chapter, and it is intended to invoke a sense of what is and what can be. This is true for the participants who so often come with very real limitations, but who become thriving artists with the right support. For the patrons who come to see the art and meet the artists, it becomes impossible to maintain old, limiting perspectives. For art therapy, these studios are places of untapped and unsuspected creative potential. I hope this chapter helps to create what can be.

References

Adamson, E. (1984). *Art as healing.* London, England: Coventure.

Allen, P. B. (1995). Coyote comes in from the cold: The evolution of the open studio concept. *Art Therapy: Journal of the American Art Therapy Association, 12*(3), 161–166.

Ault, R. E. (1989). Art therapy with the unidentified patient. In H. Wadeson, J. Durkin, & D. Perach (Eds.), *Advances in art therapy* (pp. 222–239). New York, NY: John Wiley and Sons.

Block, D., Harris, T., & Laing, S. (2005). Open studio process as a model of social action: A program for at-risk youth. *Art Therapy: Journal of the American Art Therapy Association, 22*(1), 32–38. doi: 10.1080/07421656.2005.10129459.

DeCarlo, T. (2006). Creative growth. *Raw Vision, 54,* 34–41.

Edelson, R. T. (2011). *Outsider Art, The Studio Art Movement and Gateway Arts.* http:// gatewayarts.org/wp-content/uploads/2012/08/VSA-Article-Final.pdf.

Feilacher, J. (Ed.) (2004). *Sovären das Haus der Künstler in Gugging/Soveriegn of the House of Artists of Gugging.* Heidelberg, Germany: Edition Braus im Wachter Verlag.

Franklin, M., Rothaus, M. E., & Schpok, K. (2007). Unity in diversity: A communal pluralism in the art studio and the classroom. In Kaplan, F. (Ed.), *Art therapy and social action* (pp. 213–230). London: Jessica Kingsley.

Katz, E. (1994). Creativity, art and the disabled individual. *International Journal of Arts Medicine, 3*(2), 30–33.

Junge, M. B. (2010). *The modern history of art therapy in the United States.* Springfield, IL: Charles C. Thomas.

Lentz, R. (2008). What we talk about when we talk about art therapy: An outsider's guide to identity crisis. *Art Therapy: Journal of the American Art Therapy Association, 25*(1), 13–14. doi: 10.1080/07421656.2008.10129355.

Lishinsky, S. (1980). Rehabilitative use of art in a community mental health center. In E. Ulman & C. A. Levy (Eds.), *Art therapy viewpoints* (pp. 174–186). New York, NY: Schocken Books.

Lister, S., Tanguay, D., Snow, S., & D'Amico, M. (2009). Development of a creative arts therapies center for people with developmental disabilities. *Art Therapy: Journal of the American Art Therapy Association, 26*(1), 34–37. doi: 10.1080/07421656.2009.10129316.

Ludins-Katz, F., & Katz, E. (1990). *Art & disabilities: Establishing the creative art center for people with disabilities.* Brookline, MA: Brookline Books.

McGraw, M. (1995). The art studio: A studio based art therapy program. *Art Therapy: Journal of the American Art Therapy Association, 12*(3), 167–174.

MacGregor, J. M. (1989). *The discovery of the art of the insane.* Princeton, NJ: Princeton University Press.

Morganthaler, W. (1992). *Madness & art: The life and works of Adolf Wölfli.* Lincoln, NE: University of Nebraska Press.

Naumburg, M. (1950). *Schizophrenic art: Its meaning in psychotherapy.* New York, NY: Grune & Stratton.

Peiry, L. (2001, English-language edition). *Art brut: The origins of outsider art.* Paris, France: Flammarion.

Prinzhorn, H. (1995). *Artistry of the mentally ill.* Vienna, Austria: Springer-Verlag.

Project Onward. (n.d.). Mission statement http://projectonward.org/about/mission/

Rubin, J. A. (1982). Art therapy: What it is and what it is not. *American Journal of Art Therapy, 21*(January), 57–58.

Spaniol, S. E. (2000). "The withering of the expert:" Recovery through art. *Art Therapy: Journal of the American Art Therapy Association, 17*(2), 78–79. doi: 10.1080/07421656.2000.10129506.

Timm-Bottos, J. (1995). Artstreet: Joining community through art. *Art Therapy: Journal of the American Art Therapy Association, 12*(3), 184–187.

Ulman, E. (1961). Art therapy: Problems of definition. *Bulletin of Art Therapy, 1*(2), 10–20.

Vick, R. M. (2011). Ethics on exhibit. *Art Therapy: Journal of the American Art Therapy Association, 28*(4), 152–158. doi:10.1080/07421656.2011.622698.

Vick, R. M. (2012a). Art outside the walls. *The Outsider, 17,* 11–18.

Vick, R. M. (2012b). Found in translation. *Raw Vision, 75*(Spring/Summer), 24–29.

Vick, R. M. (2013). *Adolf Wölfli: A Sad, Bad, Mad Life in Art Therapy's Prehistory.* American Art Therapy Association conference, Seattle, WA.

Vick, R., & Sexton-Radek, K. (2008). Community-based art studios in Europe and the United States: A comparative study. *Art Therapy: Journal of the American Art Therapy Association,* 25(1), 4–10. doi: 10.1080/07421656.2008.10129353

Weiss, A. S. (1992). *Shattered forms: Art brut, phantasms, modernism.* Albany, NY: State University of New York.

Wix, L. (2010). Studios as locations of possibility: Remembering a history. *Art Therapy: Journal of the American Art Therapy Association,* 27(4), 178–183. doi: 10.1080/07421 656.2010.10129388

Wolfensberger, W. (2000). A brief overview of social role valorization. *Mental Retardation,* 38(2), 105–123. doi: http://dx.doi.org/ 10.1352/0047-6765(2000)038<0105:ABOO SR>2.0.CO;2.

83

Creating Alternative Public Spaces: Community-based Art Practice, Critical Consciousness, and Social Justice

Savneet Talwar

This chapter expands the concept of art therapy beyond the narrowly defined, medicalized, and privatized encounter between the clinician and the client, and serves to demonstrate how, in responding to trauma and oppression, clinical models are not the only viable ones (Cvetkovich, 2003). In order to effectively change the lives of marginalized individuals, we need to pay attention to social justice and advocacy models. There is increasing evidence across health care disciplines of disparities in the delivery of care to minority populations (Kumagai & Lypson, 2009). In response to the growing diversity of the population of the United States, most professional health organizations—the American Art Therapy Association (AATA), American Counseling Association (ACA), American Psychological Association (APA), National Association for Social Workers (NASW)—have introduced multicultural competencies to promote effective treatment for minorities. The current model of multicultural competency centers on gaining knowledge, awareness, and skills. The foundation of this model comes from counseling and the practice of psychotherapy with individuals, which emphasize active listening, empathy and reflection on feelings. Although such qualities are important, to have a positive impact on the individuals we work with, we need to consider community-based practices that connect multiculturalism, cultural competence, and social justice.

In this chapter, I first discuss the relationship between multiculturalism, cultural competence, and social justice. I then examine the importance of critical consciousness for social justice models of working within communities and how they might relate to the training of art therapists. Finally, I offer an example of a community-based art program "Girl/Friends Institute," organized by A Long Walk Home (ALWH), to illustrate how social justice and advocacy can become a central part of art therapy services, leading to empowerment and instilling agency.

The Wiley Handbook of Art Therapy, First Edition. Edited by David E. Gussak and Marcia L. Rosal.
© 2016 John Wiley & Sons, Ltd. Published 2016 by John Wiley & Sons, Ltd.

Cultural Competence and Social Justice

The AATA ethical principle (2011) 6.0 describes cultural competence as:

> Multicultural/Diversity competence in art therapy is a capacity whereby art therapists possess cultural and diversity awareness and knowledge about self and others, and at the same time ensure that this awareness and knowledge is skillfully applied in practice with clients and client groups. Art therapists maintain multicultural/diversity competence to provide treatment interventions and strategies that include awareness of and responsiveness to cultural issues.

A number of art therapists have argued for cultural competence to be the cornerstone of art therapy education and training (Doby-Copeland, 2006; Dufrene, 1994; Hiscox & Calisch, 1998; George, Greene, & Blackwell, 2005; Talwar, Iyer, & Doby-Copeland, 2004; ter Maat, 1997, 2011). The recent article by ter Maat (2011) outlined several ways to "strengthen awareness of personal and professional competencies necessary for culturally responsible practice" (p. 4). The AATA Multicultural/Diversity competencies (2011) document highlights the importance of promoting cultural competence for understanding the self and the client's worldview, and it stressed the need for art therapists to develop appropriate interventions, strategies, and techniques in working with clients.

In order to offer culturally competent services, it is important to know both the historical context within which the concept of multiculturalism originated in the United States and its connection to social justice. Developed in the wake of the civil rights movement, diversity and multiculturalism are not just about the knowledge and skills one needs to demonstrate sensitivity, develop empathy, and sharpen listening skills; they also entail advocacy growing out of an understanding of discrimination within the personal and political realms based on issues of race, class, gender, and sexual orientation. This means that we need to locate lived experience in an intersectional, cultural, and systemic context (Talwar, 2010). When we talk about discrimination and oppression, we need to consider how lived experience contributes to the trauma discourse, since issues of race, class, gender, and sexual orientation are directly linked to the intergenerational transmission of the past into the present, as represented by such issues as slavery, harassment, violence, and the cultural memory of trauma.[1] In order to effectively address issues surrounding culture and competence, we need to examine what we mean by culture, so that we do not essentialize the individual experiences of the people we serve.

Conceptually, the term "culture" has often been relegated to simplistic categories of ethnicity and behavior, running the risk of making culture a static concept and objectifying minorities on the basis of race, appearance, language, nationality, gender, religion, and sexual orientation (Kumagai & Lypson, 2009), thus reinforcing the status quo. My goal in this chapter is not to dismiss the calls for cultural competence, but rather to urge a "critical consciousness"—an understanding of race, class, gender, and sexuality as reflections of the systems of power and subordination within which we all function. Such a stance is important not only for being culturally competent art therapists, but also for the ones who embody the role of social justice in our work with minority clients. This means that art therapists are concerned with the individual's social identity as well as his or her personal story. In this way, we form a collaboration that promotes cultural awareness, working within the boundaries of the personal and the political. As hooks (1989) stated, naming one's personal pain is insufficient, for we can only make change when it is linked to the "overall education for critical consciousness of collective political resistance" (p. 32).

The social justice paradigm means using "social advocacy and activism as a means to address inequitable social, political, and economic conditions that impede the academic, career, and personal/social development of individuals, families, and communities" (Ratt, 2009, p. 160). In this sense, human development does not simply relate to affect, behavior, or cognitive development; it also includes the culture within which individuals are socialized. When we work with people from marginalized communities, we need to take into account how issues arising from race, class, and gender have historically shaped their development. As such, a critical viewpoint is important if art therapy is to complicate its theoretical basis.

Critical Approaches to Art Therapy: Developing Critical Consciousness in Art Therapists

The term "critical" here entails a challenge to the passive acceptance of established frameworks by enquiring into their limitations and contradictions, and understanding how the theories and frameworks that inform them also serve inequality and injustice. It is important that art therapists recognize the prevailing power structures, so we can be instrumental in reducing the client's entrapment in systems of domination and dependence (Lévesque, 2007).

In the United States, art therapy has, for the most part, been shaped by psychology, which favors individualism and quantitative methods of research. Leaning toward the natural sciences, psychology has endorsed positivism in a "search for universals, for norms of emotional life and behavior, and for modes of treatment for individuals who deviate from these norms" (Watkins & Shulman, 2008, p. 4). In the past decade, some psychologists and counselors have embraced critical theory to advocate for social justice. Critiquing the universalizing nature of psychology, they challenge the passive acceptance of the naturalness of human development, diagnosis, personality structures, and forms of abnormality. They support reexamining the epistemological structures of psychological theory, and they stress the need to take into account the power structures that promote entrapment and dependence among consumers of mental health (Hare-Mustin & Marecek, 2001). In similar ways, art therapists are beginning to question the epistemological framework of art therapy (such as Frostig, 2011; Hogan, 1997; Lévesque, 2007; Whitaker, 2005), increasingly recognizing the psychosocial wellness of people who disturb the status quo.

As practicing art therapists and educators, we have an obligation to understand and evaluate the assumptions upon which art therapy has been practiced. If the goal is to provide the resources and tools that enable and empower our clients in and outside of the art therapy encounter, we need to understand the social, cultural, political, and economic influences that affect client care and treatment (Lévesque, 2007). In such an approach, the client is the expert, and as such the art therapy encounter becomes the space where histories, memories, and identities are explored. The cultural work of the art therapist is to consistently help clients increase awareness, re-inscribe their personal narratives, and destabilize the socially imposed identities that are a result of cultural marginalization, oppression, or mental health stigma. As art therapists, it is our responsibility to raise awareness, correct power imbalances, and, when necessary, be advocates for social justice for our clients.

Developing Critical Consciousness: Working with People

The term "critical consciousness" is often confused with critical thinking. According to Kumagai and Lypson (2009), critical thinking involves analysis and evaluation of the client's family history and functioning level, and then the development of a diagnosis for treatment planning. It is a cognitive process that helps practitioners improve their clinical skills and decisions, but critical consciousness is the ability to perceive social, political, and economic oppression. The term *critical consciousness*, coined by Paulo Freire (1970), suggests that individuals live in a relational world, not a vacuum. For him, true social justice is when political action is taken *with* people who are oppressed. Developing critical consciousness involves acknowledging the link between trauma, oppression, power, privilege, and the historical inequities embedded in social relationships.

From a critical thinking perspective, art therapists acknowledge that the client has been affected by one or more intersectional markers of difference—and the resulting trauma from racism, classism, gendered violence, or sexism—but a critical consciousness model entails first acknowledging the historical inequities that have shaped lived experience, then finding ways to get our clients to understand their social entrapment within cultural systems of power, and, as the goal, empowering them to take action.

According to Ward (2007), critical consciousness is about "knowing and learning how to interpret one's own experience, trust one's own voice, and give legitimacy to one's own perspective" (p. 247). Using a Freirean model, Ward developed a program for working with African American girls to identify issues of racism, gendered violence, and sexism. For her, the first step in working with the girls was to facilitate the importance of *reading* and *naming* socially marginalizing patterns: media images and stereotypes that have informed lived experiences. This means educating the girls to find the "relationship between attitudes, behaviors, feelings and ideas" (p. 255). The next step was to explore ways to respond to the socially negative images by *opposing it*. The knowledge gained from reading and naming their cultural construction, responding, and speaking up is a means of instilling agency. In this way, the girls became aware of their social marginalization, negative images, and stereotypes. Finally, the important step was to *replace* the negative images with images of pride. Critical consciousness, in this sense, is a living methodology that draws on the tensions between formal and informal knowledge. Everyday experiences are potential vehicles for informal knowledge; these experiences provoke us to question the theoretical frameworks or the formal knowledge that has defined minority experiences. It is the space between formal and informal knowledge that becomes the site for a critical self-reflexive practice. As Golub (2005) argued, social action art therapy is ideally a participatory, collaborative process that emphasizes art making as a vehicle through which communities name and understand their realities, identify their needs and strengths, and transform their lives in ways that contribute to individual, collective well-being and social justice.

Girl/Friends Summer Institute: Creating Alternative Public Spheres

The Girl/Friends Summer Institute, begun in 2009, is organized by ALWH. The institute is designed to serve African American girls from low-income communities facing racial, sexual and gender discrimination. Based on a culturally sensitive, youth-led program, its goal is to address the disproportionate impact of sexual and gender violence on low-income African American girls from an individual and systemic perspective. Under the direction of art therapist Scheherzade Tillet, the program focuses on the sexual commodification and consumerism of young African American adolescents. With the goal of raising critical consciousness on individual and social levels, the youth participants go through an intensive 3-week, 75-hour training on sexual and gender violence prevention and recovery. Using multimedia arts and art therapy for advocacy, the program addresses the social and historical factors impacting the experiences of young African American girls, developing awareness of the importance of sexual risk prevention and using the arts to raise awareness among male and female youth, led by the participants (Gipson, Tillet, & Tillet, 2011).

The first part of the program offers a critical space for the young women to examine the intersections of their personal experiences of gender, race, and sexuality. Examining their differences, aspirations, and desires, the sex education component provides the girls with the skills and language to critique the body, gendered violence, reproductive rights, and politics of representation. The second part of the program centers on building alternative public spaces[2] (Fraser, 1990) among the youth and school community. Advocacy takes the form of posters on reproductive rights, distribution of "got consent" wristbands, and making t-shirts for the clothes line project and art exhibits. A central focus is on youth leadership and peer education as a form of empowerment. As the institute moves into its fourth year, the alumni come back to participate in the capacity of youth directors assisting with programming. The program has now been instituted as a semester-long class for high school juniors and seniors, and, to reach a wider group of girls in the community, an after-school program has been added at the North Lawndale Prep Charter High School in Chicago.

According to Tillet (personal communication, July 15, 2012), Girl/Friends is not just about cultural work; at its core, it has a developmental model based on a trauma-informed practice using feminist theory that emphasizes reproductive and social justice models of empowerment. The term "reproductive justice" emerged from the experiences of women of color and their concern for the reproductive health of girls and other women of color. Emphasizing the need for a more comprehensive reproductive choice movement, Crenshaw (1989) developed an intersectional approach for the empowerment of all women, but with the understanding that the economic means of women of color, where they live, or go to school is directly linked to their sexual health and human rights. An intersectional approach asks that we take into account a woman's total reproductive health and its relationship to her living conditions and experiences at work, school, home, and on the street. The goal is not to isolate parts of a woman's representation, but instead to see women's lives and experiences as a totality. Thus, reproductive justice means advancing the discussion of women and their bodies, a discussion that must take into account the woman's community and include environmental factors of oppression, violence, and trauma experienced by women of color via race, class, gender, and sexuality.

The Girl/Friend's program focuses on offering knowledge as a form of empowerment. The participants begin by exploring their personal experiences to examine how their lives are linked with and impacted by social and political issues. By creating an alternative public space, the program not only empowers the girls, but also offers avenues for engaging the larger school community, including teachers, staff, and the male students.

ALWH published its first collection of art, poetry, and projects done by the youth leaders and participants in the community-based arts curriculum. The curriculum begins with the personal experiences of the girls. Beginning with the "Girl/Me" phase, participants actively engage in examining their sexualized, gendered, and racialized identities during this phase of the program. The work is facilitated through workshops to educate the participants about reproductive health, contraception, sexually transmitted diseases, and healthy communication skills to address the personal and social bodies. In the second phase, "Girl/Culture," the participants are asked to examine how popular culture and the media represent gendered socializing, and its impact on their communities. Through performance and monologues, they focus on their identities and representation by investigating media, popular culture images, and sexual and racial stereotypes, including competition between peers, teen dating, violence, and sexual assault. The third phase, "Girl/Power," sets out to create change and foster leadership in the Girl/Friends community. Participants get to share, co-create knowledge, and give meaning to their lived experiences in social action projects. Through social action projects such as making "got consent" t-shirts and distributing wristbands, the participants get to transform their stigmatized and stereotyped identities by engaging their community members directly. For example, distributing "got consent" wristbands to male and female students, teachers, and staff gave the youth leaders an opportunity to share the knowledge they had learned in the institute. In reshaping the youth leaders' identities, the process creates an avenue of empowerment: participants claim ownership of their bodies and learn how to speak out and advocate for social change and transformation. During the final phase of the program, "Girl/Future," the youth leaders intern at leading local agencies for ending violence (Rape Victims Advocates, Between Friends, and other domestic violence agencies). They take an active role in participating in—as well as designing—programs to end domestic and gendered violence in their communities. The program helps the participants to critically engage in becoming the "speaking subject" rather than remain the object of sociological and psychological discourse.

Conclusion

In this chapter, I present only a birds-eye view of the Girl/Friends project. When I interviewed the staff at ALWH, some themes emerged around the use of language to contextualize a social justice framework. According to Ravichandran (personal communication July 5, 2012), an important consideration for the staff was introducing the concept of "survivors" versus "victims" in re-conceptualizing violence, trauma, and the gendered identities of the youth leaders. Survivorship offers a positive image, and one that reimagines the participants' identities in a positive way. The work of ALWH does not focus on treatment but rather on social action. The positive relationships that are created among the participants through the institute help create a supportive community for the youth leaders in the present and for the future.

When art therapists translate their knowledge and experience into the public sphere with community-based art programs informed by critical methodologies, art making is no longer an intuitive process rooted in the unconscious (Frostig, 2011). Instead, community-based programs such as ALWH become a collaborative process, one that is socially conscious, open to public discourse, and invested in social change. When we locate the therapeutic in social praxis that encourages collective participation, art is no longer an object of contemplation; instead, it becomes a critical and communal process. When the participants move from listening to speaking, from private to public, from authentic to subversive, from personal to social, and from observing injustice to naming injustice, we have begun the genuine pursuit of social justice that enables agency and action in the everyday lives of the people we serve.

Endnotes

1   Marita Struken (1997) defines *cultural memory* as one that is shared outside the avenues of historical discourse. This is memory that relates to the subculture where trauma is central in the formation of identities and shared meaning.
2   Nancy Fraser (1990) argues that a public sphere is a site where social meaning is generated, circulated, contested, and reconstructed. The concept thus allows us to study the discursive construction of social problems and social identities.

References

Art therapy multicultural/diversity competencies. (December, 2011). American Art Therapy Association Inc. Retrieved from www.arttherapy.org/aata-multicultural.html.
Crenshaw, K. (1989). Demarginalizing the intersection of race and sex: A black feminist critique of antidiscrimination doctrine, feminist theory and antiracist politics. *University of Chicago Legal Forum*, 139–176.
Cvetkovich, A. (2003). *An archive of feelings: Trauma, sexuality and Lesbian cultures*. Durham, NC: Duke University Press.
Doby-Copeland, C. (2006). Cultural diversity curriculum design: An art therapist's perspective. *Art Therapy: Journal of the American Art Therapy Association, 23*(1), 81–85.
Dufrene, P. M. (1994). Art therapy with native American clients: Ethical and professional issues. *Art Therapy: Journal of the American Art Therapy Association, 11*(3), 191–193.

Ethical principles for art therapists. (Effective date: May 24, 2011). American Art Therapy Association Inc. Retrieved from www.arttherapy.org/aata-ethics.html.

Fraser, N. (1990). Rethinking the public sphere: A contribution to the critique of actually existing democracy. *Social Text, 25/26,* 56–80.

Freire, P. (1970). *Pedagogy of the oppressed.* New York, NY: Continuum.

Frostig, K. (2011). Arts activism. Praxis in social justice, critical discourse, and radical modes of engagement. *Art Therapy: Journal of the American Art Therapy Association, 28*(2), 50–56.

George, J., Greene, B., & Blackwell, M. (2005). Three voices on multiculturalism from the art therapy classroom. *Art Therapy: Journal of the American Art Therapy Association, 22*(3), 132–138.

Gipson, L, Tillet, S., & Tillet, S. (2011). A culture of safety: The development of youth-based sexual violence prevention program. *Chicago Taskforce on Violence Against Women and Young Girls.* Retrieved June 15, 2012, from https://chitaskforce.files.wordpress.com/2011/01/gipson-tillet-final.pdf.

Golub, D. (2005). Social action art therapy. *Art Therapy: Journal of the American Art Therapy Association, 22*(1), 17–23.

Hare-Mustin, R. T., & Marecek, J. (2001). *Critical psychology: An introduction.* London, UK: Sage.

Hiscox, A. R., & Calisch, A. C. (Eds.) (1998). *Tapestry of cultural issues in art therapy.* Philadelphia, PA: Jessica Kingsley.

Hogan, S. (Ed.) (1997). *Feminist approaches to art therapy.* London, UK: Jessica Kingsley.

hooks, b. (1989). *Talking back: Thinking feminist, thinking black.* Boston, MA: South End Press.

Kumagai, A. K., & Lypson, M. L. (2009). Beyond cultural competence: Critical consciousness, social justice and multicultural education. *Academic Medicine, 84*(6), 782–787.

Lévesque, F. (2007). *Critical art therapy: A third perspective.* Retrieved August 10, 2010, from www.lulu.com/product/ebook/critical-art-therapy-a-third-perspective/11771260.

Ratt, M. J. (2009). Social justice counseling: Towards the development of a "fifth force" among counseling paradigms. *Journal of Humanistic Counseling, Education, and Development, 48,* 160–172.

Struken, M. (1997). *Tangled memories: The Vietnam war, the AIDS epidemic, and the politics of remembering.* Berkley, CA: University of California Press.

Talwar, S. (2010). An intersectional framework for race, class, gender, and sexuality in art therapy. *Art Therapy: Journal of the American Art Therapy Association, 27*(1), 11–17.

Talwar, S., Iyer, J., & Doby-Copeland, C. (2004). The invisible veil: Changing paradigms in the art therapy profession. *Art Therapy: Journal of the American Art Therapy Association, 21*(1), 44–48.

ter Maat, M. (1997). A group art therapy experience for immigrant adolescents. *American Journal of Art Therapy, 21*(1), 41–48.

ter Maat, M. (2011). Developing and assessing multicultural competence with a focus on culture and ethnicity. *Art Therapy: Journal of the American Art Therapy Association, 28*(1), 4–10.

Ward, J. V. (2007). Uncovering truth, uncovering lives: Lessons of resistance in the socialization of black girls. In B. Leadbeater & N. Way (Eds.), *Urban girls revisited* (pp. 243–260). New York, NY: New York University Press.

Watkins, M., & Shulman, H. (2008). *Towards psychologies of liberation.* New York, NY: Palgrave Macmillan.

We are Girl/Friends! Art on community violence, justice and healing by Chicago teen girls. (2011). Chicago, IL: A Long Walk Home Inc. www.alongwalkhome.org.

Whitaker, P. (2005). Going through the motions: Improvisation and cooperative learning as ways of exploring contemporary subjectivity and social activism within art therapy practice (pp. 62–68). In L. Kossolapow, S. Scoble, & D. Waller (Eds.), *Arts—Therapies—Communication: European arts therapy: Different approaches.* New Brunswick, NJ: Transaction Publishers.

84

Looking Forward—Thoughts on the Future of Art Therapy—A Personal Perspective

Terry Towne

"The future is not some place we are going, but one we are creating. The paths are not to be found, but made. And the activity of making them changes both the maker and their destination."—John Schaar (1981, p. 321).

When asked to tackle the topic about the future of art therapy for this volume, *The Wiley Blackwell Handbook of Art Therapy*, I was ... well, to be honest, quite flattered, as I am not known in our professional circles as one that regularly puts her thoughts down for scholarly publications. Following that initial period of lightheadedness, I segued into a time—several months actually—during which I was engaged in, alternatively, attempts to pump myself up or believing the editors must have been crazy to assume that I had enough of the right stuff for the task. The phrase "sure, I can do this" would almost immediately be followed by panic and feelings of inadequacy. I mean, after all, haven't art therapists been talking about their future since the early days of Kramer vs Naumburg (or vice versa, if you like) ... and, honestly, what could I possibly have to add?

During the formative years of the profession of art therapy, the primary discussion about the future of art therapy centered around which theoretical framework would prevail—art in psychotherapy or art as therapy. Through that discussion (and I use the word "discussion" advisedly), heated debates raged on with supporters of each theoretical camp wanting to assert the ultimate veracity of their side of the argument. It still amazes me that there are parts of this debate that remain alive today even as the profession has embraced, to one degree or another, a plethora of new theoretical frameworks and practice styles ... but I digress.

The point I wish to make is that other, loftier, thinkers have previously examined the future of art therapy in print—and they have done it quite handily. I, as with many of them, have had a broad service-based relationship with the organizational system that, in large part, binds most art therapists together. My 40+ years as an art therapist has been spent in actively promoting art therapy through dutiful service at the local chapter level, on committees and then the board of the American Art Therapy Association (AATA). My work also led me to serve the Art Therapy Credentials Board (ATCB). In addition, I spent 10 wonderful years as a graduate-level art therapy

The Wiley Handbook of Art Therapy, First Edition. Edited by David E. Gussak and Marcia L. Rosal.
© 2016 John Wiley & Sons, Ltd. Published 2016 by John Wiley & Sons, Ltd.

educator, supervisor, and clinical director. All these varied employment and volunteer-focused activities have allowed me to engage in a process that requires simultaneous looking back and looking forward—engaging in thoughtful consideration of where we have come from and where art therapy might be headed in the future.

By way of disclaimer, I do not have a crystal ball, and you must understand that I truly believe that prognostication, in any form, is pretty much anybody's best guess. I do, however, possess a Magic 8 Ball©, and you might be surprised to know that my question "Is there a bright future for art therapy?"—which was repeated over the course of several days—was answered as follows: "it is decidedly so"; "you may rely on it"; "yes"; "concentrate and ask again" (my bad); and "it is certain." Levity aside, I believe it is incumbent on all stakeholders in our profession to think about, vigorously discuss, and develop a consensus about how we can work together toward a future that will sustain the ethical practice of art therapy; provide enhanced opportunities for employment; and bring us into strategic, mutually beneficial, long-term partnerships.

I believe there are three key challenges in making that bright future a reality: (1) establish a professional identity that can be easily described and understood by those inside and outside of the art therapy community; (2) develop effective and cohesive vision, mission, and core values statements (with specifically delineated milestones) that can be usefully articulated and supported by both internal and external stakeholders; and (3) explore and exhaust each and every opportunity to put art therapy's best foot forward through research initiatives, strategic partnerships, media exposure, and the political arena.

Identity

Replacing the theoretical debate of yesteryear are two notable discussions. The first is centered in a question about the identity of art therapy—is it a profession, or is it an idea (Allen, 2000; Hall, 2000; Lachman-Chapin, 2000; McNiff, 2000; Moon, 2000; Riley, 2000; Vick, 2000)? The second revolves around the identity of the art therapist as artist, and whether or not that identity is, somehow, being diminished (Arrington, 2001; Cahn, 2011; Lentz, 2008; Malchiodi, 1999; Wadeson, 2004). What concerns me about these discussions/debates is not that they are taking place—healthy discussion in any field has value. My concern is that these discussions have been conducted in our professional journal, *Art Therapy: Journal of the American Art Therapy Association*. I believe that publishing articles that describe or attempt to clarify our obvious confusion about our professional identity cannot be helpful as we continue our struggle to gain recognition in the larger healthcare marketplace. Again, I do not mean to imply that these discussions are not valid, but that perhaps a plenary or panel at any of our conferences would be a more appropriate place for these issues to be raised and debated.

Publishing our inability to agree on an identity is a bit like publicly airing our dirty laundry—it is out there for all to see, and fails to convey the kind of consistent and unified message about art therapy that will give us traction with allied healthcare professionals, potential professional alliances, research grant funders, and policy/statute makers. While art therapists have been publicly engaged in our own identity crisis, newer players have entered the picture and are taking the place at the table that we continue to covet. A prime example is the Society for the Arts in Healthcare, founded in 1991 (recently the name of this organization has been changed to the Global Alliance for Arts & Health), which is now well-connected and identified with the National Endowment for the Arts and Johnson & Johnson as professional allies and partners.

Although I fully acknowledge that not all art therapy professionals are members of the AATA, the profession of art therapy is inexorably linked with the national membership organization. Art therapy in the United States began to emerge as a distinct healthcare profession during the 1940s, and the formation of the AATA followed in 1969. In many ways, AATA has always been the centerpiece of the profession. Membership operations are housed within AATA, and its annual national conference is planned there. It creates educational guidelines required for entry into the profession, it provides continuing education credits to the membership, and, if managed properly, it will carry the large burden of selling art therapy to outside stakeholders in order to promote the profession to the public, employers, and policymakers. Therefore, I use the example of the AATA as it continues to hold cache—albeit cache that might be in need of an overhaul.

And why is it that many who receive graduate training in art therapy choose not to belong to the national membership organization dedicated to the profession? Perhaps it is because much of the art therapy training being done in the United States is on a dual-tract. Such tracts lead to registered and board-certified eligibility by the ATCB, as well as a state license, such as for counselors. In most cases, a state license will not include a provision for the practice of art therapy. I fully understand the need for professional regulation on the state level, and I am not naïve about the tremendous effort it can take to pass equitable legislation to cover the practice of art therapy. In 1985, I was the New York Art Therapy Association's liaison to the New York Coalition for the Creative Arts Therapies, a group that had already been hard at work with psychotherapists to promote legislation. It was not until 2005 that the New York State Legislature passed a bill establishing a number of newly regulated professions, "creative arts therapist" among them; it took 20+ years to gain recognition. Then, there is the cost of maintaining one's license and the cost of maintaining one's credentials. Cost may well be a factor that prohibits some art therapists from choosing not to be members of AATA. This larger issue is valid but is only incidental to the scope of my topic. I used AATA as a focal point, because it is the largest membership organization in the field of art therapy today.

As in any membership association, the issues of organizational and professional identity and image shape the way the members and the public perceive the purpose and function of the group. Therefore, the importance of developing a clear identity statement that describes the distinct uniqueness of art therapy—to laypersons, consumers, employers, and other professionals (including policymakers and lawmakers)—cannot be overstated. We need to ask ourselves if we have ever been fully successful in defining our organizational identity, and, if not, why?

Gioia, Schultz, and Corley (2000) defined *organizational identity* "as that which is core, distinctive, and enduring about the character of an organization" (p. 63). Ideally, an organizational identity statement would be developed by internal stakeholders, that is, those who hold membership in the AATA and are credentialed by the ATCB, in consultation with branding and marketing professionals who would have a hand in crafting the organization's image.

The identity statement would rely upon evidence-based outcomes that clarify the efficacy of art therapy in a variety of settings and would include a very brief view of the spirit of the organization (Albert & Whetten, 1985). An organizational identity that is strong will energize members as it imparts a sense of direction and purpose (Ashforth & Mael, 1996). Once a statement has been refined, a clear message about professional identity could be disseminated to art therapy practitioners to use in their search for employment, their promotion of their practice, and in discussion with members of the public and healthcare policymakers.

I posit that, if you were to put 10 art therapists in a room and ask them to define "art therapy," you would get 10 different answers that might contain some overlap. It is likely that all would contain a statement about the therapeutic value of art making but might also contain the words "psychotherapy"/"psychotherapist," "spirituality," "holistic," "mindfulness," or other terms that describe the individual practitioners' theoretical frameworks—but do these add-ons to the term "art therapy" really assist in clarifying what art therapy is for the layperson, the potential client, the politician? A Google search for "art therapy" preceded by any of the terms noted in the preceding text yields pages and pages of links. The appeal of these identifiers may assist the art therapy practitioner to "stand out in the crowd," but do they help us present ourselves as a unified profession? It is my opinion that this lack of clarity in defining the profession fails to further our desire to be better understood and more widely recognized. It does not educate an inquisitive public beyond the sometimes narrow perspective being offered by the definer.

Art therapy/art therapists may be suffering from what Dukerich, Kramer, and Parks (1998) described as *overdisidentification*. The authors described this concept as "a condition where the need for distinctiveness predominates one's need for inclusiveness," wherein "one cannot become integrated into the collective because of a need to distance oneself *from* the collective, wanting to demonstrate one's uniqueness while minimizing one's similarities" (p. 250). The visual artist makes his/her statement by conveying a personal message or commentary through his/her choice of subject matter and media. This, in part, may account for our inability to define ourselves in a professional way. Unlike the other arts therapies (dance, music, and drama), it is less common for the visual artist to collaborate, be a joiner, or be part of an ensemble. However, creating an identity for the profession of art therapy requires collaboration, consensus, and a willingness to be part of "the collective."

Vick (2000), citing Hodnett, indicated that a "profession is distinguished by (1) the ideal of service and (2) a base in a substantial body of knowledge [and may also include] cohesion, commitment to norms of service, a high percentage of members remaining in the profession through their lives, homogeneity of membership and control over professional violations" (p. 165). Vick then skillfully made the case for how the idea and profession of art therapy are inexorably intertwined. He believed that "the ability to identify and articulate [a] shared knowledge base, while still maintaining space for a diversity of viewpoints, is key to maintaining the healthy growth of a profession" (p. 166). It is imperative that we give our diversity the space it needs to flourish but not at the expense of holding ourselves back because of our inability to communicate a coherent and consistent message about who we are.

Vision, Core Values, Mission, Planning

How well do art therapists measure up in communicating to internal as well as external stakeholders regarding who we are, what we stand for, and how we view our future? In order for the AATA to flourish, it must have a vision (about what it wants to be), a set of core values, a mission statement, and plans (both strategic and operational) about how to carry out its vision and mission without losing sight of its core values.

The first step in creating excitement about an organization is the development of a vision statement—an aspirational statement about where the organization wants to go. Mikrut (January 10, 2010) stated, "the vision statement is a snapshot or summary of what the organization's end goal or final product should be" (para 2). Alcorn (1995) posited that many nonprofits have not invested the time to develop a clear and well-articulated vision, and stated, "The vision statement is enormously valuable as a stable point of reference, as a recruitment tool, and as a rallying point for existing membership and leaders" (p. 4). Kotter (1995) enumerated eight key *errors* that contribute to organizational failure. Error #3 is lacking a vision. The vision statement is a "picture of the future that is relatively easy to communicate ... [it] says something that helps clarify the direction in which an organization needs to move" (p. 63). Two cornerstones of any business, whether for-profit or not-for-profit, are the vision and mission statements.

Following the creation of the vision statement would be the development of a set of core values. Collins and Porras (1994) believed that core values exist as guidelines, and are "the essential and enduring tenets of an organization" (p. 73). Core values do not require external validation; rather, they have *intrinsic* value and importance to internal stakeholders of the organization. The vision and core values statements are also the precursors to the development of a mission statement and a cohesive and integrated organizational strategic plan. Therefore, before all else, the organization's vision must be clear and represent the aspirations of its members.

Mikrut (January 10, 2010) stated that the developing and finalizing of a mission statement are based upon a clear vision and core values; "a well-written mission statement provides a quick and clear summary of the organization's purpose for the public and is helpful in writing grants and securing funding" (para 5). Can we say, with certainty, that the mission statement of art therapy's professional membership association accomplishes this purpose?

In order to operationalize the organization's vision, core values, and mission, a well-organized strategic plan should be developed. In defining strategic plans, Alcorn (1998) recommended that organizations should create a plan that contains a minimum of three and a maximum of six strategic goals. The goals (plan) should change periodically as they are either achieved or in response to changes in the external environment, as an organization's strategic goals are time-limited initiatives. An organization accomplishes its strategic plans through an operating plan. Operating plans outline the nuts and bolts of bringing the strategic goals to fruition. Operating plans outline tasks, provide timelines, and address who will be involved in meeting the deadlines. One significant difference between the strategic plan and the operational plan is that the former is well publicized, along with the vision, core values, and mission—the latter is an internal document that serves as a roadmap for the association's day-to-day functioning.

As you are reading this overview of the cornerstones of organization structure, you might be wondering why so much attention is being paid to these particular items. The importance of these elements to an association's success must not be underestimated. In order to ensure a successful future for the profession of art therapy, close attention much be paid to revisiting each element of our organizational structure to make sure it has an aspirational vision, a dynamic mission, and a strategic plan that makes us stand out in the marketplace. The extent to which all stakeholders (members, leaders, management) of the organization are committed to each of these components of organizational success will play a large role in the future growth and success of the profession. One of the best examples in publication of a cohesive organizational structure can be found at the American Psychological Association's website. On the homepage, click on the link to "About APA," then click on the link to the strategic plan, and voila! [http://www.apa.org/about/apa/strategic-plan/default.aspx].

External Stakeholders, Media Exposure, and Strategic Alliances

The AATA has recently taken some helpful steps in pulling together an image and logotype that provides the organization with a distinctive, fresh, and professional look. Coordinating AATA's logo with its member chapters and journal is essential in pulling some disparate and old-fashioned elements together into a cohesive, identifiable whole. However, will this new look be enough to carry us to the next level in creating a future and, beyond that, a legacy for art therapy?

All institutions need regular tending, and, although a paint job or some other kind of facelift is a boost, they do not address the infrastructure of the institution. In order for stakeholders to sit up and take notice, an entity cannot simply say they are new and improved—in order for external stakeholders to pay attention, it really must be new and improved, using language that is dynamic, and reaching the specific targeted market.

Repairing an outdated organizational image requires repairs to the internal processes that have not served effectively. Once we have been able to clearly and concisely define our professional/organizational identity and have a refined brief mission, core values statement, and a unified cohesive strategic plan, we will be ready to face the future more confidently. To date, we have not been able to do this on our own, but there are professionals and professionals-in- training that might wish to partner with us on our overhaul. Trained image and consulting professionals often command top dollar, but all schools of management have a project where students take on an ailing or stagnate corporation (for-profit or not-for-profit) as a research and learning experience that is intended to be mutually beneficial. Let us find that resource.

And where should the new path that we are creating take us? When I was in graduate school at New York University, one of the very best pieces of advice I was given came from the then program director, Laurie Wilson. It proved to be such a valuable piece of advice that, more than 25 years later, I was still using it in my teaching of graduate students at the Albertus Magnus College Art Therapy Program. Laurie told me that, to be a successful art therapist, I would have to have good written and verbal skills, compassion, a strong body of knowledge in psychology, a wide range of skills in using art media and art therapy techniques—and a pioneering spirit. The implication was that art therapy was a field where few advertisements will be found in the newspapers, and folks will constantly ask you, "what's art therapy." I ask those of you reading this today—seriously—has much of that changed?

Taking serious steps to refurbish the way we look at ourselves, and by supporting and nourishing a purposeful membership and collective identity, we can be pioneers prepared to face the challenges of the future we are creating. Let us think of a future where, not just a few, but all Veterans Health Administration Medical Hospitals and Centers provide art therapy services. Let us investigate why only a handful of sites in the large chain of long-term-care facilities offer art therapy services. Let us do this work because we know that art therapy has a bright future. You can count on it.

References

Albert, S., & Whetten, D. A. (1985). Organizational identity. *Research in Organizational Behavior, 7,* 263–295.

Alcorn, M. D. (1998). http://alcornlaw.com/Docs/MDAArtVisison.pdf.

Allen, P. B. (2000). Is art therapy an idea or a profession? *Art Therapy: Journal of the American Art Therapy Association, 17*(3), 164–164.

Arrington, D. B. (2001). Guest editorial—Who's thirsty: Is our art therapy cup half empty, half full, or doth it runneth over? *Art Therapy: Journal of the American Art Therapy Association, 18*(3), 126–131.

Ashforth, B. E., & Mael, F. A. (1996). Organizational identity and strategy as a context for the individual. In J. A. C. Baum & J. E. Dutton (Eds.), *Advances in strategic management* (Vol. *13,* pp. 19–64). Greenwich, CT: JAI Press.

Cahn, E. (2011). Proposal for a studio-based art therapy education. *Art Therapy: Journal of the American Art Therapy Association, 17*(3), 177–182.

Collins, J. C., & Porras, J. I. (1994). *Built to last.* New York, NY: HarperCollins Publishers, Inc.

Dukerich, J. M., Kramer, R., & Parks, J. M. (1998). The dark side of organizational identity. In D. A. Whetten & P. C. Godfrey (Eds.), *Identity in organizations: Building theory through conversations* (pp. 245–256). Thousand Oaks, CA: Sage Publications.

Gioia, D. A., Schultz, M., & Corley, K. G. (2000). Organizational identity, image, and adaptive instability. *Academy of Management Review, 25*(1), 63–81.

Hall, N. (2000). Art therapy: Passing through the intersection. *Art Therapy: Journal of the American Art Therapy Association, 17*(4), 247–251.

Kotter, J. P. (1995). Leading change: Why transformations fail. *Harvard Business Review,* March–April, 59–67.

Lachman-Chapin, M. (2000). Is art therapy a profession or an idea? *Art Therapy: Journal of the American Art Therapy Association, 17*(1), 11–13.

Lentz, R. (2008). What we talk about when we talk about art therapy: An outsider's guide to identity crisis. *Art Therapy: Journal of the American Art Therapy Association, 25*(1), 13–14.

Malchiodi, C. A. (1999). Artists and clinicians: Can we be both? *Art Therapy: Journal of the American Art Therapy Association, 16*(3), 110–111.

McNiff, S. (2000). Art therapy is a big idea. *Art Therapy: Journal of the American Art Therapy Association, 17*(4), 252–254.

Mikrut, S. (2010, January 13). Non-profit vision statements—Core values and mission statements [Ezine article]. Retrieved from http://ezinearticles.com/?expert=Sharon_Mikrut.

Moon, C. (2000). Art therapy, profession or idea? A feminist aesthetic perspective. *Art Therapy: Journal of the American Art Therapy Association, 17*(1), 7–10.

Riley, S. (2000). Questions to which "not knowing" is the answer: An exploration of an "invented reality" called art therapy and the supporting structure known as the "profession" of art therapy. *Art Therapy: Journal of the American Art Therapy Association, 17*(2), 87–89.

Schaar, J. (1981). *Legitimacy in the modern state* (p. 321). New Brunswick, NJ: Transaction Publishers.

Vick, R. M. (2000). The idea and profession of art therapy. *Art Therapy: Journal of the American Art Therapy Association, 17*(3), 165–167.

Wadeson, H. (2004). Guest editorial—To be or not to be licensed: Is that the question? *Art Therapy: Journal of the American Art Therapy Association, 21*(4), 182–183.

Index

The Wiley Handbook of Art Therapy, First Edition. Edited by David E. Gussak and Marcia L. Rosal.
© 2016 John Wiley & Sons, Ltd. Published 2016 by John Wiley & Sons, Ltd.